1,000,000 Books

are available to read at

Forgotten Books

www.ForgottenBooks.com

Read online
Download PDF
Purchase in print

ISBN 978-1-5284-3801-8
PIBN 10910992

This book is a reproduction of an important historical work. Forgotten Books uses state-of-the-art technology to digitally reconstruct the work, preserving the original format whilst repairing imperfections present in the aged copy. In rare cases, an imperfection in the original, such as a blemish or missing page, may be replicated in our edition. We do, however, repair the vast majority of imperfections successfully; any imperfections that remain are intentionally left to preserve the state of such historical works.

Forgotten Books is a registered trademark of FB &c Ltd.
Copyright © 2018 FB &c Ltd.
FB &c Ltd, Dalton House, 60 Windsor Avenue, London, SW19 2RR.
Company number 08720141. Registered in England and Wales.

For support please visit www.forgottenbooks.com

1 MONTH OF FREE READING

at
www.ForgottenBooks.com

By purchasing this book you are eligible for one month membership to ForgottenBooks.com, giving you unlimited access to our entire collection of over 1,000,000 titles via our web site and mobile apps.

To claim your free month visit: www.forgottenbooks.com/free910992

* Offer is valid for 45 days from date of purchase. Terms and conditions apply.

English
Français
Deutsche
Italiano
Español
Português

www.forgottenbooks.com

Mythology Photography **Fiction**
Fishing Christianity **Art** Cooking
Essays Buddhism Freemasonry
Medicine **Biology** Music **Ancient
Egypt** Evolution Carpentry Physics
Dance Geology **Mathematics** Fitness
Shakespeare **Folklore** Yoga Marketing
Confidence Immortality Biographies
Poetry **Psychology** Witchcraft
Electronics Chemistry History **Law**
Accounting **Philosophy** Anthropology
Alchemy Drama Quantum Mechanics
Atheism Sexual Health **Ancient History
Entrepreneurship** Languages Sport
Paleontology Needlework Islam
Metaphysics Investment Archaeology
Parenting Statistics Criminology
Motivational

BULLETIN

OF THE

American Academy of Medicine.

VOLUME VI.

AUGUST, 1902 TO APRIL, 1905.

EASTON, PA.:
ESCHENBACH PRINTING CO.,
1905.

OF THE

American Academy of Medicine

VOL. VI.   ISSUED AUGUST, 1902.   NO. 1.

THE AMERICAN ACADEMY OF MEDICINE is not responsible for the sentiments expressed in any paper or address published in the BULLETIN.

EXAMINATIONS FOR MEDICAL LICENSURE IN 1901.[1]

CHARLES MCINTIRE, A.M., M.D., Secretary of the Academy.

For several years past, the tabulation of the results of the examinations conducted by the various state boards of examiners, has been published in the Bulletin a month or more before the annual meeting, because of the necessity of providing material for issuing that journal. This year other conditions prevailed and your secretary is able to present it in the to-be-desired manner, as a report to the Academy at its annual meeting.

The great variety of laws, and differences in the methods of procedure in the various states, together with the changes constantly taking place in one state or another make it desirable to accompany the report with a brief statement regarding the procedure in each state.

The great majority of the applicants for examination come directly from the medical schools. Hence, it is desirable to include an account of these schools. It would be better to give a somewhat full abstract of the catalogue of each college, including a full list of the faculty to make this report of the highest value for reference. This involves so much clerical work, that it was not attempted, especially as it could not be read to

[1] A condensation of a report presented to the American Academy of Medicine at its meeting at Saratoga Springs, June 7, 1902.

profit. If it is thought to be desirable it could be added later.[1]

It is to be regretted that the returns are not complete. Except in the few instances where it is especially noted, this is due to the failure to receive replies to the letters of inquiry. A great difficulty is keeping a correct list of the secretaries of the boards; they are changed, our correspondence is sent to the old address, only to find out the change incidentally in the process of time. In some states the blame of no returns cannot be put upon the present secretary, as his name was learned too late to make another inquiry. In every case, where no reply was received, a second or even a third letter has been sent.

ALABAMA.

Alabama requires an examination of every one who desires to open an office to practise medicine in the state. This examination is under the supervision of the state medical society. Practically the entire profession in Alabama is organized first into county societies and through them into the state society. The law of the state entrusts to the state society the oversight of the public health and the licensing to practise medicine. The board of censors of the state society is *ex-officio* the state board of health and also the board of medical examiners. In the same way each county has its county board of health and board of medical examiners. Any one desiring to practise medicine in any county in Alabama may come up before the county board of examiners and passing its examination may be licensed to practise in that county. Should he fail, he has the right to appeal to the state board of examiners. If he wishes he may appear for examination before the state board without first appearing before a county board. Only graduates in medicine are entitled to an examination before the county board but a non-graduate may obtain license from the state board after satisfying it of his knowledge of medicine. The examinations of the county board are forwarded to the state board for filing.

Dr. W. S. Sanders, of Montgomery, is the secretary. The fee for the examination is $10. There is no provision for accepting the license of another state.

[1] This report was projected on the plan of the article of the year previous. So many of the medical schools failed to supply the information sought, that it was decided by the Council not to publish that part of the report, but only the results of the examinations as furnished by the various boards of examiners.

EXAMINATIONS, 1901.

Name of college.	Passed.	Failed.	Total.
ALABAMA.			
Birmingham Medical College	12	0	12
Medical College of Alabama	28	1[1]	29
Montezuma Medical College	1	0	1
COLORADO.			
Denver Medical College	1	0	1
GEORGIA.			
Atlanta College of Physicians and Surgeons	0	1[1]	1
Atlanta Medical College	1	1[2]	2
Georgia College of Eclectic Medicine and Surgery	1	0	1
Georgia Eclectic Medical College	1	0	1
University of Georgia	1	0	1
ILLINOIS.			
Hering Medical College	1	0	1
KENTUCKY.			
Louisville Medical College	1	0	1
LOUISIANA.			
Tulane Medical College	6	0	6
New Orleans Medical College	0	1	1
MARYLAND.			
Johns Hopkins University	1	0	1
Baltimore Medical College	1	0	1
MISSOURI.			
Barnes Medical College	1	0	1
St. Louis Medical College	0	1[3]	1
NEW YORK.			
Columbia Medical College	2	0	2
College of Physicians and Surgeons	1	0	1
University of the City of New York	1	0	1
NORTH CAROLINA.			
Leonard Medical School, Shaw University	1	0	1
PENNSYLVANIA.			
University of Pennsylvania	1	0	1
Jefferson Medical College	1	0	1
TENNESSEE.			
Chattanooga Medical College	8	1[1]	9
Memphis Hospital Medical College	8	0	8
University of Nashville	6	1[4]	7

[1] Class of 1900.
[2] Class of 1890.
[3] Class of 1897.
[4] Class of 1898.

Name of college.	Passed.	Failed.	Total.
Vanderbilt University	14	4[1]	18
University of Tennessee	2	0	2
Meharry Medical College	4	1[2]	5
University of the South	9	0	9
Grant University	2	0	2
VIRGINIA.			
University of Virginia	3	1	4
	120	13	133

ALASKA.

There is no provision in the laws of Alaska regulating the practice of medicine, except an annual license fee of $50.00 for itinerant physicians.

ARIZONA.

Arizona requires an examination. The applicant must have graduated from a medical school; the law does not specify the length of the course. The examinations are held at Phoenix on the first Monday of January, April, July, and October, and include nine subjects: Anatomy, physiology, chemistry, obstetrics, surgery, practice of medicine, materia medica, gynecology, and neurology. An average of 75 per cent. at least on 7 of these is required for a satisfactory examination. The fee is $15.00.

Dr. William Duffield, Phoenix, is the secretary of the board. (No report of the examination has been received.)

ARKANSAS.

Two classes of practitioners are recognized in Arkansas. 1. Those who hold a diploma from a reputable medical school that requires not less than two courses of lectures in separate years. All such can secure the right to practise by exhibiting the diploma to the county clerk, and being registered in his office; the fee for registration is $1.50. 2. Those who do not possess the diploma required by the law. All those must pass an examination before a county board of examiners (for which he pays a fee of $6.00) and then register upon the certificate granted by this board. The judge of the court in each county appoints the board of examiners. They must hold at least two meetings a year.

[1] One each of classes 1878, 1887, 1900.
[2] Class of 1900.

CALIFORNIA.

An examination must be passed before the State Board of Medical Examiners. The board is a mixed one, the members being elected by the various state medical societies: five by the Society of the State of California, two by the California State Homeopathic Medical Society, and two by the Eclectic Medical Society of the State of California. The regular meetings of the board are held in San Francisco on the first Tuesday of April, August and December. The applicant for examination must have a diploma of some legally chartered medical school, complying with the requirements of the Association of American Medical Colleges at the time of graduation, or a license to practise from some examining board legally constituted to grant a license. The fee for the examination is $20 and the certificate must be registered in the office of the county clerk in which the holder intends to practise.

The law went into effect last year, superceding a practice act, which requires merely the registration of a diploma.

The members of the board are:

Dr. Cephas L. Bard, Venture.
Dr. E. C. Buell, President, Los Angeles.
Dr. George G. Gere, Treasurer, San Francisco.
Dr. D. E. Osborne, St. Helena.
Dr. Lewis A. Perce, Long Beach.
Dr. David Powell, Marysville.
Dr. Dudley Tait, San Francisco.
Dr. C. L. Tisdale, Alamede.
Dr. Charles C. Wadsworth, Secretary, San Francisco.

EXAMINATIONS.[1]

Name of college.	Passed.	Failed.	Total.
CALIFORNIA.			
Cooper Medical College	1	0	1
DISTRICT OF COLUMBIA.			
Columbian University	2	0	2
ILLINOIS.			
Chicago Homeopathic Medical College	0	1	1
Northwestern University	2	0	2
College of Physicians and Surgeons	1	0	1
Rush Medical College	0	1	1

[1] Dec. 3, 1901, and April 1, 1902.

Name of college.	Passed.	Failed.	Total.
IOWA.			
College of Physicians and Surgeons, Keokuk	0	1	1
State University of Iowa	1	1	2
KENTUCKY.			
Kentucky School of Medicine	0	1	1
MAINE.			
Bowdoin College	1	0	1
MASSACHUSETTS.			
Harvard University	1	0	1
MICHIGAN.			
University of Michigan	3	0	3
MISSOURI.			
Kansas City Medical College	0	1	1
NEW YORK.			
University and Bellevue Hospital Medical College	0	1	1
OHIO.			
Columbus Medical College	0	1	1
FOREIGN.			
University of London, England	1	0	1
University of Vienna	1	0	1
	14	8	22

COLORADO.

The graduates of medical schools recognized by the board as in good standing entitles their holders to a license to practise medicine in Colorado. Any one else desiring to practise must pass an examination before the board. Since January 1, 1900, a college, to be in good standing, must have a standard of requirements equivalent to those adopted by the Association of American Medical Colleges.

Dr. S. D. Van Meter, of Denver, is secretary of the board.

CONNECTICUT.

A license to practise medicine is issued only after an examination. The examinations are conducted by the committees selected by each of the three state societies. These committees act entirely independent of each other in the selection of questions and in their markings. The examination includes questions in anatomy, physiology, medical chemistry, obstetrics, hygiene, surgery, pathology, diagnosis and therapeutics, including practice and materia medica. A general average of 75 is required. The fee for the examination is $10; for the certificate, $2.00. Application to take the examination should be made to the secretary of the state board of health, Dr. C. A. Lindsley, New Haven.

EXAMINATIONS, 1901.

Name of college.	Passed.	Failed.	Total.
CONNECTICUT.			
Yale University	7	1	8
MARYLAND.			
Baltimore Medical College	2	3	5
College of Physicians and Surgeons	2	1	3
Johns Hopkins University	1	0	1
University of Maryland	3	3	6
MASSACHUSETTS.			
Boston University	4	0	4
Harvard University	1	0	1
MICHIGAN.			
University of Michigan	2	0	2
MISSOURI.			
St. Louis Medical College	0	2	2
NEW YORK.			
Albany Medical College	1	0	1
Long Island College Hospital	1	0	1
Bellevue Hospital Medical College	1	0	1
College of Physicians and Surgeons	5	2	7
Cornell University	1	0	1
New York Homeopathic Medical College and Hospital	5	0	5
Women's Medical College	1	0	1
OHIO.			
Western Reserve University	1	0	1
PENNSYLVANIA.			
University of Pennsylvania	1	0	1
Jefferson Medical College	1	0	1
Hahnemann Medical College	5	0	5
Woman's Medical College	1	0	1
VERMONT.			
University of Vermont	2	0	2
VIRGINIA.			
University of Virginia	3	0	3
Foreign Medical Colleges	1	4	5
Non-graduates	3	0	3
	55	16	71

DELAWARE.

License to practise medicine is issued by the Medical Council after the applicant has passed an examination before the Board of medical examiners or the board of homeopathic medical examiners. To be eligible to take the examination the applicant must be a graduate of medicine having a competent common school education and four years of medical study as interpreted by the Medical Council.

The boards meet on the third Tuesday in June and the second Tuesday in December. Application to come before either board should be made at least 10 days in advance to Dr. P. W. Tomlinson, Wilmington, the secretary of the Medical Council, and should be accompanied by the fee $10.00. The law permits Delaware to accept the licenses of other states provided the state reciprocate the courtesy.

EXAMINATIONS, 1901.

Name of college.	Passed.	Failed.	Total.
ILLINOIS.			
Hahnemann Medical College	1	0	1
MARYLAND.			
Baltimore Medical College	1	0	1
University of Baltimore	0	3[1]	3
Maryland Medical College	1	0	1
University of Maryland	2	0	2
NEW YORK.			
Albany Medical College	1	0	1
OHIO.			
Pulte Medical College	1	0	1
PENNSYLVANIA.			
Jefferson Medical College	4	0	4
Medico-Chirurgical College	1	0	1
University of Pennsylvania	1	0	1
VIRGINIA.			
University of Virginia	1	0	1
	14	3	17

DISTRICT OF COLUMBIA.

The issuing of license in the district is under the direction of the board of medical supervisors, upon the recommendation of one of the board of medical examiners. The applicant for license must be a graduate of medicine after four years' study if the diploma was issued after June 30, 1898.

Dr. William C. Woodward is the secretary of the board of medical supervisors.

EXAMINATIONS, 1901.

Name of college.	Passed.	Failed.	Total.
DISTRICT OF COLUMBIA.			
Columbian University	19	1[1]	20
National University	5	3[1]	8
Georgetown University	6	0	6
Howard University	2	0	2
ILLINOIS.			
Rush Medical College	1	0	1
IOWA.			
College of Physicians and Surgeons, Keokuk	1	1[2]	2
LOUISIANA.			
Tulane University	1	0	1
MARYLAND.			
Baltimore Medical College	1	0	1
College of Physicians and Surgeons	3	0	3
Johns Hopkins University	1	0	1
University of Maryland	2	0	2
Southern Homeopathic Medical College	1	0	1
MINNESOTA.			
Hamline University	0	1[4]	1
NEW YORK.			
New York Homeopathic Medical College and Hospital	1	0	1
OHIO.			
Medical College of Ohio	1	0	1
PENNSYLVANIA.			
Jefferson Medical College	1	1[5]	2
Hahnemann Medical College	1	0	1
TENNESSEE.			
University of the South	0	4[6]	4
VIRGINIA.			
University of Virginia	2	0	2
FOREIGN.			
University of Bologna	1	0	1
	50	11	61

Two physicians refused admission to examination.

[1] Class of 1900, passed 2nd examination.
[2] One failed twice; one was refused admission to examination.
[3] Class of 1875, 4th examination.
[4] Class of 1896.
[5] Class of 1853.
[6] One of class 1898; each appeared twice.

FLORIDA.

Florida requires passing an examination before one of several boards of examiners before the license is issued. There is a board for each of the seven judicial districts: a state homeopathic and a state eclectic board. The applicant must be a graduate of some recognized medical college.

Each board is independent of the other; there is no permanent place for keeping the records, nor cooperation in preparing questions or comparing marks, as is the rule in Alabama; the practical working of the law is unsatisfactory, and the profession of Florida has made efforts to have the law changed.

SECRETARIES.[1]

First District.—Dr. P. B. Wilson, Sneads.
Second District.—Dr. G. W. Lamar, Quincy.
Third District.—Dr. J. A. Townsend, Lake City.
Fourth District.—Dr. Neal Mitchell, Jacksonville.
Fifth District.—Dr. J. F. McKinstry, Gainesville.
Sixth District.—Dr. L. W. Weedon, Tampa.
Seventh District.—Dr. R. L. Harris, Orlando.
Homeopathic.—Dr. H. M. Bruce, Tampa.
Eclectic.—Dr. Hiram Hampton, Jr., Tampa.

GEORGIA.

There are three separate boards in Georgia, acting independently and not in unison as is the case in New York, Pennsylvania, and the District of Columbia. The applicant for examination must have been regularly graduated from a recognized medical school. The fee for the examination is $10.

Dr. J. B. S. Holmes, of Atlanta, is the secretary of the board representing the "Regular" school of medicine. Dr. R. E. Hinman, Atlanta, is secretary of the homeopathic board, and Dr. M. T. Salter, Atlanta, is secretary of the eclectic.

EXAMINATIONS, 1901.[2]

Name of college.	Passed.	Failed.	Total.
GEORGIA.			
Georgia College of Eclectic Medicine and Surgery.	10	1	11

[1] Summary of State Medical Laws, Illinois State Board of Health.
[2] Eclectic board.

Name of college.	Passed.	Failed.	Total.
TENNESSEE.			
Chattanooga Medical College	1	0	1
	11	1	12

(No applicants appeared before the homeopathic board. No report has been received from the "regular" board.)

IDAHO.

Graduates from recognized medical colleges are eligible for the examination before the State Board of Medical Examiners of Idaho. The fee for the examination is $25.00.

Dr. R. L. Nourse, Hailey, is the secretary.

EXAMINATIONS, 1901.

Name of college.	Passed.	Failed.	Total.
CALIFORNIA.			
Cooper Medical College	1	0	1
COLORADO.			
University of Colorado	2	0	2
Gross Medical College	1	0	1
ILLINOIS.			
College of Physicians and Surgeons	1	0	1
Northwestern University	1	0	1
Woman's Medical College	1	0	1
Rush Medical College	2	1	3
Homeopathic Medical College	1	0	1
Hahnemann Medical College	1	0	1
Bennett Medical College	0	1[1]	1
American Medical Missionary College	2	0	2
IOWA.			
University of Iowa	1	0	1
KENTUCKY.			
Louisville Medical College	1	1[2]	2
MICHIGAN.			
University of Michigan	1	0	1
MISSOURI.			
University Medical College	2	0	2
Barnes Medical College	1	0	1
Homeopathic Medical College	0	1[3]	1
NEW YORK.			
Albany Medical College	1	1[4]	2
Bellevue Hospital Medical College	1	0	1

[1] Class of 1900.
[2] Class of 1892.
[3] Class of 1894.
[4] Class of 1864.

Name of college.	Passed.	Failed.	Total.
OHIO.			
Eclectic Medical Institute	1	0	1
Cincinnati College of Medicine and Surgery	1	0	1
OREGON.			
Willamette University	2	0	2
PENNSYLVANIA.			
Jefferson Medical College	1	0	1
Medico-Chirurgical College	1	0	1
TENNESSEE.			
Chattanooga Medical College	0	1	1
FOREIGN.			
University of Edinburgh	1	0	1
	28	6	34

ILLINOIS.

An examination is required by the State Board of Health of Illinois of all who desire to enter upon the practice of medicine, but the law gives permission to license "graduates of legally chartered medical schools in Illinois in good standing" without an examination. The law also differs from most of the laws regulating the practice of medicine in that it does not specify the subjects for examination, but must be on such subjects that a graduate in medicine is generally required to know. The fee for the examination is $10.00 and an additional fee of $5.00 if the certificate is granted.

Power is given the board to accept licenses from other states maintaining a standard no lower than that of Illinois, if the reciprocal privilege is granted the holders of Illinois certificates.

Dr. J. A. Egan, Springfield, is the secretary of the board.

EXAMINATIONS.[1]

Name of college.	Passed.	Failed.	Total.
CALIFORNIA.			
University of California			
COLORADO.			
Denver College of Medicine			
DISTRICT OF COLUMBIA.			
Georgetown University			
Howard University			2

[1] No report of the examinations could be secured from the Illinois Board. In the "Official List of Legally Qualified Physicians, State of Illinois, March, 1902," published by the board, these figures are given as the number of candidates appearing for examination—July 1, 1899, to January 1, 1902.

Name of college.	Passed.	Failed.	Total.
ILLINOIS.			
College of Physicians and Surgeons...............			140
Northwestern University.........................			93
Northwestern University, Woman's Medical School			21
Rush Medical College............................			197
Chicago Homeopathic Medical College			36
Hahnemann Medical College and Hospital.........			56
Bennett Medical College.........................			23
American Medical Missionary College			6
College of Medicine and Surgery			14
Dunham Medical College.........................			19
Harvey Medical College..........................			22
Hering Medical College..........................			12
Illinois Medical College..........................			24
Jenner Medical College...........................			17
National Medical University......................			8
INDIANA.			
Central College of Physicians and Surgeons........			2
Medical College of Indiana.......................			3
IOWA.			
State University of Iowa..........................			3
College of Physicians and Surgeons...............			4
Keokuk Medical College			12
KANSAS.			
Kansas Medical College			
KENTUCKY.			
Hospital College of Medicine......................			6
Kentucky School of Medicine			5
Louisville Medical College........................			7
Kentucky University.............................			1
University of Louisville...........................			
MARYLAND.			
Baltimore Medical College			3
Baltimore University.............................			2
Johns Hopkins University........................			1
University of Maryland			
MASSACHUSETTS.			
Harvard University			
Tufts College			
MICHIGAN.			
University of Michigan...........................			15
Homeopathic Medical College, University of Michigan			2
Detroit College of Medicine			2
Michigan College of Medicine and Surgery.........			6
MINNESOTA.			
College of Medicine and Surgery			

Name of college.	Passed.	Failed.	Total.
MISSOURI.			
College Homeopathic Medicine and Surgery			
Kansas City Medical College			
University Medical College			
American Medical College		1	
Barnes Medical College		24	
Beaumont Hospital Medical College		1	
College of Homeopathic Physicians and Surgeons		1	
Homeopathic Medical College		1	
Marion-Sims Medical College		12	
Missouri Medical College		3	
St. Louis and Missouri Medical College		13	
St. Louis College of Physicians and Surgeons		14	
St. Louis Medical College		3	
NEBRASKA.			
John A. Creighton Medical College			
Omaha Medical College			
NEW YORK.			
Niagara University			
University of Buffalo			
Bellevue Hospital Medical College			
College of Physicians and Surgeons			
University of the City of New York			
New York Homeopathic Medical College and Hospital			
University and Bellevue Hospital Medical College			
Long Island College Hospital			
OHIO.			
Cincinnati College of Medicine and Surgery		2	
Eclectic Medical Institute		3	
Medical College of Ohio		5	
Miami Medical College		1	
Cleveland Homeopathic Medical College			
Cleveland Medical College			
Western Reserve University Medical College			
Starling Medical College			
PENNSYLVANIA.			
Hahnemann Medical College and Hospital		3	
Jefferson Medical College		7	
Medico-Chirurgical College		3	
University of Pennsylvania		4	
TENNESSEE.			
University of Tennessee			
VIRGINIA.			
University of Virginia			
WISCONSIN.			
Milwaukee Medical College			

Name of college.	Passed.	Failed.	Total.
CANADA.			
Laval University			
McGill University			2
Queen's University			3
Trinity University			6
University of Toronto			1
Western University			
FOREIGN.			
University of Erlangen, Germany			
University of Freiburg, Germany			
University of Marburg, Germany			
University of Wurzburg, Germany			
National University, Greece			1
University of Padua, Italy			1
			930

INDIANA.

With the single exception of students matriculating in an Indiana medical school before January 1, 1901, graduating and making application for license before January 1, 1905, all who desire to enter upon the practice of medicine in Indiana must pass an examination before the state board of medical registration and examination. Special power is given the board to establish a schedule of minimum requirements for medical schools, whose graduates can come up for examination. They may establish rules for the reciprocal recognition of certificates. The fee for examination is $25.00.

Dr. W. T. Goot,[1] Indianapolis, is the secretary.

EXAMINATIONS, 1901.

Name of college.	Passed.	Failed.	Total.
CALIFORNIA.			
Hahnemann Medical College	1	0	1
ILLINOIS.			
College of Physicians and Surgeons	11	0	11
Illinois Medical College	2	0	2
Northwestern University	2	0	2
Rush Medical College	10	0	10
Chicago Homeopathic Medical College	7	0	7
Hahnemann Medical College	2	1[2]	3
Bennett Medical College	3	0	3
Independent Medical College	0	1	1

[1] Dr. W. F. Curryer, the efficient secretary of the board since its creation, died suddenly on July 5, 1902.
[2] Incomplete.

Name of college.	Passed.	Failed.	Total.
INDIANA.			
Medical College of Indiana	1	0	1
IOWA.			
Keokuk Medical College	1	0	1
KANSAS.			
Kansas City Homeopathic Medical College	0	1	1
KENTUCKY.			
Hospital College of Medicine	9	0	9
Kentucky School of Medicine	10	2	12
Louisville Medical College	2	0	2
Louisville National Medical College	0	1	1
University of Louisville	4	0	4
Southwestern Homeopathic Medical College	1	0	1
MICHIGAN.			
Michigan College of Medicine and Surgery	1	0	1
University of Michigan	3	0	3
MISSOURI.			
American Medical College	1	0	1
Barnes Medical College	3	1	4
College of Physicians and Surgeons	1	0	1
OHIO.			
Eclectic Medical Institute	2	2	4
Medical College of Ohio	5	0	5
Pulte Medical College	1	0	1
Starling Medical College	1	0	1
PENNSYLVANIA.			
Hahnemann Medical College	1	0	1
TENNESSEE.			
Memphis Hospital Medical College	1	0	1
University of Nashville	1	0	1
Vanderbilt University	0	1	1
VERMONT.			
University of Vermont	1	0	1
WISCONSIN.			
Milwaukee Medical College	1	0	1
CANADA.			
Queen's University	1	0	1
Toronto University	1	0	1
	91	10	101

INDIAN TERRITORY.

Indian Territory is now in a transition state, because of the changes allotting the land to the Indians individually, and will probably adopt new laws. The old laws, differing with the different tribes were not enforcible due to the peculiar relation of the territory to the general government.

IOWA.

An examination before the state board of medical examiners is necessary to obtain a license to practise. Graduates of recognized colleges only have the privilege of examination. The fee for the examination is $25.00.

Dr. J. F. Kennedy, Des Moines, is the secretary of the board.

EXAMINATIONS, 1901.

Name of college.	Passed.	Failed.	Total.
ILLINOIS.			
Rush Medical College	0	2^1	2
Hahnemann Medical College	0	1^2	1
College of Medicine and Surgery	0	1	1
IOWA.			
College of Physicians and Surgeons, Keokuk	0	2^3	2
Iowa College of Physicians and Surgeons	0	1	1
Homeopathic Medical Department, Iowa University	0	2^4	2
MARYLAND.			
Baltimore Medical College	0	1^5	1
MISSOURI.			
Barnes Medical College	0	3^6	3
St. Louis College of Physicians and Surgeons	0	3^7	3
Homeopathic Medical College	0	1^8	1
Missouri Medical College	0	1^9	1
OHIO.			
Ohio Medical University	0	1^{10}	1
TENNESSEE.			
Meharry Medical College	0	1^8	1
	0	20	20

KANSAS.

The issuing of licenses to practise medicine in Kansas is entrusted to a state board of registration and examination. Ap-

1 One each of classes 1893, 1900.
2 Class of 1893.
3 One each of classes 1891, 1893.
4 One of class 1892.
5 Class of 1900.
6 One each of classes 1898, 1900.
7 One of class 1900.
8 Class of 1895.
9 Class of 1874.
10 Class of 1888.

plication must be made to this board, which has the power to accept a diploma of graduation or a license issued by another state as evidence of fitness to practise; or, it may insist upon an examination of the applicant to determine that fact. The board does accept certain diplomas without an examination. The fee for an examination must not exceed $15.00; for approving a diploma or state license, must not exceed $10.00.

Dr. H. W. Roby, Topeka, is the secretary.

KENTUCKY.

The state board of health issues certificates giving authority to practise medicine to such applicants who purpose to follow their profession in an orderly manner and who are graduates of such medical schools as are recognized as reputable by the board. The fee for the certificate is $2.00.

Secretary, Dr. J. N. McCormick, Bowling Green.

LOUISIANA.

The graduate in medicine must present himself before one of two boards for examination, and obtain its certificate before he can legally practise in Louisiana.

The fee for the examination is $10 00, with an additional dollar for the certificate.

Dr. F. A. Larue, New Orleans, is secretary of the board representing the Louisiana State Medical Society; and Dr. Gayle Aiken, New Orleans, of the board representing the Hahnemann State Medical Association.

EXAMINATIONS, 1901.[1]

Name of college.	Passed.	Failed.	Total.
ILLINOIS.			
Chicago Homeopathic Medical College	2	0	2

MAINE.

The board of examiners is the sole judge of the fitness of any one to practise medicine. The law states: "Each applicant must give satisfactory proof of being 21 years of age and having a good moral character, and possessing a reasonable amount of average knowledge in the branches of the science he has desired to practise in."

[1] Only the report of the Homeopathic board has been received.

Any one desiring to practise medicine in Maine must present himself for an examination in anatomy, physiology, pathology, materia medica and therapeutics, surgery, the principles and practice of medicine, and obstetrics. A general average of 75 is required, provided the markings on any single subject are not less than 60. Examinations are held in March, July, and November of each year, and the fee is $10.00.

Dr. A. K. P. Mesene, Portland, is secretary of the board.

EXAMINATIONS, 1901.

Name of college.	Passed.	Failed.	Total.
DISTRICT OF COLUMBIA.			
Howard University	0	1[1]	1
ILLINOIS.			
Northwestern University	0	1[2]	1
MAINE.			
Bowdoin College	38	0	38
MARYLAND.			
Baltimore Medical College	2	0	2
Johns Hopkins University	1	0	1
Baltimore University	5	0	5
MASSACHUSETTS.			
Harvard Medical School	6	0	6
NEW HAMPSHIRE.			
Dartmouth College	1	0	1
NEW YORK.			
College of Physicians and Surgeons	2	0	2
Cornell University	1	0	1
Long Island College Hospital	3	1[2]	4
University of the City of New York	1	0	1
Woman's Medical College of New York	1	0	1
OHIO.			
Cleveland Homeopathic Medical College	1	0	1
Miami Medical College	1	0	1
PENNSYLVANIA.			
Jefferson Medical College	1	0	1
Medico-Chirurgical College	1	0	1
University of Pennsylvania	2	0	2
TENNESSEE.			
Vanderbilt Medical College	1	0	1
VERMONT.			
University of Vermont	4	0	4

[1] Class of 1884.
[2] Class of 1892.

Name of college.	Passed.	Failed.	Total.
CANADA.			
McGill University	1	1	2
Laval University	2	0	2
	75	4	79

MARYLAND.

There are two boards in Maryland, working entirely independent of each other. One represents the Medical and Chirurgical Faculty, and the other the homeopathic state medical society. To apply for examination one must be at least 21 years old, of good moral character, have obtained a competent common school education, attended at least three courses of lectures in separate years, and have been graduated from a legally incorporated medical school. The fee for the examination is $10.00.

An applicant having a license from the board of examiners of another state, whose qualifications are equivalent to those of Maryland, may receive license to practise in Maryland upon satisfying the board of his moral character and fitness to practise, by such an examination as the board may determine upon.

The secretaries are Dr. J. McPherson Scott, Hagerstown, representing the Medical and Chirurgical Faculty, and Dr. J. S. Garrison, Easton, representing the state society.

EXAMINATIONS, 1901.

Name of college.	Passed.	Failed.	Total.
ILLINOIS.			
Rush Medical College	1	0	1
MARYLAND.			
Baltimore Medical College	9	7	16
Baltimore University	3	6	9
College of Physicians and Surgeons	9	2	11
Johns Hopkins University	4	0	4
University of Maryland	33	5	38
Maryland Medical College	9	5	14
Southern Homeopathic Medical College	11	1[1]	12
Woman's Medical College	3	0	3
NORTH CAROLINA.			
Leonard Medical School, Shaw University	1	0	1
NEW YORK.			
Bellevue Hospital Medical College	1	0	1

[1] Class of 1898.

Name of college.	Passed.	Failed.	Total.
PENNSYLVANIA.			
Hahnemann Medical College	1	0	1
University of Pennsylvania	3	1	4
Jefferson Medical College	1	0	1
Woman's Medical College	1	0	1
VIRGINIA.			
University College of Medicine	2	0	2
University of Virginia	3	0	3
CANADA.			
University of Toronto	1	0	1
Withdrawn	6	0	6
	102	27	129

MASSACHUSETTS.

The state board of registration is the sole judge of the fitness to practise. Any one may apply for an examination, which includes papers on anatomy, physiology, pathology, practice of medicine, surgery, obstetrics, gynecology, and hygiene. The fee for the examination is $10; for the certificate of registration $1. Licenses from states are not recognized.

Dr. E. B. Harvey, State House, Boston, is the secretary of the board.

EXAMINATIONS, 1901.

Name of college.	Passed.	Failed.	Total.
DISTRICT OF COLUMBIA.			
Howard University	1	0	1
Columbian University	3	0	3
GEORGIA.			
College of Physicians and Surgeons	1	0	1
ILLINOIS.			
American Medical Missionary College	2	0	2
Chicago Homeopathic Medical College	1	1[1]	2
Hering Medical College	1	0	1
KENTUCKY.			
University of Louisville	0	1	1
MAINE.			
Bowdoin College	10	0	10
MARYLAND.			
Baltimore Medical College	19	7[2]	26
Baltimore University	0	1[3]	1

[1] Class of 1890.
[2] Four of class 1900.
[3] Class of 1899.

Name of college.	Passed.	Failed.	Total.
Woman's Medical College	2	0	2
College of Physicians and Surgeons	5	2	7
University of Maryland	3	0	3
Maryland Medical College	2	0	2
MASSACHUSETTS.			
Harvard University	91	1[1]	92
College of Physicians and Surgeons	3	1	4
Boston University	21	3[2]	24
Tufts College	28	4[3]	32
MICHIGAN.			
Detroit Medical College	0	1[4]	1
Saginaw Medical College	1	1[5]	2
University of Michigan	1	0	1
NEW HAMPSHIRE.			
Dartmouth College	8	3[6]	11
NEW YORK.			
Albany Medical College	2	0	2
Bellevue Hospital Medical College	2	0	2
Columbia	2	1[7]	3
Long Island College Hospital	1	0	1
New York Medical College and Hospital for Women	1	0	1
University of the City of New York	2	2[8]	4
OHIO.			
Laura Memorial, Woman's Medical College	1	0	1
Starling Medical College	1	1[5]	2
Western Reserve University	1	0	1
Wooster Medical College	1	0	1
PENNSYLVANIA.			
University of Pennsylvania	4	0	4
Jefferson Medical College	2	0	2
Woman's Medical College	4	0	4
Medico-Chirurgical College	2	0	2
Hahnemann Medical College	2	0	2
TENNESSEE.			
Chattanooga Medical College	0	1	1
University of the South	1	1	2
Vanderbilt University	1	0	1

[1] Class of 1864.
[2] One each of classes 1896, 1899.
[3] Two each of classes 1898, 1899.
[4] Class of 1877.
[5] Class of 1900.
[6] One each of classes 1893, 1897, 1900.
[7] Class of 1896.
[8] Class of 1890.

Name of college.	Passed.	Failed.	Total.
VERMONT.			
University of Vermont	12	4[1]	16
CANADA.			
Laval University	7	4[2]	11
McGill University	3	0	3
Foreign Schools	0	2[3]	2
	255	42	297

MICHIGAN.

The board of registration in medicine issues certificates granting license to graduates of a legally incorporated, regularly established and reputable college, as "shall be approved and designated by the board of registration." All others must pass an examination before the board before registration. The fee is $10.

The following colleges are at present "designated" by the board as those whose diplomas will be accepted without examination.[4]

CALIFORNIA.
 California Medical College.
CONNECTICUT.
 Yale University.
ILLINOIS.
 Bennett College of Eclectic Medicine and Surgery.
 Chicago Homeopathic Medical College.
 Hahnemann Medical College and Hospital.
 Illinois Medical College.
 Northwestern University.
 Northwestern University Woman's Medical School.
 College of Physicians and Surgeons.
 Rush Medical College.
INDIANA.
 Physio-Medical College of Indiana.
IOWA.
 University of Iowa, Homeopathic Medical Department.
 University of Iowa.
MARYLAND.
 Johns Hopkins University.

[1] One each of classes 1897, 1899, 1900.
[2] One each of classes 1897, 1898; two of class 1900.
[3] One each of classes 1884, 1896.
[4] This list does not indicate that a diploma from a college not named may not be accepted. It is possible that no graduates may have applied for registration and the board never has passed on its qualification.

MASSACHUSETTS.
  Boston University.
  Harvard University.
MICHIGAN.
  Detroit College of Medicine.
  Detroit Homeopathic Medical College.
  American Medical Missionary College.
  Grand Rapids Medical College.
  Michigan College of Medicine and Surgery.
  Saginaw Valley Medical College.
  University of Michigan, Homeopathic Medical College.
  University of Michigan.
MINNESOTA.
  University of Minnesota, Homeopathic Medical College.
  University of Minnesota.
MISSOURI.
  American Medical College.
  Homeopathic Medical College of Missouri.
NEBRASKA.
  Lincoln Medical College.
NEW YORK.
  Cornell University.
  Albany Medical College.
  Buffalo Medical College.
  Eclectic Medical College, City of New York.
  College of Physicians and Surgeons.
  Long Island College Hospital.
  New York Homeopathic Medical College and Hospital.
  University of New York and Bellevue Hospital.
OHIO.
  Cleveland Homeopathic Medical College.
  Eclectic Medical Institute.
  Western Reserve University.
PENNSYLVANIA.
  Hahnemann Medical College.
  Jefferson Medical College.
  University of Pennsylvania.
TENNESSEE.
  Vanderbilt University.
Secretary, Dr. D. B. Harison, Sault Ste. Marie, Mich.

MINNESOTA.

Minnesota requires an examination before a state board prior to issuing the license to practise. Candidates for licensure must submit evidence of attending a medical course of not less than four courses in separate years, all of which must be given in a medical school[1] recognized by the board of examiners. A general average of 75 is necessary to pass. The fee for examination is $10.

Dr. C. J. Ringnell, 802 Andrus Building, Minneapolis, is the secretary of the board.

EXAMINATIONS, 1901.

Name of college.	Passed.	Failed.	Total.
ILLINOIS.			
Bennett Medical College	2	1	3
College of Physicians and Surgeons	1	0	1
Northwestern University	3	0	3
Northwestern University, Woman's Medical School	1	0	1
Rush Medical College	4	2[2]	6
Dunham Medical College	1	1[3]	2
Hahnemann Medical College	2	1[3]	3
Illinois Medical College	1	0	1
National Medical College	0	1[4]	1
INDIANA.			
Central College of Physicians and Surgeons	0	1[5]	1
IOWA.			
College of Physicians and Surgeons, Keokuk	1	0	1
Iowa State University	2	0	2
KANSAS.			
University of Kansas	1	0	1
MARYLAND.			
College of Physicians and Surgeons	1	0	1
Johns Hopkins University	2	0	2
MASSACHUSETTS.			
Harvard Medical College	1	0	1
Boston University	1	0	1
Tufts Medical College	1	0	1
MICHIGAN.			
University of Michigan	1	0	1
MINNESOTA.			
University of Minnesota	4	0	4
Hamline University	2	4[6]	6

[1] Students who have been admitted to advanced standing because of work done outside of a medical school, cannot take the examination.
[2] One each of classes 1896, 1897.
[3] Class of 1895.
[4] Class of 1896.
[5] Class of 1900, 2nd examination.
[6] Failed 2nd time, one each of classes 1896, 1897, 1900.

Name of college.	Passed.	Failed.	Total.
MISSOURI.			
Barnes Medical College	1	0	1
College of Physicians and Surgeons	1	0	1
St. Louis Medical College	1	1[1]	2
NEBRASKA.			
Omaha Medical College	1	0	1
NEW YORK.			
Albany Medical College	1	0	1
College of Physicians and Surgeons	1	0	1
University of the City of New York	1	0	1
OHIO.			
Miami Medical College	0	1[2]	1
Cincinnati Medical College	2	0	2
Starling Medical College	1	0	1
PENNSYLVANIA.			
University of Pennsylvania	1	0	1
Jefferson Medical College	1	0	1
Medico-Chirurgical College	0	1	1
TENNESSEE.			
University of Nashville	1	0	1
University of the South	0	1[3]	1
TEXAS.			
University of Texas	1	0	1
VERMONT.			
University of Vermont	1	1[4]	2
WISCONSIN.			
College of Physicians and Surgeons	1	0	1
CANADA.			
Laval University	1	0	1
Queen's University, Kingston	1	0	1
Trinity Medical College	3	0	3
FOREIGN.			
College of Physicians and Surgeons, Edinburgh	1	0	1
Albertina Medical College, Germany	1	0	1
Non-graduates	5	2	7
	60	18	78

MISSISSIPPI.

The State Board of Health has the oversight of the licensing to practise medicine. Any one may come up for an examina-

[1] Class 18 of 98.
[2] Class of 1871.
[3] Class of 1898, 3rd time.
[4] Class of 1899.

tion, passing which the certificate is issued. The fee for the examination is $10.25.

Secretary, Dr. J. F. Hunter, Jackson.

EXAMINATIONS.

(The Mississippi Board declines to furnish the desired information regarding their examinations.)

MISSOURI.

Any person desiring to enter upon the practice of medicine in Missouri must make application to and pass an examination before the state board of health. The fee for the examination is $15.00.

Secretary, Dr. W. F. Morrow, Kansas City.

EXAMINATIONS.

(There have been no replies to any of the letters of inquiry.)

MONTANA.

Any graduate of a recoguized medical school may come before the state board of medical examiners for examination for license. The fee is $15.00.

Secretary, Dr. W. C. Riddell, Helena.

EXAMINATIONS, 1901.

Name of college.	Passed.	Failed.	Total.
CALIFORNIA.			
University of Southern California	0	1[1]	1
ILLINOIS.			
College of Physicians and Surgeons	2	0	2
Rush Medical College	4	0	4
Hahnemann Medical College	0	1[2]	1
Dunham Medical College	1	0	1
IOWA.			
College of Physicians and Surgeons, Keokuk	0	1[3]	1
KENTUCKY.			
Hospital College of Medicine	0	1[3]	1
Kentucky School of Medicine	0	1[4]	1

[1] Class of 1896.
[2] Class of 1900.
[3] Class of 1891.
[4] Class of 1885.

Name of college.	Passed.	Failed.	Total.
MICHIGAN.			
University of Michigan	1	0	1
MINNESOTA.			
Hamline University	1	0	1
University of Minnesota	5	0	5
MISSOURI.			
Beaumont Hospital Medical College	1	0	1
Washington University	1	0	1
College of Physicians and Surgeons, Kansas City	1	0	1
Marion-Sims Medical College	0	1[1]	1
Homeopathic Medical College	0	1[2]	1
College of Physicians and Surgeons, St. Louis	0	1[3]	1
NEW YORK.			
University of the City of New York	0	1[4]	1
OHIO.			
Medical College of Ohio	1	0	1
Ohio Medical University	0	1	1
SOUTH CAROLINA.			
Medical College of South Carolina	0	1[5]	1
TENNESSEE.			
Chattanooga Medical College	0	1	1
VERMONT.			
University of Vermont	1	0	1
CANADA.			
Dalhousie University of Halifax	1	0	1
McGill University	2	0	2
University of Toronto	2	0	2
Western University, London, Ont	1	0	1
FOREIGN.			
University of Dublin, Ireland	0	1[6]	1
Durham University, England	0	1[7]	1
University of Strausburg, Germany	1	0	1
College not given	0	1	1
	26	15	41

NEBRASKA.

Diplomas of recognized colleges are accepted as evidence of the fitness to practise. Applicants for license, graduating between

[1] Class of 1896.
[2] Class of 1898, 3rd examination.
[3] Dismissed for "cribbing", class of 1895.
[4] Class of 1884.
[5] Class of 1888.
[6] Class of 1881.
[7] Class of 1895, 2nd examination.

July 1, 1891, and August 1, 1898, must have attended three courses of lectures in three separate years, and four courses, if the diplomas were given after August 1, 1898. Diplomas from foreign countries are not accepted, unless the holders of the diploma also has the legal right to practise in the country in which the diploma was issued. A certificate is issued to those possessing a diploma within the requirements of the law for which a fee of $5 is asked. This certificate must be recorded in the office of the county clerk.

Dr. Geo. H. Brash, Beatrice, is the secretary of the board.

NEVADA.

To enter upon the practise of medicine in Nevada the applicant must possess a diploma from a reputable and legally chartered medical institute of the United States which is in good standing with the board. Holders of diplomas from institutions beyond the limit of the United States must submit to an examination. The fee for issuing a license is $25.

Dr. S. L. Lee, Carson City, is secretary of the board.

NEW HAMPSHIRE.

Applicants for examination for license to practise medicine must submit evidence of a preliminary training equivalent to a high school course and graduation from a medical school after four full courses. There are three boards representing the three state medical societies, but working in harmony under the superintendent of public instruction as regent of the boards. The fee is $10.00.

Channing Folsom, Concord, is the regent.

EXAMINATIONS, 1901.

Name of college.	Passed.	Failed.	Total.
MAINE.			
Maine Medical School	5	0	5
MASSACHUSETTS.			
Boston University	3	0	3
Tufts Medical School	3	0	3
Harvard Medical School	1	0	1
NEW HAMPSHIRE.			
Dartmouth Medical School	1	0	1

Name of college.	Passed.	Failed.	Total.
OHIO.			
Eclectic Medical Institute	1	0	1
VERMONT.			
University of Vermont	2	1	3
	16	1	17

From June, 1901, to June, 1902.

NEW JERSEY.

Candidates for licensure in New Jersey must submit evidence of an academic education equivalent to a high school training, be graduated from a reputable medical school after four years of medical study, and pass an examination on (1) materia medica and therapeutics, (2) obstetrics and gynecology, (3) practice of medicine, including diseases of the eye, ear and genito-urinary organs, (5) anatomy, (6) physiology, (7) chemistry, (8) histology, pathology and bacteriology, (9) hygiene and medical jurisprudence. A general average of 75 is required.

The law permits the acceptance of licenses from other states under certain restrictions, and the board rules:

"When an applicant for the endorsement of a license issued by another state can meet, in all respects, the academic requirements of our law; show the required period of medical study prior to graduation from a legally incorporated medical college; present certified evidence of having passed a state examination in substantially the same branches and under essentially the same conditions as the law and the regulations of this board require, the best interests of the profession are served by the endorsement of such an applicant."

The fee for an examination is $25. For the endorsement approving the license issued by another state, $50.

Dr. E. L. V. Godfrey, Camden, is the secretary of the board.

Out of the 139 licenses issued during 1901, 53 were upon examination and 86 by endorsing the license of other states as follows: New York, 44; Pennsylvania, 37; Delaware, 3; and Maryland, 2.

EXAMINATIONS, 1901.

Name of college.	Passed.	Failed.	Total.
DISTRICT OF COLUMBIA.			
Howard University	2	0	2
ILLINOIS.			
College of Physicians and Surgeons	1	0	1
Rush Medical College	1	0	1

Name of college.	Passed.	Failed.	Total.
KENTUCKY.			
Louisville Medical College	1	0	1
MARYLAND.			
Baltimore Medical College	7	3	10
Baltimore University	4	4[1]	8
Maryland Medical College	1	1	2
College of Physicians and Surgeons	6	0	6
MASSACHUSETTS.			
Boston University	1	0	1
Harvard Medical School	1	0	1
MISSOURI.			
Marion-Sims College of Medicine	1	0	1
NEW YORK.			
Columbia University	4	1	5
Long Island College Hospital	1	0	1
Bellevue Hospital Medical College	1	0	1
University of the City of New York	2	1	3
New York Medical College and Hospital for Women	1	0	1
PENNSYLVANIA.			
University of Pennsylvania	5	0	5
Jefferson Medical College	10	2	12
Medico-Chirurgical College	4	6[2]	10
Hahnemann Medical College	3	1	4
TENNESSEE.			
University of the South	1	3	4
University of Tennessee	1	0	1
VIRGINIA.			
University College of Medicine	1	0	1
CANADA.			
Trinity Medical College	1	0	1
FOREIGN.			
University of Naples	1	0	1
Failed to complete examination	2	0	2
	64	22	86

NEW MEXICO.

Graduates in medicine from a college accepted by the board of health as in good standing may obtain a license to practise upon the presentation of his diploma. Any one may obtain a license to practise by passing an examination before the board. To be a college in good standing the board requires for those

[1] One of class 1899, two of 1900 (one of 1900, 4th examination).

[2] Three of class 1899 (one of 1899, 2nd examination, one 4th examination, one of 1901, 2nd examination.)

who have graduated after July 1, 1897, that the matriculants must have had a general education at least equivalent to that given by a high school, and a medical education including four courses of instruction in four years. For those graduating between July 1, 1890, and July 1, 1897, a three years' medical course is required.

Secretary, Dr. W. G. Hope, Albuquerque.

NEW YORK.

A license issued by the regents of the University of the State of New York is necessary to obtain the legal right to practise medicine in New York. To be eligible to take the examination the applicant must have followed an educational course fully equivalent to that required for the M.D. degree in any New York medical school. This requires a preliminary education, such as is given by a high school in that state, and four courses of lectures of at least six months each, in separate years, and the standing of the medical school must be adjudged by the regents as equal to the medical schools of New York. Some exceptions are made to these conditions for physicians graduating before 1902; and, by an enactment of the Legislature in 1902, "Evidence of graduation from a registered college course," may be accepted as an equivalent of the first of these four years, "provided that such college course shall have included not less than the minimum requirements prescribed by the regents for such admission to advanced standing."

The examinations are conducted by the regents' examiners. The questions are prepared by the regents from series of questions presented by the three medical examining boards, and the papers are sent to the board indicated by the applicant for marking. Each board sends its markings along with the papers to the regents, for filing and for review, recommending those to whom the regents shall issue the license to practise.

The law permits the acceptance of the license from another state if it represents an equivalent standing, but owing to technical difficulties in determining this equivalency, the provision is inoperative. The fee for the examination is $25; for certifying to a license from another state, $10.

Dr. James Russell Parsons, Jr., Albany, N. Y., is the secretary of the board of regents.

EXAMINATIONS, 1901.

Name of college.	Passed.	Failed.	Total.
CALIFORNIA.			
Cooper Medical College	1	0	1
University of California	2	0	2
COLORADO.			
Rocky Mountain University	2	0	2
CONNECTICUT.			
Yale University	8	0	8
DISTRICT OF COLUMBIA.			
Columbian University	2	0	2
Georgetown University	1	0	1
ILLINOIS.			
Rush Medical College	3	0	3
Chicago Homeopathic Medical College	2	0	2
Hahnemann Medical College and Hospital	2	0	2
Hering Medical College	1	0	1
Illinois Medical College	4	1[1]	5
Jenner Medical College	1	0	1
Northwestern University	2	0	2
Northwestern University, Woman's Medical College	1	0	1
KENTUCKY.			
Kentucky School of Medicine	1	2[2]	3
University of Louisville	0	2[3]	2
Hospital College of Medicine	1	0	1
LOUISIANA.			
Tulane University	1	0	1
MARYLAND.			
Baltimore Medical College	13	4[4]	17
Baltimore University	10	7[5]	17
College of Physicians and Surgeons	2	1	3
Johns Hopkins University	12	0	12
Maryland Medical College	1	2[6]	3
Southern Homeopathic Medical College	2	1	3

[1] Class of 1899.
[2] One each of classes 1898, 1892 (1892, 2nd examination).
[3] Class of 1898, 2nd examination.
[4] One each of classes 1895, 1900 (1900, 2nd examination).
[5] Two of class 1898; three of class 1899 (1899, two 6th, one 3rd examination) ; 1898, one 2nd, one 4th examination.
[6] One of class 1899, 2nd examination.

Name of college.	Passed.	Failed.	Total.
MASSACHUSETTS.			
Harvard Medical School	8	0	8
College of Physicians and Surgeons	0	1	1
Boston University	2	0	2
Tufts College	1	0	1
MICHIGAN.			
Detroit College of Medicine	3	0	3
University of Michigan	7	0	7
MISSOURI.			
St. Louis College of Physicians and Surgeons	1	0	1
St. Louis Medical College	1	0	1
Missouri Medical College	1	0	1
NEW HAMPSHIRE.			
Dartmouth College	3	0	3
NEW YORK.			
Albany Medical College	30	2[1]	32
Long Island College Hospital	44	11[2]	55
University of Buffalo	40	3[3]	43
Niagara University	1	0	1
Bellevue Hospital Medical College	4	0	4
College of Physicians of Surgeons	129	3[4]	132
Cornell University	31	2[5]	33
University of the City of New York	5	0	5
University and Bellevue Hospital Medical College	33	3[5]	36
New York Homeopathic Medical College	23	1	24
New York Eclectic Medical College	9	1[6]	10
New York Medical College and Hospital	10	2	12
Woman's Medical College, New York Infirmary	1	0	1
Syracuse University	15	0	15
NORTH CAROLINA.			
North Carolina Medical College	1	0	1
OHIO.			
Western Reserve University	1	0	1
Cleveland Homeopathic Medical College	2	0	2
Cleveland College of Physicians and Surgeons	1	0	1
Ohio Medical College	0	1[7]	1
Ohio Medical University	0	1[8]	1

[1] One each of classes 1898, 1900 (1898, 3rd examination).
[2] One of class 1896; two of class 1897; one of class 1900. (1896, 10th examination; one 1897, 9th examination).
[3] One of class 1899, 3rd examination.
[4] One of class 1898, 3rd examination.
[5] One each of classes 1899 1900 (1899, 2nd examination).
[6] One of class 1893.
[7] Class of 1882, 2nd examination.
[8] Class of 1898.

Name of college.	Passed.	Failed.	Total
PENNSYLVANIA.			
University of Pennsylvania	22	1	23
Jefferson Medical College	2	1	3
Medico-Chirurgical College	2	1[1]	3
Hahnemann Medical College	8	0	8
Woman's Medical College of Pennsylvania	2	0	2
SOUTH CAROLINA.			
Medical College of the State of South Carolina	2	0	2
TENNESSEE.			
University of the South	3	0	3
Vanderbilt University	0	1	1
TEXAS.			
University of Texas	1	0	1
VERMONT.			
University of Vermont	6	0	6
VIRGINIA.			
University of Virginia	4	0	4
University College of Medicine	1	0	1
WISCONSIN.			
College of Physicians and Surgeons	1	0	1
CANADA.			
McGill University	8	0	8
Queen's University	3	0	3
Trinity Medical College	6	0	6
Trinity University	4	0	4
University of Toronto	3	0	3
Victoria University	0	1	1
FOREIGN.			
University of Berlin	2	1[2]	3
University of Bonn	1	0	1
University of Kiel	1	0	1
University of Koenigsberg	1	0	1
University of Leipzig	1	0	1
University of Wurzburg	1	0	1
Royal University of Rome	0	2[3]	2
University of Bologna	1	1[4]	2
University of Naples	16	6[5]	22
University of Palermo	0	4[6]	4
University of Parma	0	1[7]	1

[1] Class of 1899.
[2] Class of 1898.
[3] One each of classes 1874, 1897.
[4] Class of 1897.
[5] Two of class 1891, one each of classes 1888, 1893, 1897, 1899 (1897, 5th examination; 1891, 1893, 1899, 2nd examination).
[6] One each of classes 1884, 1894, 1896, 1897 (1894, 2nd examination).
[7] Class of 1896.

Name of college.	Passed.	Failed.	Total.
University of Turin	1	0	1
Junta Directiva de instructions publica del distrio federal	0	1[1]	1
Imperial University of St. Valdimir	1	0	1
University of Budapest	2	0	2
University of Cracow	1	0	1
University of Prague	1	0	1
University of Vienna	4	0	4
	594	72	666

NORTH CAROLINA.

In North Carolina it is now necessary for the applicant for examination for licensure before the state board of medical examiners to submit evidence of graduation from a medical school acceptable to the board.

The board is appointed by the state medical society and meets at the place for the annual meeting of the society and not more than one week before the time for the society's meeting. The fee for the examination is $10.00.

Secretary, J. Howell Way, Waynesville.

EXAMINATIONS, 1901.[2]

Name of college.	Passed.	Failed.	Total.
ALABAMA.			
Medical College of Alabama	1	0	1
CONNECTICUT.			
Yale University	1	0	1
DISTRICT OF COLUMBIA.			
Howard University	2	0	2
GEORGIA.			
Atlanta Medical College	1	0	1
College of Physicians and Surgeons	2	0	2
University of Georgia	1	0	1
ILLINOIS.			
Chicago Homeopathic Medical College	1	0	1
KENTUCKY.			
Central University of Kentucky	1	0	1
LOUISIANA.			
Tulane University	1	0	1

[1] Class of 1877.
[2] This report is compiled from an article in the *Charlotte Medical Journal* for July, 1902. The figures given there include a period of three years. There are evidently some clerical errors in this report or in those furnished the Bulletin for previous years, as the figures do not always balance. Correction of any error will be made very gladly.

Name of college.	Passed.	Failed.	Total.
MARYLAND.			
Baltimore Medical College	1	2	3
College of Physicians and Surgeons	2	0	2
University of Baltimore	0	1	1
Maryland Medical College	0	2	2
University of Maryland	14	0	14
MICHIGAN.			
University of Michigan	1	0	1
NEW HAMPSHIRE.			
Dartmouth College	1	0	1
NEW YORK.			
College of Physicians and Surgeons	1	0	1
NORTH CAROLINA.			
Leonard Medical School, Shaw University	2	5	7
North Carolina Medical College	5	1	6
OHIO.			
University of Wooster	1	0	1
PENNSYLVANIA.			
Jefferson Medical College	3	0	3
University of Pennsylvania	4	0	4
SOUTH CAROLINA.			
Medical College of South Carolina	1	4	5
TENNESSEE.			
Memphis Hospital College of Medicine	0	1	1
University of Nashville	3	4	7
University of the South	0	1	1
University of Tennessee	0	3	3
Grant University	3	0	3
VIRGINIA.			
Medical College of Virginia	6	2	8
University College of Medicine	16	0	16
University of Virginia	3	0	3
VERMONT.			
University of Vermont	1	0	1
	79	26	105

NORTH DAKOTA.

The examining board consists of nine, one of whom must be a lawyer. Graduation from a medical school is not a prerequisite, but the applicant must submit evidence of attendance upon at least three courses of lectures of not less than six months each. The license is issued only upon passing the examinations. The fee is $20.00.

Secretary, Dr. H. M. Wheeler, Grand Forks.
(No report of examination has been received.)

OHIO.

Ohio requires passing an examination before license to practise is granted. The applicant must submit evidence of a preliminary education equivalent to a four years' high school course and graduation from a medical school recognized by the board in good standing before he is entitled to take the examination. The board has the authority to recognize licenses issued by the examiners of other states upon certain conditions. The fee for the license upon examination is $25; upon endorsement of the license from another state, $50.

Dr. Frank Winders, Columbus, is the secretary of the board.

EXAMINATIONS, 1901.

Name of college.	Passed.	Failed.	Total.
DISTRICT OF COLUMBIA.			
Columbian University	1	0	1
National University	1	0	1
ILLINOIS.			
College of Physicians and Surgeons	2	0	2
Rush Medical College	2	0	2
Chicago Homeopathic Medical College	5	0	5
Hahnemann Medical College	0	2	2
Bennett College of Eclectic Medicine and Surgery	1	0	1
Dunham Medical College	1	1	2
INDIANA.			
Physio Medical College	1	0	1
MARYLAND.			
Baltimore Medical College	1	0	1
University of Maryland	1	0	1
MASSACHUSETTS.			
Harvard Medical School	1	0	1
Boston University	1	0	1
MICHIGAN.			
Detroit College of Medicine	4	1[1]	5
Michigan College of Medicine and Surgery	0	2[2]	2
University of Michigan	6	2	8
NEW YORK.			
University of Buffalo	0	1	1

[1] Class of 1894.
[2] Class of 1899.

Name of college.	Passed.	Failed.	Total.
Woman's Medical College of New York	1	0	1
OHIO.			
Cincinnati College of Medicine and Surgery	0	1	1
Pulte Medical College	0	1[1]	1
Western Reserve University	3	1	4
Cleveland Homeopathic Medical College	1	1	2
Medical College of Ohio	2	0	2
Ohio Medical University	1	0	1
Toledo Medical College	0	1[2]	1
Starling Medical College	1	0	1
PENNSYLVANIA.			
University of Pennsylvania	5	0	5
Jefferson Medical College	4	0	4
Woman's Medical College of Pennsylvania	1	0	1
Western Pennsylvania Medical College	2	1	3
WISCONSIN.			
Milwaukee Medical College	1	0	1
CANADA.			
Western University, Ontario	1	0	1
FOREIGN.			
University of Naples	1	0	1
	52	15	67

OKLAHOMA.

Two classes are recognized by the law of Oklahoma. 1. Those possessing a diploma from a medical school recognized by the board, who are given permission to practise without an examination. 2. Those who do not possess this evidence, but who have been practising for not less than five years, who must pass a satisfactory examination before receiving permission to practise. Fee for license upon exhibition of diploma, $2.00; for examination, $30.00.

Dr. E. E. Cowdrick, Enid, is superintendent of public health and president of the board of medical examiners.

OREGON.

An applicant for license to practise medicine in Oregon must file an affidavit with the secretary of the board of medical examiners as to his medical education (a diploma is not required) and stand an examination before the board of examiners.

[1] Class of 1893.
[2] One dismissed.

Dr. Byron E. Miller, Dekum Building, Portland, is the secretary of the board.

(No report of the examination has been received from Oregon.)

PENNSYLVANIA.

The execution of the Medical Practice Act is entrusted to the Medical Council, who issues licenses to those students passing an examination before one of three boards of examiners. The questions asked by each board are the same, except on disputed topics as materia medica and therapeutics, and are prepared by the Medical Council from lists submitted by each board. The examinations are supervised by the boards themselves, and their markings are not reviewed.

The law requires a common school preparatory education which the council interprets to mean the completion of the highest grade of the public school, or a high school course, and four years of medical study, three of which must be had in a medical school. The council interprets the law to mean that the four years must be devoted exclusively to the study of medicine, which in the present day of four-year courses, makes a four years' course a requirement.

The law admits of the recognition of the license of another state provided the courtesy is reciprocated by that state. The fee for examination is $25, for the acceptance of the license of another state, $10.

Hon. James W. Latta, Secretary of Internal Affairs, Harrisburg, Pa., is the secretary of the Medical Council.

EXAMINATIONS, 1901.

Name of college.	Passed.	Failed.	Total.
CALIFORNIA.			
University of Southern California	1	0	1
DISTRICT OF COLUMBIA.			
Howard University	1	1	2
Georgetown University	3	0	3
ILLINOIS.			
College of Physicians and Surgeons	2	0	2
Hahnemann Medical College	1	0	1
Chicago Homeopathic Medical College	1	0	1
Harvey Medical College	1	0	1
Illinois Medical College	1	0	1

Name of college.	Passed.	Failed.	Total.
INDIANA.			
Indiana Medical College	1	0	1
KANSAS.			
Kansas Medical College	1	0	1
KENTUCKY.			
Hospital College of Medicine	0	2[1]	2
Kentucky School of Medicine	1	0	1
University of Louisville	1	0	1
MARYLAND.			
Baltimore Medical College	9	9	18
Baltimore University	7	7[2]	14
College of Physicians and Surgeons	10	2[3]	12
Johns Hopkins University	2	0	2
University of Maryland	1	2	3
Maryland Medical College	1	1	2
Southern Homeopathic Medical College	1	0	1
Woman's Medical College	1	0	1
MASSACHUSETTS.			
Harvard University	2	0	2
Boston University	1	0	1
MICHIGAN.			
Detroit Medical College	1	0	1
University of Michigan	2	0	2
NEW YORK.			
Bellevue Hospital Medical College	1	1	2
Columbia (College of Physicians and Surgeons)	1	0	1
Cornell University	1	0	1
NORTH CAROLINA.			
Leonard Medical School, Shaw University	1	0	1
OHIO.			
College of Physicians and Surgeons	1	0	1
Cleveland Homeopathic Medical College	9	3	12
Western Reserve University	2	0	2
Ohio Medical College	2	0	2
Medical University of Ohio	0	1	1
Starling University	1	2	3
PENNSYLVANIA.			
University of Pennsylvania	117	10[1]	127
Jefferson Medical College	70	14[4]	84
Woman's Medical College	29	2	31

[1] Second examination.
[2] Third examination.
[3] One withdrew; one, 2nd examination.
[4] Two withdrew, one was expelled.

Name of college.	Passed.	Failed.	Total.
Medico-Chirurgical College	47	17[1]	64
Hahnemann Medical College	26	3[2]	29
Western University of Pennsylvania	60	33[3]	93
TENNESSEE.			
University of the South	6	3	9
VERMONT.			
University of Vermont	1	1[4]	2
VIRGINIA.			
University of Virginia	3	1	4
University College of Medicine	3	0	3
CANADA.			
Queen's College	1	0	1
FOREIGN.			
Faculty of Medicine, Lille, France	0	1	1
University of Berlin	0	1	1
University of Austria	0	1	1
University of Palermo	1	0	1
Royal University of Naples	2	1	3
	438	119	557

RHODE ISLAND.

The law has been changed in Rhode Island whereby an examination must be passed in addition to the qualifications heretofore required. The examination is conducted by the state board of health.

Secretary, Dr. Gardiner T. Swartz, Providence.

The first examinations under the law was held in 1902.

SOUTH CAROLINA.

The graduates of the Medical College of South Carolina are licensed to practise without an examination. All others must be examined before a license is issued. The educational qualification permitting an applicant to appear for examination is graduation from a medical school recognized by the board. The fee is $5.00.

Secretary, Dr. S. C. Baker, Sumpter.

[1] One 2nd examination.
[2] One withdrew.
[3] One was expelled; one withdrew; one, 4th examination; one, 3rd examination; two, 2nd examination.
[4] Second examination.

EXAMINATIONS, 1901.

Name of college.	Passed.	Failed.	Total.
GEORGIA.			
College of Physicians and Surgeons	5	0	5
Atlanta Medical College	1	0	1
University of Georgia	4	1[1]	5
KENTUCKY.			
Hospital College of Medicine	1	0	1
MARYLAND.			
Baltimore University	1	1	2
College of Physicians and Surgeons	1	1[2]	2
University of Maryland	3	0	3
MISSOURI.			
Beaumont Hospital Medical College	0	1[3]	1
NORTH CAROLINA.			
Leonard Medical School, Shaw University	2	1[4]	3
PENNSYLVANIA.			
Medico-Chirurgical College	2	0	2
SOUTH CAROLINA.			
Medical College of the State of South Carolina	5	1[4]	6
TENNESSEE.			
Meharry Medical College	0	2[5]	2
University of Nashville	1	0	1
Vanderbilt University	1	0	1
University of the South	5	1	6
Grant University	0	1[6]	1
VIRGINIA.			
University College of Medicine	1	0	1
Medical College of Virginia	3	0	3
	36	10	46

SOUTH DAKOTA.

Graduates in medicine, having attended three full courses of medical study, no two in the same year, are entitled to registration upon presentation of their diplomas to the secretary of the state board of health, and paying a fee of $2.00.

Secretary, Dr. A. H. Rogers, Canton.

[1] Class of 1897.
[2] Class of 1874.
[3] Class of 1898.
[4] Class of 1900.
[5] One each of classes 1897, 1899.
[6] Class of 1896.

TENNESSEE.

For a year or two past the amended law in Tennessee permitted the registration of the graduates of Tennessee Medical College without an examination; this privilege expired June 1, 1902. Any one, whether graduates or not, may come before the board of examiners for an examination. The fee for the examination is $10.00; for the certificate, $5.00.

Secretary, Dr. T. J. Happell, Trenton.

EXAMINATIONS, 1902.

Name of college.	Passed.	Failed.	Total.
GEORGIA.			
Georgia College of Eclectic Medicine and Surgery	0	2[1]	2
University of Georgia	1	0	1
KENTUCKY.			
Kentucky School of Medicine	1	0	1
University of Louisville	1	0	1
LOUISIANA.			
Tulane University	1	0	1
MARYLAND.			
University of Maryland	2	0	2
MISSOURI.			
Missouri Medical College	1	0	1
NEW YORK.			
New York Polyclinic Medical College	1	0	1
College of Physicians and Surgeons	1	0	1
OHIO.			
Eclectic Medical Institute	1	0	1
PENNSYLVANIA.			
Medico-Chirurgical College	1	0	1
VIRGINIA.			
Richmond Medical College	1	0	1
University of Virginia	1	0	1
Non-graduates	25	9	34
	38	11	49

TEXAS.

Texas requires an examination before one of its three state boards, and not before the county boards as heretofore. Any one of sufficient age and character may apply for an examination before either of the three boards. Each board selects its own

[1] Class of 1901.

questions and conducts its own examinations in its own way. The fee is $15.00.

The members of the board are:

S. R. Burroughs, Buffalo, Vice-president; J. H. Evans, Palestine; D. J. Jenkins, Danyerfield; J. G. Jones, Gonzales; F. Paschal, San Antonio; J. H. Reuss, Guero; J. W. Scott, Houston; M. M. Smith, Austin, Secretary and Treasurer; J. T. Wilson, Sherman, President.

Homeopathic Board.—N. O. Brenizer, Austin, Secretary and Treasurer; A. C. Buck, Corsicana; T. J. Crowe, Dallas; M. S. Metz, McKinney; W. R. Owen, San Antonio, President; J. R. Pollock, Fort Worth; W. L. Smith, Denison; G. D. Streeter, Waco, Vice-president; G. E. Thornhill, Paris.

Eclectic Board.—W. J. Bull, Gainesville; Charles Dowdell, Innes; L. S. Downs, Galveston, Secretary; E. L. Fox, Houston; G. Helking, Bowham; G. W. Johnson, San Antonio; N. V. Mitchell, Dallas; J. N. White, Queen City.

The law was adopted in 1901 and became effective on July 9th of that year.

(No report of examinations have been received.)

UTAH.

Graduates in medicine from colleges recognized by the board are eligible for examination before the state board of medical examiners. The fee for the examination is $15.00.

Secretary, Dr. W. R. Fisher, Salt Lake City.

(No report of the examinations has been received.)

VERMONT.

Licenses to practise medicine are issued by the board of censors of the three state medical societies, who are the sole judges of the applicant's fitness, and they may examine him to ascertain this. The censors of the Vermont State Medical Society require an examination of all who apply for license. The fee is $5.00.

Secretaries, Dr. C. W. Strobell, Rutland, representing the Vermont State Medical Society; Dr. E. B. Whittaker, Barr, representing the Homeopathic Medical Society; and P. L. Templeton, representing the Eclectic Medical Society.

VIRGINIA.

Students pursuing a graded medical course may take a partial examination on such subjects as they elect and can present a certificate from the college faculty that they have satisfactorily completed their course, and need not be examined again upon these subjects, but before the license is issued only to graduates from a medical college after sustaining a satisfactory examination before the state board of medical examiners. The examination for licensure is oral as well as written. When the applicant is the licentiate from another state maintaining a standard equivalent to that of Virginia, the examination is oral and of a nature to convince the board that the applicant is fitted to practise medicine.[1] The fee is $10.00.

Secretary, Dr. R. S. Martin, Stuart.

EXAMINATIONS, 1901.

Name of college.	Passed.	Failed.	Total.
DISTRICT OF COLUMBIA.			
Columbian University	1	0	1
Georgetown College	1	0	1
Howard Medical College	5	2	7
Howard University	1	0	1
GEORGIA.			
College of Physicians and Surgeons	1	1	2
University of Georgia	0	2	2
KENTUCKY.			
Hospital College of Medicine	1	0	1
Louisville Medical College	0	1	1
University of Louisville	1	0	1
MARYLAND.			
Baltimore Medical College	1	1	2
Baltimore University	1	2	3
College of Physicians and Surgeons	5	0	5
Johns Hopkins University	1	0	1
Maryland Medical College	3	3	6
University of Maryland	10	1	11
NEW YORK.			
College of Physicians and Surgeons	3	0	3
University of the City of New York	1	0	1
NORTH CAROLINA.			
Leonard Medical School, Shaw University	2	3	5
OHIO.			
Medical College of Ohio	0	1	1

1 The board at its session June 24-26, 1901, resolved : (1) To decline to recognise the diploma of any medical college that does not conform to the requirements of the Association of American Medical Colleges. (2) That those who wish the reciprocal courtesy of the board "shall present with his petition a diploma from a reputable medical college, together with an attested certificate from a state medical examining board having the requirements of our board, and shall pass a satisfactory oral examination before a committee of the board."

Name of college.	Passed.	Failed.	Total.
PENNSYLVANIA.			
University of Pennsylvania	2	0	2
Jefferson Medical College	5	1	6
Woman's Medical College	1	0	1
SOUTH CAROLINA.			
Medical College of the State of South Carolina	1	0	1
TENNESSEE.			
Tennessee Medical College	1	0	1
Vanderbilt University	2	1	3
University of the South	8	9	17
VIRGINIA.			
Medical College of Virginia	33	8	41
University College of Medicine	38	8	46
University of Virginia	24	2	26
Non-graduates taking partial examination	63	0	63
	216	46	262

WASHINGTON.

Washington requires every one desiring to practise medicine in that state to obtain a license after an examination before a state board of medical examiners. Only graduates in medicine are eligible for an examination, and licenses from other states may be accepted by the board.

The fee for the examination is $10, which by the terms of the law is to be used to defray the expense of the board. The board is also required to keep a book wherein is recorded the names of those who come up for licenses with their qualifications and the results of the examination.

The secretary of the board is Dr. J. P. Turney, Davenport.

EXAMINATIONS, 1901.

The secretary declines to give any returns unless there is sent an "amount sufficient to at least cover cost of stenographer and stamps," because the state makes no appropriation to defray any of the expenses of our board, and to comply with the request " would necessitate a personal expense of several dollars."

WEST VIRGINIA.

The control of the practice of medicine is vested in the state board of health. Any one desirous of practising may present himself before the board and, passing the examination, receive

the certificate entitling him to practise. The fee is $10.00.
Secretary, Dr. A. R. Barbee, Point Pleasant.
(No report of the examinations has been received.)

WISCONSIN.

The Wisconsin law requires that those students now entering upon the study of medicine shall have a preliminary education necessary for entry to the junior class of an accredited high school in that state; that he shall pursue four courses of medicine of not less than seven months each in separate years and shall pass the examination before the state board of examiners. The educational qualifications are not quite so rigid for those who began their educational course before 1901. The fee is $10.00, and $5.00 additional for the certificate.
Secretary, Dr. Filip A. Forsbeck, Milwaukee, Wis.
(A report is promised, but not in time to be inserted here.)

WYOMING.

Graduates of colleges, members of the Association of American Medical Colleges, of the Homeopathic National Institute, or of the Eclectic Medical Association, or any college similar in standing in foreign countries, may receive a license to practise upon exhibition of their diploma and the payment of $5.00. All others must be examined for which the fee is $25.00.

It is interesting to note that graduates of Harvard, Columbia, and the University of Pennsylvania would be required to pass an examination in Wyoming.
Secretary, Dr. C. P. Johnson, Cheyenne.

TOTALS BY COLLEGES.

Name of college.	Passed.	Failed.	Total.
ALABAMA.			
Birmingham Medical College	12	0	12
Medical College of Alabama	29	1	30
Montezuma Medical College	1	0	1
CALIFORNIA.			
Cooper Medical College	3	0	3
Hahnemann Medical College	1	0	1
University of California	2	0	2
University of Southern California	1	1	2

Name of college.	Passed.	Failed.	Total.
COLORADO.			
Gross Medical College	3	0	3
Rocky Mountain University	2	0	2
University of Colorado	2	0	2
University of Denver	1	0	1
CONNECTICUT.			
Yale Medical School	16	1	17
DISTRICT OF COLUMBIA.			
Columbian University	28	1	29
Georgetown University	11	0	11
Howard University	9	2	11
Howard Medical College	5	2	7
National University	6	3	9
GEORGIA.			
Atlanta College of Physicians and Surgeons	9	2	11
Atlanta Medical College	3	1	4
Georgia College of Medicine and Surgery	1	0	1
Georgia College of Eclectic Medicine and Surgery	11	3	14
Medical College of Georgia	7	3	10
ILLINOIS.			
American Medical Missionary	4	0	4
Bennett College of Eclectic Medicine and Surgery	6	2	8
Chicago Homeopathic Medical College	20	2	22
College of Medicine and Surgery, Chicago	0	1	1
College of Physicians and Surgeons	21	0	21
Dunham Medical College	3	2	5
Hahnemann Medical College	9	6	15
Harvey Medical College	1	0	1
Hering Medical College	3	0	3
Illinois Medical College	8	1	9
Independent Medical College	0	1	1
Jenner Medical College	1	0	1
National College and Hospital Medical College	0	1	1
Northwestern University	10	1	11
Northwestern University, Woman's Medical College	3	0	3
Rush Medical College	28	6	34
INDIANA.			
Central College of Physicians and Surgeons	0	1	1
Medical College of Indiana	2	0	2
Physio Medical College of Indiana	1	0	1
IOWA.			
College of Physicians and Surgeons	1	2	3
Keokuk Medical College	2	4	6
Homeopathic Medical Department, State University of Iowa	0	2	2
State University of Iowa	4	1	5

Name of college.	Passed.	Failed.	Total.
KANSAS.			
Kansas City Homeopathic Medical College	0	1	1
University of Kansas	2	0	2
KENTUCKY.			
Hospital College of Medicine of Kentucky	13	3	16
Kentucky School of Medicine	13	6	19
Louisville Medical College	5	2	7
Louisville National Medical College	0	1	1
University of Louisville	7	3	10
Southwestern Homeopathic Medical College	1	0	1
LOUISIANA.			
Medical College of New Orleans University	0	1	1
Tulane University	10	0	10
MAINE.			
Bowdoin College	54	0	54
MARYLAND.			
Baltimore Medical College	67	37	104
Baltimore University	31	29	60
College of Physicians and Surgeons	46	9	55
Johns Hopkins University	25	0	25
Maryland Medical College	18	14	32
University of Maryland	74	14	88
Woman's Medical College	6	0	6
Southern Homeopathic Medical College	15	2	17
MASSACHUSETTS.			
Boston University	34	3	37
College of Physicians and Surgeons	3	2	5
Harvard University	113	1	114
Tufts College	33	4	37
MICHIGAN.			
University of Michigan	28	2	30
Detroit College of Medicine	8	2	10
Michigan College of Medicine and Surgery	1	2	3
Saginaw Valley Medical College	1	1	2
MINNESOTA.			
Hamline University	3	5	8
University of Minnesota	9	0	9
MISSOURI.			
American Medical College	1	0	1
College of Physicians and Surgeons, Kansas City	3	0	3
Kansas City Medical College	0	1	1
University Medical College	2	0	2
Barnes Medical College	6	4	10
Beaumont Hospital Medical College	1	1	2

Name of college.	Passed.	Failed.	Total.
Homeopathic Medical College of Missouri	0	3	3
Marion-Sims College of Medicine	1	1	2
Missouri Medical College	2	1	3
St. Louis Medical College	2	4	6
St. Louis College of Physicians and Surgeons	1	4	5
Washington University	1	0	1

NEBRASKA.

Omaha Medical College	1	0	1

NEW HAMPSHIRE.

Dartmouth College	14	3	17

NEW YORK.

University of Buffalo	40	5	45
Niagara University	1	0	1
College of Physicians and Surgeons	145	6	151
Columbia College	6	1	7
Cornell University	34	2	36
University of the City of New York	13	4	17
Woman's Medical College, New York Infirmary	4	0	4
New York Medical College for Women	12	2	14
Bellevue Hospital Medical College	11	1	12
New York Polyclinic Medical College	1	0	1
Albany Medical College	36	3	39
Long Island College Hospital Medical College	50	12	62
College of Physicians and Surgeons (Medical Department, Columbia)	1	0	1
Eclectic Medical College, City of New York	9	1	10
New York Homeopathic Medical College and Hospital	29	1	30
University and Bellevue Hospital Medical College	33	4	37
Syracuse University	15	0	15

NORTH CAROLINA.

North Carolina Medical College	6	1	7
Leonard Medical School, Shaw University	9	9	18

OHIO.

Cincinnati College of Medicine and Surgery	3	1	4
Eclectic Medical Institute	5	2	7
Laura Memorial, Woman's Medical College	1	0	1
Medical College of Ohio	10	1	11
Miami Medical College	1	1	2
Pulte Medical College	2	1	3
Cleveland College of Physicians and Surgeons	2	0	2
Cleveland Homeopathic Medical College	13	4	17
Western Reserve University	8	1	9
Ohio Medical College	2	2	4

Name of college.	Passed.	Failed.	Total.
Ohio Medical University	1	3	4
Columbus Medical College	0	1	1
Starling Medical College	5	3	8
Toledo Medical College	0	1	1
Wooster Medical College	2	0	2

OREGON.
Willamette University	2	0	2

PENNSYLVANIA.
University of Pennsylvania	168	12	180
Hahnemann Medical College and Hospital	47	4	51
Jefferson Medical College	107	20	127
Medico-Chirurgical College	61	25	86
Woman's Medical College	39	2	41
Western Pennsylvania Medical College	62	34	96

SOUTH CAROLINA.
Medical College State of South Carolina	9	5	14

TENNESSEE.
Chattanooga Medical College	8	4	12
Tennessee Medical College	1	0	1
Memphis Medical College	2	1	3
University of Nashville	12	5	17
Meharry Medical College	4	4	8
University of Tennessee	3	3	6
Vanderbilt University	19	7	26
University of the South	33	23	56
Grant University	5	1	6

TEXAS.
University of Texas	2	0	2

VERMONT.
University of Vermont	30	7	37

VIRGINIA.
University of Virginia	48	4	52
Medical College of Virginia	43	10	53
University College of Medicine	61	8	69
Richmond Medical College	1	0	1

WISCONSIN.
Milwaukee Medical College	2	0	2
Wisconsin College of Physicians and Surgeons	2	0	2

CANADA.
Dalhousie University	1	0	1
Laval University	10	4	14
McGill University	14	1	15
Trinity Medical College	7	0	7
Trinity University	7	0	7
University of Toronto	7	0	7

Name of college.	Passed.	Failed.	Total.
Queen's University	6	0	6
Victoria University	0	1	1
Western University	2	0	2
FOREIGN.			
Durham University, England	0	1	1
University of London	1	0	1
University of Strassburg, Germany	1	0	1
University of Vienna	5	0	5
University of Edinburgh	1	0	1
College of Physicians and Surgeons, Edinburgh	1	0	1
University of Dublin	0	1	1
Albertina Medical College, Germany	1	0	1
University of Berlin	2	2	4
University of Bonn	1	0	1
University of Kiel	1	0	1
University of Koenigsberg	1	0	1
University of Leipzig	1	0	1
University of Wurzburg	1	0	1
Royal University of Rome	0	2	2
University of Bologna	2	1	3
University of Naples	18	6	24
University of Palermo	1	4	5
University of Parma	0	1	1
University of Turin	1	0	1
University of Austria	0	1	1
University of Budapest	2	0	2
University of Cracow	1	0	1
University of Prague	1	0	1
Junta, Directiva de instructions Publica del distrio federal	0	1	1
Imperial University of St. Vincent	1	0	1
Faculty of Medicine, Lille, France	0	1	1
Royal University of Naples	2	1	3
Foreign Medical Colleges	1	6	7
College not given	0	1	1
Non-graduates	96	11	107
Withdrawn	6	0	6
Failed to complete examination	2	0	2
	2,436	522	2,958

TOTALS BY STATES.

	Passed.	Failed.	Total.
Alabama	120	13	133
Arizona	—	—	—
Arkansas	—	—	—
California	14	8	22

	Passed.	Failed.	Total.
Colorado	—	—	—
Connecticut	55	22	77
Delaware	14	3	17
District of Columbia	50	11	61
Florida	—	—	—
Georgia	11	1	12
Idaho	28	6	34
Illinois	—	—	—
Indiana	91	10	101
Iowa	0	20	20
Kansas	—	—	—
Kentucky	—	—	—
Louisiana	2	0	2
Maine	75	4	79
Maryland	102	27	129
Massachusetts	255	42	297
Michigan	—	—	—
Minnesota	60	18	78
Mississippi	—	—	—
Missouri	—	—	—
Montana	26	15	41
Nebraska	—	—	—
Nevada	—	—	—
New Hampshire	16	1	17
New Jersey	64	22	86
New Mexico	—	—	—
New York	594	72	666
North Carolina	79	26	105
North Dakota	—	—	—
Ohio	52	15	67
Oregon	—	—	—
Pennsylvania	438	119	557
Rhode Island	—	—	—
South Carolina	36	10	46
South Dakota	—	—	—
Tennessee	38	11	49
Texas	—	—	—
Utah	—	—	—
Vermont	—	—	—
Virginia	216	46	262
Washington	—	—	—
West Virginia	—	—	—
Wisconsin	—	—	—
Wyoming	—	—	—
	2,436	522	2,958

SECRETARY'S TABLE.

While it is always desirable to publish the transactions of any association promptly after the meeting, experience has proven the undesirability of attempting to make use of the August number for this purpose. The record of the very interesting and successful meeting at Saratoga will appear in the October number, with some of the papers, to be followed by the other papers in the numbers following.

The *Journal of the Association of Military Surgeons* changes from a quarterly to a monthly with the July number.

The *Chicago Tribune* commemorates its entering its new building by a special edition, issued Wednesday, July 23. There are 52 pages in the number, hence it has bigness—and several other and more excellent features to commend it.

The Maltine Company, of Brooklyn, has issued a very neat and convenient table of poisons and antidotes which it will be pleased to send to any physician on request.

We regret the necessity of recording the death of the secretary of the State Board of Medical Examination and Registration of Indiana, Dr. W. F. Curryer. He died suddenly on the 5th of July. Were the secretaries of all the boards as prompt and courteous in their correspondence, the compiler of the annual report published in this number would be able to present it without omissions.

The Denver College of Medicine and the Gross Medical College have united to form one institution. The faculties are to be congratulated, they can accomplish much more for the profession by union than by rivalry. The unfortunate part of the consolidations that have taken place during the past few years is the resulting nomenclature. For example: "The University and Bellevue Hospital Medical College," of New York ; and "The Denver and Gross College of Medicine." The sentiment of preserving the history in the names is commendable perhaps, but not convenient when one is required to transcribe them often. Like the acts of parliament, the full title should be accompanied by a brief naming.

⁎

The 7th revised edition of Polk's Medical Register of the United States and Canada has been received. It contains 3,008 pages, giving the valuable information we are accustomed to look for in "Polk". There is no change in the arrangement or make-up of the book, thus enabling us to keep using it without unlearning any old methods or acquiring new ones. Hardly a working day passes but that " Polk " is consulted in this office. Errors have been found, it is true, but the wonder is there are so few ; notwithstanding, on the whole, the information it ought to give is usually found where it ought to be. The few days use of the last edition shows a careful revision and a promise of a continuance of the help given in the past.

⁎

The American Electro-Therapeutic Association promises an interesting and profitable meeting at the Hotel Kaaterskell, Catskill Mountains, on the 2d, 3d, and 4th of September. Dr. George E. Bill, of Harrisburg, is the secretary.

⁎

The June number of the *Southern California Practitioner* is a notable one, publishing the papers included in the Symposium on Tuberculosis of the Southern California Medical Society, read at its meeting at Idyllwild in May.

⁎

P. Blakiston's Son & Co. propose publishing the *Medical Book News*, wherein the medical man may find full and prompt information of all medical books, by whomsoever published. It is to be issued every other month and will be sent without charge upon application. The number for July is the earnest of an attractive and useful periodical.

BULLETIN

OF THE

American Academy of Medicine

VOL. VI.   ISSUED OCTOBER, 1902.   NO. 2.

The American Academy of Medicine is not responsible for the sentiments expressed in any paper or address published in the BULLETIN.

THE RELIGION OF SCIENCE.[1]

By VICTOR C. VAUGHAN, M.D., LL.D., Dean of the Department of Medicine, University of Michigan.[1]

Much has been said and volumes have been written about the irreligion of scientists, and the conflict between religion and science. On the other hand, only a few have attempted to show that the man of science is a religious being and has certain definite convictions concerning his duties and obligations to his fellow man, and certain opinions concerning the development of the universe and the destiny of the race. It has seemed to me that it might not be amiss to briefly discuss from the scientific standpoint certain questions about which all of us have thought more or less, and which certainly are not devoid of interest. I am confident that every thinking man has some ideas concerning his relations to the rest of the universe. It is true that science has no creeds, and I am not egotistic enough to attempt to speak on these subjects for any one but myself. It must therefore be understood that while what I have to say is from the standpoint of one whose life has been given to scientific study, I do not seek to impose my beliefs upon my co-workers or to hold any one responsible for what I may say. Indeed, I could not claim a

[1] President's address before the American Academy of Medicine, Saratoga Springs, N. Y., June 7, 1902.

place among scientists were I to attempt to speak for others on these matters; therefore, while I shall frequently employ the third person in the remarks that I am about to make, it should be clearly understood that I am giving only my own views. In starting out upon the discussion of these matters, I desire to state most emphatically that I am wholly ignorant of even the language of the scientific psychologist of the present day, and I shall make no attempt to enter upon a philosophical dissertation. The scientific spirit, which I hope controls all my actions, leads me to approach this theme in all humility, fully conscious of the limitations imposed upon all men, and especially aware of my own meager knowledge. It has not been granted even to the greatest and wisest of men to solve the riddle of the universe, and the best among us are only seekers after the truth.

It may be that a scientific man has no right to say anything about religion. I know that this is the attitude of many of my scientific acquaintances; and I have read the very interesting paper by Leslie Stephen, in which he states that men of sense never say anything about their religion. Possibly I am altogether in error in attempting to speak upon this subject, and that the time has not yet come when even sensible men can discuss religious questions rationally. However, I have certain opinions concerning the relation between religion and science, and I hope that these opinions will be received in the same spirit in which they are offered, and that is with a desire to bring about a better understanding between the theologian and the scientist, both of whom are working honestly for the betterment of the race.

I wish it plainly understood that in this essay I do not attempt to express any opinion concerning revealed religion. On this subject it is my desire at present at least to make neither affirmations nor denials. My endeavor will be to view the subject which I shall attempt to discuss purely from the scientific standpoint, and to reach what conclusions I may uninfluenced one way or the other by current opinion on these questions. I am not conscious of possessing the slightest trace of bitterness towards either believer or unbeliever, and I have no desire to criticize any creed or to question any faith. My sole wish in writing this paper is to present the views of one trained in scientific methods regarding some of the great problems of life, and, as I have already stated, to show that there should be harmony among all good men who are striving for the accomplishment of the same purpose.

The scientific man has repeatedly been accused of being a materialist, and it is possible that this accusation may find some basis of justification in the writings of certain men who have been eminent in the scientific world, but I deny most emphatically that the majority of those who have given their lives to scientific research have been materialists. This term is one that is especially inapplicable to scientific men for they have learned to know that there are other things besides matter in the universe. The truth is that if the teachings of science could be blotted from the records of human knowledge there would be little left save materialism, and the scientist has been the most powerful foe to all materialist doctrine. Scientists have studied that imponderable, non-material something which we call energy, and which comes to us not only from the center of our own solar system, but from the most distant star. The scientist knows as no one else can that energy is as real as matter, that light, heat, electricity, and motion have an existence as real as that of the molten or gaseous elements that make up the bulk of our sun, or as that of the material which constitutes the crust of our earth. Indeed, it is the scientist who has expounded the doctrine of the conservation of energy, who has shown that energy is not only real, but is possessed of a reality that is indestructible, that it existed always and will never cease to exist. It is the scientist who has discovered the means of utilizing energy for the benefit of mankind, and he knows that the electricity that pulls the car is as real as the copper wire through which it flows. It is not only real, but the scientist measures its power with as much accuracy as he can test the tensile strength of a rope of hemp or a chain of iron. The scientist is aware not only of the existence of energy and its indestructibility, but also of its universality. He knows that not a crystal is formed without its aid and its manifestation, and that no cell in living plant or animal can come into existence or can continue its existence without the action of energy on matter. Science teaches that even in dead lifeless matter energy exists and swings every molecule in ceaseless vibration. Indeed, if we could conceive of matter devoid of energy, which I believe to be impossible, it would disappear into nothing. On this point permit me to quote from the late Dr. Fiske, who has spoken for the scientist more eloquently than I can. He says: "The conception of matter as dead or inert belongs, indeed, to an order of thought that modern knowledge has entirely outgrown. If the study of physics has taught us anything, it is that nowhere in nature is inertness or quiescence to be found. All is quivering with energy. From particle to particle without cessation the movement passes on, reappearing from moment to moment under myriad protean forms, while the rearrangements of particles incidental to the movement constitute the qualitative differences among things. Now in the language of physics, all motions of matter are manifestations of force, to which we can assign neither beginning nor end. Matter is indestructible, motion is continuous, and beneath both these universal truths lies the fundamental truth that force is persistent. The farthest reach in science that has ever been made was made when it was proved by Herbert Spencer that the law of universal evolution is a necessary consequence of the persistence of force. It has shown us that all the myriad phenomena of the universe, all its weird and subtle changes in all their minuteness from moment to moment, in all their vastness from age to age are the manifestations of a single animating principle which is both infinite and eternal."

It is pleasant to note here parenthetically that among the scientific men who have given us this grand conception of a power which pervades the whole universe, which is indestructible and eternal, there are many, like Faraday and Helmholz, whose deep religious convictions were never questioned.

Furthermore, the scientist knows and teaches that man is something more than matter, and more than a combination of energy and matter. He is aware of his own individuality, and he recognizes the fact that other men are possessed of consciousness. It was a philosopher and a scientist who said, *Cogito, ergo sum*. The scientist recognizes probably more than other men the close interdependence between mind and brain, or between consciousness and matter. He is aware of the fact that a sound mind is found only in a sound body. He observes that defective vision or imperfect hearing may produce impressions on the brain which are so faulty that erroneous conclusions are drawn from them. He finds that mechanical injury to the brain may modify, interrupt, or completely obliterate mental phenomena. He knows that disease, through its effects upon matter, may destroy reason; that narcotics, and stimulants may convert the sane, responsible individual into an insane and irresponsible person; and that even disorders of the circulation or impaired action of the liver or stomach may render healthful mental activity impossible. However, when we insist that a healthy body is essential to a sound mind we are not teaching materialism, nor are we advancing the doctrine that mind is material. I am aware of the fact that some years ago Professor Vogt stated: "The brain secretes thought as the liver secretes bile," but I have no idea that this epigram was uttered with the meaning which critics have given it. While the scientist recognizes the interdependence between brain and mind, he is aware of the fact that the latter is not a secretion of the former. While there is a close resemblance between physical or physiological phenomena on the one hand, and mental processes on the other, the two are by no means identical, and the scientist probably above all others recognizes this fact. It is true that he attempts to study mind through matter because this is the only avenue open to him. Mind manifests itself only through matter, and the close relation of the two furnishes a most interesting and profitable field for scientific investigation, but notwithstanding this fact, the law of the conservation of energy, which is one of the fundamental tenets of science, cannot be true if mind is either matter or energy. While brain changes accompany mental phenomena, and the latter are undoubtedly to some extent dependent upon the former, one is not the product of the other. According to the doctrine of the conservation of energy, energy cannot disappear in one form without reappearing in another and equivalent form. Mental phenomena cannot be measured like forms of energy. The scientist makes no attempt to measure thought, as he does heat or electricity. The amount of physical labor which a man does in a given time may be exactly measured by the increase in his tissue metabolism, but the intensity of his thought cannot be measured in any such way, and as long as this is the case we must say that mental phenomena are not comparable to forms of energy. An erroneous interpretation has been placed upon the stress which the scientist lays upon the necessity of having a sound body in order that a sound mind may manifest itself. It may be in the future that physiological psychology may make such great advances that we will be able to speak more intelligently concerning the nature of mind, but at present we must say that we know mind only as it manifests itself through matter, and that mind is neither material nor a form of energy. One of the greatest of living physiologists when asked to express his opinion concerning the nature of mind simply replied: "I do not know," and this is the position in which all of us must admit that we find ourselves.

The man of science has occasionally been denounced as an atheist. Whether this charge be true or not depends, I take it, upon the definition given to the word. The late Dr. John Fiske stated that there are three possible ways in which the universe may be regarded. First, there is no law or reasonableness in the universe save that with which human fancy may endow it. Now and then by accident there may be apparent sequences which lead us to believe that there is some purpose, but soon something else happens which shows that this is all wrong, and that the world is adrift, and is driven wherever the winds of chance may carry it. According to Dr. Fiske, this is atheism, and I suppose that there are no intelligent beings who believe in it. Second, we may regard the world as governed by laws depending upon an omnipresent energy, which is both the source and the end of all things. This, according to Dr. Fiske, is pantheism. According to this view all individuals proceed from, and ultimately return to, and are absorbed by the omnipresent energy. I will quote Dr. Fiske's words concerning the third possible conception of the universe. He says: "We may hold that the world of phenomena is intelligible only when regarded as the multiform manifestation of an omnipresent energy that is in some way,—albeit in a way quite above our finite comprehension,—anthropomorphic, or quasi-personal. There is a true objective reasonableness in the universe. Its events have an orderly progression, and so far as those events are brought sufficiently within our ken for us to generalize them exhaustively, their progression is towards a goal that is recognizable by human intelligence." This, according to Dr. Fiske, is theism.

On the other hand, Professor Harris, of Yale, in his interesting work on the self-revelation of God, classes as atheists all agnostics and all believers in any and every form of pantheism. He states: "Atheism is not commonly an assertion of positive knowledge that God does not exist. The positive assertion that there is no God is commonly the atheism of passion and hatred." He states that an agnostic is one who affirms that man has knowledge of the existence of an absolute being, but cannot know what it is further than it is the power universally present, and, as I have stated, he classes all agnostics as atheists. He defines a monist as one who believes in an absolute being that is identical with the universe itself, and he adds all monists to the list of atheists. After finding that Professor Harris puts so large a proportion of educated people among atheists, I turned eagerly to find his definition of theism, and it is as follows: "Theism, while claiming a positive knowledge of the absolute being and of what it is, affirms that the knowledge is not adequate and complete. Mystery must always lie all along the line where the absolute energizes in the finite, and the revelation of the absolute therein must at every point of time be incomplete. Hence theists do not profess to define how God creates the universe or energizes in it, and different minds may picture or symbolize the action in different ways, but this must not be confounded with pantheism. The thought remains theistic and excludes pantheism so long as it recognizes men as rational free personal beings, and also recognizes the absolute being as distinct from and transcending the universe, as conscious personal spirit, known positively, though inadequately as in the likeness of human reason, however transcending it, and as progressively realizing in the universe rational ideas and ends."

It seems to me from reading this last definition that the only difference between the atheist and the theist is that while both believe in an absolute being or a God, the former says that he is unable to predicate anything concerning the nature of this absolute being, while the other says that he has some knowledge on this subject, but admits that it is imperfect. The truth of the matter, so far as I can ascertain, is that there are at least among educated people, no atheists. The most radical difference between men is their conception of God, and in this conception there are two radically different views. Many, probably the majority of people, believe in a personal God who made the universe and all things therein, but is himself no part of it. He may be likened to a great but wise and just ruler who governs all things much after the manner of an earthly potentate, but with unlimited wisdom. As Carlisle somewhat bluntly, but, as I take it, without irreverence, put it, "an absentee God sitting idle ever since the first Sabbath at the outside of his universe and seeing it go." According to this conception of God, the only law which governs the universe is his will, and with full belief in him man may drink infected water, eat poisonous food, breathe noxious gases, and violate every law of life and still escape disease and death. This God, who is believed to be no part of the universe, may be propitiated by prayer, and by the performance of certain rites and ceremonies, and when thus gratified he may set aside every law of nature for the protection of the individual.

The other and radically different conception of God is that he is the great soul of the universe, and that the world has not been made, but that it is the product of life and growth; that it should not be compared with a watch, but with a plant, springing from the seed, growing strong in stem and rich in foliage, blossoming into flower and finally ripening the fruit. To the scientist God is law, the law of growth and development, the spirit that tends to the uplifting of all things, the quickening power which pervades all nature. The scientist has always held that law governs the universe, and if this be true he cannot in any proper sense of the term be called an atheist. He believes that law pervades everything. It controls the movements of the heavenly bodies; it has established the path of the earth around the sun; it determines the development of every form of life, and in it there is no variation. The God of the scientist does not modify the laws of nature in order to favor or to punish any individual. As the scientist sees it, the object in the development of this world is the betterment of its creatures, and he who labors with this end in view is God's helper.

The most effective way in which we can study God is by endeavoring to ascertain the laws which govern the world, and the best services that we can render Him is to obey these laws. Our race did not have its origin in a perfect pair fresh from the hands of the maker, but it has slowly developed from crude, savage ancestors, and the highest duty of man is to further with all his strength this process of developing the race.

Violation of law is sin and inasmuch as law has physical, intellectual and moral applications, sins may be committed in either or all of these directions. The man who abuses his body, yields it to degrading lusts, and debauches it in riotous living, violates law, commits sin, degrades himself, sets an unworthy example which may influence others, possibly transmits infirmities thus acquired to his descendants, and retards, much or little as the case may be, the growth of the race towards perfection. It has frequently been said that man is the crowning glory of creation, and in a general way this may be admitted, but it certainly is true that even as an animal man is still capable of much self-improvement. The individual who lives in filth from lack of energy to surround himself with better things commits a sin, and he who fails to provide for his family is, we are told, worse than an infidel. Atonement for sin can be made in only one way, and that is by renouncing the sin.

Not only individuals, but communities and nations may commit physical sin. The municipality which fails to provide wholesome drinking water for its inhabitants, and to keep its streets and alleys clean and free from contagion, is guilty of a crime, and the government that permits any class of its citizens to be so oppressed that they can not supply themselves with proper food and raiment is guilty of a criminal act. As I have already stated, there are mental and moral as well as physical sins. There are in all of these directions sins of omission and those of commission. The individual who fails to develop his mind, exercise properly his mental faculties, and increase his knowledge, is guilty of sin against the spirit of growth and development, and the government that fails to provide for the intellectual development of all its citizens cannot be held blameless, nor should it claim for itself the designation of God-serving.

So far as science has been able to solve the great riddle, it appears that the purpose in the existence of this world is the development of its inhabitants, and especially the perfection of its most complete product, which is man. Is it not true that civilized man has reached a point in this developmental process when he has become an important factor in his own growth towards perfection? Has not the creature become an active agent in the process of creation? Is not this the gospel of science? Whether there is to be a continuation of the life of the individual after death of the body or not we may not know, but we are absolutely certain that man's deeds live after he is dead. The individual lives but a span, while the race continues, and yet the growth and development of the race depends upon the individual. Unfortunately a bad man's deeds do not die with him, but are sure to live in some one else. Poisonous plants, as well as those which bear nutritious foods, have seeds and reproduce their kind, and unfortunately it often happens that the bad flourishes more abundantly than the good. Whatever be our theological beliefs, the existence of evil in the world must be admitted, and I think that all good men will agree with me when I state that the highest duty of man is to eradicate evil.

I am not going to discuss the question of free will, but it seems to me that we are compelled to admit that action can be neither moral nor immoral unless there be a certain degree of freedom of choice in the actor. A pathogenic bacillus elaborates a toxin which kills man or beast, but in the production of this poison the germ commits neither a wicked nor a righteous act. It could not behave otherwise. A plant produces a deadly alkaloid, and the beast of prey slays and devours other animals, and yet there is no moral problem involved in these acts. Moral responsibility began in man when he reached that stage in his development when by his voluntary acts he became a factor in creation. If this be true, and if the purpose of the universe be the betterment of the race, it necessarily follows that the individual who strives to lift himself and his fellow to a higher plane of living is a co-worker with God, and, on the other hand, the one who degrades himself and his fellow is an enemy to God, and with all due reverence for the great spirit or soul of the universe, it may be said, I think with truth, that the future of the human race is in the hands of man. The laws which have controlled the development of life have produced a product sufficiently perfect to become in part at least a law unto itself. God has created man and has given him dominion over the world and all that is therein, and the further advance of the race towards perfection depends upon man himself. Each individual, be his station in life high or low, is a power for good or ill, and, under certain limitations, the choice lies with himself. The creature has been elevated to the dignity and power of a creator and this imposes upon him a responsibility which he may not and cannot avoid. Man having been elevated by the process of evolution to this high and responsible position becomes a co-worker with God in the accomplishment of the great work of advancing the race towards physical, intellectual and moral perfection. If this view of the object and purpose of creation be correct, it must be admitted that the science of evolution, or the doctrine of the descent of man from the lower animals, instead of debasing the race, elevates it to a position of the highest dignity and responsibility. The most beneficent, and indeed, I might say, the most sacred labor in which man can engage is the search for truth in the understanding of the laws that govern life, and the best that man can do for his fellows is to teach them to live in conformity with these laws. All discoveries that have been made in science have brought with them at least the potentiality of the betterment of the race. It must be admitted that man has not always utilized these discoveries to the immediate improvement of the conditions of life of his fellows, but I know of no scientific advance in knowledge which has not sooner or later added to human happiness, and improved man's material and spiritual condition. The inventor who constructs a labor-saving device, potentially at least relieves certain of his fellow men from physical drudgery, and gives them opportunity and time for more elevating pursuits. The unscrupulous capitalist may seize upon this discovery and by means of it may throw a number of his employees out of the means of earning a subsistence, but this is man's sin and does not disprove the beneficence of scientific discovery. Moreover, after a period of adjustment, such inventions have, so far as I know, always benefited the race. The discovery and utilization of illuminating gas, which, by the way, had its beginnings in the scientific studies of two English clergymen, has been of great moral as well as of economical value to the world. Before cities were lighted at night even the most frequented streets were often the scenes of all kinds of crime, among which murder was included. Street illumination has done more in policing cities than could have been accomplished by an army of men. As the dark corners have been lighted up crime has disappeared or gradually receded into the still darker recesses. The value of the discovery and utilization of illuminating gas from an economical standpoint must amount to untold billions in dollars. It has enabled commerce to be carried on at night as well as by day. Illumination has permitted continuous work in manufacturing establishments of many kinds, has given employment to thousands, and the world to-day owes a debt of gratitude to Hales, Clayton, and others who in the early part of the eighteenth century were engaged in scientific research probably without ever dreaming of the great benefit which their little experiments would subsequently confer upon humanity.

The history of mankind shows that our race from its earliest beginnings has always been hampered by ignorance and its constant accompaniments, ignorance and superstition. Civilization has progressed by the slow and laborious process of extending farther and farther the limits of human knowledge. In every century there have been a few whose labors in this way have contributed to the advancement of man from the savage to the civilized state. During some periods in the history of the world the number of those engaged in acquiring knowledge and advancing the bounds of civilization has been extremely small. These are known as the dark ages of the world, when the bulk of mankind has receded rather than progressed. However, a close analysis of the history of any age will show that even during the periods of the most intense intellectual darkness there have always been some who have given their lives to the advancement of knowledge. On the other hand, there have been occasional periods of great brilliancy when scientific investigation has been popular and has met with encouragement by those occupying high positions. Fortunately for us we live in one of these brilliant periods when science is popular, and its benefits are felt and appreciated by many. As a rule the contributions of any one individual taken by themselves would be of but little value, but when added to the sum total they may become of the greatest importance. The direct application that can be made of a scientific discovery is not always a correct measure of its value. It often happens that a certain investigation leads to the discovery of a fact which at the time appears to be wholly without value, but advances made in subsequent years may convert the rough pebble, dug from the mine possibly centuries before, into a most valuable jewel. We are therefore justified in claiming that science should be pursued for its own sake, and without any reference to its future utility. Discovery must always precede application. Science must live and labor before art can exist. Pure science must always precede the application of scientific knowledge. I think that all will agree with me when I state that a scientific discovery which reduces sickness and death and gives to man longer life and greater happiness is of value to the race. A discovery which lessens crime and empties our penal institutions is by no means without value. In 1849, a physician by the name of Pollender busied himself by studying the blood of certain animals both in health and disease. He first made himself familiar with the appearance of normal blood, after which he began to observe the blood of man and animals while suffering from disease. In the course of these investigations he took the blood from cows sick with anthrax and examined it under his microscope. He observed minute rod-like bodies which he had not found in the blood of healthy cows. He repeated this observation many times, carefully comparing the blood of sick animals with those of healthy ones. Finally he concluded that these little rod-like bodies observed in the blood of the sick animals had something to do with the disease from which they suffered, and he presented to one of the journals of the time a short contribution upon this subject. However, his labors attracted but little attention. Some years later Davaine took up the same line of work and pushed it a little farther. He confirmed Pollender's observation of the presence of the rod-like bodies in the blood of animals sick with anthrax, and next he ascertained that if he took the blood containing these rod-like bodies and injected it into a healthy animal this developed anthrax, while blood which did not contain these organisms did not transmit the disease. Occasionally there had been a physician who had claimed that certain diseases must be due to minute microorganisms, or germs, but no one up to the time of Pollender had seen anything of this kind, because the demonstration of the existence of microorganisms had to await the development of the compound microscope. After Davaine this work was taken up by Pasteur, then by Koch, and a host of others until it has developed into the great science of bacteriology. Upon the discoveries made by these men and others the whole science of preventative medicine as it stands to-day has been built; and as a result, the last fifty years has been freer from epidemics than any other equal period in the history of the world.

Every time we disinfect a room after a case of diphtheria or scarlet fever we are utilizing that knowledge, the first contribution to which was made by the modest village physician Pollender in 1849. The science of bacteriology, founded upon the simple experiments mentioned above, has enabled mankind to practically stamp out certain of the infectious diseases. For instance, typhus fever, which once contributed largely to the mortality lists of every large city, now is known only in certain obscure and unclean parts of the world. The mortality in typhoid fever has been reduced from nearly 30 per cent. to less than 10 per cent. while in the same time the number of cases has been decreased in a still greater proportion. Under the knowledge which we have gained in the study of the causal relation of bacteria to disease, and which had the small beginnings already referred to, even tuberculosis,—the great white plague,—is gradually diminishing in virulence, the number of cases is decreasing, the death-rate is diminishing, and if man continues to apply the rules for its restriction which he has already put into operation, not more than two centuries at most will pass before this disease will be no more. Twenty years ago there were wild hypotheses and vague conjectures concerning the causes of certain diseases which greatly increase infantile mortality. Man looked for the cause of these diseases in the sun spots, he listened for it in the winds, he dug for it in the earth, he searched for it in the water, but bacteriological study has shown him that the great cause of cholera infantum and kindred diseases lies in milk which becomes poisonous on account of bacterial invasion and the elaboration of toxins. Already it is estimated that of children sick with this disease 30, out of every 100, more are saved now than was formerly possible. These are some of the advantages that have come to mankind from scientific research along a single line of investigation. Disease has been lessened, death has been delayed, health and happiness have been multiplied. Have not these works contributed to the development of mankind?

The discovery of the specific causes of the infectious diseases with the application of the knowledge thus gained has not only stayed the pestilence, saved untold thousands of lives, added in the aggregate centuries to human comfort and happiness, and in many other ways blessed mankind, but it has been a most potent factor in moral improvement. If one wishes to know how bad the world has been, let him read the histories of the great epidemics which swept over Europe during the period from the twelfth to the seventeenth century. The loss of life from disease was fearful, but yet more horrible are the accounts of the barbarous and atrocious crimes committed by the ignorant, degraded and superstitious people. Whole communities became thieves and murderers and perpetrated their crimes in the most brutal manner.

The telegraph and telephone have been factors in the moral improvement of the race. They greatly lessen the chance of the criminal's escape and have in this way deterred many from the commission of criminal acts. The general diffusion of knowledge from the printing press has not only been the means of intellectually advancing the race, but it may be instanced as one of the greatest moral forces which has yet been felt in the uplifting of mankind. Even the discovery of gunpowder and the improvement of fire-arms and other means of destructive warfare have caused man to be more righteous in dealing with his fellow, and war will cease when the engines of destruction become so powerful or can be used in such a way that war will mean the complete annihilation of one or both armies.

Probably there would be no advance of the race towards perfection if there were not the possibility of deterioration. To say that a thing is good is to imply the existence of things that are bad. The incentive to struggle for improvement would not be great unless there was at the same time danger of degeneration. Growth is the law of life, but growth may be in either direction. Science has emphasized this fact, and it has gone farther and demonstrated in studies of heredity that growth of the parent in either direction determines largely the starting point of the offspring. I fear that the mass of even the learned do not yet realize the import of this scientific demonstration. Generations of men die in order that other generations may live, and unless each succeeding generation starts on a higher plane than its predecessor, the world is not growing in the right direction. A proper comprehension of this fact, which has been so abundantly demonstrated in the study of evolution, should become a powerful force in the physical, intellectual and moral development of the race. The youth who yields to his passions and contracts disease is not fit to become a father, and his descendants are not likely to do better than himself, but will be prone to go from bad to worse. The man who neglects his own intellectual culture will procreate sons and daughters who will enter the race heavily handicapped, and the immoral of our generation will in their seed fill the penal institutions of the future. Moreover, the good or the bad that we may do is transmitted to future generations not only in the direct line but through others as well. Those with whom one comes in contact constitute in part his environment and influence his life and growth, and through him his neighbors' deeds may impress future generations. Science has demonstrated the indestructibility of both matter and force, and our actions are, in part at least, forms of energy, and as such they may exist even after our bodies have fallen into decay. Our deeds are pebbles dropped into the mighty ocean of life, and the scarcely perceptible ripples which arise about them will break only on the shores of eternity. Our environment is not altogether a material one. Indeed, some of its most important forces are mental and moral, and the good example of one man may not only cause his neignbor to be better, but may live in that neighbor's children and be transmitted and grow in the transmission through many generations.

Science through the doctrine of evolution has given us some proper conception of the high position to which man has been elevated and of the correspondingly great obligations which rest upon him. The spirit of growth and development has lifted man slowly and gradually from the primordial forms of life through countless generations and through varied forms and has made of him an intelligent, responsible actor in the great drama of creation. This growth towards better things must go on if the future is to be read by the history of the past, but the thoroughness and permanence with which the work is done depends upon man himself. Science teaches that man himself must by his own exertions break the bonds of ignorance and superstition which trammel him, and bear himself and his race to the heights of the great mountain of effort beyond which lies the promised land of human perfection. God will not help the indolent and vicious. He will not clean out the cesspools of filth with which the ignorant surround themselves. He will not stay the plague or cholera nor will he destroy the infection of typhoid fever with which we pollute the pure waters which he has distilled in the great laboratory within the firmament. He will not heal the sick stricken with diphtheria and smallpox. He does not select those who rule over us nor does he place either good or corrupt men in high places. These are duties assigned to the race itself. Man must work out his own salvation and if he fails to utilize the intelligence bestowed upon him in his evolution the responsibility must rest with himself. Each violation of law carries with it a penalty, and ignorance confers no immunity.

The relation of the individual to the race has been explained in large part at least by science, and this explanation furnishes the strongest incentive to righteousness in word and deed ever put before intelligent men. Science has shown in the study of heredity something of the true relation between the reproductive and the somatic cells, and has demonstrated that the former may be altered for either good or bad through the latter. This means that the mortal part of man may shape the immortal part, which for a time dwells within him, and then passes on through an endless succession of tenements of somatic cells. Will the race grow better or will it deteriorate? If it may grow better, and the individual can contribute to that betterment, then somatic life is worth living, otherwise it is not. If we admit that in man life has reached a stage of development in which the creature becomes an intelligent factor in creation, then the relation between the somatic and the reproductive cells may become a rule of conduct and a basis of morality. It should lie at the foundation of all our laws and should influence all our deeds. Shall I do this or not should be answered not by any hope of reward to the individual for doing the right nor by any fear of punishment for doing the wrong, but by the effect that the action is to have upon the actor, and through him upon the life of the race. It may be that this incentive to right doing will depend upon a finer perception and appreciation of the duties of the individual to the race than the average man can understand. The clay out of which man is made may need to be worked to a finer grain before the golden rule becomes a universal basis of conduct, and before peace dwells upon earth, and man constantly manifests good will towards his fellow man.

I stated in the beginning that I believe the average scientific man to be a religious being. Religion, as I understand it, means man's conception of the development and purpose of the universe, and of his own duties and obligations in relation thereto. Necessarily this conception is subject to changes as man develops intellectually and morally. A religion evolved by a half civilized, uneducated people must fall far short of that which satisfies the same race after centuries of growth and development. A man's religion must not and cannot be antagonistic to his intellect. This, I take it, is a cardinal point. Religion must satisfy the intellectual man and each individual must weigh the evidence and reach his own conclusions. Moreover, religion should awaken within us lofty ideals, and we should believe in it so thoroughly that it should control our words and deeds. Man should have such a conception of the origin, development and purpose of the universe and of his duties and obligations that will induce him to faithfully perform these duties, and fulfil these obligations. Unless this be the case religion is without effect upon man, and the conception of a duty without an attempt to fulfil it is a sin.

I am not narrow enough to suppose that science has been the only means of uplifting mankind and improving the race. I have in this paper emphasized scientific work because that has been my subject.

I have spoken to you a lay sermon, and I hope that whatever of truth you may find in it will be none the less acceptable for having come from other than clerical lips. You may not agree with me, but I hope that you will credit me with being a seeker after the truth. We are admonished to seek for the truth everywhere,—yes, everywhere,—and in thy search do not hesitate to enter the domain of thy enemy and if white-robed truth be there, prostrate thyself at her feet, and proclaim thyself her slave.

No one can claim the possession of absolute truth. I will close with the quotation of ideas from three authors. I say the quotation of ideas; the thoughts are theirs, the arrangement of the words is mine.

From Weisman we learn: It is the quest after perfect truth,—not its possession,—that has fallen to our lot, that gladdens us, that fills up the measure of life, yes, that hallows it.

From Hugo: To err as little as possible is the aim of good men; to err not at all is the dream of angels.

From Lessing: If the Omniscient stood before me with absolute truth in his right hand and a desire for the pursuit of knowledge in his left, even with the possibility of falling into error, and should ask me to choose, I would bow reverently and say: Give me from thy left hand; absolute truth is for Thee alone.

THE MEDICAL PROFESSION AND SOCIAL REFORM.[1]

BY EDWARD T. DEVINE, PH.D., Editor of *Charities*, and General Secretary of the Charity Organization Society of New York City.

It has been my good fortune within the past few weeks to visit the scene of one of the most notable triumphs of the medical profession—the conquest of yellow fever. The simple unpretentious laboratory in Columbia Barracks just outside Havana, the little isolation camp at a distance from the remainder of the hospital to which its yellow fever cases were formerly removed, the wire-screen cage in the middle of one of the main wards which has taken its place—the wire screen providing all the protection now deemed necessary—the enthusiasm and the justifiable satisfaction of those who participated in the discoveries and experiments with their brilliant success, their tragedies in individual cases—only so many indices of a more complete demonstration—all these produce even upon the mind of a layman an impression so profound as to be incapable of adequate expression.

Especially impressive are the physical, tangible indications of this great change wrought out in Cuba for the health and the welfare of the people. Two large wards, for example, stand side by side, one built a year later than the other. Both are some three feet above the ground. Beneath the one built first, when malaria was supposed to arise as an exhalation from the damp ground, there is a concrete floor which cost the government $2,000. The theory was that this would keep the malaria down and incidentally would permit a more complete disinfection after the flushing of the floor of the ward. Beneath the second ward there is the natural gravel which cost nothing. It is needless to say to this audience that the recoveries are as numerous in the one ward as in the other and that cases of malaria do not develop in either.

Upon the wall of the office of the Department of Sanitation there is a large chart showing the curve of the cases of yellow

[1] Read by invitation before the American Academy of Medicine, Saratoga Springs, N. Y., June 9, 1902.

fever in Cuba in 1902. Major Gorgas was chaffed by his colleagues in the military administration regarding this chart—as a bit of affectation. Yet, if so, it is surely pardonable. The chart is blank, and for the first time in 200 years the doctors are complaining that they cannot get a case of yellow fever to study. But the mind runs back to the time only a little over a year ago when Havana had already been thoroughly cleaned, even remorselessly and cruelly cleaned and the fever still recurred. That was a period of discouragement such as we cannot now easily appreciate. From our present standpoint it is obvious that it was a stage of progress, for it was a demonstration that yellow fever is not a filth disease. And there followed much more readily and universally the acceptance of the mosquito theory, and the remedy which is its corollary.

You are doubtless becoming impatient that I refer thus at length to a story which is so familiar not only to physicians and scientists, but to the public. I do so because it is one of the best instances that I can discover of that growing mutuality of interest between physicians and those who labor for the improvement of social conditions. The struggle which physicians, and health boards, and sanitarians, maintain with greater or less success to reduce the death-rate, is after all only one phase of the warfare against bad social conditions. The death-rate is only a concrete sign of the existing state of the conflict with poverty, injustice and crime with the causes of human misery. "Social salvation," remarks Mr. C. Hanford Henderson, "must come about by changing men's ideas and bodies and homes, not separately but contemporaneously." To lower the death-rate, involving as that does under existing conditions the decrease of needless suffering, the improvement of our physical bodies, and the elevation of our ideas is, therefore, an integral part of social reform, even its most spiritual signification.

In the reduction of the death-rate the first place is given instinctively to the services of the physician and the surgeon in their treatment of individual cases, and this is as it should be. The maintenance of a high professional standard in the practice of medicine is of the utmost social importance. It is not a matter which concerns primarily the individual practitioner.

For him the only thing necessary to his reputation and his pecuniary emoluments is that he shall be a little more skilful and successful than his fellow practitioners. But for the community as a whole it is the general level of the efficiency, and knowledge, and skill of those who are to be entrusted with the health and lives of the people that is of concern. Medical education therefore, and laboratory research are properly charges upon the community as a whole, and although its guidance necessarily remains in the hands of doctors of medicine, there should be quick public appreciation of every public-spirited act which makes the hospital of greater utility for purposes of instruction and the medical college of increasing breadth and efficiency.

It is both natural and at the same time worthy of special gratitude on the part of the public at large that this body, the American Academy of Medicine, includes among its special objects, the promotion of the social services rendered to the community by physicians, and the maintenance of a high standard for admission to medical colleges, and of the highest scientific standards in their curriculum. The two tasks are interdependent and both will be supported by a larger and more enthusiastic body of lay opinion than might be supposed, provided a reasonable attempt is made to explain and illustrate their necessity and their value.

This leads me directly to my principal exhortation, which is that physicians should take that part of the general public which has shown an interest in social welfare increasingly into their confidence, and should welcome more emphatically than heretofore the cooperation of the public press, of charitable agencies and public officials, including not only health boards, but those who from any point of view come into contact officially with the living conditions of the mass of the people. Such increased confidence and cooperation might profitably extend to clergymen, to employers of labor, to labor leaders and to many others whom we do not think of primarily as interested in the problems of medical science, but upon whose aid the community must rely if the conclusions of investigators and those who practise medicine are to be made the basis of universal public policy.

A friend of mine once wrote in a personal letter that in his opinion physicians are on the whole the most bigoted and narrow-minded body of men that he knew, with the single exception of clergymen. Possibly the force of this severe reflection will be somewhat mitigated by the explanation that he is interested in the manufacture and sale of a proprietary remedy. But whatever basis there is for the charge that physicians prefer to continue the guild spirit in an age to which it is ill adapted, should surely be removed. There are everywhere indications that the air of mystery surrounding the treatment of disease is clearing away, that the individual patient is frankly told much more than formerly of the nature of his disease, of the reason for this and that course of treatment.

I am far from saying that there may not still be justification for innocent temporary deception and for professional reserve, but it certainly is true that the general tendency among physicians whose standing and practice are most assured, is to speak frankly, to assume a modicum of common sense and general intelligence on the part of patients who show these qualities in other relations of life, and to rely for public respect upon their real skill in diagnosis, their acquired judgment as to treatment and remedies, and their familiarity with the literature and with the unrecorded professional experience which together place of course an impassable gulf between the competent physician and his best generally informed patient.

My present plea, and it may be that I am mistaken in believing it to be necessary, is that a similar change should come about in the attitude of the profession toward other groups of workers whose social aims are similar to those of public-spirited physicians who wish to reduce the death-rate and to lessen human suffering. There are many things which might be done by others than physicians if these others could be confident that in doing them they are moving in the right direction; if physicians would offer them the necessary direction, encouragement and support; if their personal relations with physicians were sufficiently intimate to permit the correction of errors before they had become serious and before the workers in question had done something inadvertently to invite ridicule or contempt.

The county and state organizations afford, in part, the machinery through which such increased cooperation might be secured. These organizations have rendered excellent service to the community of a negative kind in preventing loose and unsafe legislation, and have participated occasionally in positive movements for social betterment. It may be that the trade union element, the mutual benefit element, the class interest element, or whatever that element should be called which socialists are trying to develop among working men, and which is so conspicuous a feature of Wall Street, has been present also in these organizations. There is no occasion for criticism if that is the case, and yet the ideal undoubtedly calls for the organization of the professions primarily not for self-protection, but in order that through such organization more effective cooperation with the best social tendencies may be possible. It is a question only of the point of view. The test of whether it is worth while to belong to an organization is not what it contributes to one's income, but the extent to which it increases one's power for useful service to mankind.

The Rockefeller Institute and the Chicago Institute for the study of infectious diseases are made possible by special endowment. Both of them will naturally find useful materials in the experiences of the charitable institutions, the settlements, the hospitals, and certain of the city and state departments; and will in turn contribute materials for the more fruitful prosecution of the work of these agencies. Those who favor a democratic organization of society, and who like to see workers get the maximum satisfaction from their daily work, might conceivably long for the time when special endowment or subsidies for such purpose would not be necessary; when each physician who has the capacity for research and the taste for it might afford to devote some time to it; and when such special labors as require the prolonged and continuous attention of the investigator might still in some way result from the mutual sacrifices of the medical profession itself. This may appear Utopian and unreasonable, but if I were a physician some such future, it appears to me, would be my ambition.

Among all the causes of undeserved destitution, sickness is the most conspicuous. Those who are engaged in the relief of distress, unless they are mere automata, are inevitably led on to the consideration of preventive measures. It is certainly most unsatisfactory to be taking part in the relief of families who are in distress because of illness, and at the same to realize that forces are at work and conditions are present which are undermining the health of others, and leading inevitably to the situation in which relief will be required. The personal indignation which is aroused by the neglect of such forces and conditions would be a valuable ally in securing the changes which physicians well know to be essential. The social force which might easily be developed among charitable visitors, professional and volunteer, among clergymen and church visitors, among trade unionists and social reformers can scarcely be exaggerated. I know of only one occasion in which it has been even approximately brought to the point of expression. On that occasion, the recent Tenement-House reform movement in New York City, an absolute revolution in the conditions under which tenement houses may be erected, was brought about—a revolution so complete that even its most radical advocates within a year found it advisable to modify in many slight particulars the law which they had themselves formulated, and it was found that the public opinion upon which the reform rested was sufficiently permanent and well grounded to repel the most vigorous onslaughts of speculative builders whose private interests were contrary to the public interest, and who have usually under such circumstances been able to accomplish their purpose, however averse it might be to the general welfare.

One of the diseases whose insidious and evil effects are most frequently encountered by those who are called upon to inquire why a family cannot be self-supporting is malaria. It not only increases the hardship of wage-earners, causing irregularity of work and reducing physical energy, but it makes precisely the difference between self-support and dependence for many of those who are already near this dreaded border line. It attacks adults as well as children, and its full effects upon the economic position of the family may not be obvious until many years after the fever has first been acquired.

Is it not then important if we would lessen the burden of poverty, and the need for charitable relief, to do everything that science has demonstrated that it is possible to do to lessen the number of its victims? If it is true, to quote Dr. Howard's language, that perfectly satisfactory proof has been gained during the past few years that mosquitoes "are responsible for the transmission of the malarial germ from the malarial patient to healthy people," is it not incumbent upon us to utilize to the full every influence that will compel the adoption of the remedy which is thus indicated? Is not the time already longer than should have elapsed between the demonstration and the public policies which are its logical result? Should we not attack malaria in every community in precisely the spirit in which the military governor of Cuba acted upon the results of the experiments and demonstrations at Quemados? Are we likely to secure such action on the part of local health boards and physicians if the subject is treated only, or chiefly, in medical journals and in meetings like this? Should not physicians and investigators, the moment the demonstration is complete, take steps to create public opinion; to prepare newspaper articles, leaflets, pamphlets, and books that shall be at the same time scientifically accurate and to the lay mind intelligible? And should we not summon as allies in the new crusade all those who come into contact with disease, distress, and bad social conditions from other standpoints than that of the medical profession? It is generally understood that physicians must be leaders, but the point which I wish especially to make is that they cannot lead effectively unless they are in constant and intimate relations with all these other groups, relations which must be established gradually, and which should be a constant asset, immediately available when new situations of this kind arise.

Defective eyesight, decayed teeth, an imperfect carriage, are from a social point of view, not merely causes of individual suffering and occasions for the exercise of professional skill: they are also causes of poverty; causes of irregular employment; causes of undue restriction in the field of possible industrial opportunity; causes which may lead to physical deterioration in offspring. Such defects as these can be remedied, if the public sentiment of the community is alert to remedy them. Knowledge which individual parents may scarcely be expected to possess exists, nevertheless, in the community, and should find expression through the health board, through the school board, or through some other recognized agency. It may indeed be that the remedy would be found to lie chiefly in the education of parents and in the education of future generations; but whether thus indirectly or by more direct means, the prevention of disease, for which the combined efforts of physicians and of others are requisite, remains a most fundamental and a most neglected public duty.

The most striking illustration for our purpose is a movement which in this country we have as yet scarcely inaugurated, but for which there is everywhere a necessity so urgent and so apalling as to make it difficult for us to consider calmly and with due self-restraint its various aspects and the relative merits of the various remedial measures. I refer of course to the movement for the prevention of tuberculosis. It would not be appropriate to marshal here the statistics of this scourge, or to describe the beginnings that have been made by acts of legislatures and health boards, by voluntary societies formed for educational purposes, and by private philanthropy in the erection of sanatoria and the pecuniary relief of indigent sufferers. Perhaps, however, it is not carrying coals to Newcastle for me to emphasize the rapidly accumulating personal sentiment, which is the natural result of the proclamation that this disease is communicable, curable and preventable.

The transition in the public mind from submissive despair to eager hopefulness, the change from pessimism to impatient demand for fruits of the new knowledge, the slowly dawning public conviction that if tuberculosis is curable it must be cured oftener, that if it is preventable it must be prevented, that if it is communicable then there is a moral responsibility to stay the infectious plague—all this is a public awakening which may not yet be apparent if the eyes are closed, but it is a dawn of which the first faint streakings are plainly visible to those who walk upon the hilltops of suffering. It is not of our individual doing, nor shall we be able if we would to delay it. The problem for us is merely how to utilize for the good of mankind the knowledge that we have; how to extend that knowledge where it will have potent influence in the prevention of needless disease and death; how to bridge over the gap between what is written in the medical books and what is written in the sunken cheeks of the consumptives of whom one may easily now see a thousand or more in a single day if he will merely visit the hospitals of the city of New York where less than one in twenty of our entire number are to be found.

Personal interest in this subject does not often need to rest upon an altruistic basis. I do not remember that I have ever spoken about it in the smallest group without noticing some indication that it makes a direct personal appeal to at least one in the group. Nearly every family has lost a member or close friend, or looks forward with apprehension to immediately impending disaster.

It is this catholic impartiality that makes almost inevitable a concerted movement against the disease, yet the impartiality is not complete, for it feeds upon overcrowding and alcoholism and undernutrition, so that again it is found that from him that hath not is taken away even that which he hath, and that the destruction of the poor is their poverty.

The lines upon which cooperation appears to be possible at the present time between the medical profession and agencies for social betterment are at least four:

I. The promulgation through personal interviews, through public lectures, through leaflets, through newspapers and the periodical press, through clubs and classes, through the schools and colleges, and through every other practicable channel of public education of the idea that the consumptive must properly care for his sputum; that tuberculosis should be recognized and treated at the earliest possible moment; that nutritious and suitable food is essential; and that the physical presence of a consumptive who is intelligent and conscientious is not necessarily—or even probably—dangerous to others.

II. The erection of numerous and not too populous houses of rest for advanced cases—where there shall be every attempt to make easier the closing hours of life, to detect and help any hopeful case, to provide for out-of-door exercise and indoor recreation, to permit occasional or even frequent visits from friends under proper precautions; and in general to create those conditions of cheerfulness and physical comfort that will lead patients readily to enter and to remain whenever the conditions in the patient's home are such as do not permit him to remain there with comfort and safety. Such sanatoria may properly be maintained either by local taxation, or by private benevolence, and they should be numerous enough to make long journeys unnecessary, and to remove all inducement to overcrowding.

Such houses of rest may profitably be supplemented by endowments or by generous private gifts for individual patients to show how much can be done in even apparently hopeless cases if ideal conditions are attained. The interests of humanity and of science alike require numerous experiments even with advanced cases to see whether at least some of the more distressing features cannot be still further mitigated.

III. Well-equipped hospitals for the treatment of lung diseases, favorably situated as to climate, as to altitude, as to remoteness to congested populations, as to scenery, and in all other respects, in order that no known condition favorable to recovery shall be absent if it is feasible to secure it. In these hospitals which may well be comparatively few in number, there should be ample—even lavish provision for essentials of treatment. There should be no hesitation to provide everything in the way of grounds, and buildings, and maintenance, and above all no parsimony as to professional service and no lack of opportunity for laboratory research and experiment.

To the charge that this would be the creation of a favored class of public dependents, it is to be replied that these things are not done solely for the sake of the particular patients who may be cared for, but for the sake of the entire people. We are in the midst of a desperate warfare; and just as we would give every protection to a garrison that was battling for the homes and lives of all, so we would concentrate here upon the human bodies that are struggling with the bacillus, which is our common enemy, every element of strength that will enable them to resist the disease. Every patient saved, or even taught simple hygienic precautions, is multiplied into a regiment for the further conquest of new fields. If we could at one stroke cure all our consumptives, it would undoubtedly be a boon to that particular body of people; but their gain would be insignificant indeed when compared with the great gain which would accrue to those who are now sound and well, and to generations yet unborn, in the removal of what we must class as the principal cause of disease.

Liberal appropriations, therefore, to enable us finally to make headway against tuberculosis, are preeminently justified in the extraordinary position in which we are just now placed. It is not more of a scourge perhaps than formerly, although it is a question whether the increased crowding in the cities has not gone far to offset the gain in other ways. The difference is that we do know more about it; and there is added reproach in every year in which that knowledge remains merely a means of hardship to the consumptive poor through increasing their difficulties in finding and keeping employment and in moving from place to place, and does not show itself in the conquest of the plague.

Whether these more expensive and elaborate hospitals for treatable cases should be built and conducted by the state, or by the local municipalities, or by private means, is a question which may be decided differently in different communities. In New York, where the state tax has passed the vanishing point and become a fiction, while local taxation is a heavy burden, the policy which has been adopted of at least one state hospital in the Adirondacks seems clearly justified, and it is doubtful whether better results from our present point of view would not be obtained if the plan of county support of individual patients were entirely abandoned.

Similar hospitals erected and endowed by private philanthropy, making special provisions for those who can afford to pay small sums for maintenance, would admirably supplement this action of the state.

IV. Besides the educational propaganda, the houses of rest, the hospitals for incipient cases, or, as I should prefer to say, for lung diseases, or for diseases of the lungs and throat, there is indicated still a fourth line of action. We need far more knowledge than is at present available as to the relation between overcrowding and tuberculosis, not only in living and sleeping rooms, but in business offices, printing establishments and similar places of employment; as to the extent to which the disease is really what the Germans call it, a house disease, especially as to the extent to which the cheaper tenements—where, of course, the most advanced cases among the poor gravitate, since with the duration of the illness they naturally move into cheaper and cheaper rooms as wages are reduced and finally cut off entirely, and as savings are then gradually exhausted—as to the extent to which these cheaper tenements are especially infected by bacilli, and numerous other similar social aspects of the disease.

That there is frequently direct infection in business offices, even where salaries are high, hardly admits of question. That in the cities there are many rooms in basements, where the direct sunlight never enters, where ventilating systems, if they are provided, are apt not to be in working order or at least not to be working, and where employees are in too close contact is also susceptible of easy demonstration. But these things need to be made matters of record, and a basis established, first, for voluntary reform by proprietors and managers of these offices, who are often merely ignorant or thoughtless; and then, so far as the evil is not remedied voluntarily for restrictive legislation by health boards or by local or state legislative bodies. It may be also that the erection of high office buildings will be found to have some direct bearing upon the prevalence of tuberculosis. The primary task will be an inquiry as to the number of persons whose usual supply of light and air in working hours does not reach a carefully determined minimum, and as to the existing safeguards against direct infection.

When plans were submitted in New York City recently for new public bath houses, both architects and aldermen were quick to express surprise that they were to be virtually only one story in height. That the architect and the charity expert who had planned them had been determined above all to be sure that bathers should be amply supplied with air and sunlight as well as with water is a cause for congratulation, and that the wonder of the aldermen and others who objected to the plans is typical of uneducated public sentiment in general is likewise cause for regret.

We need also far more experience and knowledge than we now have as to the wisdom of aiding individual patients to remove to a more favorable climate, and as to the means of supporting them at a distance from their homes. The ethics of aided transportation of consumptives are still rather crude and undeveloped, and the complementary ethics and public policy of restricting immigration and interstate migration of consumptives also needs further elucidation. My fourth suggestion is, therefore, that there is need of investigation of certain social aspects of the disease, in which there is fully as much opportunity for cooperation between the medical profession and lay societies and individuals interested in the social welfare as in other lines that have been indicated.

In New York City, having before us the extraordinary success of the Tenement House Committee of the Charity Organization Society, it has now been decided to inaugurate a committee on the prevention of tuberculosis in the same society, in which there shall be ample representation of physicians, of men of business experience, and of men and women who have been identified with other movements for social reform, thus affording, it is hoped—we are too near the beginning for any more positive statement—that combination of scientific knowledge, of medical experience, of business efficiency, and of social enthusiasm that will permit some real contribution to the application of our existing knowledge to our recognized existing evils.

I may refer to one other subject on which the next step in reform appears to await an impetus from outside the medical profession. The practice of midwifery is virtually without regulation, except in five or six states, chiefly for the reason that physicians are reluctant to assume any responsibility for it and have apparently cherished the hope that it would either die out altogether from natural causes or that public sentiment would eventually call for legislative prohibition.

In a period of six years, from '91 to '96, inclusive, there appears in New York City to have been a slight decrease, probably about three per cent., in the number of cases attended by midwives. It is known, however, that many cases are not reported. It has been estimated again that in 1898, in New York City, midwives attended 45 per cent. of the births reported; that in 1899 the percentage remained the same, while in 1900 it increased to 49. Whichever of the two periods may afford the more accurate indication of present tendencies, it would appear that the midwife in New York City, at least, is being only very slowly, if at all, displaced by the physician. It is possible that the proportion of midwifery cases is merely kept up by the inflow of immigration. In confirmation of this view is the fact that a very large proportion of the cases occurring in the families known to the United Hebrew Charities are now treated by the physicians of a free lying-in hospital whereas only seven years ago nearly all were attended by midwives.

That the midwives are in large part totally ignorant of aseptic treatment, that many cases result fatally because of their lack of knowledge and skill, and that a very much larger number of women suffer more or less permanent injury from such defects, are incontrovertible facts. Whether the remedy lies in a prohibition of midwifery; in an increase in the amount of free treatment provided by charitable institutions; in an increase in the number of women physicians; in the official regulation and licensing of midwifery; or in the *laissez faire* policy of the present, is a problem in which social considerations are quite as important as those which are of direct professional importance to physicians.

Assuming that the number of deaths from puerperal fever is a trustworthy index of the comparative efficiency of physicians and midwives, I have caused an investigation to be made as to who was responsible for the treatment in each of the 46 deaths from this cause in the first three months of the present year in Manhattan Borough, New York City. I was surprised to find that in 21 of these cases the patient was under the exclusive charge of a physician, while in 21 cases, an exactly equal number, the patient was originally attended by a midwife, although in most of the latter cases a physician was called after the fever had developed. Eighteen of these 46 patients died in hospitals, all of these having been treated outside by physicians and removed to the hospital shortly before death. In two cases it was probable that abortion had been produced by unknown persons. In four cases the physician believed that infection was due to the nurse employed by the patient, who was ignorant or did not observe instructions. In two cases physicians had reported that midwives had been employed where investigation showed the statement to have been incorrect. It is probable that the official records at the department of health do not show all deaths from puerperal fever, since the opinion has been freely expressed that there are cases in which death occurs from this cause, but is reported to have occurred from some other cause. These statistics, although the period may be too brief to justify any generalization, point toward the conclusion that infection resulting in death occurs as frequently in the practice of physicians as in that of midwives, and they point also towards the conclusion that the regulation of midwifery and the licensing of such as have shown their competence would probably lessen or eliminate the existing evils resulting from their practice. If so, the fact that the use of the midwife is a long established custom among immigrants of several nationalities, the lower expense and the wide-spread preference for employing the services of women in this capacity would become decisive in deciding what legislation should be enacted.

Mr. Ralph Folks, who is one of the workers of the Charity Organization Society, and who has made the investigation above mentioned, will present in another place a fuller statement of the information which he has gained concerning midwifery in New York City and the remedies proposed for its abuses. My present purpose is not to present an argument in favor of any particular policy, but to suggest another illustration of a class of subjects on which frank and sympathetic cooperation might be advantageous to physicians and useful to the community.

Other illustrations of the advantage to society from such cooperation as I have tried to describe, lie at hand if they were needed. Twice in as many years the physicians of New York have joined with the reformers, the charity workers, the clergymen, the public press, and a host of good citizens to defend the charitable institutions of the state from what they believe to be vicious political attack, and the acquaintance and common experience gained in those controversies are likely to be of great service in other—let us hope more agreeable—common tasks in the future. Physicians in public office, not only in health and sanitary department, but in such allied branches of the public service as street cleaning, in administrative positions connected with charitable and correctional work, in public education and in legislative bodies give everywhere evidence of the value of medical training and experience as a preparation for such service.

As leaders of public opinion through the medical journals, through the transactions of learned societies, through public addresses, through letters to the newspapers and, especially, as I have indicated, through personal contact with men and women who have the special genius and the peculiar qualities that fit them to act as leaders, physicians count for more now than at any previous epoch.

Lest in the emphasis which I have placed upon the value of this social service and the need for more of it, I be misunderstood, permit me in closing to recur to the belief that the ordinary daily routine of a physician's private practice has also the highest social importance. I suppose that Mr. Morgan in his gift of a lying-in hospital and Mr. Carnegie in his gift of libraries, do much to promote social welfare, as many other business men might either by gifts, or by introducing some changes into their relations with their own employees. And yet if we had to choose between their contributions to human progress made in the daily conduct of their own industries and such occasional and incidental acts of altruism, we would scarcely hesitate to choose the former. It is preeminently so of the medical profession. The legitimate call of public duty will never make such demands upon individuals, and will never be addressed to so large a proportion of the profession, as to obscure the call of the individual who, whether for pay or merely in the extremity of his need, demands attention. The plea for increased cooperation confidently assumes that there will result from it not less but greater usefulness to the individual patient.

DISCUSSION.

Dr. D. L. Brower,[1] of Chicago:

Mr. President and Gentlemen of the Academy:—I am delighted to be here and to have heard this most excellent address of the secretary of the Charity Organization Society of New York City. With its conclusions in the main we must all agree, and I congratulate the author upon having expressed them in such clear language. I also desire to express my approbation of that part of the report of the Council advising the admission of such distinguished and educated laymen to associate fellowship in this organization. We belong to a profession that has been in all ages characterized by a most self-sacrificing spirit. With one breath we ask our Maker to give us our daily bread, and with the very next breath we teach the people preventive medicine. Great epidemics, as you all know, are no longer possible, for members of the medical profession have sought out the cause and have taught the people prevention. The plague which devastated Europe in the middle ages. depopulating almost large cities, makes no foothold now anywhere in civilized communities. Insanity, at one time regarded as either a diabolical possession on the one hand, or as a special evidence of Divine disfavor on the other, no longer exhibits itself publicly. Everywhere throughout the land are found institutions for their treatment.

I delight to belong to such a profession, and the expansion of this great work as suggested by the author, meets with my hearty approval. Much is being done through the efforts of this profession in teaching the court criminal jurisprudence, and in almost every community methods are being carried out for the reform of defective children. Every effort is being made by us for bettering the homes of our patients. No physician ever enters a household I think without giving instruction to the people as to the necessity of better ventilation, better preparation of food, and such things mentioned by the author. Regarding the question of deaths in midwifery service, and the service of New York physicians, I was very much surprised to hear his statements. Of course, he has the facts and I have not. In Chicago we are making special effort for the education of these midwives, for elevating their standard and requiring of them adequate education. We have there a great institution that furnishes to these women the necessary amount of medical teaching free from competent hands.

As to the dissemination of knowledge to prevent disease, I have been for many years an advocate of public lectures by doctors upon things pertaining to sanitary science. Some of my confrères think it a gross violation of our code of ethics, and a mere scheme for advertising; but, I believe it is the duty of the physician to do so at assemblies such as this and the greater one which will follow in a few days, where the effort should be made to give lectures to the laity so that each community in which the American Academy of Medicine finds a resting place shall be better acquainted with the great subject of sanitary science after we have left them than when we arrived. In my

[1] Not revised by the speaker.

own State of Illinois, it has been the rule for many years that at least one of the public addresses should be presented in such a way as to enlighten the laity of that community. I have never thought it any violation of the code of ethics from time to time as opportunity presented itself to me, by interviews with newspaper reporters, or otherwise, to give such information as I thought desirable upon common topics pertaining to this great question of preventive medicine. I think that by lectures and newspaper articles we can carry on still more energetically the great work of preventive medicine.

Dr. J. T. Searcy, Tuscaloosa, Ala.:

Dr. Devine began his paper by an allusion to the recent sanitary work in the city of Havana. Those of us, who come from the southern section of the country, have felt ourselves intensely interested in the success of that work, particularly in the ridding of the city of Havana of yellow fever. I like to hear the complimentary remarks Dr. Devine has made of the methods adopted, particularly because Dr. Reed, who was first detailed to make the experiment, once resided in my State, and Major Gorgas, who conducted the sanitation of Havana, is a personal friend from my town. I also have corresponded with Dr. Findlay, a prominent Scotch physician of Havana, who a number of years ago first promulgated " the mosquito theory " of yellow-fever infection.

I rise particularly to thank Dr. Devine for his highly suggestive address. His appeal to the profession that we get more and more into the confidence of the good people, who, along with him, in a broad and charitable way, are working for human welfare, will no doubt have its good effect. His paper shows that he himself has certainly been in such association. It is fully abreast with many advanced views of the medical profession, which tend to public welfare. It is to be hoped that all our governments will more and more recognize by proper legislation things of this kind, which are of the highest importance. The medical profession has always had as one of its objects general sociologic improvement. The removal of smallpox and of tuberculosis are not alone prominent objects, but now, as a live matter, is the abatement of yellow fever and malaria.

I am pleased to have heard the Doctor's paper, and have no doubt its effect will be to take us increasingly into the confidence and assistance of such workers as he, and will make us have closer relationship with the methods that are employed.

Dr. H. A. Tomlinson, St. Peter, Minn :

It is unpleasant and an ungracious task always, in a discussion of this kind, to call attention to the difficulties in the way, and yet it ought to be done. While we sympathize with the enthusiasm of the reader of the paper, and are in accord with him in our desire to see the ends accomplished he so earnestly advocates, we cannot forget that there are hindrances to such an association of efforts as he describes, and obstructions which are inherent in the widely divergent points of view of the profession and the laity concerning the nature of the work in which he wants them to unite. Those of us who graduated in medicine more than ten years ago, remember the valedictory by a member of the faculty on commencement day, which was largely made up of a description of the duties and privileges of the physician as a member of the community. The graduating class was always inspired and its members firmly resolved to be true to the responsibilities of their position in the community. I believe that I only voice the sentiments of those who hear me, when I say that our disappointment has been as great as our early enthusiasm was boundless. Not because we have been unwilling to do, but for the reason that the community would not let us do, and if we became insistent, accused us of unworthy motives. It takes us a long time to learn that nothing in the shape of reform or advancement in social conduct can result until public opinion is educated to the point of demanding it. We fail to remember that reform is accomplished by evolution, and not by revolution.

The writer of the paper in eulogizing the accomplishments of the army medical corps in Cuba, does not take into consideration what might have been the result if the Governor-General had been a layman, merely a military man, instead of a medical man. I am disposed to doubt if the result would have been the same. Then too, the personality of the Governor-General had something to do with the result. Such men as General "Doctor" Wood are not common.

At one time in my life I was very enthusiastic about what might be accomplished by the medical profession working with the community for its sanitary and social benefit, but my experience has been unfortunate. The rock upon which this community of effort has split, has always been the absolute assurance of the lay members of the community of their competence to determine how the medical man's work should be done. Therefore, if medical men join in such work they will save the community much trouble and themselves much heart-burning if they recognize that they must work with the layman, in the layman's own way, and determine all questions from the layman's standpoint.

From my own experience, I cannot speak with entire confidence of the advantage of newspaper exploitations of such undertakings. I have never known of a newspaper report of a medical or sanitary undertaking that was not the most completely distorted and twisted account possible. That part of the affair which is most trivial and unimportant is always made the most conspicuous, while the essence of the proceedings and the principles involved are ignored entirely. I believe, however, that much can be done by the publication and distribution of tracts, provided we do not attempt to do too much. Communities are apt to be mentally and morally lazy, and we must not expect the regeneration of mankind in from thirty to sixty days. Therefore, our efforts should be along simple lines; the instruction rudimentary and largely suggestive. Active effort on the part of a professional man always excites resentment.

The effort of the medical profession to aid in the attempt to control the spread of tuberculosis is an illustration, as well as what has been done in the past to try to do away with the physical ills which are connected with the social evil. The presence of tuberculosis in the family is looked upon very much as is insanity. It stigmatizes. Then too, in the education of public opinion we constantly run up against the influence of the personal equation. It is very difficult to get out of the mind of the individual the belief that his aggrandizement and the welfare of the community mean the same thing. It is very hard to get people to believe that there is anything beyond their own horizon. And yet if any advance is to be made it must be by the elimination of the personal equation and the thorough appreciation of the fact that the convenience or aggrandizement of the individual can not be allowed to stand in the way of the welfare of the community as a whole. Because of this short-sightedness and heedless selfishness, the existence of the plague has been denied in San Francisco. The common failure to appreciate indirect influence is one of the greatest stumbling blocks in the way of a general understanding of the economic aspect of good health in the community. The preservation of the health of the head of the family and its growing members, means not only the welfare of the family, but also money saved to the community, and the gradual elimination of the necessity for such expenditures; besides the increase in individual and collective efficiency.

The writer of the paper has so fully covered that part of the subject relating to methods that I know of nothing more to suggest.

I believe that medical men can accomplish more for the welfare of the community by not going outside of their regular path of duty, and that they can make their influence fully felt by taking advantage of those opportunities which their intimate association with the family gives to impress in concrete form the lessons which every-day experience teaches. I do not believe they will do any good on the public rostrum. Our human nature prompts us to discredit the motives of others, while the newspapers and those people whose business would be interfered with by following our advice, will accuse us of advertising.

I wish to deny that the commercial spirit exists in medical organizations. The medical profession is not a trades union, nor is it organized for its own aggrandizement. The object of all its organizations is mutual instruction and criticism. I am sorry to have to admit that efforts to accomplish commercial organization have been made, but I am glad to be able to say that they have always failed.

Dr. Walter L. Pyle, of Philadelphia :

I think the daily newspaper is the most valuable means for the general dissemination of knowledge relative to preventive medicine, but I do not think the ends can be best accomplished by a personal interview filtered through the pen of a lay reporter. Every large newspaper or press association should have a medical editor to pass upon medical matters of direct interest to the public and to write anonymous editorials and special articles on important sanitary and hygienic subjects. Emphasis should be placed upon the monetary value to the community of proper sanitary laws. Incidentally, this same editor might act as censor and eliminate many of the vile medical advertisements which, unfortunately, appear even in our best journals.

Dr. A. L. Benedict, of Buffalo :

It has sometimes been taken for granted that the members of the medical profession were pushing themselves into sociologic matters up to the very limit of officiousness, and I am glad to learn from Dr. Devine that the public take an opposite view. There are three ways in which medical matters can be brought before the laity : by public speaking; through the press; and, by word of mouth. As to public meetings for the dissemination of medical knowledge, it seems to me they are liable to be the most objectionable. A society, for instance, is formed for the dissemination of knowledge of tuberculosis. It is difficult, in any such society, to reach the kind of laity that most need our teaching, and difficult to exclude the physicians who say they are acting for the public, but who are really striving to advertise themselves.

As to word of mouth, we are all daily coming in contact with hundreds of patients and their friends through whom we can disseminate a great deal of medical common sense. Without going into personalities I make it a rule to teach patients that the man who says a person is threatened with typhoid fever, but that he will break up the fever, is a fakir. The intelligent laity are beginning to learn that quack medicines make business for the regular physician; that, as a rule, no serious case can be well treated without a diagnosis and that the latter must usually depend on a physical examination ; that it is something of the nature of a miracle for an ignorant man to be a skilful physician. I agree with the previous speakers that the daily public press is not quite the best means for disseminating medical or hygienic knowledge, as it deals with matters of immediate importance and interest. It is the weekly and monthly press that will give the best results, because opportunity is given for the presentation of carefully digested thought and the author does his own writing, instead of having his off-hand statements reported by one not familiar with the subject, and trained, by all the traditions of his profession, to interest and attract rather than to teach. Unfortunately, the popular and even semi-scientific lay magazines can not devote a great deal of space to medical matters and, as in fiction and everything else, they are influenced too much by the name of the author and not enough by the abstract excellence of the article, but the same obstacle necessarily impedes the rapid course of any reform.

Dr. Rosa Englemann, of Chicago :

It seems to me that one part of the subject has been neglected ; *viz.*, the introduction of these questions into the public schools by people fitted for this purpose; that is, by physicians. Hygiene is taught in the public schools by laymen and largely conducted on the lines of prohibition of alcoholism, and perhaps the most essential subjects of hygiene and of medicine are omitted. I think the children should be taught in the school something of the communicability and prevention of disease. We who work upon the health boards and in the slums know that there is an absolute indifference in this direction. The children would thus also take these matters to the ignorant parents.

Dr. P. Maxwell Foshay,[1] of Cleveland:

There seems to have been one point overlooked that occurs to me. I agree with the previous speakers that it is neither dignified nor becoming for individual medical men to appear in the public press as advisers of the public in matters of this sort, but I do believe that it is the province of the organized profession to deal with such problems in that way. The newspaper is the one avenue which reaches almost every citizen. If our medical societies would do, as I believe every local medical society should do, have a committee on public health to consider epidemics or matters of less importance as they claim attention, whose deliberations shall appear over the name of the committee on health of such and such medical society, much good would be accomplished. The signatures may or may not be added to the paper as seems best. In that way, the objection to the person is entirely eliminated, and at the same time the profession can make use of his knowledge and bring it into contact with the public in general. I believe that as the medical profession becomes better organized, and as each medical society has working committees, committees something like our political bodies have—House of Representatives and Senate—committees that will undertake this work year after year in a dignified manner, and give reports signed by the public health committee of such and such medical society, we can be sure that when the newspapers realize that the matters come with the endorsement of the medical profession that they will publish them without reducing the number of lines.

Dr. W. S. Hall, of Chicago:

In Chicago and its suburbs there are hundreds upon hundreds of mothers' clubs organized under the auspices of various charity and church organizations, and it is customary to invite, during the year, several medical men. One will be invited to talk to the mothers about "The Care of Young Children;" another about "What to do till the Doctor Comes," and "How to Equip a Medicine Chest," or about "Bandages and Burns." I think that is one method of giving instruction which no medical man is justified in setting aside. He ought to drop everything and go and talk to these people.

Dr. L. Connor:

Something may be learned by a little illustration of the sort of teaching that the people get when we observe that Dr. Knopf comes in this morning and opens all the windows, and that then Dr. Marcy comes in pretty soon and shuts them all down.

[1] Not revised by the speaker.

All the trouble I ever had in the world was through the attempt to make some part of the world better. This, I think, is the experience of all. Until you see in men the spirit of wanting to be better they resent the effort. Another thing of importance is that if you think it is wise to teach any part of the community, it is better to *do* those things yourself. What a man does and not what he says counts. The teachers who have moulded my own life have been those who tried to do what they taught me to do. When this profession does that it will stand for more than now. It would be recognized then as it is not recognized now. There is one thing about this public newspaper business: How is an ignorant person (and the most of the people are ignorant in the sense of being unable to appreciate medical science questions) to distinguish between the scientific fellow who wants only to help the community and the individual who wants to enrich himself at the expense of others? If that can be made clear, Dr. Foshay's suggestion may be a solution, although it is difficult to say until the method has been tried. For myself, I absolutely taboo all reporters and newspaper editors. Yet I have my warmest friends among them.

My conclusion is that it is our duty as leaders to separate ourselves from the vices of many of those behind us and exhibit the light that will lead them to safe places, by our examples, by our words, by what we write, by what we do. The doctor who will speak to another doctor, recognize him, and who will say anything in public derogatory of him, is a traitor to his profession and is helping to undo the good that either of them can do. Gentlemen, if we want to be teachers, we have got to recognize the guild of fellow teachers. When we have done that, you may be sure the others will say, "Here is a class of fellows whom we can follow."

Dr. S. A. Knopf:

I beg leave to make a motion that the Academy express its sincerest thanks to Dr. Devine, who, in the midst of his arduous duties, has come to us to present such an admirable paper. (Adopted.)

If there is anything we physicians should accept as appropriate it is the interpretation of the word "doctor." Doctor means teacher, and the mission of the true physician in this life is not only to heal, but also to teach. I do not believe in teaching only individuals; I believe also in teaching the community at large. I do not believe in teaching only ordinary people, but also the extraordinary people. I believe that physicians should teach statesmen and politicians as well as the public at large. The ignorance sometimes displayed by public men in regard to general hygiene is marvelous. Only yesterday I learned of the erection of a school building in which almost no regard was paid to light and ventilation.

It has been my privilege to work with Dr. Devine in New York on the solution of one of the most difficult social problems. Some of you, perhaps, will remember the condition of the tenement houses before the charity organizations took up the work of the tenement-house reform. You would not wonder that the death-rate was so high. I don't believe sanatoria for consumptives will ever do us the good they ought to do as long as we allow such tenement houses as have existed in New York, and still exist in many large cities. Consumption will spring up anew in the overcrowded houses that lack light and ventilation. We must begin at the primary source in our combat against this disease. We can do this through the charity organizations or similar societies. It has been done in New York and a vast improvement in the tenement houses is the result.

Concerning the duty of the physician to speak before the public I have settled opinions. I have accepted an invitation to speak next week in New York in the hall of the University Settlement. My audience, I have been told, will be exclusively working men and my subject will be "What Everybody Ought to Know about Consumption." If I am guilty of misconduct, if I violate thereby a code of ethics, I am willing to take the consequences, though I do not believe I do. On the contrary, I believe I do my duty, and that it is a sacred duty for the physician to teach the masses, as well as the individual, how to keep well.

To show you how little we physicians alone can do in regard to medicosocial diseases and how much if united to a proper lay organization, I will tell you a little experience. I have been trying for the past three months to start an anti-tuberculosis society in New York. I made an appeal to eleven of my most distinguished confrères and teachers. All were willing to create such a society and signed the appeal, but I could not get a president. I gave the appeal to my friend, Dr. Devine, with a few signatures of prominent laymen. The result is that we now have a prosperous, effective Tuberculosis Committee for the Prevention of Tuberculosis under the auspices of the Charity Organization Society, composed of some of the leading physicians, distinguished charity workers, society ladies, and business men of New York, with the Hon. Chas. F. Cox as chairman. These combined elements will do something to solve the social problem of tuberculosis.

The statement that the newspapers often report medical lectures incorrectly is true; I have also suffered from it. I have never given a newspaper interview, but when I have spoken in public the reporters have often misquoted what I have said.

What Dr. Devine has said of tuberculosis and malaria is applicable to all infectious diseases. I think every charity organization should have a board of competent physicians as advisors.

Dr. W. R. White, of Providence:

I rise for only a moment to ask Dr. Devine, if it pleases him, inclosing the discussion, to dwell a moment from his experience upon the branch of the subject introduced by Dr. Englemann. It seems to me that it is of paramount importance. The public school children, from the very class of tenements whose existence has been brought before us, are bright, eager, receptive. They constitute a medium between intelligent people and the parents in these homes. Why do not the public schools offer a channel for a great work in this direction? It seems to me that Dr. Englemann has introduced one of the most important features of this whole subject.

Dr. Fred Corss, of Kingston, Pa.:

Undoubtedly the public press is the greatest means of disseminating this knowledge, and though it is a much better instructor than our public schools, it often fails to reach the parties most in need. In illustration, in a strike in the coal fields a number of Polanders were brought in to take the place of the striking miners. Their food consisted of bacon and wheat flour. The bacon was put into a frying-pan and the wheat flour dusted in, and this was called bread. An extensive epidemic of scurvy occurred and several men became insane. The question arose of what to do? Go to the public press, and give the reporter a lecture upon scurvy and diet? These people would never read the papers. Their children were not taught in the public schools. They had never learned our language. The men were told that they must have good bread and plenty of vegetables, and the epidemic ceased when these instructions were carried out.

I agree with the other speakers upon the impropriety of giving lectures upon hygienic matters to the newspapers, and that it is unprofessional to write such except in connection with the work of the Board of Health. I have no fault to find with the papers or reporters. Their intentions are of the best. In an experience of twenty years in the school board I have never found a teacher who could teach physiology or hygiene in a way to be of any profit to the pupils. The text-books furnished by the publishing houses for the common schools are inadequate to the purpose for which they were designed.

Dr. Devine closes:

I am sorry if I did not place sufficient emphasis upon the fact that it is a tremendous advantage that a medical man was at the head in Cuba. In almost every branch of the Government is seen the splendid results of the work of General Wood.

About the newspapers, I was very far from suggesting that physicians should constantly submit themselves to interviews or should be filling the daily papers with personally signed letters. I did suggest that the relations of physicians with editors and reporters should be such as to enable editors and reporters to talk intelligently about these subjects. Perhaps the experience of one of the best known reporters of New York with a health commissioner would be interesting. The former had just gotten hold of a story which it would be very unwise to have appear in the daily papers. He thought, however, that it was too good a story to keep and said to his friend the commissioner that he did not see how he could refrain from writing it up. The commissioner said nothing about it, but a few minutes afterwards, the subject having turned into a different channel, he asked him if he would be willing to try a new magnetic battery. My friend having great confidence in the commissioner took hold of the handles and was subjected to a little shock, which became stronger until he could not let go. Before the experience was ended his word of honor was pledged that nothing should appear in the daily paper. In your relation to the reporters and editors you may have to resort to some such expedient before their education is complete. I think that particular reporter had afterwards a proper sense of propriety as to what information might be used.

I do not think that there is anything of a medical guild spirit in the medical profession as a whole. I think, however, that it is not a general indictment to say that there are individual people who do not have that breadth of view which is exhibited by many. There have been sometimes in the medical press little suggestions and paragraphs that it seems to me would not be there if it were absolutely true that there was nothing remaining that might be called a guild spirit. There appeared some time ago an editorial advising physicians not to take part in the compulsory vaccination laws, not on the ground that it would be better for the community, but because this was an unpopular movement and because there was no reason why physicians should bring upon themselves the odium that would be caused by advocating it. That, I think, is an illustration of the sort of advice that physicians should not have.

I sympathize absolutely with the suggestion about the public schools. Having taught for four years in the public schools, I recognize the opportunity that there is for making them a channel of communication between the medical profession and the homes of the poor. The best way is to have physicians serve on the school boards. In that capacity they may, at least, render even a negative sort of service by keeping out the poor text-books to which reference has been made. I should not have failed to refer to a recent excellent illustration not a week old of the kind of co-operation of which I speak in the discussion held at Detroit, on what to do for the consumptive poor, participated in by Dr. Knopf, Dr. Vaughan, and others. Sharing in discussions of that kind will do much good and no one can object to it from a professional standpoint.

I would like to state that if anything could have added to the honor of being invited to read a paper before this meeting, it is the manner in which the suggestions that I have ventured to make have been received by the Academy, and I am grateful for the suggestions that have been made for carrying out these ideas and for the interest and consideration given to that which I have tried to say.

TRANSACTIONS.

Hotel Kensington, Saratoga Springs,
Saturday, June 7, 1902.

The Academy met in its twenty-seventh annual session at 11 A.M., and was called to order by the president, Prof. V. C. Vaughan, of the University of Michigan, and went into executive session.

The minutes of the St. Paul meeting were read and adopted.
The secretary read the report of the council as follows:

Report of Council.

The Council reports the usual routine work in preparation for this meeting resulting in the program already in your possession.

An amendment to the constitution proposed at the last meeting will come before you for decision. The amendment is to permit fellows to commute their dues by the payment of a single fee. The advantages of this provision are twofold:

1. It gives the individual member an opportunity to discharge his financial obligation to the Academy and relieves him of further thought regarding the continuity of his membership.

2. It provides a more permanent roll of members. There will always be a failure on the part of some to pay the annual fee; many from simple carelessness in meeting an annual obligation for so slight an amount.

Whether the amount expressed in the amendment ($20) is the best sum should be discussed before the amendment is voted upon. The Council has had its attention called to several organizations whose annual dues are one dollar, that uniformly have made $25 the amount for a life-membership fee. These are the Association of Collegiate Alumnae (National); the Association of Alumnae of Vassar College; the Society of the Alumni of the Medical Department of the University of Pennsylvania; and the Lafayette College Alumni Association.

It will be necessary at this meeting to instruct the secretary as to the manner of keeping the separate roll of those who have neglected to pay the annual dues for three successive years, as this is the third year since the amendment to the constitution creating annual dues went into effect. The clause reads: "The neglect to pay this fee for three successive years shall cause the name of the fellow so neglecting to be entered upon a separate roll to be known as the list of suspended fellows." Shall his name be removed from the regular roll when this is done, and shall the separate roll be published when the list of fellows is published? shall the fellow entered upon this special list have any of the duties and privileges of membership? are questions that should be determined at this meeting.

There have been two local meetings held during the year. One at Columbus, O., the other at Philadelphia. Neither of the meetings was a special meeting under the provisions of the by-laws, so no minutes are to be presented. The reports of both meetings testify to a very pleasant and enjoyable social time. At Philadelphia, Dr. McIntire read a paper, by invitation, on "The Academy: Its Work in the Past and Its Possibilities in the Future."

If we had no other evidence of the increasing age of the Academy we need but inspect the increasing size of the necrologic list at each succeeding meeting. The two names first mentioned in the list of this year illustrates the difficulty of keeping the list of fellows strictly accurate, as these deaths are now first reported:

1. Adaline T. Whitney, Boston, died February 13, 1896. A.B. Vassar, 1873; M.D. Zurich, 1880; elected 1888.

2. J. M. Turner, Brooklyn, died July 2, 1896. A.B. Hamilton, 1838; M.D. Transylvania, 1841; elected 1880.

3. G. S. Machan, Providence, died April 6, 1901. A.B. Bowdoin; 1893; A.M. Bowdoin, 1895; M.D. Bowdoin, 1896; elected 1901.

4. John Spare, New Bedford, Mass., died May 22, 1901. A.B. Amherst, 1838; M.D. Harvard, 1842; elected 1881.

5. W. L. Nichol, Nashville, Tenn., died June 23, 1901. A.B. Univ. of Nashville, 1845; M.D. Univ. of Penna., 1849; elected 1889.

6. John Curwen, Harrisburg, Pa., died July 2, 1901. A.B. Yale, 1841; A.M. Yale, 1844; M.D. Univ. of Penna., 1844; elected 1877.

7. T. J. Turner (U. S. N. retired), Coldwater, Mich., died August 21, 1901. A.M. Central High School, Phila., 1853; M.D. Penna. Med. College, 1853; elected 1884; Vice-president, 1887.

8. J. M. Meyer, Danville, Ky., died September 5, 1901. A.B. Centre College, Kentucky, 1840; M.D. Transylvania, 1843; elected 1892.

9. N. S. Cheeseman, Scotia, N. Y., died September 13, 1901. A.B. Union, 1856; M.D. Union (Albany Medical College), 1860; elected 1890.

10. S. J. Jones, Chicago, died October 4, 1901. A.B. Dickinson, 1857; A.M. Dickinson, 1860; M.D., Univ. of Penna., 1860; elected 1880; Vice-president, 1885, 1886; President, 1889.

11. Jarvis S. Wight, Brooklyn, died November, 1901. A.B. Tufts, 1861; M.D. Long Island College Hospital, 1864; elected 1885.

12. A. L. Gihon (U. S. N. retired), New York, died November 17, 1901. A.B. Central High School, Phila., 1850; M.D. Phila. Medical College, 1853; elected 1883; Vice-president, 1883; President, 1884.

13. Peter R. Furbeck, Gloversville, N. Y., died January 17, 1902. A.B. Union, 1854; M.D. Long Island College Hospital, 1865; elected 1888.

14. H. R. Baldwin, New Brunswick, N. J., died February 3, 1902. A.B. Rutgers, 1849; M.D. Columbia (College Phys. and Surg.), 1853; elected 1891.

15. W. Murray Weidman, Reading, Pa., died February 8, 1902. A.B. Pennsylvania College, 1856; M.D. University of Pennsylvania, 1860; elected 1884.

16. L. B. Tuckerman, Cleveland, O., died March 5, 1902. A.B. Amherst, 1872; M.D. Long Island College Hospital, 1877; elected 1899.

17. Christian Fenger, Chicago, died March 7, 1902. A.B. University of Copenhagen, 1861; M.D. University of Copenhagen, 1866; elected 1891.

18. Z. B. Adams, Framingham, Mass., died May 1, 1902. A.B. Bowdoin, 1849; M.D. Harvard 1853; elected 1883.

[By a resolution of the Council, the report of the secretary to the Council is made a part of the report of Council and is as follows:]

The secretary desires to report to the Council that during the year, in addition to the usual routine work, $i.\ e.$, the publishing of the Bulletin, preparing for the annual meeting and the usual correspondence, etc., he has been able to accomplish several other items, which will simplify the routine and make the records in the office more easily available. He has completed the classified card catalogue of the fellows of the Academy. Each name is to be found on four separate cards. A white card is the name card, and is arranged alphabetically by names. This card gives the number, name, and date of election, with the post-office address, and colleges of graduation. A blue card is the academic college card. These are arranged alphabetically by colleges. Thus turning to Princeton, under "A," will be found all of our fellows graduated from Princeton, whose initial letter is A. A buff card does the same for the medical school, and a salmon card for the post-office address. It is possible now in a minute to tell the names of the fellows graduates of any college or medical school, or in any locality.

The individual accounts, too, are also kept by means of a card catalogue, which eliminates many sources of error.

One of the usual duties of the secretary for the last few years has been a search for names of college-bred physicians. The lists so prepared, include hundreds of names, copied on paper and filed. They are without order, and cannot be referred to except with much labor, and it is impossible to use the work of one year to check that of another. A beginning has been made during the year to make these lists of easy reference, and a card catalogue of the graduates of Yale and Union who are also physicians has been made from the latest triennials. By continuing the work as opportunity offers, fairly complete lists of college-bred physicians will be prepared, which may have other uses than those for which it was compiled.

The manuscript catalogue of fellows has made some progress, but not as much as was hoped. Your secretary finds it necessary to prepare this material himself, before it is type-written, and he has not been able to put as much time on it as was hoped.

A beginning has also been made to classify and catalogue the books and pamphlets on medical sociology in the library, partly academy, partly personal. This has been found necessary because of the increasing width of questions asked him during the year. This is placed temporarily upon the backs of printed cards, until the time comes when regular library stationery can be used.

An enumeration of a few of the inquiries received during the present calendar year may be of interest.

1. A request for a list of states making appropriations to medical colleges or hospitals, the information to be used in an address before a committee of a convention revising a state constitution. Some information was furnished. The request was the origin of a paper presented at this meeting.

2. A request from England: "In connection with the foundation of a course of lectures on the history of medicine at the Royal College of Physicians, of London, I am anxious to obtain information as to the existence of such courses in America. . . . I should be much obliged if you could give me any information or publication on the subject." Our library and catalogue enabled me to send a list of the colleges that published the name of lecturers on medical history in their catalogues.

3. Information regarding the present position of interstate reciprocity by a president of a state medical society, wishing to use the information in his annual address. The information furnished was not as complete as desired because of the lack of a catalogue.

4, 5, 6. Definite information about particular state boards of medical examiners.

7, 8. Precise information about certain medical schools.

No record has ever been kept of the number and diversity of inquiries directed to the secretary's office. These few indicate their scope.

It seems to your secretary that the Bulletin has not made the progress its importance deserves. But, in view of the fact that every year, subscriptions are permitted to expire, he fears he is placing too high a valuation upon the Bulletin. He needs to be set right as to the estimate of its real value, or to be instructed in methods to increase its circulation.

The extent of the correspondence for the year may be gleaned from the following figures: 1,550 letters were received since the last meeting and 2,654 mailed.

On motion of Drs. J. B. Roberts and Benjamin Lee, the report of the Council was adopted.

The secretary read the names of the applicants for fellowship approved by the Council. No one objecting, he was instructed to cast the ballot in their favor and they were elected.

The report of the treasurer was read and referred to a committee to audit. Drs. Edward Jackson, S. A. Knopf, and A. Stewart Lobinger were appointed as the committee.

Letters were read from Dr. Rudolph Virchow and Mr. Edward Nettleship, accepting the honorary membership to which they were elected at the last meeting.

The proposed amendments to the constitution were then considered and adopted. As amended the article reads:

ARTICLE VII.—REVENUE.

"Section 1. The sources of revenue shall be the initiation fee, dues, the transactions of the Academy, and the certificate of membership. The initiation fee of five dollars shall be paid before admission and registration. A fee of one dollar shall be due at each subsequent annual meeting; the neglect to pay this fee for three successive years shall cause the name of the fellow so neglecting to be entered upon a separate roll to be known as the list of suspended fellows; *provided*, that all fellows elected previous to, or during the meeting for 1898 shall not be liable to this penalty. If any fellow pays the sum of twenty dollars at one time, he is freed from the payment of any subsequent annual dues.

"Section 2. The money received from the payment of life dues shall be invested as the Council may direct, and the interest only can be expended."

Drs. John B. Roberts, W. S. Hall, and T. D. Davis were appointed as the Nominating Committee, and George Dock to fill the vacancy on the Committee on Honorary Membership.

The Academy at this point arose from the closed session and proceeded to the open session.

The Committee to Continue the Investigation of Reciprocity in Medical Licensure reported through Dr. Edward Jackson, of Denver. The report was referred to the Council, to act upon the recommendation and report back to the Academy.

The secretary presented a report on the "Results of the Examinations for Medical Licensure for 1901." The report was referred to the Council for publication in whole or in part.[1]

A paper entitled "The 'Personal Equation' in Marking Examination Papers" was read by Dr. Charles McIntire, of Easton, Pa., and discussed by Drs. T. D. Davis, V. C. Vaughan, S. A. Knopf, and McIntire in closing.

The Academy took recess for lunch and reassembled at three o'clock. Upon reconvening, the Academy listened to a paper on "The Family Physician of the Past, Present, and Future," by Dr. S. A. Knopf, of New York, which was discussed by Drs. H. O. Marcy, Henry L. Taylor (of the Regent's Office, University of the State of New York), H. D. Didama, W. S. Hall, Benjamin Lee, Leartus Connor, C. G. Plummer, Frederic Corss, and Knopf, closing.

Dr. Chas. M. Culver, of Albany, read a paper on "The

[1] Published in the August (1902) number of the Bulletin.

Physician as an Accountant," which was discussed by Dr. Frederic Corss.

Dr. Winfield S. Hall, of Chicago, read a paper entitled "Pure Science *vs.* Applied Science in Medicine."

Dr. A. L. Benedict, of Buffalo, presented the report of the Committee on Time Allowance in the Combined Collegiate and Medical Course.

Upon the motion to accept the report, it was discussed by Drs. A. S. Lobinger, Frederic Corss, T. D. Davis, Henry L. Taylor, L. Duncan Bulkley, E. B. Harvey, Edward Jackson, H. O. Marcy, V. C. Vaughan, and W. S. Hall, and was still under discussion at the time adopted for recess.

Dr. W. S. Hall moved that it was the "sense of the Academy that the time that should be devoted to the combination course, baccalaureate, and medical should be seven years," which was referred to the Council under the rule.

It was moved and adopted that the further discussion of the report be made a special order of business after the reading and discussion of Dr. Devine's address on Monday morning.

The Academy then took recess until eight o'clock. Upon reassembling the first vice-president, Dr. James L. Taylor, occupied the chair, and the Academy listened to the excellent address of the president on "The Religion of Science."[1]

At the conclusion of the address, the Academy adjourned until Monday morning.

HOTEL KENSINGTON, SARATOGA SPRINGS,
Monday, June 9, 1902.

The Academy met at 10 A.M. with Vice-President Taylor in the chair.

The Council made a supplemental report as follows:

The Council reports regarding the questions referred to it.

I. The resolution of Dr. Frederic Corss, reading: "That in the opinion of the Academy, alcohol should not be classified among the alimentary substances."

The Council recommends that as the question is not one of medical sociology, it does not come within the province of the Academy, and that the resolution be laid upon the table.

(The recommendation of the Academy was adopted upon mo-

[1] See page 57 of this number.

tion, and the resolution was so disposed of.)

II. The resolution of Dr. W. S. Hall was as follows: "Resolved, that in the opinion of the Academy that the combined courses, baccalaureate and medical, should occupy seven years."

The Council recommended the adoption of the following substitute:

"It is the sense of the Academy that an adjustment can be made between the baccalaureate and medical courses by which time can be saved from the present curriculum, and that efforts should be made to adjust these courses."

(On motion, the resolution proposed by the Council was substituted for the original motion and adopted.)

III. The Council recommends that the secretary's request for instruction as to the methods of placing the names of delinquents upon the lists of suspended members as required by the constitution be answered as follows:

The Academy directs that the names of suspended members shall not be published among the fellows of the Academy until they have paid in full the amount due the Academy.

(The recommendation was accepted and the secretary was so instructed by a vote of the Academy.)

IV. In view of the value of the investigation of the committee, the Council recommends the continuance of the Committee on Time Allowance in the Combined Collegiate and Medical Courses, of which Dr. A. L. Benedict is chairman.

(On motion the committee was so continued.)

V. The Council also proposes the following amendments to the constitution for your consideration. They are suggested by the conditions existing at this meeting, where we have been assisted in the discussion by those who are not physicians.

A. Add a paragraph to Article II, to be numbered 4, and to read:

"To associate those who are interested in social problems influencing or being influenced by the medical profession."

B. To insert in Section 1 of Article III after the word "fellow," the word "associate," making the section to read:

"The membership of the Academy shall consist of fellows, associate and honorary members."

C. To add sections to Article III, to be numbered 3 and 4, as follows:

"Associates shall be alumni of respectable institutions of learning having received therefrom a degree after residence and examination.

"Associates shall have all the privileges of fellows excepting the right to vote upon amendments to the constitution or by-laws, or to hold an executive office."

Renumber the present Sections 3, 4, and 5, making them 5, 6, and 7.

In present Section 5, which when renumbered would be Section 7, insert the words "and associates" after the word "fellows," in the second line, making it to read:

"The consent by ballot of two-thirds of the fellows and associates present shall be necessary for the election of fellows, associates or honorary members."

D. Insert the words "or associate" after the word "fellow" in Article VII; and the words "and associates" between the words "fellows" and "provided."

E. Insert the word "associate" after the word "fellow" in the second line of Section 2 of Article VIII.

(The proposed amendments were ordered to lay over until the next meeting according to the constitutional provision.)

Additional applicants for fellowship were elected upon the recommendation of Council.

The Committee on Honorary Members proposed Dr. William H. Welch, of Johns Hopkins University, and he was elected.

The Auditing Committee reported that the accounts had been audited, and that with the exception of a slight error in addition were found to be correct. The report of the committee was received and adopted on motion.

This completing the business, the Academy entered upon its open session, and listened to an address on "The Medical Profession and Social Reform,"[1] by Edward T. Devine, Ph.D., general secretary of the Charity Organization Society of New York City. The address was discussed by Drs. D. L. Brower, of Chicago; J. T. Searcy, of Tuscaloosa, Ala.; H. A. Tomlinson,

[1] See page 76 of this number.

of St. Peter, Minn.; Walter L. Pyle, of Philadelphia; A. L. Benedict, of Buffalo; P. Maxwell Foshay, of Cleveland; Rosa Englemann, of Chicago; W. S. Hall, of Chicago; Leartus Connor, of Detroit; S. A. Knopf, of New York, who moved a vote of thanks to Dr. Devine for his excellent paper. The motion was seconded and adopted unanimously. Wm. R. White, of Providence; Frederic Corss, of Kingston, Pa.; and Dr. Devine in closing.

The stated business of the morning—to continue the discussion on the report of the Committee on Time Allowance in the Combined Collegiate and Medical Courses—was announced, and on motion of Dr. W. S. Hall, that inasmuch as the committee has been continued, further discussion was postponed until next year.

Dr. John B. Roberts, of Philadelphia, read the next paper (in continuation of the symposium "Politics in the Medical Profession") on "The Political Side of Medicine."

After the reading of this paper the Academy took recess until three o'clock. Upon reconvening, the Academy listened to the following additional papers in the symposium:

"The Relation of the Physician to Politics," by D. C. Hawley, of Burlington, Vt.

"Compensation for Medical Service Rendered the State," by T. D. Davis, of Pittsburg.

"Medical Representation in Hospital Management," by Augustus A. Eshner, of Philadelphia.

The discussion of the papers in continuation of the symposium was participated in by Drs. P. Maxwell Foshay, of Cleveland; Charles McIntire, of Easton, Pa.; A. A. Eshner, of Philadelphia; Henry D. Holton, of Brattleboro, Vt.; S. D. Risley, of Philadelphia; L. Duncan Bulkley, of New York; and in closing by Drs. John B. Roberts, D. C. Hawley, A. A. Eshner—when Dr. Bulkley, noticing the presence of Dr. Alonzo Garçelon, asked that he might add some thoughts to the symposium, who complied with the request.

The next paper was entitled "May Hospitals Steal?" by Dr. P. Maxwell, Foshay, of Cleveland. It was discussed by Drs. A. L. Benedict, of Buffalo; Leartus Connor, of Detroit; W. L.

Estes, of South Bethlehem, Pa.; S. A. Knopf, of New York; and Foshay in closing.

Dr. S. D. Risley, of Philadelphia, read a paper on "Good Vision as a Factor in the Education Process," which was discussed by Drs. Frank Allport, of Chicago (by invitation); John E. Weeks, of New York (by invitation); Leartus Connor, of Detroit; and Risley, closing.

"State Aid for Medical Schools and Hospitals" was read by Dr. Charles McIntire, of Easton, Pa.

Dr. Rosa Englemann read a paper on "Children in Cities," which was discussed by Drs. S. A. Knopf, of New York, and Englemann, closing.

At the conclusion of the discussion the Academy went into executive session.

The Nominating Committee presented the following report through its chairman, Dr. John B. Roberts:

President—Charles McIntire, Easton, Pa.

Vice-presidents—Wm. R. White, Providence, R. I.; Geo. Dock, Ann Arbor, Mich.; Rosa Englemann, Chicago, Ill.; D. C. Hawley, Burlington, Vt.

Secretary—Alexander R. Craig, Columbia, Pa.

Treasurer—Edgar M. Green, Easton, Pa.

Assistant Secretary—John S. Davis, Univ. of Va.

It is further recommended by your committee that it be the sense of the Academy that the several vice-presidents be held responsible for the furtherance of the interests of the Academy in the region which they represent.

Your committee suggests that there be held local midwinter reunions—called and arranged by the vice-presidents—of members, to which eligible men and women shall be invited and shall have an opportunity to learn of the work of the Academy.

After some discussion the report of the committee was adopted, the officers nominated, elected and the recommendation adopted.

Several other applicants for fellowship had received the approval of the Council and the gentlemen were elected.

The Council also reported its action upon the recommendations appended to the report of the Committee to Continue the Investigation of Reciprocity in Medical Licensure.

The recommendations as formulated by the committee read:

"First. That in states which have a provision for the admission of licentiates of other state boards without examination, lists of those states the licenses of which will be so recognized be formed and published as soon as possible. And that in so forming such lists, a rather liberal spirit be shown in the determination of what constitutes equality of requirement. In no two states, not even the same state through a series of years, can it be expected that the standard of requirement will be exactly the same. Yet abuses likely to arise from any moderate difference in requirements can readily be guarded against by a demand for a moderate period (three years) of actual practice in the state from which the original license had been obtained.

"Second. That in states giving discretionary power to the examining board, the license obtained in another state, by passing a good state examination, or even the diploma of one of the better medical colleges, be accepted after five years of practice as evidence of a sufficient training in such branches as chemistry, anatomy, physiology, and pathology; and that the examination of the candidates presenting such evidence be confined to the other, or so-called practical subjects.

"Third. That in all states in which sufficient discretionary power to do these things has not been lodged with the state board of medical examiners, the effort should be made to obtain the necessary authority, guarded by an efficient, but not too oppressive, requirement of a period of actual practice in the state from which the original license was obtained.

"Fourth. That these steps shall be taken in each separate state, irrespective of formal reciprocity, or of what any state so recognized may or may not do in this direction, or of the establishment of a national board of medical examiners, or of any other desirable measures. Such measures can be promoted independently; and will be assisted rather than hindered by the carrying out of the above suggestions.

The Council recommends that these recommendations of the committee be adopted.

This was done by motion, and an additional motion proposed by Dr. John B. Roberts was also carried. Dr. Roberts said:

"If I am correctly informed, the House of Delegates of the American Medical Association will take up this same subject to-morrow. I therefore move that the secretary transmit to the secretary of the American Medical Association this recommendation of the Academy in order that it may be placed before the House of Deputies to inform the members on the various phases of the subject.

The Academy took recess until 7.30 P.M. for the social and concluding executive session.

AT THE BANQUET TABLE, HOTEL KENSINGTON,
SARATOGA SPRINGS, N. Y., June 9, 1902.

After his toast to the "Prosperous Past," the retiring president, Dr. V. C. Vaughan, of Ann Arbor, Mich., introduced the president for the coming year, Dr. Charles McIntire, of Easton, Pa., who, after speaking of "The Year to Come," called an executive session of the Academy to order for any further business that might present itself for action.

The secretary moved that a vote of thanks be passed to Dr. Culver and the members of the Committee of Arrangements, to the Committee on Program, to those who have presented papers at the meeting now closing, to the management of the Hotel Kensington, and to all who have contributed to our profit and pleasure while at Saratoga Springs. The motion was carried.

Dr. Estes, of South Bethlehem, Pa., moved that the papers and reports presented at the meeting be referred to the Council for publication. Carried.

The session was declared adjourned and the toasts continued.

The following persons were elected to fellowship during the meeting.

Walter R. Steiner, Hartford, Conn.; Lawrence W. Littig, Iowa City, Iowa; H. E. Gribbin, Augusta, Maine; James O. Lincoln, Bath, Maine; Stephen H. Weeks, Portland, Maine; Edwin B. Harvey, Westborough, Mass.; Guy Leartus Connor, Detroit, Mich., Robert Babcock, Albany, N. Y.; James Franklin Barker, Albany; E. A. Bartlett, Albany; John M. Bigelow, Albany; Lewis E. Blair, Albany; Geo. Blumer, Albany; John Davis Craig, Albany; Frederic C. Curtis, Albany; A. W.

Etting, Albany; Samuel R. Morrow, Albany; J. M. Mosher, Albany; Geo. S. Munson, Albany; M. D. Stevenson, Albany; Willis G. Tucker, Albany; Chas. A. Wall, Buffalo, N. Y.; Jane L. Greeley, Jamestown, N. Y.; Archibald Lybolt, New York; John Allen Wyeth, New York; Walter L. Huggins, Schenectady, N. Y.; Herman V. Mynderse, Schenectady; W. L. Pearson, Schenectady; Thos. Shaw Arbuthnot, Pittsburg, Pa.; Thos. Way Grayson, Pittsburg; Edward B. Heckel, Pittsburg; Stuart Patterson, Pittsburg; Stephen A. Welch, Providence, R. I.; Henry D. Holton, Brattleboro, Vt.; John Brooks Wheeler, Burlington, Vt.; Robt. F. Williams, Richmond, Va.; I. A. Shimer, United States Army, Washington, D. C.

FELLOWS AND HONORARY MEMBERS IN ATTENDANCE AT SARATOGA SPRINGS.

ALABAMA—Tuscaloosa, Dr. J. T. Searcy.

CALIFORNIA—Los Angeles, Drs. H. Bert Ellis, A. Stewart Lobinger; Pasadena, Dr. James H. McBride.

COLORADO—Denver, Dr. Edward Jackson.

ILLINOIS—Chicago, Drs. D. R. Brower, N. S. Davis, Jr., Rosa Englemann, W. S. Hall, Bayard Holmes.

IOWA—Iowa City, Dr. L. W. Littig.

MAINE—Lewiston, Dr. Alonzo Garçelon; Portland, Dr. Stephen H. Weeks.

MASSACHUSETTS—Boston, Drs. Edwin B. Harvey, Henry O. Marcy, Henry O. Marcy, Jr.; Monson, Dr. G. E. Fuller.

MICHIGAN—Ann Arbor, Drs. Geo. Dock, V. C. Vaughan; Detroit, Dr. Leartus Connor.

MINNESOTA—St. Peter, Dr. H. A. Tomlinson; Winona, Dr. H. F. McGaughey.

NEW JERSEY—Atlantic City, Drs. W. Edgar Darnall, J. A. Joy.

NEW YORK—Albany, Drs. E. A. Bartlett, C. M. Culver, J. M. Mosher, M. D. Stevenson; Buffalo, Dr. A. L. Benedict; New York, Drs. L. Duncan Bulkley, W. M. Carhart, S. A. Knopf, John A. Wyeth; Rochester, Dr. Wheelock Rider; Schenectady, Drs. Wm. T. Clute, H. V. Mynderse; Syracuse, Dr. H.

D. Didama; Troy, R. Halsted Ward.

OHIO—Cleveland, Drs. A. R. Baker, P. Maxwell Foshay; Columbus, Dr. J. E. Brown; Wheelersburg, Dr. James L. Taylor.

PENNSYLVANIA—Columbia, Dr. Alex. R. Craig; Easton, Dr. Chas. McIntire; Greensburg, Dr. W. J. K. Kline; Kingston, Dr. Frederic Corss; Lewisburg, Dr. Geo. G. Groff; Norristown, Dr. J. K. Weaver; Philadelphia, Drs. W. A. Newman Dorland, Augustus A. Eshner, W. C. Hollopeter, Benjamin Lee, G. Hudson-Makuen, Walter L. Pyle, W. Boardman Reed, Samuel D. Risley, John B. Roberts, C. A. Veasey; Pittsburg, Dr. T. D. Davis; South Bethlehem, Dr. W. L. Estes; Waynesboro, Dr. A. H. Strickler.

RHODE ISLAND—Providence, Drs. Geo. S. Matthews, S. A. Welch, Wm. R. White.

UTAH—Salt Lake City, Dr. Chas. G. Plummer.

VERMONT—Brattleboro, Dr. Henry D. Holton; Burlington, Dr. Donly C. Hawley; Woodstock, Dr. F. T. Kidder.

OBSERVATIONS IN PASSING.

It is pleasant to record that the last State Examinations Number (August, 1902) of the Bulletin has been received with favor by the journals and the profession. Possibly the only persons who look with disfavor on this annual report are those who are connected with medical schools whose equipment do not permit them to fit their graduates to ordinarily pass the ordeal of a state examination. No human progress that renders any industrial plant of less value, whether for the manufacture of medical men or nails is looked upon with favor by the owners of the plant who see in the improvement their pecuniary loss. With the nail-maker, this is a personal matter, unless as in Arkwright's time, the introduction of the improvements incites to riot. But with the doctor-manufactory it is different. The courts of the land have decided the police power should supervise the product of their manufactories, and the outcome is a matter of public safety. Hence, the greatest publicity should be given to the results of the examinations. Young men purposing to study medicine have a right to know the character of the education given by any medical school judged by the standard of the state examinations, and the laws of the various states should compel a publication of the results of all the examinations by their boards. This is the case in some states—in others, where it is not made obligatory, a public sentiment should be created compelling the fullest publicity.

Indeed, the safety of the boards themselves require it. The power given them is so great that a suspicion of its improper use will naturally follow "Star Chamber" methods. These thoughts have been suggested by the direct declination of some of the boards to furnish returns, because certain colleges object, and the tacit declination of other boards, by not answering repeated requests.

Let the profession in those states where no returns are given take their boards to task for their so doing, and the cause of state examinations will be strengthened thereby.

After extended correspondence, Dr. Craig announces that the next meeting of the American Academy of Medicine will be held at Washington, D. C., on Monday and Tuesday, May 11 and 12, 1903. The president has completed his appointments. The additional members of council are Drs. C. M. Culver, of Albany; W. L. Estes, of South Bethlehem, Pa.; G. N. Acker, of Washington; and W. H. Doughty, Jr., of Augusta, Ga.

The Committee on Program consists of Dr. Edward Jackson, McPhee Building, Denver, Chairman, with the president and secretary.

The Committee of Arrangements, Drs. G. N. Acker, Chairman; J. F. R. Appleby, G. E. Abbot, E. A. Ballock, W. H. Hawkes, Joseph Tabor Johnson, T. A. McArdle, and George L. Magruder, all of Washington, D. C.

∗

While the membership of the American Academy of Medicine is fast approaching the one thousand mark, it has never had one hundred of its fellows in attendance at any one meeting. This is due to the geographic distribution of the members. No one will dispute the statement that the usefulness of the Academy to the profession will be increased in direct ratio to the number of its members brought into touch with its activities at the meetings. But, much as this is to be desired, the vastness of our country remains to prevent the consummation of the wish.

If the mountain cannot be brought to the prophet, Mohammed is able to visit the mountain. The plan of holding local meetings of the fellows of the Academy is commendable, and it is hoped that the vice-presidents will carry out the instructions suggested by the Nominating Committee and adopted by the Academy, and more—that other meetings will be held, without the aid of a vice-president, so that the opportunity will be given for a majority of the fellows of the Academy to meet in its interests during the year.

∗

The bound volumes of the Bulletin make a handsome appearance. The cost (with the exception of Volume I), is five dollars a volume, post-paid. Volume V, the last volume, contains the numbers issued during the past two years.

**

A few months ago, the *Observer* called attention to the two prizes—one of $1000, the other of $500—offered by the Maltine Company for the best essays on "Preventive Medicine," and commended the growing spirit of public interest among commercial houses. It is mentioned again because of two additional items.

1. Two hundred and eight essays have been offered in competition for the above prizes, and Drs. Daniel Lewis, of New York, C. A. L. Reed, of Cincinnati, and John Edwin Rhodes, of Chicago, the Committee of Award, have their winter's work mapped out for them in their perusal. Their report will be of interest and, probably, of value to the profession.

2. Another offer for a prize essay is made—likewise from Brooklyn. Dr. J. B. Mattison offers a prize of $400 for the best paper on "Does the Habitual Subdermic Use of Morphine Cause Organic Disease? If so, what?

The papers, which may be in any language, must be in the hands of the chairman of the committee by not later than December 1, 1903. They become the property of the American Association for the Study and Cure of Inebriety, to be published as the committee may direct.

The committee consists of Dr. T. D. Crothers, Hartford, Conn., Editor *Journal of Inebriety*, Chairman, Dr. J. M. Van Cott, Professor of Pathology, Long Island College Hospital, Brooklyn, and Dr. Wharton Sinkler, Neurologist to the State Asylum for the Chronic Insane, Philadelphia.

**

The Bulletin, in company with a goodly number of medical journals, does not give "reading notices" to its advertisers; neither has it sought to have a large number of advertising pages. At the same time it commends the advertisements to its readers with the wish that our advertising patrons will be asked to supply your needs when they are in the line offered by them.

LITERATURE NOTES.

ANNUAL REPORT OF THE NEW YORK STATE REFORMATORY AT ELMIRA FOR THE FISCAL YEAR ENDING SEPTEMBER 30, 1901.

There is much in this report of more than passing interest. The methods employed are for the direct bettering of the prisoner, primarily through his body, in the gymnasium and drill hall, accompanied by baths—soon to be followed by mental development in school and shop; and all associated with efforts for a moral and spiritual uplift.

There is a suggestion of crime being a pathologic condition, and as such should attract the study of physicians. The report urges the necessity of the examination by competent medical authority of every condemned prisoner before the sentence is pronounced, to assist the judge in properly disposing of the case. After the reception of prisoners in a reformatory, a medical examination is needed for the proper treatment of the individual. In connection with the necessity, and the opinion maintained by some that crime is a disease, the superintendent asks: "Would it not be logical . . . to organize the staff upon a medical basis, and increase rather than decrease the number of physicians employed in reformative institutions?"

Continuing he says:

"Much good would doubtless result to the state from careful study and analysis of criminals which would be made by the physicians, as it would thus be possible to scientifically study the habits and best methods of treating them, which would in time result in a better classification and improved methods for bringing them back into society and ridding them of their antisocial tendencies. This would be along the lines which have been followed in organizing the present system of hospital treatment of the insane, and which has resulted in so much good work being done, and has also resulted in a fairly good classification of the insane, and improved methods for treating them, thus increasing the percentage of those who have been improved and rendered able to take up their home life, and lessening the burden and tax upon the people of the State for their maintenance."

_

MEDICAL COMMUNICATIONS OF THE MASSACHUSETTS MEDICAL SOCIETY. Vol. xix, No. 1. 1902. Boston, 1902. pp. 299, 32.

This volume gives the addresses and papers read at the annual meeting last June. The section of medicine devoted itself to smallpox; that of surgery to head injuries; while, on the second day, the entire society discussed "The Use of Alcohol in Medicine." None of the papers present subjects bearing directly upon medical sociology.

.

The *Hot Springs Medical Journal* comes in a new cover, which is such an improvement upon the old that not to express our pleasure at its appearance would be to fail in courtesy. It is a model of good taste.

.

THE PRESENT STATUS OF HOMŒOPATHY. Being the Presidential Address Delivered before the 58th Annual Session of the American Institute of Homeopathy, June 17, 1902. JAMES C. WOOD, M.D. pp. 16.

There is much that is commendable in this polemic pamphlet, and Dr. Wood is to be congratulated in abstaining from the use of "Allopath." It is probably as able an argument as can be made for an attack upon empiric methods in therapeutics instead of observing a Law, which confessedly cannot be proven except by empiricism. This phase of the subject does not concern the Bulletin. The social features do, and a dispassioned perusal of the pamphlet leaves the conclusion that the author is pleading for stronger fences to hedge the homeopathic physician from the full liberty of scientific research.

BULLETIN

OF THE

American Academy of Medicine

VOL. VI.   ISSUED DECEMBER, 1902.   No. 3.

THE AMERICAN ACADEMY OF MEDICINE is not responsible for the sentiments expressed in any paper or address published in the BULLETIN.

TIME-ALLOWANCE IN THE COMBINED COLLEGIATE AND MEDICAL COURSE.[1]

BY A. L. BENEDICT, A.M., M.D., Buffalo, N. Y.

Your committee wished to base its report upon the opinions of those officially connected with our educational system; and drafted the following circular letter.

To the President and Faculty:

The American Academy of Medicine, organized in 1876 for the purpose of furthering the educational and ethical status of the medical profession and composed of physicians having a college education—with some few notable exceptions—is investigating the feasibility of combined courses in arts and science and in medicine. This letter is sent to all colleges, schools of medicine and universities of the United States, except such as are not in good standing, and we bespeak your interest and cooperation, especially in the way of prompt and full replies to the questions to follow, so that accurate statistics may be collated and that the opinions of educators may be compared. In what follows, the term *college* is used in the sense of an educational institution whose curriculum is supplemental to that of the high school and leading to a bachelor's degree; the term *university* is used in the sense of a group of educational institutions including a college and one or more professional schools. The word *education* is used in the academic sense and does not here refer to professional studies.

[1] Report of a committee presented to the American Academy of Medicine, Saratoga Springs, N. Y., June 7, 1902. The report was prepared by Dr. Benedict; the other members of the committee are Drs. S. D. Risley, of Philadelphia, and Charles McIntire, of Easton.

QUESTION 1.—Is your institution a college, university or medical school? Please note any change to be made in the near future.

Q. 2.—Do you believe that a general insistence on a college education for physicians is desirable?

Q. 3.—(For medical schools and universities.) What is your present minimum of educational requirement for medical graduates?

Q. 4.—(For same.) During the last ten years, what proportion of your medical graduates have had high school and college educations, respectively? Please note any progressive change.

Q. 5.—(For medical schools and medical departments of universities.) What is the length of your present medical course? Please note any change contemplated in the near future.

Q. 6.—(For colleges.) What is the length of your course leading to a bachelor's degree? Please note any change contemplated in the near future. What is your actual practice regarding students who desire, by taking extra courses, to economize time?

Q. 7.—Do you believe that a candidate for the medical doctorate who has already received a bachelor's degree or who shall combine a college and a medical course, should have any time-allowance in his favor, or that he should be treated, in this regard, exactly as one who undertakes the medical course with merely a high school education or less?

Q. 8.—If you take the former view, do you base it on the assumption that the college course includes studies directly serviceable in the medical course or that the college-educated man can acquire technical knowledge more readily?

Q. 9.—(For medical schools and medical departments of universities.) What is your actual practice in this regard? State number of years required for combined courses, if such exist, and whether any further economy of time is allowed in special cases.

Q. 10.—(For universities.) Are your requirements of time identical for the various bachelor's degrees, in combinations of college and medical courses?

Q. 11.—(For colleges and college departments of universities.) Are your requirements of time, including cases in which special favor is shown, identical, for courses leading to the various bachelor's degrees? If not, please specify.

Q. 12.—Would you favor cooperation among colleges and segregated medical schools, so that the same time-allowance could be made for students pursuing collegiate and medical courses at different institutions, as for those pursuing combined courses at the same university? Would you conform to reasonable regulation in this regard provided such regulation were in accordance with principles established by equable representation from American colleges, medical schools and universities?

While the American Academy of Medicine has not expressed a formal opinion on any of these points and while an unbiased expression is desired from those to whom this letter is sent, yet a practical consideration of the subject must be limited by the following facts:

1. The great overcrowding of the medical profession renders it unnecessary to fear any economic embarrassment from an attempt to regulate, in any way, the requirements for the doctorate.

2. On the other hand, the general rights of citizenship and the poor requital of medical practice demand that such requirements should be of a reasonable nature.

3. The raising of the requirements of technical medical education, from two to four years, in the average medical school, within the last ten or fifteen years, tends to discourage young men from taking a college course as a basis of a medical education. A combination course, with a time-discount, partially counteracts this tendency.

4. Both from economical and ethical reasons, it is undesirable that the period of bread-winning and of responsibility should be too long deferred. If we assume that no necessity for self-support exists, during the educational period of life, the average young man will leave the high school at eighteen, the college at twenty-two, the medical school at twenty-six and the hospital at twenty-seven and, under present conditions, he will not be self-supporting till he is thirty.

5. Under present conditions, about two years of work in the medical school are practically identical, providing that a suitable election of studies in the former is made.

6. While the ideal college course is that undertaken purely as a matter of culture and without interested motives for the future, comparatively few students are so circumstanced to be able to elect their courses in this way. The great majority, even of men of influential positions, are unable to enjoy the benefit of a college education. The highest legal requirement as to the education of medical students stops with the exaction of a high-school course. A college course modified by the demands of a technical training is better than none at all.

While a categoric answer to twelve questions propounded, is especially desired, fuller discussion of the general subject will be welcomed. The collated report with discussion will be published in the transactions of the Academy and a copy will be mailed to all contributors.

Very truly yours
A. L. BENEDICT,
S. D. RISLEY,
CHARLES MCINTIRE.

Address reply to   *Committee of the American Academy of Medicine.*
DR. A. L. BENEDICT,
"The Roanoke," 156 W. Chippewa St., Buffalo.

This circular letter was sent to 143 medical schools and 302 colleges, a total of 445. The list of the U. S. Commissioner of

Education was followed, except that a few medical schools, obviously not in good ethical and educational standing, were omitted and that no colleges having less than 100 students were included; 52 replies were received from medical schools, 25 from women's literary colleges, 52 from segregated colleges for men or coeducational, and 32 from universities; Total, 161. As the replies from a university often included information from both college and medical departments, the replies received represented the cooperation of fully 40 per cent. of the institutions addressed.

Of the medical schools which gave replies as such, not counting general information received from the university offices, 30 were departments of universities, and 22 were segregated schools, including two for women only; 18 of the medical departments of universities decidedly favored a college education for physicians. From Cornell, a curious discrepancy of opinion was received. The medical preparatory school, at Ithaca, which gives only the first two years of the medical course, and which is immediately associated with the university, held that a high-school training was adequate, while the real medical department in New York City declared in favor of a college education. Disregarding qualifications, 24 of the 52 medical departments and independent schools voted for a college education; 19 against. Of the 99 replies from the standpoint of the college or of the university as a seat of general learning, 91 favored a college training for physicians and only 1 was opposed, the remainder not expressing an opinion.

As to actual practice in this regard, no independent medical school requires a college training of its students, and only 3 universities—Johns Hopkins, Baltimore, and Harvard—adhere to this high standard. The University of Minnesota requires one year in college, and the University of Michigan two years.

Most of the other medical schools make a high-school education the standard of admission, but there are numerous evasions of this requirement. For instance, in New York, in which the state takes the matter out of the hands of the medical schools and requires the furnishing of state certificates, supposed to be the representative of at least three years' work in the high school, a judicious selection of snaps allows one of very little education to begin the study of medicine. An enterprising young man got the substantial evidence of qualification to enter a medical college in nine months. During his vacation, he was carrying on the business of an eye-sight specialist and he seemed lacking, not only in the culture which is supposed to attend an education but in the rudiments of a professional instinct. At the same time, it appears that all of the medical schools which replied to our circular letter were honestly trying to adhere to a high-school education or its reasonable equivalent, as a basis of matriculation.

In answer to Q. 4 as to the respective numbers of medical graduates who had had high school and college educations, many replies ignored the important word respective and very few could give anything like accurate statistics, excepting Johns Hopkins which has the proud record of graduating in medicine none but college men. However, 19 medical departments or independent schools stated that from 12 to 90 per cent. of their graduates had high-school educations, and 27 reported 7 per cent. and upward of college-trained graduates.

None of the 52 medical schools which replied have now, less than a four years' medical course, showing that our answers are from the elite and that the diploma mills have discreetly maintained silence. It is true that the terms range from five and one-half to nine months but the longer terms include two vacations, several holidays and some waste of time at the close of the session so that there is probably pretty thorough technical training at all of these 52 schools.

The prevailing college course is, as ever, four years. Some few institutions replied that from five to seven years were required for the bachelor's degree but none of these were of wide reputation and it seems certain that this time included what most high-grade colleges require as preliminary work. Harvard, as is well-known, makes its standard bachelor's course three years, which is proper, as the modern high schools carry their work at least as far as the Sophomore admission examinations of a generation ago. Northwestern, Washington (at St. Louis), Iowa State, and Boston Universities, and Illinois College and Haverford College formally recognize the three years' course. Several other institutions probably allow the required work to be done in three years, but do not formally admit this, though urged to do so. For instance, this was formerly quite a common practice at the University of Michigan. Some colleges also allow a semester to be saved and certain universities that require four years for the bachelor's course, allow a year or more to be saved on a combined bachelor's and medical course. No college makes a difference in time for the different bachelor's degrees and the general tendency seems to be against the multiplicity of degrees of a decade or two ago, most colleges giving only two, A.B. and B. S., while a few give the one degree, A. B.

This brings us to the prime object of this commission, the matter of obtaining information on the combination of college and medical courses. Q. 7

Do you believe that a candidate for the medical doctorate who has already received a bachelor's degree or who shall combine a college and a medical course, should have any time-allowance in his favor, or that he should be treated, in this regard, exactly as one who undertakes the medical course with merely a high-school education or less?

was answered unequivocally in the affirmative by 30 medical departments or independent schools; affirmatively with some qualification by 7, which took pains to specify that the college course should have included directly serviceable studies. One, Columbia, including the College of Physicians and Surgeons, allows an economy of time only to its own students. Seven were opposed to allowing any compromise, including four universities and 3 independent medical schools, but one of these negative answers was from the Cornell preparatory medical school at Ithaca, and is in opposition to the actual practice of the university. Of the literary colleges, 65 answered unequivocally in the affirmative, 16 affirmatively with some qualification, chiefly that preliminary medical studies should be included in the bachelor's course, while 9 were opposed to any time-allowance.

Q. 8 was addressed to those who favored a time-allowance, to determine whether they had in mind the general culture and mental acuteness of a college graduate or whether they allowed for no increase in rapidity of absorption of the medical course but merely considered that certain studies might apply to both courses. From the standpoint of the medical teacher, 1 voted no, 4 favored the former and 1 the latter view, while 24 discreetly based their opinion on both views. This question was answered by several literary colleges which had not unequivocally assented to the general proposition so that 4 recognized the general superiority of training of the college graduate, 6 merely his technical training in college, while 72 accepted both factors without attempting to discriminate.

As to actual practice in this regard, 11 universities provide for a combined course of seven years; 4 allow a combined course, but not necessarily in all cases, of six years; 10 separate schools of medicine allow a graduate of a college to take the medical degree in three years. One university allows an unspecified time-discount, and 1 or 2 give credit for college courses bearing on medicine but allow no economy of time. Jefferson Medical College makes the incomprehensible statement that a combined course may be completed in five years. It is of interest to note that McGill University, at Montreal, has recently established a six years' combined course, allowing either A.B., or B.S., and M.D.

Q. 12 would obviously not be answered without qualification, expressed in many instances and implied in all. Eleven medical departments of universities favor a cooperation with segregated colleges and medical schools for a time-allowance, and 6 oppose it. Nineteen, however, would conform to equable regulation in this regard and none positively refuses. Nine independent medical schools favor cooperation and only 2 oppose it while 16 would accept regulation and only 1 refuses. Of the literary colleges and universities replying mainly from the standpoint of the college or having no medical department, 67 favor cooperation and 3 oppose it. Fifty-eight would conform to regulation and 1 refuses.

While there has not been a unanimous consent to the plan of combination courses nor to the implicit attitude of the Academy that a college education is always desirable for a physician and while a general insistence on the latter proposition is impracticable, both the number and the uniformly courteous spirit of the replies show that the Academy is interested in what educational institutions recognize as an issue of vital importance. Many replies have welcomed our interference in this matter and have said that the college has been attempting to secure results along the same general lines. There is a tendency for the college on the one hand, and the medical school on the other, to insist, each on the full carrying out of its own requirements. Probably the ideal requirement, as eloquently advocated by several of the colleges, is a bachelor's degree. On the other hand, several medical teachers have advocated that the medical course should be reduced to two years, composed of clinical and didactic instruction in the practical branches, and that the whole of the work ordinarily carried on in the first two years of the medical course should be required on admission. A few universities have anticipated this plan in a combined course or by establishing special preparatory medical departments, not necessarily in centers where clinical instruction is feasible. But the immediate execution of any such plan calls for the amendment of medical laws, wisely framed to meet present conditions but which insist on a stated time of attendance at institutions which must be known and incorporated as medical schools. A Pennsylvania college cites the case of one of its graduates who was actually paid to instruct students at a medical school which could not even credit him with the work in which he was competent to act as teacher. Thus, if the combination plan of collegiate and medical study is extended to segregated colleges and medical schools, the letter, though not the spirit of existing laws, must be modified.

No dissent is made to the statement in our circular that the medical profession is overcrowded and that no economic embarrassment need be feared from any method of restricting matriculation in medical schools nor to the statements that the elevation of matriculation requirements tends to prevent men from preceding a medical with a college course and that the combination course is, on the whole, in advance of present legal requirements. Some dissent was expressed to the other statements, for which I willingly assume personal responsibility.

The President of Harvard University seems to construe the statement that "The general rights of citizenship and the poor requital of medical practice demand that such requirements" (*i. e.*, for the medical doctorate) "should be of a reasonable nature," as a plea for a low standard. Out of its context, this would be a logical inference but it was not intended to condone a low standard or even to express the approval by the Academy of the present legal minimum of the most advanced states. At the same time, in any effort of this nature, we must not overlook the economic law that except transiently, one can not get a $5,000 man for $1,000, which is the approximate average net income in the American medical profession. However, the best way to equalize supply and demand and to bring about the necessary improvement in professional income, is to render the matriculation requirements more severe. As Harvard is the leader in the practical execution of the educational scheme of throwing as much work and time as possible on the preparatory school and of condensing the effort in the college course to three years for the average student of ability, it is obvious that we are in complete harmony of opinion.

The Rev. Prefect of studies of the Holy Cross College, is decidedly opposed to the fourth statement that:

> Both from economic and ethical reasons, it is undesirable that the period of bread-winning and of responsibility should be too long deferred. If we assume that no necessity for self-support exists during the educational period of life, the average young man will leave high school at eighteen, the college at twenty-two, the medical school at twenty-six, and the hospital at twenty-seven and, under present conditions, he will not be self-supporting until he is thirty.

He replies "Thirty is young enough for the responsibility of an M.D., and this calculation puts it at twenty-seven. One who needs a means of support at an earlier age can find others." This topic was quite thoroughly discussed at our meeting in Philadelphia in 1897. Dr. William Pepper, at that time, expressed the conviction that any educational system which did not allow an entrance upon life work by the average man, at about twenty-three, was in error. While this opinion was not unanimously accepted, it should have much weight, and I would emphasize the proposition that the average successful man, in the best sense, in any line of life work, has done the greater part of that work by the time he is thirty, although opportunity and influence do not usually allow the recognition of his value to be apparent till later. The decision of this question must rest on personal conviction, in each case : looking backward, how many of us feel that we jeopardized the health and life of our patients in our early practice, simply because of immaturity of judgment? Lack of actual knowledge, either in the general professional fund or in our personal store, must be excluded, as well as lack of tact which had merely a business bearing on our ability to acquire or hold practice. I believe that most of us will decide this question in accordance with the precedent of that Great Physician whose life work was completed when he was little past thirty.

Dr. J. C. Wilson and others, at our meeting in 1897, brought out the point that much economy of time in education might be effected by following the English plan of bringing the boy to the high school at an earlier age. The President of Northwestern University, though already following the plan of a seven years' combined college and medical course, suggests that the endeavor should be made to bring the pupil to the high school at the age of twelve, which certainly seems feasible and which would obviate the entire difficulty of allowing the professional man to enter upon his life work with a liberal education and, still, at a sufficiently early age.

From institutions of different kinds, come many valuable suggestions chief among which are two, that the requirements of the medical matriculant should be supervised so as to avoid the mere presentation of a certain bulk of high-school subjects and to insure a proper distribution of preliminary study among the sciences and classics; secondly, that it is only in a limited sense that medical schools have raised their requirements from two to four years' technical training in the last ten or fifteen years. From medical school and university alike, it is urged that the scientific branches at present filling most of the first half of the medical course, should be pursued under teachers making a lifelong occupation of such sciences, and in the atmosphere of an institution of learning, not merely of a professional apprenticeship. Let us not ignore the fact that if all medical students matriculated with a thorough knowledge of anatomy, physiology, and chemistry including their application to the normal and diseased human body, and practical familiarity with microscopic and bacteriologic technic, if, in addition they had a broadly trained intellect and a familiarity with the languages from which medicine has derived its nomenclature and is drawing its present advanced information, our medical schools could graduate a better physician in two years than they now do in four. The old system of personal apprenticeship with a preceptor was an excellent one but it reversed the proper and natural sequence of training. Would it not be a good plan to require either hospital service or service with a practitioner, for a year after the completion of the technical course?

[Note in the annexed tables the figures at the top of the columns refer to the questions as numbered in the circular letter.]

TABULATION OF REPLIES—UNIVERSITIES.

Name of institution.		4	5		
Yale University, New Haven, Conn.		literary d		4	
University of Georgia, Athens, Ga.		t		4	
Illinois Wesleyan Univ., Bloomington, Ill.		25 l. sch. 75 l college	4 years 8½ months for med.		yes
Northwestern University, Evanston, Ill.		yr. high school	¾ h. sch. ¼ coll.	4 years allowed	yes
Indiana University, Bloomington, Ind.					
University of Notre Dame, Notre Dame, Ind.		wer ept.	years 9 months lective		yes
State University of Iowa, Iowa City, Ia.				courses 4 years	yes
Central Univ. of Kentucky, Louisville, Ky.			no data	4 years 3 pass	
Boston University, Boston, Mass.				4 years	yes
Harvard University, Cambridge, Mass.					
University of Maine, Orono, Me.		75% coll. 25% h. sch.	years 9 months	4 years	yes
University of Michigan, Ann Arbor, Mich.		2 years in college			
St. John's University, Collegeville, Minn.				6 years	

TABULATION OF REPLIES—UNIVERSITIES (*Continued*).

Name of Institution.	1	2	3	4	5	6	7
University of Minnesota, Minneapolis, Minn.	U.	yes?	1 yr. coll. 4 yrs. med.		4 years	4 years	yes
Washington University, St. Louis, Mo.	U.	yes	h. sch. col. degree ex.		4 years	3-4 years	yes
University of Montana, Missoula, Mont.	U.	yes			will soon have pre-med course	4 years	yes
Nebraska Wesleyan Univ., University of Nebraska.	U.	yes				4 years	yes
University of New Mexico, Albuquerque, N. Mex.	U.	yes				4 years	yes
Colgate University, Hamilton, N. Y.	U.	yes	4 years			4 yrs. 1 yr. is practi'e	yes
Shaw University, Raleigh, N. C.	U.	yes		60 h. school 20 college		4 yrs. 6-7 mo. all'ed	no
Ohio University, Athens, O.	U.	yes				4 years	yes
Western Reserve Univ., Cleveland, O.	U.	yes				4 yrs. allow 1 yr.	yes
Ohio Wesleyan Univ., Delaware, O.	U.	yes	high school	no data	4 years	4 yrs. 2% 3½ years	no
Denison University, Granville, O.	U.	yes				4 years	yes
Oberlin College, Oberlin, O.	U.	yes				4 years	former
University of Tennessee, Knoxville, Tenn.	U.	yes				4 years	yes

TABULATION OF REPLIES—UNIVERSITIES (*Continued*).

Name of institution.		5	9	10	
St. Mary's University, Galveston, Tex.					yes
University of Vermont, Burlington, Vt.		60 high sch. 40 college	4 years		yes
University of Washington, Seattle, Wash.		prep. only	4 years occa.		yes
Lawrence University, Appleton, Wis.			4 years	yes	yes
University of Wisconsin, Madison, Wis.			4 years		yes
West Virginia University, Morgantown, W. Va.	U.		allowan'e	yes	yes

TABULATION OF REPLIES—COLLEGES.

Name of institution.	3	8
Isbell College, Talladega, Ala.	4 years, no allowance	both
Tuscaloosa Female College, Tuscaloosa, Ala.		both
St. Ignatius College, San Francisco, Cal.	5 years	both
Andrew Female College, Cuthbert, Ga.	4 yrs. from high school	both
Shorter College, Rome, Ga.	4 years	both
Luther College, Decorah, Idaho.	4-years	both
Illinois College, Jacksonville, Ill.	4 years	
St. Mary's School, Knoxville, Ill.	4 yrs., 3 yrs. same o. of hrs. allowed	both
Monmouth College, Monmouth, Ill.	3-4 years	both
Concordia College, Fort Wayne, Ind.	4 years	both
Franklin College, Franklin, Ind.	no replies	
De Pauw University, Greencastle, Ind.	4 years	both
Hanover College, Hanover, Ind.	4 years	both
Des Moines College, Des Moines, Ia.	4 years	both former yes
Simpson College, Indianapolis, Ind.	4 years	both yes

TABULATION OF REPLIES—COLLEGES (*Continued*).

Name of institution.	1	2		
Pennsylvania College, Oskaloosa, Ia.	C.	yes	allow 1 yr., 4 yrs.	yes
Cornell College, Mt. Vernon, Ia.	C.	yes	4 years	yes
Baker University, Baldwin, Kan.	C.	yes	4 years	yes
Washburn College, Topeka, Kan.	C.	yes	4 years, allow extra studies	yes
Center College, Danville, Ky.	C.	yes	4 years	no
Mansfield Female College, Mansfield, La.	C.	no	4 years	yes
Millersburg Female Coll., Millersburg, La.	C.	yes	5 years	yes
St. Mary's College, Emmittsburg, Md.	C.	yes	yes, no allowance is excluded	yes, only h. sch.
Kee Mar College, Hagerstown, Md.	C.	yes	3–4 years	yes
Radcliffe College, Cambridge, Mass.	C.	yes	yrs, 1 yr. allowed	
Mt. Holyoke, South Hadley, Mass.	C.	yes	4 years	yes?
Smith College, Northampton, Mass.	C.		4 years, discourage shorter	
Wellesley College, Wellesley, Mass.	C.	yes	?	yes?
Williams College, Williamstown, Mass.	C.	yes	4 years	
Holy Cross College, Worcester, Mass.	C.	yes	4 yrs., spe. course	yes

TABULATION OF REPLIES—COLLEGES (*Continued*).

Name of institution.	1	2	3	4	5	6	7	8	9
Kalamazoo College, Kalamazoo, Mich.	C.	yes				4 years	yes	both	yes
Charleston College, Northfield, Minn.	C.	yes				4 years	yes	credit for work	yes
East Mississippi Female Coll., Meridan, Miss.	C.	yes				4 years	yes	both	yes
Whitworth Female Coll., Rockhaven, Miss.									
Stanton Female College, Watches, Miss.	C.	no answer				no answers	no answers		
Central College, Fayette, Mo.	C.	yes				4 years	1 year allowed	both	yes
Hardin College, Mexico, Mo.	C.	yes				4 years, little allowance	yes	both	yes
Park College, Parkville, Mo.	Agr. Coll.	yes				4 years, allowance for ability	yes	both	
Wells College, Aurora, N. Y.	C.	yes				4 years	yes	former	yes
Adelphi College, Brooklyn, N. Y.	C.	yes				4 years	no	both	yes
Hamilton College, Clinton, N. Y.	C.	yes				4 years	yes	both	
Hobart College, Geneva, N. Y.	C.	yes				4 years allowed	allow one	both	yes
Barnard College, New York.	C.	no replies				no replies	no replies	no replies	
Elizabeth Coll. for Young Ladies, Charlotte, N. C.	C.	no opinions				no opinions	no opinions	no opinions	
Wake Forest College, Wake Forest, N. C.	C.	yes				4 years, allow for 95% in work	yes?	both	yes

TABULATION OF REPLIES—COLLEGES (Continued).

Name of institution.	1	2	3	4	5	6	7	8		
Hiram College, Hiram, O.	C.	yes				4 yrs., 1 yr. med. study	yes	both		
Marietta College, Marietta, O.	C.	yes				4 years	yes	latter		
Heidelberg College, Tiffin, O.	C.	yes?				4 years allowance	yes	both		
Lake Erie Coll. and Sem'y, Painesville, O.	C.	yes				4 years	yes	both		
Dickinson College, Carlisle, Pa.	C.	yes				4 years	yes	both	yes	yes
Pennsylvania College, Gettysburg, Pa.	C.	yes				4 yrs. biol ex med. course	yes	both	yes	pro ab
Haverford College, Haverford, Pa.	C.	yes				4 yrs., 3 occasionally	yes	both	yes	y
Allegheny College, Meadville, Pa.	C.	yes				4 years	yes	the latter	yes	y
Irving Female College, Mechanicsburg, Pa.	C.	yes				4 years	yes no cr. work done	both		
Westminster College, New Wilmington, Pa.	C.	yes				4 yrs. allow time	yes	both	yrs. 3 yrs for B.L.	y
Central High School, Philadelphia, Pa.	C.	yes				4 years	no	both		
La Salle College, Philadelphia, Pa.	C.	yes				4 years	yes	both		
Swarthmore College, Philadelphia, Pa.	C.	yes				4 years	yes	both	yes	y
Penn. State College, State College, Pa.	C.	yes				4 years, no change	yes	yes	yes	y
Penn. College for Women, Pittsburg, Pa.	C.	yes								

TABULATION OF REPLIES—COLLEGES (*Continued*).

Name of institution.	1	2	3	4			9	
William Jewell Coll., Liberty, Mo.	C.	yes		4 years	and biology			yes
Vassar College, Poughkeepsie, N. Y.	C.	yes		4 years	no		" "	
Washington & Jefferson Coll., Washington, Pa.	C.	yes		4 years, no cases	yes no credit work done		studies	yes
Columbia Female College, Columbia, S. C.	C.			4 years				yes
South Carolina College. Columbia, S. C.	C.	yes		4 years, owed time				
Greenville Female College, Greenville, S. C.	C.	yes			yes	both	yes	
Converse College, Spartanburg, S. C.	C.	yes		4 years	yes	both		
Kings College, Bristol, Tenn.	C.	no, if co is 4 ye		4 years	yes	both	yes	yes
Burritt College, Spencer, Tenn.	no a	swer		no answer			n answer	
Middlebury College, Middlebury, Vt.	C.	yes		4 years	yes	both	yes	yes
Southern Female College, College Park, Va.	C.	yes		4 yrs., 1 yr.	yes	both	yes	?
Hampden-Sydney College, Hampden-Sydney, Va.	C.	yes		4 years	1 yr. allowed allowed on	both	yes	yes
Earlham College, Richmond, Va.	C.	yes		4 years	sci. course	both	yes	yes
Richmond College, Richmond, Va.	C.	yes		4 yrs., credit allowed	yes	both	only B.A.	?
Beloit College, Beloit, Wis.	C.	yes		4 years	yes?	both		yes

TABULATION OF REPLIES—MEDICAL COLLEGES.

Name of Institution.			
College of Phys. and Surg., San Francisco, Cal.	high school	20 % each	both? 7 yrs.
Univ. of Colorado, Med. Dept. Boulder, Colo.	high school	50 % each for some years	7 yrs.
Yale University, New Haven, Conn.	high school and regents	39 % B.A., 36 % sch., 25 % ex	7 yrs. 1st el.
Columbian Univ., Med. Sch. Washington, D. C.	high school	5 % high schoo	alike no
Georgetown Univ., Med. Sch., Washington, D. C.	high school	78 % coll., 12½ % high school	
Howard Univ., Med. Dept., Washington, D. C.	high school dip. exam.	15 % col. degree	4 years, 7½ mo. latter
Georgia Coll. Eclectic Med. and Surg., Atlanta, Ga.	high school, 1st yr. teacher cer.	60 % high sch. 8 % coll.	1 yr. allo'd
Chicago Homeo. Med. Coll., Chicago, Ill.	high school	60 % high sch. 25 % coll.	4 years, 7½ mo. both 7 yrs.
Hahnemann Med. Coll. and Hosp., Chicago, Ill.	high school	50 % high sch. 15 % coll.	4 years both 7 yrs.
Illinois Medical College, Chicago, Ill.	high school		yrs. 6 m. both 7 yrs.
Univ. of Chicago, Rush Med. Dept., Chicago, Ill.	high school dip. exam.		4-5 yrs. both
Drake University, Des Moines, Ia.	high school or examination	no data all for 7 years, 3 yrs. prior ½	4 years or less both 4-6 years
Barnes Med. College, St. Louis, Mo.	high school	7 mo.	no allow a for deg.

TABULATION OF REPLIES—MEDICAL COLLEGES (*Continued*).

Name of institution.	1	2	3	4	5	6		9
Univ. of Kansas, Sch. of Med. Lawrence, Kan.	M.	no	high school	no data	1st 2 yrs.			6 years
New Orleans Univ., Med. Dept., New Orleans, La.	M.		Asso. Amer. Med. Coll.	3 and 4 % h. sch. 5 % college				3–4 years
Bowdoin Coll. Med. Dept., Brunswick, Me.	M.	yes?	4 years high school	10 % college	4 years, 6 mo.			7 years must study 1 . with phy.
Portland School for Med. Instr., Portland, Me.	M.	yes		50 % high sch.	4 years, 5½ mo.			
Baltimore Medical Coll., Baltimore, Md.	M.	yes	Asso. Amer. Med. Coll.	no data	4 years, 9 mo.	no		no
Baltimore Univ., Sch. of Med., Baltimore, Md	M.	yes	A.B or exam.	75 % college	4 years, 6 mo.	no		8 years credit but not time
Johns Hopkins, Med. Dept., Baltimore, Md.	M.	yes	coll. or special training	all coll. degree	4 years, 8½ mo.	yes		
Woman's Medical College, Baltimore, Md.	M.	no			4 years	yes		
Boston Univ., Sch. of Med., Boston, Mass.	M.	no	en. to college	83½ % h. sch. 16½ % college	4 years, 8 mo.	yes	former	7–8 years
College of Phys. and Surg., Boston, Mass.	M.	yes	4 years of 6 mo. each	no data, proportion increasing	4 years, 9 mo.	yes	both	4 yrs. allo'ed med. student
Coll. of Mich., Dept. of Med. and Surg., Detroit, Mich.	M.	no	high school	1st 5 yrs. 60 % last 5, 90 % h. s.	4 years		both	1 yr. credit
Hamline Univ., Coll. P. and S. Minneapolis, Minn.	M.	no	high school ex. 4 years	7–10 % coll.	4 years, 8¾ mo.	no		4 yrs. med. col. shorter course

TABULATION OF REPLIES—MEDICAL COLLEGES (*Continued*).

Name of institution.	1	2	3	4	5	6	7		9		
Univ. of Minn., Hom. Med. Dept., Minneapolis, Minn.	M.	yes?	h. sch, B.A. degree ex.	20 % college 80 % h. sch.	4 years, 8½ mo.				1 yr. formerly		n
Univ. of Minn., Med. Dept. Minneapolis, Minn.	M.	yes?	h. sch. now 1 yr. coll.	20 % college	2 years, 8½ mo.		yes	both	6-7 yrs. 6 yr. com	no?	y
Univ. of Missouri, Med. Dept., Columbia, Mo.	M.	yes	2nd year teacher's cer.	50 % college increase	4-6 yrs. 4 years, 26 wks.						
Kansas City Med. Coll., Kansas City, Mo.	M.	yes					yes	both	7 years	yes	y
Univ. of Nebraska, Coll. of Med., Lincoln, Neb.	M.	no	high school		4 years, 3½ mo.		yes	both	4 years yr. each		y
Union Coll., Med. Dept., Albany, N. Y.	M.	no		no data	4 years, 7½ mo.		yes				
Cornell Univ., Med. Dept., New York, N. Y.	M.	no	high school	no data	4 years		no own gr'd	both	7 years	yes	ye
Columbia Univ., Med. Dept., New York, N. Y.	M.				4 years, 27 weeks		allo'd ti'e		7 years cr. 1 yr.	yes	
Eclectic Med. School, Cincinnati, O.	M.	no	reg. cer. exam.	60 % h. sch. 10 % A.B.	4 years, 7 mo.		yes				
Laura Mem. Woman's Med. Coll., Cincinnati, O.	M.	yes	high school	60 % h. sch. 40 % college			yes	both		yes	y
Ohio Wesleyan Univ., Med. Dept., Cleveland, O.	M.	yes	4 years of high school	90 % h. sch. 10 % college	3-4 years		yes if part med.	both			
Western Reserve Univ., Med. Dept., Cleveland, O.	M.	yes	3 years of college	18-30 % h. sch. 40 % college	4 years, 8½ mo.		yes, 1 yr. allow	both	7 years	yes	y
Cooper Med. College, San Francisco, Cal.	M.	yes?	h. sch, yr. coll. ex.	12 % coll. 60 % h. sch. or equiv.	4 years, 30 weeks			both		as regards A.B.	y

TABULATION OF REPLIES—MEDICAL COLLEGES (*Continued*).

Name of Institution.	1	2	3	4	5	6	9
Jefferson Med. College, Philadelphia, Pa.	M.	no	high school	30½ % h. s. 27⅞ % coll.	4 yrs.	only for medical studies	5 years
Univ. of Penna., Med. Dept., Philadelphia, Pa.	M.	2 yrs. coll.	1 year high school or coll.		4 yrs., 9 mo.		7 years
Western Penna. Med. Coll., Pittsburg, Pa.	M.	yes	med. com. of Penna.	60 % h. sch. 40 % coll.	4 yrs., 8 mo.	4 years, high school	4 years
Med. Coll. State of S. Carolina, Charleston, S. C.	M.	yes	high school examination	no data	4 yrs., 6 mo.	yes	
Tennessee Med. College, Knoxville, Tenn.	M.	yes	teacher's cer. in public sch.	20 % coll.	4 yrs., 6 mo.	no, unless studies equal	
Univ. of Tennessee, Med. Dept., Nashville, Tenn.	M.	yes	teacher's 1st-yr. certificate	⅔ coll.	4 yrs., 26 w.	yes	
Vanderbilt Univ., Med. Dept., Nashville, Tenn.	M.		h. sch. coll. dip. teacher's cer.	50 % h. s. 30 % coll.	4 yrs.	yes	cues
Ft. Worth Univ., Med. Dept., Ft. Worth, Tex.	M.	yes	Asso. Amer. Med. Coll.	small but increase	4 yrs., 6 mo.	yes	4 years
Univ. of Texas, Med. Dept., Galveston, Tex.	M.	no	high school or teacher's cer.	10 % each 25 % coll.	4 yrs., 8 mo.	no if p'r't med. year allowed	1 yr. allo'd former	no
Med. Coll. of Virginia, Richmond, Va.	M.	yes	h. sch. 1 year college 1 year	no data	7 yrs., 8 mo.	year allowed	7 years
Univ. College of Medicine, Richmond, Va.	M.	yes	reg. cer., cer. of coll. A.B.; B.S.	no data	4 yrs., 9 mo.	?	no
Med. Coll. of Ohio, Med. Dpt. Univ. of Cincinnati, O.	M.	no	high school or equiv. exam.		4 yrs., 9 mo.	yes	both	have given 1 year, but state law forbid new

DISCUSSION.

Dr. A. Stewart Lobinger, Los Angeles, California:[1]

Those of us who have been teachers, feel that the question is not entirely one for the consideration of the university or the college. We have been forgetting that the curriculum in the grade schools and the high schools has been heaped up beyond measure. We give too much consideration to the refinement of the work in our colleges and academies, as well as in the medical schools, forgetting there is so much room for reform in grade and high schools. I know from my experience with the schools of Colorado[2] that there is a strong sentiment against the full curriculum given our children. The thought is to increase the future opportunities for study by putting the child in the high school at 12, and this seems to be the secret of the whole subject. It is a difficult problem to work out with the public school system, but here is reform most needed. To keep a pupil in the grade school going through a repetition of work when he should be through the high school, and then to hurry through the rest of his course is handicapping him at the wrong end of his career.

Dr. Frederic Corss, Kingston, Penna.:

I do not think the human mind develops its best activities at twenty years of age, and the boy coming out of the medical school at 20 or 22 is too young to have that quality of mind which medical studies require. What he learns is not assimilated until later. I think we should be careful not to shorten the course too much.

Dr. T. D. Davis, Pittsburg, Penna.:

It is the practice of the Jefferson Medical College to take any one with an A.B. degree; and if they have in their Senior year at the college taken an additional course in physiology and bacteriology, with the practical use of the microscope and taken chemistry, they are admitted for a three years' course. This arrangement is now likely to be forbidden under the rulings of the State Board of Pennsylvania.

I want to thank Dr. Benedict for the carefully prepared paper showing us the relation which the various institutions hold to the medical profession and how far they are willing to follow the efforts we are making to advance medical education. Also, regarding the remarks of Dr. Lobinger, I do think there ought to be reciprocity between the educational institutions of America, starting at the primary schools, going through the college and the medical school. I think it is a waste of time in this progressive age to teach chemistry to a child in the high schools, then in the college and then in the medical school. Chemistry taught at a proper

[1] Dr. Lobinger's absence in Europe prevents his revision of his remarks.—ED.
[2] Dr. Lobinger has but recently removed from Denver.

time would make men better able to practise medicine. It is a fact that very few men to-day take a full college course and graduate under the 26th year, and one year in the hospital makes him 27 before he starts on his life work. It seems to me we ought to begin farther back to prevent the duplication of studies. There ought to be some arrangement between educational institutions by which the medical course should be reduced. No man has ever failed before the Pennsylvania State Medical Examining Board who has had an A.B. on entering the medical school. It shows that the preliminary college course must have been of great advantage. A number of college graduates in a three years' course have taken the honors of their class over those who have been at medical college four years and not had a preliminary college education. I have urged before this Academy the necessity of a thoroughly equipped physician having a knowledge of logic and psychology and this ought to be required. In order to have time for these advanced studies less time must be taken in our primary schools.

H. L. Taylor, Ph.D., of the University of the State of New York:

It has been our duty during the past year to register the medical schools of the United States on the basis of the law that all matriculates subsequent to 1898 must take a four years' course before admission to the licensing examination of New York. That registration has fallen to my hands and has been actively pursued during this time. The medical law has been modified and the Board of Regents has to determine the baccalaureate courses that meet the requirements of the University for a year's allowance. We have taken advantage of this meeting and of the meetings to be held in this city to make a careful study of the subject, and at the convocation, which meets on the 30th of June, this is one of the topics to be considered. Before I ask two questions which I wish to submit, I wish to ask this Academy for the use of this paper, promising that it shall be regarded as confidential. (It was moved that this permission be granted.)

I should like to ask your opinion as to the length of a combined baccalaureate and medical course. A study which we are now making and which I have partially tabulated will be of interest. I have picked out from 34 universities with medical departments or affiliated schools as many strong institutions as I could so as to have as many political divisions represented as possible. We have incorporated a number not usually found in current literature. The first point has been to determine the length of the baccalaureate course. The B.A. degree is the basis of our study. Twenty-eight of the 34 universities are what we call "four-year-ones," which means that the college requires from that baccalaureate degree either three years of general school work and four years of college or four years of high school and three of college—a combined high school and baccalaureate course of seven years. We have, therefore, institutions strong in the baccalaureate course. Then of this group of 34 having four-year medical courses, 9 have an eight years' combined baccalaureate and medical course ; 22 have seven ; 3 have six. In the State of New York 750 high schools and academies are preparing students for college or higher work and their curriculums are constantly coming under our observation for modifications and approval. The Medical Council of the State two years ago conferred with the University in regard to a definite medical preparation course to be recommended by the University to the academies and high schools. This Council prepared a course which they wished to have adopted in the high schools of our State, and two principles were emphasized : (1) That the course should have a time limit ; that there must be eight years of pre-academic preparation and four years of high-school work; (2) that certain specific subjects should be taught. To-day New York's law requires only the quantitative test.

Out of this tabular arrangement we hope to find, (1) the number of hours on the average that should be required in each year, of the combined course ; (2) whether the combined course should include the present four-year medical course, that is, as organized to-day throughout the United States ; (3) whether all the subjects now found in the four years of medicine should be distributed somewhere in the combined course, or whether there are some items in medicine that can be dropped out. In the high schools we have been insisting that the colleges were throwing back on our shoulders the necessity of doing much of their work. It has been well said here that the high school and the common school have all they can do and that the human intellect cannot be developed and the student made ready for our present conception of collegiate work at the age of 10 or 12. Repeated studies have demonstrated that 14 years of age is an approximate age of entrance to the high school and that 18 is the average age for graduation.

Another erroneous notion has been exploded—that not five per cent. of our public school students ever enter the high school, for of the students that could enter it has been shown that 49 per cent. were in the high school. Another fact has been demonstrated, that of those who graduate from the high school a large proportion enter college. All do not go through, but they go through college or the professional school.

Assuming that the combined course is to be a seven-year one, should the combination affect the courses in such a way that no medical subjects should be found earlier in the combined course than the Senior year of the baccalaureate?

Dr. L. Duncan Bulkley, New York:

My experience has been in examining young medical men for hospital appointment, and in the education of two of my children for medicine. I can hardly oppose what seems to be the feeling of the necessity of an earlier entrance upon professional life. I do not want to feel that it cannot be done, although they are coming on very well with our present system. The more difficult entrance examinations will aid in the prevention of overcrowding the profession. Judging from the young men whom I see in the hospitals, they cannot be trusted much under 25 or 26 years of age.

Dr. John B. Roberts, Philadelphia :

I have come to the opinion that seven years is enough for the two courses—the collegiate and the medical. There is no reason why inorganic chemistry should be taught in the medical college. The student should know that before he begins his first year there. I believe that bacteriology, which is a branch of biology, can be taught better in most colleges than in most medical schools. There is no reason why bacteriology, biology, and chemistry should not begin in the Junior or Senior year of the university or college. Then a great deal of the work which is now taught in medical schools could be left out of the medical curriculum, giving time for other branches in the medical school proper. We need in the medical schools (at least, in those with which I am most familiar) somebody who holds the position which I believe the president in many colleges holds; some one to see that the various branches are coordinated. Much time is lost by allowing different professors to teach the same topics in their various courses, at points where the different branches overlap. This arises from the fact that the teaching in the medical school is not well organized as a rule, and each professor extends or restricts the boundaries of his course as he pleases. There should be some central authority over each professor to say: "You begin here and stop there." If we could cut out of the medical curriculum chemistry, biology, and bacteriology, and see that the professors did not overlap in their teaching, the scholastic degree and the medical degree could be won in seven years. It is necessary, however, that the preliminary subjects of medicine be taught in the Junior and Senior years of the college.

Dr. Harvey, secretary of the Registration Board of Massachusetts :

I am in harmony with the views expressed by several speakers regarding the medical school curriculum. If, however, certain studies now taught in the medical school can be as successfully taught during the last year in the university course I see at this moment no reason why the medical school as such may not for students so studying in the university prescribe a three-year course. Medical students should have at least four years of medicine. This we must insist on. If a student is to receive an A.B. and an M.D. at the end of seven years of student life, let three years of his time be given to a university course and four years in the department of medicine.

Dr. Leartus Connor, Detroit :

From a practical standpoint we want first to make a man of the prospective medical student and second to train him for his work as a doctor. I agree with the line of thought presented by Dr. Roberts. Much should be studied before the student gets into the medical college. It seems to me the time should be counted by so many hours of study, so many hours of definite work for a distinct purpose. The policy should be to make the most out of this boy to become a man, and to make the most out of the man to become a doctor. We should leave out the extraneous things and put in the essentials. My only hope for the medical profession is that some of the science that it studies will be put into this present problem of the scientific training of students. If it wasn't that the good Lord put into it a horse sense that enables them to throw aside some things they would be badly off. I have tried to interest my friends who are concerned with the text-books. Where is the text-book that contains only what the teacher knows, and what right has he to demand of his pupil what he doesn't know. You have a great big text-book on surgery, and you know perfectly well that no surgeon knows all there is in it. You have a great big book on anatomy and you know that no anatomist ever knows it all, and he knows much of it is not true. The same is true in all branches. The poor student has to pick the wheat from the chaff, which his teacher never could do, and almost goes crazy—and some of them do. Lots of them lose their vigor of health and mind because that which is put before them is unscientific. We are expecting of them what no man ought to expect of any boy. I had one teacher who said that he did not want us to open a book on obstetrics or on gynecology while he was our teacher; that he would tell us and demonstrate and have us use our hands as we ought to take care of our first obstetrical case and that we could study our books after we were through with the case. It is that kind of teaching for which I am pleading. I insist that the modern teaching that puts in so much laboratory work ought to be confined to definite distinct lines for specific purposes. When it is, you can rest assured that five or six years will do the work of the whole thing In the unsatisfactory way in which we are now working, we need eight years or more.

Dr. Edward Jackson, Denver :

It seems to me, taking the medical course as it is and the college course as it is, that probably seven years is the proper length for a combined course ; but a great deal could be said in favor of making it shorter. Dr. Roberts referred to the fact that so much is taught in the medical course that ought not to be taught there. It is taught there because a very large majority of medical students have not had a college or high-school course. In considering this question of a combined course we must bear in mind the need of this great majority of medical students. It is a need worthy of our attention as an organization for raising the standard of the medical profession. We do not want to put forth something that will be deficient, but it seems to me that we can state that seven years is long enough. If we can do some of the things alluded to by Dr. Connor, six years will be better. As to the selection of topics, we must, in the main, have all that is now in the medical course, though in a different way perhaps. The teaching of biology, histology, and chemistry should begin as early as the Sophomore year. But any time requirement is an extremely imperfect one. In so far as we formulate an ideal or plan that is to be generally applied, it must be made elastic. It would be as impossible to prescribe a certain time, as to prescribe the number of years for the mental development of each boy and girl along certain lines. Along with the adoption or endorsement of anything of the kind, ought to go an expressed appreciation of the necessity of elasticity.

Dr. Henry O. Marcy, Boston :

It is very easy to criticize, sometimes very hard to do ; but did it ever occur to you that we have too many doctors unless they are better ; too many surgeons, unless they are better ; too many colleges, unless they are better; too many medical schools and teachers, unless they are better? The old Roman philosopher said, train the youth carefully in mastering the things that he will be likely to use when he becomes a man. Let us have fewer colleges and demand that they shall be better ones. Then with stronger colleges and better trained men we could subdivide the work and when the men come into the medical schools, as Dr. Roberts says, the teacher should have his limitations and his enthusiasm be kept within these lines. If we had enthusiasm along these lines in the education of our youth we would have better trained physicians and surgeons. It is not alone the time limit, but how to utilize the opportunities to make the most of the man, how to help that development that will train the man into the physician. That is a part of the Academy's work, and we have been very happy in feeling that we have had a large share in shaping these questions of the future. But they are questions still. They will come up to our successors, and the better we think, the better we advise, the better will be the fruitage in the training of those who come after us.

Dr. Victor C. Vaughan, University of Michigan :

I am desirous of saying a few words upon this subject because Mr. Taylor and I have had some correspondence and in some particulars we have differed quite widely. It will be necessary for me to mention the school with which I am connected, and I desire to state in the beginning that I do this simply for the sake of clearness. In the early '80's our faculty began earnest work with the endeavor of establishing a curriculum which would combine literary and scientific with strictly medical work. We recognized the fact that the existence of the medical school with the other departments of the university on the same forty-acre campus gave us an excellent opportunity to establish such a course. Our desire was and always has been to make better and broader men in our school. We had to contend with the members of the classical department for many years before they would permit credit for medical subjects to count towards a bachelor's degree. But finally the medical faculty succeeded in its contention and I think that I am historically correct in the statement that the first combination course established in this country was inaugurated in the University of Michigan, in 1890. At that time the members of the classical and scientific faculties consented to give credit for practically all the branches that are pursued in the first two years of study in the medical department. The literary department requires one hundred and twenty hours for graduation, and ordinarily it takes a man four years to obtain this degree. But there is no set time limit. Now we have it arranged so that after a student has completed sixty or more hours in the literary department, he may go into the medical department, where he remains four years and complies with all the requirements of this department. When he obtains the additional sixty hours, which are accepted for a degree in the literary department, he goes back to that department and gets his degree. This may be at the close of his third year of studentship in the university, or it may be at the end of his fourth year. Such a student takes exactly the same work as is taken by the one who enters the medical department from any other institution. Since 1890 we have gradually increased our requirements for admission until now every medical student takes the combination course or its equivalent. It is possible that we should advance this combination course from six to seven years, but we believe that it is better to have every student taking a six years' course than it is to have ten per cent. of the students taking a seven years' course, and ninety per cent. taking only a four years' course, and I do not believe that there is another school in which a combination course is offered in which ten per cent. of its students takes such a course. It should be distinctly understood that in effecting and in establishing this combination course, the literary department has made every concession, while the medical department has made none. The result of our combination course is that practically no high schools in the country fit students for admission to our medical department. If I understand Mr. Taylor the Board of Regents of the State of New York is endeavoring to so specialize the work in the high schools that those students who look forward to the study of medicine may fit themselves for entrance upon this study in the high school. Personally I doubt the wisdom of this. I question the desirability of carrying specialization into the high school. However, I have great respect for the work done by the Board of Regents of the State of New York, and am ready to admit that the officials of his board know more about high school work than I do.

It has been argued that many of the scientific subjects now given in the first two years' work in the medical schools should be taught in the literary colleges. I doubt this very much. Take, for instance, bacteriology, which I believe should be taught as a science and not simply in its application to medicine. But bacteriology is a medical science. It had its birth in medicine. It has been fostered and developed by medicine, and there is not on this continent or in Europe, so far as I know, a literary school which teaches bacteriology with sufficient thoroughness to satisfy the requirements of a first-class medical school. Possibly there are a few literary or scientific colleges in this country that teach histology sufficiently to satisfy the demands made by a first-class medical college of its students, but such colleges are rare.

Dr. John B. Roberts:

Because they do not teach it is no reason why they should not.

Mr. Henry L. Taylor:

Could the colleges afford to put in a teacher who could teach medical bacteriology properly?

Dr. Victor C. Vaughan:

As I have already stated, our faculty may think it wise in the future to extend our combination course to seven years. In fact, our medical faculty is ready to do so at any time. I wish also to state that if a student goes through the classical and scientific department of the University of Michigan and does not take any of the prescribed medical studies and then enters the medical department, he is compelled to spend four years in the medical school before he obtains his degree. Harvard and Johns Hopkins require an A.B. degree for admission to their medical schools, and I am glad that they can do it. But we must remember that there are no other schools in this country so favorably situated financially as these are. Our obligatory six years' course went into effect in the fall of 1901. Our Freshman class entering in 1900 numbered 214, while that which entered in 1901 numbered only 113.

Dr. W. S. Hall, of Chicago:

I move that it be the sense of this Academy that the time that should be devoted to the combination course, baccalaureate and medical should be seven years. I do not want to include in the motion the other, which I think is very necessary to combine with it because it is too complicated, but simply to recommend that seven years be the time of the combined course.

The motion was seconded by Dr. Marcy, and referred to the Council.[1]

It was resolved that the further discussion be made special order immediately after the discussion of Dr. Devine's paper on Monday morning. The Academy then adjourned its afternoon session.

[1] The council recommended the following substitute, which was adopted: "It is the sense of the Academy that an adjustment can be made between the baccalaureate and medical courses by which time can be saved from the present curriculum, and that efforts should be made to adjust these courses." (ED. BULL.)

[At the executive session on Monday morning, the committee was continued, and when the time for the special order was reached, upon motion of Dr. Hall, further discussion was postponed until next year. In order to make this report as complete as possible, a closing word by the chairman of the committee is added, although it was not a part of the discussion at the meeting. ED. BULL.]

Summing up of discussion, by Dr. A. L. Benedict, of Buffalo:

The object of this whole discussion is to make the period of production as long and as valuable as possible in relation to the period of consumption of learning and preparation for life work. Several speakers have rightly emphasized the fact that the report practically ignores the quality of the work done and deals only with quantity, expressed in units of time. This is, however, inevitable for the reason that the only available test of quality of preparation is an examination, which is regarded as very imperfect by all educators. The late Martin B. Anderson used to say that "The element of time must enter into all scholarship" and while superficial and hasty preparation may render a man able to pass a certain examination, thorough preparation necessitates a pretty definite expenditure of time by all except the extremely dull and the extremely brilliant, both of which classes are undesirable as physicians.

It is undoubtedly possible and desirable that the individual who is destined to the strenuous life of medical practice should economize time and effort almost from the cradle and that he should enter the high school at the age of twelve. A little reflection will, however, convince us that such a course implies an impossible degree of forethought. The child of a family of comparatively comfortable circumstances, of education and refinement, acquires a very large proportion of his early education at home. Spelling, the art of expression; correct, if not analytic use of his own language; considerable arithmetic if he has his own spending money and is taught to keep accounts systematically; much of history and geography by travel or by learning his own family history; often a foreign language; and side-lights on all sorts of topics which facilitates his progress in school and stimulates his mental development—all these constitute a handicap of at least two years, in the comparative educational course of a child of educated parentage and surroundings and that of a less fortunate birth. But I believe that every American boy and girl, certainly the former, ought to have the democratic training of the public school, unless he is defective in health or intellect. We can not expect the public school system to establish one course for the child of the tenement and another for the child of the avenue, nor is it feasible to divide the course into short enough terms so that time can be saved without necessitating an intellectual spurt that is distinctly dangerous, for, while it would be easy for the child of fortunate circumstances to complete by the age of twelve what his less fortunate companion will have accomplished at fourteen, he can not do two years' work in one, nor even gain a term at a time under existing circumstances.

Granting that the pupil enters the high school at twelve, and is educationally prepared for college at sixteen, he is not mature enough to derive benefit from college life as at present constituted, and it is doubtful whether we would wish our colleges to be turned into boarding schools for boys.

To insure home influences for the growing youth and for the sake of economy, it seems best for each successive institution to throw as much of its work as possible upon its predecessor. Our modern high schools, with four-year courses, certainly bring the student as far as the Sophomore year of the college course of a generation ago and the reduction of the latter to three years, without detracting from the standard of the baccalaureate degree, is rational and ought to be encouraged.

Similarly, the plan already in operation at some universities, to include the first half of the four-year medical course in the college or at least in a semi-independent department at the university center ought to be encouraged by such modification of matriculation requirements, legal enactment, etc., as may be necessary.

As matters now exist, the standard college course is four years, about half the work being stated and about half elective. The former is not absolutely identical in all courses nor can the latter be chosen purely as the whim of the student may dictate. A wise compromise is required between the old-fashioned iron-clad college course and too much specialism or diletanteism. The scientific work of the medical course is just as much a matter of real education as language for the prospective journalist, Hebrew for the theologian, history and economics for the politician. While the bread-and-butter motive should not influence the college student, it is absurd to exclude a broadly educative subject simply because it will ultimately prove practically valuable.

It is thus obvious that, by a proper arrangement of the combined course in a university, a student may obtain in six years both a liberal education and a thorough medical training, equal on either aspect to that obtained by the average bachelor or medical doctor, respectively. Now it is obvious that the average man will learn more in seven years—the favorite length of the combined course—than in six, yet I believe we should urge upon universities the shorter course for the present, simply because the average man in choosing between the high-school course and a six-year-combined course which shall lead to both educational and technical degrees, will be much more likely to choose wisely, than if he is choosing between the present legal minimum and a seven-year course.

Very much has been said and written in this discussion, about the inadequacy of the college, whether existing as an independent institution or as a department of a university, to afford a satisfactory training in urinary analysis, bacteriology, etc. At a university, it is a very minor point whether the studies are pursued under medical teachers with the supervision of the literary faculty or vice versa. In the independent college, it probably is impossible to add the necessary technicalities, but this fact is not so serious as it appears to some of those that have discussed the matter from the standpoint of the medical teacher. Personally, I would go so far as to hold that the bachelor in any course, from any college of high standing, should be allowed to complete the medical course in three years, provided that he can pass the requisite examinations at reasonable intervals, simply on the ground that his mind is a better machine than that of the mere high-school graduate and can make better speed, without reference to the direct bearing upon the medical course, of his studies in the college.

The difference between college and medical courses in such subjects as physiology, anatomy, histology, chemistry, bacteriology, etc , has been greatly exaggerated. I find that medical students who have had laboratory courses in urinary and gastric analysis, staining of sputum, examination of blood, microscopic examination of urinary sediments, etc., are absolutely unable to carry out such work in actual practice and, only a few days ago, a graduate of one of the best medical schools in the country, mistook an ordinary fiber of some fabric for a long cast. On the other hand, I have taught high-school students in a week to stain, though not to examine microscopically, specimens of blood so that they could make satisfactory mounts, and also to make routine qualitative examinations of urine that could be relied upon. Even if the purely medical aspects of chemistry, histology, bacteriology, etc., were absolutely ignored in the college course, but the preparation were thorough in other respects, it would certainly be possible to add these items in a special course between the middle of June and the first of October. The deficiency in human anatomy is more serious but it certainly could be made up by the beginning of the next medical year.

We must remember that anything in the line of the present discussion is a distinct advance over any legal standard existing and over the requirements of any but a very few medical schools. We ought, at this time, to urge upon all reputable medical schools, not to accept any matriculant on teachers' certificate, regents' pass cards, etc., which do not represent, qualitatively and quantitatively, the full equivalent of a standard high-school course.

REPORT OF THE COMMITTEE ON RECIPROCITY IN MEDICAL LICENSURE.[1]

BY EDWARD JACKSON, A.M., M.D., Denver, Chairman.

A summary of the events of the past year bearing upon reciprocity in medical licensure shows some things that make for progress in that direction, and others which indicate that any good it may hold for the medical profession will be long delayed.

There is certainly a wider interest in the matter, a clearer perception that something of the kind is desirable, a more definite demand that it shall be brought about. This interest, this perception, this demand are voiced not only by a larger number of physicians, but they find expression through teachers and leaders, and even the medical examining boards have given formal recognition to this need.

On the other hand the continued discussion of "reciprocity," bringing no practical steps toward it, renders more obvious the legislative obstacles that really make it impracticable. The few state boards of examiners that have gone so far as to discuss the possibility of it, within the restricted limits of a small group of states, have gone no farther, while for the majority of states it is recognized that anything like complete reciprocity is impossible.

The suggestion of a voluntary board of national examiners, which has recently been laid before the profession, is one that merits careful attention. But it is admitted that only a part of the profession can be expected to take advantage of its certificate, which the various state boards will still be free to accept or to reject, and for those now established in practice it offers nothing.

So obvious and so great are the difficulties in the way of general reciprocity on any higher plane, that it is even urged, with some show of practical wisdom, that the only way to get "reciprocity" is to ignore all differences between the medical laws and standards of examination in the different states, and to admit the holder of the license in any state freely to practise in all states. This would be practically to exempt from examina-

[1] Presented to the American Academy of Medicine, Saratoga Springs, N. Y., June 7, 1902.

tion all who have practised elsewhere for a certain number of years, the weakest provision in some of the least efficient medical laws now in operation.

In view of the need for a better adaptation of our medical laws to the emergency of a change of residence, on the part of a physician once established in practice; in view of the danger that unwise measures are liable to be adopted to meet that need; in view of the fact that the hardship of removal arises chiefly from the necessity to review certain basic or preliminary studies that are universally more or less neglected after entrance upon actual practice, it is recommended that the following propositions be endorsed and urged upon the medical profession:

First. That in states which have a provision for the admission of licentiates of other state boards without examination, lists of those states, the licensees of which will be so recognized, be formed and published as soon as possible; and that in forming such lists a rather liberal spirit be shown in the determination of what constitutes equality of requirement. In no two states, not even in the same state through a series of years, can it be expected that the standard of requirement will be exactly the same. Yet abuses likely to arise from any moderate difference in requirement can readily be guarded against by a demand for a moderate period (three years) of actual practice in the state from which the original license had been obtained.

Second. That in states giving discretionary power to the examining board, the license obtained in another state, by passing a good state examination, or even the diploma of one of the better medical colleges, be accepted after five years of practice as evidence of a sufficient training in such branches as chemistry, anatomy, physiology, and pathology; and that the examination of the candidates presenting such evidence be confined to the other, or so-called practical subjects.

Third. That in all states in which sufficient discretionary power to do these things has not been lodged with the state board of medical examiners, the effort should be made to obtain the necessary authority, guarded by an efficient, but not too oppressive, requirement of a period of actual practice in the state from which the original license was obtained.

Fourth. That these steps shall be taken in each separate state, irrespective of formal reciprocity, or of what any state so recognized may or may not do in this direction, or of the establishment of a National Board of Medical Examiners, or of any other desirable measures. Such other measures can be promoted independently, and will be assisted rather than hindered by the carrying out of the above suggestions.

Respectively submitted,

EDWARD JACKSON,
L. DUNCAN BULKLEY,
THOS. D. DAVIS,
Committee.

DISCUSSION.

Dr. Leartus Connor, Detroit :

I think Dr. Jackson has presented the kernel of the difficulty. The trouble is in the lack of appreciation by the authorities that control legislation on these examining boards. This presentation will compel thought and out of that thought will grow the means of relieving the difficulty. When this law went into operation everybody that was a doctor was taken in, and that conglomeration included a great number who ought not to be traded off between any states. I would be very glad if, in addition to these resolutions, something to the effect that no individual should be entitled to reciprocity who does not have an education adequate to understand modern medicine or to produce it. I think it would be along the spirit of the resolutions.

Then there is another point which I think educationally would help to promote this. We have in the states a medical licensing board whose dicta furnishes the legal right to practise medicine. We have also what are called professional societies, whose business it is to cultivate professional fellowship and development, beyond and above the legal right to practise medicine. I think it is desirable to make this distinction and keep it clear to the end, that those who represent the profession, who are the state societies, and those who represent the people, who are the legal examining boards and who include all possible isms, shall be entirely separate. There is no reason why there should not be among state societies a full and fair reciprocity; and this did exist eighty years ago. A reciprocity in my own state existed with New York, Massachusetts, and Pennsylvania in that early date. That included what are now separated. It included the societies which were local. That has been changed, and we stand a mass of state organizations and a mass of local ones. One gives us the right to practise medicine, and the other determines the locality. More emphasis should be placed upon the reciprocity of state society members, so that a gentleman belonging to the Medical Society of the State of Pennsylvania, if he move to Michigan, would have only to bring his evidence of good standing. Other social bodies interchange, and it seems to me we might do that among our state societies. That would prepare the public as well as the professional mind to remove certain limitations in the way of legal reciprocity. Otherwise, I am in hearty accord with the resolutions as they stand, and move their adoption. If it is thought best, this other idea could be added.

Dr. Benjamin Lee, Philadelphia :

This report is valuable and suggestive, and contains certain recommendations. I think it has been the habit of the Academy whenever necessary to take action on a practical matter, to refer the subject to the Council before the Academy itself acted upon it. I would, therefore, amend by moving that this report be referred to the Council to report again to the Academy. The amendment was accepted as a substitute for the original motion, seconded and adopted.

[For the action taken by the Academy see the Transactions of the Academy as published in the Bulletin, for October, 1902—this volume p. 112.]

OBSERVATIONS IN PASSING.

LOCAL MEETINGS OF THE ACADEMY.

At the Atlantic City meeting of the American Academy of Medicine—the meeting for 1900—Dr. E. F. Wilson, of Columbus, O., suggested the advisability of holding local meetings of the fellows of the Academy. He asserted that most of the fellows who attended the annual meetings had an uncommonly pleasurable and profitable time. Since it is impossible to secure the attendance of a very large proportion of its membership at the annual meetings, the effort should be made to afford those who are unable to attend, an opportunity to become acquainted with the Academy spirit and receive some of the benefits of their membership by means of local meetings.

The proposal was favorably received by the Council and that year a very pleasant meeting was held in Philadelphia. One result of the meeting was a suggestion from the local committee of arrangements, that the vice-presidents each arrange for a local meeting during the year. This was presented at the meeting at St. Paul and received the approval of the Council. At the St. Paul meeting, Dr. L. B. Tuckerman, of Cleveland, suggested, as an advance on the idea, that these local meetings could be organized as chapters or branches, and thus interest a larger number, more especially among the younger physicians, whose practice as yet would not warrant their attendance upon the annual meetings and who, consequently, would not seek for admission. Dr. Tuckerman's suggestion was thought to be wise, but the Academy did not see its way clear to legislate upon the subject until further experience would make clear the legislation needed. It, however, devised a plan by which special meetings could be called where Fellows could be elected. Dr. Tuckerman took up the plan with great enthusiasm; his illness and death prevented any results. During the year 1901-1902 local meetings were held at Philadelphia and Columbus. At Columbus, it is said, a local organization was effected, but as this has not been reported to the Council it is not certainly known.

At the meeting at Saratogá Springs, last June, the nominating committee, in their report, presented a recommendation as follows: "Your committee suggests that there be held local, midwinter reunions—called and arranged by the vice-presidents—of members to which eligible men and women shall be invited and shall have an opportunity to learn of the work of the Academy." This recommendation was adopted by the Academy.

Thus far, this year, but one meeting has been reported, although several are in contemplation. On October 29th, the fellows residing in Albany met at the Ten Eyck and organized the "Albany American Academy of Medicine Club." An account of this meeting appears upon another page.

This is the first local meeting attempting a permanent organization reported officially to the secretary. It is planned to hold meetings from time to time for the discussion of Academy topics, more especially those which may be of local value.

A proper enthusiam for the American Academy of Medicine is commendable. To urge any action which will assist in increasing the personal interest of the fellows is, as a consequence, permissible. But there is a higher reason. The Academy has a right to exist only as it is useful. These local meetings will multimanifold the usefulness of the Academy, and should be sought for by every well wisher of the Academy.

•

The annual conference of the State and Provincial Boards of Health of North America, at its meeting in New Haven last October, expressed itself in no uncertain language regarding the alleged plague condition in San Francisco. When will the "business interests" of any community learn that it is only the ostrich that does not see when it hides its head in the sand.

•

The prizes for essays on "Preventive Medicine," offered by the Maltine Company, have been awarded, Dr. W. Wayne Babcock, of Philadelphia, receiving the prize of $1,000 for an essay entitled "The General Principles of Preventive Medicine." To Dr. Lewis S. Somers, also of Philadelphia—living about two squares from Dr. Babcock—is awarded the prize of $500 for an essay entitled "The Medical Inspection of Schools—A problem in Preventive Medicine." Out of 209 essays submitted, the places of residence of five of the authors are unknown. The remaining 204 came from 37 states, Alaska, the District of Columbia, and from two Canadian provinces. How many began essays that were not submitted can never be told. Probably the widest benefit will result from the wide-spread interest. Those who were in any way led to make any study because of the offer, have received a reward for their efforts and may be winners of greater prizes than the prize winners. The Maltine Company is to be congratulated on the results of its efforts.

•

We are requested by the Success Publishing Company to insert the following item:

For nearly a year past many of the doctors and dentists of this country have been victimized by a very clever swindler who has passed under several aliases, among them R. G. Stearns, R. L. Nelson, and others. He claims to represent The Success Company, publishers of the *Success* magazine, and takes orders for numerous magazines comprised in the *Success* clubbing offers. He works very rapidly, jumping from town to town, and always among doctors and dentists. All the money he obtains is appropriated, and the magazines are never ordered or received. Every effort has been made by The Success Company to apprehend this swindler, but so far without success. The Success Company requests us to notify all doctors and dentists that its representatives always bear a special dated card of introduction, and to patronize no others. It also offers a reward of $50.00 for any information which will lead to the apprehension of this swindler. He is described as follows:

From 23 to 25 years old; 5 ft. 9 in. in height; medium build; weight about 150 lbs.; dark hair (almost black) of medium length, very curly about the temples; dark gray eyes (almost hazel); rather sallow complexion, with scattered dark brown freckles; face unusually round for man of so light build; clothes not shabby, but far from new, and much worn. Black coat and vest, gray trousers (hard-twisted goods), with small stripe; black derby hat, much worn; old style turn-down collar, with made tie. General untidy appearance for a man in the soliciting business.

AMERICAN ACADEMY OF MEDICINE NEWS NOTES.//
THE LOCAL MEETING AT ALBANY.

The initial meeting of the Albany American Academy of Medicine Club was held at the Ten Eyck hotel, the evening of Wednesday, the 29th of October, 1902. It had been arranged that Dr. McIntire, the president of the National organization, the American Academy of Medicine, should grace the occasion with his presence and be useful, besides, by giving the members of the new club a better understanding of what the general organization had already accomplished and what it purposes for the future. The meeting was a reception to President McIntire, though it was designed to effect an organization as well. Mr. Parsons, secretary of the University of the State of New York, added much to the pleasure and decidedly to the profit of the occasion, as did also his associate, Dr. Taylor, by being present and seeking, as well as giving, information concerning the common interests of their Board of Regents and the American Academy of Medicine. There were present Doctors Blumer, Barker, Craig, Morrow, Munson, Tucker, and Culver. Dr. Barker was made temporary chairman and Dr. Culver secretary. On Dr. Craig's motion this temporary choice of officers was made permanent. It was, after much debate, decided to call the new organization the Albany American Academy of Medicine Club. President McIntire excited some surprise by announcing that this is the first branch of this sort formally organized; it had been supposed that the capitol city of the Empire state had for its predecessor, in this regard, the birthplace of the general Academy, Philadelphia. Its birth-year was 1876. The president and secretary were authorized to draft by-laws for the government of the new club, after which it adjourned to a pleasant banquet, of which the main features were able, instructive addresses by Dr. McIntire and Mr. Parsons.

In its *ensemble* the meeting was very gratifying to those desirous of the success of the National Academy and of the new club. C. M. CULVER, *Secretary*.

Complying with an invitation from the faculty, the American Academy of Medicine was officially represented at the inauguration of Joseph Swain, LL.D., as president of Swarthmore College, on November 15th, ex-President G. Hudson-Makuen acting as our delegate at the request of the president.

LITERATURE NOTES.

THE PUBLIC AND THE DOCTOR. By a Regular Physician. Published by DR. B. E. HADRA, Dallas, Texas. Cloth, pp. 149. Price, 50 cents.

This little book deserves a better dress and more careful proofreading. The purpose of the book is to furnish a manual on doctors and doctors, and the proper relation of the public towards either class, to be given by physicians to their patients for their instruction. It is, on the whole, a pleasantly written work and cannot but fail to be serviceable in many families, who err in their selection of a physician through ignorance. The reviewer does not agree with some of the statements, nor coincide in the wisdom of some of the opinions, but these are but minor points.

Should any of our readers find it more convenient to send to the Bulletin than to the publisher we will secure the work and forward it upon the receipt of the price.

THE MEDICAL DIRECTORY OF NEW YORK, NEW JERSEY, AND CONNECTICUT. Published by the New York State Medical Association. Vol. IV. 1902-1903. pp. 982. Price, $2.50, post-paid.

If ever any state association sets an example worthy to be followed, surely this directory is worthy of the distinction. It gives the names and addresses, with other valuable information, of 13,364 physicians, distributed as follows: 3,948 in the borough of Manhattan and Bronx, 1,323 to the borough of Brooklyn, 173 to the rest of greater New York, 5,162 in the state outside of the metropolis, 1,655 in New Jersey, and 1,103 in Connecticut. It may be obtained by addressing the Publishing Committee, 64 Madison Avenue, New York City.

THE PHYSICIANS VISITING LIST (LINDSAY AND BLAKISTON'S) FOR 1903. 52nd year of its publication. Philadelphia: P. Blakiston's Son & Co. For 25 patients per week, with pencil, pocket, etc. Leather with tuck. Price, $1.00 net.

This is the old reliable, but not an old fossil, since the editors are continually on the alert to incorporate any new feature which will add to its value. This year it has, in addition to the usual tables, an article on "Incompatibility," and a page on the "Immediate Treatment of Poisoning."

A COMPEND OF HUMAN PHYSIOLOGY ESPECIALLY ADAPTED FOR THE USE OF MEDICAL STUDENTS. By ALBERT P. BRUBAKER, A.M., M.D., Adjunct Professor of Physiology and Hygiene in the Jefferson Medical College, etc. Eleventh edition, revised and enlarged, with illustrations and a table of physiologic constants. Philadelphia: P. Blakiston's Son & Co. 1902. pp. 270. Cloth. Price, 80 cents net.

This is a revision of No. 4 of the excellent series of Quiz compends issued by this house. They have already made reputations for themselves. Dr. Brubaker has been painstaking in this revision and has been quite successful in giving an up-to-date account of his subject in a little space.

THE MATTISON'S METHOD IN MORPHINISM: A MODERN AND HUMANE TREATMENT OF THE MORPHIN DISEASE. By J. B. MATTISON, M.D. New York, published for the author: E. B. Treat & Co. 1902. Cloth, 40 pp. Price, $1.00.

This brochure is devoted to the study of the method of using the bromids in the treatment of the opium habit. It gives the results of 30 years' experience and study.

THE PHYSICIAN'S ACCOUNT BOOK, Consisting of a Manilla-bound Book and a Leather Case. By J. J. TAYLOR, M.D. Price, $1.00. Book to fill case only, 40 cents. Philadelphia: Medical Council, 12th and Walnut Streets.

This book seems to be admirably adapted to keep accounts that will be of value in collecting bills by legal processes. It is very little larger than the ordinary visiting list, takes but very little more time to make the record; hence its added value as an evidence in court more than offsets these two minor drawbacks.

UNIVERSITY OF THE STATE OF NEW YORK:
 I. REGENTS' BULLETIN, No. 58. 40th University Convocation, June 30–July 1, 1902, Price, 25 cents.
 II. NEW YORK STATE LIBRARY BULLETIN, No. 69. Comparative Summary and Index of Legislation in 1901. Price, 25 cents.
 III. IBID., No. 72. Review of Legislation, 1901. Price, 25 cents.
 IV. IBID., No. 76. Digest of Governor's Messages, 1902. Price, 25 cents.

One may be confessing ignorance of the labors of the state educational departments of other states in asserting that New York is furnishing more assistance to the searcher after truth than any other single bureau of the kind in the country. The pamphlets under review emphasize this statement:

I. We have here, among other excellent addresses and papers, several that should be mentioned : President Butler's address on "Some Fundamental Principles of American Education." President Schurman's address on "The Elective System and Its Limits," with the accompanying discussion. Regent Vanderveer's "Requirements for Admission to Medical Schools," and the discussion. These two topics are so closely allied to the report presented by Dr. Benedict and appearing in this number of the Bulletin of the American Academy of Medicine,[1] that every one interested in the subject should consult the Regents' Bulletin.

II. This is a part of the work of the New York State Library whereby the legislature of that state is helped. As fast as advance copies of the session laws of each state can be secured, the separate laws are summarized on cards and classified by subjects. These card-lists are published in an annual volume, before the meeting of the legislature, which is then informed of the legislation of all the states the previous year.

Apart from the purpose for which it is prepared, it is of general use to any one who may have occasion to know the action of the various state legislature upon any subject—medical legislation for example.

III. Using II as a basis, experts in the various departments have reviewed the legislation in the several states, thus enabling the reader to obtain a comprehensive view of the subject.

IV. This Bulletin does the same for the governor's messages as III does for the legislative enactments.

A complimentary copy has been sent us of *The Delineator*, published by the Butterick Publishing Company. *The Delineator* is now 30 years old, and commemorates that event by this enlarged Christmas number. It seems to be replete with good things for its patrons, is a marvel of typographic neatness, and enriched by

[1] Page 121.

abundance of illustration both in black and white and in colors.

TRANSACTIONS OF MEDICAL SOCIETIES :
  I. TRANSACTIONS OF THE MEDICAL SOCIETY OF NEW JERSEY, 1902. pp. 290.
  II. TRANSACTIONS OF THE STATE MEDICAL ASSOCIATION OF TEXAS. 34th Annual Session, held at Dallas, Texas, May 6-9, 1902. pp. viii + 587.
  III. TRANSACTIONS OF THE STATE MEDICAL SOCIETY OF WISCONSIN. Vol. xxxvi. 1902. pp. xv + 504.

I. It appears from the minutes that the Medical Society of New Jersey has corporate power to grant the degree of M.D.; that the New Jersey State Association of nurses are striving to secure legislative enactment for registering nurse (a project also under way in New York); and that New Jersey is taking the right stand upon recognizing the licenses of boards of examiners of other states. Should the candidate demonstrate that he has stood the test equal to the New Jersey requirements, he is accepted without an examination, without any inquiry whether the board issuing the license accepts the license of New Jersey or not. The volume also contains an excellent report on the abuses of medical charity.

II. The Texas transactions are always interesting, but contain little for the Bulletin to review. The association, in common with so many state societies, is struggling with reorganization, and has a new constitution under discussion.

III. Wisconsin still bears the palm for a handsome-looking volume. The meeting for 1902 was helpful and successful, and the papers and discussions were of value. In common with New Jersey and Texas, the Transactions record a revision of the constitution.

GYNECOLOGY, OBSTETRICS, MENOPAUSE, BEING A REVISED AND ENLARGED RÉSUMÉ OF THREE SERIAL ARTICLES APPEARING IN "THE MEDICAL COUNCIL," by A. H. P. LEUF, M.D. Philadelphia : The Medical Council. 1902. Cloth. pp. 326. Price, $2.50.

This work claims to be a treatise on the subjects mentioned in the title based upon the author's experience, adapted to the needs of the general practitioner. It is based on a series of articles published in the *Medical Council*, where they were seen and appreciated by a wide circle of readers.

STATE OF NEW YORK—STATE COMMISSION IN LUNACY. 13th Annual Report—October 1, 1900, to September 30, 1901. pp. 1470.

This volume gives a wealth of material, most of it at first

hand, helpful to the economic and sociologic study of this division of defectives.

UVEITUS—Symposium of Papers Read before the Ophthalmological Section of the American Medical Association at the Annual Meeting, Saratoga, N. Y., June, 1902. Chicago: American Medical Association Press. 1902. Cloth. pp. 91.

These truly valuable and suggestive papers have already appeared in the *Journal of the American Medical Association*. Their reprint in this handy volume will add greatly to the convenience of their re-reading.

GENERAL CATALOGUES.

I.—COLUMBIA UNIVERSITY IN THE CITY OF NEW YORK. 1754-1900. pp. 760.

II.—UNIVERSITY OF MICHIGAN. 1837-1901. pp. 706.

I.—Columbia has a wealth of history and has seen several changes in location, due to the great growth in the city of its habitation. This volume gives the lists of those who have been associated with it during these years.

II.—The history of the University of Michigan, as shown by its catalogue, while covering fewer years, includes almost as many names due to its great popularity from its organization.

Graduate lists—especially when as admirably arranged as in these catalogues, are always welcome additions to the Bulletin's library, as it enables us to keep in closer touch with the college men.

WORTH REPEATING.

From an introductory address at the University College, Liverpool, by Sir Frederick Treeves:

"All knowledge is of value in the making of a successful practitioner, and the mass of all that is to be known in the science of medicine is colossal to contemplate. It must not be assumed that the education of the physician can be founded exclusively upon text-books and treatises, even when it is supported by work in the laboratory and at the bedside. A man may possess all the learning that a well-equipped library may contain and all the erudition attentive observation in the wards may bestow and yet be short of complete success as a practitioner of his art. Absolute efficiency cannot be gauged by academic distinction nor can it be discovered by the touchstone of the examination table. In the accomplishments of the most learned physician there may be one thing lacking, the need of which may stand between him and the fullest equipment for success, and that one thing is a tactful and sympathetic knowledge of his fellow man. It is possible that a doctor may be acquainted with all that is to be known of the diseases of man and yet know too little of the man himself. Indeed, it is not too much to say that the highest qualifications of the practitioner of medicine are not to be represented by any university degree nor discovered by any system of inquisition.

"In the treatment of the sick a certain profession of dogmatism is essential. The sick man will allow of no hesitancy in the recognition of his disease. He blindly demands that the appearance of knowledge shall be absolute, however shadowy and unsubstantial may be the basis of it. Moreover, the sick man in his weakness looks to his doctor for the supporting hand and the strong arm; he is moving in the dark and he needs to be led; he is haunted by apprehension and his fears must be allayed.

"It is this succoring of the weak, this guiding of the feeble, which represents that which is best in the profession of medicine. This great privilege, this kindly power, is the heritage of all who embrace the healing art, and it is the possession, of all others, upon which the influence of the physician is based.

"The second need in the equipment of the medical man is absolute fidelity. All those who profess to attend upon the sick undertake a solemn trust which needs to be observed with punctilious care. The sick man must place implicit faith in his doctor or no faith at all. The fulness and simplicity of this confidence are the measure of the scrupulous honesty with which it must be received. In accepting this trust every physician takes upon himself a grave responsibility, and he who is most exact in the right observance of this confidence has the greatest claim to be worthy of his calling. The burden of such a trust is little appreciated beyond the confines of the medical profession, and every physician of any experience has had to learn with much bitterness how much self-denial and self-effacement this trust implies, how little the responsibility of it is appreciated, and how much injustice to the doctor its honest acceptance may involve.

"The public are apt to talk glibly of "medical etiquette" and to assume that it is founded upon some special code of ethics, and based upon a system of morals especially constructed for the advantage of the medical profession. Such criticism is unjust, as criticism usually is which is based upon imperfect knowledge. It is needless to say that there is no precept in "medical etiquette" which is other than the outcome of the simplest justice, the simplest right doing, and above all the truest care for the interests of the patient."—*British Medical Journal, Oct. 18, 1901.*

BULLETIN

OF THE

American Academy of Medicine

VOL. VI.   ISSUED FEBRUARY, 1903.   NO. 4.

THE AMERICAN ACADEMY OF MEDICINE is not responsible for the sentiments expressed in any paper or address published in the BULLETIN.

CHILDREN IN CITIES.[1]

ROSA ENGELMANN, A.B., M.D., Chicago.

Three thousand years ago Solomon said: "The destruction of the poor is their poverty."

If at the beginning of the twentieth century a 25,000,000 town as compared to a 7,000,000 rural census, finds 8,000,000 or one-fourth of the population of England and Wales "below the poverty line," instead of Booth's "Tenth submerged," thus the problem of the children of the poor is urgently paramount. About the same statistics apply to other countries and to America; but in addition America's minimum birth percentage portends near extinction of native Americans and a substitution by the children of more fertile immigrants, *viz.*, the Slav, German, Scandinavian, Italian, Irish and Hebrew.

In Chicago alone the population is increasing at the rate of "1,400 a week, rain or shine," and the birth-rate between 25,000 and 30,000 a year. Allowing for a 50 per cent. infantile death-rate, that leaves us from 12,000 to 15,000 a year new children to care for and educate into American ways of self-respect and citizenship. Such a horde of children uncared for is a menace to the integrity of the state; for "the problem of the children is the problem of the state," and since cities hold the balance of power, the children in cities are obviously important.

[1] Read at the American Academy of Medicine, Saratoga Springs, N. Y., June 9, 1902.

In a socio-economic sense the children of the rich, in such minority, need scant consideration except to be taught that social conditions need equalization and class relations simplification, and their great responsibility toward the overwhelming numbers of those below them in the social scale. They should learn the importance of humanity, fraternity, equality, duty, right, honor; not charity in its restricted sense. Since the children of the poor are to become the brain and brawn of the country we should see to it that they be given every opportunity for the highest moral, physical, and mental expansion.

We are horrified and become spasmodically generous at times of such calamities as the recent volcanic eruption, but are, on the whole, insensible to the injustice and misery of our own cities' underhalf, allowing the children to be cradled in so-called homes of filth and ignorance that cruelly drive them on to the streets first as waifs and truants, next as vagrants, and finally as wantons and criminals.

Thus the question fashions itself first and foremost into decent housing and fit environment for our poor children and next into their proper education. Credit must be given to the universal child-saving movement that, however, gives our indigent little ones only a glimpse, rather than a full heritage of what our glorious country offers.

Proper home environment of the poor can be obtained just so soon as the wealthy accept their responsibilities in the spirit of "Love ye one another," and give to the toiler a living wage, enabling him to secure a decent home in which to rear his children. When rentals become honest and there shall be a wholesale destruction of the filth and disease-breeding shacks and tenements unfit for human habitation, with the unjust revenues therefrom, and when no man avoids his moral and civic duty, nor dodges his just and proportional taxation, then will the proletariat and his children in the cities come into their kingdom of justice and plenty. With the home environment thus established we can turn now to the school, the next greatest factor in the life of the child.

One important aim of civic life should be the establishment of day schools enough and seats enough therein to place every child of every community. Idleness is the root of all evil and its final issue, illiteracy, truancy, vagrancy, viciousness, wantonness and crime. Better much than idleness is the deplorable and hopeless drudgery of countless little lives in poverty-stricken homes, sweatshops, factories, dumps, junkshops, still to be rescued from baby-tending, scrubbing, washing, label-pasting, button-sewing, pulling bastings, metal-sorting, bone-picking, bundle-carrying, errand-running, boot-blacking, paper-selling, all at starvation wages. Children's wages are often the greatest share of the family income.

Instead of night schools being established for these waifs and young toilers, compulsory attendance upon day schools should be enforced and the night schools absolutely reserved for adults.

The school age limit should be raised to the sixteenth year. Laws should be passed and enforced *extinguishing*, rather than restricting, child labor, for city statistics show such evasion of the compulsory school and factory laws, that half of the schoolboys leave school before the eleventh year, and much child employment obtains as early as the eleventh year.

A birth, instead of an age certificate that often can be secured without pay from the nearest undertaker in politics, should be required as proof of fitness for work. Punitive measures should be directed against the parents and employers for infringement of these laws instead of against the child.

The object of education, whether for black or white, country or city child, in the words of Booker T. Washington should be "directed toward earning a comfortable living and exercising thrift and economy and some leisure for the pleasures of air, earth, and water, human associates, books and amusements." There is "the necessity for the ordinary training to live." What good is a knowledge of geometry, literature, and music if a girl cannot sweep, cook, and keep her house garnished? Of what use is a knowledge of the sciences to youth and man if he does not know how, by use of hands and brain, to provide food, clothing, and shelter for those dependent upon him?

Our educational system lacks in that it does not supply industrial training enough to fit both boys and girls for useful and lucrative service, and for the obvious duty and end of life, *viz.*, legitimate fatherhood and motherhood. Teach children the laws of life and health, simple hygiene and nursing. In addiditon to the three R's, let them be taught to play and sing and to be joyous, for the majority submerged in the "three D's— dirt, discomfort, and disease"—have early developed "a capacity for sturdiness, courage, self-sacrifice, and mischief," unrealized by their more fortunate neighbors. Let them be taught natural sciences in the woods and fields or, for want of these, let both playgrounds and gardens be attached to every city public school.

Let the children be missionaries of higher ideals by bringing their parents to the ever-open assembly halls of the school for gatherings, music, and entertainments supervised by the principals and teachers of the school, the latter bringing themselves into harmony with the parents of the children into whose lives they bring so much discipline, good order and cheer. Let the school become a social economic center as well as a place for the attainment of knowledge, where neighborhood improvements and needs shall be discussed and secured by mutual cooperation and intelligence. In this way, ward politics and government would be torn from the hands of the ward heeler, and the community would obtain for itself clean, well-paved alleys and streets, public baths, small parks, gymnasiums, ball-grounds, and the abolishment of saloon and dive. No child would longer tell of a "school where dey washes 'em" nor express such an opinion as does the little Jewish fellow in his first composition: "Indians do not like to wash because they like not water. I wish I was a Indian."

Vacation schools and summer outings should become a permanent feature of our educational system rather than a temporary makeshift supported by voluntary and philanthropic contributions. We must thank the social settlements and bands of good club men and women, who have done so much to arouse public sentiment, to the importance of these educational factors, furnishing such adjuncts as crèches, kindergartens, manual training schools, penny-savings banks, boys' and girls' clubs, reading rooms and circulating libraries, good music, art exhibits, healthy amusements, etc.

Having touched upon the normal child at home and at school, we now approach the child who is either defective or has become dependent or delinquent for reasons usually over which he has no control.

The problem of the defective child such as the imbecile, the blind, the deaf, the dumb, the epileptic, can be dismissed in a few words; *viz.*, separation and supervision in proper homes and schools, both separation and training being necessary in order to prevent further procreation of their kind. We should give these unfortunates a place for development, occupation and happiness. It is surprising into what comparatively useful lives they can be trained.

Institutions placed in the country should be run on the cottage plan, with family groupings, whether or not the inmates belong to the lower-grade idiots or imbeciles, for whom shelter and kindness are indicated, or to a higher type capable of industrial development.

All epileptics should be formed into country communities where every opportunity for training and a livelihood is offered, so that eventually they may become the helpers, leaders, and teachers of their brothers in these colonies.

Since time immemorial, orphans and homeless children have been provided for in accordance with the intelligence of the age. Before and during the 18th century, defective and dependent children, whether dependent from orphanage, illegitimacy, pauperism, neglect, or cruelty of parents, became almshouse charges in associations with adult paupers and, like adults, were also subject to indenture or apprenticeship. A gradual divorce of the children from adults in almshouses took place, although the disconnected buildings still remained on adjacent ground. A more absolute divorce into establishments widely separated next occurred. Finally a distinction as to housing and care was made between defective, dependent and delinquent children and an application of educational methods adopted to their several needs is now being largely adopted.

The evolution and selection of systems for the management of dependents has in the United States resolved itself into the following classification: (A) The almshouse system, that is unfortunately retained in all but 12 of the 45 states; (B) State school and placing-out system; (C) County children's homes; (D) Support of public charges in private institutions, first, state subsidized, second, supported by public charity; (E) Boarding-out and placing-out system by first, public authorities, and second, private organizations.

The 1890 United States Census showed a reduction of children between the ages of two and sixteen years in almshouses from 4,987 to 1,770, a 36 per cent. decrease allowing for a 25 per cent. increase in the general population. Enlightened state policy and scientific philanthropy demands the absolute exclusion of children from almshouses.

In 1890, New Hampshire, not proud of its distinction of having more children in almshouses in proportion to population than any other state, removed them to asylums and private homes. Much to its shame, the legislature of Illinois at its '97 and '99 sessions eliminated from pending bills a provision prohibiting the retention of children in almshouses.

A century's experience in the care of children is a crucible in which among all systems tried, the state public school system, with its adjunct permanent placing- or boarding-out, has stood the highest test of efficiency. It is also by degrees supplanting the county system and jeopardizing its own institutional life. In fact some of the state public schools are being so rapidly emptied by the adoption, boarding- or placing-out of the children into homes, that their final closure as permanent establishments and their change into temporary shelters is imminent.

This gradual selective process in state institutions has had such an influence upon asylums and schools as to constitute a tendency toward temporary assistance for children in temporary shelters, rather than to retain them as permanent institutions; for it is proved that strictly institutional life unfits these young charges for their future struggle in the world, such children lacking initiative, independence and self-reliance. Many orphanages, homes for the friendless, and allied institutions now send their inmates to the nearest public schools and as rapidly as possible place them out under supervision in private homes. That such a placing-out and boarding system enormously diminishes the number of public charges, Michigan's state school statistics, demonstrate. The average age of admission is six to eight years. The number of admissions to the state public school was in 1900 less than in any previous year since 1879 although the general population had increased 81 per cent. from 1874 to 1900.

Out of a total of 4,807 there were remaining in the school, July 1, 1900, only 155 children. The rest are accounted for as follows:

Self-supporting	1,109
Under supervision in families	1,262
Adopted into families	484
Girls married	145
Returned to parents	575
Became of age	299
Returned to counties	611

It may be said that the influence of state schools, public asylums, and reformatories of all description is limited, because of political interference. This argument should not hold, however, since we have in our power to prevent such interference and to appoint good men and women upon our State Board of Charities and upon our National Association of Charities and Corrections.

Societies for the prevention of cruelty to animals existed eight years before one for the protection of children was organized in 1875. Humane societies have become factors controlling the disposition of defective, dependent or delinquent children, the three great classes coming before the court. They are temporary guardians until they give over their little charges to the children's aid societies, who place them in charitable and reformatory institutions.

That great strides have been made is shown by the great number of establishments existing in 1900 for juvenile dependents and offenders; *viz.*, 80,000 to 85,000 from whence in the year 1900 alone, perhaps 50,000 children were taken to be placed out in private homes.

No more pertinent comment upon the results and worth of this work can be made than the words of a western clergyman. He says of the children thus placed out: "They actually gave more than they received. They have touched the hearts of the people and opened the fountains of love, sympathy, and charity."

It is undirected as well as misdirected energy in growing youth that is productive of harm. The Earl of Meath testifies that "three-fourths of youthful rowdyism of large towns is owing to the stupidity, cruelty I may say, of the ruling powers in not finding some safety-valve for the exuberant energies of the boys and girls of their respective cities." The neglected child travels an easy road to truancy, vagrancy, beggary and thievery. Despite the prevalence of children's lodging houses, reading rooms, day and night schools, social settlements and religious meetings, troops of waifs (criminal seedlings) still exist. That there have been large returns upon the investment of children's aid societies is seen by New York City's returns from 1860–1890. Although the city's population had doubled, the commitments of girls and women for vagrancy fell from 5880 to 1980 and for girl thievery from 1 in 743 to 1 in 7500.

Of the 28,000 children committed in thirty-nine years, 32 per cent. could not read nor write. This fearful rate is now reduced to 23 per cent. In 1891 the New York Catholic Protectory statistics show that out of 3100 boys and girls committed to their care, 689 were absolutely illiterate and 2434 barely able to read and write, while the New York State Reformatory shows 75 per cent. "grossly illiterate." What a comment upon our vaunted civilization, in the acme of its material and industrial success.

As the first step towards delinquency, truancy consequently needs careful consideration and treatment. A truant is often more weak than bad, and needs but kindly help and encouragement and special methods of instruction to arrest errant attention. If the parent of a truant were punished for the child's truancy, truancy would be decidedly lessened. Should the parent be beyond reach and the child become an incorrigible truant in spite of the effort of truant officers, of whom there are far too few, then must recourse be had to a juvenile court such as now exists in 15 of our largest cities. Brought from special detention homes by probation officers to the court, the judge decides as to whether these truants or any other delinquent child shall be put upon probation, upon a suspended sentence, or given "one more chance" and a good friend to look after them before being sent to a parental school or other reformatory institution. These schools are especially adapted to the needs of these classes where not repressive or even reformatory methods are used, but where these lads and lasses are introduced to new interests, new ambitions and new powers. Chicago's system of child-saving was embodied in the new constitution of New York and other States and prevails in Massachusetts, New Jersey, and from Ohio to California, throughout our central states. This probation system was introduced in Illinois in 1889 and the results in 1901 are as follows: Chicago had tried 1204 delinquents, of whom 1071 were dependents; 315 were put on probation without commitment; 658 were put on probation after release from the John Worthy School, a jail school situated upon the house of correction grounds. Of the John Worthy School graduates, only 10.5 per cent. or 195 were again brought before the court; 517 were placed in other training schools and institutions; 778 on probation, as compared to 517 in training, not a bad showing for this method of dealing with juvenile offenders.

That much has been accomplished must be conceded if we consider that the beginning of the nineteenth century children were still committed with adults to jails and prisons. A slower evolutionary movement than that which took place for dependents is now in progress for youthful delinquents. Separate detention houses for these offenders became houses of refuge and reform, and again in their turn industrial schools, until such a change in name and purpose and development from the segregation to the cottage family, placing-out and boarding plan has been effected as to abolish the stigma of reform from the wayward child. The names of founders and charitably inclined men are given to these corrective homes, and punitive measures have been supplanted by educational ones.

A special delinquent, the wayward girl, is a question all unto itself, and a judicious policy of prevention is worth more here than later methods of cure.

The preservation of the family and clan depends upon the chastity of the women.

Prostitution is encouraged by the life of foundlings, orphans and the offsprings of the miserably poor in tenements, where there is such close contact with vice that even incest thrives. Mental and moral training is lacking when half-matured girls fall willing victims of male associates. A large number of prostitutes begin their career of shame when mere children. Much to our disgrace, they are victims of procurers; and panderers are still permitted to betray neglected children. Physical distress, even to the point of starvation, often meets the girl thrown upon her own resources for a bare living, so that when out of work, with empty purse, she is obliged to prostitute herself. This occasional prostitute is willing and does reform if a helping hand be given her.

A great percentage of prostitution obtains in minors because of ignorance, thoughtlessness, infatuation or need. There have been and still are organized societies for the debauching of little girls. In Dr. Lepileur's 1000 collected cases of prostitutes, 109 were under sixteen years of age.

Preventative measures are summed up as follows:

1. Keep the growing child from contact with vice through proper housing and lessening of family crowding, and by eviction of suspected immoral tenants upon complaint of other dwellers in the tenement.

2. Raise school-age limit and give better ethical and industrial training.

3. Teach growing boys and girls the laws of sexual life and hygiene as a preventative against the mysteries of immorality.

4. Furnish purer and more elevating forms of recreation and amusement.

5. Raise and safeguard the conditions of child and female labor.

6. Coersively confine debauched minors in houses of refuge

and reform since they are the most active source of moral and physical contagion.

To you as physicians, it is needless to say much relative to what is being done for sick children. Each and every one of you, in your communities, are the leading factors in the accomplishment of this purpose. While we have too few children's hospitals and none for the isolation of contagious diseases in Chicago, we have dispensaries, visiting nurses, volunteer summer physicians, pure milk depots, homes for destitute cripples, floating hospitals, seaside and mountain, lake and country convalescent resorts quite sufficient for the needs of our little sufferers. Such improvement all along the line has been made that Dr. Alfred Stille's arraignment in 1835 against the Philadelphia hospital is no longer relevant. He said, "100 or more children were sheltered there on their way to the early grave, to which most of them were destined." The sick child even to-day is frequently a victim of the stubborn ignorance or cupidity of its parents, to whom these babes become a source of income in that they prevent family eviction. Mandatory powers should be acquired to prevent and remove these little victims of cruelty into healthy and happy environment.

In conclusion, I wish to emphasize the credit due to woman's paramount influence in the child-saving movement. Not alone has she been the power behind her brother's and husband's throne, but she herself has been actively engaged through her church, settlement, and much-derided club-work in the formation of public opinion and absolute promotion and installation of these many public charities for children.

BIBLIOGRAPHY.

Jacob Riis—"The Children of the Poor."
Fischer—"Harvest of the City."
Homer Folks—"The Care of Destitute, Neglected, and Delinquent Children."
W. Booth—"In Darkest England."
Smedley—"Boarding-out and Pauper Schools."
Rowntree (abstract)—"Poverty, a Study of Town Life."
Smith—"The Cry of Children in Brickyards." "Jail Cradle: Who Rocks It?"
T. Wright—"The Great Unwashed."
Ellis—"Prevention Better than Cure."
The Committee of Fifteen (N. Y. City—"Social Evil."

DISCUSSION.

Dr. S. A. Knopf, New York:

I have waited until some older member should rise to discuss this problem. I am sure we are all profoundly indebted to Dr. Engelmann for this admirable paper. It has aroused in us the realization of how much is to be done, although a great deal has already been accomplished. Dr. Engelmann's paper presents many things in the ideal, but the ideal is not always attainable and we should try to ascertain what can be done now. In my experience I have found that a movement which was started in Germany, and which has since been copied in Boston has done a great deal of good in raising the physical, and even the moral condition of the children of the poor. I refer to the provision of a daily lunch for school children. Careful statistics have been kept in Germany showing the physical gain, and also that the intellectual abilities of the children were much improved. It seems to me that if we could influence our philanthropists who are so willing to give libraries and colleges, to improve the condition of the poor by giving them better homes, with more light and more air, and, if necessary, more and better food, that this social problem would soon be solved. There are certain evils that we cannot combat entirely, and we must try to ameliorate them. I most heartily endorse everything Dr. Engelmann has said, but we must try to begin on the practical side by feeding these children of the poor of whom we demand intellectual and physical results in after life.

Dr. Englemann closes:

I think I agree with Dr. Knopf perfectly as to the conditions that obtain, and all I wish to call attention to is absolutely the rule of the evil, the present social conditions and poverty. The only way to get at a question is to go to the bottom of it. I present it and offer no suggestions, except to appeal to philanthropy and a sense of justice.

GOOD VISION AN IMPORTANT FACTOR IN THE EDUCATIONAL PROCESS.[1]

By S. D. RISLEY, M.D., Philadelphia.

Since special senses are the sole avenues to the mind it is important that, in the educational process, they should be open and free from impediment. The loss, partial or complete, of one or more of these avenues renders the approach to the consciousness more difficult and in like measure diminishes the ability of the afflicted individual to apprehend the complex environments of life.

Of the group of special senses, vision, hearing, touch, taste and smell, it is probable that vision is the most important. An old German proverb says that "a blind man is a poor man." It certainly needs no argument to demonstrate this proverbial truth since whatever may be his mental grasp of apprehended truth he must contemplate without hope many heights he can never scale. He may be willing, energetic, strong of muscle and ambitious, but without sight how shall these rugged forces be directed in the straight and narrow way which leads to usefulness and material success?

It is not, however, of the blind I would speak but of the large group of individuals who are handicapped in the race for the emoluments of life by more or less serious impairment of vision.

Some years ago a clergyman brought his young daughter to me with a note from the principal of a public school, advising that a special instructor should be secured as the child was not endowed with sufficient mental capacity to pursue her studies with other children. A brief study of the eyes revealed a very high defect of refraction which made it impossible for her to recognize the letters of the alphabet. The defect was corrected by suitable correcting glasses with which she was able to pursue her studies without difficulty and soon demonstrated her mental fitness.

Statistics of school examinations, and the daily routine of the ophthalmic surgeon, have shown that a large percentage of our

[1] Read before the American Academy of Medicine, Saratoga Springs, June 9, 1902.

children start in life with congenital defects which either impair the sharpness of sight or render painful all continued use of the eyes in occupations which demand accurate vision at the near point. These anomalies of vision are the cause, in large numbers of persons, of red and weak eyes, pain in the brow and back of the head, sick headaches and many other reflex nervous symptoms. It follows that many school children who get on badly at their books, but are bright, active, energetic and successful elsewhere, remain at the foot of the class because of their defective eyes.

It is a curious fact that children are less prone to complain than are their elders; possibly from a lack of appreciation of the untoward conditions under which they labor. To many children the act of vision has always been more or less painful or unpleasant and therefore it seems to them, quite the normal condition, and so they suffer on without complaint, for how are they to know that this is not the general experience of mankind? They are, nevertheless, handicapped by this unrecognized defect and without comprehending why or wherefore find themselves distanced in the race. Need I occupy the moments allotted to me, in tracing the sociologic results of this condition, not only over the educational progress, but its secondary influence over the mental habits and essential character of a child thus burdened by the impairment of the most important special sense? The degree of success attained in any vocation is a measure of the toil and sacrifice the individual has been able or willing to expend; these are the cost of success, the price paid for the emoluments of life.

The contention of my paper is that many an individual entirely willing to pay this price is unable to do so because of impaired vision or painful eyes. Whatever may be the trend of his desires and ambitions he is, of necessity, handicapped in the struggle for their realization, and is forced to the rear of the competing throng. If by dint of great courage and force of character creditable station among his fellows and a great measure of success is won, the station is not so high or the success as great as would have been gained in the absence of the handicap;

furthermore, that if success is won, by these afflicted persons, in pursuits requiring accurate vision, it is at the price of impaired integrity of the visual organs.

We are all ready doubtless to admit that this contention is strictly true of some individuals but my design is to show that it is true of a very large percentage of persons, and hence constitutes an important factor in the socialization of highly civilized communities. I have demonstrated by statistical studies in the public schools of Philadelphia that only 11.19 per cent. of the pupils had emmetropic or model eyes, while 88.81 per cent. manifested some congenital defect. The great significance of this fact was born out in the more detailed study of the relative condition of these two classes of eyes under the strain of school work. In the first place, the model eyes remained in uniform percentage through all ages of school life, enjoyed a higher acuity of vision and were relatively free from pain and disease; while on the other hand the defective eyes, especially those with astigmatism, had a lower sharpness of sight, suffered from pain, headache and reflex nervous symptoms, red eyes, etc., and that furthermore from these was recruited a steadily advancing percentage of near-sighted eyes with their characteristic pathologic conditions, as the children advanced in age and school progress. It was obvious from these figures that there was a definite relation of cause and effect between these congenitial defects of vision and the well-known harmful results to many eyes from the strain of school life.

The injurious effect of school work on the eyes of the children, especially the steadily increasing percentage of near-sight, led earlier observers to the conclusion that it was due to faulty methods of instruction; to badly lighted and ventilated school rooms; to poorly printed books and unsuitable seats and desks. Strenuous efforts were therefore inaugurated for the improvement of the hygienic environments; but later examinations of the same children, in school houses where all these improvements had been introduced, failed to show any marked arrest of the increasing percentage of near-sight. The Philadelphia examinations were undertaken for the purpose of discovering, if possible, the cause of these injurious effects, with the result already indicated. Professional experience had taught that the correction of the errors of refraction by glasses removed not only the pain and impairment of vision, but that under their use the eyes bore the strain of near work without injury. It was rational, therefore, to urge that no child should be admitted to the schools until it had been shown by examination that the eyes were fitted to safely undertake the coming struggle with books.

The suggestion for these entrance examinations has borne fruit in many parts of the United States by the inauguration of systematic examinations and after more than twenty years has been at last introduced into the public schools of Philadelphia.

Many practical difficulties presented themselves. The necessary cost entailed by professional examinations forbade its adoption, but fortunately an expert is not needed for the detection of impaired vision. The following plan was therefore presented to the Public Education Association of Philadelphia by a subcommittee on the medical inspection of schools, and through their persistent effort was approved and adopted by the board of education, and is now in operation.

A card of test letters was published with instruction as to its employment printed on the back and distributed with a letter of instruction to all the schools. The plan required the teacher of each class to determine the sharpness of vision of each eye of every member of the class at the beginning of every school year and to record the findings on a blank furnished for the purpose. If the acuity of vision fell below a prescribed standard a card was provided to be sent to the parents of the child on which the fact of the defective eyes was briefly stated and professional examination advised.

The following is a copy of the report of the subcommittee, to the committee on the medical examination of the schools, of the Public Education Association of Philadelphia, including copies of the cards noted in the report.

Report of the Subcommittee on the Examination of School Children's Eyes.

To Miss Dora Keen, Chairman of the Committee on Medical Inspection of Schools of the Public Education Association:

Your committee begs leave to present the following report embodying their recommendations for the examination of the eyes of the school children in Philadelphia.

SYSTEM.

1. That at the commencement of each school year the eyes of each and every pupil shall be examined in the manner prescribed on the cards of instruction herewith enclosed. A. and B.

2. That the examination of the eyes of the children in each class or school-room shall be made by the teacher in charge of the class or school-room, and the result of the examinations recorded on the prescribed form furnished for the purpose, a sample of which is herewith enclosed. That these records, properly dated, shall be placed, in card index form, in the keeping of the principal of the school as a part of the school archives; to be returned to each child's teacher for the annual examination at the commencement of each succeeding school year, and to follow the child in case of promotion or transfer. Card C.

3. That when the result of the examination discloses defective vision, as set forth in the cards of instruction, the teacher shall fill up and send the parents or guardian of the child, the blank card of advice, a sample of which is herewith enclosed. Card D.

4. That new pupils entering at any time during the school term be subjected to a test of their vision in the manner prescribed, as a part of their entrance examination.

5. That in the case of very young children the examination may be deferred until they acquire a knowledge of the alphabet.

Your committee feels that argument as to the great need for these examinations of the eyes of the school children is no longer necessary. As to the feasibility of the plan they suggest, they wish to urge that the examinations in the manner prescribed do not require the services of a professional expert but can be readily performed by the teacher. Ten or fifteen children can be examined daily before the opening daily session of the school, or at its close, so that without adding greatly to the labors of the teacher, the entire class can be examined in a week or ten days, and the records carefully made and placed on file with the principal. In this way before the close of the second week of the school year the eyes of every pupil in the city will have been examined and his fitness to pursue his studies determined.

6. Should the recommendations be accepted, your committee suggests that at the beginning it would be wise to provide for a series of instruc-

tion lectures or demonstrations to the teachers in order to secure an accurate understanding of the methods set forth in the cards of instruction.

S. D. RISLEY,
B. A. RANDALL,
WM. C. POSEY,
Subcommittee.

Instruction.—To be printed on the back of

Card A.[1]

Place the scholar 20 feet distant from the card, and ascertain the smallest letters which can be read at that distance. The card should be placed in a uniformly good light. Each eye must be tested separately, the eye not being examined being excluded by holding a card over it. All pressure upon the covered eye should be avoided. If glasses are worn, vision should be tested with them. The number affixed to the smallest letter seen indicates the sharpness of sight, and this number should be recorded on the permanent record card (C), *e. g.*, if line of letters marked 40 is seen correctly, record vision as "40" for the right or left eye.

Question the pupil regarding the liability to sore or painful eyes, to headache, or blurring of the letters while reading.

If any of these be complained of, or if he fail to read the type marked XX(20) with each eye, he should be sent home with a note of information to the parent or guardian ("D"). If vision should be so low that none of the letters on the card are seen at 20 feet, it should be recorded as "less than 200."

The vision, the accommodation, and the character of any complaints referable to the eyes should be entered upon the permanent record provided for the purpose.

Card B.[2]

Ascertain the nearest point with the yard stick at which the scholar can read the smallest type clearly, each eye being treated separately.

At ten years of age or less, diamond type should be read at 3 inches or less (3″).

At fifteen years of age or under, diamond type should be read at 3½ inches or less (3½″).

At twenty years of age or under, diamond type should be read at 4 inches or less (4″).

If the scholar is unable to read this type at this distance even approximately, he should be referred home as noted on the large test card.

Record on permanent card (C) in inches the nearest point at which diamond type can be read.

[1] Card A is an arrangement of the Snellen text type.
[2] Card B has a paragraph printed with diamond type.

Card C.

Card "C" is printed on a light weight Bristol board (about a library bureau "1" card) 10 × 15 cm., and perforated for filing in a card catalogue case, with the following arrangement:

Name...CARD C.
Address..

Date.	Age.	School year.	Vision. Right.	Vision. Left.	Near point. Right.	Near point. Left.	Condition of eyes.	General health.	Remarks.
9-5, 1900	10	4	40	20	6"	3½"	*Red and watery inflamed lids.*	Good	*Suffers from frequent headaches*

This card is for permanent record, and must follow the child in case of promotion or transfer. (To be placed in card index in care of principal.)

Card D.

(To be sent to parent or guardian of any child whose vision is found to be defective.)

....(date.)
Dear.................The examination of the eyes of....................
..........shows defective sight which may hinder.............progress in the school work or lead to permanent injury to the eyes. It is therefore recommended that an eye physician be promptly consulted.

....................Teacher.
..............................School (name and location).

The cards were distributed to the schools in January, 1902, with a general letter of instruction to the principals and the examinations begun. Before many days, children bearing the card of advice presented themselves at the various clinics and consulting rooms in the city. A number of these fell into my own hands at my Wills' hospital clinic so that I had an opportunity to verify the practicability of the plan. Without exception every child presenting these cards was unquestionably in need of professional advice. By far the larger number needed glasses for the correction of some form of anomaly of refraction, and were already suffering injury from the strain of school work.

The great value accruing both to the individual and to the community from the correction of the congenital anomalies of refraction by glasses I have been able to demonstrate; consult "A System of Diseases of the Eye" Vol. II, J. B. Lippincott & Co., edited by Drs. Norris and Oliver, "School Hygiene;" also *Achives of Ophthalmology* for July, 1894, p. 247. It is there shown that in twenty years, during which ophthalmic surgeons in Philadelphia and vicinity had sedulously corrected the eyes of all persons with asthenopia, applying for relief, that the percentage of near-sighted eyes had fallen from 28.43 per cent. in the first period to 16 per cent. in the last period, a fall of approximately 50 per cent. There was also a corresponding diminution in the degree of myopia. To those who are familiar with the hampering influence of myopia over the career of the individual, or with the serious consequences of the disease in causing partial or complete blindness from choriodal atrophies, detachment of the retina, etc., these figures are of great significance. In addition to these considerations the permanent records of these examinations preserved in the school archives will, after a few years have passed, prove a source of valuable information to scientific ophthalmology in its efforts to meet the baneful influences of modern life over the integrity of the visual organs of the race.

DISCUSSION.

[The chair invited Drs. Frank Allport, of Chicago, and John E. Weeks, of New York City, to participipate in the discussion.]

Dr. Frank Allport, Chicago:

Mr. Chairman: Not being a member of this distinguished body, I had no notion whatever of taking part in any of the discussions. Inasmuch, however, as your chairman has so courteously offered me the privileges of the floor, I cannot do otherwise than accept his kind invitation and participipate somewhat in the discussion of the valuable paper which we have just heard.

Perhaps no one has done more than my friend, Dr. Risley, in advocating and successfully working for the proper examination of school children's eyes, and whatever he may have to say upon this subject must be listened to by everybody with interest and respect. The examination of school children's eyes by physicians, while ideal in its conception, is unfeasible in its practical workings. It involves too much time, trouble, expense and ill feeling, and those of us who have had something to do with such examinations in American schools within the past few years have become pretty well convinced that the only kind of an examination which stands a chance of being generally adopted, is that which is accomplished roughly, but still quite satisfactorily, by the school-teachers themselves. This method of examination is being adopted quite generally throughout the United States, and has become incorporated as a law in the state of Connecticut. It is also being used quite frequently throughout European countries, and a recent letter from India informs me that it is being used in some of the government schools in that far-off country. The methods of making these tests by school-teachers differ somewhat in different localities, but the underlying principle is always there, namely, the systematic examination of school children's eyes by school-teachers. The method used by Dr. Risley is without doubt superior, if it can be accomplished, to the one used in Chicago, Minneapolis, Milwaukee, and many other cities. It is more complete, and therefore better, but I shall be interested to learn of the ultimate history of this plan and of whether it is adopted in other cities. If it can, I shall be rejoiced, but I doubt it. It involves more labor than teachers are willing to devote to the subject, and the equipment of the different rooms in the schools with records, apparatus, etc., advocated by Dr. Risley, will, I fear, make the expense so burdensome that the average board of education will seek for cheaper means to the same end. I believe that the chief end to be accomplished in these tests is *not* the accumulation of statistics, however valuable they may be, but the *benefit to the children*, the coming generation, the hope and promise of our great Republic. If this aim is the true one, then the result can be accomplished by the asking of the simple questions, and the distribution of the warning cards to the parents of defective children, with a little moral suasion thrown in to induce such parents to accept the advice of the school authorities. This plan is perfectly simple, easily accomplished, and so cheap that 500,000 school children can be properly examined at an expense that will not exceed $150. The expansiveness of this work is colossal. I am informed that there are between 7,000,000 and 8,000,000 children attending the public schools of this country. If this is true, 5,000,000 or 6,000,000 of them have defective eyes, ears, noses and throats, which impair their health and usefulness, and impede them in the acquirement of an education, which is perhaps the most potential and influential factor in the dissipation of anarchy and crime. These facts are enormous, and face the school authorities of this country annually. They can be grappled with and conquered successfully, and a benefit accomplished that will hardly be secondary to that of vaccination, if physicians, boards of health, and boards of education, and law makers, will determine that such a desirable result shall be accomplished. This subject is, therefore, of great interest to this Academy, and to all medical organizations, and we all thank Dr. Risley for once more bringing it to our attention. I would suggest that other tests be incorporated with the visual tests. I refer to tests for hearing and for tests of the nose and throat. These matters are also of great importance, and inasmuch as they can be easily accomplished, there is no reason for omitting them.

The objections to these tests are trifling, and need hardly be dwelt upon. For instance, teachers often enter the objection that they are not competent to make tests of this nature. This is nonsense. Any teacher can ascertain how far down upon a Snellen card a pupil can read. Any teacher can ascertain whether the child habitually suffers from headache, eye tire, red eyes, crossed eyes, discharging ears, deafness, mouth-breathing, etc., and as Dr. Risley says, any one who is competent to be a teacher at all, is competent to make these simple tests. Some objectors dwell upon the fact that many parents pay no attention to the cards of warning that are sent to them by the teachers. This is doubtless true. Out of a hundred parents thus warned, a certain percentage of them will neglect the cards, but what of it? the balance *do* pay attention to them, and this balance I firmly believe constitutes a majority of the whole. We, therefore, are able to accomplish an enormous good to a great number of children, and should we falter or hesitate because a few foolish parents neglect the warning? Emphatically no. Therefore, let the good work go on. Some also see an objection in the fact that many parents send their children to department stores, jewelers, opticians, etc. This is also undoubtedly true, but it must not blind us to the fact that such a result does not occur as a rule, and that the majority of children find their way into the offices and dispensaries of reputable ophthalmologists, and many of those who at first seek unprofessional advice, once their attention has been aroused to the fact of existing trouble, frequently seek safer and wiser counsel in the end. But these and many other objections are trifling. They are mere incidents along the pathway of progress,—incidents to be overcome, and conquered, and should not deter us in advancing along those lines, which will lead us to the highest victory in the end.

Dr. J. E. Weeks, of New York:

I thank you very much for the privilege that has been accorded me. I am sorry to say that in New York the system of testing the eyes of school children has not advanced to the degree that it has reached in Philadelphia. This is largely because the ophthalmologists in New York have not been as fully alive to the desirability of such a system. The question is certainly one of great importance; the solution of the question has been reached by the labors of Dr. Risley, and his associates and by the labors of Dr. Allport, of Chicago, and his associates. I believe with Dr. Allport that school boards and boards of health should insist that tests of this nature should be made, and that the teachers should be instructed so that they could conduct the tests in a satisfactory manner. Even though the parent pay no attention to the first recommendation, repeated admonitions will convince them of the importance to the child of the examination advised.

Dr. Leartus Connor, of Detroit:

There is another phase in which vision is a factor in educational progress and that is in the fact that the teacher has good vision. I do not believe that any individual should be placed in charge of the young whose vision is not normal or as near normal as science can make it. The irritability of the nervous system from defective refraction or muscular balance, and its resulting effects upon the children, all will agree is a very important factor.

It has been proved beyond a doubt that the reason the world does not advance more is because the medical profession does not fully appreciate the importance of the definite scientific knowledge of growing children right and keeping them right in every important direction. There is nothing in medicine so magnificent as the work spread before us to-day. It is a misfortune that it takes so long to have educated doctors appreciate these magnificent things. It is difficult to teach school boards and the people, but if we could only have our brethren know and carry out this work the results would be gratifying.

Dr. Risley closes:

I have nothing special to add. I would like to say to my friend Dr. Allport that the tests for hearing were included in the plan, but did not come under the title of my paper. As to the feasibility of the plan, I will say that it had not been in operation a week in Philadelphia before a number of these cases came to my own clinic and presented the cards of advice to parents. There was considerable discussion in the committee as to how the card of instruction should be worded, and we finally decided that the name, surgeon, should not be mentioned, but the parents advised to consult an eye physician. We thought that if we chose the word surgeon they would be afraid of possible surgical interference and so would fail to follow the advice.

Dr. J. H. McBride, of Pasadena, Cal.:

It has been stated in California that in certain of the Eastern states where these investigations are being made that the public is becoming tired of them because the method is complex and expensive. I would like to ask Dr. Risley whether that is so.

Dr. Risley:

I am glad that the question has been asked. There is only one portion of this plan which is complex, that is, the permanent record of the examinations. The examinations should cover ten years of the child's school life and the record be kept in card index form and to follow the child until he enters the high school and there compared with his educational work. That is the only part which makes it seem complex, and it is a little costly to instal the plan in 75 school-houses each with a dozen rooms. As to the rest we eliminate all cost simply saying that the teachers shall do it, so what might be called the ethical side, *viz.*, the practical care for faulty eyes, is secured without cost, or with a cost so small as not to be considered.

THE FAMILY PHYSICIAN OF THE PAST, PRESENT, AND FUTURE.[1]

BY S. A. KNOPF, M.D., New York.

The family physician of the past still lives in the memory of many of us. He was not so rare an individual in years gone by as he is now. In most families the family physician was an indispensable, important, and sometimes a very dignified personage. He was a hard-working man, seldom of wealth, but universally beloved, and revered by all. He was rarely feared, except now and then by the smaller members of the family who thought to have reason to dislike him at times for his seemingly autocratic behavior. Yet, as a whole, he was the friend of all, the adviser of the family in many matters even not purely medical. He was the confessor of many a troubled heart, old and young; his remuneration was not large; he was often paid by the year a round sum, which, when there was much sickness in the family, made the average pay for a call ridiculously small. Yet he did his duty unswervingly. He would drop in to see the family whenever he was near-by or could spare the time, although he knew that all were well. In many families he had seen the children grow up from babyhood, for it was he who helped the mother when the little strangers arrived.

Could all the pleasant, touching, and heroic incidents be told in connection with the old family doctor as many of us knew him, it would be a revelation to many a young physician who now starts out in life with the sole aspiration to establish himself in a great city and become a great consulting physician; or a great surgeon—known for his operative skill, the great number of capital operations he has performed, and the great throng of students who flock hither to hear him or to see him operate. The old family practitioner, who in many instances was indeed the physician of the soul as well as of the body to those intrusted to his care, to whose true, heroic and humane picture my pen, I know, can not do justice, is gradually passing out of existence.

[1] Read before the American Academy of Medicine, at Saratoga, June 7, 1902.

I do not mean to say that there are no more family practitioners, but I believe you will all agree with me when I say that there are few of the old type of family physician left. The present family physician is not held in nearly as high esteem as our fathers and fathers' fathers in medicine were held. Furthermore, I believe, you will also bear me out when I say that there are now fewer family physicians absolutely, and relatively to number of population than there were fifty years ago.

Who shall be held responsible for this decrease in numbers of family practitioners? the decrease in esteem, this depreciation of a once so exalted position? No person, no one class, but rather scientific events and our present social conditions are the cause of his disappearance, and the disinclination of many even well-to-do families to attach to themselves a general practitioner as a family physician. The discoveries in bacteriology and in sanitary science, the wonderful strides made in surgery, the multiplication of specialties, and last but not least, the multiplicity of different systems of medicine, such as homeopathy, eclecticism, etc., not to mention Christian scientists, faithcurists, osteopaths, somopaths, and other paths, are responsible for the passing away of the older type of family physicians.

The family physician of the present is rarely held in just esteem. In some families he is called in simply to decide what specialist should be consulted; in others he is allowed to attend to minor ailments, while in serious cases the specialist is often called in without the family physician being consulted. Again, individual members of one family often manifest a preference for this or that system of medicine. Having myself had for a preceptor one of that old type of physicians who could not bear the idea that there should be any but the one regular school of medicine, and to whom the designation allopath was as distasteful as homeopath, I had imbibed his dislike, his distrust, and his disdain for any system of medicine but the regular. Shortly after graduation, I was fortunate enough to become the physician to a very nice and cultured family. I had been successful in attending the head of the family, and I flattered myself to have gained thereby the confidence of all the members. Soon, however, I found out that I never was called in when any of the children were sick. I endeavored to comfort myself with the belief that probably my youth was the cause, and that these good people did not care to trust the precious lives of their children to so young a physician. A subsequent event, however, taught me that it was not discrimination against me but rather discrimination against the school of medicine in which I had been reared and to which I was so proud to belong. One day I met a homeopathic physician coming out of the house of this family and later I received the explanation from the father to the effect that his wife would never allow her children to be treated by any physician except by one belonging to the homeopathic school. My idealistic conception of a family physician received a severe shock and has received a good many more since. I now know of a family where the husband goes to a physician of the regular school, the wife to an osteopath, the two daughters to a homeopathic lady physician, and the mother-in-law to a Christian scientist.

As I have said before there are, of course, some general practitioners who have a number of families which they attend exclusively, but even their position is not an enviable one. To be frank, as things are now I do not blame the young medical man when he dislikes the idea of becoming, and always remaining, a general family practitioner. Physicians are entitled to financial prosperity as much as any other profession or trade. Ours is a liberal profession. It has its ideals and its ethics, and has also the reputation of being the most unselfish of all professions, and I pray that it may remain forever thus. Yet, we are men, husbands and fathers, and we too would like to see our loved ones in comfort. When we lay down our burdens, or when we are called off suddenly—falling victims in the fulfilment of our duties—we too would like to feel that our wives and children shall not be in want. There is no gainsaying that, when we compare the earnings of the specialist with those of the family practitioner of the present day, the latter is at a great disadvantage. Supposing the general practitioner calls in a great surgeon to confirm his diagnosis in a case of appendicitis and an operation is decided upon; whether the patient is taken to a private hospital or operated at home, in the majority of cases he passes completely out of the hands of the general practitioner. The surgeon has his own assistants who aid him during the operation, and attend to the dressing of the wounds of the patient until his complete recovery. The great surgeon receives from $500 to $1,500 for the operation, and the family physician who was the means of saving a life by a timely calling in of the surgeon's service receives from $2 to $5 for his visits according to the circumstances of the patient. It is this great discrepancy between the remuneration of the services of a great surgeon and those rendered by the conscientious, honest, and faithful family practitioner, which makes the young man decide on a specialty while yet in the third or fourth year of college life.

I do wish to state right here that nothing is further removed from my mind than the wish to minimize the value of specialism. The field of modern medicine and surgery is so vast that not even the most brilliant mind, the most skilful operator, can master it all. As medicine and surgery stand to-day it is simply beyond the capability of human intelligence to be a great diagnostician of internal diseases, a great surgeon, gynecologist, obstetrician, oculist, laryngologist and aurist at the same time. Men who devote their whole lives, their whole energy, to the study of one of the many branches of medicine must ever be the counselors and teachers of the general practitioners.

The relation between specialist and family physician could, however, be changed to the advantage of the latter without detriment to the former. Let me take again the illustration of the great surgeon who is called in to confirm the diagnosis of appendicitis made by the family practitioner and who receives, say $500 for the operation which follows. Would it not be perfectly just if the after-treatment, such as dressing the patient's wounds and watching over him to see that no mishap occurs, would be left to the family physician, for which he would receive a remuneration a little more in proportion to the fee charged by the operator? Were such a practice in vogue I am convinced many a general practitioner would feel more kindly disposed towards some of our great operators than they do now, and the family physician of the present would rise to a higher level of importance and esteem than the public of to-day is willing to concede to him. There is much which the consultant, the great surgeon, or celebrated specialist in other branches can do to bring the standing of the family physician of the present day to a better recognition and appreciation on the part of the family by which he is engaged.

I have spoken of the family physician of the past and of the present, and now permit me to picture to you the family physician of the future, as I see him in my mind's eye, as I wish he might be while this 20th century is still called new, and as I know you all would wish him to remain as long as mankind is heir to disease. The tuberculosis problem in which I have been interested for a number of years, has taught me many things which are applicable to general medicine, to the duties and vocation of the family physician, and to the solution of the social position of the general practitioner of to-day. The one positive conclusion I have arrived at through, I believe, an earnest, unbiased and careful study of the subject, is that the tuberculosis problem will and can never be solved without the help of the family practitioner, and that consumption as a disease of the masses will never be successfully combated until the day in which every family has its family physician. No matter how strict the sanitary regulations which boards of health may issue, no matter how many sanatoria and special hospitals for the consumptive poor we may have, we must look to the family physician for the bulk of the work in fighting the "great white plague." We must look to the family physician for the discovery of the early and curable cases; we must look to him for the carrying out of the sanitary regulations; without him our sanitary ordinances will do only half the work they are intended to do. Without the family physician only the more advanced and often hopeless cases will come to our notice. Without the family physician for rich and poor, and particularly for the poor, there will be a constant supply of new tuberculous cases, created daily in the unsanitary tenements of the poor.

What has been said of tuberculosis is certainly applicable to nearly all other diseases. Most ailments increase in severity where nothing is done to check their progress. Many diseases have their etiology in ignorance, and here again you must pardon me if I use for illustration that most characteristic disease of the masses, namely tuberculosis. Malnutrition of the poor we are apt to attribute to want of food. Those of us, however, who have some experience in the tenement house life of large cities will know that there is relatively more waste of food substances in the houses of the poor than in the houses of the well-to-do. It is often nothing but ignorance on the part of the willing but untrained housewife of the laborer which makes his food expensive but not nutritious. The poor girl from the shop or factory, when she marries, does not know the art of choosing the right food and preparing it appetizingly and tastefully. The result is often not only malnutrition of husband, wife and children, but alas! also discontent, love for stimulating liquors, crime and disease. In a wealthy family, if a child or grown person grows thin in spite of plenty of food, the family physician would be consulted and not infrequently would discover the cause of malnutrition to be the fact that the food given to the patient was not of the proper kind, and with a change in the right direction the patient would improve. The poor alone have no one to turn to for advice; they only go to the dispensary when really sick; they have neither time nor are they observant enough to discover slight ailments, such as impaired digestion and lack of assimilation, conditions which are the true forerunners of consumption and other grave diseases. Again, those familiar with the life of the ordinary workingman will know how he and his family often shrink from the thought of entering a hospital. These men will make all possible sacrifices in order to keep the sick member of the family at home and provide such medical attendance for him as they are able to procure. But timely and regular attendance is rather the exception than the rule among poor families where there is a consumptive or any other kind of invalid. These poor people will first try all kinds of quack remedies, ask their druggist for advice, or, attracted by some glaring advertisements of a sure cure of consumption or all other ailments, fall into the hands of some unscrupulous charlatan.

It is evident that there would not only be a direct benefit to the families of the laboring classes from timely and judicious treatment of any of their sick members, either at home, in a hospital, or in a sanatorium, but the community at large would be a direct and indirect gainer. By providing, for example, medical attendance to families unable to pay a regular physician, or by placing the consumptive patient in time in a sanatorium, the pulmonary invalid has 75 per cent. of chances to be cured and is prevented from infecting his own kin and neighbors. Seventy-five out of a hundred consumptive patients will be prevented from becoming burdens to the community. All this would be direct gain to the community, but the indirect gain to the commonwealth by curing and making strong and useful citizens of seventy-five out of every hundred tuberculous persons, who were otherwise doomed to death in the prime of life, is well nigh beyond calculation.

There is no doubt that tuberculosis and many other diseases of the masses can and should disappear in civilized countries, and it devolves upon us medical men of the twentieth century to devise means and propose measures to our municipal authorities, state legislatures and philanthropists that will best accomplish this much-desired end. The old Scotch proverb "an ounce of prevention is worth a pound of cure" is applicable in all diseases, and particularly to phthisis pulmonalis. We all acknowledge Koch's bacillus as the true etiologic factor in tuberculosis, but we also know that in health the accidental inhalation of a few bacilli, the swallowing of some tuberculous milk, or even a scratch infected with tuberculous matter, are rarely of any consequence. The healthy nasal secretion is bactericidal, the ciliated epithelium of the upper respiratory tract is a physical hindrance to the bacilli. The gastric secretions too, in a large measure, are bactericidal, and the phagocitic power of the white blood corpuscles, in the healthy individual, is the best safeguard against the invasion of the bacilli.

It is the badly housed, underfed, overworked people, weakened by disease, intemperance and excesses, who soonest fall prey to the tuberculosis bacillus and to the germs of all other infectious diseases. The family physician employed by the municipality would insist that the dark, dreary, badly ventilated tenement house must disappear. By giving to the laboring classes better tenements, where sunshine, light and air are plentiful, with at least 600 cubic feet of space allotted to every individual, we will save many a one not only from becoming tuberculous but also from becoming a prey to other diseases.

Phthisio-genetic diseases, such as smallpox, scarlatina, measles or grip, are all diseases which, the earlier they are discovered the more chance there is of their taking a favorable course. The one who discovers them first among the well-to-do is the family physician. He may discover the early symptoms of these diseases on his regular visit before the sufferer himself has an idea of being a patient. In the family of the poor the disease must be far enough advanced for a layman to discover it before medical aid can be hoped for.

What great good can not the true family physician accomplish by a regular periodic examination of the chests of a family entrusted to his care! Venereal diseases, excesses and intemperance may be classed under one heading and may be called a trinity of evils resulting from ignorance. While the social reformer and clergyman may do their grand work in helping to combat them, the family physician has to do the bulk of the labor. He who should be, and often is, the confidential friend of every one of the family, old and young, will be best able to warn the young man of the danger which besets him when starting out in life. If a member of a family has been unfortunate enough to contract a venereal disease the family physician will see that proper treatment is instituted and all precautions taken to prevent infecting others or a reinfection of the patient himself. Again it is the family physician, friend and adviser, who may exert the most beneficent influence on old and young by pointing out to them the danger of excesses of any kind, and particularly intemperance; for let us not forget that alcoholism is not only one of the most important phthisio-genetic diseases but also the cause of a number of the most serious nervous and mental disorders, leading alas! too often to crime and moral degeneration of whole families. In some European sanatoria for tuberculous and scrofulous children, statistics show that more than 25 per cent. of the little inmates are of alcoholic parentage. You know that our insane asylums harbor from 40 to 60 per cent. of patients in whom the anamnesis shows alcoholism to be the true etiological factor.

The physician acquainted with the tendencies of the individuals entrusted to his care will know when to sound the note of warning. He will be able to combat the idea which is still very prevalent among the laity that alcohol is a good remedy for consumption, a good remedy in stomach disorders, or an indispensable stimulant to the worker. The physician will exert all his influence to show that alcohol is not a food, but, when taken in excess, a dangerous, powerful poison, destroying body and soul, undermining the strongest constitution and causing untold misery and want in many once happy and prosperous families. With such a medical adviser given him by a wise and beneficent government, the honest but poor laborer will be protected from tuberculosis and other diseases, and the moral influence which the true physician can exert in these environments must be of incalculable value to any community.

Mr. President and gentlemen, if from what I have said you have already partially divined my conception of the family physician of the future, permit me to complete, or rather summarize this conception in the following words: The family physician of the future will be the cultured, refined gentleman who through his college training has been duly prepared for the great profession he has chosen to follow. A five years' course in a medical college, not owned or controlled by a private corporation, but by an endowed independent university or state institution, and an additional year of obligatory general hospital training will have fitted him to be a sanitarian, a skilful physician, a trained general surgeon, wise enough to know when council is needed, a physician to be engaged by a number of private families among the well-to-do or by the government as a guardian of health of a certain number of indigent families. In both cases his remuneration should be large enough so that he can perform his duties without worry for his daily bread. Leisure and opportunities should be at his disposal to follow occasionally some special scientific pursuits, if he is so inclined.

The family physician of the future has to my mind a mission to perform, so high, so noble, so unselfish, that only the best of men, the greatest souls, would wish to aspire to fill such an exalted position. The work which this family physician of the future has to fulfil is greater than that of the family physician of the past or of the present. He will rise in importance and in recognition to the highest level in his social as well as in his professional relations. To him the statesman, the social economist, the philanthropist must look for help, for the family physician of the future, whether practising in the palace or in the hut, in the crowded tenements of the metropolis or among the peasants in the far-off hamlet, will be the leader in the physical and moral improvement of the race, and in making the men and women of the twentieth century true images of their Creator.

16 WEST NINETY-FIFTH STREET.

DISCUSSION.

Dr. Henry O. Marcy, of Boston:

I rise, not for the purpose of adding to the wisdom of the paper to which we have listened, but simply to render personally my thanks for the inspiration which comes from the hearing of this paper. You and I have labored in this direction for many years. We feel there is something within us aspiring to that which is higher and better in helping to make men and women mentally, morally and physiologically what they ought to be.

Mr. H. L. Taylor, of the University of the State of New York:

I would like to ask the reader of the paper if I understood him to say that alcohol was not a food?

Dr. Knopf:

Yes, in very small quantities, not more than two ounces.

Mr. Taylor:

I would like to ask if that is the judgment of the Academy. I ask because of a discussion concerning the use of stimulants and narcotics under the New York state law, and an address by Professor Atwater, of

Wesleyan University, upon the question of alcohol and its treatment in the text-books in the hands of students. In the discussion of this subject the views of a leader of the Woman's Christian Temperance work were diametrically opposed to those of Professor Atwater.

Dr. Benjamin Lee, of Philadelphia :

I trust that this discussion will not take the turn that has been given to it. It is in no way justified by the paper to which we have listened, and is not a discussion of the paper in any sense. We might spend the whole afternoon and be no nearer the solution of the problem. I do not consider that it is fair to spring a question of this kind on the Academy.

Dr. Leartus Connor, of Detroit :

I think if we study the men who lived with the old family physician, and the men who live with the present family physician we will find that they fairly match. The old family physician lived at a time when things were largely guessed at, and the personal equation was a very large factor. The present family physician lives in a time when *many* things are exact, and that is just about the difference between the two. In the country regions where there is but one doctor there are still family physicians as much as there ever were. The people themselves have gone through the same transition as we ourselves and the scientific men are now going through. They have passed through the time when the man is able to take the community by storm. They have come to learn that there is something exact in medicine. They have passed from the reign of uncertainty, and want to be under the domain of science. As a matter of fact, there are family physicians in Detroit, and I suppose there are too, in this city, who are as much a power to-day as ever. The field of medicine has immensely widened. For only half a century the ophthalmoscope has been known, and since that time nearly all the exact things in medicine have come to us. When the young men are taught how to use in a scientific manner what is known for the benefit of those committed to their care then we need not be afraid of the results. The doctor is first of all a teacher. I know there are crooked fellows in the medical profession, but there are crooked ones out of it. We can therefore leave that element out. As far as going to the Government, when the Senators return home to teach osteopathy learned in Congress we need not go to Congress for help in scientific medicine. But, scientific methods are going to rule this country, and we are apostles for them.

I have been much interested in the paper presented, which recalls the man who took care of my father's family and myself. A man 6 feet 4 inches high, weighing 250 pounds, laughing every time the fellows did right and swearing when they didn't. He had relatively little science, but had a whole lot of sharp observation and horse sense. Had he lived to-day with the development of science, with his brains and devotion to humanity, he might have been more widely known and held as high place throughout his state as he did in his own and adjacent counties. We should uphold scientific methods and teach the correct observation of phenomena, their deductions and applications to life.

Dr. C. G. Plummer, of Salt Lake City:

Mr. Taylor asked the privilege of asking a question. The privilege was granted him and I think all of us would be benefited if the question were answered, whether or not alcohol has any food value.

[A motion was made and carried, that Dr. W. S. Hall, professor of physiology in the medical department of the Northwestern University, give his opinion as to the food value of alcohol.]

Dr. W. S. Hall, of Chicago:

I did not come prepared to get into a discussion of the alcohol question. I know how interminable this discussion is, it began away back, nobody knows just where, in human history. I think we all have the greatest respect for Professor Atwater for the industry and persistence with which he has worked out the methods by which he determines exactly to a milligram the amount of material entering the human body, comparing it with that which leaves, not only by the alimentary tract, but by the pores of the skin and the lungs. I do not think that any scientific man who has read an account of these experiments will be inclined to throw any doubt upon the accuracy of, or upon his conclusions with respect to the oxidization of alcohol within the human body. The whole thing rests upon this question. What is the definition of a food? If we define a food as any substance which is oxidized within the body, then there is nothing more to say about it. It does not rest upon Professor Atwater's experiments, but upon his confirmation of experiments made by numerous other investigators. It has been conceded that alcohol is almost completely oxidized within the human body. So if we concede the fact that all substances oxidized in the human body are food, it follows that alcohol is a food, and there is no room for discussion. There is, however, not by any means a concensus of opinion as to the definition of a food. There are numerous things oxidized in the human body. Many of the toxines are oxidized. That is the way the body has of taking care of these substances. Professor Atwater takes particular pains to make this statement: That in his study of alcohol he takes no cognizance of the action of alcohol upon the nervous system or upon any other, except its action in the alimentary canal and the metabolic tissues. If we compare alcohol from the standpoint of chemistry with starch or sugar we find that it represents like these in the body a carbonaceous substance and like these it undergoes oxidation. There seems to be here a parallel which justifies the chemist to say that it is a food. Because a substance possesses characteristics similar to another substance we are not justified in concluding that it is therefore to be classed with that other substance. To show the fallacy of such reasoning, let me illustrate: All vertebrates are bilaterally symmetrical. The earth-worm is bilaterally symmetrical; therefore, the earth-worm is a vertebrate. It is just as logical to say : All foods are oxidized in the body, alcohol is oxidized in the body, therefore, alcohol is a food. It is not until we take into consideration the whole influence of alcohol that we see the many reasons why alcohol should not be classed as a food. Suppose we should make two parallel columns—things true of a food, and things true of alcohol. We would have many different points in which alcohol is diametrically opposed in its characteristics to food substance.

In Professor Atwater's own list of foods, the most complete ever published in the English, he does not mention alcohol or anything which contains alcohol as a recognized constituent.

The metabolism of food causes an increase of the body temperature, but when alcohol is taken into the body the body temperature falls. When food is taken into the body it causes an increase of muscular strength. When alcohol is taken into the body it decreases muscular strength. Food when taken into the body makes the body more steady and gives an increased nerve force. Alcohol makes the nerves less steady. If a man is to enter a race requiring accurate muscular and nerve adjustments those managing him will never permit him to take one drop of alcohol. If it were a food why should he not take it? Because there is money at stake and it is known that the dollars will be jeopardized.

These are a few of the reasons why alcohol may not, from the standpoint of the physiologist, be considered a food.

Dr. Fred Corss, of Kingston, Pa.:

It seems to me that the whole question is a perfectly legitimate one for the discussion of the Academy, and I move that the sentiment be expressed that alcohol should not be classed among the alimentary substances.

[The motion of Dr. Corss was referred to the Council. The Council recommended the tabling of the resolution as it was not purely a question of medical sociology.]

Dr. Knopf closes :

I desire first to express my appreciation for the kind reception of my paper by the Academy. Next I would like to make myself clear in regard to the use of alcohol in the treatment of consumption. It has been for years my privilege to treat a goodly number of consumptives belonging to all classes of society and I know that more mischief has been done by alcohol when considered a specific for consumption than by any other drug. There comes occasionally a time in the course of the disease when the giving of a small amount of alcohol is justified, but it is not to be given as a routine treatment in consumption either as prophylactic or curative agent. Alcohol is never a food, and the physician should prescribe it as carefully as he would any other powerful drug. I am not an extremist, but I am opposed to teaching the laity that alcohol is food. They, and particularly the poor among them, should know that a great deal more of strength-giving food can be bought for the same amount of money as they spend for alcohol with a desire for dangerous stimulation.

Nothing was farther from my intention than to criticize the general practitioner. On the contrary, my object was to raise him in the opinion of the public. I think we all should labor to elevate the social as well as the professional appreciation of the family practitioner.

THE PHYSICIAN AS AN ACCOUNTANT.[1]

By CHARLES M. CULVER, A.M., M.D., Albany, N. Y.

The American Academy of Medicine considers, from as elevated a view point as does any organization with which I am acquainted, all phases of the physician's life. It is much pleasanter for cultured medical practitioners to discuss the scientific interests of their profession than to deal with the less attractive incidents of it. While I want to resemble the fellows of the Academy, generally, in unwillingness to advocate commercialism in medicine, I am also unwilling to consider accounts as so evil as to be unworthy more attention than they often get.

The thesis defended in this paper is that enough attention ought to be paid to a physician's accounts and the method of them, that they occupy as little of his time and require as little expenditure of his energy as possible, in order that he may have as much of *both*, as he can, to devote to those functions which are specially his.

Some of the best medical doctors that have lived have disregarded, in some degree, matters of material income and perhaps it is best that they should have done so. However gifted a man may be, he is not likely to be possessed of all talents. In whatever degree the progress of medical science or art has been promoted by neglect of anything like trade considerations, such advance is matter of gratulation and the neglect hardly to be regretted. The work done under such conditions is like the treasure laid up in heaven.

If, however, system in regulation of accounts were more generally among the physician's acquirements, the dignity of the profession would, for that reason, not lose but gain.

A recent issue of one of the most known of American medical periodicals contained an editorial, of which a prominent statement was that the physician is more trusted than almost any other member of the community. It didn't say that he also

[1] Read before the American Academy of Medicine, Saratoga, June 9, 1902.

trusts more than almost anybody else, but it might have done so without exposure of its veracity to suspicion.

It is not to be claimed that bookkeeping, of the average sort, is a *pleasant* part of the physician's strenuous life, but it *is* true that it would be a much less unpleasant part, if it were so systematized and regulated that not only were time and energy being economized while it was receiving attention, but also that economy of both those valuables were augmented by the result.

No special method of bookkeeping is going to be prescribed in this paper. No one kind is best for all physicians. Each of many men follows that system which seems to him best for his use and, as a consequence, many systems are in vogue. If a person cares to be a good accountant, he may well study the matter enough to know what others, whose conclusions are likely to be valid, think best calculated to facilitate their work in that line. The most important consideration is that the books tell the truth. Lincoln said, when asked to express his opinion of a book: "If you like that sort of thing, that's just the sort of thing you like!" The dictum is applicable to the species and varieties of bookkeeping, while the genus is worthy of recommendation. No kind or amount of attention to bookkeeping, on the part of a physician, is entitled to rank as the fourth grace. It is, however, to be deplored that it can so often be truthfully said of one of our colleagues, as was lately said to me, by a patient, about his father: "He was a very good physician, but a very poor business man."

When a colleague says that he practises medicine for the money he can make in that way, we feel as if he had made a guilty confession and instinctively pity him because he did not engage in a more lucrative employment. But that a medical practitioner is likewise a careful keeper of his accounts is by no means discreditable to him. Granted that he is a worthy servant of his fellow men, in his professional capacity, it follows that he is all the better servant in proportion as he is free from embarrassment by matters that consume time and energy without being immediately connected with his work. The dignity of service is no where better exemplified than in the practice of medicine. We are not willing to wear livery nor pose as victims of self-sacrifice; yet the point that Dr. McClintock so ably maintained, at Atlantic City, at our session in 1900, that we are either altruists or truants to our profession, was well taken and is always worthy of defense. There seems to be no way of escape from keeping accounts. Let us, then, care for them in the best way, in order that they may not weigh upon us and hinder the pursuit of those ends that are primarily ours.

The last decade has witnessed many changes in business forms, and more are waiting for inauguration. In so far as improved methods are available, let us have their aid. If, all things considered, a typewritten document is better than one indicted with a pen, let's use the machine. It is not worth while to enumerate such means of economy of time or energy; the chief thing to be said of them is that we ought to hire somebody who can do the business part of our work to do it, if thereby we save chances to use the peculiar kind of education that we have acquired.

It is not a digression to note, here, that the beneficiaries from our professional work ought to be taught and encouraged to pay for medical service as nearly as possible when it is done.

While there are exceptions to this rule, as there are to most of them, there is much in favor of cash as opposed to any kind of bookkeeping that has to do with more than a cash book.

One reason why it is well to keep accounts effectively is that such action may result in more to be bequeathed. Instances of failures to do either of these things, occur to every thoughtful person who considers the matter.

As has already been hinted, this article would not even imply that selfishness is desirable, but, somewhat to the contrary, that a physician may be loyal to his profession in direct proportion as he attends carefully enough to the interests usually represented by bookkeeping accounts, that such matters do not impair his usefulness in the walks in which he is best fitted to serve his fellow men.

DISCUSSION.

Dr. Fred Corss, of Kingston, Pa.:

The prime element in bookkeeping is, of course, to get your dues, and I have found that an essential part of medical bookkeeping is to keep an account that will pass an orphans' court. In Pennsylvania it has been ruled that the bookkeeping shall be so clear that any person could reach a clear result. The kind of daily bookkeeping which is like a time-book has been ruled out of the courts of Pennsylvania. A good rule is to let your daily record be so plain that "The wayfaring man, though a fool, need not err therein." Having done that your bookkeeping will pass the court, and your pocket will be the heavier therefor.

PURE vs. APPLIED SCIENCE IN MEDICINE.[1]

By WINFIELD S. HALL, PH.D., M.D., Professor of Physiology, Northwestern University Medical School, Chicago.

1. Introductory.
    a. Science Defined.
    b. Science Classified.
        (1) Pure or Abstract Science.
        (2) Applied or Concrete Science.
2. The Pedagogic Value of Pure Science and its Place in Education.
3. The Pedagogic Value of Applied Science and its Place in Education.
4. Science in the Medical Curriculum.

INTRODUCTORY.

Science is systematized and classified knowledge of natural phenomena.

All natural phenomena,—whether of the movements of the heavenly bodies, of molecular movements, of affinities and combinations of atoms, of the manifestation of life and the development of living forms, or of the relation of individuals in human society,—*are subject to immutable laws.*

Knowledge of these phenomena is capable of orderly and logical presentation, and consists of descriptions, classifications, discussions and formulated laws.

Knowledge of the laws of nature is gained through observation. The development of science in general, and of the several sciences individually, has progressed step by step with the development of methods of observation. The science of to-day is more extended and accurate than that of a century ago because our instruments of observation,—such as telescopes, microscopes, spectroscopes, etc.,—are more accurate than were those of our great grandfathers.

All science, then, rests upon the observation of natural phenomena, and must necessarily have its foundations laid by inductive reasoning, but this method of inquiry into the realm of natural phenomena, though absolutely necessary for those who gain their knowledge of nature at first hand, is not necessary for

[1] Read before the American Academy of Medicine, Saratoga Springs, June 7, 1902.

those who gain their knowledge from the recorded observations of others.

A very common method of presenting a science is to present some of its typical and fundamental phenomena by demonstration or by laboratory exercises, and to supplement this skeletal method of observation by a systematic description and discussion of typical phenomena of the science as observed by others, following this by a formulation of its laws. As a science is thus presented by a teacher to the pupil, their discussions deal less and less with observed conditions and more and more with typical conditions,—less and less with the concrete case in which allowance must be made for errors of observation, personal equation, and individual variations from the type, and more and more with the typical case from which all these errors and variations have been eliminated.

Science thus presented may be called abstract science or pure science. The questions of pure science are hypothetical ones, and the problem deals with types, and with typical conditions. Pure science deals with theories; the knowledge gained in pure science is theoretical and one versed in the same is a theorist. The method of reasoning in science thus presented is almost exclusively deductive. On the other hand concrete or applied science deals with observed rather than typical conditions, but observed conditions differ from typical ones in being subject to errors of observation, and (in the observation of living forms) to individual variations from the type.

The method of reasoning used in applied science is inductive at first and deductive later.

THE PEDAGOGIC VALUE OF PURE SCIENCE, AND ITS PLACE IN EDUCATION.

How is mechanics taught in a liberal arts course? The teacher usually introduces the subject by definitions which set forth the scope of this field of physical science. This is followed by a series of carefully chosen experiments which illustrate fundamental laws of mechanics. These experiments may be performed by the teacher in the presence of the class or they may be made by the students in the laboratory. In either case the conditions of the experiments being under control, are made simple,—the number of variable factors is reduced to the minimum, while those variables which are operative may be determined singly, thus simplifying immeasurably the solution of the problems. Such is the foundation which is usually laid for the study of any science whether physical or biologic.

The divergence of the study toward pure science on the one hand or toward applied science on the other hand takes place at this point.

In the study of mechanics as a pure science the teacher takes his pupils to the lecture room or seminar after their brief laboratory course and they discuss the *theory* of *mechanics*.

Pure science deals with hypothetical cases in which the conditions of the case are assumed and the problem formulated. The one who solves that problem enters upon a course of reasoning which leads him, step by step, to a conclusion which represents the solution. Pure science has a pedagogic value in two ways: First, it stimulates and develops the reasoning power, and secondly, it results in formulated conclusions and principles which are capable, with more or less extensive modifications, of application to the problems of every-day life.

From the standpoint of the educator such a course affords a most important element in the training of the youth. Besides the mental training which he receives, he is introduced during his high school and college course to a number of the natural sciences,—to chemistry, physics, botany, zoology, astronomy, physiology, and sociology. It is likely that in none of these several fields of natural science, does he come into the possession of a practical, working knowledge. He does, however, gain a general knowledge of the ways in which the fundamental facts of these sciences have been observed, and he acquires a knowledge of the generalizations which have been formulated in the various sciences. His vision is thus broadened and his opinions liberalized. Such an introduction to several natural sciences may very properly make a part of a liberal education. In fact no one can be considered to be liberally educated unless he has such knowledge of at least two or three of these sciences.

PEDAGOGIC VALUE OF APPLIED SCIENCE, AND ITS PLACE IN EDUCATION.

We have pictured the usual method of presenting mechanics to a college class. How different is the method used in a school of mechanical engineering. After the preliminary laboratory and demonstration course described above as the usual introduction to any science, the student is assigned a practical problem which may take him weeks or even months to work out. It may be the construction of a lathe, a dynamo, a gas engine, or a steam engine. In any case he first works out the specifications based upon the fundamental principles which he has studied; he then makes his working drawings, which embody the specifications. After this he goes into the work shop to construct the parts of his machine in accordance with his drawings and his specifications. The parts of the theorist's engine always fit, and the completed machine always works as planned, that is, the theorist leaves no place for error of observation or of construction. How different it is in actual life, and how different will be the results which the several students of a class attain when they are assigned some practical every-day problem to solve! The skilful, well-trained youth will succeed the first time in accomplishing a perfect fit for every part of his machine, and when the parts are assembled its action is beyond criticism. The one who works beside him may have great difficulty in getting a perfect fit in the joints and bearings of his machine, and when the parts are assembled its working will not be smooth and satisfactory, its lines not graceful and its finish not perfect. The superiority of the first student is clearly apparent to every one who observes the finished piece of work. It is an example of the old adage: "By their fruits ye shall know them." The test of the man should be what he can do rather than what he can think about.

What is true of mechanics in its treatment as a pure or as an applied science is true in a general way of all sciences, whether physical or biologic.

Applied science deals with concrete problems whose conditions are determined by the experimental study of actual cases. These observations are followed by a course of reasoning similar to the reasoning of pure science, and should be checked at each step by actual observation of the conditions.

What is true of a problem in applied science in mechanical engineering is true in a general way of all problems of applied science. The student may know what the typical observation should be, but he seldom finds an absolutely typical case. This is especially true in the whole realm of biologic science, where the observer deals with living forms. No two living forms of the same species, sex, and age are absolutely alike. Each will differ from the other in minor details of structure and function, so that the observer never expects to find a typical case. He is prepared to find a case differing more or less from the typical in every item of observation. The variations may be all below or all above, or less frequently some may be below and some above the typical. The observer in applied science must also take into consideration the error of observation. The greatest care must be taken to reduce these errors to a minimum. Besides errors of observations there is the personal equation which cannot be eliminated though it may be determined in certain instances. When it is possible to so determine it the observations taken by any individual are given a weight according to the smallness of his personal error.

Attention has been called above to the fact that the theorist never has any difficulties with the working of his machine or with the application of his formula. On the other hand a slight error on the part of the worker in applied science may result in the loss of days or weeks or even months of hard endeavor. This last-mentioned phase of work in applied science is one of great importance pedagogically. The observer knows that he is on trial; that every day's work must be faultless, otherwise he may find at the end of a series of observations and elaborations that the work of days, weeks or months has been of no avail. These are the conditions in real life, conditions which we see exemplified at every turn in all lines of activity, commercial, industrial and professional.

Pure science is a most wholesome and valuable preparation for applied science. It is not, however, an indispensable preparation. Pure science without the superstructural course of applied science has no other value than simple intellectual gymnastics and a broadening of the horizon. Applied science without a foundation of pure science possesses the properties of intellectual drill possessed by pure science, but has the additional advantage of leading to results which are directly and easily applicable to every-day problems. The place for pure science is in the college of liberal arts. In professional and technical schools the conditions are favorable to the development and application of the applied sciences. In such institutions each problem of applied science leads to immediate and valuable fruitage in experience and knowledge.

SCIENCE IN THE MEDICAL CURRICULUM.

From what has preceded, it is evident that applied science possesses all the advantages of pure science, and in addition to this several advantages which pure science does not possess. The problems of medicine are problems of applied science. If the student enters upon his medical course after a preparation covering several years, during which time pure science has made an important part of his course, he will find that his scientific courses form a most valuable preparation. He will find also that he has been dealing with a purely theoretical side of science, while the medical course presents practical problems which must be solved with the minimum error if one is to succeed in the practice of his profession. There is no pure science in medicine. The typical case is the rare case. The common case is one which presents some features of the typical case combined with many features that give it an individuality and that necessitate a treatment more or less fitted to the individual case. If the student has had a long training in problems of applied science he is best fitted to cope with the difficulties which meet the clinician at every turn.

I would not make a plea for less pure science in a college course. I believe it is an important part of a liberal education. I believe, on the other hand, that an equally important part,— that no student should miss in his undergraduate work,—is a thorough drill in some small field of applied science. It is a matter of little consequence which field is chosen, whether it be mechanical engineering, field word in biology, slum work in sociology, or library work in philology. The kind of mental drill which the student gets is practically the same in each case.

The question might be asked, shall the student of medicine who enters upon his medical course without having had the benefit of a drill in pure science,—shall such a student be given work in pure science? I would answer that question emphatically in the negative. I believe that there is no time in the medical school for problems in pure science. The problems in applied science serve as a most valuable education of the powers of observation, the power of logical reasoning and the capacity to draw a safe and tenable conclusion.

STATE AID TO MEDICAL COLLEGES.[1]
By Charles McIntire, A.M., M.D., Easton, Pa.

The relation which the state government bears to the education of its citizens varies with the state. In all are to be found a more or less perfected series of common schools. In some, this common school education extends up through a university course including instruction in post-graduate work and for professional degrees. Because of the universality of public schools supported by taxation, either directly or through appropriations by the state legislature, the use of the state money to assist in maintaining schools and colleges not a part of the public school system is not thought to be a misappropriation in many of our states. In like manner the provision made for destitutes and defectives is the first step toward appropriations for hospitals and other institutions under private control.

In an argument before the Committee of Education of the Virginia Convention to revise the State Constitution, an assertion was made to the effect that it was not customary for states to make appropriations either for the assistance of medical schools or for hospitals connected therewith for teaching purposes, if they were not state institutions. Exception was taken to this assertion by another speaker, and inquiry was made of the writer for positive information on the subject. While he was able to give definite information, it was incomplete, and the investigation reported in this paper was undertaken to prepare a fairly complete report of the customs prevailing throughout the United States.

Letters were addressed to the governors of the various states and territories asking them to submit the following questions to the proper officer for a reply.

1. Does your Legislature make any appropriation for hospitals or other institutions for alleviating suffering not entirely under state control?
2. *If not*, is there any law preventing it?
3. *If so*, can you send me a recent report showing names of institutions and amounts appropriated?
4. *If so*, does the legislature include hospitals entirely under the control of medical colleges?

[1] Read before the American Academy of Medicine, Saratoga Springs, June 9, 1902.

5. Does the Legislature make any appropriations to educational institutions not entirely under state control?

6. *If so*, has it ever made such an appropriation to medical colleges?

When there were no medical colleges in a state, these questions were slightly changed.

I have to express my indebtedness to the governors of most of the states in having prompt replies sent to me. In a few states no notice was taken of the inquiry, but letters to personal friends secured the information.

In looking over the replies received we may divide all the states and territories into two general divisions. Those which are forbidden by a provision of the constitution to make any appropriation to any institution not entirely under state control; and those who are not so restrictive. The first list comprises: Alabama, California, Georgia, Louisiana, Michigan, Missouri, Montana, North Dakota, Texas, Utah, and Wyoming.

You will notice that several of these states have medical departments in their universities which are under state control.

The remaining states can be again divided into two divisions: one in which no appropriation is made although there is no law preventing it and those which make appropriations. Those who report no appropriation made, include the following states: Arizona, Arkansas, Colorado, Florida, Idaho, Illinois, Indiana, Minnesota, New Hampshire, North Carolina, Ohio, Oklahoma, Oregon, Rhode Island, South Carolina, South Dakota, Washington, West Virginia, and Vermont.

Reviewing the customs of the remaining states in alphabetic order we learn that:

Colorado makes no appropriations because the purely administrative functions of the government use all the revenue.

Connecticut is in the habit of appropriating to both hospitals and educational institutions not entirely under state control. No appropriation has ever been made to a medical school, and there is no hospital entirely under the control of its medical school.

Delaware has no medical school, makes appropriations to hospitals, etc., but not to educational institutions not entirely under state control.

Iowa, where the law does not authorize such appropriation, has made exception in making an appropriation for a maternity.

Kansas makes appropriation for hospitals other than state institutions. $16,400 was appropriated for that purpose for 1902; 27 institutions received aid in sums varying from $300 to $2,000; and a similar sum for 1903. There are no hospitals entirely under the control of medical colleges. No appropriation is made for schools or colleges not controlled by the state.

Kentucky, no information received.

Maine makes such appropriations both to hospitals and schools and has aided the medical department of Bowdoin.

Maryland makes appropriations both to educational and other institutions. Direct aid is voted to medical schools, but, probably, for the hospitals connected therewith. The state manual for 1901 gives a list of 50 institutions (not colleges) receiving an aggregate annual appropriation of $116,000 and of three others, where the state is represented on the board of managers, that receive $56,000 a year.

Massachusetts contributes to hospitals and educational institutions other than purely state institutions. But it never has aided a medical school, nor are any of its hospitals purely college hospitals. $61,000 were divided among these institutions last year.

Mississippi has no medical schools but makes appropriations to other schools and to hospitals; the latter appropriations amount to $24,000 a year.

Nevada, no report received.

New Hampshire makes an annual appropriation of $15,000 to a college which has a medical department, but probably not for the department.

New Jersey has no medical school. Its state appropriation for institutions under private control are for the chronic defective, and for educational purposes for industrial education only.

New Mexico levys a tax of $^{60}/_{100}$ of a mill on a dollar, the proceeds being divided among eight private hospitals in the territory.

New York has a constitutional provision forbidding the appropriation of state funds to hospitals, but it can make appropriation for educational institutions, but has never made such to medical colleges.

Pennsylvania is probably the banner state in the Union for its largess to hospitals, whether independent of, or connected with, medical schools.

Tennessee makes appropriations, but none to general hospitals or medical schools.

Virginia, appropriations were made under the provision of the old constitution, and are continued, I think, in the revision.

Wisconsin, no information received.

It is hoped that this tabulation will be of interest and not without value. It will certainly furnish information, should another constitutional revision convention desire it.

I wish to acknowledge the courtesy of

T. L. Sorrell, state auditor of Alabama, through Dr. J. T. Searcy, of Tuscaloosa.

Dr. Wm. Duffield, of Phoenix, Arizona, at the request of Governor Murphy.

Dr. W. P. Illing, superintendent Pulaski Co. (Ark.) Hospital, at the request of Governor Davis.

Dr. W. P. Matthews, secretary State Board of Health of California, at the request of Governor Gage.

Governor James B. Ornran, of Colorado.

John Rolman, executive secretary, Connecticut.

Caleb R. Layton, secretary of state, Delaware, at the request of the governor.

Governor W. S. Jennings, of Florida.

Mr. W. H. Warren, of Augusta, Ga.

Louis N. Ross, executive secretary of Idaho.

Dr. J. A. Egan, secretary State Board of Health of Illinois, at the request of the governor.

Charles E. Wilson, private secretary to the governor of Indiana.

D. G. Kinne, chairman of the Board of Control of Iowa, at the request of the governor.

The Auditor of Kansas, at the request of Governor Stanley.

W. G. Frazer, auditor of Louisiana, at the request of Governor Heard.

L. D. Carver, librarian of Maine State Library, at the request of the governor.

Governor John Walter Smith, of Maryland, and Robert H. Smith, Esq., of Baltimore.

T. D. Hawley, deputy auditor of Massachusetts, at the request of Governor Crane.

John F. Wilkinson, deputy auditor of Michigan, at the request of the governor.

S. W. Leavett, chairman Board of Control, Minnesota, at the request of the governor.

J. J. Conean, private secretary to the governor of Mississippi.

A. O. Allen, state auditor of Missouri, at the request of Governor Dockery.

L. R. Hass, private secretary to the governor of Montana.

R. J. Chaunce, secretary to the governor of Nebraska.

Edward N. Pearson, secretary of the state of New Hampshire, at the request of the governor.

W. S. Hancock, comptroller of New Jersey, at the request of Governor Murphy.

Edward F. Bartlett, solictor general of New Mexico, at the request of the governor.

Edward T. Devine, editor of *Charities*, New York.

Governor Chas. B. Aycock, of North Carolina.

Governor Frank Write, of North Dakota.

Dr. C. C. Brobst, secretary State Board of Health of Ohio, at the request of the governor.

Governor T. B. Ferguson, of Oklahoma.

Walter Lyon, secretary to the governor of Oregon.

Dr. F. T. Rogers, of Rhode Island.

Dr. James Evans, secretary State Board of Health of South Carolina, at the request of the governor.

Governor Chas. N. Herreid, of South Dakota.

E. K. Glenn, secretary to the governor of Tennessee.

Dr. Geo. R. Tabor, state health officer of Texas, at the request of the governor.

Hon. H. M. Wells, governor of Utah.

Dr. Henry D. Holton, of Vermont, at the request of the governor.

J. Howard Watson, secretary to the governor of Washington.

Wm. O. Dawson, secretary of state, West Virginia, at the request of the governor.

Governor DeForest Richards, of Wyoming.

OBSERVATIONS IN PASSING.

The preparation for the meetings of the organizations represented by the Bulletin are taking shape. The Association of American Medical Colleges and the Confederation of the Examining Boards meeting in New Orleans on May 4th, while the Academy will begin its session on the following Monday, May 11th, the Congress of American Physicians meeting in the same place on the following evening.

Those who are planning to present papers should notify the proper persons at once—Dr. W. S. Hall, 2431 Dearborn Street, Chicago, for the College Association; Dr. A. Walter Suiter, Herkimer, N. Y., for the Confederation; and Dr. Edward Jackson, McPhee Building, Denver Colorado, for the Academy.

⁂

Twice since the issue of the last Bulletin the management has been asked to purchase books for its patrons. If we can be of any service to others in the same way—" To hear is to obey."

⁂

The following extracts from the Annual Report of the Rhode Island Hospital, for 1902, are of interest:

"The examining agent at the out-patient department reports that during the year he questioned 5,292 new applicants, admitted 4,700, rejected 163 as not proper objects of charity, and required 429 to bring written evidence that they were proper recipients of free treatment. Of these, only 44 returned with the required credentials," p. 4, *Report of the Board of Trustees.*

"In the Royal C. Taft building for out-patients the work has been carried on as usual, and the system of admitting only such patients as are not able to employ a physician has been continued with gratifying results," p. 23.

"The influence of the hospital is being felt in wider circles each year, and aside from the direct benefit as shown by the treatment of patients, some important factors in spreading this influence are the association of the medical and nursing staff, who come in direct and intimate relation to the public at large. There are at present connected with the hospital four organizations: The Hospital Staff Association, made up of members of the visiting and out-patient staff, who, as a body, suggest and recommend changes and report to the board of trustees . . pp. 23, 24, *Report of the Superintendent.*

****

Dr. L. Duncan Bulkley is giving his fifth series of clinical lectures on Diseases of the Skin in an out-patient hall of the New York Skin and Cancer Hospital, at a quarter past four, each Wednesday afternoon. These courses are free to the medical profession.

LITERATURE NOTES.

"The object of criticism is not to criticize but to understand. More than this; as you will find it more wholesome in life and more salutary to your character to study the virtues than the defects of your friends, so in literature it seems to me wiser to look for an author's strong points than his weak ones."—Lowell.

BIOGRAPHIC CLINICS. The Origin of the Ill-Health of DeQuincey, Carlyle, Darwin, Huxley, and Browning. By GEORGE M. GOULD, M.D. Philadelphia: P. Blakiston's Son & Co. 1903. Cloth. pp. 223. Price, $1.00 net.

One may read this book as a quaint conceit of its talented and versatile author and be charmingly entertained; or he may approach it more seriously and, while being none the less pleased, may find food for thought in the suggestion of an added burden (and an added power to serve as well) to the coming physician.

The plan of the book is to write the clinical history of the men presented from the biographic data at hand; then diagnose the malady and discuss the treatment. In all of them the author sees evidence of ametropia, and their ills due largely to eyestrain. Chapters are added on "Biliousness and Headache," "Some Neglected Points in the Physiology of Vision," "The Discovery of Astigmatism and Eyestrain," and "Responsibilities." We commend the book for what it tells us and the way in which it tells it to us; we also commend it for the thought it provokes.

REPORT OF THE COMMISSIONER OF EDUCATION FOR THE YEAR 1900-1901. Vol. I, Washington, 1902. pp. cxii+1216.

The commissioner informs us of a total enrollment of 17,862 780 pupils in schools of all classes in the period covered by his report; and that the "average schooling in years (per individual of population) of 200 days each in public and private schools for the whole United States was 5.14."

In addition to the report of the commissioner thus commenting on the statistics collected, the volume contains a series of articles of interest. Those most closely allied to medical sociology are: Chap. III. Consolidation of Schools and Transportation of Pupils. Chap. IV. American Industrial Education— What Shall it Be? Chap. V. Educational Pathology, or Self-Government in School. Chap. XV. The First Comprehensive Attempt at Child Study. Chap. XXI. Temperance Instruction.

NEW DIPLOMAS OF THE FRENCH UNIVERSITIES. DOCTORATE, LICENSE DIPLOMAS, CERTIFICATES OF STUDIES, ATTESTATION OF HIGHER STUDIES, UNIVERSITY CERTIFICATES, CERTIFICATES OF ATTENDANCE, CERTIFICATES OF FRENCH LITERARY STUDIES AND OF THE FRENCH LANGUAGE FOR THE ESPECIAL USE OF FOREIGN STUDENTS. Issued by the Committee of Patronage for Foreign Students. Dole Typographie, Bernin, Girardi et Audebert, Successors. 1902.

This pamphlet is to call the attention of American students desiring to study abroad, to a new class of diplomas granted by the French universities.

"The French government has, therefore, given authority to the universities to create diplomas of a scientific nature which are called 'university diplomas,' and are given in the name of the university. These diplomas differ from the State diplomas only in this, that they do not confer any of the rights or privileges which the law attaches to the latter."

As a consequence they are relieved from the rigid conditions which made it difficult for one who had not been trained in French secondary schools to become a candidate for a university diploma. The pamphlet gives in detail the requirements for the various diplomas in the different universities of France.

Mr. Paul Melon is the general secretary of the committee of patronage for foreign students.

REPORTS OF MEDICAL EXAMINING BOARDS.

I. TWELFTH ANNUAL REPORT OF THE STATE BOARD OF MEDICAL EXAMINERS OF NEW JERSEY, 1902.

II. REPORT OF THE MEDICAL COUNCIL OF PENNSYLVANIA, MARCH I, 1900 TO MARCH I, 1902.

As the statistics of these reports are carefully tabulated in the annual article uniting the results of the examining boards of all the states, these need not be repeated here.

I. The stand taken by New Jersey regarding the licenses of other states is commendable. The board "adopted as a basis of endorsement the personal fitness and professional qualifications of the candidate plus a state certificate of license issued after examination in substantially the same medical branches and under essentially the same conditions as the law of this State and the regulations of this Board require."

The New Jersey Board thus endeavors to permit any reputable physician to open an office in New Jersey if he has substantially complied with the requirements of their law, without an additional examination and regardless of the attitude of any state towards the license issued by New Jersey.

Polk's admirable Register of the Physicians of the United States and Canada, is to be expanded in the next edition to include the physicians of North America. There have been great advances in accuracy in each succeeding issue, which will not stop, we are sure, with this increase of territory covered.

TRADE CALENDARS.

The Oakland Chemical Company issue a very neat memorandum pad which is named the "Doctor's Memory." It is a week to a page, affording ample space for noting the more important out of routine appointments.

Scott and Bowne issue their usual table pad calendar—a slip to a day, with space for memoranda. The utility of these calendars lies in the date of the day being always in sight, if all the previous slips have been removed.

The red cloth cover of the M. J. Breitenbach's Physicians' Daily Memorandum has become familiar to most of us. It gives a page to-day, with a quotation laudatory of Pepto-Mangan at the top of each page, with a fair amount of space for memoranda.

BULLETIN

OF THE

American Academy of Medicine

VOL. VI.   ISSUED APRIL, 1903.   No. 5.

THE AMERICAN ACADEMY OF MEDICINE is not responsible for the sentiments expressed in any paper or address published in the BULLETIN.

MAY A HOSPITAL STEAL?[1]

BY P. MAXWELL FOSHAY, M.D., Cleveland, Ohio.

The apparent brutality of frankness exemplified by this question suggests an unreality of the implied accusation. Unfortunately I am compelled by observed circumstances to prove that this question must be asked in all seriousness and must be answered in fairness, candor, and speed. I shall relate an instance that has fallen under my observation, prefaced by the statement that I had not the slightest personal interest in the occurrence and the further statement that personal friendship would incline me strongly to the side of those whom I feel compelled to criticize. Nor, I regret to say, is this instance a solitary one. I have notes upon a number of others, but one will just as well serve my purpose for a text as would a dozen.

The ill effect upon the public and upon the medical profession of present methods of hospital administration has long been apparent and has frequently been discussed in the journals and elsewhere. A recent authentic instance in a great hospital brings that matter again to the fore and urges a careful consideration of the real seriousness of the situation. The instance is all the more valuable as a text because the physicians involved are all incorruptible men of established character, so that it is clearly evident that it is the present system of management which is all

[1] Read before the American Academy of Medicine, Saratoga Springs, June 9, 1902.

wrong, in that it permits such things to happen and to happen frequently.

A certain large corporation has for some years had an arrangement with a physician to care for its injured employees and has paid him liberal fees for his services. The case in point was one of bone injury and the physician said an operation was necessary, stating the fee that he would ask. There was some question in the minds of the company's officers as to the necessity for the operation, and the manager of the concern related the circumstances to his personal physician who is a visiting physician to the hospital in question. Remembering that the hospital was in need of cases and of revenue, this physician suggested that the case be put in a ward at the hospital where the best treatment could be had. The ward fee was to be $7 a week, and nothing was said about the fee for the surgeon. The company sent the man to the hospital where he was operated on as a clinic case with entirely satisfactory results, by a leading surgeon, whose personal character and professional standing are a sufficient guarantee that he was an entirely innocent participator in this pretty plain instance of medical highway robbery.

What has been the result? The manager of this rich corporation is telling the officials of other corporations how he evaded the payment of a surgeon's fee in an unpromising case, and how light the total cost of this case was. Another corporation abundantly able to pay good fees has thus found a way of entirely circumventing the demands of a physician to be paid for his work, and another physician has lost a valuable portion of his practice. A most aggravating feature of the case is the fact that it is physicians of unimpeachable character who, finding unconscious refuge behind the impersonality of an "institution," thus rob their fellow physicians of their practice and their income.

This sort of occurrence, now so frequent all over the country, will inevitably disorganize the profession orelse cause it, through its medical societies, to begin an open and bitter warfare against the hospitals, unless the hospitals themselves at a very early day adopt a system which will entirely prevent their stealing cases from the individual physician who has no hospital. The members of hospital staffs must at once look into the system of receiving cases under which they work, and must provide for a careful investigation of the social origin of cases, or else they must prepare to hear from the medical societies in terms that will be very definite. The time for argument about this matter is rapidly passing away, the profession is being goaded into a fury by repeated happenings of this character, and a cataclysm is within sight. Now is the time for the hospitals to act.

The little work that I have done in attempting to improve the organization of the medical profession has brought me into contact with the resentful spirit that is engendered by occurrences of this sort in the minds of physicians who have no hospital connections. These men feel that medical societies are a hollow mockery when the most active members are part and parcel of institutions which thus unceremoniously rob the general practician of a portion of his means of livelihood. So long as the system of hospital management is so lax as to permit this sort of theft it is useless to expect that the ethics of our profession can be elevated. On the contrary this is a distinct force tending toward degradation. Real professional unity can never be attained while these things are permitted in our midst.

Coming to suggestions of possible remedies we face the fact that physicians in their hospital relations are not governed by the same code of morals which they adhere to in their relations with individual fellow practicians. And we face the further fact that the whole American system of the conduct of hospitals tends to be subversive of the interests of the medical profession. If hospitals were compelled to remunerate the members of their staffs as they do all subordinate employees, they would without much urging see that free treatment was not given to those who are able to pay. This is too great a reform to expect in our generation, however. Our *esprit du corps* has not yet arrived at that stage of development that will enable us to stand together for the accomplishment of such a reform. All that is at present practicable is to look for some readily applied remedy to the glaring defect that has been discussed in this note. It is not hard to find.

Every hospital, and this should hardly need even to be stated, should provide adequate machinery to investigate the circumstances of all who apply for free treatment. In the cities a joint bureau of investigation supported by all the hospitals and working in connection with the associated charities could in no time divide the city into convenient districts and have at hand a fairly reliable directory of all families of deserving poor. This is simple and easily done, especially when compared to the difficulties between the hospitals and the organized profession which are sure to arise if present destructive tendencies are not checked. I hope that the organized medical profession will begin by applying at first moral suasion to secure the initiation of some such plan. Failing in this, one cannot doubt that other measures will be found, and that they will not, for a time, be good for the general moral health of the profession. My plan then is for each one to become a missionary, counseling peace based upon urging the hospitals to adopt some such scheme as that herein presented. It is not new nor is it really difficult of attainment and application. It is, however, imperatively a present necessity.

DISCUSSION.

Dr. A. L. Benedict, of Buffalo:

I would like to suggest that this subject should include a wider range than the mere giving of charity to undeserving cases. Some time ago, a poor patient was referred to me by one of the city physicians for special attention in my line and, through a misunderstanding, was sent to a hospital in which I had previously served as consultant but with which I had ceased to be connected. After entering the hospital, the patient was seized by the visiting physician who simply refused to surrender it, in spite of the circumstances. The gentleman in question is a friend of mine and probably would not steal a private patient who had gotten into his office through a mistake. It is difficult to understand why there should be any difference in the ethics of paying and of charity cases, yet there seems to be a prevailing impression that any sort of dishonorable practice is allowable to secure clinical material. The only remedy for this state of affairs is to put the question squarely before each offender and make him understand that, if he persists in such practices, he must be honorable enough to confess himself dishonorable.

If any group of men choose to support a private institution, they have the right to adopt any set of by-laws that they see fit, and to treat the

patient in any way that does not jeopardize his health. The general
principle should be recognized that an institution which is supported by
public charity, whether the funds are raised by taxation or by appeal to
the public, is a public trust and not a private opportunity and that it
should be just as public to the medical profession as to the patient. Let
the hospital furnish board, interne service, medical and surgical appliances and nursing, and allow the patient the same privilege as elsewhere,
to select his attendant. Let it be understood that the physician has no
claim for services against a charity patient in a hospital ward, and let
there be, as at present, a visiting staff who shall attend to such patients
as desire their services or who cannot obtain other attendance. The great
majority of the patients would be cared for, as at present, by the regularly
appointed staff, and all criticism against the management of the hospital
on the lines indicated would be disarmed.

Dr. Leartus Connor, of Detroit:

In a large hospital, familiar to the majority present, largely endowed
and maintained by charitable contributions, the management took a
contract from an accident insurance company for the care of patients in
the wards at $4 a week when the records of the hospital showed that the
actual cost to the hospital was $7 a week. I protested that this was an
absolute steal from the benevolently inclined people of that city but I
was sneered at for my so-called Puritanism, and the matter went on. In
a town not far distant a leading physician told me this experience: A
prominent surgeon, a leader in the American Medical Association, is an
attending surgeon to the hospital and this man had put two surgical
patients into the hospital. At the head of the bed was his name, the
patient's name, and the surgical trouble for which he proposed to operate.
He was an entirely competent man. At the appointed time for the operation he went to the hospital, when he found that the attending surgeon in
the hospital had operated on both patients. Attention was called to it,
and the answer was that there must be patients for the clinics. The
further statement was volunteered that it was unsafe for a surgeon to turn
a case over and expect to get it back again. I have heard a good many
members of the profession say that they have been compelled to do operations which they did not want to do because otherwise the patients would
be stolen. I believe there is a considerable amount of truth in these
statements which is not creditable to the medical profession nor to the
hospitals with which we have to do. Dr. Foshay has pointed out to us a
grave evil. Instead of standing up for our rights, when another fellow is
knocked out we step in and take his place. We do not stand by one
another.

Dr. W. L. Estes, of South Bethlehem, Pa:

I have been in charge for many years of a general hospital, and I think
from my long service I am in a position to speak from the hospital aspect

as few other men can, and I assure you that Dr. Connor has struck the key-note of the whole trouble. Doctors will not stand by their own kind. In the hospital of which I am in charge I have the sole management as physician and surgeon-in-chief. We have established a rule, except for emergency cases, that no case shall be treated free that does not bring a certificate stating positively that he or she is unable to pay for treatment elsewhere. That rule is known throughout the whole country. I give you my word that the greatest transgressors of this rule are physicians themselves. I have upon investigation found that probably one-half of the patients who come from physicians are perfectly able to pay. The physicians would explain that the patient was not able to pay the ordinary fee. This is perfectly absurd for it is known that we are in the habit of making the fee commensurate with the ability of the patient to pay. As to an arrangement whereby any- and everybody, and any and every physician may treat cases sent to a hospital, that would be a very difficult matter. It is thinkable but scarcely possible in a managereal sense. I have seen institutions that have tried it but they have always gotten into trouble. If physicians send cases to a hospital where there are certain men on the staff whose business it is to operate and they know the rules of the institution they give up the treatment of the case and have no right to expect to continue the treatment of the patient until it leaves the hospital any more than if it were sent to an office for special treatment. To have two dozen or more physicians connected with a hospital would simply wreck the whole service in a month, because the attendants would scarcely know to whom they were responsible. It is almost impracticable to get a sufficient number of house officers to wait on every physician who would come and the house staff would thus be unable to carry on the treatment, and could not be held responsible for any emergency which might arise between the visits of the visiting physicians.

Dr. S. A. Knopf, of New York:

In regard to treating patients for nothing in hospitals I do not think there is any way out of it but not to accept any certificate at all from any individual, even from a physician. The only proper way, I believe, is the one now in vogue in some institutions in New York where they have paid visitors who make it their business to examine every case carefully by going to the home of the individual applying for help. The charity organizations are always willing to examine such cases for any physician. I think this illustrates what I said this morning, that organized charity should work for and with the medical profession. We are all willing to do charitable work, but I would strongly oppose pauperizing and giving our services for nothing to people who are able to pay. We are entitled to a reasonable compensation for our services as much as anybody, and if we help in municipal work the municipality ought to pay us as well as it pays its lawyers. I believe that every physician who benefits the community at large by treating the poor should be compensated by the community.

Dr. A. L. Benedict, of Buffalo:

The only way in which the good faith of the so-called public hospitals can be manifested is in trying the experiment of making them genuinely public. If more interne service is needed, so much the better, as this most-needed experience is, at present, available only to about one graduate out of four. If the discipline of a large hospital can not deal with the problem, it must be worked out, as it has already been commenced, along the line of the small hospital, which is private in inception but public in its development.

Dr. Foshay, closing:

I want to make my position clear. I purposely did not raise the question as between the general physician and the surgeon at all. I chose a case where another question was involved. I talked it over with the surgeon and he was shocked to know that I had been imposed upon. The fault is with the system under which the hospitals are run. I believe that most surgeons are square good fellows. The method of management needs revision, and the suggestion of Dr. Knopf of working conjointly with charity associations is a good one; it would be a simple thing to make use of the established methods of inspection by the organizations, to make clear whether patients are deserving of aid or not.

POLITICS IN THE MEDICAL PROFESSION.

I.

THE RELATION OF THE PHYSICIAN TO POLITICS.[1]

By DONLY C. HAWLEY, A.B., M.D., Burlington, Vt.

There is a sentiment in the minds of the laity and of the profession, that the physician should not take a prominent part in public affairs—in other words, that the physician should keep out of politics. It is the object of this paper to controvert this sentiment and to group a few of the reasons why it will be profitable to the public and the profession for the physician to bear his full proportion of political burdens and public honors.

In considering this subject I shall have reference to politics, not only in its broadest sense as the science of government and the art of governing, but in its narrower and generally accepted sense as the art of influencing public opinion and state policy through party organization. It is necessary to accept this narrower definition, for the reason that it is only in the field of practical politics and through party organization that one may make an impression on public affairs. I wish to be understood, however, as making no allusion to that scheming and professional kind of politics in which policy rules rather than principle, and in which men work for partisan gain rather than the public good.

In a democratic government which derives its power from the consent of the governed, and where equal rights and benefits are vouchsafed to all alike, it is the high privilege and the manifest duty of every citizen, and therefore of the physician, to bear his part of what may be called the public burden. The average citizen, including the physician, knows but little about the way his municipality is governed, how or for what purpose the people's money is expended, or what service is necessarily given by some one to keep the municipal wheels in motion.

We all wonder why this or another improvement is not forthcoming, or service promptly rendered, or nuisance abated, for-

[1] Read before the American Academy of Medicine, Saratoga Springs, June 9, 1902.

getting, perhaps, that if we performed our public duty we might be able to answer the question and supply the remedy. The physician by education, training, and daily experience is especially qualified to grasp the fundamental principles of political science and of abstract politics, and to take an active and intelligent part in practical politics. Further, a study of the science and a participation in the art of politics will be beneficial to the physician.

In every community the physician is looked upon as belonging to an educated, cultured and refined profession. He is naturally accorded a position of high respectability and of leadership, and is therefore in a position to make an impress on public opinion. The physician by his preliminary and professional training possesses a degree of mental vigor and refinement above the average citizen. Further, the physician, and especially the country physician, from the nature of his calling and environment is a close observer and generally a correct interpreter of his observations. Thrown continuously in contact with important and vital questions, and often upon his own resources alone, he learns to observe carefully and quickly, to reason rapidly, and to act at once. He is a man who is obliged to depend upon himself, to draw his own conclusions, and to work out his own problems. His daily work and experiences, therefore, tend to cultivate a keenness of insight, a power of discrimination and an independence of judgment which will enable him intelligently to grapple with the important questions which are vital to the interests of his state or his municipality.

Further, the physician is better acquainted with men, and has a deeper knowledge of human nature than the average citizen, and therefore is in a position to understand thoroughly many of the requirements of the community. From technical knowledge and experience the physician is especially qualified to render valuable service to the community in matters relating to public health and sanitation, water supply, plumbing, drainage, sewerage, ventilation, school-house construction, etc.

It is sometimes argued that the physician is not a good business man, and therefore not a proper person to be entrusted with an important office. Numberless examples of the successes of medical men in private and public life disprove any such statement, and in general this criticism is unfounded, although in many cases, no doubt, the physician is a poor collector. This, however, is due largely to the fact that the physician does not practice his profession primarily as a money-making business, and that as a consequence his transactions with his fellows are tempered by considerations which do not enter into cold and hard business.

Study of the science of politics or the philosophy of governing, which includes the history of politics and of various political systems, of constitutional law and of diplomacy, will prove interesting and profitable to the physician, and will be of benefit to him by broadening and enriching his mind. Participation in the active management of public affairs, which necessitates a study of the requirements, the relations and the rights of individuals and of communities, will tend to broaden his mental horizon and his view point, and by taking him out of the rut of daily routine work will afford a diversion at once interesting and profitable. Thus he will become a more valuable member of the political family.

It may be asked, will not an active participation in politics so divert one's attention and energies, and so absorb one's time as to lessen his interest and activity in his professional work and cause him to lose his standing in the profession, or his chances of continued professional success? I reply, that the educated physician with a well-balanced mind will not be likely to fall within such category, and further, that the physician who is great enough to avoid the entanglements of partisan politics and to give to mankind the enlightened and high-minded service of statesmanship need not for his own credit or that of the profession hesitate to become the physician statesman.

I believe it to be a good thing for the standing of the profession when any of its individual members are elevated to positions of honor and of trust by the community, and likewise for the community when physicians of the better class consent to accept such positions. Do we not every one of us recall with just pride the fact that Benjamin Rush was one of the signers of the Declaration of Independence, while many of us, no doubt, forget that he was the author of several medical volumes, essays and lectures.

The physician, as a rule, has a deep knowledge of mankind, and takes a broad view of manhood. He is better acquainted than the average man with the strength and with the weaknesses of humanity, and likewise with many of its needs. He therefore should be, and I believe usually is, a man of high ideals. Men who have ideals are morally obligated to assume the responsibility of leadership. When they fulfil this duty their influence will prove a dynamic in public opinion that will place the combined might of the community on the side of right, and will multiply the only dividends possible in town and city government, namely, improved public utilities and a higher citizenship.

II.
COMPENSATION FOR MEDICAL SERVICES RENDERED THE STATE.[1]

BY T. D. DAVIS, M.D., Ph.D., Pittsburg, Pa.

What amount is a fair professional compensation is not easily decided. *Quid pro quo* is difficult to determine justly in regard to medical services. In law the fee is frequently decided by the value of the property in litigation; by the length of time consumed; by the importance of the case; or by the *nerve* of the lawyer. This fee is usually paid without complaint simply because it would be a waste of time and temper to object. Engineers, architects, etc., charge a percentage, which is quite uniform, on the value of the work, and the cost can be estimated beforehand.

In medicine, however, there is no uniform method to estimate in money the value of services rendered. It is impossible to charge the poor and rich alike. The time-honored method of charging so much per visit, with mileage added is evidently unfair to either the patient or the practitioner. One visit differs so much from another visit in value. Mileage should differ according to weather and conveyance. Fee bills are a delusion and a snare. Old and young practitioners should not be asked to charge the same prices. Reputation has real value in medical practice. Reputation often casts the deciding vote that knowledge alone is not permitted to cast. The time consumed is hardly a fair way to estimate physicians' services, nor is physical discomforts an elevated method of deciding prices. On the other hand "a doctor is worth just what he can get," is the motto of quackery. These with other reasons may account for the fact that medicine is the poorest compensated, as far as money is concerned, of any of the learned professions.

It is certainly true that most people are willing to spend more to save their property than to save their health, yes even than to save their lives. If this is so of private individuals it is still more manifested by the governing authorities. The United

[1] Read before the American Academy of Medicine, Saratoga Springs, June 9, 1902.

States spends $75,000 to construct a single gun to destroy human life, partly under the plea of saving property, and millions are spent on floating machines of destruction, to hundreds spent for hygiene. In the army and navy the officers who are trained to destroy life are much better paid and held in higher esteem, than those who are equally as expensively trained and educated to save human lives. In the civil departments of national, state and city governments the same holds true.

The legal departments of these governments are thoroughly organized with fine talent as a rule to conduct them, and in cases of importance they can also call to their assistance the very best and even the most expensive lawyers. On the other hand, the boards of health of these same governments do not exist at all, or, to say the least, are conducted in the most penurious and indifferent manner. It is also a sad fact that they only receive anything like proper support, when it is shown that an epidemic causes pecuniary loss to the public. Money is granted more readily to stamp out smallpox than it is to prevent tuberculosis or typhoid fever. We pride ourselves, and properly so, on what our government has done for the sanitation of Cuba, but let us not forget that the governor of that island was an educated physician, or the result most likely would have been very different. Even when public sentiment is aroused and money is voted for sanitation, it is extremely difficult to have the distributing power the scientific body it should be, for too often political favorites or incompetent men are appointed rather than men of highest professional and executive skill, to devise plans and carry them into effect. It is peculiar but nevertheless true that governments will spend money freely to take care of their dead citizens or soldiers, but will give it very sparingly to take care of their living bodies. Both the public and private individuals will give generously to care for the maimed, injured or suffering, but are very stingy in giving to protect people from injury, disease or disaster.

These same traits may actuate governments in so much more liberally compensating their legal than their medical talent. That they do thus discriminate I have taken the trouble to prove by comparing the compensation of the legal and medical officers of four large cities of our country. Without taking up your time with figures in detail I simply say the salaries of the lawyers are from two to three times that of the physicians, or $6,000 for the heads of the legal departments to $2,400 for the heads of the medical departments. The city attorneys have a long list of assistants at from $2,500 to $3,500 per annum, while the assistant physicians in the health departments vary from $900 to $1,200 for the same time. In smaller cities the difference is still more marked. There is no reason for this state of affairs but that physicians underrated their own services. There is no remedy for it but through the profession. In the past it is possible many doctors underrated their services because they obtained their education in a very short time and quite inexpensively, and so valued their knowledge accordingly. Now with higher entrance requirements and four years in a medical college with all extra expenses, as a mere matter of investment a higher rate should be demanded. I have also thought possibly that a conscious lack of real training has led conscientious physicians from charging more for their services. So to-day a great deal of advice is given free by doctors, because they fail to fully realize its importance and value to the patient, as it is such elementary knowledge to the practitioner himself. Especially is this the case when simply expressing an opinion. The idea that we are a liberal profession, and also charitable, has led others to charge rates below worth of services rendered. I cannot but think also the custom of treating the clergy gratuitously both cheapens medical services and lowers the self-respect of the clergy. The supply being greater than the demand, the applicants more numerous than the positions and the willingness of the profession to accept inadequate pay has led public officials to underrate medical knowledge and thus the compensation of the medical attendants of all state institutions is very low when the training necessary and services rendered are considered.

The laborious yet gratuitous services to hospitals and eleemosynary institutions by the medical profession has also made public officials undervalue their services. I know of no just reason why a physician or surgeon should render entirely gratuitous service to a hospital when a lawyer charges the same institution. Many doctors seek these positions because of the supposed advertisement or that it may increase their practice or place them on a higher plane than their fellow practitioners or some such unworthy reason. After thirty years active work in a number of hospitals I wish thoughtfully to say that the practical advantage of such work to a diligent physician, who is not a teacher, is wonderfully overestimated by the profession. The time consumed, absence from office, and study outweigh the advantages of the large practice, while hospital methods cannot be successfully transferred to the home or private practice. I might add, it used to be the staff alone that had the privileges of hospitals, but now in order to secure his influence an outsider receives more courtesies and as many privileges as if he were serving the hospital for nothing, for there is a real rivalry between hospitals. These institutions have changed greatly. When I first served in them they were for the poor and unfortunate, with but few, if any, private rooms. Now they are but luxurious, fashionable invalid hotels with possibly charitable annexes. Yet in many cases their managers still expect gratuitous services from their staff. Why a patient who can afford to occupy a private room in a modern hospital should not render some compensation to his physician is beyond my ken. A friend of mine recently found one of his wealthiest patients in a private room in a hospital he was attending, and was required to treat him without pay! He promptly resigned from that staff. Would that all others had the same good sense and manhood. Can you wonder that the governments underpay their medical officers? So also these very hospitals by receiving state or charitable aid are able to underbid a private surgeon and force down medical fees, yet the medical profession fosters this gross injustice. The free dispensary abuse is a well-known example of the lack of business foresight in the medical profession. Its shameful abuses have been thoroughly exposed and need not be dwelt upon here. The fault is ours. The remedy is with ourselves, but so long as we hold our own knowledge and training so cheaply so long will the public authorities undervalue our services.

III
THE POLITICAL SIDE OF MEDICINE.[1]
By JOHN B. ROBERTS, M.D., of Philadelphia.

Politics in its broadest and truest sense is the science and art of business, as applied to aggregations of people. The invitation to take part in a discussion on medicine and politics has been accepted, because I have always been interested in the executive work of medical organizations, and because I believe the good citizen is the man, who exhibits a lively interest in the business activities of his country, state, and neighborhood.

A British medical man, who had shown direct personal interest in national politics, was once reminded by a fellow physician that "medicine is a jealous mistress." "True," was the reply, "but I shall give her no cause for jealousy." This gentleman subsequently became a member of the British government. I do not believe that his knowledge of medical science made him any less a wise statesman. It is probable that the sanitary and other medical acts of the British people were the better because of the influential post held by this doctor of physic.

A western newspaper said, some months ago, that the physician should not be permitted to escape his obligation to take active part in local politics; and asserted that the doctor is needed in even the higher fields of civic usefulness. This is the right view of the case.

In my medical infancy, I was taught that a physician should abstain from all public activity, except the practice of medicine. The theory was based on the belief that the field of medicine was wide enough to fully occupy him, and that, therefore, he could not hope to compete with others in intellectual matters outside of medicine and at the same time attain eminence in medicine. It was also assumed that success in practice was perhaps more sure, if the public never thought of him except as a doctor. This teaching held it unwise in a physician to give popular lectures even on medical topics, inexpedient to accept official positions in social or educational organizations, and detrimental to be known as occupied with civic questions.

[1] Read before the American Academy of Medicine, Saratoga Springs, June 9, 1902.

This doctrine held sway over me during my professional adolescence. After a time, however, I was driven by indignation at the condition of the political party, whose basic principles I espouse, to drop my attitude of indifference to all things outside of medicine. I came gradually to believe that for a doctor to neglect personal attention to civic and political problems is selfish and unjustifiable. His educational advantages, his special knowledge of sanitary requirements, his trained judgment, his self-restraint and poise in responsible situations, his familiarity with the vagaries of human nature, and the respect shown him by his fellow citizens make him eminently qualified for executive work and even leadership in civic affairs. This has recently been most conspicuously shown in this country by Dr. Justus Ohage, Health Commissioner of St. Paul, Minnesota; and in Cuba by Dr. Leonard Wood, the Governor-general.

If a young man studies medicine with the single idea of accumulating money, it may be that he will accomplish his ends more quickly by confining his exertions to the medical rut, indicated by the theory under discussion. This is, however, by no means sure. It is not unlikely that an acceptance of the duties of citizenship would enlarge his circle of friends and patients, and give opportunity for better and higher medical achievement. Narrowness of interests creates narrowness of mind; and no vocation needs broader mental grasp than medicine.

The man of education, brains and capability owes a certain part of his day to the community in which he lives and to association with which his personal success and happiness are due. If he does not give it, he is not doing his full duty to mankind. The greater the advantages he possesses, the greater the call to serve God by serving man. Few men, as a class, have greater personal capacity than physicians. Few then owe more to the state. It is possible that this due to the state should not be paid too early in the doctor's career. It may be true that in his medical adolescence he should stick to medicine almost entirely; but the time surely comes when he should aid personally in the endeavor to raise the standard of health, honesty, education and beauty in the region in which he resides. This he must strive for, even if his efforts fail to show any immediate practical result.

Time may be required to convince his community that sanitary plumbing, pure water, and compulsory vaccination pay. Men of lower ideals may deny that official dishonesty and public indecency sap the vigor of a village or town, and inevitably lead not only to higher taxes, but also to diminished personal safety. It may not be clear to all his fellows that wide-spread education of the young and systematic beautification of towns and cities attract desirable residents, raise the value of property and increase the happiness of all. Let him devote a portion of his days to the inculcation of these truths, while continuing his professional work in sick room, hospital and college. He will then find that his life is more valuable to his fellow man than that of the doctor who, from laziness, carelessness or timidity, neglects his civic duty, under the pretense that his professional work is too exacting to permit such diversion of energy. The doctor's work for the state must have, to be successful, the same quality as his work in medicine. Earnestness and sincerity, honesty and courage, intelligence and courtesy are as essential in one as the other. He must be willing in both activities to labor without thought of personal reward. To do something is a surer source of happiness than to be somebody.

If physicians take the part in civic life, which is suggested by these words, much will be done to hasten the time when we shall not feel abashed to name the place in which we live or to mention the political party we espouse. Whenever medicine has touched politics, politics has been bettered. It is almost a truism that whenever politics has touched medicine, medicine has been smirched. A corroboration of the first statement is found in the present condition of Havana, in which seaport, the United States army surgeons and the medical Governor-general have blotted out the sanitary disgrace of two centuries. The blighting effect of the injection of politics into sanitary medicine is well-known. The politicians of California denied for months the existence of the bubonic plague in San Francisco, although scientific medical men proved its existence by incontrovertible evidence. Mayor Schmitz, of the metropolis, has recently "satisfied himself" that no cases ever existed in the city, and has removed four of the members of the Board of Health because of their activity in seeking to stop the spread and existence of plague. This action reminds me of a certain laughable assertion of Mayor Ashbridge, of Philadelphia, when typhoid fever was endemic in one section of the city because of a contaminated water supply. His honor vigorously denied the existence of any unusual number of cases, claiming that in his opinion the cases called typhoid fever were really only "enteric" fever. These two examples of municipal medicine are enough to convince the most doubting that medical science, if not the medical man himself, is urgently needed in civic executive circles.

The somewhat frequent membership of physicians in school boards is an undoubted advantage to the public. This is especially true in the state of Pennsylvania, where in many of the rural districts the local school board may, under state law, assume the duties and powers of a local board of health. It is discouraging, however, to hear that a physician recently felt compelled to decline to serve longer on a certain school board in Philadelphia, because the perpetual use of improper methods by politicians interfered with the best interests of education. The children of that city suffer much in educational privileges, because of the interference of "practical" politics in school management. Teachers are appointed by "pull" and by bribes instead of on merit, schools are overcrowded and the children are given half time, because school directors are selected for political reasons. The best recommendation for school director in Republican Philadelphia is willingness to obey the machine. A considerable number, therefore, are saloon keepers by occupation and school directors by political favor.

The executive business of hospitals, of medical schools, and of societies devoted to medical subjects constitutes what is often termed medical politics. Here the doctor has frequent opportunity of showing his skill in carrying on business enterprises, and may exercise the talent of leadership. His success is probably equal to that obtained by men of equal ability in any other one walk of life. While he may lack the office training of a boy brought up in a bank or a store, his stock of general information, his knowledge of human nature, his judicial mind and his habit of scientific accuracy will soon enable him to equal, if not outstrip, his non-professional colleagues in executive grasp and precision. This assertion does not apply to the doctor, who is ignorant of scientific medicine, who never cultivates his powers of observation, who, through laziness or indifference, prescribes ready made secret nostrums of whose physiologic action he can have no real knowledge, or who flies from one new medical hobby to another.

It has been thought by some that medical men should have no voice in the management of medical schools or hospitals. They are said to be deficient in business training and methods, and it is thought that their professional relations with other medical men render them injudicious or weak disciplinarians. This view should be no more true in medicine than in legal or military circles. Courts martial are universally used to determine truth and fix responsibility in army and navy matters; and in civil life lawyers are, as other citizens, under the judicial control of members of the bar.

There is no question that much depends on the individual. Some business men know very little business, as some doctors and lawyers know very little medicine and law. A not inconsiderable experience with professional and non-professional men has shown me that the life-long pursuit of business or law does not necessarily develop energy, accuracy and honesty; nor does the same number of years devoted to the study and alleviation of disease always develop those essential traits of a successful and honorable career. Taking all things into consideration, however, I feel that the purse and the good name of an institution are safer in the hands of what I may call the composite doctor than those of the composite lawyer or business man. Special talent and special training will always tell, but no one vocation has in its ranks all the talent and all the training of the community.

My contention is that medical men are of decided advantage in the governing boards of hospitals, colleges and other institutions. They make good officers and are not as likely as others to be deceived in the qualifications of medical teachers or subordinates. The doctors frequently selected by business men as their family physicians are strong testimony to the faultiness of their discrimination in this respect. Doctors, moreover, are not more apt to be cowardly, unjust or tricky than business men. I may be prejudiced, but I am rather inclined to rate the courage, equanimity, justice and honesty of doctors above the same qualities in other men. There are undoubtedly some despicable doctors, but I have not met very many.

In a certain New England hospital, a medical officer made, some years ago, a series of vivisectal experiments on sick and dying babies. I do not know whether the man was punished by the board of trustees; but he evidently did not expect to be, for he published an account of his nefarious work, and read before a learned society a paper detailing his results. In another hospital a year ago a distinguished teacher deliberately opened a woman's gall bladder, for the sole purpose of demonstrating to some surgical guests his method of operating. Is it likely that these vivisectal operations on helpless human patients would be tolerated by a board of trustees in which medical men had seats? It may be asserted that the governing boards in these institutions never knew of the improprieties committed by their medical subordinates. True; but my reply is that boards containing a few medical men could hardly remain ignorant of such infractions of propriety.

It is not unreasonable to suppose that the justice of paying for the services of the medical staffs of hospitals will be sooner recognized, when more boards of trustees contain medical members. Hospital service, conscientiously and scientifically rendered, takes so much time that few physicians or surgeons can afford to give it without a salary. Hence much hospital work is done carelessly. Sometimes a younger man does the work, as an assistant, while the elder man gets the credit of doing charitable work without fee. The result of expecting the doctor to perform hospital service for nothing is often this: that hospitals either appoint inexperienced men with plenty of time and no private practice, or accept the gratuitous service of older and more experienced men, who slight the work, because their private patients are their first care.

According to *American Medicine* (May 25, 1901), the secretary of the Massachusetts General Hospital has calculated the annual money-equivalent of the charitable work of the staff of that institution. His computation is based upon the charges for similar services in private practice, taking low figures for the fees. The valuation for the year 1899 is as follows:

2,421 surgical operations at $25	$ 60,525
95,265 house visits at $2	190,530
104,205 out-patient visits at $2	208,410
	$459,465

It is probable that this institution follows the usual rule of American hospitals, and pays no salaries to its medical staff. At one time, perhaps still, it would not even permit the members of the medical staff to accept fees from private patients in the private rooms. The injustice of such customs and rules is evident when it is realized that a hospital could not exist without its corps of physicians and surgeons, which gives for nothing an amount of service equal in this instance to nearly a half million dollars a year. The superintendents, clerks, apothecaries, nurses, and financial agents are paid, and the members of the staff also should be paid. The salary need not be large, but it ought to be enough to insure faithful service and to compensate in some measure for the time taken from the doctor's private duties.

In 1900 the number of in-patients treated in the twelve largest general hospitals in Philadelphia was 27,132. If each of these was seen once a day by a doctor at $2 per visit the money value of such advice would be $54,264. This is a munificent daily donation to charity from the medical profession, even after deducting the amount paid by the small proportion of paying patients included in the number.

It is evident that the men who give this much of their ability to the work of hospitals should be paid at least a moderate wage.

It is equally clear that they should have representation on the governing boards.

In medical societies and college faculties the doctor has a chance to exhibit his efficiency and deficiency in political affairs. The prizes are not as high as in national or municipal politics, for salaried officers are few and fat contracts unknown. Still, the itch for office and power does cause some to descend to devious methods, and instances could be mentioned to prove that there are physicians who believe in the creed that the end justifies the means. The opportunity for correcting such evils is, however, much greater in medical than in civic circles. The majority of medical men have high ideals of conduct and under leadership will awake from lethargy to right wrong doing among their fellows. The final triumph of the general medical profession over the low-grade medical colleges shows this fact. It was the American Medical Association, the state medical societies, the American Academy of Medicine and kindred bodies, which created the sentiment that enacted laws compelling the college faculties to raise the requirements for the medical diploma.

Those of us who have practised a few decades have seen, it is true, the self-seeking medical politician attain honorable position by undesirable manipulation of men, but honor has not been obtained by the holding of the honorable post. An irregular peg does not fit well in a square hole, and the dishonored man shows early his inability to fit accurately into an honorable office. The other man, who feels that self-respect must be had though it comes high, contemplates with equanimity the misfit and smiles at the contortions of the misfitted man in his endeavor to occupy comfortably the unbecoming hole.

In the medical world, the estimate is pretty generally correct as to whom the profession should honor with its gifts of place and power. There is some degree of error, but it is by no means as great proportionally, as in the circles of business and economics. The doctor, if he live long enough, is pretty sure to have all the professional honor from his colleagues that he deserves. If he, early in life, obtain undeserved honor, he is apt to find later that, by a sort of retributive justice, his fellows learn of his defects and estimate him at his real worth. This is similar to the traditional delay of legal decisions. The medical profession comes to a just conclusion in the end, but it takes time. The estimate of the unintelligent public of professional worth may often be wrong, but that of the physician's own colleagues seldom stays wrong, even if it be wrong in the first place. He, after all, will value most the expert opinion of his fellows.

An important phase of my topic is a consideration of the actions and reactions that take place between doctors and politicians in municipal, state, and national affairs. The principal points of contact are in health boards, hospitals, medical examining and licensing boards, pension examining boards, and the army, the navy, and the marine hospital services. The entrance of scientific men into deliberative assemblies must do good, for the increasing accuracy of science cannot fail to make its impress felt in shaping legislative policy. Sanitary and hygienic problems are of ever-increasing importance in national life; and physicians have the general training which makes their views on these topics weighty. The interests of commercialism and science may seem antagonistic, but in the broadest sense they are one. To deny the existence of bubonic plague in San Francisco may seem wise to politicians; but the intelligent sanitarian knows well that it is better to admit the truth at once and stamp out the disease by immediate action. Even if that action be the destruction of Chinatown by fire, it will be cheaper and wiser than the false security bred by wilful denial of the truth. To suppress the knowledge that tetanus germs have been found in vaccine virus ought not to be the function of a medical society.

This same short-sighted policy of mere opportunists has recently been exhibited, it is said, in France. The House of Deputies has given some thought to the prevention of food adulteration and to other sanitary subjects ; and the medical deputies have been accused of being party to such sanitary legislation. It is said by the *Journal of the American Medical Association* that the result has been a demand from commercial interests that doctors and hygienists be excluded from membership in the House of Deputies. If the statement be correct, it is an odd confirmation of my belief that commercialism and politics need the physician's honest heart and clear head to prevent consummate folly.

The American Medical Association will doubtless exert a more potent influence than it has in state and national politics ; for since its reorganization it is much better fitted to make its wants known and to have its advice sought and heeded. I consider its Committee on National Legislation, which meets yearly at Washington, an instrument of increasing competency.

The state medical societies have done wonderfully good work in elevating the standard of medical education, since the Association, at its meeting at New Orleans, about eighteen years ago, sent to each of them the draft of a bill to create a state board of medical examiners. The definite proposition, endorsed at that time by the association, gave the state societies a basis of action. The state laws adopted since then vary from the original scheme, but they accomplish the purpose intended :—the removal of medical licensure from the medical college to the state government.

The movement must now be followed up until some form of reciprocity in, or transfer of, licenses be established between the states. Perhaps a certificate of a successful voluntary examination of high grade before a board of examiners representing the U. S. medical services, the American Medical Association, and the whole medical profession would be accepted by the individual states as equivalent to its own examination.

The effect of political contact upon medical matters is usually deleterious. This is often seen in the selection of the medical staff of hospitals under state or city control, the appointment of members of medical examining boards by governors, and the selection of boards of pension examiners by federal authority. It is not denied that good appointments are quite often made, but it is well known that it is the good of the party rather than the good of the service that usually regulates the selection. It is pull rather than proficiency that counts.

I know of a state board of examiners which, some years ago, had upon it as examiner in materia medica, a man who asked the physiologic action and dose of a certain much-vaunted proprietary remedy. The applicants for license had never heard its name ;

the examiner had probably recently received a sample with "literature," or had been called upon by the manufacturers' drummer. I have also known of instances where attempts were made by political forces to get examining and licensing boards to pass unqualified men.

These illustrations will perhaps suffice to justify my belief that medical science is liable to be injured by contact with politics, unless the doctors take part in politics and resolutely fight for a higher standard of public ethics. The work of pension boards and municipal and state hospitals would be much improved, if the spoils system were replaced by the merit system. It has always seemed to me a mistake that President McKinley did not leave the pension examiners under civil service rules, where they were placed, I believe, by President Cleveland.

Sir Walter Scott wrote to a friend, in 1814, at the time Napoleon was sent to Elba, that the French emperor's fate was "an awful lesson to sovereigns that morality is not so indifferent to politics as Machiavelians will assert." The present day needs some such assurance that politics must recognize the power of public morality, and I know no man better able to teach morality and ethics to the politicians than the average doctor.

IV
MEDICAL REPRESENTATION IN HOSPITAL MANAGEMENT.[1]

By Augustus A. Eshner, M.D., Philadelphia, Professor of Clinical Medicine in the Philadelphia Polyclinic, Physician to the Philadelphia Hospital, Assistant Physician to the Philadelphia Orthopedic Hospital and Infirmary for Nervous Diseases, Physician to the Hospital for Diseases of the Lungs, at Chestnut Hill.

In a spirit akin to pride, medical men have been prone to confess to a lack of business ability, until not only have they themselves come to believe in it, but they also have convinced the laity thereof. While it may be true that the physician, as a rule, dislikes the keeping of accounts and is a lenient creditor, it must not therefore be concluded that he is deficient in the higher qualities that contribute to the making of a successful business career. He may, perhaps, be unskilled in the tricks of trade, but his integrity is generally unimpeachable, he is loyal to his trust and he can be relied upon to fulfil his obligations, written and unwritten.

It should be remembered that the practice of medicine, although it has business aspects, stands upon an entirely different and much higher ethical plane than commercial pursuits generally. Medicine has always been, and let us hope it will ever continue to be, a learned profession, and those engaged in its practice must be more than mere business men and governed by other than merely commercial instincts. It would be a mistake, however, to conclude that the physician is thereby disqualified from the possession of executive or administrative ability, as well as sound business judgment. On the contrary, he is, by reason of his training, his attainments, his position and his relations with others, especially fitted for the exercise of the qualities named. Of the truth of this statement evidence exists on all sides. At the same time the physician is by reason of his pursuits and his opportunities disinclined and therefore perhaps in a sense disqualified from engaging in ordinary business activity, although there are certain fields of such activity for which often he is inclined and for which he is especially equipped and qualified. I refer particularly to hospital management. There has grown up in some quarters a

[1] Read before the American Academy of Medicine, June 9, 1902.

belief, to the development of which the medical man has himself in no small measure contributed, that the physician is unsuited by inclination, temperament, and ability even for this phase of business activity, so that by written or unwritten law he is in some places excluded from participation in those business affairs for which, as we have said, he should be and generally is most eminently fitted and qualified. To such proportions has this fallacy grown that certain lay boards of hospital management have permitted the opinion to go forth that hospital management is a matter of pure business and that the medical officers are to be looked upon as mere subordinates, to receive and to carry out the directions of their superiors, the lay managers. There has, it seems to me, occasionally been too ready assent to this proposition on the part of medical men and others, to the detriment, I am sure, of the institutions in which the ideas under consideration have prevailed.

The true and correct conception of the relations that should exist between hospital management and medical staff is that which makes one coordinate with the other and not subordinate, so that each supplements and complements the work of the other, to the end that the efforts of both will be strengthened in their mutual cooperation. Even if it be admitted that laymen are better fitted than physicians for the conduct of the business affairs of a hospital it will surely not be denied that the medical man is the better equipped for the decision of matters that must constantly arise in hospital management and in which his judgment is absolutely necessary. Such advice, it goes without saying, should be accessible within the board, or it should be sought from the members of the medical staff rather than from others. The successful administration of the affairs of a hospital therefore requires such a division of labor as assigns responsibility for all purely business matters to the lay managers and for all purely professional matters to the medical staff. In this way the two important aspects of the work of the hospital will be in the hands of experts, between whom there must, of course, exist the most perfect harmony and cordial cooperation in order to attain the best results most economically.

There are several ways in which satisfactory representation can be given the medical staff on the board of management of a hospital :

1. By electing one or more members of the staff to membership in the board ;
2. By periodic conferences between the staff and the board ;
3. By conferences between a committee of the staff and the board or a committee of the board.

As an illustration of the embarrassing complications to which a contest between a lay board of managers and the medical staff of a hospital may give rise, the recent experience of the National Hospital for the Paralyzed and Epileptic, Queen Square, London, serves as a luminous example. So pronounced indeed became the differences between the managers and the staff that the very existence of the hospital was threatened. In fact the usual grant from the Metropolitan Hospitals Sunday Fund was for a time withheld. For many years the staff of this hospital, including the names of some of the most distinguished neurologists and surgeons in the British empire, had appealed in vain for representation on the board of management, for the worthy and unselfish purpose of increasing the efficiency and the usefulness of the institution and establishing direct and cordial relations between the staff and the board. Denial of this appeal was based on the ground that the independence of the board would be endangered by the presence of medical members on it and that the philanthropic aspects of the work would be subordinated to those of a merely scientific and investigatory character. Finally the acts of a paid official, clothed with the authority of secretary and general director, as a representative of the board, became so objectionable and intolerable that the medical staff carried their appeal to the governors of the hospital, and after a long struggle succeeded in gaining their point. As a result the medical staff was accorded two representatives on the board of management, among twelve, the office of secretary-director was abolished, and the election of a senior-house physician, of a secretary and of a lady superintendent was recommended. Finally, as a fitting climax, the old board of management was turned out and an entirely new one elected in its place.

The experience thus briefly outlined should serve as a guide of action for institutions in which lay boards of managers arrogate to themselves powers that it was never intended they should exercise and undertake the performance of duties for which they are unqualified, and in connection with which the medical man must be looked upon as an expert.

The several objections that have been raised to the presence of medical men on boards of hospital management are specious and will not hold water. Thus it has been suggested that a medical man would not be unprejudiced if the acts of a medical colleague became a matter for discussion and criticism. There is no reason to believe that the medical man is less lacking than his lay colleague in the judicial quality. Indeed his scientific training is peculiarly calculated to develop this, and it is only fair to assume that he is not less capable of forming an impartial opinion on all medical matters. The objection that the presence of medical men on the board of management would result in subordinating the more humane work of the hospital to scientific and experimental observation carries its own refutation. Surely the physician is second to none in consideration of the welfare of those entrusted to his care, and patients are best treated in those institutions whose medical officers are distinguished for their scientific zeal.

That the opinions expressed in this communication are not those of medical men alone is shown in a symposium on the question of hospital management, arranged by the editor of the *Practitioner*, of London, and participated in by both laymen and physicians. It was the unqualified consensus of opinion that "some kind of representation of the medical staff on the governing body is a necessary condition of the successful management of a hospital." "Not one of the writers," the editor of the *Practitioner* goes on to say, " maintains that a hospital can be carried on by lay governors or officials without regard to the opinions and wishes of the medical staff." The Prebendary of St. Paul's, who was for ten years Chairman of the Committee on Management of King's College Hospital, thinks it essential, if the management of a hospital is to take due account of all its varied needs, that it should be kept in constant touch with the medical staff by direct and immediate communication. He holds that this can be effectually secured only by their personal representation on the governing body. In his opinion "the ideal condition of a committee of management is thus one in which men of business, who represent the practical purposes of charity, and who are accustomed to dealing with public affairs, are predominant, and in which the various professional interests, which are essential parts of a modern hospital, have a secondary but an adequate representation." The medical staff of the Royal Free Hospital is directly represented on the committee of management by two members, a physician and a surgeon, nominated annually by the Medical Committee, but elected by the governors. One of these members is also a member of the weekly board and regularly attends its meetings. This arrangement has been found of mutual advantage to both lay and medical authorities.

A member of the Managing Committee of the Children's Hospital recommends that the medical staff should form a committee of their own members to deal with professional questions that may arise among themselves or that may be referred to them by the Managing Committee. The secretary of the Seamen's Hospital lays down the principle that no hospital board can have a right sense of the duties devolving on it that does not take into its closest confidence the physicians and surgeons who have charge of the patients. This end he thinks may be attained either by having the members of the medical staff or a certain number of them sit on the board of management. His own preference is for a lay board and a council of the medical staff.

The medical contributors to the symposium are naturally in favor of some form of professional representation and they cite a large number of instances in which the wisdom of this plan is conceded by its continued and satisfactory application. In concluding his remarks on the evidence presented, the editor of the *Practitioner* holds that "it is clear that there is a consensus of opinion, lay and medical, that in the management of hospitals the medical element cannot be excluded without detriment to the interests of the sick poor, for whose relief they have been established."

DISCUSSION.

Dr. P. Max Foshay, of Cleveland, Ohio :[1]

Agreed with Dr. Roberts, any damage coming to a physician going into politics comes entirely from the motives impelling him. Men who become leaders in political movements are those who have come in contact with the members of their party and by becoming favorably known to those who are directing its affairs. Hence a physician can have greater personal influence if he will, in a proper manner, avail himself of the opportunities of cultivating the acquaintanceship of those who are influential in the politics of the place where he lives. If he does this, and keeps himself from seeking for office, his opinions, at least on medical subjects, will have weight.

Dr. Charles McIntire, of Easton, Pa :

In regard to the paper of Dr. Davis I received a letter that illustrates very well how physicians themselves prevent the profession from receiving a proper recompense for service. The letter is from a secretary of a board of medical examiners whom I asked for the results of examination.

He writes: "The state makes no appropriations to defray any of the expenses of our board, and to comply with your request would necessitate a personal expense to me of several dollars, which I do not feel I should spend for information to others who are certainly able to pay the cost of the work, if they want it. Every letter which I answer costs me two cents for postage which I pay from my private income, and when I tell you I have answered over 700 letters since, our meeting last January, involving an expense to me of $14.00 for postage alone, you will probably understand that if you want the information asked for, it will be well to send an amount sufficient to at least cover cost of stenographer and stamps."

If a person will accept an appointment from the state as secretary of the state board of medical examiners for the honor, and pay the official postage out of his own pocket, how in the name of common sense is the state to learn how to estimate the value of the service of the physician when serving in public? If all the profession in that state had the proper self-respect, either the law would be changed or there would be no examining board.

Dr. A. A. Eshner, of Philadelphia :

I should prefer to assent to Dr. Roberts' proposition in the following terms. The medical man is first a citizen and secondly a physician. Inasmuch as the administration of civic affairs constitutes an important phase of politics, if it do not comprise the entirety, and it is the bounden duty of the physician to participate in such affairs, he must, therefore, participate in politics.

[1] Condensed from stenographer's report and not revised by the author.

Dr. H. D. Holton, of Brattleboro, Vt.:

The question arises, what is the result when the medical man enters politics? Does he improve the condition of his constituents? Does he keep his own honor and standing in the community and profession, and is the result generally good? In a large city of our state, a medical man two years ago and a little over was elected mayor of the city. During his first term or about that time a large school building which is the best constructed building in the state from a sanitary standpoint, also as regards the duties which are expected to be performed in that building, was erected and completed. A library is under process of erection which is to be a model of itself. In an outbreak of smallpox during the last year that city had the benefit of a medical man in its mayor in a way that it could not have had if he had been a layman. The results in these two departments have been to the credit of the medical profession, and of much advantage to his city. The gentleman who read the first paper of the afternoon, Mayor Hawley, of Burlington, is the man to whom I refer.

Dr. S. D. Risley, of Philadelphia:

It seems to me that the gentlemen who have presented these interesting papers to us, favoring the political influence of the physician, have not done so with the idea that he shall occupy public office, but rather, that he shall exercise an active participation in civic affairs, and one at least, has given as his reason, that the physician by virtue of his station and education is better fitted than the average citizen to do so. I believe it is the duty of the physician to take active part in civic affairs. It has been my fortune to be personally well acquainted with a considerable number of men who have occupied prominent political posts and I have found them to be, on the whole, a very reasonable class of men. Whatever of fault there has been in their administration has grown largely out of low standards for action; that is to say, standards lower than would be entertained by this company of physicians. They have acted quite honestly according to their own standards. To my surprise on a number of occasions I have found that they were quite easily influenced to take another action when another view of the case was presented to them, another standard by which they could control their actions in political affairs. As an illustration, in the rural community where I have my home the greater part of the year, there was a reform party organized in the borough which had nominated a local ticket for election by the community in the hope of correcting certain alleged abuses. The gentleman who controlled the politics of the party in power came to me to inquire about my attitude. I said to him "what are you going to do about your party ticket? Are you going to renominate the men who are occupying the offices now, who obviously do not enjoy the confidence of the community?" He said, "well, what would you suggest, Dr. Risley?" I said, "suppose you call a borough meeting instead of your packed caucus or primary so-called, and let the community nominate the men for the respective office. You will have no difficulty if you place the proper men in nomination. All that the community desires is a capable and honest administration of its affairs. The town meeting was held; other citizens were nominated and as a result the township offices are held by creditable citizens. This illustrates how in my opinion the physician can use his influence in politics, but I doubt the propriety of the physician accepting political office except those allied to medicine.

In reference to Dr. Eshner's paper, I would like to say that I am thoroughly in harmony with the contention submitted. Hospitals cannot do as well without medical representation on their boards of management as with it. Any surgical or medical staff of any hospital will be constantly subjected to petty annoyance by any board which has not an adequate medical representation.

Dr. John B. Roberts, of Philadelphia, closing:

The question arises, do the people who pay us for our professional services feel that we ought to dabble or meddle in political activities of our homes? I am rather afraid that the man who takes an active part in political life, either as an office-holder, as has been so well illustrated here in one of our fellows, or as the mere adviser as in the case of that other fellow of the Academy, Dr. Risley (who caught a politician when he was scared and who, therefore, did what he was told), must expect to lose some money. I do, however, believe that it is the duty of every man in this Academy to do such work, even if it costs him money. If we do not do it, the business men who have usually lower ideals than professional men are going to allow this country to go to rack and ruin. The condition of Philadelphia and Pennsylvania politically is so horrible and I am so ashamed of that city and state that I feel it is a duty to endeavor to aid in their political regeneration.

Dr. D. C. Hawley, Burlington, Vt., closing:

The points touched upon by Dr. Risley show that his conclusions and mine are diametrically opposed. If the first part of the proposition is correct, I think the second part is correct also. If it is a man's duty as a physician to take part in the public affairs of his city, town or state, as we admit it is the duty to a certain extent of all good citizens, I believe that when he has fulfilled that part of his obligation, if the public finds him fitted by capacity, training and judgment for any office to which they choose to call him, it is his duty to accept it and render good service. I believe the community will think no less of him than if he declines upon what may be considered ethical grounds.

Dr. A. A. Eshner, of Philadelphia, closing:

I wish merely to add that there can, of course, be no objection whatever to medical men who are not members of a hospital staff being members of the board of directors. This, it seems to me, would be a distinct advantage, as in some cases it has proven to be. The main contention of the paper, however, is that there should first of all be some form of medical representation on the board of management, and that this could, in part at least, be admirably secured by selection from the staff of medical officers; or that there should be direct and immediate communication between the medical staff and the board of managers in order that the two bodies may act coordinately.

THE PERSONAL EQUATION IN EXAMINATIONS FOR LICENSURE.[1]

By Charles McIntire, A.M., M.D., Easton, Pa.

The subject of reciprocity in medical licensure, which upon first consideration seems to be a very simple one, becomes more complex as the discussion proceeds. One objection urged against the adoption of any system of reciprocity is the varying standards of the boards of medical examiners themselves, whence a paper entirely acceptable by the board of one state would not be accepted by a similar board in another state and, therefore, it would not be fair to those who passed the examination of the presumably, more difficult board to permit one to practise upon the examination of the more lenient board. It is difficult to determine the real value of the objection because, like so many other assertions based merely upon opinion, it is hard to obtain a foundation upon which to build an argument.

This paper attempts to give some facts which will enable those who are interested in the question of reciprocity to determine with greater accuracy than before the validity of the objection.

A series of questions and of answers to these questions were procured for the purpose of investigating the question purely on its merits. It is thought best not to reveal the way in which these were procured. Suffice to say, the questions have all of them been used in examinations before some state board of medical examiners, and the answers given by *bona fide* applicants for license when these questions were made use of.

It ought also be stated that in selection of the replies no effort was made to secure them from papers receiving either the highest or the lowest marks; they were taken quite at random. It was not desirable to select questions representing all the subjects of a state examination, because the school of practice of the person answering them would be revealed, and the additional labor would not make the results any more valuable for the purpose of the paper.

[1] Read before the American Academy of Medicine, Saratoga Springs, June 7, 1902.

The questions and replies were arranged in order, mimeographed, and sent to the secretaries of the various boards of medical examiners and also to a selected number of colleges.

Each set of questions was accompanied by a mimeographed circular explaining the method of research.

Efforts were made to secure markings from the eclectic and homeopathic schools and when the state board was not a mixed board from each of the boards of examiners in the state. It may also be stated that the answers were by students of different schools.

The documents thus sent out are as follows:

DEAR DOCTOR: The general question indicated by the term "Reciprocity in Medical Licensure" is a living one, and will be agitated until it is satisfactorily solved. The great danger lies in the possible adoption of ineffective plans, which will do harm. The problem is a complex one, and much of the difficulty in solution is caused by lack of definite information.

It has been assumed that the various examinations by the various state boards vary greatly in value, and the findings of one board consequently cannot be accepted by another. I doubt very much the correctness of this assumption, but believe all of the examiners will be found to mark with nearly the same degree of severity. But neither assumption proves any thing, and I have devised a plan to give us information on this subject. I earnestly invite your cooperation in carrying out this plan.

I enclose a series of questions and answers on several subjects, which I am submitting to the various state boards, with this request: That the examiners on the subject of each board will read and mark these papers, as he would the papers presented in a regular examination, and report the result to me. The questions and the answers are both honest, $i.\ e.$, the questions are selected from such as have been used by state boards, and the replies are the honest replies of young graduates in medicine, who did not know of the use of their answers. As a test of this kind must be made as impersonal as possible, I cannot give more than this personal assurance. Three answers are given to each question, but the type used easily distinguishes them. In reporting the markings, it will be necessary only to indicate the subject, the number of the question, and the marks of each reply, in the order given. Thus, "Anatomy 1-75, 84, 93," a scale of 100 or of 10 may be used.

The answers are intended to be accurate copies of the replies given. It may be that mistakes have been made in preparing the mimeograph stencils, as they were prepared somewhat hastily and are published without "proof-reading." It is but fair, then, to blame the typewriter for any errors in orthography, etc., except where such error is clearly indicated as in the answers as submitted.

There is one possible error in an investigation of this kind, the personal equation of the examiner. In an ordinary examination, that is a common factor, as the examiner's marks on the various papers are compared only with the marks of his own making. Here, however, the consciousness of a comparison may make him more critical, possibly hyper-critical, and his marks misleading. To reduce this result to a minimum, the results will be tabulated so as not to indicate the examiner or the board he represents. No opportunity for direct comparison will be afforded by any use to be made of the replies.

There is another question which this investigation may help in answering: the relative value of the college examination and the state board examination. These questions will be submitted to a representative list of colleges, with the request for the proper examiner to read and mark in a similar manner. Here too, neither the name of the examiner nor the college, will be mentioned in any use made of the information, and for the same reason.

It is planned to publish the information in the Bulletin of the American Academy of Medicine.

Again permit me to solicit your prompt and hearty cooperation, by distributing the papers to the proper person, and securing an early reply.

Very truly yours,
CHARLES McINTIRE,
Secretary.

I send duplicates of this circular to save you writing a letter of explanation.

ANATOMY.

Question 1.—Give the relation of the femoral artery at its origin, and name the branches given off as it descends the leg.

Answers:

It is one of the bifurcations of the abdominal aorta, as it bifurcates in front of the lumbar vertebra, descends through the femoral ring, passes down close to the femur, and is continued in the popliteal artery.

Above: Skin, superficial fascia, Poupart's ligament, genito-crural nerve. Externally: Anterior crural nerve (separate by partition). Internally: Femoral vein (separate by partition). Below: Rectus muscle—Branches: Superficial epigastric, superficial external iliac superficial external pudic, deep external pudic, profunda femoris (external circumflex, internal circumflex, superior perforating, middle perforating—nutrient—inferior perforating) anastomotica magnus. At the opening in the adductor magnus, it (*i. e.,* the femoral artery) becomes the popliteal.

The great sciatic nerve on the internal side, gastrochemius muscle behind, outer side with the outer head, anterior with the interoscus (sic) membranes. Muscular branch, external maleoli.

Question 2.—Give the five principal points to which the pneumogastric nerve is distributed.

Answers :

To the pharynx, tongue, larynx, esophagus, and diaphragm.

1, Lungs ; 2, stomach ; 3, heart ; 4, liver ; 5, larynx.

Heart, stomach, esophagus, trachea, larynx.

Question 3.—Describe the mammary gland.

Answers :

It is a hemispherical body (two in number) situated in the chest, in pectoral region. It is composed of lactiferous ducts, is loose connective tissue, converging in a point—the nipple. The whole is covered with skin. The nipple is a cylindrical elevation in the center of the gland, darker in color and surrounded by an areola of dark skin.

The mammary gland is a conglomerate gland, well developed in the female especially during the latter part of pregnancy and in the puerpurium. It is undeveloped in the male except under special circumstances.

The mammary gland is situated on the breast, from the third to the sixth rib, one gland on each side. The grand projects anteriorly in a protuberance known as the nipple, which is surrounded by a pigmented area known as the areola, which contains the glands of Montgomery. The ultimate divisions of the gland are known as acini. These are lined with cells which secrete the milk in form of fatty globules, surrounded by an envelope. The acini lead into ducts which gradually radiate toward the center, forming ten or so large ducts. These large ducts lead to a space directly behind the nipple.

It is a large gland situated between the deep and superficial fascia over the pectoral muscles of the breast, composed of many small glands with their ducts all leading toward the nipple. Secretes the milk. Has some intercellular tissue, also lymphatic glands are closely connected with it.

Question 4.—What nerve supplies motion to the muscles of mastication, and from what part of the skull does it emerge?

Answers :

The trifacial or fifth.

The superior maxillary division of the fifth cranial nerve, emerging from the foramen ovale of the sphenoid bone.

The fifth cranial nerve ; foramen ovale.

Question 5.—Name the elements composing, and describe the hip-joint.

Answers:

It is composed of bone, synovial membrane, and ligaments. It is situated at the lower part of the trunk, in the acetabulum of the os innominata bone. The head of the femur is held in approximation to the acetabulum by the round ligament. The whole joint is surrounded by a capsular ligament.

The ilium, the ischium, the pubis articulating to form the acetabulum in which (*i. e.*, the acetabulum) the head of the femur rests. In addition to the above bones, the following ligaments are of importance: (1) Capsular—around margin of the acetabulum and neck of femur; (2) Cotyloid—inserted in the cotyloid notch; (3) Y ligament—acetabulum to oblique line of femur; (4) Ligamentum teres from the center of the acetabulum to center of head of femur. The joint is supplied by the obturator artery and by the sciatic obturator nerve. The hip-joint is, consequently, a ball and socket joint.

The acetabulum of the innominata and the head of the femur. It is a ball and socket joint, with the ligamentum teres connecting the head with the acetabulum. Freely supplied with synovial fluid, surrounded by a capsular ligament, and many large muscles.

Question 6.—With what bones does the temporal articulate?

Answers:

The parietal, frontal, occipital, superior maxillary, malar, and sphenoid.

Occipital, parietal, sphenoid, inferior maxillary, malar.

Occipital, parietal, frontal, malar, sphenoid, inferior maxillary.

Question 7.—Give the origin of the brachial plexus of nerves and distribution of its principal branches.

Answers:

It is distributed to the neck and chest.

The brachial plexis arises from the 5th, 6th, 7th, and 8th cervical nerves, and from the first dorsal. Subscapular to the subscapular muscle; circumflex to the deltoid muscle; post-thoracic to the serratus magnus; musculospiral to the extensor muscles of the forearm (principally); ulnar to flexor muscles of forearm, in hand to little finger and half of ring finger, front and back. Median to flexor muscles of forearm; in hand, thumb and three and a half fingers on palmar surface. Half of ring finger and tip of forefinger and tip of middle finger on dorsal surface.

It arises from the 4th, 5th, 6th, and 7th cervical nerve roots, and the first dorsal root, which join to form the nerve trunks of the median (which supplies a part of the forearm and hand), ulnar (distributed to the ulnar side of the arm and hand), musculo-spiral (distributed to the back part of the arm and hand), musculo-cutaneous (which supply principally the integument of the arm).

Question 8.—Describe the uterus, giving normal size, form and relations.

Answers:

Is one of the female organs of generation, is pear-shaped, about 3 inches long and 1 1/4 wide at the top, at the broadest part. At either side of the top are given off two tubes—the Fallopian tubes. The organ is supported by six ligaments. It is situated in the lower part of the trunk and inclined forward. It is composed of a serous coat, a muscular coat, and a mucous lining. The junction of the os and the cervix is surrounded by the vagina, which is the canal to external parts, the opening of the organ begins at the os, where it is slightly broadened, then again constricted at the "neck," when it will again broaden (in the body). At the upper inside corners are openings for the Fallopian tubes.

Length, about 3 1/2 inches; length of cavity, about 2 inches; weight, about 2 ounces; cubic capacity, 1 cubic inch (increased to 400 cubic inches at term). Anteriorly, bladder; posteriorly, rectum: externally, Fallopian tubes, broad ligaments, ovaries, ureters; superiorly, intestines; inferiorly, cervix projects into vagina.

Ligaments—round (2), broad (2), utero-vesical (2), utero-sacral (2), obliterated hypogastric artery, the urachus. Blood supply—uterine cavity, branch of anterior trunk of internal iliac, ovarian artery, branch of internal pudic. Circular anastomosis around cervix. Nerve supply—sympathetic. The uterus is divided into two portions: 1. Fundus, into which are inserted the Fallopian tubes; 2, the cervix. The uterus is normally at right angles to the axis of the vagina.

Composed of muscular tissue covered by peritoneum, lined by the endometrium, has a fundus, body, neck, os uteri, and cavity. Three openings, two from the Flopian tubes, one into the vagina. Two and a half inches deep, one and a half wide, about one inch through. Piriform.

Anterior, the bladder; posterior, Duglas Culda Sack and rectum; laterally, broad ligaments, flopan tubes; above, intestines; below, into the vagina.

Question 9.—Locate and describe the fissure of Rolando.

Answers:

It begins about half way between the front of the brain (in each hemisphere) and parietal-occipital fissure, runs downward and forward to the plane of the fissure of Sylvius.

It is located between the ascending parietal and ascending frontal convolutions. It can be located externally as follows: Mark a point one-half inch behind a point one-half way between the inion and glabella, a line 3 3/8 inches in length at an angle of 67 1/2 degrees from the anterior half of the inion to glabella line will mark the fissure of Rolando.

The fissure of Rolando marks the great motor area of the brain. From above downward are the following areas: Legs, trunk, upper extremities, face.

Draw a line one and a half inch anterior from central point between the glabellum and occipital protuberance, 67 1/2° anterior from the top of the skull about two inches long. Is a deep fissure located in the motar region (sic) of the brain, is of much importance to the surgeon.

Question 10.—Name the great veins which have no valves.

Answers:

Vena cava, the pulmonary.

Pulmonary veins, portal veins, azygos veins, hemorrhoidal veins, internal jugular veins, external jugular veins, subclavian veins.

Jugular veins, disending vena cava (sic).

SURGERY.

Question 1.—Describe the best non-operative methods of reducing incarcerated inguinal hernia.

Answers:

Anesthetize the patient, flex the thighs to cause relaxation of abdominal muscles, grasp the protuding sac, push upward and backward, keeping in place by a truss.

1. Distention of the bowel by a high enuma; 2. Taxis and massage, as follows: (*a*) Flex legs on thighs; (*b*) flex thighs on abdomen, thus relaxing abdominal walls; (*c*) apply fingers at constriction; (*d*) apply thumbs at bottom of sac; (*e*) by a sort of kneading, pressing motion endeavor gently to restore the bowel to its normal position; (*f*) do not persist too long if attempt is unsuccessful.

The leg should be flexed to relax the muscles and drawn well over the other. Begin with the part that came down last to reduce, using no force, by working it back in the same direction from which it came.

Question 2.—Give the symptoms and treatment of subluxations of the inferior maxilla.

Answers:

It is often habitual. The mouth is open and fixed, the tip of the chin is further back than usual. Protect the thumbs with "finger-cots" from injury by the teeth. Stand in front of the patient, put the thumbs on the back molar teeth, the fingers at the angle of the jaw, and make pressure downward and backward with the thumbs, and forward with the fingers on the jaw.

(*a*) Deformity, it may be a unilateral or a bilateral subluxation. In both, the jaw will be somewhat projected ; in the former also somewhat turned to the opposite side ; (*b*) mouth open ; (*c*) anxious expression ; (*d*) inability to articulate distinctly ; (*e*) pain ; (*f*) immobility ; (*g*) head of bone felt in abnormal position; (*h*) A depression at normal position of head; (*i*) tenderness. Treatment: (*a*) Stand behind patient; (*b*) head of patient resting on operator's chest ; (*c*) thumbs in mouth, protecting them with towel, or place cork, or other suitable material between front teeth ; (*d*) press with thumb on lower molar teeth ; (*e*) when in place, retain for a few days by a suitable bandage, *e. g.*, Bartorn's Gibson's crossed angle of the jaw.

The jaw drops down. The mouth is opened from inability to use the jaw, place a piece of soft wood between the back teeth, grasp the bone on both sides with the hand, drawing down, forwards, and upwards. Afterwards use the four-tail bandage for a short time.

Question 3.—State the site and symptoms of Colles' fracture, and describe the most approved treatment.

Answers :

It is a fracture of the styloid process of the radius. You will have crepitus at the site of injury, a non-uniformity of the joint internally, an upward and inward deformity of the hand. Reduce by making outward distension ; place the hand in a Levis splint, with a small wad on the underside of arm above the seat of fracture.

Colles' fracture is that of both bones of the forearm about 1 1/2 inches above radio-carpal articulation. Symptoms : (*a*) Deformity, shortening. Lower fragment, above and posterior ; upper fragment, below and anterior. Consequently, silver-fork appearance. Inversion. (*b*) Mobility ; (*c*) crepitus ; (*d*) pain ; (*e*) tenderness; (*f*) swelling ; (*g*) extravasation; (*h*) ecchymosis; (*i*) impairment of function. Treatment : (*a*) Reduce fracture by extension, counter-extension and manipulation (difficult and sometimes impossible) ; (*b*) pad on dorsal surface at upper end of lower fragment; (*c*) pad on palmar surface at lower end of upper fragment ; (*d*) bond splint; (*e*) has palmar rest ; (*f*) corrects inversion; (*g*) posterior flat strip from elbow to wrist ; (*h*) arm in sling.

Fracture of the radius about one inch above the lower end. Dislocation of the parts, crepitus, pain, swelling, heat. With the hand extended, reduce the fracture by extension and manipulation. Place the arm midway between pronation and supination, using an anterior and posterior splint, which must be wide enough to prevent lateral pressure, carrying the arm in a sling.

Question 4.—Differentiate chancre and chancroid, and give the treatment for each.

Answers :

The chancre of Hunter is the one that announces an infection from syphilis. It is found at the site of infection. It is hard, indurated, depressed in the middle, with a pale, red base. Has a slight discharge, sticky and of a disagreeable odor. The treatment must be constitutional. Begin with a small dose of mercury (1/3 to 1/5 gram) of bichlorid, and gradually increase until you find out the amount that can be borne. Continue treatment for about two years.

The chancroid is the "soft chancre," has no signs of induration, and will have no, or very slight, constitutional symptoms, is caused by some septic material on an abraded surface. Treat antiseptically, wash with peroxid of hydrogen ; may sometimes be cauterized.

Chancre: Usually single; non-autoinoculable; marked induration; cup-shaped, clean; elevated; false membrane; bubo, bilatera; bubo seldom suppurates. Treatment: (a) Palliative best, merely dust with some powder as equal parts of the subnitrate of bismuth and lycopodium ; (b) curative—of little value as far as influencing the disease is concerned. If the chancre is in a prominent place, or where other persons are liable to be infected from it, it may be excised.

Chancroid : Usually multiple ; autoinoculable ; no induration (may have apparent induration from cauterization); irregular, foul ulcer; depressed; no false membrane ; bubo may be bilateral ; bubo often suppurates. Treatment : Cauterize with pure carbolic acid. If under the prepuce, cauterize the chancroid, and when healed, circumcize. If circumcized before healing, the wound is liable to infection.

Chancre is hard, red, painful, indurated base. Cut it out with a knife, dust on antiseptic powder, and dress. Give such remedies internally as iodide of potash with any other remedies as may be indicated. Chancroid is a superficial ulcer, not hard, but soft, very little inflammation. Base is not hard and red, but quite thick. Cauterize the base with nitrate of silver, and dress with antiseptic dressing.

Question 5.—Describe the most approved operation for unilateral hare-lip, and state the age at which it is preferable to operate.

Answers :

Operate at one or two years. Remove the scar which will vivify the edges, approximate the edges, and hold them in place by deep sutures and adhesive bandages.

(1) Take all aseptic precautions ; (2) anesthetize adult patient (may not be advisable in very young) ; assistant grasps lip at each side of lesion between thumbs and forefingers, thus controlling the artery ; (4) make V-shaped incision, cutting well into healthy tissue ; (5) approximate the

edges by two parallel hare-lip pins inserted to the mucous membrane so as to constrict the artery; (6) figure of eight suture around the needles; (7) Allow slight projection downward of margins of incision, thus allowing for subsequent contraction and preventing deforming depression. The deformity, *i. e.*, hare-lip should be corrected a few hours after birth, as it interferes with sucking.

Freshen the parts of the lip to be approximated, cut the tissue loose from the bones. The superior maxillary well up and back with the chisel. Place in silver wire retaining sutures, first to draw the tissues together, then approximate the skin with the enterdermic suture, draw up the silver suture to relieve tension of the other sutures and twist. Dress with antiseptic dressing. Should be done about the last part of the first year.

Question 6.—Describe an anterior luxation of the shoulder joint, and give methods of reduction.

Answers:

The nature of the accident—as a jar on the elbow of the flexed arm. There would be a flattening of the shoulder and a mal-position of the anatomical points. (1) Reduce by rotation inward and manipulation. (2) By raising the flexed arm to almost a horizontal line and straightening the elbow with combined manipulation. Keep the joint quiet.

E. g. Sub-clavicular deformity: (*a*) Depression under acromion; (*b*) head of bone in abnormal position under clavicle; (*c*) elbow backward and away from side; (*d*) immobility; (*e*) pain; (*f*) tenderness; (*g*) swelling; (*h*) extravasation; (*i*) ecchymosis; (*j*) Dugas' test—inability to place the hand on opposite shoulder and elbow to side simultaneously; (*k*) muscles on stretch—supra-spinatus, infra-spinatus, teres minor, deltoid. Treatment: Kocher's method: (*a*) Flex forearm on arm; (*b*) elbow to side; (*c*) endeavor to rotate head of humerus; if impossible, the luxation cannot be reduced by this method; (*d*) raise the arm at right angles to body, thus relaxing supra-spinatus, infra-spinatus, and deltoid; (*e*) sweep elbow down across the chest and then rotate head of humerus into place; (*f*) retain in place by a Velpau bandage. Another method is by direct extension and leverage over assistant's fist placed in axilla.

Head of humerus is felt anterior to normal position, inability to raise the arm, pain, some heat. Head of bone is rotated forward. Flex the forearm, carry inward toward the median line of body, lift the arm up, rotate it outward, and rotate the head down, back and upwards into place.

Question 7.—Detail the symptoms and describe the surgical management of a case of psoas abscess.

Answers:

The secret of the trouble is along the psoas muscle, which is along the spine or the lumbar vertebrae. There would be symptoms of an inflammatory condition, a travelling of the pus down a canal in the inguinal region, and a discharge on the inside of the thigh. Open on the thigh, clean out the tract with peroxid, and dress antiseptically.

(1) Situation, about the middle of Poupart's ligament externally to the vessels; (2) can be displaced, thus differentiating it from affections of the vessels; (3) pain; (4) tenderness; (5) swelling; (6) Fluctuation. Treatment: (1) Aspirate; (2) inject concentrated solution of boracic acid; (3) irritate sac wall with needle or trochar; (4) may inject solution of iodoform and glycerin; (5) If contents too thick for aspiration, make incision, curette, and pack with iodoform gauze. All must be done under strict aseptic precautions.

Fever, dull pain in back, increased heat over abscess, the pus follows the psoas muscles downward and points near Pourpart's ligament. Open the abscess when it points, give free drainage, cut down into the abscess and curette it out, pack with iodoform gauze, allow to drain. Internal treatment, give antiseptics; tonics to build up patient.

Question 8.—Give the treatment and complications in repair of frozen tissues.

Answers:

Treat in a cool room with cool water and alcohol; when there is good evidence of an established circulation, keep the patient warm. There is apt to be a necrosis, when amputation must be thought of, when possible on account of position.

The treatment should aim at a gradual rather than a sudden restoration of the normal temperature. To this end: (1) Friction with snow; (2) immerse in cold water, gentle friction; (3) gradually increase the temperature of the water.

Cut off the frozen tissue. The repair is by slow granulating surfaces, always amputate back of the line of frozen tissue.

Question 9.—Define the causes and state the symptoms and treatment of sinuses and fistulae.

Answers:

Can be caused by an abscess forming a tract for the discharge. The symptoms would depend on the location of the abscess. Treatment: Determine the course of the tract, open it, treat it antiseptically, and induce an obliteration in that way of the false passage.

Causes: (1) Tuberculosis, *i. e.*, swallowing of sputum; (2) hemorrhoids; (3) malignant diseases; (4) traumatism; (5) Debilitating diseases weakening the tissue. Symptoms: (1) Pain, especially in defecation; (2) discharge of pus; (3) discharge of feces if complete fistula; (4) Protrusion of skin if hard internal fistula. Treatment : (1) Make complete opening from skin to rectum; (2) Slit up tissue from fistulous tract to rectum; (3) open up all sinuses; (4) wipe entire tract with pure carbolic acid; (5) insert iodoform gauze and allow to heal from the bottom.

From bruises, fractures, or may be of normal tissue, as the sinus of the skull. When acquired, there is caries and sloughing of the bones, pus, and a lack of good granulating tissue. Deposit of foreign body with low vitality of the part forming pus through the opening and does not heal; and from internal abscess not properly treated.

Question 10.—Describe the treatment of penetrating gunshot wound of the skull.

Answers :

Shave the parts, trephine, remove all splinters of bone, etc., clean out the wound antiseptically (don't use too strong—1 to 2,500 a bichlorid solution) inside and outside; cover with iodoform gauze and bandage.

(1) Shave scalp; (2) all proper aseptic precautions. If ball still in skull; (3) allow aluminum probe to follow of its own weight the tract of ball; (4) Plan two planes at right angles to line of probe and at their junction, make a counter opening; (5) endeavor to remove ball by forceps. After ball removed; (6) drain the tract with small rubber catheter; (7) quiet, bromides, ice-cap to avoid excessive cerebral stimulation.

If ball can be located, remove by use of forceps; but if ball cannot be located, do not use the probe, wait and be guided by the symptoms that arise from the wound. Clean the wound if any evidence of sepsis and dress antiseptically; if hemorrhage shall be profuse, trephine and tie the artery.

PATHOLOGY.

Question 1.—Define sapremia, septicemia, and pyemia, and state what constitutes the specific characteristics of each.

Answers :

Septicemia is an inflammation due to some septic poison. It would be recognized by the history and the position of the morbid condition. Pyemia is an inflammation with pus. It would be recognized by seeing these two conditions and in finding streptococci in the exudate. Sapremia is a simple inflammation due to any condition that will cause an extra flow of blood to the injured part.

Sapremia, septicemia, and pyemia are toxic conditions due to the absorption of pathogenic microorganisms or their products. The three conditions may be differentiated by the following specific characteristics: (1) Sapremia—due to the absorption of the products of putrefaction; (2) septicemia—due to the absorption of the microorganisms of suppuration ; (3) pyemia—due to the absorption of the products of suppuration, *i. e.*, pus.

Are sphacelus that when they enter the blood produce septicemia. the power of producing them like form and shape. The sphacelus pyemia produces pyemia when it enters the blood, the power it has to reproduce its like.

Question 2.—Describe in detail the changes that occur in an artery, the seat of endarteritis obliterans.

Answers :

At first there will be a hyperemic condition of the lining membrane, *i. e.*, a thickening and congestion. This will give way to a "thinning-out" process, and here the place with more of a hardened, tougher, and thinner surface than the surrounding parts.

Usually a calcareous degeneration takes place in the intima, as a result, the intima is roughened and a coagulatian of blood takes place with a formation of a thrombus. This thrombus is at first red, but owing to the subsequent fatty degeneration, becomes yellowish. The walls of the artery distal to the lesion contract into a fibrous cord. Later the artery and its supply area may undergo fatty degeneration. As a result of flow of blood from neighboring capillaries or backward from the veins a hemorrhagic infarct ultimately may be formed.

The inner coat shortens, the blood forms a clot that plugs the artery, which is partly absorbed and partly formed into new tissue in the artery and receives its nutrition from the artery.

Question 3.—Give the nature and location of the morbid deposits that occur in articular rheumatism.

Answers :

The inflammation will cause a dryness in the synovial membrane of the joint, leaving a "streaky" plastic exudate and a deposit of lime salts. All the surrounding tissue will also be inflamed.

Originally deposits of uric acid and urates occur in the larger joints owing to the incomplete metabolism of the nitrogenous food. These original deposits set up an irritation and inflammation with the result that a deposit of fibrin occurs and fibrous nodular outgrowths are formed. The location of the deposits are chiefly in the larger joints or the articulating surfaces of the bones, *viz.*, in the shoulder, elbow, wrist, hip, knee, ankle. Secondary deposits often occur in the valves of the heart.

They are of a hard and painful nature occurring around joints and synovial membranes.

Question 4.—Give the pathological conditions characterizing the second stage of acute croupous pneumonia.

Answers:

In the stage of consolidation, when the exudate will be extruded into the air sacs and have filled them to a greater or less degree.

Acute croupous pneumonia, second stage, *i. e.*, consolidation. Macroscopy: (1) Lung is heavy; (2) lung sinks in water; (3) does not crepitate; (4) no frothy exudate. Microscopy—Stage of red hepitization: (1) Coagulation of exudate; (2) red blood corpuscles present; (3) lung is dark. Stage of gray hepitization—Lung is light in color because of: (1) Pressure, therefore red blood corpuscles and hemoglobin disappear; (2) presence of leucocytes; (3) fatty degeneration of exudates.

Red "heptiation" the red "corputles" become infiltrated into the air-cells producing a solidified condition of the part.

Question 5.—Describe the pathological changes and evacuated substances of ulcerative colitis.

Answers:

There will be a locally inflamed area around a circumscribed spot in the colon, which has sloughed away. The substances evacuated are the degenerated tissues of the spot.

The mucous membrane of the colon is red, swollen, and edematous. The ulcer has swollen, undermined edges, and if the process has gone so far, a smooth base composed of the outer coat of the intestine. The situation of the ulcer usually is opposite to the attachment of the mesentery. The evacuations usually are acid in reaction, copious and composed of material resembling chopped spinach. If the ulceration is extensive, the discharges may contain blood.

Inflammation, congestion of small points which slough and form ulcers extending into the muscular coats of the colon. The evacuated substances are mixed with pus, "fecies" and material of a low formation.

PHYSIOLOGY.

Question 1.—Describe the principal phenomena when muscle is physiologically active.

Answers:

The impulse is sent to the brain through the sensory nerves and is transferred to the motor area. They, by experience, send a motor impulse through the motor nerve to the seat of action and stimulate the muscle fibers to contraction.

(1) Change in form, *i. e.*, shorter and thicker; (2) change in consistency, *i. e.*, harder; (3) increase in elasticity; (4) evolution of heat; (5) production of carbon dioxid; (6) the light band of the muscle feber becomes darker; (7) chemically there is, probably, a splitting up of a highly complex proteid substance known as inogen. As a result, myosin is formed.

Nerve center to will for the muscle to act with an "afferent" nerve to carry the impression to the muscle.

Question 2.—State, in brief, the function of connective tissue, naming three varieties of this tissue.

Answers :

By its character when situated between the muscles, it allows of a contraction of the muscle, it affords a good medium, giving a certain amount of support to the larger blood vessels and nerves. Fibrous, loose, alveolar.

(1) Frame-work, *e. g.*, bones, areolar tissue; (2) protection, *e. g.*, adipose tissue, cartilage at articular surfaces; (3) warmth, *e. g.*, adipose tissue; (4) locomotion, *e. g.*, muscles; (5) conveys nutrition, *e. g.*, heart, blood vessels, blood. Examples of connective tissue: (1) Bone; (2) muscle; (3) cartilage.

Gives form to the body, holds parts together. Muscles, ligaments, bones.

Question 3.—Give the present view entertained as to the physiology of the cuneus.

Answers :

(Not answered.)

The cuneus is now supposed to be the cerebral center of vision.

Is the principal center of life.

Question 4.—Explain how absorption occurs by the lymphatics, and state what factors are operative in the process.

Answers :

By osmosis or the passage of a fluid through an animal membrane. The food from which the absorption is to occur must stand in close contact with the part of the system is to be found (which part must have a good blood supply) and from the above condition of osmosis, the lymph will be carried from the smaller to the larger vessels and into the circulation after it is purified.

Absorption occurs through the lacteals of the intestine by a process of osmosis. The food having been rendered absorbable by the process of digestion passes through the minute spaces between the cells of the basement membrane of the lacteals. (1) Minute muscles in the lacteals impel onward the absorbed material, which is known as chyle. This continued flow of the chyle onward is favored by; (2) general muscular action; (3) movements of respiration; (4) negative pressure in the thoracic duct, heart, and aorta.

A. By infiltration and absorption. B. By the lymph passing through a thin membrane (sic) into the lymph circulation. The cells of a lymph gland take from the fluids material to be converted into lymph.

Question 5.—Where and how do the various types of food, when digested, enter the blood?

Answers:

During the passage of the chyle through the small intestine, the fats having been emulsified by the pancreatic juice and the bile, and the other foods are in a state to be easily assimilated, the portions absorbed by the lymphatics are carried into the pulmonary vein, into the right side of the heart, from there into the lungs and then back into the left heart and into the general circulation.

(1) The products of fat digestion enter the blood at the left subclavian vein, *via* the thoracic duct, *via* the lymphatics and the lacteals of the intestine; (2) the products of digestion of all other types of food, organic and inorganic, are absorbable by the capillary blood vessels of the intestines and there enter the blood stream.

In the mouth, esophagus, stomach, small and large intestines, and subclavian "vain." By glands, "lymphaticts," villi, "absorptirs," and infiltration into portal veins.

While the replies have not been as numerous as one would like, still a sufficient number have been received to make the research of some value and these are tabulated below, adhering to the promise in the circular letter that they should be reported impersonally. In any list where the number, either of the board or college, is omitted, no returns on that subject were received. The same number is accorded to the same organization in all the lists.

STATE BOARD RETURNS.
ANATOMY.

	Board 1.	Paper 1.	Paper 2.	Paper 3.
Average only reported		66	83	68
Board 2.				
Average only		42	80	46
Board 3.				
Average only		64	89	73
Board 5.				
Question 1		0	95	0
" 2		50	95	80
" 3		70	85	70
" 4		70	85	90
" 5		50	90	75
" 6		85	100	95
" 7		0	95	80
" 8		60	85	85
" 9		75	95	80
" 10		60	75	25
Average		52	90	68

	Board 8.	Paper 1.	Paper 2.	Paper 3.
Question	1	50	90	30
"	2	50	90	80
"	3	60	100	80
"	4	60	90	100
"	5	80	90	80
"	6	90	100	90
"	7	60	100	80
"	8	90	100	80
"	9	70	90	60
"	10	60	80	30
	Average	67	93	71

	Board 9.	Paper 1.	Paper 2.	Paper 3.
Question	1	20	95	20
"	2	80	85	85
"	3	75	90	80
"	4	75	95	95
"	5	75	95	85
"	6	80	100	95
"	7	0	95	80
"	8	80	95	85
"	9	70	90	75
"	10	50	75	50
	Average	60	90	75

	Board 10.	Paper 1.	Paper 2.	Paper 3.
Question	1	30	90	0
"	2	90	90	80
"	3	60	90	50
"	4	50	50	80
"	5	70	90	60
"	6	80	100	90
"	7	0	100	80
"	8	50	80	50
"	9	50	80	70
"	10	50	.80	20
	Average	53	85	54

PATHOLOGY.

	Board 1.	Paper 1.	Paper 2.	Paper 3.
Average only		54	82	56
	Board 3.			
Average only		75	95	55

	Board 4.	Paper 1.	Paper 2.	Paper 3.
Question	1	15	85	0
"	2	30	50	20
"	3	40	45	0
"	4	0	75	0
"	5	10	80	0
Average		19	67	4

	Board 6.	Paper 1.	Paper 2.	Paper 3.
Question	1	75	85	
"	2	30	40	
"	3		Not marked.[1]	
"	4	40	90	50
"	5	70	80	75
Average[2]		53.75	73.75	31.25

	Board 7.	Paper 1.	Paper 2.	Paper 3.
Question	1	25	100	0
"	2	10	100	50
"	3	75	100	10
"	4	20	100	20
"	5	10	100	20
Average		28	100	20

	Board 11.	Paper 1.	Paper 2.	Paper 3.
Question	1	70	75	50
"	2	75	100	85
"	3	70	100	50
"	4	70	100	75
"	5	75	85	75
Average		72	92	67

PHYSIOLOGY.

	Board 1.	Paper 1.	Paper 2.	Paper 3.
Question	1	0	80	0
"	2	30	0	50
"	3	0	100	0
"	4	50	80	20
"	5	20	60	30
Average		20	64	20

[1] Cannot mark, not a good question, does not state whether acute or chronic disease is meant.

[2] Of the four answers marked.

	Paper 1.	Paper 2.	Paper 3.
Board 2.			
Question 1	92	94	85
" 2	60	65	62
" 3	0	100	50
" 4	75	82	86
" 5	78	84	77
Average	61	67	72
Board 3.			
Average only	35	85	55
Board 4.			
Average only	25	75	50
Board 8.			
Question 1	30	80	0
" 2	50	80	70
" 3	0	90	0
" 4	50	90	30
" 5	30	90	30
Average	32	86	26
Board 9.			
Question 1	70	80	50
" 2	80	50	50
" 3	0	0	0
" 4	50	70	90
" 5	80	90	60
Average	56	58	50
Board 10.			
Question 1	100	50	50
" 2	90	30	40
" 3	0	100	0
" 4	90	80	90
" 5	80	80	70
Average	72	68	50

SURGERY.

	Paper 1.	Paper 2.	Paper 3.
Board 1.			
Question 1	50	80	70
" 2	80	90	60
" 3	40	70	80
" 4	80	80	80
" 5	60	80	70
" 6	70	80	90
" 7	40	80	80

	Paper 1.	Paper 2.	Paper 3.
Board 1.			
Question 8	40	60	60
" 9	70	80	40
" 10	60	90	60
Average	59	79	69
Board 3.			
Average only	91	94	92
Board 6.			
Question 1	70	80	60
" 2	70	90	60
" 3	80	0	80
" 4	80	90	50
" 5	50	90	40
" 6	60	90	50
" 7	70	70	80
" 8	70	90	30
" 9	80	90	40
" 10	70	90	70
Average	70	78	56
Board 10.			
Question 1	75	85	90
" 2	90	80	75
" 3	80	90	85
" 4	90	80	85
" 5	50	85	70
" 6	80	90	75
" 7	90	50	80
" 8	60	50	40
" 9	80	85	50
" 10	70	75	80
Average	76.5	77	73

COLLEGE RETURNS.

ANATOMY.

	Paper 1.	Paper 2.	Paper 3.
College 1.			
Question 1	20	100	0
" 2	30	90	60
" 3	40	80	60
" 4	50	100	90
" 5	70	80	40
" 6	60	100	90

	Paper 1.	Paper 2.	Paper 3.
College 1.			
Question 7	0	60	50
" 8	60	80	70
" 9	50	90	40
" 10	20	50	10
Average	40	83	51
College 2.			
Question 1	10	40	0
" 2	40	80	80
" 3	30	80	70
" 4	20	50	60
" 5	30	75	60
" 6	70	100	80
" 7	0	100	90
" 8	40	70	70
" 9	30	70	20
" 10	40	70	0
Average	30	78.5	53
College 3.			
Question 1	10	70	0
" 2	60	80	80
" 3	40	80	40
" 4	20	40	70
" 5	50	70	40
" 6	70	100	90
" 7	0	50	50
" 8	70	90	50
" 9	20	80	40
" 10	20	40	10
Average	36	70	47
College 4.			
Question 1	30	90	0
" 2	50	100	90
" 3	70	90	50
" 4	50	50	80
" 5	50	80	40
" 6	60	100	80
" 7	20	80	60
" 8	70	80	60
" 9	30	90	50
" 10	50	50	20
Average	48	81	53

	College 5.	Paper 1.	Paper 2.	Paper 3.
Question	1	20	75	0
"	2	40	100	70
"	3	50	90	70
"	4	50	95	85
"	5	65	87	60
"	6	60	100	90
"	7	10	80	65
"	8	75	90	60
"	9	50	100	60
"	10	30	40	20
	Average	45	85.7	58.5

	College 8.	Paper 1.	Paper 2.	Paper 3.
Question	1	30	90	0
"	2	50	100	70
"	3	50	70	60
"	4	30	50	70
"	5	50	80	50
"	6	50	100	80
"	7	20	90	60
"	8	70	70	60
"	9	30	90	40
"	10	60	60	20
	Average	44	80	51

	College 9.	Paper 1.	Paper 2.	Paper 3.
Question	1	10	80	0
"	2	40	80	60
"	3	10	100	20
"	4	20	20	20
"	5	10	80	20
"	6	90	80.3	100
"	7	0	80	60
"	8	40	100	70
"	9	0	90	40
"	10	20	60	0
	Average	24	77.3	39

	College 10.	Paper 1.	Paper 2.	Paper 3.
Question	1	10	70	0
"	2	60	80	90
"	3	50	80	50
"	4	0	50	50
"	5	60	40	40

College 10.	Paper 1.	Paper 2.	Paper 3.
Question 6	70	100	90
" 7	0	70	50
" 8	50	70	60
" 9	30	70	0
" 10	20	20	20
Average	35	65	45

SURGERY.

College 2.	Paper 1.	Paper 2.	Paper 3.
Question 1	100	100	100
" 2	90	50	0
" 3	50	90	90
" 4	100	80	70
" 5	0	90	90
" 6	50	90	50
" 7	0	60	50
" 8	50	60	0
" 9	100	60	0
" 10	90	100	0
Average	63	78	45

College 3.			
Question 1	60	80	60
" 2	75	90	75
" 3	65	85	85
" 4	80	95	70
" 5	60	70	75
" 6	60	90	50
" 7	50	80	80
" 8	60	75	50
" 9	40	65	50
" 10	40	30	75
Average	59	75.5	66.5

College 4.			
Question 1	20	80	40
" 2	50	90	0
" 3	20	80	60
" 4	20	90	0
" 5	0	90	20
" 6	0	100	0
" 7	0	80	30
" 8	50	70	0

	Paper 1.	Paper 2.	Paper 3.
College 4.			
Question 9	10	40	0
" 10	20	60	50
Average	19	78	20
College 5.			
Question 1	70	75	70
" 2	70	80	65
" 3	50	55	70
" 4	75	85	65
" 5	60	75	50
" 6	20	80	20
" 7	65	75	70
" 8	70	75	0
" 9	65	70	0
" 10	60	75	75
Average	60.5	74.5	48.5
College 8.			
Question 1	70	80	40
" 2	80	70	60
" 3	50	80	80
" 4	70	80	60
" 5	50	90	70
" 6	50	90	50
" 7	0	80	80
" 8	70	80	0
" 9	40	80	60
" 10	50	90	80
Average	53	82	58
College 10.			
Question 1	90	95	90
" 2	80	90	85
" 3	50	70	90
" 4	90	95	90
" 5	80	85	80
" 6	50	95	50
" 7	90	90	90
" 8	85	80	70
" 9	90	90	80
" 10	85	90	90
Average	79	88	81.5

PATHOLOGY.

College 2.	Paper 1.	Paper 2.	Paper 3.
Question 1	0	90	0
" 2	0	95	10
" 3	15	90	5
" 4	7	85	20
" 5	20	90	25
Average	8.4	90	12

College 3.			
Question 1	0	90	0
" 2	20	20	30
" 3	30	80	10
" 4	40	80	70
" 5	60	80	20
Average	30	70	26

College 4.			
Question 1	30	80	
" 2	0	0	0
" 3	0	30	0
" 4	20	80	10
" 5	0	30	20
Average	10	44	6

College 5.			
Question 1	15	75	
" 2	0	0	0
" 3	25	0	0
" 4	25	75	25
" 5	25	50	25
Average	18	40	10

College 6.			
Question 1	40	100	0
" 2	40	80	30
" 3	50	90	60
" 4	40	100	40
" 5	90	50	..
Average	52	84	26

College 7.			
Question 1	0	80	
" 2	50	50	0
" 3	30	10	5

	Paper 1.	Paper 2.	Paper 3.
College 7.			
" 4	5	80	20
" 5	50	70	20
Average	27	38	9
College 8.			
Question 1	50	100	25
" 2	50	75	0
" 3	50	75	25
" 4	50	100	50
" 5	50	90	25
Average	50	88	25
College 10.			
Question 1	30	90	20
" 2	60	80	40
" 3	40	80	20
" 4	30	80	30
" 5	30	80	60
Average	38	82	34

PHYSIOLOGY.

	Paper 1.	Paper 2.	Paper 3.
College 1.			
Question 1	20	90	20
" 2[1]	..	..	..
" 3	0	100	0
" 4	70	95	10
" 5	10	100	30
Average	25	96	15
College 2.			
Question 1	40	70	0
" 2	50	20	20
" 3	0	50	0
" 4	10	90	10
" 5	0	90	10
Average	20	65	8
College 3.			
Question 1	30	90	20
" 2	40	60	40
" 3	0	100	0
" 4	50	90	40
" 5	50	100	0
Average	34	88	20

[1] Not marked because the question is vague and the writer understood it differently.

	College 4.	Paper 1.	Paper 2.	Paper 3.
Question	1	0	50	0
"	2	20	80	10
"	3	0	80	0
"	4	0	50	0
"	5	0	70	0
	Average	4	66	2

	College 5.			
Question	1	25	90	0
"	2	30	95	25
"	3	0	95	0
"	4	50	85	20
"	5	10	60	10
	Average	23	85	11

	College 6.			
Question	1	60	100	0
"	2	55	100	50
"	3	80	0	..
"	4	70	100	70
"	5	50	100	40
	Average	63	80	32

	College 8.			
Question	1	35	100	0
"	2	75	90	90
"	3	0	100	0
"	4	50	60	75
"	5	45	95	35
	Average	41	89	40

	College 10.			
Question	1	20	50	
"	2		Not marked.[1]	
"	3	0	Not marked.	0
"	4	0	60	0
"	5	20	50	20
	Average	10	52	5

[1] This question belongs rather to histology.

RECAPITULATION.
ANATOMY.

	Colleges.			Boards.		
	1.	2.	3.	1.	2.	3.
1	40	83	51	66	83	68
2	30	78.5	53	42	80	46
3	36	70	47	64	89	73
4	48	81	53	..	..	..
5	45	85.7	58.5	52	90	68
6	..	..	..	..	..	..
7	..	..	..	..	..	..
8	44	80	51	67	93	71
9	24	77.3	39	60	90	75
10	35	65	45	53	85	54
11	..	..	..	..	..	..

PATHOLOGY.

	Colleges.			Boards.		
	1.	2.	3.	1.	2.	3.
1	..	..	..	54	82	56
2	8.4	90	12	..	..	..
3	30	70	26	75	95	55
4	10	44	6	19	67	4
5	18	40	10	..	..	..
6	52	84	26	53.75	73.75	31.25
7	27	38	9	28	100	20
8	30	88	25	..	..	..
9	..	..	..			
10	38	82	34			
11	72	92	67			

PHYSIOLOGY.

	Colleges.			Boards.		
	1.	2.	3.	1.	2.	3.
1	25	96	15	20	64	20
2	20	65	8	61	67	72
3	34	88	20	35	85	55
4	4	66	2	25	75	50
5	23	85	11	..	..	..
6	63	80	32	..	..	..
7	..	..	..	..	..	..
8	41	89	40	32	86	26
9	..	..	..	56	58	50
10	10	52		72	68	50
11	..	..		..	..	..

SURGERY.

	Colleges.			Boards.		
	1.	2.	3.	1.	2.	3.
1	..	..	..	59	79	69
2	63	78	45	..	..	..
3	59	75.5	66.5	91	94	92
4	19	78	20	..	..	..
5	60.5	74.5	48.5	..	..	..
6	..	..	..	70	78	56
7	..	..	..	..	..	..
8	53	82	58	..	..	..
9	..	..	..	..	..	..
10	79	88	81.5	76.5	77	73
11	..	..	..	..	..	..

While these returns vary, as was to be expected, they are uniform in this, that with hardly an exception, one and three would have failed before every individual examiner, and would not have been licensed by any of the boards or faculties marking returns. This is a very gratifying result as, with the same set of questions, the results would be practically uniform.

It is not out of place to call attention to the criticism made on some of the questions that have been employed in actual state examinations.

Thus the second question in physiology, "State in brief the function of connective tissue, naming three varieties of this tissue," received the following criticism.

1. Not marked because the question is vague and the writers understood it differently.

2. This question belongs rather to histology.

Another writes on the questions on pathology, "The questions are in several cases not sufficiently definite."

These comments should impress upon our boards the necessity of framing clear questions in order to be fair to those who are forced to take their examinations and have so much at stake.

In conclusion, I wish to thank all who have taken the time to assist me in this investigation.

DISCUSSION.

Dr. T. D. Davis, Pittsburg:

I gathered from the first subject, anatomy, that the state boards as a rule marked these anatomical questions a little higher than the colleges. Is that carried out in physiology, etc.? It seems at all events that the medical examining boards have not made their standard higher than the medical colleges, or have not acted, in a trades-union spirit, to exclude or keep down the number of doctors, as has been charged, nor have not been working in an antagonistic spirit to the colleges.

Dr. McIntire:

I think the boards are a little more lenient than the colleges in these markings, although it would not do to generalize from these premises. I am not breaking faith when I say, in one instance, the college would not have passed their own graduate upon his answers to these questions.

Dr. Victor C. Vaughan, Ann Arbor:

This paper presents facts which are very gratifying to me, inasmuch as they demonstrate that the charge frequently made against state examining boards that they are too severe in their exactions is not true. The paper also brings out the fact that in the hurry of examining many students in the medical colleges, some of them are fortunate enough to strike questions with which they are familiar and therefore pass a satisfactory examination, whereas if more time could have been devoted to the examination, or if the student's work throughout the year, or the four years, had been taken into consideration as well as the final examination, very likely he would have failed to pass. This paper demonstrates that state boards of medical examiners are honestly striving to elevate the standard of the profession, and I wish to state that in my opinion the laws which have led to the establishment of these examining boards have done more for the advancement of medical education than the colleges have done.

Dr. S. A. Knopf, New York:

I would like to know whether there is any difference between the question asked by the regular state boards and those asked by the boards of the homeopathic and eclectic schools, and whether the questions asked by the two latter boards are of the same importance and scope as those asked by the regulars? I heard it said that some of the so-called irregular boards are more lenient in their examinations.

Dr. McIntire, closing:

Maryland, Georgia, Florida, and Louisiana are the four states in which there are separate boards, each board making their own questions and deciding for themselves. In the District of Columbia, in Pennsylvania, Delaware, and New York, and in New Hampshire, while they have separate boards, they are under the control of some supervising body and the same questions are presented to the three boards.

NATIONAL CONFEDERATION OF STATE MEDICAL EXAMINING AND LICENSING BOARDS.

The twelfth annual meeting was held in the Lecture Hall of the Y. M. C. A. Building, Saratoga Springs, N. Y., June 9, 1902.

MORNING SESSION.

The Confederation met at 10 A.M., and was called to order by the president, Dr. N. R. Coleman, of Columbus, Ohio.

Prayer was offered by the Rev. Herbert Gesner, of Saratoga Springs.

Addresses of welcome were delivered by Mr. A. P. Knapp, president of Saratoga Springs; by Dr. George T. Church, on behalf of the medical profession of Saratoga Springs; by Dr. Albert Vander Veer, of Albany, N. Y., on behalf of the Regents of the University of the State of New York; and by Dr. William Warren Potter, of Buffalo, on behalf of the State Board of Medical Examiners of New York.

The response to these addresses of welcome was made by the vice-president, Dr. Henry Beates, Jr., of Philadelphia, Pa.

The president called for the report of the secretary-treasurer.

The secretary-treasurer, Dr. A. Walter Suiter, of Herkimer, N. Y., made the following verbal report:

REPORT OF THE SECRETARY-TREASURER.

The first thing in the matter of business I have to speak of is the publication of our Transactions, and in that regard I would state that I have here copies of the Transactions for last year, which have been recently published. There was some delay in the publication of the Transactions, for reasons which it is not necessary to mention. It was thought wise to have a great many copies sent for delivery at this meeting, so that any gentleman representing any board, which is affiliated with this Confederation, has the privilege of taking a number of copies of the proceedings corresponding to the membership of the board, if he desires to do so.

As will be shown to the Executive Council by the treasurer's report, our financial condition was not such as would enable us to go on with our work without incurring some additional expense to the balance on hand; but, owing to the arrangement which we had with the Bulletin of the American Academy of Medicine, the official organ of the Confederation, we have been enabled to publish the proceedings and at the lowest possible cost. In that connection, I desire to read a communication from Dr. McIntire, which speaks for itself in regard to the matter. I call attention to this, so that it may be referred to the Executive Council and reported back to the Confederation for action.

I have a communication from the American Congress of Tuberculosis, asking that a delegate be appointed from this Confederation to that organization. Their meeting has already been held for this year, and the communication should be referred to the Executive Council.

I have also a communication from Washington, relative to the establishment of a psycho-physical laboratory, in the Department of the Interior, and it is requested that we take some action relative to the following resolution:

Resolved, "That we are in favor of the establishment of a psycho-physical laboratory in the Department of the Interior, at Washington, for the practical application of physiological psychology to sociological and abnormal or pathological data, especially as found in institutions for the criminal, pauper, and defective classes, and in hospitals, and also as may be observed in schools and other institutions."

I have another communication which I am greatly pleased to present to the Confederation. Most of the gentlemen present doubtless know that there is a proposition on foot for the establishment of a voluntary board of national medical examiners. This subject will be considered to-day, and I present this communication to the Confederation, and ask that it be referred, along with the other matters, to the Executive Council for consideration and subsequent report.

Dr. Suiter then read the following letter from Dr. Godfrey, secretary of the State Board of Examiners of New Jersey:

Camden, N. J., June 4, 1902.

DR. A. WALTER SUITER, *Secretary National Confederation State Medical Boards, Herkimer, N. Y.*

DEAR DOCTOR: I have received a communication from Dr. W. L. Rodman, of Philadelphia, and a member of the Board of Trustees of the Journal of the A. M. A., asking the support of this board in favor of his proposition for the appointment of a "Voluntary Board of National Examiners," to consist of members appointed by the A. M. A., the U. S. Service, the Confederation, etc.

I have written the Doctor that, with our present knowledge of the subject, this board cannot look upon the project favorably for the following reasons:

1. A voluntary board would have no legal standing.

2. The law of almost every state would have to be amended before its certificates could be accepted.

3. Such a board would be representative of the profession only, and not like state boards, representative of the people.

4. It would be only partially representative of the profession, since no provision is made for the different schools of medicine.

5. A voluntary board has no guarantee of continuance.

6. It would be physically impossible for any board to conduct the examinations of all the annual graduates in medicine, of whom, I believe, there are 5000 or 6000 in this country; to subdivide the board for different sections of the country would make it cumbersome.

Other reasons against the project will probably appear when the subject is discussed in the Confederation. Should the subject be brought up in the Confederation, I would be glad to have you present the above reasons as the opinion of the New Jersey Board, at the present time, why a voluntary board should not be established. It is important, I think, that the Confederation should act in the matter, since it will be brought before the House of Delegates of the A. M. A., for adoption, and is reported to have the support of prominent members of the Association and of the Confederation. With assurances of high regard, I am

Very truly yours,

E. L. B. GODFREY, M.D., *Secretary*.

The President : You have heard the report of the secretary-treasurer. If there are no objections, it will be referred to the Executive Council ; the Executive Council will report back to this Confederation in the afternoon, if possible.

The next thing in order was the annual address by the president, which was delivered by Dr. N. R. Coleman, of Columbus, Ohio. Dr. Coleman selected as the title of his address, " Uniformity in Medical Practice Acts."

On motion of Dr. Potter, the thanks of the Confederation were extended to Dr. Coleman for his very able, exhaustive, and learned address, after which the address was referred to the Executive Committee.

Mr. James Russell Parsons, Jr., Secretary of the University of the State of New York, spoke on " The Work of the Regents of the University of the State of New York."

On motion of Dr. Swartz, a vote of thanks was extended to Mr. Parsons for his admirable address.

On motion, the Confederation then adjourned until 2.30 P.M.

AFTERNOON SESSION.

The Confederation reassembled at 2.30 P.M., and was called to order by President Coleman.

The address of Mr. Parsons was discussed by Drs. Beates and Lewi.

The President: I am informed that the Executive Council has a partial report to make, and I will ask Dr. Wm. S. Foster, the chairman of the Council, to make that report now.

Dr. Foster made the following report of the Executive Council:

June 9, 1902.

The Executive Council beg to submit the following report.

The application of Geo. H. Shedd, M.D., New Hampshire Medical Examining Board for membership approved.

The application of the Missouri Medical Examining and Licensing Board for membership, per W. F. Morrow, M.D., secretary, approved.

The application of the Medical Examining Board of Virginia, per R. S. Martin, M.D., secretary, for membership approved.

Dr. Arthur MacDonald's communication in reference to Psycho-Physical Laboratory to be acknowledged by secretary.

Dr. W. L. Rodman's letter, action deferred until discussed by the Confederation.

Dr. Godfrey's letter to be considered at same time.

Evening session in Y. M. C. A. building at 8 P.M.

That the committee suggested by the president's address be appointed.[1]

Treasurer's report held over until next meeting.

W. S. FOSTER, *Chairman*.

Dr. W. F. Curryer: I move that the report be received.

Dr. Gardner T. Swartz: I second the motion.

Dr. E. B. Harvey: I understand that the Executive Council will defer its report on the letter of Dr. Godfrey until the subject-matter has been discussed by this Confederation. I would, therefore, move that so much of the report of the Executive Council as relates to the communication of Dr. Godfrey be adopted, and that the Confederation proceed at once to act upon the subject-matter of the communication, and that we now discuss it. Seconded.

The motion, as amended, was carried.

Dr. E. B. Harvey: In order to bring this matter before the Confederation at once for discussion and action, I submit the following resolution:

Resolved, " That after due consideration of the proposition for the appointment of a voluntary board of national examiners, as

[1] See p. 312.

outlined by Dr. William L. Rodman, of Philadelphia, this Confederation cannot look upon the project favorably for the following reasons:" (Here Dr. Harvey read the reasons set forth by Dr. Godfrey in his letter.)

I submit this resolution, and move its adoption by the Confederation. Seconded.

Dr. William A. Spurgeon, of Muncie, Indiana:

I am in favor of the adoption of the resolution, and yet, again, I am not fully in favor of it as it stands, for the reason that I do not believe the reasons set forth for the action of this Confederation are sufficiently full. As I take it, the American Medical Association, through its House of Delegates, will take up this question and will be influenced measurably in their action by the attitude of this Confederation with reference to this proposition, and I think that the expressions of opinion that go from this Confederation to the American Medical Association should be as full as possible, and I am inclined to the opinion, although I have not matured it, that it would be well to have a committee appointed to formulate in specific detail all of the objectionable features that would obtain in an arrangement of this kind, and consider it well and submit it through the committee from this body to the House of Delegates of the American Medical Association, in order that it may reach that Association in that form. While I think well of the resolution, and that its spirit and purpose should obtain in this case, yet I believe Dr. Harvey, who submitted it, if he was given additional time, would improve its form, make it a little more explicit, and, at the same time, embody more than appears in the resolution as it now lies upon the table. The purpose of the plan is evidently a good one. There can be no question as to the motive, as to the purpose. The object is that through the action of a national board we may have a basis for interstate reciprocity, and a kind of uniform method of getting at the capabilities of applicants for licenses to practise medicine. That is the purpose of it. There can be but one question, and that pertains to the practicability of the plan. Would it work? I don't believe it would. In the first place, the Constitution of the United States stands in the way of a legally constituted board of that character. When the committee, appointed by the American Medical Association, went to Washington City for the purpose of considering some questions with reference to securing national legislation, one of the first things they did, and a wise thing, too, was to inquire of the leading men of the Senate to know whether or not such legislation was possible, and they were informed at once it was not possible, for the reason that all legislation of this kind must come through, and by virtue of, the police power that is vested in the several legislatures, and that the Constitutional or organic law of the government would not undertake, would not permit the general government to coerce states in matters pertaining to affairs of this kind. This proposition will not be thought of favorably, because it has too many little flaws in it. It has to be voluntary, which is the only kind of national examining board can exist, by reason of the facts I have just referred to. If it is a voluntary board, then it must necessarily be made up of volunteers, men who volunteer their services to act as members of a national examining board. If it is to be a voluntary board made up of volunteers, there is not a man on the American Continent, not in the United States, who is a member of the medical profession, who would volunteer his services, and there would not be any good reason why he should or should not serve. Suppose some distinguished man here should undertake to obtrude himself upon them, he would have just as much right to voluntary membership on the board as any one else. Who is going to say no?

Here is another complication that arises: The very best men in this country to-day of the medical profession are engaged in philanthropic work, engaged in the great work of furthering the interests of humanity and of our profession, also in the unification of the profession. Some of the best, cleanest, and brightest men of the profession of medicine in America are engaged in that work, and are going to accomplish it after a while; for, as the gentleman from New York said a short time ago, in this country in all matters, the whole thing hinges on the one question of competency. That is the solution of the whole proposition, and we cannot get away from it. If a man, woman, boy, or girl is thoroughly competent, that settles the question. I cannot see how this great work, the unification of the American profession, can be accomplished by any such proposition. How would it work if we were to undertake to establish a voluntary national examining board upon the basis proposed by Dr. Rodman? The American Medical Association would start out with the proposition of designating who the men shall be. Some of them shall be members of our body; we may have one or two or three or four representatives; the army shall be represented by one or two, and the navy by two, and so that fixes it up. And the fellows who have been designated, volunteered, are mustered in to do business as a volunteer national examining board. Now, what is there to hinder the New York State Medical Society from doing the same thing? What is there to hinder the Mississippi Valley Medical Association from doing the same thing? What is there to hinder the Southern Medical Society from doing the same thing? What is there to hinder the Eclectic Medical Association, the Homeopathic, or Physio-Medical Association, any or all of them, from doing the same thing? Nothing beneath the stars, and you may have just as many volunteer national examining boards as you happen to have gatherings of medical men in this country in a little while, because it is a distinguished position. It is a position of honor, and men will say, we want to get in it. We would have division, subdivision, and wrangling over the question which is intended really for unification of the profession. Gentlemen, it defeats its own purpose. Such a board, as is contemplated by Dr. Rodman, would have no foundation in law. It would not be supported, protected, nor in any way encouraged by any kind of legal authority. It would be absolutely free and independent and have no kind of support and encouragement legally. It would not have any legal right to exist. The Constitution of the United States has provided that such a thing cannot exist except by the sanction of law, and let me say to you, when the organic law of our government states such a thing, whether by implication or positively, that a certain thing shall not obtain in this country, we had better not be in too big a hurry in giving it our sanction. Let us go a little slow about it. It would be a usurpation of authority, according to what has been said. That I would question. It is said that this volunteer national examining board is to be made up of distinguished men, men of character, and by reason of that fact, I grant you, that any state examining board in the country would make itself ridiculous if it refused to accept its certificate of qualification. That is one of the arguments advanced in favor of the national volunteer examining board; that it has distinct and independent power, and this would be used as an argument against the point I made a moment ago, that such boards would be scattered all over the country.

Gentlemen, the woods are full of distinguished medical men in this country. There is scarcely a town of any consequence that cannot turn out, in the shortest possible notice, a sufficient number of men for a national examining board, if the members of such a board are to be paid for their services. But here comes an essential difficulty in this matter. Even if that kind of national examining board should be organized, even if it can be done without begetting any of the ill consequences to which I have referred, and it was honestly at work and had made out its certificate of qualification, there is not a single, solitary, particle of value which could be attached to its certificates of qualification until those certificates had received the official endorsement of the state board to which the applicants might take their certificates. And the laws provide that the state boards themselves shall make this examination. Take the number of cases in which the laws of the states require examining boards to make the examinations themselves, hence they would not be permitted to pay any attention to certificates of qualification within or without the state from such a board except that which is accredited by law.

I do not make an argument against this matter, because I have great regard for the genius who conceived the idea. I believe it is work along the proper line; nevertheless, I think the proposition will defeat itself. It would fail to pass of its own weight. It is wholly and solely without foundation in law, and when that condition obtains the whole question is up, so far as legal matters are concerned. And this is a legal question. So its certificates would be of no account. They could not bear the seal of legal authenticity, and there would be no penalty against forgery of it. The fact of the business is that a certificate of qualification, lacking the issue of a license to practise medicine in this country, can be of no service, except it has its foundation in law. For that reason, this whole question would fall to the ground. I do not treat this question lightly, for we are seeking to remedy a condition in this country that ought to be remedied. Some of the very best men to-day in this country are professional prisoners in several of the states—a condition that ought not to obtain, and one that will be remedied, I trust, by and by, but it cannot be remedied except upon a legal basis. It has to be done by some kind of authority, and the whole question would be, without the authority of law, futile.

Dr. William Bailey, of Louisville, Ky.:

I rise to ask if the communication of Dr. Rodman contains his proposition, and if it will give us information as to what is desired. If so, I would like to have the communication of Dr. Rodman read.

The Secretary :

I will say, in reply, that there was sent with the communication a pamphlet setting forth the proposition made by Dr. Rodman, which has been published in various medical journals throughout the country, and the main proposition was, in brief, to have a voluntary board of examiners, constituted in such a manner as this : The three United States services are to be represented on this board, namely, the army, navy, and the marine hospital service, also the American Medical Association, the Association of American Physicians, a citizen, and a seventh member is to be appointed from this body. Of course, the arguments which Dr. Rodman presented in this proposition are contained in the article, which was sent along with the communication.

Dr. William Bailey :

This discussion is hardly just. I do not think that a committee appointed by the American Medical Association should be compared with a voluntary board that may be organized in any little town in this country. It is hardly just to say that this committee would be on a par with a hundred thousand men who might volunteer their services. I think that the endorsement of the American Medical Association would give the voluntary board much more influence than we can have from any outside influence. Of course, if this board examines á man, and finds him competent, it is only its endorsement of his qualifications, and it would remain for each state authority to accept the work of the board or not, and I am not sure but that many of the state boards would consent to recognize certificates given by any board that the American Medical Association would create.

Dr. N. R. Coleman, of Columbus, Ohio :

How can state boards accept the certificates of such a board when there is nothing in the law to warrant them in doing so?

Dr. Bailey :

State boards could not accept such certificates if it was contrary to the law. They require examinations themselves, and they could not do so without additional legislation. I believe that the intention of the proposition of Dr. Rodman is very good, and should not be dismissed from consideration. I take a more optimistic view of the proposition to establish a voluntary national examining board than does the gentleman from Indiana. The time and necessity for reciprocity are rapidly approaching, and I do think we ought to pass this subject by without getting more information and additional light. The matter should be thoroughly discussed before we are prepared to vote on it.

Dr. Augustus Korndoerfer, of Philadelphia :

The gentleman who has just spoken (Dr. Bailey) evidently is not aware of the strong legal impediment that stands in the way of the enactment of a board of this kind in every state, I might say, that has a medical law. Each state requires that the examining board shall have legal standing. The state of Pennsylvania cannot accept the volunteer certificate of any board, and it has no legal right to accept that certificate as being worth any more than the paper it is written on. It seems to me, we can reach the matter by asking our legislatures to enact a law, making it incumbent upon state boards to recognize certificates of qualification given by a board that is created, without legal authority from any one, but a board created in absolute contravention to the constitution of the United States, with a deliberate attempt to force upon the country a board which will take up work which the Constitution of the United States says is illegal, there is not a legislator who would dare to stand before his constituents and say ten words without feeling himself absolutely condemned, if he were to consent to a law or an amendment to be passed in his state amending the law of the state, arguing that, if possible, such an unauthorized certificate be taken in lieu of a certificate secured by a legally constituted board from some other state or his own state. It would hardly seem possible that our legislators, considering what they have done in the past in favor of developing a strict method of entrance in the medical profession, would stultify themselves by creating a volunteer medical examining board, and asking the legislatures to amend the law, which would set aside the benefits which we hope to gain through the law by accepting a volunteer certificate instead of a legal one. Our legislators would not do it. Pennsylvania would not do it, and I am reasonably certain the neighboring states would equally refuse, and it would be so in New York and in Ohio for a good while to come. And it would be so in New Jersey.

It seems to me, the best we can do is to speak a good word for the intent of this scheme and leave it to work out its course in some legal way in the future.

Dr. William S. Ely, of Rochester, N. Y.:

I am thoroughly in accord with the argument that has been advanced against the measure proposed by Dr. Rodman. I would like to know, Mr. President, whether every gentleman has read the original paper of Dr. Rodman, recommending this voluntary board. I glanced over the paper very hastily, therefore I do not feel able to determine whether the arguments advanced by Dr. Godfrey against the measure are all of equal value or not. My impression was that the board was to be formed according to the terms given in the remarks made by the secretary. As I remember in reading the article of Dr. Rodman, he went so far as to state that the first year there might not be over ten or fifteen men who would appear before the board for examination, not enough to pay the expenses, perhaps, but that gradually, year after year, there would be an increasing number to get what he calls the honorary degree or license, ranking so far above all other licenses now issued by state boards as to make the state boards willing to recognize the value of such licenses, and give these men honorary licenses in addition to their state licenses, some public recognition which would be of great advantage to the holders of them in connection with the public service or the different offices in different states. Before acting on the resolution that has been offered, I would like to be sure that every one of the objections raised by Dr. Godfrey comes within legitimate criticism of the plan proposed by Dr. Rodman. I repeat that my reading of the article was so hasty that I am not prepared to say whether all of the objections raised by Dr. Godfrey are justified or not, especially one which was read by the gentleman from Massachusetts, with reference to the enormous amount of work that would come before this board, making its practical working at first very difficult. I do not think we ought to vote on the measure without doing it intelligently.

Dr. W. F. Morrow, of Kansas City, Mo.:

This question is one of paramount importance, and if we could adopt some plan by which the examiners of the various states would work together, it would be of great benefit to the various boards of the United States. The plan that has been proposed, to my mind, would prove a failure. There is nothing to it. It has nothing behind it. By the plan contemplated, we would simply place this board in direct opposition to every state board in the United States, and the result would be a fight, having no power to act, no law by which such a board could perform its work, it would be ignored by the state boards. They would pay no attention to it, and they could not. In Missouri we have a law that compels us, as members of the state board, to examine applicants individually. If there is any reason by which we could not make an examination, then the governor by law forces the board to make an examination ; therefore, it would be impossible to consider such a board as is contemplated in this measure in any way, legally or otherwise. It appears to me, if a committee was appointed for the purpose of considering this plan, composed of the most active members of this Confederation, say a committee of five, and report to the Confederation some time to-day, we might be able to arrive at some plan by which we could accomplish some good, otherwise I cannot see how we can do anything.

Dr. Eugene Beach, of Gloversville, N. Y.:

As there seems to be some objection to the resolution offered by Dr. Harvey, it being considered inadequate, I move that the following resolution be substituted for the one offered by Dr. Harvey:

Resolved, That Dr. Rodman's proposed plan of organizing a volunteer board of national medical examiners is not at present practical; therefore, be it

Resolved, That a committee of three be appointed by the Chair for the purpose of drafting formal objections to the proposition, and that a copy of such draft be submitted to the House of Delegates of the American Medical Association after it has been presented to this Confederation. Seconded.

Dr. Harvey accepted the substitute.

Dr. Henry Beates, Jr., of Philadelphia :

I rise to a question of privilege.

The President :

Please state it.

Dr. Beates :

Does not this Confederation represent the administration of the laws of every state governing the practice of medicine? We certainly do. Therefore, have we a legal right to pass any opinion whatever upon this question ? We can neither condemn nor endorse this movement. We are legally bound to administer the laws of the states we individually represent, and we can go no further. We must be careful how in matters of sentiment we depart from the legal authority.

Dr. Joseph M. Mathews, of Louisville, Ky.:

I will not attempt a defense of the method of Dr. Rodman, nor the resolution which has been offered as a substitute for the previous one. I do not believe it will be gainsaid that every one of us in sentiment endorses the proposed plan of Dr. Rodman. I do not know the legal status of my state on this subject, nor do I know the legal status of any state on it. But we, as members of examining boards, certainly see good reasons for the establishment of such a board. Dr. Rodman has been thinking of this matter for a long time. The scheme was not gotten up in a month or six months. He spoke to me about it several years ago.

Since the article read by the secretary was printed, Dr. Rodman has modified his views materially to meet the objections that have been urged. As

Dr. Rodman is present, if we have a little time to spare, I would move that he be invited to address the Confederation for a few minutes.

Dr. McCormick:

I second the motion. Carried.

Dr. William L. Rodman, of Philadelphia, Pa.:

I appreciate very much the courtesy of being asked to make a few remarks on the subject you are discussing. I very much regret, however, that I was not here in time to hear what has been said by the different speakers, and therefore I do not know exactly what objections have been made. However, I thought I caught the drift of the discussion.

In the first place, I have been much interested in the subject of reciprocity for the past two or three years. That interest began primarily on account of the fact that I removed from Kentucky to Philadelphia, and found at once that I was compelled to go before the State Board of Pennsylvania, and pass an examination before a license could be granted to me to practise medicine. I want to say here, that I was more than courteously and generously treated by the Pennsylvania board. It was the wish of the president and of every member of that board, so far as I know, to exempt me from any examination, and to tender me the complimentary license. After getting together and consulting in the matter carefully, it was found impracticable to do so, as the law of the state is mandatory, not at all elastic, and specifically states that the applicant shall be examined in order to obtain a license to practise medicine. Although I had limited my work to surgery for many years before going to Philadelphia, and although intending to limit my work to surgery since I left Kentucky, I was compelled to submit to an examination in chemistry, materia medica, physiology, and all of the fundamental branches. I would not have any one think that I have at any time felt sore over this matter, for, as I say, I was treated with great courtesy by Dr. Beates and other members of the Pennsylvania board. But they simply had not in their power to do what I believe they would like to have done, and which should be done under similar circumstances. Therefore, I have been working at this problem for several years. I am heartily in favor of a national board of examiners by an Act of Congress. However desirable it is, it is simply impossible for us to expect a national board of examiners created by an Act of Congress. This is a matter which has been threshed over very often, and it is simply useless to pursue it any further. Many of us have written to politicians, and they have all answered in the same way, that the state is a sovereign and the national government cannot in any way impose upon state laws.

At a recent meeting of the Committee on National Legislation, I suggested, instead of a compulsory board, which was about to be recommended by the committee until they found such a board was impracticable, that there was nothing in the way of establishing a voluntary national board; and yet a license from that board would not carry with it any legal weight. I admit, there is no legal status in a board of this kind, but that it would carry with it a very considerable moral weight, and if the standard of this board is made so high, as high as that of any state board, I cannot myself see why any state board would be justified in refusing to recognize it.

I have changed my former report, as Dr. Mathews has said, because it was written hastily. After leaving Washington City and returning to Philadelphia, I realized that it was crude in several respects. If any of you gentlemen will read the current issue of the *Journal of the American Medical Association*, or the *Philadelphia Medical Journal*, you will see that the article has been amended in several very important respects. One of the most incongruous statements in the article that was read is that the words "six examiners" are used in one place, and seven in another. I said at Washington that a seventh member might be appointed, in order to recognize state boards of examiners. In the subsequent communication I say "should be appointed," because I believe the state boards have done more to elevate the standard of medical education than all other things combined. I have said repeatedly, that I know I do better work as a teacher from a knowledge of the fact that my graduates are to go before some state board, and are either given a license or cut down, and very generally when they are cut down, they deserve it. Recognizing, therefore, the work the state boards have done, and the greater work they are capable of doing in the future, I should be disposed to insist that the seventh member of this voluntary board should be a representative of your Confederation, so that the state boards of examiners and this national board may work hand in hand, in that way elevating not only the standard of medical education, but extending much needed relief to practitioners all over the country who, either through ill health, or sickness of a member of their families, may wish to move to Colorado, to California, or to any other state in the union. I feel that this is one of the most important questions that we have to consider in the profession to-day. I know of personal professional friends who have had to undergo the same experience as myself, and it is not pleasant for one who has been in the profession ten or fifteen years to have to sit between two students just out of school and pass an examination that they cannot pass themselves. We cannot expect a man who has been out of school for fifteen or twenty years to stand a creditable examination in chemistry, materia medica, obstetrics, and other branches that he has not thought much of for many years. Therefore, I would advocate a practical examination. I do not think any man has a right under any circumstances to object to an examination, but the question is, what kind of examination shall be given? If one has practised a specialty for many years, and is recognized as a specialist, if he desires to move to New York City or elsewhere, I do not think he should be required to submit to an examination in obstetrics, particularly when he does not practise that branch of medicine. Dr. Mathews, for instance, who has practised the specialty of diseases of the rectum for twenty or more years, if he should choose to go to New York City, where he might have a broader field than he has in Louisville, according to our state laws he has got to pass an examination in the fundamental branches. I do not think it is right that he should be examined in those branches in which he is not very much interested.

This scheme is a good thing for recent graduates; it is a good thing for medical education. But I realize perfectly well another statement which is correct, that 5,000 or 6,000 men could not come before the board. It is not desired that they should. This is not an average man's board, but a board for the best men coming from the best schools in the country. I cannot see any objection to this board. It has no legal status, I will admit; it is purely voluntary, therefore it works no hardships. It is simply a question of encouraging young men to take an examination which in the future may be of some advantage to them, and aid them in obtaining positions as contract surgeons in the army, navy, and marine hospital service, also upon pension boards and appointments as physicians to Indian agencies, etc.

Dr. Maurice J. Lewi, of New York:

I would suggest that the secretary read the objections offered by Dr. Godfrey, and then Dr. Rodman answer them *seriatim*.

The secretary then read the first objection, concerning which Dr. Rodman said:

I will admit that this voluntary examining board would have no legal status whatever. There is no question about that. The law of almost every state would have to be amended before the certificates of this board could be accepted. But it would seem to me an easy thing to do, if this is a desirable plan, for the physicians of the country to secure any legislation necessary affecting the medical profession. Such a board would be representative of the profession only, not like state boards representative of the people.

The secretary read objection No. 2.

In reference to this objection, Dr. Rodman said:

This voluntary board has no guarantee of continuance. Certainly not. If it does not prove to be better than anything in sight at the present time, it should not continue. We should not hesitate, however, to try it. There are no hardships imposed by it. A man can take the examination of this board if he so desires. If such a board should prove unsatisfactory after a thorough trial, it had better be allowed to pass into innocuous desuetude. But that simply depends upon the future altogether to determine. It is not desirable that all applicants should come before this board. It is a good man's board; it is not even an average man's board, and it is simply for those who are willing to strike for a high standard, and prepare themselves to pass it. If they pass the examination of this board, they should be given the privileges that usually accompany such efforts.

As to the board being non-representative, that is the easiest of all objections made. I really feel that this Confederation is to be considered very much in connection with such a board, because after all it depends upon you whether a board of this kind must either live or die. If you are not going to recognize such a board as this, there is no use in establishing it. If you are willing to recognize it, you can make such suggestions as can be met. It is easy to have eight or nine examiners, one representing the school of homeopathy, the other representing the eclectics, in that way recognizing the different schools. The examinations can be so arranged and conducted as to meet with the approval of the different schools represented. The number of the board could be increased so as to have the different schools represented, or exempt homeopaths or eclectics from examination in materia medica and therapeutics. Not being a member of this body, and not having considered homeopaths and eclectics coming up for these examinations, I do not know exactly how that could be gotten around. I do not want to make more obstacles than seem to be in the way of the board but I think that one can be easily met by exempting applicants from examination in materia medica and therapeutics, or by increasing the number of the board to nine instead of seven. The advantage of this board would be, gentlemen, that your representative, whoever he is, would be in accord with the central board; he would know exactly what was going on; he could report back to you every year what work is being done, and whether or not such a board was entitled to your support. That is the strongest feature about it. If your representative should discover that politics had crept into such a board, he could report the same back to you, and you could kill it in five minutes.

Dr. Gardner T. Swartz, of Providence, R. I.:

I would like to ask Dr. Rodman a question, namely, what special qualifications representatives of the marine hospital service, the army and navy surgeons should have in subjects pertaining to general practice. If they delegate subordinates to conduct these examinations, we should expect them to have confidence in their examinations.

Dr. Rodman:

I feel that the medical profession has always held in very high esteem the medical corps of the United States army and navy, as well as the marine hospital service. They represent, I think, that which is the highest and best in medicine in a way. Men cannot get such positions unless they are competent. We know that. They have to pass not only a rigid examination in medicine, but an examination in all of the collaterals. Therefore, it would be an easy matter to select members of the army, navy, and marine hospital service who would be as competent examiners as could be found in the United States. They have eminent surgeons and physicians, eminent pathologists and bacteriologists, and there would be an advantage of having these men at Washington, where they would be able to extend certain courtesies on account of their official position. They are willing to do this work, and they would not have to be paid a salary, because they are already paid by the United States government. I admit that it would be impossible for the surgeon-general to travel around the country, and it would be better if the best men in their respective services were detailed for the work, because the duties of the surgeon-general are onerous. I believe that there is good reason for having the three services represented.

Dr. E. B. Harvey, of Boston:

I would like to ask the distinguished gentleman this question, how would this voluntary board, the constitution of which he advocates, benefit the twenty-year practitioner like himself, who might wish to go from Kansas City or from St. Louis to Philadelphia, or from Philadelphia to New York? Again, I would like to say, does he not know that those are the men that some of the examining boards have trouble with? The examining boards recognize the ability of many of these men, and they register them in a way so as not to impose any hardship upon them. Again, the trouble examining boards have to contend with is not from the better class of men. Examining boards are not troubled with high-classed men, such as the graduates from the Johns Hopkins or McGill, but they are troubled with the low class, the middle class, the class which would not come before such a voluntary board at all. Those are the men we would like to provide for if we can by some other system than the present one.

Dr. Joseph P. Creveling, of Auburn, N. Y.:

Dr. Rodman spoke of this board being of high grade and of the great honor that would be connected with a diploma or certificate received from that board, and then in almost the next breath he speaks of only examining in certain branches, and speaks of the state board certifying to such an examination as that. Now, the law of the state of New York, and I assume of every other state, requires that the applicants shall be examined in seven branches, at least. What good would a certificate or diploma, or whatever you please to call it, from this national board be before a state board, if the national board as constituted is merely a voluntary body, and does not conform with the requirements of the state?

(Dr. Rodman did not answer the questions of Drs. Harvey and Creveling).

Dr. George W. Webster, of Chicago, Ill.:

It seems to me that the proposition of Dr. Rodman is both impracticable and wrong in principle. The doctor desires to have an easier way of having an old practitioner move from one state to another. He does not wish him to be a professional prisoner in any part of the United States, and he states that he would not examine a man, as, for instance, an ophthalmologist, in gynecology; yet he says that this board should be of such high attainments and should have an examination of such a character, that it would be accepted without question anywhere in the United States. Does he propose that we shall have one examination for the old practitioner, and one for the man who has never attended a medical college at all, and another for a man who has attended two years, another for the man who has attended for three years, and still another one for the man who has taken four years, and who is a recent graduate? If not, the method proposed does not refer to those who have practised for years, and who may desire to go from one state to another.

In the next place, this proposition is wrong in principle. If it is not right that any state shall delegate any of its authority or power to the national government, it is wrong in principle that any state shall delegate any of its authority or power to any board, whether it is a national board of health or a voluntary board of health. The thing is wrong in principle; it is contrary to law. Reciprocity can be based reasonably and practically only on this triad: first, uniformity in preliminary entrance requirements; second, uniformity in regard to the length and character of the course in instruction; third, uniformity in regard to the character of the examinations to be taken or held. If, in addition to that triad, it is possible to have desirable uniform legislation, very well. But those things are absolutely essential in obtaining reciprocity.

Dr. T. J. Happel, of Trenton, Tenn.: I move that this matter be postponed for one year. Seconded.

Dr. E. B. Harvey:

I made the original motion, or offered a resolution, for the purpose only of bringing this matter before the Confederation for discussion. The object of offering that resolution has been amply fulfilled, and it was my purpose, if any other motion was made, to ask unanimous consent to withdraw the resolution I offered. A substitute for my resolution has been offered. Now, a motion has been made by Dr. Happel to postpone this matter for one year. I believe, Mr. President, in taking action on this matter when it is at its height, when the necessity is ripe for discussion, and if this matter is ever ripe for discussion, it is to-day. To-morrow, we are told, the great American Medical Association is to discuss this matter, and take some action in regard to it. Before that Association discusses the matter, or takes any action on it, it seems to me it should have the judgment of this Confederation. Therefore, I object to postponing the matter for one year, and propose to fight it out here and now.

Dr. A. Walter Suiter, of Herkimer, N. Y.:

I want to say a word or two in that connection. As I understand it, whatever declaration this Confederation makes in the matter would have to be considered by the House of Delegates of the American Medical Association which will be in session during the current meeting. There seems to be great unanimity of opinion among the members of the Confederation with reference to the legal status of Dr. Rodman's plan, and also with reference to their judgment in regard to whether or not it should be adopted. It seems to me the members of the Confederation are as well prepared to-day in their views as to how we shall proceed to dispose of the question as they can be at any future time. I want to say to you that my experience as secretary of the Confederation is that a good deal of time is, and has been, devoted to questions of an important character by this Confederation which have been referred to committees, the members of which live at remote distances from one another so that it is difficult for them to get together and express their views, and I think it is more or less impracticable to have such matters placed in charge of committees to report at some future time. I believe that a free expression of opinion from the members of this Confederation would be as authoritative and useful now as it could be at any future time, and so I heartily endorse what Dr. Harvey has said.

Dr. W. F. Curryer, of Indianapolis, Ind.:

I have heard the arguments for and against the plan of establishing a voluntary national examining board; also the speech of Dr. Rodman, which should receive due consideration. I am firmly convinced of the impracticability of carrying out this plan. I am a member of the examining board of the state of Indiana, and I know very well how much we need reciprocity, so that an old practitioner can move from one state to another, if he so desires, either on account of ill health or otherwise. However, this problem of establishing a voluntary national examining board must be solved in a legal way. According to our state law, old practitioners must take the same examination as the fresh or recent graduates. I admit, that it is a hardship in many instances for these old practitioners to undergo the state board examination, but we are simply conforming to the law in so doing. Such a voluntary board as is proposed being illegally inoperative would be objectionable in every particular, to my mind.

Dr. E. B. Harvey:

After a brief conference with Dr. Rodman, my chief objection to the idea of postponing this matter for one year has been removed. If it is postponed for one year, I have the assurance of Dr. Rodman that it shall not come up in the house of delegates of the American Medical Association.

The President then put the motion of Dr. Happel, which was lost.

Dr. E. B. Harvey: I desire to withdraw the original resolution I offered and accept the substitute resolution offered by Dr. Beach.

Dr. Curryer: If Dr. Beach will accept an amendment, I will move that this committee report on this matter the first thing on reconvening this evening, and that a committee of five instead of three be appointed.

Dr. Beach: I accept the amendment.

The President then put the substitute of Dr. Beach, as amended, and it was carried.

The President: I will appoint on that committee Dr. E. B. Harvey, of Boston; Dr. Eugene Beach, of Gloversville, N. Y.; Dr. Wm. A. Spurgeon, of Muncie, Ind.; Dr. Augustus Korndoerfer, of Philadelphia; and Dr. Geo. W. Webster, of Chicago.

Dr. George W. Webster, of Chicago, moved the appointment of two committees, one on definition of practice of medicine, and the other on curriculum, in accordance with the suggestion contained in the president's address, and as recommended by the Executive Council. Seconded and carried.

The President stated that he would announce these committees later.

The Executive Council approved several applications for membership, and, on motion, its report was adopted.

Dr. Joseph H. Raymond, president of the Medical Council of New York, contributed a paper on "Divided Examinations for License," which was read by the secretary in the absence of the author. This paper was discussed by Drs. Harvey, Morrow, Swartz, Curryer, Lewi, Webster, and the secretary.

Dr. R. S. Martin, of Stuart, Va., read a paper entitled "What Can Be Done to Regulate the Number of Young Men Studying Medicine?" Discussed by Drs. Webster, Curryer, McCormack, Happel, Korndoerfer, Coleman, Ravogli, Beates, Bailey, and the discussion closed by the essayist.

On motion, the Confederation then adjourned until 8 P.M.

EVENING SESSION.

The Confederation reassembled at 8 P.M., and was called to order by the president.

Dr. Harold N. Moyer, of Chicago, Ill., addressed the Confederation on "The Definition of the Practice of Medicine in Medical Practice Acts." The address was discussed by Drs. Lewi, Harvey, Meserve, Spurgeon, Creveling, Curryer, Webster, and Coleman.

Dr. Wm. S. Foster, chairman of the Executive Council, reported some additional applications for membership, and, on motion, the secretary was instructed to cast the ballot for their election, which he did, and they were declared duly elected.

Dr. Foster: We wish to make a partial report on the secretary's account for the past year, and inasmuch as he has had a number of payments made to-day, we have not a full report. We find that the expenses for the past year have been $138.86, for publishing the transactions for 1901, etc., also a bill payable for $99.60, making the expenses for the past year $238.46. The income for the past year, not counting the amount that was taken to-day, has been $189.00.

On motion, the report was adopted and placed on file.

Dr. E. B. Harvey, of Boston, read the report of the special committee on a "Voluntary Board of National Examiners," as follows:

Your committee, to whom was referred the proposition originally made and discussed in the medical press by Dr. W. L. Rodman, of Philadelphia, for the establishment of a "Voluntary Board of National Examiners," with instructions to consider the same and report thereon to this Confederation as to its feasibility, begs leave to report as follows:

In the opinion of your committee, this Confederation of Examining and Licensing Boards cannot endorse nor approve such a proposition for the following reasons, to wit:

1. A voluntary national examining board would have no power, no authority, or legal right to exist.

2. No guarantee could be given of the continuance or permanency of such voluntary board, even were the laws of the several states so modified as to meet its requirements.

3. Being a voluntary board, there could be no legal manner of constituting, changing, or limiting its membership, or defining its duties.

4. Such a board would be representative of the profession only, and of the regular profession alone.

5. Without the endorsement of a state board authorized by law to grant a license to practise, a certificate of qualification from the proposed voluntary board could have no legal value whatever, and under the existing laws of the several states, the state examining boards are required to conduct the examination, and such boards cannot be paid, nor surrender such duty, even if they desire to do so.

6. To attempt the stupendous task of securing the passage of amendments to the existing laws regulating the practice of medicine in the several

states, would entail enormous labor and expense, and would probably endanger the laws themselves.

[Signed]   EDWIN B. HARVEY, Massachusetts,
GEORGE W. WEBSTER, Illinois,
AUGUSTUS KORNDOERFER, Pennsylvania,
EUGENE BEACH, New York,
W. A. SPURGEON, Indiana,
Committee.

The President: You have heard the report of the Special Committee. What will you do with it?

It was moved that the report be adopted. Seconded and carried.

Dr. E. B. Harvey: If the House of Delegates of the American Medical Association is going to discuss this matter to-morrow, I think it would be well to have a member of this Confederation to lay before the House of Delegates this report which your committee has made.

On motion, the secretary was instructed to convey to the House of Delegates of the American Medical Association the substance of the action taken by the Confederation.

Dr. Maurice J. Lewi, of New York, addressed the Confederation on the following subject: "Should There Be the Same Examination for Old Practitioners and For Recent Graduates when Applying for License to Practise Medicine?" Discussed by Drs. Webster, Curryer, Swartz, Bailey, and, in closing, by the essayist.

Dr. Henry Beates, Jr., of Philadelphia, read a paper entitled: "How May the Topics in Examinations for License Be Best Arranged by Examining Boards?" Discussed by Drs. Spurgeon and Swartz, after which the paper, on motion of Dr. Lewi, was referred to the Committee on Curriculum.

Dr. T. J. Happel, of Trenton, Tenn., read a paper on "Tennessee Methods." Discussed by Drs. Martin, Curryer, Morrow, and, in closing, by the essayist.

The President then announced the following committees:

1. Committee on Definition of Practice of Medicine—Dr. Henry Beates, Jr., Chairman, Philadelphia; Dr. H. E. Beebe, Sidney, Ohio; Dr. Wm. A. Spurgeon, Muncie, Ind.; Dr. W. F. Morrow, Kansas City, Mo.; and Dr. R. S. Martin, Stuart, Va.

2. Committee on Curriculum—Dr. George W. Webster, Chairman, Chicago, Ill.; Dr. Augustus Korndoerfer, Philadelphia; Dr. W. F. Curryer, Indianapolis, Ind.; Dr. Wm. S. Ely, Rochester, N. Y.; and Dr. Edwin B. Harvey, Boston, Mass.

The Confederation proceeded to elect officers for the ensuing year, with the following result: *President*, Dr. N. R. Coleman, Columbus, Ohio; *Vice-Presidents*, Dr. Henry Beates, Jr., Philadelphia, Pa., and Dr. James A. Egan, Springfield, Ill.; *Secretary-Treasurer*, Dr. A. Walter Suiter, Herkimer, N. Y.; *Executive Council*, Dr. Wm. S. Foster, Chairman, Pittsburg, Pa.; Dr. Joseph M. Mathews, Louisville, Ky.; Dr. Wm. A. Spurgeon, Muncie, Ind.; Dr. Wm. Warren Potter, Buffalo, N. Y.; and Dr. Augustus Korndoerfer, Philadelphia, Pa.

On motion, the time and place of the next annual meeting were left to the discretion of the president, secretary, and executive council.

There being no further business to come before the meeting, on motion, the Confederation then adjourned, *sine die*.

OBSERVATIONS IN PASSING.

The annual meeting of the Association of American Medical Colleges will be held at New Orleans, on Monday, May 4th, at 2 P.M., and will consider the following program:

1. Minutes of the Saratoga meeting.
2. The president's address, by Dr. W. L. Rodman.
3. Report of the Special Committee on Revision of Article III of the Constitution, by Drs. Ritchie, Wathen and Dodson.
4. Symposium: "To What Extent and How Rapidly Shall Our Standards of Admission to Medical Schools be Advanced?"
5. Report of secretary and treasurer.
6. Report of judicial council.
7. New business.
8. Adjournment.

****

The National Confederation of State Medical Examining and Licensing Boards.at its meeting last June, appointed a committee, consisting of one member from each State Medical Examining and Licensing Board, to frame a "Curriculum" which may be adopted by the various medical colleges of the United States. This committee is to report at the next meeting of the Confederation at New Orleans, in May.

It is the desire of the Executive Council of the Confederation to make the discussion of this report as valuable as possible, and it has planned to hold a meeting in which others than the members of the Confederation will participate. The Academy has received a very cordial invitation to meet with the Confederation in a joint session. It cannot formally accept because its meeting is in Washington on the following week; and this information was conveyed to the President of the Confederation. In reply to this letter, Dr. Coleman extends a very cordial invitation to any of the fellows of the Academy who may be in attendance upon the meeting of the American Medical Association to attend and participate in this discussion.

It is hoped that this invitation will be generally accepted and that report may be brought to the Academy meeting at Washington, where it would form a valuable part of the discussion following the symposium upon "Required and Elective Studies in the Medical Course."

∗

The medical department at Harvard has arranged for two very important changes in medical instruction. President Eliot, in his last report, says:

"The Faculty of Medicine voted in June last that beginning with the class entering the medical school in the fall of 1902, the fourth year shall be elective without any restriction. This important change was adopted after a thorough study of the subject by two committees of the Faculty.

* * * * * * * * *

"The other important experiment which has been going on in the Medical School is proceeding favorably, namely, the reduction in the number of subjects pursued simultaneously by the individual student, and the increase in the amount of time devoted to each subject while it is pursued. This system, which may be described as the block system, was first applied to the class which entered in 1899, so that three classes have already been subjected to it . . . When the class which entered in 1899 shall have graduated, it will be possible to make an instructive report on the results of the block system."

∗

We are requested to announce the meetings of the following medical societies:

The American Congress on Tuberculosis, at St. Louis, July 18 to 23.

American Electro-Therapeutic Association, at Hotel Kaaterskill, Greene Co., N. Y., September 2 to 4.

American Urological Association, annual meeting, New Orleans, May 8 and 9.

National Association of United States Pension Examining Surgeons, Washington, May 13 and 14.

∗

The Philadelphia Academy of Surgery invites essays in competition for the Samuel D. Gross Prize, of $1200, which is to be awarded on January 1, 1905. Particulars may be learned from either of the trustees, Drs. John B. Roberts, William L. Rodman, or William J. Taylor, of Philadelphia.

AMERICAN ACADEMY OF MEDICINE NEWS NOTES.

The preparations for the 28th annual meeting of the Academy are well in hand. The meeting is to be held in the large banquet hall of the Arlington Hotel, Washington, D. C. It will be convened at 11.00 A.M. on Monday, May 11th, the first hour being given to the introductory executive session, with closed doors. After this, it is expected the following time table will be adopted:

12 M. Open session.
  Report of Committee on "Time Allowance in the Combined Collegiate and Medical Course."
  Other reports.
  Scientific papers.
1.30 P.M. Recess.
3.00 P.M. Open session.
  Symposium upon "Teaching of Hygiene in the Public Schools," followed by discussion.
6.00 P.M. Recess.
8.30 P.M. Open session.
  The president's address.

Tuesday May 12th.

10.00 A.M. Executive session.
10.30 A.M. Open session.
  Scientific papers.
11.30 A.M. Symposium upon: "Required and Elective Studies in the Medical Course," followed by discussion.
  Scientific papers.
  Final executive session.
  Adjournment.

The completed program is preparing and will be sent upon request.

The Congress of American Physicians and Surgeons will convene in the Columbia Theater, Washington, at 3.00 P.M., on Tuesday, May 12th, and the effort will be made to adjourn before that time. The subject to be considered at this meeting will be "The Pancreas and Pancreatic Diseases." The president of the Congress, Dr. W. W. Keen, will deliver his address on Tuesday evening, and another general session will be held at 3.00 P.M. of Wednesday, May 13th, when "The Medical and Surgical Aspects of the Diseases of the Gall Bladder and Bile Duct" will be considered.

***

The fellows residing in Philadelphia and vicinity held their third winter meeting upon invitation of Dr. J. B. Roberts at his residence on the evening of March 21st.

Upon invitation of the Committee of Arrangements, the chair was taken by the president of the Academy.

The following papers were read: "The Objections to Prescribing Medicines of Unknown Composition," by Dr. Augustus A. Eshner; "The Propriety of Physicians Furnishing Medicines," by Dr. A. O. J. Kelly; "The Dangers of Drug-Using Without Guidance," by Dr. J. Madison Taylor.

These papers put the question of drug-using and abusing before the meeting, and the discussion that followed was entered upon heartily (some 15 or 16 participants), and was profitable to all who had the pleasure of listening, and opened up another of the many problems affecting the physician, awaiting fuller investigation for the benefit of the profession.

At the conclusion of the discussion, the fellows enjoyed a social hour as the guests of Dr. Roberts.

LITERATURE NOTES.

A COMPEND OF DISEASES OF CHILDREN ESPECIALLY ADAPTED FOR THE USE OF MEDICAL STUDENTS. By MARCUS P. HATFIELD, A.M., M.D. Third edition, thoroughly revised. Philadelphia: P. Blakiston's Son & Co. 1903. 241 pp. Price, 80 cents net.

This is No. 14 of the Blakiston series of Quiz Compends, and, except the suggestion in this name of a possible use of the book for cramming, is to be commended. Dr. Hatfield has given a concise statement of the present-day knowledge of children's diseases. It is useful to the practitioner who wishes to review the entire subject, as well as to the student who is not yet able to give the proper relative value to the fuller information of the larger books.

REPORTS OF STATE BOARDS OF CHARITIES.

I. THIRTY-FIFTH ANNUAL REPORT OF THE STATE BOARD OF CHARITIES OF THE STATE OF NEW YORK, FOR THE YEAR 1901. In two volumes with statistical appendix to Volume I bound separately. Albany: 1902. Vol. I, pp. 1046. Statistical appendix, pp. 475. Vol II, pp. 523.

II. Thirty-second Annual Report of the Board of Commissioners of Public Charities of the Commonwealth of Pennsylvania for 1901, and the Report of the Committee on Lunacy. Harrisburg: 1902. pp. 439, 219.

III. Thirty-fourth Annual Report of the State Board of Charity of Massachusetts, January, 1903. Boston: 1903. pp. viii, 476, lvii.

IV. State of Connecticut: Annual Reports of the Board of Charities to the Governor for the Years Ending September 30, 1901 and 1902. New Haven, Conn.: 1903. pp. 356.

I. There is a mass of valuable material in the volumes well worth the study. We can only sample the material in sight. Dr. Stephen Smith, the chairman of the committee having in charge the execution of the dispensary law, reports a diminution in the number of patients treated since the law went into effect. But the reduction is not as great as the investigations upon single institutions would lead one to expect. He comments thus:

"To any one familiar with conditions, and particularly to those who have studied the situation, it does not appear strange that the attendance at the dispensaries in Manhattan borough has been found increasing. One reason for the condition lies in the acute competition for cases, regardless, when generally speaking of the question whether the applicant is worthy of free treatment or not."

At another place in calling attention to the rule calling for "an investigation of doubtful applicants," he says: "In a majority of instances the investigation has consisted of simply questioning the applicant." This may account for the small reduction in the number securing medical attention at the dispensaries. Another reason is the payment of a small fee, which is growing in vogue. $17,301.89 is reported as the amount thus obtained from the dispensaries of the state from the source out of a total receipt of $134,951.48 from all sources.

Volume II is devoted to the proceedings of the second New York State conference of charities and corrections.

II. This volume gives the usual review of the condition of the institutions under its supervision.

III. The Massachusetts' Board presents a carefully prepared report of the work under the direction of the board, affording valuable information at first hand—and follows this with details of separate counties and individual institutions.

IV. The necessity for careful supervision of charitable and reform or correctional institutions is illustrated by the following paragraph in this report:

"The total sum expended in Connecticut in the department of charities and correction is a large one, $1,598,514, and yet it is not found to be excessive when compared with the amounts devoted to similar purposes in other progressive commonwealths. The state's reputation for conservatism has not prevented the advancement of certain of its institutions to a place among the best of their kind in the country, and no spirit of false economy should be permitted to retard the development of others along lines of needed improvement."

This is an expenditure of more than $1.50 per capita of the entire population of the state.

THE 1903 STANDARD MEDICAL DIRECTORY.

Possibly there is no form of publication where it is more difficult to secure completeness and accuracy than a directory, and the difficulty increases with the extent of territory covered. Were it possible, in any national directory, to cover the entire country in a single day, if the canvass were carefully done, the result would be accurate *for that day*. This is clearly impossible, and the only practicable way is to keep at it and keep improving. The first issue of the Standard, while far from fulfilling its name, gives a very excellent foundation on which to erect a very superior volume for another edition. The publishers are hard at work to this end. The new volume will consist of about 1300 pages, and, as a new feature, promises a list of physicians arranged alphabetically giving the post-office address which promises to be a great convenience.

DOES THE PRACTICE OF MEDICINE PAY? By GEORGE R. PATTON, A.M., M.D., Lake City, Minnesota. Philadelphia: P. Blakiston's Son & Co. Paper. 15 pp. Price, 10 cents.

The word "pay" in this essay is used in its commercial sense, and the elements entering into conditions enabling one to answer the question in the affirmative are very pleasantly and forcibly put by a Nestor of the profession.

Pediatrics signalizes the opening of its eighth year with a colored cover, and a change from a semimonthly to a monthly issue, publishing the same number of pages each month.

The Washington Medical Library Association began with the year the publishing of *Northwest Medicine*. The journal is under the control of medical men, is published to afford the physicians of Washington with a medium of communication, and to present the medical items of their corner of the Union to the medical world. We like the contents of the first number and its general make-up, and wish the association abundant success in its laudable enterprise.

REPORT OF THE COMMISSIONER OF EDUCATION FOR THE YEAR 1900-1901. Vol. 2. Washington, D. C. 1902. pp. 1217-2512.

In this volume are to be found the statistics, and the following summary is worth repeating:

"In the 154 medical schools there were 26,757 students, of whom 1,812 were homeopathic and 746 eclectic. This represents an increase during the year of 1,544 students. It is notable that the number of homeopathic students, which during the long period of 1877 to 1892 remained practically stationary, during the next three years was nearly doubled, and during the last six years has again become stationary. The length of the annual session in medical schools is being increased. More than one-third of them (54 out of 154) now have sessions of eight or nine months, 18 having sessions of nine months. The grounds and buildings of medical schools are reported at $14,500,000 and the endowment funds at $2,000,000, some schools failing to report this item. While a new school is occasionally started, there appears a greater tendency toward consolidation of those already founded, while occasionally one is discontinued, so that the whole number is now one less than in 1895. Although theological schools continue to be the principal recipients of benefactions, medical schools are coming into greater prominence as institutions worthy of the gifts of the wealthy."

TRADE CALENDARS.

The Lambert Pharmacal Company issue a neat leatherette desk calendar, a slip to a month, with an unobtrusive advertisement.

The McArthur's Syrup of the Hypophosphite calendar continued the form so familiar to the profession for years past.

The calendar of Fairchild Bros. and Foster is a neat piece of handsome engraving and printing.

The Provident Life and Trust Company issue a calendar with generous-sized figures, to be seen easily across the room.

BULLETIN

OF THE

American Academy of Medicine

| VOL. VI. | ISSUED JUNE, 1903. | No. 6. |

THE AMERICAN ACADEMY OF MEDICINE is not responsible for the sentiments expressed in any paper or address published in the BULLETIN.

"MUCK-RAKE" METHODS IN MEDICAL PRACTICE.[1]
BY CHARLES MCINTIRE, A.M., M.D., Easton, Pa.

As I glance at the lengthening list of the presidents of the American Academy of Medicine, and see my own name inscribed along with those chosen from among men whom the world delights to honor, I can only account for it by the benevolence of you, my friends, which permitted your sentiment to override your judgment. To some men, rich with other honors and gifts, this office may seem but a slight thing. Far different to me—that I thank you need hardly be said; that I cannot properly voice my gratitude is evident to the least observant.

It seems proper for your presiding officer in his annual address to review briefly the progress in the medico-social world during the year he is supposed to be occupying the watch-tower, as a prelude to the discussion of the selected theme for the address itself.

The familiar lines of Bishop Coxe,

> "We are living, we are dwelling
> In a grand and awful time;
> In an age on ages telling,
> To be living is sublime,"

seems to gain added force with the passing years. "What next?" was the cry expecting a negative reply, of but a few years ago. "Certainly," it was said, "no advance can be made opening up

[1] The president's address for the 28th annual meeting of the American Academy of Medicine, Washington, D. C., May 11, 1903.

new experiences. That which we have will be improved, but where can we turn for novel discoveries?" And Roentgen answered the question, by making the opaque translucent. "Surely the Ultima Thule has been reached," again was the cry —and Marconi replies in the negative as he flashes his message through space from Cape Cod to the coast of Cornwall. But these, as most wonder-exciting discoveries, added but little to the sum of previous knowledge—they were the fortunate layers of capstones merely. Their discoveries were possible only because of careful observation and experimentation by many a preceding investigator. Now that we are applying similar scientific methods of study to man and to masses of men, while great boons to humanity have not been announced as yet, the year has been full of change and progress, and in due time the layer of another capstone will appear.

Time forbids (not to mention other and more serious causes) to attempt even to catalogue all that has been done—suffice it to present a few things coming within our ken during the year.

Naturally, we first turn to educational problems and to the preliminary education of the physician. It is pleasant to record that the Ohio Examining Board has materially advanced the preliminary requirements for that state. It is likewise pleasant to see, that notwithstanding the adverse criticism of two medical journals in Cincinnati, it is apparently meeting the approval of the profession of Ohio.

The beginning of the first aphorism of Hippocrates: "Life is short, and the Art long" is truer to-day, if truth can be compared, than when it was written; and the efforts to coordinate our educational processes so as to give as much of life as possible to the practice of the art is to be commended. The question is continuing to attract the attention of educators, so that eventually much improvement will be made. A constant difficulty is the great variety of and different values (indifferent values far too often) in the course given by the degree-conferring institutions of America. The change in the law of New York, permitting students possessing a first degree, providing certain studies have been successfully pursued, to enter the second year of the medical course, has compelled the regent's office in that state to gather information as to the exact amount of work done in the various colleges in the land, leading to some surprising results. Too much praise cannot be given to Secretary Parsons and his efficient coadjutor, Dr. H. L. Taylor, for their careful collecting the facts regarding the educational systems not only of the United States but of Europe as well.

A marked utterance during the year has been that of President Wilson, of Princeton, in favor of teaching by tutors rather than by lectures. This, indeed, is in line with much of our more recent practice in medical schools.

The *Boston Medical and Surgical Journal* tells us that the students in the Medical Department of Harvard on their own initiative have arranged a course of evening lectures on the general topic of the "Relation of the Physician to the Community." This evidence of an awakening to the philosophic study of questions of social medicine must be especially gratifying to the fellows of the American Academy of Medicine.

The winter's sessions of the various State Legislatures have brought the usual crop of medical legislation—much of it praiseworthy. Arkansas, Nebraska and South Dakota will hereafter exact a license examination. Montana modifies its law to permit reciprocal relations with other boards. New Jersey amends its law to make it strictly conform to the rulings of its examining board. Illinois is striving to have a board of examiners separate from the state board of health. These are among the more important changes. Alas, that helpful legislation has been slaughtered in Colorado and Pennsylvania through the influence of physicians impelled by selfish interests!

The strength and the weakness of the state board of examiners are developing with their age. They are freely criticized, sometimes unjustly. The character of the questions asked seem to have caused more discussion than any other feature during the year. There is no reason why perfectly fair and up-to-date questions should not be framed. It is proper that no member of any medical faculty should be a member of the board ; it is true that many men are appointed for political reasons. At the same time the expert politician—a novice it may be in up-to-date medicine—can easily be supplied with proper questions by the expert teacher—a novice in political methods. There is no excuse for any but the fairest questions. The criticism of written examinations is excellent as an abstract proposition, but such examinations are necessitated by the limitations of the case. Every one refused a license would urge personal disfavor as the reason, were the examinations not conducted anonymously and a record of the examination itself preserved.

The necessity of some legal restriction in the practice of medicine is as old as Hippocrates, for we find this sentence in the first paragraph of the "Law":

"Medicine is of all the arts the most noble; but, owing to the ignorance of those who practise it, and of those who, inconsiderately, form a judgment of them, it is at present far behind all other arts. Their mistake appears to me to arise principally from this, that in the cities there is no punishment connected with the practice of medicine (and with it alone), except disgrace, and that does not hurt those who are familiar with it."

The fact that state licensure is the attempted solution evolved out of the necessities manifested during the centuries intervening since this was written, indicates there will be no step backward. We must go forward and adjust ourselves to the new conditions. This leads to the much-discussed question of "reciprocity." The most encouraging sign is that certain states, as New Jersey, Maryland and Virginia, are willing to accept the license of other boards upon some very fair and easy-to-be-performed conditions if the person wishing to transfer his license is at all worthy. The New England States have an association, but, with the exception of Maine, are at a standstill, fearing a real inequality in apparently equal conditions. The original national organization representing the examining boards, has not progressed much in this direction during the year. Two newer organizations, composed largely of the boards of the middle west, have formulated rules which they are putting in practice. The history of the development of "reciprocity in medical licensure" demonstrates the soundness of the policy suggested in a paper I had the honor to read before the National Confederation of State Medical Examining and Licensing

Boards at Atlanta in 1896. And no little thought on the subject since that time, only deepens the conviction that the true way is for each state to determine for itself apart from any thought of reciprocity—accepting the license of another state at a fair valuation, and adding thereto, if need be, additional tests to comply with its own law.

Turning from educational questions to other medico-social topics, one must note the progress in the effort to reorganize the state and county societies to bring about the solidarity of the profession contemplated by the leaders of the American Medical Association.

There is much that is Utopian in the scheme, but this should not deter the effort; the stars may not be reached should we aim at them, but a greater height will thereby be attained than were we to shoot into the ground. I am not sanguine of great benefits resulting, should the fondest dreams be realized; at the same time I feel assured of the effort accomplishing great good in other directions. The avowed purpose of the movement savors too much of selfish benefit to the profession to gain real power. The knowledge gained in the attempt will enable us to more perfectly serve and thus become truly great.

In no state has greater progress been made in this reorganization than in Michigan, because our ex-president, Dr. Leartus Connor, has put his neck to the yoke with his accustomed energy and unselfishness.

It is pleasant to report that the Rhode Island General Hospital is still efficiently guarding its out-patient department from impostors and the unworthy. Would that more hospitals would follow its example. The question of an adequate fee to the physician as related to the limited income of the average wage-earner is one that cannot be decided in a sentence. Much of the outside has been presented in the many articles on contract and lodge practice. Tempting as the subject is, it cannot be considered here.

The year has been marked also by the forelock seizure of an opportunity by one of our fellows, the distinguished president of the Congress just about to meet in this city. I refer to the letter of Dr. Keen to the honorable Senator from New Hampshire regarding vivisection, wherein an operation upon the brain of a naval cadet, which had already become public property, was used as a concrete example of the benefit of proper experimentation upon animals.

This is not the place to argue the right of man to the life of animals for a beneficent purpose. When this purpose is absent it is but impaling the fly on a pin and merits condemnation. But a sentence from a recent work, is suggestive here: "Nature does not stop to count the cost when an advance in any vital value is to be gained.[1] Does it not seem plausible that it is in harmony with nature to make use of the things of less value for the benefit of that which is worth more? And if for the benefit of man, cannot all lower life be used?

The fact that the religious newspapers published in the interest of the Methodist Episcopal Church will in the future decline to accept the so-called medical advertisements is worthy of record in this review, and the management should be made aware of the gratification of the profession upon the stand it has taken for right as opposed to commercial expediency.

The dreaming tinker in Bedford Gaol depicts a scene that suggests my theme. He says:

"The interpreter takes them apart again, and has them first into a room where was a man that could look no way but downwards, with a muck-rake in his hand. There stood also one over his head with a celestial crown in his hand, and proffered him that crown for his muck-rake; but the man did neither look up nor regard, but raked to himself the straws, the small sticks, and dust of the floor."

Do we not find muck-rakes in the hands of those of our profession—educated though they be—skilled in the art as well as learned in the science of medicine, with extensive practice among loyal patients to whom they give careful attention, who, in their individual relations to their fellow-physicians, are courteous, just, even charitable—yet seldom, if ever, are they to be found at a meeting of a medical society? From year's end to

[1] Newman Smyth's "Thorough Science to Faith," p. 216 (published February, 1902).

year's end no paper appears from their pens; no discussion is fostered by their efforts. A close student, it is possible; up, quite likely, in the knowledge of the practice of medicine, but the eyes are down; the muck-rake is gathering the straw and the chips, never seeing the larger reward, the greater glory above their heads and easily within their grasp. The reward that comes from greater service, from broader fields of influence; the glory of strengthening that profession which is honoring them and which they care so little to honor.

The oft-quoted sentence of Bacon is *apropos*:

"I hold every man a debtor to his profession; from the which as men of course do seek to receive countenance and profit, so ought they of duty to endeavor themselves by way of amends to be a help and ornament thereunto."

Wherein Bacon is more severe than Bunyan, for he who fails to make an effort to pay his debts thereby shows himself to be dishonest.

A little care is necessary at this point or, for want of a mutual understanding, we may appear to differ where we really agree. The man with the muck-rake, exhibited by the interpreter, may have been gathering a goodly pile of most valuable straw under the most adverse circumstances, but he failed to secure the richer reward within his reach. This reward was, using the word somewhat archaicly, differing in essence from the material return for his labor. The true value of the crown would not be measured by the amount of money obtainable by using it as collateral, but by the joy experienced in its possession. Let us keep in mind the fact that the imponderable essences are of greater value. Where would the world be without radiant heat, light, electrical energy, modes of motion each. You can measure light, it is true, but not with a yard stick; a vast and complex terminology has been devised to express measurements of electricity—but they are in terms of itself. If this be true in the purely physical world, much more is it in the world of human conduct. Who, for example, would place implicit confidence in a man whose rule made honesty merely a policy? But is not this an effort to express the avoirdupois of a moral quality? To weigh the imponderable? I do not see how we can escape the conclusion that our most valuable possessions are not weighable; are beyond the influence of the multiplication table, and cannot be expressed by the insignia of minted metal.

Notwithstanding the apparent domination of the world by sordid realities, it is really ruled by other forces—imagination, sentiment, the vision of the seer, distraught as he is with the miasm and dust that hides the sun, seeking to depict the ideal atmosphere purified and fair. These are the sovereigns, and under their guidance we are shown, in the language of another, that the "end of civilization is not money but men."

Sad, indeed, should these imponderable forces not be steadied by the concrete and the material, as the expansive force of steam is kept at regular work by the cylinder, the piston and the fly-wheel-material each. Sadder by far when the material gains the ascendency, causing the individual to become base. The scathing words of the Great Physician addressed to the Pharisees for tithing the ponderable mint, anise and cummin, while neglecting the imponderable judgment, mercy and faith, apply to like habits to-day. "These," said he, "ought ye to have done, and not to leave the other undone." Had the creature in the interpreter's house but asserted his manhood by the uplift of his eyes, as an $\alpha\theta\rho\omega\pi os$ and been willing to exchange his rake for the crown, the reward would have been his, and the rake; only now the straws would have been gathered for a nobler purpose. Because this is true, I assert that that man who puts all his energy in the consulting room, and lives for his patients alone, fails to reap the higher rewards that are his for the asking.

I am self-opinionated enough to believe that you agree with me in this estimate, because I am revealing the mote in the eye of our neighbor, by means of the condensing lens and oblique illumination. Your very presence at this meeting is evidence that the description does not characterize you. But, and I speak more hesitatingly, are there not possibilities of the profession's eyes containing beams? May we not, as a class, show a disposition to follow the example of the man with the muck-rake? Let us examine his conduct somewhat closely.

I. The man with the muck rake was so intent upon his calling that he was not aware of his surroundings.

Lord Bacon says: "It were good, therefore, that men in their innovations would follow the example of time itself, which indeed innovateth greatly, but quietly, and by degrees scarce to be perceived."[1]

We all have taken notice of the changes in the century so recently passed, such as the cityward trend of our population, the progress of the mechanic arts and the resulting changes in industrial life. The Scotch boy who weighted his mother's tea-kettle and harnessed steam, brought a new factor into the industrial world. A great weight was lifted from men's backs, when the spinning jenny, the power loom and other appliances replaced the direct labor of the hand. But new combinations had to be devised to meet new conditions. Working people must be congregated in large numbers to utilize the new power. Labor must be divided to secure the best results. New industrial, economic and social conditions have arisen. There is nothing novel in these statements, we all recognize them and many other great innovations that came so quietly as scarcely to be noticed. The Academy has discussed some of the changed conditions in the physician's relationship to the world, in the abuse of hospital and dispensary services, the question of provident dispensaries and contract practice, and others. But, after all, have these not been mere raked-together straw to many of us? Are we not ordering our lives by the earlier conditions?

The Rev. John Peters, D.D., in his introduction to "Labor and Capital," a book which grew out of a symposium conducted by a Metropolitan daily at the time of the great strike of the Amalgamated Association of Iron, Steel and Tinworkers in the summer of 1901, strives to sum up the opinions of those who contributed. Among other things he says:

"It is worthy of note how strong is the tendency of thinkers and practical men alike to insist that our national spirit of individualism must yield in some degree to collectivism."[2]

[1] Of Innovation.
[2] P. XXXVI.

Or, take this paragraph from "Democracy and Social Ethics," by Jane Addams, of the Hull House, Social Settlement, Chicago:

"Throughout this volume we have assumed that much of our ethical maladjustment in social affairs arises from the fact that we are acting upon a code of ethics adapted to individual relationships but not to the larger social relationships to which it is bunglingly applied. In addition, however, to the constant strain and difficulty there is often an honest lack of perception as to what the situation demands."[1]

Without accepting Miss Addams' conclusions that she is able to present a series of conditions which give color to its truth, is enough to make us wonder if with all the valuable straw we have gathered we have not failed to look up and around, and thus obtain an honest perception of the situation.

Abundant material is at hand to further elaborate this idea, but enough has been stated to give foundation to the assertion: That social innovations—progress possibly—are upon us, and these have not received the same careful attention that the innovations in medical science and art have received. Whether or not this was a neglect of a higher duty for a too exclusive attention to a lower, need not be discussed at this moment. You will at least agree with me that it is a narrowed view, a looking-down to those things which pertain to our handicraft. And President Hyde, of Bowdoin, is not speaking of physicians when he says: "The business or professional man who is that and nothing more becomes hard and inhuman, even in doing that which in itself is an inestimable service to humanity."[2]

II. And this brings us back to our man and his muck-rake, who was condemned rather for his neglect of greater rewards by the exclusive gathering of those of less value. Are we imitating him?

Again I fear we will differ in those things on which we perfectly agree, if we do not carefully define our words and place ourselves on the same level while looking across the vista in our search. Hence, I ask, what is a physician? What should he strive to be? What should be expected of him? For if we be-

[1] P. 221.
[2] "God's Education of Man," p. 185.

gin our study with widely different concepts, the same shield will be at once silver and gold.

How can we begin the search? The soul of a term is sometimes developed by a study of the history of the term itself.

A recent American author in treating of the conservatism of theologians writes: "Doctors and lawyers and scientists look with more or less distrust on all new theories."[1]

No one hesitates for a moment in understanding that the author refers to the practisers of physic, when he uses the word "Doctors." Indeed we have dictionary for it, for one of the definitions of doctor in the dictionary of the English Philological Society, reads: "A doctor of medicine; in popular, current use applied to any medical practitioner."

It is not necessary in this presence to bring evidence to show that that which now so truly stands for a vocation, implied at one time an ability to impart to others some branch of knowledge. And so the primary definition in the dictionary just quoted is: " A teacher, instructor, one who gives instruction in some branch of knowledge or inculcates opinions or principles," and it adds to this definition the words, "now rare." And since to teach, one must first possess knowledge, the word was applied to those well-known for their learning, which, in time, must be attested by the university's stamp and a doctor is one who has "attained to the highest degree conferred by a university." That the degree in medicine was early considered of value may be seen in a statement made by Whitelock, in 1654: "Many medicasters, pretenders to physic, buy the degree of doctor abroad." Truly, there is no new thing under the sun! Whether for peculiar honor or in jest, as now when the cook of a coasting vessel is known as its doctor, the followers of our profession became preeminently "doctors," I will leave to philologists to determine.

The use of doctor in English as a medical practiser goes back to a respectable age. Dryden writes (1699):

"So lived our sires ere doctors learned to kill."

And Shakespeare, a century earlier (1598) in Merry Wives (3:1):

"Shall I lose my Doctor? No! He gives me the potions."

[1] "The Old Testament and New Scholarships," Rev. J. P. Peters, D.D., p. 39.

Two hundred years earlier (1366), Chaucer says in his prologue:

"With us there was á Docteur of Phesike."

But this may mean a medical man who was doctorated.

Chaucer's title suggests us another word—physician. Would one could trace the thought that transforms the Greek $\varphi \acute{v} \sigma \iota s$ nature, into physics, physic and physician, as now used. At one time physician pertained to the student of nature, the physicist of our present-day nomenclature, than to either class indifferently.

Without further detail, does not this thought lie under the changing meaning of these words, as the force—the imbreathed spirit—which gave them meaning and caused them to enter into the life of our language as we now employ them? The medical man is one so expert in his line of study as to be able to give instruction, and inculcate opinions in that branch of study which requires knowledge of the nature of the highest type of animal life—man. And because of this he is rightly differentiated by a university and made a doctor of medicine—one able to teach man because he knows of what he is. Teaching does not necessarily imply rows of forms, the birch rod and the dunce's headpiece. Teaching has been defined as "causing another to know that which we know and which he does not, and that which we want him to know."[1] And any process which accomplishes this is teaching. But, recalling Benjamin Franklin's famous salt box, there is the teacher actual and the teacher possible. The former is hard at work at his teaching, the latter, while fitted for the vocation, is not actually following it. Let us emphasize—the doctor should have the ability to teach because he has the knowledge—the prerequisite for teaching. And this must be a knowledge of the nature of man.

The Baroness Von Hutton, in "Our Lady of the Beeches," causes "Pessimist" to write: "You in your beech forest watch the effect of nature on the human heart—not on the soul, as you imagine,"[2] and this illustrates a common belief, at least, of the threefold nature of man. The body, soul and spirit, as the theologian of the New Testament characterizes them. Let us

[1] H. Clay Trumbull, D.D., "Teachers and Teaching," p 30.
[2] P. 12.

assume the classification for convenience without discussing it. If the statement just given truly describes the physician, should his study and knowledge stop with the body merely? Shall we be content when we measure the strength of the blood stream, the rapidity of the heart action, determine the proper elaboration of the food ingested, guide a fever or use the surgeon's knife with absolute precision? Be a physician ever so expert in these things, has he compassed all the knowledge he should have to be entitled to the doctorate? Surely the hosts of alienists who are doing such noble work enable us to properly frame an answer to that question. There is a realm beyond the purely somatic that needs the services of the healer.

But more: one of the wisdom writers of the early Hebrews gave forth these words:

"Hope deferred maketh the heart sick:
But when the desire cometh, it is a tree of life."[1]

and again:

"A cheerful heart causeth good healing;
But a broken spirit drieth up the bones."[2]

This gives suggestion to the thought of possible pathologic conditions to the third side of mankind. Were this not the thought of some, how would Shakespeare make his Macbeth say:

"The labor we delight in physics pain."

Or to put in the mouth of the despairing Claudia,

"The miserable have no other medicine
But only Hope."

The nature of this side of man should also be in the ken of that one who seeks to alleviate the suffering of humanity and to cure their diseases.

If there is any truth in this thought it can be neither novel nor new. A truth so important must long ago have been observed and noted, and even now is recognized by you as long accepted.

While the material was gathering for this paper the address delivered last September before the Canadian Medical Association by our honored honorary member, Prof. Wm. Osler, appeared in the journals. It would be folly to take your time grouping details gathered from the past centuries, when a master hand epito-

[1] Prov. 13:12—R. V.
[2] Prov. 17:22—Am. Rev. V.

mizes so admirably his more extended search in the same field. His purpose differs, but the facts are the same. He says:

"The critical sense and skeptical attitude of the Hippocratic school laid the foundations of modern medicine on broad lines, and we owe it: *First*, the emancipation of medicine from the shackles of priest craft and caste; *secondly*, the conception of medicine as an art based on accurate observation, as a science, an integral part of the science of man and of nature; *thirdly*, the high moral ideals, expressed in that most 'memorable of human documents' (Gomperz), the Hippocratic oath; and *fourthly* the conception and realization of medicine as the profession of a cultivated gentleman."[1]

And the two are one, the soul of the term given to those who pursue our art as developed by the thought of the people in the making of language on the one side and the spirit dominating those to whom the term applies on the other.

Our excursion, while it had made a revolution, describes an epicycloid rather than a circle, and, if our reasoning has been sound, we can affirm that the wider outlook of the physician's duty includes not only the ministrations to relieve bodily pain and mental anguish, but to give comfort to the distempered soul as well. This latter fact is admirably illustrated in a paper presented to the Academy at the St. Paul meeting by Dr. James A. Spalding. The purpose of the paper was so entirely different that it makes the evidence of greater value. Dr. Spalding made use of a sudden loss of vision to test the methods of the optician so-called, after which he consulted a professional friend. In his narrative, he says:

"Now, I knew what was the matter with me, now I could feel as I never had before, the moral effect of what I had so often and I fear rather thoughtlessly told my patients; now for the first time in my life I better recognized a physician's responsibility towards those who consult him."[2]

There is a service which produces a "moral effect," that acts upon soul or spirit of our patients. And if we recognize the tendency of the times towards social masses, we find here too, a duty to determine the spirit moving through the masses, inspiring them

[1] Chauvinism in Medicine.
[2] This BULLETIN, V, 687.

with hope or demoralizing them with dread. We recognize the necessity of hygienic procedures, by which pure water, proper disposal of waste, fitting dwellings and the rest shall be secured for communities: our discussion this afternoon shows that we recognize the necessity of the physician's mind in the problems of mental training, as much so as it is our duty to alleviate the suffering due to mental alienation. So, too, can we lift our eyes, there is the bright crown awaiting us, if we endeavor to influence the forces working in humanity to produce the "moral effect" resulting in hopeful anticipation and not despair. That this thought is in the minds of those who, as Prof. Osler affirms, are maintaining the ancient spirit of the profession, the following from an address by Mr. Thos. Bryant, as President of the Metropolitan Counties Branch of the British Medical Association, in 1899, is offered in evidence:

" For whilst with us professional interests must naturally take first place in our thought, it should never be forgotten that the main purpose of our existence as a profession is for the public advantage, and that from such a point of view all our actions will be estimated by the world at large.''[1]

The physician who looks up and around, who reaches for the more noble rewards, must have a clear conception of the Zeitgeist. He must have not only the intelligence to enter into the experience of the captains of the age—the formers of thought, the builders of great enterprises—but he must possess that far rarer gift of sympathy enabling him to comprehend the motive, yea, the innermost spiritual breathing unformulated but real, which unconsciously shapes the outward life and manner of the other extreme of the present social order. He must comprehend the proletariat and have a working knowledge of that atavistic class reverting towards the lilies of the field—those adorned beyond the glory of Solomon, yet neither toiling nor spinning. Those of you who have read "No. 5 John Street," will remember how these classes are placed in contrast, whereby we are enabled to see some of the morbid conditions of each.

It is not for us in our professional life to enter into the political and economic discussion of the origin of these conditions—as

[1] *British Med. Journal*, 22 Jl., '99, p. 192.

men and women of affairs, we may or may not according to the bent of our fancies. But it is necessary for us to know these conditions intimately if we desire to properly solve the question of the hospital, of the free dispensary, of club practice, etc. And as we study these problems from this side, doubtless many others will develop, even of greater interest and importance. And as these questions are properly solved will the general conditions be bettered to the delight of the optimist and the discomforture of those who take pleasure in howling calamity.

If then, the physician of to-day will pause once in a while in his gathering to his store that which furnishes larger resources for diagnosis and treatment, and will look abroad, he will see opportunities for greater service and a prospect for higher rewards than ever a muck-rake could draw to his possession.

III. But again, the man with the muck rake was condemned because he put his entire energy to secure a present good, neglecting whatever greater blessing may have been offered him for the future.

The dead monarch gives place to the living sovereign. The fathers are passing on, and the sons are training for their places. Are we presenting them with muck-rakes and straw and chips alone, with a look ever downward? Or are we pointing upward to the celestial crown, theirs almost for the asking? Figure of speech aside—what is the character of the training we are seeking to impart to those upon whom the mantels will fall—whose task will be even more complex and more delicate than that assigned to ourselves? Is it to graduate men packed to the utmost with information of value, or to send them into the world fitted to acquire knowledge with ever increasing zest?

If you review the sequence of the events happening in the world, it is comparatively easy to give the chiefer ones in order. It is more difficult to get beneath and show the causes producing through the revolutions of the ages the evolution of a race. The outer and inner aspect of the same sequence of events furnishes either history or philosophy as you glide or delve. In like manner in education, there is the outer and the inner, and as the soul is of more worth than the body elsewhere, so here. If the choice must ever be made between the purely external—the acquisition of knowledge—or the purely personal—development—by all means select the latter. Fortunately an absolute divorce of this kind is not required. At the same time there is much to be approved in these words of C. H. Henderson:

"The real work of education ought to be the cultivation of the will to do, rather than the setting of tasks which would be helpful if the will were there, but which in its absence are quite meaningless or even harmful."[1]

Again, he gives us a paragraph of help in this discussion. "Every performance may be looked at from two points of view; that of the thing done and that of the doer. These are the two terms necessary to bring the thing about. We may call the one point of view the non-human, and the other the human. It seldom happens that the outlook in any performance is strictly one or the other. It usually involves a little of both. An industrial performance from the standpoint of the market, is strictly non-human, for it has to do only with the thing produced. An educational performance from the standpoint of the philosopher is strictly human for it has to do solely with the agent or doer. But industrial performances are more and more coming under the eye of the social philosopher, and are introducing the human element. In the same way educational performances are coming into touch with the market, and are submitting to the non-human standards of measurement."[2]

I fear that much of the discussion on the proper education of the physician does not preserve the golden mean so that the human and non-human purposes of Dr. Henderson are properly blended. Too much stress is laid upon the acquisition of a certain fund of facts—supposedly of use in the sick-room—the purely commercial view; while the effort at development—so that the facts acquired can be assimilated and utilized by trained thinkers possessing them—is too often given a secondary position. It is a raking-together of straw—valuable straw indeed—but the more glorious acquisition is neglected. In any discussion regarding the education of the physician it should be noted: (1) At the last analysis, the success of the physician in his daily rounds does not depend upon his educational process—please do

[1] "Education and the Larger Life," p. 87.
[2] Ibid., p. 52.

not misconstrue my words—the ultimate result is wondrously influenced by, but does not depend upon, the educational process. Sir Frederick Treves, in an introductory address at the opening of the University College at Liverpool last fall, expressed this very aptly. He says:

"A man may possess all the learning that a well-equipped library may contain and all the erudition attentive observation in the wards may bestow and yet be short of complete success as a practitioner of his art. Absolute efficiency cannot be gauged by academic distinction nor can it be discovered by the touchstone of the examination table. In the accomplishments of the most learned physician there may be one thing lacking, the need of which may stand between him and the fullest equipment for success, and that one thing is a tactful and sympathetic knowledge of his fellow man."[1]

(2) That the education is not completed when the educational system ends. This thought needs but the mention for its acceptance.

(3) Other things being equal, the man developed, with the power resulting from that development, can acquire new truths and apply them more aptly, even with a slighter foundation of facts at hand, than the man filled to repletion with facts without the developed mind to use them. Hence, if we err in commingling the studies that develop and those that chiefly impart knowledge, let us err on the side of the full development. A healthy appetite with perfect digestion is to be preferred to an engorged condition from eating a surfeit.

(4) The one object which should never be lost sight of in all our plans for the education of physicians is admirably expressed by Dr. Taylor Hudson in his president's address before the Texas Medical Society last year. He says:

"Are we not all exposed to the same danger of being shunted off onto side tracks instead of keeping the main line? Our vocation is commonly narrow and must be. Even the liberal professions, as they are called, if there be any such, for whether they are liberal or not, depends on the man; and one finds himself more physician, more lawyer, more preacher than he is a man. Our vocation gets to be bigger than we. A man is overshadowed, and his character is like a kind of vegetation under a tree,

[1] *British Med. Journal*, Oct. 18, 1902, p. 1199.

and lacks the health and fibre that sunlight gives. The remedy for this is in the manly, in distinction from merely technical or professional. * * * In other words, we must be men before we are professionals."[1]

Anything short of this gathers but stubble, and loses the opportunity to grasp diadems.

But there is another point of view of the educational problem. We cannot escape the imminence of humanity in mass—the social aggregations of the present day. How can education be applied as to best further their well-being as influenced by the medical profession.

To quote Henderson again:

"The social purpose is only realized by the idealizing and perfecting all that concerns daily human living. As a practical problem, it has to do with a man's occupation, with his food, with his dress, with his dwelling, with his health, with his organic power, with his family, with his friends, with his pleasures, with his thoughts, with his emotions,—in a word with every element that touches or makes up his life."[2]

If it be true as he says "that good and great things are only born of good and great spirit. They do not present themselves as supply to the beckoning hand of demand," and it seems plausible—then there is room for great care in the development of the modern physician, who must be able sympathetically to minister to the morbid whenever any of these functions go awry. And much of his treatment will be in educational processes themselves, whereby, for example, the masses may be taught the necessity of self-restraint as a preventive of the ills of excess—a much wider range of study and of effort than can be found in the clinical researches of the diseases produced by excess.

IV. I doubt very much if the medical profession unaided can carry on such investigations effectively, and this leads us back to our man with his muck-rake, who is condemned because he is seeking to drag everything within reach of his rake to himself, while just above him are greater joys because they must be shared with others; the mutual help of many making the crown to shine more resplendently.

[1] Transactions, Texas State Society, 1902, p. 93.
[2] Henderson, Op. cit., 51.

Of necessity, the medical man works alone in most of his labors, and he is apt to confine his efforts to his profession. He may lavish on it, but on others—unless it is the largess of the free-handed upon the sick and suffering—he lets them alone.

There is the need of his looking up and around, of joining the common brotherhood of humanity in its efforts for uplift.

Prof. Davies, lecturer on the history of philosophy, of Yale, says:

"I use the word 'education' in the large untechnical sense—not as applying to academical training only, but also as including the whole process through which society passes on its way toward a greater degree of harmony and perfection. Individualism, which has been, and is still, the American ideal of education, must be limited according to this definition, by the larger question of a man's social relations, by his political duty and by his personal efficiency in the system of things; all this as brought about by growth of personality and experience, and by the natural evolution of human life under the institutions of civilization, is what I mean by education."[1]

Education from this standpoint can not be perfected in any one except as he rubs against the social element of his environment. Hence it is not only a matter of courtesy, but a stern necessity, that conferences with non-medical men should be had by medical men in questions where there is a community of interest, and I hail with delight this feature of the last and the present meetings.

V. I would be treating the Sainted Dreamer shabbily if I were not to use his allegory to suggest another lesson. The man with the muck-rake heaped up stores of temporal things and lost his interest in things eternal.

As the study of the threefold nature of man has been urged in this paper in order that the physician might attain the highest position, in like manner is it necessary to cultivate the spiritual of his own life if he would develop in himself the highest manhood. This does not mean the proclaiming of cant nor manifestations of pure incredulity—neither condition belongs to the higher nature. But there is that life which must be spiritually discerned if at all, the facts that will not yield themselves to the tests for

[1] "Labor and Capital," p. 4.

the physical or mental, but only by the application of the rules that govern them. He, who in the last analysis does not cultivate this phase of his nature, or permits it to be developed in him to the fulness of a stature of a man in his entirety, gathers but straw with a rake and loses the crown just above him.

Possibly the custom of president's addresses is derived from the legend of the song of the swan, it is its last vital act—with the address the president's labors ceased. I do not assert it, but if it be true, the couplet of Coleridge would often apply:

> "Swans sing before they die; 'twere no bad thing
> Should certain persons die before they sing."

I fear that in my efforts as a minstrel, I have permitted the introduction of too many minor chords. Do not suppose thereby, that I wish to be pessimistic. I have only tried to hold the mirror up to nature. The mirror itself is far from perfect and the resulting images may be distorted to their hurt. Let us then with thanks to the Master Dreamer for the use of his man and rake, dismiss our model and turn our eyes outward and upward. An earlier age of English history has been the theme of a later Seer in English literature. Tennyson has immortalized the Knights of Arthur's "Round Table." The great King himself tells his Guinevere of their qualities:

> "In that fair order of my Table Round,
> A glorious company, the flower of men,
> To serve as model for the mighty world,
> And be the fair beginning of a time.
>
> * * * *
>
> To ride abroad redressing human wrongs
> To speak no slander, no, nor listen to it,
> To lead sweet lives in purest chastity.
>
> * * * *
>
> Not only to keep down the base in man,
> But to teach high thought, and amiable words
> And courtliness, and the desire of fame,
> And love of truth, and all that makes a man."

In this brighter portrait we see the embodiment of the principles underlying our calling. Yielding fair homage to all other professions, and attempting no comparisons, the practice of medicine when truly followed is the knightly profession. Here the service is for the weak against the strong, the uplifting of the oppressed, the courteous care of all. When, perchance, we find a shield emblazoned with a muck-rake, it belongs to a coward caitiff whose spurs in time will be taken from him. The profession as a profession has caught the secret of the life of the most knightly man the world has ever seen, a king whose kingdom was not of this world, whose servants did not fight—yet who more manly, who more chivalrous than he in all his acts! And the record of his purpose in life is the motto of our profession. Not embroidered upon any banner of samite, but marked by the daily deeds of the true of our guild the world over, the centuries through. "Not to be ministered unto but to minister."

TIME-ALLOWANCE IN THE COMBINED COLLEGIATE AND MEDICAL COURSE (SECOND REPORT.)[1]

BY A. L. BENEDICT, A.M., M.D., Buffalo.

As directed by the Academy at the meeting of 1902, copies of the Bulletin containing the report of your committee for last year, were mailed to such institutions as had replied to the first circular letter and to some few others, which it seemed desirable to reach. A second circular letter, which is appended, was also mailed to the same list, aggregating about 350 colleges, medical schools and universities. Either on account of failure of delivery or, more probably, of lack of attention to second-class mail matter, most of the replies received, were requests for the printed report and, while these were filled in most instances, less than fifty institutions made any reply whatever and definite acknowledgment of the Bulletin and circular letter has been made by only ten institutions.

So far as can be judged from the replies received and information previously rendered in response to the circular letter of last year, or obtained from the University of the State of New York or similar educational boards, the failure to reply to the second letter is due, not so much to indifference to the topic involved, as to the fact that most of the universities of the United States have already instituted combined courses such that a bachelor's and a medical doctor's degree may be gained in seven years after matriculation —in some instances in six—while the segregated colleges and medical schools are not yet in a position to formulate a definite plan of action.

The following excerpts from letters are of interest :

W. P. Kane, President Wabash College, Indiana : "I am in thorough sympathy with the proposition * * * to complete both courses in seven years. Most of the institutions combining college courses with professional, have this arrangement for their students. * * * An understanding should be reached also between the professional schools and the separate colleges.

[1] Report of committee to the American Academy of Medicine, at Washington, D. C., May 11, 1903. Drs. A. L. Benedict, S. D. Risley and Charles McIntire, committee. The report was prepared by Dr. Benedict.

* * * While the professional schools admit without exception the desirability of such an arrangement, there is a reluctance on the part of individual schools lest they may incur the censure of competing schools."

Rush Rhees, President University of Rochester (a segregated college from our standpoint), states that his institution is giving serious and cordial attention to the matter and would welcome our assistance.

Henry Churchill King, President Oberlin College, states that he has secured a definite arrangement with two or three medical schools and hopes that by making out a real working plan, a general system may be secured for all colleges and professional schools. He urges that the Academy elaborate a detailed plan and secure general agreement on the part of a number of the best medical schools.

John S. Stahr, President Franklin and Marshall College, Pa., expresses his sympathy with the movement and continues: " Hitherto, the medical colleges of Pennsylvania have accepted our work in this way ($i.\ e.$, so as to make a year's allowance on the medical course). Recently the University of Pennsylvania" * * * has refused "to make time allowance to college graduates, no matter how well prepared they may be." * * * "There is a bill now pending before the Legislature of Pennsylvania requiring all students to spend four years in a medical college, except in the case of institutions which have a medical department connected with their literary department. We hope this bill may be defeated."

J. L. Goodknight, Dean of Lincoln College of the James Milliken University, Illinois, states that their students may spend three years each in the college and the medical school and receive both degrees at the completion of the six years. He cites the University of Illinois and many others as pursuing the same plan. When President of West Virginia University in 1895-7, he made an arrangement for time-allowance with medical schools—there being no medical department in connection with that university—and urges the general adoption of mutual concessions.

W. S. Chaplin, of Washington University, St. Louis; J. W. Bashford, of Ohio Wesleyan University, and Henry B. Ward, Dean of the Medical College of the University of Nebraska, all favor a time-allowance. Nicholas Murray Butler, President of Columbia University, promises to give the subject his attention and several other institutions have implied as much in their request for Bulletins. Dr. Ward personally favors a six-year combined course but thinks it improbable that less than seven years would be accepted unless the student had been under the constant scrutiny of one institution. He suggests for our next meeting, a discussion of the specific character of a six-year combined course.

Curtis C. Howard, Dean of Starling Medical College at Columbus, is the only respondent from a segregated medical school. He states that Ohio grants a year's allowance in medical schools to college graduates but he emphasizes the technical deficiencies of students thus matriculated and advises that either one course or the other should be shortened to three years.

Henry L. Taylor, of the University of the State of New York, has sent advance sheets of the report on registration of medical schools and combined courses, and your committee would suggest that, if further time is devoted to this important topic, statistic information can probably be more economically and more completely obtained from this source. It may be stated that the Board of Regents of the University of the State of New York has registered a number of schools of various kinds, in different parts of the country not because all such are commended but for the sake of accumulating statistics which may ultimately lead to a better correlation of courses and so, also, as to facilitate the transfer of students from one institution to another of higher standard whereas, without registration, there would be strong temptation to the retention of students in schools of lower standard.

The following conclusions seem to be justified, regarding the problem of combined courses in arts or science and medicine:

1. It will be impracticable for many years, to insist upon the possession of a bachelor's degree as a preliminary to a medical training, although a few universities have already established this requirement and it is probable that all of the highly-endowed universities will follow within a few years.

2. It may be expected, with reasonable certainty, that all of the more densely populated states will have insisted upon a full high-school education for medical students within a few years.

3. For the same states, a four-year medical course will probably also be in effect within a few years.

4. A combination collegiate and medical course of six or seven years, will produce a much higher average attainment for the medical graduate than can be accomplished by admitting the high school and the college graduate to the medical school, on precisely the same basis.

5. The combination course is not to be considered as compromising the educational value of the college course or the technical value of the medical, provided that a suitable arrangement of details is made. In other words, at least one year and probably two years of the scientific work of the medical school has a definite cultural value so that it might fairly be elected by any

candidate for a bachelor's degree, whether he intended to study medicine or not.

6. Entirely aside from the fact that colleges and professional schools are not on the same plan of requirements, there exists a conflict of interest among the universities, segregated colleges and segregated professional schools.

7. There is a tendency, in following the selfish interests of the university, to insist that the student should pursue his entire post-academic studies at the same institution and to place the matriculant from an independent institution at a disadvantage.

8. It is difficult for the small, segregated college to meet satisfactorily, the requirements for any highly specialized course of training, although an ordinary, broad education with no ulterior object, may be acquired at such institutions.

9. The segregated medical colleges, whether in their faculty or student body, are not unanimously in sympathy with higher education, and, in some cases, not even with approved standards of technical education. In particular, the segregated medical colleges manifest the tendency to minimize the importance of mental training and broad culture and to exaggerate the importance of purely technical facts and celerity in bandaging and certain laboratory manoeuvers.

10. In certain cases, state examining boards lend their influence in such a way that the interests of the segregated colleges must suffer, as compared with those of the university or segregated medical school.

11. Purely economic considerations tend to protect the interests of the segregated medical schools, although legislation and voluntary action toward a higher standard for medical matriculants, operate to increase the proportion of college-educated men in medical departments of universities and to restrict the potential clientele of the segregated medical schools to men of secondary or even lower education.

12. Unless it be granted that the tendency to the destruction of the independent college and to the inferiority of the independent medical school is inevitable and desirable, voluntary cooperation and legislative control must be invoked in the interests of such institutions.

TRANSACTIONS.

THE ARLINGTON, Washington, D. C.,
Monday, May 11, 1903.

The twenty-eighth annual meeting of the American Academy of Medicine was called to order by the President, Charles McIntire, of Easton, Pa., at 11 A.M., in executive session.

The President said :

In opening this, the 28th session of the American Academy of Medicine, I wish to call your attention to some coincidences distinguishing each of the Washington meetings.

The first meeting in Washington—the 12th of the Academy—was held in September, 1887, at the time of the International Medical Congress. It was the first time the Academy ever met in connection with the meeting of another society. At that time the then secretary felt the depression of spirits which must come—Elijah-like—to every one who labors for social betterings. It was with difficulty he could be urged to arrange for a meeting. A meeting was secured—thirty-four were in attendance—Dr. F. H. Gerrish was elected president, who, with characteristic energy, infused new vigor in the Academy. At the next meeting in New York, more than 100 were elected to fellowship.

In 1891, the 16th meeting was held in this very building, with 46 in attendance. It was the next meeting to be held at the time and place of another society, and the first of the series held in connection with the American Medical Association. It was also the first meeting under a new secretary. The medical profession was accepting the Academy's ideas on the necessity of a preliminary education for intending medical students, to be followed by a medical course worthy the name and a state examination for licensure. It was questioned whether the Academy had not performed its mission, and an adjournment without a day be in order. The next meeting was held in Detroit, where the keen vision of Dr. Leartus Connor saw the wider field, and his voice coined the phrase : "Medical Sociology."

Again we are in Washington : it is the first meeting at the time of the Congress of American Physicians and Surgeons; a new secretary is at the desk, and questions leading to important results are before us. May the meeting for 1904 result as happily as those for 1888 and 1892!

Pardon me if I occupy a little time in indicating some of the questions which should be considered at this meeting. Our sessions are too brief to permit their postponing to the formal address assigned to me.

The first is the desirability of associating with us, in our deliberations, specialists in the various fields of research cultivated by us, and, at the same time, reserving to the profession the conserving the character of the Academy. The adoption of an amendment to the constitution phrased essentially as the substitute prepared for the amendments proposed at the last meeting, will accomplish this, I think. No one will take exception to the terms therein proposed unless because of personal ambitions or private schemes; and such would not be helpful in their association.

Then, there is the necessity of increasing the proportion of fellows actively interested in the Academy. This can be accomplished only to a limited extent by the annual meetings alone. It can be aided by properly conducted local meetings. It may be that we are not ready to advance in this direction, which is not a new idea, as I remember Dr. Steiner, one of the original members, speaking of its possibility years ago.

Again, this can be aided by improvements in the Bulletin. It is the only journal devoted to social medicine, and it should be awake to its opportunity and privilege.

In addition to the papers and transactions now appearing, it could, for example, make an annual report on medical education in the United States, giving the information for our own colleges what "Minerva" does for the "gelehrten Welt"; and give an account of our medical charities after the model of Burdett's "Year-Book of Hospitals and Charities." Then, too, it should have departments wherein the entire literature of the subject would be epitomized. These features added to its present contents might not result in financial gain, but they would make the Bulletin of great use to hosts of people.

In this connection, I desire to call your attention to the necessity of the Academy defining the mutual rights of itself and the readers of papers at its meetings. It has been assumed heretofore that the ownership of a paper read before it, was vested in the Academy and that its disposal rested with the Council; and when a paper was published elsewhere by the request of the author, it did not appear in the Bulletin. That this has not been thoroughly understood, is evidenced by the publication of some of the papers during the year. I have no recommendation to make. If we could afford to publish all the papers in one number of the Bulletin immediately after the meeting, we would be in a better position to ask for the first publication. Some regulation should be framed, made known, and lived up to.

One thing more; we have always boasted that our Nominating Committee is uninstructed and beyond the influence of outside pressure. At the last executive session held at Saratoga, there was a discussion which might be construed as a limitation to the independence of the committee. This might result most disastrously, although but the nose of the camel. No action of the Academy should free the committee from the responsibility of seeking the best available material for each office. Efficiency in service should be the only test.

It will not do to stop here ; I cannot continue without being personal. That in giving me the presidency, you have honored me far beyond my merit, no one is more conscious than myself. I hope that I not only appreciate your thought and kindness in so doing but that I am truly grateful for it as well. Indeed, I can never fully express my gratitude to the American Academy of Medicine for the added happiness it has brought into my life. Through it I have secured acquaintanceship and companionship, yea, friendship that I value beyond price. And this would not have been, had you not kept me so long, first as assistant secretary and then as secretary. The work has been congenial, and the burden, though real and often heavy to carry, has proven to be the burden of loving service. It was no more than many another would have done, and more effectually.

Now that you have expressed the approval of my effort by your present honor—for which I cannot fittingly thank you—it is the part of wisdom on the part of the Nominating Committee to forget the complimentary words of a year ago, and be guided by reason, not by sentiment. One thing is certain, the time will soon come when a change will be necessary; another thing is plausible—a new secretary, with new methods and fresh energy would be able to cause the Academy to flourish beyond our fondest hope.

So, while the Nominating Committee is to be a creature of my own, I beg of it to be true to its traditions and to select for each office that one in its judgment best fitted to be of service to the Academy.

The reading of the minutes being called for, it was resolved to omit the reading and adopt them as published in the Bulletin for October, 1902.

The secretary read the report of the Council :

The Council reports the usual routine work in the preparation of the program for this meeting which is already in your possession, and the following additional items that may be of interest :

The amendment adopted at Saratoga, permitting the commutation of dues by a single payment of twenty dollars, was made use of by a single fellow during the year.

This is the first year when the penalty could be imposed for non-payment of dues, and the Council is pleased in stating that no one is three years in arrears.

There have been two local meetings during the year. The first at Albany, where a local club was organized, on October 29, 1902. This is the first attempt for a local organization of the fellows. The second meeting was held in Philadelphia, on March 21, 1903. At this meeting interesting papers were presented by Drs. A. A. Eshner, on "The Objections to Prescribing Medicines of Unknown Composition"; A. O. J. Kelly, on "The Propriety of Physicians Furnishing Medicines"; and J. Madison Taylor, on "The Dangers of Drug-Using without Guidance."

The proposed amendments to be acted upon at the meeting have been carefully considered by the Council by correspondence during the year. Many objections were soon seen to them in the form in which they were presented, and a substitute has been prepared. The Council is divided in its opinion as to the desirability of adopting the substitute, but presents it as an improvement upon the amendments as proposed. It recommends that the substitute be accepted, and that the action of the Academy be taken upon this proposition alone.

As the treasurer's report will show, the finances of the Academy are in a much better shape than a year ago. This is the result: (1) of the payment of some bills unpaid at the time of the last report, and (2) of issuing Bulletins of a smaller size. The papers read at the last meeting were, as a consequence, scattered through the year. It is pleasing to note an increasing demand for bound volumes. That the Bulletin is appreciated in some quarters is evidenced by the following extract from a letter:

"Enclosed find $6.00, which please put to my account. I do not wish to lose any of your reports, especially those containing the statistics which you so well compile about medical colleges and medical examinations."

This was from the dean of a medical college whose subscription had not yet expired.

The president reports receiving an invitation from the faculty of Swarthmore College to send an official representative on the occasion of the inauguration of their new president. As there was not sufficient time to confer with the Council, he appointed Dr. G. Hudson-Makuen.

All of the college catalogues in the library of the Academy have been arranged according to the Dewey System of classification and catalogued upon cards, and the work is progressing on other pamphlets and bound volumes. This has greatly facilitated reference and enabled the secretary to answer many inquiries promptly.

The necrology list includes the following names; as usual, some should have been reported earlier, but the Academy's attention had not been called to their decease:

1. George F. French, Minneapolis, died July 13, 1897. A.B., Harvard, 1859; M.D., 1862. Elected 1882.

2. H. F. Ewers, Burlington, Ia., died March 30, 1899. A.B., Hamilton, 1850; M.D., Castleton, Vt., 1854. Elected 1889.

3. George E. Tyler, Denver, Col., died July, 1902. B.S., Kansas Normal College, 1890; post-graduate work in Washington; M.D., Long Island College Hospital, 1896. Elected 1901.

4. Edwin F. Wilson, Columbus, O., died August 18, 1902. A.B., Kenyon, 1882; M.D., Univ. Pennsylvania, 1885. Elected 1888; Vice-President, 1889; Member of the Council 1900.

5. T. H. Phillips, Canton, O., died August 30, 1902. A student at Washington and Jefferson; M.D., Jefferson Med. Coll., 1864; A.M., Washington and Jefferson, 1890. Elected 1897.

6. Rudolph Virchow, Berlin, Germany, died September 5, 1902. Honorary member, elected in 1901.

7. Morris J. Asch, New York, died October 5, 1902. A.B., Univ. of Pennsylvania, 1852; A.M., 1855; M.D., Jefferson Med. Coll., 1855. Elected 1879.

8. Eugene G. Carpenter, Columbus, O., died October 19, 1902. A.B., Ohio Wesleyan Univ., 1882; M.D., Coll. Physicians and Surgeons, of Baltimore, 1884. Elected 1899.

9. F. A. Packard, Philadelphia, died November 1, 1902. A.B., Univ. of Penna., 1882; M.D., 1885. Elected 1888.

10. Robert Kedzie, Agricultural College, Mich., died November 7, 1902. A.B., Oberlin, 1847; M.D., Univ. of Michigan, 1851; A.M., Oberlin, 1865. Elected 1879.

11. J. W. Lash, Chillicothe, O., died December 12, 1902. A.B., Ohio University, 1875; M.D., Columbus Medical College, 1878. Elected 1891.

12. Mary Willits, Norristown, Pa., died December 16, 1902. A.B., Swarthmore, 1876; M.D., Woman's Med. Coll. of Pennsylvania, 1881. Elected 1898.

13. C. W. Gumbes, Oaks, Pa., died January 31, 1903. A.B., Univ. of Penna., 1861; M.D., Jefferson Medical Coll., 1864. Elected 1890.

14. C. F. Ulrich, Wheeling, died February 18, 1903. A.B., Bethany, 1846; M.D., Univ. of Louisville, 1870. Elected 1897.

15. Norton Strong, U. S. A., retired, died March 23, 1903. A.B., Racine, 1873; M.D., Chicago Med. Coll., 1879. Elected 1897.

16. Edmund Ludlow, Paxton, Ill., died April 5, 1903. A.B., Northwestern Univ., 1892; M.D., 1895. Elected 1896.

On motion the report of the Council was received and adopted.

The secretary read 32 applications for fellowship in the Academy recommended for election by the Council. By unanimous vote, the secretary was authorized to cast the ballot of the Academy in favor of the applicants, which was done, and they were declared elected. The secretary read the following:

COSMOS CLUB, WASHINGTON, D. C., May 11, 1903.

MY DEAR SIR: The Board of Management of this club wishes to extend, through you, the courtesies of the club to the visiting members of the Academy of Medicine, during the present meetings.

To DR. CRAIG, *Secretary.*   Very truly yours,
    [Signed]   L. O. HOWARD, *Secretary.*

On motion, the invitation of the Cosmos Club was accepted and the secretary instructed to tender the thanks of the Academy for the courtesy.

The report of the treasurer was read and on motion referred to an Auditing Committee. The chair appointed Drs. D. C. Hawley and F. H. Gerrish on that committee.

The chair also appointed Drs. C. M. Culver, of Albany, W. L. Estes, of South Bethlehem, Pa., and H. Bert Ellis, of Los Angeles, as the committee on nominations.

The next item of business was action upon the proposed amendments to the constitution. The president announced that he was of the opinion that adopting the report of the Council replaced the amendments as proposed at Saratoga, with the suggested substitute, and, unless objection was made, he would so rule.

Copies of the substitute were distributed to the fellows, and on motion action on the amendments was deferred, being made the first order of business for Tuesday morning, in order that the fellows might inform themselves of the substitute.

NEW BUSINESS.

Dr. Edward Jackson, chairman of the Program Committee, reported an additional paper for the program, by Dr. H. Bert Ellis, of Los Angeles, on "The Necessity for a National Bureau of Medicine and Foods."

Dr. Helen C. Putnam, of Providence, offered the following:

Resolved, "That the president appoint a committee of three to report on the teaching of school hygiene at the next annual meeting of the Academy, with the probability of continuance for further service in the line of medical sociology."

The resolution was seconded and referred to the Council.

Dr. V. C. Vaughan presented the following:

Resolved, "That the president appoint a committee of three to act with the American Association for the Advancement of Science, in erecting a monument to the late Dr. Walter Reed."

The Academy rose from executive session and listened to the rest of the day's program in open session. Vice-President D. C. Hawley occupied the chair.

The report of the committee on "Time Allowance in the Combined Collegiate and Medical Course"[1] was read by the chairman, Dr. A. L. Benedict, of Buffalo. On motion the report was received and ordered to be printed in the Bulletin.

The report on "The Results of the State Examinations for Licensure for 1902" was presented by Dr. Charles McIntire. The report was on motion accepted.

Dr. H. Bert Ellis, of Los Angeles, read a paper entitled "The Necessity for a National Bureau of Medicines and Foods." The paper was discussed by Drs. A. L. Benedict, S. A. Knopf, V. C. Vaughan, T. D. Davis, and in closing, by Dr. Ellis. A motion prevailed referring the paper to the Council, with the request that it formulate a minute on the suggestions.

Dr. James H. McBride, of Pasadena, California, read a paper entitled "The Life and Education of Our Girls as Affecting Their Future," which was discussed by Drs. Walter L. Pyle, S. A. Knopf, and by Dr. McBride in closing.

At the conclusion of the discussion recess was taken until three o'clock.

Reconvening, the Academy held a symposium upon "The Teaching of Hygiene in the Public Schools." The following papers were presented:

1. "The Teaching of Personal Hygiene," by Dr. Walter L. Pyle, of Philadelphia.

2. "Physiology vs. Hygiene in Our Public Schools," by Dr. George G. Groff, of Bucknell University.

3. "The Teaching of Physiological Breathing," by Dr. G. Hudson-Makuen, of Philadelphia.

4. "The Desirable Organization for a Department of Hygiene in Public Schools," by Dr. Helen C. Putnam, of Providence.

5. "The Michigan Method," by Dr. V. C. Vaughan, of the University of Michigan.

6. "The Training of Teachers," by Dr. Thomas D. Wood, of the Teachers' Training College of Columbia University.

The discussion was opened by the Hon. William T. Harris, United States Commissioner of Education, and continued by Drs.

[1] See page 343.

T. D. Davis, S. A. Knopf, F. H. Gerrish, James H. McBride, W. R. White, A. L. Benedict, Edward Jackson, and in closing the discussion, Drs. Walter L. Pyle, G. Hudson-Makuen, Helen C. Putnam, and V. C. Vaughan.

At the conclusion of the discussion a recess was taken until 8.30, when the Academy reconvened with Vice-President Dr. William R. White in the chair, and listened to the address of the president, Dr. Charles McIntire, on "Muck-Rake Methods in Medical Practice."[1] At the conclusion of the address the Academy adjourned until Tuesday morning.

ARLINGTON HOTEL, WASHINGTON, May 12, 1903.

The Academy met at 10.25 A.M., in executive session. The proposed amendments to the constitution were taken up, the substitute reading:

SUBSTITUTE FOR AMENDMENTS OFFERED AT SARATOGA.

A. Insert "advisory" after "fellows" in Article III, Section 1, making it read:

"The membership of the Academy shall consist of fellows, advisory, and honorary members."

B. Make a new section in Article III to be numbered 3, as follows:

SECTION 3. Advisory members shall consist of those elected under the provision of Article IV of the constitution.

Renumber present sections 3, 4, and 5, making them 5, 6, and 7.

C. Article IV. Advisory members.

SECTION 1. Advisory members of the American Academy of Medicine shall be those, who, while not eligible for fellowship, are interested in its objects, elected from time to time by the Academy, to secure their cooperation and assistance in its work.

SECTION 2. Advisory members must be alumni of respectable institutions of learning, having received therefrom a degree after residence and examination.

SECTION 3. Advisory members shall be nominated to the Council by the written statement of two fellows. This statement must include the name, with the place and date of birth of the candidate; the educational institutions attended, length of residence, the degrees conferred, with the date of their conferring; positions held and present occupation and residence. The Council shall present to the Academy for its consideration, those who, in the opinion of the Council, should be elected advisory members.

[1] See page 321.

SECTION 4. The election of advisory members shall follow the rule for the election of fellows.

SECTION 5. Advisory members shall have the privileges of the floor of the Academy in all meetings, of presenting papers, of participating in the discussion of all papers and reports, and of cooperating in all investigations or researches made by the Academy. They shall have no other privileges other than those specifically given them by the constitution.

SECTION 6. The financial obligation of advisory members shall be the same as of fellows.

SECTION 7. Honorary advisory members may be elected by the fellows from among those who have made important contributions to medical sociology. They shall not exceed five for every one hundred fellows, shall be elected in the same manner as honorary fellows and shall have the same privileges.

Renumber the remaining articles.

The discussion showed grave doubts of the wisdom of the changes upon the part of many and, upon motion of Dr. Jackson, duly seconded, consideration of the amendments was postponed indefinitely.

The Council reported upon the resolutions referred to it as follows :

1. It recommends the adoption of the resolution offered by Dr. Putnam, without any reference to the possible continuance of the committee, the resolution to read :

Resolved, " That the president appoint a committee of three to investigate the teaching of hygiene in our public schools, and to report to the Academy at its next meeting.

The resolution was adopted upon motion.

As to the resolution offered by Dr. Vaughan, appointing a committee to coöperate in securing a monument in memory of Dr. Walter Reed, it recommends that since the work of Dr. Reed belongs rather to the science of biology and the allied branches than to medical sociology, no action be taken at this meeting other than to recommend the cause to the interests of the fellows as individuals.

The recommendation of the Council was adopted on motion.

As to the resolution regarding Dr. Ellis' paper, since the paper was not as yet in the possession of the Council, it can make no recommendation on the conclusions themselves. It recommends that the conclusions be referred to the Council to report at the next annual meeting.

The recommendation of the Council was adopted by a vote of the Academy.

The Council submitted additional applications for membership, recommending their election. The secretary was instructed to cast the ballot for the Academy in favor of their election, which was done and the gentlemen were elected.

The Auditing Committee reported examining the treasurer's books and the vouchers, and that they found the accounts to correspond with the report submitted. The report of the committee was, on motion, received and adopted.

The Academy at this point entered upon a scientific session. The first paper of the morning was entitled " Gonorrhoea as a Social Danger," by Dr. Prince A. Morrow, of New York, which was discussed by Drs. Gerrish, Bulkley, Benedict, and Risley.

The president interrupted the discussion to ask the pleasure of the Academy. The time assigned to the symposium of the morning was already past, and the chairman of the Program Committee had impressed the chair with the necessity of observing the time-table.

A motion prevailed for the discussion on Dr. Morrow's paper to be arrested at this point, to be resumed after the symposium of the morning.

The symposium on "Required and Elective Studies in the Medical Course," was opened by the following papers:

1. "Electives in Anatomy," by Dr. F. H. Gerrish, of Portland, Me.
2. "The Teaching of Pathology in the Medical Curriculum," by Dr. W. H. Welch, of Baltimore.
3. "Internal Medicine: To What Extent Required or Elective in the Medical Course," by Dr. S. G. Bonney, of Denver.
4. "Required and Elective Dermatology," by Dr. L. Duncan Bulkley, of New York.
5. "A Theory and a Condition as Illustrated in Ophthalmology," by Dr. Edward Jackson, of Denver.

The papers were discussed by Drs. V. Y. Bowditch, L. Duncan Bulkley, and Edward Jackson.

The last paper on the program was entitled "How the Modern Physician Can Influence in Decreasing the Birth-Rate," by Dr. Roland G. Curtin, of Philadelphia.

The Academy held an executive session at the conclusion of Dr. Curtin's paper.

The Nominating Committee presented the following report:

For President: John B. Roberts, Philadelphia.
For 1st Vice-President: Thomas D. Davis, Pittsburg.
For 2nd Vice-President: James H. McBride, Pasadena, Cal.
For 3rd Vice-President: J. T. Searcy, Tuscaloosa, Ala.
For 4th Vice-President: S. A. Knopf, New York.
For Secretary: Charles McIntire, Easton, Pa.
For Treasurer: Edgar M. Green, Easton, Pa.
For Assistant Secretary: Alex R. Craig, Columbia, Pa.

Dr. D. C. Hawley, vice-president, in the chair:

It was moved and seconded that the report of the committee be received, and that Dr. A. L. Benedict be authorized to cast the ballot of the Academy for the nominations. This was done and the chair announced the election.

The Council presented an additional name for fellowship, and the secretary was instructed to cast the ballot for the Academy, and he was declared elected.

Dr. Charles McIntire, president, in the chair:

The president appointed Drs. Helen C. Putnam, Edward Jackson, and George G. Groff as the committee to investigate the teaching of hygiene in the public schools.

Dr. Edward Jackson, chairman of the Committee on Honorary members, nominated Dr. Mary Putnam Jacobi, of New York. On motion the report was received and the secretary instructed to cast the ballot for the Academy, which was done, and Dr. Jacobi was elected.

Dr. Edward Jackson moved that the Academy tender a vote of thanks to the management of the Arlington Hotel for their courtesies, and to the retiring officers for their very efficient services. The motion was seconded and adopted.

The president-elect having been called home, could not be presented to the Academy. A motion prevailed, empowering him to make the appointments at his leisure.

On motion the Academy adjourned.

The following were elected to fellowship during the meeting:

Henry Page Abbott, Providence, R. I.
Theodore B. Appel, Lancaster, Pa.
B. J. Barker, Bath, Me.
O. G. A. Barker, Pittsburg.
J. W. Brannan, New York.
Norman Bridge, Los Angeles, Cal.
James S. Carpenter, Pottsville, Pa.
Donald Churchill, Providence.
H. A. Cooke, Providence.
F. J. B. Cordeiro, U. S. N.
G. H. Crooker, Providence.
W. B. Cutts, Providence.
Halsey De Wolf, Providence.
F. T. Fulton, Providence.
A. W. Gray, Milwaukee.
P. D. Hoover, Waynesboro, Pa.
H. J. Hoye, Providence.
Henry Kunkel, Kingston, Pa.
Isaac Leopold, Philadelphia.
M. B. Milman, Providence.
C. L. Mix, Chicago.
Wallace Neff, Washington.
W. M. Ogle, Delaware City, Del.
H. R. Price, Brooklyn.
Walter Roberts, Philadelphia.
Henry Sewell, Denver.
H. Straub Sherer, Bangor, Pa.
G. E. Shoemaker, Philadelphia.
E. E. Small, Pittsburg.
C. L. Stevens, Athens, Pa.
W. S. Thompson, Standish, Me.
S. C. P. Turner, Philadelphia.
Marx White, Minneapolis.
R. L. Wilbur, Stanford University, Cal.
Hiram Woods, Baltimore.
Walter Wyman, U. S. Public Health and Marine Hospital Service.

The following fellows and honorary members were registered at the meeting:

CALIFORNIA—H. Bert Ellis, *Los Angeles;* Jas. H. McBride, *Pasadena.*
COLORADO—Sherman G. Bonney, Edward Jackson, John Chase, *Denver.*
CONNECTICUT—Walter R. Steiner, *Hartford.*
DISTRICT OF COLUMBIA—Geo. N. Acker, E. A. Balloch, Walter Wyman, *Washington.*
MAINE—Alonzo Garçelon, *Lewiston;* F. H. Gerrish, S. H. Weeks, J. A. Spalding, *Portland.*
MARYLAND—W. W. Ford, W. H. Welch, *Baltimore.*
MASSACHUSETTS—V. Y. Bowditch, H. O. Marcy, Jr., *Boston.*
MICHIGAN—V. C. Vaughan, *Ann Arbor.*
MINNESOTA—H. A. Tomlinson, *St. Peter.*
MISSOURI—W. McN. Miller, *Columbia.*
NEW YORK—C. M. Culver, *Albany;* A. L. Benedict, *Buffalo;* L. Duncan Bulkley, S. A. Knopf, P. A. Morrow, R. W. Wilcox, *New York;* Wheelock Rider, *Rochester;* J. L. Heffron, *Syracuse.*
PENNSYLVANIA—C. L. Stevens, *Athens;* Alex. R. Craig, *Columbia;* E. M. Green, Charles McIntire, *Easton;* J. K. Weaver, *Norristown;* R. G. Curtin, Geo. M. Gould, G. Hudson-Makuen, W. L. Pyle, S. D. Risley, J. B. Roberts, J. B. Walker. *Philadelphia;* T. D. Davis, *Pittsburg;* W. L. Estes, *South Bethlehem.*
RHODE ISLAND—G. S. Matthews, H. G. Miller, Helen C. Putnam, S. A. Welch, W. R. White, *Providence.*
VERMONT—D. C. Hawley, *Burlington.*
VIRGINIA—J. S. Davis, *Charlottesville.*

OBSERVATIONS IN PASSING.
THE WASHINGTON MEETING.

The transactions of the 28th annual meeting appear on other pages of this number. It remains briefly to record the results of the meeting.

The papers and discussions were, all of them, of interest, and most of them of decided value. . As these are to be published, our readers may form their own estimates. At the same time, the subjects of some of them should receive further investigation. Among these may be mentioned:

I. The report of the committee on "Time Allowance in the Combined Collegiate and Medical Course." The conclusions of the committee should receive careful attention, and the subject should be kept before our colleges and medical schools until a scheme is devised which will enable the independent college to coordinate its course with the unattached medical school as thoroughly and effectively as is now done in many of our universities having an undergraduate department and a medical school. It is to be hoped that this subject will not be lost sight of.

II. The symposium on "The Teaching of Hygiene in the Public Schools" emphasized the importance of this subject to such a degree that a committee was appointed to continue the investigation and to report at the next meeting. It may be safely said that this committee will present more than destructive criticism upon the present methods.

III. The remaining symposium, relating to the possibility of elective in the medical course, was also timely and should be followed up by additional papers and discussion. The question of the medical curriculum demanded by the times cannot be determined except after the most careful study, viewing the subject from the standpoint of the college faculty, of the student, of the examining board, of the existing practiser, and of the public. Each class has a vital, personal interest in the subject, and the fuller the philosophic discussion, the fewer empiric experiments necessary.

The Academy is to be congratulated for its excellent work, provided thereby it will be dissatisfied with it, and standing on the actual, reach up and out for the higher possible results quite within its grasp should it but strive to reach them.

****

Now that our census office has been made continuous in its workings, there should be an effort to tabulate the vital statistics from every part of the land with accuracy. Only in this way will we be able to secure the results at all comparable with those issued by Great Britain. To make the results of the highest utility, two things are necessary. First, and most important, every state should have a compulsory registration law and provide for its execution. Secondly, there should be uniformity in the method of reporting.

The census office, in conjunction with the American Public Health Association, is striving to accomplish this by securing favorable legislation in the various states. The subject was brought to the attention of the Council of the American Academy of Medicine, at Washington. The Council, while in favor of the plan, did not see its way clear to recommend any action upon the communication presented to it, for the reason that the letter expressed a hope "that some united action will be taken by all persons interested to advance the movement in your state.

"I will be pleased to have you bring this matter to the attention of your Society, with the view of determining some definite plan of action in conjunction with other local societies to this end."

As no less than fifteen states were represented in the membership present at the meeting, the Academy was in no way able to comply with the request. But this does not prevent the active participants of its membership in the attempt to secure this much-to-be-desired legislation.

LITERATURE NOTES.

SEVENTEENTH ANNUAL REPORT OF THE COMMISSIONER OF LABOR, 1902. Trade and Technical Education. 1333 pp.

The 8th annual report of the commissioner was devoted essentially to the same subject, and this report may be looked upon as a review and a revision of the first report. The advance in trade education has been so great in the years separating the two reports as to require an entirely different treatment of the subject, so that looking at it from another view-point, this report is new and, in a sense, independent of the other report. Commissioner Wright is entitled to the thanks of all who are interested in educational matters for the varied and valuable information he has collected in this volume.

UNIVERSITY OF THE STATE OF NEW YORK. Bulletin 280, March, 1903. College Department Bulletin 20. Director's Report, 1902. Price, 20 cents.

This report gives the results of registration and licensing of the various professions and vocations placed under the supervision of the regents. The results of the medical examinations are incorporated in the annual report issued in the Bulletin. In connection with these examinations, one feature of the separate boards of examiners is worthy of mention. There were 1,043 examinations during the year covered by the report 928 before the board representing the state medical society, 88 before the board representing the homeopathic medical society, and 27 before the eclectic medical society board. The honorarium paid to each examiner varies with the fees paid by those who come before them for examination, after certain necessary expenses are deducted. Hence each examiner of the board representing the state medical society receives a little more than $1,300 for his year's labors, while less than $1,000 were available for the entire homeopathic board, and less than $200 for the eclectics.

SIR JAMES PAGET IN HIS WRITINGS: BIBLIOGRAPHY. BY HELEN C. PUTNAM, A.B., M.D. Read by appointment at the 91st annual meeting of the Rhode Island Medical Society, June 5, 1902, and reprinted from the transactions. Cloth. 24 pp.

Dr. Putnam has given us a demonstration of the proposition she quotes from Phillips Brooks—that the writings of any one makes "the subtlest form in which biography can take its shape." She has, with painstaking thoroughness, gathered his writings and given us a personal view of one of England's greatest surgeons of the last century.

TRANSACTIONS OF MEDICAL SOCIETIES.

I. TRANSACTIONS OF THE COLLEGE OF PHYSICIANS OF PHILADELPHIA. Third series, Vol. XXIV. xcii + 341 pp.

II. TRANSACTIONS OF THE MAINE MEDICAL ASSOCIATION, 1902. Vol. XIV, Part 2. 225-453 pp.

III. TRANSACTIONS LUZERNE COUNTY (PENNSYLVANIA) MEDICAL SOCIETY, FOR THE YEAR ENDING DECEMBER 31, 1902. 162 pp.

REPORTS OF STATE BOARDS OF HEALTH.

I. TWELFTH REPORT OF THE STATE BOARD OF HEALTH OF MAINE FOR THE TWO YEARS ENDING DECEMBER 31, 1901. Augusta : 1902. xviii + 304 pp.

II. THIRTY-THIRD ANNUAL REPORT OF THE STATE BOARD OF HEALTH OF MASSACHUSETTS. Boston : 1902. xlvii + 615 pp.

III. TWENTY-FIFTH ANNUAL REPORT OF THE STATE BOARD OF HEALTH OF THE STATE OF CONNECTICUT FOR THE YEAR 1902. New Haven : 1903. xxv + 264, 276 pp.

IV. TWENTY-NINTH ANNUAL REPORT OF THE SECRETARY OF THE STATE BOARD OF HEALTH OF THE STATE OF MICHIGAN, FOR THE FISCAL YEAR ENDING JUNE 30, 1901. xxxiv + 264 pp.

I. Nothing of a medico-social nature is to be found in this volume excepting, remotely, the very valuable paper on "Infant Feeding," by Dr. Young, the secretary of the board.

II. As becomes the special work of the Massachusetts, admirably conducted now over a number of years, the report gives prominence to water supply and sewage disposal. An interesting item upon malaria is to be found on page 515.

III. This report contains the results of the examinations for licensure to practise medicine, that appear in the annual tabulation prepared for the Bulletin.

IV. This report continues the excellent studies by Secretary Baker, of the prevalence of communicable diseases of Michigan, that has made the previous volumes so valuable.

The Medical Critic has placed the profession under obligations by publishing a very complete index medicus for 1902 in its April number. Of its 268 pages, 256 are taken up with the index. It seems to be carefully compiled, and convenient in arrangement.

BULLETIN

OF THE

American Academy of Medicine

VOL. VI.   ISSUED AUGUST, 1903.   NO. 7.

The American Academy of Medicine is not responsible for the sentiments expressed in any paper or address published in the BULLETIN.

THE TEACHING OF HYGIENE IN THE PUBLIC SCHOOLS.

I.

THE TEACHING OF PERSONAL HYGIENE.[1]

By WALTER L. PYLE, A.M., M.D., Assistant Surgeon to Wills Eye Hospital, Philadelphia.

Strange as it may seem, the one subject which every fair-minded person admits should be taught to school-children, namely, how to keep healthy, has been largely neglected by educational reformers. There is continual bickering and babbling about what should be taught and what omitted. Every little while a new educational fetish is urged or adopted, and each year sees the demolition of many. The pupils complain of the excessive study required, and the parents protest that their children seem to learn very little. But with all the agitation for educational reform there remains, to a great degree, the same indifference to the proper teaching of the care of the body, regarding which Herbert Spencer lectured the pedagogic world over forty years ago.

Mr. Spencer showed that knowledge may have intrinsic value, and that the value of some knowledge must be greater than that of others. In our brief lives it is most necessary to distinguish and give precedence to the useful, real, and effective over the non-

[1] Read before the American Academy of Medicine, Washington, D. C., May 11, 1903.

useful, conventional and ornamental; or, to use a Baconian phrase, "we must determine the relative value of knowledges." All knowledge passes into action, and that knowledge that leads men to better physical lives is a communal as well as an individual gain. Mr. Spencer says that in the order of their importance the leading kinds of activity which constitute human life, are :

1. Those activities which directly minister to self-preservation ;
2. Those activities which, by securing the necessaries of life, indirectly minister to self-preservation ;
3. Those activities which have for their end the rearing and disciplining of offspring ;
4. Those activities which are involved in the maintenance of proper social and political relations ;
5. Those miscellaneous activities which make up the leisure part of life, devoted to the gratification of the taste and feelings.

In other words, a rational order of subordination is : Education which prepares for a direct self-preservation ; that which prepares for an indirect self-preservation ; that which prepares for parenthood; that which prepares for citizenship ; and that which prepares for miscellaneous refinements.

It is stated with great emphasis that without doubt the actions and precautions which from moment to moment secure self-preservation are of primary importance; and that "as vigorous health and its accompanying high spirits are larger elements of happiness than any other things whatsoever, the teaching how to maintain them is a teaching that should yield in moment to no other whatever."

Fortunately knowledge subserving direct self-preservation is largely provided for by nature. The common animal instincts give warning against gross dangers. The inquisitive, timid, restless infant is chiefly concerned in hourly acquisition of the primitive faculties of co-ordination, estimation of distance, size, consistency and weight, the avoidance of things likely to cause pain, the assimilation of food, etc. Throughout childhood and youth there is a further elaboration of these primal requisites. But more than this is necessary; for, besides the mechanical dangers, there are the evils following breaches of physiologic laws. Unfortunately, so profound is the innate ignorance of these laws of life that often it is not even known that our sensations are our natural and most trustworthy guides. The less evident but no less real dangers arising from the complexities of modern social life and the attendant evil habits are continually present despite all innate instincts of warning. The pernicious influence of improper food and bad air, the abuse of stimulants and narcotics, the modern dissipations and vices, etc., can only be modified by proper and timely education.

It has been said that "health is man's birthright; that it is as natural to be well as to be born;" and that from ignorance and transgressions of physiologic and hygienic laws, arise all disease and tendency to disease. Yet, to-day, so tardy has been the recognition of the importance of instruction in the fundamental principles of applied physiology as a means to complete living, that a thoroughly well person after middle life is the exception in every community. On every side we find chronic complaint, physical weakness, weariness and overwhelming gloom, which might have been prevented by proper, timely instruction. Besides the individual suffering, time and money are ruthlessly wasted, commercial and artistic instincts are curtailed, good parenthood and citizenship are rendered impossible, appreciation of amusement is dulled, and, besides being immensely deteriorated, life is markedly shortened. "Is it not clear," asked Mr. Spencer, "that the physical sins—partly our forefathers and partly our own—which produce this ill-health, deduct more from complete living than anything else? and to a greater extent make life a failure and a burden instead of a benefaction and a pleasure?"

It is not merely the teaching of the rules of hygiene that are needed, nor the ordinary course in school-physiology. Personal hygiene is applied physiology, and a proper understanding of certain elemental truths must be acquired before they can be applied. Knowledge of the normal functions of the body and the simple methods of keeping them in healthy action is the one thing that no educated person should be excused from possessing; yet, most of our children reach maturity without sufficient parental or scholastic instruction in many essential matters of health. Men and women who would be greatly chagrined to be corrected in the pronunciation of a popular foreign proper name, or who would resent as an insult any imputation as to their lack of general culture or learning, show not the slighest embarrassment at their ignorance of the common physiologic functions of digestion, circulation, respiration, etc., or of the normal pulse-rate or the normal body-temperature. Persons of intelligence continually furnish thoughtless recommendations of purely quack remedies and unscientific instruments and apparatus; and advertisements of these articles may be seen in the best general and religious periodicals.

Unfortunately, this lack of knowledge is not confined to the laity, for we meet medical students and graduates who do not appreciate such an important physiologic truth as the compensatory strain of the ciliary muscle in the subjective correction of hyperopia and astigmatism. I have been frequently told by advanced medical students that atropin was used by oculists in testing the eyes for correcting lenses, because it dilated the pupil, with not a hint of its action on the ciliary muscle—an inexcusable ignorance of the mechanism of eye-strain. From a reading of Dr. George M. Gould's "Biographic Clinics," it seems most likely that Mr. Spencer himself, as well as his colleague, Mr. Huxley, who was especially noted for his physiologic learning, both suffered all their lives from reflexes consequent upon uncorrected or improperly ametropia.

Concerning the popular desire of the British University patrons for the classical instruction, Mr. Spencer says: "While anxious that their sons should be well up in the superstitions of two thousand years ago, they care not that they should be taught anything about the structures and functions of their own bodies— nay, would even disapprove such instruction. So overwhelming is the influence of established routine ! So terribly in our education does the ornamental override the useful !" Is this not a fairly applicable arraignment of not a few American parents, especially as to a daughter's education ? Yet, it is to the mothers of to-day that the regimen of the nursery, the rearing of children, the preparation of food, and the problems of domestic hygiene are largely left.

Most cases of illness are preventable, and Mr. Huxley says we should look upon them as criminal. Illness following disobedience of physiologic laws should be regarded as the punitive result of reprehensible conduct, and not as a simple grievance. There is such a thing as physical morality, and the preservation of health should be considered as a sacred duty. Persons who treat their bodies as they please, and transgress the rules of personal hygiene, of which they have a definite understanding, are physical sinners, and they are not only committing a sin against themselves, but often against their dependents and future generations.

Returning to the practical teaching of personal hygiene, we find that the ordinary instruction in physical education, physiology, dietetics, and exercise is not sufficient, and often faulty. It is not desirable to produce athletes, physical-culture fanatics, or practitioners of new-fangled and erratic "systems" and "pathies." What is needed is simple instruction by capable teachers in the proper care and use of the body, authoritatively based upon the best available modern anatomic, physiologic and hygienic data. We should not have "every man his own physician," as seems often the object in lectures, periodicals, and books relating to health; rather give every man fundamental knowledge that will enable him to understand, and, if necessary, formulate the requisite rules of health, and to distinguish scientific medicine from quackery. Stripped of its superfluous technicalities this knowledge may be imparted to any one of average intelligence and education, and we should strongly urge more literature and personal explanation in this direction from the medical profession. The subject is much too important to be left entirely in the hands of lay teachers and writers.

The literature for the laymen pertaining to personal hygiene is in great measure unsatisfactory and irresponsible. Many of the so-called "Health Books" are of very questionable authorship; often the compilation of a layman; perhaps an amateur pathologist, an inaccurate physiologist, a moralist of vague opinions, with unfortunately a tendency to cater to the prurient, and with unnecessary and indecent expositions of sexual matters. Such books make hypochondriacs of their readers, and if they include advice as to self-treatment, they may do great harm.

Granted that one of the most important functions of a physician is to instruct the public on necessary social and medical matters, regarding which, by nature of his profession, he is especially informed, he must proceed with great caution, neither making his science too popular nor his popular exposition too scientific. In a recent editorial in the *British Medical Journal*, there is given the following pertinent advice to medical lecturers or writers on hygienic subjects: "In addressing the laity, the physician should above all things make it clear that his function is not either primarily or secondarily that of an itinerant preacher of as much of the gospel of medicine and hygiene as he is able to put in popular form, and induce his hearers or readers to accept. Any such attitude is fatal to the respect owing him by the public, to whom he stands as a learned man. When he recognizes a morbid attitude on the part of humanity at large with regard to things hygienic, his duty is to stem and correct it where he can, but certainly not to add to it on the pretext of giving it satisfaction."

In regard to the delicate sexual problems it concludes:

"If we may speak for parents in the medical profession it is impossible to suppose that wise fathers and mothers could desire to suggest to their sons or daughters either certain problems raised, or, in many cases, the explanations proffered. There is a multitude of the best parents who think that their way is not made easier by the so-called moral reformer, but rather the reverse. And there are many of the most wholesome-minded boys and sweetest girls who hate him with a perfect hatred. The rest would probably do very well without him."

It is necessary to begin the instruction of personal hygiene before habits of carelessness and indifference are formed, and for this reason the preparatory school is by all means the place where the Gospel of Health should first be promulgated. The prevention of disease and disorders of the body ought to be among the first lessons in every rational scheme of education.

We have said much of the system, and, as yet, little of the teacher. Emerson once wrote to his daughter, "It matters little what your studies are, it all lies in who your teacher is." But, unfortunately, the ordinary teachers, like the parents, have not been trained to impart the proper knowledge of personal hygiene. I am glad to say, however, that recently, attempts have been made to correct this pedagogic fault; for instance, there has just been inaugurated at the new Teachers' College of the Columbia University in New York City, a praiseworthy attempt to train teachers "To teach health." They will not be trained as physicians or nurses, but as capable teachers of the proper care and use of the human body.

In editorial comment upon this innovation, a prominent magazine (*World's Work*, February, 1903), says: "It may not be extravagant to say that this same movement is of larger possible benefit than anything which has hitherto been done in the name of Education; for if it should ever come to pass that every pupil in the public schools should be brought naturally to a proper understanding of health and its relations to every other part of life and conduct, such a chance for the advancement of the human race would be given as no considerable section of society has yet ever had. If all easily preventable physical troubles were prevented, such an addition would be made to the energy and the good sense of the people as defies description. A merely incidental item of such social progress would be the incalculable saving of the money spent on quackery and of the waste of energy that quackery causes."

II.
PHYSIOLOGY VS. HYGIENE IN OUR PUBLIC SCHOOLS.

By GEORGE G. GROFF, M.D., Bucknell University, Lewisburg, Pa.

There is a wide-spread belief that physiology is a study which properly belongs in the curriculum of our public schools. By the term physiology is commonly meant, matter consisting largely of the elements of physiology and personal hygiene, along with some human anatomy. The text-books which have been in use in the public schools, until a very few years, have been known as works on "Anatomy, Physiology, and Hygiene." The most space and stress is laid in these books upon the anatomy and least upon the hygiene, physiology coming in for an intermediate amount of attention. In reality the order above named should be reversed. To the children of tender years, who form the great mass of those in attendance in the public schools, anatomy is not a science of moment, while hygiene, especially personal hygiene, is of the very first importance.

It is not necessary that the young child should know anything about the structure of its brain, or of its muscles, or of any of its internal organs, but it is of importance that it should know how to care for the brain, the eye, the stomach, the heart and, in a word, the body as a whole. And this can all be taught and taught well, to young children without any knowledge whatever of anatomy or physiology.

Anatomy and physiology should not be taught at all to very young children, for several reasons: 1st. The subjects are in the main beyond their comprehension. To get a clear idea of anatomical structure a person ought to know something of histology and it is practically impossible to teach histology to young children. It is not easy to teach even gross anatomy to persons of any age without proper appliances—models, charts, dry and wet preparations, etc., and without the opportunity of dissecting and observing intimately the structures of the body. And if anatomy is a difficult subject for young children, it is more true of physiol-

[1] Read before the American Academy of Medicine, Washington, D. C., May 11, 1903.

ogy, which is really one of the newest and most complex of the sciences. Physiology, moreover, is really in large part a department of chemistry, and certainly chemistry is not a study for young children.

2nd. Teachers are not generally prepared to teach anatomy and physiology. These are sciences which if taught properly require considerable special preparation. Without a dissection of the body, and without an opportunity to study chemistry in the laboratory, no teacher is very well qualified to do much work in either anatomy or physiology. It is certain that at the present time there are very few teachers in our public schools who are equipped to teach these two sciences.

3rd. The impression received by young children is often very unfavorable, when anatomic structures and physiologic processes are displayed to them. The healthy child is best off when it knows nothing of the activities of its heart, or its stomach; and to display a heart, stomach or brain to a group of young children, such as we have in our public schools, is thought by many competent teachers to be a dangerous experiment. Is is certain that among children and often among adults, harm results from morbid attention being directed to the displaying of internal organisms.

4th. Children can readily comprehend hygienic instruction without any knowledge of anatomy or physiology. It is personal hygiene in which young children need instruction. They do not need either anatomy or physiology in order to receive this hygienic information.

Physiology, as physiology, should generally not be taught below the grade of the high school, because: 1st. Teachers in grammar and primary schools have not, as indicated above, generally the knowledge of the subjects required to impart instruction in the same and without an adequate knowledge, good work cannot be done in these subjects.

2nd. Until pupils reach the high school they are commonly not prepared by mental development or through preparatory studies, for work in anatomy or physiology. It would be much better to devote the time given to this subject in primary and grammar grades to the study of personal hygiene. Too much stress cannot be laid upon teaching the child correct habits of living, although it is believed too much time may be devoted to the subject to the detriment of the pupil's welfare.

3rd. Physiology should be preceded by chemistry, and chemistry is generally not taught until the pupil reaches the high-school grade. Almost all, if not all, of the processes of metabolism occurring within the body, are chemical processes, and it is simply impossible to clearly understand these without at least some elementary knowledge of chemistry. The teacher who has not studied chemistry, can scarcely at this time be considered to be competent to teach physiology.

Personal hygiene is best taught to young children through incidental talks given at suitable times. One lesson a week ought to be sufficient in this subject. When the day is wet, children can be told of the importance of keeping their clothing dry. When the air is cold and raw, the importance of preventing the body from becoming chilled can be explained. When a heavy rain has caused the drinking-water to become turbid, danger from impure water could be explained to the class. In personal hygiene the time and manner of imparting the instruction is important, and especially should teachers be careful not to overdo the work of warning children against evident dangers, for warnings too often repeated are more liable to be neglected than if less frequently referred to.

Instruction in public hygiene (state medicine) is now almost wholly neglected, but should be extended to grammar and high-school grades. Public hygiene, also personal hygiene, may in large part be taught without any connection with anatomy and physiology, and yet there is not a book of all the hundreds in use in the public schools that contains any matter on public hygiene. It would be well for authors of publications along this line to devise a series of school books, one number to be devoted to personal hygiene, a second one to public hygiene and a third to animal physiology. Such a series could be written with no repetition of the matter in any preceding book.

The existing books on physiology now in use in the public schools are characterized by many loose, generalized statements, by inaccurate statements and by statements absolutely false. Indeed it is thought that there are no books in use in the public schools of this country, against which so many criticisms may be urged along the lines above named, as in the case of our school physiologies. To illustrate what is meant by these loose and inaccurate statements, a number from various books, now in use in our public schools, are here appended :

One of the best of these books several times makes the positive assertion that tobacco produces cancer in its users, and also that consumption is caused by alcohol. Another volume asserts that "consumption may be caused by putting on spring clothing too early in the season." One also reads that " Cider drinkers are peculiarly crabbed and cross ; " that "tobacco makes old men ill-natured ; " that " sour milk is unwholesome ; " " Cheese is indigestible ; " " Pork is a meat not fit to eat ; " and " Bile has the properties of baking-soda." " It is not proper to drink water at meals." " Fruits and vegetables in tin cans are dangerous foods." " Cider is a poison." " Insane asylums are filled with farmers' wives and daughters." " Dirt is not allowed to pass the fine hairs in the nose." Speaking of the heart, a physiology for children says: "*Frequently* the weakened walls burst, causing instant death "—delightful reading for children ! " Those muscles which are used most become *longest* and strongest." " In old persons the bones are so brittle that they break very easily." " In old pastures the bones of cattle become tender and are easily broken. The remedy is to supply fertilizers which contain lime." " In infancy, the convolutions of the brain are scarcely visible. They are also more extensive in a studious and thoughtful person than in one who does little thinking." " The snake, under his skin, has four tiny legs which, however, never grow so as to become of use to him in crawling about."

A recent book of this class, speaking of the injuries resulting from tight lacing, says that " the small chest so formed can be transmitted to offspring." It fails to note, however, that small feet so formed are not transmitted, and entirely ignores the present state of our knowledge on heredity, namely, that acquired conditions of the body are not transmitted to offspring. All of these books speak of acquired appetites as becoming transmitted —a statement incapable of proof.

The following are also from public school physiologies, and are literally quoted:

"A badly groomed horse is *never sound nor spirited*, and a dirty pig puts on one-fourth less fat than a clean one." "We should never drink any water that has flowed past any unhealthful place, or has received any foul drainage." This is good advice for the children in Philadelphia, Harrisburg, Pittsburg, Chester and other cities whose diluted sewage is the only beverage offered by the city councils. "You have heard of men who are put into prison for doing bad deeds. Nine out of every ten of these men are led to do these deeds by drinking alcoholic liquor." This statement is unproven. "Fermentation entirely alters the nature of a fruit juice." Not true at all. One book tells that "The discoverer of alcohol very properly died in a drunken stupor," when really nothing is known of the discoverer of alcohol.

"The Esquimaux who live in Greenland, drink one or two quarts of oil, and eat several pounds of candles every day." But see how a fish story will "grow," even in a scientific text-book. The next number of the "series" written by the same author, and doubtless from the same notes, we read: "An Esquimaux consumes about twenty pounds of blubber fat daily, besides drinking several quarts of train oil." What will it be in the next volume, who can tell?

As to the style and accuracy of these "scientific" treatises, the following may be taken as samples: "The eye-ball is a bag (!) almost round, thick and dull everywhere but in front, where it has a transparent cover, called the cornea, meaning a horn. This is fitted into the eye just as a watch crystal is fitted into a watch. The back chamber also holds a jelly-like fluid, called the 'glassy humor,' which allows the iris curtain to float and move freely." What a description of this organ! And there are three volumes of this stuff in the series—pages of it reading like the essays of school girls.

It is held that the time has come for medical men to call a halt in this matter. The curriculum of our public schools is far too much crowded for such matter longer to find a place in it.

III.
THE TEACHING OF PHYSIOLOGIC BREATHING.[1]
By G. HUDSON-MAKUEN, M.D., Philadelphia.

It has been estimated that there are in the United States alone more than 300,000 stammerers, and a careful study of this distressing affliction, as manifested in several hundred cases, has led me to the conclusion that its chief cause is faulty breathing in childhood. Indeed, as I have intimated in another paper, there would be no stammering if children could have the proper training in breathing during the first ten years of their lives. But serious as is the result of faulty breathing upon speech, it is still more far-reaching in its effect upon the health and general development.

Many grave diseases of childhood may be traced directly to an impoverished condition of the blood due to inadequate oxidation. Who is not familiar with the puny, anemic, open-mouthed and narrow-chested child actually and literally starving for want of that life-giving principle, so abundant in all the atmosphere about him. Oxygen is as essential to health as is good food, and it may be had for the taking. Physiologic breathing is its only price.

Breathing is instinctive and automatic. It is the first act of the individual upon coming into the world, and the last act upon going out. It may be defined as alternate contractions and relaxations of the respiratory muscles by which air is drawn through the nostrils into the lungs, where it gives up its oxygen to the pulmonary circulation and takes up effete products, and expels them from the system.

If this breathing is instinctive and automatic, you will ask, why should we call attention to it at all, and why should we teach it in the schools, and my answer is because few people practise it in a truly physiologic manner. There are many obstructions to normal breathing, and when once the natural rhythm of the breathing process is perverted it can never be entirely restored without conscious effort and well-directed practice.

[1] Read before the American Academy of Medicine, Washington, D. C., May 11, 1903.

Physiologic breathing depends upon a normal muscular development. There must be an even balance between the inspiratory and expiratory muscles. A perverted rhythm in breathing is the result of a lack of balance between these two sets of muscles, and it is always followed by an imperfect oxidation of the blood.

The normal respiratory tract is through the nostrils, and, therefore, when the nostrils are obstructed in children there is always a tendency toward an overaction followed by an overdevelopment of the inspiratory muscles. This tendency, however, of forced inspiration through the nostrils, and its resultant overdevelopment of the muscles is soon checked by a substitution of the oral channel for the nasal passages in breathing, and who of us is not familiar with the pernicious effects of this habit? Nasal obstruction then is one of the chief factors in faulty breathing.

Another important factor is the unnatural and cramped position which children are allowed to take in school, and indeed oftentimes out of school. It is not an unusual thing to see children lounging over their desks during the study period, and the attitude which many of them are allowed to assume during the writing period has reminded me of that of some of the invertebrate animals when coiled up for a sun-bath. They literally seem to have no backbone, and the organs of respiration are compressed to such an extent as to render physiologic breathing impossible, and even to interfere with the structural development of the thoracic walls. So great are the deformities acquired in this manner during early youth that no amount of exercise in later life will avail to correct them. Children even more than adults are creatures of habit, and the importance of establishing correct physical habits during school life cannot be overestimated.

I am inclined to believe that with all our much-vaunted improvements in education we are deteriorating in this one particular. We hear much talk about physical education, but is it of the right sort, and is it the result of well-directed scientific effort? Football and baseball are all right in their way, but if pupils are allowed to lounge into careless and unnatural attitudes in the school-room after these games much of their value will be lost.

My own observation is that men and women of the olden times were more graceful and erect in carriage than those of our own day, and I attribute the difference to the fact that more attention was formerly given to correct posture in sitting, standing and walking. I would have children taught the correct postures. I would have teachers insist upon their taking these postures at all times as a preliminary to physiologic breathing.

Physical obstructions to normal breathing should also be removed as early as possible. All breathing exercises are harmful when there are obstructions of any sort in the respiratory tract. We are becoming aroused to the importance of normal vision in school children, but equally important is it that we should have normal breathing, and therefore I would recommend that as we are beginning to make a systematic examination of the eyes so should we insist upon a similar examination of the respiratory tract. Obstructions in the nostrils and pharynx are probably more common in school children than is defective vision, and I am inclined to think that they are fully as productive of harm.

It has been estimated that about 70 per cent. fail to use the nose in breathing at night, and in so doing fail to get the 20 to 40 per cent. of heat, and the 60 per cent. of moisture in the respired air that should come from the nasal passages, and moreover they take into the throat countless germs that would otherwise find lodgment in the vestibules of the nostrils.

The census of 1900 shows that about 40 per cent. of the deaths occurring between twenty and fifty years were due to diseases of the respiratory tract, and I am convinced that faulty breathing is an important factor in the causation of this great mortality, and that the percentage may be much reduced by the scientific teaching of physiologic breathing.

IV.
THE DESIRABLE ORGANIZATION FOR A DEPARTMENT OF HYGIENE IN PUBLIC SCHOOLS.[1]

BY HELEN C. PUTNAM, A.B., M.D., Providence, R. I.

The head of the department of hygiene in public schools should have an academic degree, a medical degree, and experience in the intimate relation of a physician in the homes of the people; unless he has had a few years of this his efforts will be as much along theoretical lines as are those of the majority of teachers, striving to prepare children for a life whose environments, ambitions, temptations—and the results, as well as the results of their own teaching—they know only in very limited extent, much of it at second or third hand, much of it not at all. It is the history of education, in schemes for adjusting the child to its intellectual inheritances, that impulses to progress come from outside "the rank and file" of teachers. The demands of living must direct the adjustment.

In addition to these common qualifications of physicians, he needs training in his proposed specialty, school hygiene, even more than public health officials who recognize the desirability of supplementary courses or schools for sanitarians. He should have intelligent acquaintance with the history and philosophy of education, including sociology, defined by Carroll D. Wright, "the comprehension of the methods and processes by which men grow out of self and into serviceableness to their fellows." He must have sufficient knowledge of the principles of pedagogy, the methods and facts of child study and their practical applications in which German physicians have done much more than American. This means a year's work at Clark University for example.

He must have made scientific study of the theory and practice of body movements, such as a year at the Royal Central Gymnastic Institute in Stockholm provides for physicians. Our public school gymnastics, fully as much as our public school "science teaching," is lamentably handicapped by lack of scientific supervision. He

[1] Read before the American Academy of Medicine, Washington, D. C., May 11, 1903.

should supplement this with study of games (the psychology of play and fatigue he would have in his year of pedagogics). He should make a special study of methods of ventilating, plumbing, school architecture and furnishings. His advice will be needed by school committees of business men who, as a rule, from personal experience know more of the details of these latter affairs than physicians, and who incline to trust plumbers, manufacturers and architects according to their commercial standing or the value of their political influence, neither being a gauge of their intelligence in hygiene. Such men will estimate him shrewdly according to his technical knowledge and practical common sense. The influence of his position will rise or fall with the soundness of his personal attainments, with his tact, social address, and executive skill.

He should associate as assistants a staff of college women and men, of whom our leading educators earnestly desire more in elementary schools, who have taken full courses in natural sciences, including physics and chemistry, thus indicating the direction of their abilities; for it is quite hopeless to attempt to create good scientific teachers out of people whose inclinations and habits have been formed only or chiefly by literary and mathematical work. They must also have had a normal course and, if possible, one in hygiene.

His assistants for gymnastics and games, including swimming which many English day schools give children, and for cooking and some other desirable lines of domestic and municipal sanitation, should have had their training in special schools, of which there are several. *This should be liberal enough, I think, to include ideas of the possibilities of after-school hours, Saturdays and holidays (vacations).* Provision for public playground supervision could well be made from this office, for no other will have an equally intelligent and consistent interest in children's out-of-school environment.

His conception, as an expert, of his courses through the grades should enable him to assist in all technical matters and efficiently guide his staff. His should be no "arm chair" office. He himself should give the graduating classes of high and grammar schools at least a few lessons. If time does not permit both, then certainly he should meet the grammar graduates, for only one-twelfth of pupils continue into the high school; and these eleven-twelfths, both by their lesser education and their probably more harmful conditions of living, need the best wisdom he can give them. It requires special ability to hold, instruct and impress children.

Just what the department of hygiene should teach and how it should be taught, the experiments and experiences of one thus constituted will demonstrate. We can await the results with confidence, and with especial interest because it is practically an unexplored domain, upon which the amateur efforts of the general teacher have thrown little light.

School inspection for communicable diseases is undoubtedly the function of municipal boards of health, for the protection of the community; but practically it must be made by the same inspectors who report on defective eyes and other physical ailments interfering with normal progress. Shall it be by the municipal or by the school health departments?

In either event there should be full coöperation. It is possible that methods may advantageously differ between the small city and metropolis.

I believe it would be wiser to have all medical inspection of school children under the superintendence of the school physician, who would be responsible to the superintendent of health for reporting specified diseases. The reasons for this belief are:

1. Knowledge of individual health conditions is essential to the school physician's proper direction of the school surroundings.

2. The course in physical training on an effective basis will bring in almost daily contact with pupils instructors who have been especially taught to detect anemia, innutrition, defective vision, hearing and respiration, unsymmetrical and other imperfect development, these latter to a greater extent than the general practitioner, since they are those which gymnastics are especially calculated to remove or lessen. In all cases an expert is at hand to consult.

The whole body of teachers also will almost unconsciously become better informed and more alert to observe details because of the influence of such a department in their midst.

3. A staff of medical inspectors, chosen, instructed and held up to a standard by a specialist in school hygiene as municipal health officers are not, for the purpose of looking over the new children on opening days, and to be called upon for service in threatened epidemics or any especial need, will, in addition, to this preventive and direct service to the community, contribute material of scientific and educational value, trustworthy as much of the present crude and irregular work is not.

4. The treatment of cases (instead of directing to secure treatment) is undoubtedly increasing as the movement extends for school inspection according to present methods. This will always be a temptation. It weakens the sense of family and individual responsibility and so works moral harm in the community, as well as injures professional interests in more ways than one. Whether government should go so far in socialism or paternalism as to assume the actual medical care of public school children is a question probably to be negatived. The trained, constant superintendence of school inspection by a well-planned department of school hygiene is the best preventive of this mistake, and the best means of determining the merits of the proposition.

After the first years there will be much less of ordinary service because of what has already been accomplished for the large number of children in the older grades, because of the higher conditions of public health therefrom, because of the spread of information in matters of hygiene, and because of the influence toward better care of children. The wiser the organization of this work the greater those improvements will be. We notice in at least three cities the cessation of appointments of large numbers of general practitioners for short hours and nominal salaries; and, instead, a few qualified inspectors who shall give a large part of their time for a reasonable compensation. This is a logical step in the right direction. From incidental expressions of opinion in the press and elsewhere by legislators and other citizens, I believe there is a considerable amount of intelligent preference for a more careful—shall we say scientific?—introduction of sanitary measures in the schools, *i.e.*, they would give more support to a plan for providing service by physicians who had made special preparation for it.

We need to take into account the attitude of educators themselves on this question. I will begin by quoting the Commissioner of Education: "Not that I doubt the importance of hygiene, but rather that I doubt the attainments of those who *talk* so glibly about it." Many teachers are impressed with the lack of *savoir faire*, desirable from their view point, in meeting school children, exhibited by the average inspector; and, seeing the children constantly as they do, they recognize that while some cases of ill health are found by him, there are many more that go unnoticed. In fact, the practice of relying upon the teacher to pick out ailing children for the daily "clinic," the physician not seeing other pupils, a practice that quite generally obtains both in Germany and America, itself depreciates the office. I recently heard a teacher say: "How can I do anti-cigarette work among my boys when the doctor lays his cigar aside just long enough to bring in a whiff in his clothes?" It reminds one of the complaint from the district school-teacher made in Horace Mann's Common School Journal sixty-five years ago about the tobacco-chewing committeeman as a school visitor.[1]

One physician who has been active in school inspection candidly admits that health reports of the same school under different inspectors bear quite different aspects: a matter of faithfulness and capacity on the part of a poorly paid general practitioner who must earn a living outside this service to a rich community.

The present superficiality—due chiefly to lack of time, method, standard and special preparation—contributes to such quiet dissatisfaction as exists among professional friends as well as among teachers.

American teachers have not yet expressed themselves on this subject with fulness or authority. But in individual and small ways indications are found of reasonable dissatisfaction, and as many more of ignorance of the situation, and of prejudice. I have personally heard more approval of the institution of school nurse, who follows children to their homes, teaches hygiene there, and hastens their return in proper condition. Mothers, too, often express gratitude for this practical instruction. A class for training

[1] Since writing the above, information concerning more grave offenses by certain medical officials in the public schools, too regrettable to be discussed, has been given me. They were "hushed up" in the city where they occurred.

mothers of school children would be a valuable adjunct to this department. The school nurse and mothers' club are two methods.

In Germany many teachers have discussed the subject and in at least one instance have taken formal action against the kind of inspection now on trial there as well as here. Their suggested substitute is health certificates given by physicians who do not visit in the schools, leaving much more to regular school officers, including a "supervising school physician" whose province seems to be oversight of sanitary conditions. There is a quite prevalent opinion that the general practitioner is not fitted to take up this work, and at least two universities offer courses (incomplete, I think) for preparing school physicians. This is suggestive to our own universities. Their teaching of hygiene is not in advance of ours, nor their practice.

The relation of our proposed school physician to the superintendent of schools would correspond with that of college professor of hygiene or resident physician to the college president. Both, selected for intelligence as well as expert capacity, are working for the same end. The superintendent of schools is the official head of that branch of the city government. The professorships are to provide the several lines essential to public school education. The department of hygiene would be one. In time, others will evolve.

The relation of the department of instruction in "applied physiology" to "science teaching" is of practical importance. Coördination is demanded throughout school programs to economize time and strength for the best advantage of the child. It is especially practicable here. Every liberally educated "science teacher" can appreciate the possibility of selecting certain fundamental principles, processes, facts, in biology (including botany and zoölogy), physics and chemistry, that while opening the child's mind to these subjects, can be also utilized for his comprehension of such physiology as is essential to his understanding rudimentary hygiene. No one will deny that hygiene is the applied science for which every one of us has the most need. Therefore to coördinate these other sciences with this is right. Later in its education, if the child continues, the sciences will be more differentiated as its increasing capacity for more specialized service in society renders it desirable. "The story of bacteria"—(perhaps "bacteriology" is a term too dignified for the very simple instruction I have in mind)—can be made most interesting, entirely wholesome, and supremely valuable on the *practical* side in teaching cleanliness, personal reserve and purity.

We might add that with the influence of the scientific hygienist upon the teaching of the allied sciences its character would probably improve. At present scientists are almost as discouraged as physicians over the public school teaching of their specialties.

The establishment of this department can be brought about in two ways. Public sentiment, led by an educated minority, can be focused upon city government, influencing party bosses to secure an appropriation for this purpose, and upon political school officials to expend it according to popular demand. The result will be, in practically every successful attempt, much personal disgust, friction and dissatisfaction; and a compromised measure wasteful of money, and of efficiency, and deferring the well organized department to the second half of the twentieth century. There will result some education of public opinion from the agitation; but, I think, at a too great sacrifice, for public opinion will also be educated by the second method, more correctly and rapidly without the cost—a compromise and a postponement.

A department of hygiene in the public schools can be established by private endowment. To the donor would go enough of glory. It would be enough of a monument. No less good will follow the endowment of departments, erection of gymnasia, laboratories, establishment of memorial school gardens, playgrounds, swimming tanks, for the use of public school children, than follows such gifts to higher institutions of learning.

There is one objection I have known to prevail: distrust of the ability to administer such funds according to high standards by the kind of men placed in office through party elections. This is a proper objection at our present stage of municipal evolution, but it is also possible to do away with it.

We have private institutions that, because of their public service, receive governmental aid and coöperation in one way or another;

e. g., many hospitals, public libraries, technical, art, and industrial schools.

A benefactor could place the administration of a fund for a department of hygiene in the hands of *ex-officio* authorities not subject to political machinations, for the use of the public schools.

For a city of 200,000 inhabitants a fund of $300,000, yielding an income of $12,000, could be administered by a committee of five, consisting of the president, professor of pedagogy, and medical director of the gymnasium in the nearest colleges, two members elected by and from the city's largest medical society, and two advisory or associate members, the superintendents of health and of public schools.

This associated committee of seven could announce in the medical and public press that two years from date they would nominate to the city school committee a candidate for the office of school physician or professor of hygiene, for a period of five years, at a salary of $3,500 per year; that there would be an annual sum of $8,500 available for assistants, etc.

If the school committee should transfer school gymnastics to this department, where it unquestionably belongs, such amounts as have been appropriated for this or any other work so transferred, should be added to the $8,500.

This committee should stipulate the conditions of the candidacy:

1. The degree of A.B. or B.S. from a reliable college.
2. The degree of M.D. from a reliable college.
3. Five years of private (not institutional) practice.
4. Certificates from reliable institutions of having creditably completed courses in pedagogy (including child study); gymnastics (including play); school sanitation; in all equivalent to at least two years of graduate study.
5. A thesis on the methods of such a department.

Of course, the personal equation will have to be provided for.

Such an official, if elected by the constituted authorities of the city, will be wholly responsible to them. The advisory holders of the purse strings would use their discretion at the end of five years about renewing the nomination. It is not reasonable to imagine insuperable friction and collision.

A philanthropist can provide $50,000 for such an experiment for five years, with the probability of its continuance by the city when once established.

The advantage of such an endowment just now at the birth of interest in teaching hygiene is that in the hands of recognized educators and physicians it would establish a model, a standard, suggest an ideal and demonstrate its practicability. It is easier and wiser to start right than to reform a wrong start, especially in politics. A school politician of influence once advised concerning another matter: "Keep it in your own hands until it has developed to about what it ought to be, for we can't experiment. We are too much criticized. We must use cut-and-dried methods." This is one reason so many private schools excel the public. They command more special teachers, and are freer to experiment and so progress.

The advantages and even absolute necessity of special teachers—particular for the sciences—have been proven by universities, colleges, high schools, special schools, private schools for children from 9 to 14 years of age, and vacation schools. It remains for only our elementary public schools to fall in line. Scientific subjects most conspicuously need it; and of them all applied physiology is the most essential to the mass of children who leave school in their teens.

The teaching of hygiene is in as unsatisfactory and transitional a state in Europe as with us. We should "arrive" early. Why not lead instead of follow?

Let the first regular department to be established in the public schools be that of hygiene. Let the American medical profession—let the leaders in the profession—recognize this opportunity and by both logic and precedent advocate the establishment of this department, enduringly organized on a solid basis of expert knowledge.

V.

THE MICHIGAN METHOD OF TEACHING SANITARY SCIENCE OR HYGIENE IN THE PUBLIC SCHOOLS OF THE STATE.[1]

By Victor C. Vaughan, M.D., Ph.D., LL.D., Ann Arbor, Michigan.

Mr. President, Ladies and Gentlemen: In the early 80's the State Legislature of Michigan, simultaneously with the legislatures of several of the other states, passed a law making the teaching of hygiene with special reference to the action of alcohol and other stimulants and narcotics obligatory in all the schools of the state. This enactment was the result of an agitation carried on by the Woman's Christian Temperance Union. As the bill was first passed it provided that no text-book should be used except such as should be approved by the State Board of Health and the State Board of Education. In compliance with this law, the State Board of Health held a meeting for the purpose of examining the text-books presented to it for this purpose. These books were found to be so filled with inaccuracies and misstatements that the board of health was unable to approve of any book presented at that time. The book which was most urgently recommended by the Woman's Christian Temperance Union was, so far as its physiologic teaching was concerned, the most objectionable of all. For instance it stated that one of the most important constituents of milk is starch. It contained numerous similar false assertions, but it was urged that the State Board of Health adopt it because, as was stated by the representative of the Woman's Christian Temperance Union, it was all right on the alcohol question. At a second meeting of the State Board of Health held for the purpose of examining other books the work entitled "The Human Body," by the late Professor Martin, was recommended. But this did not suit the Woman's Christian Temperance Union, and the result was that at the next session of the Legislature the approval of the State Board of Health of text-books on hygiene to be used in the public schools was ren-

[1] Read before the American Academy of Medicine, Washington, D. C., May 11, 1903.

dered unnecessary. This Act still continues in force, but I believe that more harm than good has been done by it. Children were imbued with the idea that alcohol in any form and in any quantity, applied externally or internally, was a poison. I had a good illustration of this once when I was vaccinating a boy of eight or ten years of age. He was inquisitive as to the steps which I employed in the process. I first washed his arm with soap and water and then with a dilute solution of mercuric chlorid, all of which I explained to him. I then started to wash his arm with alcohol in order to remove the excess of mercuric chlorid. To this he objected very strenuously and told me that he thought that one of my age and experience should know that alcohol was a deadly poison whether applied externally or taken internally. Naturally there came to this boy in the course of time more accurate knowledge and also quite naturally, it is to be presumed, that he lost all respect for the so-called information which he had gained from his teachers. The Michigan State Board of Health, recognizing the inadequacy and possible harmfulness of the law as it stood, in 1895 induced the State Legislature to pass an enactment of which the following is a copy :

"*An Act to provide for teaching in the public schools the modes by which the dangerous communicable diseases are spread, and the best methods for the restriction and prevention of such diseases.*

"SECTION 1. *The People of the State of Michigan enact*, That there shall be taught in every year in every public school in Michigan the principal modes by which each of the dangerous communicable diseases is spread, and the best methods for the restriction and prevention of each such disease. The State Board of Health shall annually send to the public school superintendents and teachers throughout this state printed data and statements which shall enable them to comply with this Act. School boards are hereby required to direct such superintendents and teachers to give oral and blackboard instruction, using the data and statements supplied by the State Board of Health.

"SECTION 2. Neglect or refusal on the part of any superintendent or teacher to comply with the provisions of this law shall be considered a sufficient cause for dismissal from the school by the school board. Any school board wilfully neglecting or refusing to comply with any of the provisions of this Act shall be subjected to fine, the same as for neglect of any other duty pertaining to their office. This Act shall apply to all schools in this state, including schools in cities or villages, whether incorporated under special charter or under the general laws."

This is the law under which I believe that much good is now being done in the State of Michigan in the way of giving to all classes of students and those of every grade accurate information concerning the dangerous communicable diseases, how they are spread and how they may be restricted and prevented.

In accordance with this law the State Board of Health has issued an eight-page pamphlet containing the most essential information concerning the nature, spread and restriction of communicable diseases. This pamphlet also contains a diagrammatic chart showing the relative prevalence and fatality of the infectious diseases. Consumption, pneumonia, diphtheria, typhoid fever, scarlet fever, measles, whooping-cough, and smallpox are discussed briefly but accurately and in accordance with the latest scientific information concerning the etiology of disease. This pamphlet is revised each year and is placed in the hands of every teacher in the public schools of Michigan.

In addition to the pamphlet concerning the dangerous communicable diseases mentioned above, the State Board of Health issues a monthly Teachers' Sanitary Bulletin. These bulletins furnish the teachers of the state more detailed information concerning the infectious diseases and at the same time they enable the teacher to keep thoroughly posted in the progress of our knowledge concerning the etiology of diseases. The State Board of Health determines what these bulletins shall contain, publishes them and sends them free of charge to every teacher in the state. In some instances the bulletin is specially prepared by some member of the board or by some one selected for this purpose by the board. In other instances suitable articles are reprinted from medical or sanitary journals or indeed wherever they may be found. In this way matters of present and paramount interest are constantly kept before the teachers. To illustrate, I may state that during the past few months we have had quite an epidemic of hydrophobia in the state. Consequently the Teachers' Sanitary Bulletin for March, 1903, consists of a monograph by Dr.

Novy on "Hydrophobia: Its Restriction and Prevention;" other papers discuss the hygiene of school life, vaccination, the hygiene of the home, milk as a conveyor of disease, and kindred subjects.

As a result of this kind of teaching the children of the state are coming to be familiar with the latest and best scientific information of sanitary importance. These children talk about these subjects in their homes and to a certain extent educate their parents. Possibly it is too early yet to predict just what will be the result of this method of instruction, but up to the present time those of us who have provided for it and have watched its effects are inclined to congratulate ourselves upon its success.

VI.
THE TRAINING OF TEACHERS OF HYGIENE FOR PUBLIC SCHOOLS.[1]

By THOMAS D. WOOD, A.M., M.D., Professor Physical Education, Columbia University, New York City.

It is recognized more every day by intelligent, thinking people and by progressive educators that the public schools should train children more practically and successfully for the activities of every-day life, for the responsibilities of society and of citizenship, with all that they involve. So the old-time methods and subjects of school instruction are being modified. The "three R's" are being taught in a more interesting manner and in a shorter time. The child is studying the inanimate and animate world about him, and the record of this complex world in its marvelous development. The practical interests of life are being studied in the school through manual training, cooking, sewing, drawing, music, etc. The humanitarian, the esthetic and the utilitarian are alike finding their places. Much is still neglected however that is most closely related to the art of living.

Life is well defined as the correspondence of an organism to its environment. Human life involves the conscious, intelligent correspondence and adaptation of the human organism to its environment, brought about through the wise and effective supervision of the individual, properly instructed and trained.

Civilization and education proceed in development from the objective to the subjective, and the relative emphasis placed by teachers and people generally upon the subjects of study well illustrates this statement. The time and thought in school are for the most part given to the study of the environment and its indirect relations to human life, while it is too much taken for granted that the organism will instinctively or unconsciously adapt itself successfully to its surroundings. It is true indeed that the great world is infinitely larger than the individual and that most of the time and interest of the human being in school,

[1] Read before the American Academy of Medicine, Washington, D. C., May 11, 1903.

and in life in general, will naturally and desirably be taken up with the consideration of things outside of himself and outside of any consciousness of their relation to him. But for the sake of the best health and life of the individual it is necessary that he should, and consciously to a considerable extent, adjust his organism to his environment, and also, so far as may be necessary and possible, adapt his environment to his own organic needs.

It is becoming more evident to many thinking people, and especially to physicians, that more attention should be given in our schools to the study of health, hygiene and physiology—the subjects which have to do with the adjustments and relations to which I have referred. Let me state without argument the following convictions: That up to the seventh and eighth grades of the elementary school the subjects of human anatomy and physiology should not be taught as such; that these subjects, however, should be thoroughly taught in the upper grammar grades and in the high school as a part of general anatomy and physiology and for the sake of the application of the principles of hygiene and sanitation; that in the first six or seven grades of the public school, hygiene should be taught not as a special or distinct subject, but instruction in this branch should be given in all the grades through the application to life and health of the facts and principles of nature study, primitive life, domestic or home science, geography and other subjects, and that there must never be a failure to make a reasonable, helpful application of anything connected with school work, to the health and life of the pupil, and in such a way that it is distinctly understood, and will become a part of the student's life, or that the failure to put it into practice will be recognized as such.

I venture to say that there is no greater error in our modern education than the failure to realize the expression of the abstract in the concrete; the relationship of the theoretical to the practical; to apply helpfully in the life of the individual, of the home, of society, all of those things valuable for study, appropriate for instruction and capable of such useful application.

As to the training of teachers of hygiene for public schools—the instruction of the children throughout the lower grades must be given by the regular teacher. It is more important that this teacher should be an embodiment of what is sound and fine and wholesome, that she should inspire in her pupils a sane passion for all that is healthful, rational and ennobling, than that she should simply have great knowledge or a mastery of pedagogic technique.

She must be mature in judgment as well as in body and in heart, and she should have a philosophy of life based upon a knowledge of biology and of human conditions which will give her a true appreciation of the relative values of human life in the large, and of the details of each day.

The training of this teacher of hygiene should begin with his or her own school life and proceed with the progress through the grades in which hygiene is taught in a rational and satisfactory manner. However, as it is almost impossible to find a school in which this subject of such vital importance receives adequate attention, we may not, in this generation of teachers at least, expect to find many who have had that best of all preparations for the teaching of health and hygiene, *viz.*, the instruction and development from childhood in a school atmosphere where this subject has the place which it deserves.

Many of the grade teachers will study in the high school, and if this course of study contains as much instruction in physics, chemistry, biology, physiology, hygiene and sanitation as all of the students should receive for the practical purposes of life, those who teach later will have had a very good foundation for the instruction of their pupils in matters relating to health. It is practically most important, however, that the normal schools and all institutions which train teachers should provide instruction in, and give due emphasis to, the subjects bearing upon hygiene. For the proper training of teachers in general there should be in every normal school and college a course in school hygiene which would prepare the teacher to deal adequately with the different aspects of health. Such courses are being introduced into some of the normal schools of Europe, more particularly in Germany. They are given in a few places in this country and must have a general recognition in the near future.

The best teaching of hygiene in the lower grades can not be given by the use of text-books, but it is all important that there should be many helpful books providing the teachers with scientific material in such form that they can readily adapt it to the needs of children of different ages and various conditions of life. Again, teachers will be greatly helped by books suggesting the application of many subjects and facts to health teaching, and pointing out the desirable correlation between hygiene and other subjects in the course of study.

While most of the instruction in hygiene in the public schools must be given by the general teacher if given at all, and while as a rule it is better that the grade teacher should give this direct instruction to the pupils, still it is important for several reasons that there should be special teachers of hygiene in the high schools as well as in all higher educational institutions, and special supervisors of hygiene in the elementary and grammar schools.

For reasons which are interesting but too complicated to develop at this time, there is and will be for some time a tendency to slight the teaching of hygiene in the work of the school. In the competition and pressure of subjects in the school curriculum; in the confusion and congestion of conscious interests in the minds of both teacher and pupil, hygiene will usually be crowded out of its rightful place. It is important, then, to have the special teachers and supervisors protect this subject, present its claims and procure its reasonable recognition as well as to supervise and direct the hygiene instruction given in various ways.

There will be few places at first where a special teacher or supervisor of hygiene will be employed under this title to give his or her first thought or entire time to this work. In some of the large cities the school physician or a medical supervisor may attend adequately to this interest. But this will not often be the case unless the physician has an extraordinary interest in the teaching of hygiene in the schools or unless he is employed on such terms that it is not necessary for him to devote much time or energy to the practice of medicine. Again, it is not practicable, for some time at least, to expect the teacher of science or biology to do justice to the subject of health. These teachers have been trained too largely in the methods and with the interests of pure science and, although their subjects are related so closely to health and hygiene, it is the exceptional teacher in this line who has a genuine instinct and feeling for hygiene and makes the application of his own subjects to health in a satisfactory manner.

In some places, of course, this special teaching or supervision of hygienic instruction will be provided for by the specialists referred to, but it seems probable that most of this special work in public education will be provided for by another class. There is in this country, not only in our higher educational institutions, but in our public schools as well, a rapidly growing demand for special teachers and supervisors of physical education, and hundreds of these are already employed in the public school service. If these teachers have any genuine interest in their own special field of education they are primarily devoted to the health and rational organic development of their pupils. They are to be sure, in most cases, too narrowly concerned and employed in the gymnastic and athletic training of their students and this, as a rule, without sufficient general or professional education even for the special work which they are trying to do. But it seems desirable to take advantage of the existence of this already large body of special teachers with their interests directed toward health; to enlarge considerably the context of the term physical education so that it will include not only physical training but school hygiene, the investigation of the health and physical condition of the pupils, and the supervision of the teaching of hygiene in the different grades.

This enlargement of the scope of "physical education" would not only provide for school hygiene and its various phases and for the instruction in the subject of hygiene throughout the schools, but it would be of great advantage to physical training in its present field. It would further unify most advantageously the different health interests of the schools, and, most important of all in some respects, it would raise the standard and the requirements for the general and professional training of teachers and supervisors in this line. This department of education might be called physical education, hygiene or something else, but it would have to do with all the health interests of education. It would have a dignity which physical training has not as yet. It would require a preparation (general and special) as broad, as thorough and as severe as that of any other educational specialist, if not more so. It would attract many well-trained physicians and able teachers who have already had preparation, if not experience, in other lines of educational work, to say nothing of students of promise and ability who would find this department competing with old and well-established branches of education. It would, I believe, provide most practically and successfully for the teaching of hygiene and for the training of special teachers and supervisors of this subject.

The general college or university course is not a sufficient preparation for this hygienic specialist, although it is important that he, or she (for the majority of these will be women, for some time at least) should have collegiate training. The medical course is not enough although many of the important positions in this field will be advantageously filled by medical graduates.

The special teacher and supervisor of hygiene should have a broad general education with a thorough grounding in science. To this should be added a special training in biology, anatomy, physiology, psychology, hygiene, sanitation, school hygiene, nature study and special branches of these subjects which are being developed. If a medical training and experience can be added to this preparation it will be of great advantage, but much of the technical training desirable for this field can best be provided in the colleges and universities where special teachers and supervisors of various branches are trained by professional courses of instruction adapted to their several needs. Here, the student should get a comprehensive idea of the history and principles of education, a clear and sympathetic understanding of the general purposes and methods of educational effort and, through contact with specialists in many lines, a better appreciation of the nature and scope of his own work, its place in the general scheme of education and its relation to other branches and subjects.

The professional training of teachers in such a course as I have suggested should include not only excellent theoretical instruction but practical work in laboratory and gymnasium and actual teaching of hygiene under careful criticism.

There is here, a new grouping of interests in education, and in a sense a new specialty in the field of teaching. In this way, as has already been suggested, the teaching of hygiene in the schools may most successfully be accomplished.

The effective teaching of health requires not only a wise and skilful selection and adaptation of subject-matter but also a perfect educational method. No subject can fail more seriously in the schools, if improperly handled, than this vital subject of hygiene. No phase of education is more fundamental and important. No line of teaching requires more careful, more extensive or more thorough preparation, or a finer grouping of qualifications of health, intellect and character in the teacher.

DISCUSSION.

Hon. William T. Harris, U. S. Commissioner of Education:

It gives me very great pleasure to hear these papers and to note the good, sound things stated. I think that if the matter of teaching hygiene in the schools were in the hands of the regular physicians there would be a great improvement brought about. We look to the physician as the true healer in this matter of hygiene. There seems to be no systematic instruction even in the normal schools in the principles of hygiene. Many years ago Horace Mann took up the matter of hygiene and made one of his reports on that subject, and that report gave a great deal of encouragement to quacks, and the report itself is more or less full of quackery.

I want to say something with reference to the so-called physical training in the schools, and the few things I have to say I shall read from a printed speech of mine. Physical exercise after a hard lesson can not be a good thing if it is too vigorous. The will-power is the same, whether attention is given to grammar or to calisthenics, and calisthenics is not a rest from grammar in this respect. The child with his will-power already strained in the grammar class is thus greatly injured by the close attention he gives to the directions of the teacher of physical exercise, and the only result of calisthenics in these cases is to aid a tendency toward nervous dyspepsia. We have voluntary and involuntary powers, and I do not know of any system of instruction in physical training which starts out with that clear distinction in dealing with hygiene. The involuntary powers must be let alone, and the less you use your will-power the better you digest. I started out with nervous dyspepsia early in youth and when, years after, I entered college I heard the gospel of physical training as a cure. I practised in the gymnasium until I gained four inches around the chest. I wondered why I did not have strong health, and why I had indigestion. I left college at the middle of the third year and went to Missouri, and I found there a great many people drinking lager beer. It was a disagreeable liquid to hold in my mouth. But I sometimes drank half a glass of beer on Saturday evening at a club after two hours' study of arithmetic, and found that on those nights I slept better and was almost free from dyspepsia the next day. I have tried a small dose of beer—half a pint or less, three times a week just before retiring as an effective medicine in case of dyspepsia. Of course I am not advocating the drinking of beer as a habit. I believe in total abstinence for all healthy people and for almost all sick people.

The effect of physical training is to put the will into the muscles. It is to give one such control over all his muscles that each act performed by the body is performed by the use of all the muscles which nature has provided for the purpose. The farmer or the blacksmith develops a few muscles and neglects others. The gymnasium is supposed to cultivate many muscles which remain rudimentary in the ordinary man. The imprudent gymnast is careless about the hygienic precautions in relation to eating and sleeping.

This gymnastic and calisthenic training, so-called, are violent demands upon the will-power and a rapid drain of the nervous energy. Hence physical exercise directly after a hard lesson is not a proper sequence. The will-power which has been drained by the mental work is reduced to complete exhaustion by the violent physical exercise.

"Every pound of energy expended on work, either of mind or of body," says Dr. Sargent, "must be made good by food, rest, or sleep."

"The employment of the muscles in exercise not only benefits their especial structure, but acts on the whole system. When the muscles are put in action, the capillary blood vessels with which they are supplied become more rapidly charged with blood, and active changes take place, not only in the muscles, but in all the surrounding tissues. The heart is required to supply more blood, and accordingly, beats more rapidly in order to meet the demand. A larger quantity of blood is sent through the lungs, and larger supplies of oxygen are taken in and carried to the various tissues. The oxygen, by combining with the carbon of the blood and the tissues, engenders a larger quantity of heat, which produces an action on the skin, in order that the superfluous warmth may be disposed of. The skin is thus exercised, as it were, and the sudoriparous and sebaceous glands are set at work. The lungs and skin are brought into operation, and the lungs throw off large quantities of water, containing in solution matters which, if retained, would produce disease in the body. Wherever the blood is sent, changes of a heathful character occur. The brain and the rest of the nervous system are invigorated, the stomach has its power of digestion improved, and the liver, pancreas, and other organs perform their functions with more vigor. By want of exercise, the constituents of the food which pass into the blood are not oxidized, and products which produce disease are engendered. The introduction of fresh supplies of oxygen induced by exercise oxidizes these products and renders them harmless. All other things being the same, it may be laid down as a rule that those who take the most exercise in the open air will live longest."

But the student who reads of these direct effects without, at the same time, carefully learning the indirect effects of physical training on digestion and sleep, and mental work or worry, will almost inevitably neutralize all the good that comes from physical exercise.

Within the school the pupil is supposed to be under a severe strain of discipline and attention to study. Regularity, punctuality, silence, conformity to rules as to sitting or standing, strict self-control on the part of the pupil, and a forced attention to his lesson or to the recitation of his fellow pupils, or to the explanations of his teacher—all this produces a great tension of physical and mental powers. If it were continued too long, congestion would be produced, affecting the heart or brain or digestive functions or some local nerve center. Past experience, noting this fact, has endeavored to avoid the danger by establishing recess. The pupils are all dismissed from the school building and removed from the school restraints for an interval of a few minutes. The pupil leaves the close air of the school-room and rushes out into the pure air, suddenly relieved from the cramp of muscles in sitting in a particular position on a hard seat, and relieved, likewise, from the cramp of nervous energy that has been diverted from natural functions of digestion, circulation, and secretion, and concentrated on the conscious processes of attention and obedience to the external commands of the teacher or to his own self-imposed industry.

The chief use of the recess is its complete suspension of the strain on the will-power, and the surrender to caprice for a brief interval. Any form of calisthenics or gymnastic exercise is, therefore, a diversion of the recess from its normal function. It is the substitution of one kind of tension of the will for another. The tension of the will requisite to perform properly the requirements of school discipline and instruction is such as to withdraw the nervous energy from those great centers of secretion and circulation, stomach, heart, kidneys, liver, and lungs. Congestion, as before said, is easily initiated, and if continued, will produce functional derangements connected with the organs of digestion and circulation. The seeds of indigestion, renal weakness, liver complaint, constipation, even of fearful scourges like Bright's disease, may be sown in the system in early years by injudicious confinement in the school-room.

The great physical need of the pupil is relaxation; the pupil needs to stretch his cramped muscles and send the blood in torrents through his limbs, which become torpid with unuse. The pupil is in want of fresh air and of the deep inflation of the lungs that exercise in the open air gives. He ought to use his voice, too. It is proposed to substitute calisthenics for the purpose of supplying all these wants; throw open the windows and let in fresh air; have a system of well-devised movements which will give the needed circulation of the blood.

Calisthenic exercise serves a good place in the school-room, but its most important function is not a physiologic one. It is true that the blood is caused to circulate more vigorously through the limbs and those parts of the body that have become partly torpid with sitting or standing still. But the chief demand upon the pupil in calisthenics is a requirement of him to strain his attention and exercise his will. It is a will-training to a greater extent than a physiologic training. The great distinction between work and play is this one: In play, the mind is spontaneous, governed entirely by its own inclination; in work, the will-power is exercised to conform its individuality to some externally prescribed course of action. Calisthenic exercise is severe work and not by any means a relaxation. But the child needs relaxation, and not merely a change of work, although the change is of some benefit. Exercise of the limbs, in accordance with a prescribed formula, is not the thing that nature requires.

The child has been exercising his will in the four directions of self-control. To be regular, punctual, silent, and industrious, now giving his attention to the mastery of some subject by himself, and anon, following with alertness and critical acumen the recitation of some fellow pupil, or some explanation or direction by the teacher. Calisthenics does not afford relief to the will-power. We have seen that all exercise of the will in the act of fixed and unremitting attention has a powerful influence over the digestive, circulatory, and secretory functions of the body. This influence, if not intermitted, will cause derangements of these functions. A run in the open air, a saunter at will, or a vigorous game with one's fellows, free from restraint of authority—any exercise, in short, of the spontaneous choice of the pupil, will give this desirable relief to the heart, the stomach, the glands, and the ganglia.

Physical exercise affects directly the muscular system, but the muscular system is not all of the body, nor, indeed, itself directly the generator of what is called nervous energy. There is a nutritive process of digestion, and a distributive process of circulation through the heart and lungs and liver, the two forming a building-up function which restores, repairs, and increases the organism and removes the waste. There is, besides, a nervous organism which receives impressions from without and conveys impulses that react on the environment.

Physical exercise indirectly acts on the digestion and the circulatory system and on the nerves of sensation, and its relation to those other bodily functions is nearly or quite as important as the direct relation of exercise to the muscles and the acquiring of strength.

During the first fifty years of agitation on the subject of bodily training, connected with the rise of Turner Societies in Germany, and the preaching of the gospel of bodily culture as auxiliary to intellect and will by Spurzheim, his disciples, George Combe, Horace Mann, and their numerous followers, we may say, without hesitation, that the doctrine of physical exercise was passing through its stage of superstition and quackery. There was a sharp dividing line between the believers in hygiene and the old school of physicians, and this separation led quite naturally to dismal results. The doctors opposed, with blind conservatism, the new apostles, and the latter justified the attitude of the former by a radicalism equally blind and fanatical.

Physical exercise is now directed by educated physicians in our colleges. It is a new movement of the highest importance, the establishment of a resident physician in each of our colleges as supervisor of gymnastics and recording inspector of physical development among the students. It means a synthesis of science with reform and the end of the era of quackery in hygiene.

Our civilization is so bent on the conquest of nature and the production of wealth, that it perpetually drains its supply of nervous energy and produces disaster along this line. Here is the special problem of our time for hygiene to meet: How to restore and conserve nervous energy.

There are, as we have seen, three factors here: First, the one of food and its proper assimilation; second, the factor of rest and sleep; third, the factor of exercise—muscular and mental. It is obvious enough that digestion requires nervous energy, just as muscular and mental labor does. Hence, digestion must be given time to accumulate its nerve force. It must not be encroached on by bodily exercise or by mental exercise. But what is the average amount of time required for this, and should it be total cessation from bodily and mental labor, or is light labor of both, or either, best for the digestive process?

If the chapters could be written which should describe the grave mistakes committed by amateurs in the use of physical exercise as a hygienic measure, they would furnish a sufficient warning for the present generation. They would describe various experiments of using midnight hours for walks and rides in the open air. The student used all his day for intellectual work, and supposed that an hour or two of exercise taken at a late hour of the night would answer his needs. Another experiment selected its period of exercise in the early morning, curtailing the period of sleep in order to secure the requisite time before breakfast. Violent physical exercise taken early in the morning is very exhaustive of nervous energy, and probably in most instances the student has cultivated nervous dyspepsia, quite as much as he has cultivated his muscles. We have all read in the biography and autobiography of Thomas Carlyle the mention of his walks late in the night. Every one has had something of this kind in his own experience, or in the experience of persons of his acquaintance. It was only yesterday that a distinguished laborer in the cause of education told me of his own follies in this matter. Led on by reading injudicious writings on this subject of hygiene, he had so curtailed his night's rest for the sake of morning exercise that nervous collapse resulted. His physician prescribed as the only possible remedy a long period of total rest. The hours of sleep at night were nearly doubled, and a relaxation from study in the daytime was insisted upon. Relief came as a consequence.

Besides the mistake of cutting off the sleeping hours at the beginning or at the end for the sake of physical exercise, there is an equally harmful mistake of bringing the hour of exercise close to the hours for meals. Just preceding or just succeeding a meal, any exercise of sufficiently energetic a character to cause the blood to leave the organs of digestion and fill the muscles of the body or the brain is injurious and tends to produce dyspepsia. The stomach needs the greater share of the nervous energy and likewise of the arterial circulation. Dr. Sargent thinks that violent exercise should not be taken at a period so long as three hours after a meal, on account of the danger of faintness, which neutralizes the good results of such exercise. Provided the person has just taken violent exercise, the blood is diverted to the muscles and brain and away from the stomach. The taking of food at this time, when the nervous system is depleted of its vitality, is considered unfavorable to the best action of the digestive functions.

We remember, too, that cold bathing, which has been so often commended with a great lack of discrimination, is another source of injury to the health when it is resorted to by persons with nervous temperaments or feeble constitutions, and at a time when the system has been depleted of its vital energy by work or exercise, or when the digestive organs are occupied with recently taken food.

The old rule made by a farmer population to encourage early rising, which mentions as its effect to health, wealth, and wisdom as its product, has made mischief with conscientious students, who have supposed that early rising in itself is a good thing, even when not preceded by the precautions named in the adage, namely, "early to bed."

It is a very important matter to consider that physical exercise has its best effect when carried on socially in the form of plays and games, or contests with one's fellows. The stimulus which is derived from emulation and interest in one's fellow students has to be compensated for by a sheer exertion of the will in the case of calisthenic exercises, and in the case of prescribed athletic training by the use of weights, ladders, and the other appliances of the gymnasium.

Dr. T. D. Davis, of Pittsburg :

I recently attended a symposium in which attention was given to the great advantage of manual training in the public schools. A little later I was at the national convention of kindergarteners, in Pittsburg, in which the importance of nature study, etc., was discussed, and later I attended a convention where music in the public schools was the principal theme. For some time, in our city, we have heard a great deal of physical culture, extending all the way from a dancing class to an athletic association, and the dear temperance people want us to give a great deal of time to teaching the evils of alcohol. If so much attention is given to these, I am wondering where the three Rs are to come in. We have heard many things of profound importance in regard to the teaching of hygiene in our high schools. You see how it runs riot in physiology, and instead of being a benefit I think many of the books are a detriment. I was one of the first to introduce physical culture in our schools. It is taught as suggested by Dr. Makuen by instructions upon how to breathe, how to sit, how to hold one's self, etc. We use no paraphernalia whatever, and our system is especially suited for public schools and never need take more than five or ten minutes, and this instead of the old time recess. The trouble is in trying to foist on the public school everything that comes along. While we can discuss the advantage of a proper knowledge of hygiene the question is, how much of it can be taught in the little time allowed for special studies in the public schools? And even if taught, how much practical use would it be? No one violates the rules of hygiene more than do doctors! On this there is a great variety of opinion. The most practical thing I have heard this afternoon is that which they are doing in Michigan; these little bulletins sent out, brief, yet clear, and carefully selected, the teachers reproducing them in the course of their teaching to bring out the fundamental principles, are ideal. I can see absolutely no objection to this; if you can get your teachers to understand the subject and realize its importance and to teach it so that the children will practise it, no doubt great good would be accomplished. I think the method is a wonderful advance and practical in the extreme. It is far better than sending out gilt-edge books and having instructors. It appeals to me as such a great advantage that I think I shall use my influence in introducing the method in our own schools.

Dr. S. A. Knopf, New York:

All the papers which we have just listened to are so highly interesting that I wish we had time to discuss each one as freely as it deserves. The only criticism I have to offer, if such it can be called, is that too much has been said on the theory and not enough on the practice of hygiene. You cannot teach children under the age of 12 much of the theory of hygiene, but you can give them practical lessons. A child even of five years of age can be taught never to kiss any other child on the mouth, or allow itself to be kissed except on the cheek; not to scratch itself with its dirty finger nails, or to put its fingers in its mouth; not to spit on a slate, on the floor, sidewalk, or playground; not to swap apple cores, candy, chewing gum, whistles, etc.

The recommendations set forth in Dr. Makuen's paper I heartily endorse. In my practice among the tuberculous and the predisposed I find many who do not know what I mean when I tell them to take a deep breath. I have known adults and children who have been taught physical exercises, gymnastics, and calisthenics, but could not breathe properly. School children should not only be taught this, but also how to sit, walk, and stand correctly.

Dr. Putnam has given us her views on the necessity of attaching a medical staff to every school. All of us who know how a school without a school physician may become the source of dangerous and fatal epidemics of infectious children's diseases, will most heartily approve of Dr. Putnam's suggestions. In connection with this subject permit me to tell you of an experiment which was recently tried in New York. Besides the school physician we detailed a number of trained nurses to help teach practical lessons in the prevention of the disease not only to the children but also to the parents. Thus, for example, in a case of pediculosis we do not content ourselves with sending the child home to tell the mother about it, but a nurse is sent to visit the home of the child and teach the mother how to clean the head from all lice and how to prevent a recurrence of the parasite. This is what I call teaching the practice of hygiene to mother and child alike through the medium of the medical staff of the school.

One word as to the teaching of hygiene in medicine through the aid of the Michigan Teachers' Bulletin. This is an admirable method of keeping the teachers abreast with the advancement in preventive medicine, and I consider myself indeed privileged and honored to have been enabled to contribute a little article on the subject of tuberculosis to this excellent magazine. Since our distinguished friend, Professor Vaughan, asks for suggestions I would venture to say that the usefulness of the Bulletin would be vastly enhanced if, instead of limiting its circulation to teachers, it should also reach the more advanced pupils of the public schools. The time must come when the teaching of physical culture and school hygiene must be obligatory in all our public schools, and the teachers of those branches should be especially trained physicians.

Dr. F. H. Gerrish, Portland, Me.:[1]

I think Dr. Davis has not borne in mind the essential in teaching children they should know how to keep well. If the teaching of reading, writing and arithmetic is worth more than that, I have yet to learn it. I should say that the teaching of hygiene is an essential.

I think Dr. Putnam's suggestion of the method of instruction in hygiene in the schools is very interesting, and I think it not impossible that somebody

[1] Published without revision by Dr. Gerrish.

may be found—some multimillionaire—who will give the necessary amount to make the experiment of this proposed method. Whatever method is tried, I am sure that the worst trouble about its operation will be the very pernicious theory at work all over the country. If there were no teaching of hygiene at this time, it would be comparatively easy to institute a good method. But, as Dr. Vaughan has said, there is a method prevailing already. How pernicious it is, no one can understand who has not examined some of the books recommended. The chief trouble about any method of teaching hygiene is to be found in the requirements of the present laws regarding its teaching.

Dr. James H. McBride, of Pasadena, Cal.:[1]

With reference to slovenly attitudes of children in schools, I believe that slovenly muscular attitudes lead to slovenly mental attitudes. Many a boy is dull at his books because he has not been taught to sit up and keep his muscles in harmony with his mental condition when engaged in studying his lessons. It has been considered a fact that people who teach in school do not take the same amount of physical exercise, and do not need it as do those occupied otherwise, and that teachers cannot take much exercise without being exhausted by it.

In reference to the share which doctors might take in the teaching—what I say does not apply to members of this Academy—no person in the community knows less about hygiene than the average physician. It seems to me that a school of hygiene for doctors would be a good thing.

Dr. W. R. White, Providence:

Granting that the remarks of the last speaker are correct, that the average physician is a poor hygienist, there is nothing impracticable in the suggestions of Dr. Putnam's paper. Her argument is that the head of this department of our public school system shall be liberally educated, shall have an established medical practice, and have had special study in the other school departments. It seems to me the experiment she has described is extremely practical. Considering the susceptibility to disease of little children, to have an educated mind brought to bear on this subject is most important. I think the time is coming when the school physician will have his proper place, when he will be paid for having learned to discriminate. If, as our distinguished speaker states, it is irrational to conduct calisthenic exercises immediately after exercises that tax the will-power, the medical man should be the one to know that, and to antagonize the system. It seems to me that the position would be based upon practical utility and conservatism, and that from a philanthropic standpoint the influence of this department of hygiene would be most valuable. The instruction which this head of the department would give to teachers, enabling them to distinguish early enough the symptoms of certain diseases, would be of the utmost importance.

[1] Published without the revision of Dr. McBride.

Dr. A. L. Benedict, of Buffalo:

We have to distinguish sharply between hygiene and the teaching of hygiene. Both are important subjects and it is very difficult to avoid confusing them. I do not see how a competent man who has been five years in private practice could afford to do the work suggested by Dr. Putnam at such a salary as is ordinarily paid by cities. In regard to the teaching of hygiene, it has been well brought out that you cannot teach scientific hygiene to little children, for it cannot be taught without a basis of physiology and anatomy. The children can be taught the ordinary rules of health by personal admonition, but they cannot be given formal instruction, and it is very questionable whether any special time should be set aside for class instruction in hygiene. I think the instruction to little children should be given in the home and by the parents. The common schools give us a very valuable opportunity to reach the children and through them to reach the homes. The children who are not cleanly, and especially those who bring with them animal parasites and communicable diseases, should be sought out, but the actual prophylaxis and treatment should not be part of the school work but should be relegated to an expert who may be a member or employee of the board of education or of the board of health, as seems more convenient in any locality.

Dr. Edward Jackson, of Denver:

We must bear in mind more and more that for a large proportion of children the school education is the greater part of education, and the school life is the best life that they know. For many children the school is less an institution for teaching the three Rs, and more an institution for civilizing a new generation, for bringing to a higher civilization the descendants of those who have not yet enjoyed such a civilization. In that work the teaching of health is an ultimate and supreme object. But not the teaching of hygiene as a special technical branch, which deals with the periods of incubation of certain diseases, or the particular way in which certain bacteria are transmitted. In these discussions personal hygiene is too much lost sight of. It may be easier to teach how certain contagious diseases can be prevented than to teach how children may be trained in developing their own powers and in keeping them at their best. And yet, it seems to me, that the latter is the very much more important branch of the subject.

As has been indicated by some of the papers, this must be chiefly done through the teachers of the public schools. The thing is to get some one to teach the teachers. Dr. Putnam has suggested an experiment that I think we would all like to see tried, and Dr. Wood has indicated certain lines on which the teachers can be approached. In both instances the important thing is to get the right kind of supervisor of this teaching. If that is done the teaching of hygiene can be brought to a much higher plane in a very few years. The present teaching has been referred to as a hindrance. But it is not on a whole. What has been done may much of it be wrong, but it has accomplished this : It has turned the attention of the teachers, of the community, and of the medical profession to the teaching of hygiene in the public schools. It ought to be a matter of shame to all of us that the laws requiring the teaching of hygiene in the public schools have been framed and passed and enforced in nearly all of the states of this country, not by persons who had an intelligent comprehension of what the teaching of hygiene should be, but by those who had no comprehension of such whatever, who were simply fanatics about the use of alcohol. Still they have turned attention to the subject, and with that done, very much can be accomplished by intelligent effort. The teachers, as a rule, are deeply dissatisfied with the present method of teaching hygiene, and with what they are expected to do. We can find among them most efficient allies. We must work for the removal of the defects in existing laws and the intelligent supervision of the teaching.

Dr. Walter L. Pyle, of Philadelphia, closing :

I have been much interested in the diversity of this discussion. The subject is one that has been very dear to me. There has been a tardy recognition of Herbert Spencer's statement that there can be no sound scheme of education that does not first of all preach the gospel of health. In my experience the usual mistake in this direction is in the teaching of intricate anatomic details, and undue attention to the pernicious effects of alcohol and tobacco. These two things seem to occupy the minds of the people who discuss the subject. Most of the health books are unscientific and full of most ridiculous statements by laymen inspired by fanatics rather than scientists. Children should, of course, be told that alcohol and tobacco are pernicious in their effects, but one-half of the health primers should not be taken up with these statements. The matter impressed me so forcibly that I determined to edit a popular book upon personal and domestic hygiene, with each section written by an acknowledged medical authority. To prevent over-lapping I sent out to different contributors a copy of my scheme, inviting them to write upon the subjects in their respective chapters. The result was a book that every educated layman could appreciate. All through the book there was a decided and purposive repetition of warnings against the abuse of alcohol and tobacco. The first comment I had from an educator was that it was too liberal in its views relative to the use of alcoholic beverages to be adopted in public schools.

It is not necessary to teach the intricate details of physiology and anatomy in imparting the truths of personal hygiene, and there are certain elemental facts which can be taught very early in the public schools, almost in the first class.

With regard to the Teachers' College, I am sorry that Dr. Wood is not here. I think the project is one of the greatest reforms of the day, and I am sorry that the title and synopsis of his paper are not more descriptive.

Another fallacy in the teaching of personal hygiene is the important place given to calisthenics. Exercise is a nerve effort, and often nerve and will force are unduly wasted just as Dr. Harris has stated. An excellent way to make a child nervous is to give him too much calisthenics. Dr. Harris has brought out a strong point regarding the encroachment of the voluntary powers upon the involuntary, and I am glad to see it emphasized by a layman.

The idea of having a tired child using up his nerve force in calisthenics instead of the normal play recess is atrocious. The basic principles of health can be taught to almost everybody and it is the physician's duty to explain to the general public the necessary points in hygiene.

Dr. G. Hudson-Makuen, of Philadelphia, closing :

A few years ago Professor E. W. Scripture, of Yale, made some interesting experiments along the line of physical exercise among students. He had them lift a weight by the flexion of the forearm a definite number of times every day for several months, and at the end of the period the flexion, both of the practised and the unpractised arm, was measured, and it was found that the increase in strength in the arm that had not been practised was almost as great as that of the one which had been practised. In other words, the specialized forearm exercise developed a general increase of strength effecting the whole muscular and nervous system. It was the development of general *nerve power* that made the unpractised arm as strong as the practised one. These results seem to me to have an important bearing upon this matter of physical education in schools. The value of calisthenic exercises is not so much in the effect they have upon the muscles as it is in the effect they have upon the mind. Moreover these exercises do not exhaust the child's will-power; it does not take any will-power for a child to go through physical exercises in imitation of the teacher, but more than anything else in schools they tend to develop the faculty of attention, of imitation, and of concentration, and will-power is the outgrowth and natural consequence of the development of these three faculties.

You cannot keep a child from thinking, but you can teach him how to think, and you can develop the higher faculties of the brain by physical exercises. I believe that calisthenics and play have in them elements of physical development not found in the ordinary school work.

Dr. Helen C. Putnam, of Providence, in closing :

I am very glad this proposition has been so favorably discussed. In reply to one criticism: The average income (uncertain) of private practitioners in Europe and America ranges from $600 to $1,000. He would be doing well who fitted himself for an assured $3,500, aside from the good he would be accomplishing. It compares favorably with that of college professors, and of superintendents of schools. This is a suggestion only for a population of 200,000.

Specialists in other sciences attribute the indifferent success of public-school teaching in their lines to the same incompetent teaching ; a lack of sufficient laboratory bias and breadth of knowledge to accomplish what might be in a short time, and to make the subject as interesting, useful, educative as it should be.

We are expecting of these teachers, the majority under 35 years of age, the great majority having not more than a high or a normal school preparation, for $300 to $700 a year[1]—a few $1,000 or $1,200, rarely any one more—we are expecting from each one the government of a crowded, heavy-atmosphered room, the conduct of classes after expert methods in seven or eight topics, oversight of hygiene and morals, personal sympathy ; in addition, music, art, gymnastics, and excellent teaching of natural sciences. This is a program that a little later in the child's life requires a force of a score of many degreed experts and financial outlay accordingly. No *man* of corresponding or higher grade could possibly do what we expect from every woman who teaches. Consider to what grammar masters have simplified their subjects. These demands upon women are unreasonable.

It will be in 50 years, I venture, looked back upon with profound astonishment, both that we secured so much work in so many lines, and that any public could have required such work.

Another consideration is that centuries of teaching mathematics and languages through the various grades has systematized that work and it is therefore easier for the average instructor.

Hygiene, more than any other subject, is for purposes of instructing children in an experimental stage. This is a stumbling block in addition to its inherent complexities. A master hand is needed to clear the path.

[1] I have since learned that the average of salaries of women teachers in the public schools of the United States is $270 !

GONORRHEA INSONTIUM, ESPECIALLY IN RELATION TO MARRIAGE.[1]

By Prince A. Morrow, M.D., New York, N. Y.

I have employed the term "gonorrhea insontium" to designate a certain class of infections which are distinguished by the conditions under which contagion takes place. From a strictly scientific standpoint, such a differentiation is, of course, inadmissible; gonococcic infection is the same, irrespective of the conditions under which it originates. The qualificative "insontium" implies, therefore, an ethical, rather than a medical, distinction. Further, its use embodies the popular conception that the existence of gonorrhea carries with it certain stigma; that it is in some sort an opprobrium and a reproach to the bearer and furnishes presumptive proof, at least, of immorality. It is worthy of note that venereal diseases are the only ones that have this moral, or rather immoral, aspect. Without attempting to explain or justify the grouping of a particular class of diseases upon a purely ethical basis, it may be said that as long as gonorrhea is classed by popular opinion as a shameful disease, we should recognize a distinction between cases in which the disease is contracted by voluntary exposure to contagion, under conditions which society qualifies as immoral, and cases in which contagion is conveyed under conditions which are sanctioned as lawful, honorable and virtuous.

The term "syphilis insontium" has been long consecrated by usage to embrace the innocent victims of this disease. In this category are classed not only cases of conjugal contamination and inherited syphilis, but a vast number of cases of extragenital infections occurring in family life and through various industrial occupations and professional relations. The literature of syphilis insontium is large and constantly increasing, so that, at the present day, syphilis is not regarded as necessarily a venereal disease.

Gonorrhea more nearly conforms to the type of a venereal

[1] Read before the American Academy of Medicine, at Washington, D. C., May 12, 1903.

disease, having its almost exclusive origin in the venereal act; yet it is often innocently acquired. Certainly no moral stigma should attach to the innocent victims of this disease when contracted under the sanctity, and what should be the safeguard, of the marriage relation.

COMPARATIVE SIGNIFICANCE OF GONORRHEA AND SYPHILIS AS SOCIAL DANGERS.

While gonorrhea cannot claim the multiple and varied modes of syphilitic contagion and is not susceptible of hereditary transmission, yet, owing to its much greater frequency, its prolonged latency, the insidious character of its infection in married life, and its effects upon the health and conceptional capacity of the woman, it is quite as formidable a social plague as syphilis.

Unquestionably, the most sombre chapter of syphilis insontium is the murderous influence of the disease upon the offspring, but the no less pernicious effects of gonorrhea upon the procreative function, its inhibitory influence upon the perpetuation of the species, which is the primary and fundamental basis of the institution of marriage, are by no means adequately appreciated. Syphilis destroys the product of conception or blights its growth and normal development. Gonorrhea is more radical and effective in its action; it renders null and void the procreative process by mechanical obstruction of the seminiferous tubes or oviducts or by rendering sterile or unproductive the culture field of the ovum. Gonorrhea absolutely prevents what syphilis maims or destroys.

We have long been accustomed to look upon syphilis as a serious social peril, both from its individual risks and from its morbid irradiations into the family and social life; hence the relations of syphilis with marriage have been most carefully studied, the degree and duration of its infective capacity have been approximately fixed, and the conditions of admissibility of the syphilitic to marriage have been rigorously formulated. On the other hand, we have been accustomed to look upon gonorrhea as a local disease, trivial in character, of limited duration, and its important relations with marriage have been, until within recent times, unrecognized and, even now, are too often entirely ignored.

When syphilis is introduced into the family, the situation, though bad enough, is not without hope. All the possibilities promised by marriage are not irrevocably lost. After the first series of explosive violences are expended upon the offspring, there is still hope that under the attenuating influence of time and treatment the virulence of the diathesis will be exhausted, and the results, so far as the procreation of healthy children is concerned, may be as if the disease had never existed. But the introduction of gonorrhea into married life entails consequences infinitely more disastrous to the health and life of the mother. She may be rendered a life-long victim, and her hope of children absolutely extinguished. When the gonorrheal infection invades the annexial organs, determining obliterations, adherences, deviations, etc., these changes are final and irremediable; the woman becomes irrevocably sterile, not to speak of the danger to her life which, in many instances, can only be averted by the sacrifice of her reproductive organs.

We are accustomed to look upon syphilis as the most active cause of depopulation, but gonorrhea is the much more powerful factor. Janet, in discussion "Social Defence against the Venereal Peril," recently (1902) declared "that gonorrhea with tuberculosis, perhaps more than tuberculosis, is the great pest of our age. If we compare, from a social point of view, the importance of gonorrhea with that of syphilis, gonorrhea is to syphilis as 100 is to 1, not only from the standpoint of the number of persons attacked, but also from the standpoint of the gravity of the lesions and their perpetuity. Gonorrhea modifies in a manner, often permanent, the genital organs of patients, renders them infinitely dangerous for the women they approach, causes all the metrites and annexial inflammations which to-day give to surgeons three-quarters of their work, and conducts finally both men and women to sterility."

The predominance of gonorrhea as a cause of depopulation is not surprising, in view of the fact that it primarily and specifically affects the organs of generation. In the male this is so essentially true that almost every inflammatory process affecting the genito-urinary organs is at once referred to gonorrhea as the exciting cause. In the woman the whole brunt of the disease falls upon the reproductive apparatus. All modern writers upon diseases of women recognize that gonorrhea is the chief determining cause of the inflammatory diseases peculiar to woman. Syphilis, on the contrary, while it owes its genesis in the majority of cases to inoculative contact of the genital organs, is in no sense a genito-urinary disease. "It is only genital in its approach, and not at all in its manner of expression" (Keyes). Syphilis is a disease of the general system; its most essential lesions are in organs quite remote from the genital sphere; its effects upon the generative organs are the result of the nutritive disorders which affect the general system.

We may ask, why this disparity in the relative importance assigned to syphilis and gonorrhea in their relations to marriage? One reason is the greater dread which syphilis has always inspired, on account of the more formidable character of its manifestations compared with the relatively mild and apparently harmless symptoms of gonorrhea. The true explanation of this disparity must be sought for in lack of the coordinate development of our knowledge of these diseases, or rather in the limitations of our knowledge respecting the pathogenic rôle of the gonococcus, and especially the fact that gonorrhea in women has never been carefully and completely studied until within recent years. The attention of pathologists was almost exclusively devoted to masculine gonorrhea; our knowledge of feminine gonorrhea is essentially a modern acquisition. Many inflammatory affections of the female genital organs were referred to simple causes or regarded as peculiar to woman by virtue of her physical organization and the physiologic functions peculiar to her sex. The modern period of our knowledge begins with the discovery of the gonococcus.

In this paper, attention will be briefly directed to the three principal modes in which gonorrhea insontium is manifest in married life: (1) The individual risks to the health and life of the woman; (2) its effect upon her conceptional capacity; (3)

its effect upon the infant in the production of abortion and ophthalmia neonatorum. To these dangers may be added (4) the vulvovaginitis of young girls which often results from the introduction of gonorrhea into the family.

RISKS TO THE LIFE AND HEALTH OF THE WOMAN.

With the discovery of the gonococcus by Neisser it became possible to trace the pathogenic influence of the germ by its identification in many local and systemic disorders which it occasioned. Even before the discovery of the gonococcus, Noeggerath, with a prescience which can be considered scarcely less than intuitive, recognized the pathogenic influence of gonorrhea upon the pelvic organs of women, and, reasoning from effect to cause, boldly incriminated the latent urethritis of the male as the active factor in the production of these inflammations and the oft-resulting sterility. The vagaries of Noeggerath, as they were then considered, have become, with some modifications, the accepted facts of science to-day. Indeed, subsequent investigation has rather broadened than restricted the pathogenic influence of the gonococcus in the causation of pelvic inflammations.

As it is intended to touch lightly upon the pathology of gonorrhea, only the profound manifestations of the disease will be here considered.

In women the primary infection is more often localized in the deep parts, which is explained by the physiology of coitus, the germs being deposited in the uterine neck at the moment of ejaculation. Our knowledge of the habitual cervical localization of primary gonorrheic infection is essentially modern. To this lack of knowledge must be attributed the fact that the frequency of gonorrhea in women was so long overlooked, unrecognized, and unstudied. Undoubtedly it represents the most serious form of gonorrhea in women, not only from the standpoint of its insidious infection, its failure of recognition and treatment, but from the fact that it constitutes a point of departure for infection of the fundus of the womb and the annexial organs.

Another peculiarity of gonorrhea in women is the torpid, nonacute character of the primary process. In the majority of cases the infection is established insidiously without acute symptoms, either of a subjective or an objective character, so that, as a rule, gonorrhea in females presents itself as a chronic affection, either from the rapid subsidence of the acute symptoms or because it may develop *d'emblée* as a chronic process.

It is asserted that the abundant seromucous secretions (the little lochia) which immediately follow the menstrual period constitute an admirable culture field for the gonococci; not only is there multiplication of gonococci, but there is a tendency to invade the body of the womb, owing to the modifications in the uterine mucosa, and perhaps, also, to the more open and patulous condition of the os internum, which opposes less resistance to the entrance of the microbes.

When a gonorrheic woman becomes pregnant, the disease, hitherto passive, undergoes a modification more or less marked in its virulence and course. Strumbuhl and others have remarked the frequency with which the first clinical signs of gonorrhea are coincident with conception. Gottschalk and Immerwahr report cases where, under the influence of pregnancy, there was such a multiplication of diplococci in the cervical secretions that the slide preparations gave the illusion of a pure culture.

While there is no positive means of ascertaining how far the gonorrheal process may gain in extension during the course of pregnancy, there can be no doubt that with the termination of pregnancy, whether it be in abortion or in accouchement at full term, there is communicated a powerful pathogenic impulse to the upward ascension of the infection. In the large majority of cases, pregnancy is the pivot upon which hangs the destiny of the woman, so far as the extension of the infection to the womb and its annexa is concerned. All investigators who have had occasion to examine the lochial fluids unite in attesting that immediately after confinement, even as early as the second day, there is an extraordinary multiplication of the gonococci. The lochial fluid is an excellent culture medium, and the gonococci are found almost in pure culture. Not only are the gonococci multiplied in number and exalted in virulence, but the way is opened for ascending infection and the soil prepared by the process of parturition.

INFLUENCE OF GONORRHEA UPON CONCEPTIONAL CAPACITY.

The influence of gonorrheal infection in woman upon her conceptional capacity and upon the course and termination of pregnancy is of especial interest from the view point of race perpetuation. It has long been known that gonorrhea has an inhibitory influence upon the reproductive capacity of a woman. Noeggerath has asserted that 50 per cent. of sterility in women is caused by gonorrhea. Neisser declares more than 50 per cent. of the voluntary childless marriages and limitations of the number of children are due to gonorrhea and its sequelae in men and women. Lier-Ascher found that, out of 227 women, 121 were sterile because of gonorrhea. Numerous other authorities might be quoted, showing that a large percentage of sterility, as well as of abortions, are due to gonorrheal endometritis of the cervix and body of the uterus.

In explanation of the pathogenesis of sterility, much importance was formerly attached to the morbid condition of the mucosa of the uterus, which rendered it inapt for the germination of the ovum. At the present time we recognize that in almost all cases the production of sterility in the female admits of a purely mechanical explanation. It is caused by the blocking-up of the channels of communication between the ovary and the uterine receptacle of the ovum, thus preventing germinative contact with the spermatozoids. Before these profound alterations in the channels take place, the gonorrheic woman may conserve her conceptional capacity. A woman with gonorrhea of the cervix may readily conceive; conception may take place when the gonorrhea is acute, with a profuse purulent discharge. Fecundation may even take place when the uterine mucosa is infected. Gonorrheal salpingitis does not necessarily inhibit conception unless the channel of communication through the *ostium uterinum* is closed. Brothers reports two cases of women with pus tubes (bilateral salpingitis), the husbands at the time suffering from gonorrhea, who gave birth to several children. Unfortunately, in the majority of cases the first pregnancy, terminating either in abortion or accouchement, opens the gates to the infection which may have long existed in the cervix or the external genital canal, and admits its ascension to the ovaries, tubes, and peritoneum and the production of the changes which constitute a mechanical obstacle to the passage of the ovum. These changes are, as a rule, permanent and irremediable. It thus happens that the aptitude of the gonorrheic woman for conception is often extinguished by the first pregnancy, the first child representing the sum total of her productive energy. The sterility of the gonorrheic woman is thus relative rather than absolute. It is, in the expressive German phrase, *ein kinder sterilität*—a one-child sterility.

The influence of gonorrhea upon the course and termination of pregnancy is of importance in this connection. Sänger contends that the abortive influence of gonorrhea is quite as pronounced as that of syphilis. While this statement is perhaps overdrawn, yet clinical evidence shows most conclusively that there is an abnormal frequency of abortions among gonorrheic women who have become pregnant. Noeggerath found that of 53 women who became pregnant during the course of gonorrhea, 19 aborted. Fruhinsholtz found that of 101 pregnancies occurring in gonorrheic women, 71 went to full term, 23 terminated in abortion, and 7 by premature accouchement. In a number of these cases the presence of the gonococci was demonstrated in the residual placental *débris*, furnishing presumptive proof that it was the direct cause of the abortion.

The frequency with which these annexial complications are caused by gonorrhea is variously estimated by different authorities. Verchin states that in all his operations for salpingitis the cause could be attributed to a gonorrhea, or at least to the consequences of gonorrhea. In Pozzi's operations at the Lourcine Hospital nearly all were for gonorrheal salpingitis. In the report of the special committee of the American Medical Association, in 1901, which gave the opinion of the leading gynecologists in this country and Europe as to the "proportion of cases of pelvic inflammation coming under your care which were attributable to gonorrheal infection," there was found to be a wide difference of opinion as to the proportion attributable to this cause. Some operators gave their opinion that 90 per cent. were of gonorrheic origin. Price says that, in over a thousand sections for pelvic inflammation, 95 per cent. were attributable to gonorrhea, and that in these 95 per cent. the history was reliable and clear. Pozzi and Frederic gave a percentage of 75. A few of the estimates fall below 20, and the majority range from 23 to 95 per cent. The average of the entire statistics is 47 per cent. The exceedingly small percentage given by some of the reporters may have been due to the failure to make the bacteriological test for the gonococci, or perhaps, in some instances, to a lack of technical skill or to faulty methods in making this investigation. As Petersen says, "the more the disease is studied in women and the greater the improvement in bacteriological methods, the higher is to be found the percentage."

These statistics, be it understood, give no accurate idea of the prevalence of inflammatory diseases of the female generative organs due to gonorrhea; the percentages are for the most part based on cases requiring operative interference. They take no cognizance of the large number of gonorrheally infected women who, for various reasons, are not subjected to operation, and who continue under the care of the family physician, dragging out a miserable existence of semi-invalidism, subject to painful or difficult menstruation, with suppurative exacerbations, no longer able to walk freely, and condemned to pass their days of suffering in a reclining position, until, after several years, it may be, of this suffering, worn out and desperate, they apply to the surgeon for relief.

The bearing of these observations upon the question of the low fecundity of married women is obvious. In this country the question of the low birth-rate has assumed the importance of a national problem which has engaged the thoughtful attention and study of some of our most distinguished educators, sociologists and statesmen. Its designation as "race suicide" would favor the assumption that the low birth-rate is in all cases voluntary and independent of physical causes relating to the health or productive capacity of the married partners. There is ample reason for believing, however, that in a large proportion of cases the low birth-rate is not a result of choice but of incapacity. In this country the information derived from the Census Bureau Reports is worthless as a basis for the appreciation of this question, as they do not give proportion of sterile marriages to the whole number of marriages or to the general birth-rate or fecundity of the population. In certain European countries, where the statistics are compiled with more accuracy and with special reference to certain economic interests which are ignored by our Census Bureau, it has been found that the proportion of sterile marriage is about one in eleven.

The census report of 1900 has not yet furnished data as to the conjugal condition of the population.

The census of 1890 gives 32,000,000 married people, which would represent 16,000,000 marriages; at least one out of every seven is sterile. In different parts of this country the proportion is one in four or one in five.

No one knows better than the writer of this paper that the proportion of sterile marriages due to gonorrhea is an unknown and unknowable quantity; that it is impossible to present figures that aim even at approximate accuracy; but, from the mere statement of the fact that there is such a vast amount of sterility, and that gonorrhea is a common and most efficient cause, we can but conclude that the proportion due to this factor must be considerable.

There are so many pathogenic causes of a local or constitutional nature assigned as the cause of sterility, so much artificial sterility in which the marriage is childless by the choice of the parties conjoined who take precautions to frustrate or defeat nature by avoiding pregnancy, that it is impossible to determine whether the sterility is from incapacity or from choice. In looking over the statistics of the birth-rate in this country, we are impressed with the large percentage of marriages in which one child represents the total fecundity. Now, this is most significant in view of the fact that this is precisely the form of sterility for which gonorrhea is directly responsible, *viz.*, one-child sterility.

Abstraction made of every other possible factor of sterility and minimizing gonorrhea as a predisposing agent to the lowest possible degree, yet there must remain a vast contingent of sterile marriages which are caused directly and solely by gonorrheal infection. If "premeditated childlessness is a crime against society," as recently asserted by a high government authority, what shall be said of enforced childlessness, of the sterility which is not of choice but of compulsion; of the sad fate of women balked of their desire to have children by the disease of their husbands?

It is only in the confessional of the consulting room that one learns of the intense, unsatisfied craving on the part of many women for children, and of the wretchedness and disappointment they suffer when condemned to pass their existence in a childless wedlock. The instinct and craving for maternity becomes in some women a veritable obsession. They will at any cost of time and pain and suffering submit to any treatment which promises relief—curetting, division of the cervix, and even more formidable operations upon their pelvic organs. And the satire of it all is that in many cases the husband, inflated with the sense of his own virility, is himself responsible for the sterility!

The proportion of sterility due to the husband is said by Gross to be 17 per cent. Brothers, in his investigations, found that it was 20 per cent. Engelmann is inclined to place it at one in four, or 25 per cent. And it is to be remembered that almost the entire proportion of sterility in woman is due to gonorrhea communicated to her by her husband.

OPHTHALMIA NEONATORUM.

The social dangers which follow the introduction of gonorrhea into marriage are not limited to its effect upon the health or life of the mother, nor yet to its inhibitory influence upon her conceptional capacity, but are manifested still farther in the infective risks the mother herself conveys to her offspring.

In the vicious circle created by the process of parturition in the gonorrheal woman, the being she brings into the world is not only the innocent occasion of her pelvic accidents, but in turn becomes the recipient of the germs of the maternal disease, which may cause irreparable injury to one of the most precious organs of special sense, the eye.

The child, in its passage through the maternal parts, is compelled to undergo a veritable baptism of virulence. In the course of its passage, the face of the child and especially the eyes are liable to be soiled with the uterine, vaginal, and the vulvar liquids, containing gonococci. The opening of the eyes of the infant, occurring as a rule when the child comes into the world permits the penetration of the secretions into the conjunctival sac. The gonococci find in the delicate mucosa of the eyes a favorable soil for inoculation. The prolonged sojourn of the infant in the lower strait also favors this inoculation. In primipara, in whom the process of parturition is prolonged, the infant is more apt to contract contagion. After birth, the infectious secretion may be carried into the eyes through the intermediary of sponges, wash-cloths, or by the fingers of the accoucheur or nurse. When one eye remains uninfected, it may be inoculated with the purulent secretion of the other.

Gravity.—It is estimated that from 10 to 20 per cent. of all blindness is caused by gonorrheic infection. Of all causes of blindness, purulent conjunctivitis is the most powerful factor. According to Neisser, there are in Germany, at the present time, 30,000 blind, whose loss of sight is due to gonorrheal ophthalmia. In many institutions for the blind, no fewer than 60 per cent. of the inmates have lost their sight from gonorrheal infection. In the institutions of Paris, the percentage is estimated at 46; in Switzerland, 20; in Breslau, 13; in this country from 25 to 50.

Frequency.—In the report of the Committee of Seven, which records 1,941 cases of gonorrhea in women occurring in private practice in this city one year, there were found 265 children with purulent ophthalmia. In the same year there were found in one of the eye hospitals of this city 136 cases of purulent ophthalmia.

In maternity hospitals, the frequency of this accident has been reduced by the employment in women known to be suffering from gonorrhea of strict antiseptic prophylactic measures, such as vaginal douches, etc., up to the moment of accouchement.

Although purulent ophthalmia of the new-born has been largely shorn of its horror by the introduction of the Credé method, yet even now many children suffer the lifelong misfortune of deprivation of sight from maternal infection during the process of parturition. Even at the present day in Germany the gonorrhea of the new-born causes each year about 600 cases of blindness. It is said that in the blind population of Switzerland, one in every five is due to purulent conjunctivitis.

Unfortunately, when gonorrhea is localized in the cervix uteri, clinical evidence and bacteriological proof of its existence may be exceedingly difficult or impossible. The occurrence of purulent ophthalmia in the new-born may be accepted as proof-positive of the infection of the mother.

The symptomatology of purulent conjunctivitis is too familiar to require description. The chief danger so far as the effect upon the visual function is concerned, resides in the corneal complications and their consequences. If treatment is instituted before the cornea becomes seriously implicated, the results are always more favorable.

Horner found 161 cases of ophthalmia neonatorum, 53 of which were brought to him after the cessation of the active inflammatory process for corneal lesions more or less grave; of these 53, 14 were completely blind, 25 were partially blind, and in 15 there were corneal opacities which impaired vision. In the remaining 108 cases which were brought to him in active evolution, 40, or 37 per cent., presented corneal lesions before treatment, and three during treatment. He observed that the greater number of patients in whom the cornea was attacked suffered from a more or less complete diminution of visual capacity.

Hirshberg, in 200 cases of gonorrheal ophthalmia, found that 53, or 27 per cent., suffered from initial corneal lesions; six of these terminated in complete blindness. In 378 cases of purulent conjunctivitis treated by Heim, 317 were cured completely, and

61 had permanent lesions with impaired vision. Eperon, in 161 cases occurring in private practice, had only 11 bad results. Of these 11, 7 presented, when first seen, grave and irreparable lesions of the cornea, most of which were produced by a too active treatment with caustic solutions.

The dangers of purulent conjunctivitis from maternal infection are not limited to the child. Nothing is more infectious than ophthalmia neonatorum. It often happens that the attendants, the nurse, or the members of the family are infected, and it is to be observed that, while the infection may be comparatively benign in the infant and yield readily to the Credé method, with complete conservation of the integrity of the sight, the infection transmitted to the attendants most often results in a virulent inflammation which may entirely destroy the eyes. It is probable that the infection of the eyes of the child during confinement is in many cases less active; the inoculated pus may be attenuated by the fluids with which it is mingled. Oftentimes it is the pus of a chronic metritis which possesses only a modified virulence. When transferred to the more favorable soil of the conjunctival membrane of the child, it acquires an exalted virulence and becomes capable, when again transferred to a new medium, of determining the highest grade of inflammation. Gonorrheal conjunctivitis of the adult may terminate in perforation with destruction of vision or it may lapse into a chronic stage.

The Credé method of treating ophthalmia neonatorum must be regarded as one of the most valuable acquisitions to modern therapy, since, through the introduction of this prophylactic measure, the destructive efforts of the gonococcus upon the eyes of the new-born have been materially reduced. On account of the pain and irritation caused by the 2 per cent. solution of silver nitrate and its caustic, penetrating action, there is a tendency on the part of ophthalmologists to substitute a milder solution of the silver nitrate or one of the silver salts, such as protargol, argyrol, or argamentine. The use of a few drops of a 10 per cent. solution of argyrol is claimed to be an infallible preventive, which is entirely free from the irritating effects caused by the silver nitrate.

DANGERS TO THE ENTOURAGE.

Vulvovaginitis of Young Girls.—Another danger introduced into family and social life by gonorrhea is caused by a certain class of inoculations to which the term gonorrhea insontium applies with special fitness.

One of the characteristics of gonorrhea is its susceptibility of being communicated by mediate contagion. No fact is better established than that coitus is not essential to infection. The numerous facts of experimental inoculation show conclusively that the virus of gonorrhea may be transferred by means of any indifferent object upon which it has been deposited and inoculated when brought into contact with a mucous surface susceptible to its action. Even before the discovery of the gonococcus, it was known that the pus of gonorrhea might be isolated and collected, or, when accidentally adherent to any foreign body, might be unconsciously inoculated. Numerous well-authenticated cases of water-closet infection have been recorded. Rossolimos cites cases in which it was derived from the night-vase, towels, etc. The common use of vaginal douche tubes may be the cause of gonorrheal transmission; the fingers, thermometers, towels, sponges, etc., may be the medium of transference of the virus. The period during which the dried pus deposited on a foreign body conserves its virulence is not absolutely determined.

It is evident, therefore, that a case of gonorrhea in a family may be the source of multiple contagions. Of most interest in this connection is the class of contagions which, through their habitual localization, have received the name of vulvovaginitis. The innocent victims of this form of contagion are usually children from two to six years of age. It may be present in the new-born or at any age below puberty.

Frequency.—There are no statistics available from which we can estimate the frequency of this accident; undoubtedly it is much larger than is commonly supposed. In the report of the Committee of Seven, there were found 218 cases of vulvovaginitis in private practice in this city among 1,941 cases of gonorrhea in women.

While it is admitted that not all the cases of purulent discharge from the genitals of young girls are of gonorrheal origin, yet the other factors, the irritation of pin-worms, uncleanliness, certain diathetic states, attempted violation, etc., pay an etiologic rôle quite insignificant in comparison with the gonococcus.

In this connection it may be stated that the vulvovaginitis of young girls has most important medico-legal relations. Formerly these cases were almost universally attributed to violation. The assumption that any purulent discharge from the genital mucous membrane of a young girl is necessarily the result of criminal intercourse has often led to the unjust accusation and punishment of innocent persons for attempted violation. One knows the facility with which children are disposed to accuse and lie, especially if they have bad habits to conceal. The physician should always be exceedingly reserved in giving an opinion in such cases, as the suggestion that a purulent discharge in a young girl was caused by violation might lead to the gravest consequences. We now recognize that gonorrhea in children is vastly more often due to accidental mediate transmission than to attempted intercourse.

Our knowledge of the gonorrheic origin of vulvovaginitis is essentially a modern acquisition. It is only within the last ten or fifteen years, since the methods of distinguishing between simple and specific inflammation have been more generally understood and employed, that vulvovaginitis is recognized as a true gonorrheal infection. One has only to examine our text-books on diseases of children, prior to 1890, in order to appreciate this fact. Koplik (1893) did much to disseminate in this country a knowledge of the specific origin of this disease and the comparative frequency of its occurrence.

Calven Brach examined 21 children with vulvovaginitis; in 20 he found the gonococcus; 7 had been violated; 3 had contracted the disease at the hospital; 10 others had shared the bed of the mother suffering from gonorrhea, or there lived in the same family some person affected with gonorrhea. Kalven, in the examination of 30 girls, aged from seven months to eleven years, found gonorrhea in 24. In 6, the inflammation was of a simple character. Fischer found the gonococcus in 50 out of

59 cases. Vaillon and Halle found gonorrhea in 25 cases out of 27.

Etiology.—Infection of the child may occur (1) during the process of parturition; (2) from inoculative contact of the genitals of the child with a person suffering from gonorrhea; or (3) from mediate contagion by means of various articles upon which the virus may have been deposited.

Inoculation may take place from contact of the vulva of the child with uterine secretions mixed with pus containing gonococci. A breech presentation favors the ready penetration of the gonococci into the genial tract. This is more apt to be the case when the labor is prolonged.

In the large majority of cases the patient has had actual contact with persons suffering from gonorrhea. It may be from sleeping in the same bed with the father or mother, in other cases with a brother, sister, or nurse who is suffering from the infection. Spaeth found that in 90 per cent. of all cases of specific vulvovaginitis in children coming under his notice, the mothers suffered from leucorrhea or uterine discharge. These family epidemics are very frequent. The youngest child is not usually the one first contaminated. The comparative infrequency of this accident before the second year, as a rule, is explained by the fact that this period corresponds to the time during which the child occupies the cradle alone.

In other cases the contagion is conveyed mediately by the use of sponges, towels, or by the use of a common bath. There are numerous cases of mediate contagion recorded from vulvovaginitis from the use of pencils or other articles soiled with the discharge. In one case a little girl who had received in the eye, while playing, the finger of one of her playmates who was afflicted with vulvovaginitis, suffered from a characteristic purulent conjunctivitis in which gonococci were abundantly found.

Epidemics of specific vulvovaginitis have been recorded by numerous observers in children's hospitals. In almost all cases the origin of the epidemic could be traced to a child who had entered the hospital with a specific vulvovaginitis.

Epidemics of vulvovaginitis have been observed from the

common use of public baths by children. Suchard reports a remarkable epidemic of vulvovaginitis in young girls at Lavey, which continued for twelve or fifteen days until the use of the public bath was forbidden. Another remarkable epidemic was reported by Skutch as occurring in the city of Posen, where 236 children, whose ages varied from six to fourteen years, developed in the course of a fortnight vulvovaginitis of gonorrheal origin which was proved to be due to the use of the public bath.

Localization.—The term vulvovaginitis does not strictly indicate the exclusive localization of the infection. While the vulva is primarily affected, the infection may invade not only the vagina, but the urethra and cervix. Contrary to what is observed in the adult, Bartholini's glands are rarely the seat of the infection. The vagina of the child, however, is quite susceptible to the action of the gonococcus, but the inflammation is as a rule of comparatively short duration. Just as in the adult, the gonorrheal process tends to localize itself in the urethra or in the cervical neck.

While the urethra is also frequently the seat of the process, it is, however, not so persistent and gives rise to no serious symptoms.

The cervical localization of the gonorrhea of young girls is now recognized as much more common than was formerly supposed. In the majority of cases in which the duration of the inflammatory process has been prolonged, the mucosa of the cervix will be found congested and inflamed, and pus is seen to exude from the cervical opening. Koplik found that, in all the cases examined by himself with a small urethral speculum, pus escaped from the external os. The participation of the uterine mucosa in the inflammatory process may be considered quite habitual.

The extension of the infection to the body of the uterus and the consequent evolution of pelviperitonitis, though comparatively rare, is no less well authenticated. There are numerous cases in which the tubes, ovaries, and peritoneum were found to be involved in the pathological process. Currier suggests that many cases of undeveloped uteri resulting in dysmenorrhea and sterility may be due to gonorrheal infection in infancy. It is also probable that many cases of metritis and salpingitis occurring in virgins and young women at the age of puberty, or later, and the origin of which was indeterminate, may be ascribed to an antecedent vulvovaginitis which may have been overlooked or forgotten.

Specific infectious vulvovaginitis and that due to simple causes have certain clinical characteristics in common—redness, swelling, and purulent discharge. They can, as a rule, be distinguished by clinical evidence; the results of treatment also serve to differentiate them. In gonorrheal vulvovaginitis the discharge is thick, greenish yellow, and abundant. In simple vulvovaginitis the discharge is thin, serous, viscous, or yellowish gray. The latter has a tendency to clear up promptly under the influence of cleanliness and simple aseptic washes. If these simple means do not promptly succeed in curing the trouble, further attempts should be made to ascertain its possible specific nature. The gonococcus may be found in almost all cases if examination is made at a favorable moment.

It is worthy of note that gonorrheal vulvovaginitis may be the source of serious autoinfection—the patient transferring the gonorrheal virus from the vulva to the eyes.

The tendency of the child to carry the hand to the genital parts explains the frequent transference of the infection. Gonorrheal ophthalmia is recognized as a most frequent complication of vulvovaginitis. Ceseri reports certain cases of this kind out of 26 cases of vulvovaginitis. Weidmark has observed 19 cases of this complication. Gonorrheal rheumatism is also a frequent complication of vulvovaginitis. Beclèrc has reported several cases which demonstrate the coincident occurrence of gonorrheal rheumatism and vulvovaginitis in infants. The comparative frequency of this complication is not, however, possible to determine.

It is no exaggeration to state that every year in this country thousands of young, innocent women are infected by their husbands who, in many cases, do not dream that they carry to the marriage bed the germs of a disease destined to wreck the health or lives of their partners. These women are condemned to invalidism, to various inflammatory disorders of the pelvic organs, to sterility, to castration, by the act of men who have vowed to love, cherish and protect them. It is not because men are so lacking in conscience and sensibility that they perpetrate these crimes; it is largely from ignorance and lack of knowledge as to the nature and danger of gonorrheal infection, for which the medical profession is largely responsible. After all, the views of the laity upon many medical subjects are but the reflected opinions of the medical profession. The time is not long past when the existence of an intermittent gleet was not thought to be an obstacle to marriage. Many physicians were accustomed to recommend what was called "the sexual hygiene of married life" as the best cure for these intermittent discharges. It is not surprising that the laity are unsuspicious of the pathogenic significance or the potentiality for mischief of a disease which the physician regarded as practically cured.

WHAT ARE THE REMEDIES?

Since prostitution is the fountain-head of this disease, it might seem that the only effective remedy would be to attack the evil at its source. All experience proves, however, that prostitution must be looked upon as a necessary evil in our social system, which cannot be uprooted or destroyed, and it must be remembered that it is not the prostitute, but the husband and father, who carries the poison home and distributes it to his family.

Many sociologists, with a fatuous belief in the efficacy of legislation to suppress and control prostitution, look upon legal enactments as our only social defence against the venereal plague. Much has been written and much has been said about the efficacy of moral and religious influence in the uprooting of vice, upon the beneficial effects of the regulation of prostitution or its suppression by state and municipal legislation; but the fact is irrefutable that no legislative force, whether practicable or not, no police intervention, whether justifiable or the reverse, promises to be immediately available. In this country at least, recognition of the evil to the extent of license and control is barred by public sentiment. The policy of the movement encounters a strong hostility from the public. We have to fall back upon methods which are practicable and available. The true remedy, the only remedy at present available to modify or minimize the appalling evils, moral and physical, which flow from venereal diseases, is the education of the public, the general dissemination of knowledge respecting the dangers and modes of contagion of venereal diseases. It is not by legislative enactments, but by the persuasive force of enlightenment, by combating the dense ignorance which prevails among the laity, and especially among the young upon whom the incidence of these diseases most heavily falls that these evils can be corrected. If a young man is instructed into a knowledge of the fact that venereal disease is the almost invariable concomitant of licentious living, that such indulgence is not wholesome for him, that it carries with it consequences to himself and to others, consequences which may impair his health, vitiate his manhood and lead to a forfeiture of all those hopes and aspirations which are to be fulfilled in a safe, fruitful, and happy marriage—he will pause and consider, etc. Human nature is so constituted that from the days of Adam until now the mandate "Thou shalt not," etc., has ever proved the strongest incentive to disobedience.

What the laity needs, then, is such enlightenment. (1) An entire reconstruction of the traditional view that gonorrhea is a trivial disease, easily cured and entailing no serious after-consequences. (2) A knowledge of the fact that apparent cures are most often deceptive, that the chief danger of the disease is its potentiality for mischief after apparent cure. (3) That the gonococci are endowed with remarkable longevity; that they may persist in a latent state, susceptible of being awakened into activity and virulence, months or years after active symptoms have ceased. (4) That the necessary and indispensable condition of the admissibility to marriage of the gonorrheic is a clean bill of health, the absence of gonococci from the urethral secretions, demonstrated by the most exacting bacteriological tests.

The results of the false impressions instilled into the minds of young men, that sexual indulgence is essential to health should be corrected. It is through the medical profession that this saving and salutary influence of enlightenment must come. The family physician is peculiarly adapted, by his intimate relation with his patients, the freedom which his vocation allows him to talk on topics ordinarily forbidden, and his relation as friend as well as professional adviser, to impart this information and explain matters relating to sexual hygiene in a manner always decent, but sufficiently plain.

DISCUSSION.

Dr. F. H. Gerrish, Portland, Me.:[1]

I wish to express the very great satisfaction I have had in listening to this most able and interesting paper. The subject is one of the highest importance for us as physicians and as sociologists. I have myself been greatly interested in it for a number of years. A quarter of a century ago, I read an essay—the annual address—before the Maine Medical Association on the subject of the duties of the medical profession upon prostitution and its allied vices; and, while at that time we did not know as much as we do now of the virulency and danger of gonorrhea, we did know that it was a menace to people in various ways, and the ground that I took then was equally the ground taken by Dr. Morrow now: The necessity of the education of the young, purely but plainly with reference to sexual matters. Then and now I believe that this is the one way out of this great difficulty.

Last year, at the meeting of the Maine Medical Association, of which at that time I had the honor of being president, in my address I recommended that a committee should be appointed to report this year upon the advisability of securing legislation which should place gonorrhea and syphilis upon the list of those diseases required to be reported to the boards of health as contagious diseases. That report will be made next month and I am informed will be in favor of such legislation. Whether such legislation can be obtained remains to be seen, but I had largely in mind the educational influence in agitating for the legislation. I do not think that legislation will affect morals directly, but indirectly the educational value is often very great.

Dr. L. Duncan Bulkley, of New York:

I do not think that we can overestimate the importance of the paper presented to us. I have to acknowledge that the conviction has come a little slowly upon my mind in regard to the importance of gonorrhea as compared to that of syphilis, in its influence upon the human race. Some ten years ago when I read a paper upon syphilis, and urged legislative enactment, whereby syphilis should be placed upon the list of contagious diseases, in the discussion Dr. Keyes, of New York, made a statement that startled me.

[1] Published without the revision of Dr. Gerrish'.

Said he, "gonorrhea is many times more dangerous to public health than syphilis." Since then I have watched results and I am quite convinced that his opinion is correct. While I was hardly prepared to accept all the statements of Dr. Morrow's paper with regard to the immense amount of sterility and abortions due to gonorrhea, I presume the statements are true, and if so, it is indeed desirable to have them gathered into one paper. It is a subject that distinctly and peculiarly comes under the attention of this Academy of Medicine, in its relation to sociology. We all agree that active legislative laws against prostitution will never succeed in this country. "Thou shalt not" will only make them want to do it the more. I think we should from this time forth use our influence day by day in having men understand the dangers they run when they give way to their lusts. We should become imbued with the idea of being medical missionaries in society. In my office I have had men say to me, "Why, I don't think anything more of gonorrhea than I do of a cold. Every one has it, or expects to have it." It is more frequent than any of us imagine.

I think the writer has well brought out the point of gonorrhea of women as being seldom recognized. In man it is recognized because of the pain in micturition. That does not exist in women. There is only a slight degree of leucorrhea, to which little attention is paid and the majority of cases in women are left unchecked for years. We know that it sometimes runs itself out.

Perhaps the Academy knows that the matter has been taken up in New York with Dr. Morrow as chairman of a committee (of which I have the honor to be a member) to investigate the subject in New York City. At the meeting of the American Medical Association, last year at Saratoga, in the Skin Section there was a paper and some discussion with regard to the prophylaxis of venereal diseases, and a committee was appointed to visit the Section on Hygiene and present the matter. I happened to be appointed on that committee. We visited the Section on Hygiene and they appointed a Joint Committee, and the Joint Committee framed a resolution which went before the House of Delegates upon the prophylaxis of venereal diseases. A report was made this year. The committee was continued and at the last meeting of the House of Delegates that committee was continued as a Central Committee with instructions to organize a Congress on the Prophylaxis of Venereal Diseases, which will probably be held during the St. Louis Fair. That committee is to be enlarged by members from all states, each state having its representative appointed by the president of the state medical society.

Dr. A. L. Benedict, of Buffalo:

What Dr. Bulkley has said reminds me of my own experience. I have found syphilis a very rare trouble; or if it is more common, it is so well cured and so innocuous that I do not recognize it. Even in practice limited to the digestive organs, syphilitic cases ought to be as frequent as in the average population. In abdominal work in women especially, we have complications in the pelvis calling for operation, the result of gonorrhea. There are two points to which I would like to refer: (1) The radical cure of these cases. There exists among gynecologists at present a desire to save ovaries. I believe it is a pretty general rule that it is better to take out both ovaries in these cases, to exterminate the whole field of danger when there is a possibility of infection, and that this danger should usually outweigh the laudable endeavor to avoid sterility or the fear of loss of the rather theoretic internal ovarian secretion. (2) The obligation to examine for the gonococcus. I remember in my practice the case of a young working girl with movable kidney in which there was a pus tube. The gynecologists said, of course it was gonorrhea. I believe that a man taking that ground is bound to do a great injustice to many innocent women. During the Pan-American Exposition a young man came into my office. He had what appeared to be gonorrhea. On examination there was no gonorrhea present, but simply a septic inflammation. In general practice I have seen cases in which married men had urethritis, but without gonorrhea. The social complications of a false diagnosis can be readily imagined, and I believe in every case the matter should be absolutely settled. I remember a case occurring recently of a young girl with cystitis. The whole history pointed toward gonorrhea, which was denied. Examination showed colon-bacillus infection of the bladder.

I would like to ask Dr. Morrow if he believes the responsibility for gonorrhea is traced back to the West Indies as has been stated.

Dr. S. D. Risley, of Philadelphia:

I am glad that Dr. Benedict alluded to the other forms of infection rather than those due to the gonococcus of Neiser. I regret very much that the part of the paper relating to ophthalmia neonatorum was not read, since it is well known there are such cases not gonorrheal in character; that is, there are other forms of infection which are very persistent in the eyes of the newborn child, usually not so virulent as those of the gonococcus. I agree with Dr. Benedict that a bacteriologic examination should be made before an opinion of that specific form of infection is made.[1]

[1] The discussion on Dr. Morrow's paper was unfortunately abruptly closed by the arrival of an hour fixed for the discussion of another subject.

OBSERVATIONS IN PASSING.

The Second Annual Report of the New York State Hospital for the Care of Crippled and Deformed Children gives account of a praiseworthy effort to build up self-respecting wage-earners out of very defective material.

The crippled children are placed under such treatment as a very competent surgical staff may direct. The results have been very gratifying, the helpless are cured, or at least so improved as to make their defect much less pronounced, thereby increasing their chances to earn a livelihood.

***

The Annual Report of the New York State Reformatory describes an entirely different work, with the same object in view, and a much more extensive proportion. A statement on the reverse of the title-page informing us that "this volume in editing, typography, illustration, and binding is solely the product of inmates' labor," when taken in connection with the excellence of the work, shows that some of the inmates have acquired skill in these trades.

This institution receives from the courts certain prisoners, and endeavors to reform them by the use of such means as will lift them up physically, mentally, and morally. There are schools for the illiterate, trades instruction for non-skilled (there being now 32 trades taught), gymnasium, military drill, etc., and the outcome is very gratifying.

***

At the recent convocation of the University of the State of New York, Dr. Helen C. Putnam, upon invitation of the regents, presented her plan for organizing the department for the instruction of hygiene in the public schools. As Dr. Jackson said in the general discussion at the Washington meeting, the previous agitations on the subject leading to the present laws has awakened public thought on the subject. Let the physicians of the land aid in directing this awakened thought, and great good will result even to the cause which led to the first agitation on the subject.

BULLETIN

OF THE

American Academy of Medicine

Vol. VI.   Issued October, 1903.   No. 8.

The American Academy of Medicine is not responsible for the sentiments expressed in any paper or address published in the Bulletin.

ELECTIVE STUDIES IN THE MEDICAL COURSE.

I.

ELECTIVES IN ANATOMY.[1]

By Frederic Henry Gerrish, M.D., Portland, Maine.

My views on electives in the medical course will probably be regarded by many as hopelessly old-fashioned, and as indicative of an unprogressive spirit; but I shall endeavor to give good reasons for the faith that is in me.

Quite frequently we see in one or another medical journal an editorial on "the passing of the general practitioner," and it is always a lamentation that the "family doctor" is, in the opinion of the editor, rapidly becoming merely a guide, whose service to his patrons consists in advising them what specialist to employ for the treatment of the ailment which may exist on any particular occasion. We are told of a lady, who was about to make a long visit in one of our great cities, and who was charged to see a noted oculist, if she had trouble with her eyes, a famous aurist should her ears be in need, a great gynecologist in certain contingencies, a well-known laryngologist, if her voice required attention, another specialist for ailments of her stomach, and so on. The long list having been rehearsed, the lady asked, "And to

[1] Read before the American Academy of Medicine, Washington, D. C., May 12, 1903.

whom shall I go, if I am sick?" This, of course, is the *reductio ad absurdum* of the matter. No one seriously questions the advantage of having experts in the various lines of medical work, or doubts that the great advances in our knowledge come from those who focus their attention upon some limited portion of the field. That the number, both absolutely and relatively, of those who devote their energies to special studies is increasing admits of no question, and is not to be deplored; but that more than a minority will ever do so is practically impossible. It is not true in the most densely populated countries, and *a fortiori* it can never be the fact in America, for the area of our country is so vast that outside of great communities the population must be widely scattered and unable to support a number of medical men sufficiently large to permit any considerable division in the kind of their work. This great land must always depend for its medical service very largely upon the all-round doctor, and the frequent displays of grief at the extinction of the family physician are entirely misplaced—the funeral sermon need not be prepared until the corpse is much more nearly ready than is the case at present.

We may fairly start, then, with the assumption that the enormous majority of medical men are going to be general practitioners from the necessities of the case. Consequently it is the plain and primary duty of a medical school to give its students such an equipment as will qualify them to become all-round doctors—not the peers of specialists in any namable line, but capable of doing in their field of action that quality of work which reasonableness and a righteous law demand. It will immediately be objected that this plan makes provision for those only who contemplate general practice, and ignores the needs of the minority who purpose devoting themselves to specialties. This objection, however, seems to me to be based upon an incomplete conception of the methods by which the best specialists are educated. A physician, who has taken advantage of a wide opportunity for observation of specialists in any line, must have been impressed with the difference between those of them who have begun their medical career with some time spent in general practice, and those who, from the start, have consecrated their talents, however great, to work in a narrow field. The former class continually has in mind the co-relation of the condition of the whole system and manifestations of disease in any particular organ; the latter frequently fails to interpret aright the local symptoms, because his thoughts are so completely engaged with the morbid exhibition to which his attention is specifically invited. The medical school does the highest service to the student, who means to be a specialist, by insisting that he shall equip himself first for general practice; and it would be well for the community if every young graduate could be persuaded to go into general medical work for a few years, at least, so that his views of the inter-relationship of functions, both physiologic and pathologic, might be widened and strengthened.

Thus far my remarks may be interpreted to mean opposition to electives in any branch of the medical curriculum, and I shall not attempt to avoid that imputation. Having been a teacher of various branches in medicine for a third of a century, I have had a considerable opportunity for knowing medical students; and I have no hesitation in saying that very few of them are competent, in the early part of their course, to judge of their own capabilities or the needs of the community for medical service. A large part, dazzled by the brilliancy of surgery, register a vow in the early months that they will be great operators, not appreciating the fact that only a small minority of the medical men in any land can find enough major surgery to keep them busy. The ambitions of the novice are usually frost-bitten before he reaches his fourth year, and he is fairly content if he can discover a community in which he has a tolerable prospect of getting a living in what he had previously considered the much humbler realm of general practice. After a time he is likely to come to the conclusion, which, in my opinion, is perfectly sound, that there is required for first-class achievement in all-round practice a much higher grade of talent, a greater resourcefulness, and finer moral fiber than for success in any specialty. Thus the average medical student demonstrates in his course that he is not competent to make a wise selection of the branches which it is best for him to study. If he could have his way, he would neglect essentials, and devote himself to some department in which he would have practically but little probability of success from any point of view.

If my argument has a basis of truth, a knowledge of the structure of the entire body is fundamentally important for the medical man. As commonly taught, many unimportant details are insisted upon, which are promptly forgotten as soon as the examinations are passed. But even when unessential matters are eliminated, there remains so much anatomy to be learned as to require all of the time which this department of the curriculum can fairly claim. Consequently, it is injudicious to encourage the undergraduate to attempt additional anatomical work. If, from his interest in this branch, he takes extra hours in it, he must do so at the expense of required tasks in some other line, or else overtax himself—neither of which things is either wise or just. But, when he has attained the doctorate, he has a sufficient knowledge of all the departments to qualify him to judge whether or not it is best for him to pursue his studies in anatomy any further, and he may then give rein to his taste, and take means to broaden and deepen his learning in this direction, without endangering the desirable symmetry of his professional development or impairing his potential capacity as a practitioner of the healing art.

II.
INTERNAL MEDICINE—TO WHAT EXTENT REQUIRED OR ELECTIVE IN THE MEDICAL COURSE?[1]

BY S. G. BONNEY, A.M., M.D., Dean and Professor of Medicine, Denver and Gross College of Medicine.

In order to more clearly define the applicability of the elective system to internal medicine, it is almost necessary to consider first its general relation to a medical course and to review briefly the trend of medical educative thought.

The sociologic and economic conditions of the country do not at present, as formerly, require a large number of physicians to supply, from time to time, the needs of the smaller communities. There is on the contrary an appeal for relief from the incubus of the insufficiently prepared practitioner, in order that more encouraging inducements may be offered to the type of the educated physician. From a strictly business standpoint, these inducements to spend years of preparatory study are now becoming not particularly attractive to those contemplating general medicine in view of the active competition incident to the overcrowding of the profession. Failure to remain in medical practice is said to attend the efforts of nearly one-third of all graduates of recent years.

Despite the recent advances in medical teaching, consisting in part of more rigid requirements for admission, the lengthening of the period of study and the enlargement of the curriculum, all tending to impose legitimate restrictions upon the number of students, and notwithstanding, also, the well-known uncertainties of success in practice, there is, nevertheless, no material diminution in the number of young men willing and anxious to undertake the laborious task of systematic medical study. This implies a certain change in the motives and aspirations of the more liberally educated medical students of to-day, some of whom are induced to begin the study of the purely scientific aspect of medicine with its opportunities for original research and investigation,

[1] Read before the American Academy of Medicine, Washington, D. C., May 13, 1903.

while others are attracted early to the possible attainment of special knowledge and skill in certain departments with the hope of subsequent contribution to the science of medicine, rather than the acquirement of a large general practice. These natural tendencies in students have been further influenced by necessary and progressive changes in the course of medical instruction.

As a result of the greatly enlarged curriculum and the enormous increase of medical knowledge, the student is brought to a realization in the beginning of his career, that he will be utterly unable to acquire even a superficial knowledge of all branches, and that he may hope to attain a degree of proficiency only in a small proportional part of his profession.

The inevitable result is an appreciation of the necessity for specialization in some form. In spite of the admitted objections to the greater development of specialism, the fact remains that it is distinctly in accord with popular and professional demand. A high degree of special attainment based upon broad fundamental knowledge has ever been the chief factor in advancing the science and art of medicine. Save in the remotely settled districts, the day of the general practitioner, in his ordinary acceptance, is nearly at an end, and in his place are to be found men, who, if they are less courageous, less self-reliant than the time-honored country doctor, are nevertheless, more cognizant of their limitations.

To encourage intelligent specialism, to afford an opportunity to excel in certain departments, and at the same time to guard against superficial and disproportionate work, constitutes an important province in the modern medical school. To this end a full interpretation of the elective system has been offered, not with a view of aiding premature specialization, but more to permit an early beginning of a thorough preliminary preparation leading to subsequent advanced work either in internal medicine or other specialties.

The elective system may be defined as that method of instruction which permits the exercise under a supposedly wise direction of the student's choice of study according to his conception of his peculiar needs and purposes, and his inherent adaptability for certain work. That a flexible curriculum is correct in principle and has been shown by experience to be a distinct advance in colleges of liberal arts and preparatory schools, no observer of pedagogic conditions will deny. This, however, in view of the greater responsibility involved in medicine, does not necessarily constitute evidence in favor of its general adoption as a system of medical education. It may be said to possess definite advantages in certain institutions and be capable therein of its most complete and satisfactory elaboration according to the size, facilities, and purposes of the school. Manifestly, precisely similar conditions may not be in force in other colleges, and an equal observance, therefore, of the elective system rendered impractical, or if attempted to the same degree, productive only of harm.

It follows that the extent of the applicability of the system to any school must vary according to the peculiar scope and working ideals of the institution. It is recognized that the purposes of some of the modern university medical schools are much more comprehensive than merely to educate doctors. The preparation and training of practical physicians, as exemplified in undergraduate instruction, forms but a single integral part of their real mission or ambition. Their energies are devoted in part to the rendering of post-graduate instruction, the pursuit of original research on the part of the professors and selected students, the investigations of new discoveries and new phases of medical learning, and to the possible enlargement of the practical scope of pure science. It is in these institutions that the elective system is of the utmost advantage in offering opportunity for the attainment of the highest degree of technical learning, and it is to be commended in its fullest interpretation, if practised under the restraining, governing, and advisory counsel of the proper officials of the faculty. Such institutions are scarcely to be subjected, however, to the same principles of thought accorded to the medical school proper, whose sole object is to shape the early education of working doctors. Even in such institutions the elective system may be said to present certain features of advantage if applied with discrimination to the latter portion of the course, presupposing a thorough preparation in the required fundamental studies, and subject in each instance to the well-considered approval of the medical authorities. The degree to which such satisfying results may obtain must vary according to the peculiar conditions in force in each institution, thus rendering any school in this respect a law unto itself. The size of the school, the number of students, the amount of endowment, and the proportionment of electives affords no reliable measure of its real efficiency. A small school is not necessarily of low standard provided it possesses ample laboratory and hospital facilities, and embraces in its faculty men of sufficient preliminary education, of ripe experience, and possessed of proper enthusiasm and high ideals. In like manner it is not simply the method or system of instruction, elective, required, didactic or clinical, that determines in full the career or usefulness of the student, as much as the manner in which the subject is interpreted and the degree of inspiration awakened by the instructor. The practical utility of the elective system varies not only with reference to the institution where it is employed, but also according to the extent of its application to the various departments. As practised in a few institutions it permits not only the choice of the subject, but of the instructor as well, and the manner in which instruction shall be given.

What are some of its recognized general advantages in a well-balanced and duly proportioned course of instruction?

(1) The adaptability of the particular study to the peculiar requirements and mental receptivity of the student based on the known divergence in character and degree of individual capacity.

(2) The consequent increased interest on the part of the student in not being compelled to devote valuable time to some irrelevent and, to him, apparently unimportant branch.

(3) The greater degree of technical efficiency attained by those anticipating a specialty through the additional time afforded for such preliminary preparation.

(4) The improved opportunities for observation and study afforded to those contemplating general medicine, in being relieved of too rigid requirements in a few of the distinctly refined specialties.

(5) The shortening of the period of time demanded in prepara-

tion for practical work, this not to imply, however, the completion of special education in a four years' course.

(6) The inspiration and incentive derived on the part of the instructor from the fact that his students are at once earnest and enthusiastic, and that he, himself, is given immediate active recognition.

(7) The opportunity afforded in the larger institutions for the more intimate contact of instructor and student. This closer association and exchange of thought incident to the smaller colleges is of great utility in the imparting of knowledge.

These general advantages of the elective system though scarcely worthy of detailed elaboration may obtain in all instances if under the actual and not nominal supervision of a board of control.

There are objections, however, to be made and answered as to the practical employment of the system. The basis of these objections is found to exist purely through a possible laxity or carelessness on the part of the faculty in the exercise of their advisory, or, if necessary, arbitrary function.

(1) The necessity exists on the part of the faculty for infinite patience and time in the deliberate consideration of each student's needs and purposes, in order to insure a proper selection of study. This is sometimes difficult of practical attainment and demands that the work of review and counsel be apportioned to a duly constituted committee who shall be held responsible for results.

(2) There is a possibility of error in the choice of method of instruction, the tendency being perhaps to neglect didactic and recitation teaching for the apparently more natural or practical instruction at the bedside. Here the text is found in the patient rather than the disease. While this constitutes the essential thought in actual practice, it is insisted that its proper judicial fulfilment could not be there attained save by a course of preliminary instruction relative to the disease itself. The student is enabled to profit by the clinical work as illustrative of what has been previously acquired from the comprehensive and well-rounded lecture or recitation. The bedside teaching develops careful methods of examination and closeness of observation, be-

sides emphasizing in a practical way the lessons of the didactic lecture and text-book. It should be carefully guarded, therefore, that in the student's choice of method, each coordinate branch of instruction be given within certain fixed limits its due and justly accorded place.

(3) The selection of a prospective specialty may be made at too early a period in the course of medical instruction, thus involving the possibility of an unwise choice before the student has had sufficient opportunity to properly appreciate his own inclinations and special fitness. As a matter of fact, however, the student is usually prepared to judge somewhat as to his tastes and desires, relative either to scientific or practical work upon the completion of his required fundamental studies. If teaching of scientific subjects or laboratory investigation is selected as the most suitable field for future work the decision is better made then than at the time of graduation. If a course of special practical study is avowedly instituted in the midst of his period of undergraduate instruction, it is certainly destined to result more satisfactorily if pursued under the direction of the faculty, than if practised as formerly according to the fancies and prejudices of the student who has always been found to entertain notions of his own concerning the line of work he is supposedly designed to follow.

(4) The likelihood is suggested that measures looking toward too early specialization may produce superficial and embryonic results. Should the training and instruction in special work preparatory for practice be permitted to end upon graduation, against which possibility there is unfortunately no distinct remedy, the objection is only too well sustained. If, however, post-graduate work is insisted upon as a *sine qua non* before entering upon special practice, it must follow that the selected grouping of studies in undergraduate instruction has only served to render more thorough and complete the preliminary preparation for specialism. It is evident that a properly regulated course of electives constitutes one of the most conspicuous advances in modern medical teaching. Its degree of usefulness varies according to the extent of its application and control peculiar to each department of a medical course.

How far shall this apply to internal medicine? The relation of internal medicine to the elective system is radically different from that of all other coordinate branches of medical instruction, in that it occupies a position singularly unique and distinctive in its scope and requirements. Its practical working basis may be said to consist of a modified form of individual and original research supplemented by inductive clinical reasoning. It is not even an applied science in the sense of the suggested assumption of fixed definite evidence or demonstrable truth. Its sphere of action may be regarded rather as a thinking, reasoning empiricism, involving speculative deductions along the projected lines of laboratory and pathologic investigation, extended to the border limits of actual experience. In the practice of internal medicine the cases are not presented in classified form, catalogued and indexed, but rather furnish in themselves the source and inspiration for needful study and detailed investigation, in order to harmonize apparent differences and properly elucidate the relations of perplexing complications.

Rational medical interpretations are directly resultant upon the closeness of the observations, the accuracy of the premises and the soundness of the logical reasoning, rather than upon the application of the known laws of pure science, or recourse to a mental accumulation of authoritative data.

The field of knowledge of internal medicine may be said to comprise an enormous mass of discrete, disordered and unsettled medical information to which are added the confusing results of original research, new discoveries and fresh observations. The correct expounder of changing medical opinion must possess above all the attributes of experienced clinical wisdom not to be obtained through the possession of the highest degree of technical knowledge nor the retention of a great mass of precise facts capable of laboratory demonstration, but rather acquired through proper methods of observation, suitable habits of thought and processes of reasoning. These are accorded in a satisfying degree only to the well-balanced and judicial mind, disciplined thoroughly through the medium of an education by no means entirely technical. The ability to select scientific facts with wisdom and discrimination and to interpret them with accuracy, to recognize error and pretense, to form rational conceptions and to exercise intelligent conservative judgment, requires at present, no less than formerly, a degree of broad and liberal culture in its fullest sense as supplementary to a natural mental endowment.

The proposition is now advanced: Can this intensely practical and vitally important branch of medical education be justly subjected to the elastic principles of the elective system? The question may be said to apply first, to those contemplating internal medicine, and secondly, to those anticipating special work. For the future practitioner in internal medicine, it must be apparent that the most complete and best proportioned system of preparatory education is none too good. He has never been trained too thoroughly. It is also insisted that the teaching faculty is by far a better judge as to what should constitute a comprehensive and well-rounded course of instruction in this department. The teaching of internal medicine comprises such various subdivisions of the subject, such diversity of method and such a large staff of instructors as to allow, under the elective system, a very wide latitude as to the relative amount of attention assigned to the several collateral branches. It is easy to conceive how a student might elect certain of these and be given credit for the required amount of time in internal medicine and even pass brilliant examinations, yet to have sadly neglected other equally important portions of the work. To preclude this possibility the student should be compelled to devote a certain definite time to each of the various methods and means of instruction, none of which are entirely without their proportionate value. The fact that there exists a wide difference of opinion among teachers of medicine as to the best methods of imparting knowledge to senior classes affords no justification in itself for permitting students to select the manner in which to pursue the study of a given subject, but rather suggests the wisdom of demanding at least a degree of familiarity with all branches of the department. A well-balanced and required system of didactic, recitational and bedside instruction with original conference work according to the seminar method offers to students the best that can be afforded in undergraduate work.

While the elective system offers opportunity to special students for original and advanced work in medicine, the necessity and practical advantage of this is hardly apparent. The prescribed course during the four years in this department of the modern medical school offers a sufficient degree of advanced study if properly taken advantage of to satisfy the actual demands of the most exacting student. If more than this be attempted along certain lines of undergraduate instruction in medicine, it must be at the expense of other work in the same branch or else through the sacrifice of even a superficial attention to the so-called specialties. The educated physician in internal medicine should possess at least a general knowledge of the special branches. In view of these considerations there does not seem to exist good and sufficient reasons to justify the application of the elective system in internal medicine to those contemplating general medicine.

To what extent shall the prospective specialist be permitted to exercise his prerogative under the elective system as applied to internal medicine before graduation? It may perhaps be the opinion of some medical educators that a certain given course for such students be offered as a minimum requirement and that by this means more time be afforded for work in their chosen field for original research. To this, however, objection is here made on the following grounds:

(1) That expert practical knowledge in any specialty presupposes and demands a good working familiarity with the theory and practice of medicine, and this is not to be learned any too thoroughly in a completed system of undergraduate work.

(2) That the finished work in any specialty should never be attempted in a medical school regardless of its scope or facilities, the only field for the attainment of a sufficient degree of special knowledge to justify practice being found in post-graduate work, reinforced by clinical experience.

(3) That the demand for original research among undergraduates is more fancied than real, the actual purpose of the student at this time being to absorb much, rather than to attempt to contribute a little.

(4) That in view of the uniformly earlier attainment of social, professional, and financial success of the specialist and greater

ease of living, the law of compensation justly requires a much longer period of earnest, studious preparation.

(5) That the present overcrowding of the profession morally necessitates the imposition of rigid restrictions to graduation as well as to admission, and the possession of the highest possible degree of proficiency in order to compete successfully with those unhandicapped by knowledge or conscience.

For these reasons there does not appear in the interests of the would-be specialists any special necessity for the application of the elective system to this department.

It is hoped that these mere suggestions may sustain the thought that a consistent regard for the highest ultimate welfare of all students and practitioners of medicine requires that the elective system, although of great recognized value as applied to a portion of the course of instruction, should bear no considerable relation to the study of internal medicine in American medical colleges.

III.
REQUIRED AND ELECTIVE DERMATOLOGY.[1]
By L. Duncan Bulkley, A.M., M.D., New York.

Although diseases manifesting themselves on the skin, being fully exposed to view in all their stages, should be those with which medical men would be supposed to be best acquainted, the fact is notorious that this class of affections is among those about which the least is known, practically, by the general medical profession at large.

The reason for this does not seem to be from the want of actual observation and study, for from the earliest records of medicine we find quite as clear descriptions of this class of diseases as of those affecting other organs. Nor does it appear to be from a want of recent application to the branch of dermatology by those specially qualified to study and develop it; for the literature in this direction is hardly exceeded in amount by that in any other branch of medicine; there have been, also, nearly two dozen medical journals, published at different times, devoted to this branch; likewise many societies exist, local, national, and international, where this class of affections has been exclusively considered, in addition to innumerable presentations of the matter before general medical societies, while most excellent text-books and monographs have continually appeared.

The fault seems to lie much deeper, and I believe will be found mainly in the attitude of the colleges toward this branch of medicine.

It must be granted, however, at the outset, that the intricacies of nomenclature and classification which have been developed at times, by certain writers, have contributed somewhat to the difficulty of acquiring this branch. It must also be granted that many, or even most, of the diseases of the skin are not fatal and do not seriously incapacitate those affected by them, and so perhaps, might not seem to so urgently call for medical care.

[1] Read before the American Academy of Medicine, Washington, D. C., May 12, 1903.

But, on the other hand, no one who has seen much of the practice of dermatology will question the very serious amount of annoyance and distress often occasioned by the various changes which take place in the skin, while, in many instances, dermatology is a most important field of study and practice from its intimate relations to general practice. Many instances of this could be cited, brief mention of a few must suffice.

Thus, syphilis is much more prevalent than many realize, especially as innocently acquired, and the importance of early recognition and prompt and rigorous treatment can hardly be overestimated. In many instances failure or neglect has caused the infection of innocent victims, and serious disfigurement or damage to important organs, or even grave nervous troubles and death have resulted from inability or failure to appreciate the situation.

The exanthemata will also often afford puzzles which an acquaintance with dermatology only will solve. In the matter of drug eruptions, the physician will often be at a loss unless acquainted with dermatology.

But even in the line of the ordinary affections of the skin, such as eczema, urticaria, acne, psoriasis, etc., the practising physician will often be at a great disadvantage unless he has a fair acquaintance with this branch, not only in the direction of affording the most service to his patient, but also as to the general relations of the same. Not infrequently eczema will be the first tangible evidence of a general nervous break down, which should be heeded in order to save the patient from further serious trouble; an urticaria may perhaps be the first urgent symptom which points to intestinal indigestion; or an acne the indication of physical weakness or possibly of sexual disorder, and so on. The general practitioner, therefore, can never afford to neglect to cultivate dermatology and expect to do the best for his clientele.

One further thought in this direction is that the training of close observation, and often of minutiæ belonging to the study and practice of dermatology, will often serve well in many other lines of practice, of which many illustrations could be given, did time and space permit.

Dermatology is essentially a clinical branch, and for its acquirement much practical observation is necessary, and unquestionably some considerable time must be devoted to it in the college curriculum if the student is to gain any reasonable knowledge of this branch. In order to teach it properly, the department should be equipped with a proper collection of colored plates, photographs, and, if possible, models of the diseases involved, as well as a good supply of clinical material.

Owing to its practical importance to the practitioner, students should be required to attend clinical lectures on this subject certainly the last two years, and should also have class instruction, with examinations at least half yearly. Those contemplating special practice in dermatology should be encouraged to take special courses from the instructors during the last two years, and, of course, afterward in post-graduate institutions.

But the more scientific aspects of the study should be cared for as well, and in order to properly understand the subject there should also be a good knowledge of microscopy and bacteriology. It is surprising how relatively ignorant many in the profession appear to be of even the comparatively simple study and recognition of the vegetable parasites on the skin. For this purpose these subjects should be taught early in the course, in connection with ordinary laboratory work.

It has already been mentioned that it is believed that the reason of the present lack of knowledge in the profession in regard to diseases of the skin is due mainly to the attitude, in times past, of the colleges toward this branch of medicine; in the apathy concerning it of those in authority.

In some of the leading colleges there have been special clinical professors of this branch for some years, but in few is attendance compulsory, and there is often little or no class instruction and adequate examinations are not required. But in looking over the curriculum of many colleges there is no mention whatever of this branch, while in some its teaching is associated with that of some other branch or branches, and no suggestion is made of special instruction, and no text-books are recommended.

It is useless and hopeless to expect or believe that a knowledge of diseases of the skin will be acquired unless proper and adequate instruction is given, and apparently it is equally useless to believe that the colleges will awaken to the necessities of the case unless greater pressure is brought to bear upon them by the profession at large.

Let us hope that the American Academy of Medicine, which has already accomplished so much good in many directions, may be the means of causing them to realize the importance of a good knowledge of diseases of the skin to those who shall graduate in the future.

IV.
TRAINING FOR A SPECIALTY—THE THEORY AND THE CONDITION AS ILLUSTRATED BY OPHTHALMOLOGY.[1]

By EDWARD JACKSON, M.D., Denver, Colo.

The popular theory of how the specialist should be trained is well understood and generally acquiesced in. He should pursue the usual undergraduate course in medicine, get what hospital experience he can, and enter upon general practice without thought of a specialty. After some years of general practice should he find that he is especially interested in a particular class of diseases, or especially successful in their treatment, he may begin to think of restricting his practice to that particular line of work and becoming a full-fledged specialist.

That is the theory. What is the condition as illustrated in the ophthalmic practice of this country?

The emphasis laid upon the importance of knowing something about all the other branches of medical practice seems to prevent appreciation of the importance of the ophthalmologist knowing the special facts of ophthalmology. This was fairly illustrated a few years ago, when the professor of ophthalmology in one of our medical schools in good standing (not a member of this Academy but eligible to it) reported that he had seen three cases of glioma of the retina all occurring in patients over fifty years of age—a statement as startling as would be a claim that congenital dislocation of the hip often begins after middle life.

Another result of this training is illustrated by the long account of a very peculiar case given me by a practitioner of twenty years' experience in general practice, who had only recently launched himself as a specialist. That his case was one of hysteria (as he afterwards admitted it to be) he had never suspected. But from the subjective symptoms he had dug out of his patient, by prolonged, laborious investigation, he was going to disprove well-established laws of physiology and physics.

[1] Read before the American Academy of Medicine, Washington, D. C., May 12, 1903.

But the most hopeless phase of the attempt to take up new lines of professional work, after most of one's aptitude and all his habits of study have been lost, was illustrated by a doctor who had been over twenty-five years in practice. He was of more than average intelligence, and wide general information. He had been the president of his state medical society, one of the largest in the country, and for several years had been known as a specialist on diseases of the eye. He explained to me that he did not believe there was any such thing as mixed astigmatism, that an eye could not be both hyperopic and myopic at the same time.

He illustrated the utter inability of the mind untrained in that particular direction to grasp a fundamental mathematical conception. And also the dogmatism which develops in the mind of the active medical practitioner, who ceases to be a student. His sense of self-sufficiency could set at naught the authority of great names like Helmholtz and Donders, and with it the whole current of professional learning. With such a cast of mind once developed, what possibility is there for taking up a line of thought and study which is as different from that of the ordinary medical practitioner as the deciphering of Babylonian tablets or the determination of the path of a comet?

From time to time I have been asked for advice, as to the general matters or particular cases, by those who have entered upon the practice of ophthalmology in conformity with this particular theory. To point out and analyze in dreary repetition, the evidences their letters present of ignorance, bewilderment and utter inability to cope with the task to which the writers have addressed themselves, might occupy the whole of our session to-day.

Considering the serious condition that has developed out of the theory in question, we might well wonder why it became current. Probably it came as a first grudging concession of the movement towards specialization within the medical profession. To that rising tide it was the "thus far, and no farther" of the medical and surgical monarchs of the day.

But we need not impugn the motives of the leaders of the profession, who expounded and enforced this theory. They simply did not know what they were expressing an opinion upon, and under these circumstances an opinion may be honest, plausible, and supported by excellent reasoning, yet still be absolutely erroneous.

Consider the assumptions implied in this theory. (1) That all medical knowledge and skill, that are of practical importance, are attainable by the average individual. That what may not be so mastered is comparatively unimportant refinement, or can only be expected of the rarely gifted master minds. That since the average medical student can know it all, he should know it all. (2) That the specialties have no real domain of special knowledge and skill which may be transmitted by training, but that so far as the specialist is worthy of any recognition, his endowments are congenital, or flow out of his individual mind and character. (3) That when the specialist attempts to enter upon his particular line of practice, without these years of general practice, he merely intends to content himself with a little fragment of that knowledge, which is possessed by all well-informed, general practitioners; that in taking up a specialty he greatly narrows his mental horizon and interests.

In this last assumption lies the error which vitiates much that has been written or spoken regarding specialism. Specialization in medical practice is essentially related to expansion, not to narrowing. It is the rapid expansion of the field of medical activity that has compelled specialization. The individual worker may lessen his field of endeavor in one direction, but only that he may expand it in another. Expansion is the cause, the necessary narrowing but an incidental effect.

Science has outstripped the capacity of the individual mind. Only by subdivision of labor are the highest efficiency and farther progress possible. What Fellow of this Academy claims that he can detect beginning infiltration in a lung, do a good abdominal section, identify the various pathogenic bacteria, correct clubfoot, accurately measure errors of refraction, train to efficiency imperfectly used organs of voice and speech, and judiciously apply the Roentgen rays in diagnosis and treatment? We need not pause for reply. No truthful man will ever again claim mastery in all departments of the healing art.

But we cannot give up our new found knowledge, our increased ability to cope with disease. Neither will we, because of the limitations of the average mind, confine their benefits to those who can command the services of exceptional talent. The specialist is wanted not merely as a leader and consultant, a special luxury at the command of the rich. He is needed to treat the mass of the people because he can do it more efficiently. This is true now, and every new discovery increases the need and renders the situation more acute. Any scheme of medical education worth our consideration must provide for it. How?

As I am well aware, the branch used for illustration, ophthalmology, is exceptional in the extent of the territory it has added to the general domain of medicine, in the peculiarity of the problems it takes up, and in the means it employs for their solution. But in this it illustrates more clearly the tendencies of our time and renders more tangible the problems of the future.

The situation is, that no medical school now gives anywhere near the training for ophthalmic practice that the same time and effort ought to furnish. The average medical graduate is far less fitted for the practice of ophthalmology than for the practice of internal medicine. But would you devote undergraduate schools to internal medicine, and leave ophthalmology to post-graduate schools without any organized curriculum? You can no more require a good working knowledge of internal medicine as a preliminary to the study of ophthalmology, than you can require a working knowledge of ophthalmology as a preliminary to the study of internal medicine. Persistence in the attempt to do either will break our profession into separate and unrelated groups of workers, as it is tending to do already. The recognition of a heart murmur has no more general importance than the recognition of a vascular lesion in the retina, commmonly less. The one is as much a special procedure as the other. There is no justification for the precedence given to the former in the medical curriculum.

As soon as you specialize by not giving in that curriculum the training required for all branches of our profession, you introduce specialism by exclusion. You educate a class who may be called general practitioners, but who are not general practitioners because they are ignorant of one part of the work of a truly general practitioner. The work of our profession is suffering more from this specialization by ignorance than from specialization by choice.

The plan that seems chiefly relied on to meet the expansion of modern medicine, is to expand the curriculum. Is a new bacterium or plasmodium discovered—extend the curriculum; a new form of disease isolated and characterized—extend the curriculum; a new department of physical or biologic science brought to serve the purposes of medical art—extend the curriculum. In this way the present rate of medical expansion could probably be met by doubling the length of the medical course about once in ten years.

But, unfortunately, this simple plan ignores the finite character of the human mind, ignores the limitations of the individual life and energy, ignores the laws which determine practical efficiency in any line of human effort. The time for improving medical education, by now and again adding a year to the required period of study, has passed. The period of undergraduate work now advised, four years for the general collegiate training and four years in the professional school, is certainly as much as can wisely be devoted to it by the mass of students, if it be not already excessive.

Consideration of the most developed branch of medical practice shows the necessity for a careful recasting of the medical curriculum along these lines:

1. We should bring together, not certain "fundamental branches," but the fundamental, widely-related and highly educational facts, methods, and manipulations from all branches, and shape them into a course in which every student of medicine should be thoroughly trained.

2. It should be recognized that this required course will not fit one to enter upon any particular branch of medical practice, as he should be fitted before receiving the medical degree.

3. There must be offered additional courses among which the student may choose, each of which will fit the student for a particular line of practice, one or more of which shall be required of each candidate for graduation.

It will be urged, this is a recognition of specialism. It is: Specialization in the medical profession is a fact. It is a fact of swiftly increasing importance. Failure to recognize it will bring separation and disorganization. Custom, prejudice, the inability of established leaders to appreciate the new conditions that develop around them, will delay the recognition long enough, and upon that recognition depend the future unity and the highest efficiency of the medical profession.

DISCUSSION.

Dr. H. P. Bowditch, of Boston :

I have listened with great interest to the papers, and I would like to say at the outset that I agree with Dr. Gerrish in his opinion that the time for the general practitioner has not yet gone by. I believe that the general practitioner will be with us for many years to come. I do not, however, regard this as an argument against the advantages of an elective system, for I believe that an elective system affords the best opportunities for securing good general practitioners. Every first-class medical school must teach everything that any student or graduate may reasonably desire to know. To give all this information to every student would require the lengthening of the course of study to ten or fifteen years. The only alternative is some sort of an elective system. The only question is, how that elective system can be best organized. In the Harvard Medical School, we have recognized the fact that we have been teaching *some* of our undergraduates a certain number of things which *all* the undergraduates do not require to know. We have now so condensed our required instruction that we get it all into three years, but Dr. Gerrish may be right in saying that, in some schools, the elective courses should be limited to graduate classes. We think, however, that we can condense into three years the medical knowledge requisite to make a safe practitioner of medicine. We consider that the man who has studied medicine three years at Harvard knows enough to recognize and treat the ordinary diseases and to call in a specialist when his own knowledge fails. But, we say that if he wants the Harvard M.D. degree he must study another year, and in that year, if he wants to be a general practitioner, we advise him to take the electives in the various clinical branches and not to trouble himself at all about specialties, but to get as much hospital training as possible before graduation. In this way, we believe, he will in four years obtain the best possible training for the general practitioner. If, on the other hand, he does not want to be a general practitioner, we advise him either to take preliminary courses in any of the specialties or to devote himself to work in some of the various laboratories. When he has done that we will give him the degree of Harvard M.D. How this plan can be brought into relation with graduate work is not yet determined. It seems to me that the experiment is in the right direction and will lead to beneficial results, whether we have to modify the plan in the future or not. It is important to note that this plan does not *require* a student to specialize in his fourth year but only *permits* him to do so if he wishes to.

Dr. L. Duncan Bulkley, of New York:

I have nothing to say, except that I think the specialists fully appreciate all that has been said to-day about the necessity of their having a broad education. I agree with the statement that those who study their specialties in the broadest way are those who have not only had a broad education but also some general practice.

Concerning the general practitioner, of course, we regard him very highly. I am reminded of Dr. Fisher, of Sing Sing, who in a speech described the work of the general practitioner, and cited a case. He brought his hearers to a high degree of interest, and then exclaimed, "There is where you want brains."

Dr. Edward Jackson, of Denver, in closing:

There is one phase of this subject which has not had justice done to it in this symposium. It has only been referred to I think by Dr. Welch. It is the educational value of electives. Whether a man is in general practice or any line of special practice, his first business as a practitioner of medicine is that of an original investigator. If he does not do some work of original investigation in every case, he is a poor representative of the medical profession. Training for medicine must be training for original investigation. Unless there is some opportunity for a man to choose his own work and follow it because he is interested in it, and thus develop aptitude and taste for investigation; the medical course will prove, no matter how much it may give him in the way of knowledge, harmful rather than helpful to him in his function to the community. Probably this side of electives in the medical course is more important than any other side that has been developed this morning, and I do not like to have the discussion closed without mentioning it.

THE LIFE AND HEALTH OF OUR GIRLS IN RELATION TO THEIR FUTURE.[1]

By JAMES H. McBRIDE, M.D., Los Angeles, Cal.

The first need of life is a good physique. Whether one's work is in the field, or the college, or the home, health, vigor, and endurance determine the amount and quality of it. Whatever a few sickly geniuses may have accomplished, the average man or woman needs the physical capital of a sound body.

Though the world's work is increasingly mental work, the tests of efficiency being more and more mental tests, there was never a time when physical robustness counted for more than at the present day.

The mind has had exclusive attention in systems of education. They have dealt with nothing but the intellect. We are now beginning to recognize the importance of the body in the intellectual scheme, and of the brain in relation to the body, and of the mind as the supreme function of the body.

Life is a conflict, and its vigor, harmony, and achievement come of this. Agencies within the body and without are working against survival and tend to lessen life or destroy it. If the defenses of the body against disease were abandoned for a day, we should die. Our destruction would also be certain, though slower, if the higher contests of life were abated. Conflict is the price of existence. Life of the right sort consists in doing things, in overcoming. This requires robust qualities of mind and body, and these express the energy that days and years have developed and compacted into structure. From childhood to maturity we are determining the quality of health and character. At every stage of life we are what our past has made us.

The brain is the organ of thought, but the entire body is concerned in the mental functions. This is so because at every step in the evolution of the organism from lower life, with every addition to the nervous mechanism, there were corresponding new connections of brain and body in ever-increasing complexity. All ages of life have gone to this. All relations, all experiences,

[1] Read before the American Academy of Medicine, Washington, D. C., May 11, 1903.

all conflicts, tragedies, triumphs, and failures, all survivals of individuals and of function went to the making of these relations that life exhibits.

The interdependence of brain and body is a primary fact of life, and a commonplace of physiologic psychology. The solidarity of the organism is shown in the relation between the size of the heart and brain. It is not probable that any part of the body functionates without influencing the brain. If a limb is amputated in early life, the nerve cells of the center controlling it will not develop well. If the muscles of one arm are developed by exercise, the other arm grows stronger. If one hand gains in skill by special exercise, the other gains in a regular and measurable proportion. Mosso has shown that during mental effort blood leaves the extremities and flows toward the brain. We seem to think to our finger ends.

The one thing more than any other that has dominated man's life and made him what he is, is action. The results of action were woven into the fabric of man's brain by the experiences of countless generations of ancestors. In the primitive man, thought always expressed action; it was out of the necessities of action that thought came into existence. Our thinking has in it a muscular or motor element. It recapitulates those primitive motor co-ordinations that were in the making of it.

It is not difficult to see that the athlete's actions are the expression of his thoughts. The connection is familiar. It is a like truth and a larger one that all thinking, even the reasoning of the philosopher, has in it a subconscious rehearsal of old motor associations, through which thought came into existence; ancestors laid the foundation in their motor thinking for all the fine reasoning of their wise and spectacled descendant. In the primitive man the motor relationships of thought were simpler; in the more highly developed, height upon height has been reared for more complex reasoning, and yet the motor element is still there, though it is veiled and takes place in invisible physiologic pantomime. Stanley Hall says, "We think in terms of muscular action." With all mental processes there is this motor filiation, and as thought succeeds thought a thousand actions of the body are gone through with in physiologic shorthand.

An educational system should have two main objects: First, to make a sound and healthy body; second, the formation of character through mental and moral discipline. As all character comes of moral experiment, so the efficient body comes of experiment in doing things, in all possible discipline that gives the body strength, symmetry, poise.

The Greeks were wiser than we. They saw that the proper foundation for mental training was training of the body. In our system of education we have heretofore worked at the top and neglected the foundation. In our strenuous preoccupation with the mind we have forgotten the body.

Dr. D. A. Sargent, of Harvard, says concerning the neglect of physical training in our public schools: "There is not a single exercise in the school curriculum that requires them to lift their hands above their heads, or to use their hands and fingers, except to turn a page or thumb a piece of chalk." Again he says: "Under such conditions, with no attempt made at classification according to physical needs, with every one doing the same thing without any moral enthusiasm on the part of the teacher, without hope of approval or reward on the part of the pupil, without even the inspiring strains of music to relieve the monotony, our public-school children are put through what some persons choose to call educational gymnastics."[1]

There are evidences of an awakening interest in this country in the physical side of child life. Gymnasiums are now in use in the public schools in a number of our cities, though relatively the number is small. It is a most gratifying sign also that our colleges and universities have gymnasiums with skilled directors, and, in the colleges for young women, special attention is now directed to the physical development of the students.

The proportion of young people who go to colleges and universities is, however, a mere fraction. The vast majority of our young people never go even to a high school, nor is anything whatever done with a view to physical development. We leave their bodies to the caprices of natural activity and the chances of occupation. Much of those old constructive forces that belonged to the virile life of primitive man, forces that were packed into

[1] *American Physical Educational Review*, March, 1900.

every fiber by ages of harsh experience, that were majestic in their power and still potential in every child as a splendid physical capital, are not utilized by our methods.

In regard to the life of young women, we are liable to be misled into thinking that more of them have an interest in outdoor life and sports than is the case. The young women who play golf and tennis are relatively conspicuous, and when we see them we congratulate ourselves and are inclined to brag a little because of the growing fondness of young women for outdoor life. We forget their obscure sisters, the great majority of girls and young women who rarely or never play tennis or basket-ball or golf. Those who engage in these or any outdoor sports are a mere fraction of the total number. Unfortunately these latter, in common with the others, almost universally wear the conventional style of dress, that is, they compress their bodies with unyielding garments, and they will, of course, have the usual proportion of weak muscles and displaced organs.

Physicians alone know how much misery is caused by the unhygienic dress of women. That all protests have in the past been fruitless might easily have been foreseen. It took epidemics that killed their thousand, not sermons on hygiene, to make men establish quarantine. Health regulations have rarely been adopted because of instruction in hygiene,—they have been enforced by the necessity of self-protection. The promise of better health for women from proper dress is quite vague. The classes who illustrate the advantages of it are not models of form and gracefulness, while the appeal of fashion and the desire to conform and please come of a normal and wholesome instinct. It is not probable that women will be greatly influenced in their dress by any appeals made on the ground of health or comfort. Hygienic dress for women will come as they discover that in their new competition with men, just now beginning, they will fall short of the best possible success to the degree that they lack the staying qualities that men have. They will then adopt hygienic dress from necessity.

The worst feature of woman's dress is the corset. The following is a hint of what it means in the life of women: In an

Eastern college[1] for young women, there were 35 in the graduating class. Of these, 19 dressed after hygienic models and wore no corsets; 16 dressed in the usual style. Eighteen of the class took honors—of these 13 wore no corsets. Of the seven who were chosen for Commencement parts, six wore no corsets. Of those who carried off prizes for essays during the year, none wore corsets. Of the five chosen for class-day orators, four wore no corsets. Query: If the wearing of a single style of dress will make this difference in the lives of young women, and that, too, in their most vigorous and resistive period, how much difference will a score of unhealthy habits make, if persisted in for a lifetime?

The vital capital of a generation depends primarily upon what the parents transmit. A sound constitution may be wrecked by abuse and the offspring be thereby affected unfavorably. The bodily vigor of the parent, which is largely under individual control, influences offspring quite as much as the inborn parental qualities that are inheritable. The first demand of parenthood is health. A strong and robust body may battle successfully against a bad heredity. If men and women would live as they ought to live for a few generations, half the morbid heredity would be eliminated. This is a capital fact in the possible improvement of the race. The effort of society should be to make men and women of this day physically sound, and ultimately make the race so. Heredity, which is the most important single factor of life, would then always work toward racial betterment. As it is now, if all disease and crime were swept away, mankind is living so badly that the crop of the diseased and criminal would soon be large again. The inheritance of both health and disease has generally had obscure beginnings in far-off relationships. The insanity of to-day is in its genesis largely an affair of the previous generation and others farther back. Influences that weakened the vital resistances of ancestors sent into the world unstable brains that were unequal to the adverse conditions of life. The heredity of each one is complex and infinite. Ages upon ages of human experiences, with their strength and their weakness, are packed into our bodies. They act and think and speak in us. We are children of thousands of ancestors whose multiplied lives reach back across

[1] Dr. Lucy M. Hall in *Outlook*.

the centuries. In the deeper, physiologic sense the race inheritance is the larger.

The common impression that play develops the body sufficiently is an error. Play is the natural language of the growing body, and is vitally important to children. It has the advantage of furnishing the greatest amount of exercise with the least expenditure of mental effort. It appeals especially to the automatisms, and so while it exercises, it diverts and rests. Play, however, does not supply all the training that is demanded. Neither does work. Work is excellent, not alone because it does in some measure promote development, but because it has in it a moral discipline. It cannot supply alone a certain kind of discipline that is needed. The gymnasium of the garden and field has helped to give robustness to generations, but it develops the body unequally. Neither does it supply the finer and more accurate muscular adjustments, with the associated mental drill that special training supplies. Life demands this special training more and more as social organization increases in complexity, both in its intellectual and industrial relations. There is no more profitable drill than that which is obtained in this way. Attention, alertness, interest, courage, quickness of decision, the larger forces of character are here being made in the individual as by a ruder training they were made in the race.

Awkwardness, lack of skill in doing things is waste. Accuracy, ease, gracefulness are economies. Special training of the body brings the power of self-control in action—an important matter in character-making. To do things speedily and accurately, to do them in one way and that the best, this is self-control of a high order. Self-control does not consist in keeping still. It consists in that wise self-direction that men of action show, and that makes their lives significant.

No girl should be allowed to grow up without special physical training. This should be supplied when the body is growing and the physiologic habits are being established. If the body is not made strong and is not well developed before 20, it will not be after that time. The size of the muscles is determined during the growing period, as is the skill in using them. Special exercise in later life may develop temporarily neglected muscles, but as soon as the exercises are abandoned they will return to their former size. If they are well developed during the growing period, the larger size is a permanency, and the vigor that goes with this means not only physical capital, but a mental resource.

There is no more important fact relative to the life-work than that all activities of the body tend to develop the brain and the mental power as well. Child play and games, the romp and frolic of boys and girls, and all games of skill involve those primary co-ordinations that are racial in origin, and that are a preparation for the higher and more complex co-ordinations of later life. Every game well learned, every kind of work involving skill that is well mastered, means new brain structure brought into activity that serves as a foundation for mental acquisition later. Every game that a boy learns makes a smarter boy of him if he utilizes the skill for the best purposes. Girls need not play all the games that boys do, but there is no reason why they should not be as robust as boys, and no reason why they should not have the physical training that makes strong bodies.

I am now directing the physical training of a little girl of 12. She is most active and has never been seriously ill. Her tastes are for outdoor life, and they have been encouraged. She climbs trees, runs over the hills, hunts flowers and insects, studies birds and loves nature. She is thoroughly healthy in mind and body. When I examined her at 11 years of age, I found her trunk and arm muscles were mere bands. They were certainly a poor report of her activities. She is now taking systematic training. She does not inherit large muscles, and there will be no attempt to make an athlete of her. To do this would be to rob other parts of the body. What she needs is compactness and solidity with moderate size and a certain skilfulness. Her life history will be practically determined by what is done with her body during the next five years. One could easily write a prescription for early invalidism in this child, and have it filled in thousands of homes of the land. Have her wear the conventional dress, crowd her in school and college and neglect her physical development, and at twenty we have the tragedy.

The physical development of girls is not so simple a matter as that of boys, for the girl's body is more complex and the development period has more risks in it. An inactive life is quite as bad for the girl as for the boy, and overstudy or stress of any kind is more serious in its consequences for the growing girl. Girls learn quite as fast as boys, or even faster, and the effects of overstudy are often not apparent until after they have left school. The phrase "overstudy" is often misused. If adults and children work under proper conditions they are rarely injured by any amount of mental labor. If men who work with their brains and students who apply their minds intensely would take proper rest, food and exercise, there would be no danger of overworking. When people thus engaged break down in health they should charge their failure to a neglect of the essentials of healthy living. Many young women injure their health in school not because they study too hard, but because they fail to observe a few simple laws of health that could be summarized in a page.

A girl of twelve coming under my observation studied hard at school and became morbidly anxious about her studies. She slept little, had almost constant headache, no appetite, was bloodless, emaciated and poorly developed. She was ordered from school for three months, and was required to play outdoor games and take much exercise. When school was resumed, her exercise and general hygiene were carefully directed. In six months she was strong and without an ailment, and now, four years afterwards, she is in perfect health, though she has not missed a day from school. The result showed that she had not studied too hard, but that her physical development had been neglected.

The student girl should take active outdoor exercise every day under proper conditions of dress. Girls are liable to overdo at outdoor exercise and at gymnastics. This is especially liable to be the case with those who need exercise most. Intelligent direction is necessary for most of them. Mothers who are fearful their daughters will break down from overstudy need have no fears if the young women care for their physical life. Systematic and persistent exercise out doors will usually insure good health for girls and young women who are studying. A few weeks or months of outdoor life or of active training is not sufficient. This would be a parody on what should be a life habit, as much as eating and sleeping. Plato provided that two years out of the three from seventeen to twenty—certainly, the best years for study—should be entirely devoted to the gymnasium.

Plato had limitations in his experience, for he had never ridden on a fast train, nor talked from New York to San Francisco, nor searched for God's stars through modern smoke, but he knew the secret of health and the real source of man's power. He looked to the triumph of life, not to the petty victory of examination day.

We often hear it said that woman's organization is more delicate than man's, but this delicacy is partly if not wholly the work of civilization. Centuries of repression and hindrance, of hobbling and swaddling have gone to the making of her physical frailty, what there is of it. We admire the frail type of beauty with its appealing suggestions of dependence. The Amazonian mother whose hardy progeny will be the captains of the next generation draws no eye. Considering that civilization tends to refine away feminine vigor, and that there are yet many women who are physically strong, shows what miracles nature can work, and it certainly is a prophecy for racial betterment. In the wild state woman shows no serious physical frailty. She carries the burdens of the tribe, and her fiber is as tough as that of man. We need have no fear of the fate of the race if the living are kept healthy. Here as elsewhere, quality is more important than quantity. Through the law of the survival of the fittest, there comes ultimately the survival of the best. In nature's large economy, it is surely true that the race that becomes extinct deserves its fate.

The building of a strong body with the establishment of good health means to achieve that which runs through all normal life, good physiologic habit. All life is, in last analysis, habit; there are not only habits of mind, but habits of body over which we have but indirect control. The functional life of any organ tends to repeat itself, and this repetition is habit. If by a wise way of living one has established the best possible functional life in the organs, this becomes the standard for the body and the energies are on a level with the physiologic habits that have thus been formed.

Doctors know how easy it is to set up morbid, grumbling habits in some organ or organs, that may continue for years or even a lifetime. Every part of the body has a certain capacity to resist disease or unfavorable conditions, and if this resistance is once broken down by some neglect or disorder of any particular organ, the vital capacity of that part is ever after of an imperfect kind. Half our work as doctors is in treating disorders that are the result of some part of the system having been injured by sickness or neglect, and which ever after is an invalid organ, drawing a heavy pension from the system for its disability.

The systematic physical activity and the good personal hygiene in early life that go to make one strong have also the advantage that these practices become life habits that cannot be broken without discomfort. The desire for healthy exercise becomes a kind of hunger of the body that must be satisfied.

There are very many people who from lack of early physical perfection live always on a lower plane than would otherwise have been the case. They are not sick—they are simply less alive than they ought to be. Their physical development was never properly completed, and the functions of the body have never realized their full capacity.

All the achievement of men and women is based largely upon capacity for sustained exertion. To be capable of this, one needs a body that from proper drill in the formative period of life has the habit of energetic and swift response to demands. A poorly developed body means less work and an inferior quality of work, less courage, less persistence. It means, in some cases, to put among the common places a career that with robust health might have risen to great achievement.

Boys are better developed than girls because they lead more active lives than girls. There is no reason why a boy should be physically more active than a girl. There is no reason why the man should be better developed physically than the woman. Our methods should produce the best possible development of both.

The animal enjoyment a boy finds after a day in school in

wild, rough play puts fresh life into him and new thoughts into his head, while the girl, early impressed with a sense of the importance of decorum and with the ghost of propriety ever before her, goes home quietly, and the studies of the day still recurring in the tired brain like an echo, her mind is occupied by them in spite of herself. Study pursued under such circumstances may be ruinously harmful, when the same amount might do little or no harm, if done with proper regard to the necessity for exercise and diversion.

There is very much in the life of young women of the present time that tends to arrest the development and result in lowering of the life capacity. They get through girlhood successfully, but the stress of married life or independent employment is too much for their frail bodies and they become invalids or semiinvalids, capable of enduring little, doing little or enjoying little, and spend their lives on the border land of the physically necessitous.

The girls of the present day, who are brought up under more comfortable conditions than their grandmothers, have gained much, no doubt, in the change of conditions; but they have lost something, in that in many homes there is less of healthy exercise, less of that kind of work that developed the body and also developed simple and healthy tastes. There is, as a result of this, poorer physical development, less feeling of responsibility in the home on the part of the young ladies, and not so great a sense of duty. When every member of the family had every-day, specific duties, work to do that had to be done, work that exercised the body as well as the moral sense in discharging a duty, such life, dreary and harsh as it sometimes was, and often barren of most of those things that we regard as common comforts, had at least the great advantage of providing work that furnished physical exercise, and that was also done under the sense of obligation. There is a moral and physical healthfulness in such a life that goes to the making of strong and simple characters and that puts purity of blood and vigor of constitution into descendants.

Many women, in my experience, break down because, or partly because, they have not a certain kind of training fitting them for the responsibilities of life. No young woman should grow up to a marriageable age without having been initiated gradually into the work and responsibilities that belong to a wife and the keeper of a home. A lack of this kind of training is the cause of much nervous invalidism. One who has grown up without proper training in these matters is much more liable to have a distaste for such duties than if she had been taught from girlhood to consider them as a matter of course. New and untried duties are always hard, and they are doubly hard if one dislikes them, for a distaste for work involves ruinous friction. The number of young women who soon after marriage break down from the unexpected strain of new duties is very large. The mother of a young woman who had become a nervous invalid within two years after marriage said to me there was no apparent cause for her daughter's illness, as she had been shielded from everything from childhood. This was apparently not because the young lady was delicate, but because an indulgent and unoccupied mother chose to keep her daughter in the condition of a child. The real cause of her trouble was plain enough; she had never known what work or care or responsibility was and the little stress of caring for a home made an invalid of her.

One may well ask why any healthy girl should be shielded. What she needs is not shielding but intelligent and sympathetic direction in work that tends to develop a sense of duty and an exercise of judgment. What is a home for to a young woman, if it is not a school that in some measure anticipates by preparation the later and larger discipline which should come to all, a school from which she is graduated into the sober and exigent realities of womanhood.

Why, indeed, should any one be shielded? Were Maria Mitchell and Lucretia Mott shielded? Were our grandmothers, who lived simple and toilsome lives, prepared therefor by being shielded? Was it ever the case anywhere that a person who had been shielded grew to be a forceful character or proved a success in presence of the swift and onerous demands of life?

Every girl should at least be prepared for the eventualities of married life. Not all women marry, but no woman is a loser who has the training that prepares her for all possible responsibilities of womanhood. Whatever tends to develop in woman all the characteristics of womanhood is an advantage to her. We cannot ignore the fact that there lies at the basis of woman's nature the eternal law of womanhood, and that whatever she may do, whatever station she may fill, she is none the worse but infinitely the better for being a thorough woman.

It is worth remarking that happiness depends more largely upon health than people know. Whatever the causes of unhappiness may be in general, I believe that imperfect health, not that which puts one to bed, but that of low vitality and sluggish function which makes endurance unreliable and the performance of tomorrow uncertain, this kind of imperfect health is chargeable with much of the unhappiness that there is in the world.

With a desire to get the views of educators and physicians on the subject of the life and health of American girls, I recently addressed the following question to 20 physicians, school-principals and teachers. "Do you believe that American girls of this generation will be physically stronger than their mothers?"

I have only space to quote the reply of Prof. H. E. Kratz, Superintendent of the Schools of Calumet, Michigan. Professor Kratz is an educator of national reputation, one of those who had the insight to recognize early the primary importance of the physical side of the life of school children. He has made careful investigations on this subject and has written articles of permanent value in regard to child growth and health.

He says: "Your question is one that cannot be answered offhand, and even then not definitely or positively. There are some things that would indicate that the girls of to-day are not as strong, physically, as their mothers were at their age.

"I believe there is a growing tendency on the part of parents in this country to shield their girls from the hardships and severe experiences to which they were exposed. A mistaken kindness seeks to protect them from all adverse influences. Of course, strong character and strong bodies are not as readily developed under such conditions. I believe there is also an attitude on the part of the boys and girls to demand more from their parents, taking it as their right to escape these severer experiences of life which go to make up strong men and women. There is, therefore, a tendency to hot-house growth, and this will of course neither develop strong bodies nor strong minds.

"On the other hand, we are waking up more to the need of physical training in the public schools, particularly in the cities. The matter is in its infancy, but the time I believe is not far distant when our high schools and at least upper-grade schools will all have well-equipped gymnasiums, and more careful attention will be paid to the physical development. Quite a number of the best-equipped high schools are already well equipped along these lines, but the great mass of the girls and boys are not yet provided with such physical training as they need.

"As the city population is so rapidly increasing in proportion to the rural, the necessity is growing greater for better provision in the line of physical training, as in the cities the opportunities for physical training and the limited number of duties which can be imposed upon the children are a great handicap.

"The universities, as you rather intimate, are making, as a rule, excellent provision for physical training, but of course the number of girls in universities is small as compared with the large number elsewhere.

"On the whole, I am rather inclined to the opinion that the girls of to-day are not as strong physically as their mothers."[1]

The overwrought and intense manner of many American women is partly due, I suppose, to the contagiousness of custom; but it is also due to jerky and imperfect co-ordination of undeveloped muscles and oversensitive nerve centers. Well-developed and vigorous nerve centers command the muscles to orderly, smooth and graceful movement, whereas those not so developed leave the

[1] Dr. Mary E. B. Ritter, in a paper read before the California State Medical Society in 1903, gave the results of the examination of 660 Freshman girls at the University of the State of California, at Berkeley. Of this number, 176 or 26²/₃ per cent. are subject to headaches; 193 or 29¹/₄ per cent. are habitually constipated; 86 or 13 per cent. are subject to indigestion; 3 or ¹/₂ per cent. had defined tuberculosis; 7 or ⁹/₁₀ per cent. had goitre; 57 or 9 per cent. were markedly anemic; 105 or 16 per cent. had abnormal heart sounds; 62 or 9¹/₃ per cent. had rapid or irregular pulse; 193 or 29¹/₄ were subject to backaches; 443 or 67 per cent. were subject to menstrual disorders; 10 or 1¹/₂ per cent. gave histories of having broken down in grammar or high school, two from "nervous prostration." In contrast to these figures, 149 or 22⁸/₁₀ per cent. reported themselves as free from all aches or pains or functional disturbances.

muscles to ill-regulated and haphazard action. This is made worse when one falls into the too common American habit of fictitious animation, stilted attitudes of mind and body, and artificial and fussy manners that arouse tense, cramp-like muscular states that are wastefully exhausting, so that gripped hands, scowling features, anxious eyes, irregular movements leak away the energy as fast as it accumulates. Many women seem to think that interest calls for a display of intensity, eagerness, an affectation of excitement. They are vastly mistaken. Healthy interest is quiet-mannered; it is low-voiced; it demands no fuss; it involves no strain.

Our intense and hurried American life which indicates mental tension and unhealthy excitement can be cured by cultivating composure and stopping our high-pressure methods of doing things. The greatest need for healthy human lives is plain, simple, and homely interests. Those who do not have them lack an essential condition of sound character.

The interests of American women are too often mere excitements, and these are always unhealthy. They are unfavorable to quiet and systematic living and lead to selfishness and discontent. I believe much of the poor health of women is due to their habits of excitement. They lose thereby the nack of taking things with composure and self-restraint; the most ordinary occurrences stir up an intensity of feeling and a certain amount of mental tension that are uncalled for and are unhealthy. The woman who is thoroughly healthy lives a frictionless and a fuller life; she is cheerful, she is satisfied with those simple and homely things upon which the most of happiness and the healthier happiness depends. She is more charitable, she has more faith in life and more confidence in human nature. She does not "endlessly question whether she has done just the right thing." She does not make her consciousness a reception hospital for wounded feelings, and in seeing things in just proportion she distinguishes between the occurrences of moment and the trivial incidents of life.

We Americans, both men and women, have too much self-consciousness; we are overanxious about appearances and effects; our dash and intensity and eagerness are artificial and wasteful.

Healthy-mindedness is outward-mindedness; it is forgetful of self in a quiet interest in things to be quietly done. It means that calmness, not excitement, indicates strength; that force of character is not shown by haste, but rather by deliberateness; not how speedy, but how careful; not how much, but how well.

There is too much eagerness and fussy restlessness in our life. Expression is entirely out of proportion to impression. Though the greater part of life consists in doing something, it does not follow that we should be forever on the run. The work of life is not wholly in action. Self-restraint, calmness, a certain repose have a large share in the enterprise.

In all physiologic processes, there is a certain amount of energy put by as a reserve. If this were not so, every action or every thought would leave us bankrupt of vitality. If we are to have proper self-direction and concentration of effort, there must be structures and centers that are resting, having reserves of unused energy. Through this comes self-direction and restraint of tendencies and impulses. In the healthy and well-developed body, unconscious restraints are always being applied in order that irregular action and waste be prevented. Those who fail here wear too much expression in their faces, and are restless and anxious-minded. They scatter their energies in useless muscular tensions and in ill-regulation of thought and action. One often sees in plain country folk a calmness of expression and a quiet manner that is in beautiful and restful contrast to the knit brows and eager manner of the city resident.

To insist upon the completest womanhood is not to demand that every woman should marry. The idea that woman's only function was that of reproduction was primitive; it was a belated survival of the period of the tent and the war club. There are other things for many women besides marriage and maternity.

There is no danger of race extinction; Nature has taken out insurance against that. The problem is not to get more people— it is rather to improve those we have, and leave room also for those who come after us to live better and ampler lives. The cry for more people and dense populations is animal and material. Is not the struggle already hard enough and bitter enough? Do we want more of the necessitous; more mothers weary and worn with grinding toil, more stunted children, more fathers heartsick and hopeless with the fight of poverty? It will, however, always remain true that the one, best work for most women will be in the home, where as wives and mothers they will have the making of men and the shaping of men's destiny. Though there are other worthy aspirations that woman may have, there are none higher than this. No oratory that she can pronounce, no pictures that she can paint, and no books that she can write, exceed in worth to the world a life like this. By leaving her impress upon her children, she lives again in them and in their descendants, and in them too she carries forward the ideals, and perpetuates the great traditions of the race.

DISCUSSION.

Dr. S. A. Knopf, of New York:

I am a little more optimistic than the reader of the paper, because I really think that our American women have improved and not degenerated in physical development. Let us compare the measurements of the native American woman in the better classes of twenty-five years ago with those of to-day and we will see that they have improved in height, chest-expansion, and average health.

The same, however, can not be said of our laboring girls and women. Their growth and development is often dwarfed because they work in unhygienic environments and live in unscientific tenements. The primary cause, however, of this physical degeneracy among the laboring women must be sought in child labor, which is still in many states the curse of our nation. The little girl who must labor in the mill instead of roaming about and playing in the open air can never become a physically strong woman. There is much work in this respect before us members of the Academy who are interested in medical sociology and in the physical and moral development of our nation. The curricula in many of our schools are also too overburdened and the intellectual education of our children is pushed to such an extent that the physical development must necessarily suffer.

In conclusion, let me express my appreciation of the admirable paper which Dr. McBride has presented to us, and also ask that the discussions may be continued in order that we all may benefit by the expression of the opinions of others.

Dr. McBride in closing:

There is little to be said. The existence of child labor as related by Dr. Knapp is a national disgrace. One cannot think of the matter with patience. It is true in some sense that there is more interest in the health of school children and the young generally than formerly. We are only, however, at the beginning. I think it is safe to say that in 95 per cent. of our public schools the physical training of the pupils is absolutely ignored.

OBSERVATIONS IN PASSING.

Why is it that mankind generally, when in a discussion, are apt to hurl offensive epithets at the heads of their opponents? For example, in the present discussion on the proper teaching of hygiene, why insist that the honorable women who are earnestly trying to stem the evils of intemperance, are "fanatics." When Curran disputed with the fish-wife, he defeated his opponent by calling her a parallelepipedon, but that instance is a solitary exception.

This question was caused by reading an article on "Separate and Mixed Boards," in an exchange. The writer claims to belong to one of the "Schools" of Medicine, and there is no epithet hurling in mentioning that fact, and he uses these words among others: "To be domineered over and dictated to by a clique of medical bigots"

It may be quite true in medicine as it certainly is elsewhere, that a majority develops the worst form of tyranny, and it would be but the manifestation of ordinary, every-day human nature for the majority of medical men to domineer and dictate to the minorities. If it is true, it is a pity—we deplore the fact. But does the calling of that majority "A clique of medical bigots" aid to right the wrong? Is it even excusable to say "you're another," because their high-mightiness, the medical aristocrats (pardon the lapsus, allopaths were meant) have been fond of coining quaint and grotesque epithets and hurling them promiscuously upon all who could not say "Shibboleth?" Candidly, would not every particle of right be conserved if the picturesque element were abandoned and facts with logically deduced conclusions employed instead?

A State examination for licensure in medicine is to afford the people of that State protection from incompetent practisers of medicine. A physician is licensed for the same reason that steamboat engineers are licensed—to secure men who have a working knowledge of the machine entrusted to their care.

It is not hurling epithets when the writer of this expresses it as an opinion gained from some study of the subject, when he says that with separate boards, the grading of those boards representing the minorities of the profession are uniformly higher, which means that the weaker men can the more readily pass their tests, and the people are not so well protected. If this opinion is a fair deduction from the facts, it is an argument for a mixed board much more effective than any compound, descriptive, invective, that can be framed.

****

The National Dental Association at a recent meeting, held at Asheville, N. C., took the following action :

Resolved, That it is the sense of the National Dental Association that each medical college in the United States should include in its curriculum a lectureship on "Oral Hygiene, Prophylaxis, and Dental Pathology."

A course of instruction as suggested by this resolution will give valuable information. Whether it is practicable to add another subject to courses already overcrowded, admits of debate. The question is an inherently complex one, and the knot, difficult enough to untie at the best, has become a tangle by the pulling of many outside influences. An Alexander is needed to sever the rope. Possibly the proper use of the electives, as hinted at in the symposium published in this number, might aid in reducing the tangle.

****

The same circular, conveying this resolution, also mentions that the National Dental Association is endeavoring to introduce the teaching of oral hygiene in the public schools. Capital! if the instruction is to be a part of the general instruction on hygiene. We commend the perusal of the papers in the symposium on "Teaching of Hygiene in the Public Schools" read before the Academy at its last meeting to those interested in this subject.

****

The Society of American Authors are engaged in the laudable endeavor to secure a lower rate of postage for manuscript. That it is possible to send the manuscript for a magazine article to London—to Yokohama, for that matter—for less postage than would be required to send it from Boston to New York, is one of the several anomalies of the postal laws. It would seem but fair that our domestic postal service should not impose greater charges than that of the Universal Postal Union, and that every one, to the extent of his influence, should cooperate with the Authors' Association.

⁎

The American Confederation of Reciprocating Examining and Licensing Medical Boards will hold a meeting at the Southern Hotel, St. Louis, On Tuesday, October 27th, at two in the afternoon. Invitations are practically extended to every one interested in reciprocity in state licensure to be present. This organization is solving the exchange of licenses, by exchanging them when practicable, and permitting them to be used as credentials of value when a full exchange is not legally possible. In this way it is forming a nucleus which will attract other states, as soon as the exhibition of the desirability of an exchange is so demonstrated as to permit the removal of the present legal obstacles.

⁎

The Conference of State and Provincial Boards of Health of North America will hold its next meeting in Baltimore, on October 23 and 24, 1903, with headquarters at "The Stafford."

LITERATURE NOTES.

A COMPEND OF HUMAN ANATOMY. BY SAMUEL D. L. POTTER, M.A., M.D., M.R.C.P. London. Seventh edition. Revised and enlarged, with 138 wood engravings; also numerous tables and 16 plates of the arteries and nerves. Philadelphia: P. Blakiston's Son & Co., 1012 Walnut Street. 1903. Cloth. 372 pp. Price, 80 cents net.

Through the opportunity afforded a revision by the frequent editions of this manual, the author has given a concise, and, as far as we have examined it, accurate work of anatomy. It makes an excellent text-book, permitting the teacher to enlarge upon the information given as the exigencies of the class-room demand.

A COMPEND OF THE DISEASES OF THE SKIN. BY JAY F. SCHAMBERG, A.B., M.D. Third edition. Revised and enlarged, with 106 illustrations. Philadelphia: P. Blakiston's Son & Co., 1012 Walnut Street. 1903. Cloth. 291 pp. Price, 80 cents net.

Dr. Schamberg has given a very readable, brief treatise on dermatology in this little volume. When one recalls the dry-as-dust tomes of a generation ago and compares them with the clearly expressed and comprehensive text-books of to-day, it almost excites a feeling of regret that one was not able to make the acquaintance of so important a subject in so pleasing a manner. That the printer is able to reproduce the photographer's art by means of "half-tones" adds greatly to this.

We notice one curious *lapsus pennæ* on p. 118, "Among these may be mentioned the *acids* of *alkalies*." (Italics ours.)

THE CRUSADE AGAINST TUBERCULOSIS—CONSUMPTION A CURABLE AND PREVENTABLE DISEASE—WHAT A LAYMAN SHOULD KNOW ABOUT IT. BY LAWRENCE F. FLICK, M.D. Philadelphia: David McCay, Publisher, 1022 Market Street. Cloth. 295 pp. Price, $1.00 net.

The preface of this book states "Much unnecessary fear of the contagion of tuberculosis has been stirred up. . . . For the purpose of bringing about a better understanding of things, . . . this little volume is offered to the public."

Dr. Flick's long study of the subject makes him a proper person to properly set forth these subjects in such a manner as the non-medical reader may obtain a clear comprehension of the subject. He treats of the various topics in some 40 or 50 chapters such as "What Consumption is," "What Tuberculosis is," "Climate as a Factor in Consumption," "The Workshop in the Spread of Tuberculosis," "The Natural Course of Tuberculosis," "How to Avoid Getting Consumption."

There is a need for popular volumes on prevailing maladies, and we hail a work of this kind written by a master hand.

JOURNAL OF SOCIAL SCIENCE CONTAINING THE PROCEEDINGS OF THE AMERICAN ASSOCIATION. No. XLI. August, 1903. Boston papers of 1903. Published for the American Social Science Association. Damrell and Upham and the Boston Book Company, Boston, Mass. 1903. Cloth. 139 pp.

Of the four papers presented to the department of health, that of Professors Sedgwick and Hough on "What Training in Physiology and Hygiene May We Reasonably Expect of the Public Schools?" is of especial interest, as it could have been made another paper in the series presented at the last meeting of the Academy. The conclusions do not entirely coincide with these papers, but they do not conflict with them, and afford additional evidence of the accuracy of those conclusions which are in accord.

BULLETIN

OF THE

American Academy of Medicine

VOL. VI.   ISSUED DECEMBER, 1903.   NO. 9.

The American Academy of Medicine is not responsible for the sentiments expressed in any paper or address published in the BULLETIN.

HOW THE PHYSICIAN MAY INFLUENCE THE DECLINING BIRTH-RATE.[1]

BY ROLAND B. CURTIN, M.D., Ph.D., of Philadelphia.

The subject of this paper was suggested by the decreasing number of the children annually born in the United States. This has repeatedly been brought to notice; but more recently has it been made prominent by the thought emphasized by President Roosevelt.

The writer was much struck by a paper read in France in 1896, in which the author demonstrated by statistics that the two great republics of the world, France and the United States of America, were the only countries that would lose in population if immigration should be stopped. Not that these two countries alone show a decrease, because the same is true of the whole civilized world, but not to such an extent as is found in France and America. Upon looking over the statistics of the older states of our country, we find the greatest loss is among the old, influential or rich families; so much so that family after family averages one, one and a half, or two children to each couple. Quite recently in Wilkes-Barre, Pennsylvania, a census was taken and it was found that in the seventh ward where live most of the wealthier inhabitants there was but a single birth for the six months ending

[1] Read before the American Academy of Medicine, at Washington, D. C., May 12, 1903.

June 30, 1903. The average in the wards where the working people lived was high. In Forty Fort where many of the citizens are descendants of the old Connecticut settlers there was in the same period not a single birth. I know of a town in New England with a population of four hundred and fifty persons among whom are fifty married couples capable of producing children. In this town the school contains a single scholar and no more in sight to be educated.

The greatest number of children come from the unassimilated foreign population. Therefore it occurs to me that the balance of political power will, in a short time, be in the hands of these children, and not in the hands of that "strain" which has brought our country to its present position among nations. It therefore seems proper to inquire into the facts and see if among the many causes any can be found for which the physician alone is responsible. Perhaps this "racial suicide" question may influence our future position among the nation of the world. It has been said by a wise observer that the nations who care least for their children first stand still, then retrograde.

A family limited to one child usually shows a spoiled, overdressed child, unhealthy intellectually, and so selfish as to be of little comfort or use to their families or the country. Such children are apt to be petted, spoiled, peevish, without self-denial or straight-forward manhood. Are such citizens the ones to force their way to the front in science, art, or commerce? Neither will the progeny of those that have never had the education before and after birth be able to cope with foreigners educated, generation after generation, for their life occupation. They will work in after while; but they will at once be pushed to the front, before they are prepared for the work. It commonly takes two or three generations in America to fit this material for the work of properly guiding and governing.

Ad. ; Smith, long ago, said that poverty seems to be favorable to generation. Such being the case, we should educate these poor children, as they will soon play an important part as our country's fight for first place, that is, to take the place of the children of the rich, who, petted, mentally and physically emasculated, selfish, and conceited, are poor material for the first rank in either war or peace.

Among the causes of the diminished birth-rate not generally mentioned are the changes in the method of living. The apartment house, which is growing in favor, is a bad school for good wives and mothers, especially those that are young. Children are not wanted in such quarters. The population in these apartment houses, as a rule, turn a cold shoulder upon the woman who is a fond mother, or commiserate her for her enslaved position. The servant-girl question often drives families to these houses. Another cause is the nervous trades, which bring on exhaustion and unfit women for maternity, and housekeeping. Clerks, stenographers, shop and factory girls are to be included in this category.

Another cause is the pursuit of manly callings by women. First, it makes them feel independent of marriage. Secondly, they take the work from the men, so that the men cannot afford to support a wife.

The undomestic parents are another cause of this evil. Very lately I saw the happy mother of a large family who told me that she was fifty years old, and that she had slept away from her home only one night in all that time. She was like Sarah, a biblical character, who we are told, was always found in her tent. A woman not like Sarah told me to call on Sunday as that was the only day she was at home.

With these few remarks by way of introduction, I shall proceed to tell what the doctor has to do with it. To begin with, he can do a great deal of good or a great deal of harm. The doctor's advice is generally very potent with loyal patients; therefore, let it be of a high moral character. The explanations that have been given for existing conditions are numerous; but, as yet, I have never heard any one speak of the part that the doctor takes in this great tragedy. By high prices, he may increase the family expenses to such an extent as to plunge the young husband in debt, often depriving the family of the necessaries of life, driving it to a boarding-house, and altogether discouraging the couple, or causing dissentions that may separate them. We must admit that at the present time there are many conditions that contribute to the increase of the expenses of the family. At the time when I first went into practice, the charge for a labor was from $10 to $25; only a few physicians charged more. The nursing cost but little, and the outfit was made by the wife. Now we have to confront a fee from $25 to $250; nurse's wages and board for eight weeks, $240; mother's outfit, $15 to $50; child's $35 to $100. Think of what this bill would be to a clerk that is living up to his means in keeping house. The above does not include many other expenses incidental to the confinement, and the doctoring of the enlarged family afterwards. I fear that soon all the confinements will be made in hospitals, in order to reduce the expenses.

It is not unusual for a doctor to tell a woman, after a hard labor, in which the child is still born, that she cannot have a living baby; and he may also tell her that she will die in her next confinement. I have seen such cases, when the words of the doctor has not dissuaded the woman; the second labor was easy, and the child was born alive. Again I have known of a case in which the mother had a learned obstetrician measure her daughter with a pelvimeter, and he decided that the daughter could not be safely delivered. She married later, and was quite easily delivered of a small child. I have known of women that have been deterred from marrying late, because the doctor had said that it was dangerous to marry after a certain age.

Tell your patients that a break in the matrimonial cycle is an invitation to ill health, and that the full cycle of matrimony is conducive to long life, health and beauty, when not too excessive.

Late marriages are apt to lead to the transmission of acquired and hereditary diseases and habits, such as nervous diseases, gout, intemperance, etc.

Some of the writers on hygiene for our schools have much to answer for by giving information that leads to evil. The subject should be looked at from all sides; many conditions are to blame.

I have said nothing about the criminal doctor who does wholesale murder, nor have I spoken of those who tempt such villians by their gold to disobey the laws of God and man. The physician that deals out information to the laity as to the unlawful methods of avoiding conception is a culprit before his God, the laws of man, and the moral law.

A woman once told a friend of mine, a physician, that when she conceived she had gone to her family doctor and complained of uterine symptoms, asking for a uterine examination; and that the introduction of the sound and a local application had always relieved her.

My reasons for writing on this subject is that I see a growing laxity principally among the younger men of the profession. I would caution such persons to carefully avoid the danger line which, once crossed, is seldom retraced.

What I have said is based upon an experience in a large city and the large cities usually set the fashions for the smaller cities, and they for the towns and the people of the country.

CONCLUSIONS.

The doctor may influence the birth-rate:

(1) By increasing the expenses of confinement.
- (*a*) By charging high prices;
- (*b*) By expensive nursing;
- (*c*) By expensive outfits.

(2) By giving discouraging advice.
- (*a*) By advising the drying up of the milk, and substituting expensive bottle-feeding.
- (*b*) By instructing patients how to avoid conception.

(3) By careless intra-uterine instrumentation.

(4) By removing the essential organs of generation.

(5) By the false hygienic teaching in our schools.

NECESSITY FOR A NATIONAL BUREAU OF MEDICINES AND FOODS.[1]

By H. Bert. Ellis, M.D., Los Angeles, California.

For at least a quarter of a century, the philanthropic ambition of the manufacturer of pharmaceuticals, to make life easier for the physician by improving upon the pharmacopeia and by putting up medicines ready mixed and possessing virtues unknown in other makes of similar mixtures, has been quite manifest. The pharmacopeia has been regarded as an excellent historical work, to be consulted occasionally for reference but not for use, and its abbreviated title, in the form of " U. S. P.," has certain esthetic properties that appeal to some manufacturers so strongly that they add the letters to the labels of certain of their products. As indicating any definite thing, however, they are about as misleading as the mystic C. P. on the label of a reagent; it may or may not be chemically pure (the strong probability is that it is not), and the U. S. P. preparation may or may not conform to the standards of the pharmacopeia.

The attitude of many, if not most of the prominent manufacturing houses is about this, they say : " We have discovered a process by which we can treat the crude drug in a more satisfactory manner than in that called for by the pharmacopeia, and by our process we extract the essentials more completely and more carefully, so that our product is much better than that indicated in the pharmacopeia. It is also better than any similar product manufactured by any other house, for no other house can use our method."

Every manufacturing house makes practically the same statement, and each has its own method and its own standard, and consequently its own product differs not only from that of every other house, but probably all differ, more or less, from the standard of the pharmacopeia, which the physician, in theory, is following. Examination shows that fluid extracts made by different houses and all branded U. S. P. will not mix together and differ widely in the amount of the extractive matter they

[1] Read before the American Academy of Medicine, Washington, D. C., May 11, 1903.

contain; tinctures made from the solid or fluid extracts of various houses vary from 10 to 60 per cent. in the amount of the alkaloidal principle in solution. Yet they may all be branded U. S. P.

What is the pharmacist to do? He can not determine which is actually the best preparation to carry, nor can he keep all brands in stock. Suppose all the brands of a given product are honestly made by these various processes and are honestly put out by the manufacturers as being U. S. P. or better. The fact remains that they are unlike, each differing from every other brand and nearly all differing from the pharmacopeial standard. The result is that a given prescription filled at one time with ingredients of one brand will not be the same or have the same therapeutic effect as when at another time it is filled with ingredients of another brand having a different "standard." In consequence the physician, who knows what he prescribes, does not know what the patient actually takes.

The list of chemicals ordinarily and commonly found adulterated, and their adulterants, would be far too long to be cited here, but it is an imposing array. And of the adulterants commonly used, many are by no means harmless, but are harmful in a marked degree. What physician, for instance, would care to freely apply aristol, knowing that it might contain 65 per cent. free alkali? Or who would care to make use of phenacetin in fairly large doses, knowing that it might be adulterated with 90 per cent. acetanilid? The conditions are such that little dependence may be placed upon the legend of the label, no matter what the name of the manufacturer may be.

Now let us look at another very large and vexing question— the enormous number of "proprietary" remedies. First, however, it will be well to define the terms employed. In strict compliance with the definition of the word, "Squibb's chloroform," "Merck's cocaine," "Wyeth's quinine," listerine, antikamnia, phenacetin, and "Paine's celery compound" are all proprietary remedies, for the property rights in each case are owned by a given individual or corporation, and the articles may not be made or sold as such by any other individual or corporation. Probably ninety-nine out of a hundred physicians, if asked to name the "patent medicines" in the list given, would mention listerine, antikamnia, and Paine's celery compound. They would be wrong in every one, for the only patent medicine in the list is phenacetin. Those just named are not "patent" at all; they are simply nostrums, protected by trade-mark and copyright, and the composition of any or all of them is unknown and may be varied at will by the manufacturer. The composition of a true patent medicine is filed at the patent-office and may be known to any one; the name applied to the thing is free to commerce and to science on the expiration of the patent right. Some of the most conservative upholders of a high standard of the ethics of therapeutics have agreed that any remedy of which the actual composition is known, may be ethically employed and prescribed by physicians, and the members of the Pharmacopeia Revision Committee have, I understand, taken the same position and will probably admit to the next edition of that work, a number of the true patent medicines.

No difficulty presents in dealing with nostrums, true patent medicines, and such simple preparations as were mentioned for illustration, in which the name of the maker has come to be indicative of a high-grade preparation. It is the very large class of proprietary preparations put out by leading manufacturers and advertised to physicians by personal solicitation and otherwise, that is perplexing and troublesome. If the manufacturer publishes the formula of a given preparation, giving the active ingredients and their quantities, couched in the ordinary terms of chemistry and pharmacy, and if there is strong probability that the formula so given is correct, so that every physician may know exactly what his patient is taking, the remedy is one that may be ethically employed or prescribed by any physician. If the formulas of preparations of this class could be certified as correct, and if the manufacturer's misuse, for advertising purposes, of statements given by physicians could be controlled and kept within proper professional limits, the objection to physicians recommending such remedial agents would be largely removed.

This may be done in a strictly professional manner, through the medium of a properly constituted board of experts representing the two great interests involved—medicine and pharmacy. It would not be possible for the manufacturer to do this work, for his statements would probably always be looked upon askance by a large number of physicians. No single individual could do the work, for his motives would be questioned. But a carefully selected board, which had no interest at stake, could undertake and successfully carry on the work, if such a board received general professional support.

A board, or bureau, of this sort could certify to the truthfulness of the label placed upon any product whose manufacture was placed under its supervision, and which it would check from time to time, by analysis or assay of samples bought on open market. It could also censor the advertising statements of the manufacturers whose goods were certified by it, and in this way prevent the improper use of medical comment upon certified articles. All physicians would benefit by knowing exactly the composition of those mixtures which it might be desirable to use, and also by receiving unbiased statements emanating not from the commercially interested manufacturer, but from a professional board of scientific men of high repute. Trade literature would soon be replaced by these reliable and truthful statements, and thus one other evil would in time disappear. The benefit to the manufacturer of any good and legitimate preparation would at once be noticed, for the formula of such a preparation would be vouched for by a disinterested board, and the advertising statements regarding it, having passed the censorship of such a board, could and soon would be relied upon and treated with respect and consideration by a large number of physicians who now pay no attention whatever to trade literature, for the reason that it is essentially one-sided and therefore probably unreliable.

It is also proposed that this bureau shall undertake the work of proper inspection of such food stuffs as might be accepted for that purpose by the board of control, certifying to their purity or composition. The conditions in the food stuff business are as bad, if not worse, than they are in the matter of chemicals and pharmaceuticals. The products of certain houses may be accepted as reliable owing to the reputation that has come to attach to the name; but these are few in number and there is an element of doubt even in these cases, in the mind of the average buyer. Adulteration of foodstuffs is carried to a point that would scarcely be believed by one not acquainted with actual conditions; the sale, wholesale and retail, of adulterants is quite a business in itself.

That the correction of the many and very serious evils here merely outlined is much to be desired, is admitted by every one, and by many it is considered as of first importance that some steps be taken looking to their correction. Proper control of these and similar questions should be a government function; but the government can not command, it can only condemn. It is largely on this account that many of the largest and best manufacturers of reputable standing and honest intent have persistently opposed all the national pure-food and drug bills that have been introduced into congress during the past fourteen years.

The last pure-food and drug bill—the one that passed the house but got lost in that celebrated chamber of antiquities called the senate—was supported by most of the nostrum manufacturers, many manufacturers of pharmaceuticals of questionable standard, and a large number of foodstuff manufacturers whose products are decidedly not above question; opposed to the bill were most of the large manufacturers of foodstuffs and pharmaceuticals whose products are considered to be of high grade. Why? For one reason, because the proposed law as drawn, did not apply at all to nostrums or pharmaceutical preparations other than those found in the pharmacopeia—the products from which most manufacturing houses derive the major portion of their income; probably there is no pharmaceutical manufacturing house in the country that does or could pay a dividend of 1 per cent. from the profits derived from the manufacture of pharmacopeial products alone. For another reason, because under the proposed law the power to condemn any and all products was placed in the hands of a single individual, and manufacturers of even the highest repute were afraid that at some time or other this power might get into the hands of some one who might be "influenced."

It seems possible to modify a suggestion made by Dr. F. E. Stewart before the American Medical Association in 1881, and to make a practical solution of the question at least possible. Such an assumption is based on the belief that many manufacturers of products under discussion are honest and desire to place on the market only products of certain standard and of honest quality, and that the aggregate annual value of such products would be very considerable. Certified milk is no longer a theory in many localities, and the benefits to the public and to the dealers have been made manifest. Why not carry out the same principle, modified where necessary, in the domain of drugs and foodstuffs? Why not try to associate those manufacturers whose primary intent is to be honest and to put up only honest goods, supervise their work, and their advertising, and see that it is properly done from a professional and ethical standpoint?

The heart of the proposed plan for a National Bureau of Medicines and Foods is to bring into voluntary association with the professions of medicine and pharmacy, such manufacturers as really desire to put up only standard and honest goods and to deal with the professions interested in a truly professional and ethical manner. It is proposed that there shall be a board of ten directors, five of whom shall be elected by the American Medical Association and five by the American Pharmaceutical Association. This board would not be subsidized by the manufacturers, for the members would receive no salaries, and merely traveling expenses and *per diem* when called upon to attend meetings of the board or its committees. The board would pass upon all products submitted to the bureau for inspection and certification, and would formulate all rules for the manufacture of certified products, which rules the manufacturer would contract to follow. It would further undertake to see that all such rules were followed by the manufacturers. It might also undertake to see that reliable information concerning certified products was placed in the hands of those interested—the professions of medicine and pharmacy, and the general public—in a manner that would be advantageous to the physician and to the pharmacist, because the information would be unbiased, and profitable to the manufacturer, because it would place such reliable statements in the hands of the consumers of his goods.

Several good lawyers have given their attention to the legal status of such a proposed bureau, and they are unanimous in the opinion that its position would be very strong. It could not be compelled to certify anything not complying with its standards nor following its rules, and thus could not be forced into expensive litigation on that point. It could also frame its charter and by-laws in such a way as to control its associate members (the manufacturers), and to discipline them for breach of contract in not abiding by the rules formulated for their guidance and agreed to by them. At first it would accept for certification only such products as could be handled with perfect safety, such articles as are subject to analysis or assay, and would have for its associate members only such concerns as it deemed absolutely reliable in their intent to be strictly honest in the quality of the goods they put out. Such a bureau would, under no circumstances, condemn anything. It would simply certify to the standard of identity, purity, quality or strength, or compliance with a given formula, of each package of each and every article that it could vouch for.

The Pharmacopeia Revision Committee is at present considering an exceedingly important question: The standardization and admission to the pharmacopeia of diphtheria antitoxin. The difficulty is this; if a standard is fixed and antitoxin is placed in the pharmacopeia, the pharmacist who dispenses it becomes responsible for the standard. But he cannot determine the standard of the antitoxin he sells, and for which he is made responsible, without opening the sealed package in which it is put up by the manufacturer. Immediately the seal is broken, the antitoxin becomes valueless; consequently, he cannot determine the standard of that for which he is made responsible. If the control of the whole matter were placed in the hands of such a professional bureau as is proposed, its solution would present no difficulty. The Revision Committee would indicate the standard for U. S. P. antitoxin, and the bureau would undertake to have duly qualified experts at hand wherever antitoxin might be produced, who should determine the standard of each batch and certify only to such batches as complied with the pharmacopeial standard. Each package would then bear a label of the bureau, certifying to the standard of the contents. Any such statement made by the manufacturer, could not be relied upon, for he is commercially interested; the statement of a wholly disinterested, unprejudiced and unbiased board of scientific men could, however, be officially recognized.

The most sanguine adherent of the proposed bureau would hardly claim that it will do away with all dishonesty. There will always be dishonesty and trickery in the world and in medicine. Doubtless the time will never come, when the manufacturer who so desires cannot find some physician who, for the regular fee of $25, will write an article extolling the virtues of anything indicated by the manufacturer.

But it is claimed that much good can be done. It is believed if the professions of medicine and pharmacy will unite to demand that certain standards shall be maintained and that they shall receive proper and ethical treatment at the hands of those whose products they sell, they will get what is demanded and they will go far toward raising themselves from the lowly and unpleasant position in which they are to-day. If, however, the professions of medicine and pharmacy prefer to remain as they are; if they prefer to have manufacturers dictate what they shall prescribe or use on the one hand, and what they shall carry in stock and sell on the other hand, they have simply to continue in the present state of inactivity. They may rest absolutely assured that the condition will not be changed by any periodically threatened legislation, nor by any attempt on the part of one or two manufacturers.

Hard work and concentrated effort are required in the winning of anything worth having; present evils, we may be sure, will not be remedied without unremitting effort and an unrelaxing grasp of the situation. A simple declaration of belief, a statement of what is considered proper professional attitude toward proprietary remedies, and all the memorials addressed to congress that could be drawn in a hundred years will have no effect in correcting the abuses which the profession of medicine now calmly suffers. Only an organized and determined effort to see that these abuses are corrected, will avail in the slightest, but I am absolutely certain that such an effort could be successful. The objects outlined may be attained; the vexing questions may be settled; all these things may be done in a thoroughly proper and professional manner by means of an association of interests such as is proposed in this National Bureau of Medicines and Foods.

Whether this work will be done, depends upon how real the demand for relief is. If the demand is only strong enough to make the statement: "Yes, things are wrong; let us memorialize congress," nothing will ever be done. If it is sufficiently strong to make these two great associations, the American Medical and the American Pharmaceutical Associations, the one representing medicine and the other standing for the best in pharmacy, actually undertake to see that something tending toward relief shall be done, then relief is at hand. Then the successful organization of such a proposed bureau would be assured, for all that the manufacturer needs to cause him to undertake this work is to be assured that it is really demanded.

It is possible to find honest men to formulate the rules of such a bureau and to establish proper standards; it is possible to find honest men to see that they are maintained; it is possible to find honest men to carry on the business of the bureau and to see that it is kept out of trouble through the exercise of good business judgment and common sense; it is possible to find the means for defraying the expenses of doing the work; it simply remains to be seen whether the physicians and pharmacists of the country, represented in their national associations, really want these things done and will stand together and demand that they shall be done.

DISCUSSION.

Dr. A. L. Benedict, of Buffalo:

It seems to me that Dr. Ellis has struck the key-note of this problem. Whenever we come to consider a matter of this sort we are opposed by the fact that about one hundred and ten years ago the framers of our Constitution laid down certain state and a very few national rights, and the meaner and smaller and the less account a state is, the more the citizens in that state stand up for their state rights. As in many other instances, we are met with the obstacle that there is no national authority to take up this issue. There is just one society which could act with force in this matter. That is the American Medical Association. What we want is not a certificate regarding the ethics of preparations mentioned, but to know what is in the preparations. In one sample of liquid peptonoids which was examined there was scarcely a trace of nutritive material. I have no question but that the manufacturers acted in perfectly good faith, and I believe there was some defect in the manufacture, for subsequent samples have proved rich in nutriment. There are dozens of manufacturers who would be glad to submit to tests and who do have their goods tested by reliable chemists, but the information is not authoritative. We want some source of information to which physicians can apply for definite information. If we could have a board established by the American Medical Association it would help us. The paper is extremely important and the matter should be discussed so that we can come to some tangible basis. If we could have such a board in the immediate future it would save us trouble and save lives. Thousands of lives are lost every year in this country simply because we do not know our digitalis. There is no agreement as to what the active principle of digitalis is. We want not information as to whether it is pure, but we want to know what is in it. We can then make our own judgments as to purity, quality and strength.

Dr. Victor C. Vaughan, of Ann Arbor:

It seems to me that this paper opens up a subject that is very important, and I should dislike very much to see the American Academy of Medicine take decided action in the matter. This was brought before the House of Delegates in the American Medical Association and there was no action taken on it, and the committee was continued. I should be perfectly willing to do that here, but I think it would be an unfortunate thing for the Academy of Medicine to endorse it. The proposition is capable of good and it is also capable of great harm. I think that if we would teach against the wholesale administration of drugs it would be far better than any such proposition as this. The more intelligent a physician is, within certain limits, the less the number of drugs that he gives, and if we only give those drugs which would benefit the patient it would be easy enough to control their manufacture. On the other hand, as I understand it, if a man wants to come out with some prepared foods, or wine of pepsin, etc., he will simply go to this board and the board will say that the wine of pepsin is what it is said to be, the approval of the profession is stamped upon a product that cannot be worth anything under any conditions. The purer the article is the worse it is. Wine of pepsin is absolutely worthless as a digestive substance, and so it is with many other articles. The quicker we stop endorsing these things the better will it be for the profession and for the patient. There never was a life saved by these preparations, and to put the stamp of approval of the medical profession on them would, it seems to me, be disadvantageous altogether. I am not condemning Dr. Ellis' paper, but asking that we go slowly, that we may consider the matter more thoroughly. I am not so sure that government control would not be the proper thing. The German government controls the preparation of antitoxin, and they do not have in Germany such disasters as we had some time ago in St. Louis. I think the government ought to control some of the preparations at least. It is a big subject, and too important a one to rush into without more consideration.

Dr. T. D. Davis, of Pittsburg:

I think we all realize the importance of this subject, especially when we look on our office desks and see the scores and scores of samples of all kinds of things which have been left there, with the voluminous literature which attends them. The question is one of commercialism *vs.* science, and whenever this obtains it is a one-sided proposition. Take, for instance, what Dr.

Vaughan has said—that the matter should be under government supervision. All the patent medicines are put out under the auspices of the government and granted upon the advice of so-called experts. Patent medicines are now pretty much a thing of the past, because a copyright of the name can be secured, but the formula does not have to be published at all; and the so-called proprietary medicines in most cases, are named and issued simply to gull the profession. In regard to the proposition that the American Medical Association help in this matter, I think the association will have to cast the beam out of its own eye before it goes for this mote. Its journal is full of the advertisements of these very things we want to get rid of. I am heartily in accord with the report if it could be carried out practically, but when commercialism is opposed to science, I am very much afraid that in the long run commercialism will get the better of the science even under a carefully selected board.

Dr. A. L. Benedict:

I think we lose sight of the fact that it is not a matter of ethics. The matter is one which we have been discussing as long as we have been practising. A friend of mine, one of the best therapeutists in my part of the country, will not use drugs unless he gets them from one particular drug store, and he claims this is the only way to get results. I think Dr. Vaughan has confused the matter of education and ethics with this practical one of certification. I never made a gastric analysis except in five cases in which there was need of pepsin, yet tons of it are sold every year. If we do prescribe wine of pepsin we ought to know what is in it. Of course, we cannot make a satisfactory chemic examination of digitalis, but there is a fairly reliable physiologic test of digitalis; some is good and some of it will simply take away the chances of the patient's life. There are cases in which we want proprietary foods. Patients will take them when they will not take solid food. We want to know whether they are pure and what is in them.

Dr. Ellis, in closing:

I simply wanted to present the subject for consideration and have a little discussion. The idea of the bureau is not to take up a thing which the government should control. For many years there have been bills presented to Congress and they are no nearer being passed now than when presented. I think we can accomplish something by the method which I have proposed. We would be working in harmony with the government, and effective legislation on this matter might be brought about.

EXAMINATIONS FOR MEDICAL LICENSURE IN 1902.[1]

BY CHARLES MCINTIRE, A.M., M.D., Secretary of the Academy.

It has not been thought necessary to incorporate in this report more than an outline of the requirements demanded by the various States of the candidate seeking licensure in medicine, since these have been given from time to time in previous reports, the last time in the report for last year. All changes in the laws, as far as known, are noted, and, when possible, the full text of the law given. For the most part, the tabulations of the results of the examination has been revised by the official board.

ALABAMA.

Examination essential; graduation from medical school optional.
Legislation since the last report.
* Dr. William H. Sanders, State House, Montgomery, is the secretary.

I.

THE OSTEOPATHIC BILL.

SECTION 1. Any person holding a diploma from a legally incorporated school of osteopathy recognized as of good standing by the Alabama State Osteopathic Association, and wherein the course of study comprises a term of at least twenty months, or four terms of five months each, in actual attendance at such school, and which furnishes instruction in the following branches; to-wit, anatomy, hygiene, medical jurisprudence, symptomatology, minor surgery, physiology, chemistry, histology, pathology, gynecology, obstetrics, and the theory of osteopathy, and one full term of practice of osteopathy, shall, upon the presentation of such diploma to the State Board of Medical Examiners, and satisfying such board that he is the legal holder thereof, be granted, by such board, an examination of the following branches; to-wit, (1) anatomy, physiology, hygiene, medical jurisprudence, physical diagnosis, urinalysis, and toxicology; and (2), gynecology, midwifery, and osteopathic principles and diagnosis.

The examination of such applicant shall be conducted by said State Board of Medical Examiners, in all respects as examinations are now conducted by them, except that the questions as to the subjects enumerated under Clause 2, above, shall be propounded by and the answers thereto shall be graded by a practising osteopath in this State, who shall be appointed by the governor immediately on the passage of this Act, and who shall be known as State

[1] A report presented to the American Academy of Medicine at its meeting in Washington, May 11, 1903.

Osteopathic Examiner, and whose term of office shall be three years, and until his successor is appointed by the governor. Any vacancies in said office shall be filled by appointment by the governor. The fee for said examination, which shall accompany the application, shall be fifteen dollars; ten dollars of which shall be appropriated as such fee is now appropriated in cases of application for licenses to practise medicine, and five dollars shall be paid to said State Osteopathic Examiner.

In order to receive the certificate hereinafter provided for, the same general average shall be made by such applicant on his said examination as is now required under the rules of the State Board of Medical Examiners, provided that osteopaths who resided in the State on January 1, 1903, and who are graduates of legally incorporated schools of osteopathy, as above recognized, shall be entitled to receive the certificate hereinafter provided for, upon the payment of the fee prescribed, without passing such examination.

Upon passing a satisfactory examination, as above prescribed, the said Board of Medical Examiners shall issue a certificate to the applicant therefor, signed by the President of said Board, which certificate shall authorize the holder thereof to practise osteopathy in the State of Alabama. It shall be lawful for the holder of such certificate to practise osteopathy in the State of Alabama.

SEC. 2. The certificate provided for in the foregoing section shall not authorize the holder thereof to prescribe or use drugs in his practice, nor to perform major or operative surgery.

SEC. 3. Any person holding such certificate may apply to the State Board of Medical Examiners to be examined in surgery upon passing an examination in which such applicant may, in addition to osteopathy, practise surgery in this State.

SEC. 4. That all laws and parts of laws in conflict herewith, and particularly Section 5333 of the Code, in so far as it conflicts herewith, be and the same are hereby repealed.

II.

A bill prescribing the subjects for examination, entitled

An Act to prescribe the Branches of Medical Learning upon Which Applicants for the Privilege of Treating Diseases of Human Beings in this State Must Be Examined, and to provide for the Issuance of Certificates of Qualification Therefor.

SECTION 1. Be it enacted by the Legislature of Alabama, That any applicant for a certificate of qualification to treat diseases of human beings by any system of treatment whatsoever, shall, according to the rules prescribed and standards established by the Medical Association of the State of Alabama, be examined by one of the authorized Boards of Medical Examiners of this State in the following branches of medical learning; to-wit, chemistry, anatomy, physiology, the etiology, pathology, symptomatology, and diagnosis of diseases; obstetrics and obstetrical operations; gynecology; minor and major surgery; physical diagnosis; hygiene; and medical jurisprudence; and should said applicant be found proficient in said branches of medical learning a certificate of qualification in such form as shall be prescribed by said Medical Association of the State of Alabama shall be issued to him, which shall entitle him to treat any and all diseases of human beings in this State in any manner that he may deem best.

SEC. 2. Be it further enacted, That when an applicant states in writing that he neither studied nor proposes to practise major surgery, said applicant shall be exempt from examination in said branch of major surgery, and should he be found proficient in the other branches of medical learning named in Section 1 of this Act, a certificate of qualification in form to be likewise prescribed by the Medical Association of the State of Alabama shall be issued to him, which shall entitle him to treat all diseases of human beings in this State in such a manner as he may deem best, except by the practice of major surgery.

SEC. 3. Be it further enacted, That all laws and parts of laws in so far as they conflict with the provisions of this Act, be and the same are hereby repealed.

Approved February 26, 1903.

EXAMINATIONS, 1902.

Name of college.	Passed.	Failed.	Total.
ALABAMA.			
Birmingham Medical College	4	0	4
Medical College of Alabama	15	0	15
DISTRICT OF COLUMBIA.			
Columbian University	1	0	1
GEORGIA.			
Atlanta College of Physicians and Surgeons	20	0	20
Atlanta Medical College	1	0	1
Georgia College of Eclectic Medicine and Surgery	3	0	3
University of Georgia	1	0	1
ILLINOIS.			
Hahneman Medical College	1	0	1
Northwestern University	1	0	1
KANSAS.			
Kansas Medical College	0	1[1]	1
KENTUCKY.			
Hospital College of Medicine of Kentucky	2	0	2
Louisville Medical College	1	0	1
University of Louisville	0	1[2]	1
LOUISIANA.			
Tulane University	2	0	2
MARYLAND.			
College of Physicians and Surgeons	2	1[3]	3

[1] Class of 1897.
[2] Class of 1894.
[3] Class of 1893.

Name of college.	Passed.	Failed.	Total.
Maryland Medical College	3	0	3
University of Maryland	1	0	1
MASSACHUSETTS.			
Boston University	1	0	1
NEW YORK.			
Columbia	1	0	1
University of New York	1	0	1
NORTH CAROLINA.			
Leonard Medical College	3	0	3
OHIO.			
Eclectic Medical Institute	1	0	1
Medical College of Ohio	0	1[1]	1
Pulte Medical College	1	0	1
PENNSYLVANIA.			
Jefferson Medical College	2	0	2
University of Pennsylvania	1	0	1
TENNESSEE.			
Chattanooga Medical College	6	0	6
Grant University	4	1[1]	5
Meharry Medical College	2	3[2]	5
Memphis Hospital Medical College	7	0	7
University of Nashville	4	0	4
University of the South	4	0	4
University of Tennessee	3	1[3]	4
Vanderbilt University	4	0	4
VERMONT.			
University of Vermont	0	1[4]	1
VIRGINIA.			
University of Virginia	1	0	1
Non-graduates	3	6	9
	107	16	123

ALASKA.

There are no laws regulating the practice of medicine in Alaska.

ARIZONA.

The law under which Arizona was working was declared to be unconstitutional, and nothing was done during the year. A new

[1] Class of 1897.
[2] Class of 1898, 2, 1902.
[3] Class of 1893.
[4] Class of 1900.

law to comply with the decision of the courts has been adopted; the Act is as follows:

Be it enacted by the Legislative Assembly of the Territory of Arizona:

SECTION 1. That it shall be unlawful for any person to practise medicine within the Territory of Arizona until he or she have obtained a license therefor, as hereinafter in this Act prescribed.

SEC. 2. No person shall receive a license to practise medicine within the Territory unless he or she shall have:

First. Obtained a diploma to practise medicine, or some department thereof, regularly issued by a medical college, lawfully organized under the laws of the state or territory wherein such college shall have been located at the time of the issuance of such diploma; and,

Second. Obtained a certificate entitling him or her to practise medicine, as prescribed in Section 4, Chapter 1, Title 53, being paragraph 3529 of the Revised Statutes of Arizona, 1901, or shall have passed a satisfactory examination prescribed by the provisions of an Act of the Legislative Assembly of Arizona, entitled "An Act to amend an Act to regulate the practice of medicine in the Territory of Arizona," approved March 18, 1897; or

Third. Practised medicine within the Territory of Arizona continuously for five successive years preceding the date fixed for the taking effect of this Act; or,

Fourth. Upon examination by the Board of Medical Examiners of Arizona, shown to the satisfaction of the Board that he or she possesses sufficient knowledge and skill to properly practise medicine; and,

Fifth. Become a *bona fide* resident of Arizona, and shall have passed the age of twenty-one years and shall have a good moral character.

SEC. 3. There shall be and there is hereby established in Arizona, a board to be known as the "Board of Medical Examinations of Arizona." Said Board shall consist of five members, who shall be nominated and, by and with the consent of the Legislative Council, appointed by the Governor. Such members shall, at the time of their appointment, be each a *bona fide* citizen of the United States, and have been a resident of the Territory of Arizona for at least three consecutive years continuously next preceding the time of his appointment; and at the time of his appointment shall be and shall have been for at least three consecutive years theretofore actually engaged in the practice of medicine in the Territory of Arizona. The term of office of said members of said Board shall be for five years, except that of the members first appointed under the provisions of this Act, one of whom shall be appointed for one year, one for two years, one for three years, one for four years, and one for five years. Three of the members of said Board shall be physicians of the regular school of medicine, one of the homeopathic school of medicine and one of the eclectic school of medicine. The Board shall, upon its organization, and thereafter once in each year, elect one of its members as president and one of its members as secretary thereof, whose respective terms of office as president and secretary shall be one year. The president shall preside at the meetings of the Board and shall, by his signature, authenticate all licenses issued under the provisions of this Act. The secretary shall keep the records of the Board, have the custody of its books, papers and seal; shall countersign all licenses issued under the provisions of this Act, and shall act as the treasurer of the Board. Said Board shall make reasonable rules and regulations for the transaction of its business, not inconsistent with law or the purposes and intent of this Act. The Board shall meet in regular session quarter-yearly, at a regularly designated place of meeting, at Phoenix, Arizona, and at such other times as it may from time to time appoint.

SEC. 4. Any person desiring to obtain a license to practise medicine within this Territory shall make application therefor to the Board of Medical Examiners of Arizona. The application shall be in writing and state the name of the applicant, his age, his residence, the name and location of the college whence his diploma issued, the length of time, if at all, he has practised medicine, and where, giving specifically the places where he has practised medicine; and the dates between which he practised at each place, and the particular school and department of medicine he practised; and contain such other information as may be prescribed by the rules and regulations of the Board. Each application for license shall be verified by the oath of the applicant, taken before some officer authorized by the laws of Arizona to administer oaths. The application shall be accompanied by the diploma of the applicant, or by a copy thereof, authenticated to the satisfaction of the Board. The applicant shall also present with his or her application the affidavits of at least three or more residents of the county and state wherein the applicant formerly resided and practised medicine, stating, within their own knowledge, the name of the applicant, the length of time they have known him or her, his or her residence, the length of time he or she has resided there, and, if applicant shall have practised medicine in Arizona, the length of time and place or places where he or she has so practised, and that the applicant is a person of good moral character. If the applicant shall have received a certificate under the provisions of Paragraph 3529, Revised Statutes of Arizona, 1901, or shall have passed a satisfactory examination prescribed by an Act of the Legislative Assembly of the Territory of Arizona, entitled "An Act to amend an Act to regulate the practice of medicine in Arizona," approved March 18, 1897; or, if the applicant shall have practised medicine within the Territory of Arizona continuously for five successive years next preceding the date fixed for the taking effect of this Act, he or she shall present with his or her application proper and satisfactory evidence thereof; the applicant shall at the time of the presentation of his or her application for a license to practise medicine, pay to the secretary of the Board of Medical Examiners the sum of two dollars ($2). If it shall appear that the applicant has not obtained the certificate mentioned in Paragraph 3529, Revised Statutes of Arizona, 1901, or passed the satisfactory examination prescribed by the provisions of an Act of the Legislative Assembly of Arizona, entitled,

"An Act to amend an Act to regulate the practice of medicine in Arizona," approved March 18, 1897, and shall not have practised medicine within this Territory continuously for five years next preceding the date fixed for the taking effect of this Act, then no license shall issue to him or her, until he or she shall have, upon examination by the Board, shown to the satisfaction of the Board that the applicant possesses sufficient knowledge and skill to properly practise medicine.

SEC. 5. The examination provided for in the preceding section shall be made by said Board as soon after the application shall have been presented as it may be conveniently done, and after notice to the applicant of the time and place thereof. The examination shall be conducted under such reasonable rules and regulations as the Board may prescribe therefor, and with the design and purpose of ascertaining the fitness of the applicant for the practice of medicine in this Territory.

If the applicant request it he or she shall have the privilege of being examined in the branches of the science and the practice of medicine other than physiology, anatomy, pathology, chemistry, practice, surgery, obstetrics and gynecology, by the member or members of the Board, if there be any, of the particular school of medicine specified in his or her diploma, and if the examination in such other branches be satisfactory to the members or member conducting said examination, it shall be approved by the Board and to the extent thereof be deemed to be to the Board's satisfaction. Before any examination the applicant shall pay to the secretary of the Board, in addition to the fee hereinbefore required, the further fee of ten dollars ($10.00).

SEC. 6. When it shall be made to appear to the satisfaction of the Board that the applicant possesses the qualifications in this Act prescribed to fit him or her to practise medicine in this Territory, and that he or she has complied with the provisions of this Act, a license shall thereupon issue to the applicant. The license shall be signed by the president and countersigned by the secretary of the Board, and have impressed upon it the seal adopted by the Board. It shall recite that the person therein named has complied with the provisions of this Act, and that he or she is entitled to practise medicine in the Territory of Arizona, and shall be in such form as the Board may adopt.

SEC. 7. Upon proper proof to the Board of Medical Examiners of Arizona that the holder of any license issued under the provisions of this Act has been guilty, since the issuance thereof, of any grossly immoral or unprofessional conduct, or of any other conduct rendering him or her unfit to practise medicine in this Territory, or has been convicted of any felony, said Board shall, after due notice to such holder and full opportunity to him or her to defend against or refute such charges, revoke and cancel such license, and it shall thereafter be unlawful for such person to practise medicine in this Territory until he or she shall again be licensed thereto under the provisions of this Act.

SEC. 8. The members of the Board of Medical Examiners of Arizona shall receive for their compensation and reimbursement of all expense incurred by the Board or its members in the discharge of the duties imposed by this Act, the fees paid by the applicants for license and examinations, the same to be apportioned and applied by the Board.

SEC. 9. The secretary of the Board shall keep a register of those to whom license to practise shall be issued under the provisions of this Act. Such record shall be kept in a substantially bound book, in which shall be entered in alphabetical order the name of licensees, their place of business, the date of issuance of license, and such other memoranda as the Board may direct. The secretary shall also keep a proper and accurate account of all moneys received and disbursed by him. He shall also properly endorse, file and safely keep all applications for license and accompanying papers, and papers used in the examination of applicants for license, and turn over all said books and papers to his successor in office.

SEC. 10. Any person shall be regarded as practising medicine within the meaning of this Act who shall within this Territory (a) by advertisement, or any notice, sign or other indication, or by any statement, printed, written or oral, in public or in private, made, done or procured by himself or herself, or any other, as his or her request, for him or her, claim, announce, make known or pretend his or her ability or willingness to diagnosticate, or prognosticate any human diseases, ills, deformities, defects, wounds or injuries; (b) or who shall so advertise or make known or claim his or her ability and willingness to prescribe or administer any drug, medicine, treatment, method or practice, or to perform any operation, manipulation, or apply any apparatus, or appliance for cure, amelioration, correction, reduction or modification of any human disease, ill, deformity, defect, wound or injury, for hire, fee, compensation or reward, promised, offered, expected, received or accepted, directly or indirectly; (c) or who shall within this Territory diagnosticate or prognosticate any human diseases, ills, deformities, defects, wounds or injuries, for hire, fee, reward or compensation, promised, offered, expected, received or accepted, directly or indirectly; (d) or who shall within this Territory prescribe or administer any drug, medicine, treatment, method or practice, or perform any operation or manipulation, or apply any apparatus or appliance for the cure, alleviation, amelioration, correction, reduction or modification of any human disease, ill, deformity, defect, wound or injury, for hire, fee, compensation or reward, promised, offered, expected, received or accepted, directly or indirectly; (e) or who shall act as the agent of any person, firm or corporation, in the practice of medicine as hereinbefore set forth; (f) except it be in the advertisement or practice of dentistry, midwifery, or pharmacy, or in the usual business of opticians, or of venders of dental or surgical instruments, apparatus and appliances.

SEC. 11. The provisions of this Act shall not be construed to modify or in any wise to effect the provisions of the laws of this Territory relating to the practice of dentistry.

Sec. 12. Any person or persons violating any of the provisions of this Act, upon conviction thereof, shall be fined in any sum not less than one hundred dollars ($100) nor more than one thousand dollars ($1,000), or by imprisonment in the County jail for a period of not less than three months nor more than one (1) year, or both such fine and imprisonment at the discretion of the laws.

Sec. 13. All laws in conflict or inconsistent with this Act are hereby repealed.

Sec. 14. This Act shall be in force and effect from the date of its approval by the governor; provided, however, that persons having already complied with previous laws regulating the practice of medicine in the Territory of Arizona shall have until the first day of June, 1903, within which to file their applications for license and procure same, and until such time no penalty shall be imposed upon such lawful practitioners for a violation of the provisions of this Act.

Approved March 19, 1903.

ARKANSAS.

The legislature for 1903 adopted a new Act, under which the practice of medicine will be regulated hereafter. It provides for three Boards of Examiners independent of each other. Any person desiring to practise medicine must make application to the secretary of the board of his choice, and submit to an examination on anatomy, physiology, chemistry, materia medica, theory and practice of medicine, surgery and obstetrics. If he passes, he will receive a certificate which must be recorded in the office of the clerk of the county in which he resides.

The fee for the examination is $10; the penalty for practising without a recorded license is a fine of from $25 to $500, or imprisonment for from ten to ninety days, or both.

Members of the Board—The State Medical Board of the Arkansas Medical Society, William Crutcher, M.D., Pine Bluff; Adam Guthrie, M.D., Prescott; O. E. Jones, M.D., Newport; M. L. Norwood, M.D., Lackesburg, *Treasurer;* G. V. Paynor, M.D., Green Forest; J. P. Runyan, M.D., Little Rock, *Secretary;* C. R. Shinault, M.D., Helena, *President.*

Eclectic State Medical Board—W. M. Allison, M.D., Bee Branch; W. C. Hudson, M.D., Mulberry, *Treasurer;* W. S. May, M.D., Gordon; W. H. Simmons, M.D., Rector; R. L. Smith, M.D., Russelville, *President;* J. W. Tibbles, M.D., Grange; J. L. Vail, M.D., Little Rock, *Secretary.*

Homeopathic State Medical Board—Victor Hallman, M.D., Hot Springs, *Secretary.*

TEXT OF THE LAW.

AN ACT to regulate the practice of medicine and surgery, and providing for the appointment of three Boards of State Medical Examiners, and defining their duties.

Be it enacted by the General Assembly of the State of Arkansas :

SECTION 1. That the medical examiners herein provided for shall consist of three Boards ; one of physicians and surgeons, recommended by " The Homeopathic Medical Society of Arkansas ;" one of physicians and surgeons recommended by " The Arkansas State Eclectic Medical Society ;" and one of physicians and surgeons, recommended by "The Arkansas Medical Society."

There shall be seven (7) members of each Board, appointed so as to have one member from each congressional district upon each Board. The appointment shall be made by the governor from a list of names presented by the respective medical societies.

SEC. 2. That the members first appointed on the Boards shall be divided into two (2) classes, the first class to consist of four (4) members appointed for two (2) years; the second class of three (3) members shall be appointed for four (4) years, and thereafter all appointments shall be for four (4) years.

Vacancies in the said Boards shall be filled as they occur by appointments from lists furnished as provided. No member shall be appointed for more than two terms in succession ; and no member, or professor, or teacher in a medical college or school, or university, having a medical department, shall be appointed upon the Boards.

SEC. 3. Within the thirty days after their appointments, the respective Boards shall meet and organize by electing a president, secretary and treasurer of their respective Boards.

The treasurer of the said Boards shall give bond in such amount as may be designated by the Board, conditioned for the faithful disbursement of all moneys coming into his hands as such treasurer.

Each of the said Boards shall have a common seal. The president and secretary shall have power to administer oaths for the purpose of this Act. The members of the Boards shall, before entering upon the discharge of their duties, take the oath prescribed by the Constitution of this State for State officers.

SEC. 4. The said Boards shall hold four regular stated meetings per year; to-wit, the second Tuesdays in January, April, July and October, at such places as a majority may agree upon, consulting the convenience of the Boards and applicants for examination and certificates.

Special meetings may be held upon the call of the president whenever it is deemed necessary or expedient. Said Boards shall keep a record of their proceedings, together with a correct list of all applicants for license to practise medicine, in any of its branches, with name, sex, color, age, nativity, time spent in the study of medicine, and, if possessing a diploma, the name and locality of the institution granting same, stating the system of medicine followed by each.

This record shall also state whether the applicant was rejected or licensed; said record shall be *prima facie* evidence of all matters required to be kept therein, and a certificate issued under the seal of said Board, and signed by the president and secretary thereof, and shall be *prima facie* evidence in any of the courts of this State of any matter appearing upon said records.

SEC. 5. The Boards shall be styled and known as the "Homeopathic State Medical Board," the "Eclectic State Medical Board," and the "State Medical Board of the Arkansas Medical Society."

The "Homeopathic State Medical Board" shall examine all applicants who propose to practise the homeopathic system of medicine; the "Eclectic State Medical Board" shall examine all applicants who propose to practise the eclectic system of Medicine; and the "Board of Arkansas Medical Society" shall examine all other applicants.

The Boards shall act separately and independently of each other, and wherever this Act refers to and defines the duties of the Board, it shall be construed as referring to their acting separately, as well as independently of each other.

SEC. 6. Every person now practising medicine in this State shall, within ninety days after the passage of this Act, prepare a written statement, giving his name, post-office address and county; when and where he received authority to practise medicine in this State; where his diploma or certificate is on record; and, if a diploma, from what school or medical college issued; such statement shall be sworn to before some officer authorized to administer oaths, and shall be forwarded to the secretary of the Board representing his school of medicine.

If it shall appear from such statement that such person was regularly authorized to practise medicine under the then existing laws, the said Board shall register the name of such person in their list of accredited physicians, and issue to such person a certificate that his name has been placed upon such list. If it shall appear from the statement that such person has not been legally authorized to practise medicine, or that his diploma is not from a reputable medical school or college, or, if from any other source of information, it shall appear that the statement is false, the Board shall refuse to issue to such a person a certificate, and shall notify such person in writing of their refusal and the reason therefor. If such person shall show to the satisfaction of the Board by affidavits or otherwise that he has complied with the laws of this State regulating the practice of medicine, they shall in that event issue to him a certificate. Upon the failure of such person to make the proof required by this section, he shall, before continuing in the practice, make application and stand examination required by the following provisions of this Act.

SEC. 7. Any person who shall wilfully and knowingly make any false statement to the Board concerning his authority to practise medicine shall be deemed guilty of perjury and punished, as now provided by law for those found guilty of perjury, and may be indicted and tried for such offense, either in the county where the affidavit to such statement was made, or where such person resides.

SEC. 8. Every person residing in this State, or coming into it, of the age of twenty-one years, who has not heretofore been licensed to practise medicine under the existing laws, making application to register under the provisions of this Act for the purpose of practising medicine and surgery in this State, shall first make application to the secretary of the Board, and his application shall be accompanied by a fee of ten dollars ($10), this fee being for examination and registration before this Board. Such examination may be written or oral at the discrimination of the Board, and shall be of an elementary and practical character, including anatomy, physiology, chemistry, materia medica, theory and practice of medicine, surgery and obstetrics.

If, in the opinion of the Board, the applicant possesses the necessary qualifications, the Board shall issue to him a certificate.

SEC. 9. Every person receiving a certificate from the Board, whether practising now or hereafter licensed to practise, shall have such certificate recorded in the office of the county clerk where he is practising or proposes to practise; and, when such person moves to another county for the purpose of continuing the practice of medicine, he shall file for record with the county clerk of the county to which he moves, a certified copy of his certificate.

SEC. 10. That to prevent delay and inconvenience, any member of the Board applied to may grant an applicant a temporary permit to practise, upon the payment of the fee required of applicants, and after a satisfactory examination, such permit shall not continue in force longer than until the next regular meeting of the Board, and shall in no case be granted within six months after the applicant has been refused a certificate by the Board.

No additional fee shall be charged the applicant by the Board who has previously paid the amount for a temporary permit. All amounts paid to members of the Boards for temporary permits, shall be by such members paid to their respective treasurers.

SEC. 11. Every person who shall practise, or shall attempt to practise medicine in any of its branches, or, who shall perform or attempt to perform any surgical operation for any person, or upon any person within this State without first having complied with the provisions of this Act, shall be deemed guilty of misdemeanor, and upon the conviction thereof, shall be punished by a fine of not less than twenty-five dollars ($25), nor more than five hundred dollars ($500); or by imprisonment in the county jail for a period of not less than ten days, nor more than ninety days; or, by both fine and imprisonment; and each day of such practice shall constitute a separate offense.

Provided, however, That this shall not apply to persons now engaged in the practice of medicine until ninety days after the passage of this Act, the time allowed them for procuring their certificate.

Sec. 12. Any itinerant vender of any drug, nostrum, ointment or application of any kind, intended for the treatment of disease or injury, or, who may, by writing, print or other methods, profess to cure or treat diseases or deformity by any drug, nostrum, manipulation, or other expedient, in this State, shall be deemed to be inviolation of this law and punished as provided. This does not apply to persons who obtain certificates, as herein provided.

Sec. 13. Any person shall be regarded as practising medicine, in any of its departments, within the meaning of this Act, who shall append M.D. or M.B. to his name; or repeatedly prescribe or direct for the use of any person or persons, any drug or medicine or other agency for the treatment, cure, relief of any bodily injury, deformity or disease.

Provided, That nothing in this Act shall be so construed as to prevent any person from administering domestic remedies without receiving any compensation therefor, and nothing herein shall apply to the so-called midwife.

Sec. 14. The secretary of the Board shall provide the Board with blank books, certificates, and such stationery as is necessary for the transaction of the business pertaining to their duties. All money received by the Board shall be disbursed by the treasurer upon the warrant of the secretary, countersigned by the president of the Board.

The members of the Board shall receive as a compensation for their services the sum of ten dollars ($10) per day for every day actually engaged in the discharge of their duties under this Act, and the secretaries shall receive such additional salary as may be fixed and agreed upon by the Boards.

The members of the Board shall pay their own traveling expenses and hotel bills. The members of the Boards shall look to and be dependent entirely upon the fees provided for herein for their compensation, and all other expenses in connection with their duties.

It shall not be lawful for the said Boards, or any members therefor, in any manner, whatever, or for any purpose, to charge or obligate the State for the payment of any money whatever. If, after paying all legitimate obligations of the Board, for stamps, printing, salary of secretary, etc., there should not be sufficient sums on hand to pay each member his *per diem* in full, the amount shall be prorated; but, if at the end of the year, there should be a greater revenue derived than sufficient to meet all obligations, such surplus shall remain in the treasury to be used in expenditures of the Boards during the following year.

Sec. 15. The Boards shall annually file with the governor a report of their transactions during the year, giving the names of all to whom they have granted certificates during the year, naming the system of medicine practised by each, and shall in such report show the amount of money received; and from what source, the amount expended, and for what purpose, and shall embody in their report any other matters or facts deemed expedient, and make such recommendations for the improvement of the practice of medicine in this State as may be deemed advisable.

If the Boards shall have sufficient funds on hand to pay for same, they shall have said reports printed in pamphlet form and furnish each physician in this State with a copy thereof.

SEC. 16. All laws or parts of laws in conflict with this Act are hereby repealed, and this Act shall take effect and be in force ninety days after its passage.

Approved February 17, 1903.

CALIFORNIA.

California has a single Board of Examiners before whom all desiring to practise medicine must present themselves. Only graduates in medicine from a school whose standing is equivalent to that required by the Association of American Medical Colleges can present themselves.

Members of the Board—E. C. Buell, Los Angeles; George G. Gere, *Secretary*, 825 Market St., San Francisco; D. E. Osborne, St. Helena; Lewis A. Perce, Long Beach; David Powell, *President*, Marysville; Dudley Tait, *Vice-President*, San Francisco; Walter S. Thorne, San Francisco; C. L. Tisdale, *Treasurer*, Alameda; Ray L. Wilbur, Palo Alto.

EXAMINATIONS, 1902.

Name of college.	Passed.	Failed.	Total.
CALIFORNIA.			
Cooper Medical College	6	0	6
College of Physicians and Surgeons	2	7	9
Hahnemann Medical College	4	1[1]	5
University of California	20	1	21
University of Southern California	1	0	1
CONNECTICUT.			
Yale University	2	0	2
ILLINOIS.			
American Medical Missionary College	0	1	1
Chicago Homeopathic Medical College	1	0	1
Chicago Medical College	1	0	1
College of Physicians and Surgeons	0	1	1
Hahnemann Medical College	1	1[2]	2
Northwestern University	1	1	2
Northwestern University of Woman's Medical School	1	0	1
INDIANA.			
Medical College of the University of Indianapolis	1	0	1
IOWA.			
College of Physicians and Surgeons	0	1[2]	1

[1] Class of 1901.
[2] Class of 1878.

Name of college.	Passed.	Failed.	Total.
KENTUCKY.			
Kentucky School of Medicine	0	1[1]	1
University of Louisville	0	1[2]	1
MARYLAND.			
Baltimore University	0	1	1
Johns Hopkins University	4	0	4
MASSACHUSETTS.			
Harvard University	1	0	1
MICHIGAN.			
University of Michigan	0	1[3]	1
Detroit College of Medicine	1	0	1
MISSOURI.			
Ensworth Medical College	0	1[4]	1
Kansas City Medical College	0	1[4]	1
Barnes Medical College	0	1[5]	1
St. Louis Medical College	0	2[6]	2
NEW YORK.			
Bellevue Hospital Medical College	1	0	1
Columbia University	1	0	1
University City of New York	2	2[7]	4
OHIO.			
College of Physicians and Surgeons	0	1[5]	1
Ohio Medical University	0	1[8]	1
Starling Medical College	0	1	1
PENNSYLVANIA.			
Hahnemann Medical College	1	0	1
Jefferson Medical College	2	1	3
Woman's Medical College	1	1[9]	2
VIRGINIA.			
University of Virginia	1	0	1
CANADA.			
University of Toronto	1	0	1
FOREIGN.			
University of Groningen	0	1[10]	1
	57	31	88

[1] Class of 1885.
[2] Class of 1892.
[3] Class of 1878.
[4] Class of 1894.
[5] Class of 1898.
[6] One class of 1859.
[7] One of each class 1886, 1879.
[8] Class of 1881.
[9] Class of 1872.
[10] Class of 1891.

COLORADO.

Graduates from medical schools whose curriculum complies with the requirements of the Association of American Medical Colleges may be licensed without an examination; all others who desire to settle in Colorado must pass an examination.

Board of Examiners—Drs. C. K. Fleming, Denver; John Inglis, Pueblo; Sol. G. Kahn, Leadville; P. J. McHugh, Fort Collins; T. W. Miles, *President*, Denver; George C. Stemen, Denver; Charles F. Stough, Fort Collins; D. A. Strickler, Denver; S. D. Van Meter, *Secretary and Treasurer*, 1723 Tremont Street, Denver.

CONNECTICUT.

Since the last report, Connecticut has changed its law, requiring the possession of a diploma from a reputable medical school before one can present himself before either one of the committee for examination.

Application to take the examination should be made to the secretary of the State Board of Health, Dr. C. A. Lindsley, New Haven.

EXAMINATIONS, 1902.

Name of college.	Passed.	Failed.	Total.
ALABAMA.			
Medical College of Alantma	0	1	1
COLORADO.			
Gross Medical College	1	0	1
CONNECTICUT.			
Yale	12	0	12
GEORGIA.			
College of Physicians and Surgeons, Atlanta	1	0	1
ILLINOIS.			
Hering Medical College	1	0	1
College of Physicians and Surgeons Chicago	1	0	1
IOWA.			
Keokuk College of Medicine	0	1	1
KENTUCKY.			
University of Louisville	1	0	1
MARYLAND.			
Baltimore Medical College	1	2	3
Baltimore University	1	0	1
Johns Hopkins University	2	0	2
MASSACHUSETTS.			
Harvard University	1	0	1

Name of college.	Passed.	Failed.	Total.
Boston University	1	1	2
Tufts Medical College	2	1	3
MINNESOTA.			
University of Minnesota	1	0	1
NEW HAMPSHIRE.			
Dartmouth	1	0	1
NEW YORK.			
Long Island Medical College	1	1	2
Bellevue Hospital Medical College	2	0	2
Cornell	2	0	2
College of Physicians and Surgeons, New York	11	0	11
New York Homeopathic Medical College	1	0	1
New York University	1	0	1
Syracuse University	1	0	1
University and Bellevue Hospital Medical College	5	0	5
OHIO.			
Starling Medical College	0	1	1
PENNSYLVANIA.			
Hahnemann Medical College	3	0	3
Jefferson Medical College	3	0	3
Medico-Chirurgical College	1	1	2
University of Pennsylvania	3	0	3
Woman's Medical College	2	0	2
TENNESSEE.			
University of the South	0	1	1
VERMONT.			
University of Vermont	5	0	5
CANADA.			
McGill University	1	0	1
Trinity University	0	1	1
	69	11	80

DELAWARE.

Delaware requires a preliminary education, four years of medical education, and graduation from a medical school, and the passing of an examination before one of the two Boards, before the Medical Council will issue the necessary license, unless the applicant is already licensed in another state, when, under certain conditions, the license will be accepted as evidence of fitness to practise.

Applications for licensure must be made to Dr. P. W. Tomlinson, Wilmington, the secretary of the Medical Council.

EXAMINATIONS, 1902.

Name of college.	Passed.	Failed.	Total.
DISTRICT OF COLUMBIA.			
Georgetown University	1	0	1
MARYLAND.			
Baltimore University	2	1[1]	3
PENNSYLVANIA.			
Hahnemann Medical College	4	0	4
Jefferson Medical College	2	0	2
Medico-Chirurgical College	2	1	3
University of Pennsylvania	3	0	3
TENNESSEE.			
University of Tennessee	1	0	1
FOREIGN.			
University of Naples	1	0	1
	16	2	18

DISTRICT OF COLUMBIA.

The examinations in the district are conducted by three boards of examiners under the direction of a Board of Medical Supervisors (Dr. William C. Woodward, secretary). Graduation in medicine is a prerequisite to take the examination, and the medical course must be, at least, of four years to those graduating after June 30, 1898.

EXAMINATIONS, 1902.

Name of college.	Passed.	Failed.	Total.
DISTRICT OF COLUMBIA.			
Columbian University	20	0	20
Howard University	3	0	3
National University	6	2[2]	8
University of Georgetown	2	0	2
ILLINOIS.			
American Medical College	0	1	1
Hahnemann Medical College	1	0	1
College of Physicians and Surgeons	1	0	1
MARYLAND.			
Baltimore Medical College	1	0	1
Johns Hopkins	2	0	2
NEW YORK.			
Columbia	2	0	2
PENNSYLVANIA.			
Hahnemann Medical College	1	0	1

[1] Class of 1898.
[2] One class 1901, 3rd examination; one withdrew, 2nd examination.

Name of college.	Passed.	Failed.	Total.
Jefferson Medical College	2	0	2
University of Pennsylvania	1	1[1]	2
Woman's Medical College	1	0	1
TENNESSEE.			
University of the South	1	1[2]	2
	44	5	49

FLORIDA.

The medical law in Florida remains in its ancient inefficient condition. There are seven Boards, one for each judicial district; and two Boards for the state at large, one each for the homeopaths and eclectics. The number of physicians entering Florida in any one year is too small to cause such cumbersome machinery to work smoothly, and it has been found impossible to secure the results of the examinations.

GEORGIA.

Georgia has three Boards of Examiners, working entirely independently of each other. A person desiring to practise medicine in Georgia, must pass an examination before the Board of his choice. Application should be made to the secretary.

The "Regular" Board is composed of Drs. I. H. Gross, *Secretary and Treasurer*, Athens; J. B. S. Holmes, *President*, Atlanta; E. A. Jelks, Quitman; F. D. Patterson, *Vice-President*, Cuthbert; F. M. Ridley, La Grange.

The Homeopathic Board is composed of Drs. M. A. Cleckley, Augusta; R. B. Cuthbert, *Vice-President*, Rome; R. E. Hinman, *Secretary and Treasurer*, Atlanta; John Z. Law, Atlanta; C. M. Paine, *President*, Atlanta.

Dr. M. T. Salter is the secretary of the Eclectic Board.

EXAMINATIONS, 1902.

Name of college.	Passed.	Failed.	Total.
ALABAMA.			
Birmingham Medical College	1	0	1
DISTRICT OF COLUMBIA.			
Howard University	3	0	3
National Medical University	0	1	1
GEORGIA.			
Atlanta College of Physicians and Surgeons	53	1	54
University of Georgia	36	3	39

[1] Class of 1898.
[2] Class of 1901, 4th examination.

Name of college.	Passed.	Failed.	Total.
IOWA.			
Iowa University	1	0	1
KENTUCKY.			
Kentucky School of Medicine	1	0	1
University of Louisville	1	0	1
LOUISIANA.			
New Orleans University	1	0	1
Tulane	1	0	1
MARYLAND.			
Baltimore Medical College	2	0	2
College of Physicians and Surgeons	1	0	1
Woman's Medical College	1	0	1
University of Maryland	4	0	4
MICHIGAN.			
University of Michigan	2	0	2
MISSOURI.			
Barnes Medical College	1	0	1
NEW YORK.			
University of the City of New York	1	0	1
NORTH CAROLINA.			
Leonard Medical College	3	0	3
PENNSYLVANIA.			
Hahnemann Medical College	2	0	2
TENNESSEE.			
Chattanooga Medical College	5	0	5
Grant University	1	0	1
Vanderbilt University	2	0	2
University of Tennessee	3	0	3
Meharry Medical College	6	0	6
University of the South	1	0	1
VIRGINIA.			
University of Virginia	2	0	2
	135	5	140

IDAHO.

To obtain a license to practise medicine in Idaho, one must have been graduated from a reputable medical college and pass the examination of the State Board of Medical Examiners.

Dr. R. L. Nourse, Hailey, is the secretary of the board.

EXAMINATIONS, 1902.

Name of college.	Passed.	Failed.	Total.
CALIFORNIA.			
University of California	0	1[1]	1

[1] Class of 1888.

Name of college.	Passed.	Failed.	Total.
ILLINOIS.			
College of Physicians and Surgeons	3	0	3
Rush Medical College	4	0	4
INDIANA.			
Fort Wayne College of Medicine	1	0	1
MICHIGAN.			
University of Michigan	0	1[1]	1
MISSOURI.			
University of Kansas City	1	0	1
College of Physicians and Surgeons	0	1[2]	1
College of Physicians and Surgeons, St. Louis	0	1[3]	1
PENNSYLVANIA.			
University of Pennsylvania	1	0	1
TENNESSEE.			
University of Chattanooga	0	1[4]	1
University of Nashville	0	1[4]	1
	10	6	16

ILLINOIS.

The examinations in Illinois are under the direction of the State Board of Health. Graduates of recognized medical schools only are eligible for examination.

Dr. J. A. Egan, Springfield, is the secretary of the Board.

EXAMINATIONS, 1902.

Name of college.	Passed.	Failed.	Total.
DISTRICT OF COLUMBIA.			
Georgetown University	1	0	1
ILLINOIS.			
American Medical Missionary College	4	0	4
Bennett Medical College	18	0	18
Chicago Homeopathic Medical College	6	0	6
College of Medicine and Surgery	1	0	1
Dunham Medical College	4	0	4
Hahnemann Medical College and Hospital	8	6[5]	14
Harvey Medical College	20	0	20
Hering Medical College	2	0	2
Illinois Medical College	10	2[6]	12
Jenner Medical College	1	1[4]	2

[1] Class of 1892.
[2] Class of 1882.
[3] Class of 1893.
[4] Class of 1901.
[5] Two, classes of 1884, 1899, one of 1901; one withdrew.
[6] One, class of 1900, one of 1903 withdrew.

Name of college.	Passed.	Failed.	Total.
National Medical University	4	1	5
Northwestern University	12	0	12
Northwestern University Woman's Medical School	1	0	1
Rush Medical College	103	1	104
College of Physicians and Surgeons	40	3	43
INDIANA.			
Medical College of Indiana	1	0	1
IOWA.			
Keokuk Medical College	4	4[1]	8
KENTUCKY.			
Hospital College of Medicine	5	0	5
Kentucky University	1	0	1
Louisville Medical College	1	0	1
MARYLAND.			
Baltimore Medical College	1	0	1
Baltimore University	1	0	1
Johns Hopkins	1	0	1
MICHIGAN.			
University of Michigan	2	0	2
Detroit College of Medicine	1	0	1
Michigan College of Medicine and Surgery	1	0	1
MINNESOTA.			
University of Minnesota	1	0	1
MISSOURI.			
American Medical College	2	0	2
Barnes Medical College	1	2	3
Marion-Sims College of Medicine	3	0	3
Missouri Medical College	1	0	1
St. Louis College of Medicine	7	0	7
St. Louis Medical College	1	0	1
St. Louis and Missouri Medical College	1	0	1
Washington University	2	0	2
NEBRASKA.			
John A. Creighton Medical School	2	0	2
NEW YORK.			
New York Homeopathic Medical College and Hospital	1	0	1
OHIO.			
Eclectic Medical Institute	3	2[2]	5
Miami Medical College	1	0	1
Cleveland Medical College	1	0	1
Western Reserve University	1	0	1
Columbus Medical College	1	0	1
Starling Medical College	1	0	1

[1] One withdrew.
[2] Both class of 1900.

Name of college.	Passed.	Failed.	Total.
PENNSYLVANIA.			
Hahnemann Medical College	2	0	2
Jefferson Medical College	2	0	2
University of Pennsylvania	4	0	4
TENNESSEE.			
Meharry Medical College	1	0	1
WISCONSIN.			
Milwaukee Medical College	1	0	1
CANADA.			
Laval University	1	0	1
McGill University	1	0	1
University of Toronto	1	0	1
FOREIGN.			
University of Geneva	1	0	1
University of Naples	1	0	1
University of Bucharest	1	0	1
University of Parma	2	0	2
University of Christiana	1	0	1
Imperial University of Kazan	1	0	1
	304	22	326

INDIAN TERRITORY.

The old tribal laws were inoperative, and the work of reorganization is not yet complete, making, practically, no medical practise act in the territory.

INDIANA.

Indiana admits to examinations only those who have graduated from a medical school maintaining the Board's standard. With the exception of those students who matriculated in Indiana before January 1, 1901 (and even these must apply for license before January 1, 1905), all intending practicers must pass the examination.

Dr. W. T. Gott, Indianapolis, is the secretary.

EXAMINATIONS, 1902.

Name of college.	Passed.	Failed.	Total.
ILLINOIS.			
American Medical Missionary College	1	0	1
Bennett Medical College	3	0	3
Chicago Homeopathic Medical College	1	0	1
Chicago Medical College	1	0	1
College of Physicians and Surgeons	6	0	6

Name of college.	Passed.	Failed.	Total.
Hahnemann Medical College	4	0	4
Illinois Medical College	1	0	1
Rush Medical College	15	0	15
INDIANA.			
Fort Wayne Medical College	1	0	1
Medical College of Indiana	2	0	2
IOWA.			
College of Physicians and Surgeons, Keokuk	0	1	1
Keokuk Medical College	1	0	1
KENTUCKY.			
Hospital College of Medicine	6	0	6
Kentucky School of Medicine	1	2	3
Louisville Medical College	4	0	4
Louisville National Medical College	2	0	2
University of Louisville	4	1[1]	5
MASSACHUSETTS.			
Boston University	1	0	1
Harvard Medical College	1	0	1
MICHIGAN.			
University of Michigan	5	0	5
Michigan College of Medicine and Surgery	1	0	1
MISSOURI.			
Kansas City Homeopathic Medical College	2	0	2
Barnes Medical College	2	1	3
Marion-Sims Medical College	1	0	1
Missouri Medical College	1	1[2]	2
Homeopathic Medical College	1	0	1
NEW YORK.			
College of Physicians and Surgeons	1	0	1
University and Bellevue Hospital Medical College	1	0	1
OHIO.			
Cincinnati College of Medicine and Surgery	0	1	1
Eclectic Medical Institute	6	0	6
Laura Memorial Woman's Medical College	1	0	1
Medical College of Ohio	7	1[3]	8
Miami Medical College	4	0	4
Western Reserve University	2	0	2
PENNSYLVANIA.			
Jefferson Medical College	3	0	3
University of Pennsylvania	1	0	1
Woman's Medical College	2	0	2
Western Pennsylvania Medical College	1	0	1

[1] Class of 1898.
[2] Class of 1878.
[3] Class of 1877.

Name of college.	Passed.	Failed.	Total.
TENNESSEE.			
University of Nashville	2	0	2
Vanderbilt University	1	0	1
VIRGINIA.			
University of Virginia	1	0	1
FOREIGN.			
Royal University, Budapest	0	1	1
	101	9	110

IOWA.

An examination before the State Board of Medical Examiners is necessary to obtain a license to practise. Graduates of recognized colleges only have the privilege of examination.

Dr. J. F. Kennedy, Des Moines, is the secretary of the board.

EXAMINATIONS, 1902.

Name of college.	Passed.	Failed.	Total.
COLORADO.			
Gross Medical College	1	0	1
ILLINOIS.			
American Medical Missionary College	1	0	1
Bennett Medical College	2	0	2
Chicago Homeopathic Medical College	4	0	4
College of Physicians and Surgeons	36	0	36
College of Medicine and Surgery	0	1^1	1
Hahnemann Medical College	11	1	12
Dunham Medical College	0	1^1	1
Illinois Medical College	1	0	1
National Medical College	1	0	1
Northwestern University	13	0	13
Northwestern University Woman's Medical School	2	0	2
Rush Medical College	21	0	21
INDIANA.			
Fort Wayne Medical College	1	0	1
Physio-Medical College	0	1^2	1
IOWA.			
College of Physicians and Surgeons, Des Moines	9	0	9
College of Physicians and Surgeons, Keokuk	0	1^3	1
Keokuk Medical College, College of Physicians and Surgeons	35	2^1	37
Keokuk Medical College	0	1^3	1

[1] Class of 1901.
[2] Class of 1876.
[3] Class of 1893.

Name of college.	Passed.	Failed.	Total.
Iowa University, Homeopathic Department	6	1[1]	1
Iowa University	40	0	40
Sioux City College of Medicine	8	0	8

KANSAS.
Kansas Medical College	1	0	1

KENTUCKY.
Louisville Medical College	1	0	1
University of Louisville	1	0	1

MASSACHUSETTS.
Tufts	1	0	1

MICHIGAN.
University of Michigan	2	0	2
Detroit Medical College	1	0	1

MINNESOTA.
University of Minnesota	0	1[2]	1

MISSOURI.
American Medical College	1	1[3]	2
Barnes Medical College	1	4[4]	5
Marion-Sims Medical College	1	0	1
St. Louis College of Physicians and Surgeons	6	1[5]	7
St. Louis and Missouri Medical College	1	0	1
Missouri Medical College	0	1[6]	1

NEBRASKA.
J. A. Creighton Medical College	5	0	5
Omaha Medical College	7	0	7

NEW YORK.
College of Physicians and Surgeons	2	0	2

OHIO.
Eclectic Medical Institute	1	0	1
Medical College of Ohio	2	0	2
Miami Medical College	1	0	1
Homeopathic Hospital College	1	0	1
National Normal University	0	1[1]	1

PENNSYLVANIA.
Jefferson Medical College	4	0	4
Medico-Chirurgical College	2	0	2
University of Pennsylvania	2	0	2
Woman's Medical College	1	0	1

[1] Class of 1892.
[2] Class of 1895.
[3] Class of 1896.
[4] One each of classes 1898, 1900, 1901.
[5] Class of 1901.
[6] Class of 1872.

Name of college.	Passed.	Failed.	Total.
TENNESSEE.			
Meharry Medical College	0	1[1]	1
University of Tennessee	1	0	1
WISCONSIN.			
Wisconsin College of Physician and Surgeons	1	0	1
Milwaukee Medical College	1	0	1
CANADA.			
Trinity University	1	0	1
	241	19	260

KANSAS.

The Kansas State Board of Registration and Examination requires the applicant for licensure to present evidence of having completed the medical studies required by the medical practise act (graduation from a medical school after at least three years' study, the terms in each year being not less than six months, long, if the applicant graduated before April 1, 1902; graduates after that date must have had four terms of at least six months no two in the same year) and pass an examination.

Dr. D. F. Lewis, Topeka, is the secretary.

EXAMINATIONS, 1902.

Name of college.	Passed.	Failed.	Total.
ILLINOIS.			
College of Physicians and Surgeons	2	0	2
Hahnemann Medical College	1	0	1
Northwestern University	4	0	4
Rush Medical College	5	0	5
INDIANA.			
Indiana Medical College	1	0	1
Hospital Medical College	1	0	1
KANSAS.			
Kansas Medical College	2	0	2
MARYLAND.			
Maryland Medical College	1	0	1
Southern Homeopathic Medical College	1	0	1
MASSACHUSETTS.			
New England University	0	1[2]	1
MICHIGAN.			
University of Michigan	1	0	1
Detroit College of Medicine	1	0	1

[1] Class of 1895.
[2] Class of 1876. So in returns.

Name of college.	Passed.	Failed.	Total.
MISSOURI.			
University of Missouri	1	0	1
Kansas City Homeopathic Medical College	1	0	1
College of Physicians and Surgeons, Kansas City	1	0	1
University Medical College	3	0	3
Woman's Medical College	1	0	1
Central Medical College	1	0	1
Ensworth Medical College	2	0	2
American Medical College	2	0	2
Barnes Medical College	1	0	1
Marion-Sims-Beaumont Medical College	1	0	1
Missouri Medical College	1	0	1
College of Physicians and Surgeons, St. Louis	1	0	1
NEBRASKA.			
Cotner University	0	1[1]	1
Creighton Medical College	1	0	1
OHIO.			
American Health College	0	1[2]	1
Eclectic Medical Institute	1	0	1
Laura Memorial, Woman's Medical College	1	0	1
PENNSYLVANIA.			
Jefferson Medical College	0	1[3]	1
Western Reserve Medical College	1	0	1
CANADA.			
McGill University	1	0	1
Non-graduates	1	7	8
	42	11	53

KENTUCKY.

The law of Kentucky entrusts the licensing of physicians to its State Board of Health. The evidence of fitness is the possession of a diploma from a medical school acceptable to the board. The provisions of the Kentucky law give to the board greater powers over those who have been licensed by it, than do most laws, so that while weak in its admittance clause, the Kentucky law fulfils the purpose of a medical practise act, *i. e.*, the protection of the people from incompetent practicers, more effectually than the laws of most states.

Dr. J. N. McCormack, Bowling Green, is the secretary.

[1] Class of 1896.
[2] Class of 1895. Fraudulent.
[3] Class of 1895.

LOUISIANA.

There are two independent Boards of Examiners in Louisiana, one of them representing the homeopathic members of the profession. Candidates for examination must have a diploma from a medical school recognized by the Board before coming up for examination.

The secretaries are Dr. F. A. Larue, 624 Gravier Street, and Dr. Gayle Aiken (Homeopathic), 1102 St. Charles Avenue, both in New Orleans.

EXAMINATIONS, 1902.

Name of college.	Passed.	Failed.	Total.
ARKANSAS.			
Arkansas University	1	0	1
ILLINOIS.			
Rush Medical College	2	0	2
GEORGIA.			
College of Physicians and Surgeons	3	0	3
INDIANA.			
Fort Wayne Medical College	1	0	1
KENTUCKY.			
Kentucky School of Medicine	1	1[1]	2
Kentucky University	1	0	1
University of Louisville	1	0	1
LOUISIANA.			
New Orleans University	2	5[2]	7
Tulane	29	3	32
MICHIGAN.			
Detroit College of Medicine	1	0	1
MISSOURI.			
University Medical College	1	0	1
Washington University	1	0	1
NEW YORK.			
Columbia	2	0	2
PENNSYLVANIA.			
University of Pennsylvania	1	0	1
TENNESSEE.			
Grant University	0	1	1
Memphis Hospital Medical College	20	2	22
University of Nashville	2	0	2
University of the South	7	1	8
University of Tennessee	1	0	1
Vanderbilt University	1	0	1

[1] Class of 1896.
[2] Class of 1901.

Name of college.	Passed.	Failed.	Total.
VIRGINIA.			
University of Virginia	1	0	1
	79	13	92

MAINE.

Since the last report, the requirements have been changed in Maine, so that now the applicant for licensure examination must have been graduated from a medical school acceptable to the board.

Dr. A. K. P. Meserve, Portland, is the secretary.

EXAMINATIONS, 1902.

Name of college.	Passed.	Failed.	Total.
DISTRICT OF COLUMBIA.			
Columbian University	1	0	1
ILLINOIS.			
Hahnemann Medical College	1	1	2
Northwestern University	1	1[1]	2
KENTUCKY.			
Louisville Medical College	0	1	1
MAINE.			
Eclectic Medical College	0	1[2]	1
Medical School of Maine	3	0	3
MARYLAND.			
Baltimore Medical College	2	0	2
College of Physicians and Surgeons	2	0	2
MASSACHUSETTS.			
Boston University	2	0	2
College of Physicians and Surgeons	2	0	2
Harvard	4	0	4
Tufts	2	0	2
MICHIGAN.			
University of Michigan	2	0	2
NEW HAMPSHIRE.			
Dartmouth	3	1	4
NEW YORK.			
Long Island College Hospital	1	0	1
Columbia	6	0	6
Cornell	1[3]	0	1
PENNSYLVANIA.			
Eclectic Medical College	1	0	1
Hahnemann Medical College	1	0	1

[1] Class of 1892, 2nd examination.
[2] Class of 1884.
[3] One reciprocal registration.

Name of college.	Passed.	Failed.	Total.
Jefferson Medical College	1	0	1
University of Pennsylvania	3	0	3
VERMONT.			
University of Vermont	2	0	2
CANADA.			
Laval University	2	0	2
	43	5	48

MARYLAND.

The two Boards in Maryland work independently of each other. The applicant must make application to the Board of his choice submitting evidence of his graduation from a medical school requiring the standard of the Association of American Medical Colleges or of the American Institute of Homeopathy; foreign credentials must be a full license to practise in the country granting them. Exceptions to these conditions are made in favor of physicians who have practised in another state for a period of not less than three years prior to April 11, 1902, students who were in second year of their medical course at the time of the passage of the Act, and accepted licentiates from other states.

Those who are properly qualified must pass an examination. Licentiates of the District of Columbia are entited to licensure without examination, and the Boards may enter into reciprocal relations with other states for the same privilege.

Dr. J. McP. Scott, Hagerstown, is secretary of the Board representing the Medical and Chirurgical Faculty, and Dr. Joseph S. Garrison, Easton, that of the State Homeopathic Society.

EXAMINATIONS, 1902.

Name of college.	Passed.	Failed.	Total.
DISTRICT OF COLUMBIA.			
Howard Medical College	1	0	1
Howard University	1	1	2
GEORGIA.			
Georgia College Eclectic Medicine and Surgery	1	0	1
ILLINOIS.			
Hahnemann Medical College	1	0	1
LOUISIANA.			
Charity Hospital	0	1	1
MARYLAND.			
Baltimore Medical College	6	4	10

Name of college.	Passed.	Failed.	Total.
Baltimore University	0	9	9
College of Physicians and Surgeons, Baltimore	13	0	13
Johns Hopkins	7	1	8
Maryland Medical College	3	7	10
University of Maryland	32	12	44
Woman's Medical College	3	0	3
Southern Homeopathic Medical College	8	0	8
NEW YORK.			
Niagara Medical College	0	2	2
NORTH CAROLINA.			
Leonard Medical School, Shaw University	1	1	2
PENNSYLVANIA.			
Jefferson Medical College	4	0	4
Woman's Medical College	1	0	1
Hahnemann Medical College	3	0	3
VIRGINIA.			
University of Medicine	0	1	1
WASHINGTON.			
Columbia	1	0	1
Non-graduates	0	23	23
	86	62	148

MASSACHUSETTS.

Any one 21 years of age or over, of good moral character, may apply to the Board of Registration for examination. If this be passed satisfactorily to the board, a license to practise is issued.

Dr. E. B. Harvey, State House, Boston, is the secretary of the Board.

EXAMINATIONS, 1902.

Name of college.	Passed.	Failed.	Total.
COLORADO.			
Gross Medical College	1	0	1
University of Colorado	1	0	1
CONNECTICUT.			
Yale	3	0	3
ILLINOIS.			
American Medical Missionary College	1	0	1
Chicago Homeopathic Medical College	0	1[1]	1
Chicago University	0	1[2]	1
Hering Medical College	1	0	1
College of Physicians and Surgeons	1	0	1
Rush Medical College	2	0	2

[1] Class of 1890.
[2] Class of 1900.

Name of college.	Passed.	Failed.	Total.
KENTUCKY.			
Kentucky School of Medicine	1	0	1
University of Louisville	0	1	1
MAINE.			
Bowdoin	4	1	5
MARYLAND.			
Baltimore Medical College	14	3[1]	17
Baltimore University	6	4[2]	10
Johns Hopkins University	6	0	6
College of Physicians and Surgeons	5	1[3]	6
University of Maryland	2	0	2
Woman's Medical College	1	0	1
MASSACHUSETTS.			
Boston University	18	0	18
Harvard	79	1[4]	80
College of Physicians and Surgeons	4	2	6
Tufts	30	1[5]	31
MICHIGAN.			
University of Michigan	3	0	3
Saginaw Valley Medical College	2	0	2
MISSOURI.			
Missouri Medical College	1	0	1
NEW YORK.			
Albany Medical College	1	0	1
Long Island College Hospital	4	1[6]	5
Bellevue Hospital Medical College	3	0	3
Cornell	1	0	1
New York Medical College Hospital for Women	1	0	1
New York University	4	0	4
Columbia	15	1	16
NEW HAMPSHIRE.			
Dartmouth	10	2[7]	12
OHIO.			
Cleveland Homeopathic Medical College	1	0	1
Starling Medical College	1	0	1
PENNSYLVANIA.			
Electic Medical College	1	1[8]	2
Hahnemann Medical College	1	0	

[1] One each of classes 1892, 1901.
[2] One each of classes 1895, 1901.
[3] Class of 1892.
[4] Class of 1870.
[5] Class of 1899.
[6] Class of 1901.
[7] One, class of 1893.
[8] Class of 1867.

Name of college.	Passed.	Failed.	Total.
Jefferson Medical College	4	0	4
Medico-Chirurgical College	2	0	2
University of Pennsylvania	6	0	6
Western Pennsylvania Medical College	1	0	1
TENNESSEE.			
Summertown Medical[1]	1	0	1
University of the South	3	1[2]	4
Vanderbilt University	0	1[3]	1
VERMONT.			
University of Vermont	16	5[4]	21
CANADA.			
Laval University	3	3	6
McGill University	2	1[5]	3
Foreign	14	3[6]	17
Non-graduates	50	124	174
	271	135	306

MICHIGAN.

On September 16, 1903, a new law went into effect in Michigan which requires an examination for every one intending to practise in Michigan.

The secretary of the Board is Dr. B. D. Harrison, Sault Ste. Marie.

TEXT OF THE ACT.

An Act to amend Section 1, 3 and 7 of Act number 237 of the public Acts of 1899, entitled "An Act to provide for the examination, regulation, licensing and registration of physicians and surgeons, and for the punishment of offenders against this Act, and to repeal Acts and parts of Acts in conflict therewith."

The People of the State of Michigan enact:

SECTION 1. Sections 1, 3 and 7 of Act number 237 of the public Acts of 1899, entitled "An Act to provide for the examination, regulation, licensing and registration of physicians and surgeons and for the punishment of offenders against this Act, and to repeal Acts and parts of Acts in conflict therewith," are hereby amended so as to read as follows:

SEC. 2. The Governor shall appoint, by and with the advice and consent of the Senate, ten resident electors of the State, who shall constitute a Board of Registration in Medicine. Not more than five of the persons

[1] So in return.
[2] Class of 1901.
[3] Class of 1894.
[4] One each of classes 1897, 1900; two, class of 1900.
[5] Class of 1898.
[6] One each of classes 1883, 1899, 1900.

so appointed shall be from the school of medicine known as regular; not more than two of the persons so appointed shall be from the school of medicine known as homeopathic; not more than two of the persons so appointed shall be from the school of medicine known as eclectic; and not more than one of the persons so appointed shall be from the school of medicine known as physio-medical, and the Governor may select such appointees from the latest lists filed in the office of the Secretary of State at Lansing by each of the four legally incorporated State Medical Societies of the schools of medicine as herein mentioned aforesaid, such lists to be certified to under oath of the president and secretary of each society respectively, and such lists to contain at least treble the number of names as each society has representatives on the Board. But in the event that one or more of the societies above named, through their presidents or secretaries, shall from any cause neglect, omit or refuse to file as aforesaid, such lists or list, then and in that case the Governor shall appoint or fill the vacancies in said Board without reference to such list or lists which the aforesaid society or societies have for any cause neglected, omitted or refused to file with the Secretary of State, as herein mentioned aforesaid; but the number of representatives from each of the schools of medicine shall be the same as provided for in this Act. All persons so appointed shall be legally registered physicians of the State, shall be graduates in good standing of reputable medical colleges, and shall have been actively engaged in the practice of medicine in this State for at least six years immediately preceding the time of such appointment. The ten persons so appointed shall be appointed in two classes, each class to consist of five persons. The first class shall consist of those physicians appointed by the Governor under Act number 237, laws of 1899, October 1, A.D., 1901, who shall serve during the time for which they were so appointed, namely: To October 1, 1905; and the second class shall be appointed to hold office for four years beginning with the first day of October of the present year, and both classes shall hold office until their successors are appointed; and thereafter the Governor shall appoint, before the first day of October of each biennial period, five persons qualified as aforesaid, in each class, to hold office for four years from the first day of October next ensuing. No member of said Board shall belong to the faculty of any medical college or university. The Governor shall also fill vacancies occasioned by death or otherwise, and may remove any member for the continued neglect of duties required by this Act. Vacancies in said Board shall be filled in accordance with the provisions of this Act for the establishment of the original Board, and a person appointed to fill a vacancy shall hold office during the unexpired term of the member whose place he fills. The business of said Board shall be transacted by and receive the concurrent vote of at least seven members.

SEC. 3. On and after the date of the passage of this Act, all men and women who wish to begin the practice of medicine and surgery in any of its branches in this State, shall make application to the State Board of Registration in Medicine, to be registered and for a certificate of registration. This registration and certificate shall be granted to such applicants as shall give satisfactory proofs of being twenty-one years of age and of good moral character, but only upon compliance with at least one of the following conditions contained in subdivisions one, two and three of this Section:

First. That applicant shall be registered and given a certificate of registration if he shall satisfactorily pass an examination before the Board upon the following subjects: Anatomy, physiology, chemistry, pathology, materia medica and therapeutics, toxicology, histology, practice of medicine, surgery, obstetrics, gynecology, mental and nervous diseases, diseases of the eye, ear, nose and throat, bacteriology, hygiene, public health laws of Michigan and medical jurisprudence, said examination to be conducted as follows:

(*a*) The applicant shall pay a fee of $25 prior to examination: *Provided*, That the examination fee for graduates of any medical school in the State of Michigan, approved by said Board, shall be the sum of $10.

(*b*) The examination shall be in writing, oral, or both.

(*c*) The questions on all subjects, except in materia medica and therapeutics and practice of medicine, shall be such as may be answered alike by all schools of medicine.

(*d*) The applicant shall, if possible, be examined in materia medica and therapeutics and practice of medicine by those members of the Board or by a qualified examiner appointed by the Board, belonging to the same school as the applicant, and no applicant shall be rejected because of his adherence to any particular system of practice.

(*e*) An average percentage of at least 75 per cent. of correct answers shall be required from every candidate. No additional fee shall be charged by this Board for the registration of those who successfully pass such examination: *Provided, however,* That such applicant for examination shall have a diploma from a legally incorporated, regularly established and reputable college of medicine within the states, territories, districts and provinces of the United States, or within any foreign nation (provided such foreign nation accord a like privilege to graduates of approved medical colleges of this State) having at least a four years' course of seven months in each calendar year, as shall be approved and designated by the Board of Registration in Medicine: Also *Provided,* That such applicant shall have, previous to the beginning of his course in medicine, a diploma from a recognized and reputable high school, academy, college or university, having a classical course, or shall pass an examination equivalent at least to the minimum standard of preliminary education adopted and published by the Board before examiners appointed by and in accordance with the regulations of aforesaid Board, and at such time and place as the Board may designate: *Provided,* A student entering a college in Michigan, having a preliminary examination of a standard approved by the Board of Registration in Medicine shall not be required to take this examination : *Provided*, That this requirement of preliminary education shall not apply to those students who, on the date of the passage of this Act, were regularly registered as students of legally organized and reputable medical colleges approved of by said Board : And *provided*, also, That the requirement of medical education shall not apply to those graduates of legally organized and reputable medical colleges approved of by said Board who had graduated from such colleges, previous to the date of the passage of this Act ; and students complying with the other provisions of this section who on January 1st of the present year were regularly registered as students of legally organized and reputable medical colleges of this State, approved of by said Board, may obtain a certificate of registration as graduates of such colleges and without examination by the Board upon payment of a fee of $10. The Board of Registration in Medicine shall, from time to time, adopt and publish a minimum standard of medical education, and no medical college shall be approved and designated by said Board under this subdivision one, of Section 3, unless, in the judgment of the Board, it conforms with such standard.

Second. The applicant shall be registered and given a certificate of registration if he shall present a certified copy or certificate of registration or license which has been issued to said applicant in any foreign nation where the requirements of registration shall be deemed by said Board of Registration in Medicine to be equivalent to those of this Act : *Provided*, Such country shall accord a like privilege to holders of certificates from this Board. The fee for registration from applicants of this class shall be $25.

Third. The applicant shall be registered and given a certificate of registration if he shall present a certified copy of certificate of registration or license, which has been issued to said applicant within the states, territories, districts or provinces of the United States where the requirements for registration shall be deemed by the Board of Registration in Medicine to be equivalent to those of this Act, and shall otherwise conform to the rules and regulations agreed upon between the State Board of which he is a licentiate and said Board relative to the recognition and exchange of certificates between states : *Provided*, Such states shall accord a like privilege to holders of certificates from this Board. The fee for registration from applicants of this class shall be $25.

Fourth. If any person shall unlawfully obtain and procure himself to be registered under this section, either by false and untrue statements contained in his application to the Board of Registration in Medicine, or by presenting to said Board a false or untrue diploma or license, or one fraudulently obtained, he shall be deemed guilty of a felony, and on conviction thereof shall be punished by a fine of not less than $300 nor more than $300, or imprisonment at hard labor for not less than one year, nor more than three years, or both, at the discretion of the court, and shall forfeit all rights and privileges obtained or conferred upon him by virtue of such registration as a physician or surgeon.

Fifth. Any person who shall swear falsely in any affidavit or oral testimony made or given by virtue of the provisions of this Act, or the regulations of the Board of Registration in Medicine, shall be deemed guilty of perjury, and upon conviction thereof shall be subject to all the pains and penalties of perjury.

Sixth. The Board of Registration in Medicine shall refuse to issue a certificate of registration provided for in this section to any person guilty of grossly unprofessional and dishonest conduct of a character likely to deceive the public, and said Board shall, after due notice and hearing, revoke a certificate issued subsequent to the date of the passage of this Act, or subsequent to the date of the passage of Act number 237 of the public Acts of 1899, for like cause or for offenses involving moral turpitude, habitual intemperance, the drug habit, or for fraud or perjury in connection with obtaining a certificate of registration, or for a certificate obtained or issued through error, when such offenses shall have been legally established in a court of competent jurisdiction: And *Provided*, further, After the passage of this Act, the Board may at its discretion revoke the certificate of registration, after due notice and hearing of any registered practitioner who inserts any advertisement in any newspaper, pamphlet, circular, or other written or printed paper, relative to venereal diseases or other matter of any obscene or offensive nature derogatory to good morals.

SEC. 4. Any person who shall practise medicine or surgery in this State without first complying with the provisions of this Act, or any person who shall violate its provisions (except as heretofore provided in Section 3 of this Act), shall be deemed guilty of a misdemeanor, and upon conviction thereof shall be punished by a fine of not more than $100, or by imprisonment in the county jail for a period of not more than ninety days, or by both such fine and imprisonment, for each offense. It shall be the duty of the prosecuting attorneys of the counties of this State to prosecute violations of the provisions of this Act.

MINNESOTA.

The applicant for examination for licensure must be a graduate of a medical school acceptable to the Board of Examiners, of which Dr. C. J. Ringnell, 802 Andrus Building, Minneapolis, is the secretary.

EXAMINATIONS, 1902.

Name of college.	Passed.	Failed.	Total.
ILLINOIS.			
Bennett Medical College	2	0	2
Chicago Homeopathic Medical College	3	0	3

Name of college.	Passed.	Failed.	Total.
College of Physicians and Surgeons	10	5	15
Hahnemann Medical College	2	2[1]	4
Northwestern University	5	0	5
Rush Medical College	23	0	23

INDIANA.
Central College of Physicians and Surgeons	1	0	1

IOWA.
College of Physicians and Surgeons, Keokuk	2	1[2]	3
Iowa State University	3	0	3
Sioux City College of Medicine	1	1[3]	2

KANSAS.
Kansas Medical College	1	0	1
University of Kansas	1	1[4]	2

KENTUCKY.
Hospital Medical College	1	0	1
Kentucky School of Medicine	2	1	3

MARYLAND.
Johns Hopkins	1	0	1
University of Baltimore	1	0	1
University of Maryland	1	1	2

MASSACHUSETTS.
Harvard	1	0	1

MICHIGAN.
University of Michigan	7	2[5]	9
Saginaw Valley Medical College	1	0	1

MINNESOTA.
Hamline University	24	4[6]	28
University of Minnesota	65	0	65

MISSOURI.
Barnes Medical College	0	1[7]	1
Homeopathic Medical College	1	0	1
Marion-Sims Medical College	0	1	1

NEW YORK.
New York Homeopathic Medical College	1	0	1

OHIO.
Eclectic Medical Institute	1	0	1

PENNSYLVANIA.
Hahnemann Medical College	2	1	3
Jefferson Medical College	1	0	1

[1] Class of 1897.
[2] Class of 1898.
[3] Class of 1894.
[4] Class of 1899.
[5] Two, class of 1877.
[6] Two, class of 1896.
[7] Class of 1901.

Name of college.	Passed.	Failed.	Total.
Medico-Chirurgical College	1	0	1
University of Pennsylvania	1	0	1
TENNESSEE.			
University of the South	1	0	1
WISCONSIN.			
College of Physicians and Surgeons	2	0	2
CANADA.			
Laval University	1	0	1
McGill University	1	0	1
Trinity University	3	0	3
FOREIGN.			
Kiel University	1	0	1
University of Christiana	1	0	1
Undergraduates	0	5	5
	176	26	202

MISSISSIPPI.

Mississippi requires the intending practitioner to come up for an examination before the State Board of Health. This examination is the only test.

Secretary, Dr. J. F. Hunter, Jackson.

EXAMINATIONS, 1902.

The following report of the examination was received from the secretary:

Our Board met in the City of Jackson, on May 13th and 14th, and examined applicants for license to practise medicine. We had 153 applicants and 77 were passed.

MISSOURI.

Missouri, like Mississippi, has no educational requirement beyond the passing of an examination before its State Board of Health.

Dr. W. F. Morrow, secretary, Kansas City.

EXAMINATIONS, 1902.[1]

Name of college.	Passed.	Failed.	Total.
CALIFORNIA.			
California Medical College	1	0	1
GEORGIA.			
University of Georgia	1	0	1
ILLINOIS.			
Hahnemann Medical College	3	0	3
Rush Medical College	2	0	2
Woman's Medical College	1	0	1

[1] These results have not been officially verified by the Board, and are taken from the *Journal of the American Medical Association.*

Name of college.	Passed.	Failed.	Total.
IOWA.			
Keokuk Medical College	1	2	3
KANSAS.			
University of Kansas	1	0	1
MICHIGAN.			
University of Michigan	1	0	1
MISSOURI.			
Missouri Medical College	1	0	1
Kansas City Homeopathic Medical College	1	1	2
Kansas City Medical College	9	0	9
Medico-Chirurgical College, Kansas City	4	0	4
University Medical College	4	2	6
Central Medical College	2	1	3
Ensworth Medical College	2	1	3
American Medical College	1	0	1
Barnes Medical College	16	7	23
Marion-Sims-Beaumont Medical College	22	1	23
Homeopathic Medical College	0	1	1
St. Louis College of Physicians and Surgeons	10	10	20
St. Louis Medical College	1	0	1
Washington University	6	1	7
NEBRASKA.			
Lincoln Medical College	1	0	1
NEW YORK.			
Columbia	1	1	2
PENNSYLVANIA.			
University of Pennsylvania	1	0	1
TENNESSEE.			
Meharry Medical College	1	0	1
FOREIGN.			
Royal College of Physicians and Surgeons	1	0	1
	95	28	123

MONTANA.

Montana exacts the completion of a medical course satisfactory to its board and passing an examination before the license to practise is given.

Secretary of the Board, Dr. W. C. Riddell, Helena.

EXAMINATIONS, 1902.

Name of college.	Passed.	Failed.	Total.
ILLINOIS.			
Chicago Homeopathic Medical College	1	0	1
Chicago Medical College	1	0	1

Name of college.	Passed.	Failed.	Total.
Hahnemann Medical College	0	1[1]	1
Northwestern University	1	0	1
College of Physicians and Surgeons	1	0	1
Rush Medical College	3	0	3

IOWA.
College of Physicians and Surgeons, Keokuk	0	1[2]	1

KENTUCKY.
Hospital College of Medicine	1	0	1
Kentucky School of Medicine	1	0	1

MARYLAND.
Baltimore University	1	0	1

MICHIGAN.
University of Michigan	1	0	1

MINNESOTA.
University of Minnesota	3	0	3

MISSOURI.
Beaumont Hospital Medical College	1	0	1
College of Physicians and Surgeons, St. Louis	0	1[3]	1
Homeopathic Medical College	1	0	1
Marion-Sims Medical College	2	0	2
College of Physicians and Surgeons, Kansas City	1	0	1
Missouri Medical College	0	1[4]	1

NEBRASKA.
Creighton Medical College	1	0	1

NEW YORK.
New York University	0	1[5]	1

OHIO.
Ohio Medical University	0	1[6]	1

PENNSYLVANIA.
Medico-Chirurgical College	0	1[7]	1

SOUTH CAROLINA.
Medical College of South Carolina	1	0	1

CANADA.
Dalhousie University	1	0	1
McGill University	2	0	2
Toronto University	1	0	1
Victoria University	1	0	1
Western University	1	0	1

[1] Class of 1900.
[2] Class of 1891, failed twice.
[3] Class of 1895.
[4] Class of 1889.
[5] Class of 1884.
[6] Class of 1901.
[7] Class of 1900.

Name of college.	Passed.	Failed.	Total.
FOREIGN.			
Dublin University	0	1[1]	1
University of Durham	1	0	1
Strassburg University	1	0	1
	29	8	37

NEBRASKA.

Hereafter Nebraska will exact an examination in addition to the diploma heretofore required.

Dr. George H. Brash, Beatrice, is secretary of the Board.

TEXT OF ACT.

SECTION 1. There shall be established in the State of Nebraska a Board to be styled the State Board of Health. Said Board shall consist of the Governor, Attorney General and Superintendent of Public Instruction, and the Governor shall be *ex-officio* chairman of said Board.

SEC. 2. Said Board shall meet upon the call of the Governor and within thirty days after the approval of this Act and shall meet thereafter as often and at such times as the Governor may from time to time designate.

SEC. 3. Said Board shall within sixty days after the approval of this Act appoint four secretaries who shall be graduated physicians of at least seven years consecutive practice who shall be at the time of their appointment actually engaged in practice in the State of Nebraska, one of whom shall be appointed for the term of one year, one for the term of two years, one for the term of three years, and one for the term of four years, and thereafter it shall be the duty of said Board to appoint or reappoint one secretary every year as the term of those theretofore appointed shall expire, but each secretary shall continue in office until his successor shall have been appointed. Said appointments shall be made so, that of said secretaries two shall be physicians of the called regular school, of one of the so-called eclectic school, and one of the so-called homeopathic school.

SEC. 4. Said secretaries shall have power, and it shall be their duty to assist and advise said Board in the performance of its duties as prescribed by this Act, to summon witnesses and take testimony in the same manner as witnesses are summoned and depositions taken under the Code of Civil Procedure, and to report said testimony to the Board together with their findings of fact and recommendations on all matters coming before said Board requiring evidence for their determination except as hereinafter provided.

SEC. 5. It shall be the duty of said Board to see that all the provisions of this Act are strictly enforced, to grant certificates as herein provided, and to cause to be prosecuted all violations of this Act. Said Board shall have and use a common seal and may make and adopt all necessary rules, regulations and by-laws not inconsistent with the constitution and law of this state or of

[1] Class of 1881.

the United States to enable it to perform its duties and transact its business under the provisions of this Act.

SEC. 6. A majority of said Board shall constitute a quorum for the transaction of business.

SEC. 7. It shall be unlawful for any person to practise medicine, surgery or obstetrics, or any of the branches thereof, in this State, without first having applied for and obtained from the State Board of Health a license so to do. Application therefor shall be in writing and shall be accompanied by the examination fees hereinafter specified and with proof that the applicant is of good moral character. Applications from candidates who desire to practise medicine and surgery in any or all their branches shall be accompanied by proof that the applicant is a graduate of a medical school or college in good standing, as defined in Section (8) of this article. When the application aforesaid has been inspected by the Board and found to comply with the foregoing provisions, the Board shall notify the applicant to appear before it for examination at the time and place mentioned in such notice. Examinations may be made wholly or in part in writing by the Board, and shall be of a character sufficiently strict to test the qualifications of the candidate as a practitioner. The examination of those who desire to practise medicine and surgery in any or all their branches shall embrace those subjects and tropics, a knowledge of which is commonly and generally required of candidates for the degree of doctor of medicine, by reputable medical colleges in the United States. All examinations provided for in this Act shall be conducted under rules and regulations prescribed by the Board, which shall provide for a fair and wholly impartial method of examination. It is also provided that examinations on practice of medicine and therapeutics shall be conducted by the member or members, of the Board of Secretaries, who are of the same school of medicine as that of the applicant. And it is further provided that the said State Board of Health may, at their discretion, admit, without examination, legally qualified medical practitioners, who hold certificates to practise medicine in any State with equal requirements to those of the State of Nebraska.

SEC. 8. The term medical school or college in good standing, shall be defined as follows; to wit, a medical school or college requiring a preliminary examination for admission to its course of study in all the common branches, and in Latin and the higher mathematics, which requirements shall be regularly published in all the advertisements and in each prospectus or catalogue issued by said school, which medical school or college shall also require as a requisite for granting the degree of M.D., attendance upon at least four courses of lectures of six months each, no two of said courses to be held within one year, and having a full faculty of capable professors in all the different branches of medical education; to wit, anatomy, physiology, chemistry, toxicology, pathology, hygiene, materia medica, therapeutics, obstetrics, bacteriology, medical jurisprudence, gynecology, principles and practise of medicine and surgery, and specially requiring clinical instruction in the two last-named of not less than four hours per week in each during the last two courses of lectures; *Provided*, That this four years clause shall not apply to degrees granted or to be granted, prior to August, 1898.

SEC. 9. It shall be the duty of all persons intending to practise medicine, surgery or obstetrics in the State of Nebraska before beginning the practice thereof, in any branch thereof, to present his diploma to said Board, together with his affidavit that he is the lawful possessor of the same, that he has attended the full course of study required for the degree of M.D., and that he is the person therein named. Such affidavit may be taken before any person authorized to administer oaths, and the same shall be attested under the hand and official seal of such official if he has a seal, and any person swearing falsely in such affidavit shall be guilty of perjury and subject to the penalty therefor.

SEC. 10. If upon investigation of the proofs submitted to the Board, and after the examination, as hereinbefore provided, the applicant shall be found entitled to practise, there shall be issued to said applicant the certificate of said Board under its seal and signed by its secretaries stating such fact, and it shall be the duty of the applicant before practising to file such certificate or a copy thereof in the office of the county clerk of the county in which he or she resides or in which he or she intends to practise; such certificate or copy shall be filed by the county clerk and by him recorded in a book kept for that purpose, properly indexed, to be called the "Physicians' Register" and for such services the county clerk shall receive from the applicant the same fees as are allowed to the register of deeds for the recording of conveyances.

SEC. 11. It shall be the duties of said secretaries to keep a full record of all the Acts and proceedings of said Board and of all certificates granted thereby together with the proof upon which certificates are granted, but when said proof in any case shall have been on file in the office of said Board for ten days said certificate may be issued by said secretaries without a vote of the Board, if no protest has been filed and if in their opinion said proof complies with the provisions of this Act.

SEC. 12. Any person who shall have obtained a certificate provided by this Act and shall remove to another county, shall, before entering upon the practice of his profession in such other county, cause said certificate to be filed and recorded in the office of the county clerk of the county to which he has removed.

SEC. 13. The Board may refuse certificates to persons guilty of unprofessional or dishonorable conduct, and it may revoke certificates for like cause; provided always that they have given the person an opportunity to be heard in his or her defense.

SEC. 14. No person shall recover in any court of this State any sum of money whatever for any medical, surgical or obstetrical services unless he shall have complied with the provisions of this Act and is one of the persons authorized by this Act to be registered as a physician.

SEC. 15. Any person not possessing the qualifications for the practice of medicine, surgery or obstetrics required by the provisions of this Act, or any person who has not complied with the provisions of this Act who shall engage in the practice of medicine, surgery or obstetrics, or any of the branches thereof in this State, shall be deemed guilty of a misdemeanor and on conviction thereof shall be fined in any sum not less than fifty dollars ($50) nor more than three hundred dollars, ($300) and costs of prosecution for each offense and shall stand committed until such fine and costs are paid.

SEC. 16. Any person shall be regarded as practising medicine within the meaning of this Act who shall operate or profess to heal or prescribe for or otherwise treat any physical or mental ailment of another. But nothing in this Act shall be constructed to prohibit gratuitous services in case of emergency, and this Act shall not apply to commissioned surgeons in the United States Army and Navy, not to nurses in their legitimate occupations, nor to the administration of ordinary household remedies.

SEC. 17. Any itinerant vender of any drug, nostrum, ointment or appliance of any kind intended for the treatment of any disease or injury, or who shall, by writing, printing or any other method, publicly profess to cure or treat diseases or injury or deformity by any drug, nostrum manipulation or other expedient shall be deemed guilty of a misdemeanor, and upon conviction thereof shall be fined in any sum not less than fifty dollars ($50), nor more than one hundred dollars ($100) or be imprisoned in the county jail for a period of not less than thirty (30) days, nor more than three (3) months or both in the discretion of the court, for each offense.

SEC. 18. Every holder of a diploma from a recognized medical college within the State of Nebraska, making application for an examination and a certificate under the provisions of this Act, shall pay to the Board of Secretaries, prior to his examination, the sum of ten dollars ($10.00). All other persons making such applications shall pay to said Board the sum of twenty-five dollars ($25.00). All such fees shall be equally divided among the four secretaries of the Board as full compensation for their services and expenses. For the taking of any testimony, each of the secretaries shall be entitled to charge and receive such fees as are provided for notaries public for similar services. No part of such fees shall be paid out of the state treasury.

NEVADA.

To enter upon the practice of medicine in Nevada, the applicant must have been graduated from a medical school in the United States in good standing with the Board. Graduates of foreign medical schools must, in addition, submit to an examination.

Dr. S. L. Lee, Carson City, is secretary of the Board.

NEW HAMPSHIRE.

New Hampshire has three Boards of Medical Examiners working in harmony under the supervision of the Superintendent of Public Instruction, who is *ex-officio* regent of the Boards. Only those who have complied with certain requirements can come up for examination. The applicant must be over twenty-one years of age, of good moral character, have a preliminary education equivalent to a registered academy or high-school course, have studied medicine for four full years, at least six months of each year being spent in a medical school, and have received a diploma therefrom. By a change of the law it is now required of those physicians to practise in the summer hotels of New Hampshire to take the same examination as those physicians who reside in the state all the year.

Hon. Channing Folsom, Department of Public Instruction, Concord, is the regent.

EXAMINATIONS, 1902.[1]

Name of college.	Passed.	Failed.	Total.
CONNECTICUT.			
Yale	1	0	1
MAINE.			
Bowdoin	1	0	1
MARYLAND.			
Baltimore Medical College	3	1	4
MASSACHUSETTS.			
Harvard	6	0	6
Boston University	1	0	1
Tufts	1	0	1
NEW HAMPSHIRE.			
Dartmouth	6	0	6
NEW YORK.			
Long Island College Hospital	1	0	1
New York Homeopathic Medical College	0	1[2]	1
PENNSYLVANIA.			
Medico-Chirurgical College	2	0	2
Jefferson Medical College	1	0	1
VERMONT.			
University of Vermont	4	1[3]	5
CANADA.			
Lavall University	0	1	1
McGill University	3	0	3
	30	4	34

[1] Includes examination of March, 1903.
[2] Class of 1899.
[3] Class of 1901.

NEW JERSEY.

The examinations for licensure in New Jersey are under the supervision of a single Board of Examiners. There have been some changes in the law which have revised the standard of qualifications. The new qualifications are:

"The academic requirements will be a certificate or diploma issued after four years of study, either in a normal, manual training or high school of the first grade, in this State (New Jersey) or in a legally constituted academy, seminary or institute of equal grade, or a student's certificate of examination for admission to the Freshman class of a reputable literary college or an academic education considered and accepted by the State Superintendent of Public Instruction as fully equivalent.

"The medical requirements will be four full school years of medical study, of at least nine months each, including four satisfactory courses of lectures of at least seven months each, in four different calendar years, in a legally incorporated medical college or colleges, prior to receiving the degree of doctor of medicine."—*From a circular issued by the Board.*

Dr. E. L. B. Godfrey, Camden, is secretary of the Board.

EXAMINATIONS, 1902.

Name of college.	Passed.	Failed.	Total.
CONNECTICUT.			
Yale	2	0	2
DISTRICT OF COLUMBIA.			
Columbian University	1	0	1
Howard University	1	0	1
MARYLAND.			
Baltimore Medical College	8	1	9
Baltimore University	3	3[1]	6
College of Physicians and Surgeons, Baltimore	7	0	7
Johns Hopkins	1	0	1
Maryland Medical College	1	0	1
MASSACHUSETTS.			
Boston University	1	0	1
Harvard	1	0	1
NEW HAMPSHIRE.			
Dartmouth	1	0	1
NEW YORK.			
Bellevue Hospital Medical College	1	0	1
Columbia	4	1[2]	5
Cornell	1	0	1
University and Bellevue Hospital Medical College	3	0	3

[1] Two of class 1898, one of class 1900, 5th examination.
[2] Class of 1881.

Name of college.	Passed.	Failed.	Total.
NORTH CAROLINA.			
Leonard Medical School	1	1	2
PENNSYLVANIA.			
Hahnemann Medical College	1	2[1]	3
Jefferson Medical College	9	2	11
Medico-Chirurgical College	4	0	4
University of Pennsylvania	2	0	2
Woman's Medical College	2	0	2
TENNESSEE.			
University of the South	2	1[2]	3
VERMONT.			
University of Vermont	1	0	1
VIRGINIA.			
Medical College of Virginia	1	0	1
FOREIGN.			
University of Montpelier, France	1	0	1
University of Naples, Italy	2	1[3]	3
University of Turin, Italy	1	0	1
	63	12	75

NEW MEXICO.

The law of New Mexico permits the licensing of graduates from a medical college of good standing as defined by the Act.

Members of the Board—B. D. Black, M.D., Las Vegas, *Secretary;* George C. Bryan M.D., Alamogordo; M. F. Desmarais, M.D., Santa Rosa, *Vice-President;* G. W. Harrison, M.D., Albuquerque, *President;* William D. Radcliffe, M.D., Belen, *Treasurer;* J. J. Shuler, M.D., Raton; J. H. Sloan, M.D., Santa Fe.

TEXT OF THE ACT.

Be it Enacted by the Legislative Assembly of the Territory of New Mexico:

SECTION 1. That a Board of Health is hereby established which shall be known as the New Mexico Board of Health, and be composed of seven reputable physicians of known ability who are graduates of medical schools of good standing, who are registered practitioners in, and who are *bona fide* residents of New Mexico. The Governor of New Mexico shall appoint the members of said Board, and shall fill any vacancies occurring therein, and shall remove from said Board any member who fails to fully perform his duties on said Board. The members of said Board shall be appointed for a term of two years, and qualify as the Board of Regents of the University of New Mexico is required to do.

SEC. 2. The Board shall organize and select one of its members as president, one as vice-president, one as secretary, and one as treasurer, within

[1] Class of 1899, one, 4th examination, one, 3rd examination.
[2] Class of 1901, 3rd examination.
[3] Class of 1888.

four months after the appointment of its members. Said Board shall hold meetings in the City of Santa Fe, in the Capitol building, in the rooms provided for it by the Capitol Custodian Committee, on the first Mondays of each and every June and December. Said Board may hold a special meeting in cases of emergency, said special meeting to be called by the president of the Board, and the object of the meeting fully stated. A majority of the members of this Board shall constitute a quorum for the transaction of all business.

SEC. 3. The said Board shall, upon the production of evidence satisfactory to it, license any reputable person who is a graduate of a medical college in good standing, as defined by this Act, to practise medicine, surgery and obstetrics in New Mexico. A medical college in good standing for the purposes of this Act is declared to be one of at least ten years continuous existence, one which now requires a high school certificate or its equivalent, for admission to it, and one which now or hereafter requires an attendance on, and gives four full courses in four separate years, and one which has ample clinical facilities such as are furnished in large cities. And said Board shall at its December meeting in each year prepare and cause to be printed and distributed for the information of those interested, a copy of this law and a list of the medical colleges in the United States of America recognized by it to be in good standing under this section. And such Board shall recognize any honorary or emeritus degree conferred upon any eminent foreigner by any such college as fully and to the same extent as if the applicant were a regular graduate thereof. The president and secretary of said Board shall be and are hereby empowered to administer oaths to applicants and all witnesses and others appearing before said Board in any application or proceeding provided for herein, and any person making a false oath or affidavit before said Board, shall be guilty of perjury, and be subject to punishment for that crime. The secretary of said Board shall issue a temporary license to any person complying with the provisions of this Act, who has paid the fee to the secretary.

SEC. 4. Every person holding a certificate of said Board of Health, shall have the same recorded in a book provided for that purpose in the office of the probate clerk of the county wherein the practitioner resides, within thirty days after said certificate is issued, and the date of the recording shall be endorsed on said certificate. Said certificate, or a copy of the registration, must be again recorded in any county to which the practitioner may remove permanently. And the fact that no such certificate shall be found recorded in the county where any person is practising or offering to practise medicine shall be accepted by the court as *prima facie* evidence that no such certificate has been issued, and shall throw the burden of proving that he has a certificate upon the defendant in any suit or prosecution begun against him for the violation of the provisions of this Act.

SEC. 5. It is hereby made the duty of this Board to refuse to license any person guilty of immoral, dishonorable or unprofessional conduct, and said

Board shall also revoke and annul any certificate which has been issued by said Board, or any previous Board, upon satisfactory proof being made to the said Board, that the holder of said certificate or diploma has been guilty of immoral, dishonorable or unprofessional conduct. Five days' notice shall be given in writing to the person accused of improper conduct, with a copy of the charge against him, requiring him on a day named to appear before the Board, and show cause why his license should not be revoked or canceled. When any such license has been revoked or canceled by said Board, the said Board shall send notice in writing under the hand of the secretary, which notice shall be filed for record and recorded in the book in which the physicians' licenses are recorded, in the office of the Probate Clerk of the county in which the person, whose license has been revoked, resides. Any person whose certificate has been revoked or canceled by said Board, under the provisions of this Act, who shall hereafter practise or attempt to offer to practise medicine in New Mexico shall thereby become guilty of a misdemeanor and shall be punished as provided in Section 9 of this Act.

SEC. 6. For the purposes of this Act the words "practice of medicine" shall mean to open an office for such purpose or to announce to the public or to any individual in any way, a desire or willingness or readiness to treat the sick or afflicted, or to investigate or diagnose, or offer to investigate or diagnose, any physical or medical ailment or disease of any person, or to suggest, recommend, prescribe or direct, for the use of any person, any drug, medicine, appliance or other agency, whether material or not material, for the cure, relief or palliation of any ailment or disease of the mind or body, or for the cure, or relief, of any wound, fracture or bodily injury or deformity, after having received, or with the intent of receiving therefor, either directly or indirectly, any bonus, gift or compensation.

Provided, That nothing in this Act shall be construed to prohibit gratuitous services in cases of emergency, or the domestic administration of family remedies, or women from practising midwifery, and this Act shall not apply to surgeons of the United States in the discharge of their official duties.

SEC. 7. Each applicant for a license to practise medicine in New Mexico shall pay the secretary of this Board a fee of twenty-five ($25.00).

SEC. 8. Any vender, except licensed druggists, of any drug, nostrum, ointment or appliance of any kind intended for the treatment of disease or injury or who shall, by writing or printing, or any other method, profess to cure or treat disease or deformity by any drug, nostrum, manipulation or other expedient, shall pay a license of one hundred dollars ($100.00) per month into the treasury of said Board, upon which said payment, such vender shall be licensed by said Board to sell drugs, nostrum, medicines and ointments. And any person so vending or attempting to sell either from his home or office or from vehicles or by traveling through the country, on foot or horseback, any such drugs, medicines or ointments, without paying such license, shall be deemed guilty of a misdemeanor, and upon conviction thereof, shall be punished by a fine not to exceed one hundred dollars

($100.00) or imprisonment in the county jail not to exceed ninety days, or by both such fine and imprisonment, in the discretion of the court.

SEC. 9. Upon payment to the Board of the fees provided for in Section 7 of this Act, said Board may grant licenses to licentiates of other states and territories, which have like requirements as this Act provided for, and when said states and territories also honor our licenses or certificates, to the same extent as they now recognize our licenses and no further. Any person who shall practise medicine, or attempt to practise medicine, without first complying with the provisions of this law, and without being the holder of a certificate entitling him to practise medicine in New Mexico, shall be deemed guilty of a misdemeanor, and upon conviction thereof, shall be punished by a fine not to exceed one hundred dollars ($100.00), or imprisonment in the county jail not to exceed ninety days, or by both such fine and imprisonment, in the discretion of the court.

SEC. 10. One-half of every fine collected under the provisions of this Act, shall go and be paid by the court in which conviction is had, to the sheriff, deputy sheriff, constable or other person who makes complaint, and arrests and causes to be prosecuted, the persons so convicted. The other half of all such fines and all fees herein provided to be paid, shall go and be the property of the said Board of Health and shall by the treasurer of said Board be kept in some bank designated by said Board. He shall give bond to the Board in the sum of one thousand dollars ($1,000.00) conditioned for the faithful performance of his duty as treasurer, and that he shall pay over any and all sums of money received by him as such upon the proper order therefor. Such bond shall be given by some Fidelity or Surety company authorized to do business in this territory, and the premiums paid therefor, shall be paid by the Board as one of its necessary expenses. All the expenses of the members of said Board necessarily and properly incurred in attending the sessions of said Board, and for necessary supplies, shall be paid out of the said fund upon the order of the president and the secretary of said Board. The treasurer of the Board shall keep a correct and itemized account of all moneys received and disbursed, and shall make a report to the Board at each meeting. The secretary of said Board is required to report the doings and proceedings of said Board, together with the amount of all moneys by it received and disbursed, and on what account, with items, on the first day of December in each year, to the Governor of New Mexico.

SEC. 11. Said Board of Health is hereby authorized and empowered to make all necessary rules and regulations for carying out the provisions of this Act.

SEC. 12. Section 3 of Chapter 18 of the Session Laws of 1901, and all Acts and parts of Acts in conflict with this Act are hereby repealed, and this Act shall take effect and be in force thirty days after its passage.

Approved March 12, 1903.

NEW YORK.

New York requires a preliminary education fully equivalent to the high-school course established by the regents of the University of New York, four courses in a recognized medical school, covering four years of study (but will accept graduation from approved literary or scientific colleges to count for the first year medical study) before one can apply for a licensure examination. There are three Boards working in harmony under the supervision of the board of regents.

James Russell Parsons, Jr., State House, Albany, is the secretary of the regents.

EXAMINATIONS FOR THE YEAR ENDING JULY 31, 1902.

Name of college.	Passed.	Failed.	Total.
CALIFORNIA.			
Cooper Medical College	1	0	1
University of California	1	0	1
CONNECTICUT.			
Yale	7	0	7
DISTRICT OF COLUMBIA.			
Columbian University	1	0	1
Georgetown University	1	0	1
Howard University	2	0	2
GEORGIA.			
Atlanta College of Physicians and Surgeons	2	0	2
ILLINOIS.			
American Medical Missionary College	1	0	1
College of Physicians and Surgeons	1	0	1
Hahnemann Medical College	3	0	3
Illinois Medical College	0	1[1]	1
Rush Medical College	2	1[2]	3
Northwestern University Woman's Medical School	2	0	2
KENTUCKY.			
Kentucky School of Medicine	1	1[1]	2
University of Louisville	2	1[3]	3
LOUISIANA.			
Charity Hospital Medical College	1	0	1
Tulane University	1	0	1
MAINE.			
Bowdoin	1	0	1
MARYLAND.			
Baltimore Medical College	6[4]	2[3]	8

[1] Class of 1899.
[2] Class of 1898.
[3] Class of 1901.
[4] One examined 1900, license held for completion of examination.

Name of college.	Passed.	Failed.	Total.
Baltimore University	3	5[1]	8
College of Physicians and Surgeons	3	0	3
Johns Hopkins	12	0	12
Maryland Medical College	1	1[2]	2
University of Maryland	2	0	2
Southern Homeopathic Medical College	1	0	1

MASSACHUSETTS.

Boston University	5	0	5
College of Physicians and Surgeons	0	1[3]	1
Harvard	8	0	8
Tufts	0	1[3]	1

MICHIGAN.

University of Michigan	6	0	6
Detroit College of Medicine	2	1[3]	3

MINNESOTA.

University of Minnesota	1	0	1

MISSOURI.

College of Physicians and Surgeons	1	0	1

NEW HAMPSHIRE.

Dartmouth	1	0	1

NEW YORK.

Albany Medical College	25	3[4]	28
Long Island College Hospital	38	4[5]	42
University of Buffalo	47	2[6]	49
Bellevue Hospital Medical College	6	0	6
Columbia	106[7]	6[8]	112
Cornell	47	1	48
New York Eclectic Medical College	6[1]	2	8
New York Homeopathic Medical College	21	1	22
New York Medical College and Hospital for Women	5	1[9]	6
University of the City of New York	2	0	2
University and Bellevue Hospital Medical College	35	1[10]	36
Syracuse University	23	2	25

NEW HAMPSHIRE.

Dartmouth	1	0	1

[1] Two of classes 1899, 1901, one, class of 1898.
[2] One, class of 1901.
[3] One, class of 1900.
[4] One each of classes 1898, 1900.
[5] One each of classes 1897, 1899.
[6] One, class of 1901.
[7] One examination not complete.
[8] One, class of 1898, two, class of 1901.
[9] Class of 1901.
[10] Class of 1899.

Name of college.	Passed.	Failed.	Total.
OHIO.			
Eclectic Medical Institute	1	0	1
Medical College of Ohio	3	1[1]	4
Cleveland College of Physicians and Surgeons	0	1[2]	1
Cleveland Homeopathic Medical College	2	0	2
Ohio Medical University	1	0	1
PENNSYLVANIA.			
Hahnemann Medical College	8	0	8
Jefferson Medical College	6	1[3]	7
Medico-Chirurgical College	5	1[3]	6
University of Pennsylvania	22	0	22
Women's Medical College	4	0	4
SOUTH CAROLINA.			
Medical College of South Carolina	1	0	1
TENNESSEE.			
Memphis Hospital Medical College	1	0	1
Vanderbilt University	2	0	2
University of the South	0	1[4]	1
VERMONT.			
University of Vermont	4	0	4
VIRGINIA.			
University of Virginia	4[5]	0	4
Medical College of Virginia	2	0	2
CANADA.			
Dalhousie University	1	0	1
Queen's University	3	0	3
Laval University	0	1[6]	1
McGill University	7	0	7
Ontario Medical College for Women	1	0	1
Trinity Medical College	3	0	3
University of Toronto	3	0	3
FOREIGN.			
University of Havana	1	0	1
Faculty of Medicine	1	0	1
University of Paris	2	0	2
University of Berlin	4	0	4
University of Leipzig	2	0	2
University of Munich	1	0	1
University of Athens	1	0	1
University of Bologna	0	1[3]	1

[1] One, papers canceled for attempted fraud.
[2] Class of 1893.
[3] Class of 1897.
[4] Class of 1901.
[5] One, requirements not fully met.
[6] Class of 1895.

Name of college.	Passed.	Failed.	Total.
University of Genoa	2	1[1]	3
University of Naples		12[2]	19
University of Palermo		3[3]	7
University of Parma		0	1
University of Pisa		0	1
Royal University of Rome		0	2
University of Bucharest		0	2
Imperial University of Kharkov		0	1
University of Tomsk		0	1
University of Urief		1	1
College of Physicians and Surgeons, Edinburgh		0	2
	564[4]	61	625

NORTH CAROLINA.

The graduate of any medical school requiring not less than three courses of at least six months each may apply for an examination before the board.

Dr. George W. Presse, Charlotte, is the secretary.

EXAMINATIONS, 1902.

Name of college.	Passed.	Failed.	Total.
COLORADO.			
University of Colorado	1	0	1
DISTRICT OF COLUMBIA.			
Howard University	0	1[5]	1
GEORGIA.			
Atlanta Medical College	1	0	1
College of Physicians and Surgeons, Atlanta	1	2[6]	3
Southern Medical College	1	0	1
University of Georgia	3	0	3
KENTUCKY.			
Louisville Medical College	1	0	1
University of Kentucky	1	0	1
University of Louisville	1	0	1
LOUISIANA.			
Tulane University	1	0	1
MARYLAND.			
Baltimore Medical College	1	0	1

[1] One of class 1898.
[2] One each of classes 1876, 1878, 1894, 1895, 1897, 1898, 1899; three, class of 1900; two papers canceled for fraud.
[3] One each of classes 1896, 1898.
[4] 6 examinations requirements not fully completed.
[5] Class of 1900.
[6] One, class of 1895.

Name of college.	Passed.	Failed.	Total.
College of Physicians and Surgeons	2	0	2
Johns Hopkins	1	0	1
Maryland Medical College	1	0	1
University of Baltimore	0	2[1]	2
University of Maryland	13	0	13
MICHIGAN.			
University of Michigan	2	0	2
MISSOURI.			
College of Physicians and Surgeons	1	0	1
NEW HAMPSHIRE.			
Dartmouth	1	0	1
NEW YORK.			
Columbia	1	0	1
University and Bellevue Hospital Medical College	2	0	2
Woman's Medical College New York	1	0	1
NORTH CAROLINA.			
Leonard Medical College	5	2[2]	7
North Carolina Medical College	14	2[3]	16
PENNSYLVANIA.			
Jefferson Medical College	3	0	3
University of Pennsylvania	1	0	1
SOUTH CAROLINA.			
South Carolina Medical College	1	0	1
TENNESSEE.			
Memphis Hospital Medical College	0	1	1
Tennessee Medical College	0	1	1
Grant University	3	2[4]	5
University of Nashville	2	0	2
University of South	1	0	1
VIRGINIA.			
Medical College of Virginia	3	0	3
University College of Medicine	1	1[5]	2
University of Virginia	1	0	1
	72	14	86

NORTH DAKOTA.

The applicant for examination must submit to the Board of Examiners evidence of attendance of at least three courses of lectures of not less than six months each.

Dr. H. M. Wheeler, Grand Forks, is the secretary.

[1] Classes of 1891, 1900.
[2] One, class of 1901.
[3] One, class of 1898.
[4] Both, class of 1900.
[5] Class of 1900.

EXAMINATIONS, 1902.

Name of college.	Passed.	Failed.	Total.
ILLINOIS.			
College of Physicians and Surgeons	1	0	1
Rush Medical College	2	1	3
University of Illinois	2	0	2
INDIANA.			
Central College of Physicians and Surgeons	1	0	1
IOWA.			
College of Physicians and Surgeons	1	0	1
University of Iowa	1	0	1
KENTUCKY.			
Louisville Medical College	1	1[1]	2
MASSACHUSETTS.			
Harvard	1	0	1
MICHIGAN.			
University of Michigan	2	0	2
Detroit Medical College	1	1	2
Grand Rapids Medical College	1	0	1
MINNESOTA.			
University of Minnesota	2	1	3
College of Physicians and Surgeons	2	0	2
Hamline University	4	0	4
MISSOURI.			
Barnes Medical College	3	0	3
CANADA.			
Trinity University	4	0	4
Queen's Medical College	1	0	1
	30	4	34

OHIO.

Ohio provides a preliminary examination for intending medical students. Those who have not taken this must present evidence of having pursued a four years' high-school course; the medical education includes a four years' course in a college accepted by the board.

Dr. Frank Winders, Columbia, is the secretary.

EXAMINATIONS, 1902.

Name of college.	Passed.	Failed.	Total.
ILLINOIS.			
American Medical Missionary College	1	0	1
Chicago Homeopathic Medical College	1	0	1
College of Physicians and Surgeons	5	0	5

[1] Class of 1894.

Name of college.	Passed.	Failed.	Total.
Dunham Medical College	1	0	1
Illinois Medical College	1	0	1
National Medical University	1	0	1
Northwestern University Medical College	1	0	1
Rush Medical College	6	0	6

INDIANA.

Fort Wayne College of Medicine	0	2	2
Medical College of Indiana	1	0	1

KENTUCKY.

Kentucky School of Medicine	0	1	1

MARYLAND.

Baltimore Medical College	2	1	3
College of Physicians and Surgeons, Baltimore	2	0	2
Johns Hopkins	2	0	2

MASSACHUSETTS.

Harvard	3	0	3

MICHIGAN.

University of Michigan	13	3[1]	16
Detroit College of Medicine	2	0	2

MISSOURI.

Kansas City Homeopathic Medical College	1	0	1
Barnes Medical College	0	2	2
Marion-Sims Medical College	1	0	1

NEW YORK.

University of Buffalo	1	0	1
Columbia	1	0	1

OHIO.

Miami Medical College	1	0	1
College of Physicians and Surgeons, Cleveland	2	0	2
Homeopathic Hospital College of Medicine	0	1	1
Western Reserve Medical University	0	1[2]	1
Ohio Medical University	1	1	2
Medical College of Ohio	2	0	2
Starling Medical College	1	0	1

PENNSYLVANIA.

Jefferson Medical College	2	0	2
University of Pennsylvania	7	0	7

CANADA.

Western University Medical College	1	0	1
Woman's Medical College	1	0	1
Trinity Medical College	1	0	1

[1] One each of classes 1872, 1874, 1878.
[2] Class of 1886.

Name of college.	Passed.	Failed.	Total.
FOREIGN.			
Edinburgh University	1	0	1
Royal University of Science	0	1[1]	1
	66	13	79

OKLAHOMA.

A new law is now in force in Oklahoma, making an examination a prerequisite for license.

Dr. E. E. Cowdrick, Enid, is the secretary.

TEXT OF THE LAW.

Be it Enacted by the Legislative Assembly of the Territory of Oklahoma:

SECTION 1. There is hereby established a territorial Board of Health, composed of three persons, residents of this Territory, regularly practising and legally qualified physicians in good standing, to be appointed by the governor and approved by the council. The term of office of each member shall be two years, and one member shall be designated by the governor as superintendent, who shall be *ex-officio* secretary of the Board. The Board shall elect one of its members as president and the other as vice-president.

SEC. 2. The president, when present, and the vice-president when the president is absent, shall preside at the meeting of the Board. The secretary shall keep a record of the proceedings of the Board and of his own proceedings as superintendent of the Board of Health. The Board of Health shall hold meetings every three months, due notice of the time and place to be given by the secretary.

SEC. 3. It shall be the duty of the Board of Health to examine applicants and grant licenses to those found to be qualified, and entitled to the same, to quarantine against outside territory known to be infected with contagious or infectious diseases, to condemn and destroy impure and diseased articles of food offered or exposed for sale in the territory and to act in conjunction with the county and municipal Boards of Health.

SEC. 4. The salary of the superintendent of the Board of Health shall be $800 per annum, and he shall be allowed for records, supplies, printing and traveling expenses actually and necessarily expended not to exceed $500 per annum, which shall be paid upon sworn itemized statements. The president and vice-president of the Board shall receive no compensation except fees for examination of applicants for license to practise medicine and surgery, which shall be equally divided between them, and actual and necessary traveling expenses, not to exceed $100 each per annum.

SEC. 5. No person hereafter shall practise medicine or surgery in this Territory without first obtaining a license from the territorial Board of Health. Application for license shall be made in writing, together with a fee of $5, accompanied by a proof of good moral character, and proof of ten

[1] Class of 1894.

years' continuous practise, or proof of graduation from a reputable medical college. When the application has been inspected by the Board and found to comply with the foregoing provisions, the Board shall notify the applicant to appear for examination at a time and place designated in such notice. Examinations shall be made in whole or in part in writing and be sufficiently strict to test applicant's qualifications to practise medicine. All members of the Board shall be present and participate in such examination. It shall be the duty of the person holding such license to register in the office of the register of deeds, in a book kept for that purpose, in the county in which the person resides or intends to practise. *Provided*, That an osteopath shall not be required to pass an examination in materia medica or therapeutics.

Sec. 6. Any person practising or offering to practise medicine or surgery in any of their branches, without first having obtained a license from this Board, shall be deemed guilty of a misdemeanor and upon conviction thereof shall be fined in any sum not less than $50 nor more than $100, or by imprisonment in the county jail for a period of not less than thirty days, nor more than six months, or by both such fine and imprisonment at the discretion of the court, and all costs incurred therein.

Sec. 7. The provisions of this Act shall not affect the rights of persons now legally practising medicine, osteopathy or surgery in this Territory; nor shall it prohibit the application of domestic remedies by one member of a family to another thereof; nor administering of remedies by another in case of emergency, without compensation; nor shall it comply to any commissioned medical officer of the United States army, navy or marine hospital service, in the discharge of his official duties; nor to any legally qualified dentist, when engaged exclusively in the practice of dentistry; nor to any physician or surgeon from another State or Territory who is a legal practitioner of medicine or surgery in the State or Territory which he resides, when in actual consultation with a legal practitioner of this Territory, nor to any physician or surgeon residing on the border of a neighboring State or Territory and duly authorized under the law thereof to practise medicine or surgery therein, whose practice extends into the limits of this Territory: *Provided*, That such practitioner shall not open an office or appoint a place to meet patients or receive calls within the limits of the Territory; nor to any osteopath who shall pass examination in the subject of anatomy, physiology, obstetrics, and physical diagnosis in the same manner as required of other applicants before the territorial Board of Health, and who has thereupon received a certificate from the Board which, when filed with the register of deeds, as is required in the case of other certificates from the Board shall authorize the holder thereof to practise osteopathy in the Territory of Oklahoma, but shall not permit him to administer drugs nor to perform major surgery.

Sec. 8. The county Boards of Health shall consist of three persons: a legally qualified physician appointed by the territorial superintendent, who shall be superintendent and secretary of the county Board of Health, the chairman of the county commissioners who shall be president, and a legally qualified physician appointed by the Board of county commissioners who shall be vice-president. The superintendent of county Boards of Health shall have power to abolish nuisances that are dangerous to the public health, to isolate persons afflicted with dangerous or contagious diseases, and to do such other things with the approval of the Board as may be deemed necessary for the preservation of the public health. Such superintendent shall be paid for expenses actually and necessarily contracted in the discharge of his duties, together with fees for duty performed : *Provided*, That the sum total of such expenses and fees shall not exceed $100 per annum. Such bills of expense and fees shall be filed with the county clerk and allowed by the Board of County Commissioners, as other bills are allowed by them. *Provided, further*, That should an emergency exist on account of the prevalence of any dangerous epidemic, such county Board of Health may make such provisions for the isolation and care of the sick as may be required, by and with the consent and approval of the county commissioners.

SEC. 9. Chapter 8 of the statutes of Oklahoma 1893, together with all Acts and parts of Acts in conflict herewith are hereby repealed.

SEC. 10. This Act shall take effect and be in force from and after its passage and approval.

Approved March 12, 1903.

OREGON.

Applicants for license to practise medicine must file an affidavit stating the time spent in the study of medicine, and pass an examination before the Board of Examiners.

Dr. Byron E. Miller, Dekum Building, Portland, is the secretary of the Board.

(No reports of the examinations in Oregon for 1902 have been obtainable.)

PENNSYLVANIA.

The examinations for licensure in Pennsylvania are conducted by the Boards of Examiners, working in harmony under the supervision of the Medical Council. The rules of the Medical Council require a preliminary training of a high-school course, or passing a state examination on subjects equivalent to such a course, graduation from a medical school after a four years' course and passing the examination of one of the Boards of Examiners.

Hon. James W. Latta, Secretary of Internal Affairs, Harrisburg, is the secretary of the Medical Council.

EXAMINATIONS, 1902.

Name of college.	Passed.	Failed.	Total.
COLORADO.			
University of Denver	1	0	1

Name of college.	Passed.	Failed.	Total.
DISTRICT OF COLUMBIA.			
Georgetown University	3	1	4
Howard University	3	1[1]	4
National University	1	0	1
ILLINOIS.			
Chicago Homeopathic Medical College	1	0	1
College of Physicians and Surgeons	4	0	4
Dunham Medical College	2	1	3
Hahnemann Medical College	1	0	1
Illinois Medical College	1	0	1
Northwestern University	2	0	2
Rush Medical College	1	0	1
INDIANA.			
Indiana Medical College	0	1	1
University of Medicine, Indianapolis	1	0	1
KENTUCKY.			
Hospital College of Medicine	1	0	1
Kentucky School of Medicine	0	1	1
University of Louisville	1	1[2]	2
MARYLAND.			
Baltimore Medical College	14	4[3]	18
Baltimore University	4	3[4]	7
College of Physicians and Surgeons	13	0	13
Johns Hopkins	1	0	1
Maryland Medical College	2	5[5]	7
University of Maryland	4	1	5
MICHIGAN.			
University of Michigan	1	0	1
OHIO.			
Eclectic Medical Institute	7	0	7
Pulte Medical College	1	0	1
University of Cincinnati	1	0	1
Cleveland Homeopathic Medical College	3	0	3
Ohio Medical University	1	0	1
Starling Medical College	1	1[1]	2
PENNSYLVANIA.			
Hahnemann Medical College	43	4[6]	47
Jefferson Medical College	95	5[7]	100

[1] 2nd examination.
[2] 5th examination.
[3] One, 3rd examination.
[4] One, 2nd examination.
[5] One withdrew; two, 2nd examination.
[6] Two, 2nd examination.
[7] One withdrew; one, 7th examination; one, 8th examination.

Name of college.	Passed.	Failed.	Total.
Medico-Chirurgical College	77	10[1]	87
University of Pennsylvania	104	7[2]	111
Woman's Medical College	19	0	19
Western Pennsylvania Medical College	53	13[3]	66
TENNESSEE.			
University of Tennessee	1	1	2
University of the South	5	3[4]	8
VERMONT.			
University of Vermont	1	0	1
VIRGINIA.			
University College of Medicine	1	0	1
CANADA.			
McGill University	1	0	1
FOREIGN.			
Charing Cross Medical School, London	1	0	1
Faculty of Medicine, France	1	0	1
University of Naples	1	3[5]	4
	479	66	545

RHODE ISLAND.

Any reputable physician desiring to practise in Rhode Island may obtain a license to practise from the State Board of Health after passing a satisfactory examination before the Board.

Dr. Gardiner T. Swartz, Providence, is the secretary.

EXAMINATIONS, 1902

Name of college.	Passed.	Failed.	Total.
DISTRICT OF COLUMBIA.			
Georgetown University	1	0	1
MAINE.			
Bowdoin	3	0	3
MARYLAND.			
College of Physicians and Surgeons	1	0	1
Baltimore Medical College	3	1	4
Baltimore University	1	3	4
University of Maryland	2	0	2
MASSACHUSETTS.			
College of Physicians and Surgeons	1	0	1
Harvard	6	0	6
Tufts	2	1	3

[1] One, 2nd examination; two, 3rd examination; one, 4th examination; one withdrew.
[2] One expelled; one, 2nd examination; two withdrew.
[3] One, 2nd examination; four, 3rd examination; one, 4th examination.
[4] One, 2nd examination; one, 6th examination.
[5] One withdrew; one, 2nd examination.

Name of college.	Passed.	Failed.	Total.
MICHIGAN.			
Saginaw Valley Medical College	0	1	1
NEW HAMPSHIRE.			
Dartmouth	2	2	4
NEW YORK.			
Columbia	4	0	4
University Medical College	1	0	1
PENNSYLVANIA.			
Hahnemann Medical College	1	0	1
Jefferson Medical College	1	0	1
Medico-Chirurgical College	1	0	1
VERMONT.			
University of Vermont	1	0	1
CANADA.			
Laval University	1	1	2
FOREIGN.			
University of Naples	1	0	1
Non-graduates	2	3	5
	35	12	47

SOUTH CAROLINA.

South Carolina requires those who desire to practise to have been graduated from a medical school; if the school of graduation is situated in South Carolina, no examination is required; if it is not, there must be in addition an examination.

Dr. S. C. Baker, Sumter, is the secretary.

This change in the law of South Carolina removes it from that class of states where an examination is required in every instance, and from a tabulation of the examinations in this report.

SOUTH DAKOTA.

South Dakota has changed its law and will hereafter require an examination before the license to practise is issued.

Dr. H. E. McNutt, Aberdeen, is the secretary.

TEXT OF THE LAW—ESTABLISHING A BOARD OF MEDICAL EXAMINERS.

An Act to establish a Board of Medical Examiners, making an appropriation for the same, regulating the practice of medicine, surgery and obstetrics, providing for licensing physicians and surgeons and providing for penalties for violations of such regulations of the practice of medicine, surgery and obstetrics.

Be it Enacted by the Legislature of the State of South Dakota:

SECTION 1. BOARD CREATED. There is hereby created a Board of Medical Examiners for the purpose of examination, regulation, licensing and registration of physicians and surgeons in the State of South Dakota. Said Board shall consist of seven members, who shall have been residents of the State of South Dakota for not less than five years preceding their appointment not more than two of whom shall be from the same county.

SEC. 2. GOVERNOR TO APPOINT. The governor shall immediately upon the taking effect of this Act appoint seven skilled and capable physicians who shall constitute said Board, two of whom shall hold their office for one year, two for two years, and three for three years from the date of their respective appointments, and until their successors are appointed, and the governor shall each year thereafter on or before the third day of July appoint for the term of three years two or three as the case may be, skilled and capable physicians to fill the vacancies caused by the expiration of the terms of such members as above provided. The governor shall fill by appointmen: all vacancies occasioned by death or otherwise.

SEC. 3. BOARD—OF WHOM CONSIST. The said Board shall consist of nct more than four members from the school known as regular, not more thai two from the school known as homeopath, and not more than one from th: school known as eclectic. Five members of this Board shall constitute 1 quorum for the transaction of business.

SEC. 4. MEETING OF—ELECTION OF OFFICERS—BOND OF. The Board shall meet at Huron, South Dakota, at a date to be named by the governo:, for organization in 1903, and shall elect from their number a presiden:, vice-president, and secretary who shall also act as treasurer and all officers shall be elected annually thereafter. Said Board shall procure a common seal. The secretary and treasurer shall execute a bond, to the State of South Dakota, in the penal sum of two thousand dollars ($2,000) with two or more sufficient sureties. Said bond shall be conditioned upon the faithful discharge of his duties, and shall be approved by the governor.

SEC. 5. MEETINGS—WHEN HELD. The Board shall hold two regular meetings each year, beginning on the second Wednesday of July, and the second Wednesday of January of each year, and such additional meetings at such times and at such places as the Board may deem advisable. The Board shall have power to make rules and regulations for the government of the said Board and its officers, and for the proper discharge of its duties.

SEC. 6. RECORD MUST BE KEPT. Said Board shall keep a record of all proceedings thereof, and also a record or register of all applicants for a license together with his or her age, time spent in the study of medicine, and the location and name of all the institutions granting to such applicants degrees or certificates of lectures in medicine or surgery such register shall also show whether such applicant was rejected or licensed under this Act, said record or register shall be *prima facie* evidence of all matters therein recorded No member of the said Board shall belong to the faculty of any medical college or university nor shall any one of them be financially interested in the manufacture or sale of drugs, or the practice of pharmacy.

SEC. 7. APPLICATION FOR LICENSE—QUALIFICATION OF APPLICANT. On and after the taking effect of this Act all persons desiring to begin the practice of medicine or surgery or obstetrics in any of their branches in this State shall make application to said Board for a license to practise medicine, surgery or obstetrics in the State of South Dakota. Such license shall be granted to such applicants who shall give satisfactory proofs of being at least twenty-one (21) years of age and of good moral character, but only on compliance of the following conditions; the applicant shall be given such license if he shall pass an examination before the Board upon the following subjects: anatomy, physiology, chemistry, pathology, therapeutics, practice of medicine, surgery, obstetrics, gynecology, diseases of the eye and ear, bacteriology, medical jurisprudence, and such other branches as the Board may deem advisable, and in addition thereto shall present evidence of having attended four full courses of lectures of at least twenty-six (26) weeks each in a legally organized and reputable medical college recognized by the Board of Medical Examiners, no two courses being in the same year and of having received a diploma from a legally organized and reputable medical college which shall be in good standing as shall be determined by the Board, and said diploma must be submitted to the Board for inspection and verification provided that the four courses of lectures of six months each shall not apply to applicants who graduated prior to 1898.

SEC. 8. EXAMINATION—HOW CONDUCTED. Said examination shall be conducted as follows: First, the applicant shall, before being permitted to take the examination, pay the secretary of the Board an examination fee of twenty dollars ($20). Second, the examination shall be in writing, oral or both as the Board may determine. Third, the questions on all subjects except therapeutics and practice of medicine shall be such as may be answered alike by all schools of medicine. The applicant shall, if possible, be examined in therapeutics and practice of medicine by those members of the Board belonging to the same school as the applicant and a license and certificate shall not be refused any applicant because of his adherence to any particular school of medicine. The average percentage of at least 75 per cent. of correct answers shall be required of every applicant. Any applicant who shall not pass the said examination, shall be eligible to a second examination at the next regular meeting of the Board or at such time as the Board may designate without an additional examination fee.

SEC. 9. LICENSE. Said Board shall grant a license to practise medicine and surgery and obstetrics in all their branches in the State of South Dakota to each applicant who has satisfactorily passed the said examination and has fulfilled all other requirements of this Act. Said license can only be granted by the consent of not less than five (5) members of the said Board and which said license shall be signed by the president and secretary of the said Board and attested by the seal of the Board. All examination papers together with the lists of questions answered shall be kept for reference and inspection for a period of not less than three (3) years.

SEC. 10. LICENSE WITHOUT EXAMINATION—WHEN. The said Board may, in its discretion, accept and license upon the payment of the license fee without examination of the applicant, any license which shall have been issued to him by the Examining Board of the District of Columbia, or any State or Territory of the United States, provided, however, that the legal requirements of such Examining Board shall have been at the time of issuing such certificate, or license in no degree or particular less than those of the State of South Dakota at the time when such certificate or license shall be presented for registration to the Board created by this Act; and *Provided, further*, That the provisions of this section contained shall be held to apply only to such of said Medical Examining Boards as accept and register the certificate or license granted by this Board without examination by them of the persons holding such certificates or license. Each applicant upon making application under the provision of this section shall pay to the secretary of the Board a license fee of twenty dollars ($20).

SEC. 11. BOARD MAY REFUSE TO GRANT LICENSE. The Board shall have the power and authority to refuse to grant a license under this Act for unprofessional, immoral or dishonorable conduct on the part of the applicant. The action of the Board in refusing to grant a license under this Act shall be final.

SEC. 12. MAY REVOKE LICENSE. The Board shall have the power and authority to revoke any license of any physician or surgeon heretofore or hereafter granted or issued upon complaint made to it on oath by one responsible person if it shall satisfactorily appear to the Board, either, first, that such physician or surgeon has been guilty of unprofessional, immoral or dishonorable conduct; or second, that such physician or surgeon has been convicted of a felony; or third, if such physician or surgeon publicly professes or claims to cure, or treat disease, injury or deformity in such a manner as to deceive the public; or fourth, gross professional incompetency; *Provided*, That such license shall not be revoked except after a hearing before the Board of Medical Examiners at which at least five members of such Board shall be present and of which hearing the person holding the license to be revoked shall have had not less than ten days' written notice of the time and place of said hearing and only upon due proof of the facts stated in the complaint.

SEC. 13. UNPROFESSIONAL OR DISHONORABLE—MEANING OF. The words unprofessional or dishonorable conduct as used in Sections 11 and 12 of this Act are hereby declared to mean, first, procuring or aiding or abetting a criminal abortion. Second, the employing of what is known as cappers or steerers. Third, the obtaining of any fee on the assurance that a manifestly incurable disease can be permanently cured. Fourth, wilfully betraying a professional secret. Fifth, all advertising of medical business in which untruthful or improbable statements are made or which are calculated to mislead or deceive the public. Sixth, all advertising of any medicine, or any means whereby the monthly periods of women can be regulated or the menses reestablished if suppressed. Seventh, conviction of any offense involving moral turpitude. Eighth, habitual intemperance.

SEC. 14. PERSONS AGGRIEVED MAY APPEAL. All persons feeling aggrieved by the action of the Board in revoking their license may appeal to the circuit court of the county in which the person whose license is revoked resides, in the same manner as now provided by law in cases of appeal from the decision of a Board of county commissioners, and the perfection of such appeal shall operate as a stay to the revocation of said license until the final determination thereof by the court; *Provided, however*, That at any time during the pendency of such appeal the said Board may appeal to the court for a temporary injunction restraining the apellant from the practice of medicine, surgery or obstetrics, until the final determination and judgment on such appeal which said injunction may in the discretion of the court be issued without the requirement of any bond.

SEC. 15. LICENSE MUST BE RECORDED. The person receiving a license to practise shall have the same recorded in the office of the register of deeds in the county where he resides and practises. The said register of deeds shall in July and January of each year furnish the secretary of the State Board of Medical Examiners a list of all licenses so recorded.

SEC. 16. MONEYS MUST BE PAID TO STATE TREASURER. All moneys received by the said Board shall be paid to the State treasurer and shall be credited to the general fund of the State, and a receipt in duplicate for the same shall be filed with the secretary of said Board of Medical Examiners, and in the office of the State auditor.

SEC. 17. COMPENSATION OF MEMBERS OF BOARD. Each member of the Board shall receive as compensation the sum of five dollars ($5) per day for each day actually in attendance upon the meetings of the Board and five cents for every mile necessarily traveled and his necessary expenses while attending such meetings. The secretary of the Board of Medical Examiners shall receive as compensation for his services the sum of eight hundred dollars ($800) per annum, which salary shall be in full for his services as a member of the Board. All bills for stationery, postage and other necessary expenses shall be approved by said Board and sent to the auditor of the State who shall draw his warrant upon the State treasurer for the amount due.

SEC. 18. MEDICAL BOARD FUND ESTABLISHED. There is hereby established a fund to be known as the Medical Board fund, and the sum of four thousand dollars ($4000) is hereby appropriated out of the moneys in the State treasury not otherwise appropriated to meet the expenses of carrying out the provisions of this Act for two years, namely, two thousand dollars ($2000) for the year beginning February 15, 1903, and ending February 14, 1904, and two thousand dollars ($2000) for the year beginning February 15, 1904, and ending February 14, 1905. And the State treasurer is hereby directed and required to set such sum apart to the credit of such fund subject to the orders and disbursements as herein provided for. The money in the said fund shall only be paid out by the State auditor's warrant on said fund, on an order drawn by the secretary of the said Board and countersigned by the president.

SEC. 19. ITINERANT PHYSICIANS MUST PROCURE ITINERANT LICENSES. Any physician practising medicine, surgery or obstetrics, or professing or attempting to treat, cure or heal diseases, ailments or injuries by any medicine appliance or method who goes from place to place, or from house to house, or by circulars, letters or advertisements, solicits persons to meet him or her for professional treatment at places other than his office at the place of his permanent residence is hereby declared to be an itinerant physician, and shall in addition to the ordinary physician's license as in this Act provided procure an itinerant's license from the State Board of Medical Examiners for which he shall pay to the secretary of the Board the sum of five hundred dollars ($500) per annum upon the payment of said sum of five hundred dollars ($500) the Board shall issue to the applicant therefor, a license to practise within the State as an itinerant physician for one year from the date thereof. The Board may for the same reasons as specified in Sections 11, 12 and 13 of this Act refuse to issue such itinerant's license, or having issued it, may revoke it for the same reasons as specified in Sections 11, 12 and 13 hereof.

SEC. 20. PENALTY FOR PRACTISING WITHOUT A LICENSE. Any person practising medicine, surgery or obstetrics in any of their branches as an itinerant physician as in Section 19 hereof defined without having procured such itinerant license, shall be guilty of a misdemeanor and upon conviction thereof shall be punished by a fine of not less than five hundred dollars ($500) nor more than eight hundred dollars ($800) or imprisonment in the county jail not less than thirty days nor more than ninety days, or by both such fine and imprisonment.

SEC. 21. UNLAWFUL TO USE TITLE AND PRESCRIBE—WHEN. When a person shall append or prefix the letters M.B., or M.D., or the title Dr. or Doctor or any other sign or apellation in a medical sense to his or her name or shall profess publicly to be a physician or surgeon, or who shall recommend, prescribe or direct for the use of any person any drug, medicine apparatus or other agency for the cure, relief or palliation of any ailment or disease of the mind or body, or for the cure or relief of any wound, fracture or bodily injury, or deformity after having received or with the intent of receiving therefor, either directly or indirectly, any bonus, gift or compensation, shall be regarded as practicing within the meaning of this Act.

SEC. 22. THIS ACT NOT APPLICABLE WHEN. This Act shall not apply to the commissioned surgeons of the United States army, navy or marine hospital service in actual performance of their duties, nor to regularly licensed physicians or surgeons from outside this State in actual consultation with physicians of this State nor to dentists or osteopaths in the legitimate practice of their profession nor to Christian Scientists as such, who do not practise medicine, surgery or obstetrics by the use of any material, remedies or agencies, nor to resident physicians and surgeons of this State regularly licensed and practising in this State at the time of the taking effect of this Act.

Provided, however, That the license heretofore or hereafter granted to any physician or surgeon may be revoked for the same reason, and in the same manner as stated and provided in Sections 12 and 13 hereof.

SEC. 23. PRESENTATION OF FRAUDULENT DIPLOMAS—PENALTY. Any person who shall present to the Board of Medical Examiners a fraudulent or false diploma, or one of which he is not the rightful owner for the purpose of procuring a license as herein provided or who shall file or attempt to file with the register of deeds of any county in the State a license of another representing the same to be his own, or shall falsely personate any one to whom a license has been granted or who shall file or attempt to file with the register of deeds of any county in this State, a license of another with the name of the party to whom it was granted or issued erased, and his own name inserted in its place or who shall file or attempt to file with the Board of Medical Examiners any false or forged affidavits of identification, shall be guilty of a misdemeanor, and upon conviction thereof shall be punished by a fine of not less than fifty dollars ($50) nor more than one hundred dollars ($100) or by imprisonment in the county jail for a period of not more than thirty days or by both such fine and imprisonment.

Any person who shall practise medicine or surgery or obstetrics in any of their branches in this State without having obtained a license as in this Act provided shall be guilty of a misdemeanor, and upon conviction thereof shall be punished by a fine of not less than fifty dollars ($50) nor more than one hundred dollars ($100) or by imprisonment in the county jail for a period of not more than thirty days or by both such fine and imprisonment ; *Provided*, That the provisions of this section shall not apply to the provisions of Sections 19 and 20 of this Act, nor modify or change the penalties prescribed in Section 20 hereof.

SEC. 24. DUTY OF STATE'S ATTORNEY. It shall be the duty of the State's attorney to prosecute any and all violations of this Act committed in his county.

SEC. 25. REPEAL. All Acts and parts of Acts in conflict with the provisions of this Act are hereby repealed.

SEC. 26. EMERGENCY. An emergency is hereby declared to exist, and this Act shall take effect and be in force from and after its passage and approval.

Approved March 5, 1903.

TENNESSEE.

The only requirement to receive a license to practise in Tennessee is to pass an examination before the State Board of Medical Examiners.

Dr. T. J. Happel, Trenton, is the secretary.

EXAMINATIONS, 1902.

Name of college.	Passed.	Failed.	Total.
GEORGIA.			
Atlanta Medical College	0	1	1
University of Georgia	1	0	1
Eclectic College of Medicine and Surgery	0	1	1
KENTUCKY.			
Kentucky School of Medicine	1	0	1
University of Louisville	1	0	1
LOUISIANA.			
Tulane	1	0	1
MARYLAND.			
University of Maryland	2	0	2
MISSOURI.			
Missouri Medical College	1	0	1
NEW YORK.			
Columbia	1	0	1
New York Polyclinic	1	0	1
OHIO.			
Eclectic Medical Institute	1	0	1
PENNSYLVANIA.			
Medico-Chirurgical College	1	0	1
VIRGINIA.			
Richmond Medical College	1	0	1
University of Virginia	1	0	1
Non-graduates	23	13	36
	36	15	51

TEXAS.

Texas has three Boards of Examiners, working independently of each other, before either of which any one over 21 years of age and of good moral character, may apply for an examination.

Secretaries, Dr. M. M. Smith, Austin; Dr. N. O. Berizer (Homeopathic Board), Austin; Dr. L. S. Downs (Eclectic Board), Galveston.

EXAMINATIONS, 1902.

The results of the examinations have not been procurable.

UTAH.

Utah has a single Board of Medical Examiners, and requires the applicant to possess a diploma from a medical school in good standing in the State where it exists, and to pass an examination.

Dr. W. R. Fisher, Salt Lake City, is the secretary.

EXAMINATIONS, 1902.

Name of college.	Passed.	Failed.	Total.
CALIFORNIA.			
College of Physicians and Surgeons	2	0	2
Cooper Medical College	1	0	1
COLORADO.			
Denver Medical College	2	0	2
DISTRICT OF COLUMBIA.			
University of Georgetown	1	0	1
ILLINOIS.			
College of Physicians and Surgeons	2	0	2
Northwestern University	1	0	1
IOWA.			
Iowa College of Physicians and Surgeons	1	1[1]	2
KANSAS.			
University Medical College	1	0	1
MARYLAND.			
College of Physicians and Surgeons	1	0	1
MINNESOTA.			
University of Minnesota	1	0	1
MISSOURI.			
Hahnemann Medical College	1	1[1]	2
St. Louis College of Physicians and Surgeons	0	1[2]	1
Missouri Medical College	1	0	1
NEW YORK.			
Bellevue Hospital Medical College	2	0	2
OHIO.			
Starling Medical College	1	0	1
Western Reserve University	0	1[3]	1
FOREIGN.			
Berlin University	1	0	1
	19	4	23

VERMONT.

Each of the three State Medical Societies appoint a Board of Censors. Beyond the fact that the applicant is a graduate of a medical school, each Board is the sole judge of the applicant's fitness and may be examined. The Boards avail themselves of the permission.

Secretaries, Dr. S. W. Hammond, Rutland (Vermont State Medical Society); E. B. Whittaker, Barr (Homeopathic Medical Society); P. L. Templeton, Montpelier (Eclectic Medical Society).

[1] Class of 1901.
[2] Class of 1891.
[3] Class of 1898.

EXAMINATIONS, 1902.

Name of college.	Passed.	Failed.	Total.
MARYLAND.			
Baltimore Medical College	3	1	4
MASSACHUSETTS.			
Tufts	1	0	1
MICHIGAN.			
University of Michigan	1	0	1
NEW HAMPSHIRE.			
Dartmouth	1	0	1
NEW YORK.			
Columbia	1	0	1
PENNSYLVANIA.			
Woman's Medical College	1	0	1
TENNESSEE.			
University of the South	1	1[1]	2
VERMONT.			
University of Vermont	9	0	9
CANADA.			
Laval University	2	2[2]	4
McGill University	1	0	1
	21	4	25

VIRGINIA.

A single Board supervises the licensing to practise in Virginia, which is only done after an examination; graduation from a medical school is now required in Virginia, and the Board does not recognize a school which does not conform to the requirements of the Association of American Medical Colleges. The examination may be divided—part of it taken at the end of the second college year (which gives no right to practise) and the rest at the completion of the course. A graduate from a medical school who has passed a State Board Examination in another State and been licensed to practise therein may be licensed in Virginia, by passing such an examination as will convince the Board of his ability to properly care for any patients that may be entrusted to him.

Dr. R. S. Martin, Stuart, is the secretary.

EXAMINATIONS, 1902.

Name of college.	Passed.	Failed.	Total.
DISTRICT OF COLUMBIA.			
Columbian University	2	0	2

[1] Class of 1901.
[2] One, class of 1901.

Name of college.	Passed.	Failed.	Total.
Georgetown University	1	0	1
Howard University	2	1	3
GEORGIA.			
College of Physicians and Surgeons	2	1	3
University of Georgia	1	0	1
ILLINOIS.			
College of Physicians and Surgeons	1	0	1
University of Illinois	0	1	1
KENTUCKY.			
Kentucky School of Medicine	2	1[1]	3
Louisville Medical College	1	0	1
University of Louisville	0	1	1
Hospital College of Medicine	1	0	1
MARYLAND.			
Baltimore Medical College	2	3	5
Baltimore University	1	2	3
College of Physicians and Surgeons, Baltimore	1	0	1
Johns Hopkins	1	0	1
Maryland Medical College	2	1	3
University of Maryland	5	2[2]	7
Woman's Medical College	1	0	1
MISSOURI.			
College of Physicians and Surgeons, St. Louis	2	0	2
NEW YORK.			
Long Island College Hospital	1	0	1
Buffalo University	1	0	1
Syracuse University	1	0	1
Columbia	3	0	3
University of the City of New York	1	0	1
NORTH CAROLINA.			
Leonard Medical College	6	5	11
Shaw University	1	0	1
OHIO.			
Medical College of Ohio	1	0	1
PENNSYLVANIA.			
Hahnemann Medical College	0	1	1
SOUTH CAROLINA.			
Medical College of South Carolina	1	1	2
TENNESSEE.			
Tennessee Medical College	1	0	1
University of the South	6	3	9
TEXAS.			
University of Texas	1	0	1

[1] Presented another's diploma.
[2] One withdrew.

Name of college.	Passed.	Failed.	Total.
VIRGINIA.			
University of Virginia	11	2	13
Medical College of Virginia	13	2	15
University College of Medicine	12	3	15
FOREIGN.			
University of Berlin	1	0	1
	89	30	119
Non-graduates	143	1[1]	144

WASHINGTON.

Candidates for examination to obtain a license to practise medicine in Washington, must have been graduated from some duly authorized medical college.

Dr. P. B. Swearingen, Tacoma, is the secretary.

EXAMINATIONS, 1902.

Name of college.	Passed.	Failed.	Total.
CALIFORNIA.			
Cooper Medical College	6	1[2]	7
University of California	1	0	1
COLORADO.			
Denver University	0	1	1
University of Colorado	2	0	2
DISTRICT OF COLUMBIA.			
Georgetown University	1	0	1
GEORGIA.			
College of Physicians and Surgeons	1	0	1
University of Georgia	1	0	1
ILLINOIS.			
American Medical Missionary	2	0	2
Chicago Homeopathic Medical College	3	2[2]	5
College of Physicians and Surgeons	9	2[3]	11
Dunham Medical College	1	0	1
Hahnemann Medical College	3	0	3
Illinois Medical College	0	1	1
Northwestern University	6	2[4]	8
Woman's Medical College	1	0	1
Rush Medical College	13	4[5]	17

[1] Incomplete.
[2] One, class of 1885.
[3] One each of classes 1889, 1901.
[4] One each of classes 1897, 1899.
[5] One each of classes 1879, 1885; two, class of 1897.

Name of college.	Passed.	Failed.	Total.
INDIANA.			
Fort Wayne Medical College	1	0	1
Physio-Medical College	0	1[1]	1
IOWA.			
Iowa College of Physicians and Surgeons	1	1[2]	2
Keokuk Medical College	0	1[3]	1
Iowa State University	1	0	1
Sioux City Medical College	1	0	1
KANSAS.			
Kansas Medical College	3	0	3
University of Kansas	1	0	1
KENTUCKY.			
Hospital College of Medicine	1	0	1
Kentucky Medical College	1	0	1
Louisville Medical College	3	1[4]	4
University of Kentucky	1	0	1
University of Louisville	0	1[5]	1
MARYLAND.			
College of Physicians and Surgeons	1	0	1
MASSACHUSETTS.			
Harvard	4	0	4
MICHIGAN.			
University of Michigan	16	2	18
Detroit Medical College	3	2[6]	5
MINNESOTA.			
Minneapolis University	1	0	1
Minnesota State University	1	0	1
University of Minnesota	6	0	6
MISSOURI.			
Kansas City Medical College	2	1[7]	3
Kansas City University	0	1[8]	1
Homeopathic Medical College	0	1[8]	1
College of Physicians and Surgeons	0	1[9]	1
Beaumont Medical College	2	0	2
Marion-Sims Medical College	2	0	2
St. Louis College of Physicians and Surgeons	1	0	1
St. Louis Medical College	1	0	1

[1] Expelled for cribbing.
[2] Class of 1874.
[3] Class of 1897.
[4] Class of 1882.
[5] Class of 1901.
[6] One each of classes, 1896, 1897.
[7] Class of 1889.
[8] Class of 1898.
[9] Class of 1893.

Name of college.	Passed.	Failed.	Total.
NEBRASKA.			
Lincoln Medical College	0	1[1]	1
Omaha Medical College	3	1[2]	4
NEW YORK.			
Long Island Medical College	1	0	1
Bellevue Hospital Medical College	3	0	3
Columbia	1	0	1
Cornell	1	0	1
New York Homeopathic Medical College	1	0	1
University of New York	2	0	2
OHIO.			
Eclectic Medical Institute	0	2[3]	2
Medical College of Ohio	1	0	1
Cleveland Medical College	0	1[4]	1
Western Reserve University	1	0	1
Homeopathic Medical College	1	0	1
Ohio Medical University	1	0	1
Starling Medical College	0	1[1]	1
OREGON.			
University of Oregon	5	0	5
PENNSYLVANIA.			
Hahnemann Medical College	1	1[5]	2
Jefferson Medical College	7	4	11
University of Pennsylvania	4	0	4
TENNESSEE.			
University of Nashville	1	0	1
Tennessee Medical College	1	0	1
Vanderbilt University	1	0	1
VERMONT.			
University of Vermont	1	0	1
VIRGINIA.			
Virginia Medical College	1	0	1
WISCONSIN.			
Milwaukee Medical College	0	1[1]	1
College of Physicians and Surgeons	1	0	1
CANADA.			
McGill University	2	0	2
Manitoba Medical College	1	0	1
Trinity Medical College	2	1[1]	3
University of Toronto	1	0	1

[1] Class of 1897.
[2] Class of 1894.
[3] One each of classes, 1871, 1882.
[4] Class of 1883.
[5] Class of 1901.

Name of college.	Passed.	Failed.	Total.
FOREIGN.			
University of Copenhagen	0	1[1]	1
Tokio University, Japan	1	0	1
	150	40	190

WEST VIRGINIA.

The State Board of Health issues a license to practise medicine in West Virginia to any person who can pass its examination.

Members of the State Board of Health—Drs. H. A. Barbee, *Secretary and Executive Officer*, Point Pleasant; J. L. Dickey, Wheeling; A. N. Frame, *President*, Parkersburg; D. P. Morgan, Clarksburg; S. N. Myers, Martinsburg; J. E. Robins, Claremont; C. W. Spangler, Maybury; A. G. Staunton, Charleston; S. W. Varner, Glenville; A. R. Warden, Grafton.

EXAMINATIONS, 1902.

Name of college.	Passed.	Failed.	Total.
DISTRICT OF COLUMBIA.			
Columbian Medical College	2	0	2
Howard University	2	0	2
ILLINOIS.			
Illinois Medical College	2	0	2
Northwestern University	1	0	1
Rush Medical College	1	0	1
IOWA.			
Keokuk College of Physicians and Surgeons	2	0	2
KENTUCKY.			
Hospital College of Medicine	1	0	1
Kentucky School of Medicine	2	2[2]	4
Louisville Medical College	1	1[3]	2
University of Louisville	4	0	4
MARYLAND.			
Baltimore Medical College	18	0	18
Baltimore University	1	2[4]	3
College of Physicians and Surgeons	8	2	10
Johns Hopkins	1	0	1
Maryland Medical College	9	0	9
University of Maryland	3	1	4
Woman's Medical College	1	0	1
MISSOURI.			
Barnes Medical College	1	1	2
Washington University	0	1	1

[1] Class of 1901.
[2] One, class of 1901.
[3] Second examination.
[4] One employed a substitute and was detected.

Name of college.	Passed.	Failed.	Total.
NEW YORK.			
University of Buffalo	1	0	1
NORTH CAROLINA.			
Leonard Medical College	2	0	2
OHIO.			
American Eclectic College	1	0	1
Ohio Medical College	1	0	1
Eclectic Medical Institute	2	0	2
Pulte Medical College	1	0	1
Ohio Medical University	1	0	1
Starling Medical College	4	0	4
PENNSYLVANIA.			
Hahnemann Medical College	2	0	2
Jefferson Medical College	4	0	4
University of Pennsylvania	2	0	2
Western Pennsylvania Medical College	8	1[1]	9
TENNESSEE.			
University of Nashville	1	0	1
Meharry Medical College	1	0	1
University of Tennessee	1	0	1
University of the South	1	0	1
VIRGINIA.			
University of Virginia	4	0	4
Medical College of Virginia	4	0	4
University College of Medicine	7	0	7
Virginia Medical College	3	0	3
Non-graduates	5	14	19
	116	25	141

WISCONSIN.

Wisconsin has adopted a new law since the last report.

TEXT OF THE ACT.

An Act relating to the State Board of Medical Examiners, and to the registration and licensing of persons engaged in the practice of medicine, surgery, or osteopathy in the State of Wisconsin.

The People of the State of Wisconsin, Represented in Senate and Assembly, do enact as follows:

SECTION 1. The Governor shall appoint a Board of Medical Examiners to be known as the Wisconsin State Board of Medical Examiners, consisting of eight (8) members. Such appointments shall be made from separate lists presented to him every second year, one list of ten (10) names presented by the Wisconsin State Medical Society, one list of ten (10) names presented

[1] Class of 1868.

by the Homeopathic Medical Society of the State of Wisconsin, one list of ten (10) names presented by the Wisconsin State Eclectic Medical Society, and one list of five (5) names presented by the Wisconsin State Osteopathic Association. In case any of said societies or associations fail to present such list of names, the governor may fill vacancies in the Board by appointment from the last list filled by such association or society previous to the occurrence of such vacancy. The appointment of each member of said board shall be for the term of four (4) years and until his successor is appointed and qualified; the proportion of the different schools of medicine as herein provided, shall be preserved. No instructor, stockholder, member of, or person financially interested in any school, college or university having a medical department, or of any school of osteopathy, shall be appointed a member of said board. Three members of said board shall be allopathic, two shall be homeopathic, two eclectic and one osteopathic, and all shall be licentiates of said board, and no member shall serve for more than two consecutive terms, provided nothing contained in this Act shall be construed as terminating or in any manner interfering with the term of any member of the present State Board of Medical Examiners, but each of said members shall serve out his present term as a member of said Board.

SEC. 2. Said Board shall annually, at its July meeting, elect from its members a president, secretary and treasurer, and shall have a common seal. The president and secretary may administer oaths for the accomplishment of the objects of the Board. Said Board shall hold regular meetings on second Tuesday in each January at Milwaukee and the second Tuesday of each July at Madison, and such other meetings at such other times and places as it may from time to time determine. The Board shall keep a record of all its proceedings and also a register of all applicants for license, together with a record showing their ages, time spent in the study of medicine and the name and location of all institutions granting to such applicants, degrees or certificates of lectures in medicine, surgery or osteopathy. Said register shall also show whether such applicant was rejected or licensed, and said books and register shall be prima facie evidence of all the matters required to be kept therein.

SEC. 3. All persons commencing the practice of medicine, surgery or osteopathy in any of their branches in this state, shall apply to said Board at the time and place designated by said Board, or at any regular meeting thereof for license so to practise, and shall present to said Board a diploma from a reputable college of medicine and surgery or osteopathy. A college to be deemed reputable by this Board shall require at least four courses of not less than seven months each before graduation, no two of such courses to be taken within any one twelve months, and that shall require for admission thereto a preliminary education equivalent to that necessary for entrance to the junior class of an accredited high school in this state, including a one year's course in Latin, and that shall after the year 1906 require for admission to such a school a preliminary education equivalent to graduation from an accredited high school of this state, and shall submit to an examination in the various branches of medicine and surgery usually taught in reputable medical colleges, or if the applicant be an osteopath he or she shall present a diploma from a regularly conducted college of osteopathy maintaining a standard in all respects equal to that hereby imposed on medical colleges as to preliminary education, said college after 1904 to give three courses of eight months each, no two courses to be given in any one twelve months, and after the year 1909 such college shall give four courses of seven months each, as hereinbefore provided for medical colleges, and shall pass the regular examination of such Board in anatomy, histology, physiology, obstetrics, gynecology, pathology, urinalysis chemistry, toxicology, dietetics, physical and general diagnosis, hygiene, and theory and practice of osteopathy. The examination in materia medica, therapeutics and practice shall be conducted by members of the Board representing the school of practice, which the applicant claims or intends to follow. After examination, as hereinbefore provided, the Board shall, if it find the applicant qualified, grant a license to said applicant to practise medicine and surgery in all their branches in this state, or a license to practise osteopathy therein, which license can only be granted by the consent of not less than six members of said Board, and which, after the payment of fees as hereinafter provided, shall be signed by the president and secretary thereof, and attested by the seal of the Board. Osteopaths, when so licensed, shall have the same rights and privileges and be subject to the same laws and regulations as practitioners of medicine and surgery, but shall not have the right to give or prescribe drugs or to perform surgical operations. The fee for examination shall be fixed by the Board, but shall not exceed $15.00 in each case, with $5.00 additional for the license if issued. Such fee or fees shall be paid by the applicant to the treasurer of the Board and may be applied toward defraying any proper and reasonable expenses of the Board; provided, however, that any student who is exempted as a matriculant of any medical college of this state under chapter 306 of the laws of 1901, whose name is now on file with the Wisconsin State Board of Medical Examiners, shall on the presentation of a diploma from any Wisconsin college, and on the payment of the fees specified in this Act, and having satisfied said Board that he or she is a person of good moral character, be licensed to practise without further examination by such Board, provided that said college maintains its standard herein required. Every person practising medicine or surgery in the state of Wisconsin, who, at the time of the passage and publication of this Act, has not received a license from said Board, and who shall after such passage and publication present a diploma from a reputable medical college and give satisfactory evidence of having been a reputable practitioner of medicine and surgery in the state of Wisconsin continuously since the first day of July, 1897, shall be granted a license without examination upon the payment of a fee not exceeding $5.00, as determined by said Board. Any person applying for such license shall if he or she be possessed of a certificate of registration issued under and according to the provisions of chapter 87 of the laws of 1899, present such certificate to said Board with the diploma and application of such license, and surrender said certificate on the issuance of said license, the registration fee paid for same shall be deducted from the last-named fee. Any practitioner of medicine or osteopathy holding a certificate from any other state board imposing requirements equal to those established by the Board provided for herein, may on presentation of the same with a diploma from a reputable medical or osteopathic college, be admitted to practise within this state without an examination, at the discretion of the Board, on the payment of the fee fixed by the Board, not exceeding the sum of $25.00.

SEC. 4. All money received by the Board shall be kept by the secretary thereof who shall also act as treasurer, out of the funds coming into their possession from the fees mentioned in the preceding section; the Board may pay all legitimate and necessary expenses incurred by them, their agents or employees in the discharge of the duties of the Board, and the members may receive for their services a sum to be determined by the Board, not exceeding five dollars for each day actually spent in attending to the business of the Board; the secretary shall receive a salary to be fixed by said Board, not to exceed one thousand dollars per annum. Such salary, compensation and expenses shall be paid from the fees received by the Board, and no part thereof shall be paid out of the state treasury. The secretary shall furnish to the Board such bond as they may from time to time direct. It shall be the duty of said Board to make a report of their proceedings to the governor at the end of each biennial period, together with an account of all moneys received and disbursed by them, and all moneys in excess of actual expenses shall be paid into the state treasury, secretary of said board securing a receipt therefor, said moneys there to remain as an emergency fund which may be withdrawn in whole or in part by said Board in case of necessity with the consent of the governor. Said biennial period shall begin December 31, 1904. The provisions of this Act shall not apply to commissioned surgeons of the United States army, public health and marine hospital service, or to physicians and surgeons of other states or countries in actual consultation with resident physicians of this state.

And provided further, that any practitioner of medicine or surgery, holding a license from the State Board of Medical Examiners of any adjoining state, dated since January 1st, 1901, shall on presentation of the same within one year from the taking effect of this Act, accompanied by a certificate from the secretary from the State Board of Medical Examiners of the state issuing the license that such applicant is a reputable practitioner of medicine and surgery, be licensed to practise medicine and surgery in this state, without an examination, at the discretion of the Board on payment of the fee.

SEC. 5. Every person hereafter practising medicine, surgery or osteopathy in this state shall be required to have the license herein provided for, or heretofore issued by the Wisconsin State Board of Medical Examiners, or a certificate of registration issued pursuant to the provisions of chapter 87 of the laws of 1899, and any person having or hereafter receiving a license according to the provisions of this Act, or having such certificate of registration, shall record the same with the county clerk of any county in which said person shall practice and pay to said clerk or clerks a fee of fifty (50) cents each for recording the same, and said clerk shall enter a memorandum thereof, giving the date of said license or certificate, the name of the person to whom it was issued, school of practice chosen, and the date of such recording in a book to be provided and kept for that purpose. Any such person who shall fail to record his or her license or registration certificate, as herein provided, shall not exercise any of the rights or privileges conferred by such license or certificates. And any person beginning such practice without having obtained such license contrary to law, or any person who, not having such license or certificate of registration herein referred to, shall advertise or hold himself or herself out to the public as a physician, surgeon, osteopathist or specialist in any of the branches of medicine, surgery or osteopathy, or who shall use the title of "Doctor," or shall append to his or her name the letters "M.D." or "M.B.," meaning doctor or bachelor of medicine, or "D.O.," meaning doctor or diplomat of osteopathy, or any other letters of designation meaning any of the titles enumerated in this section, shall be punished by a fine of not less than $50.00 nor more than $100.00 for each offense, or by imprisonment in the county jail for a term not exceeding three months, or by both such fine and imprisonment. Any person practising medicine, surgery or osteopathy, or without authority assuming the title of "doctor of medicine," "doctor or diplomat of osteopathy," "bachelor of medicine," or "physician," or "surgeon," or "osteopathist," or "osteopath," shall not be exempted from, but shall be liable to all the penalties and liabilities for malpractice, which physicians, surgeons or osteopathists are liable to, and ignorance on the part of any such person shall not lessen such liability for failing to perform, or for negligently or unskilfully performing or attempting to perform any duty assumed, and which is ordinarily performed by physicians, surgeons or osteopathists. If any person licensed or registered by said board shall be convicted of any crime committed in the course of his professional conduct, the court in which such conviction is had, may in addition to any other punishment imposed pursuant to law, revoke such license or certificate. Said board shall have the power to adopt such rules for its government and may require the filling out of such blanks by applicants, as it may deem necessary in order to ascertain the true character and qualifications of an applicant for license, and the board may in its discretion refuse to grant license to any person who does not furnish satisfactory proof of good moral and professional character.

SEC. 6. Every person shall be regarded as practising medicine or osteopathy within the meaning of this Act, who shall append to his or her name the letters "M.D.," "M.B.," or "D.O.," Doctor, Dr., or any other letters or designation with intent to represent that he or she is a physician, surgeon or osteopathist, or who shall for a fee prescribe drugs or other medical or surgical treatment or osteopathic manipulation for the cure or relief of any wound, fracture, bodily injury, infirmity, or disease, provided, however, that nothing in this Act contained shall be construed to apply to any dentist or resident refracting optician engaged in the practice of his or her profession.

SEC. 7. It shall be the duty of the Board of Medical Examiners to investigate all complaints in regard to the violation, or disregard of, or non-compliance with the provisions of this Act, and to bring all such cases to the notice of the proper prosecuting officers, and it shall be the duty of the district attorney of the proper county to prosecute all violations of this Act.

SEC. 8. No person practising medicine, surgery or osteopathy shall have the right to collect, by law, any fees or compensation for the performance of any medical or surgical services, or fees for any service as an osteopathist, or to testify in a professional capacity as a physician, or surgeon, or insanity expert in any case, unless he or she holds a license from the Wisconsin Board of Medical Examiners, or the certificate of registration hereinbefore referred to, with a diploma from a reputable medical college or society or a certificate of membership in a medical society, and has been duly recorded as a practitioner in the state of Wisconsin; provided, that nothing in this Act contained shall be construed as restricting any court in a criminal action from receiving the testimony of any person as a witness.

SEC. 9. All Acts or parts of Acts in any wise conflicting with the provisions of this Act are hereby repealed.

SEC. 10. This Act shall take effect and be in force from and after its passage and publication.

Approved May 22, 1903.

EXAMINATIONS, 1902.

Name of college.	Passed.	Failed.	Total.
COLORADO.			
Gross Medical College	1	0	1
DISTRICT OF COLUMBIA.			
Howard University	1	0	1
ILLINOIS.			
American Medical College	1	0	1
Bennett Medical College	2	0	2
Chicago College of Medicine and Surgery	0	1	1
Chicago Homeopathic College	3	1	4
Chicago Medical College	2	1[1]	3
College of Physicians and Surgeons	16	0	16
Hahnemann Medical College	4	0	4
Harvey Medical College	0	2[2]	2
Illinois Medical College	1	1	2

[1] Class of 1897.
[2] Class of 1901.

Name of college.	Passed.	Failed.	Total.
Northwestern University	17	0	17
Rush Medical College	29	1	30
University of Illinois	1	0	1
IOWA.			
Keokuk Medical College	1	1	2
University of Iowa	2	0	2
KENTUCKY.			
Academy of Medicine[1]	0	1	1
Louisville Medical College	3	0	3
University of Louisville	1	0	1
MARYLAND.			
Johns Hopkins	1	0	1
Maryland Medical College	1	0	1
MICHIGAN.			
University of Michigan	1	0	1
MINNESOTA.			
University of Minnesota	2	0	2
College of Physicians and Surgeons	0	1	1
MISSOURI.			
Marion-Sims-Beaumont College of Medicine	3	0	3
St. Louis College of Physicians and Surgeons	1	0	1
NEBRASKA.			
Omaha Medical College	0	1[2]	1
NEW YORK.			
Columbia	1	0	1
University of New York	1	0	1
OHIO.			
Miami Medical College	1	0	1
PENNSYLVANIA.			
Hahnemann Medical College	3[3]	0	3
Jefferson Medical College	1	0	1
University of Pennsylvania	2	0	2
CANADA.			
Trinity Medical College	2	0	2
FOREIGN.			
University of Munich	1	0	1
	106	11	117

WYOMING.

A graduate in medicine from a medical college or member of the Association of American Medical Colleges, the Homeopathic

[1] So in returns.
[2] Class of 1893.
[3] One conditioned.

Institute, or the National Eclectic Medical Association, or any college of similar standing in foreign countries, may receive a certificate giving the right to practise medicine upon presentation of the diploma. All others must pass an examination.

Dr. C. P. Johnson, Cheyenne, is the secretary.

RECAPITULATION BY COLLEGES.

Name of college.	Passed.	Failed.	Total.
ALABAMA.			
Birmingham Medical College	5	0	5
Medical College of Alabama	15	1	16
ARKANSAS.			
Arkansas University	1	0	1
CALIFORNIA.			
California Medical College	1	0	1
College of Physicians and Surgeons, California	5	7	12
Cooper Medical College	14	1	15
Hahnemann Medical College	4	1	5
University of California	22	2	24
University of Southern California	1	0	1
COLORADO.			
Denver Medical College	2	0	2
Denver University	1	1	2
Gross Medical College	4	0	4
State University, Colorado	2	0	2
University of Colorado	2	0	2
CONNECTICUT.			
Yale	27	0	27
DISTRICT OF COLUMBIA.			
Columbian University	28	0	28
Georgetown University	12	1	13
Howard University	17	3	20
National University	7	3	10
GEORGIA.			
Atlanta College of Physicians and Surgeons	82	4	86
Atlanta Medical College	2	1	3
Georgia College of Eclectic Medicine and Surgery	4	1	5
Southern Medical College	1	0	1
University of Georgia	43	3	46
ILLINOIS.			
American Medical Missionary College	11	1	12
American Medical College	1	1	2
Bennett Medical College	27	0	27
Chicago Medical College	5	1	6

Name of college.	Passed.	Failed.	Total.
College of Medicine and Surgery, Chicago	1	2	3
Chicago Homeopathic Medical College	23	4	27
Chicago University	0	1	1
College of Physicians and Surgeons, Chicago	139	10	149
Dunham Medical College	8	2	10
Hahnemann Medical College	42	22	64
Harvey Medical College	20	2	22
Hering Medical College	4	0	4
Illinois Medical College	17	5	22
Jenner Medical College	1	1	2
National Medical University	6	1	7
Northwestern University	66	4	70
Northwestern University Woman's Medical College	6	0	6
Rush Medical College	226	6	232
University of Illinois	3	1	4

INDIANA.

Name of college.	Passed.	Failed.	Total.
Central College of Physicians and Surgeons, Indiana	2	0	2
Fort Wayne Medical College	5	2	7
Hospital Medical College	1	0	1
Medical College of the University of Indianapolis	1	0	1
Medical College of Indiana	5	1	6
Physio-Medico College	0	2	2
University of Medicine, Indianapolis, Indiana	1	0	1

IOWA.

Name of college.	Passed.	Failed.	Total.
College of Physicians and Surgeons, Keokuk	4	4	8
Iowa College of Physicians and Surgeons, Des Moines	12	3	15
Iowa University, Homeopathic Department	6	1	7
Keokuk Medical College	7	10	17
Keokuk Medical College, College of Physicians and Surgeons, Iowa	35	2	37
Sioux City College of Medicine	10	1	11
University of Iowa	43	0	43

KANSAS.

Name of college.	Passed.	Failed.	Total.
Kansas Medical College	7	1	8
University of Kansas	4	1	5

KENTUCKY.

Name of college.	Passed.	Failed.	Total.
Academy of Medicine, Kentucky	0	1	1
Hospital College of Medicine, Kentucky	18	0	18
Kentucky School of Medicine	14	11	25
Kentucky University	4	0	4
Louisville Medical College	17	4	21

Name of college.	Passed.	Failed.	Total.
Louisville National Medical College	2	0	2
University of Louisville	17	7	24
LOUISIANA.			
Charity Hospital Medical College	1	1	2
Tulane University	35	3	38
New Orleans University	3	5	8
MAINE.			
Bowdoin	12	1	13
Eclectic Medical College	0	1	1
MARYLAND.			
Baltimore Medical College	97	23	120
Baltimore University	25	35	60
College of Physicians and Surgeons	62	3	65
Johns Hopkins	43	1	44
Maryland Medical College	24	14	38
Southern Homeopathic Medical College	10	0	10
University of Maryland	67	17	84
Woman's Medical College	7	0	7
MASSACHUSETTS.			
Boston University	30	1	31
College of Physicians and Surgeons	7	3	10
Harvard University	116	1	117
New England University	0	1	1
Tufts	39	4	43
MICHIGAN.			
Detroit College of Medicine	13	5	18
Grand Rapids Medical College	1	0	1
Michigan College of Medicine and Surgery	2	0	2
Saginaw Valley Medical College	3	2	5
University of Michigan	68	9	77
MINNESOTA.			
College of Physicians and Surgeons, Minnesota	2	1	3
Hamline University	28	4	32
University of Minnesota	84	2	86
MISSOURI.			
American Medical College	6	1	7
Barnes Medical College	26	19	45
Beaumont Medical College, Missouri	3	0	3
Central Medical College	3	1	4
College of Physicians and Surgeons, Missouri	2	2	4
Ensworth Medical College, Missouri	4	2	6
Hahnemann Medical College, Missouri	1	1	2
Homeopathic Medical College of Missouri	3	2	5

Name of college.	Passed.	Failed.	Total.
Kansas City Homeopathic Medical College	5	1	6
Kansas City Medical College	11	2	13
Kansas City University	0	1	1
Marion-Sims College of Medicine	35	2	37
Medico-Chirurgical College, Kansas City	4	0	4
Missouri Medical College	7	3	10
Physicians and Surgeons, Kansas City	2	0	2
St. Louis College of Physicians and Surgeons	21	14	35
St. Louis Medical College	10	2	12
St. Louis and Missouri Medical College	2	0	2
University of Kansas City	1	0	1
University Medical College, Missouri	8	2	10
University of Missouri	1	0	1
Washington University	9	2	11
Woman's Medical College, Missouri	1	0	1

NEBRASKA.

Cotner University	0	1	1
John A. Creighton Medical College	8	0	8
Lincoln Medical College	1	1	2
Omaha Medical College	10	2	12

NEW HAMPSHIRE.

Dartmouth	25	5	30

NEW YORK.

Albany Medical College, New York	26	3	29
Bellevue Hospital Medical College	18	0	18
Columbia	164	9	173
Cornell	53	1	54
Long Island College Hospital	47	6	53
Niagara Medical College, New York	0	2	2
New York Homeopathic Medical College	25	2	27
New York Polyclinic	1	0	1
New York College and Hospital for Women	6	1	7
New York Eclectic Medical College	6	2	8
Syracuse University	25	2	27
University and Bellevue Hospital Medical College	46	1	47
University of Buffalo	50	2	52
University of City of New York	16	3	19
Woman's Medical College, New York Infirmary	1	0	1

NORTH CAROLINA.

Leonard Medical College	22	9	31
North Carolina Medical College	14	2	16

OHIO.

American Health College	0	1	1
American Eclectic College	1	0	1
Cincinnati College of Medicine and Surgery	0	1	1

Name of college.	Passed.	Failed.	Total.
Cleveland College of Physicians and Surgeons	2	1	3
Cleveland Homeopathic Medical College	3	0	3
Cleveland Medical College	1	1	2
College of Physicians and Surgeons, Ohio	0	1	1
Columbus Medical College	1	0	1
Eclectic Medical Institute	22	4	26
Homeopathic Hospital College, Ohio	2	1	3
Laura Memorial, Woman's Medical College	2	0	2
Medical College of Ohio	17	3	20 *
Miami Medical College, Ohio	8	0	8
National Normal University	0	1	1
Ohio Medical University	4	3	7
Pulte Medical College	3	0	3
Starling Medical College	9	4	13
University of Cincinnati	1	0	1
Western Reserve University	5	1	6

OREGON.

Name of college.	Passed.	Failed.	Total.
University of Oregon	5	0	5

PENNSYLVANIA.

Name of college.	Passed.	Failed.	Total.
Eclectic Medical College, Pennsylvania	2	1	3
Hahnemann Medical College	79	9	88
Jefferson Medical College	159	14	173
Medico-Chirurgical College	97	13	110
University of Pennsylvania	170	8	178
Western Pennsylvania Medical College	63	14	77
Women's Medical College	34	1	35

SOUTH CAROLINA.

Name of college.	Passed.	Failed.	Total.
Medical College of South Carolina	4	1	5

TENNESSEE.

Name of college.	Passed.	Failed.	Total.
Chattanooga Medical College	11	1	12
Grant University	8	4	12
Meharry Medical College	11	4	15
Memphis Hospital Medical College	28	3	31
Summertown Medical College	1	0	1
Tennessee Medical College	2	1	3
University of Nashville	12	1	13
University of South	33	13	46
University of Tennessee	10	2	12
Vanderbilt University	11	1	12

TEXAS.

Name of college.	Passed.	Failed.	Total.
University of Texas	1	0	1

VERMONT.

Name of college.	Passed.	Failed.	Total.
University of Vermont	44	7	51

VIRGINIA.

Name of college.	Passed.	Failed.	Total.
Medical College of Virginia	27	2	29

Name of college.	Passed.	Failed.	Total.
Richmond Medical College	1	0	1
University College of Medicine	21	5	26
University of Virginia	26	2	28
WISCONSIN.			
Milwaukee Medical College	2	1	3
Wisconsin College of Physicians and Surgeons	4	0	4
CANADA.			
Dalhousie University	2	0	2
Laval University	10	8	18
Manitoba Medical College	1	0	1
McGill University	22	1	23
Ontario Medical College for Women	1	0	1
Queen's Medical College	1	0	1
Queen's University	3	0	3
Trinity Medical College	7	1	8
Trinity University	9	1	10
University of Toronto	7	0	7
Victoria University	1	0	1
Western University Medical College	1	0	1
Western University	1	0	1
Woman's Medical College	1	0	1
FOREIGN.			
Charing Cross Medical School, London	1	0	1
College of Physicians and Surgeons, Edinburgh	2	0	2
Dublin University	0	1	1
Edinburgh University	1	0	1
Faculty of Medicine	2	0	2
Imperial University of Kharkov	1	0	1
Imperial University of Kasan	1	0	1
Kiel University	1	0	1
Royal College of Physicians and Surgeons	1	0	1
Royal University of Science	0	1	1
Royal University of Rome	2	0	2
Royal University of Budapest	0	1	1
Strassburg University	1	0	1
Tokio University, Japan	1	0	1
University of Athens	1	0	1
University of Berlin	6	0	6
University of Bologna	0	1	1
University of Bucharest	3	0	3
University of Christiana	2	0	2
University of Copenhagen	0	1	1
University of Durham	1	0	1
University of Genoa	2	1	3
University of Geneva	1	0	1

Name of college.	Passed.	Failed.	Total.
University of Groningen	0	1	1
University of Havana	1	0	1
University of Leipzig	2	0	2
University of Munich	2	0	2
University of Montpellier	1	0	1
University of Naples	13	16	29
University of Palermo	4	3	7
University of Paris	2	0	2
University of Parma	3	0	3
University of Pisa	1	0	1
University of Tomsk	1	0	1
University of Turin	1	0	1
University of Urief	0	1	1
" "	14	3	17
Non-graduates	84	172	256
	3,781	729	4,510

RECAPITULATION BY STATES.

	Passed.	Failed.	Total.
Alabama	107	16	123
California	57	31	88
Connecticut	69	11	80
Delaware	16	2	18
District of Columbia	44	5	49
Georgia	135	5	140
Idaho	10	6	16
Illinois	304	22	326
Indiana	101	9	110
Iowa	241	19	260
Kansas	42	11	53
Louisiana	79	13	92
Maine	43	5	48
Maryland	86	62	148
Massachusetts	271	135	406
Minnesota	176	26	202
Missouri	95	28	123
Montana	29	8	37
New Hampshire	30	4	34
New Jersey	63	12	75
New York	564	61	625
North Carolina	72	14	86
North Dakota	30	4	34
Ohio	66	13	79
Pennsylvania	479	66	545

	Passed.	Failed.	Total.
Rhode Island	35	12	47
Tennessee	36	15	51
Utah	19	4	23
Vermont	21	4	25
Virginia	89	30	119
Washington	150	40	190
West Virginia	116	25	141
Wisconsin	106	11	117
	3,781	729	4,510

OBSERVATIONS IN PASSING.

From a circular received from the census bureau, it appears that a more uniform method of nomenclature will be adopted in the very near future in the United States for reporting vital statistics. The information contained in this circular has already appeared in full in the more frequently appearing journals, and need not be reprinted here. The readers of the Bulletin are in hearty accord with the plan and are fully acquainted with the suggestions, we are sure.

_

In like manner the resolutions adopted by the Mississippi Valley Medical Association at its recent meeting at Memphis, both on toy-pistol tetanus, and the necessity of eye examination of children have received wide publicity. The association is to be commended for giving prominence to these important subjects. The next meeting will be held in Cincinnati on October 11 to 13, 1904.

_

The subject for the Enno Sander Prize Essay for 1904, offered by the Association of Military Surgeons of the United States is "The Relation of the Medical Department to the Health of Armies."

Dr. James Evelyn Pitcher, Carlisle, Pa., secretary of the association, will furnish any information concerning the conditions. The competitors are limited to those who are eligible to active or associate membership in the association.

_

Parke Davis & Co. have lost a valued and valuable coadjutor in the death of William Matthew Warren. Medical journalism also suffers, since Mr. Warren was the publisher of that series of journals fostered by that firm, and which, under his care, maintained their dignity and professional tone notwithstanding their affiliation with a commercial house.

_

Dr. L. Duncan Bulkley is giving his sixth series of clinical lectures on diseases of the skin, at the New York Skin and Cancer Hospital.

LITERATURE NOTES.

A Hand-Book of the Diseases of the Eye and Their Treatment. By Henry R. Swanzy, A.M., M.B., F.R.C.S.I., Surgeon to the Royal Victoria Eye and Ear Hospital. Eighth Edition, revised, with 168 Illustrations and Zephyr card of Holmgren's tests. Philadelphia: P. Blakiston's Son & Co. 1903. Cloth. pp. 580. Price, $2.50 net.

That a work of this kind should reach an eighth edition is, of itself, evidence of its value. In this edition many changes have been made in order to incorporate the newer things in ophthalmology.

A notice "to the student" that he "should read carefully Chapters I, II, and III, omitting at first the fine print, either before or immediately on joining the ophthalmic hospital or department," shows the purpose of the book. For the purpose it is excellently conceived and admirably executed. The proof-reading has been carefully done; we notice on page 96 a slip where ʒi should read ℥i, which would be of little moment were the book not intended for students (seventh line from the bottom). In the index, too, some of the titles are misplaced as where hemophthalmos follows homatropin.

The Practice of Medicine—A Text-Book for Practitioners and Students with Special Reference to Diagnosis and Treatment. By James Tyson, M.D., Professor of medicine in the University of Pennsylvania. Third Edition. Thoroughly revised and in parts rewritten —with 134 illustrations including colored plates. Philadelphia: P. Blakiston's Son & Co. 1903. pp. 1240. Cloth. Price, $5.50.

In the preface of the first edition of the book Prof. Tyson said: "It represents almost purely personal work. . . . It does not pretend to be based on my personal practice only. In these days of specialized work this would be impossible, though with most of even the rare forms of disease in every section I have had some experience." It is this clearly expressed stating, by a man whose experience has been so extensive as to properly judge the relative value of the literature of each department, that makes this a work of value. No one can treat exhaustively the subjects under consideration in a volume of this size. It is not the argument of the advocate, nor even the presentation of the case to a jury by the judge, that is needed. Rather the decision of the judge, where he, too, decides upon fact as well as law. This Prof.

Tyson's book does. He treats the subjects concisely yet with enough elaboration to furnish a clear mental concept of each disease. His style is lucid, easily read and attractive. In this third edition he fairly presents the present state of modern medicine. The rôle of the anopholes and stegomyia genera of the mosquito is explained, while the possibility of the house fly conveying contagion is not overlooked.

The illustrations illustrate, and the publisher has left nothing to be desired in press work or general appearance of the work.

PRACTICAL GYNECOLOGY—A COMPREHENSIVE TEXT-BOOK FOR STUDENTS AND PHYSICIANS. By E. E. MONTGOMERY, M.D., LL.D., Professor of Gynecology, Jefferson Medical College. Second Edition, revised, with 539 illustrations, the greater part of which have been drawn and engraved specially for this work, for the most part from original sources. Philadelphia: P. Blakiston's Son & Co. 1903. Cloth. pp. 900. Price, $5.00 net.

The first edition of this work appeared in 1900. The necessity for a second edition in so short a time speaks for itself as to the value of the work and the esteem with which it has been held. Prof. Montgomery has made use of the opportunity to improve wherever experience showed the desirability even to rewriting, to bring the subject-matter up to date, and to add to the wealth of the illustrations.

THE PRACTICE OF OBSTETRICS DESIGNED FOR THE USE OF STUDENTS AND PRACTITIONERS OF MEDICINE. By J. CLIFTON EDGAR, Professor of Obstetrics and Clinical Midwifery in the Cornell University Medical College; attending obstetrician to the New York Maternity Hospital, with 1221 illustrations, many of which are printed in color. Philadelphia: P. Blakiston's Son & Co. 1903. pp. 1111. Cloth, $6.00, sheep or half morocco $7.00 net.

Those of us who have followed Prof. Edgar's development as a teacher of obstetrics in his various contributions on the subject, will expect great things in this book, and, in this, they will not be disappointed. The subject is carefully presented from a practical and clinical standpoint. The method of presentation is well thought out, the language clearly expresses the thought of the man thoroughly conversant with his subject, and the illustrations are just at hand when a clearer understanding of the text can be given by an illustration.

The mechanical part of the book is a worthy setting of the excellent material furnished by the author.

PHYSICIAN'S POCKET ACCOUNT BOOK. BY J. J. TAYLOR, M.D. Published by the Medical Council, 4105 Walnut St., Philadelphia. Price, $1.00.

This book differs from the ordinary visiting list, but may be used in its place, its chief advantage being, that one entry is needed for the busy doctor to keep his books, and that entry is such as to be accepted in the courts as evidence in case of a dispute over a bill.

FUNCTIONAL DIAGNOSIS OF KIDNEY DISEASE WITH ESPECIAL REFERENCE TO RENAL SURGERY, CLINICAL EXPERIMENTAL INVESTIGATIONS. BY DR. LEOPOLD CASPER (Privatdocent an der Universität) and DR. PAUL FRIEDERICH RICHTER (Assistant der III Med. Klinik) in Berlin. Translated by DR. ROBERT C. BRYAN, Adjunct Professor Genito-urinary Diseases, University Medical College of Richmond, Va., and DR. HENRY L. SANFORD, Resident Surgeon Lakeside Hospital, Cleveland. Philadelphia: P. Blakiston's Son & Co. 1903. Cloth. pp. 233. Price, $1.50 net.

We have given the title-page of this work in full, because it so admirably describes its scope. This is a subject which should receive the careful consideration of every surgeon who does any operative work upon the kidneys. The researches of the learned authors are of enough importance to be consulted in this connection, and those members of the profession who do not keep themselves informed of the German medical literature are indebted to the translators for this volume.

ILLINOIS STATE BOARD OF HEALTH. REPORT ON MEDICAL EDUCATION AND OFFICIAL REGISTER OF LEGALLY QUALIFIED PHYSICIANS. 1903. Embracing Medical Practice in Illinois; Medical Colleges in Illinois and Faculties; Medical Societies in Illinois and Officers; Pension Examining Boards in Illinois; Requirements for Practice in the United States; Medical Colleges in the United States; Official Register of Physicians; Springfield, Illinois, State Register. 1903. pp. clxix + 380.

The Illinois Board of Health was the pioneer in literature of this kind and at one time, the reports prepared by Dr. Rauch were the only works available for information regarding medical schools and practise Acts, and even yet, one finds references to these early reports. The present report well sustains the reputation of the earlier reports. Through the kindness of Dr. Egan, the secretary of the board, we were furnished advance sheets and made use of them in confirming the accuracy of the Bulletin report published in this number. Where the statements differed, pains were taken to go to original sources for information, and the results demonstrated the painstaking care of the compiler.

Apart from the official register, the Bulletin strives to offer similar information for the whole country as fully as does Illinois for its State, the great expense attendant upon gathering and collating such information only preventing its more frequent presentation.

LESSONS ON THE EYE FOR THE USE OF UNDERGRADUATE STUDENTS. BY FRANK L. HENDERSON, M.D., Ophthalmic Surgeon to St. Mary's Infirmary, and the Christian Orphan's Home; consulting oculist to the St. Louis City Hospital, etc. Third Edition. Philadelphia : P. Blakiston's Son & Co. 1903. Cloth. pp. 205. Price, $1.50.

We wish to commend this book in the highest terms. It is what it claims to be. It is possible for a medical student to master the contents of this book, be subject to a series of recitations and a term examination within the time that could fairly be given to the subject. Having done so, he has the foundation on which to build his future studies, either in the clinic or by reading larger and fuller treatises. A series of text-books on the various specialties patterned after this would have great pedagogic value.

TEXT-BOOK OF DISEASES OF THE EYE FOR STUDENTS AND PRACTITIONERS OF MEDICINE. BY HOWARD F. HANSELL, A.M., M.D., Clinical Professor of Ophthalmology, Jefferson Medical College, and WILLIAM M. SWEET, M.D., Demonstrator of Ophthalmology Jefferson Medical College. With 256 illustrations, including colored plates. Philadelphia: P. Blakiston's Son & Co. 1903. Cloth. pp. 532. Price, $4.00 net.

This is an excellent text-book for the student of ophthalmology, and is equally valuable for those students, not specializing on ophthalmology, and for general practitioners who wish an up-to-date work on eye diseases. The subject is treated clearly, and originally. It is not meant by this that nothing but original material has been used ; contrariwise the literature of the subject is kept well in mind and made use of; but the book is cast upon a model differing from the usual form of the text-book, and thereby the value of the book has been increased. Like most human efforts, the book is not without error—*vide* " tincture of hyoscyamin," on page 431, a quite evident *lapsus*, but as reviewers do not live in glass houses, cannot be passed by. The mechanical part of the book is worthy of all commendation.

THE PHYSICIAN'S VISITING LIST (Lindsay and Blakiston's) for 1904. Fifty-third year of its publication. Philadelphia: P. Blakiston's Son & Co. $1.00 to $2.25, depending upon size.

A visiting list that has been issued for fifty-three years must have more than usual elements of popularity and usefulness. While in general it maintains the form so well-known, each year there are slight innovations—betterings, so that, while ancient it is by no means antiquated.

AMERICAN ACADEMY OF MEDICINE—NEWS NOTES.

The president has appointed Dr. C. M. Culver, of Albany, Dr. W. S. Hall, of Chicago, and Dr. Leonard Freeman, of Denver, as the additional members of the council.

The Program Committee has Dr. D. C. Hawley, of Burlington, Vt., as its chairman. Fellows desiring to contribute papers should communicate their intention to Dr. Hawley at their early convenience. The Program Committee always strives to avoid a crowded program and reserve the right to decline any paper to prevent the crowding of the program or to promote its harmony.

Two of the sessions will be given to symposia on

I. The Relations of Physicians to Dentists and Pharmacists.

II. Are Modern School Methods in Keeping with Physiologic Knowledge?

This will leave two entire sessions for reports and general papers, with the president's address at an evening session.

BULLETIN

OF THE

American Academy of Medicine

VOL. VI.   ISSUED FEBRUARY, 1904.   NO. 10.

The American Academy of Medicine is not responsible for the sentiments expressed in any paper or address published in the Bulletin.

HANDBOOK OF THE AMERICAN ACADEMY OF MEDICINE. 1903-1904.

INTRODUCTION.

The purpose of this handbook is to give a list of the Fellows of the Academy, the constitution and by-laws, and such other information as may be of general interest.

PLACES AND TIMES OF MEETINGS.

1. 1876.—September 6, Philadelphia.
2. 1877.—September 11, 12, New York.
3. 1878.—September 17, 18, Easton, Pa.
4. 1879.—September 16, 17, New York.
5. 1880.—September 28, 29, Providence, R. I.
6. 1881.—September 20, 21, New York.
7. 1882.—October 26, 27, Philadelphia.
8. 1883.—October 9, 10, New York.
9. 1884.—October 28, 29, Baltimore.
10. 1885.—October 28, 29, New York.
11. 1886.—October 12, 13, Pittsburg.
12. 1887.—September 3, Washington.
13. 1888.—November 13, 14, New York.
14. 1889.—November 13, 14, Chicago.
15. 1890.—December 2, 3, Philadelphia.
16. 1891.—May 2, 4, Washington.
17. 1892.—June 4, 6, Detroit.
18. 1893.—June 3, 5, Milwaukee, Wis.

19. 1894.—August 29, 30, Jefferson, N. H.
20. 1895.—May 4, 6, Baltimore.
21. 1896.—May 2, 4, Atlanta.
22. 1897.—May 29, 31, Philadelphia.
23. 1898.—June 4, 6, Denver.
24. 1899.—June 3, 5, Columbus, O.
25. 1900.—June 2, 4, Atlantic City, N. J.
26. 1901.—June 1, 3, St. Paul, Minn.
27. 1902.—June 7, 9, Saratoga Springs, N. Y.
28. 1903.—May 11, 12, Washington.
29. 1904.—June 4, 6, Atlantic City, N. J.

PRESIDENTS.

1876	*Traill Green	Easton, Pa.
1877	*Traill Green	Easton, Pa.
1878	*Frank H. Hamilton	New York.
1879	*Lewis H. Steiner	Baltimore.
1880	*F. D. Lente	New York.
1881	*E. T. Caswell	Providence.
1882	*Traill Green	Easton, Pa.
1883	Henry O. Marcy	Boston.
1884	Benjamin Lee	Philadelphia.
1885	*Albert L. Gihon	U. S. N.
1886	†R. Stansbury Sutton	Pittsburg.
1887	*L. P. Bush	Wilmington, Del.
1888	F. H. Gerrish	Portland, Me.
1889	Leartus Connor	Detroit.
1890	*S. J. Jones	Chicago.
1891	*Theophilus Parvin	Philadelphia.
1892	P. S. Conner	Cincinnati.
1893	J. E. Emerson	Detroit.
1894	George M. Gould	Philadelphia.
1895	*J. McFadden Gaston	Atlanta.
1896	Henry M. Hurd	Baltimore.
1897	J. C. Wilson	Philadelphia.
1898	L. Duncan Bulkley	New York.
1899	Edward Jackson	Denver.
1900	G. Hudson-Makuen	Philadelphia.
1901	S. D. Risley	Philadelphia.
1902	V. C. Vaughan	Ann Arbor, Mich.
1903	Charles McIntire	Easton, Pa.
1904	John B. Roberts	Philadelphia.

* Deceased. † Resigned.

HONORARY MEMBERS.

(Limited to five to every one hundred Fellows.)

Date of election.	Name.	Residence.
1879	*Agnew, D. Hayes (*1892)	Philadelphia, Pa.
1896	Babcock, J. W	Columbia, S. C.
1882	*Campbell, Henry F. (*1891)	Augusta, Ga.
1888	Championiere, Lucas J	Paris, France.
1886	Davis, N. S	Chicago, Ill.
1888	Didama, Henry D	Syracuse, N. Y.
1882	*Flint, Austin (*1886)	New York, N. Y.
1897	Flint, Austin, Jr	New York, N. Y.
1889	Grant, Sir James Alexander	Ottawa, Canada.
1879	*Gross, Samuel D. (*1884)	Philadelphia, Pa.
1887	*Hewitt, W. M. Graily (*1893)	London, England.
1884	*Holmes, Oliver Wendell (*1894)	Boston, Mass.
1903	Jacoby, Mary Putnam	New York, N. Y.
1889	Jordan, David Starr	Leland Stanford, Jr., University, Cal.
1887	*Le Fort, Leon (*1893)	Paris, France.
1888	Lord Lister	London, England.
1887	Martin, August	Berlin, Germany.
1890	*Millard, Perry H. (*1897)	St. Paul, Minn.
1885	Mitchell, S. Wier	Philadelphia, Pa.
1887	Mooren, Albert	Düsseldorf, Germany.
1901	Nettleship, E	Nutcombe Hill, England.
1895	Osler, William	Baltimore, Md.
1895	Park, Roswell	Buffalo, N. Y.
1896	Peterson, Frederick C	New York, N. Y.
1887	Philips, Chas. D. F	London, England.
1896	Potter, Wm. Warren	Buffalo, N. Y.
1897	Ransahoff, Joseph	Cincinnati, O.
1888	*Rauch, John H. (*1893)	Chicago, Ill.
1887	*Semmola, M. (*1896)	Naples, Italy.
1883	*Sims, J. Marion (*1883)	New York, N. Y.
1885	*Smith, Henry H	Philadelphia, Pa.
1884	Sternberg, Geo. M	Surgeon-General, U. S. A.
1895	Stockton, C. G	Buffalo, N. Y.
1887	Unna, P. G	Hamburg, Germany.
1901	*Virchow, Rudolph (*1902)	Berlin, Germany.
1902	Welch, William H	Baltimore, Md.
1888	*Wells, Sir T. Spencer (*1897)	London, England.

FELLOWS.

* Deceased. ‡ Letter to last address returned; present whereabouts unknown. Names in italic have commuted dues by a payment of $20.

Date of election.	Name.	P. O. Address.
1882	Abbot, Griffith E	Leominster, Mass.
1903	Abbott, Harlan P	393 Broad, Providence, R. I.
1885	Acker, George N	913 16th, Washington, D. C.
1883	*Adam, Z. B. (*1902)	Framingham, Mass.
1880	*Agnew, Cornelius R. (*1888)	New York, N. Y.
1892	Alden, Chas. H	U. S. A.
1893	Alderson, M. E	Russellville, Kentucky.
1897	Alleman, H. M	Hanover, Pa.
1894	Allemann, L. A. W	64 Montague, Brooklyn, N. Y.
1881	*Allen, Charles L	Rutland, Vt.
1880	*Allen, Nathan (*1889)	Lowell, Mass.
1878	*Allen, William H. (*1850)	Philadelphia, Pa.
1885	*Alleyne, J. S. B. (*1895)	St. Louis, Mo.
1892	Allyn, G. W	432 Penn Ave., Pittsburg, Pa.
1888	Allyn, H. B	501 S. 42d., Philadelphia, Pa.
1890	Alt, Adolf	3036 Locust, St. Louis, Mo.
1899	Amberg, S	1304 Madison Ave., Baltimore, Md.
1880	Amory, Robert	279 Beacon, Boston, Mass.
1879	Andrew, George L	6123 Sheridan, Chicago, Ill.
1884	Andrews, Edmond	65 Randolph, Chicago, Ill.
1884	Andrews, Edward W	65 Randolph, Chicago, Ill.
1887	Andrews, Frank T	65 Randolph, Chicago, Ill.
1892	Angle, Edward J	1400 O, Lincoln, Nebraska.
1903	Appel, Theodore B	305 N. Duke, Lancaster, Pa.
1879	Appleby, James F. R	1430 33rd, N. W., Washington, D. C.
1902	Arbuthnot, Thos. S	5th Ave. and Maryland, Pittsburg, Pa.
1879	*Asch, Morris J. (*1903)	New York, N. Y.
1900	Aschman, Gustavus A	Wheeling, W. Va.
1877	Atkinson, William B	1400 Pine, Philadelphia, Pa.
1898	Atwater, James B	Westfield, Mass.
1896	Babcock, Robert H	103 State, Chicago, Ill.
1898	Bagot, William S	Stedman Block, Denver, Colo.
1901	Baker, Albert R	604 New England Bldg., Cleveland, O.
1888	Baker, Clarence A	312 Congress, Portland, Me.
1890	Baker, George Fales	1818 Spruce, Philadelphia, Pa.
1891	*Baldwin, Henry R. (*1902)	New Brunswick, N. J.
1877	Baldwin, Neilson A	1572 3rd, Brooklyn, N. Y.
1895	Balloch, Edward A	1013 15th, N. W., Washington, D. C.
1892	Bannister, Henry M	828 Judson Ave., Evanston, Ill.
1894	Bardwell, E. O	Emporium, Pa.
1903	Barker, Byron F	Bath, Me.
1902	Barker, James F	54 Clinton Ave., Albany, N. Y.

1903	Barker, Olin G. A	1114 Westinghouse Bldg., Pittsburg, Pa.
1898	*Barlow, Walter J*	328 Wilcox Block, Los Angeles, Cal.
1883	Barnum, Eugene E	Lancaster C. H., Va.
1897	Barreto, O. de Mello	Sao Paulo, Brazil.
1896	Bartholow, Paul	1525 Locust, Philadelphia, Pa.
1882	Barton, James M	1337 Spruce, Philadelphia, Pa.
1889	Bates, Joseph H	Neponset, Ill.
1883	*Baxter, J. W. (*1890)	U. S. A.
1897	Beach, William H	954 W. North Ave., Allegheny, Pa.
1878	*Beard, George M	New York, N. Y.
1882	Beck, Richard H	Hecktown, Pa.
1889	Beebe, Warren L	St. Cloud, Minn.
1891	Behrens, Bernt M	375 Syndicate Block, Minneapolis, Minn.
1889	Bell, Finis E	Mattoon, Ill.
1891	Bemus, Morris N	303 N. 2nd, Jamestown, N. Y.
1897	Benedict, A. L	156 W. Chippewa, Buffalo, N. Y.
1877	*Benham, S. W	Pittsburg, Pa.
1879	*Bennett, William C	Danbury, Conn.
1878	Bermingham, Edward J	75 W. 45th, New York, N. Y.
1890	*Bidwell, Walter D. (*1896)	Colorado Springs, Colo.
1897	Bieser, Augustus E	256 W. 54th, New York, N. Y.
1889	*Bigelow, George F. (*1893)	Boston, Mass.
1892	Biggs, Herman M	5 W. 58th, New York, N. Y.
1877	Billings, John S	32 E. 31st, New York, N. Y.
1897	Birney, David B	1810 De Lancey Pl., Philadelphia, Pa.
1884	Bishop, Rufus W	70 State, Chicago, Ill.
1893	Blackader, A. D	236 Mountain, Montreal, Canada.
1892	*Blake, Chas. E. (*1894)	San Francisco, Cal.
1899	Blake, Francis W	187 E. State, Columbus, O.
1902	Blumer, George	Sierra Madre, Cal.
1889	Boise, Eugene	2 Ottawa, Grand Rapids, Mich.
1879	Bombaugh, Chas. C	856 Park Ave., Baltimore, Md.
1898	Bonney, Sherman G	726 14th, Denver, Colo.
1890	Boone, Sherman W	Presque Isle, Me.
1889	Boothby, James M	Dubuque, Ia.
1886	*Borland, Matthew H	Pittsburg, Pa.
1894	Bourne, Geo. William	Kennebunk, Me.
1879	*Bowditch, Henry I. (*1892)	Boston, Mass.
1882	Bowditch, Vincent Y	506 Beacon, Boston, Mass.
1892	Bradford, E. F	24 Elm, Mechanic Falls, Me.
1889	Bradford, Thomas B	828 Washington, Wilmington, Del.
1894	Bradford, William H	365 Congress, Portland, Me.
1900	Brainerd, Henry G	315 W. 6th, Los Angeles, Cal.
1889	Braisted, William C	U. S. N.
1903	Brannan, John W	11 W. 12th, New York, N. Y.
1891	Brasseur, John B	Stephenson, Mich.

1901	Bray, Chas. W	Biwabik, Minn.
1894	*Braymer, O. W. (*1898)	Camden, N. J.
1884	Brekes, David	319 E. 51st, New York, N. Y.
1899	Brewster, Mary Jones	8 Bedford Terrace, Northampton, Mass.
1903	Bridge, Norman	217 S. Broadway, Los Angeles, Cal.
1886	*Briggs, Chas. E. (*1894)	St. Louis, Mo.
1897	Brinsmade, Wm. B	123 Joralemon, Brooklyn, N. Y.
1890	*Bristol, Bennet J. (*1903)	Webster Groves, Mo.
1897	Bristow, Algernon T	234 Clinton, Brooklyn, N. Y.
1894	Brock, Henry H	662 Congress, Portland, Me.
1889	Brockman, David C	Ottumwa, Ia.
1892	Brodie, Benjamin P	Detroit, Mich.
1883	Bronson, Edward B	123 W. 34th, New York, N. Y.
1901	Brower, Daniel R	34 Washington, Chicago, Ill.
1896	Brown, Adelaide	1212 Sutter, San Francisco, Cal.
1883	*Brown, Alfred (*1899)	Hellertown, Pa.
1896	Brown, Charlotte B	1212 Sutter, San Francisco, Cal.
1879	Brown, Francis H	Hotel Lyndeboro, Boston, Mass.
1894	Brown, Frank I	South Portland, Me.
1899	Brown, John E	239 E. Town, Columbus, O.
1890	*Browning, William W. (*1900)	Brooklyn, N. Y.
1877	*Bruce, George D. (*1891)	Pittsburg, Pa.
1901	Brunner, William E	514 New England Bldg., Cleveland, O.
1901	Bruyere, John	123 Perry, Trenton, N. J.
1881	*Buel, Henry W. (*1893)	Litchfield, Conn.
1898	Buel, John L	Litchfield, Conn.
1889	Buist, John R	151 N. Spruce, Nashville, Tenn.
1877	*Bulkley, Jonathan E	Wilkes-Barre, Pa.
1879	Bulkley, L. Duncan	531 Madison Ave., New York, N. Y.
1899	Bullard, Frank D	245 Bradbury Block, Los Angeles, Cal.
1886	*Bunting, Ross R. (*1900)	Philadelphia, Pa.
1888	*Burbank, Augustus H	Yarmouthville, Me.
1881	*Burchard, Thomas R	New York, N. Y.
1897	Burgin, Horman	63 W. Chelton Ave., Germantown, Pa.
1882	*Bush, Lewis P. (*1892)	Wilmington, Del.
1892	Butler, Glentworth R	229 Gates Ave., Brooklyn, N. Y.
1879	*Cabell, James L	Univ. of Va., Charlottesville, Va.
1882	Cadwalader, Charles E	240 S. 4th, Philadelphia, Pa.
1901	Cadwallader, Edith W	Woman's Hosp., N. Coll. Ave., Phila., Pa.
1901	Cahill, John T	344 Haverhill, Lawrence, Mass.
1882	Campbell, W. Francis	86 Green Ave., Brooklyn, N. Y.
1895	Capron, Franklin P	118 Angell, Providence, R. I.
1898	Carhart, Wm. M. d'A	252 Madison Ave., New York, N. Y.
1899	*Carpenter, Eugene C. (*1902)	Columbus, O.
1903	Carpenter, John S	Pottsville, Pa.
1879	*Carpenter, John T. (*1899)	Pottsville, Pa.

1894	Carpenter, W. T.	Iron Mountain, Mich.
1881	Carr, George W	27 Waterman, Providence, R. I.
1889	Carter, James M. G	236 County, Waukegan, Ill.
1888	*Cary, George (*1899)	Houlton, Me.
1892	Castle, Curtis H	Merced, Cal.
1882	Castle, Franklin D	418 So. Broad, Philadelphia, Pa.
1879	*Caswell, Edward T	Providence, R. I.
1892	Cato, Frank Lee	De Soto, Ga.
1890	Cattell, Henry W	3709 Spruce, Philadelphia, Pa.
1900	Chaddock, Charles D	3750 Lindell Boulevard, St. Louis, Mo.
1895	Chapin, Charles V	City Hall, Providence, R. I.
1896	*Chapman, Frank B. (*1897)	Middletown, Mass.
1892	Chapman, Norwood H	Monte Vista, Colo.
1898	Chase, John (*1901)	414 Kitteredge Bldg., Denver, Colo.
1890	*Cheeseman, Nathaniel S.	Scotia, N. Y.
1895	Chesebro, Edmund D.	Elmwood Ave. and Hawthorne, Providence, R. I.
1884	*Chestnut, John H. W. (*1900)	Philadelphia, Pa.
1878	Chrystie, Thomas M. L	1748 Broadway, New York, N. Y.
1903	Churchill, Donald	369 Broad St., Providence, R. I.
1878	Cisna, William R	Penna. Co., Chicago, Ill.
1897	Clark, Chas. F.	Brooklyn, N. Y.
1887	Clarke, Augustus P	825 Mass. Ave., Cambridge, Mass.
1879	Cleeman, Richard A	2135 Spruce, Philadelphia, Pa.
1898	Clough, Augustus A	1349 California, Denver, Colo.
1891	Cluness, William R	Stockton and Sutter, San Francisco, Cal.
1883	Clute, William T	520 Liberty, Schenectady, N. Y.
1890	Coan, Titus M	70 Fifth Ave., New York, N. Y.
1884	*Coblentz, Joseph, (*1899)	Vaughan, Wash.
1894	Cochrane, Jasper D	Saco, Me.
1888	*Cocks, David C., (*1890)	New York, N. Y.
1901	Coggeshall, Frederic	1077 Boylston Ave., Boston, Mass.
1897	Cogswell, Charles H	409 Marlboro, Boston, Mass.
1894	Cohen, Solomon S	1525 Walnut, Philadelphia, Pa.
1895	Collins, George L	223 Benefit, Providence, R. I.
1877	*Collins, James (*1895)	Philadelphia, Pa.
1896	Collins, Rufus G	5059 State, Chicago, Ill.
1899	Connell, Charles W	Fall River, Mass.
1886	Connell, J. G	3519 Fifth Ave., Pittsburg, Pa.
1880	Conner, Phineas S	159 W. 9th, Cincinnati, O.
1902	Connor, Guy L	91 Lafayette Ave., Detroit, Mich.
1878	Connor, Leartus	103 Cass, Detroit, Mich.
1885	Cook, Charles E	Mendota, Ill.
1877	*Cook, Joseph S. (*1903)	Washington, N. J.
1903	Cooke, Henry A	234 Benefit, Providence, R. I.
1889	Cooperrider, Charles A	370 S. 4th, Columbus, O.
1903	Cordeiro, F. J. B	U. S. N.

1898	Corson, Elton S	Toungoo, Burma.
1898	Corss, Frederic	Kingston, Pa.
1888	Cotton, David S	Portsmouth, O.
1897	Coverly, John H	191 Washington Park, Brooklyn, N. Y.
1882	Cowan, George	Danville, Kentucky.
1884	Cowles, Edward	McLean Hosp., Waverly, Mass.
1897	*Craig, Alexander R*	232 Cherry, Columbia, Pa.
1901	*Craig, John J*	Columbia, Pa.
1902	Craig, Joseph D	12 Ten Broeck, Albany, N. Y.
1883	*Crane, Charles H (*1883)	U. S. A.
1897	Criado, Louis F	430 W. 116th, New York, N. Y.
1890	Crile, George W	"The Osborn," Cleveland, Ohio.
1888	Crocker, Frank H	Machias, Me.
1903	Crooker, George H	159½ Benefit, Providence, R. I.
1892	Crossland, Jefferson C	Zanesville, O.
1888	Culbertson, Emma B	33 Newberry, Boston, Mass.
1897	Culbreth, David M. R	203 E. Preston, Baltimore, Md.
1899	Culver, Charles M	36 Eagle, Albany, N. Y.
1888	Cummings, Charles E	Seattle, Wash.
1888	Cummings, George H	699 Congress, Portland, Me.
1901	Curtin, Roland G	22 S. 18th, Philadelphia, Pa.
1902	Curtis, Frederic C	Albany, N. Y.
1886	Curtis, Lester	35 34th Pl., Chicago, Ill.
1877	*Curwen, John (*1901)	Harrisburg, Pa.
1888	Cutter, Charles K	178 School, Somerville, Mass.
1903	Cutts, William Bryant	509 Westminster, Providence, R. I.
1900	Daland, Judson	317 S. 18th, Philadelphia, Pa.
1881	Dana, Charles L	50 W. 46th, New York, N. Y.
1889	*Dana, William L (*1897)	Portland, Me.
1899	Dandridge, Nathaniel P	422 Broadway, Cincinnati, O.
1891	Darey, J. Herbert	Northwood, Iowa.
1898	Darnall, William E	1719 Pacific Ave., Atlantic City, N. J.
1879	Darrach, James	5021 Green, Germantown, Pa.
1889	*Davies, John E (*1900)	Madison, Wis.
1888	Davies, Oscar C. S	243 Water, Augusta, Me.
1897	Davis, Gwilym G	255 S. 16th, Philadelphia, Pa.
1895	Davis, John S	Charlottesville, Va.
1901	Davis, John S., Jr	Union Protestant Hospital, Baltimore, Md.
1885	Davis, Nathan S., Jr	65 Randolph, Chicago, Ill.
1886	Davis, Thomas D	261 Shady Ave., Pittsburg, Pa.
1895	Day, Frank L	240 Benefit, Providence, R. I.
1880	Deal, Lemuel J	2106 Hancock, Philadelphia, Pa.
1889	Dearborn, Alvah B	Somerville, Mass.
1889	Denison, Charles	823 14th, Denver, Colo.
1888	Dennett, Wm. S	8 E. 49th, New York, N. Y.
1897	Dennis, Frederic S	542 Madison Ave., New York, N. Y.

1892	De Spelder, Elias	Drenthe, Mich.
1882	Devendorf, C. A.	508 Woodward Ave., Detroit, Mich.
1889	Dewees, Wm. B	542 S. Santa Fe Ave., Salina, Kas.
1900	Dewey, Richard	Wauwatosa, Wis.
1903	De Wolf, Halsey	212 Benefit, Providence, R. I.
1900	Dickey, John L	Cor. 12th and Chapline, Wheeling, W. Va.
1879	*Dickson, J. N.	Pittsburg, Pa.
1897	Diefenderfer, Harold	6303 Monroe Ave., Chicago, Ill.
1897	Diehl, Alfred E	361 Pearl, Buffalo, N. Y.
1888	Diven, Samuel L.	95 N. Hanover, Carlisle, Pa.
1889	Doane, L. Leo	303 Chestnut, Meadville, Pa.
1900	Dock, Geo	14 Cornwell Place, Ann Arbor, Mich.
1896	Dodds, J. Chambers	Tolono, Ill.
1878	*Dodge, Daniel A	Brooklyn, N. Y.
1896	Dorland, W. A. Newman	128 S. 17th, Philadelphia, Pa.
1895	Doughty, Wm. H., Jr	822 Greene, Augusta, Ga.
1892	Dow, Frank F	68 Vick Park, Rochester, N. Y.
1897	Drown, Thos. M	South Bethlehem, Pa.
1879	Drysdale, Thos. M	1307 Locust, Philadelphia, Pa.
1883	*DuBois, Francis L (*1895)	U. S. N.
1881	Dudley, E. C.	1617 Indiana Ave., Chicago, Ill.
1886	Duff, John M	4502 5th Ave., Pittsburg, Pa.
1891	Dundor, Adam B	118 S. 4th, Reading, Pa.
1878	*Dunglison, Richard J. (*1901)	Philadelphia, Pa.
1898	Dunham, Edward K	338 E. 26th, New York, N. Y.
1899	Dunham, John D	228 E. Town, Columbus, O.
1890	*Dunlap, W. Herbert (*1895)	Syracuse, N. Y.
1883	*Dunster, E. S.	Ann Arbor, Mich.
1889	Dunton, Wm. R	5059 Germantown Ave., Philadelphia, Pa.
1894	Durand, Henry S	87 S. Fitzhugh, Rochester, N. Y.
1882	Dwight, Henry E	336 S. 15th, Philadelphia, Pa.
1878	*Dyer, Ezra	Newport, R. I.
1891	Edgar, J. Clifton	54 E. 34th, New York, N. Y.
1892	Edwards, Arthur A	2816 Indiana Ave., Chicago, Ill.
1897	Einhorn, Max	20 E. 63rd, New York, N. Y.
1898	Elliot, George T	36 E. 35th, New York, N. Y.
1897	Ellis, H. Bert	243 Bradbury Block, Los Angeles, Cal.
1885	Elmer, Henry W	65 W. Commerce, Bridgeton, N. J.
1888	Elmer, Matthew W	Bridgeton, N. J.
1880	*Elmer, William	Bridgeton, N. J.
1880	Elmer, Wm., Jr	44 W. State, Trenton, N. J.
1900	Elmere, J. A	Jefferson Med. Coll., Philadelphia, Pa.
1879	*Elsberg, Louis (*1885)	New York, N. Y.
1902	Elting, Arthur W	247 State, Albany, N. Y.
1880	Ely, James W. C.	61 Waterman, Providence, R. I.
1897	Ely, Thomas C	2041 Green, Philadelphia, Pa.

1883	Emerson, Justin E	128 Henry, Detroit, Mich.
1890	Emerson, Nathaniel B	Honolulu, Hawaiian Islands.
1879	*Engel, Hugo (*1897)	Philadelphia, Pa.
1892	*Engleman, Geo. J (*1903)	Boston, Mass.
1898	Englemann, Rosa	51st and Lake Ave., Chicago, Ill.
1892	Erwin, R. W	Bay City, Mich.
1897	Eshner, Augustus A	224 S. 16th, Philadelphia, Pa.
1898	Esterly, Daniel E	723 Kansas Ave., Topeka, Kan.
1892	Estes, W. L	South Bethlehem, Pa.
1877	Evans, Horace Y	N. E. Cor. 17th and Green, Philadelphia, Pa.
1888	*Eveleth, John M (*1894)	Hallowel, Me.
1900	Everitt, Ella B	1807 Spruce, Philadelphia, Pa.
1889	*Ewers, Henry F (*1899)	Burlington, Ia.
1889	Ewing, Arthur E	2670 Washington Ave., St. Louis, Mo.
1892	Ewing, W. Brown	Wernersville, Pa.
1888	Fairbairn, Henry A	213 McDonnough, Brooklyn, N. Y.
1881	*Farnham, Horace P	New York, N. Y.
1883	Farnsworth, Philo J	Clinton, Iowa
1893	Favill, Henry B	100 State, Chicago, Ill.
1879	*Fegley, Orlando (*1900)	Allentown, Pa.
1892	Felch, Theodore A	304 W. Euclid, Ishpeming, Mich.
1891	Felter, Mahlon	1626 5th Ave., Troy, N. Y.
1891	*Fenger, Christian (*1902)	Chicago, Ill.
1878	Fisher, Frank	1832 Arch, Philadelphia, Pa.
1878	*Fisher, George J (*1893)	Sing Sing, N. Y.
1889	Fisk, Samuel A	37 18th Ave., Denver, Colo.
1889	Fiske, George F	438 La Salle Ave., Chicago, Ill.
1890	Fitz, Edward S	328 S. Rose, Kalamazoo, Mich.
1892	Fleming, George W	Shelbyville, Ind.
1889	*Flint, Kendall (*1892)	Haverhill, Mass.
1890	Flintermann, Johann	Woodward Ave., Detroit, Mich.
1888	Flood, Everett	Palmer, Mass.
1897	Fly, Edward M	National City, Cal.
1890	Flynn, William	Marion, Ind.
1893	Focht, William H	64½ E. Perry, Tiffin, O.
1896	Ford, De Saussure	Augusta, Ga.
1878	*Ford, William H (*1897)	Philadelphia, Pa.
1901	Ford, William W	1616 W. Calvert St., Baltimore, Md.
1892	Fordyce, John A	66 Park Ave., New York, N. Y.
1897	Forwood, William H	U. S. A. (retired)
1899	Foshay, P. Maxwell	89 Euclid Ave., Cleveland, O.
1890	Foskett, George M	235 Pleasant, Worcester, Mass.
1888	Foster, Addison H	779 W. Monroe, Chicago, Ill.
1888	Foster, Charles W	Woodfords, Me.
1897	Foster, William S	252 Shady Ave., Pittsburg, Pa.

1877	*Foulke, Lewis W (*1887)	Chillicothe, O.
1882	*Foulkes, James F.	Oakland, Cal.
1878	Fox, George H.	18 E. 31st, New York, N. Y.
1877	*Franklin, Gustavus S (*1901)	Chillicothe, O.
1884	Free, Spencer M.	DuBois, Pa.
1897	Freeman, Leonard	California Bldg., Denver, Colo.
1882	*French, George F (*1897)	Minneapolis, Minn.
1893	French, Samuel W.	1216 Grand Ave., Milwaukee, Wis.
1889	*French, William F (*1898)	Noroton, Conn.
1898	Fretz, John Edgar	112 N. 3rd, Easton, Pa.
1901	Friedenwald, Julius	7 W. Franklin, Baltimore, Md.
1901	Friedlander, Alfred	22 W. 7th, Cincinnati, O.
1882	*Frost, Carlton P (*1896)	Hanover, N. H.
1878	*Friutnight, J. Henry (*1900)	New York, N. Y.
1888	Fry, Frank R.	2610 Locust, St. Louis, Mo.
1888	Fuller, Charles	Lincoln, Me.
1897	Fuller, Geo. E.	Monson, Mass.
1903	Fulton, Frank T.	169 Angell, Providence, R. I.
1888	*Furbeck, Peter R (*1902)	Gloversville, N. Y.
1882	Garçelon, Alonzo	Lewiston, Me.
1890	Gardiner, Edwin J.	170 State, Chicago, Ill.
1892	*Gaston, J. McFadden (*1903)	Atlanta, Ga.
1898	*Gaylord, John F (*1903)	Plymouth, Mass.
1882	*Gerhard, Abraham S (*1891)	Philadelphia, Pa.
1878	Gerhard, Jerome Z.	27 S. 3rd, Harrisburg, Pa.
1883	Gerrish, Frederic H.	675 Congress, Portland, Me.
1892	Gerster, Arpad G.	34 E. 75th, New York, N. Y.
1888	Gibson, Arthur C.	111 State, Bangor, Me.
1887	*Gibson, Wm. J (*1893)	Philadelphia, Pa.
1883	*Gihon, Albert L (*1901)	U. S. N.
1897	Gilchrist, T. Caspar	317 N. Charles, Baltimore, Md.
1888	*Given, Obadiah G.	Carlisle, Pa.
1890	Gleason, E. Baldwin	1204 Walnut, Philadelphia, Pa.
1897	Goldspohn, Albert	519 Cleveland Ave., Chicago, Ill.
1888	Goodale, Geo. L.	Cambridge, Mass.
1901	Goodale, Joseph L.	397 Beacon, Boston, Mass.
1890	Goodale, Walter T.	Saco, Me.
1898	Goodwin, Ralph S.	Thomaston, Conn.
1890	Gorgas, Ferdinand I. S.	845 N. Eutaw, Baltimore, Md.
1892	Gould, George M.	1631 Locust, Philadelphia, Pa.
1878	*Govan, Wm. (*1894)	Stony Point, N. Y.
1889	Graham, David W.	672 W. Monroe, Chicago, Ill.
1884	*Graham, F. Ridgely (*1895)	Chester, Pa.
1892	Grant, H. Horace	1916 Market, Louisville, Ky.
1903	Gray, A. W.	174 Wisconsin, Milwaukee, Wis.

1902	Grayson, Thos. W	Westinghouse Building, Pittsburg, Pa.
1902	Greeley, Jane L	Jamestown, N. Y.
1889	Green, Edgar M	340 Spring Garden, Easton, Pa.
1884	*Green, Jas. S (*1892)	Elizabeth, N. Y.
1883	Green, John	2670 Washington Ave., St. Louis, Mo.
1891	*Green, John Traill (*1892)	Tucson, Ariz.
1876	*Green, Traill (*1897)	Easton, Pa.
1893	Gregory, Louis L	514 Evanston Ave., Chicago, Ill.
1902	Gribbin, H. E.	Augusta, Me.
1888	Grim, H. A	Allentown, Pa.
1892	Groff, Geo. G	Lewisburg, Pa.
1892	Grosvenor, J. W	118 Plymouth Ave., Buffalo, N. Y.
1890	*Gumbes, Chas. W (*1903)	Oaks, Pa.
1889	Guthrie, J. Renwick	Dubuque, Ia.
1884	Hadden, Alexander	155 E. 51st, New York, N. Y.
1892	Hahn, Henry H	Youngstown, O.
1891	Halberstadt, Andrew H	Pottsville, Pa.
1888	Hale, George W	235½ N. Summer, Nashville, Tenn.
1894	Hall, J. N	308 Jackson Bldg., Denver, Colo.
1896	Hall, Winfield S	2431 Dearborn, Chicago, Ill.
1882	Halsey, Calvin C	Montrose, Pa.
1880	Ham, Albert E	199 Benefit, Providence, R. I.
1901	Hamburger, Louis P	1412 Eutaw Place, Baltimore, Md.
1899	Hamilton, Charles S	1 N. 4th, Columbus, O.
1877	*Hamilton, Frank H (*1886)	New York, N. Y.
1899	Hamilton, William D	1 N. 4th, Columbus, O.
1894	Hammond, William P	47 Monument Sq., Charlestown, Mass.
1892	Hanna, W. M	Henderson, Ky.
1885	Hansell, Howard F	1528 Walnut, Philadelphia, Pa.
1897	Hardie, Thomas M	34 Washington, Chicago, Ill.
1891	Hare, George A	Fresno, Cal.
1882	Harlan, George C	1515 Walnut, Philadelphia, Pa.
1899	Harlow, George A	New Insurance Bldg., Milwaukee, Wis.
1880	*Harlow, Lewis D (*1895)	Philadelphia, Pa.
1882	Harper, Thomas S	Hotel Windsor, Philadelphia, Pa.
1897	Harriman, Wilbert E	Ames, Ia.
1879	*Harris, Elisha (*1884)	New York, N. Y.
1891	*Harris, William H (*1893)	Louisville, Ky.
1889	Harrison, Wallace K	52 Walton Place, Chicago, Ill.
1889	Harsha, Wm. M	58 State, Chicago, Ill.
1880	*Hartley, Theophilus S	Ridgeway, Pa.
1902	Harvey, E. B	Westborough, Mass.
1878	Harvey, Olin F	Wilkes-Barre, Pa.
1884	Hatfield, Marcus P	70 State, Chicago, Ill.
1878	*Hatfield, Nathan	Philadelphia, Pa.

1890	Haven, Alfred C	Lake Forest, Ill.
1898	Haven, Foster S	143 W. 61st, New York, N. Y.
1898	Hawkes, Forbes	42 E. 26th, New York, N. Y.
1890	Hawkes, Wm. H	1317 Columbia Road, Washington, D. C.
1898	Hawkins, Thos. H	1740 Welton, Denver, Colo.
1900	Hawley, D. C	204 Pearl, Burlington, Vt.
1897	Hay, Eugene C	Hot Springs, Ark.
1898	Hayes, Wm. Van V	10 E. 43rd, New York, N. Y.
1901	Head, Geo. D	300 Walnut, S. E., Minneapolis, Minn.
1893	Head, Louis R	Madison, Wis.
1888	Heath, Frederic C	19 W. Ohio, Indianapolis, Ind.
1902	Heckel, Edward B	524 Penn Bldg., Pittsburg, Pa.
1889	Heffron, John L	528 S. Salina, Syracuse, N. Y.
1900	Heidingsfeld, M. L	22 W. 7th, Cincinnati, O.
1888	*Helm, Wm. H (*1898)	Sing Sing, N. Y.
1889	Hemenway, Henry B	Evanston, Ill.
1888	Herbst, Henry H	28 N. 5th, Allentown, Pa.
1890	Herdman, William J	328 E. Huron, Ann Arbor, Mich.
1889	Herrick, Fréd. S	Brooklin, Me.
1889	*Herrick, Henry J (*1901)	Cleveland, O.
1880	Hersey, George D	148 Broad, Providence, R. I.
1898	Hershey, Edgar P	408 California Bldg., Denver, Colo.
1899	Hertzler, Arthur E	Halstead, Kas.
1878	Hess, Robert J	610 Fairmount Ave., Philadelphia, Pa.
1898	Hessler, Robert	Logansport, Ind.
1901	Hildreth, John L	14 Garden, Cambridge, Mass.
1888	Hill, Gershom H	Equitable Bldg., Des Moines, Ia.
1888	Hill, Horace B	Augusta, Me.
1897	*Hill, Horace G (*1901)	Philadelphia, Pa.
1896	Hinsdale, Guy	Hot Springs, Va.
1888	*Hitchcock, Alfred (*1900)	Farmington, Me.
1888	Hitchcock, Charles W	29 Henry, Detroit, Mich.
1888	Hitchcock, Edward, Jr	Ithaca, N. Y.
1888	*Hitchcock, Francis E (*1896)	Rockland, Me.
1881	*Hodgdon, Richard L (*1893)	Arlington, Mass.
1878	*Hodge, H. Lenox (1881)	Philadelphia, Pa.
1898	Hoff, John Van R	U. S. A.
1884	Holland, James W	2006 Chestnut, Philadelphia, Pa.
1897	Hollopeter, William C	1428 N. Broad, Philadelphia, Pa.
1897	Holmes, A. Mansfield	205 Jackson Block, Denver, Colo.
1893	Holmes, Bayard	104 E. 40th, Chicago, Ill.
1882	*Holmes, Edward L (*1900)	Chicago, Ill.
1902	Holton, Henry D	Brattleboro, Vt.
1903	Hoover, P. D	Waynesboro, Pa.
1882	Hopkins, George G	350 Washington Ave., Brooklyn, N. Y.

1888	Hough, Garry de N	542 County, New Bedford, Mass.
1891	House, Charles F	Painesville, O.
1903	Hoye, H. J	194 Broad, Providence, R. I.
1882	*How, Lyman B (*1893)	Manchester, N. H.
1890	Hubbard, William N	17 E. 38th, New York, N. Y.
1889	Hubbell, Charles L	Williamstown, Mass.
1885	Huger, William H	Charlestown, S. C.
1902	Huggins, Walter L	104 Jay, Schenectady, N. Y.
1901	Humer, Guy L	Johns Hopkins Hosp., Baltimore, Md.
1888	Hunt, Charles O	Portland, Me.
1888	*Hunt, Henry H (*1894)	Portland, Me.
1889	Hunter, Charles H	12 Syndicate Block, Minneapolis, Minn.
1890	Hurd, Arthur W	Buffalo, N. Y.
1889	Hurd, Henry M	Johns Hopkins Hospital, Baltimore, Md.
1878	Hutchins, Alexander	796 DeKalb Ave., Brooklyn, N. Y.
1890	Hutchinson, Woods	310, "The Failing," Portland, Ore.
1884	Hyde, James W	100 State, Chicago, Ill.
1890	Irish, John C	219 Central, Lowell, Mass.
1879	*Irwin, Crawford (*1900)	Hollidaysburg, Pa.
1888	Isham, Geo. S	64 Bellevue Pl., Chicago, Ill.
1889	*Jackson, A. Reeves (*1892)	Chicago, Ill.
1882	Jackson, Edward	McPhee Bldg., Denver, Colo.
1900	Jackson, John H	Fall River, Mass.
1889	Jacobs, Luther D	Emporia, Kas.
1884	*Jaggard, Wm. W (*1896)	Chicago, Ill.
1892	Jenkins, Wilbur O	14 S. 7th, Terre Haute, Ind.
1886	Jennings, Samuel D	Sewickley, Pa.
1878	Jewett, Chas	330 Clinton Ave., Brooklyn, N. Y.
1894	Jewett, Chas. S	892 Main, Buffalo, N. Y.
1888	Johnson, Anna H	Redlands, Cal.
1898	Johnson, Frank M	117 Beacon, Boston, Mass.
1884	Johnson, Frank S	2521 Prairie Ave., Chicago, Ill.
1897	Johnson, Geo. W	733 Grace, Chicago, Ill.
1884	*Johnson, Hosmer A	Chicago, Ill.
1892	Johnson, John G	493 Woodward Ave., Detroit, Mich.
1882	Johnson, Joseph Tabor	1728 K, N. W., Washington, D. C.
1888	Johnson, Russell H	Summit, Chestnut Hill, Philadelphia, Pa.
1897	Johnson, Woodbridge O	Fu San, Korea.
1895	*Johnston, R. Erskine (*1901)	Danville, Pa.
1889	Johnstone, A. W	Danville, Ky.
1889	Jones, C. George	Jacksonville, Ill.
1899	Jones, Harry H	626 E. Market, York, Pa.
1899	Jones, Howard	Circleville, O.
1880	‡Jones, H. Webster	
1880	*Jones, Samuel J (*1901)	Chicago, Ill.

1897	*Jordan, James R (*1898)	Montgomery, Ala.
1889	Joy, Henry L	Marshall, Mich.
1900	Joy, J. Addison	Atlantic City, N. J.
1878	Judson, Adouiram B	1 Madison Ave., New York, N. Y.
1886	Kearns, W. D	1734 Penn Ave., Pittsburg, Pa.
1879	*Kedzie, Robert C (*1902)	Agricultural College, Mich.
1899	Keen, Wm. W	1729 Chestnut, Philadelphia, Pa.
1895	Keene, Geo. F	Cranston, Howard P. O., R. I.
1891	*Keeney, James F (*1894)	U. S. N.
1892	Kelley, Richmond	First and Jefferson, Portland, Ore.
1894	Kellogg, E. Wells	420 Mitchell, Milwaukee, Wis.
1900	Kelly, A. O. J	1911 Pine, Philadelphia, Pa.
1883	Kemper, Andrew C	303 Broadway, Cincinnati, O.
1889	Kennedy, Josiah F	State House, Des Moines, Ia.
1884	*Kerr, James W	York, Pa.
1889	Kessel, George	Cresco, Ia.
1876	*Keyser, Peter D (*1897)	Philadelphia, Pa.
1898	Kickland, William A	Fort Collins, Colo.
1889	Kidder, F. Thomas	Woodstock, Vt.
1893	Kiefer, Guy L	497 St. Antoine, Detroit, Mich.
1890	Kiefer, Hermann	89 E. Forest Ave., Detroit, Mich.
1877	*Kieffer, Stephen B	Carlisle, Pa.
1889	*Kimball, Arthur H	Battle Creek, Mich.
1888	Kinch, Charles A	285 W. 70th, New York, N. Y.
1889	King, Alfred	610 Congress, Portland, Me.
1899	King, William H	412 S. 15th, Philadelphia, Pa.
1899	Kinsman, David N	255 E. Long, Columbus, O.
1886	Kline, W. J. K	Greensburg, Pa.
1892	Knapp, Charles P	Wyoming, Pa.
1898	Knight, C. A	Peekskill, N. Y.
1889	Knight, Charles H	147 W. 57th, New York, N. Y.
1897	Knopf, S. A	16 W. 95th, New York, N. Y.
1888	*Knox, James S (*1892)	Chicago, Ill.
1893	Knox, Samuel B. P	912 Anacapa, Santa Barbara, Cal.
1884	*Kollock, Cornelius (*1897)	Cheraw, S. C.
1889	Kreider, George N	522 Capitol Ave., Springfield, Ill.
1897	Kunkel, George B	Harrisburg, Pa.
1903	Kunkel, Henry	Kingston, Pa.
1899	Kyle, D. Braden	1517 Walnut, Philadelphia, Pa.
1889	Kynett, Harold H	1728 Spring Garden, Philadelphia, Pa.
1896	*Lackersteen, Mark H (*1897)	Chicago, Ill.
1898	LaForce, Wm. B	Ottumwa, Ia.
1882	*Landis, Henry G	Columbus, O.
1889	Landon, Henry B	6 Fay Block, Bay City, Mich.
1892	Lansing, James B. W	Tenafly, N. J.

1890	Laplace, Ernest	1828 S. Rittenhouse Sq., Philadelphia, Pa.
1876	*Larison, Geo. H (*1892)	Lambertville, N. J.
1891	*Lash, Josiah W (*1902)	Chillicothe, O.
1879	Lathrop, Horace	Cooperstown, N. Y.
1897	Lathrop, Ruth Webster	Care Woman's Med. Coll., Phila., Pa.
1901	Leach, Sydney	Tuscaloosa, Ala.
1879	Leaman, Henry	832 N. Broad, Philadelphia, Pa.
1888	Learned, Wm. T.	422 Franklin, Fall River, Mass.
1877	Lee, Benjamin	1420 Chestnut, Philadelphia, Pa.
1880	*Lee, Chas. C (*1893)	New York, N. Y.
1890	Lee, Elmer	127 W. 58th, New York, N. Y.
1901	Le Levre, Egbert	52 W. 56th, New York, N. Y.
1894	Leffmann, Henry	119 S. 4th, Philadelphia, Pa.
1901	Leighton, Charles M	365 Congress, Portland, Me.
1894	Leland, George A	669 Boylston, Boston, Mass.
1879	*Lente, Frederick D	New York, N. Y.
1903	Leopold, Isaac	1518 N. Franklin, Phila., Pa.
1888	Lester, John C	119 Schermerhorn, Brooklyn, N. Y.
1884	*Levis, Richard J (*1890)	Philadelphia, Pa.
1893	Lewis, A. B.	Hamilton, Kas.
1889	Lewis, Charles H	301 First, Jackson, Mich.
1890	Lewis, Daniel	252 Madison Ave., New York, N. Y.
1887	Lewis, Edwin R	Washington, D. C.
1897	Lewis, Henry F	4426 Lake Ave., Chicago, Ill.
1891	Lewis, James R	Grinnell, Ia.
1897	Lichty, John A	4634 5th Ave., Pittsburg, Pa.
1901	‡Light, Gertrude U	
1902	Lincoln, James O	Bath, Me.
1881	*Lincoln, Nathan S (*1898)	Washington, D. C.
1883	*Lincoln, Rufus P (*1900)	22 W. 31st, New York, N. Y.
1877	*Lindsley, J. Berrien (*1897)	Nashville, Tenn.
1890	Lippincott, J. Aubrey	435 Penn Ave., Pittsburg, Pa.
1882	*Little, William S	Philadelphia, Pa.
1902	Littig, Lawrence W	Iowa City, Ia.
1893	Littlefield, George H	361 Neponset Ave., Boston, Mass.
1902	Lobinger, A. Stewart	Los Angeles, Cal.
1897	Loeb, Hanau W	3559 Olive, St. Louis, Mo.
1885	Logan, Henry V	306 N. Washington Ave., Scranton, Pa.
1893	Longsdorf, Harold H	Dickinson, Pa.
1897	Lott, William C	4001 Walnut, Philadelphia, Pa.
1878	*Love, John J. H (*1897)	Montclair, N. J.
1896	*Ludlow, Edmund (*1903)	Paxton, Ill.
1902	Lybolt, Archibald	280 W. 127th, New York, N. Y.
1881	Lyman, Henry M	70 State, Chicago, Ill.
1879	Lyons, Frederick A	50 E. 63rd, New York, N. Y.
1884	McArdle, Thomas E	707 12th, N. W., Washington, D. C.

1901	McBride, James H	Pasadena, Cal.
1881	*McBride, Thomas A	New York, N. Y.
1889	McCaskey, George W	107 W. Main, Fort Wayne, Ind.
1897	McClintock, Charles T	270 Woodward Ave., Detroit, Mich.
1888	McCollister, Elisha A	Lewiston, Me.
1894	McCulloch, C. Carter	U. S. A.
1892	McCulloch, J. T	Freeport, Pa.
1898	McDonnell, Ralph A	1142 Chapel, New Haven, Conn.
1901	McDonough, Edward J	624 Congress, Portland, Me.
1901	McGaughey, Hugh F	216 Centre, Winona, Minn.
1877	McIntire, Charles	52 N. 4th, Easton, Pa.
1888	McKennan, T. M. T	810 Penn Ave., Pittsburg, Pa.
1878	McKenzie, William	Conshohocken, Pa.
1884	McMurtry, Louis S	Louisville, Ky.
1893	McNutt, H. E	Aberdeen, S. D.
1892	McWilliams, Samuel A	3456 Michigan Ave., Chicago, Ill.
1889	*MacDonnell, R. Lea (*1891)	Montreal, Canada.
1901	*Machan, George Stover (*1901)	Providence, R. I.
1890	MacLaren, Archibald	350 St. Peter, St. Paul, Minn.
1898	MacLaren, William S	Litchfield, Conn.
1900	Magill, William S	355 W. 145th, New York, N. Y.
1887	Magruder, George L	815 Vermont Ave., N. W., Washington, D. C.
1889	Major, George W	"Mozufferpore", East Liss, Hants, England.
1897	Makuen, G. Hudson	252 S. 16th, Philadelphia, Pa.
1887	Manges, Morris	941 Madison Ave., New York, N. Y.
1889	Marble, John O	55 Pearl, Worcester, Mass.
1897	Marchand, Jacob F	133 N. Cleveland Ave., Canton, O.
1879	Marcy, Henry O	180 Commonwealth Ave., Boston, Mass.
1900	Marcy, H. O., Jr	180 Commonwealth Ave., Boston, Mass.
1889	Marshall, Cuvier R	2243 N. 17th, Philadelphia, Pa.
1889	Marshall, George M	1819 Spruce, Philadelphia, Pa.
1885	Marshall, George W	Milford, Del.
1899	Marshall, John S	Presidio, San Francisco, Cal.
1895	Martin, Francis C	Roxbury Station, Boston, Mass.
1891	Martin, James N	Ann Arbor, Mich.
1885	Maryott, E. Edgar	92 Main, Springfield, Mass.
1891	Mason, Jarvis K	Suffield, Conn.
1888	Mason, Wm. C	Bangor, Me.
1895	Massie, Joseph P	17 E. Grace, Richmond, Va.
1889	‡Matthews, F. M	
1897	Matthews, George S	419 Cranston, Providence, R. I.
1879	Matthewson, Arthur	139 Montague, Brooklyn, N. Y.
1890	Matzinger, Herman G	Buffalo, N. Y.
1890	Maurer, J. M	502 E. Sunbury, Shamokin, Pa.
1897	May, Chas. H	698 Madison Ave., New York, N. Y.

1890	Mayberry, Chas. B	Retreat, Pa.
1899	Medbery, Josiah	31 E. Chestnut, Columbus, O.
1877	Meisenhelder, Edmund W	320 W. Market, York, Pa.
1889	Merriman, Henry P	2239 Michigan Ave., Chicago, Ill.
1889	Merritt, Emma S	2323 Washington, San Francisco, Cal.
1892	Merz, Chas. H	Sandusky, O.
1898	Metcalf, Henry S	Mt. Carroll, Ill.
1891	Mettler, L. Harrison	4228 Greenwood Ave., Chicago, Ill.
1892	*Meyer, J. M (*1901)	Danville, Ky.
1890	Mial, Leonidas L	145 W. 12th, New York, N. Y.
1903	Milan, Michael B	26 Bainbridge, Providence, R. I.
1883	Miles, Geo. W	Oneida, N. Y.
1889	*Millard, Henry B (*1893)	New York, N. Y.
1881	Miller, Horace G	262 Benefit, Providence, R. I.
1897	Miller, Walter McN	Columbia, Mo.
1889	Mills, Hiram R	Port Huron, Mich.
1884	*Miner, Joshua L (*1889)	Wilkes-Barre, Pa.
1885	Mitchell, Alfred	Brunswick, Me.
1879	*Mitchell, Chauncey L	Brooklyn, N. Y.
1892	Mitchell, Giles S	277 W. 8th, Cincinnati, O.
1892	Mitchell, Matthew R	605 Kansas Ave., Topeka, Kas.
1903	Mix, Charles L	3134 S. Park Ave., Chicago, Ill.
1897	Montgomery, Edward E	1703 Walnut, Philadelphia, Pa.
1899	Moore, Dickson L	141 E. State, Columbus, O.
1901	Moore, Hugh M	Oxford, O.
1882	*Moore, J. Fred (*1893)	Brooklyn, N. Y.
1878	Moore, James W	Easton, Pa.
1890	Moore, John H	Bridgeton, N. J.
1884	Morehouse, Geo. R	2033 Walnut, Philadelphia, Pa.
1889	Morris, Elliston J	128 S. 18th, Philadelphia, Pa.
1880	Morris, J. Cheston	1514 Spruce, Philadelphia, Pa.
1899	Morris, J. W	142 Forest Ave., Jamestown, N. Y.
1883	Morrow, Prince A	66 W. 40th, New York, N. Y.
1884	*Morton, Douglas (*1892)	Louisville, Ky.
1880	*Morton, Lloyd	Pawtucket, R. I.
1881	Morton, Wm. J	36 W. 56th, New York, N. Y.
1889	Moses, Thos. F	Waltham, Mass.
1901	Mott, John S	522 Rialto Bldg., Kansas City, Mo.
1897	Moulton, A. R	49th and Market, Philadelphia, Pa.
1894	Moulton, Charles F	W. Roxbury, Mass.
1882	*Muhlenberg, Francis (*1894)	Lancaster, Pa.
1882	Muhlenberg, Wm. F	Reading, Pa.
1882	*Mulford, Isaac B	Camden, N. J.
1889	*Mulhall, Joseph C (*1900)	St. Louis, Mo.
1902	Munson, George S	30 Eagle, Albany, N. Y.

1900	Murray, W. R.	409 Dayton Bldg., Minneapolis, Minn.
1890	Musser, Charles S.	Aaronsburg, Pa.
1902	Mynderse, Herman V.	Schenectady, N. Y.
1897	Nancrede, Charles B.	910 Cornwell Place, Ann Arbor, Mich.
1888	Needham, George G.	218 E. 19th, New York, N. Y.
1903	Neff, Wallace	1337 K, N. W., Washington, D. C.
1882	Nelson, Daniel T.	2400 Indiana Ave., Chicago, Ill.
1889	Nelson, Edwin M.	965 Hamilton Ave., St. Louis, Mo.
1884	*Nelson, Samuel N (*1893)	Revere, Mass.
1898	Newcomb, James E.	118 W. 69th, New York, N. Y.
1879	*Newcomet, Henry W.	Philadelphia, Pa.
1900	Newhart, Horace	837 Andrus Bldg., Minneapolis, Minn.
1897	Newman, Henry P.	438 La Salle Ave., Chicago, Ill.
1895	Newton, Edwin D.	Athens, Ga.
1889	*Nichol, Wm. L (*1901)	Nashville, Tenn.
1895	Niesley, Chas. M.	Manhasset, N. Y.
1900	Nisbet, J. Douglas	10 E. 43rd, New York, N. Y.
1890	Noble, Henry S.	Middletown, Conn.
1901	Noble, Mary R.	118 E. Monument, Colorado Springs, Col.
1888	O'Brion, Chas. C	Groveton, N. H.
1888	O'Donovan, Chas., Jr.	311 W. Monument, Baltimore, Md.
1880	*O'Leary, Chas. (*1897)	Providence, R. I.
1894	O'Neill, James B.	519 Congress, Portland, Me.
1885	Oakes, Wallace K.	60 High, Auburn, Me.
1903	Ogle, W. M.	Primero, Colo.
1898	Olds, Frank W.	Williamstown, Mass.
1894	Oliver, C. A.	1507 Locust, Philadelphia, Pa.
1898	Osborn, Geo. W.	339 Broad, Bridgeport, Conn.
1885	*Osgood, Wm. (*1894)	North Yarmouth, Me.
1884	Otis, Edward O.	308 Commonwealth Ave., Boston, Mass.
1878	Ott, Isaac	Easton, Pa.
1889	Overfield, Adam	Houghton, Mich.
1885	Packard, Chas. A.	Bath, Me.
1888	Packard, Frederick A.	258 S. 18th, Philadelphia, Pa.
1889	Packard, John H.	1924 Spruce, Philadelphia, Pa.
1889	*Page, H. R.	Des Moines, Ia.
1897	Paine, Arthur R.	211 Lafayette Ave., Brooklyn, N. Y.
1879	*Pancoast, Wm. H (*1897)	Philadelphia, Pa.
1888	Park, John G.	Lunatic Hospital, Worcester, Mass.
1897	Parker, Wallace A.	Springfield, Mass.
1898	Partree, Homer T.	Blandford, Mass.
1880	*Parvin, Theophilus (*1898)	Philadelphia, Pa.
1889	Patterson, E. Blanchard	Manistique, Mich.
1903	Patterson, Stuart	5541 Ellsworth Ave., Pittsburg, Pa.
1883	Patzki, Julius H.	U. S. A. (Retired).

1899	Pease, Edward Allen	483 Beacon, Boston, Mass.
1891	Peck, Geo.	926 N. Broad, Elizabeth, N. J.
1898	Peck, Geo. B.	865 N. Main, Providence, R. I.
1895	Peckham, Frank E.	53 Governor, Providence, R. I.
1898	Pegram, John C., Jr	234 Benefit, Providence, R. I.
1901	Penrose, Clement A.	21 W. Mt. Royal Ave., Baltimore, Md.
1889	Penrose, Chas. B.	1720 Spruce, Philadelphia, Pa.
1882	*Pepper, Wm. (*1898)	Philadelphia, Pa.
1880	Perkins, Francis M.	1428 Pine, Philadelphia, Pa.
1882	Perry, Chas. R.	900 Main, Worcester, Mass.
1891	Peterson, Reuben	4621 Woodland Ave., Chicago, Ill.
1892	Phillips, Ellis	347 E. Long, Columbus, O.
1892	Phillips, G. W.	Vinal Haven, Me.
1897	*Phillips, Thos. H (*1902)	Canton, O.
1891	Phillips, W. W. L.	52 W. State, Trenton, N. J.
1882	Pickett, Thos. E.	Maysville, Ky.
1895	Pilcher, Jas. E.	Carlisle, Pa.
1879	Pilcher, Lewis S.	145 Gates Ave., Brooklyn, N. Y.
1879	*Pinkney, Howard (*1888)	New York, N. Y.
1898	Platt, Walter B.	802 Cathedral, Baltimore, Md.
1897	Plummer, Chas. G.	Mercantile Block, Salt Lake City, Utah.
1892	Pontius, Paul J	1629 Chestnut, Philadelphia, Pa.
1882	Porter, Geo. L.	266 State, Bridgeport, Conn.
1880	Porter, Geo. W.	8 Greene, Providence, R. I.
1885	Post, M. Hayward	2641 Washington Ave., St. Louis, Mo.
1897	Post, Silas Benham	222 N. Cleveland Ave., Canton, O.
1900	Powell, W. M.	31 S. Indiana Ave., Atlantic City, N. J.
1888	*Pratt, H. D. V., Jr. (*1899)	Elmira, N. Y.
1888	Presbrey, Silas D.	103 Weir, Taunton, Mass.
1903	Price, Henry R.	163 Hancock, Brooklyn, N. Y.
1890	Prince, Arthur E.	Springfield, Ill.
1897	Probasco, J. B.	175 E. Front, Plainfield, N. J.
1894	Pudor, Gustav A.	Portland, Me.
1893	Puls, Arthur J.	116 Mason, Milwaukee, Wis.
1898	Pulsford, Henry A.	South Orange, N. J.
1895	Pusey, Wm. A.	103 State, Chicago, Ill.
1894	Putnam, Harry L.	Houlton, Me.
1892	Putnam, Helen C.	127 Angell, Providence, R. I.
1895	Pyle, Walter L.	1806 Chestnut, Philadelphia, Pa.
1888	Rae, Alexander	20 Clinton, Brooklyn, N. Y
1889	Ranney, Ambrose L.	156 Madison Ave., New York, N. Y.
1897	Ravogli, Augustus	5 Garfield Place, Cincinnati, O.
1877	*Rea, James C.	Pittsburg, Pa.
1884	*Read, Ira B.	New York, N. Y.
1889	Reddy, Herbert L.	61 Beaver Hall Hill, Montreal, Canada.

1882	*Reed, Joseph A		Dixmont, Pa.
1897	Reed, Robert J		Wheeling, W. Va.
1882	*Reed, Thos. B		Philadelphia, Pa.
1900	Reed, W. Boardman	1833 Chestnut,	Philadelphia, Pa.
1888	Reed, William G		Sturbridge, Mass.
1889	Reeve, Richard A	22 Shuter,	Toronto, Canada.
1900	Reiley, E. A		Atlantic City, N. J.
1879	*Reiley, George W (*1892)		Harrisburg, Pa.
1888	*Rex, George A (*1895)		Philadelphia, Pa.
1888	Rice, W. E		Bath, Me.
1888	*Rich, Joshua B (*1896)		Worcester, Mass.
1896	Richardson, Maurice H	224 Beacon,	Boston, Mass.
1891	Rider, Wheelock	53 S. Fitzhugh,	Rochester, N. Y.
1885	*Ring, Charles A (*1903)		Portland, Me.
1888	*Ring, Frank W		New York, N. Y.
1899	Risley, Samuel D	1824 Chestnut,	Philadelphia, Pa.
1898	Ritchie, Harry Parks	105 Lowry Arcade,	St. Paul, Minn.
1894	Robbins, J. E		Danville, Pa.
1879	Roberts, John B	1627 Walnut,	Philadelphia, Pa.
1903	Roberts, Walter	33 S. 19th,	Philadelphia, Pa.
1885	Robinson, Daniel A	142 Hammond,	Bangor, Me.
1892	Robinson, R		East Brady, Pa.
1884	Robison, John A	297 Ashland Boulevard,	Chicago, Ill.
1897	Roche, C. Percy de la	1518 Pine,	Philadelphia, Pa.
1893	Rochester, De Lancey	469 Franklin,	Buffalo, N. Y.
1879	Rockwell, A. D	113 W. 34th,	New York, N. Y.
1891	Rogers, Arthur C		Faribault, Minn.
1897	Rogers, Daniel W	2204 Michigan Ave.,	Chicago, Ill.
1897	Rogers, Frederick T	117 Broad,	Providence, R. I.
1898	Rogers, John B		North Bloomfield, Cal.
1895	*Rohe, George H (*1899)		Sykesville, Md.
1878	Roosa, Daniel B. St. J	20 E. 30th,	New York, N. Y.
1897	Rothrock, John L	235 Lowry Arcade,	St. Paul, Minn.
1899	Ruddick, William H	502 E. Broadway,	S. Boston, Mass.
1889	Rutherford, Clarendon	102 Fullerton Ave.,	Chicago, Ill.
1878	*Ryerson, Thomas		Newton, N. J.
1889	Salisbury, James Newton		Russellville, O.
1878	*Sandt, John (*1889)		Easton, Pa.
1879	*Sanford, Leonard J (*1896)		New Haven, Conn.
1878	Santee, Eugene J	532 N. 6th,	Philadelphia, Pa.
1891	Sargent, Dudley A	Hemenway Gymnasium,	Cambridge, Mass.
1891	Sartain, Paul J	212 W. Logan Sq.,	Philadelphia, Pa.
1889	Satterthwaite, Thomas E	17 E. 44th,	New York, N. Y.
1898	Savage, Watson L	308 W. 59th,	New York, N. Y.
1890	Sayre, Reginald H	285 5th Ave.,	New York, N. Y.

1889	Schauffler, Edward W.	900 Walnut, Kansas City, Mo.
1901	Schauffler, William G.	Lakewood, N. J.
1892	Scheel, A. M.	Belleville, Ill.
1878	Schenck, P. L.	60 St. Mark's Ave., Brooklyn, N. Y.
1882	*Schenck, Tunis (*1899)	Bath Beach, N. Y.
1898	Scheppegrell, Wm	Medical Bldg., New Orleans, La.
1898	Schneideman, Theodore B.	112 S. 18th, Philadelphia, Pa.
1877	Schoonover, Warren	115 E. 59th, New York, N. Y.
1877	*Schultz, Solomon S (*1891)	Danville, Pa.
1895	Schweinitz, Geo. E. de	1705 Walnut, Philadelphia, Pa.
1890	Schwenk, Peter N. K.	810 N. 7th, Philadelphia, Pa.
1878	Scott, J. McPherson	Hagerstown, Md.
1882	Scott, Xenophon C.	127 Euclid Ave., Cleveland, O.
1888	Scribner, Ernest V.	Worcester, Mass.
1888	Seaman, Wm. S.	16 W. 52nd, New York, N. Y.
1896	Searcy, J. T.	Tuscaloosa, Ala.
1897	Sechrist, Cora S.	176 Euclid Ave., Cleveland, O.
1882	*Seely, W. W (*1903)	Cincinnati, O
1876	Sell, Edward H. M.	137 W. 94th, New York, N. Y.
1884	*Shakespeare, Edward O (*1900)	Philadelphia, Pa.
1895	Shannon, John R.	Cabaniss, Ga.
1877	*Shapleigh, Elisha B (*1892)	Philadelphia, Pa.
1885	Shapleigh, John B	3621 Washington Ave., St. Louis, Mo.
1896	Shastid, Thos. H	1129 Michigan Ave., Ann Arbor, Mich.
1886	Shaw, Wm. C.	1009 Wylie Ave., Pittsburg, Pa.
1877	*Shearer, James M	Dillsburg, Pa.
1890	Shearer, Niles H.	York, Pa.
1882	Sheldon, Chas. S.	Madison, Wis.
1901	Sheldon, H. W.	Negaunee, Mich.
1897	Sheppard, John E.	130 Montague, Brooklyn, N. Y.
1903	Sherer, H. Straub	Bangor, Pa.
1889	Sherrill, Edwin S.	270 Woodward Ave., Detroit, Mich.
1902	Shimer, Ira A.	U. S. A.
1903	Shoemaker, George E.	3727 Chestnut, Philadelphia, Pa.
1878	Shoemaker, John V.	1519 Walnut, Philadelphia, Pa.
1890	Shoemaker, Levi L	Wilkes-Barre, Pa.
1878	Shrady, Geo. F.	8 E. 66th, New York, N. Y.
1878	Shrady, John	149 W. 126th, New York, N. Y.
1897	Shurly, Burt R.	32 Adams Ave., W. Detroit, Mich.
1876	*Sibbet, Robert Lowry (*1898)	Carlisle, Pa.
1899	Silver, Edward V.	Salt Lake City, Utah.
1890	Simmons, Arthur R	224 Genesee, Utica, N. Y.
1889	Simmons, Chas. E.	742 Lexington Ave., New York, N. Y.
1897	Simmons, Warren S., Jr	338 Lafayette Ave., Brooklyn, N. Y.
1888	Simmons, Wm. H.	Bangor, Me.

1897	Simons, Chas. E.	1302 Madison Ave., Baltimore, Md.
1888	Simpson, Frederic T.	122 High, Hartford, Conn.
1890	*Sinne, H. H (*1891)	Trenton, N. J.
1890	Sleeper, Frank E.	Sabatis, Me.
1892	Sloan, Henry H.	498 W. North Ave., Chicago, Ill.
1886	*Sloan, James G (*1897)	Monongahela City, Pa.
1903	Small, Edward H.	Penn and Negley Aves., Pittsburg, Pa.
1888	Small, Freeman E.	198 High, Portland, Me.
1878	*Smith, Albert H.	Philadelphia, Pa.
1889	Smith, A. Lapthorn	250 Bishop, W. Montreal, Canada.
1888	Smith, Andrew R. G.	North Whitefield, Me.
1893	Smith, Bryant	136 Wisconsin, Milwaukee, Wis.
1888	Smith, Charles D.	126 Free, Portland, Me.
1880	*Smith, Charles G.	Chicago, Ill.
1898	Smith, Edward W.	34 W. Main, Meridan, Conn.
1891	Smith, George E.	23 Woodland Ave., Oberlin, O.
1895	Smith, Henry H.	43 Elm St., New Haven, Conn.
1891	Smith, Joseph R.	U. S. A. (Retired).
1883	Smith, Thomas J.	Bridgeton, N. J.
1888	Smith, Thomas P.	Saccarappa, Me.
1889	Smith, William H.	Shell Rock, Ia.
1882	Smith, William T.	Hanover, N. H.
1891	Smock, Ledru P.	3330 Chestnut, Philadelphia, Pa.
1897	Snipe, Langdon T.	Bath, Me.
1893	Snively, I. Newton	1617 N. Broad, Philadelphia, Pa.
1879	*Snively, Joseph C.	Brooklyn, N. Y.
1879	*Snow, Edwin M.	Providence, R. I.
1900	Snyder, Thos.	1919 Main, Niagara Falls, N. Y.
1901	Somerville, Wm. G.	Tuscaloosa, Ala.
1895	Southard, Wm. F.	603 Sutter, San Francisco, Cal.
1885	Spalding, James A.	627 Congress, Portland, Me.
1881	*Spare, John (*1901)	New Bedford, Me.
1899	Spaulding, Frank W.	Clifton Springs, N. Y.
1892	Speed, J. N.	Rushville, Ill.
1891	Springer, Willard	810 Washington, Wilmington, Del.
1878	Stahley, Geo. D.	Gettysburg, Pa.
1888	Stanwood, Robert G.	231 Orange, Newark, N. J.
1889	Staples, Allen	Dubuque, Ia.
1889	*Staples, Geo. M (*1895)	Dubuque, Ia.
1894	Staples, Henry L.	Syndicate Blk., Minneapolis, Minn.
1897	Stein, Simon G.	Muscatine, Ia.
1876	*Steiner, Lewis H (*1892)	Baltimore, Md.
1902	Steiner, Walter R.	4 Trinity, Hartford, Conn.
1884	Stellwagen, Thos. C.	1809 Chestnut, Philadelphia, Pa.
1903	Stevens, Cyrus L.	Athens, Pa.

1883	*Stevens, Chas. W (*1901)	Charlestown, Mass.
1902	Stevenson, M. D.	61 S. Ferry, Albany, N. Y.
1884	*Stevenson, J. M (*1896)	Pittsburg, Pa.
1895	Stewart, W. Blair., cor. N. Carolina & Pacific Aves., Atlantic City, N. J.
1876	*Stewart, Wm. S (*1903)	1801 Arch, Philadelphia, Pa.
1883	Stoddard, E. V.	68 S. Washington, Rochester, N. Y.
1889	Stone, Wm. G.	Montclair, N. J.
1892	Storer, Samuel T.	New Concord, O.
1900	Stout, G. C.	34 S. 15th, Philadelphia, Pa.
1892	Stout, Joseph	Ottawa, Ill.
1901	Strathern, Fred. P.	Bennett Bl., St. Peter, Minn.
1877	*Strawbridge, James D.	Danville, Pa.
1897	Strickler, Abraham H.	Waynesboro, Pa.
1897	*Strong, Norton (*1903)	U. S. A.
1889	Strong, Thomas D.	Westfield, N. Y.
1879	Stuart, Francis H.	123 Joralemon, Brooklyn, N. Y.
1879	Stubbs, George E.	1616 Walnut, Philadelphia, Pa.
1898	Stuver, Emanuel	Fort Collins, Colo.
1900	Summa, Hugo	2249 St. Louis Ave., St. Louis, Mo.
1888	Swan, Charles E.	Calais, Me.
1900	Swartz, Gardner T.	70 Waterman, Providence, R. I.
1892	Swift, Elisha P.	Florence, Wis.
1888	Swift, William N.	378 County, New Bedford, Mass.
1892	Sykes, Richard L.	Columbus, Miss.
1883	Tadlock, A. B.	Tetalama, Cal.
1892	*Talley, Alexander N (*1897)	Columbia, S. C.
1895	Taneyhill, George L.	1103 Madison Ave., Baltimore, Md.
1889	Tappey, Ernst T.	270 Woodward Ave., Detroit, Mich.
1898	Taylor, Henry Ling.	60 W. 55th, New York, N. Y.
1897	Taylor, Hugh M.	6 N. 5th, Richmond, Va.
1889	Taylor, James L.	Wheelersburg, O.
1894	Taylor, J. Madison.	1504 Pine, Philadelphia, Pa.
1878	*Taylor, Wm. F.	Philadelphia, Pa.
1878	*Thacker, John A (*1891)	Cincinnati, O.
1889	Thayer, Addison S.	730 Congress, Portland, Me.
1892	Thayer, H. W.	Corry, Pa.
1878	Thomas, James C.	107 W. 47th, New York, N. Y.
1888	Thombs, Samuel B.	Knightville, Me.
1890	Thompson, Geo. E.	599 Tremont, Boston, Mass.
1889	Thompson, John F.	601 Congress, Portland, Me.
1903	Thompson, William S	Standish, Me.
1897	Thomson, Archibald G.	1426 Walnut, Philadelphia, Pa.
1897	Thomson, Wm.	1426 Walnut, Philadelphia, Pa.
1897	*Thorner, Max (*1899)	Cincinnati, O.
1886	Thrasher, A. B.	157 W. 9th, Cincinnati, O.

1901	Tiffany, Frank M	Stamford, Conn.
1898	Tinker, Martin B	Johns Hopkins Hospital, Baltimore, Md.
1883	Todd, William S	Ridgefield, Conn.
1888	Tolman, Julia	695 Massachusetts Ave., Arlington, Mass.
1901	Tomlinson, Harry A	St. Peter, Minn.
1892	Tomlinson, Joseph	Roadstown, N. J.
1894	Totman, David M	303 Montgomery, Syracuse, N. Y.
1877	Treichler, C. Galen	Honeybrook, Pa.
1897	Tressel, John H	Alliance, O.
1888	Trowbridge, Edward H	54 Pleasant, Worcester, Mass.
1890	Trowbridge, Grosvenor R	1331 Main, Buffalo, N. Y.
1888	Tucker, Edward T	258 Pleasant, New Bedford, Mass.
1902	Tucker, Willis G	Albany, N. Y.
1899	*Tuckerman, Louis B (*1902)	Cleveland, O.
1879	Turnbull, Charles S	1719 Chestnut, Philadelphia, Pa.
1880	*Turner, Joseph M (*1898)	Brooklyn, N. Y.
1897	Turner, Oliver W	Augusta, Me.
1903	Turner, S. C. P	1506 Walnut, Philadelphia, Pa.
1891	Turner, Sylvester W	Chester, Conn.
1884	*Turner, Thomas J (*1901)	Coldwater, Mich.
1893	Tuttle, Albert H	735 Main, Cambridge, Mass.
1898	Tuttle, George M	49 W. 38th, New York, N. Y.
1901	*Tyler, George E (*1902)	Denver, Colo.
1897	*Ulrich, Charles F (*1903)	Wheeling, W. Va.
1899	Upham, J. H. J	106 E. Broad, Columbus, O.
1892	Vail, J. B	322 W. Market, Lima, O.
1897	Van Benschoten, William C	63rd and Monroe Ave., Chicago, Ill.
1889	*Van Bibber, W. C	Baltimore, Md.
1877	Vanderveer, John R	Monroe, N. Y.
1890	Van Duyne, John	318 James, Syracuse, N. Y.
1888	Van Hook, Weller	4043 Grand Bldg., Chicago, Ill.
1891	Van Pelt, Chas. L	Toledo, O.
1888	Van Santvoord, Richard	106 W. 122nd, New York, N. Y.
1879	Van Valzah, W. W	40 E. 25th, New York, N. Y.
1891	Vaughan, Victor C	15 S. State, Ann Arbor, Mich.
1898	Veasey, Clarence A	116 S. 19th, Philadelphia, Pa.
1890	*Vermyne, J. J. B (*1898)	Boston, Mass.
1882	Vinton, Chas. H	Wernersville, Pa.
1892	Voldeng, M. Nelson	Hospital for the Insane, Cherokee, Ia.
1886	Von Klein, Carl H	248 E. Erie, Chicago, Ill.
1878	*Wagner, Chas. K (*1898)	Newark, N. J.
1888	Waldron, Martha M	Hampton, Va.
1889	Walk, James W	737 Corinthian Ave., Philadelphia, Pa.
1899	Walker, Gertrude A	308 S. 13th, Philadelphia, Pa.
1900	Walker, J. B	1617 Green, Philadelphia, Pa.

1888	Walker, John E	Thomaston, Me.
1895	Walker, Samuel J	105 Pine, Chicago, Ill.
1902	Wall, Charles A	306 Hudson, Buffalo, N. Y.
1889	Ward, R. Halsted	53 4th, Troy, N. Y.
1897	Warden, Carl C	133 N. Spruce, Nashville, Tenn.
1889	Warner, Helen F	53 Adams Ave., W. Detroit, Mich.
1884	*Warren, Chas	Washington, D. C.
1888	Warren, Stanley P	99 Free, Portland, Me.
1892	Warren, Wadsworth	32 Adams Ave., Detroit, Mich.
1884	Watson, Wm. Perry	101 Bentley Ave., Jersey City, N. J.
1882	Waugh, Wm. F	1416 E. Ravenswood Park, Chicago, Ill.
1883	Weaver, J. K	612 DeKalb, Norristown, Pa.
1888	*Webster, Chas. E (*1892)	Portland, Me.
1888	*Weed, Chas. L	Philadelphia, Pa.
1902	Weeks, Stephen H	Portland, Me.
1884	*Weidman, W. Murray (*1902)	Reading, Pa.
1892	Weitz, Joseph A	Montpelier, O.
1897	Welch, John C	Bellevue, Pa.
1902	Welch, Stephen A	253 Washington, Providence, R. I.
1888	Wells, George M	Wayne, Pa.
1897	Wentworth, Wm. W	230 W. 65th, Chicago, Ill.
1895	Wentz, Alexander C	Hanover, Pa.
1888	Weston, Edward B	3975 Drexel Boulevard, Chicago, Ill.
1888	Wheeler, Geo. A	Castine, Me.
1902	Wheeler, John B	Burlington, Vt.
1898	Wheelock, Wm. E	Morristown, N. J.
1890	Whitcombe, Chas. R	Hotel Pelham, Boston, Mass.
1903	White, Marx	Univ. of Minnesota, Minneapolis, Minn.
1895	White, Wm. R	7 Green, Providence, R. I.
1882	Whitebeck, J. Ward	209 East Ave., Rochester, N. Y.
1888	*Whitney, Adaline S (*1896)	Boston, Mass.
1882	*Whittaker, James T (*1900)	Cincinnati, O.
1899	Whittier, Francis F	Brookline, Mass.
1894	Whittier, Frank N	Brunswick, Me.
1877	*Wickes, Stephen	Orange, N. J.
1885	*Wight, Jarvis S (*1901)	Brooklyn, N. Y.
1903	Wilbur, Ray L	Stanford University, Cal.
1889	Wilcox, Dorvil M	Falls Village, Conn.
1890	Wilcox, Reynold W	679 Madison Ave., New York, N. Y.
1888	Williams, A. O	Ottumwa, Ia.
1902	Williams, Robert F	508 E. Grace, Richmond, Va.
1892	Williams, T. R	DeLancey, Pa.
1898	Williamson, Edward L	163 W. 74th, New York, N. Y.
1898	*Willits, Mary (*1902)	Norristown, Pa.
1888	*Wilson, Edwin F (*1902)	Columbus, O.

1884	*Wilson, Henry P. C., Jr. (*1897)	Baltimore, Md.
1888	Wilson, James C.	1509 Walnut, Philadelphia, Pa.
1900	Wilson, W. Reynolds	112 S. 20th, Philadelphia, Pa.
1890	Wing, Edgar D.	Galesburg, Ill.
1886	Wing, Elbert	Los Angeles, Cal.
1880	*Wing, Theodore T.	Susquehanna, Pa.
1892	Wirt, William E.	477 Prospect, Cleveland, O.
1879	Witthaus, Rudolph A.	410 E. 26th, New York, N. Y.
1882	Wolff, Henry A.	233 5th Ave., New York, N. Y.
1897	*Wood, Casey A*	103 E. Adams, Chicago, Ill.
1889	*Wood, Robert W (*1892)	Jamaica Plains, Mass.
1892	*Woodbridge, Luther D (*1899)	Williamstown, Mass.
1888	Woodman, Walter	64 Sparks, Cambridge, Mass.
1898	Woodruff, Thomas A.	103 E. Adams, Chicago, Ill.
1903	Woods, Hiram	842 Park Ave., Baltimore, Md.
1888	Woodside, Albert	St. George, Me.
1892	*Woolley, C. N.	Newburg, N. Y.
1884	Wordin, Nathaniel E.	174 Fairfield Ave., Bridgeport, Conn.
1891	Wright, Adam H.	30 Gerrard, E. Toronto, Canada.
1899	Wright, Thompson B.	Circleville, O.
1902	Wyeth, John A.	19 W. 35th, New York, N. Y.
1901	Wyman, B. L.	212½ N. 20th, Birmingham, Ala.
1903	Wyman, Walter	Marine Hospital Service, Washington, D. C.
1893	*Wyman, Samuel E.	Cambridge, Mass.
1884	*Young, I. Gilbert (*1899)	Philadelphia, Pa.
1886	Zenner, Philip	335 W. 9th, Philadelphia, Pa.
1888	Ziegler, Samuel L.	1504 Walnut, Philadelphia, Pa.

Number of honorary members......... 23
" " fellows......... 853

Total membership............ 876

The fellows are urgently requested to advise the secretary at once of any error or omission and to keep him informed of any changes from time to time.

Article I. Title.

This Association shall be known as the AMERICAN ACADEMY OF MEDICINE.

Article II. Object.

The object of the Academy shall be—

1. To bring those who are alumni of classical, scientific, and medical schools into closer relations with each other.

2. To encourage young men to pursue regular courses of study in classical and scientific institutions before entering upon the study of medicine.

3. To extend the bounds of medical science, to elevate the profession, to relieve human suffering, and to prevent disease.

Article III. Membership.

SEC. I. The membership of the Academy shall consist of fellows and honorary members.

SEC. II. The fellows shall be alumni of respectable institutions of learning, having received therefrom—

(1) The degree of Bachelor of Arts, or Master of Arts, after a systematic course of study, preparatory and collegiate; but when a candidate has not received either of these degrees in course, other evidences of a preparatory liberal education, which shall be considered as equivalent to the same by the council, may be accepted in lieu of a degree by the Academy;

(2) The degree of Doctor of Medicine, after a regular course of study, not less than three years, under the direction and instruction of preceptors and professors; or

(3) When a candidate is an alumnus of a foreign institution, or institutions, not granting the degree of Bachelor or Master of Arts, or of Doctor of Medicine, a certificate, or certificates, or a license, which shall be considered as equivalent by the council, may be accepted in lieu thereof by the Academy.

(4) The fellows shall be reputable graduates in medicine.

SEC. III. Honorary members shall consist of gentlemen in the medical profession, at home and abroad, who have made important contributions to medical science.

SEC. IV. The honorary members shall not exceed five for every one hundred fellows. They shall be entitled to attend the meetings of the Academy and participate in the proceedings, but shall have no right to vote or hold office.

SEC. V. The consent, by ballot, of two-thirds of the fellows present, shall be necessary for the election of fellows or honorary members.

Article IV. Officers.

The officers of the Academy shall be a president, four vice-presidents, a secretary, an assistant secretary, and a treasurer. These shall be elected by ballot from the fellows, to serve one year, or until others are elected. The president is ineligible for two successive terms.

Article V. Council.

The council shall consist of the officers of the Academy, ex-presidents, and one fellow for every twenty or fraction thereof in attendance. The latter shall be appointed annually by the president.

Article VI. Meetings.

The Academy shall hold one regular meeting each year.

Article VII. Revenue.

Sec. I. The sources of revenue shall be the initiation fees, dues, the transactions of the Academy, and the certificates of membership. The initiation fee of five dollars shall be paid before admission and registration. A fee of one dollar shall be due at each subsequent annual meeting; the neglect to pay this fee for three successive years shall cause the name of the fellow so neglecting to be entered upon a separate roll to be known as the list of suspended fellows: *Provided*, That all fellows elected previous to, or during, the meeting for 1898 shall not be liable to this penalty. If any fellow pays the sum of twenty dollars at one time, he is freed from the payment of any subsequent annual dues.

Sec. II. The money received from the payment of life dues shall be invested as the council may direct, and the interest only can be expended.

Article VIII. Discipline.

Sec. I. The fellows of the Academy in their relations with each other and with their fellow men agree to be governed by the principles embodied in the present code of ethics of the American Medical Association, and by the constitution and by-laws of the Academy.

Sec. II. A complaint being duly made to the council by two fellows against any fellow or honorary member for a violation of the constitution or by-laws of the Academy, the ethical principles therein recognized, or the laws of morality, shall be heard and considered by the council, notice of the same, including the time and place of hearing, being served on the accused by the secretary at least four weeks beforehand that he may present his defense; and the sentence of the council, whatever it may be in such case, shall be final.

Article IX. Quorum.

Five fellows of the Academy shall constitute a quorum at any regularly called meeting.

Article X. Certificate.

A Latin certificate of fellowship, bearing the seal of the Academy and the signature of the officers, shall be issued to any fellow on payment of its actual cost.

Article XI. Delegates.

Delegates may be sent by vote of the Academy, or by the council when the Academy is not in session, to medical associations in foreign countries; and delegates may also be received from such associations.

Article XII. Amendments.

Every proposal to alter or amend the constitution of the Academy, shall be made in writing and entered on the minutes. If two-thirds of the fellows present at the next regular meeting vote for such alteration or amendment, it shall be adopted.

BY-LAWS.

Article I. Duties of the Officers.

Sec. I. The president shall preside at the meetings of the Academy and of the council, preserve order, announce the admission of fellows and members, appoint all committees not otherwise ordered, fill vacancies which may occur in the council and in committees, and name the time and place of meeting for the council. When requested by a majority of the officers to call a special meeting of the council, he shall direct the secretary to call such meeting, and shall indicate the special subjects to be considered. He shall deliver an address before the Academy at the close of his term of office, and perform such other duties as the constitution, by-laws, and parliamentary usages require.

Sec. II. The vice-presidents, when called upon, shall assist the president in the performance of his duties. In his absence, or at his request, one of them, in the order of seniority, shall take his place in the Academy or in the council, and may deliver the annual address.

Sec. III. The secretary shall have charge of the records and the correspondence of the Academy. He shall receive all proposals for membership presented in due form and shall lay them before the council. He shall receive the initiation fees and give vouchers for them. He shall pay the same to the treasurer and shall take his receipt therefor. He shall enter in the register of the Academy the names of all the fellows admitted from year to year with their post-office address, place of nativity, time of birth, degrees, the institution conferring them, and the dates thereof; and in another column the time of their demise, when that shall occur. He shall enter in another part of the register the names of the honorary members. He shall keep an accurate and legible account of the acts of the Academy and of the council, and shall preserve the same carefully and deliver them to his successor when elected. He shall edit the transactions in a manner and style agreed upon by the council. He shall give due notice in the medical journals of the meetings of the Academy. He shall notify committees of their appointment, and shall, in connection with the presiding officer, certify all acts of the Academy and of the council.

Sec. iv. It shall be the duty of the assistant secretary to assist the secretary in the meetings of the Academy as well as in the meetings of the council, and in his absence to take his place.

Sec. v. The treasurer shall collect and take charge of the funds of the Academy. He shall pay out of these only such sums as are ordered by the Academy or by the council, and shall take vouchers for the same. He shall annually present a statement of the finances of the Academy, which shall be referred to a committee of three fellows to be audited. He shall hold the funds of the Academy in trust, and shall give security for faithful performance of his duties when the receipts shall exceed $500 annually. He shall also take charge of its transactions and distribute them on the receipt of the price of the volume, and may sell them to any person. He shall deliver all funds in his possession to his successor, when elected.

Article II. Duties of the Council.

Sec. i. The council shall convene at the call of the president, and shall consider and act upon all proposals for membership presented in due form, as indicated in the by-laws, signed by at least one fellow, and countersigned by the secretary. If the council is satisfied that the qualifications of the candidate are such as are required by the constitution, it shall report the same to the Academy, with the words "Approved by the council" endorsed on the proposal. In the case of those who may not be reported, or who do not receive a vote of two-thirds of the Academy, no minute shall be kept.

Sec. ii. It shall be the duty of the council to consider and recommend plans for promoting the objects of the Academy; to superintend its interests; to make arrangements for the meetings; to determine finally all questions of medical ethics arising among the fellows and members; to decide upon, and superintend, all its publications; to authorize the disbursement of unappropriated funds in the treasury for the payment of current expenses; and to perform such other duties as may from time to time be committed to it by the Academy.

Article III. Communications.

Sec. i. Papers on medical subjects may be read before the Academy, provided they have been deposited with the secretary of the council at least thirty days before the time of the regular meeting, and have also been approved by the council.

Sec. ii. All motions or resolutions, excepting those which relate to ordinary and routine business, shall be referred to the council without debate. Unless otherwise instructed by the Academy, the council shall report the resolution back with its recommendation at the next executive session following the introduction of the resolution.

Article IV. Time and Place of Meeting.

Sec. i. The Academy shall hold a regular meeting annually, the place and time to be determined upon at the previous regular meeting; but both place and time may be changed by the council for reasons that shall be specified in the announcement of the meeting.

SEC. II. The council may call special meetings of the Academy whenever, in its judgment, it is necessary; and it shall call a special meeting whenever it is requested to do so by twenty-five fellows of the Academy.

SEC. III. At any special meeting only such business can be transacted as is mentioned in the call for the meeting.

SEC. IV. The minutes of all special meetings shall be sent to the secretary of the Academy within thirty days after the meeting of the Academy for its information and, with the exception of the fellows elected, be subject to its revision or veto. The transactions of all special meetings shall be a part of the proceedings of the year designated by the previous annual meeting.

ARTICLE V. THE ORDER OF BUSINESS.

The order of business shall be fixed by the council.

ARTICLE VI. AMENDMENTS.

Every proposal to alter or amend the by-laws shall be made in writing; and if such alteration or amendment receive the unanimous consent of the fellows present, it shall be adopted; but if objections be made, the alteration or amendment shall lie over until the next regular meeting, when, if it receive the vote of two-thirds of the fellows present, it shall be adopted.

OBSERVATIONS IN PASSING.

In reading the proof of the results of the examination before the board of examiners, the lack of uniformity in the nomenclature of the degree giving institutions was very apparent. The reports were compiled and submitted to the secretaries of the various boards for revision, using the naming from the data furnished, in order to enable the secretary to quickly verify the tabulation. Afterwards there was an effort to make the designation of the various colleges uniform. It has not been accomplished to our satisfaction.

If the secretaries of the various boards will insist upon each applicant for examination using the corporate name of his college on his blank making application, the results would be more satisfactory. There are many schools known by more than one name, as College of Physicians and Surgeons, of New York, and Columbia; Medical School of Maine and Bowdoin; in every instance the more general name, *i. e.*, of the college, and not the department, should be used.

We hope to profit by the experience, and devise a scheme to obviate this lack of uniformity to be used in the next report.

****

It never pays to *think* one is right, unless the thought is verified by the facts in the case. Thus there is printed on page 497 of the last number of the Bulletin a bill purporting to be an "osteopathic bill" for Alabama, which was thought to have been adopted at this office. There were no reasons why we should have thought so, had the transactions of the State Medical Society been read with care. However, it will serve to point a moral. The bill on pp. 497, 498 is the osteopathic bill as presented by the adherents of that cult, and in the form it passed the House of Representatives. The bill on pp. 498, 499 is the substitute reported back by a portion of the Senate's Committee, after the profession of the State had been heard from, and which eventually became the law.

At the beginning of the year we look for reminders of and help for the new year and we are not disappointed.

Scott and Browne and the Pope Manufacturing Company furnish pad calenders, a slip for a day with space for memoranda. M. J. Breitenbach Company cling to their red cloth yellow paper desk memorandum book now so familiar. In like manner, the Eisner & Mendelson Company have sent us their vest-pocket diary, having the same size and appearance as those of previous years. The Consolidated Stock and Petroleum Exchange, of New York, send a similar book but longer, making it more convenient for vest-pockets of the average depth. The Mellier Drug Company, of St. Louis, has issued a celluloid cover diary memorandum for several years past; it follows the same style in its reminder for 1904.

**

THE 1904 MEETING.

Preparations are steadily making for the meeting at Atlantic City. The Committee of Arrangements has selected the Shelburne for the headquarters. We were at the Shelburne in 1900, and the recollection of that visit will cause the approval of the committee's action on the part of those who attended that meeting. A reduction of rates has been secured on all the rooms; but as the price of rooms varies, it will be better for each to arrange beforehand for accommodation.

The Committee on Program report the promise of several very valuable papers, and the outlook for a profitable meeting is excellent. There is still space for a few papers and as the committee is often compelled to make a selection, in order not to overcrowd the program on the one hand, and to preserve its harmony on the other, it is urged upon all who may desire to contribute papers to notify the chairman of the committee (Dr. D. C. Hawley, Burlington, Vt.) as soon as possible.

For convenience, the scheme for the meeting is published again. It is suggested that the papers cluster around two topics.

I. The Relation of Physicians to Dentists' and Pharmacists.

II. Are Modern School Methods in Keeping with Physiologic Knowledge?

Under this second topic the committee suggests as sample subjects the following:

Is the solid session best from a health standpoint?

The proper school age, and the age at which pupils should graduate.

Is equal treatment of the sexes best, or do girls require a different treatment from boys?

Do our modern school methods tend to the too early and rapid mental development of our boys and girls at the expense of proper physical and moral development?

Is mental overstrain at puberty likely to undermine the nervous system of the girls?

School systems should be so flexible that every girl might remain at home if necessary for three or four days each month during the menstrual period without fear of falling behind in her classes.

Proper education, not more education, demanded for our girls from a physical, intellectual and moral standpoint.

Are art, music and the modern languages more necessary to women than to men?

Does too much exceptional culture for women tend to remove from the rank of motherhood those most likely to produce children of high-class brain power?

Papers on general subjects are also solicited to be used in the sessions not devoted to the specially appointed discussions.

LITERATURE NOTES.

COMPEND OF DISEASES OF THE EAR, NOSE AND THROAT. BY JOHN JOHNSON KYLE, B.S., M.D. 85 illustrations. Philadelphia: P. Blakiston's Son & Co. 1900. pp. 280. Price, 80 cents net.

This is another of that excellent series of manuals, named "Quiz Compends" by the publisher. Capable of being misused, as are most things, they have a wide sphere of usefulness under ordinary using. This volume is an excellent example of the best of its class.

A NON-SURGICAL TREATISE ON DISEASES OF THE PROSTATE GLAND AND ADNEXA. BY GEORGE WHITFIELD OVERALL, A.B., M.D. Chicago: Rowe Publishing Company. pp. 207.

This book gives the results of the author's studies over a period of years on the employment of medical means, chiefly electric, for these diseases. It is a book worthy the perusal of every one whose practice includes such complaints.

REPORTS OF BOARDS OF CHARITIES AND CORRECTIONS.

I. THIRTY-SIXTH ANNUAL REPORT OF THE STATE BOARD OF CHARITIES OF THE STATE OF NEW YORK, 1902.
    Vol. I.—Text and Appendix Papers. pp. vii, 575. Appendix to Vol I,—Statistics. pp. xi + 774.
    Vol. II.—Manual and Directory. pp. vii, 1114.
    Vol. III.—Proceedings of the New York State Conference of Charities and Corrections at the third annual session, Albany, 1902. pp. ii + 326.

II. SIXTEENTH BIENNIAL REPORT OF THE MICHIGAN STATE BOARD OF CORRECTIONS AND CHARITIES, 1901-1902. pp. xiii + 231.

III. THIRTY-FOURTH ANNUAL REPORT OF THE BOARD OF STATE CHARITIES AND CORRECTIONS OF RHODE ISLAND. pp. 159. Illustrated by a number of half-tone cuts.

IV. FOURTEENTH ANNUAL REPORT OF THE STATE COMMISSION IN LUNACY OF THE STATE OF NEW YORK. Oct. 1, 1901, to Sept. 30, 1902. pp. ix + 1091.

I. These volumes convey a wealth of information regarding the institutional work of the empire state. The magnitude o this can be estimated from a few figures gathered from the report. Total valuation $5,307,894.05; total receipts for the year $1,588,245.62; total expended for all objects $1,474,829.49, the population on October 1, 1902, being 7,137. These figures do not include the county institutions.

At the state conference, the principal topics discussed were the Mentally Defective; the Care and Relief of Needy Families in Their Homes; Relief of the Sick Poor; Dependent, Neglected, Delinquent and Defective Children; The Institutional Care of Destitute Adults; and The Treatment of the Criminal. Speakers of known ability took part in the discussion of each of these topics, making this volume especially valuable.

II. This report is confined to an account of the doings of the various Michigan institutions, and makes a valuable volume for information, when statistics are to be compiled.

III. The Board of Rhode Island has enriched the report with a number of process cuts. It too deals with the workings of the institution of that state during the year.

IV. New York is paying more attention to the medical work of her insane hospital, as well as the study of problems of mental pathology in the laboratories connected with her hospitals.

Colorado Medicine is one of the youngest of our medical journals. It is the official organ of the Colorado State Medical Society, and for that sake alone should receive a cordial welcome. It is under the supervision of Drs. Edward Jackson, who is the editor, S. E. Solly and Robert Levy, which assure its character and worth. The first two numbers give earnest of a valuable addition to our periodic literature.

There are exchanges and exchanges and it might cause a smile at the crudity of our judgment were we to attempt to publish a catalogue under this classification. We have no hesitancy in saying that among the exchanges we value has been the *Journal of Comparative Neurology*, under the editorial management of C. L. and C. Judson Herrick, and published at Denison University, Granville, O. A prospectus before us announces an enlargement of the scope of the journal with a strengthening of the editorial staff, and a change from a quarterly to a bi-monthly issue. It will hereafter be known as *The Journal of Comparative Neurology and Psychology* and will be issued at $4.00 a year. We can unqualifiedly recommend the journal to all who labor on subjects treated upon by it. Address Prof. C. Judson Herrick at Granville, O.

And this reminds us of another exchange, not from any similarity of contents, but because it can safely be mentioned as especially valuable. The *Literary Digest* is a weekly of a type that no busy man desirous of information about the world in which his own world of active life exists, can do without. It stands among the first, if not in a class by itself, of papers of its type.

THE MILK SUPPLY OF 200 CITIES AND TOWNS. BY HENRY E. ALVORD, C.E., AND R. A. PEARSON, M.S., U. S. Department of Agriculture, Bureau of Animal Industry. Bulletin, No. 46. Washington: Government Printing Office. 1903. Paper. pp. 210.

The daily press have the habit of commenting adversely on the immensity of the output of the Government Printing Office. If all the material issued compared in value to the various bulletins of the scientific bureaus, the criticism would be captious. The milk supply for domestic use is a question of vital value, and one very excellent way to learn how to control it, is to learn how other people are trying to solve the problem. This volume helps materially in securing this knowledge.

HOSPITAL REPORTS.

I. PHILADELPHIA HOSPITAL REPORTS. Vol. V, 1902. Edited by HERMAN B. ALLYN, M.D. Philadelphia. 1903. Cloth. pp. 178.

II. MT. SINAI HOSPITAL REPORTS. Vol. III, 1901-1902. Edited by N. E. BRILL, A.M., M.D. New York. 1903. Paper. pp. 572.

III. 45TH ANNUAL REPORT OF ST. LUKE'S HOSPITAL. New York. 1902-1903. Paper. pp. 144.

IV. ANNUAL REPORT OF THE RHODE ISLAND HOSPITAL. 1903. Paper. pp. 127.

V. MEMORIAL HOSPITAL. Richmond, Va. 1903.

VI. EASTON HOSPITAL FOR YEAR ENDING JUNE, 1903.

I and II publish a number of interesting and valuable papers by the staffs; the others give only the happenings at the hospitals and the statistics. These are rather the more valuable for reference in medico-sociologic studies. All hospital reports are preserved and catalogued and can be made available for research work at any time. The Bulletin will gladly receive such reports from every hospital.

ANNUAL REPORT OF THE SUPERVISING SURGEON-GENERAL OF THE MARINE HOSPITAL SERVICE OF THE UNITED STATES FOR THE FISCAL YEAR 1900. pp. 736.
Ibid, for 1901. pp. 652.

These reports give a faint idea of the immensity of the work assigned to the service and the admirable way in which it is done.

VALID OBJECTION TO SO-CALLED CHRISTIAN SCIENCE. By REV. ANDREW F. UNDERHILL, Rector of St. John's Church, Yonkers, N. Y.

The Arlington Chemical Company has presented this pamphlet, containing a very excellent article on Christian Science, which it avers is neither Christian nor scientific. Possibly it will convince no one against his will, but to an open mind it is capable of great influence for the truth.

BULLETIN

OF THE

American Academy of Medicine

VOL. VI.   ISSUED APRIL, 1904.   No. 11.

The AMERICAN ACADEMY OF MEDICINE is not responsible for the sentiments expressed in any paper or address published in the BULLETIN.

LAWS IN THE UNITED STATES, A.D. 1903, RELATING TO COMPULSORY INSTRUCTION IN SCHOOLS IN PHYSIOLOGY AND HYGIENE WITH SPECIAL REFERENCE TO THE EFFECTS OF ALCOHOLIC DRINKS AND NARCOTICS ON THE HUMAN SYSTEM.

To the American Academy of Medicine:—

The Committee on the Teaching of Hygiene in Public Schools respectfully submits as a preliminary report the accompanying compilation of the laws now existing in all states and territories, relating to so-called "temperance physiology."

HELEN C. PUTNAM,
EDWARD JACKSON,
GEORGE G. GROFF.

March 8, 1904.

UNITED STATES.

TERRITORIES, DISTRICT OF COLUMBIA, MILITARY AND NAVAL ACADEMIES, INDIAN AND COLORED SCHOOLS IN THE TERRITORIES.

From United States Statutes at Large, p. 69.

Be it enacted by the Senate and House of Representatives of the United States of America in Congress assembled:

SECTION 1. That the nature of alcoholic drinks and narcotics, and special instruction as to their effects upon the human system, in connection with the several divisions of the subject of physiology and hygiene, shall be included in the branches of study taught in the common or public schools, and in the Military and Naval Schools, and shall be studied and taught as thoroughly, and in the same manner, as other like required branches are in said schools, by the use of text-books in the hands of pupils where other branches are thus studied in said schools, and by all pupils in all said schools throughout the Territories, in the Military and Naval Academies of the United States, and in the District of Columbia, and in all Indian and colored schools in the Territories of the United States.

Sec. 2. That it shall be the duty of the proper officers in control of any school described in the foregoing section to enforce the provisions of this act; and any such officer, school director, committee, superintendent, or teacher who shall refuse or neglect to comply with the requirements of this act or shall neglect or fail to make proper provisions for the instruction required and in the manner specified by the first section of this act, for all pupils in each and every school under his jurisdiction, shall be removed from office, and the vacancy filled as in other cases.

Sec. 3. That no certificate shall be granted to any person to teach in the public schools of the District of Columbia or Territories, after the first day of January, anno Domini eighteen hundred and eighty-eight, who has not passed a satisfactory examination in physiology and hygiene, with special reference to the nature and the effects of alcoholic drinks and other narcotics upon the human system.

Approved, May 20, 1886.

ALABAMA.

From General Public School Laws of Alabama, 1901.*

Page 6.

3546. *Duties of Superintendent of Education.*— * * * (3) He shall make provision for instructing all pupils in all schools and colleges supported, in whole or in part, by public money, or under State control, in hygiene and physiology, with special reference to the effects of alcoholic drinks, stimulants, and narcotics upon the human system.

Page 20.

3577. No certificate shall be granted hereafter to any new applicant to teach in the public schools of Alabama who has not passed a satisfactory examination in the study of the nature of alcoholic drinks and narcotics and of their effects upon the human system in connection with the several divisions of physiology and hygiene.

3578. Every teacher shall give instruction as to the nature of alcoholic

* The state boards of education of practically all states issue biennially, or at other short intervals, pamphlets containing the laws in force relating to their departments. Our references are to these pamphlets, unless otherwise specified.

drinks and narcotics and their effects upon the human system, and such subjects shall be taught as regularly as any other in the public schools and in every grade thereof.

ALASKA.

(See United States, Territories, &c., p. 635.)

ARIZONA.

From Public School Laws of Arizona, 1901.

Title 17.—Education.

Page 8.

13. Every applicant for a first-grade Territorial certificate must be examined by written and oral questions in algebra, geography, history and civics, physiology, hygiene, with special reference to the nature and the effects of alcoholic drinks and other narcotics and stimulants upon the human system. * * * Applicants for a second-grade certificate shall not be required to pass an examination in algebra or natural philosophy.

Page 31.

85. Instruction must be given in the following branches, viz.: Reading, writing, orthography, arithmetic, geography, grammar, history of the United States, elements of physiology, hygiene, including the nature of alcoholic drinks and narcotics and special instruction as to their effect upon the human system, elements of book-keeping, industrial drawing, and such other studies as the Territorial Board of Education may prescribe, but no such other studies can be pursued to the neglect or exclusion of the studies enumerated.

Page 38.

112. Any teacher * * * who shall fail to comply with any of the provisions mentioned in this Title, shall be deemed guilty of unprofessional conduct, and it shall be the duty of the proper authority to revoke his or her certificate or diploma.

(See also United States, Territories, &c., p. 635.)

ARKANSAS.

From Digest of Laws relating to Free Schools in the State of Arkansas, 1901, pp. 25-6.

Be it enacted by the General Assembly of the State of Arkansas:

SECTION 1. That physiology and hygiene, which must in each division of the subject thereof include special reference to the effect of alcoholic drinks, stimulants, and narcotics upon the human system, shall be included in the branches of study now and hereafter required to be regularly taught and studied by all the pupils in the common schools of this State.

Sec. 2. It shall be the duty of the boards of directors and county examiners to see to the observance of this statute and make provisions therefor; and it is especially enjoined upon the county examiner of each county that he include in his report to the State superintendent of public instruction the manner and extent to which the requirements of section 1 of this act are complied with in the schools and institutions of his county.

Sec. 3. After two years from the passage of this act no license shall be granted to any person to teach in the public schools of this State who has not passed a satisfactory examination in physiology and hygiene, with special reference to the effects of alcoholic drinks, stimulants and narcotics upon the human system.

Sec. 4. That this act take effect and be in force from and after the first day of July, 1899.

CALIFORNIA.

From School Law of California, 1903, pp. 38-9.

Sec. 1665. Instruction must be given in the following branches in the several grades in which they may be required, viz.: Reading, writing, orthography, arithmetic, geography, nature study, language and grammar, with special reference to composition; history of the United States and civil government; elements of physiology and hygiene, with special reference to the effect of alcohol and narcotics on the human system; music, drawing, and elementary bookkeeping, humane education; *provided, that* instruction in elementary bookkeeping, humane education, elements of physiology and hygiene, music, drawing and nature study may be oral, no text-books on these subjects being required to be purchased by the pupils; *provided further,* that County Boards of Education may, in districts having less than one hundred census children, confine the pupils to the studies of reading, writing, orthography, arithmetic, language and grammar, geography, history of the United States and civil government, elements of physiology and hygiene, and elementary bookkeeping until they have a practical knowledge of these subjects; * * *

Sec. 1667. Instruction must be given, in all grades of school and in all classes during the entire school course, in manners and morals, and upon the nature of alcoholic drinks and narcotics and their effects upon the human system.

COLORADO.

From the School Law of the State of Colorado as amended to date. 1903.

Page 63.

Sec. 78. The public schools of this state shall be taught in the English language, and the school boards shall provide to have taught in such schools the branches specified in Section 15 ["physiology"] of said [this] chapter, and such other branches of learning in other languages as they may deem expedient, including hygiene, with special reference to the effects of alcoholic stimulants and narcotics upon the human body [1887 last clause added]; and shall cause to be given in each school week two lessons of not less than ten minutes' duration each on the subject of humane treatment to animals [1901]; * * *

Page 79.

ALCOHOLIC DRINKS AND NARCOTICS.

An Act to provide for the study of the nature of alcoholic drinks and narcotics and their effects upon the human system, in connection with the several divisions of the subject of physiology and hygiene by the pupils in the public schools of the state. Approved April 4, 1887. In force July 4, 1887. [L. '87, p. 378.]

Nature and Effects of Alcoholic Drinks and Narcotics Be Taught.

SECTION 1. That the nature of alcoholic drinks and narcotics and special instructions as to their effects upon the human system, in connection with the several divisions of the subject of physiology and hygiene, shall be included in the branches of study taught in the public schools of the State, and shall be studied and taught as thoroughly and in the same manner as other like required branches are in said schools, by the use of text-books, designated by the board of directors of the respective school districts, in the hands of pupils where other branches are thus studied in said schools, and by all pupils in all said schools throughout the State. (L. '87, p. 378, Sec. 1; Mills Ann. St., Sec. 4046.)

Failure to Enforce Provisions of Act—Penalty.

SEC. 2. That it shall be the duty of the proper officers in control of any school described in the foregoing section to enforce the provisions of this act; and any such officer, school director, committee, superintendent or teacher, who shall refuse, fail or neglect to comply with the requirements of this act, or shall neglect, refuse or fail or [to] make proper provisions for the instruction required, and in the manner specified by the first section of this act, for all pupils in each and every school under his or her jurisdiction shall be removed from office, and the vacancy filled as in other cases.

CONNECTICUT.

Laws relating to Schools, Connecticut School Document, No. 3, 1904.

Pages 14-15.

SECTION 43. Hygiene, including the effects of alcohol and narcotics on health and character, shall be taught as a regular branch of study to pupils above the third grade in public schools; and, in grades above the fifth, text-books treating of the effects of alcohol and narcotics on the human system shall be used. This section shall apply to classes in ungraded schools corresponding to the grades designated herein, but shall not include high schools. Normal and teachers' training schools shall give instruction on the subjects prescribed in this section and concerning the best method of teaching the same.

SEC. 44. Whenever the comptroller shall be satisfied that any town or district has failed to comply with the requirements of section 43, he may withhold from such town or district the whole or any part of the school dividend.

Page 57.

SEC. 194. * * * No certificate to teach in grades above the third in graded schools nor in classes corresponding to such grades in ungraded schools shall be granted to any person who has not passed a satisfactory examination in hygiene, including the effects of alcohol and narcotics on health and character. * * *

DELAWARE.

From Delaware School Laws for Free Public Schools, 1898.

Page 24.

SEC. 16. * * * It shall be the further duty of each of said committees and boards of education to see that all pupils in all the free schools in the district are instructed in physiology and hygiene, with special reference to alcoholic drinks, stimulants, and narcotics upon the human system, and to see that all the said schools are sufficiently supplied with such text-books relating to such subjects as are furnished the district in the distribution of free text-books hereinafter provided. Any teacher in any of the free schools of the State, failing to so instruct all the pupils under his governance, shall, unless ordered to the contrary by a school officer having authority over him, be liable to a fine of $25, to be recovered before any justice of the peace of the proper county by any informer; and any school officer ordering a teacher under him not to instruct the pupils as aforesaid shall be liable to like fine, recoverable as aforesaid by any informer.

Page 38.

SEC. 24. * * * Every person who is of a good moral character, and who shall in examination answer 90 per centum of the questions asked in * * * physiology and hygiene, with special reference to the effect of alcoholic stimulants and narcotics upon the human system, * * * shall receive from the superintendent a first grade certificate, * * *.

[Similar examination in physiology and hygiene is required for second grade and provisional certificates.]

DISTRICT OF COLUMBIA.

(See United States, District of Columbia, p. 635.)

FLORIDA.

From Digest of the School Laws of the State of Florida, 1900, p. 18.

Sec. 40. Each board of public instruction is directed—* * *

14th. To prescribe, in consultation with prominent teachers, a course of study for the schools of the county and grade them properly, and to require to be taught in every public school in the county over which they preside elementary physiology, especially as it relates to the effects of alcoholic stimulants and narcotics, morally, mentally, and physically; and all persons applying for certificates to teach shall be examined upon this branch of study under the same conditions as other branches required by law. (Rev. Stat., Sec. 242, 10th.)

GEORGIA.

From Acts and Resolutions of the General Assembly, 1901, p. 54.

No. 367.

An Act to provide for the teaching of physiology and hygiene (physiology, which shall include with other hygiene the nature and effects of alcoholic drinks and other narcotics upon the human system) in the public schools in Georgia; to provide a penalty in case any board of education, in city or county, fails to provide for the teaching of the same, and requiring all teachers to stand a satisfactory examination upon said subject as for other subjects.

Section I. Be it enacted by the general assembly of the State of Georgia, and be it hereby enacted by authority of the same, That the nature of alcoholic drinks and narcotics, and special instruction as to their effects upon the human system, in connection with the several divisions of the subject of physiology and hygiene, shall be included in the branches of study taught in common or public schools in the State of Georgia, and shall be studied and taught as thoroughly and in the same manner as other like required branches are in said schools.

Sec. II. It shall be the duty of county and city superintendents of schools receiving aid from the State to report to the State School Commissioner any failures or neglect on the part of the board of education; to make provisions for instructions of all pupils in any and all of the schools under their jurisdiction, in physiology and hygiene (physiology, which shall include with other hygiene the nature and effects of alcoholic drinks and other narcotics upon the human system) and the board of education of each county of this State shall adopt proper rules to carry the provisions of this law into effect.

Sec. III. No license shall be granted any person to teach in the public schools, receiving money from the State, after the first Monday in January,

1903, who has not passed a satisfactory examination in physiology and hygiene (physiology, which shall include with other hygiene the nature and effects of alcoholic drinks with other narcotics upon the human system).

SEC. IV. Be it further enacted, That all laws in conflict with this Act are hereby repealed.

Approved, December 17, 1901.

HAWAII.

(See United States, Territories, &c., p. 635.)

IDAHO.

From the General School Laws of the State of Idaho, 1901, p. 29.

SEC. 1028. *Certificates, to whom granted.*—The county superintendent shall grant certificates in such form as the State superintendent shall prescribe to those persons only who shall have attained the age of eighteen years, who have attended the said public examination and shall be found to possess good and moral character, thorough scholarship, and ability to govern and instruct the school, but no certificate shall be granted to any person, except to applicants for primary certificates, who shall not pass a satisfactory examination in * * * physiology, and hygiene, with particular reference to the effects of alcoholic drinks, stimulants, and narcotics upon the human system, * * *.

ILLINOIS.

From Illinois School Law, 1901, pp. 91-2.

AN ACT *to amend "An Act relating to the study of physiology and hygiene in the public schools," approved June 1, 1889, in force July 1, 1889. Approved June 9, 1897, in force July 1, 1897.*

SECTION 1.—*Be it enacted by the People of the State of Illinois, represented in the General Assembly*: That, "An Act relating to the study of physiology and hygiene in the public schools," approved June 1, 1889, in force July 1, 1889, be amended so as to read as follows:

That the nature of alcoholic drinks and other narcotics and their effects on the human system shall be taught in connection with the various divisions of physiology and hygiene as thoroughly as are other branches in all schools under State control, or supported wholly or in part by public money, and also in all schools connected with reformatory institutions.

All pupils in the above mentioned schools below the second year of the high schools and above the third year of school work, computing from the beginning of the lowest primary year, or in corresponding classes of ungraded schools, shall be taught and shall study this subject every year from suitable text-books in the hands of all pupils, for not less than four lessons a week for ten or more weeks of each year, and must pass the same tests in this as in other studies.

In all schools above mentioned all pupils in the lowest three primary school years, or in corresponding classes in ungraded schools, shall each year be instructed in this subject orally for not less than three lessons a week for ten weeks in each year, by teachers using text-books adapted for such oral instruction as a guide and standard.

The local school authorities shall provide needed facilities and definite time and place for this branch in the regular course of study.

The text-books in the pupils' hands shall be graded to the capacities of the fourth year, intermediate, grammar and high school pupils, or to corresponding classes as found in ungraded schools.

For students below high school grade such text-books shall give at least one-fifth their space, and for students of high school grade shall give not less than twenty pages to the nature and effects of alcoholic drinks and other narcotics. The pages on this subject, in a separate chapter at the end of the book, shall not be counted in determining the minimum.

SEC. 2. In all normal schools, teachers' training classes and teachers' institutes, adequate time and attention shall be given to instruction in the best methods of teaching this branch, and no teacher shall be licensed who has not passed a satisfactory examination in this subject and the best methods of teaching it.

Any school officer or officers who shall neglect or fail to comply with the provisions of this act shall forfeit and pay for each offense the sum of not less than five dollars nor more than twenty-five dollars.

INDIANA.

From School Law of Indiana, 1901, pp. 205-6.

228. *Effect of alcoholic drinks and narcotics.* 1. The nature of alcoholic drinks and narcotics and their effects on the human system in connection with the subjects of physiology and hygiene, shall be included in the branches to be regularly taught in the common schools of the State and in all educational institutions supported wholly or in part by money received from the State; and it shall be the duty of the Boards of Education and boards of such educational institutions, the township trustees, the Board of School Trustees of the several cities and towns in this State to make provisions for such instruction in the schools and institutions under their jurisdiction, and to adopt such methods as shall adapt the same to the capacity of the pupils in the various grades therein; but it shall be deemed a sufficient compliance with the requirements of this section if provision be made for such instruction orally only, and without the use of text-books by the pupils. (Revised Statutes 1897, section 6201.)

229. *Teachers examined concerning.* 2. No certificate shall be granted to any person (on) or after the first day of July, 1895, to teach in the common school or in any educational institution supported as aforesaid who does not pass a satisfactory examination as to the nature of alcoholic

drinks and narcotics and their effects upon the human system. (R. S 1897, section 6118.)

230. *Failure to teach effects—Dismissal.* 3. Any Superintendent or Principal of, or teacher in any common school or educational institution supported as aforesaid who wilfully refuses or neglects to give the instruction required by this act shall be dismissed from his or her employment. (R. S. 1897, section 6202.)

INDIAN TERRITORY.

(See United States, Territories, &c., p. 635.)

IOWA.

From Iowa School Laws and Decisions, 1902.

Page 117.—*The Normal School.*

Sec. 2677. *Branches of study.*—Physiology and hygiene shall be included in the branches of study regularly taught to and studied by all pupils in the school, and special reference shall be made to the effect of alcoholic drinks, stimulants, and narcotics upon the human system; and the board of trustees shall provide the means for the enforcement of the provisions of this section, and see that they are obeyed. (25 G. A., ch.1, Sec. 1.)

Pages 11-12.—*Examination of Teachers.*

Sec. 2736. *Subject.*—The examination shall include competency in and ability to teach * * * physiology and hygiene, which latter, in each division of the subject, shall include special reference to effects of alcohol, stimulants and narcotics upon the human system. * * *

Page 14.

Sec. 2737. *Certificate-revocation.*— * * * The superintendent shall revoke the certificate of any teacher who shall fail or neglect to comply with the provisions of law relating to the teaching of physiology and hygiene, and such teacher shall be disqualified for teaching in any public school for one year thereafter.

Page 16.

Sec. 2739. *Reports.*—The county superintendent shall annually, on the first Tuesday in October, make a report to the superintendent of public instruction, giving a full abstract of the several reports made to him by the secretaries and treasurers of school boards, stating the manner in and extent to which the requirements of the law regarding the instruction in physiology and hygiene are observed, and such other matters as he may be directed by the State superintendent to include therein, or he may think important in showing the actual condition of the schools in his county. * * *

Page 17.

Sec. 2740. *Enforcing laws.*—The county superintendent shall see that all provisions of the school law, so far as it relates to the schools or school officers within his county, are observed and enforced, specially those relating to the fencing of school house grounds with barb wire and the introduction and teaching of such divisions of physiology and hygiene as relate to the effects of alcohol, stimulants, and narcotics upon the human system, and to this end he may require the assistance of the county attorney, who shall at his request bring any action necessary to enforce the law or recover penalties incurred. (21 G. A., ch. 1, Sec. 2; 20 G. A., ch. 103, Sec. 2.)

Pages 45-6. *Board of Directors.*

Sec. 2775. *Instruction as to stimulants, narcotics, and poisons.*—It shall require all teachers to give and all scholars to receive instruction in physiology and hygiene, which study in every division of the subject shall include the effects upon the human system of alcoholic stimulants, narcotics, and poisonous substances. The instruction in this branch shall, of its kind, be as direct and specific as that given in other essential branches, and each scholar shall be required to complete the part of such study in his class or grade before being advanced to the next higher, and before being credited with having completed the study of the subject. (21 G. A., ch. 1.)

KANSAS.

From School Laws of Kansas, 1901, p. 75.

Sec. 206. *Examination of teachers in physiology and hygiene.*—No certificate shall be granted to any person to teach in any of the public schools of this State after the 1st day of January, 1886, who has not passed a satisfactory examination in the elements of physiology and hygiene with special reference to the effects of alcoholic stimulants and narcotics upon the human system; and provision shall be made by the proper officers, committees, and boards for instructing all pupils in each public school supported by public money and under State control upon the aforesaid topics. (Laws, 1885, ch. 169, sec. 1; Gen. Stat., 1889, sec. 5667.)

KENTUCKY.

From Kentucky Common School Laws, 1900, p. 15.

Sec. 21. *Course of study.*—The instruction prescribed by the board shall embrace spelling, reading, writing, arithmetic, English grammar, English composition, geography, physiology and hygiene, civil government, United States history, and history of Kentucky. After July 1, 1893, the nature and effects of alcoholic drinks and narcotics upon the human system shall, in all schools supported wholly or in part by the State, be taught as thoroughly as other required studies to all pupils studying physiology and hygiene as a part of this branch.

LOUISIANA.

From State School Law, adopted by Regular Session of the General Assembly, 1902.

Page 21.

SEC. 23. Be it further enacted, etc., That the branches of orthography, reading, writing, drawing, arithmetic, geography, grammar, United States history, the laws of health, including the evil effects of alcohol and narcotics, shall be taught in every district. * * *

Page 29.

SEC. 51. Be it further enacted, etc., That to obtain a third grade certificate the applicant must be found competent to teach spelling, reading, penmanship, drawing, arithmetic, English grammar, geography, the history of the United States, the Constitution of the United States, the Constitution of the State of Louisiana, physiology and hygiene, with special reference to the effects of stimulants and narcotics upon the human system, and the theory and art of teaching.

[Sections 52 and 53 require the above subjects and certain additional ones for second and third grade certificates.]

Page 30.

SEC. 58. Be it further enacted, etc., That each teacher of any school in this State supported wholly or in part from public money shall, before receiving any remuneration for services rendered in said capacity, file a certificate with the person by whom such payments are authorized to be made to the effect that such teacher has faithfully complied with all the provisions of this Act during the entire period for which such payment is sought, and in the manner specified in this Act; and no money shall be paid to any teacher who has not filed such a certificate.

Page 31.

SEC. 61. Be it further enacted, etc., That the teacher shall faithfully enforce in the school the course of study and the regulations prescribed in pursuance of law; and if any teacher shall wilfully refuse or neglect to comply with such requirements, the parish superintendent, on petition or complaint which shall be deemed sufficient by the board, may remove or dimiss him or her. * * *

MAINE.

From Laws of Maine Relating to Public Schools, 1901, pp. 22-3.

II. On satisfactory evidence that a candidate possesses a good moral character, and a temper and disposition suitable to be an instructor of youth, they shall examine him in reading, spelling, English grammar, geography, history, arithmetic, bookkeeping, civics, and physiology with special reference to the effects of alcoholic drinks, stimulants and narcotics upon the human system; * * *

III. * * * No certificate shall be granted any person to teach in public schools of this state after the fourth day of July, eighteen hundred and eighty-five, who has not passed a satisfactory examination in physiology and hygiene, with special reference to the effects of alcoholic drinks, stimulants and narcotics upon the human system.

V. They shall make provisions for instructing all pupils in all schools supported by public money, or under state control, in physiology and hygiene, with special reference to the effects of alcoholic drinks, stimulants, and narcotics upon the human system.

MARYLAND.

From the School Laws of Maryland, 1902, p. 19.

40. The nature of alcoholic drinks and narcotics, with special instruction as to their effects upon the human system, in connection with the several divisions of the subject of physiology and hygiene, shall be included in the branches of study taught in the common schools, and shall be taught to and studied by all pupils whose capacity will admit of it, in all departments of the public schools of the State, and in all educational institutions supported wholly or in part by money from the State; and the said study shall be taught to and studied by said pupils in said schools as thoroughly and in the same manner as other like branches are there taught and studied, with text-books in the hands of pupils, where other like branches are thus studied; and said text-books must be published, printed, and sold in the State of Maryland.

41. It shall be the duty of boards of county school commissioners and of the board of commissioners of public schools of Baltimore city, county examiners, superintendents of public schools of Baltimore city, and boards of all educational institutions receiving aid from the State, to enforce the provisions of the preceding section. [Laws of 1886, ch. 495.]

MASSACHUSETTS.

From the Revised Laws of the Commonwealth of Massachusetts Relating to Public Instruction, 1902.

Page 11.

SECTION 1. Every city and town shall maintain, for at least thirty-two weeks in each year, a sufficient number of schools for the instruction of all the children who may legally attend a public school therein, * * * . Such schools shall be taught by teachers of competent ability and good morals, and shall give instruction in * * * physiology and hygiene, and good behavior. In each of the subjects of physiology and hygiene, special instruction as to the effects of alcoholic drinks and of stimulants and narcotics on the human system shall be taught as a regular branch of study to all pupils in all schools which are supported wholly or partly by public money, except schools which are maintained solely for instruction in particular branches. * * *

Pages 25-6.

SECTION 1. Every child between seven and fourteen years of age shall attend some public day school in the city or town in which he resides during the entire time the public day schools are in session, * * * . The attendance of a child upon a public day school shall not be required if he has attended for a like period of time a private day school approved by the school committee of such city or town in accordance with the provisions of the following section, or if he has been otherwise instructed for a like period of time in the branches of learning required by law to be taught in the public schools, or if he has already acquired such branches of learning, * * * .

SEC. 2. For the purposes of the preceding section, school committees shall approve a private school only when the instruction in all the studies required by law is in the English language, and when they are satisfied that such instruction equals in thoroughness and efficiency and in the progress made therein the instruction in the public schools in the same city or town; * * * .

MICHIGAN.

From the General School Laws of Michigan, 1901.

Pages 20-1.

(58.) SECTION 4680. SEC. 15. The district board shall specify the studies to be pursued in the schools of the district [districts], and in addition to the branches in which instruction is now required by law to be given in the public school of the state, instruction shall be given in physiology and hygiene, with a special reference to the nature of alcohol and narcotics, and their effects upon the human system. Such instruction shall be given by the aid of text-books in the case of pupils who are able to read, and as thoroughly as in other studies pursued in the same school. The text-books to be used for such instruction shall give at least one-fourth of their space to the consideration of the nature and effects of alcoholic drinks and narcotics, and the books used in the highest grade of graded schools shall contain at least twenty pages of matter relating to this subject. Text-books used in giving the foregoing instructions shall first be approved by the state board of education. Each school board making a selection of text-books under the provisions of this act shall make a record thereof in their proceedings, and text-books once adopted under the provisions of this act shall not be changed within five years, except by the consent of a majority of the qualified voters of the district present at an annual meeting, or at a special meeting called for that purpose. The district board shall require each teacher in the public schools of such district, before placing the school register in the hands of the directors [director], as provided in section thirteen of this act, to certify therein whether or not instruction has been given in the school or grade presided over by such teacher, as required by this act, and it shall be the duty of the director of the district to file with the township clerk a certified copy of such certificate. Any school board neglecting or refusing to comply with any of the provisions of this act shall be subject to fine or forfeiture the same as for neglect of any other duty pertaining to their office. This act shall apply to all schools in the state, including schools in cities or villages, whether incorporated under special charter or under the general laws. (Act 165, 1887.)

Pages 53-4.

(153.) SEC. 4775. SECTION 1. *The People of the State of Michigan enact*, That from and after June thirtieth, eighteen hundred and ninety, each school board of the state shall purchase, when authorized, as hereinafter provided, the text-books used by the pupils of the schools in its district in each of the following subjects, to wit: Orthography, spelling, writing, reading, geography, arithmetic, grammar (including language lessons), national and state history, civil government, and physiology and hygiene; but text-books once adopted under the provisions of this act shall not be changed within five years: Provided, That the text-book on the subject of physiology and hygiene must be approved by the state board of education, and shall in every way comply with section fifteen of act number one hundred and sixty-five of the public acts of eighteen hundred and eighty-seven, approved June ninth, eighteen hundred and eighty-seven: And provided further, That all text-books used in any school district shall be uniform in any one subject.

Page 90.

(256.) SEC. 1827. SEC. 16. The said board shall examine all text-books in physiology and hygiene offered for use in the public schools of this state, and approve those only which comply with the law relative to the space required to be devoted to the consideration of the nature and effects of alcoholic drinks and narcotics, as provided in act one hundred and sixty-four of the public acts of eighteen hundred and eighty-seven. It shall also be the duty of said board to distribute to the various educational institutions of the state such specimens of copper, iron and other ores and rocks prescribed for such distribution under the provisions of section three of act nine of the public acts of eighteen hundred and seventy-seven, being compiler's section eight hundred and forty-one of Howell's annotated statutes.

[The act of 1887 referred to is act 165 instead of 164. It amends Sec.

15, Ch. 3, of the general laws of 1881 relative to public instruction and will be found in Section 4680. See Comp. Section 58.]

MINNESOTA.

From Laws of Minnesota relating to the Public School System, 1901, p. 111.

Title xxvii. Moral Science, and Physiology and Hygiene.

SECTION 365 (1894, SEC. 3892). *In physiology and hygiene.*—It shall be the duty of the boards of education, and trustees in charge of schools and educational institutions supported in whole or in part by public funds, to make provision for systematic and regular instruction in physiology and hygiene, including special reference to the effects of stimulants and narcotics upon the human system.

SEC. 366 (1894, SECS. 3893, 3894). *Teachers to be examined and give instruction in.*—It shall be the duty of all teachers in public schools of the state to give systematic and regular instruction in physiology and hygiene, including special reference to the effects of stimulants and narcotics upon the human system; and any neglect or refusal on the part of such teachers to provide instruction as aforesaid shall be deemed sufficient cause for annulling his or her certificate by the county superintendent or other competent officer. No certificate shall be granted any person to teach in the public schools of this state * * * who has not passed a satisfactory examination in physiology and hygiene, with special reference to the effects of stimulants and narcotics upon the human system.

(It is for the board of education in a fair endeavor to observe the requirements of the law, and, subject, of course, to your review, to determine to what extent, in what grades, and by what means instruction upon the subject named shall be imparted.—*Childs*, June 4, 1895.)

SEC. 367 (1895, SEC. 3895). *Duty of county superintendent.*—It shall be the duty of the county superintendent of schools to report to the superintendent of public instruction any failure or neglect on the part of any board of education or trustees of a school or institution receiving aid in whole or in part from the state, to make provision for the instruction aforesaid, and such failure or neglect being satisfactorily proven by the county superintendent or by other persons, it shall be sufficient warrant upon which the superintendent of public instruction may withhold the apportionment of the current school fund from such district; *provided*, that not more than one-fourth of said apportionment shall be withheld upon the first offense, one-third upon the second, and one-half upon any subsequent offense.

(The withholding of an apportionment is a harsh measure and should not be inflicted upon a district unless it is obvious that the infraction has been wilful.—*Childs*, May 13, 1895.)

Sec. 368 (1894, Sec. 3896). *Text-book.*—The superintendent of public instruction and the presidents of the normal schools of this state are directed to recommend some suitable text-book, and to furnish the same at cost to the several school districts of this state, for the study of physiology and hygiene, with special reference to the effects of stimulants and narcotics upon the human system.

MISSISSIPPI.

From School Laws of Mississippi, 1900.

Page 27.

Sec. 4019. The branches of study upon which teachers are required to be examined constitute the curriculum of the free public schools.

Sec. 4022. To obtain a first grade license the applicant must be examined on spelling, reading, practical and mental arithmetic, geography, English grammar and composition, United States history, history of Mississippi, elements of natural philosophy, civil government, elements of physiology and hygiene, with special reference to the effects of alcohol and narcotics on the human system; and to obtain a second grade license the applicant must be examined on * * * primary physiology with special reference to the effects of alcohol and narcotics on the human system; but a teacher otherwise qualified shall not be refused a certificate to teach for the next two years by reason of a want of sufficient knowledge on the subject of physiology.

Sec. 4023. To obtain a third grade license the applicant must be examined on the subjects required for second grade and must make thereon an average of not less than sixty per centum, with not less than forty per centum on any subject.

Page 43.

State board of examiners. (Act approved March 18, 1896.)

Sec. 7. Any teacher may secure a State license by passing a satisfactory examination, in the presence of the county superintendent or other authorized agent of the State board of examiners, in * * * elements of physiology and hygiene, with special reference to the effects of alcohol and narcotics on the human system, * * * .

MISSOURI.

From School Laws of the State of Missouri, 1899.

Page 46.

Sec. 9799. Physiology and hygiene, including their several branches, with special instruction as to the effects of alcoholic drinks, narcotics and stimulants on the human system, shall constitute a part of the course of instruction and be taught in all schools supported wholly or in part by public money, or under State control. [R. S. 1889, Sec. 8024, amended, Laws, 1897, p. 233.]

Page 82.

Examination for teachers' certificates.

SEC. 9958. * * * Teachers shall be granted a third grade certificate who are of good moral character and who shall pass a satisfactory examination upon the following branches: * * * physiology and hygiene with special reference to the effect of alcoholic drinks and stimulants and narcotics generally upon the human system. * * *

[Examinations for first and second grades include the foregoing with other subjects.]

MONTANA.

From School Laws, 1903, p. 26.

Senate Bill No. 14.

"An Act to amend Section 1861 of the Political Code of the State of Montana relating to the Course of Study in Public Schools."

Be It Enacted By the Legislative Assembly of the State of Montana:

Section 1. That Section 1861, Article 8, Chapter 6 of the Political Code be amended so as to read as follows:—

Section 1861. All common schools shall be taught in the English language: And instructions shall be given in the following branches, viz.: Reading, penmanship, written arithmetic, mental arithmetic, orthography, geography, English grammar, physiology and hygiene. With special reference to the effect of alcoholic stimulants and narcotics on the human system. History of the United States and of Montana. Also a system of humane treatment of animals as embodied in the laws of Montana. Such instruction to consist of, at least, two (2) lessons of not less than ten minutes each per week. The principal or teacher in every school shall certify in each of his or her reports that such instruction has been given in the school under his or her control. Attention must be given during the entire school course to the cultivation of manners. To the laws of health. Physical exercise. Ventilation and temperature of the school room.

Section 2. All Acts and parts of Acts in conflict herewith are hereby repealed.

Section 3. This Act shall be in full force and effect from and after its passage and approval by the Governor.

Approved Feb. 24th, 1903.

[So printed in official pamphlet.]

NEBRASKA.

From the School Laws and School Land Laws of Nebraska, 1901, p. 59.

Sec. 5a. *Scientific temperance instruction.*—Provisions shall be made by the proper local school authorities for instructing the pupils in all schools supported by public money, or under State control, in physiology and hygiene with special reference to the effects of alcoholic drinks and other stimulants and narcotics upon the human system.

Sec. 6. *Examination.*—No certificate shall be granted to any person to teach in the public schools of the State of Nebraska after the first day of January, eighteen hundred and eighty-six, who has not passed a satisfactory examination in physiology and hygiene with special reference to the effects of alcoholic drinks and other stimulants and narcotics upon the human system.

NEVADA.

From State of Nevada School Laws, 1897, p. 5.

State board of education. (Statutes 1895, p. 81.)

Sec. 4. The powers and duties of the board shall be as follows:

First. To prescribe and cause to be adopted a uniform series of text-books in the principal studies pursued in the public schools, to wit: Reading, writing, arithmetic, spelling, language, grammar, geography, history of the United States, physiology and drawing. Special prominence shall be given in all public schools to the effect of alcoholic stimulants and of narcotics upon the human system. No school district shall be entitled to receive its pro rata of the public school money unless such text-books on the above subjects as have been prescribed by the State board of education shall be used in all the public schools pursuing subjects covered by said text-books; * * * .

NEW HAMPSHIRE.

From School Laws of the State of New Hampshire, 1903.

Pages 28-9.

Section 6. Chapter 92. (*As amended by chapter 40, Session Laws of 1895, and chapter 31, Session Laws of 1903.*) They shall prescribe in all mixed schools and in all graded schools above primary, the studies of physiology and hygiene, having special reference to the effects of alcoholic stimulants and of narcotics upon the human system, and shall see that the studies so prescribed are thoroughly taught in said schools and that well approved text-books upon these subjects are furnished to teachers and scholars, * * * . Candidates shall be examined in the subjects prescribed by law, or by the school board in accordance with law.

Section 2, chapter 40, Laws of 1895. If any member of the school board shall neglect or refuse to comply with the provisions of the first paragraph of section 6 he shall forfeit the sum of two hundred dollars.

Page 42.

Sec. 2, Chapter 94. (*As amended by chapter 35, Session Laws of 1895,* *and chapter 33, Session Laws of 1903.*) The superintendent of public instruction * * * shall investigate the condition and efficiency of the system of popular education in the state, especially in relation to the amount and character of the instruction given to the study of physiology and hygiene, having special reference to the effects of alcoholic stimulants and of narcotics upon the human system, and shall recommend to school boards what he considers the best text-books upon those subjects and suggest to them the best mode of teaching them, and shall pursue such a course for the purpose of awakening and guiding public sentiment in relation thereto as may seem to him best, * * * and he shall biennially make a report, containing * * * a detailed report of his own doings.

NEW JERSEY.

From New Jersey School Laws, 1902, pp. 104-5.

237. The nature of alcoholic drinks and narcotics and their effects upon the human system shall be taught in all schools supported wholly or in part by public moneys as thoroughly and in the same manner as other like branches shall be taught, by the use of graded text-books in the hands of the pupils when other branches shall be thus taught, and orally only in the case of pupils unable to read. In the text-books on physiology and hygiene the space devoted to the consideration of the nature of alcoholic drinks and narcotics and their effects upon the human system shall be sufficient for a full and adequate treatment of the subject. The failure or refusal of any district to comply with the provisions of this section shall be sufficient cause for withholding from such district the State appropriation.

238. No certificate shall be granted to any person to teach in the public schools, except to persons applying for special certificates to teach music, drawing, manual training, or other subjects not included in the usual school curriculum, who shall not have passed a satisfactory examination in physiology and hygiene with special reference to the nature of alcoholic drinks and narcotics and their effects upon the human system.

NEW MEXICO.

(See United States, Territories, &c., p. 635.)

NEW YORK.

From the Consolidated School Law of the State of New York, 1902.

Pages 24, 26, 28.

Title V. School commissioners; their election, powers and duties.

Sec. 13. Every commissioner shall have power and it shall be his duty: * * *

5. To examine, * * * persons proposing to teach common schools within his district, * * * . No certificate shall be granted to any person to teach in public schools of this state who has not passed a satisfactory examination in physiology and hygiene, with special reference to the effects of alcoholic drinks, stimulants and narcotics upon the human system. * * *

Pages 48-50.

Title VII, Article 6. Of trustees, their powers and duties.

Sec. 47. It shall be the duty of the trustee or trustees of every school district, and they shall have power: * * *

11. To establish rules for the government and discipline of the schools in their respective districts; and to prescribe the course of studies to be pursued in such schools. Provision shall be made for instructing pupils in all schools supported by public money, or under state control, in physiology and hygiene, with special reference to the effect of alcoholic drinks, stimulants and narcotics upon the human system.

Page 77.

Title VIII. Of union free schools. Article 4. Of the powers and duties of boards of education.

Sec. 15. The said board of education of every union free school district shall severally have power, and it shall be their duty: * * *

5. To make provision for the instruction of pupils in physiology and hygiene with special reference to the effect of alcoholic drinks, stimulants and narcotics upon the human system.

Pages 104-6.

Title XV. Article 6. Physiology and hygiene in the public schools.

Sec. 19.[*] The nature of alcoholic drinks and other narcotics and their effects on the human system shall be taught in connection with the various divisions of physiology and hygiene, as thoroughly as are other branches in all schools under state control or supported wholly or in part by public money of the state, and also in all schools connected with reformatory institutions. All pupils in the above-mentioned schools below the second year of the high school and above the third year of school work computing from the beginning of the lowest primary, not kindergarten year, or in corresponding classes of ungraded schools, shall be taught and shall study this subject every year with suitable text-books in the hands of all pupils, for not less than three lessons a week for ten or more weeks, or the equivalent of the same in each year, and must pass satisfactory tests in this as in other studies, before promotion to the next succeeding year's work; except that where there are nine or more school years below the high school, the study may be omitted in all years above

[*] As amended by section 1, chapter 901, laws of 1896.

the eighth year and below the high school, by such pupils as have passed the required tests of the eighth year. In all schools above mentioned, all pupils in the lowest three primary, not kindergarten, school years or in corresponding classes in ungraded schools shall, each year, be instructed in this subject orally for not less than two lessons a week for ten weeks, or the equivalent of the same in each year, by teachers using text-books adapted for such oral instruction as a guide and standard, and such pupils must pass such tests in this as may be required in other studies before promotion to the next succeeding year's work. Nothing in this act shall be construed as prohibiting or requiring the teaching of this subject in kindergarten schools. The local school authorities shall provide needed facilities and definite time and place for this branch in the regular courses of study. The text-books in the pupils' hands shall be graded to the capacities of fourth year, intermediate, grammar and high school pupils, or to corresponding classes in ungraded schools. For students below high school grade, such text-books shall give at least one-fifth their space, and for students of high school grade, shall give not less than twenty pages, to the nature and effects of alcoholic drinks and other narcotics. This subject must be treated in the text-books in connection with the various divisions of physiology and hygiene, and pages on this subject in a separate chapter at the end of the book shall not be counted in determining the minimum. No text-book on physiology not conforming to this act shall be used in the public schools, except so long as may be necessary to fulfil the conditions of any legal adoption existing at the time of the passage of this act. All regents' examinations in physiology and hygiene shall include a due proportion of questions on the nature of alcoholic drinks and other narcotics, and their effects on the human system.

Sec. 20.* In all normal schools, teachers' training classes and teachers' institutes, adequate time and attention shall be given to instruction in the best methods of teaching this branch, and no teacher shall be licensed who has not passed a satisfactory examination in the subject, and the best methods of teaching it. On satisfactory evidence that any teacher has wilfully refused to teach this subject as provided in this act, the state superintendent of public instruction shall revoke the license of such teacher. No public money of the state shall be apportioned by the state superintendent of public instruction or paid for the benefit of any city until the superintendent of schools therein shall have filed with the treasurer or chamberlain of such city an affidavit and with the state superintendent of public instruction a duplicate of such affidavit that he has made thorough investigation as to the facts, and that to the best of his knowledge, information and belief, all the provisions of this act have been complied with in all the schools under his supervision in such city during the last preceding legal school year; nor shall any public money of the state be

* As amended by section 1, chapter 901, laws of 1896.

apportioned by the state superintendent of public instruction or by school commissioners or paid for the benefit of any school district, until the president of the board of trustees, or in the case of common school districts the trustee or some one member of the board of trustees, shall have filed with the school commissioner having jurisdiction an affidavit that he has made thorough investigation as to the facts, and that to the best of his knowledge, information and belief, all the provisions of this act have been complied with in such district, which affidavit shall be included in the trustees' annual report, and it shall be the duty of every school commissioner to file with the state superintendent of public instruction an affidavit in connection with his annual report showing all districts in his jurisdiction that have and those that have not complied with all the provisions of this act, according to the best of his knowledge, information and belief, based on a thorough investigation by him as to the facts; nor shall any public money of the state be apportioned or paid for the benefit of any teachers' training class, teachers' institute or other school mentioned herein, until the officer having jurisdiction or supervision thereof shall have filed with the state superintendent of public instruction an affidavit that he has made a thorough investigation as to the facts, and that to the best of his knowledge, information and belief, all the provisions of this act relative thereto have been complied with. The principal of each normal school in the state shall, at the close of each of their school years, file with the state superintendent of public instruction an affidavit that all the provisions of this law, applicable thereto, have been complied with during the school year just terminated, and until such affidavit shall be filed no warrant shall be issued by the state superintendent of public instruction for the payment by the treasurer of any part of the money appropriated for such school. It shall be the duty of the state superintendent of public instruction to provide blank forms of affidavit required herein for use by the local school officers, and he shall include in his annual report a statement showing every school, city, or district which has failed to comply with all the provisions of this act during the preceding school year. On complaint by appeal to the state superintendent of public instruction by any patron of the schools mentioned in the last preceding section, or by any citizen, that any provision of this act has not been complied with in any city or district, the state superintendent of public instruction shall make immediate investigation, and on satisfactory evidence of the truth of such complaint, shall thereupon and thereafter withhold all public money of the state to which such city or district would otherwise be entitled, until all the provisions of this act shall be complied with in said city or district, and shall exercise his power of reclamation and deduction under section nine of article one of title two of the consolidated school law.

NORTH CAROLINA.

Laws of 1891. *Chapter* 169.

An Act to provide for the study of the nature of alcoholic drinks and narcotics, and of their effect upon the human system, in the public schools.

The General Assembly of North Carolina do enact:

SECTION 1. That the nature of alcoholic drinks and narcotics, and special instruction as to their effects upon the human system, in connection with the several divisions of the subject of physiology and hygiene, shall be included in the branches of study taught in the common or public schools of the state of North Carolina, and shall be studied and taught as thoroughly and in the same manner as other like required branches are in said schools, by the use of text-books in the hands of pupils and orally in case of pupils unable to read, and shall be taught by all teachers and studied by all pupils in all schools in this state supported wholly or in part by public money.

SEC. 2. That the text-books used for the instruction to be given in the preceding section for primary and intermediate grades shall give at least one-fourth of their space to the consideration of the nature and effect of alcoholic drinks and narcotics, and the text-books used in the highest grades of the public schools shall give at least twenty pages to the consideration of this subject.

SEC. 3. That no certificate to teach in the public schools of this state shall hereafter be granted to any applicant who has not passed a satisfactory examination in the study of the nature of alcoholic drinks and narcotics and of their effects upon the human system, in connection with the several divisions of the subject of relative physiology and hygiene.

SEC. 4. That it shall be the duty of the proper officers in control of any school described in the first section of this act to enforce the provisions of this act, and any such officer, school-director, committee, superintendent or teacher who shall refuse or neglect to comply with the requirements of this act, or shall neglect or fail to make proper provisions for the instruction required and in the manner specified by this act for all pupils in each and every school under his control and supervision, shall be removed from office and the vacancy filled as in other cases.

SEC. 5. This act shall be in force and effect from and after the first day of August, eighteen hundred and ninety-one. (Ratified the 27th day of February, A. D., 1891.)

From Public School Laws of North Carolina, p. 40.

An Act to establish a text-book commission (ratified February 8, 1901).

SEC. 2. * * * It shall not be lawful for any school officer, director, or teacher to use any other books upon the same branches other than those adopted by said State text-book commission. Said uniform series shall include the following branches, to wit: * * * physiology, hygiene, nature and effect of alcoholic drinks and narcotics * * * .

NORTH DAKOTA.

From the General School Laws of the State of North Dakota, 1903.

Page 26.

SEC. 648. *Teacher's certificate may be revoked, when.*—He [county superintendent of schools] shall see that the pupils are instructed in the several branches of study required by law to be taught in the schools as far as they are qualified to pursue them. If any teacher neglects or refuses to give instruction as required by law in physiology and hygiene, and the nature and effect of alcoholic drinks, narcotics and stimulants, the county superintendent shall promptly revoke such teacher's certificate and cause him to be discharged. If the teacher, so neglecting or refusing to give instructions in such branches, holds a state certificate, the county superintendent shall immediately certify such refusal or neglect to the superintendent of public instruction.

Page 69.

SEC. 750. *Branches to be taught in all schools.*—Each teacher in the common schools shall teach pupils when they are sufficiently advanced to pursue the same following branches: Orthography, reading, spelling, writing, arithmetic, language lessons, English grammar, geography, United States history, civil government, physiology and hygiene, giving special instruction concerning the nature of alcoholic drinks, stimulants and narcotics, and their effect upon the human system; physiology and hygiene and the nature of alcoholic drinks, stimulants and narcotics, and their effect upon the human system shall be taught as thoroughly as any branch is taught by the use of a text-book to all pupils able to use a text-book who have not thoroughly studied that branch and orally to all other pupils. When such oral instruction is given as herein required, a sufficient time, not less than fifteen minutes, shall be given to such oral instruction for at least four days in each school week. Each teacher in special school districts and in cities organized for school purposes under special law shall conform to and be governed by the provisions of this section.

OHIO.

From Ohio School Laws, 1900, pp. 142-3.

SECTION 1. The nature of alcoholic drinks and other narcotics, and their effects on the human system, in connection with the various divisions of physiology and hygiene, shall be included in the branches to be regularly taught in the common schools of the State, and in all educational institutions supported wholly or in part by money from the State; and it shall be the duty of boards of education and boards of such educational institutions to make suitable provisions for this instruction in the schools and institutions under their respective jurisdiction, giving definite time and place for this branch in the regular course of study, and to adopt such methods as will adapt the same to the capacity of pupils in the various grades and to corresponding classes as found in ungraded schools; the same tests for promotion shall be required in this as in other branches.

SEC. 2. In all teachers' institutes, also in all normal schools and teachers' training classes which shall hereafter be established by the State, adequate time and attention shall be given to instruction in the best methods of teaching this branch. No certificate shall be granted to any person to teach in the common schools or in any educational institution supported as aforesaid who does not pass a satisfactory examination on this subject and the best methods of teaching the same. It shall be the duty of the State commissioner of common schools to see that the provisions in this section relating to county teachers' institutes, and schools and classes established by whatever name hereafter for training teachers, and the examinations of teachers, are carried out; and said commissioner shall each year make full report of the enforcement of said section in connection with his annual report.

SEC. 3. Any school official, or any employee in any way concerned in the enforcement of the act, who wilfully refuses or neglects to provide for or to give the instruction required by this act shall be fined, and shall pay for each offense the sum of twenty-five dollars Mayors, justices of the peace, and probate judges shall have concurrent jurisdiction with the common pleas court to try the offenses described in this act, and all fines or penalties collected under this act shall be paid into the general county school fund of the county in which such fine or penalty was collected.

OKLAHOMA.

(See United States, Territories, &c., p. 635.)

OREGON.

From Oregon School Laws, 1901, pp. 53-4.

Title VIII. School Teachers.

SEC. 56. A teacher's duty while in charge of the school shall be as follows: * * *

3. To labor during school hours to advance the pupils in their studies; to create in their minds a desire for knowledge, principle, morality, politeness, cleanliness and the preservation of physical health; and it is hereby made the duty of every teacher to give, and of every board of school directors to cause to be given, to all pupils suitable instruction in physi-

ology and hygiene, with special reference to the effects of alcoholic drinks, stimulants and narcotics upon the human system. Such instructions in physiology and hygiene shall be given orally to pupils who are below the fourth grade, and shall be given by the use of text-books to all pupils above the fourth grade, and such instruction shall be given as thoroughly to all pupils as instruction in arithmetic or geography is given. Each teacher of a public school, before leaving the school register with the school clerk, shall certify therein whether instruction has been given in the school or grade presided over by such teacher, as required by this act, and no public money shall be paid over to the treasurer of a district unless the register of such district contains a certificate of the teacher that instruction has been given in physiology and hygiene, with special reference to the effects of alcoholic drinks, stimulants and narcotics upon the human system, as required by this act.

PENNSYLVANIA.

From the Common School Laws of Pennsylvania, 1902, pp. 299-302.

Act April 2, 1885, Sections 1-3, Public Laws, page 7.

CCCVII. That physiology and hygiene, which shall, in each division of the subject so pursued, include special reference to the effect of alcoholic drinks and stimulants and narcotics upon the human system, shall be included in the branches of study now required by law to be taught in the common schools, and shall be introduced and studied as a regular branch by all pupils in all departments of the public schools of the Commonwealth, and in all educational institutions supported wholly or in part by money from the Commonwealth (r).

CCCVIII. It shall be the duty of county, city, borough superintendents, and boards of all educational institutions receiving aid from the Commonwealth, to report to the Superintendent of Public Instruction any failure or neglect on the part of the boards of school directors, boards of school controllers, boards of education, and boards of educational institutions receiving aid from the Commonwealth, to make proper provision in any and all of the schools or districts under their jurisdiction for instruction in physiology and hygiene which, in each division of the subject so pursued, gives special reference to the effects of alcoholic drinks, stimulants, and narcotics upon the human system as required by this act; and such failures on the part of directors, controllers, boards, of education, and boards of educational institutions receiving money from the Commonwealth thus reported or otherwise satisfactorily proven, shall be deemed sufficient cause for withholding the warrant for State appropriation of school money to which such district or educational institution would otherwise be entitled (s).

CCCIX. No certificate shall be granted any person to teach in the public schools of the Commonwealth or in any of the educational institutions receiving money from the Commonwealth, after the first Monday of June, Anno Domini one thousand eight hundred and eighty-six, who has not passed a satisfactory examination in physiology and hygiene, with special reference to the effects of alcoholic drinks, stimulants and narcotics upon the human system.

RHODE ISLAND.

From State of Rhode Island, Laws pertaining to Education, 1900, p. 55.

CHAPTER 60, SECTION 7. The school committees of the several towns shall make provision for the instruction of the pupils in all schools supported wholly, or in part, by public money, in physiology and hygiene, with special reference to the effects of alcoholic liquors, stimulants and narcotics upon the human system.

SOUTH CAROLINA.

From the School Law of South Carolina, 1901, p. 22.

SEC. 27. It shall be the duty of the County Board of Education and of the Boards of Trustees hereinafter provided for to see that in every school under their care there shall be taught, as far as practicable, orthography, reading, writing, arithmetic, geography, English grammar, the elements of agriculture, history of the United States and of this State, the principals of the Constitution, and laws of the United States and of this State, morals and good behavior, algebra, physiology and hygiene, and especially as to the effects of alcoholic liquors and narcotics upon the human system. English literature, and such other branches as the State board may from time to time direct.

SOUTH DAKOTA.

From School Laws, State of South Dakota, 1903, p. 24.

SECTION 2378. Instructions shall be given in the common schools of the state in the following branches, in the several grades in which each may be required, viz.: Reading, writing, orthography, arithmetic, geography, primary language and English grammar, history of the United States, physiology and hygiene, with special instruction as to the nature of alcoholic drinks and their effect upon the human system, and civil government.

TENNESSEE.

From the Public School Laws of Tennessee, 1903, p. 21.

SECTION 32. (4) Amendment taking effect January 1, 1896 (Acts 1895, Chap. 180): In addition to the branches in which instruction is now given in the public schools of this State, Physiology and Hygiene, with a special reference to the nature of alcoholic drinks and narcotics, and smoking cigarettes, and their effects upon the human system, shall also be taught as thoroughly as other required branches, and shall be made a regular course of study for all pupils in all schools supported entirely or in part by public money.

(5) No certificate shall be granted to any person to teach in the public schools of this State after the first of January, 1896, who has not passed a satisfactory examination in Physiology and Hygiene, with special reference to the effects of alcoholic drinks and narcotics, and cigarette smoking upon the human system.

TEXAS.

From School Laws of Texas, 1901.

Page 9.

SEC. 19. All public schools in this State shall be required to have taught in them orthography, reading in English, penmanship, arithmetic, English grammar, modern geography, composition, physiology and hygiene, including the effects of alcoholic stimulants and narcotics on the human system, mental arithmetic, * * * . (Art. 3909a, R. S., as amended by the 27th Leg.)

Page 32.

SEC. 69. An applicant for a third grade certificate shall be examined in * * * elementary physiology and hygiene and the laws of healt , with special reference to narcotics, * * *. (1) An applicant for a second grade certificate shall be examined in the subjects prescribed for a third grade certificate, and, in addition thereto * * * physiology and hygiene * * *. (2) An applicant for a first grade certificate shall be examined in the subjects prescribed for third and second grade certificates, and in addition thereto, in * * * the effects of tobacco and alcoholic intoxicants upon the human system. (Art. 3974, R. S., as amended by the 26th Leg.)

UTAH.

From School Law of Utah, 1901, p. 32.

It shall be the duty of all boards of education and trustees in charge of schools and educational institutions supported in whole or in part by public funds to make provision for systematic and regular instruction in physiology and hygiene, including special reference to the effects of stimulants and narcotics upon the human system. [R. S., sec. 1829.]

VERMONT.

From General Laws of the State of Vermont, Relating to Public Instruction, 1903, p. 22.

SECTION 683. In every town there shall be kept for at least twenty-eight weeks in each year, at the expense of said town, by a teacher or teachers of competent ability and of good morals, a sufficient number of schools for the instruction of all the children who may legally attend all the public schools therein; and all pupils shall be thoroughly instructed in * * * elementary physiology and hygiene, with special reference to the effect of alcoholic drinks and narcotics on the human system, * * * . [In the law relating to district schools "elementary physiology and hygiene" is not followed by this clause.]

VIRGINIA.

From Virginia School Laws, 1901, pp. 60-61.

97. *Subjects to be taught.*—In every public free school shall be taught orthography, reading, writing, arithmetic, grammar, geography, physiology and hygiene, civil government, drawing, history of the United States and history of Virginia. In teaching physiology and hygiene approved text-books shall be used, plainly setting forth the effects of alcohol and other narcotics on the human system, and such effects shall be as fully and thoroughly taught as are other branches of the said last-named subjects.

WASHINGTON.

From School Laws of the State of Washington, 1903.

Title III. The Common School System. Chapter 1.—District Schools.
Page 37.

SEC. 65. All common schools shall be taught in the English language, and instructions shall be given in the following branches, viz.: * * * physiology and hygiene with special reference to the effects of alcoholic stimulants and narcotics on the human system, * * *.

Chapter XI.—*Penalties*, pp. 78, 79, 81, 82.

SEC. 162. (4) Upon complaint in writing being made to any county superintendent by any district clerk, or by any head of a family, that the board of directors of the district in which said clerk shall hold his office, or said head of family shall reside, have failed to make provisions for the teaching of hygiene or have failed to require it to be taught, with special reference to the effects of alcoholic drink, stimulants and narcotics upon the human system, as provided by law, in the common schools of such districts, it shall be the duty of such county superintendent to investigate at once the matter of such complaints, and if found to be true, he shall immediately notify the county treasurer of the county in which such school district is located, and after the receipt of such notice, it shall be the duty of such county treasurer to refuse to pay any warrants drawn upon him by the board of directors of such district subsequent to the date of such notice and until he shall be notified to do so by such county superintendent. Whenever it shall be made to appear to the said county superintendent, and he shall be satisfied that the board of directors of such district are complying with the provisions of law in this matter, and are causing physiology and hygiene to be taught in the public schools of such district as hereinbefore provided, he shall notify said county treasurer, and said treasurer shall thereupon honor the warrants of said board of directors.

Sec. 163. (5) Any county superintendent of common schools who shall fail or refuse to comply with the provisions of the preceding section shall be liable to a penalty of one hundred dollars, to be recovered in a civil action in the name of the state, in any court of competent jurisdiction, and the sum recovered shall go into the state current school fund; and it shall be the duty of the prosecuting attorneys of the several counties of the state to see that the provisions of this section are enforced.

Sec. 164. (6) In case the district clerk fails to make the reports as by law provided, at the proper time and in the proper manner, he shall forfeit and pay to the district the sum of twenty-five dollars for each and every such failure. He shall also be liable if, through such neglect, the district fails to receive its just apportionment of school monies, for the full amount so lost. Each and all of said forfeitures shall be recovered in a suit brought by the county superintendent or by any citizen of such district, in the name of and for the benefit of such district, and all monies so collected shall be paid over to the county treasurer and shall be by him placed to the credit of the general fund of the district to which it belongs.

Sec. 166. (8) Any teacher who wilfully refuses or neglects to enforce the course of study or the rules and regulations required by the State Board of Education, or by any other lawful authority, shall not be allowed by the directors any warrant for salary due until said teacher shall have complied with said requirements.

Sec. 174. (16) Any district using text-books other than those prescribed by the State Board of Education or by other lawful authority, or any district failing to comply with the course of study prescribed by the State Board of Education or by other lawful authority, or any district in which warrants are issued to a teacher not legally qualified to teach in the common school of the said district, shall forfeit twenty-five per cent. of their school fund for that or the subsequent year, and it is hereby made the duty of the county superintendent to deduct said amount from the apportionment to be made to any district failing in either or all of the above requirements, and the amounts thus deducted shall revert to the general school funds of the state, and the county treasurer shall return the same to the State Treasurer for reapportionment.

WEST VIRGINIA.

From the School Law of West Virginia, 1903, p. 18.

11a. I. That the nature of alcoholic drinks and narcotics, and special instruction as to their effects upon the human system, in connection with the several divisions of the subject of physiology and hygiene, shall be included in the branches of study taught in the common or public schools, and shall be taught as thoroughly and in the same manner as other like required branches are in said schools, and to all pupils in all said schools throughout the State.

II. It shall be the duty of the proper officers in control of any school described in the foregoing section to enforce the provisions of this act; and any such officer, school director, committee, superintendent or teacher who shall refuse or neglect to comply with the requirements to this act, or shall neglect or fail to make proper provisions for the instruction required and in the manner specified by the first section of this act, for all pupils in each and every school under his jurisdiction, shall be removed from office, and the vacancy filled as in other cases.

III. No certificate shall be granted to any person to teach in the public schools of the State, after the first of January, anno domini, eighteen hundred and eighty-nine, who has not passed a satisfactory examination in physiology and hygiene, with special reference to the nature and the effect of alcoholic drinks and narcotics upon the human system.

WISCONSIN.

From School Laws of Wisconsin, 1901, pp. 51-52.

Physiology and hygiene. SECTION 447a. Provision shall be made by the proper local school authorities for instructing all pupils in all schools supported by public money or under state control, in physiology and hygiene with special reference to the effects of stimulants and narcotics upon the human system. The text-books used in giving such instruction shall have the joint approval of the state superintendent and the state board of health.

(This section contemplates instruction in physiology and hygiene, for all pupils sufficiently advanced in age and scholarship, with special reference to the effects of stimulants and narcotics upon the human system. Under the guidance of an approved book, oral instruction in this topic may be given to pupils that are too immature to be benefited by the use of a textbook.

The effectiveness of the work in this branch, so far as its oral presentation is concerned, will depend on the simplicity of the instruction, and the good judgment of the teacher in avoiding abstruse and offensive statements. In all instruction given under this law the subject of anatomy should be considered as taking a secondary place.)

SEC. 450. Every applicant for a certificate shall be examined in the subjects hereinafter mentioned, for the several grades respectively as follows: For the third grade, in orthoepy, orthography, reading, penmanship, arithmetic, English grammar, geography, the history of the United States, the constitution of the United States, the constitution of the state of Wisconsin, physiology and hygiene, with special reference to the effects of stimulants and narcotics upon the human system, * * *.

[These and additional examinations are required of teachers of first and second grades.]

WYOMING.

From School Laws of the State of Wyoming, 1901, pp. 38-9.

SEC. 612. Physiology and hygiene, which shall include in each division of the subject special reference to the effects of alcohol and narcotics upon the human system, shall be included in the branches taught in the common schools of the State, and shall be introduced and taught, either orally or by text-book, in all departments of the public schools above the second primary grade and in all educational institutions supported wholly or in part by the State. (R. S. 1887, sec. 3969.)

SEC. 613. It shall be the duty of the several county and city superintendents of the schools in the State, and of the secretary of the board of directors of all other educational institutions receiving aid from the State, to report to the State superintendent of public instruction any failure or neglect on the part of any board of trustees of any school district, or the board of directors of any educational institution receiving aid from the State, to make proper provision for the teaching of the branches mentioned in the last preceding section in any or all of the schools or other educational institutions under their charge, or over which they have jurisdiction, and such failure on the part of the above-mentioned officers, so reported and satisfactorily proved, shall be deemed sufficient cause for withholding the warrant for the district appropriation of school money to which such school district or educational institution would otherwise be entitled. (R. S. 1887, sec. 3970.)

SEC. 615. No certificate shall be granted hereafter to any person to teach in the schools of Wyoming, who shall not pass a satisfactory examination in physiology and hygiene, with special reference to the effects of alcoholic drinks, stimulants, and narcotics upon the human system. (R. S. 1887, sec. 3972.)

OBSERVATIONS IN PASSING.

A CORRECTION.

Our attention has been called to an error in the last report on the results of the examinations before the various medical examining boards. It occurs in the statistics for California (p. 511), where a failure is charged to the Ohio Medical University, with the statement that he belonged to the class of 1881. Further investigation shows the person failing did graduate in 1881, and as the Ohio Medical University graduated its first class in 1893, it is self-evident that it should not have been charged to that institution, and, for the benefit of the other and older medical schools in Ohio, he was not an alumnus of any Ohio school. Where the error was made cannot now be discovered as the manuscript has not been preserved. The placing of the error, however, is immaterial; we regret its occurrence and hope to exercise even greater care in future compilations.

****

The American Neurological Association will meet in St. Louis on September 15th, 16th and 17th, and its meetings will be followed (beginning September 19th) with the session of the various medical departments of the congress of arts and sciences. The American Electrotherapeutic Association meets in St. Louis at about the same time September 13th to 16th.

****

The national consumer's league has issued a very useful pamphlet on child labor legislation, analyzing and tabulating the provisions of the acts of the various state legislatures. On the last page it rearranges a table published in the last census, giving the *total* number of illiterate children between 10 and 14 years, in the order of the number. In this list Wyoming heads the list with but 72, while Alabama is at the bottom of the column with 66,072.

****

The publishing of the laws regulating the teaching of hygiene in the public schools of the various states in this number of the Bulletin, will prove a great convenience to those who are interested in this subject. It was done because the academy's committee at the beginning of its work, was not able to find such a compilation. Two have been published during the year, each a part of a large volume, not easily obtainable, and both having omissions which are supplied in our summary. The number of extra copies of the Bulletin is always limited, but while the supply lasts, copies will be sent to any address upon receipt of the price of a single number of the Bulletin, 50 cents. Post stamps will be accepted.

****

The preparations for the next meeting are well in hand. With the Shelburne as headquarters, comfort is assured. The preliminary circular has been issued. Copies of the program, when issued, will be sent to those who request them. The Trunk Line Association give a very favorable concession, and it is hoped that the meeting will be well attended. If you advise the secretary of your purpose to attend, you will be kept informed of all arrangements.

LITERATURE NOTES.

BIOGRAPHIC CLINICS—VOLUME II. THE ORIGIN OF THE ILL HEALTH OF GEORGE ELIOT, GEORGE HENRY LEWES, WAGNER, PARKMAN, JANE WELCH CARLYLE SPENCER, WHITTIER, MARGARET FULLER OSSOLI AND NIETZSCHE. By GEORGE M. GOULD, M.D. Philadelphia: P. Blakiston's Son & Co. 1904. Cloth. 392 pp. Price, $1.00.

Dr. Gould has continued his strikingly original studies and has given us another charming volume. In the preface he alludes to the reception of the first volume by the medical press, and is disappointed because his conclusions were not received with enthusiastic concurrence. It is not within the bounds of the Bulletin to discuss why this was so; it is only mentioned to note that path-finders, the constructive idealist, always are so received. It is a higher compliment than a universal hand-concussion of the claqueurs. We commend this volume entirely apart from the main thesis as worthy of reading; it is equally commended for the demonstrations given of the thesis, the true purpose of the book.

ARE WE TO HAVE A UNITED MEDICAL PROFESSION? BY CHARLES S. MACK, M.D., Laport, Ind. Paper. 44 pp. Price, 25 cents, to be obtained of the author.

The author of this pamphlet makes a distinction between what is so frequently tagged "regular medicine," and homeopathy of which he is a champion. He calls the former "rational medicine." Do not for a moment suppose that he wants us to call homeopathy "irrational medicine," but rather, although he does not use the term, superrational medicine. Homeopathy transcends rational medicine as the supernatural soars above natural processes. "The particular cure of which *similia similibus curantur* is the law * * * is an immediate[1] change from that which is abnormal to what is a normal (or approximately normal) condition of vital processes." "One cannot in rational practice attempt this cure, for in rational practice there must always be sought an immediate end *in itself* knowable, as a change in the vital processes is not; it is knowable only in its effects."

These two quotations ought to give the thought of the author for most of his pamphlet is taken up in ringing the changes upon them. From this it appears that homeopathy can not be discussed rationally, since it "transcends the possibilities of rational medicine," and can, consequently be accepted only by the use of those faculties which enable one to lay hold upon the supernatural and the superrational; it must be an exercise of faith. When one observes how easily faith may become credulity, one can see the danger in this line of conduct in a medical man. It also prevents a criticism of the pamphlet by any agnostic for he does not possess the qualifications to appreciate the statements made. It also explains why so many difficulties arise when the elect and the philistine come into contact.

ANNUAL REPORT OF THE COMMISSIONER OF EDUCATION FOR THE YEAR 1902. 2 vols. pp. cxii, 1-1176; 1177-2447.

Attention is called to the following items of special interest to physicians in this report. Chapter 11, p. 509ff medical inspection of schools abroad. A section of Chapter 22, p. 868. The medical institute for women at St. Petersburg. Chapter 27, child

[1] Immediate is used here in its sense of acted upon without the intervention of anything, and with no thought of time.

study in Chicago. Chapter 36, p. 1499ff, professional schools (including statistics). Chapter 42, p. 2043ff, schools for nurses; Chapter 45, 47, p. 2115ff, schools for the defective classes and kindred topics.

This report makes a fitting companion to the earlier volumes of the valuable series, volumes that one does not care to do without, when facts and figures bearing upon our educational problems are desired.

THE MAN WHO PLEASES AND THE WOMAN WHO CHARMS. BY JOHN A. CONE. New York: Hinds and Noble, 31 W. 15th St. Cloth. pp. 131. Price, 75 cents, postpaid.

This is not an ordinary manual of deportment, although it treats of that subject; but a series of very readable essays which can be read with both pleasure and profit by the cultured as well as those who are seeking it.

PREVENTIVE MEDICINE—TWO PRIZE ESSAYS: "THE GENERAL PRINCIPLES OF PREVENTIVE MEDICINE," BY W. WAYNE BABCOCK, M.D.; "THE MEDICAL INSPECTION OF SCHOOLS: A PROBLEM IN PREVENTIVE MEDICINE," BY LEWIS S. SOMERS. Brooklyn, N. Y.: The Maltine Company. Paper. pp. 230, 54.

These are the essays awarded the prize offered by the Maltine Company, and are reprinted, the first, from the *Brooklyn Medical Journal*, the other, from the *Medical News*. It is to be hoped that these essays, now they are published in book form will have a much wider circulation even than that afforded by the journals in which they were printed, and that they will be carefully read by many who have not been studying the advances in preventive medicine as thoroughly as those in therapeutics. They cannot help doing a world of good.

TRANSACTIONS OF SOCIETIES.

I. NATIONAL ASSOCIATION OF UNITED STATES PENSION EXAMINING SURGEONS. Vol. I. Second Annual Meeting. Washington, D. C. May 13, 14, 1903. Published by the Association. 1903. pp. 215.

II. TRANSACTIONS OF THE MAINE MEDICAL ASSOCIATION. 1903. Vol. xiv. Part III. pp. 457–636.

III. MEDICAL COMMUNICATIONS OF THE MASSACHUSETTS MEDICAL SOCIETY. Vol. xix. No. II. 1903. pp. 301–618; 33–60.

IV. TRANSACTIONS OF THE MEDICAL SOCIETY OF NEW JERSEY. 1903. pp. 439.

V. Transactions of the Rhode Island Medical Society. Vol. VI. Part IV. pp. 419–562.
VI. Transactions of the State Medical Association of Texas, 35th Annual Session. 1903. pp. 635.
VII. Transactions of the New York Academy of Medicine. 1896-1901. pp. 471.
VIII. Transactions of the College of Physicians of Philadelphia. 3d series. Vol. 25. pp. 194.
IX. Transactions of the Luzerne County [Penna.] Medical Society for 1903. Vol. xi. pp. 184.

I. This volume gives the papers read at Washington last May. They are quite fairly confined to the discussion of problems presented to the pension examination surgeon, and demonstrate the need of some place where such problems can be discussed. As the membership is limited by qualifications other than those pertaining purely to medicine, that place must be a separate organization and not the section of some larger medical society.

II. This volume gives the transactions of the 51st meeting and is rich in historic matter, and will make a valuable work of reference.

III. This volume contains a series of three papers on privileged communications, one by a physician, the remaining two by lawyers that add to the literature on this subject.

IV. There is a wealth of medico-sociologic material in this volume. There are reports by committees on the "Abuse of Medical Charity;" on "Legislation;" on "Present Methods of Education from the Standpoint of the Physician." The address of the president (Dr. E. L. B. Godfrey, of Camden, the efficient secretary of the New Jersey Board of Medical Examiners) is entitled "The Educational Standards of the Medical Profession of New Jersey, Past and Present." Besides, there are papers on "The Organization and Operations of Hospitals and Other Charitable Institutions in the State of New Jersey;" and on "Court Testimony of Medical Experts in Mental Diseases."

V. The president's address on "Heredity and Its Lessons," and a paper on "The Trade and the Professions," wherein are some exceedingly plain but pertinent strictures upon the conduct of physicians, are the only papers pertaining to social medicine in this volume.

VI. This is the last volume that will appear under the editorial control of the late Dr. H. A. West, for several years, the efficient secretary of the Texas society. He will be a personal loss to the reviewer, since he was always ready and cordial in replying to questions relating to the laws regulating medical practice in Texas, before the days of state boards.

VII. We have not received the handsome appearing pages of the New York Academy transactions for some years. This volume published a full account of its semicentennial celebration in 1897.

VIII. These transactions contain their usual wealth of material, but none of it relates to social medicine.

IX. This volume illustrates what can be done by a county medical society, apart from a large city, if it only has the will to do it.

THE PERPETUAL VISITING AND POCKET REFERENCE BOOK, INCLUDING INFORMATION IN EMERGENCIES, FROM STANDARD AUTHORS. St. Louis, Mo. Dios Chemical Company. 1904. Price, 10 cents for postage.

This book is published as an advertisement by the firm issuing it, and is among the best of its class as we remember them. At the bottom of each page there is a concise bit of advice to the physician, most frequently laudatory of certain "ine" preparations, but not always. Thus a little social medicine is inculcated in, "Avoid dining out with your patients;" "Do not allow indiscreet friends to go about over-praising you." From them any medical aphorisms we quote two : "Lemons act favorably in purpura ;" "Strophulus, a common popular skin disease in infants." This is the first intimation that there was a fad for any cutaneous trouble other than that reputed to be affected by the Scotch.

The *Maryland Medical Journal* lost its February number in the great fire in Baltimore. Incidentally, this was caused by the tardiness of receiving a paper which had already been read. It is not often that belated papers cause so much loss ; it is not uncommon for them to be causes of annoyance and friction.

Fortunately duplicate proofs were on file beyond the fire line; most of the matter was reset, in Philadelphia, and a commendable number issued more promptly than the ordinary issuing of some of our exchanges.

THE DAILY MEDICAL. Medical Publishing Co. 154 E. 72d Street, New York: One dollar a year.

On the whole, we rather like this venture, it gives a great deal one does not care for; it gives some things in a way that savors of non-medical editing (as when it explains that inflammatory rheumatism is a very painful affection), but it does gather many items of interest to us, of a kind which have not heretofore come within the view of the weeklies. In like manner, many of the articles of no interest to us are of value to others. If the publishers can afford to issue it at a dollar a year, most physicians will receive a big return for the investment. Since writing the above, the *Daily* has stopped its visits. Should this notice become an epitaph, it is to be regretted, as it was a promising infant.

CONTRIBUTIONS TO BIOLOGY FROM THE HOPKINS SEASIDE LABORATORY OF THE LELAND STANFORD JR. UNIVERSITY.

XXXI. THE PALEONTOLOGY AND STRATIGRAPHY OF THE MARINE PLIOCENE AND PLEISTOCENE OF SAN PEDRO, CALIFORNIA. BY RALPH ARNOLD. pp. 420.

XXXII. THE FISHES OF PANAMA BAY. BY CHARLES H. GILBERT AND EDWIN C. STARKS. pp. 304.

It will be left to the proper journals to review these handsomely printed volumes. Attention is called to them here because they illustrate a phase of university work frequently forgotten. The opportunity for research, the development of science, and acquiring of information for their own sakes, apart from any immediate "practical" application, forms an invaluable deposit to the credit of that type of mind which is engaged in the merely utilitarian. May the opportunities for like study as produced these excellent contributions be multiplied.

BULLETIN

OF THE

American Academy of Medicine

VOL. VI.   ISSUED JUNE, 1904.   NO. 12.

The AMERICAN ACADEMY OF MEDICINE is not responsible for the sentiments expressed in any paper or address published in the BULLETIN.

THE DOCTOR'S DUTY TO THE STATE.[1]

BY JOHN B. ROBERTS, A.M., M.D., Philadelphia.

The doctor's highest duty is to be honest and to fight for honesty in his profession and in the state. He should abhor cowardice in others, as in himself, for cowardice is the parent of dishonesty. The professional coward and the commercial coward have aided efficiently, if perchance unwittingly, the present degradation of the body politic and the body medical. Moral cowardice is a characteristic of both corporations and individuals in this twentieth century, and is the result of the worship of the "Almighty Dollar," which has usurped the place of "Self-respect" in men's minds.

The sociologic character of the work of this Academy and its educational requirement for fellowship authorize the introduction here of topics of an economic, or politico-social, nature. No excuse need therefore be made for my choice of subject. To those who may object to the criticisms of my profession, my city or my state, I reply that I know of no better way to remedy evils than to recognize their existence. An honest and just investigation of suspected corruption and an honest and brave avowal of discovered wrong are the first steps towards amelioration of evil. He, who is afraid to see, and dare not mention, the misdoings of himself and his colleagues, is his profession's worst son. He, who cries out for concealment under the plea of loyalty, is no

[1] The President's Address for the 29th Annual Meeting of the American Academy of Medicine, Atlantic City, N. J., June 4, 1904.

better than the scheming political leader, whose cowardice and insincerity call forth the reprobation of upright citizens. It needs no argument to prove that cowardice begets lying and that a liar is essentially a coward. Reformation comes from honest introspection, which begets respect and honor from the outside world.

David's description of a citizen of Zion is "he that walketh uprightly, and worketh righteousness, and speaketh the truth in his heart." The upright gait, the righteous labor and the truthful spirit are as needful now as in the times of the great King.

The superior training of doctors of medicine, their unusual opportunities to know the needs of a community, their wide acquaintance with citizens, their many chances to play the part of missionary, and their personal influence with active men make their responsibility to the state great. Even greater is the responsibility, and greater is the duty, that rests upon a fellow of this Academy, because its claim to existence is founded upon a broad cultivation of the humanities, in addition to medical education.

The doctor is excused from jury duty and is entitled to withhold medical confidences under certain circumstances. He should, therefore, be willing to render a return for these privileges in a higher civic courage and usefulness. It is not only his religious or ethical duty to be honest and brave; but his civic duty as well. In these days, moreover, a mere passive virtue is not sufficient.

The doctor must fight for honesty in others also and strike real knock-down blows at political and professional chicanery, if he wishes to do his whole duty to the public. There are in all vocations, weaklings who do nothing but accept the benefits which their environment brings them. They make no return to their generation and when dead leave no special vacancy in the economic household. Such impassive units are of little real worth. Although they may do no active harm, they increase the deadweight of indifference, which must be lifted, if the righteousness of the world is to increase and the happiness of humanity to be brought to its fulfilment. It has always been this inertia that has retarded progress, and permitted wrong to flourish.

The physician should be on guard lest in civic matters he become tainted with this form of inert conservatism. It is easy to plead professional engagements and personal modesty as excuses for lack of energy in uprooting hygienic and political evils.

A physician does not do his duty to his fellow citizens by merely treating their typhoid fevers, while making no effort to compel the local rulers to supply pure drinking-water to the home. He knows the cause of this disease, and it is his bounden duty to actively labor for a pure water supply. Similar activity in urging measures to prevent the spread of smallpox and other contagious diseases is a recognized part of his professional work. The doctor may not escape this responsibility, because his sluggish temperament and unused conscience permit him to see with equanimity ignorant men and innocent children suffer and die. If he is mentally or physically lazy, let him select some position in the world, where such inactivity and uselessness are less censurable.

Some may exclaim that these matters are not the business of the practising physician, but belong to the civic officials. Such excuses for dereliction of civic and professional duty should always arouse active condemnation. The doctor knows the results of scientific study of hygienic questions and should insist upon their application to the citizen's person and possessions. A member of a community, who is favored by education, experience, and social position, owes more to the common good than one less fortunate in these attributes. The more one has, the more one owes to his fellows. Let us all accept the responsibility of our profession, if we accept its honors and emoluments.

This claim upon the doctor is individual and may not be shirked. To delay for societies, institutions, or combinations of men to make the start is not justifiable. A brave knight goes to battle alone. He does not wait for companions to give him courage and afford succor. Delay often means failure. Prompt action often gives the only possible success. After all, history shows that organized bodies follow a single brave spirit. The great reforms have always been started by the alert brain or agile body of one man. He, who works for the love of the duty to be done, soon finds followers. He who tremblingly waits for company in good deeds has a sorry achievement to his credit. The one-man fights for righteousness have made the modern better than the ancient world.

Much unpaid work is to be done on this earth. I like to think that a great deal of it is done by doctors. The public knows that physicians do much for the sick without money recompense. Much is to be done in civic affairs, which brings no reward and no glory. This is just as much the doctor's duty as to cure the poor and friendless, or to ease their road to the grave.

How often financial success blunts the conscience and lessens the activity of medical men! What a misconception of duty this! The less one has to think of the necessities of his wife and children, the more free is he to devote his energies to the public service. It is often pretty easy to pardon the impecunious man, who for his household's sake is driven to accept a "dirty dollar" for some improper service to a sly tempter. No excuse seems adequate, however, when a similar dereliction is committed by a physician of means, education and intelligence. His brains and intellectual training should show him the true path, which may be invisible to his muddlepated colleague; the absence of financial stress makes his failure to do the right inexcusable. It is unreasonable to expect us all to be measured by the same standard of ethics or morals. The fellows of this Academy, for instance, are rightly expected to do better, and be better, than men of less intellectual opportunity. So also, those of means, whether professional men or business men, should be held to a stricter ethical responsibility than those who have a daily struggle to feed their children. In the abstract, right is right, wrong is wrong, and duty is duty, without regard to collateral circumstances; but I cannot bring myself to believe that so much is to be expected from the naturally weak and accidentally fettered, as from those who are strong and free. Strength and freedom give power; and power always brings responsibility. This is the reason that I urge our 800 fellows to consider the doctor's duty to the state.

In my city the business men will not work to free the state from the political ills that affect it; and I therefore call thus earnestly for political deliverance at the hands of the doctors. The attitude of indifference, to election frauds, legislative corruption and police blackmail, on the part of the business community, is easily intelligible to students of economic conditions. Much of the bribery in council chambers and legislative assemblies is the direct result of business competition. A railroad or a hospital desires to obtain a franchise, a grant of land, or an appropriation, to make it more prosperous than its competitor or rival. Its directors, believing that the end justifies the means, ignore the principles of ethics, because it is success that appeals to them, and bribe the men who vote, with cash from the treasury of the corporation, or, even worse, give them a rake-off of 10 per cent. from the appropriation obtained from the public coffers. Many illustrations of this kind of bribery and robbery are familiarly discussed in our daily contact with society. Yet the directors, who permit this thing to be done, pose as good citizens and expect us to greet them with deference and respect.

It is not difficult to understand the hold on these same directors, which the political bosses have, when they desire to raise a large corruption fund to pay for illegal voters and repeaters on election day. It is not surprising that such contemptible citizens and successful directors pay blackmail to both the larger political parties. Are they any better or any worse than the carter who gives the policeman $10 to permit his cart to obstruct the public highway, night after night, to save stable rent; or the brothel-keeper, who pays a monthly stipend to the police captain, to be undisturbed in her trade?

The managers of the great corporations are the chief causes of civic corruption. I have some respect for the ignorant dwellers in the tenements and alleys, who obey the ward leaders, probably their only friends in time of sickness, and accept for their vote a drink of whiskey, a silver coin or a bag of flour. Their subservience has at least the flavor of gratitude. The business man with full bank account, cultivated surroundings and clear insight, who allows his legislative agent to bribe members of council, assembly or congress, with money, stock or unworthy patronage, deserves the contempt of true men. It is no valid excuse to plead that these things are done, without his knowledge, by the executive officers of his railroad or institution. If he be a director, let him take the responsibility, as well as the honor, pertaining to his position, and prevent such acts on the part of the subordinates. Shifting responsibility may quiet his uneasy, though feeble, conscience, but it does not lessen the contempt felt by others for such unworthy citizenship.

It is not fair to suggest that cases of this kind are found only among business men, and that the liberal professions are free from this political taint. The law and the clergy doubtless have their unworthy followers. That the medical profession has not succeeded in keeping all such evil practices out of its ranks is known too well. The promoters and trustees of some medical schools and hospitals are not a whit behind railroad and telephone magnates in seducing the political leaders to appropriate public funds for private use. Some of us have seen the coarsest forms of political trickery invade even medical organizations, with which no laymen are connected.

These illustrations serve to confirm the belief that human nature is the same in all avocations. They impel us to use due diligence to discover, and fight, the unworthy ones in our midst, who thus degrade the whole profession by failing to recognize their duty to the state.

You may think these general statements, made by reason of perusal of sensational newspapers. I assure you that I, as an election official, have personal knowledge of political corruption of the worst kind in the Eighth Ward of Philadelphia. My testimony under oath to the Court of Common Pleas has shown that I know something of the topic of which I am now speaking. My interest in professional organizations and in sociological studies has enabled me to see many things bearing on the relations of medical men to each other and to the state. Knowledge thus obtained makes me ashamed of some of my fellow doctors as well as of some of my fellow citizens in business walks. Men, desirous of seeing municipal government free from fraud and bribery, send generous contributions for that end with the condition that their names be kept unknown. Others decline to allow their names to be used publicly, lest the political machine interfere with their private business. The honest citizen in Philadelphia to-day is held in bondage as complete as that of the negro of the Southern States in 1861.

This cowardice, of business men and even of the judges, is

scarcely to be wondered at when the condition of affairs is examined. A four-story residence, with a brown stone front, on a lot 23 feet by 175 feet, situated on Walnut Street, is assessed at $60,000, while a four-story residence, with a red stone and brick front, on a lot only 22 feet by 125 feet, and with much less backbuilding, situated in the same square of Walnut Street, is assessed at $65,000. Every intelligent man one meets will say, "That's easy to understand. The first belongs to Governor B., the other to Dr. A."

The guilty election officers of the fifth division of the eighth ward are allowed to pursue election frauds undisturbed, for months after three judges have heard from a reputable citizen sworn testimony of their corrupt practices. Proprietors of disorderly houses easily obtain straw bail. Our friends point out to us "speakeasies," where liquor is illegally sold, concerning which the police apparently have no knowledge.

Upright citizens are ashamed of the machine-made judges, who seem in cases of a political character to strain every nerve to find technical quibbles in favor of the accused, with the result that justice to the state is practically impossible. Is not this due to the fact that judges know that their tenure of office depends on obedience to the political machine? This same machine it is that creates the courts, selects the judges, picks out officials which the judges subserviently appoint, and raises the judge's salaries after they have been "good." These things are now so notorious that it is the judge, who fails of renomination whom the community honors. His rejection by the machine is an evidence that he has been a courageous and faithful judge. His retention would mean that he had made himself "solid" with the political bosses, who control the machine and who expect favors at his hands.

The public has not failed to observe that political cases, in which there is a reasonable general belief that the accused is guilty, are often tried before judges, whose recent political affiliations make them possibly amenable to pressure at the machine's hands. Has the people not been surprised more than once at the rulings of the judge in favor of the accused politician?

It does not conduce to honesty in the young to see one of the Middle States represented in the United States Senate by a man, who seemingly escaped punishment, when on trial for illegal use of the state's money, only because the acts were done so long ago that the evidence must be ruled out. It needs the doctors and all citizens to cry out for public honesty, when a Western State is now represented in the United States senate by a senator who is serving a term in jail! How can we expect Philadelphia boys to believe in decency when one of its wards has been repeatedly represented in the state legislature by a man who was the backer, if not in part a proprietor, of a bawdy house?

It is time for physicians to wake up and in a body insist upon that public honesty and decency, which the business men, the lawyers, and the clergymen seem afraid to demand from the rulers of the cities, in which we live. Business men are the main bribers of politicians and the greatest buyers of legislation. They are, therefore, the chief element in the political corruption of the day. They are worse traitors to the country than the politicians, who accept the bribes and deliver the franchises and other legislative privileges, for they often pose as "respectable citizens." Their hypocrisy is used to cover ill deeds.

A blunt and fearless political boss, who boldly robs the public in the manner of a highwayman, is less to be despised than the sneaking business man who, through his legislative agents, secretly pays the boss to rob the people, while he himself wears a sanctimonious face and is "shocked" at the prevailing corruption. The insincerity and dishonesty of a large contingent of the business world make one feel that the chief satisfaction in human intercourse is to be found in association with little children, whose straightforward honesty is proverbial.

Nothing impresses the unthinking world so much as success, and nowadays money-making and money-having seem to cover many forms of dishonesty. It has recently been delightful to see the faith of business men and financiers, in successful politicians rewarded by great losses of money. So long as these politicians amassed wealth by robbing only the city and state, their compatriots in business respected, trusted, and even bowed down to them. This unreasoning mental attitude recently gave fine opportunity for the same political schemers to unload worthless securities on their financial acquaintances. Many men have now learned the needed lesson that a public thief will become a private thief, if he only have opportunity and a reasonable assurance of escape from punishment. A business man recently said that it was his opinion that a large proportion of men in business were honest only because it paid. So long as honesty is required, many men will be honest; so soon as business furnishes the same opportunity for unpunished fraud as does politics, men in all walks of life will emulate our political bosses in knavery, robbery and blackmail.

The doctor, by being honest in his dealings with his patients, can do much to raise the public standard of truthfulness, and thus serve the state. It is a common belief that doctors are inclined to tell untruths, in order to save the sensibilities of their patients. This practice does unfortunately seem to be not uncommon among a certain kind of doctors; but it does not represent the real spirit of our profession. A patient who has once been deceived by a doctor's lies, is not apt to put much faith in his subsequent statements. Dr. Cabot, of Boston, wrote an important article on this subject a few years ago. His advocacy of truth and his belief that truthfulness is the best policy deserve high praise.

When one places the life of his wife, his child or himself in the hands of a physician, he has a right to expect honesty and truthfulness in the man so honored. I have no patience with dishonest doctors, who expect success and respect at the hands of their patients, and yet treat them with secret nostrums of unknown strength, deceive them with false words, and allow them to dictate the methods of treatment. If a doctor cannot induce his patient to do what is proper in treatment, he has no right to temporize and follow the patient's desires rather than what he knows to be the only right line of treatment. It is much more honest to say to the unbelieving and contemptuous sick man, "If I have the responsibility, I must have the control. You must get some other doctor, if you will not obey me."

It is no wonder that many patients treat physicians with little consideration and respect. The unscientific methods, careless attention to details, and weak conduct of many doctors are enough to make the public fly to osteopaths, Christian scientists and other quacks, who seem to at least have the virtue of believing in their own nonsense. A weak-kneed, wobbly-minded doctor cannot expect to arouse sentiments of confidence; he is necessarily doomed to a life of professional failure.

An honest physician need not be as blunt as a boor, but he must be forceful, truthful, confident, and self-respectful. It will not take long for the local public to recognize the work of such a man as a citizen and the young will grow up to respect and emulate him in civic value. This is part of the doctor's duty to the state.

The doctor should teach the laity that mental hygiene, or discipline, is as essential to proper living and happiness as physical hygiene. The theologians for centuries taught us to train the spirit to save the soul, while the physicians laid too much stress perhaps on the physical side of human nature. It is now seen that the mutual relations of a sound mind and a sound body are of primary importance in the saving of the soul as well as in saving the body. Hygiene of the body gives a spirit of religious toleration and calm, and fits man for the next world as well as for this. So also, hygiene of the mind gives a healthy digestion and a good income-making body and fits man for this world as well as the next. Many of the mental and physical wrecks in our homes and hospitals, which may truly be said to be "possessed of a devil" would have been useful members of the body social, had they had proper mental culture from childhood. Such control must be obtained by psychic gymnastics, instituted by parents during the early years of childhood. Nervous children are the get of nervous households. It should be as disgraceful to be called "nervous" as to be called "bandy-legged" or "cock-eyed." If parents would practice self-control, their children would emulate this virtue, just as well-shaped athletic parents have children, who aspire to their parents' physical beauty and prowess.

It is the doctor's duty to teach the state's inhabitants this fact, and not encourage hysteria, neurasthenia, and general "cantankerousness" by foolish sympathy, unwise talk or ignorant diagnoses of "railway spine." Many wrecked lives and useless citizens are made by unwise advice given by doctors, into whose hands persons with slight injuries first fall for treatment. Many damage suits could be avoided with justice to the injured and to the agents responsible for the injury, if all doctors realized the importance of mental control. Many "railway spines" and traumatic neuroses are caused by the doctor's unscientific and unreasoning sympathy.

The doctor's duty to the state includes instruction to his patients in mental hygiene, and the prevention of unnecessary litigation. It is easy to develop a neurasthenic crank out of a patient, who has received an insignificant injury, and it is easy to make a hysterical valetudinarian out of a useful citizen by magnifying his dangers and feeding his imagination with depressing possibilities. It is the doctor's public duty to see that such sad occurrences do not result from his maladroitness.

Instances could easily be given to prove this contention. Take as an example a railroad company that was in my opinion practically robbed of between $15,000 and $20,000 for an insignificant injury, which ought not to have brought to the patient more than a few hundred dollars at the very most. I recollect well a firm that was forced to pay $5,000 or $6,000 for an injury to an employee, which was of comparatively little moment. The woman when brought into court after months of delay was a neurasthenic wreck, due not to the injury but to injudicious friends, lawyer, and perhaps doctors. A prompt settlement of the claim, which in justice to all should have been by a small amount of money, would have saved the girl's health. What can the worried and distressed patient do, if the doctor does not protect her from her own family's anxiety and cupidity and the lawyers' greed? The doubtful professional character of lawyers' contingents fees in damage suits should be affirmed by good citizens. It requires an unusually honest man, be he lawyer or doctor, to resist the temptation to magnify the patient's sufferings when his own pay depends on the jury's verdict.

In connection with the same topic may be mentioned the wrong done to the public by what may be called "alarmist" practitioners. Some doctors make such a "mountain" out of a "molehill" of illness that they become known to their professional colleagues and even to their patients and their patients' friends as those who perpetually cry "wolf, wolf," when there is no "wolf." This conduct is partly due to narrowness of professional experience, partly to temperament, but the laity often attribute it to a desire to scare the patient into a mental attitude, which will allow frequent visits and large bills. With all deference to the specialties, I cannot help feeling that the limited outlook, which special practice furnishes, contributes to this evil as much perhaps as real ignorance of etiology, symptomatology, therapeusis and prognosis.

A graduate, who has become a specialist a few months after commencement day, may with perfect truthfulness on his part assert that a furuncle of the auricle, a follicular tonsillitis, a foreign body in the cornea, a bean in the nose, or a small crop of herpes over one of the ribs is a serious condition demanding rest in bed, a trained nurse at $20 per week, and daily visits at $5 per visit. His assertion is, however, as untrue, in the majority of cases, as the statement of the ignoramus who calls a febrile attack due to indigestion a case of typhoid fever, and says that it was aborted in three days by his treatment.

Even specialists of eminence are not free from this injustice to the public, which keeps patients unnecessarily from business, depleting their pocket-books, and adding to the anxiety of their households. It is in some cases a pardonable error, for to examine for years only eyes, or ears, or throats or skin must make a doctor's horizon as small as that of the old-fashioned dentist, whose profession was much more that of a mechanic than a physician. Recent years have fortunately given the state specialists in dentistry and other departments of medicine, who know the collateral branches of the healing art. The general surgeon and physician too are now learning the necessity of at least some working knowledge of the specialist's science and art.

An important duty of the doctor is to support the present state supervision of medical practice. The various state laws governing medical licensure are far from perfect, but they result in much better protection of the citizen than did the commercial medical schools of ten or twenty years ago. Many of you remember the struggle to wrest from medical teachers the power to create medical practitioners with almost no real knowledge of medicine.

The medical schools of that day were, in many instances, conducted merely as money-makers for the professors. The chief output was a crop of half-educated men with a moderate knowledge of the art of medicine, but almost none of medical science.

It is gratifying to remember that it was the medical profession itself, which ended this system by obtaining laws to give state boards of medical examiners control of the entrance to medical practice. Now, the medical schools educate, but the states, through their respective examining boards, fix the standard of education and control the license to practise. It is the duty of the doctor as a citizen to strengthen the hands of these boards, because they give the public an opportunity to know which physicians have sufficient education to render them likely to be safe practitioners.

It is undoubtedly possible for a man to pass the examinations of a board, and yet be a dangerous practitioner, either because of his rascality or his lack of common sense. Still, this menace to the public safety is infinitely less than was the case when students entered medical college, ignorant of the common school branches, attended two five-month courses of lectures, and were given the medical degree after a farcical examination, conducted by the teachers whose income depended upon the size of their classes. In those days a considerable number of students deliberately selected the medical schools known to have the easiest examinations.

The present system of state license is a hardship, when a doctor removes from one state to another, and the demand for reciprocity in medical licensure is therefore reasonable. Even this defect in the method of protecting the public from medical ignorance, however, is inconsequential, when compared with the evils of the former system of commercial college control of medical practice.

Fellows of this Academy were active in the campaign to destroy low-grade medical schools, by the establishment of state examinations, and that work has been pretty satisfactorily accomplished. Professors, who fought the enactment of laws to protect the public from their ignorant pupils, still probably evade the law when possible, or perchance endeavor to bring political pressure to bear on the examiners. I have known political pressure to be exerted to influence medical examiners to pass unqualified men, but, in the instances with which I am acquainted, the bravery and honesty of a few doctors frustrated the scheme.

These facts show why it is the doctor's duty to the state to support the medical examining boards, to work to have honest men appointed upon them, and not to be too censorious of their shortcomings. We, who have not served on these boards, know little of the worry, the work, and the weariness entailed by honest service in them. The man, who unreasonably or unjustly decries the system and its exponents, is doing an economic wrong similar to that of those few honorable but short-sighted doctors, who for years played into the hands of the profession's enemies by opposing state control of medical licensure.

The manner, in which state laws compelled low-grade medical colleges to adopt entrance examinations, lengthen terms, and exact efficient final examinations, has fully justified the prophecies of the advocates of state control.

It is difficult to understand the mental quality of an educated physician, who believes that he is acting honestly toward his patients, when he accepts his therapeutic teaching from the advertisements of secret remedies and writes his prescriptions after consultation with the drummer of a drug firm. I formerly supposed that the sale of large quantities of these secret medicines was due to their use by ignorant physicians who had graduated from low-grade medical schools. Careful observation has convinced me of the error of this view. Some years ago, I read in a cyclopaediac work on one of the specialties an elaborate article by one of my hospital colleagues, in which "A———" was suggested in the treatment of a certain disease. I saw recently a letter written by a professor in a great University Medical School, in which he advised that a patient, whom I had referred to him, be given "P———." Not very long ago, I heard a metropolitan professor of surgery discant on the value of "H——— ;" and about a year since one of my patients told me that she had been advised to take "M———," by a hospital physician of Philadelphia. These facts suffice to show that intelligent physicians, and even teachers, have been led into the illegitimate practice of treating patients with remedies of whose composition they are ignorant.

It is clearly improper for a doctor to prescribe a certain remedy for a patient, when he does not know, and is not permitted to find out, the character and the amount of the powerful drugs it contains. It is also, in my opinion, detrimental to professional integrity for medical journals, conducted under professional auspices, to accept advertisements of pharmaceutical products of secret composition.

Both of these questions have been vigorously discussed in medical circles during recent years. As to the first proposition there can be but one answer, which is that a doctor has no right to use a powerful therapeutic weapon, unless he knows its possibilities for good and evil. These possibilities he cannot know unless he is able to learn how much acetanilid, strychnin, arsenic, mercury or other active ingredient it contains. The propriety of medical journals, published by doctors, increasing the dangerous use of these secret remedies by accepting their advertisements cannot be successfully maintained. In a discussion among some officers of a medical journal, a distinguished professor of medicine once said: "Other journals take them, why shouldn't our journal?" The reply to this query is: "Some doctors accept commissions for steering patients to operating specialists, why not we also?" If the vice of prescribing medicines of unknown composition is to be rooted out, honest doctors must jointly repudiate any such illicit combination with commercial journalism, and individually refuse to prescribe remedies of whose composition they are kept in ignorance.

It is said that in Japan the importation of secret proprietary medicines containing a poison, from which accidents might result, is absolutely prohibited, and that the retailer must be informed as to the ingredients, proportions and doses. (*American Medicine*, May 9, 1903, from *Canadian Journal of Medicine and Surgery*.) Such a law would render valuable service to the public of America. Osler in an address before the Canadian Medical Association in 1902, spoke of these nostrums being "foisted on the profession by men who trade on the innocent credulity of the regular physician, quite as much as any quack preys on the gullible public."

It must be a very ignorant or dishonest doctor, and not an innocently credulous one, who treats his patients with the secret nostrums brought to his notice by interested salesmen.

Such a travesty of medical science deserves the condemnation of every honest doctor. It is the duty of every honest consultant to express his adverse opinion, when such course of treatment is suggested in the consultation room. It may be true that men of distinction use remedies of unknown composition; it may be true that medical journals, owned by doctors or by great medical schools and organizations, accept advertisements of these abominations; but such conduct only serves to show to what degradation a lax ethical spirit may bring even those whom we would like to respect.

The secret-remedy evil is degrading the medical faculty at this hour very much as the low-grade medical school debauched the profession two or three decades ago. The cause is the same: laziness and love of money. The cure is the same: an aroused professional sentiment It was the leaven of honesty in the hearts of the doctors at large, which compelled avaricious professors and low-grade medical schools to cease deluging the public with unsafe and ignorant medical practitioners. It took energy, courage and unselfishness to carry on the work. Honest men were compelled to antagonize friends, to fight against their *almae matres*, to relinquish opportunity of professorial position, and to be misunderstood by other honest men. What matter, when the goal was to preserve the state and uphold the honor of the medical guild?

You and I have now a similar, but mightier, task. Then we fought colleges with self-satisfied faculties and thousands of dollars invested in teaching plants. Now, we have to battle against professional dishonesty, therapeutic credulity, and millions of dollars invested in the manufacture of secret nostrums by quick-witted business men.

The task is made more difficult by the fact that a very large number of these vaunted remedies and foods owe their popularity to the alcohol they contain. Dr. Charles Harrington made, a few years ago, a chemical analysis of many of these products. His paper (*Boston Medical and Surgical Journal*, March 12, 1903, quoted in *American Medicine*, March 21, 1903, p. 469) showed that one of these foods contained in volume 23.03 per cent. of alcohol, another 10.60 per cent., another 14.81 per cent., another 15.81 per cent., another 15.58 per cent., another 18.95 per cent., and another 19.72 per cent. He found the nutriment contained in the maximum daily amount, which was recommended of these so-called foods, was only 1.25 ounces, but the contained amount of alcohol was equivalent to six ounces of whiskey.

A much-advertised remedy was found by the Massachusetts State Board of Health to contain 23.46 per cent. by weight of alcohol, another 15.33 per cent., another 16.77 per cent., and another 5.87 per cent. The New York *Evening Post* (quoted by *American Medicine*, March 21, 1903) mentions a "tonic" which contained 41.6 per cent. of alcohol, and refers to other remedies, called by names suggestive of vegetable composition, containing 26.2 per cent., 18.8 per cent., and 21 per cent. of alcohol.

It is not difficult to understand the ease with which makers of these remedies obtain certificates of their remedial value from preachers, statesmen and women, but one would expect medical men to be too wary to be caught in the trap. Their endorsement by physicians always suggests to me ludicrous credulity, therapeutic ignorance, or downright bribery.

Many of the pain-curing secret remedies, used by the laity and prescribed by dishonest doctors, contain acetanilid, phenacetin, and similar agents, in unknown quantity. The danger to life assumed by the administration of these powerful drugs, in indefinite amounts, is so great that a thinking man must stand aghast at the temerity of physicians, who prescribe mixtures of unknown composition for the relief of headache, neuralgia and other ills. Acetanilid and its congeners are known to depress the heart and may have a hemolytic, or disorganizing, effect upon the blood itself. (*University of Pennsylvania Medical Bulletin*, 15, 462, 1903, quoted by *Journal of the American Medical Association*, March 21, 1903, 786). The *Journal of the American Medical Association* (January 16, 1904, 177) expresses the belief that a recent increase in the number of sudden deaths from heart disease in New York City was due to the unusual consumption of acetanilid.

It is not surprising that addiction to the use of acetanilid, alcohol, and cocaine is frequent among persons of unsuspected impropriety in this regard. The unnecessary taking of medicine for all kinds of real and imaginary minor ills is common. The storekeeper and the druggist, whose function is to sell goods, naturally encourage the consumption of proprietary medicines and vaunt their remedial qualities. The doctor should protect the public from such insidious intoxicants and poisons by refusing to condone their use or prescribe them.

The remedy for the evil lies in the development of a feeling of individual responsibility in the medical faculty. Let every doctor refuse to accept samples of secret medicines, refuse to waste time talking therapeutics with smooth-tongued salesmen, refuse to debauch medical science by believing the mendacious advertisements called by the trade "literature," and treat his patients honestly by giving them, what they pay for, the best result of his own knowledge and experience.

I think with pleasure of the discomfiture of a drummer for a much-advertised lithia water, when I told him in my office that I did not expect to prescribe the said water, because Professor M———, of the University of————, had analyzed a number of the lithia waters on the market and had told me that he could find no lithia in any of them. The stereotyped reply, to all agents of secret nostrums, that I do not prescribe medicines of whose composition I am kept in ignorance, has saved me many hours for more advantageous professional work than conversation with men whom I despise.

It is possible that efficient aid may be obtained, in our crusade against this evil, through congressional legislation. The law which gives the Public Health Service a limited supervision over the manufacture of, and interstate traffic in, viruses, serums, antitoxins and the like, and the proposed Heyburn Pure Food and Drug Bill are steps in the right direction.

In all these questions of such moment to the state, the essential element is the honesty of the individual members of society. It is said that "corporations have no souls." The proverb is justified by the fact that men, who constitute corporations, put their individual consciences and ideals of right aside, as soon as their actions are assignable to a body of men instead of to its individual members. As incorporation limits individual financial responsibility, so it acts as a narcotic to individual rectitude. This is seen in larger fields of action, as in governments, which will steal harbors from heathen Chinese, rob African farmers of their country and freedom, and under the color of diplomacy emulate even the father of lies.

Though corporations and governments have no souls they, fortunately for the preservation of civilization and religion, are sure to suffer the penalty of their misdeeds. In this, at least, they are no more apt to escape punishment than men. Economic laws avenge economic follies and sins with much the same resistless energy as is seen in the operations of the natural law and the moral law.

The doctor sees the sins of youth bear fruit in old age, and the sins of the father visited upon the children down to the third and fourth generation. He, as others, sees in history the same process exhibited in the remote effects of corporate and governmental vice. He knows how murder committed under military sanction is only a little less debauching than murder committed under the sanction of a lynching bee; he knows how political robbery and ballot frauds lead to a deterioration of the public morality and health; and he realizes from observation that nothing is so relentless as the orderly course of the laws of nature and of nature's God.

To whom then shall the state look for preservation of its health, to whom shall the state call for help in time of trouble, in whom shall the state place its hope for deliverance from political corruption? The honest citizen; and the honest doctor is his best representative.

TRANSACTIONS.

THE SHELBURNE, ATLANTIC CITY, N. J.
SATURDAY, June 4, 1904.

The twenty-ninth annual meeting of the American Academy of Medicine was called to order by the president, John B. Roberts, of Philadelphia, at 11 A.M.,—the Academy sitting in executive session.

The minutes of the last session were read and approved.

The report of the council was read by the secretary, and is as follows:

Little has happened during the year for the council to report. There have been no local meetings, whence the entire effort has been expended on the preparations for this meeting. About the usual changes have been made in the roll, with an average net increase in membership.

It may be interesting in this connection to mention that our roll contains 224 names that have received the asterisk, and that of the seven who in 1876 met to organize the Academy, but two are living, Dr. E. H. M. Sell, of New York, being the only one of the founders still a Fellow of the Academy.

The nature, variety and value of the papers and reports that have been submitted regularly to the Academy for a number of years, seem to show that we have found our place, and are filling it with commendable energy. It is interesting to note how we appear to act as a vanguard. When the Academy began to insist upon a proper preliminary education for physicians, the profession received the message with shoulder shrugs. To-day, the Academy's position is almost universally conceded. In like manner, when the Academy took up the study of medico-social topics in a scientific manner, it was thought to be merely dilettanteism; but, if imitation be the highest praise, a glance at almost any program for a medical society meeting will show the universality of that praise. There is material enough in sight to absorb the activities of the Academy for some time to come, and this part of our life requires no special recommendation from the council.

From time to time the Academy has been helped by the participation of the non-medical in our discussions. Last year, after a full and careful deliberation, it was decided that it was not best to permanently incorporate a non-medical class into our membership. But the following plan suggested by a portion of an address before the Convocation of the Regents of the University of the State of New York last June might be worthy of consideration.

By this plan, the Academy would issue invitations to certain selected organizations of a sociologic trend, to send delegates to our annual meetings, who, upon presentation of their credentials and registration (without a fee), will be presented to the Academy as Corresponding Members with the privileges of the floor at the open sessions for that meeting only.

While in attendance at this convocation, the secretary had opportunity to examine the excellent records kept in the regent's office as to the actual work done in the various colleges of the United States. It was learned that many of them grant the first degree on very slight attainments. The council suggests that it would be well for the Academy to consider the desirability of appointing a committee to prepare a list of colleges whose course is really worthy of the first degree. Graduates from these colleges would be accepted by us for fellowship, while those who made application having degrees from institutions not on this list would require the scrutiny now given to those who do not possess a degree. While the probabilities are that very few applications would be received from the weaker institutions, we might assist in advancing the value of the A.B. and similar degrees, as we have helped in giving the doctorate a higher academic value.

Perhaps the most serious problem to be solved by the Academy is the financial. Not that we are financially embarrassed, or are in debt, but the treasury is kept in this condition by the expenditure of considerable labor. The council is aware that the question is an old one, growing out of a faulty condition that prevailed for a number of years, that our present method was reached after long and careful deliberation as the only one practicable, and a method that would correct the earlier mistake in time. We do not propose any change (it would be unwise to do so). Our calling your attention to the subject is to suggest that means be taken to hasten the good time that is to come. One thing is evident from the great diversity of interests involved in medical sociology and because our efforts are largely altruistic, the volume of correspondence must continue to be large, and it can be wisely extended. As an illustration of the amount of correspondence now thought to be necessary, the secretary expended $101.50 for postage stamps alone during the past year. Hence the office expenses of the Academy will necessarily be high, as clerical help must be employed. $1200 is the minimum annual income that should be considered. It would be very helpful, if every member were to receive the Bulletin without paying an additional subscription. It will be unwise to make any change in the amount of the dues. During the year a plan was carried out which practically canvassed those members who were elected to fellowship under the earlier pledge of the initiation fee being the only financial obligation. This has enabled the council to classify these members elected before 1899 who are exempt from the penalty of non-payment of dues. . . . It also enabled it to estimate with some degree of accuracy what increase in membership will be necessary to furnish the Academy with an income sufficient to enable it to reduce the subscription of the Bulletin to one dollar and furnish it to all members on the payment of their dues. If we double our membership, this can be done. It may seem chimerical to expect so large an increase of members in a short period. But every year one or two of the fellows make special efforts to secure additions to our roll, and these usually report from three or four to a score of applications. Every fellow has three separate fields to cultivate for new fellows : The eligibles among his neighbors, his college and his medical school. A general enthusiastic effort on the part of those who register at this meeting would so increase our numbers at the next meeting that it would require little effort to secure the number desired for our present purpose by 1906. Without setting any definite number before us as our goal, or letting down the bars in any way, we urge the fellows to make an increased and persevering effort to enlarge our membership until the income will be sufficient to permit the dues to be the subscription to the Bulletin as well.

In 1901 a committee was appointed to receive and report one name from the recommendations for honorary membership at each meeting. This committee has held over from meeting to meeting. The council suggests that it would be more in harmony with the other committees, were it made a standing committee to be appointed by the president from year to year, and recommends that you take the necessary action to authorize it.

We submit the annual necrology; the list seems to grow longer year by year.

1. T. J. Burchard, New York, date of death not known. A.B. College of the City of New York, 1869; M.D. Bellevue Hospital Medical College, 1872. Elected to the Academy, 1881.

2. W. J. Gibson, Philadelphia, died February, 1893. A.B. Princeton, 1880; M.D. Columbia, 1882. Elected to the Academy, 1887.

3. Charles W. Stevens, Charlestown, Mass., died January 25, 1901. A.B., Harvard, 1860; M.D., Harvard, 1870. Elected to the Academy, 1883.

4. John F. Gaylord, Plymouth, Mass., died April 14, 1903. A.B., Yale, 1876; M.D., Yale, 1878. Elected to the Academy, 1898.

5. Joseph S. Cook, Washington, N. J., died July 4, 1903. A.B., Union, 1853; M.D., University of Pennsylvania, 1856; A.M., Lafayette, 1865. Elected to the Academy, 1877.

6. Charles A. Ring, Portland, Me., died July 8, 1903. A.B., Bowdoin, 1868; M.D., Bowdoin, 1872. Elected to the Academy, 1885.

7. W. W. Seely, Cincinnati, died November 7, 1903. A.B., Yale, 1862; M.D., Medical College of Ohio, 1864. Elected to the Academy, 1882.

8. J. McFadden Gaston, Atlanta, Ga., died November 15, 1903. A.B., South Carolina College, 1843; M.D., Medical College of South Carolina, 1846. Elected to the Academy, 1892; Vice-President, 1893; President, 1894.

9. George J. Engelman, Boston, died November 17, 1903. A.B., Washington University, 1867; M.D., University of Berlin, 1871. Elected to the Academy, 1892.

10. W. S. Stewart, Philadelphia, died November 28, 1903. A.B., Jefferson, 1860; M.D., Jefferson Medical College, 1863. One of the Founders of the Academy; Vice-President, 1876.

11. B. J. Bristol, Webster Groves, Mo., died November 28, 1903. A.B.,

Yale, 1854; M.D., Long Island College Hospital, 1866. Elected to the Academy, 1890.

12. Edmund Andrews, Chicago, died January 22, 1904. A.B., University of Michigan, 1849; M.D., University of Michigan, 1852; LL.D., University of Michigan, 1888. Elected to the Academy, 1884.

13. A. C. Gibson, Bangor, Me., died February 2, 1904. A.B., Bowdoin, 1883; M.D., Bowdoin, 1885. Elected to the Academy, 1888.

14. W. H. Hawkes, Washington, D. C., died March 13, 1904. A.B., Brown, 1867; M.D., University of Pennsylvania, 1874. Elected to the Academy, 1890.

15. A. R. Simmons, Utica, N. Y., died March 27, 1904. A.B., Amherst, 1871; M.D., Columbia, 1875. Elected to the Academy, 1890.

16. C. G. Chaddock, St. Louis, died April 1, 1904. No academic degree; M.D., University of Michigan, 1885. Elected to the Academy, 1900.

17. Charlotte Blake Brown, San Francisco, died April 19, 1904. A.B., Elmira Female College, 1866; M.D., Woman's Medical College of Pennsylvania, 1874. Elected to the Academy, 1896.

18. Luther D. Jacobs, Emporia, Kan., died April 28, 1904. A.B., Pennsylvania College, 1863; M.D., University of Pennsylvania, 1866. Elected to the Academy, 1889.

19. Giles Mitchell, Cincinnati, died May 5, 1904. A.B., University of Indiana, 1873; M.D., Medical College of Ohio, 1875. Elected to the Academy, 1892.

20. John M. Duff, Pittsburg, died May 14, 1904. A.B., Western University of Pennsylvania, 1872; M.D., Jefferson Medical College, 1874. Elected to the Academy, 1886.

On motion the report of the council was received and its recommendations adopted.

The council also recommended that the Academy elect to fellowship a number of applicants whose qualifications had been approved by it. The secretary was unanimously instructed to cast the ballot of the Academy electing them.

The report of the treasurer was presented to the Academy:

TREASURER'S REPORT.

Balance		$ 8.32
RECEIVED.		
Initiation fees		175.00
Bulletin:		
Subscription and extra copies	$528.45	
Advertising	204.67	
Reprints	68.10	
		801.22
Certificates		12.00
Dues		228.10
Dues, Life Commutation		80.00
Interest on Life Commutation		2.46
Interest on Reserve Deposit		6.61
Miscellaneous		11.50
Total received		$1325.21

EXPENDED.

Bulletin:
- Printing $595.93
- Postage 10.86
    - ——— 606.79
- Printing other than Bulletin...................... 48.15
- Secretary's traveling expenses..................... 15.65
- Secretary's office expenses......................... 364.35
- Stenographer's fee.................................. 50.00
- A. L. Benedict (Chairman) 8.50
- Transfer to Permanent Fund 100.00
- Printing certificates 20.00
- Miscellaneous....................................... 18.11
- Total expended............................. ———$1231.55

Balance................................... 93.66

On motion the report was referred to an Auditing Committee. The Chair appointed Drs. W. L. Estes, of South Bethlehem, Pa., and C. M. Culver, of Albany, on that committee.

The president appointed the Nominating Committee as follows: George E. Fuller, Munson, Mass., Chairman; Guy L. Connor, Detroit; Edward Jackson, Denver; C. L. Stevens, Athens, Pa.; and J. W. Grosvenor, Buffalo.

He also announced the following committee to tabulate the academic value of the first degree, as recommended in the report of the council: W. S. Hall, Chairman, Chicago; D. C. Hawley; Burlington, Vt.; W. Jarvis Barlow, Los Angeles; Charles McIntire, Easton; C. L. Van Pelt, Toledo.

At this point the Academy arose from the executive session and entered upon an open session.

The special report of the council on the paper of Dr. H. Bert Ellis, of Los Angeles, presented at the last meeting was read by the secretary.[1]

The report was discussed by Dr. H. Bert Ellis, Leartus Connor, and Philip Mills Jones, of San Francisco, secretary of the Joint Committee on Medicine and Foods of the American Medical Association, and the American Pharmaceutical Association. Dr. Jones had been invited to participate in the discussion upon motion of Dr. Ellis.

On motion, the report of the Committee to Investigate the

[1] To be published in a future number of the Bulletin.

Teaching of Hygiene in the Public Schools, was postponed until the special hour, Monday morning (11 A.M.).

The secretary read a partial report of the results of examination before the State Boards of Medical Examiners for 1903. He was requested to complete and publish the report.

The Academy took recess at this period until 3 o'clock.

At the afternoon session, the following papers, composing the symposium on "The Relation of Physicians to Dentists and Pharmacists," were read.

1. "The Relations of Dentistry and Medicine," by Edward C. Kirk, Philadelphia. Upon invitation of the committee.

2. "The Relations of Physicians to Dentists," by John M. Marshall, U. S. A. Read by Dr. A. L. Craig in the absence of Dr. Marshall.

3. "Ethical Pharmacy," by A. L. Benedict, Buffalo.

4. "A Protest against Proprietary Products," by A. Mansfield Holmes, Denver.

5. "Synonyms in the New United States Pharmacopeia," by Joseph G. Remington, Philadelphia. By invitation of the Committee on Program, read by Dr. A. L. Craig in the absence of Professor Remington, who was detained by serious illness in his family.

6. "Science vs. Shekels," by Charles McIntire, Easton, Pa.

These papers were discussed by W. R. White, of Providence; Eugene S. Talbot, of Chicago (by invitation); L. Duncan Bulkley, of New York; H. O. Marcy, of Boston; S. A. Knopf, of New York; J. W. Grosvenor, of Buffalo; Leartus Connor, of Detroit; and by Dr. Kirk in closing.

The Academy took recess at the close of the discussion until 8 o'clock, when it listened to an able address by the president, with Vice-President T. D. Davis in the chair, entitled "The Duty of the Doctor to the State."[1]

At the conclusion of the address, H. Bert Ellis moved a vote of thanks to Dr. Roberts for his admirable address. It was seconded and adopted by a hearty and unanimous vote. The Academy then adjourned until Monday morning.

[1] See p. 673, this number.

THE SHELBURNE,
June 6, 1904.

The Academy met in executive session with Dr. T. D. Davis, vice-president, in the chair.

The Council reported that they had investigated additional applications for membership, and the names of those who were recommended by them. By a unanimous vote the secretary was instructed to cast the ballot for the Academy and the gentlemen were elected.

The Council also reported receiving the resignations of Drs. F. C. Curtis, of Albany, J. L. Hildreth, of Cambridge, Mass., W. A. Posey and W. F. Waugh, of Chicago, and recommended the Academy to accept them. On motion the resignations were accepted.

The Auditing Committee reported auditing the books of the treasurer and finding them correct.

At this point the Academy arrested the executive session, and listened to the report of its committee to "investigate the teaching of hygiene in the public schools" with open doors.

Dr. Helen C. Putnam, the chairman of the committee, reported upon the laws of the various states, and the text-books, and Dr. Edward Jackson upon medical inspection. The reports were but reports of progress and were discussed by Drs. Leartus Connor, J. T. Searcy, De Lancey Rochester, H. O. Marcy, J. W. Grosvenor, W. S. Hall, E. H. M. Sell, T. N. Hall, T. D. Davis and was closed by Dr. Putnam for the committee.

Dr. W. S. Hall at the end of his discussion offered the following:

Resolved: I. That the AMERICAN ACADEMY OF MEDICINE recommend to the publishers of school text-books of physiology and hygiene, that these text-books be revised not less frequently than once in three years, in order that they may be kept illuminated by the full light of our latest researches in science and most advanced theories of pedagogy.

II. That the AMERICAN ACADEMY OF MEDICINE express to the educators of this country: (1) their belief in the advantages of special teachers for physiology and hygiene in all those schools where special teachers are employed for other branches; and (2) their belief that every teacher should be thoroughly instructed in this important branch as a regular part of the normal course.

The resolution was seconded and referred to the council, as was also the motion continuing the committee until its work was completed.

The Academy took recess until three o'clock.

The Academy reconvened in open session with Dr. J. H. McBride, vice-president, in the chair, and entered upon the consideration of the symposium, "Are Modern School Methods in Keeping with Physiologic Knowledge?"

The following papers were read:

"Is the Present Method of Educating Girls Consistent with Their Physiologic Development, and Is It for the Welfare of the Race?" A. Lapthorn Smith, Montreal.

"Is Equal Treatment of the Sexes Best, or Do Girls Require the Same Treatment as Boys?" S. H. Weeks, Portland, Me. (read by the secretary).

"The Gynecologic Aspect of Mental Overstrain at Puberty, and Its Influence on Development." W. E. Darnall, Atlantic City.

"The Effect of Modern School Methods upon the Health of the Teacher." Jane L. Greely, Jamestown, N. Y.

The discussion was opened by W. S. Hall, of Chicago, and continued by T. D. Davis, Leartus Connor, V. C. Vaughan, and J. A. McBride, A. Lapthorn Smith and Jane L. Greely closing the discussion.

A paper entitled "The Correspondence Method of Treating Disease" was read by F. T. Rogers, of Providence, and discussed by A. Ravogli, of Cincinnati, G. T. Swartz, of Providence, and W. M. Beach, of Binghampton, F. T. Rogers closing the discussion.

"How May the Public School Be Helpful in the Prevention of Tuberculosis?" was the title of the last paper by S. A. Knopf, of New York. It was discussed by J. W. Grosvenor, of Buffalo, and S. A. Knopf.

The Academy at this point went into executive session and listened to the report of the Nominating Committee. The report was accepted and the secretary instructed to cast the ballot for the Academy. This was done and the following were elected: *President*—W. S. Hall, Chicago; *Vice-Presidents*—H. Bert Ellis, Los Angeles; R. A. Reeve, Toronto; L. S. McMurtry, Louisville;

Maurice Richardson, Boston; *Secretary*—Charles McIntire, Easton, Pa.; *Treasurer*—E. M. Green, Easton, Pa.; *Assistant Secretary*—A. R. Craig, Columbia, Pa.

The council made its final report:

The council wishes to report upon the motion of Dr. W. S. Hall. Since the report of the committee was preliminary and presented no definite conclusions, it was moved by Dr. Hall, the maker of the suggestion, that the question be referred to the committee with the request that the principles involved be formulated in their final report.

On the motion to continue the committee until it had completed its work, the council recommends its adoption.

The report of the council was, on motion, adopted.

Edward Jackson, the chairman of the Committee on Honorary Members, presented the name of Sir Patrick Manson, M.D., F. R. S., Lecturer, London School of Tropical Diseases, for honorary membership because of his work on the mosquito theory of malaria, which has not received the public recognition deserved by the great importance of that discovery. The secretary was instructed to cast the ballot for Dr. Manson, which was done and he was elected.

On motion of Dr. G. Hudson-Makuen duly seconded, a vote of thanks was given the management of " The Shelburne " for the excellent way in which the Academy was entertained.

On motion of Dr. S. A. Knopf, duly seconded, the president with the officers and committees were thanked by the Academy for the preparation for and conduct of the meeting.

The Academy then took recess until 8.00 o'clock for the social session.

The Academy reconvened at 8.00 o'clock in social session, partaking of a most excellent banquet later in the evening.

During the evening Dr. Roberts introduced Dr. W. S Hall, the newly elected president. On motion, the president was authorized to make his appointments at his convenience, and on motion, the Academy adjourned.

The following were elected to fellowship during the meeting:

J. U. Barnhill, Columbus, O.
J. W. Beach, Binghampton, N. Y.
C. S. Caverly, Rutland, Vt.
J. B. Chapin, Philadelphia.

Edward Mayer, Pittsburg.
H. D. Michler, Easton, Pa.
A. I. Miller, Brattleboro, Vt.
D. C. Miller, Mason and Dickson, Pa.

C. G. Coakley, New York.
W. P. Conaway, Atlantic City.
Ray Connor, Detroit.
A. Davidson, Los Angeles.
Wm. McC. Davis, Pittsburg.
T. G. Dunlap, Atlantic City.
J. C. Egbert, Wayne, Pa.
George Fetterolf, Philadelphia.
M. Figueira, Brooklyn.
C. E. Gilbert, Atlantic City.
D. V. Gleysteen, Alton, Ia.
J. M. Hamilton, Rutland, Vt.
L. J. Hammond, Philadelphia.
C. M. Hazen, Bon Air, Va.
L. E. Holmes, Asheville, N. C.
H. N. Hoople, Brooklyn.
W. A. Howe, Phelps, N. Y.
A. G. Hurd, Medbury, Mass.
P. M. Jones, San Francisco.

W. J. Morton, New York.
M. G. Motter, Washington, D. C.
L. C. Peters, Philadelphia.
J. H. Pleasants, Baltimore.
F. M. Pottenger, Los Angeles.
G. H. Powers, San Francisco.
L. A. Purington, Yarmouth, Me.
John Ruhräh, Baltimore.
Gould N. Shelton, Shelton, Conn.
L. M. Spalding, Boston.
H. P. Stearns, Hartford, Conn.
E. S. Sternberger, New York.
B. H. Stone, Burlington, Vt.
Franz Torek, New York.
H. R. Watkins, Burlington, Vt.
C. M. Williams, New York.
J. H. Woodward, New York.
J. H. Wright, Columbus, O.

The following fellows were registered in attendance.

ALABAMA—J. T. Searcy, *Tuscaloosa*.

CALIFORNIA—W. Jarvis Barlow, H. G. Brainerd, H. Bert Ellis, *Los Angeles*; J. H. McBride, *Pasadena*; P. M. Jones, *San Francisco*.

COLORADO—S. G. Bonney, J. N. Hall, T. H. Hawkins, A. M. Holmes, Edward Jackson, Henry Sewall, *Denver*.

DELAWARE—Willard Springer, *Wilmington*.

ILLINOIS—R. H. Babcock, Rosa Engelmann, P. Maxwell Foshay, W. S. Hall, Casey M. Wood, *Chicago*.

IOWA—L. W. Littig, *Iowa City*.

KENTUCKY—M. E. Alderson, *Russellville*.

MARYLAND—Julius Friedenwald, John Ruhräh, G. Lane Taneyhill, *Baltimore*.

MASSACHUSETTS—E. B. Harvey, H. O. Marcy, H. O. Marcy, Jr., *Boston*; G. E. Fuller, *Munson*; S. D. Presbrey, *Taunton*.

MICHIGAN—W. J. Herdman, V. C. Vaughan, *Ann Arbor*; Guy L. Connor, Leartus Connor, Charles Hitchcock, C. T. McClintock, *Detroit*.

NEW JERSEY—W. E. Darnall, J. A. Joy, W. Blair Stewart, *Atlantic City*; H. W. Elmer, *Bridgeton*; W. G. Schauffler, *Lakewood*; William Elmer, *Trenton*.

NEW YORK—C. M. Culver, *Albany*; G. W. Beach, *Binghampton*; H. N. Hoople, *Brooklyn*; A. L. Benedict, J. W. Grosvenor, De Lancey Rochester, *Buffalo*; M. B. Tinker, *Ithaca*; M. N. Bemus, Jane L. Greely, *Jamestown*; L. Duncan Bulkley, S. A. Knopf, E. H. M. Sell, *New York*; W. A. Howe, *Phelps*; R. H. Ward, *Troy*.

OHIO—M. L. Heidenfeld, Augustus Ravogli, *Cincinnati*; J. U. Barnhill, *Columbus*; H. M. Moore, *Oxford*; C. L. Van Pelt, *Toledo*.

PENNSYLVANIA—C. L. Stevens, *Athens*; A. R. Craig, *Columbia*; R. M. Green, Charles McIntire, *Easton*; W. J. K. Kline, *Greensburg*; Frederic Corss, Henry Kunkel, *Kingston*; J. K. Weaver, *Norristown*; R. G. Curtin, G. M. Gould, Benjamin Lee, G. Hudson-Makuen, W. L. Pyle, Boardman Reed, S. D. Risley, J. B. Roberts, P. J. Sartain, C. P. Turner, *Philadelphia*; T. D. Davis, W. S. Foster, J. M. T. McKennan, *Pittsburg*; A. H. Halberstadt, *Pottsville*; A. B. Dundor, *Reading*; W. L. Estes, *South Bethlehem*; J. C. Egbert, *Wayne*.

RHODE ISLAND—G. S. Matthews, Helen C. Putnam, F. T. Rogers, G. T. Swarts, W. R. White, *Providence*.

VERMONT—H. D. Holton, *Brattleboro*; D. C. Hawley, *Burlington*; C. S. Caverly, *Rutland*.

WEST VIRGINIA—G. A. Aschman, *Wheeling*.

CANADA—A. Lapthorn Smith, *Montreal*.

OBSERVATIONS IN PASSING.
THE ATLANTIC CITY MEETING.

Before the impressions of our last meeting have faded, it is well to attempt to record them. Doubtless the Academy would have had a profitable meeting anywhere, but in few places, if in any, are the creature comforts so unostentatiously ministered as to combine the pleasurable and the profitable into a unit of delight as was done by the management of "The Shelburne." The pleasant meeting room, in full view of the ocean, the roar of whose waves making the only noise to disturb the meeting, contributed not a little to this result.

The report on the teaching of hygiene in public schools, opens a field of study of importance that may well occupy the attention of the Academy for some time to come. The committee was continued, and we may expect additional contributions of value to the literature of this subject.

The symposium of the relation of dentists and pharmacists to the medical profession would have been more effective were they separated, as the character of the relation between medicine and the other callings differs with each. Nevertheless, the papers and discussion will be worthy of careful reading. The remaining symposium on modern school methods was disappointing because the papers did not fully cover the ground. Indeed the young woman received proportionally too much attention. The papers and discussion were of real value, but much of the general topic remains to be discussed. There is room for a large amount of investigation here. Any one undertaking it with any degree of thoroughness can not help being richly repaid.

Dr. Rogers' paper exposed the methods of the unscrupulous, while Dr. Knopf's gives a wider circulation to his excellent ideas as to the assistance that schools can give to prevent the spread of the white plague.

Of the executive business two of the most important items were the appointment of a committee to investigate the comparative academic value of the first degree of the various colleges, and empowering the council to invite organizations of a sociologic trend to send accredited representatives to specified meetings of the Academy to have the privileges of the floor in the open session.

Dr. Winfield S. Hall, of Chicago, professor of physiology in the medical department of the Northwestern University, was selected as president.

Forty-five fellows were elected and the registration of fellows reached 94, the largest in the history of the Academy.

The place for the 1905 meeting is not yet decided. It is hardly possible that the Academy will meet with the American Medical Association.

***

The officials to whose care the preparations for the XV International Congress of Medicine is entrusted ask us to permit the following, which we most cheerfully do, and without editing.

XVTH INTERNATIONAL CONGRESS OF MEDICINE—LISBON, APRIL, 1906.

We have received the first number of the Journal of the XVth International Congress of Medicine, that will take place in Lisbon on the 19th to 26th of April, 1906. This number contains the statute of the Congress, the organization of the sections and of the national committees of the different nations. One must remark in the statute the 2d article, that only admits in the Congress, beyond the doctors, the scientific men presented by the National or Portugese committees.

The contribution is of 25 francs or 20 marks or 1 pound sterling.

The work of the Congress is distributed in 17 sections:

1—Anatomy (Descriptive and compared anatomy, anthropology, embyology, histology).
2—Physiology.
3—General pathology, bacteriology and pathological anatomy.
4—Therapie and pharmacology.
5—Medicine.
6—Pediatry.
7—Neurology, psychiatry and criminal anthropology.
8—Dermatology and syphiligraphy.
9—Surgery.
10—Medicine and surgery of the urinary organs.
11—Ophthalmology.
12—Laryngology, rhinology and stomatology.
13—Obstetrics and gynecology.
14—Hygiene and epidemiology.
15—Military medicine.
16—Legal medicine.
17—Colonial and naval medicine.

The Executive Committee of the Congress has the intention to print, before the reunion, all the *official reports ;* it is necessary that they shall be given before the 30th of September, 1905, to the general secretary. For the free communications it is necessary that they should be given before the 31st of December, 1905, if the authors want that the conclusions should be printed before the opening of the Congress.

The official language is the French. In the general assemblies, as in the sections, the English, German, and French may be used. We see that the Committee of the Congress has excluded the Portugueese from the languages permitted; this has only been done with the intention of diminishing the number of languages spoken ; there can be no jealousy when the legislator begins by sacrificing himself.

The president of the Committee of Organization is the doctor M. da Costa Alemão ; the general secretary is the doctor Miguel Bombarda ; all the adhesions must be addressed to this doctor (Hospital de Rilhafolles, Lisbon).

LITERATURE NOTES.

The Booklovers Magazine for May, 1904, contains among other capital articles, one of the late Senator Quay, of Pennsylvania, which becomes especially timely because of his decease since the magazine appeared. It is well worth the perusal, even by those who have no special interest in the man himself. As usual the Booklovers is crowded with a wealth of illustration.

Polk's Medical Register and Directory of North America for 1904 (the eighth revised edition) has been received and, like everything else in the American medical world, is growing to colossal proportions. While cast on the lines of the previous editions there appears to be a number of minor improvements to increase its usefulness as a work of reference. In its accuracy it seems to equal the previous editions, which is no faint praise. The surprise is not that there are errors in the work and many of them, but that in the aggregate, the errors are so few and cause so little inconvenience. Polk's "is an office necessity in these days of communication among physicians."

THE OPHTHALMIC YEAR BOOK. A DIGEST OF THE LITERATURE OF OPHTHALMOLOGY WITH INDEX OF PUBLICATION FOR THE YEAR 1903. BY EDWARD JACKSON, A.M., M.D. The Herrick Book and Stationery Company, Denver, Colorado. 1904. pp. 260. Price, $2.00.

This is a book for the ophthalmologist, and its perusal will give him a fair acquaintance with the literature of 1903 that pertains to actual advancement in his branch, and furnish him with the information enabling him to secure more complete details upon any subject in which he is especially interested.

WATER SUPPLY AND IRRIGATION PAPERS. Department of the Interior, United States Geological Survey. Washington Printing Office. 1903.

Nos. 83, 84, 85. REPORT OF PROGRESS OF STREAM MEASUREMENTS FOR THE CALENDAR YEAR 1902. BY F. H. NEWELL. pp. 304, 200, 250.

No. 86. STORAGE RESERVOIRS ON STONY CREEK, CALIFORNIA. BY BURT COLE. pp. 62.

No. 87. IRRIGATION IN INDIA. BY HERBERT M. WILSON. pp. 238.

No. 88. THE PASSAIC FLOOD OF 1902. BY G. B. HOLLISTER AND M. O. LEIGHTON. pp. 56.

These pamphlets form the part of a very valuable series issued under the supervision of Charles D. Wolcott, the director of the survey, and illustrate one of the beneficent functions of the Government Printing Office, which we are too apt to associate with franked speeches appearing as transactions of Congress by a vote of "leave to print."

REPORTS OF STATE BOARDS OF HEALTH.

I. TWENTY-SIXTH ANNUAL REPORT OF THE STATE BOARD OF HEALTH OF THE STATE OF CONNECTICUT FOR THE YEAR 1903. New Haven, Conn. 1904. pp. 331, 276.

II. EIGHTEENTH ANNUAL REPORT OF THE STATE BOARD OF HEALTH AND VITAL STATISTICS OF THE COMMONWEALTH OF PENNSYLVANIA. Harrisburg. 1903. pp. 782.

I. Connecticut's board does not think that the death-rate is an accurate criterion of the sanitary administration because so many deaths are the result of disobedience of the personal laws of health that are not under the control of the health authorities.

BULLETIN

OF THE

American Academy of Medicine

VOL. VI.   ISSUED AUGUST, 1904.   NO. 13.

THE AMERICAN ACADEMY OF MEDICINE is not responsible for the sentiments expressed in any paper or address published in the BULLETIN.

RESULTS OF THE EXAMINATIONS FOR MEDICAL LICENSURE IN THE UNITED STATES FOR 1903.[1]

BY CHARLES McINTIRE, A.M., M.D., Secretary of the Academy.

This is the sixth annual report of the series. Early in the history of the Academy, before the days of examining boards, the secretary was instructed to present an annual report on medical legislation, which Dr. Dunglison was very faithful in doing. For a long time he was able to report only attempts to secure legislation, mostly unsuccessful. It was before the days of our publishing our own papers, and the reports, if preserved, are scattered in various medical journals. They would afford a valuable contribution to the history of medical legislation if obtainable.

For two or three years before the first of the present series of reports, our Bulletin classified the states according to the character of the medical licensure law, publishing explicit directions of procedure in each instance. Quite naturally, a publication of the results in those states admitting to practice by examination followed.

These reports have never been complete. It has been impossible to secure the cooperation of the secretary of every board. It speaks well for the interest taken in the development of professional standing on the part of the members of the various boards that so many are willing to cooperate. The compiler of

[1] Report of the secretary presented at Atlantic City, June 4, 1904.

the report wishes to express his appreciation of the assistance so generously given. It is true that the results published are for the benefit of our profession; were it not so, the labor bestowed upon the preparation would be effort thrown away. When we glory in our profession, we naturally look at those whose lives have made it glorious. When, in less enthusiastic mood, we look upon the seamy side, we find a sufficient number of examples of dishonorable practice to make us pessimistic; and the true estimate of the profession, it is to be found in neither extreme. While the vast majority of our number are honorably following the best tradition of our profession, they are doing so without ostentation and are inclined to be indifferent to the conduct of others. This fact explains why so many and so great evils have crept into the practice of medicine, and the great difficulty in securing reform, for those who are prone to devious ways are far from quiet.

One of the great evils thus permitted was the insufficient "school" education of the physician, and by "school" it is desired to include the entire process conducted in educational institutions whether primary, liberal or professional. Not that school processes alone will make skilful practices, or honorable physicians. It will, however, cut out a vast number of incompetents and unworthy, and reduce the proportion of the undesirable. Herein lies the advantage of an examining board, and the individual who objects probably does so because of a pinched foot in the board's shoe.

The great governing factor in American life is public opinion. The board will fail unless backed by the enlightened public opinion of the mass of the profession. Not a year passes but somewhere, an attack is made upon some medical examining act, to let down the bars so that incompetents can enter. Unless the profession is kept informed of the working of the board, and its interest kept alive, the baser element will gain in ascendency.

Unless, for example, it can be shown that the proportion of graduates of some particular medical school that fail in their state examinations is far beyond the average, that school can continue to beguile students by specious circulars and special promises. It is to furnish this publicity that these reports are compiled, and it is because of the direct strengthening of the boards themselves, we are free to ask their cooperation as the results are for the benefit of the profession not only, but a direct help to the boards themselves, none the less real, because intangible.

The totals reported for the previous years have been:

	Passed.	Failed.	Total.	Per cent. licensed.
1898	2,328	562	2,890	80.6
1899	2,645	560	3,205	82.5
1900	3,000	504	3,504	85.3
1901	2,436	522	2,958	82.3
1902	3,781	729	4,510	83.8

One difficulty in preparing these returns is the various names given to medical schools. Thus the College of Physicians and Surgeons, of New York, and the medical department of Columbia University are the same, and there are a number of schools that have changed their names more than once in a not overly prolonged existence. The effort is made to call the school by its latest name unless there are some reasons for using the older name. And also, when a school is in any way affiliated with a university, the name of the university is employed; thus it is *University of Chicago* and not *Rush Medical College*.

The principal tabulation is given under the individual colleges. In the tabulation by states, the totals only are given. This seems to be the most satisfactory method of presenting the facts.

QUALIFICATIONS FOR THE LEGAL PRACTICE OF MEDICINE IN THE VARIOUS STATES AND TERRITORIES.

NOTE—The requirements in many of the states specify that the medical school must be recognized by the board as in good standing. It has not been thought necessary to particularize the standard required by each board. The advertised standard of the Association of American Medical Colleges will usually meet these requirements, and a letter addressed to the secretary of the board will secure definite information as to a specified college in that state.

The subject of reciprocity or acceptance of state licenses by another state is treated in a supplementary paragraph.

ALABAMA.

A certificate of qualification will be issued to such as pass an examination before one of the authorized boards of examiners. There is a board of examiners for each county, which can issue a certificate for the county only, and a state board whose certificate gives the right to practise in any county. Only graduates from recognized schools of medicine may be examined by a county board, while any one may present himself for examination before the state board, and passing the examination, will be given the legal permission to practise medicine. If any one does not wish to practise major surgery, it may be omitted from the subjects for examination, and a corresponding certificate issued upon passing the examination.

Dr. W. H. Sanders, Montgomery, is the secretary of the state board of examiners, to whom letters of inquiry should be addressed.

ALASKA.

There is no law regulating the practice of medicine in Alaska.

ARIZONA.

The applicant for a license must have graduated from a medical college lawfully organized, and pass an examination before the state board of medical examiners.

Secretary of the board, Dr. William Duffeld, Phoenix.

ARKANSAS.

Passing an examination before one of the three boards of medical examiners and registering the license issued in the county court. Secretaries: Dr. J. P. Runyan, Little Rock, for the state board of the Arkansas Medical Society; Dr. J. L. Vail, Little Rock, for the eclectic state medical board; Dr. Victor Hallman, Hot Springs, for the homeopathic state medical board.

CALIFORNIA.

The provision of the California law which permits only graduates of medical schools whose standing is equivalent to that of the Association of American Medical Colleges to come up for examination has been decided to be constitutional by the supreme court. To practise legally in California one must secure a license after an examination before the state board.

The secretary of the board is Dr. G. G. Gere, 825 Market St., San Francisco.

COLORADO.

Colorado has not as yet been able to change her law and accepts the diploma of certain colleges whose curriculum complies with the requirements of the Association of American Medical Colleges, without an examination.

Dr. S. D. Van Meter, secretary, 1723 Tremont St., Denver.

CONNECTICUT.

A diploma in medicine is a prerequisite for examination. There are three boards one a homeopathic, another an eclectic. Each board acts independently, framing its own questions, but the returns are all made to the state board of health, for the issuing of licenses, etc.

Dr. C. A. Lindsley, secretary of the state board of health, New Haven, is the official to whom letters of inquiry should be addressed.

DELAWARE.

There are two boards of examiners in Delaware, one homeopathic, working in harmony under the oversight of the medical council. The law specifies a moderate degree of preliminary education, four years' study of medicine, and passing the state examination.

Dr. P. W. Tomlinson, Wilmington, is the secretary of the medical council.

DISTRICT OF COLUMBIA.

Candidates for licensure in the district must have graduated from a reputable medical school, and if graduating after June 30, 1898, after pursuing a four years' course. There are three boards of examiners working in harmony under the oversight of the board of medical supervisors.

Dr. Wm. C. Woodward, Washington, is the secretary.

FLORIDA.

There is a board of examiners for each of the seven judicial districts, besides a homeopathic and an eclectic board for the state-at-large. Any one is qualified to take the examination.

Secretaries:[1]
    1st Judicial District, Dr. Louis de M. Blocker, Pensacola.
    2nd   "   "   Dr. J. F. Williams, Monticello.
    3d   "   "   Dr. J. A. Townsend, Lake City.

[1] Report State Board of Health, Illinois; Medical Education, 1903, p. cxxi.

4th Judicial District, Dr. J. H. Durkee, Jacksonville.
5th   "   "   Dr. G. E. Welch, Paletka.
6th   "   "   Dr. L. A. Bize, Tampa.
7th   "   "   Dr. R. L. Harris, Orlando.
State Homeopathic Board, Dr. C. W. Johnson, Jacksonville.
State Eclectic Board, D. D. E. Saxton, Tampa.

GEORGIA.

Graduates of recognized medical schools are eligible for examination before one of the three boards of examiners of Georgia. These boards are independent of each other, without the supervision of a single licensing commission as in some states.

Secretaries: Dr. I. H. Goss, Athens; Dr. R. E. Hinman, 153 Whitehall St., Atlanta (homeopathic board); Dr. W. V. Robertson (president), 77½ Peachtree St., Atlanta (eclectic board).

IDAHO.

Only graduates in medicine are eligible for examination in Idaho, and the college issuing the diploma must be in good standing with the state board of medical examiners.

Dr. R. L. Nourse, Hailey, is the secretary of the board.

ILLINOIS.

The educational standard is graduation from a medical school in good standing with the board. If the applicant has graduated since January 1, 1900, he must have attended four courses of lectures in separate years. In addition, the applicant must pass an examination before the state board of health.

Dr. J. A. Egan, Springfield, is secretary.

INDIAN TERRITORY.

Congress at its last session passed a registration law for Indian Territory, which hereafter will regulate the practice of medicine in this territory.

TEXT OF THE LAW.

An Act regulating the practice of medicine and surgery in the Indian Territory.

Be it enacted by the Senate and House of Representatives of the United States of America in Congress assembled. That hereafter no person shall practise medicine and surgery, or either, as a profession in the Indian Territory without first being registered as a physician and surgeon, or either, in the office of the clerk of the United States court in the district in which he or she offers to practise.

SEC. 2. That each district clerk in the Indian Territory shall keep in his office a well-bound book, in which he shall register the names of such persons as shall be lawfully qualified, as hereinafter provided, and who shall apply for registration, as physician and surgeon, or either, with the date of such registration.

SEC. 3. That hereafter any person who may wish to practise the science of medicine or surgery, or both, in the Indian Territory shall be allowed to register as such who shall file with the clerk of the United States court of any district in the Indian Territory a certificate of qualification signed by a majority of the board of medical examiners of the district in the Indian Territory in which he or she offers to register : *Provided*, That any person living in a district in which no board is organized may apply to the board of some other district in the Indian Territory.

SEC. 4. That immediately after the passage of this act the United States judge in each district in the Indian Territory shall appoint for his district a board of medical examiners, consisting of three persons, who shall be citizens of the district and learned in the science of medicine and surgery, of good moral character, graduates of some reputable medical college recognized by either of the American medical college associations who shall thereafter be duly registered under this Act, who shall hold their office for a period of four years, or until their successors are duly appointed and qualified ; and should a vacancy occur in any of said boards at any time, the same shall be filled by appointment made by the United States judge of the district in which the vacancy occurs.

SEC. 5. That the members of said board shall, before entering upon the discharge of their duties, take the official oath required to be taken by officers of the Indian Territory.

SEC. 6. That at the first meeting of the members of such boards, after they shall have been appointed, preparatory to the transaction of business assigned them under this Act, they shall organize by electing one of their members as president and another as secretary, and adopt a seal.

SEC. 7. That physicians and surgeons who shall be engaged in practice at the time of the passage of this Act shall each, within six months thereafter, present to said board their diplomas, together with affidavit in each case that the affiant is the lawful possessor of the same and he is the person named therein. Such as have no diplomas shall within the same time submit sworn applications, setting forth the extent of their medical education and their experience as practitioners, and shall be subject to a careful examination by the board.

SEC. 8. That the regular meetings of each board shall be held quarterly at the court house of that district on the first Monday in January, April, July and October in each year, and when so assembled said board shall faithfully and impartially examine all such persons as shall appear before them for that purpose touching their qualifications to practise medicine and surgery, or either, and all such persons as shall satisfy such board of examiners, or a majority of them, that he or she is of good moral character and duly qualified in knowledge and capacity to practise medicine and surgery, or either, shall receive from such board a certificate of qualification as physician and surgeon, or either, as the case may be, which certificate shall entitle such person to registration under the provisions of sections two and three: *Provided further*, That no person desiring to practise medicine under this Act shall be excluded therefrom on account of any particular system or school of medicine that he or she may desire to practise.

SEC. 9. That the board may refuse certificates to persons guilty of unprofessional or dishonorable conduct, and it may revoke certificates for like causes: *Provided always*, That they have given the person an opportunity to be heard in his or her defense.

SEC. 10. That any person desiring to be examined at any other time than the regular quarterly meeting shall notify the president of the board of such desire, whose duty shall be to assemble the board as soon as practicable and examine applicant.

SEC. 11. That the district clerk shall give to every person registered under this Act a certificate of registration over his signature and official seal, and such certificate shall authorize any such person to practise as physician or surgeon, or both, as the case may be, in any district in the Indian Territory, provided he or she registers said certificate with the clerk of the United States court for each district in which he or she desires to practise.

SEC. 12. That the clerk shall receive as his fee for all services required of him under this Act in each case the sum of $1.50.

SEC. 13. That any two members of said board shall constitute a quorum for the transaction of all such business as shall come before it, and each applicant for examination shall pay in advance to the secretary, to be divided equally among the members of such board, the sum of $10, which shall be their only compensation.

SEC. 14. That all physicians and surgeons holding diplomas desiring to practise the science of medicine and surgery in the Indian Territory shall submit the same to the board of examiners for the district in which they desire to practise for examination and approval, for which said applicant shall pay a fee of $1 to said board, and upon approval by said board of said diploma shall not be required to undergo the examination herein provided for; and said board shall issue to said applicant a certificate of approval, which certificate shall be registered in the clerk's office for the district in which said board holds jurisdiction: *Provided, however*, That no person holding a diploma issued after July 1, 1904, shall be permitted to practise medicine or surgery for pay in the Indian Territory except that the diploma be issued by a medical school or college requiring a preliminary examination for admission to its course of study in all the common branches and the higher mathematics, which requirements shall be regularly published in all the advertisements and in each prospectus or catalogue issued by said school, which medical school or college shall also require as a requisite for granting the degree of doctor of medicine attendance upon at least four courses of lectures of six months each, no two of said courses to be held within one year, and having a full faculty of capable professors in all the different branches of medical education, to-wit, anatomy, physiology, chemistry, toxicology, histology, pathology, hygiene, materia medica, therapeutics, obstetrics, bacteriology, medical jurisprudence, gynecology, principles and practice of medicine and surgery, and specially requiring clinical instruction in the last two named of not less than four hours per week in each during the last two courses of lectures.

SEC. 15. That any person who shall prescribe or administer medicine for or who shall in any manner treat disease, wounds, fractures, or other bodily injury for pay shall be deemed physicians and surgeons under this act.

SEC. 16. That any person who shall hereafter engage in the practice of medicine and surgery, or either, in the Indian Territory, in violation of the requirements of this act, shall be deemed guilty of a misdemeanor, and upon conviction in any court having jurisdiction thereof under the laws of the United States governing the practice of medicine and surgery in the Indian Territory shall be fined in any sum not less than $25 and not more than $100; and each day said physician or surgeon shall practise medicine or surgery without being registered as hereinbefore required shall be deemed a separate offense: *Provided, however*, That nothing in this act shall be constructed to prohibit gratuitous service in cases of emergency or the domestic administration of family remedies. And this act shall not apply to surgeons in the service of the United States in the discharge of their official duties, or to physicians or surgeons from other territories or states when in actual consultation with a physician or surgeon duly registered as provided herein. And *provided further*, that osteopath, massage, Christian science, and herbal treatment shall not be affected by this act.

Approved, April 23, 1904.

Secretaries: Central District—Dr. B. W. Caldwell,[1] Hugo; Northern District—Dr. B. F. Fortner, Vinita; Southern District—Dr. E. E. Chivers, Mannsville; the members of the board for the Western District is composed of Drs. R. M. Counterman, Eufaula, J. M. Lemon, of Okmulgee, and M. F. Williams, Muskogee,[2] appointed on July 11th, and had not organized when the information was sent.

INDIANA.

With an exception for certain students in Indiana medical schools who apply for license before January 1, 1905, all persons entering upon the practice of medicine in Indiana, must be graduates of medical schools recognized by the board as maintaining

[1] Journal of the American Medical Association, July 2, 1904.
[2] Muskogee Phoenix, July 12, 1904.

the established standard, and must pass an examination before the board of examiners.

Dr. W. T. Gott, Indianapolis, is the secretary.

IOWA.

Iowa requires the possession of a diploma from a medical school recognized as in good standing by the board—and for those who have graduated after January 1, 1899, evidence of having taken four courses in medicine in separate years—as a qualification to come before the board for an examination.

Dr. J. F. Kennedy, Des Moines, is the secretary of the board.

KANSAS.

While the Kansas law permits the board of registration and examination to accept diplomas of such colleges as may be determined to be of good standing as evidence of fitness to practise medicine, the board wisely insists upon an examination of all who desire licensure. The applicant for examination must have a diploma from a medical school, secured after a three or a four years' course depending whether it was granted before or after April 1, 1902.

Dr. D. F. Lewis, Topeka, is the secretary.

KENTUCKY.

The law of Kentucky entrusts the licensing of physicians to its state board of health. The evidence of fitness is the possession of a diploma from a medical school acceptable to the board. The provisions of the Kentucky law give the board greater powers over those who have been licensed by it, than do most laws, so, while weak in its admittance clause, the Kentucky law as administered is one of the most effective in all the states.

Dr. J. N. McCormack, Bowling Green, is secretary.

LOUISIANA.

Louisiana requires the applicant for examination to be a graduate of a college recognized by the board. There are two boards of examiners working independently of each other.

The secretaries are Dr. F. A. Larue, 624 Gravier Street, and Dr. Gayle Aiken (homeopathic), 1102 St. Charles Avenue, both in New Orleans.

MAINE.

The educational requirement in Maine is graduation from a medical school recognized by the board, and passing an examination upon the usual medical studies.

Dr. A. K. P. Merserve, of Portland, is the secretary.

MARYLAND.

The applicant for examination in Maryland must submit evidence that he possesses a competent common school education and is a graduate of a medical school requiring the standard of the Association of American Medical Colleges, or of the American Institute of Homeopathy. Foreign credentials must be those which permit the holder to practise in his own country. There are two boards working independently, and the qualified applicant must pass an examination before the board of his choice to obtain a license.

Secretaries: Dr. J. Mc. P. Scott, Hagerstown, and Dr. Joseph S. Garrison (homeopathic), Easton.

MASSACHUSETTS

The state board of registration in medicine is the sole judge of the fitness of an applicant to practise medicine in Massachusetts. Any one may attempt the examination. The effect of this law is to increase the labors of the board, for very few not possessing a diploma in medicine are licensed.

Dr. E. B. Harvey, State House, Boston, is the secretary.

MICHIGAN.

Michigan now requires a preliminary education equivalent to a high school course, graduation from a medical school requiring four separate courses of at least seven months each, and passing an examination before the state board before a license to practise is issued.

Exception is made to these requirements to applicants graduating before the passage of the law.

Dr. B. D. Harrison, Saulte Ste. Marie, is the secretary.

MINNESOTA.

Minnesota was the first state to establish a state board of medical examiners, all previous medical practice acts simply approving diplomas of acceptable medical schools. It now requires a diploma from a recognized college of medicine as a qualification to come up for examination.

Dr. C. J. Ringell, 807 Andrus Building, Minneapolis, is the secretary.

MISSISSIPPI.

The examination by the state board of health is the only requirement to receive a license to practise.

Dr. J. F. Hunter, Jackson, is the secretary.

MISSOURI.

The requirements for Missouri are essentially those for Mississippi.

Dr. W. F. Morrow, Kansas City, is the secretary.

MONTANA.

The applicant for a license must submit evidence of having attended a medical college for four years (at least six months in each year), and have been graduated by an institution accepted by the board and submit to an examination.

Dr. William C. Riddell, Helena, is the secretary.

NEBRASKA.

An examination before the state board of medical examiners is now required of all who desire to practise in Nebraska. Candidates for examination must submit evidence of graduation from "a medical school or college of good standing."

Dr. George H. Brash, Beatrice, is the secretary.

NEVADA.

Nevada requires the applicant to be a graduate of a medical school in good standing with the board with no examination if the college is situated in the United States. Should the applicant hold a foreign diploma he must submit to an examination.

Dr. S. L. Lee, Carson City, is the secretary.

NEW HAMPSHIRE.

The requirements to practise medicine in New Hampshire include a preliminary education equivalent to a registered academy or high school course; a diploma in medicine after four years' study with four courses of not less than six months each, and submitting to a state examination. There are three boards of examiners working in harmony under the supervision of the Superintendent of Public Instruction, who is *ex-officio* regent of the boards of examiners.

Hon. Channing Folsom, Department of Public Instruction, Concord, is the regent.

NEW JERSEY.

New Jersey's educational requirements include a preliminary education equivalent to the four years' course of a high school of the first grade; four years' study of medicine, including four courses of not less than seven months each in a legally incorporated medical college, before receiving the degree in medicine. Applicants having these qualifications can submit themselves to an examination.

Dr. E. L. B. Godfrey, Camden, is the secretary.

NEW MEXICO.

The board of health of New Mexico is empowered to license physicians who have graduated from medical colleges who are in good standing as defined by the Act. The board is required to prepare a list of such colleges at its December meeting each year.

Dr. B. D. Black, Las Vegas, is the secretary.

NEW YORK.

New York requires a preliminary education fully equivalent to the high school course of New York, four courses in a recognized medical school covering four years of study (but will accept graduation from approved literary or scientific colleges for the first year of medical study), and a medical diploma as qualifications to apply for a state examination.

There are three boards of examiners acting under the supervision of the state of New York education department.

Charles F. Wheelock, State House, Albany, is the chief of the examination department.

NORTH CAROLINA.

North Carolina requires the applicant to pass an examination before the state board to secure a license to practise. Only those who possess a diploma from a recognized medical school or a license from another state are eligible to take the examination.

The secretary is Dr. George W. Pressly, Charlotte.

NORTH DAKOTA.

North Dakota does require of all who come up for examination to present evidence of attending three courses of lectures of not less than six months each, but does not require a diploma.

Dr. H. M. Wheeler, Grand Forks, is secretary.

OHIO.

Students intending to practise in Ohio, should take the preliminary examination provided by the board before entering upon the medical college course. If this is not done, the applicant must present evidence of having pursued a four years' high school course, in addition to a four years' medical course in a college accepted by the board.

Dr. Frank Winders, Columbus, is the secretary.

OKLAHOMA.

Oklahoma now requires every applicant for license to practise medicine to pass an examination before the board of health. Only those who are graduates of a reputable medical college or who have been in continuous practice for ten years are eligible for the examination.

Dr. E. E. Cowdrick, Enid, is the secretary.

OREGON.

Oregon requires an examination before a license is issued. Applicants must file a statement of the time actually spent in the study of medicine.

Dr. Byron E. Miller, Dekum Building, Portland, is the secretary.

PENNSYLVANIA.

The medical practice act of Pennsylvania creates three boards of medical examiners and a medical council under whose supervision the boards conduct the examination. The rules of the council prescribe a preliminary education equivalent to that given by a full high school course, four courses of medical instruction in a recognized medical school and a diploma in medicine, as the qualifications for coming up for an examination.

The Hon. N. C. Schaeffer, LL.D., Superintendent of Public Instruction, State Capitol, Harrisburg, is the secretary of the medical council.

RHODE ISLAND.

Any reputable physician passing an examination before the state board of health may be licensed to practise in Rhode Island.

The secretary of the board is Dr. Gardner T. Swartz, of Providence.

SOUTH CAROLINA.

The last legislature has given a new law for South Carolina, embracing some new features, notably the exemption of examination from the *Junior Curriculum* upon certain conditions. This may remove the objection of graduates of some years' standing as to the lack of justice in the ordinary state examination.

Dr. W. M. Lester is secretary, and Dr. Mary R. Baker, assistant secretary, both in Columbia.

TEXT OF THE LAW.

AN ACT TO REGULATE THE PRACTICE OF MEDICINE IN SOUTH CAROLINA, TO PROVIDE FOR A STATE BOARD OF MEDICAL EXAMINERS AND TO DEFINE THEIR DUTIES AND POWERS.

SECTION 1. *Be it enacted* by the General Assembly of the State of South Carolina, That on and after the approval of this Act, no person shall practise medicine or surgery within the state unless he or she is twenty-one years of age, and either has been heretofore authorized so to do, pursuant to the laws in force at the time of his or her authorization, or is hereafter authorized to do so by subsequent subdivisions of this Act.

SEC. 2. Any person shall be regarded as practising medicine, within the meaning of this Act, who shall treat, operate on, or prescribe for any physical ailment of another, except those engaged solely in the practice of osteopathy. But nothing in this Act shall be construed to prohibit service in cases of emergency, or the domestic administration of family remedies.

SEC. 3. There shall be established a state board of medical examiners, composed of eight reputable physicians or surgeons, one from each of the seven congressional districts, and one from the state at large, to be nominated by the State Medical Association, and appointed and commissioned by the governor. The term of office of the members of the board shall be for a period of two years, and until their successors in office shall have been appointed and qualified. Any vacancy in said board of examiners by death, resignation or otherwise, shall be filled in the same manner as above specified: *Provided*, That the governor shall have the right to reject any or all of the members nominated, upon satisfactory showing as to the unfitness of those rejected. In case of such rejection, former members of the board shall hold over until their successors can be chosen in the manner as above provided.

The members of the board first appointed under the provisions of this section shall be divided into two classes. The first class to consist of the four members from the odd number congressional districts of the state, and the second class of the remaining four members, the three from the even number congressional districts with the one from the state at large. The first class shall hold office under the said first appointment for the period of two years, until 1905; the second class for one year from the date of their appointment, until 1904. Thereafter the term of office of the first class shall expire on each odd number year of the calendar, and those of the second class on each even number year of the calendar : *Provided, further*, That the first nomination herein provided for, shall be held at the next annual meeting of said State Medical Association, and the members of the present board shall continue in office until their successors are appointed and have qualified, as hereinbefore provided. The governor shall appoint three competent homeopathic physicians from the state at large, who shall constitute a state board of homeopathic medical examiners, whose term of office, powers, duties, modes of procedure and compensation shall be the same as those of the regular state board herein provided for : *Provided*, That no applicant who has failed or who may hereafter fail in his examination by the state board of medical examiners, shall be allowed to present himself or herself before the state board of homeopathic examiners for examination : *Provided, further*, That no graduate of any medical college requiring less than a four years' course of study will be eligible for examination before this board.

SEC. 4. Said board of medical examiners shall meet regularly at Columbia, S. C., on the fourth Tuesday in April of each year, and continue in session until all applicants are duly examined.

A majority of said board shall constitute a quorum for the transaction of business.

At their first meeting they shall organize by the election of a chairman and a secretary, who shall also be treasurer, and said board shall have power to call extra meetings, when necessary, and to make all necessary by-laws and rules for their government.

SEC. 5. It shall be the duty of said board, when organized, to examine all candidates for examination, as hereinafter provided and described, and to pass upon their qualifications and fitness to practise medicine in this state, and to give to each successful applicant a certificate to that effect, upon the payment of $5 to the treasurer of said board. Such certificate of qualification shall entitle the holder or holders thereof, respectively, to be registered as a lawful practising physician by the clerk of court of the county in which he or she, or they, may reside, upon payment to said clerk of court of a fee of

25 cents for each registration. No physician will be considered as a legally qualified practitioner, or as having fully complied with the law, until he shall have obtained said registry. In the interim between the meetings of the board, the president and secretary of the board shall be allowed to grant temporary license to practise medicine until the next regular meeting of the board, to such persons as would, under the above sections, be eligible for examination. Said temporary license shall not entitle the holder to registry with the clerk of court of the county in which he resides, but at the next regular meeting of the board, the applicant must come up for the regular examination for permanent license.

SEC. 6. All persons who hold diplomas from any medical college or schools of established reputation, given prior to the passage of this Act, and who present certificates of their good moral character, and of their sobriety, from some reputable person or persons known to the board, and who give evidence of sufficient preliminary education (equivalent to the possession of a teacher's first-grade certificate), shall be eligible for examination before the board, irrespective of their time of attendance upon medical lectures; but no person who shall graduate after the passage of this Act, shall be eligible to appear before the board for examination unless he or she shall give evidence, in addition to sufficient preliminary education, that he or she has attended four full courses of lectures of at least twenty-six weeks each, no two courses being in the same year, and has received a diploma of M.D. therefrom.

SEC. 7. The curriculum of the state board of medical examiners shall be divided into two sections; the first comprising the junior or primary branches of medical education, hereafter to be designated as the *Junior Curriculum*. The second, comprising the senior and clinical portion of medical education, hereafter to be designated as the *Senior Curriculum*. The *Junior Curriculum* shall comprise the following branches, namely:

1. General anatomy.
2. Physiology and histology.
3. Materia medica and medical botany.
4. Chemistry, organic and inorganic, and medical physics.
5. Bacteriology and pathology.

The *Senior Curriculum* shall comprise:

1. Anatomy, regional or surgical.
2. Practical hygiene and sanitary science, state medicine.
3. Practical uranalysis, urinary microscopy.
4. Therapeutics and toxicology.
5. Surgery, general and special, surgical procedure.
6. Practical medicine and diseases of children.
7. Practical obstetrics and gynecology.
8. Medical jurisprudence.

Said examinations shall be conducted either in writing or orally, or both, at the discretion of the board.

SEC. 8. All applicants before the board, holding a diploma from a four-year graded medical college of established reputation, whether in or out of the state, who have pursued a study of four separate courses, and have attained a mark of not less than 75 per cent. on each individual branch of their curriculum, as evidenced by certificate from the dean of their college, shall be exempted from examination in the Junior Curriculum, and shall be examined only on those subjects contained in the Senior Curriculum, as heretofore outlined. Those applicants who hold diplomas issued by chartered medical colleges, but whose term of attendance has been less than four years, as above stated, must pass upon both the Junior and Senior Curriculum, as must also those attending a four years' course who cannot produce a certificate showing that they have attained a mark of 75 per cent. on all the branches of their college curriculum.

SEC. 9. The board shall be empowered without examination to indorse, upon receipt of the license fee of $5, the licenses issued by other state boards having an equal standard: *Provided*, Said other boards accord to the licenses of the South Carolina State Board the same courtesy; and said other state board licenses, when indorsed, shall entitle the holder to registry in this state, and to all the rights and privileges thereby granted.

SEC. 10. The standard required by the state board of medical examiners shall be an average of not less than 75 per cent. on all the branches examined upon, and not less than 60 per cent. on the individual branch.

SEC. 11. The board shall keep a record of all the proceedings thereof, and also a record or register of all applicants for a license, together with his or her age, time spent in the study of medicine, and the name and location of all institutions granting such applicant's degrees or certificates of lectures in medicine or surgery. Said books and register shall be *prima facie* evidence of all the matters therein recorded.

SEC. 12. The members of said examining board shall receive for their services the same per diem and mileage as is paid to the members of the general assembly, for each day engaged, said compensation to be paid from the state treasury, upon the certificate of the president of the board, countersigned by the secretary. The license fees collected from applicants shall be turned into the state treasury. There shall be set aside from said fees each year, the sum of $50 (if so much be needed), as a contingent fee, for the purpose of supplying the secretary with necessary stamps and stationery, and to print the proceedings of the board.

SEC. 13. It shall be unlawful for any person or persons to practise medicine in this state who has failed to comply with the provisions as above recited, and any one violating the provisions of this Act shall be deemed guilty of a misdemeanor, and for each offense, upon conviction by any court of competent jurisdiction, shall be fined in any sum not less than $50, nor more than $300, or imprisonment in the county jail for a period of not less than thirty, nor more than ninety days, or both, at the discretion of the court, one-half of said fine to go to the informant, and the other half to the state:

Provided, That dentists and midwives, and those engaged solely in the practice of osteopathy, shall not be subject to the provisions of this section. Nothing contained in this Act shall in any way affect or apply to physicians and surgeons who have already registered in accordance with the law now of force, nor shall it apply to commissioned medical officers of the United States army or navy, or the United States Marine Hospital Service, nor shall it include physicians or surgeons residing in other states and called in consultation in special cases with physicians or surgeons residing in this state, nor to physicians or surgeons residing in this state, nor to physicians, graduates of any reputable college, who have been practising medicine for five years: *Provided*, That nothing contained in this Act shall in any way affect any person having a diploma from any legally chartered and regularly conducted school of osteopathy: *Provided, further*, That nothing in this Act shall be so construed so as to allow osteopaths to prescribe medicines and practise surgery: *Provided, further*, That the said osteopaths submit their diplomas or certificates of graduation from such college to the state board of medical examiners, who shall grant a permit to practise osteopathy without examination upon the payment of a fee of $5 to the said board.

SEC. 14. In no case, wherein the provisions of this Act shall have been violated, shall any person so violating be entitled to receive a compensation for services rendered. But all persons now practising, in accordance with the law now of force, or who may hereafter practise medicine or surgery, as herein provided, shall be entitled to charge, sue for, and collect for their services.

SEC. 15. Upon the refusal of the said board to grant a license to any applicant, an appeal may be had to the governor, who may order a reexamination of the applicant, to be held in the presence of the dean of the faculty of any medical college in this state, and a committee composed of seven practising physicians.

SEC. 16. All Acts and parts of Acts inconsistent herewith are hereby repealed.

Approved the 27th day of February, A.D. 1904.

SOUTH DAKOTA.

Graduates of medical schools recognized by the board of examiners are eligible for the examinations before the state board of examiners, to secure a license to practise in South Dakota.

Dr. H. E. McNutt, Aberdeen, is the secretary.

TENNESSEE.

There are no educational limitations in Tennessee. The applicant must pass an examination before the state board of health, to secure the necessary license.

Dr. T. J. Happel, Trenton, is the secretary.

TEXAS.

Any one twenty-one years of age or over presenting evidence of good moral character is eligible for examination before one of the three boards of examiners, empowered to issue a license to practise. These boards are entirely independent of each other.

Secretaries: Dr. M. M. Smith, Austin; Dr. N. O. Berizer (homeopathic board), Austin; Dr. L. S. Downs (eclectic board), Galveston.

UTAH.

A graduate in medicine from a medical school in good standing in the state where it exists may appear before the Utah board of medical examiners for his license examination.

Dr. W. R. Fisher, Salt Lake City, is the secretary.

VERMONT.

To practise in Vermont one must have a diploma in medicine and a license obtained by examination from the board of censors of one of the three state medical societies.

Secretaries: Dr. W. S. Hammond (Vermont State Medical Society), Rutland; Dr. E. B. Whittaker (homeopathic medical society), Barre; Dr. P. L. Templeton (eclectic medical society), Montpelier.

VIRGINIA.

A graduate of a medical school, whose standard complies with the requirements of the Association of American Medical Colleges, is eligible for the examination before the state board of examiners.

Dr. R. S. Martin, Stuart, is the secretary.

WASHINGTON.

To obtain a license to practise in Washington, one must have a diploma in medicine and pass the examination before the state board of examiners.

Dr. P. B. Swearingen, Tacoma, is the secretary.

WEST VIRGINIA.

There are no educational requirements for those who wish to practise in West Virginia.

The fitness is determined solely by an examination before the state board of health, which must be passed to obtain a license.

Dr. H. A. Barbee, Point Pleasant, is the secretary.

WISCONSIN.

Wisconsin provides a preliminary education and graduation from a medical school complying with the requirements of the board as qualifications for coming before the board of examiners for the license examination.

Dr. Filip A. Forsbeck, Milwaukee, is the secretary.

WYOMING.

The Wyoming board issues a license to practise to those who are graduates of any medical school that is a member of the Association of American Medical Colleges, the Homeopathic Institute, or the National Eclectic Medical Association,—or, should the applicant be the graduate of a foreign medical school, it must be equal in its standing.

Dr. C. P. Johnson, Cheyenne, is the secretary.

RECIPROCITY.

Every limitation of a more complex civilization causes friction at the first. Whittier's bare-foot boy had his feet cramped, when it became necessary for him to wear shoes. The American doctor, who could claim to be such because he displayed a sign making the claim, resents the invasion upon his personal liberty, when he is compelled to procure a diploma, even if only by purchase. In like manner the medical graduate resents the state examination, and the licentiate of a state board his inability to wander at will upon the strength of his one license. Hence, early in the history of our medical practice acts, the question of exchange of licenses among different states became a very living question.

None of the earlier laws made provision for any transfer. Possibly the first state to do so was New York, which feature was copied by the laws of New Jersey, Pennsylvania, District of

Columbia and other states until now, it is usual to find a clause permitting the reciprocal exchange of licenses in most laws.

It is comparatively easy to frame a clause in a legislative Act permitting reciprocity; it is far different and much more difficult to put the reciprocity clause into operation. Naturally, each law provides that the license to be accepted must represent the same qualifications and there must be a return of the courtesy, or it would not be reciprocity. The National Confederation of Medical Examining and Licensing Boards early attacked this question, only to develop the difficulties in the way, and gave up the discussion as at present useless until certain other conditions were secured. To some of these conditions it has been devoting its strength during the more recent meetings.

Thinking the way to reciprocate was to reciprocate, members of certain other boards organized another society with a strikingly similar name—the American Confederation of Reciprocating Examining and Licensing Medical Boards. The boards of Wisconsin, Indiana, Michigan, Ohio, Iowa, Georgia,[1] Kansas, Illinois, Nebraska, Kentucky, Maryland,[2] New Jersey and the Eclectic Board of Pennsylvania are members according to the last report.

The basis for reciprocal registration under which this Confederation is now working is the following:

(A) As a prerequisite to reciprocal registration, the applicant shall file in the office of the board of the state of which he is a licentiate such evidence as will enable the said board to certify that he is of good moral and professional character. Such certificate shall be filed with his application for reciprocal registration in another state.

(B) (Qualification 1).—A certificate of registration showing that an examination has been made by the proper board of any state, on which an average grade of not less than 75 per cent. was awarded, the holder thereof having been at the time of said examination the legal possessor of a diploma from a medical college in good standing in the state where reciprocal registration is sought, may be accepted in lieu of examination as evidence of qualification. Provided that in case the scope of the said examination was less than prescribed by the state in which registration is sought, the applicant may be required to submit to supplemental examination by the board thereof in such subjects as have not been covered.

(C) (Qualification 2).—A certificate of registration or license issued by the proper board of any state may be accepted as evidence of qualification

[1] Whether only one or the three boards is not stated.
[2] Whether one or both boards is not stated.

for reciprocal registration in any other state. Provided that the holder of such certificate has been engaged in the reputable practice of medicine in such state at least one year ; and also provided that the holder thereof was at the time of such registration, the legal possessor of a diploma issued by a medical college in good standing in the state in which reciprocal registration is sought, and that the date of such diploma was prior to the legal requirement of the examination test in such state.

The difficulties of securing reciprocity have caused other plans to be adopted. The Virginia board was the first to accept the license from another state as presumptive evidence of the sufficiency of the applicant's preparation, and contented itself with an examination along clinical lines. If this examination is satisfactory, the applicant is licensed. There are legal difficulties in the way of adopting this plan, but it presents the most promising method of satisfactorily solving the vexed question. It has been tried with success by Maryland and New Jersey, and is worthy of more attention than it has heretofore received. The new law of South Carolina is in harmony with this idea, but with a slightly different plan.

At the last meeting of the Confederation of State Medical Examining and Licensing Boards (at Atlantic City, June 6, 1904), the secretary of the New Jersey board, Dr. E. L. B. Godfrey, presented the following resolutions. The Confederation was not ready to act upon them and ordered them printed, that they might receive more careful study. It is to be hoped that the Confederation can see its way clear to recommend a plan based on the principles here set forth, as they permit a proper removal from one state to another without undue hardship on the part of the physician, while retaining for the boards their rights and responsibilities.

WHEREAS, National legislation cannot affect the question of state jurisdiction in medical practice without the surrender of definite state sovereignty, and

WHEREAS, State medical examination is the basis for state medical license, or the indorsement of a license issued after an approved examination of another state, and each state is the judge of the qualifications of its medical licentiates, and

WHEREAS, It is manifestly unjust and a cause of open complaint by the profession to compel an experienced physician, licensed after a state examination, to undergo a second examination (practically a reexamination in the same elementary branches) upon removing from one state to another, when the requirements for medical license in the two states are substantially the same, or lower in the state from which indorsement is asked; therefore

Resolved, That it is the sense of this Confederation that, among those states whose standards of requirements are equal or substantially the same their licentiates by examination who can meet the moral, academic, medical and examining requirements of the state whose indorsement is asked, are entitled to and should be indorsed, irrespective of reciprocity.

Resolved, That when the standard of requirements of any two states are unequal, it is in the interest of the profession that the state having the lower requirements should indorse the examined licentiates of the state having the higher requirements, irrespective of reciprocity, when such candidates can meet every legal and educational requirement of the indorsing state.

Resolved, That reciprocity limited by statue to reciprocating states, which demands equal rights and privileges in return as conditions of indorsement, with the purpose of compelling recognition of its own licentiates, is detrimental to and retards the progress of the profession, because :

1. It restricts the extension of indorsement by its limitations.
2. It causes hardship to the profession because of its uncertain tenure.
3. It excludes indorsement from states having higher requirements by reason of which reciprocity cannot be effected.
4. It refuses recognition to distinguished physicians of non-reciprocating states.
5. It recognizes neither the merit of a state examination nor that of the licentiate as compared with reciprocity.
6. It tends to maintain standards at the level of the lowest reciprocating state, and offers no inducement for a state to raise its standards above those of its reciprocating neighbors.
7. It practically involves an omnibus indorsement, without inquiry as to the status of the individual candidate, and without discrimination, since all licentiates of a state stand legally upon an equal footing.
8. It is impractical for adoption by any considerable number of states, because of the difference in state laws, standards and population.

Resolved, That reciprocity based upon a voluntary agreement of state boards is, like statutory reciprocity, impractical, because :

1. There is no uniformity in state laws and no ability to enforce them.
2. When differences arise between examining boards, in respect to the status of colleges, the grade of examinations or the eligibility of candidates rejected by one board for examination by another, there is no law, national, interstate, or state, to adjust the differences or to enforce the agreement which may be broken at the pleasure of either board and without redress.

Resolved, That interstate indorsement, authorized by statute and exercised at the discretion of a state medical licensing board, irrespective of reciprocity, based upon the substantial equality of educational requirements, upon a state examination satisfactory and approved as to kind and grade, and upon the individual merit and the professional qualifications of the candidate for indorsement, is far better than indorsement based upon either statutory or voluntary reciprocity, and tends more than either to further the cause of higher medical education and the autonomy of the profession throughout the country.

1. It is good state policy since it neither denies citizenship nor the right to practise to any physician entitled through merit to its privileges.

2. It makes the state the sole judge of the qualifications of its licentiates by enforcing the same requirements for indorsement as for examination for license, thus placing all licentiates on the same footing.

3. It accepts a state examination for what it represents as an examination but not as more important than the merits and qualifications of the candidates for indorsement.

4. It tends to raise and maintain a high standard of education by making a license from a state with high requirements more widely acceptable for indorsement than one from a state of low requirements, and thus admits of early national application.

5. It requires legal evidence of individual merit as well as professional qualifications for approval for indorsement, and thus tends to reduce to a minimum the indorsement of irregular, itinerant practitioners.

6. It puts a premium on character and education and renders the best practitioners eligible for indorsement in every state.

7. It indorses both the state and the individual candidate, and failure of a state to reciprocate, therefore, does not afford either a legal or valid reason for rejecting any of its licentiates who can meet every requirement of the statute.

8. It may accept any of the examined licentiates of a state for endorsement, or only those examined and licensed under the most recent requirements.

Resolved, That a state that will not indorse the examined licentiate of another state where the standards are co-equal, or of a state where the standards are higher, stands as a hindrance to medical progress, because:

1. It does not recognize the efficiency once proved by examination in a state of co-equal or higher requirements.

2. It limits the working sphere of the profession.

3. It exacts the same requirements for license from the physician, duly licensed after an examination in a co-equal state and experience by years of practice, that are exacted from the inexperienced graduate.

Resolved, That indorsement, therefore, irrespective of reciprocity, should be granted to examined licentiates of states whose standard of requirements are co-equal or higher, when the candidate for endorsement can meet in all respects the requirements of the statute governing the practice of medicine.

RECIPROCITY IN THE VARIOUS STATES.

The following states have no legal provision for accepting a license from the board of another state: Alabama, Arizona, Arkansas, Florida, Georgia, Idaho, Louisiana, Massachusetts, Minnesota, Mississippi, Missouri, North Carolina, North Dakota, Oklahoma, Rhode Island, Tennessee, Utah and West Virginia.

The following states have a pure reciprocity clause, *i. e.*, the acceptance of the license from another board depends upon a mutual exchange between the two boards; where the names of individual states in *italics* follow the name of the state, they indicate the states with which it is in reciprocal relation:[1] California, Delaware (*Maryland, New Jersey*) District of Columbia, Illinois (*Maine, Michigan, Nebraska, New Jersey, Ohio, Virginia, Wisconsin*), Iowa, Maine (*Illinois, Michigan, New Jersey*), Michigan (*Illinois, Maine, New Jersey, Ohio*), Montana, New Hampshire, New York, Ohio, Oregon, Pennsylvania, South Carolina, South Dakota, Texas, Wisconsin.

The following states have special provisions:

Connecticut.—The examining boards may issue a certificate of approval to any applicant from another state showing an examination certificate of equal grade, upon which a license will be issued.

Indiana will accept the license of another state in lieu of an examination, when evidence is submitted that the applicant is a graduate of a medical school in good standing with the Indiana board, and that the license was granted after an examination where the general average was not less than 80 per cent., provided if all the subjects required by the Indiana board were not included in the examination for license, a supplemental examination in these subjects be taken.

Kansas will issue a temporary permit to licentiates of other states.

Maryland licenses the licentiates of the District of Columbia upon certification of the license by the district board of medical supervisors, has the authority to accept the license of another state, if that state reciprocates, or may grant a special examination to the licentiate of another state to determine his fitness.

Nebraska, the board may, at its discretion, "admit without examination, legally qualified medical practitioners, who hold

[1] The names of these reciprocating states were not obtained directly from the boards; neither their accuracy nor the completeness is asserted.

certificates to practise medicine in any state with equal requirements to those of the state of Nebraska."

New Jersey does not reciprocate, but accepts the license of another state in lieu of an examination under certain conditions. But most of the states whose license is acceptable to New Jersey, accept that of New Jersey as evidence of passing a state examination. As this method, which is practically the method of Virginia and Maryland, is worked up more thoroughly in its details in New Jersey than elsewhere, they are copied here:

SYNOPSIS OF REQUIREMENTS.[1]

Synopsis of Requirements for Endorsement of Medical Licenses Issued by Other States.

Medical licenses issued after examination by other states may be endorsed by New Jersey, in lieu of examination; *provided*, that the standards of academic, medical and examining requirements of the state issuing the license are substantially the same as those of New Jersey; and *provided further*, that the candidate for endorsement complies with the conditions required from candidates examined by this state as follows:

I. CONDITIONS OF ENDORSEMENT.

1. Candidates must present a certificate of academic education to attach to and file permanently with their applications in one of the following forms:

(*a*) A certificate of graduation or a certified copy of diploma, issued after four years of study either in a normal, manual training or high school of the first grade in this state, or in a legally constituted academy, seminary or institute of equal grade.

(*b*) A student's certificate of examination for admission to the Freshman class of a reputable college, bearing the seal of the institution attended, or duly attested before a notary.

(*c*) A certificate from the State Superintendent of Public Instruction of New Jersey, stating that the candidate's academic education is considered and accepted by him as fully equivalent to either of the above requirements, upon approval of credentials or examination.

2. Candidates must have studied medicine not less than four full school years of at least nine months each including four satisfactory courses of lectures of at least seven months each, in four different calendar years in a legally incorporated American or foreign medical college or colleges, prior to receiving the degree of doctor of medicine.

3. Candidates must have passed a state examination in substantially the same medical branches, and under essentially the same rules and regulations as required by this board for examination, and must have received a state license upon an average marking of at least 75 per cent.

[1] 13th Annual Report, 1903, p. 29.

4. Candidates must present with their applications a certificate of moral character either from an incorporated medical society, signed by the president or secretary thereof over the seal of the society, or from two legally qualified physicians, residents of the same locality as the candidate, duly attested by a notary.

5. Candidates must present a letter from a registered, reputable physician of New Jersey, recommending them for endorsement by this board.

II. APPLICATION FOR ENDORSEMENT.

Application for endorsement must be made upon a blank form provided by this board and obtained of its secretary, and must be filled out in conformity with the above conditions: Bear the seal of the medical institution from which the candidate was graduated, with the certificate of the dean or other executive officer, stating number and length of courses of lectures, and date of graduation; bear a verbatim copy of the applicant's state medical license over the seal of the state examining board issuing the same, together with the affidavits of the president and secretary thereof, as to the date of the examination, number of license, subjects examined and total average attained, and must be returned to the secretary of this board for approval and filing, with the affidavit of the candidate and a certified check or postal money order for the regular fee of $50.

Graduates of foreign institutions must file with their applications, a certified copy, with translation, of their academic and medical diplomas, made by and under the seal of their respective consuls-general, showing that the candidate possesses the full right to practise medicine in all its branches in the country in which the diploma was issued to which the candidate must make affidavit that he is the person named therein.

The endorsement of a college diploma, or a foreign license cannot be accepted in lieu of a state examination. Candidates must designate the state license to be endorsed, and the acceptance of an application for endorsement cannot be determined until the forms provided by this board have been properly filled out and submitted for approval.

Virginia accepts the license of another state in part. The applicant must show that he has fulfilled the educational requirements, and submit to an oral examination, but is exempted from the stated examination.

Washington—The power is given the board to accept the licenses from other states, when they represent an equal grade.

The states not mentioned include those accepting recognized diplomas without a license examination.

RESULTS OF THE EXAMINATIONS.

The results of the examinations are tabulated first by states, and then by the colleges graduating the applicants for examination. In the second tabulation, only those colleges are given which are now actively engaged in teaching. It is to be regretted that the results do not include the returns from all the states, as the value of the statistics would be increased many fold.

I. By States.

State.	Passed.	Failed.	Total.	Percentage passed.
Alabama	116	21	137	85
Alaska[1]	...	...	...	...
Arizona[2]	...	...	...	...
Arkansas[3]	9	3	12	75
California	182	63	245	74
Colorado[4]	...	...	...	...
Connecticut	57	16	73	78
Delaware	7	4	11	64
District of Columbia	64	14	78	82
Florida[5]	...	...	...	...
Georgia[6]	71	12	83	86
Idaho	32	14	46	70
Illinois	459	47	506	90
Indian Territory[7]	...	...	...	...
Indiana	135	19	154	88
Iowa	268	22	290	92
Kansas	45	5	50	90
Kentucky[4]	...	...	...	...
Louisiana[8]	130	24	154	84
Maine	73	0	73	100
Maryland	95	33	128	74
Massachusetts	323	120	443	73
Michigan	23	3	26	88
Minnesota	162	37	199	81
Mississippi[9]	...	...	...	...
Missouri	176	40	216	81
Montana	17	9	26	65
Nebraska[10]	1	0	1	100

[1] Alaska has no medical law.
[2] No returns received.
[3] No returns from the eclectic board. Examination by the board representing the Arkansas State Medical Society obtained from *Journal of the American Medical Association* and are not revised by the secretary of the board.
[4] Licenses on diplomas.
[5] No attempt was made to secure the returns from Florida because of the uniform failure of former attempts. The law is chiefly at fault.
[6] No returns obtainable from the eclectic board.
[7] No efficient practice act in 1903.
[8] No report from homeopathic board, probably no examination.
[9] No returns obtainable.
[10] The law for examination did not take effect until August 1, 1903.

State.	Passed.	Failed.	Total.	Percentage passed.
Nevada[1]	...	...	...	...
New Hampshire	33	4	37	89
New Jersey[2]	203	0	203	100
New York	633	51	684	93
North Carolina	77	26	103	75
North Dakota	49	8	57	86
Ohio	99	10	109	91
Oklahoma[3]	...	...	...	...
Oregon	58	7	65	89
Pennsylvania	479	95	574	83
Rhode Island	52	15	67	78
South Carolina	47	4	51	92
South Dakota	34	7	41	83
Tennessee	78	7	85	92
Texas[4]	143	26	169	85
Utah	23	3	26	88
Vermont[5]	47	4	51	92
Virginia	134	43	177	76
Washington[6]	119	22	141	85
West Virginia	128	58	186	69
Wisconsin	67	3	70	96
Wyoming[1]	...	...	...	...
Totals	4948	899	5847	85

It should be noted when these figures are compared, that those states where the percentage is the lowest, the law permits non-graduates to come up for examination.

II. By Colleges.

Alabama.

BIRMINGHAM MEDICAL COLLEGE, Alabama.

B. L. Wyman, M.D., Dean. Graduates in 1903, 22.

EXAMINATIONS.

	Passed.	Failed.	Total.
Alabama	21	1	22
Tennessee	1	0	1
	22	1	23

Percentage passed, 96.

[1] Licenses on diplomas.
[2] The annual report makes no mention of any rejections.
[3] No information obtainable.
[4] Results of the board representing the Texas State Society obtained from the *Journal of the American Medical Association*; of the eclectic state society, through the courtesy of the secretary of the board. No returns received from the homeopathic board.
[5] No returns from the eclectic board.
[6] Examination for January through the courtesy of the secretary. That for June from the *Journal of the American Medical Association*.

UNIVERSITY OF ALABAMA, Mobile.
Geo. L. Ketchum, M.D., Dean. Graduates in 1903, 12.

EXAMINATIONS.

	Passed.	Failed.	Total.
Alabama	15	1	16
Illinois	1	0	1
Louisiana	2	0	2
South Dakota	1	1	2
Tennessee	1	0	1
Texas	1	0	1
	21	2	23

Percentage passed, 91.

Arkansas.

UNIVERSITY OF ARKANSAS, Little Rock.
F. L. French, M.D., Secretary. Graduates in 1903, 12.

EXAMINATIONS.

	Passed.	Failed.	Total.
Alabama	1	0	1
Texas	2	0	2
	3	0	3

Percentage passed, 100.

California.

CALIFORNIA MEDICAL COLLEGE, San Francisco.
D. MacLean, M.D., Dean. Graduates in 1903, 7.

EXAMINATIONS.

	Passed.	Failed.	Total.
California	0	1	1
Washington	0	1[1]	1
	0	2	2

Percentage passed, 0.

COLLEGE OF PHYSICIANS AND SURGEONS, San Francisco.
D. A. Hodghead, M.D., Dean. Graduates in 1903, 28.

EXAMINATIONS.

	Passed.	Failed.	Total.
California	17	5	22
Oregon	2	0	2
Utah	1	0	1
Washington	1	0	1
	21	5	26

Percentage passed, 82.

[1] Class of 1902.

COOPER MEDICAL COLLEGE, San Francisco.
Henry Gibbons, Jr., M.D., Dean. Graduates in 1903, 45.

EXAMINATIONS.

	Passed.	Failed.	Total.
California	33	3	36
Minnesota	1	0	1
Oregon	1	0	1
Pennsylvania	1	0	1
Washington	5	1[1]	6
	41	4	45

Percentage passed, 91.

HAHNEMANN MEDICAL COLLEGE, San Francisco.
James W. Ward, M.D., Dean. Graduates in 1903, 12.

EXAMINATIONS.

	Passed.	Failed.	Total.
California	7	2	9
Oregon	1	0	1
Utah	1	0	1
	9	2	11

Percentage passed, 82.

OAKLAND COLLEGE OF MEDICINE AND SURGERY, Oakland.
Edward N. Ewer, M.D., Registrar. Graduates in 1903, 0.

UNIVERSITY OF CALIFORNIA, San Francisco.
Arnold A. D'Ancona, M.D., Dean. Graduates in 1903, 26.

EXAMINATIONS.

	Passed.	Failed.	Total.
California	17	1	18
New York	1	0	1
Utah	1	0	1
Washington	1	0	1
	20	1	21

Percentage passed, 95.

UNIVERSITY OF SOUTHERN CALIFORNIA, Los Angeles.
Walter Lindley, M.D., Dean. Graduates in 1903, 27.

EXAMINATIONS.

	Passed.	Failed.	Total.
California	22	0	22

Percentage passed, 100.

[1] Class of 1897.

Colorado.

DENVER HOMŒOPATHIC COLLEGE, Denver.
  James P. Willard, M.D., Dean. Graduates in 1903, 6.
UNIVERSITY OF COLORADO, Boulder.
  Luman M. Giffin, M.D., Dean. Graduates in 1903, 8.

EXAMINATIONS.

	Passed.	Failed.	Total.
California	1	0	1
Idaho	3	0	3
	4	0	4

Percentage passed, 100.

UNIVERSITY OF DENVER, Denver.
  S. G. Bonney, M.D., Dean. Graduates in 1903, 33.

EXAMINATIONS.

	Passed.	Failed.	Total.
Illinois	1	0	1
Iowa	1	0	1
New York	1	0	1
North Carolina	2	0	2
Pennsylvania	1	0	1
Utah	1	0	1
Virginia	1	0	1
	8	0	8

Percentage passed, 100.

Connecticut.

YALE, New Haven.
  Herbert E. Smith, M.D., Dean. Graduates in 1903, 27.

EXAMINATIONS.

	Passed.	Failed.	Total.
California	1	0	1
Connecticut	15	3	18
Kansas	1	0	1
Massachusetts	1	0	1
New Hampshire	1	0	1
New Jersey	3	0	3
New York	5	0	5
Pennsylvania	1	0	1
Rhode Island	1	0	1
South Dakota	1	0	1
	30	3	33

Percentage passed, 91.

District of Columbia.

COLUMBIAN UNIVERSITY, Washington.
W. F. R. Phillips, M.D., Dean. Graduates in 1903, 34.

EXAMINATIONS.

	Passed.	Failed.	Total.
District of Columbia	21	1	22
Indiana	1	0	1
Maryland	1	0	1
New York	1	0	1
Ohio	1	0	1
Pennsylvania	5	0	5
Virginia	4	1	5
Washington	1	0	1
West Virginia	1	0	1
Wisconsin	1	0	1
	37	2	39

Percentage passed, 95.

GEORGETOWN UNIVERSITY, Washington.
Geo. M. Kober, M.D., Dean. Graduates in 1903, 22.

EXAMINATIONS.

	Passed.	Failed.	Total.
California	1	0	1
District of Columbia	7	0	7
Illinois	1	0	1
New Jersey	2	0	2
New York	2	0	2
Ohio	1	0	1
Pennsylvania	2	0	2
Rhode Island	1	0	1
Tennessee	1	0	1
Washington	1	0	1
	19	0	19

Percentage passed, 100.

HOWARD UNIVERSITY, Washington.
Robert Reyburn, M.D., Dean. Graduates in 1903, 29.

EXAMINATIONS.

	Passed.	Failed.	Total.
California	1	0	1
District of Columbia	8	5	13
Illinois	0	1	1
Maryland	2	0	2

	Passed.	Failed.	Total.
New Jersey	1	0	1
North Carolina	1	0	1
Virginia	2	0	2
West Virginia	3	1	4
	18	7	25

Percentage passed, 72.

NATIONAL UNIVERSITY, Washington.

EXAMINATIONS.

	Passed.	Failed.	Total.
District of Columbia	5	3	8
Washington	1	0	1
	6	3	9

Percentage passed, 67.

Georgia.

ATLANTA COLLEGE OF PHYSICIANS AND SURGEONS, Atlanta.
W. S. Kendrick, M.D., Dean. Graduates in 1903, 34.

EXAMINATIONS.

	Passed.	Failed.	Total.
Alabama	2	0	2
Georgia	31	9	40
New York	1	1[1]	2
North Carolina	1	2	3
South Carolina	3	0	3
Tennessee	1	0	1
Texas	3	0	3
Virginia	2	0	2
	44	12	56

Percentage passed, 79.

GEORGIA COLLEGE OF ECLECTIC MEDICINE AND SURGERY, Atlanta.
W. M. Durham, M.D., Proctor. Graduates in 1903, 2.

EXAMINATIONS.

	Passed.	Failed.	Total.
Alabama	2	0	2
New York	1	0	1
North Carolina	0	1	1
Rhode Island	0	1	1
Tennessee	0	1	1
Texas	1	0	1
	4	3	7

Percentage passed, 57.

[1] Class of 1894.

UNIVERSITY OF GEORGIA, Augusta.
De Saussure Ford, M.D., Dean.   Graduates in 1903, 7.

EXAMINATIONS.

	Passed.	Failed.	Total.
Georgia	2	1	3
New York	1	0	1
North Carolina	1	1	2
South Carolina	2	1[1]	3
Texas	1	0	1
	7	3	10

Percentage passed, 70.

Illinois.

AMERICAN COLLEGE OF MEDICINE AND SURGERY, Chicago.
J. D. Robertson, M.D., Secretary.   Graduates in 1903, 10.

EXAMINATIONS.

	Passed.	Failed.	Total.
Illinois	6	0	6
Indiana	0	1	1
	6	1	7

Percentage passed, 86.

AMERICAN MEDICAL MISSIONARY COLLEGE, Chicago.
E. L. Eggleston, M.D., Secretary.   Graduates in 1903, 22.

EXAMINATIONS.

	Passed.	Failed.	Total.
California	1	1	2
Illinois	3	0	3
Iowa	1	0	1
Kansas	1	0	1
Massachusetts	1	0	1
New York	1	0	1
Tennessee	2	0	2
	10	1	11

Percentage passed, 91.

BENNETT COLLEGE OF ECLECTIC MEDICINE AND SURGERY, Chicago.
A. L. Clark, M.D., Dean.   Graduates in 1903, 18.

EXAMINATIONS.

	Passed.	Failed.	Total.
Illinois	8	2	10
Indiana	2	0	2

[1] Class of 1899.

	Passed.	Failed.	Total.
North Dakota	0	1	1
Oregon	1	0	1
South Dakota	1	0	1
Texas	0	1[1]	1
Wisconsin	2	0	2
	14	4	18

Percentage passed, 78.

CHICAGO HOMEOPATHIC MEDICAL COLLEGE, Chicago.
W. M. Stearns, M.D., Dean. Graduates in 1903, 37.

EXAMINATIONS.

	Passed.	Failed.	Total.
Arkansas	1	0	1
California	1	1	2
District of Columbia	1	0	1
Georgia	1	0	1
Idaho	1	0	1
Illinois	17	0	17
Indiana	1	0	1
Iowa	3	1	4
Kansas	2	0	2
Minnesota	2	0	2
Montana	1	0	1
New York	2	0	2
Ohio	1	0	1
Washington	1	0	1
Wisconsin	1	0	1
	36	2	38

Percentage passed, 95.

COLLEGE OF MEDICINE AND SURGERY, Chicago.
Florence Dressler, M.D., Secretary. Graduates in 1903, 12.

EXAMINATIONS.

	Passed.	Failed.	Total.
Illinois	9	4	13
Michigan	1	0	1
Pennsylvania	1	0	1
Texas	0	1[2]	1
	11	5	16

Percentage passed, 69.

[1] Class of 1894.
[2] Class of 1899.

HAHNEMANN MEDICAL COLLEGE, Chicago.
W. Henry Wilson, M.D., Registrar. Graduates in 1903, 69.

EXAMINATIONS.

	Passed.	Failed.	Total.
California	5	1	6
Idaho	1	0	1
Illinois	45	2	47
Indiana	3	0	3
Iowa	9	1	10
Kansas	0	1	1
Minnesota	4	2	6
Montana	0	1	1
New Jersey	2	0	2
New York	0	1[1]	1
Pennsylvania	3	0	3
Vermont	1	0	1
Washington	2	0	2
Wisconsin	2	0	2
	77	9	86

Percentage passed, 90.

HARVEY MEDICAL COLLEGE, Chicago.
Frances Dickinson, M.D., Dean. Graduates in 1903, 20.

EXAMINATIONS.

	Passed.	Failed.	Total.
Arkansas	1	0	1
Idaho	1	1	2
Illinois	16	0	16
Indiana	2	0	2
South Dakota	1	0	1
Wisconsin	0	2	2
	21	3	24

Percentage passed, 88.

HERING MEDICAL COLLEGE, Chicago.
H. C. Allen, M.D., Dean. Graduates in 1903, 22.

EXAMINATIONS.

	Passed.	Failed.	Total.
Illinois	6	0	6
Indiana	1	0	1
Iowa	1	0	1
Kansas	2	0	2

[1] Class of 1879.

	Passed.	Failed.	Total.
North Dakota	1	0	1
Washington	1	0	1
Wisconsin	1	0	1
	13	0	13

Percentage passed, 100.

ILLINOIS MEDICAL COLLEGE, Chicago.
B. B. Eads, Dean. Graduates in 1903, 47.

EXAMINATIONS.

	Passed.	Failed.	Total.
Illinois	12	2	14
Indiana	2	0	2
Iowa	1	0	1
Kansas	1	0	1
Louisiana	1	0	1
New York	0	1[1]	1
Ohio	2	0	2
Pennsylvania	1	4[2]	5
Rhode Island	2	2	4
Texas	2	1	3
Utah	1	0	1
Washington	1	1[3]	2
West Virginia	2	1[1]	3
Wisconsin	1	0	1
	29	12	41

Percentage passed, 71.

JENNER MEDICAL COLLEGE, Chicago.
C. Shorman, M.D., Dean. Graduates in 1903, 13.

EXAMINATIONS.

	Passed.	Failed.	Total.
Illinois	11	2	13

Percentage passed, 85.

NATIONAL MEDICAL COLLEGE, Chicago.
D. L. Rogers, M.D., Registrar. Graduates in 1903, 17.

EXAMINATIONS.

	Passed.	Failed.	Total.
Illinois	6	3	9
Wisconsin	1	0	1
	7	3	10

Percentage passed, 70.

[1] Class of 1899.
[2] Class of 1900.
[3] Class of 1902.

NORTHWESTERN UNIVERSITY, Chicago.
N. S. Davis, M.D., Dean. Graduates in 1903, 127.

EXAMINATIONS.

	Passed.	Failed.	Total.
Alabama	2	0	2
California	5	0	5
Idaho	2	0	2
Illinois	39	0	39
Indiana	2	0	2
Iowa	45	0	45
Kansas	3	0	3
Minnesota	8	0	8
Montana	2	0	2
New Jersey	1	0	1
North Dakota	5	0	5
Washington	5	2[1]	7
Wisconsin	10	0	10
	99	2	101

Percentage passed, 99.

UNIVERSITY OF CHICAGO, Chicago.
Frank Billings, M.D., and John M. Dodson, M.D., Deans. Grad. in '03, 220.

EXAMINATIONS.

	Passed.	Failed.	Total.
Arkansas	1	0	1
California	3	4	7
Idaho	2	1	3
Illinois	119	0	119
Indiana	15	0	15
Iowa	24	1	25
Kansas	5	0	5
Louisiana	1	0	1
Minnesota	12	2	14
Montana	3	0	3
New York	3	0	3
North Dakota	3	0	3
Ohio	5	0	5
Oregon	5	0	5
Pennsylvania	3	0	3
South Dakota	5	0	5
Texas	6	0	6
Utah	7	0	7

[1] Classes of 1897 and 1899.

	Passed.	Failed.	Total.
Washington	9	4[1]	13
Wisconsin	15	1	16
	206	13	219

Percentage passed, 94.

UNIVERSITY OF ILLINOIS, CHICAGO.
William E. Quine, M.D., Dean. Graduates in 1903, 216.

EXAMINATIONS.

	Passed.	Failed.	Total.
Arkansas	1	0	1
California	4	4	8
Idaho	2	0	2
Illinois	54	11	65
Indiana	7	0	7
Iowa	41	1	42
Kansas	1	0	1
Minnesota	12	6	18
Montana	2	0	2
New York	1	0	1
North Dakota	4	1	5
Ohio	3	0	3
Oregon	4	0	4
Rhode Island	1	0	1
South Dakota	1	0	1
Tennessee	2	0	2
Utah	1	0	1
Washington	9	0	9
Wisconsin	16	0	16
	176	23	199

Percentage passed, 88.

Indiana.

CENTRAL COLLEGE OF PHYSICIANS AND SURGEONS, Indianapolis.
John F. Barnhill, M.D., Secretary. Graduates in 1903, 22.

EXAMINATIONS.

	Passed.	Failed.	Total.
Indiana	1	0	1
Texas	1	0	1
	2	0	2

Percentage passed, 100.

[1] Classes 1879, 1885, 1896, and 1897.

ECLECTIC MEDICAL COLLEGE, OF INDIANA, Indianapolis.
W. M. Brown, M.D., Dean.   Graduates in 1903, 5.

EXAMINATIONS.

	Passed.	Failed.	Total.
Indiana	0	1	1
Texas	1	1	2
	1	2	3

Percentage passed, 33.

FORT WAYNE COLLEGE OF MEDICINE, Fort Wayne.
C. B. Stemen, M.D., Dean.   Graduates in 1903, 5.

EXAMINATIONS.

	Passed.	Failed.	Total.
California	1	0	1
New York	0	1[1]	1
	1	1	2

Percentage passed, 50.

PHYSIO-MEDICAL COLLEGE OF INDIANA, Indianapolis.
C. T. Bedford, M.D., Secretary.   Graduates in 1903, 9.

EXAMINATIONS.

	Passed.	Failed.	Total.
Iowa	1	0	1
Tennessee	0	1	1
	1	1	2

Percentage passed, 50

UNIVERSITY OF INDIANAPOLIS, Indianapolis.
Henry Jameson, M.D., Dean.   Graduates in 1903, 76.

EXAMINATIONS.

	Passed.	Failed.	Total.
Georgia	1	0	1
Indiana	3	0	3
Texas	1	0	1
	5	0	5

Percentage passed, 100.

[1] Class of 1882.

Iowa.

DRAKE UNIVERSITY, Des Moines.
D. S. Fairchild, M.D., Dean. Graduates in 1903, 11.

EXAMINATIONS.

	Passed.	Failed.	Total.
Iowa	9	2	11
New York	1	0	1
	10	2	12

Percentage passed, 83.

KEOKUK MED. COLLEGE OF PHYSICIANS AND SURGEONS, Keokuk.
C. E. Ruth, M.D., Secretary. Graduates in 1903, 56.

EXAMINATIONS.

	Passed.	Failed.	Total.
District of Columbia	1	0	1
Idaho	1	0	1
Illinois	11	2	13
Indiana	0	2	2
Iowa	32	1	33
Kansas	1	1	2
Minnesota	2	0	2
Montana	0	1	1
North Dakota	0	3	3
Washington	1	0	1
	49	10	59

Percentage passed, 83.

SIOUX CITY COLLEGE OF MEDICINE, Sioux City.
J. N. Warren, M.D., Secretary. Graduates in 1903, 23.

EXAMINATIONS.

	Passed.	Failed.	Total.
Illinois	1	0	1
Iowa	13	0	13
Minnesota	0	1	1
South Dakota	2	1	3
	16	2	18

Percentage passed, 89.

UNIVERSITY OF IOWA, Iowa City.
James R. Guthrie, M.D., Dean. Graduates in 1903, 35.

EXAMINATIONS.

	Passed.	Failed.	Total.
California	3	1	4
Idaho	1	1	2

	Passed.	Failed.	Total.
Illinois	4	0	4
Iowa	34	1	35
Kansas	1	0	1
Minnesota	2	1[1]	3
New Jersey	1	0	1
North Dakota	1	0	1
Oregon	1	0	1
South Dakota	0	1	1
	50	5	55

Percentage passed, 91.

UNIVERSITY OF IOWA (Homeopathic), Iowa City.
George Royal, M.D., Dean. Graduates in 1903, 11.

EXAMINATIONS.

	Passed.	Failed.	Total.
Iowa	12	0	12

Percentage passed, 100.

Kansas.

COLLEGE OF PHYSICIANS AND SURGEONS, Kansas City.
J. E. Sawtelle, M.D., Dean. Graduates in 1903, 10.

KANSAS MEDICAL COLLEGE, Topeka.
John E. Minney, M.D., Dean. Graduates in 1903, 12.

EXAMINATIONS.

	Passed.	Failed.	Total.
Idaho	0	1	1
Oregon	1	0	1
Pennsylvania	1	0	1
Texas	2	0	2
	4	1	5

Percentage passed, 80.

UNIVERSITY OF KANSAS, Lawrence.
C. E. McClung, M.D., Dean. Graduates in 1903, 0.

Kentucky.

CENTRAL UNIVERSITY OF KENTUCKY, Louisville.
P. Richard Taylor, M.D., Dean. Graduates in 1903, 69.

EXAMINATIONS.

	Passed.	Failed.	Total.
Alabama	2	1	3
Illinois	2	0	2
Indiana	8	0	8

[1] Class of 1891.

	Passed.	Failed.	Total.
Iowa	1	0	1
Kansas	1	0	1
Louisiana	1	0	1
North Carolina	0	1	1
Ohio	0	1	1
South Carolina	1	0	1
Texas	2	0	2
West Virginia	2	1[1]	3
	20	4	24

Percentage passed, 83.

KENTUCKY SCHOOL OF MEDICINE, Louisville.
W. H. Wathen, M.D., Dean. Graduates in 1903, 56.

EXAMINATIONS.

	Passed.	Failed.	Total.
California	1	0	1
Idaho	0	3	3
Illinois	2	0	2
Indiana	19	7	26
Iowa	0	1	1
Louisiana	0	2	2
Maine	1	0	1
Massachusetts	2	1[2]	3
Ohio	0	1	1
Pennsylvania	0	1	1
Vermont	0	1	1
Virginia	1	0	1
Washington	0	1[3]	1
West Virginia	0	3[4]	3
	26	21	47

Percentage passed, 55.

KENTUCKY UNIVERSITY, Louisville.
Thomas C. Evans, M.D., Dean. Graduates in 1903, 57.

EXAMINATIONS.

	Passed.	Failed.	Total.
Alabama	2	1	3
Illinois	1	0	1
Indiana	6	0	6

[1] Class of 1900.
[2] Class of 1903.
[3] Class of 1897.
[4] Class of 1901.

	Passed.	Failed.	Total.
Kansas	1	0	1
North Carolina	2	0	2
Texas	1	0	1
Washington	1	0	1
West Virginia	1	0	1
	15	1	16

Percentage passed, 94.

LOUISVILLE MEDICAL COLLEGE, Louisville.
Irvin Abell, M.D., Secretary. Graduates in 1903, 53.

EXAMINATIONS.

	Passed.	Failed.	Total.
Alabama	6	1	7
Georgia	1	0	1
Idaho	1		
Illinois	1	0	1
Indiana	3	3	6
Kansas	1	0	1
Louisiana	3	1	4
New York	2	0	2
North Carolina	2	1	3
Oregon	3	0	3
Pennsylvania	1	1[1]	2
South Dakota	1	0	1
Tennessee	4	0	4
Texas	2	0	2
Virginia	2	1	3
Washington	2	2[2]	4
West Virginia	1	0	1
	36	11	47

Percentage passed, 77.

LOUISVILLE NATIONAL MEDICAL COLLEGE, Louisville.
W. A. Burney, M.D., Dean. Graduates in 1903, 4.

UNIVERSITY OF LOUISVILLE, Louisville.
J. M. Bodine, M.D., Dean. Graduates in 1903, 34.

EXAMINATIONS.

	Passed.	Failed.	Total.
Alabama	1	0	1
California	0	2	2
Indiana	3		

[1] Class of 1902.
[2] Classes of 1898 and 1900.

	Passed.	Failed.	Total.
Louisiana	2	0	2
Massachusetts	1	0	1
New Jersey	2	0	2
New York	1	0	1
North Carolina	2	0	2
Ohio	0	1	1
Pennsylvania	1	1	2
Texas	3	2[1]	5
West Virginia	0	2[2]	2
	16	9	25

Percentage passed, 64.

SOUTHWESTERN HOMEOPATHIC MEDICAL COLLEGE, Louisville.
A. L. Monroe, M.D., Dean. Graduates in 1903, 5.

Louisiana.

NEW ORLEANS UNIVERSITY, New Orleans.
H. J. Clements, M.D., Dean. Graduates in 1903, 5.

EXAMINATIONS.

	Passed.	Failed.	Total.
Louisiana	2	5	7

Percentage passed, 29

TULANE UNIVERSITY, New Orleans.
Stanford E. Chaille, M.D., Dean. Graduates in 1903, 82.

EXAMINATIONS.

	Passed.	Failed.	Total.
Alabama	5	1	6
California	0	1	1
Georgia	1	0	1
Indiana	1	0	1
Louisiana	66	0	66
Rhode Island	1	0	1
Tennessee	1	0	1
Texas	3	0	3
Virginia	1	0	1
	79	2	81

Percentage passed, 97.

[1] Class of 1894.
[2] Class of 1903.

Maine.
BOWDOIN, Portland.
Alfred Mitchell, M.D., Dean. Graduates in 1903, 20.

EXAMINATIONS.

	Passed.	Failed.	Total.
California	1	1	2
Maine	21	0	21
Massachusetts	1	1[1]	2
New York	0	1[2]	1
Rhode Island	1	0	1
Washington	1	0	1
	25	3	28

Percentage passed, 89.

Maryland.
BALTIMORE MEDICAL COLLEGE, Baltimore.
David Streett, M.D., Dean. Graduates in 1903, 93.

EXAMINATIONS.

	Passed.	Failed.	Total.
California	1	0	1
Connecticut	5	2	7
Delaware	2	0	2
District of Columbia	0	1	1
Illinois	3	0	3
Indiana	2	0	2
Kansas	1	0	1
Louisiana	1	0	1
Maine	2	0	2
Maryland	21	4	25
Massachusetts	16	3[3]	19
New Hampshire	2	1[4]	3
New Jersey	9	0	9
New York	9	0	9
North Carolina	4	0	4
Ohio	3	0	3
Pennsylvania	13	10	23
Rhode Island	2	3	5
Vermont	7	2	9
Virginia	1	2	3
West Virginia	10	1[5]	11
	114	29	143

Percentage passed, 73.

[1] Class of 1891.
[2] Class of 1892.
[3] Class of 1902, 1903 (2).
[4] Class of 1903.
[5] Class of 1899.

BALTIMORE UNIVERSITY, Baltimore.
Hampson H. Biedler, M.D., Dean.   Graduates in 1903, 26.

EXAMINATIONS.

	Passed.	Failed.	Total.
Delaware	0	1	1
Illinois	2	1	3
Maine	2	0	2
Maryland	0	5	5
New Jersey	2	0	2
New York	3	1[1]	4
North Carolina	1	0	1
Pennsylvania	6	5[1]	11
Vermont	1	0	1
Virginia	2	2	4
West Virginia	3	2[2]	5
	22	17	39

Percentage passed, 56.

COLLEGE OF PHYSICIANS AND SURGEONS, Baltimore.
Thomas Opie, M.D., Dean.   Graduates in 1903, 76.

EXAMINATIONS.

	Passed.	Failed.	Total.
Alabama	2	0	2
California	0	1	1
Connecticut	1	6	7
District of Columbia	0	1	1
Georgia	2	0	2
Illinois	1	0	1
Kansas	1	0	1
Maine	3	0	3
Maryland	10	3	13
Massachusetts	5	3[3]	8
New Jersey	9	0	9
New York	3	0	3
North Carolina	1	0	1
Oregon	1	0	1
Pennsylvania	9	1	10
Rhode Island	5	0	5
Tennessee	1	1	2
Virginia	1	1	2

[1] Class of 1900.
[2] Class of 1903.
[3] Classes of 1902 and 1903 (2).

	Passed.	Failed.	Total.
Washington	1	0	1
West Virginia	11	0	11
	67	17	84

Percentage passed, 80.

JOHNS HOPKINS UNIVERSITY, Baltimore.
William H. Howell, M.D., Dean. Graduates in 1903, 49.

EXAMINATIONS.

	Passed.	Failed.	Total.
California	3	0	3
District of Columbia	7	0	7
Georgia	2	0	2
Illinois	4	0	4
Iowa	1	0	1
Maine	1	0	1
Maryland	10	1	11
Massachusetts	5	0	5
Minnesota	1	0	1
New York	6	0	6
North Dakota	1	0	1
Ohio	3	0	3
Rhode Island	1	0	1
South Dakota	1	0	1
Virginia	2	0	2
Wisconsin	3	0	3
	51	1	52

Percentage passed, 98.

MARYLAND MEDICAL COLLEGE, Baltimore.
J. William Funck, M.D., Dean. Graduates in 1903, 59.

EXAMINATIONS.

	Passed.	Failed.	Total.
Alabama	0	1	1
Maine	2	0	2
Maryland	5	9	14
Massachusetts	2	2[1]	4
New York	2	0	2
Pennsylvania	5	3	8
South Carolina	1	1[2]	2
Texas	1	0	1
Vermont	0	1	1

[1] Class of 1903.
[2] Class of 1902.

	Passed.	Failed.	Total.
Virginia	4	3	7
West Virginia	9	2	11
	31	22	53

Percentage passed, 60.

UNIVERSITY OF MARYLAND, Baltimore.
D. Dorsey Coale, M.D., Dean. Graduates in 1903, 96.

EXAMINATIONS.

	Passed.	Failed.	Total.
Delaware	0	2	2
District of Columbia	1	0	1
Georgia	3	0	3
Maine	1	0	1
Maryland	34	7	41
Minnesota	2	0	2
New Jersey	2	0	2
New York	3	0	3
North Carolina	11	3	14
Ohio	2	0	2
Pennsylvania	5	4	9
South Carolina	6	0	6
Tennessee	2	0	2
Texas	1	0	1
Virginia	7	3	10
Washington	1	0	1
West Virginia	5	0	5
	86	19	105

Percentage passed, 82.

SOUTHERN HOMŒOPATHIC MEDICAL COLLEGE, Baltimore.
Geo. D. Shower, M.D., Dean. Graduates in 1903, 3.

EXAMINATIONS.

	Passed.	Failed.	Total.
Georgia	1	0	1
Maryland	3	0	3
Massachusetts	0	1[1]	1
	4	1	5

Percentage passed, 80.

[1] Class of 1903.

WOMAN'S MEDICAL COLLEGE, Baltimore.
R. H. Thomas, M.D., Dean. Graduates in 1903, 2.

EXAMINATIONS.

	Passed.	Failed.	Total.
Delaware	1	0	1
Illinois	1	0	1
Massachusetts	1	0	1
New Jersey	1	0	1
	4	0	4

Percentage passed, 100.

Massachusetts.

BOSTON UNIVERSITY, Boston.
J. P. Sutherland, M.D., Dean. Graduates in 1903, 36.

EXAMINATIONS.

	Passed.	Failed.	Total.
California	1	0	1
Connecticut	3	0	3
Maine	1	0	1
Massachusetts	25	4[1]	29
Montana	0	1	1
New Hampshire	2	0	2
New York	3	0	3
North Carolina	0	1	1
Pennsylvania	2	0	2
Texas	1	0	1
Virginia	1	0	1
Washington	1	0	1
	40	6	46

Percentage passed, 87.

COLLEGE OF PHYSICIANS AND SURGEONS, Boston.
John H. Jackson, M.D., Registrar. Graduates in 1903, 19.

EXAMINATIONS.

	Passed.	Failed.	Total.
Connecticut	0	1	1
Maine	2	0	2
Massachusetts	7	4[2]	11
New Jersey	2	0	2
New York	1	1[3]	2

[1] Classes of 1898, 1899, 1902 and 1903.
[2] Class of 1902 (2), 1903 (2).
[3] Class of 1899.

	Passed.	Failed.	Total.
Virginia	0	1	1
West Virginia	1	0	1
	13	7	20

Percentage passed, 65.

HARVARD UNIVERSITY, Boston.
William L. Richardson, M.D., Dean. Graduates in 1903, 114.

EXAMINATIONS.

	Passed.	Failed.	Total.
California	3	0	3
Connecticut	3	0	3
Georgia	1	0	1
Indiana	1	0	1
Maine	8	0	8
Massachusetts	80	0	80
Montana	1	0	1
New Hampshire	9	0	9
New York	9	1[1]	10
North Dakota	1	0	1
Ohio	1	0	1
Oregon	3	0	3
Pennsylvania	1	0	1
Rhode Island	9	0	9
Washington	2	0	2
	132	1	133

Percentage passed, 99.

TUFTS COLLEGE, Boston.
Harold Williams, M.D., Dean. Graduates in 1903, 35.

EXAMINATIONS.

	Passed.	Failed.	Total.
California	0	1	1
Connecticut	0	1	1
District of Columbia	1	0	1
Louisiana	1	0	1
Massachusetts	41	2[2]	43
New Hampshire	1	1[3]	2
New York	1	0	1
Rhode Island	0	1	1
Vermont	1	0	1
	46	6	52

Percentage passed, 84.

[1] Class of 1902.
[2] Classes of 1899, 1903.
[3] Class of 1903.

Michigan.
　　DETROIT COLLEGE OF MEDICINE, Detroit.
　　　H. O. Walker, M.D., Secretary. Graduates in 1903, 62.

EXAMINATIONS.

	Passed.	Failed.	Total.
California	2	2	4
Indiana	1	0	1
Minnesota	1	0	1
New Jersey	1	0	1
New York	1	0	1
Ohio	3	0	3
Oregon	2	0	2
Pennsylvania	1	0	1
Rhode Island	1	0	1
Vermont	1	0	1
Washington	5	0	5
Wisconsin	2	0	2
	21	2	23

　　　Percentage passed, 91.

　　DETROIT HOMEOPATHIC COLLEGE, Detroit.
　　　A. D. MacLahlan, M.D., Dean. Graduates in 1903, 14.

EXAMINATIONS.

	Passed.	Failed.	Total.
Connecticut	1	0	1
Maryland	1	0	1
	2	0	2

　　　Percentage passed, 100.

　　GRAND RAPIDS MEDICAL COLLEGE, Grand Rapids.
　　　C. H. White, M.D., Dean. Graduates in 1903, 16.

EXAMINATIONS.

	Passed.	Failed.	Total.
Indiana	1	0	1
Ohio	1	0	1
Oregon	1	0	1
	3	0	3

　　　Percentage passed, 100.

　　MICHIGAN COLLEGE OF MEDICINE, Detroit.
　　　Hal C. Wyman, M.D., Dean. Graduates in 1903, 34.

EXAMINATIONS.

	Passed.	Failed.	Total.
Ohio	1	0	1

　　　Percentage passed, 100.

UNIVERSITY OF MICHIGAN, Ann Arbor.
V. C. Vaughan, M.D., Dean.   Graduates in 1903, 92.

EXAMINATIONS.

	Passed.	Failed.	Total.
California	5	4	9
Idaho	2	0	2
Illinois	7	0	7
Indiana	3	0	3
Iowa	6	0	6
Louisiana	2	0	2
Maine	1	0	1
Massachusetts	2	0	2
Minnesota	3	0	3
Montana	1	1	2
New Jersey	3	0	3
New York	10	1	11
North Carolina	1	0	1
North Dakota	3	0	3
Ohio	8	0	8
Oregon	4	0	4
Pennsylvania	3	0	3
Rhode Island	1	0	1
South Dakota	1	0	1
Tennessee	1	0	1
Virginia	1	0	1
Washington	7	0	7
Wisconsin	1	0	1
	76	6	82

Percentage passed, 93.

UNIVERSITY OF MICHIGAN (Homeopathic), Ann Arbor.
W. B. Hinsdale, M.D., Dean.   Graduates in 1903, 13.

EXAMINATIONS.

	Passed.	Failed.	Total.
Pennsylvania	1	0	1
Washington	0	1	1
	1	1	2

Percentage passed, 50.

Minnesota.

HAMLINE UNIVERSITY, Minneapolis.
George C. Barton, M.D., Dean.   Graduates in 1903, 34.

EXAMINATIONS.

	Passed.	Failed.	Total.
Indiana	1	0	1

	Passed.	Failed.	Total.
Minnesota	27	6	33
North Dakota	6	0	6
South Dakota	1	1	2
Wisconsin	1	0	1
	36	7	43

Percentage passed, 84.

UNIVERSITY OF MINNESOTA (Homeopathic), Minneapolis.
Eugene L. Mann, M.D., Dean. Graduates in 1903, 6.

EXAMINATIONS.

	Passed.	Failed.	Total.
Minnesota	6	2	8
New York	1	0	1
	7	2	9

Percentage passed, 78.

UNIVERSITY OF MINNESOTA, Minneapolis.
Parks Ritchie, M.D., Dean. Graduates in 1903, 70.

EXAMINATIONS.

	Passed.	Failed.	Total.
California	2	0	2
Idaho	2	0	2
Iowa	1	0	1
Minnesota	65	5	70
Montana	1	0	1
New York	1	0	1
North Dakota	11	0	11
Oregon	1	0	1
South Dakota	1	0	1
Washington	9	0	9
Wisconsin	3	0	3
	97	5	102

Percentage passed, 95.

Missouri.

AMERICAN MEDICAL COLLEGE, St. Louis.
M. M. Hamlin, M.D., Dean. Graduates in 1903, 18.

EXAMINATIONS.

	Passed.	Failed.	Total.
Idaho	0	1	1
Illinois	3	0	3
New York	1	0	1

	Passed.	Failed.	Total.
Texas	3	0	3
Utah	0	1	1
	7	2	9

Percentage passed, 78.

BARNES MEDICAL COLLEGE, St. Louis.
Pinckney French, M.D., Secretary. Graduates in 1903, 100.

EXAMINATIONS.

	Passed.	Failed.	Total.
Alabama	1	0	1
California	1	1	2
Georgia	1	. .	1
Idaho	2	1	3
Illinois	10	10	20
Iowa	2	2	4
Texas	3	1[1]	4
Washington	2	0	2
West Virginia	2	0	2
Wisconsin	1	0	1
	25	15	40

Percentage passed, 62.

CENTRAL MEDICAL COLLEGE, St. Joseph.
C. A. Tygart, M.D., Secretary. Graduates in 1903, 23.

EXAMINATIONS.

	Passed.	Failed.	Total.
Idaho	1	1	2
Washington	1	0	1
	2	1	3

Percentage passed, 66.

ECLECTIC MEDICAL UNIVERSITY, Kansas City.
Theodore Doyle, M.D., Dean. Graduates in 1903, 15.

ENSWORTH MEDICAL COLLEGE, St. Joseph.
Jacob Geiger, M.D., Dean. Graduates in 1903, 14.

EXAMINATIONS.

	Passed.	Failed.	Total.
Kansas	0	1	1
Washington	0	1[2]	1
	0	2	2

Percentage passed, 0.

[1] Class of 1899.
[2] Class of 1887.

HOMŒOPATHIC MEDICAL COLLEGE OF MISSOURI, St. Louis.
L. C. McElvee, M.D., Dean. Graduates in 1903, 13.

EXAMINATIONS.

	Passed.	Failed.	Total.
Illinois	1	1	2
Indiana	2	0	2
Washington	1	1[1]	2
	4	2	6

Percentage passed, 67.

KANSAS CITY HAHNEMANN MEDICAL COLLEGE, Kansas City.
S. H. Anderson, M.D., Dean. Graduates in 1903, 17.

EXAMINATIONS.

	Passed.	Failed.	Total.
Kansas	2	0	2
Oregon	0	1	1
	2	1	3

Percentage passed, 67.

KANSAS CITY MEDICAL COLLEGE, Kansas City.
R. M. Schauffler, M.D., Secretary. Graduates in 1903, 24.

EXAMINATIONS.

	Passed.	Failed.	Total.
Iowa	0	1	1
Kansas	3	1	4
Minnesota	1	0	1
Montana	0	2	2
North Dakota	1	0	1
Ohio	0	1	1
Pennsylvania	0	1	1
Utah	1	0	1
Washington	4	0	4
	10	6	16

Percentage passed, 63.

MARION-SIMS-BEAUMONT MEDICAL COLLEGE, St. Louis.
H. W. Loeb, M.D., Dean. Graduates in 1903, 88.

EXAMINATIONS.

	Passed.	Failed.	Total.
Alabama	6	2	8
Illinois	18	1	19
Indiana	3	0	3
Iowa	1	0	1

[1] Class of 1898.

	Passed.	Failed.	Total.
Kansas	2	0	2
Louisiana	1	0	1
Minnesota	0	2	2
North Dakota	0	1	1
Oregon	1	0	1
Pennsylvania	1	0	1
South Dakota	1	0	1
Utah	1	0	1
Washington	1	0	1
	36	6	42

Percentage passed, 86.

MEDICO-CHIRURGICAL COLLEGE, Kansas City.
George O. Coffin, M.D., Dean. Graduates in 1903, 19.

ST. LOUIS COLLEGE OF PHYSICIANS AND SURGEONS, St. Louis.
Waldo Briggs, M.D., Dean. Graduates in 1903, 62.

EXAMINATIONS.

	Passed.	Failed.	Total.
Illinois	10	5	15
Indiana	2	0	2
Iowa	3	1	4
Kansas	1	0	1
North Carolina	1	0	1
North Dakota	1	0	1
South Dakota	0	1	1
Utah	0	2	2
Washington	2	1[1]	3
West Virginia	1	1[2]	2
	21	11	32

Percentage passed, 66.

UNIVERSITY MEDICAL COLLEGE, Kansas City.
Samuel C. J. Bryant, M.D., Dean. Graduates in 1903, 63.

EXAMINATIONS.

	Passed.	Failed.	Total.
California	1	0	1
Idaho	3	2	5
Indiana	1	0	1
Iowa	1	4	5
Kansas	3	0	3

[1] Class of 1893.
[2] Class of 1903.

	Passed.	Failed.	Total.
Louisiana	1	0	1
Montana	0	1	1
Oregon	2	0	2
Washington	0	1[1]	1
	12	8	20

Percentage passed, 60.

UNIVERSITY OF MISSOURI, Columbia.
A. W. McAlester, M.D., Dean. Graduates in 1903, 12.

EXAMINATIONS.

	Passed.	Failed.	Total.
New York	1	0	1
North Dakota	1	0	1
South Dakota	1	0	1
Texas	1	0	1
	4	0	4

Percentage passed, 100.

WASHINGTON UNIVERSITY, St. Louis.
Robert Luedking, M.D., Dean. Graduates in 1903, 53.

EXAMINATIONS.

	Passed.	Failed.	Total.
California	2	2	4
Idaho	1	0	1
Indiana	1	0	1
Iowa	2	0	2
New York	1	0	1
North Carolina	1	0	1
Texas	1	0	1
Washington	3	0	3
	12	2	14

Percentage passed, 85.

WOMAN'S MEDICAL COLLEGE, Kansas City.
Nannie P. Lewis, M.D., Dean. Graduates in 1903, 1.

EXAMINATIONS.

	Passed.	Failed.	Total.
Idaho	1	0	1

Percentage passed, 100.

[1] Class of 1889.

Nebraska.

JOHN A. CREIGHTON UNIVERSITY, Omaha.
D. C. Bryant, M.D., Dean. Graduates in 1903, 29.

EXAMINATIONS.

	Passed.	Failed.	Total.
California	1	0	1
Idaho	1	0	1
Illinois	2	0	2
Iowa	5	2	7
	9	2	11

Percentage passed, 82.

COTNER UNIVERSITY, Lincoln.
M. B. Ketchum, M.D., Secretary. Graduates in 1903, 16.

EXAMINATIONS.

	Passed.	Failed.	Total.
South Dakota	1	0	1
Texas	2	0	2
Washington	0	1[1]	1
	3	1	4

Percentage passed, 75.

UNIVERSITY OF NEBRASKA, Omaha.
Paul H. Ludington, M.D., Dean. Graduates in 1903, 38.

EXAMINATIONS.

	Passed.	Failed.	Total.
California	0	1	1
Iowa	4	1	5
Kansas	1	1	2
Minnesota	1	0	1
North Dakota	1	0	1
South Dakota	1	1[2]	2
Utah	1	0	1
Washington	2	0	2
	11	4	15

Percentage passed, 73.

New Hampshire.

DARTMOUTH, Hanover.
William T. Smith, M.D., Dean. Graduates in 1903, 14.

EXAMINATIONS.

	Passed.	Failed.	Total.
Iowa	1	0	1
Maine	2	0	2

[1] Class of 1897.
[2] Class of 1899.

	Passed.	Failed.	Total.
Massachusetts	8	0	8
Michigan	0	1	1
Minnesota	1	0	1
New Hampshire	5	0	5
Ohio	1	0	1
Oregon	1	0	1
Rhode Island	2	1	3
Vermont	2	0	2
Washington	0	1[1]	1
	23	3	26

Percentage passed, 88.

New York.

COLUMBIA, New York.

Graduates in 1903, 168.

EXAMINATIONS.

	Passed.	Failed.	Total.
California	5	0	5
Connecticut	6	0	6
District of Columbia	2	0	2
Idaho	1	0	1
Maine	2	0	2
Massachusetts	3	1[2]	4
New Hampshire	2	0	2
New Jersey	26	0	26
New York	121	7	128
North Carolina	3	0	3
Rhode Island	2	0	2
South Dakota	2	0	2
Texas	1	0	1
Utah	1	0	1
Vermont	1	0	1
Washington	1	0	1
West Virginia	2	0	2
	181	8	189

Percentage passed, 96.

CORNELL, New York.

Wm. M. Polk, M.D., Dean. Graduates in 1903, 60.

EXAMINATIONS.

	Passed.	Failed.	Total.
Alabama	1	0	1
Connecticut	1	0	1

[1] Class of 1875.
[2] Class of 1903.

	Passed.	Failed.	Total.
Illinois	1	0	1
New Jersey	5	0	5
New York	50	0	50
Pennsylvania	1	0	1
Rhode Island	1	0	1
Washington	1	0	1
	61	0	61

Percentage passed, 100.

ECLECTIC MEDICAL COLLEGE OF THE CITY OF NEW YORK, New York.
Geo. W. Boskowitz, M.D., Dean. Graduates in 1903, 13.

EXAMINATIONS.

	Passed.	Failed.	Total.
New Jersey	1	0	1
New York	16	1[1]	17
	17	1	18

Percentage passed, 94.

LONG ISLAND COLLEGE HOSPITAL, Brooklyn.
Joseph H. Raymond, M.D., Dean. Graduates in 1903, 40.

EXAMINATIONS.

	Passed.	Failed.	Total.
California	0	1	1
Connecticut	1	0	1
Indiana	1	0	1
Massachusetts	1	0	1
New Hampshire	1	0	1
New Jersey	4	0	4
New York	42	3	45
Washington	1	0	1
	51	4	55

Percentage passed, 93.

N. Y. HOMŒOPATHIC MEDICAL COLLEGE AND HOSPITAL, New York.
W. H. King, M.D., Dean. Graduates in 1903, 29.

EXAMINATIONS.

	Passed.	Failed.	Total.
California	0	1	1
Connecticut	2	0	2
Maryland	1	0	1
Massachusetts	1	0	1
New Hampshire	1	1[2]	2

[1] Class of 1902.
[2] Class of 1889.

	Passed.	Failed.	Total.
New Jersey	5	0	5
New York	22	1[1]	23
North Carolina	0	1	1
Ohio	1	0	1
Pennsylvania	1	0	1
Rhode Island	0	1	1
Vermont	2	0	2
	36	5	41

Percentage passed, 90.

N. Y. MEDICAL COLLEGE AND HOSPITAL FOR WOMEN, New York.
M. Belle Brown, M.D., Dean.   Graduates in 1903, 8.

EXAMINATIONS.

	Passed.	Failed.	Total.
Connecticut	1	0	1
Massachusetts	1	0	1
New Jersey	2	0	2
New York	8	0	8
Rhode Island	1	0	1
	13	0	13

Percentage passed, 100.

SYRACUSE UNIVERSITY, Syracuse.
Henry D. Didama, M.D., Dean.   Graduates in 1903, 29.

EXAMINATIONS.

	Passed.	Failed.	Total.
Massachusetts	1	0	1
New York	26	0	26
Rhode Island	1	0	1
	28	0	28

Percentage passed, 100.

UNION, Albany.
Albert Vander Veer, M.D., Dean.   Graduates in 1903, 33.

EXAMINATIONS.

	Passed.	Failed.	Total.
California	1	0	1
Massachusetts	1	0	1
New York	32	3[2]	35
Oregon	1	0	1
Vermont	1	0	1
	36	3	39

Percentage passed, 92.

[1] Class of 1901.
[2] Class 1897, 1903 (2).

UNIVERSITY AND BELLEVUE HOSPITAL MED. COLLEGE, New York.
Edward G. Janeway, M.D., Dean. Graduates in 1903, 73.

EXAMINATIONS.

	Passed.	Failed.	Total.
Alabama	1	0	1
Georgia	2	0	2
Indiana	1	0	1
Massachusetts	5	0	5
Nebraska	1	0	1
New Hampshire	2	0	2
New Jersey	12	0	12
New York	48	7	55
North Dakota	1	1	2
Ohio	1	0	1
Rhode Island	2	0	2
Vermont	3	0	3
	79	8	87

Percentage passed, 91.

UNIVERSITY OF BUFFALO, Buffalo.
Matthew D. Mann, M.D., Dean. Graduates in 1903, 45.

EXAMINATIONS.

	Passed.	Failed.	Total.
California	1	0	1
New Jersey	1	0	1
New York	41	3[1]	44
Ohio	1	0	1
West Virginia	1	0	1
	45	3	48

Percentage passed, 94.

North Carolina.

NORTH CAROLINA MEDICAL COLLEGE, Davidson.
J. P. Monroe, M.D., President. Graduates in 1903, 10.

EXAMINATIONS.

	Passed.	Failed.	Total.
North Carolina	9	1	10
South Carolina	2	0	2
Virginia	1	0	1
	12	1	13

Percentage passed, 92.

[1] Classes of 1893, 1899, 1903.

SHAW UNIVERSITY, Raleigh.
James McKee, M.D., Dean. Graduates in 1903, 23.

EXAMINATIONS.

	Passed	Failed	Total
Alabama	0	1	1
Georgia	3	0	3
Massachusetts	1	0	1
New Jersey	2	0	2
North Carolina	2	2	4
Rhode Island	1	0	1
South Carolina	5	1[1]	6
Virginia	6	7	13
West Virginia	1	4[2]	5
	21	15	36

Percentage passed, 59.

UNIVERSITY OF NORTH CAROLINA, Chapel Hill and Raleigh.
F. P. Venable, Ph.D., LL.D., President. Graduates in 1903, 4.

EXAMINATIONS.

	Passed	Failed	Total
North Carolina	4	0	4

Percentage passed, 100.

Ohio.

CLEVELAND COLLEGE OF PHYSICIANS AND SURGEONS. Cleveland.
N. Stone Scott, M.D., Dean. Graduates in 1903, 22.

EXAMINATIONS.

	Passed	Failed	Total
Pennsylvania	1	0	1
Washington	1	0	1
	2	0	2

Percentage passed, 100.

CLEVELAND HOMEOPATHIC MEDICAL COLLEGE, Cleveland.
Gaius J. Jones, M.D., Dean. Graduates in 1903, 40.

EXAMINATIONS.

	Passed	Failed	Total
Alabama	0	1	1
Illinois	1	0	1
Kansas	1	0	1
New York	2	0	2
Ohio	6	2	8

[1] Class of 1902.
[2] Classes of 1897, 1902 (2), 1903.

	Passed.	Failed.	Total.
Pennsylvania	4	4	8
West Virginia	1	0	1
	15	7	22

Percentage passed, 70.

ECLECTIC MEDICAL INSTITUTE, Cincinnati.
F. J. Locke, M.D., Dean. Graduates in 1903, 45.

EXAMINATIONS.

	Passed.	Failed.	Total.
California	0	1	1
Illinois	2	1	3
Indiana	4	2	6
Iowa	0	1	1
Kansas	1	0	1
Ohio	1	0	1
Pennsylvania	6	0	6
Texas	2	0	2
Washington	0	1[1]	1
West Virginia	2	1[1]	3
	18	7	25

Percentage passed, 72.

MIAMI MEDICAL COLLEGE, Cincinnati.
J. C. Oliver, M.D., Dean. Graduates in 1903, 40.

EXAMINATIONS.

	Passed.	Failed.	Total.
Illinois	1	0	1
Indiana	2	0	2
Iowa	1	0	1
Michigan	1	0	1
Ohio	3	1	4
Pennsylvania	1	1	2
	9	2	11

Percentage passed, 82.

OHIO MEDICAL UNIVERSITY, Columbus.
George M. Waters, M.D., Dean. Graduates in 1903, 58.

EXAMINATIONS.

	Passed.	Failed.	Total.
Indiana	2	1	3
Maryland	0	1	1
Ohio	6	0	6

[1] Class of 1900.

	Passed.	Failed.	Total.
Pennsylvania	7	1	8
Tennessee	1	0	1
Texas	1	0	1
	17	3	20

Percentage passed, 85.

PULTÉ MEDICAL COLLEGE, Cincinnati.
J. D. Buck, M.D., Dean. Graduates in 1903, 10.

EXAMINATIONS.

	Passed.	Failed.	Total.
California	1	0	1
Indiana	1	0	1
Maryland	1	0	1
Massachusetts	0	1[1]	1
Oregon	0	1	1
Pennsylvania	1	0	1
	4	2	6

Percentage passed, 67.

STARLING MEDICAL COLLEGE, Columbia.
Starling Loving, M.D., Dean. Graduates in 1903, 49.

EXAMINATIONS.

	Passed.	Failed.	Total.
Indiana	1	0	1
North Dakota	0	1	1
Ohio	7	0	7
Oregon	0	1	1
Pennsylvania	3	1	4
Utah	1	0	1
Washington	0	1[2]	1
West Virginia	5	0	5
	17	4	21

Percentage passed, 81.

UNIVERSITY OF CINCINNATI, Cincinnati.
P. S. Conner, M.D., Dean. Graduates in 1903, 54.

EXAMINATIONS.

	Passed.	Failed.	Total.
California	2	0	2
Illinois	1	0	1
Indiana	6	0	6
Kansas	1	0	1
New York	2	0	2

[1] Class of 1902.
[2] Class of 1897.

	Passed.	Failed.	Total.
Ohio	8	1	9
South Carolina	1	0	1
Tennessee	0	1	1
Texas	0	1	1
Washington	3	0	3
West Virginia	5	0	5
	29	3	32

Percentage passed, 91.

TOLEDO MEDICAL COLLEGE, Toledo.
Park L. Myers, M.D., Secretary. Graduates in 1903, 14.

WESTERN RESERVE UNIVERSITY, Cleveland.
B. L. Milliken, M.D., Dean. Graduates in 1903, 26.

EXAMINATIONS.

	Passed.	Failed.	Total.
California	1	1	2
District of Columbia	0	1	1
Indiana	1	0	1
Iowa	1	0	1
Massachusetts	1	0	1
New Jersey	1	0	1
Ohio	4	0	4
Pennsylvania	1	0	1
	10	2	12

Percentage passed, 83.

Oregon.

UNIVERSITY OF OREGON, Portland.
Simeon E. Josephi, M.D., Dean. Graduates in 1903, 10.

EXAMINATIONS.

	Passed.	Failed.	Total.
Oregon	10	0	10
Wisconsin	2	0	2
	12	0	12

Percentage passed, 100.

WILLAMETTE UNIVERSITY, Salem.
W. H. Byrd, M.D., Dean. Graduates in 1903, 7.

EXAMINATIONS.

	Passed.	Failed.	Total.
New York	1	0	1
Oregon	5	0	5
	6	0	6

Percentage passed, 100.

ivania.

HAHNEMANN MEDICAL COLLEGE AND HOSPITAL, Philadelphia.
Charles M. Thomas, M.D., Dean.   Graduates in 1903, 69.

EXAMINATIONS.

	Passed.	Failed.	Total.
Connecticut	3	0	3
District of Columbia	4	0	4
Indiana	2	0	2
Maine	1	0	1
Maryland	1	0	1
Massachusetts	1	0	1
Minnesota	1	0	1
Montana	1	0	1
New Jersey	13	0	13
New York	3	0	3
Ohio	2	0	2
Pennsylvania	56	0	56
Virginia	1	0	1
Washington	1	0	1
West Virginia	1	0	1
	91	0	91

Percentage passed, 100.

JEFFERSON MEDICAL COLLEGE, Philadelphia.
James M. Holland, M.D., Dean.   Graduates in 1903, 166.

EXAMINATIONS.

	Passed.	Failed.	Total.
Alabama	3	0	3
Arkansas	1	0	1
California	2	0	2
Connecticut	3	1	4
Delaware	0	1	1
Georgia	2	0	2
Idaho	2	1	3
Illinois	2	0	2
Indiana	5	0	5
Iowa	2	0	2
Kansas	1	0	1
Louisiana	2	0	2
Maine	2	0	2
Maryland	2	1	3
Massachusetts	3	0	3
New Hampshire	1	0	1
New Jersey	30	0	30
New York	7	0	7

	Passed.	Failed.	Total.
North Carolina	1	0	1
Ohio	6	0	6
Oregon	1	0	1
Pennsylvania	98	16[1]	114
Rhode Island	3	1	4
South Dakota	1	0	1
Texas	3	0	3
Utah	1	0	1
Washington	2	0	2
West Virginia	2	0	2
Wisconsin	2	0	2
	190	21	211

Percentage passed, 90.

MEDICO-CHIRURGICAL COLLEGE OF PHILADELPHIA, Philadelphia.
Seneca Egbert, M.D., Dean. Graduates in 1903, 93.

EXAMINATIONS.

	Passed.	Failed.	Total.
California	1	0	1
Delaware	2	0	2
Indiana	1	0	1
Massachusetts	1	0	1
Minnesota	1	0	1
New Hampshire	1	0	1
New Jersey	14	0	14
New York	2	0	2
Ohio	1	0	1
Pennsylvania	75	13	88
Rhode Island	0	1	1
South Carolina	1	0	1
Tennessee	2	0	2
Utah	1	0	1
West Virginia	1	0	1
	104	14	118

Percentage passed, 88.

UNIVERSITY OF PENNSYLVANIA, Philadelphia.
Charles H. Frazier, M.D., Dean. Graduates in 1903, 111.

EXAMINATIONS.

	Passed.	Failed.	Total.
California	6	1	7
Delaware	2	0	2

[1] Second examination (5).

	Passed.	Failed.	Total.
District of Columbia	3	0	3
Georgia	1	0	1
Indiana	1	0	1
Kansas	1	0	1
Louisiana	1	0	1
Maine	4	0	4
Maryland	1	0	1
Massachusetts	3	0	3
Minnesota	1	0	1
New Jersey	27	0	27
New York	37	0	37
North Carolina	3	0	3
North Dakota	1	0	1
Ohio	6	0	6
Oregon	1	0	1
Pennsylvania	58	2	60
Virginia	2	0	2
Washington	3	0	3
West Virginia	7	0	7
	169	3	172

Percentage passed, 98.

WESTERN UNIVERSITY OF PENNSYLVANIA, Pittsburg.
J. C. Lange, M.D., Dean. Graduates in 1903, 79.

EXAMINATIONS.

	Passed.	Failed.	Total.
New Jersey	1	0	1
New York	2	0	2
Ohio	2	0	2
Pennsylvania	70	21	91
Virginia	1	0	1
West Virginia	3	0	3
	79	21	100

Percentage passed, 79.

WOMAN'S MEDICAL COLLEGE OF PENNSYLVANIA, Philadelphia.
Clara Marshall, M.D., Dean. Graduates in 1903, 30.

EXAMINATIONS.

	Passed.	Failed.	Total.
District of Columbia	1	1	2
Massachusetts	2	0	2
New Hampshire	1	0	1
New Jersey	5	0	5

	Passed.	Failed.	Total.
New York	6	0	6
Ohio	2	0	2
Pennsylvania	17	1	18
South Carolina	1	0	1
South Dakota	1	0	1
Virginia	1	0	1
	37	2	39

Percentage passed, 95.

South Carolina.

MEDICAL COLLEGE OF SOUTH CAROLINA, Charleston.
Francis L. Parker, M.D., Dean. Graduates in 1903, 21.

EXAMINATIONS.

	Passed.	Failed.	Total.
California	1	0	1
Connecticut	1	0	1
North Carolina	1	1	2
South Carolina	20	0	20
	23	1	24

Percentage passed, 96.

Tennessee.

CHATTANOOGA NATIONAL MEDICAL COLLEGE, Chattanooga.
F. W. Haigler, M.D., Dean. Graduates in 1903, 1.

EXAMINATIONS.

	Passed.	Failed.	Total.
Texas	2	1	3

Percentage passed, 67.

GRANT UNIVERSITY, Chattanooga.
E. A. Cobleigh, M.D., Dean. Graduates in 1903, 41.

EXAMINATIONS.

	Passed.	Failed.	Total.
Alabama	9	2	11
Arkansas	1	0	1
Georgia	1	0	1
Kansas	1	0	1
Maine	1	0	1
North Carolina	1	2	3
Pennsylvania	1	0	1
Texas	1	0	1
	16	4	20

Percentage passed, 80.

KNOXVILLE MEDICAL COLLEGE, Knoxville.
H. M. Green, M.D., Secretary. Graduates in 1903, 6.

MEMPHIS HOSPITAL MEDICAL COLLEGE, Memphis.
W. B. Rogers, M.D., Dean. Graduates in 1903, 195.

EXAMINATIONS.

	Passed.	Failed.	Total.
Alabama	8	1	9
Georgia	0	1	1
Alabama	8	1	9
Louisiana	25	6	31
North Carolina	2	1	3
Tennessee	22	2	24
Texas	2	1	3
	59	12	71

Percentage passed, 83.

TENNESSEE MEDICAL COLLEGE, Knoxville.
Henry J. Kelso, M.D., Secretary. Graduates in 1903, 8.

EXAMINATIONS.

	Passed.	Failed.	Total.
Georgia	1	0	1
Louisiana	1	0	1
North Carolina	2	5	7
South Carolina	1	0	1
Tennessee	7	0	7
Texas	0	1	1
Washington	2	0	2
	14	6	20

Percentage passed, 70.

UNIVERSITY OF NASHVILLE, Nashville.
Wm. G. Ewing, M.D., Dean. Graduates in 1903, 50.

EXAMINATIONS.

	Passed.	Failed.	Total.
Alabama	7	0	7
Georgia	2	0	2
Louisiana	7	1	8
North Carolina	0	1	1
Oregon	1	0	1
Tennessee	4	1	5
West Virginia	1	0	1
	22	3	25

Percentage passed, 88.

UNIVERSITY OF THE SOUTH, Sewanee.
John S. Cain, M.D., Dean. Graduates in 1903, 38.

EXAMINATIONS.

	Passed.	Failed.	Total.
Alabama	2	0	2
Arkansas	1	0	1
California	0		
Connecticut	0		1
Georgia	4	0	4
Louisiana	6	3	9
Maine	1	0	1
Maryland	0	1	
New York	2		2
Pennsylvania	1	2	3
Rhode Island	1	0	1
Tennessee	1	0	1
Virginia	6	5	11
West Virginia	3	0	3
	28	14	42

Percentage passed, 67.

UNIVERSITY OF TENNESSEE, Nashville.
Paul F. Eve, M.D., Dean. Graduates in 1903, 33.

EXAMINATIONS.

	Passed.	Failed.	Total.
Alabama	3	1	4
Kansas	1	0	1
Louisiana	3		3
New Jersey	1		1
North Carolina	2		3
Tennessee	7		7
Texas	6	0	6
Virginia	1	0	1
	24	2	26

Percentage passed, 92.

VANDERBILT UNIVERSITY, Nashville.
Wm. L. Dudley, M.D., Dean. Graduates in 1903, 34.

EXAMINATIONS.

	Passed.	Failed.	Total.
Alabama	5	3	8
California	1	1	2
Georgia	2	0	

784

	Passed.	Failed.	Total.
Louisiana	1	1	2
Maine	1	0	1
Massachusetts	1	1[1]	2
Minnesota	1	0	1
Montana	1	1	2
New York	1	0	1
North Carolina	1	0	1
Oregon	0	1	1
Tennessee	12	0	12
Texas	4	1[2]	5
Virginia	0	1	1
Washington	1	0	1
	32	10	42

Percentage passed, 76.

WALDEN UNIVERSITY, Nashville.

G. W. Hubbard, M.D., Dean. Graduates in 1903, 41.

EXAMINATIONS.

	Passed.	Failed.	Total.
Alabama	5	1	6
California	1	1	2
Georgia	5	1	6
Illinois	1	0	1
Iowa	0	1	1
Louisiana	0	2	2
South Carolina	2	0	2
Tennessee	2	0	2
Texas	1	0	1
	17	6	23

Percentage passed, 73.

Texas.

BAYLOR UNIVERSITY, Dallas.

E. H. Cary, M.D., Dean. Graduates in 1903, 3.

EXAMINATIONS.

	Passed.	Failed.	Total.
Texas	1	0	1

Percentage passed, 100.

DALLAS MEDICAL COLLEGE, Dallas.

EXAMINATIONS.

	Passed.	Failed.	Total.
Texas	3	0	3

Percentage passed, 100.

[1] Class of 1894.
[2] Class of 1885.

FORT WORTH UNIVERSITY, Fort Worth.
  Bacon Saunders, M.D., Dean. Graduates in 1903, 5.

EXAMINATIONS.

	Passed.	Failed.	Total.
Louisiana	1	0	1

Percentage passed, 100.

PHYSIO-MEDICAL COLLEGE OF TEXAS, Dallas.
  R. L. Spann, M.D., Secretary. Graduates in 1903, 3.

EXAMINATIONS.

	Passed.	Failed.	Total.
Texas	4	0	4

Percentage passed, 100.

UNIVERSITY OF TEXAS, Galveston.
  W. L. Prather, M.D., President. Graduates in 1903, 35.

EXAMINATIONS.

	Passed.	Failed.	Total.
North Carolina	1	0	1
Texas	18	0	18
	19	0	19

Percentage passed, 100.

Vermont.

UNIVERSITY OF VERMONT, Burlington.
  B. J. Andrews, M.D., Secretary. Graduates in 1903, 31.

EXAMINATIONS.

	Passed.	Failed.	Total.
California	0	1	1
Connecticut	4	1	5
Maine	1	0	1
Massachusetts	11	6	17
Michigan	1	0	1
Minnesota	0	1	1
New Hampshire	3	0	3
New Jersey	1	0	1
New York	5	1[1]	6
Rhode Island	4	1	5
Utah	1	0	1
Vermont	25	0	25
	56	11	67

Percentage passed, 84.

[1] Class of 1898.

Virginia.

MEDICAL COLLEGE OF VIRGINIA, Richmond.
Christopher Tompkins, M.D., Dean. Graduates in 1903, 35.

EXAMINATIONS.

	Passed.	Failed.	Total.
District of Columbia	0	1	1
Massachusetts	0	1[1]	1
New Jersey	1	0	1
North Carolina	4	0	4
Virginia	23	8	31
Washington	1	0	1
West Virginia	10	0	10
	39	10	49

Percentage passed, 80.

UNIVERSITY COLLEGE OF MEDICINE, Richmond.
J. Allison Hodges, M.D., Dean. Graduates in 1903, 44.

EXAMINATIONS.

	Passed.	Failed.	Total.
North Carolina	8	1	9
Pennsylvania	2	0	2
Virginia	32	3	35
West Virginia	5	0	5
	47	4	51

Percentage passed, 92.

UNIVERSITY OF VIRGINIA, Charlottesville.
Dr. James M. Page, Chairman. Graduates in 1903, 25.

EXAMINATIONS.

	Passed.	Failed.	Total.
Alabama	6	0	6
District of Columbia	2	0	2
Georgia	1	0	1
Maryland	1	0	1
New Jersey	1	0	1
New York	3	0	3
North Carolina	1	0	1
Pennsylvania	2	0	2
South Carolina	1	0	1
Tennessee	2	0	2
Texas	1	0	1
Utah	1	0	1

[1] Class of 1900.

	Passed.	Failed.	Total.
Virginia	23	3	26
West Virginia	3	0	3
Wisconsin	1	0	1
	49	3	52

Percentage passed, 94.

Wisconsin.

MILWAUKEE MEDICAL COLLEGE, Milwaukee.

Wm. H. Earles, M.D., President. Graduates in 1903, 43.

EXAMINATIONS.

	Passed.	Failed.	Total.
Illinois	2	0	2
North Dakota	1	0	1
Pennsylvania	1	0	1
South Dakota	1	0	1
	5	0	5

Percentage passed, 100.

WISCONSIN COLLEGE OF PHYSICIANS AND SURGEONS, Milwaukee.

W. H. Washburn, M.D., Secretary. Graduates in 1903, 23.

EXAMINATIONS.

	Passed.	Failed.	Total.
Minnesota	1	1	2
Montana	1	0	1
	2	1	3

Percentage passed, 66.

Non-graduates.

EXAMINATIONS.

	Passed.	Failed.	Total.
Alabama	2	5	7
Arkansas	2	3	5
Michigan	5	2	7
Oregon	0	1	1
Texas	43	14	57
West Virginia	22	34	56
	74	59	133

Percentage passed, 56.

CANADA.

Manitoba.

UNIVERSITY OF MANITOBA, Winnipeg.

H. H. Choun, M.D., Dean. Graduates in 1903, 17.

EXAMINATIONS.

	Passed.	Failed.	Total.
Iowa	1	0	1

Percentage passed, 100.

Quebec.
  McGILL UNIVERSITY, Quebec.
    T. G. Roddock, M.D., Dean. Graduates in 1903, 100.

EXAMINATIONS.

	Passed.	Failed.	Total.
California	2	1	3
Illinois	0	1	1
Kansas	1	0	1
Maine	6	0	6
Massachusetts	7	0	7
Michigan	1	0	1
Minnesota	2	0	2
Montana	2	0	2
New Hampshire	1	0	1
New York	5	0	5
North Dakota	1	0	1
Rhode Island	2	0	2
Washington	6	0	6
	36	2	38

Percentage passed, 92.

  UNIVERSITY BISHOPS COLLEGE, Quebec.
    F. W. Campell, M.D., Dean. Graduates in 1903, 5.

EXAMINATIONS.

	Passed.	Failed.	Total.
Pennsylvania	1	0	1
Wisconsin	1	0	1
	2	0	2

Percentage passed, 100.

  UNIVERSITY LAVAL, Quebec.
    Graduates in 1903, 17.

EXAMINATIONS.

	Passed.	Failed.	Total.
California	0	1	1
Illinois	1	0	1
Maine	6	0	6
Massachusetts	8	2[1]	10
Minnesota	1	0	1
Montana	1	0	1
New Hampshire	0	1[2]	1

[1] Classes 1901 and 1903.
[2] Class of 1902.

	Passed.	Failed.	Total.
Rhode Island	1	0	1
Vermont	1	0	1
	19	4	23

Percentage passed, 83.

ONTARIO MEDICAL COLLEGE FOR WOMEN, Toronto.

EXAMINATIONS.

	Passed.	Failed.	Total.
New York	1	0	1

QUEEN'S UNIVERSITY, Kingston.
J. C. Connell, M.D., Dean. Graduates in 1903, 48.

EXAMINATIONS.

	Passed.	Failed.	Total.
Iowa	1	0	1
Michigan	1	0	1
New York	5	0	5
North Dakota	1	0	1
Vermont	1	0	1
	9	0	9

Percentage passed, 100.

UNIVERSITY OF TORONTO, Toronto.
R. A. Reeve, M.D., Dean. Graduates in 1903, 90.

EXAMINATIONS.

	Passed.	Failed.	Total.
Indiana	2	0	2
Iowa	1	0	1
Maryland	1	0	1
Michigan	6	0	6
Minnesota	2	0	2
New York	5	0	5
	17	0	17

Percentage passed, 100.

TRINITY MEDICAL COLLEGE, Toronto.

[Trinity Medical College gave a diploma, but bestowed no degrees. Most of its students secured a degree in medicine from Trinity University, which did not maintain a medical faculty. It is possible that some of those given in this tabulation should be attributed to Trinity University.]

EXAMINATIONS.

	Passed.	Failed.	Total.
Indiana	1	0	1
Michigan	4	0	4

	Passed.	Failed.	Total.
Minnesota	2	0	2
New York	2	0	2
Washington	3	1[1]	4
	12	1	13

Percentage passed, 92.

TRINITY UNIVERSITY, Toronto.

EXAMINATIONS.

	Passed.	Failed.	Total.
New Jersey	1	0	1
New York	1	0	1
Pennsylvania	1	0	1
	3	0	3

Percentage passed, 100.

UNIVERSITY VICTORIA COLLEGE, Coburg.

EXAMINATIONS.

	Passed.	Failed.	Total.
Michigan	1	0	1
Rhode Island	0	1	1
	1	1	2

Percentage passed, 50.

WESTERN UNIVERSITY, London.
W. H. Moorhouse, Dean. Graduates in 1903, 18.

EXAMINATIONS.

	Passed.	Failed.	Total.
Michigan	3	0	3
North Dakota	1	0	1
	4	0	4

Percentage passed, 100.

FOREIGN QUALIFICATIONS.

The results of the examinations of those possessing Foreign Qualifications (other than Canada) are arranged by countries and not by universities, as we are not as interested in the individual educational institutions abroad.

EXAMINATIONS.

Austria.

	Passed.	Failed.	Total.
California	0	1	1
Illinois	3	0	3

[1] Class of 1897.

	Passed.	Failed.	Total.
New York	2	0	2
Texas	2	0	2
	7	1	8

Percentage passed, 88.

Belgium.

	Passed.	Failed.	Total.
Iowa	1	0	1
Louisiana	0	1	1
	1	1	2

Percentage passed, 50.

Denmark.

	Passed.	Failed.	Total.
California	0	1	1
Iowa	1	0	1
	1	1	2

Percentage passed, 50.

France.

	Passed.	Failed.	Total.
California	0	1	1
New York	1	0	1
	1	1	2

Percentage passed, 50.

Germany.

	Passed.	Failed.	Total.
California	2	0	2
Illinois	1	0	1
New York	7	2	9
Oregon	0	1	1
Virginia	0	2	2
Wisconsin	1	0	1
	11	5	16

Percentage passed, 69.

Great Britain.

	Passed.	Failed.	Total.
California	2	0	2
Connecticut	1	0	1
Iowa	1	0	1
New York	2	0	2
Rhode Island	1	0	1
Utah	1	0	1
	8	0	8

Percentage passed, 100.

Greece.

	Passed.	Failed.	Total.
Illinois	1	0	1

Percentage passed, 100.

Hungary.

	Passed.	Failed.	Total.
Indiana	1	0	1

Percentage passed, 100.

Italy.

	Passed.	Failed.	Total.
California	0	2	2
Illinois	9	2	11
New York	25	10	35
Ohio	1	1	2
Pennsylvania	1	2	3
Rhode Island	2	2	4
	38	19	57

Percentage passed, 67.

Mexico.

	Passed.	Failed.	Total.
Texas	1	0	1

Percentage passed, 100.

Norway.

	Passed.	Failed.	Total.
Iowa	1	0	1
Minnesota	0	1	1
North Dakota	3	0	3
South Dakota	1	0	1
	5	1	6

Percentage passed, 83.

Portugal.

	Passed.	Failed.	Total.
Rhode Island	1	0	1

Percentage passed, 100.

Roumania.

	Passed.	Failed.	Total.
New York	5	1	6

Percentage passed, 83.

Russia.

	Passed.	Failed.	Total.
Michigan	2	0	2
New York	6	0	6
	8	0	8

Percentage passed, 100.

Sweden.

	Passed.	Failed.	Total.
California	0	1	1
Indiana	1	0	1
	1	1	2

Percentage passed, 50.

TEN YEARS' WORK OF A BOARD OF MEDICAL EXAMINERS.

[As a very fitting accompaniment to a report on the results of most of the state boards of examiners for one year, is this tabulation of the results of ten years' work by a single board. It would have been of greater value did it include all of the Pennsylvania statistics for the decade; possibly its publishing will cause the other boards to prepare similar reports. The secretary of the board, Dr. Guernsey, has made the profession his debtor by this great labor. No one unacquainted with tabulations of this character can appreciate the amount of work required to secure the desired results. We thank the compiler for his request that we publish the statistics.—*Ed. Bull.*]

STATISTICS OF THE BOARD OF HOMEOPATHIC MEDICAL EXAMINERS OF PENNSYLVANIA—JUNE, 1894–DECEMBER, 1903, INCLUSIVE.

At the annual meeting of the board of medical examiners representing the Homeopathic Medical Society of Pennsylvania, statistics of the work done by said board during the ten years of its existence, 1894–1904, were presented in his annual report by the secretary, Dr. Joseph C. Guernsey, as follows:

"We now come to a portion of this report to which I invite your closest attention. Ten years ago "The Medical Act" of Pennsylvania became operative, under the provisions of which this board was created to perform a special function. Considering it a matter of interest to know precisely what work has been accomplished since its organization, April 3, 1894, to the present time, June, 1904, your secretary has prepared the following statistics.

"Table A shows the number of "applicants" at each examination held by this board since June, 1894; the gevral average of those examined (which includes successes and failures); and the rank of each examination. You will see that twenty-one examinations have been held; the highest general average was 87.45 obtained in June, 1901; the lowest general average of any class examination was 71.33 in December, 1897.

A.

Date.	Number examined.	General average.	Rank.
June, 1894	43	77.02	18th
October, 1894	5	78.98	16th

Date.	Number examined.	General average.	Rank.
February, 1895	8	82.49	10th
June, 1895	38	82.44	11th
December, 1895	13	85.92	4th
June, 1896	64	82.37	13th
December, 1896	8	84.07	5th
June, 1897	57	86.13	3rd
December, 1897	9	71.33	21st
June, 1898	57	76.87 (Failed 22)	20th
December, 1898	20	82.60	9th
June, 1899	51	79.99	14th
December, 1899	11	82.39	12th
June, 1900	30	82.64	8th
December, 1900	10	77.42	17th
June, 1901	38	87.45	1st
December, 1901	9	77.32	19th
June, 1902	52	86.32	2nd
December, 1902	6	79.02	15th
June, 1903	60	84.02	6th
December, 1903	12	83.68	7th
Total, 21	Total, 601	……	……

Table B shows all the medical colleges from which the applicants came; the number of applicants from each college; the number passed and failed also the percentage passed and failed from each college; finally, the number of applicants, and their colleges, who "withdrew" from an examination prior to its completion.

B.

JUNE, 1894–DECEMBER, 1903, INCLUSIVE.

College.	Number examined.	Number passed.	Number failed.	Percentage passed.	Percentage failed.	Number withdrew.
1 Boston University School of Medicine...	12	10	2	83.33	16.67	…
2 Chicago Homeopathic Medical College	14	12	2	85.72	14.28	…
3 Cleveland Homeopathic Medical College	76	53	23	69.74	30.26	2
4 Cleveland University of Medicine and Surgery[1]	24	12	12	50.00	50.00	…
5 Dunham Medical College and Hospital, Chicago	2	1	1	50.00	50.00	…
6 Hahnemann Hospital College, San Francisco	1	0	1	0.0	100.00	1

[1] Now known as the "Cleveland Homeopathic Medical College."

College.	Number examined.	Number passed.	Number failed.	Percentage passed.	Percentage failed.	Number withdrew.
7 Hahnemann Medical College and Hospital, Chicago	10	8	2	80.00	20.00	...
8 Hahnemann Medical College, Philadelphia	435	390	45	89.66	10.34	3
9 Hering Medical College, Chicago	2	2	0	100.00	0.0	...
10 Homeopathic Medical College, University of Michigan, Ann Arbor	1	1	0	100.00	0.0	...
11 New York Homeopathic Medical College and Hospital	4	4	0	100.00	0.0	...
12 New York Medical College and Hospital for Women	3	3	0	100.00	0.0	...
13 Pulté Medical College, Cincinnati	6	5	1	83.33	16.67	...
14 Southern Homeopathic Medical College and Hospital, Baltimore	8	5	3	62.50	37.50	...
15 Southwestern Homeopathic Medical College, Louisville, Ky	1	1	0	100.00	0.0	...
16 Western Homeopathic College, Cleveland[1]	1	1	0	100.00	......	...
17 Trinity University, Toronto	1	1	0	100.00	......	...
	601	509	92	84.69	15.31	6

"Table C shows the very lowest personal averages; to wit, all those below 50 and the colleges from which the recipients were graduated.

"Surely no one fact proclaims with more eloquence the need of examining boards to spur medical colleges to better work than these averages. I rejoice to say that there is an apparent improvement on the part of medical colleges in teaching and preparing their students for the practice of medicine; for, while from 1894 to 1900 students were permitted to graduate so illy instructed as these averages show, from June, 1900, to June, 1903, the lowest average was 58.28—a decided gain! In June, 1903, however, an applicant again received an average below 50—*viz.*, 49.14.

"One of two things seems evident: Either those who are poorly qualified fear to try the Pennsylvania State Medical Examining Board; or, the colleges are doing better preparatory work. Whichever is the case, Pennsylvania reaps the benefit.

[1] Now known as the "Cleveland University of Medicine and Surgery."

C.

Date.	General average.	College.
October, 1894	45.43	Cleveland Univ. Med. and Surg.
December, 1895	49.00	" " " " "
December, 1895	40.43	Hahnemann, Philadelphia.
June, 1896	48.28	" "
December, 1897	47.71	Cleveland Hom. Med. Coll.
June, 1898	41.28	Hahnemann, Philadelphia.
June, 1899	47.71	Cleveland Hom. Med. Coll.
June, 1899	46.00	Southern Baltimore.
June, 1900	43.29	Hahnemann, Philadelphia.
June, 1903	49.14	Cleveland Hom. Med. Coll.

"We now turn to the bright side of our figures and view, in Table D, the very *highest personal* averages since 1894, taking all those above 95—in itself a very high mark—name of recipient and college of graduation.

D.

Date.	Name.	General average.	College.
Feb., 1895	G. A. Van Lennep, M.D.	96.71	Hahnemann, Philadelphia.
June, 1895	R. J. Abele, M.D.	98.86	" "
Dec., 1895	A. Cookman, M.D.	99.71	" "
June, 1896	A. Korndoerfer, Jr., M.D.	98.71	" "
Dec., 1896	Anna D. Varner, M.D.	96.57	Cleveland Hom. Med. Coll.
June, 1897	John E. Dehoff, M.D.	97.28	Southern, Baltimore.
June, 1898	Oscar E. Boericke, M.D.	95.43	Hahnemann, Philadelphia.
Dec., 1899	R. H. Woodruff, M.D.	96.00	" "
June, 1901	Roy C. Cooper, M.D.	96.43	Boston Univ. School Med.
June, 1902	John E. James, Jr., M.D.	98.28	Hahnemann, Philadelphia.

Table E presents a general summary of all the foregoing.

E.

June, 1894—June, 1904.

Total number of examinations in ten years	21
" " " applicants examined " "	601
" " " " passed " "	509
" " " " failed "	92
General average of all applicants examined " "	82.33
" " " " " passed " "	85.48
" " " " " failed " "	64.89
Total number examined in ten years	Men 565, Women 36
" " failed once	" 48, " 5
" " " twice	" 8, " 3
" " " three times	3
" " " four "	" 2
Highest, personal, general average	Men 99.71
" " " "	Women 96.57
General average attained by 565 men, ten years	82.65
" " " 36 women "	77.26

"The above statistics are absolutely correct, each figure and detail having been proven and verified. They have cost much time and great labor but I felt that in no way could the ten years' existence of this board be better exhibited and emphasized than in stating just what work it has accomplished. Whether it would be advisable to publish them in medical journals is a matter for our consideration. I am in favor of doing so. By the Medical Act of Pennsylvania all records of the medical examinations are kept on file and are open for public inspection. Any person can go through the records at Harrisburg and can collect and publish any or all of the facts here given. I would rather have them come from us direct in their present accuracy and entirety than some day to have an outsider publish a garbled and incorrect version."

JOSEPH C. GUERNSEY, A.M., M.D.,
Secretary.

After hearing the above report the Board of Homeopathic Medical Examiners of Pennsylvania unanimously voted that Dr. Joseph C. Guernsey be authorized to publish the statistics as given above.

OBSERVATIONS IN PASSING.

It is gratifying to learn that the medical practice act of California has been declared constitutional by the courts. The question arose upon the right of the legislature to define the standard of medical schools whose diplomas would give the holder the right to come up for an examination in the terms of the Association of American Medical Colleges. It is also noted with pleasure that South Dakota has secured the conviction of a person practising without a license. Every legal decision strengthening medical practice acts throw a greater responsibility upon those who are executing them. First and last, and all the time, the laws are for the benefit of that part of the community who are patients.

****

The greater attention paying to the undesirability of prescribing ready-to-use medicines is not to the liking of the makers thereof. Judging from some utterances published in one of our medical monthlies, and reprinted for wider distribution, it is hoped to cloud the vision of the prescriber by cuttle-fish methods. Patriotism is commendable, and there are worse habits than those of the jingo; but neither patriotism nor jingoism is concerned in the question of therapy and the prescribing of drugs. The befogging the question by raising such an issue arouses suspicion of the presence of something which has not been kept aseptic in the country of the Danes.

*

The Southern Surgical Gyneocological Association proposes to unveil a statue to the late Dr. William E. B. Davis—of pleasant countenance and precious memory—of Birmingham, Ala., at its next meeting in December. Dr. Davis was the founder of the association that thus seeks to keep in memory the services of one who deserves to be remembered for the services he was enabled to render to man.

*

The Exposition at St. Louis is said to be well worthy a visit, that it has many excellencies in addition to its size. Among the numerous circulars received by the Bulletin, those relating to the

Philippine exhibit have awakened the greatest interest. Yankee ingenuity and Yankee enterprise have produced an exhibit of our wards in the Orient which is admirable from any point of view. The islands themselves will be benefited by the education of our people concerning them and, *pari pasu*, the islanders who are here will be able to understand the United States a little better. It affords a profitable amusement for the merely curious, an excellent opportunity for study to those so inclined, and an aid to the thoughtful citizen in forming his opinion as to the political future of the Philippines.

Another feature, lasting but a week—September 19th to 25th—will be the Congress of Arts and Sciences; a full program can probably be obtained from the president of the Congress, Prof. Simon Newcomb, at Washington. We regret its size prevents its copying.

The Congress is divided into seven divisions with 24 departments divided into numerous sections; among these, medicine, sociology and education find place, with much to interest our readers.

We are assured by the president of the Congress that a most hearty welcome will be extended to any of the Academy who will be in attendance.

***

The Medical Temperance Association and the American Association for the Study of Inebriety united in a single organization on June 8, 1904, under the name American Medical Society for the Study of Alcohol and Other Narcotics. Its purpose is to encourage and promote more exact scientific studies of the nature and effects of alcohol in health and disease; to secure more accurate investigations of the diseases associated with or following from the use of alcohol and narcotics; to correct the present empirical treatment of these diseases by secret drugs and so-called specifics, and to secure proper legislation for the care, control and treatment of spirit and drug takers. Dr. T. D. Crothers, of Hartford, Conn., is the secretary, who will gladly furnish any information to those interested.

LITERATURE NOTES.

THE SURGERY OF THE HEART AND LUNGS. BY B. MERRILL RICKETTS, PH.B., M.D. New York: The Grafton Press. pp. 510. Cloth, $5.00; half leather, $7.50.

One wonders that 510 pages should be needed for the discussion of this subject, until one sees how completely the author discusses the subject, including a long record of experiments and of cases *in extenso*. Then the wonder becomes admiration, in treating so completely those subjects so interesting and important to up-to-date surgeons.

In the chapter on the anatomy of the heart, the author calls attention to the absence of cardiac ganglia in the interventricular septum and the apex of the heart, and this explains why some wounds of the heart are instantly fatal and others are not. This is followed by chapters on malformation, malposition, injuries, suturing, and the various diseases in reference to their surgical possibilities. The division treating of the lungs in like manner receives careful and extended consideration, with full bibliography at the end of each chapter, and the record of experimental research.

In the chapter on pneumotony, no reference is made to Mata's method of forced insufflation of the lungs to obviate collapse, and bare mention is made of this all-important and almost constant result of opening a chest which has no intrapleural adhesions, or which contains but little fluid in the pleural cavity. The excellent papers and their discussion at the Saratoga meeting of the American Medical Association are also overlooked.

Taking the work as a whole it is to be commended to the profession as an excellent up-to-date discussion of heart surgery and a fair exposition of the surgery of the lungs—a most valuable book of reference for the surgeon's library.

A TEXT-BOOK OF HUMAN PHYSIOLOGY. BY ALBERT P. BRUBAKER, A.M., M.D., Professor of Physiology and Hygiene in the Jefferson Medical College—with colored plates and 354 illustrations. Philadelphia: P. Blakiston's Son & Co. 1904. Cloth. pp. 699. Price, $4.00 net.

We are pleased with the appearance of this work. The field of physiology is so extensive that it is difficult to condense into a volume the size of this, a well-balanced and fair description of the science, that will be at once readable, reasonable and fairly up to date. Professor Brubaker is to be complimented on having overcome the difficulties and given a book to be commended.

The publishers should receive their share of praise for the mechanical part, which makes a worthy setting for an admirable treatise.

THE DOCTOR'S RECREATION SERIES.

I. THE DOCTOR'S LEISURE HOUR. FACTS AND FANCIES OF INTEREST TO THE DOCTOR AND HIS PATIENT. Arranged by PORTER DAVIS, M.D. pp. 352.

II. THE DOCTOR'S RED LAMP. A book of short stories concerning the doctor's daily life. Selected by CHARLES WELLS MOULTON. pp. 343.

These are the first two volumes of a series of a dozen volumes about the doctor, issued under the general editing of Charles Wells Moulton. The price of each volume in cloth is $2.50 and in half morocco $4.00.

Any one who loves a handsomely appearing book is at once favorably disposed to these volumes. A good quality paper, gilt top and deckel edge. The page has a generous margin, the type is of a good size and the impression clear. Everything combines to invite the reader to devour the contents. Each volume contains several illustrations of merit.

The first volume is a thesaurus of ancedotes and bon mots concerning the medical profession. Like most collections, the individual specimens vary in value and worth. They are classified, which will enable one to make them more readily available should one desire to refresh his memory that he may quote them. The compiler has done well in his compilation, and in making easily accessible these scattered stories.

Volume two is made up of a choice selection of short stories about the doctor. The owners of the copyrights have been gracious, the editor has been judicious, and we have a volume of the "little classics" type about the doctor in literature. Here we find Conan Doyle's "The Doctors of Holyland," Lucy S. Furman's "The Curing of Kate Negley;" Butler Monroe's "Dr. Pennington's Country Practice;" and others by Ian Maclaren, Ruth McEnery Stuart, Maud Wilder Goodwin and others.

The prospectus for the entire series promises other volumes of even greater interest.

How Abstinence Pays is a booklet prepared by Chas W. Scovel, A.M., and George P. Donehoo, Ph.M., D.D., to bring to popular attention the conclusions of a paper by Roderick Mackenzie Moore, Actuary of the United Kingdom Temperance and General Provident Institution on the "Comparative Mortality, among Assured Lives, of Abstainers and Non-abstainers from Alcoholic Beverages," which was read before the British Institute of Actuaries, on Nov. 30, 1903. The figures as quoted show a marked difference in favor of the abstainer over the non-abstainer who was temperate enough to permit of his insurance. The price of the pamphlet is five cents and can be obtained from Mr. Scovel, Keystone Building, Pittsburg.

Pennsylvania has a new journal—*Sanitation*—which is the official bulletin of the state board of health of Pennsylvania, and the associated health authorities and sanitarians of Pennsylvania. It is a handsome-appearing journal and promises to be worthy of its title.

The New Jersey State Medical Society abandons its volume of transactions and the first number of its *Monthly Journal* is on our table. It promises well.

The *Colorado Medical Journal*, for March, 1904, is enlarged by the addition of 162 extra papers and is devoted to the consideration of various phases of tuberculosis. It contains 28 separate articles by physicians of repute from various parts of the Union. It makes a valuable contribution to the literature of the subject. The price of this number is one dollar, and can be obtained from the publishers, Denver, Colorado.

BULLETIN

OF THE

American Academy of Medicine

VOL. VI.   ISSUED OCTOBER, 1904.   NO. 14.

The American Academy of Medicine is not responsible for the sentiments expressed in any paper or address published in the BULLETIN.

THE RELATION OF PHYSICIANS TO DENTISTS AND PHARMACISTS.

I.

THE RELATIONS OF MEDICINE AND DENTISTRY.[1]

BY EDWARD C. KIRK, D.D.S., Sc.D., Dean of the Dental Department, University of Pennsylvania.

The claim which dentistry makes for recognition as a department of the science and art of healing is one which probably needs no argument to support it. The fact that its objective ends are the cure of disease, and the restoration of normal function are sufficient and self-evident foundations upon which to base the claim. Its peculiarities of origin and development have, however, caused dentistry to occupy an anomalous position, with respect to those other allied departments of the art of healing to which collectively is applied the comprehensive term medicine. In their origin both medicine and dentistry were probably coeval for among all the ills which flesh is heir to, primitive man doubtless suffered from dental diseases and sought relief therefrom as he did from his other infirmities at the hands of those able to give it, and it was in response to the demands for such relief that the healing art came into being.

The earliest records show that certain classes of dental diseases were treated by physicians. The writings of Hippocrates,

[1] Read by invitation before the American Academy of Medicine, Atlantic City, June 4, 1904.

Galen, Scribonius, Largus, Celsus and their early followers contain descriptions of diseases of the teeth, and directions for their treatment from a purely medico-therapeutic standpoint, showing that treatment of dental diseases including extraction of teeth was a recognized part of the earliest medical and surgical practice.

Loss of teeth or their partial destruction by caries necessitated a mode of treatment which practitioners of medicine were not prepared to supply. The kind of skill required in these restorative operations was that possessed by the artisan, and especially by the goldsmith and jeweler, hence, it occurred that the making of prosthetic fixtures for the restoration of lost dental organs became engrafted upon the calling of the artisan or mechanic. Recent studies by Dr. Vincenzo Guerini, of Naples, who has given much time to the subject of dental archeology, have brought to light the fact that prosthetic dentistry was practised by Etruscan specialists in the art who introduced it into Rome five or six centuries before the Christian era and about four centuries before the advent of Archagathus who, according to Pliny, was the first physician to practise in Rome.

It will thus be seen that dentistry has had a dual origin : Its problems in pathology have kept it in constant and vital relation with medicine, while its requirements in the restorative phase of its art have necessitated its relation with the craft of the artisan, and it is this latter feature so essential to its practice which has in the course of its evolution developed dentistry as a profession having a separate system of preparatory education, a special literature and a professional organization independent of medicine.

The separate professional organization of dentistry became a necessity from the unwillingness of medical institutions to furnish the instruction necessary for the technical education of dental practitioners. The request was made and formally refused with the result that in 1839, the first dental college in the world for the systematic training of dentists was established in Baltimore, and the divorcement of dentistry and medicine was then officially proclaimed.

The new enterprise did not escape opposition and criticism ; its graduates were authorized to call themselves doctors of dental surgery, and by many holders of the medical degree this assumption of the doctor title by the dental graduate was regarded as an invasion of medical rights, which brought down a storm of criticism upon the new profession. The institution was, however, supported by the general body of dentists, its classes increased and the coincident founding of a well-ordered periodical devoted to the interests of dentistry together with the organization of dental societies soon established the profession of dentistry upon a sound continuing basis.

The evolution of all that concerns the science and art of healing during the sixty-five years which have intervened since the birth of the dental profession has wrought some interesting changes in the relationships of medicine and dentistry, as a result of the development which both have undergone.

The most evident change which has occurred is the enormous increase that has taken place in the volume of data with which the healing art is concerned. Scientific research into the composition, structure and function of the human body and its reactions to those modifying influences which constitute disease have so enlarged the scope of medicine that it is now admittedly impossible for a single human mind to successfully compass more than one of its departments. Hence, the development of medical specialism as an accepted mode of practically dealing with the problems of healing. It has come to be generally recognized that in order to be classed as an expert one must needs be a specialist whereas at the period when dentistry was launched as a separate calling, specialism in medicine was so little recognized as to be regarded as unethical. This growth of medical thought toward the recognition of the legitimacy of specialism has led the medical practitioner in the course of time to regard somewhat less critically the special practice of the dentist.

The most potent factor which has brought about the present sympathetic relationship of medicine and dentistry is the expansion of the curriculum of dental education so as to include the fundamental branches of medical training and the consequent production of a class of dental practitioners whose professional ideal is harmonious with that of other practitioners of the healing art in all of its departments.

There, however, remains the fact that the dentist lacks the

training which leads to the medical degree and while his training is such as entitles him to consideration and approval and due recognition for his attainments, the criticism is yet made that he is not a physician, that his training is not a medical training, and that his degree is the badge of a partial culture.

In the analysis of criticism of this character the fundamental principle of all education must be given due recognition, *viz.*, that education is ultimately ultilitarian in its object. Both physician and dentist are enlisted in the service of humanity; it is for that service that they exist and it is for that service they are trained. It is true that the dentist lacks the educational training that leads to the medical degree and therefore in a technical sense is not a physician. It is, however, not true that he lacks medical training. The professional education of the dentist to-day is based upon a curriculum which experience has shown to be best adapted to the necessities of his calling. Its foundation is constructed of all of those elementary subjects which constitute the basis of the medical curriculum. In university dental schools the instruction in the branches fundamental to the medical course is for two years taken concurrently by the dental and medical classes, and the requirements in these subjects are identical for both, with a few minor exceptions. Upon this medical foundation is erected the superstructure of the special scientific and technical training of the prospective dental practitioner. The further pursuit of the purely medical curriculum and the attainment of the medical degree by the dental student has been found to be impracticable for two reasons.

First because the acquirement of technical skill in dental art necessitates the development of a degree of manipulative ability, which cannot easily be acquired unless its training be undertaken during the period of adolescence. Manual training must always constitute an essential part of the dental curriculum throughout its entire extent. It has been the experience of the majority of those practically concerned with dental education that where training for the development of manual skill is deferred until early middle life or even past the twenty-fifth year the attainment of a high degree is almost impossible. In the course of a discussion of the subject at a meeting of the International Dental Federation, held at Cambridge, England, in 1901, Sir Michael Foster, Deputy Vice-Chancellor, of Cambridge University, and the distinguished professor of physiology in that institution said that he "had for many years past urged that the education of the surgeon should not be delayed too long, because it was impossible after certain years to acquire that suppleness and dexterity of touch which was necessary for success. The mind grows old very slowly and can be educated even late in life, but the body becomes old very soon and it is necessary to train it while it is really young." The plan of making the dentist a medical specialist *de facto* by first pursuing the complete medical course and taking the degree in medicine and then adding thereto the special dental training and its degree has been frequently tried, but the practical results have been on the whole unsatisfactory, mainly because the training in dental manipulative procedures has been postponed so long as to make a high degree of practical manual efficiency impossible. Practitioners so trained have not as a class rendered as efficient dental service as those who have received their dental training earlier in life, and have acquired a broader training in medicine later.

The second reason why the dentist is not technically a medical specialist is that the curriculum of his professional education is now four years in length,[1] and to acquire both medical and dental degrees would involve an expenditure of time and money, undesirable and unnecessary for the average practitioner.

I have dealt somewhat at length with the educational aspect of the question for it is upon that feature that the relationships of dentistry and medicine are based. I have endeavored to make clear the reasons why dentistry, though essentially a department of the healing art, is not, strictly speaking, a speciality of medicine; because it has had its origin and development outside the family of recognized medical specialties. It has, however, grown from a common root, developed side by side with medicine and is growing, as it were, into the medicine of the future.

The art of dentistry especially in America, has had a wonderful and active growth; perhaps in no calling of an allied character

[1] Since this paper was written the length of the standard dental curriculum has been reduced to three years. It is believed, however, that this reduction of the times of the course is but temporary.—E. C. K.

has greater ingenuity, resourcefulness and skill been developed than in all that pertains to the technical procedures of dental art, but the problems of pathology confront the dentist in his calling as they do the specialist who is concerned with any other part of the human body. The dentist is therefore a healer.

The therapy of dental and oral disorders requires something more than prosthetic treatment. Indeed the possibilities of dental mechanic art seem to have reached the stage where they are adequate to meet all conditions to which they are applicable, and it is to the vital side of the problem that dentistry has been and is now addressing itself. The issues with which the dental practitioner is called upon to deal are rarely directly those of life and death as in the case of the practitioner of medicine and surgery, but his problems are those which are intimately associated with bodily health and always of personal comfort. They involve an intimate knowledge of the principles of physiology and pathology as well as of the gross and minute anatomy of the structures of the oral cavity and those surrounding it, together with a general knowledge of the structure of the body as a whole.

To the solution of the problems of etiology which oral and dental diseases present must be brought the same breadth of knowledge and intellectual training as is required for the solution of disease problems of other parts of the body. General recognition of this requirement has developed the spirit of investigation and research work among the scientific workers in this department so that in its advancement dentistry has kept pace with the vanguard in medical research.

The idea of a purely local relation for dental and oral disease is fast disappearing and giving place to a more rational understanding of the interdependence of these pathologic phenomena and faulty bodily nutrition. Even so distinctly localized a disease as dental caries is in the light of recent scientific research, coming to be viewed as an expression of a diathetic fault or an error in metabolism by which the buccal secretions are charged with a waste product which constitutes the most acceptable pabulum for the development of the caries producing fungi. There is much evidence to sustain such a view, and if further research should demonstrate its validity the prophylaxis of dental caries would necessarily involve dietetic and constitutional treatment arranged with a view to correcting the metabolic error. The chemistry of faulty nutrition has received much valuable aid from the light thrown upon its problems through study of the oral fluids. Michaels, of Paris, has, as a result of his investigation, announced the proposition that the composition of the saliva varies constantly with certain recognized pathologic states. The work of others tends to confirm the general accuracy of Michaels generalization, and there is being developed a scientific ordering of the data of sialosemeiology destined to be of the utmost importance in the diagnosis of various types of general malnutrition. Indeed, it may be claimed that the study of the chemistry of the saliva affords a more accurate picture of the status of nutrition than does the urine, in view of the fact that the saliva contains those crystallizable substances which are dialyzed directly from the blood through the glands into the mouth in a fluid which is not an excretory waste product as in the urine.

The investigations of dental pathologists into the bacteriology of the oral cavity have shown not only that the mouth is the prolific breeding-ground of many varieties of pathogenic bacteria which are constant inhabitants of the mouth, but the still more important fact that the mouth is the portal of entry by which the majority of disease-producing germs find entrance into the body-at-large. The studies which have been made in oral bacteriology for the purpose of determining the etiology of mouth lesions have led to much deeper problems than are presented by the purely local features of these disorders. The constant presence of specific pathogenic bacteria in many locally healthy mouths has aroused inquiry into the questions of susceptibility and immunity and the more intricate problems of nutrition and the chemistry of abnormal metabolism as factors of disease predisposition. To these vital questions dentistry is not only giving practical attention but is contributing a fair quota of data toward their solution.

The general proposition that the mouth and its contained organs may furnish objective evidence of constitutional disease is well recognized, but the diagnostic value of such evidence has had mainly an empirical basis. Dentistry is addressing itself to the scientific solution of these oral pathologic phenomena and placing their data more and more within the category of ascertained facts to be practically utilized in diagnosis.

The trend of this type of dental research is to bring into closer relationship the practitioner of dentistry and the practitioner of medicine, and there is urgent need of this more intimate relationship in view of the more efficient service to humanity which it would insure.

Under the present circumstances the dentist is not qualified to form correct judgments as to the problems which confront the practitioner of medicine and with which he is presumably qualified to deal, yet the circumstances of his contact with humanity are such as to place him in a position where his knowledge of the diagnostic importance of oral phenomena will often enable him to recognize serious bodily disease before the patient is himself aware of it, and consequently before the thought of seeking medical advice has occurred to him.

Appreciation of the fact by the medical profession that the training of the dentist qualifies him to recognize and intelligently interpret the meaning of these oral diagnostic phenomena would enure to the advantage of both professions as well as to their respective patients; or, viewing the matter from the opposite standpoint, there is fully as urgent a need that the practitioner of medicine and of surgery should acquire a closer contact with what assistance dentistry is able to give in the solution of disease problems.

Two cases have recently presented themselves at the dental clinic of the University of Pennsylvania which illustrate this necessity. Both patients were suffering from a suppurative process which was discharging through a fistula in front of the angle of the lower jaw. The first case had been treated for some weeks in the surgical out-patient department of a hospital. A free incision along the lower border of the body of the mandible had been made and the bone several times curetted under the belief that the condition was an osteomyelitis with resultant necrosis. The currettement was continued until the roots of a molar were exposed by removal of its outer alveolar plate. In this condition the case was referred to the dental clinic where it was found that the disorder was simply a dento-alveolar abscess in which the accumulated pus had burrowed a fistulous outlet upon the face. Extraction of the tooth brought about a cure at once.

The second case was precisely similar, but was diagnosed as a tubercular abscess of one of the chain of cervical lymphatics and was referred by a specialist in tuberculosis to a dermatologist for treatment. The dermatologist made X-ray applications for three weeks with no improvement. The patient applied to the dental clinic for other treatment and an oral examination revealed that a lower first molar with putrescent pulp was the exciter of the infection which led to the discharge of pus upon the face. The diagnosis was verified by injecting an antiseptic fluid through the pulp chamber, and root canal of the molar under slight pressure with the result that the fluid escaped from the external facial orifice of the fistula. This case promptly yielded to treatment without extraction.

The need for such mutual understanding of the possibilities of both medicine and dentistry as will prevent mistakes of this character seems self-evident. The periodical literature of both professions indicates that as the expansion of what may perhaps be expressed as "the sphere of influence" of each proceeds, the points of contact between them become more numerous. Indeed there are many instances where no line can be sharply drawn between them.

While much has been said and considerable attention has been given to the discussion of what may be designated the political or organic relations of the professions of medicine and dentistry; and while it is doubtless right and proper that some formal definition of these relations should be attempted, yet from the point of view of your essayist it seems to be infinitely more important that there should be a general recognition of the need for a closer interrelationship between medicine and dentistry based upon their possibilities for mutual helpfulness. And a careful consideration of this possibility should convince us all of its advantage both to the science and art of healing and to humanity.

II.
THE RELATIONS OF PHYSICIANS TO DENTISTS.[1]

BY JOHN S. MARSHALL, M.D., Examining and Supervising Dental Surgeon U. S. Army, President of Examining Board.

Mr. President and Fellows of the American Academy of Medicine: The invitation of your chairman of the Program Committee to prepare a short paper upon "The Relations of Physicians to Dentists" was received with pleasure and also with surprise: with pleasure, because of the opportunity afforded me to do something in the way of contributing to the work of the Academy, and with surprise that there should be any doubt or even an implied doubt about these relations.

From my own standpoint as a medical graduate who has devoted the greater part of his professional career to the specialty of dental surgery as practitioner and teacher, there has never been the least doubt as to my relations, either *professionally* or *ethically* with my brethren, the physicians or the dentists.

From the standpoint of my personal observations, however, I am forced to recognize the fact that there is a question in the minds of a good many medical practitioners as to whether or not the dentist is entitled to be classed as a medical specialist; whether they can recognize him as such, and consult with him upon the same professional and ethical grounds that are accorded to specialists in other departments of medicine and surgery. To properly understand this subject, these relations must be viewed from the professional and the ethical standpoints.

THE PROFESSIONAL STANDPOINT.

In order to clear the ground of any false premise we must propound and answer the following questions:

First—What constitutes a physician in the broad acceptance of the term?

Second—What constitutes a dentist?

These questions we will try to answer by quoting the accepted definitions of these terms as found in the dictionaries in common use, but it will be necessary to first look at the definitions of the terms *medicine* and *surgery*.

[1] Read before the American Academy of Medicine, Atlantic City, N. J., June 4, 1904.

Medicine—"A science which relates to the prevention, cure or alleviation of disease."

Surgery—The art of healing by manual operation; that branch of medical science which treats of manual operations for the healing of diseases or injuries of the body; sometimes that branch of medical science which has for its principal object the cure of external injuries."—(*Webster's Unabridged Dictionary*).

Medicine—"A science, the object of which is the cure of disease and the preservation of health. Occasionally, it is used to comprehend all branches of the healing art; at others, to comprise one great division, in contradistinction to surgery and obstetrics. Medicine, in this sense, includes many branches, the chief of which are anatomy, physiology, pathology, hygiene, materia medica and pharmacy."

Surgery—"That part of the healing art which relates to external diseases, their treatment, and, especially to the manual operations adopted for their cure."—(*Dunglison's Medical Dictionary*).

DEFINITIONS OF THE TERM—PHYSICIAN.

"A natural philosopher, an experimenter in physics. A person skilled in physics, or the art of healing; one duly authorized to prescribe remedies for, and treat diseases, a doctor of medicine."—(*Webster's Unabridged Dictionary*).

"An investigator of nature. Properly speaking, one who has received his degree from an incorporated institution, as doctor of medicine, but often applied in the United States to any one who practises physics. The French formerly used the word *physicien* in the same sense. It is now appropriated by them to the natural philosophers."—(*Dunglison's Medical Dictionary*).

In these definitions of the term *Physician*, it is used in its broad sense, as generally employed in the United States, namely; a practitioner of medicine and surgery, one who holds the degree of *Medicinae Doctor*, while the definitions of the term *Medicine* in its broadest sense, includes every department of the healing art. *Surgery*, specifically, includes all those departments of the healing art which deal with injuries and diseases that are susceptible to treatment and cure by operative or manipulative procedures.

DEFINITIONS OF THE TERM—DENTIST.

Dentist.—"One whose business it is to clean, extract or repair natural teeth, and to make and insert artificial ones; a dental surgeon."

Dentistry—"The art or profession of a dentist."—(*Webster's Unabridged Dictionary*).

Dentist—"One who devotes himself to the study of the diseases of the teeth, and their treatment."

Dentistry—"Odontotechny, odontiatria, odontotherapia, dental surgery; the art of dentist."—(*Duglinson's Medical Dictionary*).

In these definitions the terms *Dentist* and *Dentistry* are used in their most *restricted* sense.

Dentistry, as practised to-day, is a much more comprehensive art, calling, profession, or specialty, than is described in the foregoing definitions. Dentistry has, in reality, grown to be an important specialty of medicine and surgery which has outgrown its early limitations.

The terms dentist, "Zahnartz" or tooth doctor no longer indicates the scope of the field of operations occupied by the dental surgeon.

The terms *Stomatalogy* and *Stomalogist* have been suggested as substitutes for dentistry and dentist, as it is thought these more nearly define the special field of operation of the dental surgeons of to-day. These terms, however, fall short of indicating the actual extent or limitations of the specialty.

If I were asked to define the extent and limitations of dentistry or stomatology, I should state it as "That department of medicine and surgery which relates to the study of the diseases, injuries and irregularities of the teeth, their treatment and preservation, the replacing of lost teeth by artificial substitutes, and the treatment of the diseases, injuries and deformities of the oral cavity, the jaws, and the accessory sinuses.

With this last and broader definition before us, I would invite your attention, very briefly, to the present system of dental education, as a means of indicating the professional status of this specialty.

In the best dental colleges, the students applying for admission are required to present the same credentials of preliminary education, as is required by the best class of medical colleges, or submit to an examination to prove their qualifications.

The courses of instruction for the first two years are practically the same as for medical students, the terms are of the same length; namely, seven to nine months in each year, and cover a period of four academic years.

The courses of instruction in the schools of the better class are fairly uniform, and cover the following fundamental sciences as taught in the medical colleges:

Anatomy, human and comparative.
Embryology, including the development of the teeth.
Histology, vegetable and human.
Physics, applied, including electricity.
Chemistry, including metallurgy.
Physiology, including chemico-physiology.
Bacteriology, including surgical and special mouth bacteriology.
Materia medica and therapeutics, including anesthesia.
Electro-therapeutics.
Pathology, general and special dental pathology.
Physical diagnosis.
General surgery, including the technique of sterilization and antisepsis.

To these are added those subjects which particularly pertain to the practice of this specialty; namely,

Odontology, human and comparative.
Dental techniques, prosthetic.
Dental techniques, operative.
Principles of operative dentistry, including construction of porcelain inlays.
Principles of prosthetic dentistry, including crown and bridge work and the construction of interdental splints.
Orthodontia.
Modeling (in clay) of the entire bones of the head, and of the teeth, enlarged.
Oral surgery.

To this is added an immense amount of laboratory and clinical instruction in prosthetic and operative dentistry and oral surgery, the time of the students being fully occupied, as a rule, from nine in the morning until five or six in the afternoon.

It will thus be seen that the dental surgeon is well grounded in the fundamental sciences of medicine and surgery, and fully qualified, theoretically and practically, for all of his professional duties, and may proudly stand by the side of his brethren in the other specialties of medicine without fear of being shamed whenever or wherever the crucial test of professional knowledge and practical ability shall be applied.

Fifty years ago it was a rare fortune to find a practitioner of dental surgery who was a graduate of a literary college or of a medical school. To-day there are scores and hundreds in the profession who hold the degree of B.A., or B.S., and a considerable number who have also earned the M.D. degree.

The dental surgeon may, therefore, be classed as a specialist in medicine, and I have no hesitation in saying that I believe him to be as thoroughly well qualified to assume the duties and responsibilities of his specialty when first graduated from his college as are the young men who have recently graduated from the medical schools, or the theological seminaries.

Dentistry is an *art* and a *science*. So closely related and associated is it with medicine and surgery that it cannot be separated from them.

The *art* of dentistry, like that of surgery, is made up of manual operations and manipulations. It consists of the ability to treat diseases and injuries by manipulations and operations, more or less mechanical in their nature, and to construct and restore by art, the teeth and portions of the face or jaws lost by disease or injury.

The *science* of dentistry, like that of medicine, consists of the knowledge and the ability to apply it, of the fundamental sciences of anatomy, physiology, chemistry, histology, bacteriology, pathology, materia medica and therapeutics. It consists of knowing *how* and *why* certain diseases of the mouth produce abnormal manifestations in the general system, or certain systemic diseases produce oral manifestations. Why, for instance, pregnancy sometimes causes an acute pulpitis (toothache) or a gingivitis, or produces pyorrhea alveolaris? Why the extraction of a tooth for a pregnant woman may sometimes result in an abortion? Why in malarial districts it is never wise to cap an exposed pulp? Why irritation of a tooth pulp will sometimes cause a progressive amaeurosis, or an impacted third molar cause deafness, neuralgia in the various branches of the trifacial nerve, or reflex neurosis in remoter parts of the body? Why an acute dento-alveolar abscess may produce septicemia or a chronic abscess cause pyemia? Why an unhygienic condition of the mouth may be responsible for certain gastric and intestinal disorders, or inflammation of the pharynx, tonsils or larynx? Why devitalized teeth of the upper jaw are often the cause of antral diseases, or why diabetes mellitus, Bright's disease, uterine irritations or displacements may sometimes produce gingivitis, stomatitis or pyorrhea alveolaris, etc., etc.

The professional relations of the physician and the dentist should therefore be of the same character as that which obtains between other specialists and the general practitioner. They can be, should be, and are, when consulting, of mutual help to each other, each dependent upon the other for special knowledge and skill in the diagnosis and treatment of diseases within their special fields of practice.

The growth of specialism within the last twenty-five or thirty years, has made it simply impossible for any one individual to become skilful in all of the specialties, hence we are obliged to depend upon each other for the proper care and treatment of our patients when they are suffering from diseases or injuries which do not come within our particular specialty or present peculiarities which call for consultation.

Please understand I am not now making a plea for the recognition of the dentist as a specialist in medicine. The dentist has already obtained this recognition by the force of his special knowledge and technical skill, a recognition which has been freely accorded to him by the American Medical Association and the International Medical Congresses, and, I believe, by the individual fellows of the American Academy of Medicine. The mere fact that the dentist does not, in many instances, hold the M.D. degree should not debar him of his just rights to fellowship as a member of the medical profession. He is a *physician*, as the accepted definitions of the term make clear,—holding a legally recognized degree, and, under it, entitled to practise in his special department of medicine and surgery.

THE ETHICAL STANDPOINT.

From the ethical standpoint the reputable dentist is as rigid in his motions, in relation to professional ethics, as any other class of specialists. I have endeavored to show that professionally he is by education a specialist in medicine, fully prepared and qualified for his particular duties, and that the practice of dentistry or stomatology is founded upon the recognized principles and methods of modern medicine and surgery.

Dentistry is not a *pathy* nor an "exclusive method of practice," but a broad and liberal profession, claiming to "try all things and to holding fast to that which is good," in its effort to prevent and combat disease.

The fact that dental surgeons holding the D.D.S. degree only, have been eligible to membership in the American Medical Association, and the International Medical Congresses for several years, removes any question as to their medical status and places them in the same relations to the medical body in general as that of the ophthalmologist, laryngologist or rhinologist.

The development of the science of medicine and surgery during the last twenty-five or thirty years has been so great and the advancements along special lines so numerous, that specialism in practice has become a necessity. The day has passed when the general practitioner was all-sufficient, and specialism has become the order of the day.

The oldest of these specialties, in the modern sense, is dentistry. It has developed along independent lines, being the first specialty to establish an independent school and confer a special degree. The wisdom of this action was at one time seriously questioned but the development of this and other specialties requiring long and delicate technical training of hand and eye, has proved that that training could not have been imparted in the ordinary medical colleges, and thus the wisdom of founding the dental schools, has been established.

I am not in sympathy, however, with the idea which prevails in some quarters that because dental education is conducted in separate schools and the faculties confer a special degree, therefore "dentistry is a separate profession." Separate schools were a necessity for the development of technical skill and the younger specialties like ophthalmology, laryngology and rhinology have recognized the advantage of these schools for technical training and, as a consequence, post-graduate schools have been organized in all of our large cities for teaching these and other specialties.

Dental surgery has also developed so greatly along particular lines during the last twenty-five years that it is already breaking up into specialties, and we find one dentist limiting his practice to operative dentistry, another to prosthetic dentistry, another to orthodontia and still another to oral surgery.

Like general medicine and surgery, it has grown to such proportions that no one individual can become expert in all of these departments, hence specialism is the natural solution of the difficulty.

The general practitioners of medicine and the specialists in all the departments of the "Healing Art" are therefore dependent and interdependent upon each other for counsel and advice in all serious cases or those which are obscure in symptoms, or outside the limitations of their special field of practice and only by the recognition of the possession of such knowledge and attainments by the specialists, can the best interests of our patients be subserved, or our own honorable position as a broad-minded, liberal, and skilful profession be maintained.

Physicians and surgeons have learned to respect the cultured dentist for his diagnostic ability and operative skill, and do not, in these days, hesitate to consult with him even though the only professional title he possesses is that of doctor of dental surgery.

In reality there is no more reason why a physician should hesitate to consult with a dental surgeon in relation to the diagnosis and treatment of diseases within the field of his special practice because he does not hold the degree of doctor of medicine, than that he should hesitate to consult with a physician holding the English title of M.R.C.P. or a surgeon holding the title of M.R.C.S. Neither of them are *doctors* of medicine, yet they are legally qualified to practise physic and surgery respectively in their own country, and their qualifications are recognized in the states of the Union.

The whole question, therefore, from the ethical standpoint, of the relations of physicians to dentists depends upon our willingness to recognize the dental surgeons as medical specialists, and

I do not see how we can withhold such recognition after the favorable action of the American Medical Association and the International Medical Congresses. In all the nations of Europe dentists are classed as medical specialists, while in our own country, which has been the cradle and the school of modern dentistry,—a specialty which has brought renown upon our system of professional education and made the name of American dentist honored the world over—we have not at this late day, *unanimously* accorded him that honorable position in the ranks of medicine and surgery which, by his learning and skill, he has fairly won, and the beneficence of his calling entitles him to occupy.

SYNONYMS IN THE NEW UNITED STATES PHARMACOPOEIA.[1]

By Joseph P. Remington, Ph.M., Chairman, Committee of Revision U. S. Pharmacopoeia.

The nomenclature of a science or an art reflects the progress of such science or art made from the time that its foundations were laid. Porter, in his "Human Intellect," has thoroughly expressed the value of nomenclature, when he says: "The technical nomenclature of a single science, when finished and arranged, is a transcript of all the discriminating thoughts, the careful observations, and the manifold experiments by which the science has been formed."

This exalted view of nomenclature, at first sight, would appear difficult of application to medicine and pharmacy in their present condition, and still it is not too much to say that a comparison of the nomenclature used in the first edition of the United States Pharmacopoeia in 1820, with that of the present pharmacopoeia of 1890, would show that much progress has been made through the adoption of certain cardinal principles which are well recognized, and have at last become thoroughly established among English-speaking nations.

One of the most difficult problems connected with the framing of an International Pharmacopoeia would be the adoption of a nomenclature acceptable to all civilized countries. "But," exclaims the scholar, "why should this be difficult? Latin is the language of science, it is a dead language, and why cannot the various nations meet in an International Congress and settle upon a nomenclature which would be authoritative and acceptable to all?" The answer is, that there are radical differences in the views which are held by those in authority in the various countries, and through long custom a terminology has been established, which is in general use by physicians and pharmacists, and it would be exceedingly difficult to effect any change that would not be regarded as revolutionary. We may take for illustration one chemical salt—"common baking-soda." This, in the United States and British Pharmacopoeias is known as *Sodii Bicarbonas*;

[1] Read by invitation before the American Academy of Medicine, Atlantic City, N. J., June 4, 1904.

in the Russian, *Natrium Bicarbonicum*: in the Swedish, Dutch, Danish and Norwegian, *Bicarbonas Natricus*; Austria and Hungarian, *Natrium Hydrocarbonicum*; Italian, *Bicarbonato di Sodio*; Spanish, *Carbonato (Bi) Sodico*; Belgian, *Bi-carbonas Sodae*: Helvetian and German, *Natrium Bicarbonicum*; Portugese, *Bi-carbonato de Soda*; French, *Carbonate (bi-) de Soude*; Chilian, *Bicarbonato di Soda*: Venezuelan, *Bicarbonato de Sodio*.

But if such differences exist in the names of the Latin titles of largely used pharmacopoeial substances, the synonyms which have come to be known as the ordinary vernacular names, used by the uneducated class, present a study most bewildering to the scholar, but exceedingly interesting to trace to their original sources.

But the object of this paper is to draw attention to the subject of the nomenclature of the forthcoming pharmacopoeia, and particularly to the use of synonyms. It may not be known to all the members of this Academy that our present pharmacopoeia recognizes several names for the same substance. If we turn to the substance known commercially as arsenic, we find five different names, *Acidum Arsenosum*, the Latin title; arsenous acid, the English name; As_2O_3, the chemical formula; arsenic trioxide and white arsenic are both synonyms—the first used by the chemist who wishes to be exact, the other by non-technical people, dealers and importers. The medical and pharmaceutical professions are accustomed to see the abbreviated form *Ac. Arsen.* in prescriptions, and it will probably require some years to become accustomed to the name which has been adopted for the forthcoming pharmacopoeia, *Arseni Trioxidum*. But it is necessary to recognize the correct chemical name for this substance, for modern chemical views prove that it is not an acid, but a trioxide of arsenic.

Again, the largest consumption of arsenic in all countries, is not as a medicine, but in the arts. I need but mention Paris green, and the enormous quantities used in exterminating that pest of the farmer, the potato beetle (*Doryphora decemlineata*.)

It is just because of the varied use to which are put so many chemical substances used in medicine, that difficulties have arisen in selecting the terminology to be used in the new book. One of the principal objects of a pharmacopoeia is to establish standards for the purity of official substances. The arsenic which comes to this country from abroad, and is intended to be used for the grosser products, need not be separated from some natural impurities with which it is always associated. The manufacturer of a compound which is intended to be used as an insecticide merely needs to know the percentage of arsenic trioxide in the crude substance, but the pharmacist must not only know to the fraction of a per cent. the purity of the product which he is to use in preparations upon which often hang the issues of life, but he must know the physical and medical properties of the contaminations.

Within the last few years, owing to the passage of what are known as "pure food and drug laws," in the various states, the United States Pharmacopoeia has come into great prominence for it has been made the standard for purity upon which the laws are based. Heretofore, there seemed to be no great necessity for drawing the line sharply between the standard for articles used for foods and medicines, and those for substances used in the arts. But prosecutions have been instituted under these food and drug laws, and judges have ruled that inasmuch as the law made the United States Pharmacopoeia the standard, it must apply to all substances bearing the name. These decisions have produced most embarrassing situations throughout the country. Honest druggists and merchants have been penalized for selling products which were not up to the official standards, and which were not used nor intended for use in medicines. A good illustration is afforded by hydrochloric acid. The synonym for this is muriatic acid, and this is frequently used for renovating brick fronts. It is manifestly absurd to require the degree of purity for such an acid as would be required for medicinal use or as a chemical reagent. In the forthcoming pharmacopoeia this difficulty will be remedied by inserting a clause in the introductory notices that the tests in the book are to apply *only to the substances used as medicines.* The public is protected, because the tests which follow under the article compel the standard to be maintained, and if the druggist dispenses the cheap, impure product for medicinal purposes or internal use when he should not, the fault can easily be detected.

But the use of synonyms in the pharmacopoeia has led to many embarrassments. Some druggists have sold, under the name of the synonym "laudanum," a preparation deficient in strength, and some have actually kept two tinctures of opium for sale, one the official tincture of opium for prescription use, and another labeled "Laudanum;" the latter is often sold in round green glass vials by cross-roads, general store merchants, to the public, and taken in doses of a teaspoonful without serious injury. The better class of druggists will not conduct business in this way, and those who do, excuse their action by saying that they could not think of selling official tincture of opium under the name of laudanum, to be sold by the country merchants, because serious results would follow on account of the dose of the weak laudanum having become so well established.

If we take for another example the well-known ointment popularly sold as "cold cream," it will be found that this ointment has been made for many years, often by perfumers, and has come to mean an oleaginous, soft ointment containing rose water, but frequently made by a process entirely different from that of the official formula. Many illustrations could be supplied, which would show the necessity for physicians adhering closely to official titles in writing prescriptions. If the synonym "cold cream" is abandoned in the pharmacopoeia, no excuse will remain for the pharmacist dispensing anything else but ointment of rose water, or *unguentum aquae rosae*, when this title is used in the prescription or physician's order.

The first object of a pharmacopoeia is to establish uniformity in the various preparations, so that no matter in what part of the country a physician may prescribe an official article under the official name, he will be sure to get it, because the liability to prosecution from the state officers will compel greater care on the part of the pharmacist. In looking over the prescription files of a druggist, one is surprised to note the great want of care on the part of physicians in the use of synonyms. Many prescriptions for articles are found written with unofficial titles, and in many cases some unrecognized synonym is used. Fluid extract of Indian hemp has been used as a name and fatal results have followed, because the physician intended fluid extract of *apocynum* and fluid extract of *Cannabis indica* was dispensed, Indian hemp being a synonym for both. For many reasons the Committee of Revision has decided to discourage, in every way, the use of synonyms, and the number will be greatly reduced, taken out of the text of the book, and used probably only in the index. It will be observed that it would not be wise at this time, to abandon all control over synonyms by dropping them entirely from the book. The latter course would permit a druggist to use some preparations not up to the standard of the pharmacopoeia (for he might think that he could make a preparation which would be cheaper, and in his opinion, better), and he could dispense such upon a prescription, even when the physician expected that the official article would be employed. When, on the other hand, a synonym is recognized in the pharmacopoeia, it is understood that the official requirements apply to the synonym with as much force as they do to the official product. If a physician, however, uses a synonym which is not in the book, the pharmacist may use his specially prepared product, for it is outside the pale of pharmacopoeial authority.

In conclusion, the writer would earnestly call the attention of physicians to the importance of carefully noting any changes in official nomenclature, and the necessity for greater care in using official titles in writing prescriptions, when they intend the standard preparation to be dispensed.

[NOTE—The remaining papers of the Symposium with the discussion will appear in the December Bulletin of the American Academy of Medicine.]

REPORT OF THE COUNCIL ON DR. ELLIS' PAPER.[1]

At the meeting in Washington last year, Dr. H. Bert Ellis read a paper entitled "The Necessity for a National Bureau of Medicine and Foods." The paper was referred to the council by a vote of the Academy with a request that a minute be formulated on the suggestions. Upon this reference, the council reported:

"As to the resolution regarding Dr. Ellis' paper, since the paper is not as yet in the possession of the council, it can make no recommendation on the conclusions themselves. It recommends that the conclusions be referred to the council to report at the next annual meeting."

This recommendation was adopted by the Academy, and, in compliance with this action, this report is submitted to you at this time.

Dr. Ellis' paper was published in the Bulletin for December last, enabling the Fellows to become acquainted with it. The proposition suggests a commission of certification of several diverse classes of products, which may be divided into three groups:

(1) Professedly officinal preparations.
(2) Preparations of vague composition.
(3) Food products.

The point is well taken in the paper that the function of a government commission is to condemn, whence the standard is maintained, under government supervision, by the dread of discovery and its attendant penalties. Dr. Ellis' proposal rather follows the example of a stock exchange, and its listed securities, and there is much that is commendable in the idea, the example cited of certified milk being to the point.

If we could have a commission, able enough to properly decide, of sufficient integrity to be above influence of any kind; judicial enough to be free from prejudice; tactful enough to secure sympathetic cooperation and support, a deal of good could be accomplished by it.

The very extent of the field to be occupied, necessitates the greatest care not alone in the development of the scheme, but

[1] Presented to the Academy, at Atlantic City, June 4, 1904. Dr. Ellis' paper was published in the Bulletin for December, 1903, Vol. VI, p. 486.

more particularly, in the presentation of it, so that its purpose may be easily comprehended, that the arguments, *pro and con*, may not drift into glittering generalities or misapprehensions. It would make it a simpler proposition if food products were omitted because of the difficulty of properly limiting the articles to be certified. The term includes a range of products from triscuits to bovril. Of all classes of manufacturers, none would hail the possibility of a certificate more than the numerous makers of preparations of vague composition—those preparations whose exploiting agents glibly tell the contents, but with equal candor, when pressed for the proportions, admit them to be the secret of the firm. A preparation of this kind, no matter what its vaunted merit, ought to excluded from the attention of the commission, until a full formula is published on the label of the original package. Otherwise, there would be a constant contest between shrewdness and integrity that would make the life of the proper kind of a commission unendurable, and the whole scheme be likely to fail.

Limiting the field of oversight of the commission by these exclusions, what are the possible objections to it?

First—The amount of work required of the commission. Extensive laboratories would be required, engaged in continually examining the preparations certified, which must be purchased at haphazard in the open market; an office with a series of records and no little correspondence must be maintained and a carefully conducted publicity department installed. All this must be under the immediate supervision of the commission itself. It could not be left largely to subordinates, the commission simply signing reports accepted on faith.

A commission of this kind could not command the proper sort of men unless a considerable salary accompanied the appointment, and this apart from the principle so often affirmed by the Academy that physicians should not belittle the value of their services by giving public professional services without adequate compensation.

Secondly—With a fitting salary attached to the office, there is the greater temptation for the self-seeker to make use of his influence to secure an appointment, and thus open the way for members of the commission from among men who would be willing to be retained by the maker of off-standard products. For, be it remembered, were all the manufacturers careful to comply with the standard, there would be no need of certification, and some of the men who do not maintain the standard, err through design, and would stop at little to secure their ends.

Third—The expenses of the commission increase the difficulty because of the only feasible way to secure the money to meet them. The similarity to listed and non-listed stocks has already been mentioned; the parallel can be carried further. The money for the commission must be given by those firms enjoying the privilege of a certification. The employees of the commission would not be greater sinners or weaker than most of mankind, should they be apt to be lenient towards those who were providing them their livelihood.

Hence, notwithstanding the council commends the abstract proposition in Dr. Ellis' paper, it concludes that as at present developed, it is fraught with too many difficulties to be satisfactorily employed, besides being open to possibilities of great abuses.

It recommends that further thought be given to the plan, hoping a thoroughly practical scheme can be worked out, and that in the meantime, the Academy take no action.

DISCUSSION.

Dr. H. Bert Ellis, Los Angeles, Cal.:

I do not see that the council could have reported much differently. A scheme has been figured out by which a committee appointed by the American Medical Association think that this matter can be accomplished without involving in difficulties the national association. There is no question but that something should be done to relieve the busy practitioner, in fact, all practitioners, from the great mass of patent medicines, or proprietary medicines and of inaccurately made drugs or preparations of drugs, and it is incumbent upon somebody to start a movement which will have this end in view. If things are allowed to run as they have been for the last ten years we will be overwhelmed by unknown qualities.

Dr. Leartus Connor, Detroit, Mich.:

With Dr. Ellis' statement of facts I am heartily in accord, but of the proposed methods for practical work I am in doubt. The Michigan State Medical Society at its last meeting, unanimously voted to have its delegates to the House of Delegates of the American Medical Association urge the establishment of a clearing-house for medical products of unknown composition under the direction of its board of trustees. It recognizes the fact that even the very elect are deceived in the tools that they use by the push of commercial houses. As a matter of human nature you will not get much support of a proposition in which the individual is not benefited. So, the Michigan State Medical Society will urge that the board of trustees of the American Medical Association be requested to establish a commission to serve without salary, to establish and maintain laboratories and employ exports to ascertain the composition of unknown medicinal compounds and publish the same in the association journal. The object is to get knowledge, and place it before the profession for its guidance. If such action were taken by this meeting, in good faith, I am sure that a large per cent. of those not in the association would be attracted thereto. This matter should be considered by the American Medical Association, because all the states have larger financial, and other resources than any one, and all are equally walking in darkness. Its adoption of the idea would brighten the pathway, cheer the heart, and secure the cooperation of every one spending his life for truth and fact. Engaged in this work of getting light we would forget a thousand things that interfere with organization.

Dr. Philip Mills Jones, San Francisco, Cal.:

I am very glad indeed to hear Dr. Connor accentuate the value and promise of still greater value to the medical profession of ascertaining plain unadulterated facts. We have had an increasing quantity of fiction year by year until now it is almost a flood. For two years there has been a committee at work appointed to secure any possible means of relief. To this committee was submitted the plan of organizing a bureau for doing this work as it is done in England and France. A number of the committee think that a private corporation would be a good thing; but others think that the matter should be controlled by the two great associations represented in the question, medicine and pharmacy. As I remember the paper of Dr. Ellis, it gave an indefinite outline of the plan proposed, without any details. It would be impossible to enter into the minor details, but one or two questions that have been raised by the council have been considered by our joint committee for a year and a half. In the matter of secrecy, it was agreed that the certificate of incorporation of the proposed bureau should contain the requirement that no preparation having a secret formula could at any time be considered. In the matter of resources and funds, the simile of listed securities is a very good one indeed. About them everything is supposed to be known. That is exactly the conclusion that our committee has come to in the consideration of this matter, that nothing should be handled about which everything is not known. The department of agriculture has gone into these things. Its report on the milk supply was conspicuous in not condemning unsanitary conditions, but in approving the certification of proper dairies, not in driving out the poor thing, but in giving value to that which came up to the requirement. The only practical and feasible method is not to condemn by published statement or inference, but to endorse that thing upon which the profession can rely. The funds for carrying on the work must come from those benefitted by it; but, as any manufacturer in the country may submit a product and have it taken care of if found to comply with the requirements, there can be no question of partiality towards those who pay. The matter of payment would be reduced to a minimum. Some of the large manufacturers say they will not sacrifice the vast amounts of money they have expended in building up the false impression that only the goods of their particular house can be relied upon; others only need to be shown that the work is undertaken in a proper way, when they will welcome it. Our committee is unanimous in believing that a large number of the best manufacturers when such work is undertaken will be glad to welcome it.

The report of the council was adopted on motion.

OBSERVATIONS IN PASSING.
MEDICAL RECIPROCITY AGAIN.

The secretary of the American Confederation of Reciprocating Examining and Licensing Medical Boards in a very courteous manner takes the Bulletin to task for endorsing the resolutions presented by New Jersey to the other Confederation of Medical Examining Boards, which does not have "Reciprocating" in its name, and encloses a reprint of a communication to the *Journal of the American Medical Association* for August 13, 1904.

It is confessed that the words of commendation were written after this article had been read carefully, because the writer did not accept the soundness of some of the conclusions.

That a dozen states are at present "reciprocating" is a matter for congratulation. Whether they are "better" states or not, can only be determined when the states with which they are compared are designated.

This fact does not alter another fact, that certain other states (probably because they are not better states) are not able to enter into this fraternal relation and without any assumption of superiority as the cause for their action. The method suggested by the New Jersey Board is a method which can be accepted by medical boards of the states of every degree of excellence, without interfering with the special conditions of the state law (legislative vagaries often) and at the same time give the applicant for a license the full benefit of his previous examination, if he has passed an examination. By this method the spirit of the state licensure Acts, that each individual desiring to practise in the given state is personally scrutinized, is conserved.

The chief exception to the resolutions is that it does not provide for the licensing of a physician who began practising before the adoption of the state examination Act. The criticism avers that a man who would have secured a right to practise in any state—for example, New York—had he, when he graduated in medicine, taken up his residence in that state, still has the right to enter upon practice, should he now desire to remove from the state where he secured a legal right to practise upon the qualifications come from those benefitted by it; but, as may submit a product and have it taken requirements, there can be no question The matter of payment would be redr manufacturers say they will not s have expended in building up their particular house can be that the work is undertaken Our committee is unanimo manufacturers when such

The report of the

given him without

The man forfeited and he had ample opportunity ...ation of the Act before the law. He now is amenable to are the common rights of those e in that state.

every practiser of twenty years' efforts as when he began. He may not be a the profession, and it is a good thing that Again, it may not be fair to the local pro- ...ger men, to permit them to be crowded by an ...ans from another state, whose only qualification to the licensing body is years of practice.

...ted that it is a hardship to the individual who for ...ons desires to change his residence. To a man who ...ed any standing at all, any removal must be a hardship, must be included with the rest, until such a time when examination may be permitted to physicians with years of ...ence.

...ile there is not only no objection to state exchanging licenses ...e it is possible, but it is positively commendable for them to ...so, the endorsement of license permits a much wider applica- ...on, removing many a hardship from the younger physician especially, who may not have been fortunate in his first selection of a locality, and it is to be hoped that the plan will be accepted, even by those states who are members of the confederation of reciprocating boards, for their dealings with those boards not yet progressive enough to join with them in the reciprocating idea.

∗

We are pleased to see that Dr. L. Duncan Bulkley plans to give his sixth series of clinical lectures on "Diseases of the Skin" in the outpatient hall of the New York Skin and Cancer Hospital, Corner Second Avenue and 19th Street, New York. The lectures will be held Wednesday afternoons at 4.15 o'clock, beginning on November 2nd. The course is free to the medical professions and Dr. Bulkley will be pleased to have any of our readers visiting

**

...Co. are planning an historical exhibi-
... objects relating to medicine, chemistry,
...lied sciences, in London in the near future.
...ed to have objects of the sort loaned to them.
...rm will secure particulars.

LITERATURE NOTES.

...L OF PHYSIOLOGICAL AND CLINICAL CHEMISTRY. BY ELIAS H. BARTLEY, B.S., M.D., PhG., Professor of Chemistry, Toxicology and Pediatrics in the Long Island College Hospital. Second Edition. Revised and enlarged, with 47 illustrations. Philadelphia: P. Blakiston's Son & Co. 1904. pp. 188. Price, $1.00 net.

The author in his preface gives a definition of a medical school, which, if adopted, would assist in the discussion of many problems relating to medical education, especially those pertaining to preliminary training. He defines it:

"A medical college is a technical school for the training of young men or women in the science of the prevention or the diagnosis and treatment of disease."

And he deduces from this definition:

"The chemical teaching should, therefore, be directed to this purpose, and should consist in teaching the fundamental principles and the application of these principles to the science of medicine, especially to the diagnoses and treatment of diseased conditions."

The author carries out the plan very nicely. After a few exercises in experimental physiologic chemistry, he treats in turn of the chemistry of the blood, the urine, the gastric contents, the feces and of milk—gives methods for analysis, and enough information of the clinical significance to join the information with that given in the text-books on other subjects. It is not captious criticism that suggests a revision of the page headings in a new edition. Thus at the top of one page is to be found "Diagnosis of Renal Diseases," followed on succeeding pages by "Carbohydrates," when the pages themselves are devoted to the determination of carbohydrates in urine, and not to a discussion of their clinical chemistry.

IN THE YEAR 1800—BEING THE RELATION OF SUNDRY EVENTS OCCURRING IN THE LIFE OF DOCTOR JONATHAN BRUSH DURING THAT YEAR. BY SAMUEL WALTER KELLEY, M.D. 1904. Saalfeld Publishing Company, Akron, O. pp. 421. Price, $2.50.

This is the third volume of the doctor's recreation series, and to our mind is of far more interest and value than either volume previously issued. Dr. Kelley is to be congratulated if this be his maiden effort in the field of fiction. It is an historic novel, wherein the medical thought and medical action of the time is very cleverly wrought into an interesting story. We will not spoil the tale by attempting a synopsis of it here.

THE URINE AND CLINICAL CHEMISTRY OF THE GASTRIC CONTENTS, THE COMMON POISONS AND MILK. BY J. W. HOLLAND, M.D., Professor of Medical Chemistry and Toxicology, Jefferson Medical College, Philadelphia. Forty-one illustrations. Seventh edition, revised and enlarged. Philadelphia: P. Blakiston's Son & Co. 1904. pp. 172. Price, $1.00 net.

This volume is prepared for the use of medical students, its size will permit it to be carried in the coat pocket, it opens on end and is printed on one side only, making it convenient to take notes. The book is admirably adapted for its purpose. The descriptions of processes are clear and easily followed, its tests are selected with judgment, and the teachings evolved from the results sane and sound.

THE SIXTH ANNUAL REPORT OF THE INDIANA STATE BOARD OF MEDICAL REGISTRATION AND EXAMINATION FOR THE YEAR ENDING DECEMBER 31, 1903. State Printer, Indianapolis. 1904. pp. 271.

This report gives the Indiana medical law as now in force; colleges not recognized, rules of the board, minimum requirements for colleges to be recognized, duties of county clerks, the financial report, examination questions, the rules for reciprocity, results of the examinations, synopsis of medical licensing laws in the United States, and a list of the licensed physicians in Indiana.

BULLETIN

OF THE

American Academy of Medicine

VOL. VI.   ISSUED DECEMBER, 1904.   NO. 15.

The American Academy of Medicine is not responsible for the sentiments expressed in any paper or address published in the BULLETIN.

THE CORRESPONDENCE METHOD OF TREATING DISEASE.[1]

BY F. T. ROGERS, M.D., Providence, R. I.

That imitation is the sincerest flattery none need question and, were proof needed, a glance at the advertising pages of any of the current monthlies would suffice to show that, whoever may have been the originator of the scheme to treat diseases by correspondence, he has scores of imitators.

If there was not profit in it there would not be ten of these advertising fakirs where a few years ago there was but one, if there was not a good profit in it they could not afford to pay the current advertising rates in some of the mediums used, and of the value of advertising in creating and maintaining a market for any product nothing need be said. We are all familiar with the phenomenal financial success of certain large advertisers and read with a certain amount of awe of the enormous sums which they yearly devote to the exploitation of their wares, so that, granting that there are men shrewd enough to profit by these successes and the probabilities of large pecuniary returns, there is needed to make the scheme feasible merely a medium to reach the people and a gullible public.

Fortunately for these quacks the medium is found in every newspaper, periodical and monthly published; even those editors who decry most loudly other impositions on the public and who

[1] Read before the American Academy of Medicine, Atlantic City, June 6, 1904.

pride themselves upon the purity of their pages apparently welcome these frauds who have no saving grace beyond possibly a promptness in paying their bills, and unfortunately the gullible public is ready for them. The more improbable their claims, the more eager are they to avail themselves of the offer.

For some years I have read these advertisements with interest, have admired the display of knowledge of the frailties of human nature exhibited by their authors and marveled that such sweeping statements regarding the nature of disease and its cure could find credence in the mind of any one save the ignorant, and have wondered just how these fakirs proceeded to profit by their scheme which was apparently so fair and so free.

So I was afflicted with various disorders and, seeking help, I wrote to many of these quacks and was overwhelmed with shame that I was such an easy mark, for their scheme is simplicity itself and owes its success to that one factor. I learned some things I did not know before, however, and I have been prompted to report my findings to this body because here, to my mind, lies the remedy and I ask your indulgence to a recital of a few facts and a suggestion, not to a mass of platitudes or of theories regarding what I believe to be a great public evil.

The method of one is essentially the method of all and I can describe it no better than to report to you how I was cured of baldness.

This advertisement appeared in a monthly which makes great claims for the purity of its pages and the responsibility of its advertisers.

"FALLING HAIR AND BALDNESS can be relieved. *There is one way to tell* the reason of baldness and falling hair, and that is by a microscopic examination of the hair itself. The particular disease with which your scalp is afflicted must be known before it can be intelligently treated.

"Send a few fallen hairs from your combings to Prof. ———, the celebrated bacteriologist, and he will send you absolutely free a diagnosis of your case, a booklet on the care of the hair and scalp, and a sample box of the remedy which he will prepare for you."

This letter was sent: "My hair is very thin and when it gets just so long it falls out. I saw your advertisement in the ——— *Magazine* and I send you some of the hairs. Please send me some of your medicine and tell me what is the matter."

To be sure that the sample of hair sent could by no means offer a suggestion of such a disorder I took a long hair from a young lady who has an abundant growth and cut it into lengths of a half-inch, then I added a few short hairs pulled from the back of my daughter's terrier on whom no suspicion of baldness rests, and this was what I received:

DIAGNOSIS NO. 45612.
Be sure to give this number in ordering.

Diagnosis of Hair.
Microscopic examination made by J. H. A.
Revelations—Ulcerated Root Sheath.
Fall of hair—Progressive.
Stage of hair—Diseased Roots.
Disease—Folliculitis.
Curable or not? Yes.
Cost of full course of treatment for this case, $2.50.
Estimated term of treatment—three months.

And this letter:

"*Dear Sir:* Your favor with enclosure of hair at hand. A careful microscopic examination has revealed the fact that the disease of which you complain is due to Folliculitis—that is an inflammation of the hair Follicle. This disease is caused by a parasite (or Bacilli) that first attacks the sebaceous glands which furnish the lubricant or oil for the hair. These glands are soon destroyed and the inflammation rapidly extends to the inner membrane lining of the hair Follicle where small quantities of pus are secreted which destroy the hair bulb, causing the hair to slip from the collapsing walls of its Follicle.

"The microscopic revelations in your case indicate that the disease in its present stage will soon yield to treatment, and will result in a renewed growth of strong and healthy hair.

"I prescribe the following course of treatment for your case: First wash the hair and scalp with pure imported German Shampoo which is included in the treatment—directions will be found on the box when you receive it. Then rub the Treatment which I will prepare for your case into the roots of the hair every other day. Massage your scalp well with the tips of your fingers the day following the use of the Treatment which is perfectly harmless. I enclose herewith a small box of a preparation which you should rub into the roots of your hair until you receive the full course of treatment. This will prepare the roots of your hair for the Treatment. With my scientific Treatment specially prepared for each individual case, in my laboratory,

I guarantee to stop falling hair, grow new hair where the diseased hair has fallen no matter how long standing the disease has been. Dandruff disappears in ten days after my treatment is begun. No more itching or irritated scalp after the first few applications of my remedy. One full Course of Treatment will last you for three months and grow new hair an inch a month.

"Awaiting your reply, I am
Very truly yours,
——————."

The sample to be used every other day till the full treatment was received was a small tin box one-half inch in diameter and of the thickness of a postage stamp, containing an ointment sufficient in quantity to cover thinly a ten-cent piece.

A letter written by a friend in another city described his trouble as follows: "I have been bald for years, only a few straggling hairs showing which are apparently healthy and grow to a considerable length. What is the matter?"

The diagnosis, letter and treatment were identical.

No reply was made and in a few weeks came letter No. 2:

"*Dear Sir:* A short time since, at your special request, I made a scientific microscopic examination of the hair I received from you and sent you a small box of a preparation to use until you should receive the full course. If you have used it you well know how much it has improved the condition of your scalp. My records show that your case will result seriously providing a Full Course of my Treatment is not commenced at once. I sincerely trust that you realize how important this matter is to you, providing you desire a perfectly healthy scalp and vigorous hair. You no doubt know that the sample sent you was not enough to effect a permanent cure, although you may have noticed great improvement in the condition of your hair. My treatment never fails. Faithful application according to directions sent with each course of treatment, will completely eradicate dandruff, stop falling hair and grow new hair.

"If your case is not attended to at once serious results will certainly follow and you will become partially or totally bald. Prevention is better than a cure and you should begin your treatment at once. I am, as a professional man, interested in your case, and have decided to offer you my full $2.50 Course of Treatment for $2.00, transportation charges paid, including a box of German Shampoo. This special offer is so low that it will at once appeal to you.

"I made this offer because I realize that with your influence in your neighborhood you can do me, as well as your friends who may be afflicted with dandruff, falling hair or any disease of the scalp, the greatest service by telling them what the Treatment has done in your case.

"With my scientific Treatment specially prepared for each individual case in my own laboratory, I guarantee to stop falling hair, grow new hair where the diseased hair has fallen, on any head no matter how long standing the disease has been, and no matter how bald the head has become. I guarantee you a cure no matter what remedies you have used without result. The basis of my remedy is a powder extracted by burning coal with lime by my own secret process, and this is the only remedy known to medical science that will produce the desired results. That is why physicians who do not know of my remedy are apt to think baldness is incurable. One full course of treatment will last you for three months, and cure every ordinary disease of the scalp, and will grow new hair about an inch a month.

"Send $2.00 at your earliest convenience, so that the good already accomplished by the sample sent you may not be entirely lost, and I will send you my Full $2.50 Course of Treatment, transportation charges paid.

"P. S.—When you order please state for my convenience that your diagnosis number can be found in book 436."

Pray notice several points of an artist in this scheme, *i.e.*, an apparent scientific diagnosis appealing strongly to the average man, the number appended, 45612, and the record book 436 showing the large number of patients, the flattery of an appeal to a neighborhood influence and the warning of serious and incurable trouble. I was for a moment actually worried for fear I was getting bald although second thought convinced me that if the eminent bacteriologist had even looked at the hair sent he would have found no hair bulbs at all save those from the dog and he is not worrying.

It is, however, in the domain of general medicine that these artistic advertising liars are seen to the best advantage. It is so easy to magnify common and unimportant symptoms into evidences of serious disease, so easy to frighten by word pictures of impending consumption, insanity and death the poor invalid who does not get well under the care of a physician (and there are such) that the field of operation is greatly enlarged.

An extensive advertiser who claims to be a "Specialist in Diseases of Men (sealed) and Women, for Dyspepsia, Rheumatism and Diseases of the Heart and Kidneys," caters to the failing of most people who are always eager to get something for nothing by offering to furnish advice and medicine free.

"LEARN HOW TO GET WELL. My Book will tell you how to get well at my risk. Tell me in strictest confidence about your ailment. I will advise you. I will tell you of a druggist near you who will let you have six bottles of Dr. ———'s Restorative,

A Month At My Risk. If I succeed you pay $5.50. If you say to the druggist 'it did not help me' he will bill the cost to me. I will tell him to do so."

Two letters were sent to this man from different addresses. In one I said: "Can you cure me of heart disease and dropsy. The doctors say I can't get well. Please send me your book and an order for medicine." In another a request was made for medicine to cure ulcer of the stomach with vomiting of blood.

A stereotyped reply was received to each and no distinction was made between the two cases. He says:

"I enclose you herewith my special pamphlet and the first few pages in it will fully explain my guarantee.

"On the back of this pamphlet I have written the names of the nearest dealers who issue these warrants, and I have to-day written each of these dealers, authorizing them to furnish you the medicine on my offer of a month's treatment at my risk. Bear in mind, please, that in writing the druggist my only motive was to secure for you every accommodation or privilege that is given to any one. I positively never even hint to the dealer anything concerning the nature of the ailment about which a patient writes me. This is something I always hold as strictly confidential.

"I have given your dealer my agreement that if this month's test should fail I will pay him for the medicine you take. Your deposit will be entirely returned to you. Your dealer will see that the treatment I advise shall not cost you a penny if you think it does not reach your case.

"Your case should not be exceptionally difficult. I firmly believe that desirable results will come if you will be fair to yourself. Read carefully, please, pages one and two of my booklet. I want you to understand what I have accomplished in finding and strengthening these weak nerves. I labored long and hard for this. Do not expect results with impossible quickness, however, but in justice to yourself be reasonable. Difficulties may, of necessity, mean some delay, but there is not an average of one case in forty which will not yield to this treatment. And there are few of these troubles that can be permanently cured without any treatment, which alone reaches these controlling nerves.

"I cannot better show my unbounded confidence than I do by assuming the entire risk. No other physician has ever done that, in chronic diseases, with any other remedy in the history of medicine. I do this because I have learned in a lifetime's experience what this treatment can do, while those who suffer know nothing about it. I wish to make the arrangement so fair that none who need it can reasonably neglect it.

"If you desire any special advice after commencing the treatment, please command me. Should you have any difficulty in securing the remedy on the terms I have offered, please write me at once, and I will see that you get it in some way.

"I am glad to learn of your case and I fully believe that within a few weeks you will be very glad that this matter was presented to you."

One would think from the advertisement that the medicine was to be free, but such is not the case. You are requested to buy the medicine, and if after you have taken three bottles you have not received benefit your money will be returned to you. A so-called warrant is attached, but really amounts to nothing, and with the proverbially easy-going nature of the public, the occasional request for the return of the price is probably complied with, but as a rule the patient realizes that he has been buncoed, and keeps silent.

If no attention is paid to this letter there soon comes letter No. 2:

"*Dear Sir*. Receiving no reply to my letters, I judge that you have decided not to take my treatment at present. The decision is unfortunate, but I am sure you will eventually change it. If you are ever to receive a permanent cure, you will find, I think, that it will come in the way I propose.

"Whatever other medicines you test, there is none which will be offered you, as mine is, on a guarantee signed by your dealer. You must take the risk yourself. And the longer you continue unsuccessful treatments, the better you will appreciate what I tell you. Common treatment can't cure such cases; and relief, if it comes, doesn't usually last long.

"Whatever other experiments you make, remember that I have made them before you. You could not in a century make so many tests as I have, for you have but one case to treat, while I have had thousands. For such cases there is nothing known to medicine which I have left untried.

"If you could know me personally you would accept and believe what I tell you. You would hardly go on spending time and money on treatments which I have already proved ineffective. But your own experiments will eventually prove to you that I am right; and when you reach that conclusion my offer will still be open to you. I am ready at any time to grant you the fullest privilege of my guarantee. Your dealer will at any time sign the agreement. The risk shall be entirely mine; the benefit yours.

"Many, many sick people accept this offer of mine every week, and an average of thirty-nine in forty are cured! You will in time hear of these in your own vicinity, and you will then think more seriously of what I have said.

"Above everything, don't become discouraged, for a way to cure is open when you are ready for it. I tell you positively, after a lifetime of experience, that your case is curable, and my remedy will cure it. And I fully believe that you can find no other way so satisfactory, so safe."

Again a third attempt is made to get your money by letter No. 3, with which is enclosed a directed postal card. In it he says:

"*Dear Sir:* I wish to ask if you have secured the prescription about which you wrote me the other day; and if you have started the treatment. I keep a careful record of my patients, and watch the progress of each case by keeping in touch with them. To this end, I shall esteem it a favor if you will let me know if the treatment is started. Or if you have met with any difficulties in obtaining the remedy under the guarantee that I offered. Please let me know that.

"I find little difficulty in curing the diseases I treat. The failures are so rare that I feel almost certain of a cure when once the treatment is begun. But there is a difficulty in securing the confidence of those who need help; those who have been so often disappointed, and perhaps deceived, that faith is lost in everything. Even with my guarantee—my agreement, signed by the patient's own dealer—that the treatment shall be free if it fails, I find that some who need the treatment most still hesitate.

"Is this the case with you? If so, won't you be frank enough to tell me why you hesitate? Can you think of any way in which I could make this opportunity more fair?

"Suppose it was a friend who suffered; and a physician went to him and said: 'Here is my prescription which I have spent a lifetime in getting right. With it I have cured perhaps a quarter million cases like yours. I have so much confidence in it that I have told your dealer to let you take it thirty days at my risk, and I have given him my agreement that if it fails I will pay for it.'

"Would you not think your sick friend both reckless and unwise if he neglected such an offer? You would ask how he hoped to get well, and to what else he could turn. Don't you think that some friend who knew of this offer would feel the same about you?

"Now that you have kindly written me, I wish to exert every effort to cure you. For this reason I enclose you a self-addressed postal, and ask you to please let me know if you have obtained the treatment; and, if not, will you let me know why?"

In self-preservation the medical profession should rise *en masse* and overthrow this man who so annihilates disease and cures incurables or else our occupation will soon be gone.

With slight variations in detail with varying expression and delicacy of touch this theme is played by the hundreds of fakirs who thrive on American credulity. From scores of letters I learn that the methods are the same. They are all imitators of some pioneer who has achieved greatness.

Yet occasionally there comes a variation which is the evidence of genius. Most of the letters plainly show that they are a stereotyped form, the name of the inquirer being in type but a Chicago dissolver of cataracts has left spaces where the name can be inserted so deftly that you flatter yourself that it is a personal letter you are receiving.

"I hope you did not write out of mere curiosity, Mr. Rogers," he writes, "for I have never failed in making a permanent cure with my new Dissolvent Method when any sight remained," and this in reply to a query whether he could cure complete blindness from optic atrophy of a year's standing.

Sharpers do not try to sell a gold brick twice to the same person and these men of the same ilk do not hope to get more than the first advance from the hopeless cases but in this great country the supply is practically unlimited and, as some one has truthfully and coarsely stated, "a sucker is born every minute."

Perhaps the most novel exponent of this method is the man who promises to make you taller by several inches by means of a specially devised instrument which changes the cartilages in the body besides several other desirable things, but the gist of the whole matter is $10. You are requested to pay for a cheap exerciser an exorbitant price, expecting an impossible result.

So did time permit I could relate dozens of experiences with similar quacks and frauds but they are all alike. If you believe their claims you can be cured of all the ailments flesh is heir to, you can if blind be made to see, if deaf be made to hear, you can be accurately fitted to glasses to correct ametropia, you can remedy all bodily deformities and grow as tall as you would like.

Some of the claims are so monstrous, so palpably absurd, that it is a wonder that any one can be found to give credence to them. Says one: "There are two sets of nerves in the body, the outside nerves and the inside nerves." "Ninety-nine per cent. of all disease is functional. Organic disease is rare." "Cross-eyes can be cured in two minutes without pain or operation. Cataracts can be absorbed. Spectacles are never needed." Electricity applied to the kneejoint will increase the height an inch. Cartilage is half bone and half muscle." And so on *ad infinitum*.

The claims of these men are substantiated by testimonials from grateful patients. Some of them are undoubtedly honest in their statements but are mistaken in their condition. More are given without due consideration of the subject because asked to do so and because they like to see their names in print, but most of them are absolute fabrications. I have written to them, I have written to physicians residing in their locality, I have personally investigated some near at home and I believe unqualifiedly that they may be classed either as the statement of one who is ignorant of his exact condition both before and after the so-called treatment, they are a bid for some commissions from these quacks for sending new patients (for they make tempting offers for new victims), or they are fictitious.

I have personally seen those who have been cured of cataract who never had cataract, those who have been cured of epilepsy who have attacks of grand mal every six weeks and petit mal almost daily. I know of an instance where a patient gave a testimonial stating how she had been cured of Bright's disease who died in coma before the testimonial was printed, of a man who was cured of nephritis and albuminuric retinitis yet who was totally blind before he succumbed to the disease. I know personally of a false statement as to facts made in the hopes of inducing others to take the treatment for the sake of the commission offered.

Of the third class it needs but a glance to detect the fraud. In a circular before me I find testimonials from people residing in Afton, Indian Territory; New York, Iowa; Steeles, Louisiana: Turon, Kansas; Ulm, Minnesota; Taylor, North Dakota. Find these places on the map or in any atlas. Investigate the congressman for the fourteenth district, whose picture adorns the front page of the newspaper. He is either a mythical personage or his name is spelled wrongly or his address erroneous. A loophole is usually left for curious investigators, but the perpetrators bank on the proverbial disinclination to such action and believe that most inquirers will assume the truthfulness of the testimonial without further questioning.

This evil has extended to the real purveyors to the profession and manufacturing pharmacists who cater to the trade of physicians, looking with envious eyes upon the apparent success of quacks, have begun to advertise their wares as cure-alls for various ailments while still soliciting the physician to prescribe their preparations. The May number of *Harper's*, *McClure's* and *Pearson's* contain the advertisements of thirty of those quacks and of formerly reputable houses exploiting the virtues of some particular preparation. Has the profession no pride that it continues to patronize manufacturers who thus violate all proprieties? Yet I have seen on the prescription books of druggists in my city prescriptions written by educated physicians, members of state and national societies calling for Peruna, Green's Nervura, Hood's Sarsaparilla and Scott's Emulsion. I wondered that any of the laity could believe the absurd claims yet in a recent open letter to the medical profession regarding a pharmaceutical product there occurs this absurd statement:

"It is a scientific compounding of enzymes by methods which unite them into a complex element in which vitality is preserved and is restored in the circulation. It is representative of an 'internal secretion' possessing great vitalizing properties, acting especially upon the physiological function of metabolism and cell osmosis. It also has the property of restoring the balance between supply and waste; of transforming the toxic waste to harmless excretory products, and in a large proportion of systemic defects this means removal of cause. It restores the resistant elements of the blood, which creates immunity and destroys infection. Briefly stated, it does therapeutically what no remedy or method of treatment has done hitherto."

And this bids for patronage:

"Physicians will appreciate our good-will in the new label on the packages to be issued hereafter. The proprietary label is not adhered, but can be instantly removed, leaving a blank prescription label for the directions of the physician. There will be nothing on the bottle to identify it, aside from the prescriber's signature. This is only another proof of our expressed purpose to protect physicians from counter-prescribing, and an earnest of our good-will."

Probably this bombastic and meaningless conglomeration of English words finds among the profession some who are impressed by it and who use the product, knowing as little of its nature as the proprietor itself.

It is asked what harm is done save to exemplify the adage that a fool and his money is soon parted. Talk with your brother practitioners. Recall your own cases of consumptives grasping at a forlorn hope and by some nostrums so checking secretion and disturbing nutrition that all possible gain from good food and fresh air is denied them; of cases of metrorrhagia at the menopause under uterine tonics till carcinoma of the uterus is too advanced for relief; of the young who absorb enough rot about loss of vitality and shrunken parts to render them neurasthenic and subject to all sorts of imaginary ailments; of the blind who, buoyed by false hopes, have allowed glaucoma to progress till hopeless; of the thousands who seek their alcoholic stimulants and narcotics in the much vaunted patent medicines, and then tell me if this is not a real evil, if it is not a task imposed on us as medical men and honest men to do all in our power to correct it.

Reputable periodicals should not admit to their columns such stuff, the mails should not be the medium by which it is spread broadcast and I believe the remedy lies in one word—Publicity. Educate our patients to the foolishness of such claims, publicly denounce the methods employed, criticize unsparingly the editor who for a few dollars plays a part in this shameful proceeding and by word, pen and example flay at every opportunity these monsters, who by false pretenses and absurd promises are a menace to public welfare.

DISCUSSION.

Dr. Augustus Ravogli, Cincinnati:

I agree with the opinion of the essayist that quacks and advertisers are the ruin of a great many patients, but in the present condition the law cannot easily be reached. I am a member of the State Board of Medical Examiners of Ohio. I have prosecuted over forty and have obtained sentence in nearly every case. A great many, however, are out of reach, because they do not prescribe but only sell a patented medicine. I believe that the legislature ought to enact a law forbidding the sale of medicines without the prescription of a regular physician. I believe that a law of this kind will be exceedingly useful to diminish these advertised medicines.

Another point is that there are some who are regularly recognized as doctors and have their license, that keep several institutions in different cities. A patient is met by an attendant in the office who says, he is the doctor's assistant and will submit the case to the professor who is performing an operation. In this way they deceive the public and avoid the law. We need to have a stringent law to stop this deception, or we must have patience until we can obtain through severe examinations the elimination of this pest of the medical profession and of the public in general.

Dr. G. T. Swartz, of Providence:

I think that what the gentleman has said regarding the law in this connection is very true. As secretary of the Board of Registration of Rhode Island, in attempting to prosecute people, I have found certain parties utilizing the post-office to obtain fees in this way. A lady would call at the post-office and collect the contributions, from her private box, then repair to the money order department and have the coupons cashed. She then would immediately take a train to another city, making it impossible to prove that she was practising in Rhode Island. Her advertisement would be in the daily papers, and her post-office address in our city, but she could not be proved to have opened an office in the state. I have interested the postal authorities hoping to obtain some assistance, but they found that they were unable to prosecute inasmuch as she returned a certain equivalent for the money given. I do not see how to solve this problem.

Dr. Beach, of Binghampton, N. Y.:

I would like to say in regard to this paper that I know of a very successful manufacturer of patent medicine who has become police commissioner. Since entering upon this position, testimonials have been published by his chief of police and some of his subordinates to the effect that they have been cured by this patent medicine of kidney diseases and other troubles.

THE RELATION OF PHYSICIANS TO DENTISTS AND PHARMACISTS.[1]

IV.

ETHICAL PHARMACY.[2]

By A. L. Benedict, A.M., M.D., Buffalo.

The typic city drug store represents a bizarre combination of businesses. It is usually a public telephone station, often a branch post-office, express office, place to pay gas bills, sometimes a branch circulating library and laundry. One can buy candy, hair brushes, tooth brushes, soap, valentines, knives, and various other articles of merchandise, tobacco, soda water and other soft drinks, and occasionally, strong liquors as beverages. At some stores, one can even obtain a light lunch, at others, pet animals, gold fish, etc. In short, if you want anything and do not know exactly where to seek it, it is a good rule to ask at the drug store. There is no particular ethical objection to the drug store serving as a miscellaneous caterer to the wants of the public although the physician, who is wont to take his medical equipment rather seriously and exclusively, never quite recovers from the incongruity of such signs as "prescription counter in the rear," "prescriptions a specialty," etc. It certainly would surprise the public if, after our name on a sign, we displayed some such notice as this: "A specialty made of attending to patients."

However, the public is not allowed to forget that the drug store exists for the purpose of selling remedial agents. More or less startling and often life-size display cards remind us of the virtues of plasters "which feel good on the back," and which serve partially to hide the charms of ladies and gentlemen in undress. Menstrual pads make an attractive window dressing especially, if flanked with an illustrated reminder of tablets which work while we sleep and break the monotony of a night's rest in a sleeping car. Gigantic green frogs amuse the children and remind adults of the frog in their throats, while vaginal syringes are instructive to the young and afford a subject for thought on the part of the statistician who is interested in our falling birth-rate. A

[1] Continuation of the Symposium from the October number.
[2] Read before the American Academy of Medicine, Atlantic City, N. J., June 4, 1904.

paste-board trained nurse can be made to advertise pretty nearly anything and, if she can do some automatic feats with an atomizer or a sprinkler, she is doubly charming.

On entering the store, we find that the front shelves and, indeed, sometimes all that are visible, between the soda fountain and the prescription department, are devoted to an object lesson in the uselessness of our own profession. It even seems strange that there should be a prescription department at all, when all the ills to which humanity is heir, can be relieved by the purchase of the appropriate remedy, neatly and not very expensively compounded and with explicit directions for the guidance of patients, either on the label or included with valuable information as to the sun, moon, and stars, or a complete joke book or collection of popular songs.

However, the patient who runs this gauntlet of proprietary medicines and who escapes the druggist's own advice as to headaches, rheumatism, bronchitis, etc., is welcome to present his prescription at the desk and, if we have been careful to avoid the metric system and have limited ourselves to cod-liver oil, calomel and tincture of opium and similar staples, he can get it filled with slight risk of error and with reasonable promptness. If however, we have written for some such troublesome preparation as oil of phosphorus, or bromin, or for some new drug not yet in constant demand, the patient may have to wait till it is sent for and, unless, one practises in New York, Philadelphia, Chicago and a very few other centers of trade, several days may elapse before the order is filled.

Why, as a profession, do we endure all this from a profession which is avowedly, a specialization of our own, for the purpose of supplying medicines and medical appliances? Because, in the first place, we cannot help ourselves and because, secondly, in the majority of instances, the druggist is, at heart, not only a good fellow but an intelligent and conscientious man who can not help himself either but is hampered by all sorts of customs, who is under the screws of wholesale dealers of all shades of respectability and who is subject to the same, if not greater, competition in an overcrowded profession, which we realize in our own experience.

If the druggist did not sell stamps, soda water, hair brushes and act as agent for the gas company, the express companies, the telephone company, the laundry, and even for Uncle Sam's post-office, his store would fail in popularity. We can have no reasonable objection to the sale of soap and tooth powder. It is only a step to porous plasters and antiseptics, and only another step to headache powders, liniments, cough syrups and cathartics. The patient will not, under existing conditions, take our prescriptions to a man who will not sell him his own selection of drugs and aid him in that selection. Many druggists are courteous enough to look embarrassed when we happen to be in the store to see if he can fill a prescription for something a little out of the ordinary, and a man comes in and announces that he wants something for his liver or to take to his little boy with croup. Some have become so accustomed to such occurrences that they overlook even this deference to our suppositious function and privilege.

I am convinced that the druggist can not help himself out of his present predicament, without the initiative of the medical profession. Some druggists want this assistance, some do not. Some openly declare that they do not care to bother with prescriptions. One man, of whom I know personally, issues cards of this form with every prescription. "This prescription is a valuable formula for ———. Yourself or any of your friends can get it on payment of ———." Thus, every physician whose prescription reaches this store, becomes the originator of a quack medicine, without any of the emoluments of quackery. On the other hand, there are pharmacists of good standing, who are not adapted to teaching positions, who cannot write text-books or secure official appointments of one kind or another, who love their chosen profession and who are practically debarred from practice unless they submit not only to an irksome commercialism, but to methods that they recognize as unethical and, potentially, at least, as dishonorable and murderous.

The solution of the whole problem is perfectly simple in theory, and it has been carried into practice with some degree of success in occasional instances. Find a pharmacist who is qualified in his profession, who wishes not only to make a specialty of prescription-compounding, but who will limit himself to such work.

Having found one such man in a city, apply exactly the same rule to him and his competitors that should be applied to the genuine and to the fake specialist in any other line of medical subdivision. If the ophthalmologist, laryngologist, or neurologist is posing as a specialist and, at the same time, competing with the general practitioner in his own legitimate field, while some other specialist is doing honest work in his specialty, the responsibility rests with the general profession, for no specialist can succeed with a double-barreled gun if the general practitioners refuse to start the game for him. In the case of the druggist, the offense against the ordinary laws of specialism is even more flagrant, for the druggist is neither competent nor legally qualified to compete with the medical profession.

A study of the directory of any city will show that there is one drug store to every five to ten physicians. Many of these stores have a force of five or more pharmacists, few have less than two, including advanced students. It is absurd to suppose that the legitimate profits on prescriptions, even including the earnings and profits on agencies, soda water, etc., can support any such ratio of pharmacists. The bulk of the support of the so-called pharmacal profession is the patent medicine business and the illegal practice of medicine. Curiously enough, my personal experience has been that the very men who are interested in pharmacal education, who are officially represented with our own profession in the codification of drugs and who make the best speeches as to the dignity of the profession of pharmacy, have been the most flagrant violators of the principles of ethics and have made the most glaring mistakes in the practice of their profession. Understand me, however, to refer merely to isolated examples and to make no general charge against either the profession of pharmacy in general or its most representative portion.

The solution of the problem proposed must, if successfully carried out, involve a marked diminution in the numbers of pharmacists in good standing, and a practical separation of the pharmacist as a professional man from the soda water, agency-conducting, retail quack and counter-dispensing business man. Such separations are always wholesome. We can fight or ignore quackery and illegal practice. In the long run, it makes more work for the regular profession than it removes by competition and while it is our obvious duty to combat it in the interests of the community, we are not called upon to place ourselves in a false light and reduce our influence for good, by unwise attempts at interfering with a too powerful influence.

While there is no particular objection to the various, extra-medical side lines carried on in the average drug store, it is obvious that, unless some druggist already in business, were willing to eliminate from his store the entire middle portion and the show window, it would be practically impossible to continue them. The only ethical pharmacy on a practical working basis that I have ever actually seen, consisted of a comparatively small room in a medical office building. There was no pretense at catching custom by attractive displays and the drug stock itself was not imposing but I was assured that it contained almost everything prescribable by a man in regular practice, including most of the newer chemicals and the really valuable, ethical proprietary preparations. It was supported by about twenty physicians, and prescriptions were filled not only well but comparatively cheaply, and to the satisfaction of the intelligent laity. Presumably, other druggists did not like it but, if not, they had every freedom of competing on the same basis.

Some question may be asked as to the business relations of physicians to such a pharmacy. My own idea is that there should be none, further than the informal understanding that the physicians should, so far as possible, send their prescriptions to the man who refrains from extra-professional and unprofessional drug business and also, so far as possible, keep them from passing into the hands of druggists competing on present methods. It may be objected that such a course will lead to the suspicion of interested motives. Undoubtedly, this suspicion will arise as it does under existing circumstances and, I am informed, with ample basis of truth in some instances. Druggists, on whose word I can rely, have stated that they have been practically forced to pay commissions although one cannot respect the stamina of a druggist who would yield to such a demand much more than the integrity of the physician who would make it. However, the charge of dishonorable motives is readily met in any particular case and as the language appropriate in such an emergency would not be appropriate to this occasion, it is unnecessary to enter into details.

V.
SCIENCE vs. SHEKELS.[1]
By Charles McIntire, A.M., M.D., Easton, Pa.

Science would have rather a sorry time of it without shekels. Harnessed together, they can make a very fair team. It is best to have them tandem, with science leading. But, when a choice must be made—either science or shekels—then there is a very imminent possibility of the mischief to play. To most men the choice comes sooner or later and, while the method of its coming is seldom twice alike in its details, upon broad lines they are surprisingly similar.

This contest between science and shekels is one of the greatest stumbling blocks in the way of the proper relation between the physician and the pharmacist. This paper will attempt to call attention to a few conditions where the physician fails.

We must always remember the uncertainty of medicine. Few would dare to apply the mathematical reasoning ascribed to a medieval physician who was sure he could cure the Duke who was ill with an ailment that puzzled his medical attendants. "Ninety and nine out of every hundred afflicted with this disease die," said he. "The Duke will be my hundredth case; the rest have all died." To every practiser, at one time or another, comes a patient with a condition that, in its essence, is uncertain, with the resulting necessity either of confessing ignorance, or of temporizing, whence an ancient direction to medical students: "Treat the symptoms as they arise." It is possible that temporizing may be a wise procedure in some instances; that is not the question before us now. This particular problem comes more frequently in proportion to the lack of technical ability on the part of the physician. Because of this, from the earliest times, there has been dependence upon famous recipes, such remedies as have come down to us in the synonyms that Prof. Remington has discussed. Recall the special formulae—secret preparations frequently—that have worked their way into professional favor. These are used, sometimes to veil ignorance, sometimes to cater to one's ease—since it expends less thought energy to employ a ready-to-use remedy.

[1] Read before the American Academy of Medicine, Atlantic City, N. J., June 4, 1904.

It is playing upon this trait of the physician's character that causes our reception rooms to be visited by gentlemanly-enough fellows, representatives of This, That & Co., ready-to-use medicine-makers, who have a full line to suit the ills of flesh, being able to fit the short and stout as well as the tall and slim with some remedy in their stock. Or, possibly, a new garment auto-adjustable to nearly every shape and size is offered. It permits the sending to our offices circulars (probably better tracts on medical ethics) advising us of the wonderful curative properties of some happy combination under a name coined by a wondrous imagination. A London surgeon of a statistical turn made a record of a year's collection and publishes the results in the *British Medical Journal* in the number for May 7, 1904, p. 1085. It makes an interesting article.

Here is a sample from a circular recently received:

"———— is a highly concentrated compound of six substances skilfully blended, and has an aromatic, piney fragrance.

"It contains no poison, opiates, drugs or narcotics, nor does it contain ether or chloroform. Not only is it an efficient persuader of natural sleep by inhalation, but it is also soothing, and tends to relieve catarrhal conditions of the mucous membrane.

"———— is harmless when used as directed and its formula has the sanction and approval of medical men to whom it has been submitted."

There is more of it but this is enough for our purpose. Would any one be busied in distributing printed matter of this kind if registered medical men, when at the end of their tether, would not be willing to make a trial of it, because it is easier so to do than to work out some remedy for themselves? It is shekels to go on with a treatment; it is shekels less laboriously gathered to take the other fellow's word (even if the communication is unsigned) than to dig out the truth for one's self.

These habits of using ready-to-wear medicines, or specifying the particular manufacturer for standard products, make it necessary for the druggist to increase the money outlay in keeping up a stock. When one fellow makes something which proves to be a good thing (at least a shekel-gatherer), some other house has an itching palm for a share of the shekels, and another preparation of a similar nature finds its way to the physician's office table, left in person by the suave agent, who chaunts its virtues charmingly. Hence Dr. A. swears by Forest, Wayman & Co.'s. Aromatized Solution of Podophyllin, while Dr. B. insists upon Dull and Bloom's Compound Elixir of May Apple, the probable actual difference between the two in therapeutic action being about as much as there is between tweedledum and tweedledee. Both preparations must be kept and, if by any chance he fails to keep his stock replenished and would give Dr. B.'s patient Dr. A.'s favorite, he is guilty of the heinous crime of substitution. Is not the person who places the stumbling-block in the way, an accessory before the act?

Do not misconstrue my position. I do not believe that any pharmacist has the right to fill a prescription other than it is nominated in the bond. My contention is that the conditions nominated in that instrument are needlessly severe in many instances, and the temptation is to avoid those conditions which would not exist in a less rigorous but equally valuable document.

But it is not only in the half concealed formula preparations where the druggist is burdened. In the line of officinal compounds, one demands a fluid extract prepared by one house; another insists on that of entirely a different manufacturer. This choice is brought about by a different set of causes than the other, but both alike are fostered by the polite agent striving to aid his employer to gather shekels.

Considerable ingenuity is employed to have the physician assume the rôle of the cat in pawing chestnuts from the coals. Notwithstanding the apparent liberality of these propositions, the appeal always places shekels before science. Within the current year, I have received several suggestions upon the following plan. With the advertisement of the article, there are two private mailing cards addressed to the house. One is to be sent directly to the firm by the victim—pardon me, I should say the doctor—, the use of the other is made clear in the following instructions :

"*Dear Doctor:* " In order to give you an opportunity to further test the advantages of our ————, we make you the following liberal proposition : Fill out the attached cards, mail No. 1 to us and hand Nos. 2 and 3 to your druggist. Upon the receipt of the order for one dozen from your druggist, we will send with his order one-fourth dozen free for your use."

Presumably enough men are found who, in order to get three packages free, will ask the druggist to clutter his shelves with the twelve, to pay a handsome return on the cards sent out. Is it any wonder that the druggist must abandon the legitimate and take up a vaudeville character of merchandise, to enable him to keep in stock the 10,010 articles required of him by an over-exacting profession? and, as time rolls on, that he imitates his physician patrons by keeping largely that which will bring shekels, even at the expense of science?

Would it not be better for the physician to say: "Mr. Druggist, I want the best and purest the market supplies. When I prescribe the fluid extract of ergot, I will expect a preparation that will do its work. You are the man to make the selection. I do not care whether it is made by Jones, Brown or Robinson; if it is not up to the mark, I will tell you and will want to know the reason why." This treatment of druggists would soon divide them into two classes; the one would be furnishing reliable remedies; the other, if you do your duty, like Ephraim of old when bound to his idols, would be left alone. Put the druggist on his honor, and those who are desirous of science and shekels will not fail you, while those, to whom it is shekels and let science take care of herself, will companion with such of our own profession as tread the same road.

Incidentally this plan of action would accomplish two other benefits: It would spare our time from the visits of the representatives of the manufacturers and save them the expense of "sampling" the profession. It would work ill in depriving a number of gentlemanly fellows of their accustomed means of earning a livelihood.

A few months ago, I was speaking to a physician—a neighbor—mentioning that he might receive a visit from the agent of Dash, Blank & Co., who was sampling Antihotine. He remarked that he always used Obflammatine, because he owned some stock in the company making it. In April of this year, I received a circular from a banking firm, offering stock in a pharmaceutical company established for the manufacture of the standard preparations, where 20 per cent. discount was offered to stockholders on all purchases. Here, again, are opportunities for shekels to get the better of science. A true pharmacist will delight in the manufacture of as many preparations as his facilities will permit.

I have in mind a store in a community of about 30,000 that makes in its own laboratory most of the preparations whose formulae are known, and you can rely upon their products, for they know what they are giving. Such a spirit should be encouraged, but, while those doctors whose earnings permit a surplus, should be entitled the privilege of receiving as large a return on invested money as they can secure, at the same time it is questionable whether the shekels should be secured by investments tempting one to use certain remedies because of a monied interest in them.

Here, then, is the end of it all: Pharmacists are not perfect, but are influenced by like passions as ourselves; neither are they totally depraved. It were much better to fan the flame of right-doing from right motives, however feeble, than to hurl rocks of abuse from a singularly conspicuous house of glass, because they yield to the temptation of putting shekels in advance of science. It will also be commendable if we set them an example by always properly harnessing our own team.

DISCUSSION.

Dr. William R. White, Providence, R. I.:

I do not hesitate now to congratulate the Chairman of the Committee on Program, of which I have the honor to be a humble member. I think Dr. Hawley has given us for this first afternoon a most admirable program, and I congratulate the writers and readers of the papers. Every one of these subjects is broad enough to occupy a long time for its consideration. It gave me special pleasure to hear from the distinguished dental professor from Philadelphia, and I am sure that that pleasure was shared by every one present. It seems to me that the importance of the subject is absolutely beyond question. The only incomprehensible thing is that physicians and surgeons and dentists have so long kept apart, that there has not been a better understanding of the mutual dependence of the one so-called profession on the other, not only from a professional standpoint but from a humanitarian standpoint. We are all servants of the public. It seems to me that we have been very slow in coming to the position of promulgating the suggestion that there should be a closer relationship between men of the two professions.

I was very much interested in the two cases quoted by Dr. Kirk. They were two instances in which the primary trouble was located in the region of a tooth. Fortunately, they fell finally into the right hands and were recognized. Some cases go on to a more serious result, possibly fatal, and the real condition is never realized. If you will pardon me I will refer to a case of this kind reported before the Providence Medical Association, by Dr. Wm. B. Wilson, one of our bright young men. He has given me permission to relate the case here.

J. G., aet. 65; chills and fever one week previous to my first visit, accompanied by backache, headache and general malaise and some toothache; poorly nourished, but aside from an endocardial murmur the condition was fair. I was having at this time several cases of malarial fever and concluded this was such a case. After a short time other causes were suggested. Examination of the mouth showed about a dozen teeth in the upper jaw from which the gums had retracted and at the junction of the gum and tooth pus was oozing. A dentist was called in consultation. (This was only three days after Dr. Wilson first saw the case.) "He advised removal of teeth. Under ether, they were extracted and the mouth washed. On the following day there was a chill, followed by pain in the right side of the head and tenderness in the parotid region on the same side. On the next day his general condition was worse. Five days after extraction of the teeth I opened the parotid, under anesthesia. The patient died seven days after the operation. Each root had a little sac containing pus."

It seems to me that that case was a very suggestive one, and that there a life was sacrificed just as a great many lives are sacrificed, because the case was not reported early by some one, and proper treatment applied. Evidently, there was a man from the working classes whose teeth had been neglected, as teeth are in that class of people. With results so serious as were manifested in this case, it seems to me that the medical profession cannot too promptly make a point of being more acute in differentiating troubles which may originate in the mouth, and in calling in the scientific dentist for his technical skill. It seems that here is a demand for humanitarian work, and it is not inappropriate before this Academy to suggest the line.

Not long ago I attended a game of baseball and my position was near to a crowd of young fellows from our factories. Occasionally, a joke would go around and mouths would fly open, and from the closeness of my contact with these I had a chance to make an oral inspection at pretty close hand, and to me it was a pronounced object lesson. I was impressed by the fact that somebody's children had been neglected by somebody. Of course, their fathers and mothers were poor people and they were ignorant of the importance of the care of the teeth and its bearing upon appearance and health, and these children grew up as children in that class do. There needs to be some of the work which is done in Germany and in other European countries, where dental inspection of school children has been in practice for several years, and I am glad to see that the same method is being introduced in some of the cities of this country. Boston has already begun and St. Louis is looking closely to it. It was somebody's duty to guard those children against that condition. They were pretty good-looking fellows, but with the opening of their mouths there was a change in your impression. There were toothless gums, discolored teeth and artificial teeth.

Although the practical part of this work devolves upon our dental friends, it is incumbent upon the medical profession to do something for the establishment of dental clinics in cities and towns where the children of the poorer classes can be treated in season to avoid the destruction of this part of their anatomy which is so essential to their looks and health.

In regard to the amalgamation of these now separate professions under one head, I do not feel able to speak. The doctor gives clearly the reasons why graduates in dentistry are not eligible to receive the full degree of M.D., and why, perhaps, they are not exactly eligible to election to medical societies. It seems to me it is far more important that the two professions should work together better and that dentists should be invited to meet with physicians more in consultation. During all the time I have been connected with the Rhode Island Medical Society only on one or two occasions has a dentist addressed us. I have known members of the state society to be invited to attend the meetings of the Rhode Island Dental Society.

I was much impressed with Dr. Kirk's plea for a more thorough study of the function and condition of the saliva. It brought home to me the thought that I have an adult member of my family who has a certain condition of her gums and teeth which renders it necessary for her to go to her dentist regularly, a thoroughly scientific man, who does something to prevent her teeth from loosening. I believe that dentist is preserving my wife's teeth. That same person is subject to attacks of neuralgia, the cause of which I have not been able to make out. I am wondering whether there is any possible connection. The neuralgia is usually located in the frontal region.

In regard to the other subject considered in this symposium, I think we can never have a better state of things, unless we physicians exercise our influence in our communities for the establishment of such a drug store as suggested by Dr. Benedict. I do not know how practical the experiment might prove to be. I wish a man like Dr. Benedict and a resident of a city like Buffalo, would take the initiative, that he would enlist a sufficient number of the scientific practitioners in his city and start a drug store that would be worthy of the name where the dispensing of pure medicines would not be secondary to the present fantastic features of the ordinary pharmacy of the city. If this were done, and a subsequent report made of increasing success, this would be a means of other cities taking up the work.

Of all the professors in my college days there was one man who left his impression upon my mind in a most marked degree. It was Dr. Henry M. Field, Professor of Materia Medica and Therapeutics, Dartmouth Medical College, who afterward moved to California. He was a scientific therapeutist. He was a devout believer in the action of medicines and a teacher of the desirability and necessity of prescribing drugs with reference to obtaining their therapeutic effect. He believed that one should know what the medicines were capable of doing, what was to be gained from them, and to be sure of the purity of the drug itself.

Eugene S. Talbot, Chicago :[1]

From what the essayists have shown in these papers to-day, it must be evident that the specialty of medicine called dentistry is not the most un-

[1] By invitation of the Program Committee.

important department of medicine. The late Professor Samuel D. Gross, of Philadelphia, seconding the recommendation for the establishment of a new section of dentistry in the American Medical Association in 1880, at Richmond, Virginia, said, "many men come into the world and go out of it without the aid of a physician but not a person but requires the assistance of the dentist sooner or later."

Sixty-five years ago, a few medically educated men desired to teach dentistry in a medical college. They made known their wishes to a medical college faculty who refused to comply with their request for the reason that dentistry was not a specialty of medicine but purely a mechanic art. The function of dentistry then was filling teeth, extraction and insertion of artificial dentures. The establishment of the first dental college was the outgrowth of that refusal. In casting aside dentistry, physicians did not realize that they had done the wisest and best thing for this branch of medicine. The mechanics of dentistry had not been worked out. It was necessary that the entire energy of the profession should be concentrated upon the mechanic side. Mechanical dentistry, like all mechanic arts, is limited and reached its highest development some years ago. The narrow teaching of a mechanic has taught us to view the jaws and teeth too narrowly. The teeth are now known to be a deeply related, not a shallowly separate part of the human body and that their well-being depends upon its health.

The two most important diseases which dentists treat (decay and interstitial gingivitis from which all suffer) are most often influenced by systemic changes. All other diseases of the teeth and associate parts belong to the domain of medicine and surgery.

So far as insterstitial gingivitis is concerned, the dentist must be a better diagnostician than the physician. The alveolar process being the most sensitive structure in the human body is hence an index to more grave systemic conditions.

The changes in the system which bring about this disease such as those shown in intestinal fermentation, high or low specific gravity of urine, indicanuria, excessive acidity of the urine, gases in the bowels, acidity of the stomach are trivial matters to the general practitioner, except when serious complications arrive. Long before gout, rheumatism, kidney lesions, arterosclerosis and the like manifest themselves, interstitial gingivitis is well established and teeth often loosen and drop out. The general practitioner and specialist watch the gums and alveolar process for systemic effects in prescribing mercury. They also examine the gums and alveolar process of men and women working in metals and drugs. For like reasons, the earlier symptoms of more grave diseases, which ultimately destroy life, must here be met.

The dentist of the future must hence be as well grounded in the fundamental principles of medicine as other specialists which should be taught in a regular medical college with medical students. This is done (so far as I know) in universities having dental departments. The term "dentist," as applied six or eight decades ago, is now outgrown. Increasing knowledge of pathology has driven dentists from the narrow limits of the tooth itself into the adjoining tissues. Dentists are stomatologists for the same reason that there are gynecologists, otologists, etc.

The general welfare of a patient is based upon a healthy mouth. This should be the first thought of the physician or surgeon. How an operation along the alimentary tract can be expected to be successful with pus germs circulating throughout the canal from diseased gums is a mystery. How far pernicious anemia may be the result of pyorrhea alveolaris, I am unable to say, but pus germs taken into the stomach at every swallow are certainly not conducive to good blood, health or happiness. Patients suffering with indigestion and those trying to recover from other diseases obtain better results from drugs if the mouth and chewing apparatus be placed in a normal healthy condition.

For these reasons medical colleges should have a chair upon stomatology where sixteen to twenty lectures should be given upon the pathology and treatment including oral hygiene of the mouth and teeth. Twenty-four years ago, such chairs were established in the seven medical colleges in Chicago, one of which I have held up to the present time.

While medical teaching has been and is being greatly improved it has much to learn from the dental teaching whose candidate performs all operations successfully before he can be graduated.

Dentistry is the only specialty in medicine that is taught separately and independently of other specialties and in which a special degree is conferred. The average dental graduate is better equipped to practise his specialty than other graduates. He should, therfore, be called in consultation like other specialists but until he has a medical degree his position will remain inferior to other consultants. M.R.C.P. and M.R.C.S. imply a general medical education.

Dr. L. D. Bulkley, New York :

The care of the mouth in connection with medicine is a subject to which I have paid a great deal of attention, having to look at the mouth so continually with regard to syphilis, in regard to the action of mercury, and many other things, so I have come to look upon the mouth and the condition of the mucous membranes as an exceedingly important part of my examination of the health of the individual. Dr. Talbot brought up the question : How can the organism be healthy when it is constantly swallowing pus? This organism must have something to do with the vitality of the individual, yet many people I have seen every day with discharging cavities of pus from dead teeth or the ordinary pyorrhea alveolaris. It has been my fortune to be appointed to one of the large dental societies of New York, to address the members, and I have brought with me plates and models in regard to the syphilitic lesions of the mouth. Dentists ought to be made acquainted with these lesions in the mouth, due to syphilis. Several dentists have acquired lesions on their fingers from not knowing that patients had syphilis.

In regard to the care of teeth in children, I think if dentists would refer their patients to physicians to treat some of these various conditions it would be much better, and they would escape much discomfort by judicious internal treatment. Time and again I have seen loosening teeth tighten up under appropriate treatment combined with local treatment. In regard to the growth of teeth in children I know they can be changed by the food, diet, and proper administration of internal medicine. Physicians should pay more attention to the relation of the teeth to epithelioma and have irritating teeth taken out at an earlier period.

Dr. Henry O. Marcy, Boston :

It has been wisely said that all truth is valuable. I am reminded of a new application of the saying as I note that the caricaturist of to-day is teaching better than he knows when he pictures our strenuous chief executive, with such excellent teeth. The two professions are coming closer together. I am reminded by Dr. Kirk's paper of an opportunity which I had of examining many skulls of prehistoric type from South America, and I was surprised to find in adult skulls whole rows of perfectly sound teeth. Illustrative cases have been given, showing that the dentist and physician should work in harmony. I would like to refer to a case in which a nearly fatal mistake by an excellent dentist was made in removing a very bad wisdom tooth. Peroxide of hydrogen was forcefully injected. It entered freely into the inferior dental canal. The most excrutiating pain followed entirely round the jaw. For weeks, the suffering was intense. The life of the patient was jeopardized. Necrosis of the entire alveolar process and part of the wall of the external ramus followed. Despite all possible care, operation followed operation with life-long suffering. The injection had carried the infection before the pressure of the gas in such a way as to disseminate it through the entire canal. Two exceptional cases came under my surgical attention sometime since. In one, a man past seventy, a tumor for some years had been developing, causing severe pain in the lower jaw. It was supposed to be cancer by experienced practitioners. I chiseled out a fully developed tooth, lying longitudinally. Its removal gave entire relief.

The second case was a woman of advanced years. For months she had suffered severely from a painful tumor of the lower jaw near the median line. This also had been diagnosticated cancer and inoperable. A large tooth had developed laterally. It was removed with much difficultly, but a perfect cure flolowed. Both these patients had been without teeth for years. The dental and oral surgeon contributes very much of value for the benefit of his brother of larger pretension, but often of lesser knowledge.

Dr. S. A. Knopf, New York :

One word which covers the relation between medicine and dentistry has not been used, the word interdependence. I do not believe there is a physician in general practice who has not been compelled, in the interest of his patient, to consult with a dentist or to advise his patient to see one. I am equally convinced that a conscientious dentist is obliged sometimes to call in either a surgeon or a physician for consultation. In my work which is limited to tuberculous patients I have learned valuable lessons concerning the need of the dentist. In my service at the hospital as well as in my outdoor clinic I have a great many poor consumptives, and among them there are always a good number of cases where I know I can do them no good, unless the hospital board allows me to order a new set of teeth. Often their digestion is faulty for no other reason than lack of teeth. It seems to me that the care of the teeth is of equal importance and should be taught to medical students. I believe that some mixed infections in pulmonary tuberculosis can be traced to decayed teeth. It is as important to examine the teeth of school children as it is to examine their eyes or chests. I hope the time will come when every family in the United States will be provided with a family physician and with a family dentist.

In relation to the use of patent medicines referred to in other papers read to-day, permit me to quote from a communication which I have prepared for another section. The amount of alcohol in patent medicines which are used by millions of American citizens and taken in tablespoonful doses two and three times a day, ranges from 12 to 47.5 per cent. I think that if this Academy stands for anything it stands for higher education and higher ideals of the professional man, but also for the enlightenment of the masses in regard to the danger of self-drugging. Our statesmen, lawyers, jurists, ministers, etc., often have no hesitation to put down their names endorsing preparations of the composition of which they have not the slightest idea. I think it is within the province of this Academy to send out a warning to all who are guilty of such dangerous practices.

Dr. J. W. Grosvenor, Buffalo, N. Y.:

I wish to make an inquiry. It is important that the poor, both children and grown people, who are unable to pay dentists for their services, should be able to seek advice and proper treatment from some source; one of the speakers spoke of the need of forming clinics for this purpose; I have supposed that in every dental college the poor could be treated; I want to ask whether this is not the case? In Buffalo, N. Y., there is such a free clinic.

Dr. Leartus Connor, Detroit:

It is good sense that a general consult his aids in planning his campaign or in executing it. Obviously, in this instance the dentists are our aids. They tell us that diseased adenoids and tonsils modify the arches of the roof of the child's mouth, so disturb the position of the teeth. Others tell us that cases of endocarditis, otitis media, defects of articulation, blunted senses, impaired mental and physical vigor, indigestion, constipation, night terrors and many other disorders spring from the hypertrophy of these bodies. I suspect that in a careful study we shall find that infections from the tonsils and adenoids have much to do with diseases of the teeth as well as their malposition. Admitting these and associated facts, we realize the pernicious effects of retaining these sources of infection a single hour. The same thing applies to pharmacists. If the doctor would only take the educated pharmacist by the hand there would be gain. We need each other, and until we seek one another in a friendly spirit we shall fail of our greatest possibilities. The man who furnishes us our surgical appliances is also worthy of our cooperation. He is an out-post of the general army fighting against disease. If intelligent individuals who seek the higher good would come together and talk over their points of necessary contact, other questions would adjust themselves.

Dr. Kirk closes:

I have always felt that there was a very close relationship between medicine and dentistry and I have had this afternoon a practical realization of that relationship. I never felt more at home in my life than at this moment and in this presence. It has been very gratifying to have had the benefit of this discussion from the medical standpoint and to see there is a realizing sense of the importance and necessity for all of us who have the same objective ideal, the cure of disease, getting together and comparing results. As a dentist, I want to endorse everything Dr. Bulkley has said with reference to the importance of just the line of work to which he has given attention. The cases which I have reported occur because of the lack of that relationship which I have advocated and which Dr. Connor has so strongly brought out. I want to correct what may be a misapprehension, that I have made any plea or suggestion for a political or organic relationship between dentistry and medicine. I do not advocate that idea; there are those in dentistry who do, but what I do stand for is that close affiliation of these branches of the healing art which means mutual helpfulness. The time is coming when we will have an official organization of medical specialism which will place the several departments of the healing art on about the same educational basis.

I have enjoyed the discussion greatly, and believe it will be productive of great good to our patients and to ourselves.

OBSERVATIONS IN PASSING.

After much correspondence and long discussion, it has been decided to hold the next annual meeting of the American Academy of Medicine in Chicago on Thursday and Friday, November 9 and 10, 1905. The last time that the Academy met apart from the meeting of any other medical organization was in 1894, when it met at Jefferson, N. H., and had a most excellent meeting. Previous to 1891, the Academy always met in the fall, and apart from the meeting of any other society. On November 13 and 14, 1889, it held a very pleasant and successful meeting in Chicago.

There are many possibilities which, if utilized, will make the next meeting memorable. The program can hardly fail of being excellent. The continuation of the report of the Committee on Teachin Hgygiene in the Public Schools will open up subjects deserving of careful discussion. The preliminary report of another committee upon the somewhat unattractive subject of the value of the first degree in our literary and scientific schools could better be read by title than occupy the time of the Academy, were it not that it must present the timely subject of the preliminary training for the medical course, whether accompanied by a degree or not. The discussion on these two subjects is enough to make the meeting attractive. In addition to this and the papers upon independent topics that may be accepted, the Committee on Program will endeavor to arrange a symposium on "The Influence of Recreation upon the Individual and the Community from the Medical and Sociological Standpoints." Any presentation of this subject, however mediocre, will furnish fuel to keep a council camp-fire burning a long while, and the general discussion can hardly fail to be of value; but mediocre papers are not to be expected. We can trust the keen censorship of the chairman of the committee to prevent that. How much more valuable then will the presentation of this very timely subject be?

∗

President Hall requested Dr. D. C. Hawley, of Burlington, Vt., to continue as chairman of the Committee on Program, a position he filled so successfully last year, and he has consented to serve. Fellows desirous of presenting papers at the next meeting are requested to correspond with Dr. Hawley.

∗

We are in receipt of a "folder" lauding a book called "The All-Around Specialist." From an examination of it we infer that "specialist" is used here in the sense that is employed by the self-laudatory advertisements in the daily press, when the object is to impress the dear public who are gullible. Hence one is not surprised at even these surprising statements. The italics are ours.

"The *science* of refraction is *fully discussed* in this chapter. The directions are so plain and simple that any person having no knowledge of this subject can quickly become proficent in the fitting of glasses. . . . There is a profit of from *five* to *ten* dollars on *every pair* of glasses that are furnished."

"RETINOSCOPY.

"The rapidly growing popularity of this method of estimating the refraction of eyes and the perfect ease with which it can be accomplished by following a few simple rules have prompted the author to add the subject to this book. The directions are so simple and complete that any physician can *easily* become proficient in the use of the retinoscope, thus enabling him in a few moments to correctly estimate the refraction of a child or an idiot —where questioning is impracticable."

∗

The Committee on Appropriations of the Colorado State Medical Society recommended at the last meeting that "car-fare and Pullman fare of delegates to the American Medical Association be paid by the state society." The recommendation was adopted. This is a move in the right direction. When the business world learns that physicians estimate each other's time as of value so as pay them a money consideration for services rendered medical associations, the sooner will they be willing to recompense physicians properly for services rendered the public. It would be still better if all the ordinary traveling expenses of the delegate be met by the society.

LITERATURE NOTES.

BOOKS RECEIVED.

[All books received for editorial comment will be entered on this list as they are received. An effort will be made to give an unbiased notice of each book as promptly as possible by some one competent to formulate the opinion.]

REFRACTION AND HOW TO REFRACT. THORINGTON. Third Edition. Blakiston. $1.50 net.

THE SURGICAL TREATMENT OF BRIGHT'S DISEASE. EDEBOHLS. Frank F. Lisiecki. $2.00.

BRIGHT'S DISEASE AND DIABETES. TYSON. Second Edition. Blakiston. $4.00 net.

A BOOK ABOUT DOCTORS. JEAFFRESON. Doctor's Recreation Series. Vol. IV. Saalfield Publishing Co. $2.50.

A QUIZ COMPEND ON MEDICAL LATIN. ST. CLAIR. SECOND EDITION. Blakiston. $1.00 net.

APPENDICITIS. BAYARD HOLMES. Appleton. $2.00.

GENERAL CATALOGUE OF MEDICAL BOOKS. Interleaved. Blakiston. Cloth, 25 cents.

THE PHYSICIAN'S VISITING LIST. Blakiston.

THE PERPETUAL VISITING AND POCKET REFERENCE BOOK—with calendar for 1905. St. Louis. Dios Chemical Co. Price 10 cents, post-paid.

THE PHYSICIAN'S POCKET ACCOUNT BOOK. J. J. TAYLOR, M.D. Philadelphia. The Medical Council.

A BOOK ABOUT DOCTORS. BY JOHN CORDY JEAFFRESON. 1904. Akron, O.: The Saalfield Publishing Co. pp. 516. Price, $2.50.

This is the fourth volume of the doctor's recreation series and a reprint. Some years ago while nosing around a second-hand bookstore in New York, the writer of this note happened upon a copy of this book, which he at once purchased and afterwards— many times afterwards—enjoyed.

It treats essentially of the habits, manners and peculiarities of the English medical profession, from the gold-headed stick and wig down to the middle of the nineteenth century. We hope the enterprise of the Saalfield Company in again putting this fund of information in reach of the profession will be amply rewarded.

A Treatise on Bright's Disease and Diabetes with Especial Reference to Pathology and Therapeutics. By James Tyson, M.D., Professor of Medicine in the University of Pennsylvania, etc. Second Edition, illustrated. Including a section on "Ocular Changes in Bright's Disease and in Diabetes," by George E. De Schweinitz, M.D., Professor of Ophthalmology in the University of Pennsylvania, etc. Philadelphia: P. Blakiston's Son & Co. 1904. pp. 381. Price, $4.00 net.

The first edition of this work was issued in 1881, and has been out of print for a long time. This second edition is in fact a new volume, making use of all the results of the many researches made in the intervening years. It goes without saying that Prof. Tyson's interpretation of the facts makes a volume of interest and value; that his opinions are worth reading and heeding. The additional chapters on the ocular changes by Professor De Schweinitz, increase the value of an already valuable work, and make it a book for the ophthalmologist as well as for the general practitioner.

A Compend of Medical Latin Designed Expressly for the Elementary Training of Medical Students. By W. T. St. Clair, A.M. Second Edition Revised. Philadelphia: P. Blakiston's Son & Co. 1904. pp. 131. Price, $1.00 net.

This is one of Blakiston's justly famous series of Quiz-Compends, and this particular volume is fully abreast in its excellencies with the others of the series. At the same time we hope that in the very near future the condition will be such that the book may be regarded as one of the curiosities of medical literature, when there can not be found a student in medicine of the class for whom this book is prepared. "The author's aim in publishing this little book, is to present to the student of medicine, in a plain and practical way, the fundamental principles upon which the medical language is built. The student who comes to the study of medicine with little or no knowledge of Latin, its technical language, will find in this little book a patient and careful helpmate to guide him safely through the perplexing mazes of the special terms and phrases used in medicine, *i. e.*, Medical Latin."—*Preface*. The book does this admirably; our expectation is that the student of no knowledge in Latin will disappear.

REFRACTION AND HOW TO REFRACT, INCLUDING SECTIONS ON OPTICS, RETINOSCOPY, THE FITTING OF SPECTACLES AND EYE-GLASSES, ETC. By JAMES THORINGTON, A.M., M.D. Third Edition. Philadelphia: P. Blakiston's Son & Co. 1904. pp. 314. Price, $1.50 net.

If one excepts the point of view of the author, one can find nothing to condemn in this manual. The descriptions are clear, the teaching sound, there are many items of information which would escape the reader of the usual text-books on ophthalmology, to his loss. The point of view to which exception is taken is the lack of knowledge of elementary physics on the part of medical students, for whom the book is intended primarily. If there be such, and there must be for this work is evidently a product of experience, they ought not to be tempted to master the principles of physiologic optics, before they are grounded in physical optics. We regret that this is not demanded. The part of the book which treats of the principles of optics fails at times to be accurate in statement because of the attempt to express the truths in a popular manner. Thus on page 54 are the words: "Looking at a perpendicular straight line." Nowhere in the context can be found any statement showing to what this line is perpendicular; a vertical line is meant. Another example is found on page 132. "This makes half a circle (hemisphere) of 180°." A half circle is not a hemisphere, and if a half-circle can be projected other than 180° it will revolutionize the *mathematica ars*. Other examples could be given as where it is asserted a perpendicular forms right angles, page 19, and the definition of prism on page 23. Fortunately in those portions of the book which are of real value, no such carelessness in diction is discoverable. Prof. Thorington has erred through a false philanthropy. He wished to teach the art of refracting to students who were unacquainted with the science of refraction, and, instead of insisting they should climb up to a proper understanding, he has endeavored to write down to their understanding.

VISITING LISTS.

I. THE PHYSICIAN'S VISITING LIST. (Lindsay and Blakiston's) for 1905.

II. THE PERPETUAL VISITING AND POCKET REFERENCE BOOK WITH CALENDAR FOR 1905. (Dios Chemical Company, St. Louis.)

III. THE PHYSICIAN'S POCKET ACCOUNT BOOK. (The Medical Council, Philadelphia.) pp. 224. Leather. Price, $1.00.

I. It is enough to say of this list, now in the 54th year of its publication, that it annually renews its youth while retaining the excellencies of its age, and, as it has been for two generations, is still in the first class of books of its kind, with very few associates.

II. The publishers of the book will send it to any address for ten cents, and it is available as a visiting book despite its low price. On account of its price it is not fair to compare it with other books.

III. This book instructs the physician to keep his accounts in such a manner as to make them acceptable to the courts should he have recourse to them for collection, and at the same time in so simple a manner as to require no more writing than many of the other systems in vogue. It is well worth the investigating by those who do not keep a regular set of books.

The new journal, *Ophthalmology*, deserves a notice in our pages because it is an attempt to present to the profession a journal of real worth and of elegant appearance, and its initial number is handsome enough and valuable enough to disarm adverse criticism that of its 188 pages, but 57 are given to original articles; most of the remainder is given to abstracting current literature. Would it not be possible for all the journals on a given subject to form a syndicate and prepare an abstract that could be used after the fashion of the patent insides of a country weekly. One can not read all the articles, and most of us are indebted to the abstracter beyond our ability to pay. At the same time there is a danger of being buried in the depths of the abstracter, if one attempts to read more than one journal. (Quarterly $5.00 a year, 105 Grand Ave., Milwaukee, Wis.)

BULLETIN

OF THE

American Academy of Medicine.

VOL. VI.   ISSUED FEBRUARY, 1905.   NO. 16.

THE AMERICAN ACADEMY OF MEDICINE is not responsible for the sentiments expressed in any paper or address published in the BULLETIN.

ARE MODERN SCHOOL METHODS IN KEEPING WITH PHYSIOLOGIC KNOWLEDGE?

I.

IS THE PRESENT METHOD OF EDUCATING GIRLS CONSISTENT WITH THEIR PHYSIOLOGIC DEVELOPMENT? AND IS IT FOR THE WELFARE OF THE RACE?

BY A. LAPTHORN SMITH, B.A., M.D., M.R.C.S., Eng. Fellow of the British and American Gynecological Societies; Honorary Fellow of the Italian Gynecology Society; Professor of Gynecology in the University of Vermont; Professor of Clinical Gynecology in Bishop's University, Montreal; Surgeon-in-Chief of the Samaritan Hospital for Women; Gynecologist to the Western General Hospital and to the Montreal Dispensary, and Consulting Gynecologist to the Women's Hospital, Montreal, Canada.

As the highest aim of our profession is to prevent disease by teaching the people the laws of health, the writer felt that it was a duty as well as a pleasure to comply with the request of the American Academy of Medicine to write a paper on this topic. The mere fact that this question was chosen as the topic for a symposium or group of papers shows that there was in the minds of the members of the committee, all of whom are physicians with a large experience of human ills, a grave doubt whether the present tendency towards pushing the education of girls to the highest possible point is consistent with their physiologic development and for the welfare of the race. The task was an agreeable one, for the writer's own professional experience had already forced him to the conclusion that the health of the future mothers of the race was not as good as it should be, and that there were causes for the same which could and should be removed. That there is more sickness among the women of to-day than there was among their mothers and grandmothers, seems to be the general opinion of a great many physicians who give special attention to this branch of medicine. In fact it is notorious among the laity themselves that there is a great deal more ill health among women now than there was fifty years ago, and the patients both male and female are constantly asking us what is the reason that there are so many sick and complaining women? I say that patients in general, and not female patients alone, are making this inquiry, for young men by the hundreds of thousands who should be married and at the head of happy homes full of children, and who are remaining single until long after the age at which they should be married and who are doing so at an enormous loss to their moral and physical welfare, give this as their principal excuse, that the average experience of their friends who have married, has been that the educated women of the present generation are physically unfit to be wives and mothers.

The writer recognizes several sources of error which must be allowed for before making sure that this conclusion is correct. First, the men, who, by great care in selecting, or by chance, have secured a healthy wife say nothing about their happiness, for they take it as a matter of course, as if it were something that should be so, instead of being something remarkable, while the men whose wives begin complaining a few days after their marriage, and continue to complain until death comes to their relief, are almost sure to tell their friends about their misfortune, and in return for the sympathy which they deserve and receive, they advise their bachelor friends to remain single.

The other source of error arises with the specialist, who because all the women who come to him are sick and give a history of never having had a day's health since their marriage, would come to the conclusion therefore that all married women are ailing. In other words that because he never sees or knows any women professionally, who are not ailing, well women do not exist.

There is still another source of error coming from the married state itself which must not be charged to the woman or her education, but to the men, for no matter how perfect a woman's health may be before marriage, she may still prove a failure as a wife and a mother if she acquires gonorrhea with its pus tubes and pelvic peritonitis.

There is still another source of error which may or may not be due to the woman's education, namely the inducing of abortions. These, of course, wreck a woman's health, and make her a failure as a wife and a mother, but in the majority of cases it is because she is already a failure in health that she resorts to this crime, for with few exceptions, it is only sick married women who dread pregnancy and the raising of a happy family.

Now after making due allowance for these sources of error the writer still believes that the majority of educated women on this continent reach a marriageable age in such poor condition of health that it is a real hardship for them to perform the normal natural duties of wifehood and motherhood, and of raising an ordinary sized family.

We need hardly spend any time in arguing that the cheerful and happy performance of these duties is the manifest destiny of women, and that any general disinclination to undertake them, or any attempt to shirk them when undertaken, will inevitably throw the whole world's machinery out of gear, and bring disaster upon her and upon the race. Nature indeed has a summary way of punishing either men or women, who from motives of selfishness or from physical inability, do not marry and raise a family; she simply extinguishes that breed and replaces it on the earth by a race of people less highly educated, but which knows enough to propagate itself.

It is true that an infinitesimal number of people, mostly women, deny that it is the destiny of women to become wives and mothers, and would even lead them in a rebellion against nature, telling them that these duties are degrading, and that they should abandon the profession of home-making and launch out into political or business life. But the whole common sense of the world is against them, because it sees that when they do succeed, as they undoubtedly do, their success absolutely fails to bring them the happiness and the satisfaction which the poorest laborer's wife obtains from her houseful of hungry but happy little ones.

The writer admits that every child should receive an elementary education, which should, up to puberty, be the same for boys and girls, provided that it be given in such a manner as to not interfere with their physical development. A large part of every day should be spent in the open air, either at drill or in play, and there should be no homework to keep them up late at night, which is one of the great mistakes in modern methods of bringing up children. Our mothers and grandmothers, when children, were in bed at eight o'clock at the latest, while our children are allowed, on various pretexts, to remain up until ten or eleven. Does it not seem folly to allow or urge a child to fill its brain so full of work during the evening that it keeps on working all night, even repeating its lessons during its restless sleep? A great improvement has taken place during the last few years by the introduction of manual training or Sloyd for boys, and in a few schools the girls are being taught cooking and domestic science; of this, however, I will have more to say later.

At the age of puberty, boys and girls should have a different course of education; the menstrual function makes great demands upon the girl's strength, and if her brain is worked up to its fullest capacity, then the organs of generation must suffer, and the foundation is laid for life-long female troubles, such as ovarian neuralgia, etc. This is the experience of every gynecologist with whom I have spoken on the subject, namely, that the average girl has not enough blood to meet the enormous demands of the brain required by modern education, and at the same time to allow her organs of generation to grow as they should. This seems to the writer to be the explanation of the large number of cases of infantile uterus we meet with in grown-up women. This infantile uterus either will not conceive, or if it does, it will almost surely be torn at the first labor. It is the general opinion, therefore, that every month, girls should be excused for a few days during which they should either rest if they are pained, or stay out in the sun or fresh air without anything to call the blood away to the brain. According to present methods of education nothing is allowed to interfere with the process of developing the brain by rigorous attendance at classes and the study of the multiplicity of unnecessary subjects. But by the method which the writer and many of his colleagues would advocate, nothing should be allowed to interfere with the girl's physical development, all the education in the world being of no account whatever, compared with the possession of robust health. It is a pleasure to notice that in many schools on this continent a great deal of attention is being given not only to the teaching of hygiene but also to the practice of it by allowing the girls to engage in outdoor games which are of the greatest possible value in developing the muscles. In the writer's opinion, there should be a complete change in the subjects taught to girls during the last few years at school; algebra, Euclid, botany, chemistry, mythology, astronomy, Greek and Latin, should be cut out, and the time devoted to dressmaking, millinery, cooking and domestic economy, including the care of the baby, the making of the home, and even the care of the husband. In fact, when a girl leaves school at sixteen or seventeen she should be thoroughly prepared to become the best possible wife and mother at eighteen. In the writer's opinion this is the age at which every woman ought to be married, instead of waiting until twenty-six or twenty-eight. What has made the average marrying age gradually rise from eighteen to twenty-eight during the last hundred years? What has made the divorce rate gradually increase during the same time? Simply because women have been gradually educated to want more and to be able to do less, so that marrying a poor young man for love is no longer possible or even desirable. A highly educated woman of eighteen has intellectual and other requirements which few men under thirty-five or forty can afford to give her; the consequence is that for the next ten years she ruins her remaining health by all-afternoon card parties and all-night dancing parties in darkened and badly ventilated rooms under the idea that she is having a good time, while the man whom she should have been glad to marry, is losing not only his body but also his soul in the many ways which are only too well-known to all. When such an old maid and such an old bachelor get married, which they unfortunately sometimes do, what do they want with children? They have been living for themselves all their lives and it is too late to learn to live for others now. If they had been married at eighteen and twenty-five, respectively, they could have adapted themselves to each other and the six or eight children would have been so many bonds to unite them more firmly until they were parted by death. The writer knows several hundred women with large families who are perfectly happy but not one of them is highly educated. Is it any wonder then that he is in favor of less high education, of more manual training, of simpler methods of living, earlier marriages and more children. It may be justifiable for men to exchange a little of their health for higher education, although even in their case it is doubtful, for many of our most successful men left school with much health but little education; but as far as the race is concerned health is not so important for the man as for the woman, for in God's providence she has to furnish all the material for the growth of the child before birth and for a year or more after. If her own brain requires an extraordinary supply of phosphates there will be none left for her little one.

I have already shown how higher education renders wifehood and motherhood distasteful, owing to defective development of the sexual organs; let me now call attention to the fact that it is making these duties and privileges exceedingly difficult. Higher education of women is making motherhood more difficult, not only because it is increasing the ability of the nerves to perceive pain more keenly, but because the pains of labor are actually greater than they were a century ago; as the writer said in his paper before the Southern Surgical and Gynecological Association some ten years ago, "Under civilization, a new type of disease has sprung up among women who are accustomed to have everything done for them and to do little themselves; persons who think and feel a great deal, but act little. Oversensitive nerves and weak muscles are partly inherited and partly the result of training; of a training which instead of making a child into a good animal, has been, perhaps not intentionally, directed towards developing the mind and hindering the growth of the body; a training which develops complexity of nervous structures instead of nervous energy. It is the result of a childhood spent in learning a great deal and doing a very little. Instead of training women to be strong, tall, and muscular, with good appetites and the power of sleeping well, the whole tendency of modern education is to depress and mortify the flesh in order to exalt the spirit.

The result is that anything the muscles have to do is done with great difficulty, while whatever the nerves have to do is done too well. It is not surprising then that such a complex process as labor, depending as it does upon the nervous and muscular system, should be affected injuriously by an education whose sole aim seems to be to exalt the nerves and depress the muscles. The process of dilatation of the os uteri, which among uneducated women goes on quietly and without sufficient pain to prevent them from attending to their occupations, becomes in the highly educated woman, a long and agonizing process, owing to her increased sensibility. There is a great outcry with very little work. Owing to defective nutrition, the amniotic membrane breaks at the very beginning of labor, so that the waters escape and dilatation must take place by the direct pressure of the child's head, instead of by the beautifully equalized hydrostatic pressure. The pressure of the child's head being greater at certain points than at others, the stretched cervix is lacerated. In the writer's opinion laceration of the cervix could not possibly occur if the cervix were normal, and if dilatation were performed by the bag of waters and if neither fingers nor instruments were introduced within it. If the bag of waters were strong enough to remain intact until the perineum is also dilated, as he has seen it occur among the uneducated classes in Canada, rupture of the perineum would not happen either. This too early spontaneous rupture of the amniotic sac means a dry labor, and a dry labor is a very exhausting one, which is too often followed by the application of the forceps before dilatation is complete. This in turn generally means a badly ruptured cervix and perineum.

At the Boston meeting of the American Gynecological Society a few weeks ago, one of the speakers with a large obstetric practice admitted that it was impossible for the majority of his patients to have a normal labor, on account of the severity of the pain and the weakness of the muscles.

There is yet another way in which the sedentary life, which the higher education of women entails, renders maternity difficult, namely, by reducing the size of the pelvis. It is a law of physiology that the more muscles are used, the larger they grow; and not only the muscles but the bones to which those muscles are attached also develop. When children are kept many hours a day sitting at a desk, their abdominal muscles are not used and consequently they atrophy; in girls this is a serious matter, for the round muscles of the uterus only contract when the abdominal muscles do so, being supplied by the same nerves. As the keeping of the uterine fundus forward where it ought to be, depends upon the contractile power of these little cords, and as the slightest exertion will push the uterus back if these cords fail to do their work, weakness of the round muscles almost surely entails retroversion. Of course, retroversion means that the bowels come upon the anterior surface of the uterus and drive it downwards, until it is lying on the pelvic floor, almost at the outlet of the vulva. If, on the other hand, the round muscles are used hundreds of times a day, as they undoubtedly are when girls are running and playing and jumping, they become well developed, and so strong that they can pull the fundus forward, in normal anteversion, until it touches the pubic symphysis, before the bowels have time to be forced by intraabdominal pressure in front of it. The uterus can stand an unlimited amount of pressure on its back because the symphysis pubis then receives the weight of it, while it can bear very little on its anterior surface because there is nothing to stop it from falling backwards, until it is lying helplessly on the pelvic floor. As a rule, retroversion incapacitates a woman from performing her duties, and yet how common this condition is, may be judged from the fact that the writer has had to operate on over five hundred cases besides five hundred others whom he has cured by pessaries and other means. That the trouble is increasing as education increases may be inferred from the fact that twenty-five years ago it was so rare for a young girl to have any diseases of the womb that we seldom felt justified in making a vaginal examination, while now so large a proportion of the cases are young girls that we are justified in examining them whenever hygienic treatment fails to cure them in a reasonable time.

In conclusion, I am happy to say that owing to recent improvements in methods, my remarks do not apply with so much force to the great colleges for women, such as Bryn Mawr, Vassar, and Wellesley, where special attention is paid to the physiologic development of the girls, but even they have at least the defect of making the women, who graduate from them, superior to the men whom they should marry, so that failing the realization of their ideal, they do not marry at all. My remarks apply with greatest force to the girls in the high schools, many of whom are competing for positions as teachers, and of whom the mental strain is making physical wrecks. It would be far better in the writer's opinion for those girls to qualify themselves for becoming wives and mothers, and to leave the teaching, of boys at least, to men who would then be paid much better salaries, enabling them to marry, and have happy homes.

248 Bishop Street, Montreal.

II.

"IS EQUAL TREATMENT OF THE SEXES BEST, OR DO GIRLS REQUIRE THE SAME TREATMENT AS BOYS?"[1]

By Stephen H. Weeks, M.D., of Portland, Maine.

Observe please, that the subject of my paper is in the form of a question.

"Is Equal Treatment of the Sexes Best, or Do Girls Require the Same Treatment as Boys?" This paper forms one of a series on the general topic: "Are Modern School Methods in Keeping with Physiologic Knowledge?"

By school methods is meant, of course, the methods of education; and I ask, what is education? Mr. John Stuart Mill once said "Education, in its larger sense, is one of the most inexhaustible of all topics. Though there is hardly any subject on which so much has been written by so many of the wisest men, it is as fresh to those who came to it with a fresh mind, a mind not hopelessly filled with other people's conclusions, as it was to the first explorers of it; and, notwithstanding the great mass of excellent things which have been said respecting it, no thoughtful person finds any lack of things, both great and small, still waiting to be said." Education in its most extended signification is the art of developing and cultivating the various physical, intellectual, esthetic and moral faculties, and may then be divided into four branches: physical, intellectual, esthetic and moral. This definition is by no means complete, but is used merely as indicative of the manner in which this subject has generally been discussed.

Education is further divided into primary education, or instruction in the first elements of knowledge, received by children in common or elementary school or at home; secondary, that received in grammar and high schools or in academies; higher, that received in colleges, universities and post-graduate schools; and special or professional, that which aims to fit one for the particular vocation or profession in which he or she is to engage.

At the very beginning of this paper, I wish to say that a radical difference, both psychical and physical, exists between the male

[1] Read before the American Academy of Medicine, Atlantic City, N. J., June 6, 1904.

and the female, and no amount of training, under the modern interpretation of the equality of the sexes, can ever remove this distinction, without at the same time destroying the true grace and dignity of the female character. Hannah More recognized the eternal distinction between the sphere of a man and the sphere of a woman and would educate her for the sphere in which she must forever move,—a sphere settled by the eternal laws of nature and duty. She says:

"Is it not more wise to move contentedly in the plain path which providence has obviously marked out for the sex, rather then to stray awkwardly, unbecomingly, unsuccessfully, in a forbidden road; to be good originals, rather than bad imitators; to be excellent women, rather than indifferent men? "So that if we deny to women the talents which lead them to excel as lawyers, if we question their title to eminence as mathematicians, if they are less conversant with the powers of Nature, the structure of the human frame, and the knowledge of the heavenly bodies than philosophers, physicians and astronomers, let them take comfort, that in their very exemption from privileges which they are sometimes disposed to envy, consist their security and their happiness."

Madam de Maintenou was the first great woman who gave a marked impulse to female education in our modern times. Her wisdom, tact and experience were not lost upon Hannah More who exercised, as no other woman, so broad and deep an influence on the public mind, in the combined character of woman of society, author and philanthropist.

The idea of separate schools for boys and girls is not exclusively a modern one. It prevailed in Greece and in Rome. Under the empire there was, at Athens, an academy with ten professors, where many Roman youths were taught; girls, too, received a careful training during the last of the empire, there being schools for them alone.

In Norway since the year 1814, much attention has been paid to education. Their higher schools differ from the common schools, in that more attention is paid to the modern languages, and the instruction in the other branches is more complete; some of the schools are for boys alone, some are for both boys and girls, and two are for girls exclusively. In Sweden, are found the usual classes of schools; among them are nine normal schools, seven of which are for males, and two for females. During the years devoted to primary education or instruction in the first elements of knowledge, received by children at home, or in common or elementary schools, the girls may receive the same treatment as the boys. After a girl has reached the period of puberty, she has a very important physiologic function to perform, which recurs every month, and which lasts from five to seven days. During this time she should be in bed, and her course of study should be so arranged, that she may do so, without falling behind her classes or being obliged to make up lost work.

Among the diseases most frequently dating back to this period are to be enumerated chorea, dysmenorrhea, hysteria, epilepsy, headache, worry, insomnia, and other neuroses wholly or partially of reflex origin, all frequently involving an hereditary element, but yet largely dependent on overexcitation of the brain and spinal cord.

When we come to the subject of the higher training of young women, three questions present themselves for consideration.

1. Shall a girl receive a college education?
2. Shall she receive the same kind of college education as a boy?
3. Shall she be educated in the same college?

As to the first question: It must depend upon the character of the girl. Precisely so with the boy. The needs of the times are imperative. The highest product of social evolution is the growth of the civilized home—a home, that only a wise, cultivated, and high-minded woman can make. To produce such women is one of the worthiest functions of higher education. No young woman capable of becoming such, should be condemned to anything lower.

Four of the best years of one's life spent in the company of noble thoughts and high ideals, cannot fail to leave their impress. To be wise and at the same time womanly, is to wield a tremendous influence that may be felt for good in the lives of generations to come.

It is not forms of government which make or unmake men, it is the character and influence of their mothers and wives. The higher education of women means more for the future than all conceivable legislative reform. Its influence does not end with the home; it means higher standards of manhood, greater thoroughness of training, and the coming of better men; let us educate our girls as well as our boys for the respective spheres in which they are to move, because a generous as well as a proper education should be the birthright of every daughter of the Republic as well as every son.

2. Shall we give our girls the same education as our boys? If we mean by the same, an equal degree of breadth and thoroughness, and an equal fitness for high thinking and wise acting,—yes, let it be the same.

If we mean: Shall we reach this end by exactly the same course of studies? then my answer must be no. For with different persons, the same course of study will not yield the same results. The old college course met the needs of no one, and so was adapted to all alike. The great educational awakening of the last twenty-five years in America lay in breaking the bonds of this old system.

The essence of the new education is individualism: its purpose is to give to each young man and to each young woman that training which will make a man of him, and a woman of her. In the college and university of to-day, the greatest liberty in the choice of study is given to the student: the professor advises, the student chooses, and the flexibility of the courses makes possible the proper culture of every form of talent. This power of choice carries with it the duty of choosing aright. The ability to choose makes a man of the college boy, and a woman of the college girl and transfers college work from an alternation of tasks and play, to its proper relation to the business of life.

The best education for a young woman is surely not that which has proved unfit for a young man. She is an individual as well as he, and her work gains as much as his by its relation to her life. An institution which meets the varied needs of varied men may also meet the varied needs of varied women, for the intellectual needs of the two sexes are not so different in many important respects.

The special or professional needs, so far as they differ, will bring their own satisfaction. Those who have had to do with the higher training of women know that the severest demands can be met as well by young women as by young men. In this, however, those who have taught both, must agree; the training of women is just as serious and important as the training of men, and no training which falls short of the best, is adequate for either.

The next important question which presents itself. Shall young women be taught in the same classes as young men? My answer is no. At the present time there is a strong tendency in favor of the affirmative answer to this question. There is a strong feeling, especially in the Western colleges and universities, toward coeducation. It is claimed that better men are made where the two sexes are not separated. By those who favor coeducation, it is claimed that it is of great advantage to both men and women during their education, to meet on a plan of equality.

Women are brought into contact with men who can do things, whose sense of reality is strong, and who have definite views in life. This influence affects them for good. In like manner, association with wise, sane and healthy women is of value to young men.

At the present time, the demand for the higher education of women is met in three different ways:

1. In separate colleges for women, where the courses of study are more or less parallel with those given in colleges for men: In some of these, the teachers are all women, in some they are mostly men, and in others there is a more or less equal division.

2. In annexes for women to men's colleges: In these, part of the instruction given to the men is repeated for the women, though in different classes or rooms; and there is more or less opportunity for them to use the same libraries and museums.

3. By coeducation: In this system, young men and young women are admitted to the same classes, are subjected to the same requirements, and are governed by the same rules. This system is now fully established in the State institutions of the North and West, and in most of the other colleges in the same region.

Rev. Wm. DeWitt Hyde, D.D., president of Bowdoin College,

says: "Of the three methods to which you refer, I am inclined to the opinion, that coeducation is the worst, coordinate education is better, and separate education is best."

The University of Chicago has abandoned coeducation, during the first two years of its course.

A woman's college is more or less distinctly a technical school. It is a school of training for the profession of womanhood. It encourages womanliness of thought as differing more or less from the plain thinking which is called manly. In woman's education, the tendency is toward the study of beauty and order. Literature and language take precedence over science. Expression is valued more highly than action.

I am heretic enough to inquire whether our athletics are the panacea we have been inclined to think them. There is much truth in what Prof. Stanley Hall said about the education which a boy gained on the hills here. I am heretic enough to inquire whether too much time is not spent in athletics by our young men and young women.

Leaving the question unanswered, I will ask another: Shall we give the girl the same athletic training as the boy? The fact that young women have been going in for some of the more strenuous forms of athletics of late, has called out very forcible expressions of opinion from the prominent educators of the country. Among these who have vigorously condemned the more violent forms of sport as totally unfitted to young women, are President Eliot, of Harvard, and Miss Lucile E. Hill, physical director at Wellesley. Both are agreed that athletic games which demand a large amount of physical force and nervous energy, are very sure in the long run to be extremely harmful to the average woman. Miss Hill even goes so far as to include basketball in the list of undesirables. It is probably true that both young men and women in some instances carry the athletic idea too far. In football, a game constantly assailed but too popular to be done away with off hand, we are undoubtedly carrying physical development, at times, to a point that endangers the future health of the player. What is needed for both young men and women is the application of the laws of physical well-being to all their sports. When we cease to encourage those physically unfit for the more violent forms of sport to engage in them regardless of consequences, we shall come nearer to escaping both serious danger and deserved criticism. In case of women there is need for greater caution: the athletic young woman is all right in her place; assuredly she is not, upon the football field, nor in matched games of basketball, and the greatest questions are presented as to either the fitness or safety of such sport. I have extended this paper beyond its proper limit, and will now close by saying that our real interests lie in better and more noble training of our young people, in making our young men more manly, our young women more womanly, and our land more godly.

III.

THE GYNECOLOGIC ASPECT OF MENTAL OVERSTRAIN AT PUBERTY, AND ITS INFLUENCE ON DEVELOPMENT.[1]

BY WM. EDGAR DARNALL, A.M., M.D., Atlantic City, N. J.

The period of puberty is the most critical time in the whole life of the female, because this time of most rapid development of both mind and body may be the starting point for the physical perfection of womanhood or the first beginning of a physical wreck. "Many a young life is battered or forever crippled in the breakers of puberty. If it cross these unharmed and is not dashed to pieces on the rocks of childbirth, it may still ground on the ever recurring shallows of menstruation, and lastly upon the final bar of the menopause, ere protection is found in the unruffled waters of the harbors beyond the reach of sexual storms."

The girl while passing through this period is peculiarly susceptible to mental, moral, and physical influences, and during this period may receive the first blow. Ere the girl is fully aware of the change that has taken place, or is warned by her mother of its significance, she has heedlessly exposed herself to injury, and the results may sap her energies through life. It is most important, therefore, that her environment and tendencies should be studied with discreet carefulness.

The average pubescent girl is at school and, under the modern high-pressure system of education, is straining every nerve to keep up with her duties. Her physical development is slighted, and what vitality she has is all used up in mental effort. It is forgotten that cultivation of the mind and the cramming of the intellect do not comprise the whole of education, and that unless the body is developed along with the mind more harm than good may be done. The demand for rapid education is the curse of the age. The crowding of children through long years of work often sacrifices health, permanently, for promotion. The work of maturity is demanded by educators, where maturity does not exist.

From the ninth to the sixteenth year is the period of most rapid growth in height and weight, and sexual development begins.

[1] Read before the American Academy of Medicine, Atlantic City, June 6, 1904.

From now until the pubertal change is fully established there may be manifestations of physical, emotional and intellectual turmoil characterized by the various neuroses as, hysteria, chorea, epilepsy, somnambulism, neurasthenia, romancing, cardiopathies, gastric, hepatic, renal, vesical, genital, metabolic, pulmonary trouble, convulsions, nervous laughs, nervous coughs, anemias, deformities, etc. The neuroses may be of a purely psychic type as, hallucinations, ecstasy, delusions, night terrors, idiocy, imbecility, the various types of insanity, stupor, love, jealousy, anger, hate, theft, rape, arson, homicide, suicide, alcoholism, and the various forms of mental disturbance other than insanity. There may be periodic headache, capricious appetite and muscular twitchings.

During this period the body is developing so fast that brain weight is actually lost by the lessening of the usual blood supply to the brain, which is diverted to nourish rapidly growing organs. The child brain under these circumstances is easily fatigued. What is acquired by a brain that is tired is soon lost, memory becomes impaired, vital force is required faster than it is generated; the work of to-day is done on to-morrow's credit, and the system of the child becomes wholly at a loss to protect itself against disease and accident. "I am convinced," says Pearce, "that from the neurologist's standpoint such children in the cities would do better to have only one session in school, than be compelled to rush to a midday meal, then back again within an hour to recitation, which necessarily requires the freest circulation in the brain to the detriment of digestion, which, of course, is ill carried on under such abnormal circumstances. Over half the general aches and pains, including headaches, are due to disturbance of metabolism from various causes."

The physiologic processes of puberty make greater demands of the girl than they do of the boy, and yet in addition to performing the same work in school as her more rugged brother, her parents are not only anxious that she shall excel in the regular studies, but that she shall also acquire accomplishments such as music and painting at an early age. Is it any wonder then that under this system of high pressure and overstimulation the overworked girl, robbed of rest, sleep and exercise, fails to develop physically into perfect womanhood? These years of endless antagonism between brain growth and body growth, years perhaps the most important in her whole life, are very needful for the perfect development of the reproductive organs and the establishment of their functions. On them may hang the whole future health and happiness of the woman and her usefulness as a member of society.

Let me illustrate for a moment what I mean: to-day girls are absolutely started to school before they can dress themselves. They sit in miserably ventilated rooms from six to eight hours with perhaps a few minutes' recess, when they hurriedly eat a cold lunch. At twelve years of age they are studying English, mathematics, and a host of other things. The girl reaches home in the afternoon tired and worn out from efforts that have been too much for her. She must go at once to her music and practise for two hours, or until she becomes so nervous that the notes fail to strike harmony. Supper is announced. Afterwards she must begin her preparation for the next day's work, often being forced to study as late as ten or eleven o'clock. Then, of course, her tired brain and body are too exhausted for sleep. This is not an overdrawn picture, and every physician knows that it is not right to subject a girl verging on menstruation, or one in whom nature is making a desperate effort to maintain this function, to such an exhausting strain as this.

Visit the female colleges and you will be impressed with the large numbers of pale-faced girls whose roseate blushes of youth have been chased away by nervous exhaustion, born of the shadows of midnight toil; bright eyes have been dulled by brain fag, and sweet temper transformed into irritability, crossness and hysteria, while the womanhood of the land is deteriorating physically and filling our hospitals with invalids, neurasthenics, and sexual incompetents. After this weary worn-out rest-needing girl is released from school she launches into the dissipations of society. She may be highly cultured and shine in society, but her future husband will discover too late that he has married a large outfit of headaches, backaches, and spineaches instead of a woman fitted to take up the duties of life.

Accompanying this prolonged strain of school life there is

usually a combination of other causes also involved in the school breakdown. Home life is often badly regulated, and the parents or guardians must in many cases share a part of the blame, on account of carelessness and unwise indulgences at home. Scant attention is given to the functions of the bowels and bladder. Gross carelessness is the rule. There is an utter disregard in many cases for the menstrual week, when by their own feeling and sensations women ought to know that they are unfit for exhausting brain work, or fatiguing body work. The religious systems of Moses and Zoroaster made provision for this period, and even savage Indian women show more wisdom at this period than the product of modern civilization. The tepee of the menstruating Indian is built so low that she is compelled to lie down. Again the stomachs of girls are often spoiled by an unwholesome diet of sweetmeats, pickles and highly seasoned food, and the bad habit of nibbling between meals. Too long confinement in impure air inadequate supplies of light, little exercise, and poor sanitation complete the evils that other factors have contributed to.

Schmidt-Mounard found in the schools of Leipzig that headaches, sleeplessness and nervous ailments were frequent, especially among girls. Those schools, however, in which attention was given to gymnastics and other forms of exercise had a much smaller proportion of children suffering from these complaints than those in which it was not.

The adolescent period has been termed "the golden period of life when the faculties of both soul and body reach their acme." "It is," writes Alice Smith, "the transitional period when youth begins to look out upon society with the dawning insight of maturity. It is the time when childish illusions are dispelled, and the time when broad educational influences are most needed." The work should not be such as will overtax either the mental or the physical powers. Girls, especially, should be exempt from gymnastic work and other heavy physical effort during the menstrual period lest they bring about pelvic disease, and severe mental strains lest they fail to properly develop and functionate. "The gymnastic ideal should be to develop a splendid physique, a sound condition of the body, which means the uniform development of the organism in all its organs and parts." There should be a perfect adjustment of structure to function, a conserving of energy against the strain of future emergencies, and a creation of perfect metabolism, *i. e.*, the balancing of nutrition and waste.

While the inflexibility of school requirements acts as one of the factors in maintaining and perhaps in creating this unhealthful physical state among girls, in many instances, yet we are well aware that there are also other and potent causes for it, such as the unsuitable dress of the average female, social excesses, indiscretions in diet, neglect of sleep and the bodily needs, which contribute to the result in a large degree. Could the teacher understand the nature and the signs of the extra physical strain to which so large a per cent. of the female pupils are periodically subjected, and were she free to temper the demands of the curriculum to meet the condition, much and serious injury might be avoided. Certainly one of the strongest factors in bringing about a reduction of nerve energy and laying the foundation of a future psycho-neurosis is menstrual disorder and an unhealthy condition of the generative organs. The bane of the existence of the school girl worn out from her overwrought and overstimulated life, is dysmenorrhea. Chapman thinks that fully 75 per cent., who have reached the age of puberty, would give a history of scant and painful menstruation. Engelmann, in a tabulated list of 5000 cases among school girls, found 66 per cent. suffering from menstrual troubles. As a result of observations made on 2000 girls in the schools of New England, Jane Kelley Sabine found 75 per cent. with menstrual troubles, and 90 per cent. with leucorrhea and ovarian neuralgias. 60 per cent. had to give up work for one or two days in each month. The fact of the pain being increased with hours of intensity of study, with worry and emotion, and being diminished or ceasing entirely without treatment of any kind during vacation time is a fitting commentary on the underlying causes. These are nervous menstrual pains oftentimes due to a spasmodic action of the uterine muscular tissue. They are augmented by physical exertion and mental strain. The mental or nervous element is a more prominent factor than we usually take it to be and shows the importance of general management of the girl and the elimination of all injurious conditions of worry and debility, mental or physical, for psychical conditions and nerve influences undoubtedly have much to do with this function.

"Statistics have clearly shown the tremendous susceptibility and the almost feverish activity of the system in the prepubertal period, the period of developing womanhood; susceptibility indicated by heightened morbidity, and nerve excitement by increase of stuttering and hysteria; heightened physiologic activity by increased growth; and resistance to disease by lowered mortality; all gradually wane as the vital energies are claimed more and more by the reproductive function, and reach their lowest ebb with the advent of puberty, again rising after menstruation is established, and it is at this period of still unstable equilibrium that we find the school girl."

Similar conditions less intense recur before each menstrual period. Investigation has proven the increased pulse rate, blood tension and temperature, increased nerve excitation and muscular power, with a depression consequent upon the appearance of the flow, the system slowly regaining its normal tension with slight rise shortly after cessation, and these scientific facts are verified and emphasized by the status of young womanhood of to-day, which reflects the present conditions of life and indicates the susceptibility of the physiologic function in the early years of puberty and during menstruation.

This mental depression is evident in the listlessness, indifference and inability to master tasks easy at other times noted by every observant educator as indicating the presence of the flow and the period of its first advent. It is at this period that overstrain most readily occurs. The powers of attention and concentration are most quickly exhausted and the brightest mind, the most sensitive high-strung nervous organization, is as a rule most responsive and most liable to impairment during the first menstrual periods. The nervous system in the healthy and vigorous frequently shows an excitability, which may not pass beyond psychic limits, but in the less strong, often, symptoms which are pathologic, are developed and the connection between the menstrual epoch and the mental status becomes pronounced. The younger the girl, the nearer the period of puberty, the more impressionable is her nervous system and her susceptibilities for influences good or evil so that the greatest amount of harm is wrought in the first year of her functional life.

Dr. W. Gill Wylie pointedly expresses the truth when he says "that the American horse receives on the average better treatment than the young woman of America from the time of early girlhood until the age of development has passed. The stock breeder never forces the young animal during the period of development, realizing that it is the time the greatest care should be taken, while American parents especially of the middle classes, with great ambition for their children, and the desire that they develop intellectually beyond their own standard, allow their heads to be crammed with knowledge so rapidly that the brain cannot assimilate it, and the result is that all the strength of development is devoted to the brain, and physique finds expansion as best it can. New England furnishes the extreme type of this woman, supposedly more perfect than in any other section, intellectually above the average, but with a physique below par, with greatly reduced reproductive powers, all due to the forcing of study at the age of development."

This forced education, therefore, at or subsequent to the time of puberty, leads to flabby muscular development, poorly developed lungs, weak heart and arteries, feeble digestion, anemia, malnutrition of the nervous system, nervous irritation and an increase in neurasthenia, chorea, hysteria and final collapse.

Careful observation will show that a large proportion of the women who make up the neurotic class, have arrested development of the sexual organs in varying degrees. The human brain is approximately one-forty-fifth of the body weight. It demands about one-seventh of the blood to supply its needs. If the education be forced at the developmental period of puberty the brain needs more to meet the strain. The growing uterus and adnexa must suffer therefore in consequence of the withdrawal of blood and the nutrition it should receive. The result is a defect that is very common, the failure of the uterine cervix to develop. It retains its infantile characteristics. Under these circumstances the uterus is usually abnormally anteflexed; the canal of the uterus is less patulous than normal, with a very small os. The cervix is long and conical in shape and the uterine functions imperfectly discharged. These women nearly always suffer with scanty and painful menstruation, while amenorrhea, menorrhagia and metrorrhagia, endometritis and leucorrhea are common. The entire uterus as well as the tubes and ovaries may be involved in this imperfect development, and may remain more or less rudimentary. Under the strenuous responsibilities of life it is this class of patients who are most likely to break down and suffer from neurasthenia, and hysteria, and if of an unstable stock, even develop insanity. Much of such lack of development and final breakdown undoubtedly, has its beginning back in the forcing process of school days, the insufficient attention to physical development, which is allowed to struggle for recognition as best it may, the abuse of the corset and other vicious habits of dress and person.

As preventive measures much can be done by a watchful study of the girl for overwork, by restricting the studies during the establishment of puberty, and if this cannot be done, by taking her from school altogether until menstruation is established. Ambition to excel must be curbed when it is pressing too hard with school duties. Better sacrifice the first place in the class, or fail on an examination than get through at the expense of a poorly developed body, a nervous breakdown, and a dwarfed womanhood.

Especial attention should be paid to a proper regulation of habits at home. All stimulants and excitement, such as late hours, children's parties, and the many artificialities of our so-called modern civilization which tend to bring about a premature maturity, should be avoided. Childhood is the time of active development and growth, and as sleep is nature's great upbuilder and restorer, children should have an abundance of it, especially while their vital capacities are being drained by exacting school duties. Especial care must be given to the general health, daily evacuation of the bowels, and frequent emptying of the bladder. Proper diet should be looked after, hurried eating and eating between meals absolutely forbidden, nick-nacks and sweetmeats restricted, while plenty of outdoor exercise and healthy recreation should be engaged in.

Even more care is to be employed as the period of puberty advances,—that period when the woman's womanhood is struggling with all its energy for recognition, and when the rapid growth of pelvic organs is making exacting demands upon her strength, vitality, and nervous system that must be met. If her supply of vital force is expended in mental pursuits her physique must suffer. Undue excitement, mental worry, or anything that may divert the vital forces from the great work they are performing in the development and perfecting of her womanhood must be jealously guarded from the pubescent girl, for in all her entire life this short period is the most important to her, mentally, morally and physically, and her whole future happiness may hang upon it.

Not until teachers and parents remember that health is more important than knowledge; not until schools realize the futility of the forcing process of education, and guard the health of their girls by diminishing rather than increasing the work of the pubescent period; not until they appreciate more fully that a sound mind depends upon a sound body, can we hope to diminish the pitiable army of suffering neurotics and sexual incompetents, who so largely constitute the womanhood of the land, and who are to be the mothers of the men of our country.

BIBLIOGRAPHY.

Carstens, J. H.: *Journal of the American Medical Association*, October 17, 1903.

Chapman, G. C.: *Alabama Medical and Surgical Age*, March, 1896.

Darnall, Wm. Edgar: *American Gynecological and Obstetrical Journal*, June, 1901.

Dickinson, R. L.: *New York Medical Journal*, November 5, 1887.

Englemann, G. J.: *Journal of the American Medical Association*, February 9, 1901.

Engelmann, G. J.: *Transactions of the American Gynecological Society*, 1900.

Gossett, W. B.: *Louisville Journal of Medicine*.

Kellogg, J. H.: *Transactions of the Michigan State Society*, pp. 41, 1891.

Kirk: "Handbook of Physiology," pp. 178.

Miller: *Journal of the American Medical Association*, January 9, 1897.

Montgomery, E. E.: "Text Book of Gynecology," pp. 159.

Martin's: "Human Body," Ap. p. 15.

Noble, C. P.: *Pennsylvania Medical Journal*, November, 1900.

Pearce, F. S.: *Journal of the American Medical Association*, November 14, 1903.

Sabine, J. K.: Paper before Society for Medical Improvement, December 16, 1901.

Schmidt-Mounard: "Treatment," November, 1900.
Stuver, E.: *Medical News*, August 19, 1899.
Smith, Alice M.: *American Medicine*, November 7, 1903.
Thomas and Munde: "Diseases of Women," pp. 89.
Wilkinson, D. L.: *Journal of the American Medical Association*, November 14, 1903.
Wylie, W. Gill: In *New York World*.
Zinke, E. G.: *Journal of the American Medical Association*, February 9, 1901.

IV.

THE EFFECT OF MODERN SCHOOL METHODS UPON THE HEALTH OF THE TEACHER.[1]

BY JANE L. GREELEY, M.D., Jamestown, N. Y.

A good tool, properly used, may be counted upon for reasonably prolonged service. It does not chip at the edge, nor bend, nor grow irremediably dull while the blade is yet scarcely worn. If it must be discarded early, one of two things is wrong—either the temper of the steel was poor, or it was applied to unfit work in an unfit way.

If it is true, as an inquirer will soon learn from agencies and school boards, that the average teacher is no longer considered a desirable candidate for a position after ten or fifteen years of service; if it is true that the physical and nervous condition of the average teacher after that time makes vigorous and successful work in any other calling doubtful; if elasticity goes, and the mark of prolonged tension appears in physiognomy and habit; then either the original stock is weak—which we do not concede for the average,—or modern school methods are not ideal in their effect upon the agent who administers them. Let it be granted at the outset that there are many exceptionally wise superintendents and school boards, many, very many, wise and successful and sound teachers, yet of the average I believe that these statements may truthfully be made. To a certain extent the same facts are true in not a few professions and occupations. The assumption is none the less lawful, that every man's work ought so to be carried on that with reasonable pause for renewal of energy, he may continue it with increasing success at least well through the meridian of life. Or, if it is of necessity quickly exhausting, it should be so recognized and its value and recompense set accordingly. It is impossible not to feel that there is something wrong, somewhere, at the bottom of the rapid deterioration of nerve-force which many teachers show. It is not easy to fix upon any cause, much less to suggest any remedy, but an inquiry may serve to indicate a worthy subject for thought. For purposes of discussion we may consider the average grade teacher of the modern

[1] Read before the American Academy of Medicine, Atlantic City, June 6, 1904.

public school, the teacher through whose hands pass by far the largest proportion of the great army of scholars.

The length of the school year is certainly not in itself a proper cause for complaint. Few professions or occupations can give twelve weeks out of fifty-two for relaxation, with, moreover, a working week of but five days out of seven. Our long vacations are a matter of surprise to the Germans who with their different temperament and different climate carry on their work as easily with half our rest-time. But aside from the American tendency to rapid wear in all lines, why is it that a succession of ten years of forty five-day weeks tells on the fiber of the average teacher as it does?

Our inquiry must concern itself chiefly with women (although to a degree the same wear is apparent in all teachers), for the vast majority of public school teachers are women, and while general conditions remain as they are the same fact will remain true. I do not believe that simply because they are women they cannot endure reasonably difficult work for a lifetime, but, at all events, if society claims this particular service from them, as it certainly does, they should not be worn out unreasonably fast. What are the elements of their task?

In the first place, teaching, itself, under the most favorable conditions is a work peculiarly exhausting. It involves a specially complex mental activity in that the subject in hand must be viewed not only from the standpoint of perfect comprehension but in a sense from the respective standpoints of fifty differing minds, the swift and the slow, the clear and the cloudy, all to a degree inadequate at the start. The very gist of successful help is the ability to see exactly where the difficulty lies. So to present a subject that the ignorant mind may slowly and firmly lay hold upon it to retain it forever as an integral part of itself is a task to weary in time a mental Hercules. In proportion as the knowledge lies close to the fundamental structure of the mind is it difficult to analyze and impart. Herein is the peculiarly hard task of the teacher of the early grades. Consider the amazing genius of Miss Sullivan, the teacher who opened to Helen Keller's mind the universe of matter and thought. To describe color to the blind, sound to the deaf, abstract conceptions to a brain that had no names for even material things—it was skill almost beyond comprehension. What of the cost in nerve force of a few hours of such labor? To analyze knowledge which is wellnigh fundamental and place it in the grasp of a mind for the first time will never be easy. Is it strange that Saturday and Sunday scarcely suffice to relieve that absolutely drained-dry feeling of Friday night? Add to the purely intellectual effort, the sense of responsibility for the proper development of the child's mind and character, the stimulating of the indifferent, the discerning allowance for the timid, the control of the wayward, and the ever-shifting, manifold task becomes a strain upon the steadiest nerves.

Now as to the range of detail. The schedule of work required in the grades of an up-to-date city school is a document at once impressive and depressing to one trained in old-fashioned ways. To what might one not have attained, grounded after this fashion! But two questions creep in with insistent force. Is it, after all, in the interest of the best growth of the child to have so much highly nourishing food carefully minced and fed to him? What superhuman endowment of brains is requisite on the part of the teacher to cover for him such wide fields of thought—to be master of *all* the natural sciences, well-read in history, versed in literature, keen in mathematics, appreciative in the arts, practical in economics, faultless in applied psychology? The requirements for an ideal teacher of the early grades are appalling, not so much perhaps those measured by examination as those put upon her by her own ambition and conscience and therefore implying double the tension and strain. Surely no one has much more of the wearing struggle to attain to the impossible than the ambitious grade teacher.

Consider how immature mentally and physically are many of them as they take up the work, often under twenty, just out of high school or hard-pressed normal course, knowing little of human nature, eager only to get and to give the greatest possible amount in the shortest possible time. Blossoming time in America comes too soon in many lines, but in none more distinctly than in pedagogy. The young teachers enter upon their campaign of peculiarly intricate labor upon costly material before they have had time to develop philosophy or judgment on the one hand, or a sound body on the other. True, if teaching was postponed two or three years many would not enter upon it at all by reason of marriage or the exigencies of self-support. Is it practicable for women to undertake slow preparation for any work when a certain proportion of them are likely to marry without carrying it on far? That may be a problem, but another will balance it. Is it worth while to do anything superficially because one may not always continue to do it? To be sure, thorough preparation means higher recompense, but if we demand great things of our teachers we ought to pay for the quality of preparation and service we require. The work is too important to be a mere stopgap, or means of quick return for unripe effort. It is a high profession, to be chosen with due regard to personal fitness, to be followed with thought of long endurance, and to be recompensed with fit reward for the demands it makes. Some day the public will appreciate the economy of heavy expenditure in the manufacture of citizens.

The present normal course claims to emphasize, and does emphasize, as the chief aim of teaching the development of the child's mind rather than the imparting of facts. And yet I question whether the average teacher understands how to *let* a mind grow and consequently how to relieve her own of a considerable element of tension. Perhaps she cannot be taught this in normal days and yet I believe she should have more training in the philosophy of patience, better comprehension of the fact that the personality of the instructor and the poise and temper of his mind have more vital bearing upon the welfare of his pupil than the eager storing-up of facts. It is Mark Hopkins at one end of a log that makes the best university. If the training of teachers brought about a certain depth of philosophy in place of a part of their enthusiasm for results, it would add five years to the endurance of their nervous systems and a world of benefit to their students. Some attain it and are successful and sound of nerve for a lifetime.

If I were to choose those who should have charge of the making of teachers I would select not so much, men of broad information and enthusiasm for detail as men of mellow philosophy who understood human nature and the worth of teachers sound of body and nerve and would train them to remain so. They would appreciate the greatest single educational factor in the reach of the scholar—the personality of the teacher—and would allow no accumulation of detail to overwhelm or damage this.

In too many cases this personal element is given little room for exercise by reason of the inflexible requirements of the schedule. Often the attempt to bring scholars up to these takes spontaneity from the work and adds an element of strain from the beginning of the year to its end. How the benefit from uniformity of standard can be spared, I confess I do not see, but that the striving to attain it pervades the teacher's work to a degree far from helpful in its effect upon her is true.

In reply to the question "What part of your work is most tiring?" the answer will not seldom come—"Detail work outside the line of regular instruction." The tendency toward tabulating and compiling in the management of the modern school, useful as it is for purposes of comparison, has much against it in this respect. The grade teacher must keep record of attendance, attainments, family history, physical defects, books issued, thermometer readings, and so on *ad infinitum*—useful facts every one, but a wearying total for a tired teacher, especially when the number of students under her charge is 50 or 60 instead of the 30 or 40 which make a reasonable group to manage. Add to this written work or manual work to be inspected and appraised and the multiplicity of detail becomes a burden, and there is an inevitable loss of enthusiasm and buoyancy in carrying on the essential work of teaching.

Until ideal conditions of work prevail, what may be done to lengthen the period of a teacher's highest usefulness? First, teach her how to relax in her work; second, teach her how to relax outside of it. Perhaps she knows the necessity in theory, not often does she understand it in practice. She needs to be reminded not to waste energy even in small ways, to seize brief opportunities for relief of tension, to fight against hurry and worry, to turn the key upon school-care outside of certain limited hours. She needs to be reminded that brain and nerve cells waste with exercise and need wise food and pure air and long sleep for rebuilding.

Teach her the true use of a vacation. How seldom does she

understand genuine recreation! Often she spends her summer occupied with general domestic duties not wholly laid aside even in term time, or claims that she is sufficiently rested by "doing as she pleases." Sometimes she is so wholly lacking in common sense as to give two months to attending a summer school to wear deeper the brain-paths left by her daily treadmill. Rarely does she know the wisdom of change of scene and interest, pure fun and frolic, and contact with things in nature that grow and breathe and say nothing. I have heard it said of the New England character that it lacked ability to play hard. The same thing is true of many school-teachers—they are too desperately in earnest. A wise prescription for many of them would be "develop a saving sense of humor." Recall for a moment those extraordinarily successful as teachers and note this priceless characteristic.

All this is commonplace advice, but our educators are material too valuable to be used up quickly and needlessly. In the wise future we shall see them adding year by year to physical vigor as well as to mental ability, appreciated and paid in proportion to their ripe experience and mature wisdom in the manufacture of sound, high-principled and intelligent citizens.

DISCUSSION.

Dr. W. S. Hall, of Chicago:

I am constrained to begin with the last paper, partly because it is freshest in my mind and partly because Dr. Greeley has struck the key-note to modern pedagogy and has struck the key-note to the changes which modern school methods must undergo. I think the medical profession has emphasized the shortcomings of some of our educational methods. The results of these methods have already been clearly set forth in the papers presented. I will commend them generally and speak somewhat more in detail of this paper of Dr. Greeley.

I wish that paper might be printed in several thousand copies and sent to educators all over America. If I could single out the one thing that struck me as most important it is the little expression which Miss Greeley did not intend to emphasize highly: "Letting the mind grow." How frequently we see a boy or girl slightly backward in physical development, and precocious in mental development, the parents wisely deciding to keep the child out of school until the eighth or tenth year. At the tenth or twelfth year the child is up with its regular grade. Its mind has been growing and developing. On entering the school environment with the more advanced mental capacities it quickly and easily passes over the work usually taken up in the first years.

Again, a child becomes overworked at school and the parents regretfully take it out of school for a year. It is vegetating during that year, but its mind is probably gaining more than if in school. In my own family our girl of ten years seemed to be overworked and we kept her out the whole Spring term. The following autumn she easily carried the usual work not falling behind her class; because she had had a thorough upbuilding in mind and body. Teachers generally realize this and feel that they would like to let their pupils *grow* but the *system* will not permit it.

The importance of manual training has been emphasized by several of the papers and has been spoken of by Miss Greeley. All that is necessary is to emphasize the paramount importance of that. I am informed that in my own city an equipment for manual training can be introduced into the schools for a thousand children for $1200 per annum. To get the manual training installed the money will have to be raised by subscription; but it will be made up, because there are enough people who realize the importance of this hand-brain development. That is the line which the future education must take, for without the development of the hand there can be no symmetrical development of the brain.

Dr. T. D. Davis, Pittsburg:

One of the troubles of our public schools is the fact that there are so many scholars of different grades of advancement and of different intellects in the same room, who must be taught in the same classes and the teacher is expected to bring all to the level of the highest. Another difficulty is that the parents load their children down with so much to do outside of school, instead of allowing them to have all their time at home for recreation and some study. I have had to investigate a number of complaints concerning teachers giving their scholars too much night work, and have always found that the trouble was with the parents requiring the child to do too much at home in addition to the school work, such as attending dancing school, taking music lessons, preparing for Sabbath school and other entertainments, social engagements and many other things that occupied the time that should have been given to recreation. It is an easy matter to blame the child's physical troubles on the school. It seems to argue great application and studiousness of the child. I have known young misses who have become strong and healthy by going away from home to a private school where they were not subjected to these outside engagements and yet the curriculum was more severe than in the public schools that they had been attending.

A point that cannot be emphasized too strongly is the necessity of the public school-teacher having possibly more than forty scholars under her care and being expected to bring them all up to the same level in a definite length of time. It is almost beyond human power to do this if they do not have the cooperation of the parents at home; and especially when "a child is taken out of school in order that its brain may grow" and on being put back is expected to equal the others, at the end of the session, who have remained and been judiciously taught. This great hardship reflects on the teacher, but is probably not taken into account by the parent.

As a rule children are not sent to school too young. It has been my observation, that the drones and hold-backs in the schools are children who have been kept at home until they were eight or nine years of age by foolish parents and break down trying to catch up with those of their own age. It is all right to point to the wonderful teaching of Laura Bridgeman and Helen Keller, but if their teachers had been compelled to teach a definite amount in a certain period of time or been liable to lose their positions if they did not do so, through some ignorant school director, their mental and nervous systems could not have endured the strain.

Dr. Leartus Connor, Detroit:

In the very interesting papers that we have heard there comes the picture of a great Juggernaut, a great machine under which every child that comes to the public schools must pass. The machine starts with the proposition that mentral training only is desirable, that the ultimate aim is to turn out of this machine, only doctors, lawyers, preachers, or similar scholars. The intention is not to have the boy grow to the largest stature of manhood, or the girl to the largest type of womanhood. If it were, the common sense of the teacher would eliminate that which would damage and bring in that which would help. No two children were ever made alike, and yet we have an inflexible system for their education and the children often come to grief. The most of them should never have been lawyers, doctors or preachers, exclusive brain workers, but the system under which they were placed compelled them, nothing else was respectable. The state didn't set its impress on anything else. It didn't encourage anything else. Hence the degradation of physical labor. We see "hope" in the manual training schools and departments for training children to "do things." The state needs physical workers as well as mental and the schools should train both.

Dr. J. H. McBride, Pasadena, Cal.:

In the syllabus of Dr. Smith's paper, he says that all higher education is injurious to the health and if I have understood him, he has maintained this in his argument.

I think that there are facts that controvert this. The record of Wellesley and Vassar show that the graduates of these institutions enjoy quite as good health as the average and those of them who marry, have a greater average number of children than other women. It is the experience in the California Universities, Stanford and Berkeley, that the health of the young women who go there is better when they graduate than when they enter.

There is no reason furnished by physiology why a woman's health should be injured by acquiring knowledge, if she studies under proper conditions, and the conditions under which women study in college are being rapidly improved.

There is good evidence that education, if conducted under proper conditions, helps to physical development. The Greek system proved that this was possible. At Annapolis they have naval cadets, at Newport there are naval apprentices. The Cadets receive gymnastic training in addition to the naval drill and five hours study daily, which is a severe mental drill. At Newport the apprentices who are simply intended for sailors have no mental training but their entire régime is otherwise like that of the Annapolis Cadets.

At the end of the four years training it has been found that the Cadets who have studied five hours a day are taller than the apprentices at Newport and that they also have a larger chest girth and weigh more, showing that the total vital capacity is on the side of the boys who had the mental training.

Concerning the health of school-teachers referred to by Miss Greeley, it is an important subject but there is not time here to discuss it. Teachers live too much indoors. They not only use the mind to the neglect of the body but they use the mind in an endless repetition year after year, a monotony that is itself injurious to the health. Variety of mental occupation and varied interests are conducive to good digestion, red blood and vigorous muscles and if our teachers had this with added physical activity that each one might easily have, the nervous breakdowns that not infrequently occur among them would be very rare.

If there is any person in the world who specially needs to have abounding health and physical vigor, it is the teacher. Without this vigor, work will be done under pressure, and with the friction that wears.

Dr. Smith closes:

In answer to the criticisms of my paper, I made an exception in favor of the great boarding schools, and I would like to add the universities. The health of girls improves very much in good boarding schools or universities owing to the regular life and the absence of those extra things put upon them at home. Many a time I have been the means of stopping children from going on with music at the expense of their health. I think the family doctors could do much in this direction. My remarks in the paper applied mostly to the girls of the public schools where the competition is so keen. I used to tell the teachers that if my own children ever got to the top of the class I would take them away for a year. Children should not be urged beyond their strength.

We hear much of "Why is the church losing its influence?" My answer is, because highly educated women cannot be satisfied with the home that the average young man can afford to give them, and men who cannot marry as a rule cannot go to church. If you want the churches filled get women to make marriage attractive. They can do it if they want to, but not by higher education.

OBSERVATIONS IN PASSING.

The postponement of the annual meeting until the late fall should not prevent any activities for the advance of the interest fostered by the American Academy of Medicine. The meeting should be a memorable one in every respect. When it met in Chicago in 1889, 32 were registered in attendance, and 100 were elected to fellowship. With the growth of the Academy since then, it is not expecting too much to double both these figures. It is too early to make plans for attendance; it is none too early to begin a campaign to secure new members. Let every fellow call to mind graduates of his own college who are eligible, and present the claims of the Academy to them for the purpose of securing an application for fellowship.

What are these claims? It is necessary to formulate a preliminary statement. A college course is not essential for procuring information, for securing of knowledge, or even for acquiring an education. There are many who are the peers of any college-bred man in these things. But in a college education, if the man has been benefitted by his college life, he attains a college spirit which no other environment can give and which cannot be imitated. There is an enthusiasm, a bouyancy, not for selfish ends but for achievement which is *sui generis*. Again, the medical profession in its best types is intensely conservative, a condition to be at once admired and deplored. It maintains a proper dignity, which is well, it permits the flourishing of the hangers-on to the profession which is ill. Were the solidity of the conservatism tempered by the enthusiasm of the constructive idealist working with facts, not fancies, many of the ills that now torment the profession would follow the path that typhus and yellow fever, or other diseases of like nature, have trodden because of the investigation of the sanitarian.

These are the days, when the solution of the problem of society is attempted in a scientific spirit, and the life of a physician is so woven in the fabric of society, that, more than any other profession, does its success depend upon proper relations to it. While these problems are attacked in a desultory manner by many, there is little of patient scientific investigation. To these questions the American Academy of Medicine is devoting its attention. Every college-bred physician who has not lost the college spirit will find some phase of the many-sided problem of interest, and the patient investigation of the many will result in the accurate delimitation of the practice of medicine in the social structure. The problems are as interesting, as practical and as valuable in their sphere as the discovery of the cholera microbe or the plasmodium of malarial fever. The resulting benefits result rather to the profession as a profession than to the individual, and are removed from modern commercialism, but here again they appeal to the spirit of a college training. Indeed, the founders of the Academy, while led by other reasons in defining the qualification for membership, were directed wisely, since the field of study which has opened to the Academy, can only be conducted by that force most markedly manifested in the college spirit. Here then, is an association of physicians, whose investigations are along lines in harmony with other researches undertaken in the college spirit, and whose conclusions are for the furtherance of the medical profession in everything which makes for excellence; an association which does not conflict with any other organization, but is rather of assistance to them; an association particularly attractive to every college man who has taken in its spirit and its purpose. These are the claims we can present for the active cooperation of every college-educated physician of our acquaintance. If properly presented by those now enrolled, the increase of membership at the next meeting will be far beyond two hundred.

**

The fourth official bulletin of the XVth International Medical Congress, which is to be held in Lisbon in April, 1906, gives evidence of the activity of the committee in charge. At this early date, the scientific value of the Congress appears to be assured not only from the number of papers already promised, but as well by the persons who have promised them. The twelfth section has been divided into two sub-sections, on laryngology, rhinology and otology and on stomatology. Dr. John H. Musser is the chairman of the committee representing the United States.

The first letter opened in 1905 contained a circular headed in "scare-lines," "THE DRUG-FIEND MAKERS, THE ROTTENEST OF QUACKS," containing an attack upon some business house alleged to be engaged in disreputable practices but unsigned. Everything said about the firm may be true, but what words can fairly express the despicable meanness of the man who is unwilling to be responsible for his statements, and stabs in the dark?

∗

The fourth annual report of the New York State Hospital for the Care of Crippled and Deformed Children records the continuance of the good work of this excellent institution. It is gratifying to note that a property has been purchased for its permanent location at West Haverstraw, which will be occupied in the Spring.

The hospital cottages for children at Baldwinville, Mass., are of a wider scope, but in the same direction of affording help to children. The twenty-second annual report of the corporation is on our table, detailing the benefits resulting from its ministration.

LITERATURE NOTES.

THE SURGICAL TREATMENT OF BRIGHT'S DISEASE. BY GEORGE M. EDEBOHLS, A.M., M.D., LL.D., Professor of the Diseases of Women in the New York Post-graduate Medical School and Hospital. New York: Frank F. Lisiecki, 9 Murray Street, publisher. pp. 333. Price, $2.00.

Dr. Edebohls' idea of treating chronic nephritis by decapsulation of the kidney, while an extension of the suggestion already published by Reginald Harrison, was the first authoritative and systematic recommendation for surgical treatment of chronic Bright's disease.

The interest this method has excited in the medical world proves the value attached to a measure which seems to promise more than any other known method of treating conditions which have hitherto been followed by certain speedy death.

As Dr. Edebohls says in his preface, "The time is not ripe for a complete systematic presentation of the subject of the surgical treatment of Bright's disease. The present work is therefore to give facts and information especially as regards results . . . concerning the new treatment."

The book is made up of a collection of monographs written by Dr. Edebohls and published in various journals on the subject of renal decapsulation, arranged in chronologic order, and of the collected histories of 72 cases, all the cases he had operated on from Bright's disease up to the end of the year 1903.

The work is an interesting and a profitable one to all physicians. Whether one agrees with Dr. Edebohls or not in his recommendation to treat chronic nephritis by surgical measures, the record of the observations and reasoning leading up to his method, the dispassionate presentation of the facts with the array of cases and their results, make this pioneer volume a valuable one.

A DICTIONARY OF NEW MEDICAL TERMS, INCLUDING UPWARDS OF 38,000 WORDS AND MANY USEFUL TABLES, BEING A SUPPLEMENT TO "AN ILLUSTRATED DICTIONARY OF MEDICINE BIOLOGY, AND ALLIED SCIENCES," BY GEORGE M. GOULD, A.M., M.D., based on recent scientific literature. 1905. Philadelphia: P. Blakiston's Son & Co. pp. 571. Price, $5.00.

Dr. Gould states in his preface that over 30,000 new terms have been devised for the medical sciences since the last revision of his illustrated dictionary. This fact explains why we are so often disappointed in consulting a dictionary; it is so often as bare of the particular word whose meaning is unknown, as Mother Hubbard's cupboard in the nursery rhyme. While the coining of terms has not ceased with the issuing of this volume, we are 30,000 and more to the good by its issuing. The profession should thank Dr. Gould for including in this supplement not only the newer terms, but many others that are passing out of use, or have already become antiquated, one can do no research work without meeting them. Because they are obsolete, the precise meaning has escaped our memory, and it is just as useful to have these as the newest creation of the word-coiner. The appearance of the page resembles the dictionary to which it is a supplement. Every one who owns a Gould Dictionary should possess himself of this volume; and those who have one of the other excellent medical dictionaries can use this in connection with his favorite nearly as well.

The publishers announce the binding of this supplement in a single volume with the dictionary, which is convenient for those who wish to purchase both dictionary and supplement.

THE DOCTOR'S WINDOW—POEMS BY THE DOCTOR, FOR THE DOCTOR, AND ABOUT THE DOCTOR. EDITED BY INA RUSELLE WARREN. 1904. Akron, O.: The Saalfield Publishing Co. Cloth. pp. 288. Price, $2.50.

This is the fifth volume of that very satisfactory series publishing by the Saalfield Publishing Company. Satisfactory is used advisedly, for each volume is maintaining the promises of the prospectus, whereby there is a feeling of satisfaction and not disappointment. The editor of this volume, while quite happy in her selection, is not using the word poem in the subtitle critically to characterize a very enjoyable collection of verse including some poems. There are about 125 selections in all, including many that are well known from Chaucer to James Whitcomb Riley, and others by men of less renown, which will make the collection the more valuable, since these selections are not so available in the ordinary library.

The new series of the *Eclectic Medical Gleaner*, published under the auspices of the Lloyd Library, appears in a new dress, changed beyond recognition. It is typographically among the handsomest journals coming to our notice; that it will be conducted upon lines of a high ideal goes without saying with the Lloyd Library sponsorship. Still we miss the scintillations of the former editor, handsome-appearing and handsome-acting as the first number of the new series is.

The *Interstate Medical Journal*, for January, follows its excellent custom, giving a series of articles reviewing the literature for 1904, and indicates the progress made in medicine during the year. It is well worth the reading.

The October (1904) number of the *National Druggist*, of St. Louis, issues a comprehensive account of the drug exhibit of the exposition, and is adorned with such a wealth of illustration as to make it a work of art.

The *St. Louis Courier of Medicine* is publishing a series of articles on the care of premature infants, based on the experience of Dr. Zahorsky, who had medical control of the "Incubator on the Pike" during the latter part of the Exposition. The articles are worth the reading.

The *Arena* begins a series of articles on the political corruption in Pennsylvania, a prolific theme, and as the author, Mr. Rudolph Blankenburg, has been in the front rank of the "Anti's," there should be revelation helpful to the purification of the corrupting.

The *Annals of Surgery* for December, is remarkable for several noteworthy items: it completes the 40th volume and the 20th year of its publication, and under the same editorial supervision; it contains 270 pages of letter press, quite a volume in itself, and does not abate from the usual high standard of its papers, in thus increasing their number. Editor, publisher and reader are to be alike congratulated.

GENERAL CATALOGUE OF MEDICAL AND SURGICAL WORKS. Philadelphia: P. Blakiston's Son & Co. Cloth, pp. 109, interleaved. Price, 25 cents.

This is not an ordinary book catalogue, but quite a complete list of the medical books on the market, printed in a neat volume about 6 x 3½ inches in size and neatly bound. Its size and binding permits it to be kept near at hand, where it will furnish the list of books obtainable, when one wishes to make a purchase, without seeking for and searching through a number of pamphlets. The blank pages permit of manuscript additions to the list as the books are announced from time to time.

VITAL STATISTICS OF THE CITY OF CHICAGO FOR THE YEARS 1899-1903 INCLUSIVE. Chicago. 1904. pp. 128.

Dr. Reynolds, the efficient Health Officer of Chicago, has tabulated and published the vital statistic returns of that city in a form that will make their consultation much more convenient, and add to their value.

NOTES FOR THE GUIDANCE OF AUTHORS IN THE SUBMISSION OF MANUSCRIPT TO PUBLISHERS. 1905. New York. The MacMillan Company. Paper. pp. 66. Price, 25 cents.

These "Suggestions have been compiled with the aid of the

heads of the various departments of the MacMillan Company," and are valuable because clearly expressed and to the point. If every person who is contemplating the preparation of a paper for a medical society, which paper afterwards is to be published, would possess himself of a copy of the booklet and heed its suggestions, it would be to the advantage of all who are concerned in the publishing.

HOW TO STUDY LITERATURE—A GUIDE TO THE INTENSIVE STUDY OF LITERARY MASTERPIECES. BY BENJAMIN A. HEYDRICK, A.B. (Harvard), Professor of English Literature—State Normal School, Millersville, Pa. Third edition revised and enlarged. New York: Hinds, Noble and Eldredge, 31-35 W. 15th Street. pp. 150. Price, 75 cents.

"This book is intended to aid in the study of literature," and it is planned admirably to start one upon such a study. It calls attention to the various classes of literary expression, and gives outlines for the study of the various forms, giving concrete examples in directing the study of definite selections. Should a student make use of this book and read the author's suggestions, he will be in a position not only to enjoy but to profit by his future reading.

BULLETIN

OF THE

American Academy of Medicine.

VOL. VI.   ISSUED APRIL, 1905.   No. 17.

The American Academy of Medicine is not responsible for the sentiments expressed in any paper or address published in the BULLETIN.

HOW MAY THE PUBLIC SCHOOL BE HELPFUL IN THE PREVENTION OF TUBERCULOSIS?[1]

By S. A. KNOPF, M.D., New York, Vice-president of the American Academy of Medicine; Associate Director of the Clinic for Pulmonary Diseases of the Health Department; Visiting Physician to the Riverside Sanatorium for Consumptives of the City of New York; Consulting Physician to Sanatorium Gabriels, Gabriels, N. Y., the Consumption Hospital of West Mountain, Scranton, Pa., Binghampton, N. J., etc.

A little over a year ago I had the honor to deliver a lecture on a subject similar to the present one, before the Teachers' College of the Columbia University of the City of New York. It was entitled "The Duties of the School Teacher in the Combat of Tuberculosis as a Disease of the Masses." My audience was composed of graduates and undergraduates in pedagogy, and I was more than pleased and gratified to see the deep interest manifested in the subject by the young men and women present. A few weeks later my lecture appeared in *American Medicine* and has since been reprinted in the *Journal of Education* and in the *Teachers' Sanitary Bulletin*, and the Department of the Interior, Office of Indian Affairs, has asked me for permission to reprint it for distribution in the Indian schools. This shows that the interest in the subject is spreading, and the time for the public school to take up the question of how to be helpful in the prevention of tuberculosis seems eminently ripe. This I may plead as an excuse for bringing the subject before the American Academy of Medicine as a medicosociological question well worth our consideration. It

[1] Read before the American Academy of Medicine, at Atlantic City, June 6, 1904.

is my sincere hope that the discussion of this paper by the Academicians who have made school hygiene, preventive medicine, and tuberculosis a special study will bring out many valuable points of interest to us and of interest to the cause.

To be as concise as possible, I have divided my address into four parts, namely, the duties of the school board, the duties of the superintendent, the duties of the school-teacher, and those of the school physician, relating to the prevention of tuberculosis.

The school board, or board of education, as it is called in some localities, should, in choosing a site for a school, bear in mind that, whenever possible, a somewhat elevated region, where the streets are wide and the surrounding houses not too high and not too close together, and where the traffic is not too heavy, should be selected for building a public school. About the construction of a modern and model schoolhouse much could be said. The essentials of such construction are well-known to all sanitarians and up-to-date architects. In relation to the prevention of tuberculosis I would suggest only a few points. Where the site or locality does not permit of having a large playground, a roof garden which can be covered in winter is absolutely necessary. Instead of our American windows, which can only be opened to one-half of their extent, I should wish to see French windows in every schoolhouse, or in the wall sliding windows or those that turn on a pivot, all of which permit twice the amount of foul air to go out and of good air to come in that our ordinary windows do. Heating and general ventilation of schoolrooms should, of course, be of the most improved kind. The walls and woodwork of schoolrooms should be plain, to make the accumulation of dust virtually impossible and the cleaning easy. All corners should be rounded off, and the walls painted. The interior equipment—that is to say, the school furniture, benches, and desks—should be so arranged that they can be easily moved or folded together, so that a thorough cleaning of the floors is made possible after each daily session. It goes without saying that the drinking-cup should be replaced by the hygienic drinking fountain, which makes the use of a cup unnecessary, and thus eliminates one method of transmission of microbic disease.

Every public school should have a well-equipped gymnasium

and a swimming tank with constantly running fresh or salt water, warmed to a suitable temperature in winter. Each pupil should be given the opportunity to bathe several times during the week. To learn to swim should be made obligatory and every class should be supervised by a competent swimming master. Leaving aside the great hygienic gain to be derived from such an installation, especially when the pupils are recruited from homes where bathrooms are rare and where regular bathing is considered superfluous, the swimming lessons will be of value to every boy and girl, and in case of such disaster as the recent Slocum tragedy there will be a much smaller loss of life. There is hardly a college in existence in America where the gymnasium and the swimming tank do not form an important part of the equipments, and a college without them would surely suffer in prestige. The public school where the children of the masses receive their education should not be behind the private college in its equipments.

I am convinced not only that the public school which has a well-equipped swimming establishment and which makes regular bathing and instruction in swimming obligatory for every pupil will have fewer cases of infectious and contagious diseases, particularly scrofula and tuberculosis, but that the intellectual and moral status of its pupils will also be higher.

The duties of the superintendent of a public school in the prevention of tuberculosis are manifold. In arranging the curriculum he should bear in mind never to push the intellectual training to the detriment of the bodily development or physical welfare of the children in his school. There has been, and is yet, altogether too much overtaxing of the brain and the nervous system of our boys and girls in public and also in private schools. Our gynecologists and nerve specialists have given us enough illustrations of the detrimental effects of the overtaxing and overstraining of the mind and the nervous system of young girls at the age of their development into womanhood. Those of us who have given tuberculosis a somewhat closer study also know that it is often at the period of entering puberty that the predisposed individual becomes most susceptible to the invasion of the bacillus, particularly when additional strain is put upon the physical or mental system. This holds good of both sexes. A judiciously divided curriculum, intercepted with gymnastics, swimming, and as much outdoor instruction as possible, would seem to me a most important factor in the prevention, not only of tuberculosis, but of all indoor diseases and nervous troubles.

By outdoor instruction I mean not only botanizing tours and geological excursions, but also outdoor singing and outdoor recitation. In my text-book on tuberculosis,[1] as well as in my article on the subject in the *Twentieth Century Practice of Medicine*,[2] I quoted Barth, of Köslin, who had made a careful study of the effects of singing on the action of the lungs, on diseases of the heart, on the pulmonary circulation, on the blood, the vocal apparatus, the upper air passages, the ear, the general health, the development of the chest, and on the activity of the digestive organs. As a result of his studies he came to the conclusion that singing should be considered one of the exercises most conducive to health. I am willing to go even further and say that outdoor singing and outdoor recitation, when the weather is neither too windy nor too cold, is a most excellent means of preventing the development of pulmonary diseases. You have all heard of the numerous cases of open-air speakers, such as political campaigners, evangelists, etc., having developed their respiratory capacities and strengthened their lungs as a result of their peculiar profession. Some even profess to have been cured of consumption as a result of their outdoor speaking. The German military authorities, who have the reputation for instituting all exercises which tend to prevent disease and invigorate the soldiers, have of late much encouraged singing during the marching of the troops.

To every class in the public school should be given opportunity in fairly good weather to have recitation and singing at least once a day in the playground, adjoining garden, or roof garden. Breathing exercises should, of course, be instituted at least for a few minutes at a time for all classes. This should be done either in the open air or when the windows are wide open, and a number of times each day. The simple breathing exercises which I recommend as a prevention of pulmonary diseases, I have pub-

[1] "Pulmonary Tuberculosis, Its Modern Prophylaxis and the Treatment in Special Institutions and at Home," p. 86, P. Blakiston's Son & Co., Philadelphia.
[2] "Tuberculosis, Diagnosis, Prognosis, Prophylaxis, and Treatment," *Twentieth Century Practice of Medicine*, 20, 230.

lished and illustrated in my books, as well as in various articles, and also in my popular essay on tuberculosis,[1] and I don't feel that it will be necessary to describe them again here. The selection of rational text-books on physiology and general hygiene must be left to the good judgment of the board of education and the superintendent.

The duties of the superintendent and those of the schoolteacher are, of course, interdependent. The former makes out and supervises the curriculum, the latter carries it out. The lessons in physiology and hygiene must be adapted to the age and understanding of the pupils. The schoolteacher should, of course, be familiar with all the practical and feasible methods in vogue in regard to the prevention of tuberculosis as an infectious and communicable disease. The source of infection from indiscriminate expectoration, from coughing and sneezing in people's faces, from kissing on the mouth, and other unhygienic habits can be taught in simple words to the children of even the primary classes. A good method to impress these simple rules on schoolchildren, and thus protect them from contracting tuberculosis during school life, is to have printed leaflets given to every child. These leaflets should contain the "do's" and "do nots" which are the alphabet in the prevention of tuberculosis in kindergartens, private and public schools, and college. I have compiled these simple rules, and with your permission will read them:

Do not spit, except in a spittoon or a piece of cloth or a handkerchief used for that purpose alone. On your return home have the cloth burned by your mother, or the handkerchief put in water until ready for the wash.

Never spit on a slate, floor, sidewalk, or playground.

Do not put your fingers into your mouth.

Do not pick your nose or wipe it on your hand or sleeve.

Do not wet your fingers in your mouth when turning the leaves of books.

Do not put pencils into your mouth or wet them with your lips.

Do not hold money in your mouth.

Do not put pins into your mouth.

Do not put anything into your mouth, except food and drink.

Do not swap apple cores, candy, chewing gum, half-eaten food, whistles, bean-blowers, or anything that is put in the mouth.

Peel or wash your fruit before eating it.

[1] "Tuberculosis as a Disease of the Masses, and How to Combat It," M. Firestack New York.

Never cough nor sneeze in a person's face. Turn your face to one side, and hold your hand or handkerchief before your mouth.

Keep your face and hands and finger-nails clean; wash your hands with soap and water before each meal.

When you don't feel well, have cut yourself, or have been hurt by others, do not be afraid to report to the teacher.

These leaflets should be read and re-read by the pupils and explained and commented upon by the teacher. Children should be not only allowed, but rather urged, to take these leaflets home and show them to their parents. Thus, these little ones may become missionaries in homes where cleanly habits and domestic hygiene have been heretofore unknown.

In schools where slate- and lead-pencils are given to the children and collected after school hours, these articles should be disinfected before they are again distributed to the pupils. Not only the spread of tuberculosis, but far more contagious diseases, such as measles, diphtheria, and scarlet fever, may be prevented among school-children by this simple precaution. The custom in vogue in some schools of having every child use a suitable envelope, so as always to have the same pencil, while preferable to no precaution at all, is, in my opinion, not nearly so safe as a thorough disinfection.

Another method of teaching school-children the prevention of tuberculosis has been inaugurated in France in a most ingenious way. My distinguished teacher, Professor Letulle, suggested to the Minister of Education of France that the covering of the books used by school-children should serve as a means of instructing the pupils concerning the prevention of tuberculosis. He himself wrote the two pages of instruction for that purpose. The outside cover represents the exterior of a sanatorium, and the text is illustrated by a number of pictures. Permit me to give you here the translation of the subjects which are treated in a most concise and comprehensible way on these two pages:

"The air we breathe and the respiratory organs.

"Tuberculosis decimates humanity.

"Tuberculosis is contagious.

"Tuberculosis and its microbe.

"Robert Koch, the discoverer of the microbe of tuberculosis (consumption).

"Tuberculous infection from man to animal and fr
to man.

"Tuberculosis can be prevented.

"Sure way to prevent consumption.

"Never use strong drinks.

"Tuberculosis can be cured.

"Tuberculosis is a social disease."

An important point in the prevention of the disease
sideration among school-children is, to my mind, that t
teacher should be familiar with the objective signs and
of tuberculosis and the characteristics of a person pred
consumption. Thus, for example, if the child is a mouth
owing to vegetation in the retronasopharynx, the teacl
call the attention of the school physician or parents to t
condition, as predisposing to nasal and bronchial cat:
possibly pulmonary complications. The school-teacher
familiar with the meaning of such objective symptoms,
sistent cough, feverish face, becoming easily tired, or a
increased excitability, and on the discovery of these
take such steps as are indicated. As is well-known, tu
of the bones and joints is relatively and absolutely more
in children than pulmonary complications. Lameness
tiring of arms or legs is often the beginning sympto
tuberculosis. A slight pressure in the region of the joi
a sudden severe pain. If the spinal column is affected,
toms will depend upon the location of the vertebra wl
tacked by the disease. For example, if this should be
gion of the neck, there will be difficulty in swallowing,
ing, or a frequent dry cough. If any of the vertebræ
gion of the chest is affected, a feeling of constriction lil
band around the chest will be observed, accompanied
digestive troubles. If the seat of the disease is the lowe
of the spinal column, there will be irritation of the bla
lower bowels, an inclination to much urinating, and
pains toward the hips.

If any such symptoms are discovered by the school-tea
school physicians and the parents should be notified.

Scrofulous children are found particularly frequently in

tricts of the poor, and the teacher should know that scrofulosis is only a lighter type of tuberculosis, but it is tuberculosis, and that it can be successfully treated and cured by fresh air, sunshine, good food, and improving the general hygienic environments. The scrofulous child is usually pale, with flabby skin and muscles. The glands around the neck are swollen, and skin disease, sore eyes, and running ears are frequent symptoms. The little patient usually manifests a phlegmatic condition, but we might also find some that are nervous and irritable. The latter often have a particularly white, delicate skin, which makes the veins visible. Fever may be observed in some scrofulous children. In view of the happily very curable nature of scrofulous affections, the importance of the early recognition and of the timely and judicious treatment is, of course, self-evident.

In speaking of scrofulous and tuberculous children of the poor I must revert once more to the duties of the school board; for what can the teacher or the superintendent do with the underfed children of the poor attending our public schools? Breathing exercises will not supplement their lack of food, but, if anything, they will increase the appetite of the pupil, and a cracker and an apple are not enough for a growing boy or girl and altogether too little to make their cheeks red. I would therefore suggest to the board of education a philanthropic enterprise in which the generous and good-hearted people of every city would most gladly join. It may thus become possible to provide these half-starved little ones with a luncheon of a few meat sandwiches and one or two glasses of good milk, and I am convinced that fewer will develop tuberculosis and scrofulosis, and they will do better work at school and at home.

To avoid a pauperizing tendency, a few pennies may be charged for these lunches. This practice is in vogue in the city of Boston, Mass., and works most satisfactorily. After a few weeks of such persistent administration of good luncheons the previously underfed children improve in appearance and often gain from two to three pounds in weight.

Lastly, we come to the duties of the school physician. They have already been pointed out in part in speaking of the duties of the schoolteacher in referring to the physician all suspected pupils for careful examination. A second duty of the school physician should be the constant supervision of the sanitary condition of the school-buildings; regular visits to the gymnasium and the swimming school; and, lastly, the most important function of all, the periodical examination of the chests of all pupils, teachers, and employees of the school. The weeding-out of all such individuals as might constitute a source of infection, or those whose treatment becomes an imperative necessity, the advice to be given to parents of a tuberculous child, will make the school physician a most important factor in the solution of the tuberculosis problem.

It goes without saying that the school physician, who must devote so much time to this duty in order to do it faithfully, should receive ample remuneration for his services.

It is with great satisfaction that I saw among the news items of the *Medical Record* of April 30th that the San Francisco Board of Health had inaugurated the systematic examination of school-children. To the honor of the profession let me add that the first examination was made by a voluntary corps of fifty physicians.

In the prevention of tuberculosis in childhood I have always looked upon the suppression of child labor as one of the *prima facie* necessities. While it is with a sense of deep humiliation that we must acknowledge that this curse to childhood is not yet entirely done away with in all our states, it is gratifying to note the ever-increasing progress toward its suppression.

However, there is one kind of child labor which the law can only reach with difficulty, except as it has the cooperation of the schoolteacher and the school physician. I refer to those cases where cruel or thoughtless parents impose upon their often delicate children the fulfilment of household duties or the performance of manual labor which would task the strength of a grown person. The timid child will probably never complain, but when the teacher or school physician suspects that the paleness, the stooping shoulders, and the tired, sad look are the result of excessive manual labors imposed upon the child by parents or guardians, it is his duty to investigate and interfere. All of you who have worked among the poor will remember the pale-faced little mothers taking care of two or three younger sisters or brothers and carrying the baby for hours in their frail arms. Even the widowed father has no right to impose such burdens on his little daughter. With tact and judicious advice, or with the help philanthropic organizations offer to parents, the conditions can sometimes be remedied; but I know from experience that occasions arise when the majesty of the law alone will protect the child from being used as a little beast of burden, made a physical wreck before the age of puberty, or neglected and treated so that it will become a sure candidate for consumption in its early teens.

What shall be done with a tuberculous child whose presence in the public school may be a danger to his comrades, besides making his own recovery much more difficult? Municipalities and philanthropists should, after the example of the people in Europe, create seaside or country sanatoria where the tuberculous children may not only have the best possible chance of becoming cured, but also receive the necessary education. In France, Germany, Italy, and Holland all the sanatoria for tuberculous and scrofulous children are in reality school sanatoria, and the intellectual development of the children goes hand in hand with their restoration to health. The unfortunate school-teacher, who often through overwork and close confinement has contracted the disease, which in the adult is often more readily recognized, and as a result usually has to resign, might find here an opportunity to earn his or her living anew, at least during the convalescent stage. The curative results in the sanatoria for scrofulous and tuberculous children are simply surprising; in some of them they have been as high as 70 and 80 per cent. of absolute cures.

In conclusion, let me express the wish that American municipalities and philanthropists may soon realize that public school sanatoria for the treatment of tuberculous and scrofulous children are an urgent necessity in nearly all our large American cities. They will have to serve as places for cure of the thousands of tuberculous children, many of whom, without this, will ultimately develop the more severe type of the disease, and will become burdens, if not to their parents, to the community at large. With ample provisions for the cure and with the fulfilment of the duties of the school boards, superintendents, teachers, school physicians, and parents, it is my firm belief that the public school can be made one of the most important factors in the prevention of tuberculosis as a disease of the masses.

16 WEST NINETY-FIFTH STREET.

CONSIDERATIONS REGARDING MEDICAL INSP[ ]
IN THE PUBLIC SCHOOLS.[1]

By EDWARD JACKSON, M.D., Denver, Colorado.

We study disease that life and health may be p
Medicine began with men already stricken by wound or
infection, and the things looked to for their direct relief.
vanced to warning them of impending danger, whetl
pestilence or tainted food or brittle arteries. The line
tinued advance is toward development of the greatest
ties of life and health by knowledge applied to the whol
of living. Hygiene understood, taught, practised, mac
nant in the public schools is the next step in this progres

School hygiene must include attention to actual disea:
the schools and provision for its treatment; the immed
pression of epidemics; the recognition of all physica
among the pupils, with steps to help secure their cc
as far as possible; maintenance of the best sanitary cc
throughout the whole school environment of the child; t
ing by verbal instruction, exercises and habitual pr
general and individual hygiene; and the inspiring in ever
the same reverence for health that we seek to instil wit
to patriotism or moral obligation.

Without claiming that this work of fundamental and t
importance is to be done wholly by the medical profess
obvious that it must at many points be guided by and
upon that mass of knowledge which has been and is lab
accumulated by the medical profession, and much of
available from no other source.

Medical inspection or medical supervision of schools is t
agency through which our knowledge of vital processes
ease is to be applied. We say medical supervision, for
spection ending in itself would be a farce. There must
seeing and doing. Inspection takes value and significar
as it becomes the first step toward modifying what it di
But for efficiency the circuit from seeing to doing must b

[1] Read before the American Academy of Medicine at Atlantic City, N. J., J
in connection with the first partial report of the committee to investigate the
hygiene in the public schools.

ened as much as possible. So far as may be the eyes to see, the knowledge to appreciate and the judgment and authority to act should be vested in the same person, and in the immediate future this person will generally be the medical inspector. Generally but not always. Even at the present time the recognition of certain physical defects and the dealing with them is, in many places, left largely or wholly to the teacher; and in some cities the director or teacher of gymnastics is more likely to develop into the true school physician, than is the medical inspector strictly so-called. Therefore, in the present report we desire to call attention to the work to be done, and the ideals to be aimed at without elaborating any detailed system of organization, or distributing the specific duties among the school officers to whom they might be assigned. It is this design that is responsible for this apparent confusion of school inspection and supervision, of using as synonyms medical inspector and school physician, when evidently these terms may be properly used to indicate distinct officers.

The work of medical inspection in the schools is directed obviously to three purposes: (A) The detection and limiting the spread of contagious diseases. (B) The study of physical defects and other departures from normal health in the scholar, with indication of the remedy. (C) Supervision of the scholar's environment; and to these may be added when we have fully qualified inspectors holding the right relations with other school authorities (D) some supervision of the instruction regarding hygiene.

The qualifications which this work demands of those who are to carry it on are:

1. *Skill in diagnosis*, the broadest and most difficult department in practical medicine. The diagnosis of disease is something that cannot be learned in fragments. Only to an extremely limited extent, and then with great uncertainty can any one disease be recognized, except by the person who can recognize all diseases. There are refinements of diagnosis which remain perforce chiefly in the hands of specialists, but every diagnostician knows that each extension of his ability to recognize a new pathologic condition increases the certainty and exactness of his diagnosis of every condition. There is no diagnosis which is not

differential. The recognition of the condition present demands that a host of other conditions be also borne in mind.

2. At least *outline knowledge of what is required to meet each pathologic condition discovered.* Even if medical inspection in the schools dealt merely with contagious diseases, the duty would be well performed only by one who had received the greater part of a thorough medical education. In New York City, where the inspector is not allowed to mention the name of any physician or dispensary to the scholar, or even in general to make the slightest suggestion or criticism of treatment, they have been compelled to give with the exclusion cards full printed directions regarding the management of pediculosis, and to have a corps of trained nurses to send into the children's homes to see that certain skin diseases are efficiently treated.

But the dealing with contagious disease is only of minor importance in school hygiene. It helps greatly to restrict the general morbidity of the community, but affects less the health of actual pupils than do conditions like eye-strain or imperfect general nutrition, that do not exclude the patient from the schoolroom. If the object of school hygiene is the health of the children, almost every morbid condition that may affect the body should be recognized by the medical inspector and the needs of each particular case and the possible ways of meeting them intelligently appreciated.

3. *The medical inspector of schools must have a broad, definite, practical knowledge of hygiene, including the factors which produce disease and those which guard against it.* He must have some special knowledge with regard to the heating, lighting and ventilation of rooms and buildings, the disposal of refuse, disinfection, the general endurance of children and the signs of fatigue. The best medical supervision will go even further than this and include an understanding of developmental and corrective physical training.

Enough has been said to indicate that the medical inspector is simply a new specialization in the broad field of medicine. The training of the medical school, the actual treatment of patients, the quickening influence of medical journals and medical societies, are all essential to qualify one for such a line of work. Indeed, the efficiency of the inspector and the value of his work will depend to a considerable extent upon actual personal acquaintance with his colleagues in the medical profession, who practice in the district from which the scholars are drawn. He can only do his best to secure the health of the school, when, with the full advantage of the esprit d'corps of the medical profession, he is free to intrude as a friendly consultant upon any physician from whose families the scholars under his care may be drawn, with a freedom that is only possible to a recognized and friendly member of our profession.

The thing that is required of us as members of the medical profession to-day is a frank, hearty recognition of this new specialty. Recognition of its importance, its scope, the difficulties necessarily encountered by those entering upon it, with the possibilities it offers of useful employment for a certain number of educated physicians, and of benefit to all other branches of the profession and the public at large.

By drawing attention to existing remediable deformities and departures from normal health, there will be created a demand for skilled professional service, of the highest value to the community, and so of direct profit to our profession. The difficulties that have beset other specialists await the medical inspector, sometimes lessened, sometimes increased by the fact that he is working under the authority and in the pay of the general public, but always requiring the same intelligent appreciation of the rights of others, the same avoidance of unfriendly criticism, the same persistent endeavor to maintain a friendly relation that will bear the inevitable friction of contact through unintelligent and fault-finding patients. Let us recognize how much the medical inspector of schools has in common with the rest of us, entitling him or her to full participation in every privilege of our profession. Let us also recognize that if well-qualified for the special work, he or she possesses a certain amount of special knowledge that the mass of the profession cannot lay claim to; and which entitles him to speak with authority in certain situations.

The duties of a medical inspector of schools, or the school physician, may be considered a little more minutely. Inspection which is to guard against contagious diseases depends for its effi-

ciency upon early recognition and prompt action.
short of daily inspection of all schools is a very poor p
against acute infectious diseases. The plan which brin
the school physician each morning, every child sus;
acute illness, is the only one that can receive the approv
telligent sanitarians. The instant dismissal of the chi
home, and the more searching investigation of the ca
home, either by the family physician or the inspecto
health authorities, is probably the most practical way o
with the cases of acute infectious disease. Chronic ir
also, must be followed beyond the schoolroom, either
the family physician or the health authorities, or, where
by the staff of school nurses. Something must be don
the mere declaration that the child is unfit to attend
medical inspection is to command the confidence of a
people.

Acute illness not contagious in character should also b
upon by the school physician to the extent of deciding
the interests of the patient demand his exclusion from sc
these cases there is the greatest need for a good under
between the school physician and the practitioner und
care the child should properly come.

Chronic diseases and deformities, congenital or acquii
require more careful investigation, but they allow of mc
Before going into any case minutely the school physic
properly satisfy himself as to whether the disease or fau
velopment is receiving intelligent attention from som
member of our profession, and if such be the case he sh
frain from any investigation of it, except in conjunction w
colleague.

In many chronic cases the school physician should
another very important function. Through him the prac
in charge of the case should be able to secure that mod
of school routine which the interests of his patient require.
times it will be a matter of special light or seating, or k
work in the school; sometimes the arrangement for a
course of physical training or the modification of the c
school instruction to meet the needs of the particular chil

through the school physician we can expect that more and more the individual peculiarties of the scholar shall receive recognition, in the tasks he is put to for the purpose of drawing out and developing his powers. In this direction there is opportunity for original scientific work of great importance. Progressive educators feel keenly that popular machine methods of instruction are defective, and look to those who best understand physiologic and pathologic processes for guidance and help in their attempts at improvement.

Defects of sight and hearing which directly hamper the child in its school work, and which are liable to arise or increase during school life, should be systematically sought for, at least once a year, among all pupils. The return of a child to the schoolroom, after exclusion for illness of any sort, should be the occasion for careful examination, which may reveal recently acquired defects of these special senses, but such defects may arise quite apart from illness that would interrupt school attendance.

Even the school physician who may be quite unfitted to give instruction in hygiene, may be able to offer helpful criticism of the teaching of hygiene that goes on in the school. On this account such teaching should be at least partly under his supervision if he does not take a more active part in it.

There can be no doubt that the medical inspection of schools, like other special work in medicine, will be best done by a distinct class of practitioners who devote their whole time to this and similar work. To have it in the hands of those who are in no way professional rivals will avoid the friction and opposition almost certain to arise where a physician also in private practice is called upon, in his capacity of school physician, to form a medical opinion regarding patients of a fellow practitioner.

This kind of complete specialization is greatly to be desired and in the main aimed at. But in a period of development and transition the most desirable cannot always be attained. In some places it will be possible to have the functions of school physician and health officer combined in one who has withdrawn from private practice. But where a competent school physician can only be found among those actively engaged in practice, one should be chosen largely because he has the respect and confidence of

his colleagues, and an unaggressive temper that wi
secure that co-operation which is absolutely essential tc
results.

Special training for the duties of school physician v
as has already been indicated, with a complete course ir
ard medical college. To this must be added a certain r
years, say three, of general medical practice. We ca1
ceive of any other way of acquiring, at the present t
diagnostic skill which is the first essential in medical i
of schools. Beyond this there must be a pretty thorou;
in hygiene, both personal and public hygiene, includ
practical skill in bacteriology.

Courses of the kind required already exist in connec
some of our larger universities and medical schools,
these require some further development before they
meet the needs of the school physician. To this should
a good practical course on physical training, such as is n
in a few of our best institutions, and which should be c
every one of them claiming the title of college or univers

The current literature of this special department of mt
already considerable. The appended bibliography
chiefly the titles of papers that have appeared in Engl
January 1, 1903. The periodical literature appearing i1
and German is in some respects more extensive and 1
portant. Those who can avail themselves of it will
brought together in the Index Medicus chiefly under t i
ings: Hygiene of Person and Hygiene of Schools. In l
future the work of the school physician will doubtless bec :
subject of special text-books.

BIBLIOGRAPHY.

Andrew, F.: "Paper in Opposition to the Introduction of Mili.
into Public Schools," *J. State Med.*, London, 1904, 12, B 1-83.

Baker, L. K.: "Sanitary Legislation Affecting Schools," *Clevel* 1
J., 1903, 2, 571-575.

Bancroft, Jessie H.: "The Place of Automatism in Gymnastic E1
Am. Phys. Educat. Rev., Brooklyn, 1903, 8, 218-231.

Berry, F. May D.: "The Education of Physically Defective Childr
the London School Board," *Lancet*, 1903, 2, 17-29.

Beszant, Miss S. B.: "The Teaching of Hygiene," *J. San. Inst.*,
1903-4, 24, 788-797.

Boyd, J. J.: "School Notification of Infectious Disease," *Public Health*, London, 1903-4, 16, 94-98.

"Brief Statement of the Results Obtained by the Commission of the British Dental Association Appointed to Investigate the Condition of the Teeth of School Children," *British Dental J.*, London, 1903, 24, 809-816.

Bracken, C. W.: "Practical Hygiene in Elementary Schools," *J. State Med.*, London, 1903, 11, 314-325.

Bronner, A.: "On the Importance of Examining the Eyes and Ears of all Children, Not Only Those of the Board Schools," *J. San. Inst.*, London, 190, 1, 189-198.

Bryce, P. H.: "The Ethical Value of Education in Preventive Medicine," *Canad. J. Med. and Scin.*, Toronto, 1903, 12, 1-9.

Burnell, T.: "The Teaching of Hygiene in Elementary Schools," *J. State Med.*, London, 1903, 11, 326-330.

"Discussion in Applied Hygiene for School Teachers," *J. San. Inst.*, London, 1903, 24, 27-40.

Ehinger, C. E., "Physical Examination in Normal Schools and Public Schools," *Am. Phys. Educat. Rev.*, Brooklyn, 1903, 8, 237-244.

Emerson, Florence G.: "Medical School Inspection in Greater New York," *Brooklyn Med. J.*, May, 1904.

Foster, B.: "Some Problems of Preventive Medicine," *Am. Med.*, Philadelphia, 1903, 5, 422-466.

Great Britain. Royal Commission on Physical Training. (Scotland). Report of the . . . 2 V., London, 1903. Neil & Co., 199, p. 1 diag. 648 p. 101.

Groff, G. G.: "Physiology *vs.* Hygiene in Our Public Schools," This Bulletin (Easton, Pa.), 1902-3, 6, 370-374.

Hall, G. S.: "Child Study at Clark University, an Impending New Step," *Am. J. Psychol.*, Worcester, 1903, 14, 96-106.

Hancock, H. Irving: "Japanese Physical Training," New York and London, 1904. G. P. Putnam's Sons. 19 + 171 pp., 12 plates.

Hay, M.: "Notification of Measles and Whooping Cough," *Public Health*, London, 1902-3, 15, 382-397.

Hermann, C.: "The Present Method of Medical School Inspection in Greater New York," *N. Y. Med. J.*, 1903, 27, 401-403.

Jackson, E.: "Testing of Vision in the Public Schools," *Colorado Med.*, Denver, 1903-4, 1, 97-102.

Johnson, H. P.: "Medical School Inspection in the City of New York," Tr. M. Soc. of N. Y., Albany, 1903, pp. 183-189.

Knott, J.: "Brain Fag, and Its Effects on the Health," *N. Y. Med. J.*, 1903, 78, 986-989.

Little, A.: "Care of the Eyes of the Children Attending Elementary Schools," *J. San. Inst.*, London, 1903-4, 24, 814-824.

Lloyd, R. J.: "The Education of Physically and Mentally Defective Children," *Westminister Rev.*, London, 1903, 159, 662-674.

Lydston, G. F.: "Briefs on Physical Training," *Am. Med.*, Philadelphia, 1903, 5, 300, 342, 383, 419, 463.

Mackenzie, W. L.: "Medical Inspection of Schools and School Children, with Special Reference to the Royal Commission on Physical Training," *County and Municip. Rec.*, Glasgow and Edinburgh, 1903, 1, 486.

Macpherson, J. D.: "Popular Medical Education, Its Aid in Limiting the Spread of Disease," *Buffalo Med. J.*, 1902-3, 42, 709-722.

Moore, S. G.: "The Advantages To Be Gained by the Teaching of the Elements of Hygiene in Schools," *J. State Med.*, London, 1903, 11, 309-313.

Nesbitt, D. M.: "Warming and Ventilating of Public Schools," *J. San. Inst.*, London, 1903-4, 24, 825-833; 3 plans, Idiag.

Newsholme, A.: "School Hygiene, the Laws of Health in Relation to School Life." New Ed. London, 1903. S. Sonnenschien & Co., Vol. VI, pp. 12 + 311.

Newton, R. C.: "Some Practical Suggestions on Physical Education in the Public Schools," *Med. News*, New York, 1903, 83, 1115-1117.

Powers, L. M.: "Some Observations Made on the Inspection of Schools," *S. California Pract.*, Los Angeles, 1903, 18, 292-297.

Putnam, Helen C.: "The Desirable Organization for a Department of Hygiene in Public Schools," This Bulletin (Easton, Pa.), 1902-3, 6, 378-386.

Richards, H.: "The Education Bill, and the Sanitary Control of Schools," *Med. Mag.*, London, 1903, 12, 77-82.

Richards, H. M.: "The Sanitary Control of Schools with Reference to the Education Bill," *Public Health*, London, 1902-3, 15, 121-136. "Some of the Medical Problems of Public Elementary Schools," *J. San. Inst.*, London, 1903-4, 24, 775-782.

Robertson, J. C.: "The Introduction of Military Drill into Public Schools," *J. State Med.*, London, 1904, 12, 75-80.

Rothwell, Annie: "Hygiene in Elementary Schools, and Its Bearing in Home Life," *J. San. Inst.*, London, 1903-4, 24, 773.

Savage, W. B.: "Physical Education, Past and Present," *Am. Phys. Educat. Rev.*, Brooklyn, 1903, 8, 209-217.

Schmidt, H. F.: "School Hygiene and the Need of Medical Supervision in All Our Schools, *N. Y. State Med. J.*, New York, 1904, 4, 24-28.

Sedgwick, W. T., and Hough, T.: "What Training in Physiology and Hygiene May We Reasonably Expect in the Public Schools?" *Science*, New York and Lancaster, Pa., 1903, n. s., 18, 333-360.

Sheard, C.: "Infectious Diseases among School Children, *Can. Lancet*, Toronto, 1903-4, 37, 621-625.

Sherer, J. W.: "School Hygiene of the Eye," *St. Louis Cour. of Med.*, 1903, 29, 369-379.

Smith, Alice M.: "A Study of School Hygiene, Development of Children and Preventive Medicine," *Am. Med.*, Philadelphia, 1903, 6, 743.

Somers, B. S.: "The Medical Inspection of Schools; A Problem in Preventive Medicine," *Med. News*, Jan. 17, 1903.

Swain, R. L.: "The Brain of Children and Some Suggestions from the Standpoint of the Physician as to How It Should Be Regarded by the Teacher," *Am. Med.*, Philadelphia, 1903, 6, 950-955.

Todd, F. C.: "School Sanitation Relative to Sight and Hearing," *St. Paul Med. J.*, St. Paul, 1903, 5, 274–280.

Tomlinson, J.: "The Present Methods of Education from the Standpoint of the Physician," *Am. Med.*, Philadelphia, 1903, 6, 196.

Towne, S. R.: "Medical Inspection of Schools," *Western Med. Rev.*, Lincoln, Neb., 1903, 8, 33–36.

Vaughan, V. C.: "The Michigan Method of Teaching Sanitary Science or Hygiene in Public Schools of the State," This Bulletin (Easton, Pa.), 1902-3, 6, 387–390.

Walker, J. R.: "The Care of the Eyes during School Life," *Occidental Medical Times*, San Francisco, 1903, 17, 409–413.

Ward, J. W.: "Medical Inspection of the Public Schools," *Pacific Coast Journal Homeop.*, San Francisco, 1904, 12, 34–38.

Ward, T. D.: "The Training of Teachers of Hygiene for Public Schools," This Bulletin (Easton, Pa.), 1902-3, 6, 391–409.

Warner, F.: "The Inadequate Teaching of Hygiene in Public Schools," *Columbus Med. J.*, 1903, 27, 261–271.

Wilcox, DeW. G.: "Further Investigation Regarding the Physical Effects of Regent's Examination upon School Children," *Trans. Homeop. Med. Soc.*, New York, Rochester, 1903, 38, 65–81.

Wintsch, C. H.: "Medical School Inspection," *N. Am. J. Homeop.*, 1903, 51, 210–217.

OBSERVATIONS IN PASSING.

A CRITICISM ON LICENSE TO PRACTISE LAWS.

Dr. Norman Bridge, of Los Angeles, in a letter to the members of the Medical Examining Board of California, writing in protest to the board's action regarding an individual, calls attention to a serious blunder in many of our medical laws. This is not the place to discuss the merits of the particular action of the board objected to, as it is of local importance. The general proposition suggested is of general value. Dr. Bridge writes:

There is, I believe, no warrant of law for the board to go behind the action of a college in granting a particular diploma. The college is, and the law contemplates that it shall be, the sole judge of the fitness of a candidate for its diploma. The board may investigate a college to see if its requirements are up to standard, and may for cause against it refuse to admit all its graduates for examination. But it has no right to throw out a particular person whom an accredited college has honored with its degree, on the ground of alleged taint in the giving it. To say that the board can inquire as to whether a college has relaxed a rule as to time with a particular student is to say that it may inqure whether a certain professor has been unduly lenient in his final examination of that student or has excused him from too many lessons—or as to any other of a hundred different matters of college management that it is the function of the faculty to attend to. Such a contention would be manifestly absurd, as such a performance would be illegal and impertinent.

Whatever may be the true interpretation of the California law, there are states where the boards can and do examine the holder of a particular diploma to see if it has met the Procrustean requirements of the medical practice act. No one can accuse the Bulletin of the American Academy of Medicine of being opposed to state examination for licensure, so that any criticism of medical laws is the criticism of a friend and not the captious opposition of a foe. In this very thing the laws are uniformly weak: A rigid course as to years, months, weeks, days and hours is prescribed. Every one must be run in the self-same mould. Medical schools, in the eyes of the law, are looked upon as shrewd schemers whose chief occupation is to find loop-holes to permit their students to creep into the fold. It must be confessed that the medical schools have sometimes so acted as to require the exercise of large-hearted charity not to so consider them. But all medical schools do not act so; there are some that are honorable. It may be possible to find a medical faculty that has the true welfare of the profession at heart, and would scorn to seal with its degree, one who was not fairly prepared. If such a faculty can be found, it will have another plank in its platform: The highest development of the individual is by adapting the educational process to his individual characteristics. And still another: If a student has acquired the knowledge of a subject, the method of his acquiring that knowledge is of secondary importance. Hence a student may be fairly admitted to advance standing although he did not follow the usual course to reach it. As a precaution, it may be well to mention that the above proposition does not advocate the pursuit of unusual methods to secure knowledge; it applies only to those who have already secured it, possibly by a much greater expenditure of time and application than the usual way would have taken.

These hard and fast rules in the practice acts do not tend to the highest development of the profession. They tend to the mediocre and routine. It was much better to give the medical schools some liberty. Should any school abuse this liberty let it alone receive the anathema. For a long time the profession was apathetic and evils could flourish; now that it is awakened to the necessity of thorough training a better product will be obtained by the cooperative effort of college and boards of examiners.

∗

The fifth number of the journal of the Fifteenth International Congress of Medicine, which is to be held at Lisbon, in April, 1906, shows commendable progress in the preparations. Already (February 20, 1905) some 205 papers have been promised for the various sections, many of them from eminent medical men— and the number of general addresses is nearing completion.

∗

The next meeting of the American Electro-Therapeutic Association will be held in New York, September 19 to 21, 1905.

∗

The first annual report of the Henry Phipps Institute for the study, treatment and prevention of tuberculosis, located in Philadelphia, requires a volume of 265 pages, and when one examines the report, the conclusion is reached that there are none too many. Of all the ills that prey upon mankind, this one, perhaps, is most dependent upon sociologic factors, and is one place at least, where the physician and the sociologist tread the same path in their strictly professional routine. The problems so intimately related here, are not entirely separated elsewhere, and the study of the obvious, clears the vision for the investigation of those whose relationship is not so clearly seen, but whose interdependence is just as real. Apart then from the scientific value of the work of the Phipps Institute, and of the evidences of philanthropy, there is the other benefit, of demonstrating the subtle relationship of disease and society, and of the necessity of the study of social problems by the physician to aid him in his warfare with disease.

LITERATURE NOTES.

APPENDICITIS AND OTHER DISEASES ABOUT THE APPENDIX. BY BAYARD HOLMES, B.S., M.D. New York: D. Appleton and Co. 1904. pp. 368, and 7 plates, two of which are in color. Price, $2.00. Sold by subscription only.

This book begins the second part of Dr. Holmes' writing on surgical emergencies in his "Text-book of Surgery for Practitioners of Medicine," and it is the first division of "Abdominal Surgery."

Seven chapters of the thirteen which compose the book, or 241 pages, are devoted to a very thorough consideration of appendicitis, its history, pathology, symptoms, diagnosis and treatment; these are discussed separately and fully.

One chapter is given to the various forms of peritonitis, a short chapter is devoted each to intussusception and to perforating typhoid ulcer. After these follows a chapter on general bibliography and lastly one of "adages" pertaining to the subjects discussed.

The book is well illustrated both by plates and by cases. The graphic colored plates called "the ideal mankin" with luminosities to call attention to the especial seat of pain and its radiations in the various abdominal diseases are very interesting and useful.

Dr. Holmes' dogmatism, especially in the paragraph in which he sums up under the head "conclusions," after his chapters on appendicitis, may possibly offend the sense of some conservative surgeons. In teaching, one must be dogmatic, however.

The book as a whole well sustains Dr. Holmes reputation of an able surgeon, a clear thinker and a luminous writer.

THE INFLUENCE OF GROWTH ON CONGENITAL AND ACQUIRED DEFORMITIES. By ADONIRAM BROWN JUDSON, A.M., M.D., profusely illustrated. New York: William Wood & Co. 1905. pp. 276.

While it may neither add to nor diminish the scientific accuracy of this book, the charming style in which it is written adds greatly to one's pleasure in reading it. Indeed one hardly credits in advance the possibility of receiving the same gratification in reading this admirable work on orthopedics, that one does in reading an essay on some literary theme. As to the subject-matter, Dr. Judson shows himself so thoroughly conversant with his subject, and withal presents his own conclusions so clearly, that one can ask for little more in that respect. The "make-up" of the book is well worthy the firm publishing it.

REPORTS OF MEDICAL EXAMINING BOARDS.

I. FOURTEENTH ANNUAL REPORT OF THE STATE BOARD OF MEDICAL EXAMINERS OF NEW JERSEY. 1904.

II. FIRST BIENNIAL REPORT OF THE STATE BOARDS OF MEDICAL EXAMINERS OF THE STATE OF SOUTH DAKOTA. 1904.

III. NINTH ANNUAL REPORT OF THE BOARD OF REGISTRATION OF MEDICINE, STATE OF MAINE. December 31, 1903.

IV. LIST OF REGISTERED PHYSICIANS IN ARKANSAS. January 10, 1905.

I. New Jersey has developed a very excellent law. It conserves the welfare of the people, which is the prime purpose of such laws, protects the licensed physician from competition from men of less educational qualifications, and recognizes the licenses issued by other states at their true value, without the vexatious disputes about reciprocity.

It is gratifying to note that 22 per cent. of the licentiates held literary or scientific degrees, which is an advance on a few years since. 76 per cent. of the physicians now practising in New Jersey are licentiates of the board. This is evidence of the time soon approaching when all physicians will have had a state license and the problem of removing from one state to another simplified. As the results of the examination are tabulated in the annual report published in the Bulletin, they will not be reviewed at this time.

II. This report is a strong contrast to the one just reviewed in that it is beginning the effort, while New Jersey has had the experience of years to determine its course. Hence, it is fitting, in the first report, to find a clear statement of the conditions that have led up to the necessity of the state examining boards. The work of the board opens well for the future of the profession in South Dakota.

III. It is much to be regretted that Maine has not published all of its reports, the last one published previously being the fifth report of the board. The tabulation of the examinations has already been published in the Bulletin. The report contains the minutes of the meeting of the board, the registration act, the regulations adopted by the board and a list of the physicians of Maine.

IV. The Arkansas medical practice act required the registration of all who were legally entitled to practise at the time of the passage of the act, so this pamphlet gives the official list of all legally practising physicians in Arkansas up to the date of its issuing.

TRANSACTIONS OF MEDICAL SOCIETIES.

I. TRANSACTIONS OF THE MAINE MEDICAL ASSOCIATION. 1904. Vol. XV. Part I. pp. 215.

II. TRANSACTIONS OF THE MEDICAL ASSOCIATION OF THE STATE OF ALABAMA, MONTGOMERY. 1904. pp. 580.

III. PROCEEDINGS OF THE CONNECTICUT MEDICAL SOCIETY, 1904. 1904. Published by the Society. pp. 576.

I. This volume records the happenings of the 52nd annual meeting, June 1 to 3, 1904. It contains three papers of interest to the medical sociologist. "The Care of the Feeble Minded," by Dr. Bigelow T. Sanborn; "Medical Mistakes," a very readable paper full of suggestion and food for thought, by Dr. James A. Spalding, a Fellow of the American Academy of Medicine; and "The Medical Registration Law," by Dr. A. K. P. Meserve, who was secretary of the Maine Board of Medical Examiners, from its organization until his death, a month or more ago.

II. No state society keeps a closer watch over the profession in its borders than does that of Alabama, and judging from its transactions, with the happiest results, as when it can be said of some county societies that every eligible physician is a member, and there is no illegal practitioner in the county unprosecuted. The following extract from the report of the junior vice-president, Dr. John Robert Graves Howell, of Dothan, is worthy the careful consideration of thoughtful men everywhere.

Some men decline to make an effort to get certain men to join the county society on the ground that they are not fit material. I do not agree with that idea, for the worst man can be improved in every respect and nothing else will do the work like membership in the county and state organization. This gives them contact with men whose influence is uplifting beyond conception.

I find that the best way on earth to get bad qualities out of my fellow practitioner is to get them out of myself and let him see how admirable it is. My plea to the 599 physicians in the southern district is: Never lose an opportunity to make a member a better member, and never neglect to induce those on the outside to unite with us.

III. The Connecticut society adopted a motion to instruct the Committee of Arrangements for the next meeting to "abolish all exhibits in connection therewith."

The report of the medical examiners give some figures of interest. Several of those who were examined in Connecticut, were also examined in other states, and a comparison of the grades received before the several boards is given:

A Connecticut average	82.5	New York average	86.5
B " "	84.8	" " "	91.8
C " "	77.5	" " "	85.0
D " "	82.9	Pennsylvania "	83.8
E " "	75.6	" "	82.7
E New Jersey average	83.2		

These figures possibly sustain the contention of the committee that the Connecticut marking is as severe as the other states, although it does not prove it by any means. It does show a greater uniformity in marking than one would expect, and should aid the approach of the good time when the license of another state will be accepted at a fair valuation.

Sanitation for January contains an excellent article on the new filter beds for Philadelphia, fully illustrated.

Vol. I, No. 1, of the *Georgian Practician* has been received. This first number sets a high standard, which we hope will be maintained. One of the noticeable features of the newer journals is the great improvements made by our printers, and the *Practician* is no exception. It is published at Savannah, at two dollars a year.

The *Arena* is continuing its history of the development of Quayism in Pennsylvania, which is but one of many caustic articles in each number. Many of its articles are idealistic, a very fair proportion constructive and helpful.

The *Literary Digest* continues to furnish a breadth of news of the world's progress and newspaper thought that makes it a particularly valuable journal for the busy man who wishes to know of the happenings in the world and the comments thereon outside his own field of reading.

The *American Journal of Surgery and Gynecology* will drop the latter part of its title with the April number. It will be published under the management of Dr. Joseph MacDonald, Jr., so long connected with the *International Journal of Surgery*. Dr. Walter M. Brickner will edit the journal, assisted by a brilliant corps of collaborators.

Index to Vol. VI.

Accountant, The Physician as an. By C. M. Culver................ 207
Alcoholic Drinks and Narcotics, Laws in the U. S. A. D., 1903, Relating to Compulsory Instruction in Schools in Physiology and Hygiene with Special Reference to the Effects of, on the Human System..... 635
Anatomy, Electives in. By Frederic H. Gerrish.................. 435
American Academy of Medicine—Hand-book 1904, 597; News Notes, 316, 596; Transactions Saratoga Meeting, 1902, 102; Washington Meeting, 1903, 347; Atlantic City Meeting, 1904...................... 694
Are Modern School Methods in Keeping with Physiologic Knowledge? Symposium.. 871
Benedict, A. L. Ethical Pharmacy, 848; Time Allowance in the Combined Collegiate and Medical Course, 121; Time Allowance in the Combined Collegiate and Medical Course, Second Report............. 343
Birth Rate, How the Physicians May Influence the Declining. By Roland G. Curtin.. 481
Bonney, S. G., Denver. Internal Medicine, To What Extent Required or Elective in the Medical Course................................ 439
Boys, Is Equal Treatment of the Sexes Best, or Do Girls Require the Same Treatment as,? By Stephen H. Weeks...................... 880
Breathing, The Teaching of Physiologic. By G. Hudson-Makuen....... 375
Bulkley, L. Duncan, New York. Required and Elective Dermatology.... 449
Children in Cities. By Rosa Engelmann............................ 169
Cities, Children in. By Rosa Engelmann.......................... 169
Collegiate (Course) Time Allowance in the Combined Collegiate and Medical. By A. L. Benedict, 121; Second Report................. 343
Compensation for Medical Services Rendered the State. By T. D. Davis 238
Consideration Regarding Medical Inspections in the Public Schools. By Edward Jackson.. 923
Constitution.. 625
Correspondence Method of Treating Disease, The. By F. T. Rogers..... 835
Culver, C. M., Albany, N. Y. The Physician as an Accountant........ 207
Curtin, Roland G., Philadelphia. How the Physician May Influence the Declining Birth-rate.. 481
Darnell, William Edgar, Atlantic City, N. J. The Gynecologic Aspect of Mental Overstrain at Puberty and Its Influence on Development.. 887
Davis, T. D., Pittsburg. Compensation for Medical Services Rendered the State... 238
Dentistry and Pharmacy, The Relations of Physicians to—A Symposium 803
Dentistry, The Relation of Medicine and. By Edward C. Kirk........ 803
Dentists, The Relation of Physicians to. By John S. Marshall......... 812

Dermatology, Required and Elective. By L. Duncan Bulkley.............. 449
Devine, Edward T., New York City. The Medical Profession and Social Reform.. 76
Disease, The Correspondence Method of Treatment. By F. T. Rogers. 835
Doctor's Duty to the State, The. By J. B. Roberts............................. 675
Education, Good Vision an Important Factor in the Educational Process. By S. D. Risley.. 181
Effect of Modern School Methods on the Health of the Teacher, The. By Jane L. Greely... 897
Electives—in Anatomy. By Frederick H. Gerrish, 435; in Dermatology. By L. Duncan Bulkley, 449; In Medicine. By S. G. Bonney.......... 439
Ellis, H. Bert, Los Angeles. Necessity for a National Bureau of Medicines and Foods.. 486
Engelmann, Rosa, Chicago. Children in Cities..................................... 169
Eshner, A. A., Philadelphia. Medical Representation in Hospital Management... 253
Ethical Pharmacy. By A. L. Benedict.. 848
Examinations—For Medical Licensure in 1901. By Charles McIntire, 1; 1902, 497; Results of the, for 1903. By Charles McIntire, 709; The Personal Equation in, for Licensure. By Charles McIntire............ 262
Foods, Medicines and, Necessity for a National Bureau of. By H. Bert Ellis... 486
Foshay, P. Maxwell, Chicago. May a Hospital Steal?......................... 227
Family Physicians of the Past, Present and Future. By S. A. Knopf.... 193
Gerrish, Frederic H., Portland, Me. Electives in Anatomy.................. 435
Girls—Is Equal Treatment of the Sexes Best, or Do, Require the Same Treatment as Boys? By Stephen H. Weeks, 880; Is the Present Method of Education, Consistent with Their Physiologic Development? and Is It for the Welfare of the Race? By A. Lapthorn Smith, 871; The Life and Health of Our, in Relation to Their Future. By James H. McBride.. 460
Gonorrhea Insontium, Especially in Relation to Marriage. By Prince A. Morrow... 410
Good Vision an Important Factor in the Educational Process. By S. D. Risley.. 181
Greeley, Jane Lincoln, Jamestown, N. Y. The Effect of Modern School Methods in the Health of the Teacher... 897
Groff, G. G., Lewisburg, Pa. Physiology vs. Hygiene in Our Public Schools... 370
Guernsey, J. G., Philadelphia. Ten Years' Work of a Board of Medical Examiners... 793
Gynecologic Aspect of Mental Overstrain at Puberty, and its Influence on Development, The. By William Edgar Darnall................................. 887
Hall, W. S. Chicago. Pure vs. Applied Science in Medicine................. 211
Hawley, Donly C., Burlington, Vt. The Relation of the Physician to Politics... 234

Health, the Life and, of Our Girls in Relation to Their Fut
  James H. McBride..................
Hospital, Management, Medical Representation in. By A. A.
  253 ; May a, Steal. By P. Maxwell Foshay..................
How May the Public School Be Helpful in the Prevention of '
  losis? By S. A. Knopf..................
How the Physician May Influence the Declining Birth-rate. B
  G. Curtin..................
Hygiene, Physiology and, Laws in the U. S. A. D. 1903, Re
  Compulsory Instruction in Schools in, with Special Refe
  the Effect of Alcoholic Drinks and Narcotics on the Humar
  635; Physiology vs., in Our Public Schools. By G. G. Gr
  The Desirable Organization for a Department of, in the
  Schools. By Helen C. Putnam, 378 ; The Teaching of, in (
  lic Schools, a Symposium, 363 ; The Teaching of Perso
  W. L. Pyle, 363 ; The Michigan Method of Teaching, in th
  Schools of the State. By V. C. Vaughan, 387; The Tra
  Teachers of, for Public Schools. By Thomas D. Wood......
Internal Medicine—To What Extent Required or Elective in t
  ical Course? By S. G. Bonney..................
Is Equal Treatment of the Sexes Best, or Do Girls Require tl
  Treatment as Boys? By Stephen H. Weeks..................
Is the Present Method of Educating Girls Consistent with Their
  logic Development? And Is It for the Welfare of the Race i
  Lapthorn Smith..................
Jackson, Edward, Denver, Col. Consideration Regarding Mec
  spection in the Public Schools, 923 ; Report of the Comm
  Reciprocity in Medical Licensure, 155 ; The Training for a S]
  the Theory and the Condition as Illustrated by Ophthalmol
Kirk, Edward C., Philadelphia. The Relations of Medicine ar
  tistry..................
Knopf, S. A., New York. How May the Public School Be He
  the Prevention of Tuberculosis, 913. The Family Physicia
  Past, Present and Future..................
Laws in the U. S. A. D. 1903, Relating to Compulsory Instru
  School, Physiology and Hygiene with Special Reference
  Effect of Alcoholic Drinks and Narcotics in the System.......
Licensure, Examination for Medical. By Charles McIntire, in
  in 1902, 497; in 1903, 709 ; The Personal Equation in Exami
  for. By Charles McIntire..................
Life and Health of Our Girls in Relation to Their Future, Tl
  James H. McBride..................
List of Fellows..................
Literature Notes........119, 163, 224, 317, 360, 479, 592, 631, 669, 7

Makuen, G. Hudson, Philadelphia. The Teaching of Physiologic Breathing.. 375
Marshall, John S., U. S. A. The Relation of Physicians to Dentists..... 812
Marriage, Gonorrhea Insontium, Especially in Relation to. By Prince A. Morrow.. 410
May a Hospital Steal? By P. Maxwell Foshay................................. 227
McBride, James H., Los Angeles, California. The Life and Health of Our Girls in Relation to Their Future.................................... 460
McIntire, Charles, Easton, Pa. Examination for Medical Licensure in 1901, 1; in 1902, 497; "Muck Rake" Methods in Medical Practice, 321; Results of the Examinations for Medical Licensure, 1903, 709; Science vs. Shekels, 857; State Aid to Medical Colleges, 218; The Personal Equation in Examinations for Licensure......................... 262
Medical Colleges, State Aid to. By Charles McIntire........................ 218
Medical Course, Time Allowance in the Combined Collegiate and. By A. L. Benedict, 121; Second Report.. 343
Medical Examiners—Ten Years' Work of a Board of. By J. G. Guernsey 793
Medical Inspection in the Public Schools, Consideration Regarding. By Edward Jackson.. 923
Medical Practice Acts 1903, Indian Territory, 714; South Carolina........ 723
Medical Licensure, Examination for. By Charles McIntire, in 1901, 1; in 1902, 497; in 1903, 709; Reciprocity in, Report of the Committee on. By Edward Jackson.. 155
Medical Practice "Muck Rake" Methods in. By Charles McIntire...... 321
Medical Profession, The, and Social Reform. By Edward T. Devine..... 76
Medical Representation in Hospital Management. By A. A. Eshner..... 253
Medical Services, Compensation for, Rendered the State. By T. D. Davis.. 238
Medicine (See Internal Medicine); Pure vs. Applied Science in. By W. S. Hall, 211; the Political Side of. By John B. Roberts........... 242
Medicines and Food, Necessity for a National Bureau of. By H. Bert Ellis.. 486
Medicine and Dentistry, The Relations of. By Edward C. Kirk............ 803
Mental Overstrain, The Gynecologic Aspect of, at Puberty, and Its Influence on Development. By William Edgar Darnall..................... 887
Michigan Method of Teaching Sanitary Science or Hygiene in the Public Schools of the State. By V. C. Vaughan.. 387
Morrow, Prince A., New York. Gonorrhea Insontium, Especially in Relation to Marriage.. 410
Narcotics, Alcoholic Drinks and, Laws in the United States A. D. 1903 Relating to Compulsory Instruction in Schools in Physiology and Hygiene with Special Reference to the Effect of, on the Human System... 635
"Muck Rake" Methods in Medical Practice. By Charles McIntire...... 321
National Confederation of State Medical Examining and Licensing Boards—Transactions.. 292

Necessity for a National Bureau of Medicines and Foods. By H. Bert Ellis.. 486
News Notes.. 162
Observations in Passing.......... 116, 159, 223, 314, 359, 434, 477, 591, 629, 668, 705, 798, 831, 865, 906
Ophthalmology, The Training for a Specialty, the Theory and Condition as Illustrated by. By Edward Jackson... 453
Physicians, The Relation of, to Dentists. By John S. Marshall............. 812
Personal Equation in Examinations for Licensure. By Charles McIntire... 262
Personal Hygiene, The Teaching of. By W. L. Pyle........................... 363
Pharmacy, Ethical. By A. L. Benedict... 848
Pharmacy, The Relation of Physicians to Dentistry and—a Symposium. 803
Physician as an Accountant. By C. M. Culver..................................... 207
Physician, How the, May Influence the Declining Birth-rate. By Roland G. Curtin.. 481
Physician, The Family, of the Past, Present and Future. By S. A. Knopf.. 193
Physician, The Relation of the, to Politics. By Donly C. Hawley......... 234
Physicians, The Relation of, to Dentistry and Pharmacy—a Symposium 803
Physiology and Hygiene, Laws in the U. S. A. D. 1903, Relating to Compulsory Instruction in Schools in, with Special Reference to the Effects of Alcoholic Drinks and Narcotics on the Human System 635
Physiology, Are Modern School Methods in Keeping with Physiologic Knowledge—a Symposium 871
Physiology vs. Hygiene in Our Public Schools. By Geo. G. Groff........ 370
Physiologic Breathing, The Teaching of. By G. Hudson-Makuen 378
Political Side of Medicine. By John B. Roberts.................................... 242
Politics, The Relation of the Physician to. By Donly C. Hawley......... 234
President's Address 1902. The Religion of Science. By Victor C. Vaughan, 57; 1903, " Muck Rake " Methods in Medical Practice. By Charles McIntire, 321; 1904, The Doctor's Duty to the State. By J. B. Roberts... 675
Puberty, The Gynecologic Aspect of Mental Overstrain at, and Its Influence on Development. By William Edgar Darnall........................ 887
Public Schools, The Teaching of Hygiene in—a Symposium................. 363
Public Schools, Physiology vs. Hygiene in Our. By G. G. Groff........... 370
Pure vs. Applied Science in Medicine. By W. S. Hall........................ 211
Putnam, Helen C., Providence. The Desirable Organization for a Department of Hygiene in the Public Schools.................................... 378
Pyle, Walter L. Philadelphia. The Teaching of Personal Hygiene........ 363
Reciprocity in Medical Licensure, Report of the Committee on. By Edward Jackson... 155
Reciprocity the Medical Licensure.. 729
Relations of Medicine and Dentists, The. By Edward C. Kirk 803
Relations of Physicians to Dentists, The. By John S. Marshall............ 812
Relations of Physicians to Dentists and Pharmacists—a Symposium 803

Religion of Science. By Victor C. Vaughan.................................... 57
Report of the Committee on Reciprocity in Medical Licensure. By Edward Jackson... 155
Required and Elective Dermatology. By L. Duncan Bulkley............... 449
Required and Elective Studies in the Medical Course. Symposium...... 435
Remington, Joseph P., Philadelphia. Synonyms in the United States Pharmacopeia.. 821
Report of Council on Dr. Ellis's Paper... 826
Results of the Examinations for Medical Licensure in the United States for 1903. By Charles McIntire.................................... 709
Risley, S. D., Philadelphia. Good Vision an Important Factor in the Educational Process... 181
Roberts, John B., Philadelphia. The Doctor's Duty to the State, 675; the Political Side of Medicine.. 242
Rogers, F. T., Providence, R. I. The Correspondence Method of Treating Diseases 835
Sanitary Science, the Michigan Method of Teaching in the Public Schools of the State. By V. C. Vaughan............................ 387
Saratoga, Transactions of Meeting at, 1902..................................... 102
School, How May the Public, Be Helpful in the Prevention of Tuberculosis? By S. A. Knopf... 913
Schools, Considerations Regarding Medical Inspection in the Public. By Edward Jackson.. 923
Schools, Laws in the U. S., A. D. 1903, Relating to Compulsory Instruction in, in Physiology and Hygiene with Special Reference to the Effect of Alcoholic Drinks and Narcotics on the Human System...... 635
School Methods, Are Modern, in Keeping with Physiologic Knowledge? —Symposium... 871
School Methods, The Effect of Modern, on the Health of the Teacher. By Jane L. Greeley... 897
Schools, The Desirable Organization for a Department of Hygiene in the Public. By Helen C. Putnam 378
Schools, the Michigan Method of Teaching Sanitary Science or Hygiene in the Public, of the State. By V. C. Vaughan.............. 387
Schools, The Training of Teachers of Hygiene for Public. By Thomas D. Wood... 391
Science, Pure vs. Applied, in Medicine. By W. S. Hall..................... 211
Science, The Religion of. By Victor C. Vaughan............................. 57
Science vs. Shekels. By Charles McIntire..................................... 853
Secretary's Table... 55
Sexes, Is Equal Treatment of the, Best, or Do Girls Require the Same Treatment as Boys? By Stephen H. Weeks..................... 880
Smith, A. Lapthorn, Montreal, Canada. Is the Present Method of Educating Girls Consistent with Their Physiologic Development? And Is It for the Welfare of the Race?.............................. 871

Social Reform, The Medical Profession and. By Edward T. Devine..... 76
Specialty, the Training for a. The Theory and the Conditions as Illustrated by Ophthalmology. By Edward Jackson.................. 453
State Aid to Medical Colleges. By Charles McIntire..................... 218
State, Compensations for Medical Services Rendered the. By T. D. Davis 238
State, the Doctor's Duty to the. By J. B. Roberts 675
Synonyms in the United States Pharmacopeia. By Joseph P. Remington 821
Teacher, the Effect of Modern School Methods on the Health of the Teacher. By Jane L. Greeley.. 897
Teachers of Hygiene, The Training of, for Public Schools. By Thomas D. Wood 391
Teaching of Hygiene in Public Schools—a Symposium...................... 363
Teaching of Physiologic Breathing, The. By G. Hudson Makuen......... 375
Teaching Sanitary Science or Hygiene. The Michigan Method of, in the Public Schools of the State. By V. C. Vaughan..................... 387
Ten Years' Work of a Board of Medical Examiners. By J. G. Guernsey 793
The Teaching of Personal Hygiene. By W. L. Pyle............................ 363
The Desirable Organization for a Department of Hygiene in the Public Schools. By Helen C. Putnam.. 378
The Relation of the Physician to Politics. By Donly C. Hawley............ 234
Time Allowance in the Combined Collegiate and Medical Course. By A. L. Benedict... 121
Time Allowance in the Combined Collegiate and Medical Course, Second Report. By A. L. Benedict.. 343
Training for a Specialty, The Theory and the Condition as Illustrated by Ophthalmology, The. By Edward Jackson............................... 453
Training of Teachers of Hygiene for Public Schools, The. By Thomas D. Wood 391
Treating Disease, The Correspondence Method of. By F. T. Rogers..... 835
Tuberculosis, How May the Public School Be Helpful in the Prevention of? By S. A. Knopf.. 913
United States Pharmacopoeia, Synonyms in. By Joseph P. Remington 821
Vaughan, V. C., Ann Arbor, Mich. The Michigan Method of Teaching Sanitary Science or Hygiene in the Public Schools of the State, 387; The Religion of Science.. 57
Vision, Good, An Important Factor in the Educational Process. By S. D. Risley 181
Washington, D. C. Transactions of Meeting at 1903........................... 347
Weeks, Stephen H., Portland, Me. Is Equal Treatment of the Sexes Best, or Do Girls Require the Same Treatment as Boys?................. 880
Wood, Thomas D., New York. The Training of Teachers of Hygiene for Public Schools.. 391
Worth Repeating 167